Dictionary of the Decorative Arts

John Fleming and Hugh Honour

Dictionary of the Decorative Arts

Harper & Row, Publishers
New York, Hagerstown, San Francisco, London

John Fleming and Hugh Honour

Dictionary of the Decorative Arts

Harper & Row, Publishers
New York, Hagerstown, San Francisco, London

This work was originally published in Great Britain
under the title
The Penguin Dictionary of Decorative Arts.

DICTIONARY OF THE DECORATIVE ARTS

For information address Harper & Row, Publishers, Inc.,
10 East 53rd Street, New York, N.Y. 10022.

FIRST U.S. EDITION
ISBN: 0-06-011936-5
LIBRARY OF CONGRESS CATALOG CARD NUMBER: 76-50163

Designed by Gerald Cinamon

To Lettice and in memory of Allen

Cross-references are indicated by the use of SMALL CAPITALS

Ceramic Marks *881*

Hall-marks on Silver *890*

Makers' Marks on Silver and Pewter *893*

Photographic Acknowledgements *896*

This dictionary was planned as a companion volume to the *Penguin Dictionary of Architecture* which we wrote in collaboration with Sir Nikolaus Pevsner (1966, illustrated edition 1975). It is concerned with furniture and furnishings – i.e. movable objects other than paintings and sculpture – in Europe from the Middle Ages onwards and in North America from the Colonial Period to the present day. We have gone beyond these limits of place and time only in order to include accounts of craftsmen and types of objects that have played a part in the development of the decorative arts in the West, e.g. Chinese and Japanese ceramics. We have excluded articles of personal adornment, musical instruments, scientific instruments, clocks (but not their cases), manuscripts and printed books (but not their bindings).

There are four types of entry in the dictionary: definitions of stylistic and technical terms; accounts of materials and processes of working and embellishing them; biographies of leading craftsmen and designers; and brief histories of the more notable factories in which objects for household use and decoration have been made.

The very brief bibliographies at the end of entries are intended as guides for those in search of more detailed information and a wider range of reproductions. They do not attempt to be exhaustive. To save space we have omitted standard works of reference which, if cited, would have been repeated in entry after entry – U. Thieme and F. Becker (eds.), *Allgemeines Lexikon der bildenden Künstler*, Leipzig 1907–50; W. B. Honey, *European Ceramic Art, from the End of the Middle Ages to about 1815*, London 1952; P. MacQuoid and R. Edwards, *Dictionary of English Furniture from the Middle Ages to the Late Georgian Period*, London 1954; H. Hayward (ed.), *World Furniture*, London 1965; R. J. Charleston (ed.), *World Ceramics*, London 1968.

We should particularly like to thank Sir Francis Watson who kindly read and commented on our first draft entries on French subjects, Professor Ulrich Middeldorf who gave us advice on a wide range of subjects and Mr Peter Ward-Jackson who helped us with ornamental designers. To Betty Ettles we are indebted for timely editorial help. Our debt to Gerald Cinamon is difficult to express adequately for the book owes so much to his skill as a designer.

John Fleming/Hugh Honour

Wood-cut initial from Historia romana
by Appian of Alexandria,
printed by Erhard Ratdolt, Venice, 1477

Aalto, Hugo Alvar Henrik (1899–1976). Finnish architect and designer, he is famous for his bent plywood furniture. His first buildings were in a modernized version of the classical architecture of mid-C19 Finland but by 1927 he had adopted the International Modern style for his now famous library at Viipuri. Shortly after this, when building a convalescent home at Paimo between 1929 and 1933, he began to concern himself with furniture design. His first important design was for a convertible sofa-bed, made in 1930, with a thickly upholstered seat and back mounted on a very simple chromium-plated tubular steel frame. In 1932 he used tubular steel in conjunction with laminated plywood for a chair. The following year he founded the Artek firm in Helsinki to manufacture and market fabrics, light fittings and furniture made to his designs. He referred to them as 'architectural accessories', which suggests their decorative as well as practical function (in contrast to the term used by LE CORBUSIER for his furniture, *équipment*). Aalto was quick to realize that, from a psychological as well as an economic point of view, wood was a more appropriate medium than metal for the construction of furniture. In birchwood, hitherto used only for making skis, he found his ideal material. It has a beautiful grain, a golden colour, and can be polished to a silky texture. This organic beauty makes it more easily acceptable than cold steel. When laminated as plywood it is as resilient as steel. And it is much cheaper, easier to manufacture, and lighter in weight.

Inspired to some extent by THONET's bent beechwood chairs, by the tubular steel chairs of Mart STAM and Marcel BREUER and, in a practical way, by the process of manufacturing skis, Aalto developed a number of laminated birchwood chairs in the 1930s. In one, a long curving panel of laminated wood is suspended in a framework of thicker laminated strips. The framework is solid and only the panel resilient. He achieved greater springiness by adopting the cantilever principle and suspending a scrolled panel, forming both seat and back, between two

Alvar Aalto:
chair designed for Paimo Sanatorium, Finland, 1929–32 (Musée des Arts Décoratifs, Paris)

U-shaped loops of thicker laminated strips. For non-resilient furniture – e.g. three-legged stools and tables – he devised a leg composed of several pieces of laminated wood which fan out to support the top, making a joint that is as elegant as it is strong and durable. The tables are thus composed not so much of four legs as of upturned Us which can support tops of either wood or glass. His stools of the 1930s have circular plywood tops treated as separate members but in 1947 he devised another type in which the tops of the legs fan out to form the seat.

Although he adopted wood as his medium, Aalto abandoned not only carved ornament but all the traditional techniques of joinery. His designs are perfectly adapted to mechanized production and could hardly be realized by any other means. For, unlike most architect-designers, he has been as much concerned with mass production for the largest possible market as with the problem of furnishing his own buildings. For individual clients he has designed only slightly more elaborate and luxurious versions of his mass-produced pieces. He has also concerned himself with special problems in furniture design – small and durable furniture for kindergartens, seats that may easily be stacked for storage (his three-legged stool is particularly well-adapted for stacking in large numbers) and tall low-backed bar-stools.

Alvar Aalto: vase of amber-coloured cast glass, made by Karhula-Iittala, Finland, 1937 (Museum of Modern Art, New York)

Aalto's furniture, like his architecture, reveals a level-headed regard for simple practical needs, a highly developed sensitivity for linear elegance and an innate feeling for natural forms and textures. In a world that had proved to be less enthusiastic about machine aesthetics than RIETVELD and his friends had expected, it satisfies a natural craving for the organic, in both materials and shapes. It is significant that in the 1930s he also designed some excellent glass of which certain bowls are among the earliest examples of 'free form' in a utilitarian object.

Lit: G. Labo, *Alvar Aalto*, Milan 1948; Karl Fleig (ed.), *Alvar Aalto*, London 1963; *Möbel aus Holz und Stabl: Alvar Aalto, Mies van der Rohe*, Exh. Cat., Gewerbemuseum, Basel 1957.

Abaquesne, Masseot (*fl.*1526–57). He was a French potter, working at Rouen and specializing in tile pavements painted with elaborate heraldic designs, allegorical figures and italianate grotesques. He also produced italianate drug jars vigorously decorated with heads and foliage painted in a pallid colour scheme dominated by cool blues and yellows. He died before 1564, by which date his son **Laurent** was in charge of his workshop which the latter carried on until about the end of the C16.

Lit: M. J. Ballot, *La céramique française: Bernard Palissy et les fabriques du XVIe siècle*, Paris 1924: A. Lane, *French Faience*, London 1948.

Abbotsford Ware, *see* WEMYSS WARE.

Abildgaard, Nikolai Abraham (1743–1809). Leading Danish Neo-Classical painter. He designed and made for his own use, *c.*1800, some remarkably elegant Grecian furniture including chairs copied exactly from Greek C5 B.C. vases and decorated with painted panels also imitating red figure vases (Museum of Decorative Arts, Copenhagen). Also designed some much less archaeologically correct furniture for Prince Christian Frederick of Denmark (*c.*1807).

Lit: L. Swine, *Abildgaard Arkitektur og Dekoration*, Copenhagen 1926.

Absolon, William (1751–1815). English 'outside painter' of pottery (working like a German HAUSMALER) who from 1790 had a studio in Yarmouth where he painted flowers, landscapes, heraldic achievements, etc. on cream-coloured earthenware from the STAFFORDSHIRE (including TURNER, and WEDGWOOD) and LEEDS potteries. He also decorated glass. Many of his works are signed or marked with a painted arrow: there is a notable collection of pieces in the Norwich Castle Museum.

Lit: W. Freeth in *The Connoisseur* XXIII (1909), p. 251; W. A. Thorpe in *The Collector* X (1930), pp. 30, 100.

Abtsbessingen pottery A small factory in Thuringia producing faience of good quality, said to have been founded in 1739 (though no records date from before 1753) and continuing until the late C18 or early C19. Products included tureens, tea-kettles, tankards, vases, pyramids of flowers for table decorations and boxes fashioned like pug-dogs, often finely painted in high-temperature colours. It was under the patronage of the Schwarzburg family, and some products are decorated with their coat of arms from which the factory mark, a fork, was also derived.

Lit: M. Sauerlandt in *Der Cicerone* III (1911), p. 7.

Acajou Moucheté Spotted MAHOGANY known in England as 'fiddle-back' mahogany.

Acanthus Classical ornament based on the thick, prickly, scalloped leaves of the Acanthus plant, notably on the capitals of the Corinthian and Composite Order. In French it is often referred to as 'chicorée' though this is a misnomer.

Acanthus ornament: engraving by Pietro Antonio Priseo, 1624

Lit: F. Rothe, *Das deutsche Akanthusornament des 17 Jahrhunderts*, Berlin 1938.

Acier, Michel-Victor (1736–95). He was a modeller at the MEISSEN PORCELAIN FACTORY and became, after 1764, joint *Modellmeister* there with Johann Joachim KÄNDLER. He was brought from France in order to revive the factory's export trade after the Seven Years' War by introducing up-to-date French designs. His work is sentimental or sometimes moralizing, very different from Kändler's. He is credited with the introduction of lace-work in porcelain. He retired in 1781.

Åckermark, Peter, *see* SÖLVESBORG POTTERY.

Acorn cup A silver covered cup in the form of a giant acorn generally with a trunk-like stem, made in England in the late C16 – early C17. Like the somewhat similar gourd cup, it reflects the taste of this period for natural forms.

Acorn cup, gold, London, c.1610, from Stapleford Church, Leics. (British Museum)

Acroteria Plinths for statues or ornaments placed at the apex and ends of a PEDIMENT; also, more loosely, both the plinths and what stands on them.

Act of Parliament clock, *see* CLOCK.

Adam, Robert (1728–92). British Neo-classical architect, interior decorator and designer of furniture, metalwork, carpets, chimney-pieces, etc. for which his name is still a household word. He created (in partnership with his brother **James**, 1732–94) the Adam style which swept over England in the 1760s and 70s and quickly spread to France and the U.S. He trained under his architect father in Edinburgh, then studied in Rome (1754–8) where he knew PIRANESI, Clérisseau and other French Neo-classical artists and designers and acquired a vast repertory of classical motifs. But his style developed in a very personal manner. It is lighter, more delicate and less solemn than that of his French contemporaries (e.g. NEUFFORGE) being nearer to the Rococo in its airy gossamer prettiness and delight in sophisticated ornament, though fully Neo-classical in its motifs, its linearity and its cool restraint. His aim was, in his own words, 'to transfuse the beautiful spirit of antiquity with novelty and variety'. This he achieved occasionally by basing designs on antique marbles (e.g. a Roman sarcophagus suggested the shape and decoration for a bench for Lansdowne House), more frequently by applying classical architectural enrichments to furniture rather more solid and rectilinear than that of the Rococo period. His early furniture, designed for Kedleston, 1759–60, is heavy in STUART's manner. But imported LOUIS XVI STYLE furniture of the mid-1760s appears to have opened his eyes to a more elegant and polished approach to the Antique and his style quickly matured. His furniture always depended less upon form than ornament,

Robert Adam: commode designed 1773 for Osterley Park (Osterley Park, Middx.)

Adam design for dining-room furniture, from
The Works of Robert & James Adam, *London 1771*

eventually declined into exaggerated delicacy and over-sophistication, and sometimes deserved Horace Walpole's opprobrious epithets – 'filigrane and fan painting, gingerbread and snippets of embroidery'. It is usually either gilt or painted white with gilt mouldings, more rarely in the ETRUSCAN STYLE which he invented. Its extreme delicacy and intricacy was facilitated by his use of synthetic materials (e.g. composition on wire) for ornament, especially for pendant and tracery motifs which he greatly favoured. He was at his best with mirrors which he used as a field for filigree ornament. He designed mainly wall furniture (mirrors, girandoles, pier tables and commodes) and decorative pieces (urns, torchères, tripods, etc.). And he appears to have invented the sideboard. The best Adam style furniture was made by CHIPPENDALE but does not seem to have been designed by Adam himself. At various stages of his career he designed a few pieces of GOTHIC REVIVAL furniture. A similar stylistic development marks his designs for plasterwork, especially ceilings, of which several exquisite examples survive. The carpets which were woven to his designs by Thomas MOORE echoed the tight geometrical patterns surrounded by Antique style *rinceaux* of the ceilings, also their fresh colour schemes of pinks, greens, blues and white. His few designs for silver suggest that he – or perhaps one of the Italian draughtsmen whom he employed – was more influenced by contemporary Roman work with its touch of Piranesi-like fantasy, than the more severe Neo-classical patterns popular in France. A great quantity of silver made in England in the 1770s and 80s shows his influence – his love of forms derived from Antique vases and urns, his use of such motifs as the husk, anthemion and palmette, Vitruvian scroll, festoons, paterae, etc. The same forms and motifs appear in much of the metalwork of Matthew BOULTON and cast iron stoves and fireplaces by the Carron Ironworks, for which he provided designs. WEDGWOOD pottery also shows his influence though he appears to have had no direct contact with the firm. The Adam style was diffused by his published *Works in Architecture* (1773; 2nd vol. 1779; 3rd vol. 1822) and by the publications of his assistants, notably PERGOLESI and George Richardson. It fell under heavy fire in the more severely classically minded REGENCY PERIOD but returned to favour in the 1860s when his designs were much imitated.

Lit: E. Harris, *The Furniture of Robert Adam*, London 1963; R. Rowe, *Adam Silver, 1765–1795*, London 1965; D. Stillman, *The Decorative Work of Robert Adam*, London 1966; M. Tomlin, *Catalogue of Adam Period Furniture*, Victoria & Albert Museum, London 1972.

Adamesk, *see* TYNESIDE POTTERIES.

Adams & Company A prominent American glasshouse, it began in 1851 when **Adams, Macklin & Co.** took over the **Stourbridge Flint Glass Works** begun by John Robinson at Pittsburgh in 1823. It produced flint glass tablewares and pressed, engraved and later lime glasswares, also cut glass and, in the 1870s, opal wares. It was still in business in 1889.

Lit: A. C. Revi, *American Pressed Glass and Figure Bottles*, New York 1964.

Adams, L., *see* STIPPLE ENGRAVING.

Adams, William There were a number of STAFFORDSHIRE POTTERY makers of this name, mostly related to each other. 1. **William Adams** (d.1805) of Greengates, Tunstall, who had been a pupil of WEDGWOOD and made good quality deep blue jasper wares and cream-coloured earthenwares. He was succeeded by his son **Benjamin** (d.1820). 2. **William Adams** (1748–1831) of Brick House, Burslem and Cobridge, who was a general potter. 3. **William Adams** (1772–1829) of Stoke who made blue-painted wares in the early C19, especially for the American market. His son **William Adams** (1798–1865) made similar wares.

Lit: P. W. L. Adams, *A History of the Adams Family of North Staffordshire*, London 1914; R. Nicholls, *Ten Generations of a Potting Family*, London 1931.

Adamsez, *see* TYNESIDE POTTERIES.

Adlerglas or **Adlerhumpen** A type of German drinking glass – tall, cylindrical-shaped, with or without a cover, and decorated in enamel with a double eagle of the Holy Roman Empire bear-

Adlerglas of German enamelled glass, dated 1604 (Victoria & Albert Museum)

ing on its wings the 56 armorial bearings of the families composing the empire. They were extremely popular from the mid C16 onwards.

Lit: A. von Saldern, *German Enamelled Glass*, New York 1965.

Adzed surface Slightly undulating surface of wood finished with an adze, a type of axe with the blade set at right angles to the handle.

Aegeri, Karl von, *see* EGERI, Karl von.

Aegricanes Technical (Greek) name for the goat's or ram's head, much used in antiquity for the decoration of altars, revived as an ornamental device in the Renaissance and used on furniture in the late C18.

Aelst, Pieter van, *see* BRUSSELS TAPESTRY FACTORY.

Affenkapelle or **Monkey Orchestra** A German type of SINGERIE in porcelain, introduced at MEISSEN *c.*1750–60 probably by J. J. Kändler. Monkey musicians had appeared in Singerie paintings, e.g. by D. Teniers II. Affenkapelle porcelain groups consist of about twenty figures. The Meissen groups were frequently imitated at other European porcelain factories.

Lit: C. Albiker, *Die Meissner Porzellantiere im 18. Jahrhundert*, Berlin 1959.

Affleck, Thomas (1740–95). Leading American cabinet-maker. Born in Scotland, he emigrated in 1763 and settled in Philadelphia where he became an outstanding exponent of the American Chippendale style. He was more restrained and less Rococo than his contemporary Benjamin RANDOLPH. He continued making Chippendale style furniture into the FEDERAL period.

Lit: Joseph Downs, *American Furniture, Queen Anne and Chippendale Periods, in the Henry Francis Du Pont Winterthur Museum*, New York 1952; M. S. Carson in *The Connoisseur* CLXIX (1968) pp. 187–91.

Afshari carpets, *see* PERSIAN CARPETS.

Agata Late C19 American type of coloured glass shaded from white to rose. It was made by the NEW ENGLAND GLASS COMPANY and other factories.

Agate glass An imitation of semi-precious stones, such as chalcedony, jasper and onyx as well as agate, made by mingling molten glass of two or more colours and fashioning vessels or decorative objects from the mixture. Very popular in Venice (where it was called *Calcedonia*) and Germany (where it is called *schmelzglas*) in the Renaissance. Similar in appearance to PÂTE DE VERRE which is made by a different process.

Agate ware Pottery intended to look like agate, made from clays of different colour combined to suggest the veining of a hard stone. Made in Ancient Roman times and very popular in C18 England when it was produced by STAFFORD-

SHIRE potters, notably T. WHIELDON and J. WEDGWOOD.

Airtwist decoration Spiral patterns drawn out of air bubbles, within the stems of C18 and later wine-glasses, especially English.

Airtwist decoration in the stem of an English mid-C18 wine glass (Victoria & Albert Museum)

Ajouré A French term applied to pierced or perforated metalwork.

Akerman, John (*fl.*1719–48). He advertised diamond-cut flint glass in 1719 in London where he was a glass merchant employing several cutters both English and, probably, German. He also sold ceramics. He was Master of the Glass Sellers' Company 1740–48.

Ak-Hissar carpets, *see* TURKISH CARPETS.

Alabaster A fine-grained form of gypsum or limestone, generally white but sometimes reddish or yellowish and translucent if cut in thin laminae. (It was sometimes used for small church windows in the Middle Ages, notably in Italy.) It is easy to carve and consequently rather fragile, and has been used as a medium for sculpture since early times. In England it was much used for small carvings of religious subjects from *c.*1340 until the Reformation, especially Nottingham Alabasters. It became a popular medium once again in late-C18 Italy and various ornamental objects such as vases, pedestals, clock-cases, etc. have been carved out of it ever since.

Alabastron A small cylindrical bottle with a rounded base and spreading rim, made to hold cosmetics in Ancient Egypt and Greece, originally of alabaster, later of glass, pottery or other substance.

Alafia This word – Arabic for benediction – is often used decoratively in stylized Arabic lettering on HISPANO-MORESQUE WARES from the C15 onwards, notably those made at VALENCIA.

Alb A white tunic, reaching to the feet and enveloping the person, worn by priests at religious ceremonies and, occasionally, by consecrated kings. It was decorated with richly embroidered APPARELS at the wrists and along the bottom.

Albany slip A slip of dark brown clay, found near Albany, New York, and frequently used on salt-glazed stoneware from the early C19 onwards.

Albarello (strictly *alberello* but the corrupt form is more usual). A cylindrical drug pot with neck and foot slightly narrower than the body which is often gently waisted. The neck is grooved with a flange round which a parchment cover could be tied. Occasionally it is supplied with strap-shaped handles. The form (and probably the name) originated in Persia in the C12 and became very popular in Europe from the C15, first in Spain (HISPANO-MORESQUE POTTERY) and then in Italy. Vessels of this form were later made by the many potteries which derived from Italian maiolica, in France, the Netherlands, Spain, Portugal, England and Germany. The form remained popular into the C18 especially in Italy

Albarello made at Faenza potteries, c15 (Musée de Cluny, Paris)

where it was revived as a mainly decorative type of vessel in the c19.

Lit: H. Wallis, *The Albarello. A Study of Early Renaissance Maiolica*, London 1904; L. Campanile, *I vasi di Farmacia*, Milan 1973.

Albertolli, Giocondo (1742–1839). He was a leading Neo-Classical ornamental designer, notable for his work as an interior decorator in Milan (Palazzo Reale) and Florence (Palazzo Pitti) and for his volumes of engraved designs which were very influential, even on cabinet makers, notably MAGGIOLINI. He was trained at Parma where he came into contact with the French architect and designer E.-A. Petitot. In 1775 he became professor at the Milan Accademia di Belle Arti and directed the school of ornament there until 1812. His engraved designs were published as *Ornamenti diversi . . . .* 1782; *Alcune decorazione di nobili sale*, 1787; and *Miscellanea per i giovani studiosi del disegno*, 1796. He also published *Corso elementare di ornamenti architettonici*, Milan 1805.

Lit: P. Mezzanotte in *Dizionario Biografico degli Italiani*, Rome 1960, vol. I.

Albini, Franco (b.1905). Italian architect and industrial designer, best known internationally for his revolutionary museum designs and furnishings, e.g. Museo del Palazzo Bianco, Genoa (1951) and Museo del Tesoro di San Lorenzo, Genoa (1954–6). He designed a metal chair in 1936 but all his best furniture dates from after 1950 when he won international acclaim (with Gino COLOMBINI) at the Low Cost Furniture Competition in New York. His recent work includes an excellent dismountable table (1957), circular armchair (designed with Franca Helg 1960) and a metal frame and upholstered foam rubber chair (1962).

Albissola Potteries A group of c17 and c18 maiolica factories near SAVONA. The best was that owned in the mid c18 by **Luigi Levantino**, which produced wares decorated in a lively sketchy manner often reminiscent of Magnasco. Pottery is still made at Albissola. The factory mark is very uncertain.

Lit: C. Barile, *Antiche Ceramiche Liguri, Maioliche di Albissola*, Milan 1965; G. Farriș and V. A. Ferrarese in *Atti della Società Ligure di Storia Patria*, N.S. IX (1969), pp. 13–43.

Alcaraz carpets From the late c15 to the mid c17 Alcaraz was, with CUENCA, the main centre for SPANISH CARPETS. Early products are sombre in colour, usually with a red ground, geometrical in decoration and rather coarse in execution – woollen pile on an undyed woollen foundation, tied with single warp knots, i.e. Spanish knots. From the mid c15 onwards the influence of TURKIȘH CARPETS and of Italian velvets becomes evident in design and in the c17 various types of Turkish carpets were imitated, notably Ushak, Holbein and Lotto types.

Alcora pottery Outstanding c18 Spanish faience factory founded *c*.1727 near Valencia by Don Pedro d'Alcantara, Conde de Aranda and staffed partly from MOUSTIERS. Early products included

Alcora tin-glazed earthenware plaque of 'Christ disputing with the doctors', mid c18 (Temple Newsam House, Leeds)

plates and plaques painted with grotesques in the manner of BERAIN, busts of negroes and pyramidal table-centres surmounted by *putti*. An unusually bold handling of the Rococo style marks the products of the period 1749–89 – statuettes of women in high mantillas, elaborate table fountains, large busts and, notably, wall plaques painted in the full range of HIGH-TEMPERATURE COLOURS at their most brilliant with scenes after French and Italian prints surrounded by glistening white, richly modelled Rococo frames. English Neo-classical wares were imitated 1789–*c.*1800 and Staffordshire statuettes 1810–58. (For factory mark *see* p. 881.)

Lit: M. Escriva de Romani, Conde de Casal, *Historia de la Ceramica de Alcora*, Madrid, 1919; H. Honour in *Apollo* LXII (1955), pp.14–17.

Aldine bindings Early gold-tooled bookbindings made in Venice and elsewhere in N. Italy, usually decorated with simple geometrical patterns of strapwork or with rectangular panels of gold fillets, with the book title or author's name stamped in the middle. Stylized arabesques or a small trefoil leaf (called an 'Aldine fleuron') were often used in the angles.

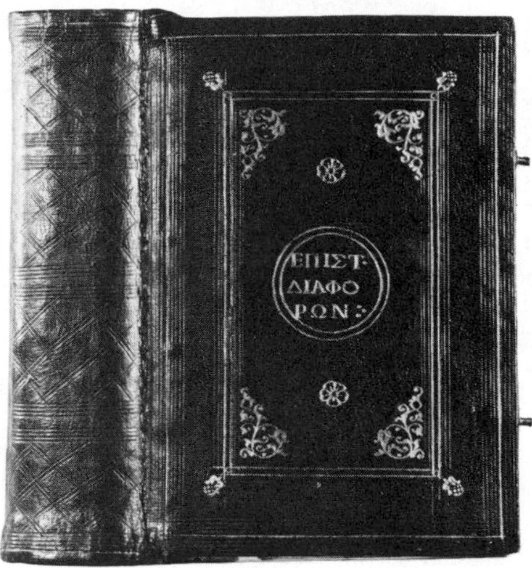

Aldine binding, dated 1499 (Victoria & Albert Museum)

Aldovrandi, Carlo, *see* BOLOGNA POTTERIES.

Ale glass A type of c18 English drinking glass, for beer or ale. It has a long, rather narrow trumpet-shaped bowl, with stem and spreading foot. When the stem is short it is called a Short Ale or a Dwarf Ale.

Lit: P. C. Trubridge in *The Glass Circle* I (1972), pp. 46–57.

Alençon lace Some thirty Venetian lacemakers were brought to France by Colbert in 1665 and settled at Alençon in 1675. They established a LACE industry there under government protection. In the course of the c18 the industry declined but was revived under Napoleon and again during the Second Empire. The name *point d'Alençon* is applied to needlepoint lace with a uniform *fond* and *réseau*, much use of *modes* and rather bold main elements each of which is outlined with a conspicuous *cordonnet*; but such lace was made in many places besides Alençon.

Point d'Alençon lace, c19 (Victoria & Albert Museum)

Lit: G. Despierres, *Histoire du Point d'Alençon*, Paris 1886; B. Palliser, *History of Lace*, rev. M. Jourdain & A. Dryden, London 1902.

Alentours A type of border for tapestries, first produced at the GOBELINS TAPESTRY FACTORY in 1714 in the Don Quixote set designed by Coypel with *alentours* by Belin de Fontenay. Thereafter it was extensively developed at the Gobelins and exploited elsewhere as well. Whereas earlier tapestry borders had simulated picture frames, *alentours* simulated a rich damask panel decorated with *trompe l'oeil* garlands of flowers, ribbons, birds, etc., and it filled the greater part of each hanging. A figurative scene, usually designed by another artist, appeared as a framed picture hung in the centre. The best known examples are those with figurative scenes designed by Boucher and *alentours* by Maurice Jacques. *Alentours* had several practical advantages. They reduced costs because an *alentour* could be carried out by less highly skilled craftsmen than those who made figures, and they introduced some flexibility since they could be readily adapted to clients' requirements as to size. *Illustrated next page.*

Alhambra vase, *see* MALAGA POTTERY.

Alicatados Spanish term meaning 'cut work', applied to near Eastern and Spanish panels of tilework composed of pieces of white and coloured tile sawn into regular shapes after firing and arranged in (generally geometrical) patterns.

Alla Porcellana, *see* PORCELLANA.

Allen, Robert (1744–1835). He was manager of the LOWESTOFT PORCELAIN FACTORY from 1780

Alentours designed by Belin de Fontenay, Gobelins tapestry 'Don Quixote', 1714, after C.-A. Coypel (Quirinal Palace, Rome)

until it closed *c.*1800 when he continued to work independently as a porcelain painter, decorating wares made at ROCKINGHAM and also some imported from China.

Allgood, Thomas, Edward & John, *see* PONTYPOOL JAPANNING FACTORY.

Allison, Michael (d.1855). One of the best furniture-makers working in the Federal style active in New York where he is listed in the directories 1800–1847. He was a contemporary and rival of D. PHYFE. His furniture is rich but restrained, with large expanses of highly figured mahogany veneer and very little decoration, usually no more than stringing, small inlays and pediments of open, pierced design. He began in the Hepplewhite style (e.g. sideboard in Los Angeles County Museum) but later worked in the Sheraton style (e.g. Canterbury and table-desk in H. F. du Pont Winterthur Museum).

Lit: G. Norman-Wilcox in *The Connoisseur* CLXXI (1969), pp. 203–7.

Alloy An amalgam containing either a base metal mixed with a precious metal, e.g. gold and silver coins, or different metals fused together (to form brass, bronze, etc.).

Allwine, Lawrence (*fl.c.*1786). He was an American chair-maker, specializing in Windsor chairs, usually painted or gilded. He invented a fast-drying varnish named after him 'Allwine Gloss'.

Almorratxa or **Morratxa** A type of Spanish glass rose-water sprinkler. The body is usually ovoid or pear-shaped resting on a high spreading foot. The vessel is filled through the neck. Four slender upright spouts for sprinkling rise from the shoulder. It is found especially in Catalonia.

Almorratxa: Catalan glass, c17 or c18 (Victoria & Albert Museum)

Alpujarra A type of Spanish peasant bedspread or rug, made in Alpujarra near Granada. It is probably Moorish in origin. Rather coarse and heavy, it has some 20 loops per square inch. Most alpujarras are in two colours but some have as many as ten. The fringe is woven separately.

Altare glasshouse Founded near Genoa probably in the C11. Little is known of its products but it played a part of great importance in the history of European glass since its craftsmen (unlike those of the VENETIAN GLASSHOUSES) were from 1495 required to do a spell of work abroad, and some of them helped to found glasshouses in France and the Netherlands.

Lit: R. Schmidt, *Das Glas*, Berlin 1922; W. B. Honey, *A Handbook for the Study of Glass Vessels*, London 1946; I. Schlosser, *Das alte Glas*, Brunswick, 1965.

Altdorfer, Albrecht (*c.*1480–1538). German Renaissance painter and engraver. His numerous prints include some designs for silver which typify the style of the early Renaissance Nuremberg craftsmen, e.g. handsomely proportioned covered cups simply decorated with gadrooning and an occasional acanthus leaf, described as Renaissance because of the absence of Gothic features rather than because of the presence of Classical or Italianate ones. He also made ornamental engravings which probably served as models to furniture makers.

Lit: L. Lorenze in *Repertorium für Kunstwissenschaft*, XXVIII, 1905; H. Hildebrandt, *Die Architektur bei Albrecht Altdorfer*, Strassburg 1908; F. Winzinger, *Albrecht Altdorfer*, Munich 1963.

Altmann, Johann Gottlieb, *see* BUNZLAU POTTERIES.

Alumina pottery, *see* COPENHAGEN PORCELAIN FACTORY.

Amber 1. A yellowish, translucent fossil resin found chiefly on the southern shores of the Baltic. It has been used since the Middle Ages for jewellery, decorative objects such as vases, and for decorating furniture.

2. An alloy of 4 parts gold and 1 part silver.

Amberg, Adolf (1874–1913). German sculptor and metalworker trained at the Berlin Kunstgewerbeschule, then at the Académie Julian in Paris and the Berlin Academy. He was employed 1894–1904 by the firm of Bruckmann & Sohn of Heilbronn designing silver table-wares and ornamental pieces, notably a large silver fountain called 'German Music' executed in collaboration with the architect Otto Rieth and shown at the Paris International Exhibition of 1900. In 1904–5 he executed the models of numerous exotic male and female figures for the 'Marriage Procession' table-centre made by the BERLIN PORCELAIN FACTORY.

Adolf Amberg: Indian girl with peacock, Berlin Porcelain, modelled 1904/5 (Karl H. Bröhan Collection, Berlin)

Lit: Porzellan-Kunst: Sammlung Karl H. Bröhan, Exh. Cat., Schloss Charlottenburg, Berlin 1969.

Amberg pottery A Bavarian faience factory founded by Simon Hetzendörfer in 1759 and continuing to operate until 1910. Most products were simple household wares of white faience, sometimes decorated in colours, during the earlier years, and of cream-coloured earthenware from *c.*1790 onwards. But at least one finely decorated piece is known – a tankard in the Bayerisches Nationalmuseum in Munich. In the C19 the factory made reproductions of LUDWIGSBURG porcelain models. (For factory mark *see* p. 881.)

Lit: A. Stohr, *Deutsche Fayencen und deutsches Steingut*, Berlin 1919; K. Hüseler, *Deutsche Fayencen*, Stuttgart 1956–8.

Amberina A type of late C19 American glass of the fancy or ornamental type known as Art Glass to which AGATA, FAVRIL, PEACHBLOW, etc., also belong. Amberina is a clear lead glass, pale amber to ruby in colour, and was used for table-wares as well as ornaments. It was first made by the NEW ENGLAND GLASS COMPANY in 1883 and later produced also by the LIBBEY GLASS CO.

Amboyna wood A hard wood with a close grain and a beautifully curled and mottled figure, not unlike THUYA WOOD. It is light red-brown to orange in colour and comes from the amboyna tree, *pterospermum indicum*, found in the Moluccas. It has been much used in marquetry.

Amelung, Johann Friedrich (*fl.*1784–95). A native of Bremen who emigrated to the U.S. and, with the financial assistance of a group of Bremen merchants, founded in 1784 the Amelung Glasshouse at New Bremen near Fredrickstown, Maryland. (It was also known as the New Bremen Glasshouse, the Etna Glass Works and the American Glass Manufactory.) This was a fairly large establishment staffed mainly by German immigrants. It produced a fine if slightly smoky crystal glass and an engraved covered goblet of this material was sent back to Bremen in 1788 as a proof of achievement. A similar goblet engraved with the name of a Baltimore merchant is in the Maryland Historical Society, and others are recorded. Coloured glass vessels were also made. But the factory was mainly occupied in making window glass, looking-glass, bottles and lenses. The factory was not, however, a financial success and it closed in 1795.

Lit: H. and G. S. McKearin, *Two Hundred Years of American Blown Glass*, New York 1950.

Amelung Glasshouse, *see* AMELUNG, J. F.

Amen glass A type of JACOBITE GLASS made to commemorate the rising of 1715, it is a footed stem glass decorated with a diamond point engraved prayer ending with Amen, and with the letters I.R. elaborately scrolled with a concealed figure of eight and a crown.

American Pottery Company A factory founded at Jersey City, New Jersey, in 1833. It was the first in America to succeed in producing printed wares to compete with those imported from England. The designs were often of local and sometimes topical appeal. It also made wares, especially jugs, decorated in relief and covered with a thick brown ROCKINGHAM glaze. The factory closed in 1854.

Amphora A tall two-handled vessel with a wide foot and spreading neck, used by the ancient Greeks and Romans for oil, wine, etc.

Ampulla A small vessel or vial, usually of glass, for oil or perfume as used by the ancient Romans for toilet purposes or for anointing the dead. It usually had a round body and narrow neck. The name and form survived as a liturgical vessel in the Western Church and some notable examples were used in coronations (though not always preserving the original form).

Amstel porcelain factory In 1784 the **Oude Loosdrecht** factory (formerly the WEESP PORCELAIN FACTORY) closed and moved to Oude Amstel near Amsterdam where it continued under the direction of **F. Dauber** until 1799. It was then sold, moved to Nieuwer Amstel and closed in 1820. Its products are undistinguished. (For factory mark *see* p. 881.)

Lit: E. Schrijver *Hollands Porcelein*, Bussum 1966.

An Hua decorations Literally 'secret decorations' – i.e. those incised or painted in white slip on Chinese porcelain in such a way that they can be seen only when the piece is held up to the light, like a watermark in paper. They first appear in the Yung-lo period (1403–24).

Anatolian carpets, *see* TURKISH CARPETS.

Andalusian glasshouses The most interesting group of Spanish factories established in a region where glass has been in constant production since Roman times. The main centres were at Castril de la Peña and neighbouring villages of Don Fadrique and Pinar de la Vidriera. The material is rarely colourless and generally of a bluish or brownish olive tone. Inspiration was derived from HISPANO-MORESQUE art and, after the c15, Venetian glass. Forms are often fantastic with much use of applied threads pincered into ridges and points. Vases of basically Persian shape, with a narrow waist, a neck flaring out

Andalusian glass vase, c17
(Victoria & Albert Museum)

into a mouth as wide as the base and a pair of large wing-shaped handles, were a speciality and are still being made.

Lit: Alice Wilson Frothingham, *Spanish Glass*, London 1964.

Andiron A metal object, usually a horizontal bar supported on feet with an upright decorative frieze at the front, to hold burning logs above the level of the hearth. In French a '*chenet*'. It is generally simple and utilitarian but sometimes very elaborately wrought in the style of the time, from Gothic to Neo-Classical, and normally made of iron but for the greater houses also of bronze, brass or even silver. Louis XIV had many *chenets* made of silver and in c18 France the decorative part was frequently of gilt bronze. They were much more frequently made in pairs than singly. Pairs of small andirons are called fire-dogs, and from the Renaissance onwards were often used in conjunction with a pair of purely decorative andirons.

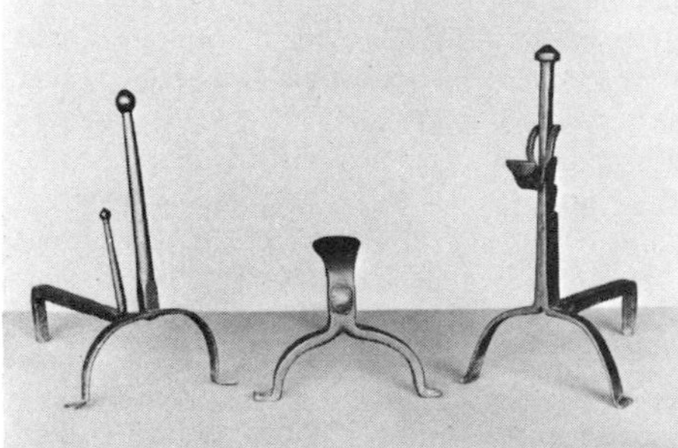

Andirons from Sussex, c18 (Victoria & Albert Museum)

Andreoli, Giorgio, called **Maestro Giorgio** (*fl.*1492–*c.*1553). He was a notable maiolica painter working at GUBBIO who specialized in LUSTRE painting and was particularly successful in combining a rich ruby lustre with a golden yellow. He came from Intra in N. Italy but was settled at Gubbio by 1498 with his brother **Salimbene** (d.*c.*1522). His early work is difficult to identify. Pieces bearing his mark date from 1518 to 1541. At first he painted original compositions, generally religious subjects, but later he relied largely on engravings after Raphael. His son **Vincenzo** (d.1576) is also known to have worked as a potter.

Lit: J. Chompret, *Répertoire de la majolique italienne*, Paris 1949; B. Rackham, *Italian Maiolica*, London 1952.

Andiron of gilt bronze, French, late c18 (Louvre)

Giorgio Andreoli: maiolica plate, Gubbio, early c16 (Musée de Cluny, Paris)

Andries, Guido (*fl.*1512–*c.*1541). He was the leading potter in Antwerp where he is recorded in 1512 making tin-glazed earthenware. He may have been identical with the 'Guido da Savino' mentioned in 1556–9 by PICCOLPASSO as having emigrated from Castel Durante to Antwerp. His factory in Antwerp was carried on by his sons **Lucas, Frans** and **Joris Andriessen**. Another son, **Jasper Andries**, is recorded in Norwich *c.*1567 and London.

Angarano pottery A subsidiary of the nearby NOVE POTTERY AND PORCELAIN FACTORY. Cream-coloured earthenware figures and groups were made in the 1770s.

Angell, Joseph III (*c.*1816–*c.*1891). Proprietor of a firm of London silversmiths which he inherited in 1849. At the Great Exhibition of 1851 he showed a number of vessels, table-centres, etc., very richly decorated with much chased and relief work and enamelling. A casket with medallions of Anthony and Cleopatra designed by him is in the Victoria & Albert Museum.

Angermair, Christof (d.1632/3). Notable German Baroque ivory carver of virtuoso skill in rendering minute detail. His masterpiece is the elaborate coin-cabinet in the Bayerische Nationalmuseum, Munich.

Lit: H. Kreisel, *Die Kunst des deutschen Möbels*, Munich 1968.

Angoulême Pottery French faience factory established in 1748 by **Bernard Sazerac** (d.1774) and active until the late C19. It began by imitating the wares of ROUEN and MOUSTIERS. Large figures of lions, dogs, sphinxes, etc., probably intended for garden ornaments, are among the more interesting products. An employee of this concern, **Pierre Fleurat**, founded a second factory in 1782.

Lit: J. Chompret *et al.*, *Répertoire de la faïence française*, Paris 1933–5.

Animal carpets A type of Persian carpet of which the famous Hunting Carpets form part, *see* PERSIAN CARPETS.

Annealing A toughening process by exposure to continuous and slowly diminishing heat, it is used especially in the making of glass which would otherwise be very brittle, but metals and porcelain and pottery are also sometimes subjected to annealing.

Anreiter von Zirnfeld, Anton (*c.*1725–1801). He was a notable porcelain painter, working at DOCCIA and the VIENNA PORCELAIN FACTORY. He was the son of **Johann Karl Wendelin Anreiter von Zirnfeld** (*c.*1702–47), a HAUSMALER working in Vienna until 1737 when Carlo Ginori engaged him as chief painter for the Doccia factory. After beginning at Doccia under his father, Anton returned to Vienna in 1746 and was chief painter at the Vienna factory from 1754 to 1801. Like his father he specialized in delicately painted landscapes and also executed figure subjects.

Lit: A. Lane, *Italian Porcelain*, London 1954; L. Ginori-Lisci, *La porcellana di Doccia*, Milan 1963.

Ansbach pottery & porcelain factory A faience factory was founded *c.*1708–10 by **Matthias Baur** and a Delft-trained potter **J. K. Ripp** (who went to the NUREMBERG POTTERY FACTORY in 1712). Early products were blue and white (the ground is bluish) decorated in the 1720s in a restrained version of the *style rayonnant* of ROUEN. After

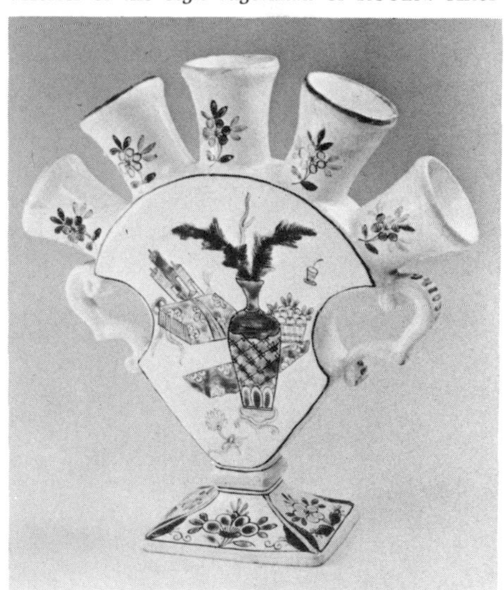

Ansbach tin-glazed earthenware, 'Green Family' tulipière, c.1730–45 (Kunstgewerbemuseum, Berlin)

1730 production was greatly influenced by **Johann Georg Christoph Popp** who became manager in 1747. He was responsible for the 'Green Family' Ansbach wares which made the factory's name. These were jugs, tankards, etc., in traditional south German forms but decorated in high-temperature colours with imitation Chinese *famille verte* designs. Sometimes the decorations were imitated from IMARI wares. The factory declined after Popp's death in 1791. It later became a State concern producing white earthenware until it closed in 1839.

A porcelain factory was opened in 1757 as an extension of the faience factory and various craftsmen came to Ansbach from the MEISSEN PORCELAIN FACTORY including JOHANN FRIEDRICH KÄNDLER. Nevertheless the style of Ansbach products was closer to that of the Berlin factory than to Meissen. The finest rank among the best German porcelain. It closed in 1860. (For factory mark *see* p. 881.)

Lit: M. Krieger, *Ansbacher Fayence und Porzellan, Gesamt Katalog der Sammlung Adolf Bayer*, Ansbach 1963; A. Bayer, *Die Ansbacher Fayence Fabrik*, Brunswick 1959; A. Bayer, *Ansbacher Porzellan*, Ansbach 1933.

Anse de Panier French term for the handle of a basket, applied to similarly shaped decorative motifs especially in C16 metalwork, and to C18 chair backs of segmentally arched outline.

Anthemion Greek word for a flower, used to describe a band of architectural enrichment on a cornice, the necking of an Ionic capital, etc., consisting of alternating palmettes and lotus motifs or two types of palmette (one of open, the other of closed form). This type of ornament was much used in the late C18 when the elements were arranged not only one beside the other in a horizontal band (as in Greek architecture) but also one above another in vertical strips. A type of PALMETTE resembling honeysuckle flowers is sometimes called an anthemion.

Anthemion

Antifixae Classical architectural roof ornament used on pedimented furniture in the Neo-Classical, Regency and Empire styles.

Antimacassar A small covering to protect the back of an upholstered chair or sofa from contact with the sitter's head. It was widely used in the later C19, often taking the form of a white crochet-work panel. The name derives from Macassar oil, then commonly used as a hair dressing. In the U.S. it was later called a 'tidy'.

Antique, The Term used since the Renaissance to describe Greek and Roman art. The term 'after the Antique' refers to decorative motifs, etc. copied from Greek or Roman originals. But any object made more than a century ago may be called *an* antique.

Antler furniture, *see* HORN FURNITURE.

Antonibon, Giovanni Battista, *see* NOVE POTTERY AND PORCELAIN FACTORIES.

Antwerp lace A strong rather heavy looking pillow lace made from the C17: a two handled vase is the dominant decorative motif. Several other types of lace were made at Antwerp, notably MECHLIN. *See also* LACE.

Lit: P. G. Trendell, *Victoria & Albert Museum Guide to the Collection of Lace*, London 1930.

Antwerp potteries The main centre for tin-glazed earthenware in the Netherlands in the early C16. The production of 'maiolica' in Antwerp appears to have been started in 1508 by Guido ANDRIES who probably emigrated from Castel Durante. Other prominent potters included Hans or Jan Floris, Jan BOGHAERT and Barnaert Vierleger. Their work is distinguished by the use in its decoration of strap-work and scrolled devices of the *ferronerie* type associated with the Antwerp designers Cornelis FLORIS and Cornelis Bos. The Antwerp potteries gradually lost their lead after 1568 and during the next century were succeeded by DELFT.

Lit: B. Rackham, *Early Netherlands Maiolica*, London 1926; J. Helbig in *Bulletin des Musées Royaux d'Art et d'Histoire*, 1947.

Antwerp tapestry factories They were active from the C15 onwards and in the C16 produced floral borders and *verdures* for Brussels and Oudenarde tapestries. The finest Antwerp tapestries were made in the C17, often very reminiscent in their design of paintings by Rubens and Jordaens (*see* WAIUTERS, Michel).

Aogai Japanese lacquer inlaid with mother-of-pearl derived from the Haliotis shell.

Apengeter, Hans, von Sassenlant (*fl.*1327–44). German bronze and brass worker and one of the very few to sign his work. He made bells, candlesticks, door-handles, etc., e.g. the seven-armed bronze candelabra (1327) in Kolberg cathedral, the brass baptismal basin (1332) in the Marienkirche in Lübeck, and the baptismal basin (1340 or 1344) in the Nikolaikirche, Kiel. Born in Halberstadt, he worked in Lübeck from 1332 to 1342 – also elsewhere in north Germany, notably Rostock, Wismar, Stettin, Göttingen and Hildesheim.

Apostle spoon A silver spoon with the top of the handle fashioned as a tiny statuette of an Apostle, very popular in England 1490–1675 and also made on the continent, mainly in Germany. Sometimes (but not always) they were made in sets of thirteen, a dozen topped with figures of the Apostles and one, the Master spoon, with a figure of Christ. *Illustrated next column.*

Lit: C. G. Rupert, *Apostle Spoons*, Oxford 1929.

Apparel A medieval term, revived in the C19, for embroidered panels applied to such vestments as ALBS. They were often very rich, with gold and silver thread, etc., and sometimes with pearls and jewels.

Applique French term for a sconce or other fitting attached to a wall or to a piece of furniture.

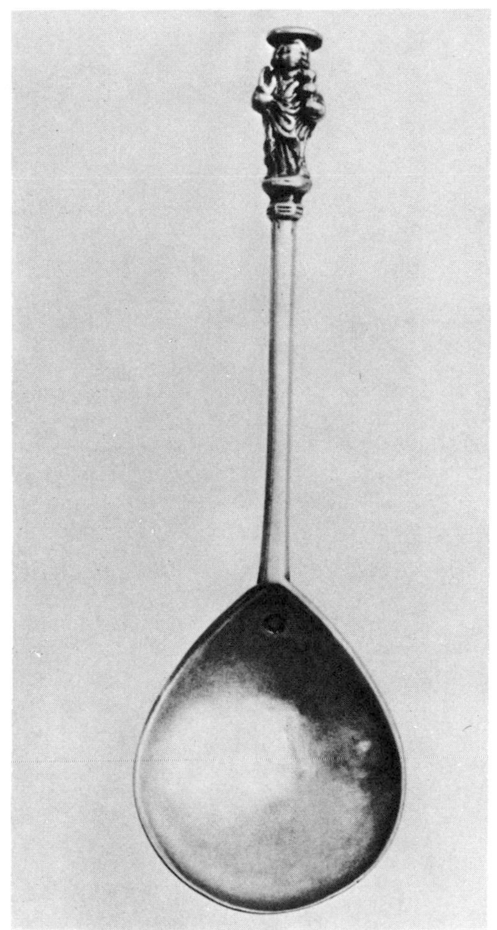

Apostle spoon, silver, London 1504 (Ashmolean Museum, Oxford)

Appliqué or **applied work** Textile technique whereby patterns or representational scenes are formed by attaching pieces of fabric to another fabric of contrasting colour and texture. The Bayeux tapestry (C11) is the most famous example. *Illustrated next page.*

Aprey pottery factory Founded by **Jacques Lallement Baron d'Aprey** in 1744, it was taken over *c.*1769 by **François Ollivier** from the NEVERS POTTERY FACTORY until 1792 and the

Appliqué silk panel, French, c17 (Musée des Arts Décoratifs, Paris)

best wares date from this period, especially those in the Strassburg 'porcelain style' in enamel colours, e.g. by Jacques Jarry who was employed between 1772 and 1781 and was famous for his decorations of birds and flowers, and Antoine Mege who was employed from 1776 onwards and painted birds and landscapes. After the Revolution the factory continued making common faience until 1885. (Porcelain is said to have been made at Aprey but this is uncertain.) (For factory mark *see* p. 881.)

Lit: P. Deveaux, *Les faïences d'Aprey*, Paris 1908; E. Tilmans, *Faïences de France*, Paris 1954.

Apron piece Ornamental member below the seat rail of a chair or settee, or below the under-framing of a cabinet-stand, side-table, etc. It is sometimes called a *lambrequin* or a *label*.

Apt pottery factory Founded at Le Castelet near Apt by **César Moulin**, it remained in his family until 1852. Meanwhile other pottery factories opened in or near Apt which still remains an important centre for pottery-making. The most characteristic wares of the original factory are in a yellow and brown marbled pottery (perhaps imitated from Wedgwood's AGATE WARE). Figures and groups as well as useful wares were made. The best known C19 factories were those of Elzéar Bennet and La Veuve Arnoux.

Lit: A. Lesur & Tardy, *Les poteries et les faïences françaises*, Paris 1957–60; M. Ernould-Gandouet, *La Céramique en France au XIX siècle*, Paris 1969; E. Fabre in *Keramos* 25 (1964), pp. 39–61.

Aquamanile A medieval bronze ewer for ablutions at table, often of zoomorphic shape. The finest date from the C13 and were made by MOSAN METALWORKERS in the form of lions (often with dragons crouching on their backs to serve as handles), mounted knights, monsters or Campaspe riding on the unfortunate Aristotle.

Aquamanile: brass. Hildesheim, mid C13, workshop of the 'Meisters der Domtaufe' (Kunstgewerbemuseum, Berlin)

Arabesques Intricate and fanciful surface decoration based on rhythmic linear patterns of scrolling and interlacing foliage, tendrils, etc., usually covering the entire surface with a network of fine ornament in zigzags, spirals, knots, etc. Human figures are not used – as they are in GROTESQUES.

The origin of arabesques is disputed but it would appear to have been in Saracenic ornament, especially that found on objects decorated by Moslem craftsmen in Europe, e.g. VENETIAN SARACENIC METALWORK. Such objects are decorated with intricate interlaced patterns (either strapwork or foliated) of a type known then as Arabesque or Moresque. Similar decorations were used for book-bindings, textiles and pottery, and engraved designs were published from *c.*1530 onwards by

Arabesque decorations on a cup designed by Holbein, from an etching by Hollar (Victoria & Albert Museum)

such designers as Francesco Pelegrini, Jean Gourmont, Holbein, Jamnitzer and Firens. The development of arabesques is exactly contemporary with that of STRAPWORK by ROSSO at Fontainebleau, but the exact nature of the connection between them is unknown.

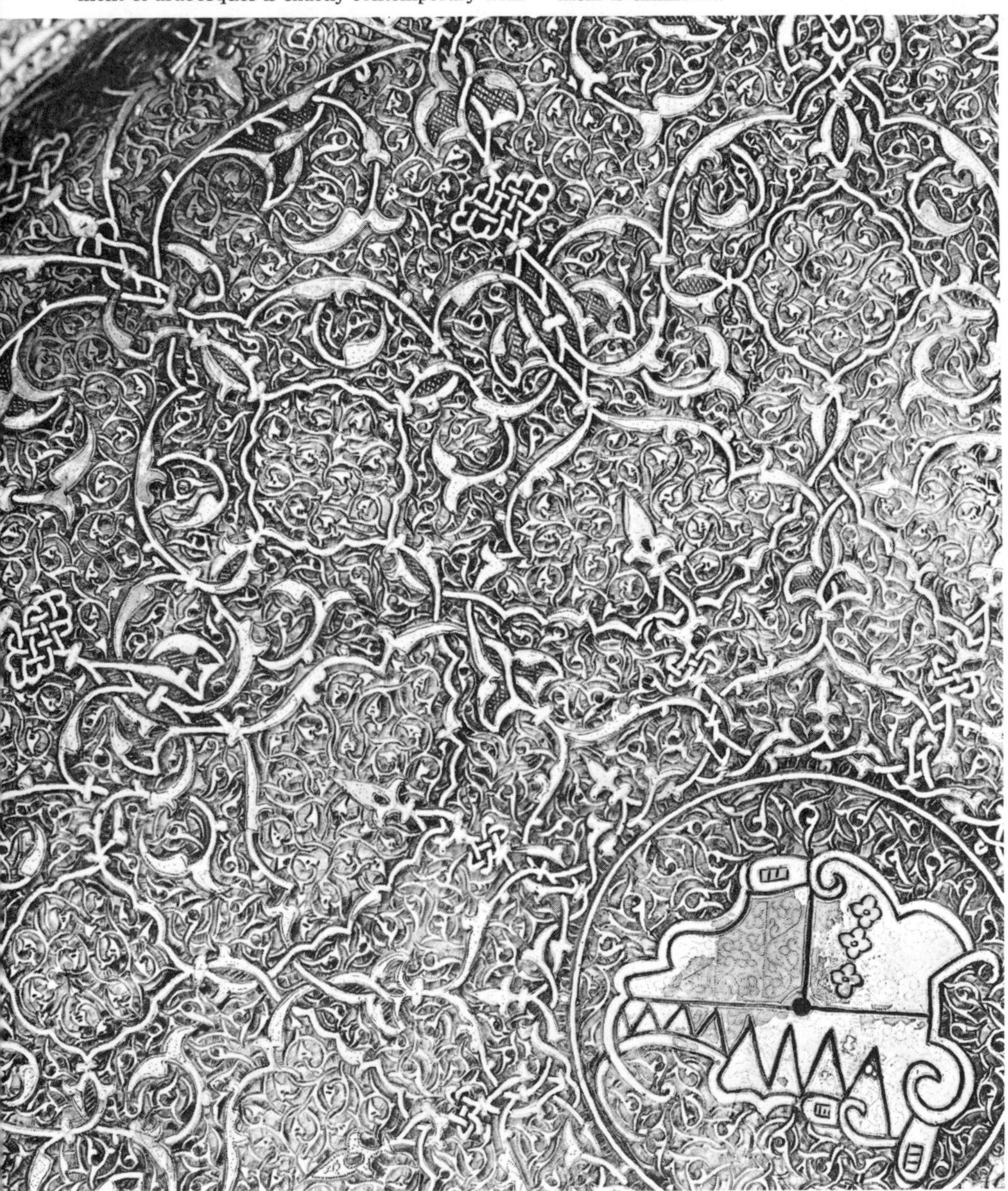

Arabesque decoration on Venetian-Saracenic damascened brass dish, early c16, detail (Victoria & Albert Museum)

Arabesque by Jean Gourmont (d.1551)

Lit: P. Ward-Jackson, 'Some main streams and tributaries in European ornament 1500–1750, Part 2: The Arabesque' in *Victoria & Albert Museum Bulletin*, July 1967.

Arabia pottery Leading Finnish pottery factory, founded outside Helsinki in 1874 as a subsidiary of the Swedish RÖRSTRAND POTTERY. It began by producing table and kitchen wares in undecorated, glazed stoneware and then bone china. In 1884 it became an independent company, though Rörstrand continued to hold the majority of shares until 1916. From 1895 it produced some distinguished ART NOUVEAU vases designed and painted by Thure Oberg (1871–1935) – the best Finnish examples of this style. The factory was modernized in 1922 and began to produce good, frankly modern household wares in the 1930s. Kaj FRANCK became the chief designer in 1946 and it now produces some of the best available modern pottery and porcelain, e.g. the 'Kilta' series of heat-proof earthenware cooking and table wares in a range of plain colours (designed 1948 and marketed from 1953), and the somewhat similar dark brown 'Liekki' wares designed by Ulla Procopé 1957 (in this series the lids of cooking vessels may also be used as serving dishes). The factory has also provided facilities for artist potters (e.g. Toini Muona and Kyllikki Salmenhaara, both making thrown stoneware) and marketed their wares.

Arabia stoneware by Kaj Franck, 1955 (Kunstindustrimuseet, Copenhagen)

Arbalète French word for a cross-bow used to describe profiles of similar contour. A commode that is double-bowed in front is said to be *en arbalète* or *en arc d'arbalète.*

Arcaded decoration Early type of ornamentation, common on chests, representing a series of arches on columns or pilasters.

Arcaded decoration on c12 chest from Valère Castle (Musèe cantonal de Valère, Switzerland)

Arcanist A carrier of the secret (or *arcanum*) of the materials and processes used in the manufacture of hard-paste PORCELAIN.

Archambo, Peter (d.1767). He was an English silversmith of French origin and is first recorded in 1720 when his mark was entered at Goldsmiths Hall, London. He began with a plain, simple style but by 1733 had adopted a French Rococo manner. His son **Peter** (d.1768) was apprenticed to Paul de LAMERIE in 1728 and was in partnership with **Peter Meure** 1749–55. (For his mark *see* p. 893.)

Architrave Correctly the lowest section of an ENTABLATURE, but also, loosely, the moulded frame surrounding a doorway, window or other opening.

Ardabil carpets Two of the most famous of all PERSIAN CARPETS, measuring more than 10 × 5 metres, of an intricate floral pattern with a large central medallion from which lamps are 'suspended', completed 1539–40 and said to have been housed in the mosque at Ardabil in N.W. Persia until the late C19. As both had been damaged, portions of one were used to repair the other which was acquired by the Victoria & Albert Museum in 1893. The central part of the other is in the Los Angeles County Museum and a border fragment is in the Textile Museum, Washington D.C. The design has often been copied on a smaller scale. *Illustrated next column.*

Lit: D. Sylvester, *Islamic Carpets from the Joseph V. McMullan Collection,* Exh. Cat., Arts Council, London 1972; R. Stead, *The Ardabil Carpets,* Malibu 1974.

The Ardabil Carpet, 1539–40 (Victoria & Albert Museum)

Ardus pottery factory Started in *c.*1739 by François Duval with staff from the MONTPELLIER POTTERY FACTORY, it became a 'manufacture royale' in 1749 and was leased by Lestrade and Lapierre, later of MONTAUBON. Early wares are in a Moustier-Bérain style. After 1770 enamel decoration was introduced. Latterly it produced *faïence-fine* and closed in 1786.

Lit: E. Forestié, *Les anciennes faïenceries de Montauban, Ardus,* etc. Montauban 1929; E. Tilman, *Faïence de France,* Paris 1954.

Arfe (or **Arphe**), Enrique de (*c.*1470–*c.*1545). The founder of the most notable family of Spanish goldsmiths. He was born in Germany and probably trained at Cologne, but settled in Spain by 1500. Shortly after that date he was working on a vast silver *custodia* or portable tabernacle for León Cathedral (finished 1522, destroyed 1809). He later supplied similar tabernacles in an exuberant flamboyant Gothic style for the cathedrals of Cordova and Toledo. The latter is 10 feet high, weighs 172 kg. and has 260 statuettes. It is a mesh of gothic archways, set with pearls, etc. His

Enrique de Arfe: silver-gilt custodia, *1518 (Cordova Cathedral)*

son **Antonio** (1510–*c.*1566) adopted the Renaissance or rather the Plateresque style with a lavish use of classical motifs heaped one on top of another as in the large silver tabernacles in Santiago Cathedral (1539–45), Fuente Ovejuna (Cordova) and Medina de Riosco (Valladolid). The third generation is represented by Antonio's more famous son **Juan de Arfe y Villafane** (1535–1603) who made the large tabernacles for Avila Cathedral (1564–71), Seville Cathedral (1580–87) but much altered) and the processional cross for Burgos (1592). His was a severely classicizing style the merits of which he proclaimed in his writings, warning his compatriots against the use of Flemish and French pattern books. He wrote a treatise on the art of the goldsmith *Quelatador de la plata oro y piedras* (1572), a description of his Seville tabernacle (1587) and a treatise on proportions, partly in verse, *De varia comensuracion para esculptura y Architectura* (1585). He was much employed by Philip III.

Lit: F. J. Sanchez Canton, *Los Arfes*, Madrid 1920; Charles Oman, *The Golden Age of Hispanic Silver 1400–1665*, London 1968.

Argentine German or NICKEL SILVER: it was also called Argentan.

Argyle or **Argyll** An English C18 type of gravy warmer in the form of a coffee-pot, usually of metal but also of pottery (e.g. Wedgwood creamware). The gravy was kept warm by a hot-water jacket system. It is first recorded *c.*1760. The origin of the name is obscure. It is said to be connected with the 4th Duke of Argyll.

Argyll: late C18 Sheffield Plate (Victoria & Albert Museum)

Lit: H. Newman in *Apollo* LXXXIX (1969), pp. 98–105.

Arita porcelain factories The first and best group of Japanese porcelain factories, founded at Sarayama near Arita, on Kyushu, by a Korean potter **Ri Sampei** who in 1616 discovered a source of *kaolin* at Izumiyama and moved an entire Korean village of potters (some 900 people) to the district. The first products have a fine white body decorated with linear and floral designs in underglaze cobalt blue, rather like late MING provincial Chinese porcelain which was also imitated in Korea. Such wares were extensively exported to Europe by the Dutch who, from 1641, had a trading post nearby at Deshima. They included tankards and jugs of European form intended for the European market. (Similar wares were made at Mikawachi and exported from HIRADO.) Enamelled wares in the KAKIEMON style were made in the district from the mid C17 onwards and much richer IMARI WARES intended for export to Europe from slightly later. In the C18 the Arita factories seem to have imitated the products of the KUTANI PORCELAIN FACTORY for the home market. Much of the finest Japanese porcelain was made *c.*1716–35 in kilns at Okawachi near Arita, founded *c.*1660 and exclusively patronized by members of a local noble family, Nabeshima – mainly plates very boldly painted with landscapes, flowers, birds, etc., sometimes interlaced patterns recalling the rich designs of silk kimonos, in underglaze blue combined with overglaze enamels. Porcelain factories still flourish in and around Arita.

Lit: Soame Jenyns, *Japanese Porcelain*, London 1965.

Imari porcelain vase with brocaded decorations, made at Arita, C17–18, (Victoria & Albert Museum)

Armada chest Fanciful C19 name for a heavy iron-bound coffer used for the storage of valuables, generally of German make and rarely dating from before the C17.

Armadio Italian for cupboard. In origin a CASSONE with doors instead of a lid, later (C16) developing into a two-storied piece with pilasters and other massive and monumental architectural elements. Frequently made for sacristies.

Armoire A cupboard, usually of a somewhat monumental character, decorated with pilasters, etc. But the word is often applied to the upright or drop-front secretaire (*secrétaire en armoire*) which looks like a cupboard when closed. *Illustrated opposite, left.*

Armoire à deux corps French term for a piece of case furniture consisting of two cupboards, each with two doors, set one above the other, the front and sides of the upper one being recessed. It generally has an architectural framework with pilasters and a crowning pediment. *Illustrated opposite, right.*

Armorial porcelain Any porcelain plates, tureens, etc., on which a coat of arms is the main decorative motif, but especially CHINESE EXPORT PORCELAIN.

Armoire, c16 French (Hospice, Villaneuve les Avignon)

(Right) Armoire à deux corps, c17 French (Louvre)

Arnhem pottery The best Dutch tin-glazed earthenware factory apart from those at DELFT. It was active 1755–73 and began by producing imitations of Delft wares. Later products included some pieces decorated in high-temperature colours with scenes after the Rococo prints of J. E. Nilson, others influenced by the Swiss faience factories, and a group of wares painted with enamel colours like those of STRASBOURG. A few figures, often incorporated with little bowls to serve as salt-cellars, were made in the late 1750s and early 1760s. From the late 1760s black basaltes and cream-coloured wares were also made.

Lit: J. M. Noothoven van Goor in *Keramos* 1 (1958), pp. 7–26 and 2 (1958), pp. 3–21.

Arnoux, Léon, *see* MINTON'S POTTERY AND PORCELAIN FACTORY.

Arraiolos carpets A Portuguese type of needlework wool carpet made at Arraiolos, between Lisbon and Elvas, since the Middle Ages. Up to the c18 they usually derive from Persian carpets in design and colouring but later they became more original with colours restricted to blues and yellows. Examples are in the Museu de Arte Antiga, Lisbon, the Palácio Nacional de Queluz, and the Victoria & Albert Museum, London. *Illustrated next page.*

Lit: J. Barreira (ed.), *Arte portuguesa,* I n.p., pp. 265–320; Robert C. Smith, *The Art of Portugal,* London 1968.

Arras Old English name for a tapestry, named after the N. French town which exported many hangings to England.

Arras porcelain factory Began producing soft-paste porcelain in 1770 but closed in 1790. Tablewares only were made, very simply decorated in blue or crimson monochrome with sprigs of flowers or chinoiseries. More elaborate, Sèvres-style decorations, with gilt borders, are found on c19 forgeries using old Arras porcelain. (For factory mark *see* p. 881.)

Arraiolos carpet
(Museu Nacional de Arte Antiga, Lisbon)

Arras tapestry factories Established in the late C13 and apparently the most important in Europe by the mid C14 (though no works survive from this early period). After 1384, when Arras was annexed to the Duchy of Burgundy, they were lavishly patronized by the Burgundian Court and also profited from the alliance between England and Burgundy which permitted them to import English wool and export tapestries across the Channel. But the only product that can be ascribed to Arras with confidence is the set with the story of *St Piat and St Eleuthère* of 1402 (Tournai Cathedral), woven in wools of no more than twelve different shades. A work of striking Gothic realism, it shows groups of rather grumpy-faced figures against a background of castellations and tightly packed half-timbered houses. Other tapestries usually attributed to Arras include a Passion series (Saragossa Cathedral: Musée Cinquantenaire, Brussels; Vatican Museum) and several secular subjects: a *Trojan War* cycle, *The Story of Clovis* and, best of all, the *Chatsworth Hunts* (Victoria & Albert Museum) of *c.*1425–50 – a set of four large panels each some 13 × 40 ft, depicting courtiers in clothes of a fantastic stylishness, pursuing various beasts and birds amongst forests of tiny trees and over ground studded with fresh spring flowers. These may, however, have been woven at the TOURNAI TAPESTRY FACTORIES, which were open to similar artistic influences and also supplied the Burgundian Court. By the mid C15 the Arras factories began to decline as Tournai took the lead, but they remained active until the early C16.

Arras tapestry: detail of the Chatsworth Hunts, *c.1425–50 (Victoria & Albert Museum)*

Lit: H. Göbel, *Wandteppiche*, Leipzig 1923–34; R.-A. Weigert, *French Tapestry*, London 1962; D. Heinz, *Europäische Wandteppiche*, Brunswick 1963; G. Wingfield-Digby, *The Devonshire Hunts Tapestries*, London 1971.

Arrasene A fine wool or silk chenille thread used in embroidery especially in the C19.

Arretine potteries Arretium (modern Arezzo) was an important centre for the production of 'red gloss' pottery (TERRA SIGILLATA) especially in the late C1 B.C. when the workshop of Marcus Perennius Tigranus, who probably came from the E. Mediterranean and many of whose workers bore Greek names, set new standards for the technical quality and design of wares ornamented with figurative subjects in crisp relief. There were many other potteries in the district producing similar wares until *c*.30 A.D.

Lit: R. J. Charleston, *Roman Pottery*, London 1955.

Arris Sharp edge at the join of two surfaces forming an angle, as on a prism.

Arrow vase A Chinese type of vase with a long cylinder neck at the top of which are two tubular loops or lugs. It was used as the target in the 'arrow game' – arrows being aimed into the mouth and lugs.

Art Deco The fashionable style of the inter-war period (1918–39) which supplanted ART NOUVEAU and co-existed with the Machine Age

Art Deco plate by J. Luce, c.1925 (Musée des Arts Décoratifs, Paris)

Art Deco cigarette case, silver, lacquer and egg-shell, by Raymond Templer, c.1930

styles of LE CORBUSIER, RIETVELD, F. L. WRIGHT, and the BAUHAUS. It developed out of the modernist, anti-historical, elements in Art Nouveau but displayed rather less regard to refinement of craftsmanship and naturalistic ornament, and much more to the demands of mechanized production and machine-like forms. Though its origins may be traced back to the first years of the century, it owes its name to the first major international exhibition of decorative arts to be held after the first World War – *L'Exposition Internationale des Arts Décoratifs et Industriels Modernes* held in Paris in 1925. Le Corbusier and Jeanneret contributed a *Pavillon de l'Esprit Nouveau* but this was relegated to the periphery and aroused little except scornful comment. Pride of place was given to interiors decorated by R. MALLET-STEVENS, furniture by P. CHAREAU, P. FOLLOT, A. GROULT, A.-A. RATEAU, E.-J. RUHLMANN and Messrs SUE ET MARE, glass and jewellery by R. LALIQUE, silver by J.-E. PUIFORCAT, and metalwork by J. DUNAND. Other notable practitioners included the stage designer and graphic artist Romain de Tirtoff known as Erté (b.1893), the couturier

Art Deco side-table and lamp, by Donald Deskey (Radio City Music Hall, New York)

Art Deco tea service, Shelley Pottery Ltd, c.1930 (Victoria & Albert Museum)

Paul Poiret, the glassmaker M. MARINOT, the designer Maurice Dufrène (1876–1955) and, outside France, the English pottery designer Clarice Cliff and the American designer Donald Deskey (b.1894) who was responsible for the interior and fittings of Radio City Music Hall, New York. Most of the big manufacturers of household and decorative objects took up the style, notably BACCARAT, CHRISTOFLE, DAUM FRÈRES, DOULTON PORCELAIN CO., JENSEN. But the most familiar manifestations of the style are cheaply and often poorly made pieces of furniture (especially wireless sets), ceramics, metalwork, etc., which share with the more notable products only a taste for modernistic (but non-functional) form, with much streamlining, geometrical patterns of zig-zags and circles, and strident colour schemes. Dismissed, even in the 20s and 30s, as trash or *Kitsch* by admirers both of the older forms of decorative arts and of Bauhaus design, the vogue for Art Deco began only in the 1960s when it was taken up by collectors (who sought the finer items) and American painters (who drew inspiration from the cheaper and more popular).

Lit: B. Hillier, *Art Deco*, London and New York 1968; *idem*, *The World of Art Deco*, Exh. Cat., Minneapolis Institute of Arts, 1971; T. Walters, *Art Deco*, London 1973.

Art furniture A term first used in England in the 1860s by C. L. EASTLAKE in *Hints on Household Taste* (1868) and in the name of the Art Furniture Company which manufactured pieces designed by E. W. GODWIN. It was generally applied to furniture, often architect-designed, which manifested a reaction against the popular taste for neo-Rococo rosewood and mahogany pieces and a preference for simple outlines, walnut and oak with the unvarnished exposure of the natural grain. Decorative details were at first generally medieval, later Japanese. Some pieces seem to anticipate the work of the ARTS AND CRAFTS MOVEMENT of the 1880s and ART NOUVEAU of the 1890s.

Lit: N. Pevsner, *Studies in Art, Architecture and Design*, vol. II, London 1968.

Art Nouveau A self-consciously 'new' decorative style which originated in the 1880s, reached its height of popularity *c.*1900 and expired, an unlamented casualty, in the 1914–18 war. The name derives from that of a shop opened by S. BING in Paris in 1895. In Italy it is called 'stile Liberty' after the London shop of A. L. LIBERTY, in Germany and Scandinavia 'Jugendstil' after a magazine *Jugend*, and in France by a variety of names, mostly opprobrious. It is characterized by the ubiquitous use of limply swaying, curving lines, by tentacular tendrils and flower and leaf motifs, by deliquescent human figures (usually female with much flowing hair) in very shallow relief, and by a tendency towards extreme asymmetry. A premium was put on originality and craftsmanship – semi-precious stones became popular in jewellery (e.g. LALIQUE), pewter and other base metals returned to favour for table wares. Though ostensibly a non-revivalist style it owed a great deal to the past, both immediate (JAPONAISERIE and ARTS AND CRAFTS MOVEMENT) and more remote (CELTIC). Its earliest dated manifestations are the title page of a book on Wren's churches (1883) and some textile designs by MACKMURDO who may have been influenced by the BIZARRE SILKS fashionable in the age of Wren (i.e. late C17–early C18). In France, GALLÉ and other members of the School of NANCY owed much to ROCOCO models (e.g. LAMOUR's ironwork in Nancy itself). MACKINTOSH and the GLASGOW SCHOOL drew inspiration from Celtic art: and Dutchmen, like LION-CACHET and NIEUWENHUIS,

Art Nouveau candelabra, ivory and silver, by Egide Rombaux & Franz Hoosemans, Brussels 1900 (Kunstgewerbemuseum, Berlin)

Art Nouveau chair, designed by H. Guimard, c.1900 (Musée des Arts Décoratifs, Paris)

same group includes the Austrian OBRIST, the Belgian HORTA, the Dane BALLIN and the Italian BASILE. But GUIMARD in his use of flowing non-representational ornament anticipated certain developments in C20 abstract sculpture, if not decorative designs, and VALLIN eventually abandoned the School of Nancy for functional furniture. The British designers – BAILLIE SCOTT, BRANGWYN and Mackintosh – developed an angular and rather Puritan style which pointed the way towards the simplicity of C20 INDUSTRIAL DESIGN, influencing the more progressive and enterprising

Art Nouveau sideboard by Ferdinand Brunot, 1901–2 (Musée de l'École de Nancy, Nancy)

probably looked back to C17 silver in the AURICULAR STYLE. These national influences coalesced thanks to such periodical publications as *Jugend* and *The Studio*, and to several notable International Exhibitions (Liège 1895, Venice 1899, Vienna 1900, Turin 1902). But there were two divergent tendencies within the movement itself, one purely decorative and backward-looking, the other progressive. The former is predominant in most French exponents of the style, e.g. CHARPENTIER, DAUM, GAILLARD, GALLÉ, LACHENAL, MAJORELLE, MUCHA, PROUVÉ. (Majorelle also made reproduction Rococo furniture.) The

Austrians HOFFMANN and OLBRICH and the German ENDELL. In Denmark JENSEN began as an Art Nouveau silversmith but soon emerged as the designer of the prototypes of much modern tableware. But it was the Belgian Henry VAN DE VELDE who proved to be the most important and vital link between both the Arts and Crafts, Art Nouveau and modern industrial design.

Lit: H. Selig (ed.), *Jugendstil*, Heidelberg-Munich, 1959; R. Schmutzler, *Art Nouveau*, London 1964.

Artigas, José Llorenz or **Joseph-Llorenz** (b.1892). Studio potter born and trained in Barcelona but working from 1924 in Paris where he began by producing handsomely designed but undecorated stoneware. For his later, decorated wares he collaborated with painters, first with Raoul Dufy (1932–3), but notably with Joan Miró.

Arts and Crafts Movement An attempt to revive handcrafts and improve standards of decorative design in late Victorian England, inspired by the teaching of William MORRIS and Ruskin. Its main organizer was C. R. ASHBEE, its propagandist Walter CRANE. 'The true root and basis of all Art lies in the handicrafts,' Crane wrote. He believed that 'genuine and spontaneous art is a pleasurable exercise' and considered it his mission to 'turn our artists into craftsmen and our craftsmen into artists'. The whole movement was thus affected by the romantic socialism of Ruskin (especially *Unto This Last*) and Morris. Hence the establishment of guilds (Century Guild, Art Workers' Guild, Guild of Handicrafts, etc.) and the tendency for craftsmen to flee from the great capitalist centres to the country – Ashbee, GIMSON and LETHABY all settled in the Cotswolds. In the 1880s the various craftsmen developed individual styles. Some broke away from the Gothic Revival in favour of the simplicity, lightness and elegance of the QUEEN ANNE STYLE; others made a more original attempt to express the fellowship of craftsmen by producing richly decorated furniture on which workers in pewter, brass, ivory, leather, etc., aided the cabinet-maker. Most of them succumbed to ART NOUVEAU influence in the 1890s. Not until the later 1890s did austere, cottagey solidity (inspired by Philip WEBB) become the movement's hall-mark. The craftsmen exhibited widely in Europe and exerted some influence on design (especially in Germany) but after 1900 the movement came to be regarded as a cul-de-sac. Despite their Socialist ideals they could provide no more than a few sensitively designed objects for a few sensitive (and fairly wealthy) patrons. The task of providing the millions with well-designed articles was left to the industrial designers who came to terms with the machine, though they often derived inspiration from the Arts and Crafts movement (especially in Germany, *see* BAILLIE SCOTT). Their influence was much greater in the U.S.A., where an Arts and Crafts movement began in the 1870s and grew steadily more prominent until World War I (*see* W. H. GRUEBY, E. HUBBARD, NEWCOMB COLLEGE POTTERY, ROOKWOOD POTTERY, G. STICKLEY).

Lit: Gillian Naylor, *The Arts and Crafts Movement*, London 1971; J. D. Kornwulf, *M. H. Baillie Scott and the Arts and Crafts Movement*, Baltimore-London 1971; *The Arts and Crafts Movement*, Exh. Cat., London 1973; R. Judson Clark, *The Arts and Crafts Movement in America 1876–1916*, Exh. Cat., Princeton-Chicago 1972–3.

Ash, Gilbert (1717–85). Leading early New York furniture-maker, perhaps trained in Philadelphia. He specialized in chairs. Several labelled and one signed piece have survived. His son **Thomas** (d.1815) advertised in New York in 1775 as a Windsor Chair Maker.

Lit: Joseph Downs, *American Furniture: Queen Anne and Chippendale Periods in the Henry Francis Du Pont Winterthur Museum*, New York 1952.

Ashbee, Charles Robert (1863–1942). He was trained as an architect (under G. F. Bodley) and became an influential designer and writer and leader of the ARTS AND CRAFTS MOVEMENT of which he became the principal organizer. In 1888 he founded the Guild and School of Handicraft at Toynbee Hall in the East End of London. For it he designed furniture in a lighter version of the

C. R. Ashbee: silver salt set with semi-precious stones, 1900 (Jerdein Collection, London)

MORRIS style and also silver and metalwork in a style which would now be called ART NOUVEAU though Ashbee himself would have denied the name. His work and that of the School was exhibited widely both in England and abroad, at Vienna, Munich, Düsseldorf and Paris. In 1891 Ashbee moved the School and Guild to Essex House in Mile End, London, and in 1902 it moved out of London to Chipping Campden in the Cotswolds where he founded the School of Arts and Crafts (1904–14) which attempted to revive both handicrafts and husbandry. In 1909 he published *Modern English Silverwork*. But he began to lose his faith in handicrafts and in 1910 stated that 'modern civilization rests on machinery, and no system for the encouragement or the endowment of the teaching of the arts can be sound that does not recognize this'. He was one of the first in Europe to understand and admire F. L. WRIGHT whom he knew and visited as early as 1901. He wrote the introduction to a book on Wright published in Berlin in 1911 (by Wasmuth), presenting him as a 'machine architect'. But in 1915 he gave up and went to Cairo University as a lecturer in English. Nevertheless, he made a significant break with Victorian traditions and a younger generation was to profit from his example.

Lit: Shirley Bury in *Victoria & Albert Museum Bulletin* III (1967); Hugh Honour, *Goldsmiths & Silversmiths*, London and New York 1971.

Ashbury metal A very hard alloy of tin with antimony and zinc: a type of PEWTER. It was used mainly for spoons, snuff-boxes, etc.

Askew, Richard (*fl.*1772–95). He was a porcelain painter working at the CHELSEA factory until 1772 and then at the DERBY factory. In 1794–5 he was working in Birmingham. Decorations of figure subjects in pink monochrome and in colours have been attributed to him but no signed examples are known.

Aspetti, Tiziano (1565–1607). Notable Venetian sculptor, much influenced by Alessandro Vittoria and best known for his long-limbed bronze statuettes of mythological, allegorical and religious subjects. Numerous small bronzes of this type, as well as door-knockers and fire-dogs, have been attributed to him.

Assay groove A zig-zag or wriggled groove found on the underside of a piece of silver (continental or Scottish but rarely English) made when a sample of the metal was taken for assaying. Sometimes it resembles a letter N or Z but no significance can be attached to its form.

Assisi work Modern name for a type of embroidery made in various places, including Italy, since the C16, with the pattern reserved in plain linen and the rest of the ground covered with long-armed cross-stitch in red or other coloured thread. It is sometimes said to have been produced first in the convents of Assisi but this is unlikely. It appears to be so called because such embroidery has been made at Assisi in recent times.

Astbury, John (1686–1743). Notable STAFFORDSHIRE potter. He is said to have learnt the technique of making red stoneware from the ELERS brothers, but is better known for his LEAD-GLAZED EARTHENWARE, especially brown vessels decorated with reliefs of trailing vines, hops, etc. stamped from pads of white clay and applied to the surface (similar wares were made by T. WHIELDON), rather more refined than most earlier Staffordshire pottery but still distinctly rustic. He also produced some charmingly naive statuettes of musicians, men on horseback, etc., usually modelled in two or more types of clay of contrasting colours. The most typical wares are always unmarked. Some wares of *c.*1760–80 have 'ASTBURY' impressed.

Lit: B. Rackham, *Early Staffordshire Pottery*, London 1951.

Astbury-Whieldon figures The name given to lead-glazed STAFFORDSHIRE pottery statuettes of a type associated with the names of J. ASTBURY and T. WHIELDON. *Illustrated opposite.*

Astragal A small semi-circular moulding or bead: also, loosely, the glazing bars of case furniture.

Athénienne Lidded urn supported on a classical tripod adapted as a wash-hand basin, plant stand, perfume burner or candelabra. Invented 1773 by an amateur, **J. H. Eberts**, it was one of the most self-consciously archaeological examples of the Louis XVI STYLE. *Illustrated opposite.*

Astbury-Whieldon:
Lady on Horseback, *lead-glazed earthenware, Staffordshire pottery, c.1740 (Victoria & Albert Museum)*

ATHENIENNE
Nouveau Meuble
Servant
de Console
de Pot a Fleurs
de Cassolette
de Terrasse
de Rechaud
de Reservoir
Inventé et Gravé par I.H.E.

Athénienne: Engraving published by Eberts as an advertisement for the original athénienne, c.1773

Lit: S. Eriksen & F. Watson, *Burlington Magazine*, CV (1963), p. 108.

Atlantes Supports in the form of male figures (usually nude or only partly clad) occasionally found on C17 and C18 furniture.

Atterbury & Company T. Atterbury founded a glasshouse in 1859 at Pittsburgh, Pennsylvania, which was first called the White House Works and then Atterbury & Company. It produced blown and pressed table-wares.

Aubusson carpet factories Carpets with a knotted pile like those of the SAVONNERIE FACTORY were made at Aubusson from 1742 and at Felletin nearby from 1786; BRUSSELS CARPETS were also made. But the Aubusson factories are famed mainly for smooth-faced tapestry woven carpets which they produced in the late C18 and in great quantity in the C19 when the vogue for tapestry hangings was at a low ebb. They are in the Louis XVI and Empire styles, with symmetrical designs incorporating classical motifs, often relieved by large, blowsy bunches of roses, etc. Colours are soft and light – buffs, chocolate-browns, rose-pinks, pale yellows, dove-greys, etc. – producing an extremely delicate and sophisticated but usually rather feminine, boudoir effect.

Lit: M. Jarry, *The Carpets of Aubusson*, Leigh-on-Sea 1969.

Aubusson tapestry factories A group of workshops in Aubusson and the nearby village of Felletin (between Clermont-Ferrand and Limoges) established by the early C16. Aubusson differed from the other French tapestry factories (BEAUVAIS and GOBELINS) in that the weavers worked in their own homes and not at a central factory. The first products of interest were religious and mythological scenes and VERDURES of the mid C17. The workshops were given an official charter in 1665 but most of the weavers were Huguenots and defected after the revocation of the Edict of Nantes (1685). A revival began in 1732; copies were made of Gobelins and Beauvais tapestries, notably *The Hunts of Louis XV* (after Oudry) and *The Chinese Hangings* (after BOUCHER). But the best and most famous products were the hangings and furniture covers depicting scenes from the

Fables of La Fontaine. Other designs were derived from contemporary prints – *The Four Ages* (after Lancret), *Sea Pieces* (after Vernet), etc. Reproductions of earlier tapestries were made in the c19. A c20 revival was inspired mainly by Jean LURÇAT who began to supply cartoons for Aubusson in 1939. Other modern artists whose cartoons have been woven include Marcel Gromaire (b.1892), Marc Saint-Saens (b.1903), Lucien Coutaud (b.1901), Raoul Dufy (1877–1953) and Graham Sutherland (b.1903). The cartoons have generally been simplified by the weavers who have also been allowed some scope in interpretation. Under the influence of French Medieval tapestries, and to some extent Pre-Columbian textiles, the colour range has been drastically reduced and coarser materials have been employed.

Aubusson tapestry, Felletin workshops, signed by I. Dennat, c18 (Victoria & Albert Museum)

Aubusson tapestry, designed by F. Leger and made by Tabard Frères et Soeurs, Aubusson 1952 (Kunstindustrimuseet, Copenhagen)

Lit: H. Göbel, *Wandteppiche*, Leipzig 1923–34; R.-A. Weigert, *French Tapestry*, London 1962.

Audran, Claude III (1657–1734). The last great Louis XIV designer and decorator. He was born in Lyons, the son and nephew of notable engravers, went to Paris 1692, and entered the service of the Crown 1696. The arabesque and singerie decorations which he executed in several royal palaces were slightly freer than BÉRAIN's and may have exerted some influence on WATTEAU, though he did not develop further towards the Rococo. He designed the *alentours* for the Gobelins *Portières des dieux* (1699–1711) and the attractive *Mois grotesques* (1708) which provide the best record of his transitional style. *Illustrated opposite.*

Lit: Claude Audran, Exh. Cat., Bibliothèque Nationale, Paris 1950. R.-A. Weigert, *French Tapestry*, London 1962.

Auffenwerth, Johann (d.1728). An Augsburg enameller and the first *Hausmaler* known to have worked for the MEISSEN PORCELAIN FACTORY. A few signed examples of his painting on porcelain survive (e.g. in the British Museum) but some of those attributed to him may be by B. SEUTER. Two of his daughters were decorators of porcelain, **Anna Elisabeth** (b.1696) and **Sabina** (b.1706); the work of the former is known from two coffee cups, that of the latter from a coffee service decorated with chinoiseries in iron-red, purple and gilt.

Lit: S. Ducret in *Keramos* 50 (1970), pp. 3–29; T. H. Clarke in *Keramos* 60 (1973), pp. 17–40, and 61 (1973), pp. 62–4.

Augusta, Cristóbal de (*fl.*1569–84). Spanish potter from Estella in Navarre who settled in

C. Audran: design for a ceiling, watercolour, c.1700–1710 (Nationalmuseum, Stockholm)

Seville by 1569 when he married the daughter of a leading maker of maiolica tiles Roque Hernández. In 1577 he completed a large (156-tile) panel of the *Virgin of the Rosary* (Museo de Bellas Artes, Seville). The same year he began to supply tiles for the decoration of reception rooms in the Alcázar with continuous wall panels simulating tapestry with strapwork and grotesque ornament separated by TERM figures – all in a distinctly Flemish style. He continued to supply tiles for the Alcázar until 1584. A number of tile panels in churches in and near Seville have been attributed to him.

Lit: A. W. Frothingham, *Tile Panels of Spain*, New York 1969.

Auguste, Robert-Joseph (*c.*1723–1805). He was one of the best silversmiths during the Louis XVI period but nothing is known about him until 1756 when he is recorded as a journeyman. The following year he was made a *maître* by royal command. Much of the most costly work he did for Mme de Pompadour and Louis XVI has been destroyed, including the gold crown, chalice and other regalia for the King's coronation in 1774. He is best known today for his table silver such as the still Rococo pieces he made in 1768 now in the Danish royal collection and the Antique Revival dinner service he made in 1775–6 for Gustav III (Swedish royal collection). He made similar services for Catherine the Great, the King of Portugal and other royal clients. All his work of this period has a sophisticated classical elegance, austere, and adorned with the barest minimum of ornament. After the retirement of ROETTIERS he became the leading silversmith in Paris. In 1788 he was made supplier and manager of the Paris mint where he collaborated with DENON. His son **Henri** (1759–1816) appears to have taken over his silver workshops in about 1785 and he continued to make elaborate dinner services, notably one acquired by George III in 1787 and still in the royal collection. It is more massive and less smooth than his father's work. Henri Auguste's best silver is in a full-blown Empire style, e.g. the ewer and swan-handled basin used at Napoleon's coronation and the magnificent *surtout de table* given by the City of Paris to Napoleon on the same occasion, which includes two superb classicizing *nefs* (now in Château de Malmaison). Despite

R.-J. Auguste: silver aiguière *for Napoleon (Château de Malmaison)*

Imperial patronage he did not prosper and in 1809 went bankrupt. He died in Haiti. (For his mark *see* p. 893.)

Lit: Y. Bottineau & O. Lefuel, *Les Grands Orfèvres*, Paris 1965; F. J. B. Watson, *The Wrightsman Collection: I Furniture*, vol. ii, New York 1966.

'Augustus Rex' mark, *see* FREDERICK AUGUSTUS I.

Auliczek, Dominicus (1734–1804). He succeeded BUSTELLI as *modellmeister* at the Nymphenburg Porcelain Factory, becoming factory inspector in 1773 until dismissed in 1797. He specialized in hunting-groups and groups of fighting animals, sometimes after prints by Riedinger, but also executed groups of gods and goddesses in a classicizing style.

Lit: F. Bukàček, *Domenicus Auliczek*, Poličce 1939.

Ault, William, *see* LINTHORPE POTTERY.

Aumbry Originally, in medieval times, a receptacle for provisions to be given away as alms. But the term was soon applied to any type of closed cupboard, whether enclosed in or hung on a wall, and also to coffers. Nowadays it is generally reserved for an enclosed recess for sacred vessels in the wall of a church.

Aumonier, Frederic, *see* WOOLLAMS & COMPANY.

Aurene glass A type of iridescent glass developed at the STEUBEN GLASS WORKS by F. CARDER from 1904 onwards, somewhat similar to Tiffany's Favrile glass though the shapes of the vessels are more traditional. The colouring – gold, blue, green, red and brown – was obtained by the combination of metallic and non-metallic glasses. Pieces were sometimes sprayed with a solution of stannous chloride which gives them a velvety texture.

Auricular style Also called Lobate Style, in Dutch *Kwabornament* and in German *Knorpelwerk*. Dutch C17 silver style characterized by curious slithery curving forms like the interior of a shell or the lobes of an ear (hence its name) and such fantastic motifs as dolphins whose tails gradually merge into ripples of water and eddying waves which develop into the faces of grinning monsters or sinuous nudes. The silver is so softly and smoothly modelled that it appears to be in a molten state. The style, derived mainly from Dutch Mannerist engravings and German silver, was first developed by Paulus van VIANEN before 1607 and transmitted 1614 to his elder brother and nephew. Other notable practitioners include Thomas BOGAERT and Johannes LUTMA. M. Mosyn published a series of designs for Auricular plate in Amsterdam *c.*1650. Auricular motifs also appeared in the carved ornament on C17 Dutch and German furniture, especially chairs inspired by

Auricular style: design by M. Mosyn, c.1650

the designs published by a cabinet-maker of Frankfurt-am-Main, Friedrich Untensch in *Neues Zieratenbuch* (*c.*1650).

Lit: W. K. Zülch, *Entstehung des Ohrmuschelstils*, Heidelberg 1932.

Austin, Jesse, *see* PRATT, Felix.

Automata Animated figures made in Europe probably since C5 B.C. and certainly since the Hellenistic period. They became very popular in Byzantium. Most medieval examples are associated with clocks (like that of 1356–61 still working in the Frauenkirche, Nuremberg) and have a religious significance. But from the C14 they were also in demand as table ornaments to amuse and astonish the guests at a banquet. Very elaborate ones were made in C16 Germany, like the jewel-encrusted silver gilt group of Nessus and Deianera (Grünes Gewöolbe, Dresden) which ran on wheels and shot arrows, or the *Ship of Charles V* (Musée de Cluny, Paris) which moves with a rocking motion while an organ plays, sailors clamber about the rigging and courtiers file past the Emperor who raises his sceptre and bows to each one. In the C16 a wide range of fantasies were made, often with tiny mechanisms, in France, Switzerland and England (where James Cox was the master of the craft). Gem-studded golden caterpillars that could wriggle across a table, enamelled mice that could run and rear themselves on their hind legs, tiny boxes from which birds would appear, warbling and fluttering their wings, were among the many popular types. Their production has never ceased though they have generally been made mainly for children since the early C19.

Lit: A. Chapnist, E. Droz, *Automata*, New York 1958. J. Prasteau, *Les automates*, Paris 1968.

Auvera, Johann Wolfgang van der (1708–1756). German Rococo sculptor born in Würzburg where his father (Jakob) was Court Sculptor. He was sent by the Prince-Bishop to study in Vienna from 1730 to 1736. He was responsible for the woodwork in the mirror room (Spiegelkabinett) of the Würzburg Residenz – destroyed in World War II – though some pieces of carved furniture which he executed for the same room survive, notably console tables with very rich bases and *verre églomisée* tops. They are among the finest examples of German Rococo furniture. He also carved some large-scale figurative sculpture.

J. W. van der Auvera: side-table, c.1744 (Residenz, Würzburg)

Lit: H. Kreisel, *Die Kunst des deutschen Möbels*, vol. II, Munich 1970.

Avelli, Francesco Xanto (*fl.*1528–45). Notable and

Avelli dish, after Raphael, signed and dated 1533, Urbino maiolica (Victoria & Albert Museum)

prolific Italian maiolica painter working at URBINO in the ISTORIATO style. He was strongly influenced by N. PELLIPARIO but employed a darker, richer colour scheme. He derived his compositions from prints after Raphael and other masters, and favoured scenes from mythology, contemporary poetry and contemporary events, often accompanied by a few lines of verse. He sometimes signed his work.

Lit: J. Chompret, *Répertoire de la maiolique italienne*, Paris 1949; J. Prentice von Erdberg in *Journal of the Walters Art Gallery, Baltimore*, XIII (1950–51), pp. 30–37.

Aventurine A dark brown glass with gold specks in it, made by mixing copper crystals with the molten glass and so called because of its accidental discovery (or re-discovery) at Murano in the C16. It is also sometimes used as a glaze. A similar or identical process had been used in antiquity. A similar effect was also obtained from the C16 onwards in other mediums, notably lacquer of both Japanese and European origin, yellow, red or dark brown in colour. With lacquer the effect is sometimes obtained by sprinkling minute clippings of gold wire over the surface during application. J.-F. Watin's *L'Art du Peintre, Doreur, Vernisseur* . . . , Paris 1828, gives a detailed description of how to make the European variety.

Avisse, Jean (1723–after 1796). He belonged to a family of Parisian *menuisiers*, became a *maître* in 1745 and was immediately successful, probably because of his modest prices as well as his excellent craftsmanship. He worked in both the Louis XV and Louis XVI style and was patronized by the Crown and by some of the most fashionable *tapissiers* in Paris. Examples of his work are in the Mobilier National and the Musée des Arts Décoratifs, Paris.

Lit: F. J. B. Watson, *The Wrightsman Collection: Furniture*, New York 1966.

Avisseau, Charles-Jean (1795–1861). French potter with a factory at Tours, producing ceramics inspired by HENRI DEUX ware and PALISSY. His Palissy-like wares are the best; they have a finer finish than the originals but tend to be much more busily decorated with snakes, snails, lizards, etc.

C.-J. Avisseau: lead-glazed earthenware dish dated 1857 (Musée Sallies, Bagnières de Bigorre)

Lit: A Lesur & Tardy, *Les poteries et les faïences françaises*, Paris 1957–60.

Avon pottery Of the several potteries at Avon, near Fontainebleau, one functioning in 1620, apparently under the direction of **Barthélemy de Blénod,** was responsible for producing lead-glazed earthenware figures and groups of great charm, marked with an incised BB in monogram. They include figures of a nurse, a kneeling Magdalen, bagpiper, hurdygurdy player and a child carrying puppies away from a bitch who

Avon pottery: lead-glazed earthenware group of a boy with dogs, early c17 (Louvre)

tugs at his coat. Examples are in the Louvre and the Victoria & Albert Museum. The factory mark is very uncertain. In 1850 Jacob PETIT moved his porcelain factory to Avon from Fontainebleau.

Lit: M. J. Ballot, *Bernard Palissy et les fabriques du XVIe siècle*, Paris 1924.

Axminster carpet The name given to three distinct types of mechanically woven carpet with worsted pile, produced at the WILTON CARPET FACTORY, KIDDERMINSTER CARPET FACTORY and elsewhere (but *not* at the Axminster Carpet Factory). *Chenille Axminster*, first made in 1839 on hand-operated looms, is a two-process fabric with an unlimited range of colour. Chenille cloth is woven in a weft loom and then cut into separate strips, which take a V shaped section by the folding upwards and spreading of the severed ends of the woollen weft, and look rather like furry caterpillars (French: *chenilles*). These strips are woven into a fabric with catcher-, chain- and stuffer-warps. Power weaving was first used for this type of carpet 1876–84, but even so the fur had to be combed into place by hand. The development by **H. Skinner** of Yonkers, New York, of a new type of power loom in 1876 (introduced into England 1878) made possible the production of another type of carpet, closer in character to the knotted carpet (*see* CARPET). This is called *'Spool' Axminster* from its being woven on a spool-loom using a series of wide spools, wound with yarn, dyed in stripes according to the pattern to be woven, from which tufts are inserted around the weft to form the surface. A third type, *'gripper' Axminster*, is made on a loom, patented by Brinton and Greenwood in 1890, which uses JACQUARD mechanism to feed pile yarn in tufts between the warp threads. The range of colours used for the pattern is, however, limited.

Axminster carpet factory Founded in 1755 at Axminster, Devonshire, by **Thomas Whitty** to produce hand-knotted pile carpets. Little is known of its first products except that they were expensive and intended for the luxury market. Carpets of the early c19 include a chinoiserie carpet with dragons and serpents (1817, Royal Pavilion, Brighton) and a Turkish style carpet (1823, Sir John Soane's Museum, London). The factory closed down in 1835 and its equipment was transferred to the WILTON CARPET FACTORY.

Lit: B. Jacobs, *Axminster Carpets 1755–1957*, Leigh-on-Sea 1970.

Azulejos Spanish and Portuguese for 'tiles'; but in English the word is generally used to designate large panels of tiles applied to the exterior walls of buildings. The word is probably of Arabic origin but its derivation is disputed.

Calligraphic initial, cut in wood, from Christophe Plantin's Printing Office, Antwerp, c.1567

Baby cage A light framework on casters in which a child may learn to walk, otherwise called a go-cart.

Baccarat glasshouse Founded near Lunéville 1765. During its most notable period, 1822–58, products included fine crystal glass table-wares and vases, *opaline* vessels in a wide variety of delicate colours, and the much prized *millefiore* paper-weights for which it is mainly famous. It has continued to produce glass of good quality, if seldom of very inspired design, to the present day.

Lit: P. Hollister, *The Encyclopedia of Glass Paperweights,* New York 1969.

Bacchereto, *see* FLORENCE POTTERIES.

Bacchus, George, & Sons Glasshouse in Birmingham trading under this name from 1840 (previously Bacchus, Green & Green to 1834, then Bacchus & Green). In the 1830s it made the first pressed glass in England and from the 1850s imitations of cut glass. It also made cased glass of which several examples were prominently exhibited at the 1851 Exhibition. Cut, engraved and coloured table-wares were also produced.

Baccin, Giovanni Maria, *see* NOVE POTTERY AND PORCELAIN FACTORIES.

Bachelier, Jean-Jacques (1724–1805). French painter and ornamentalist who played a very important role in the development of the Vincennes – SÈVRES PORCELAIN FACTORY from 1748 to 1793, being in charge of painting throughout this period (in conjunction with **Lagrenée** 1785–93) and of modelling 1751–7 and 1766–74. He was largely responsible for the delicate Louis XVI style of painting characteristic of the factory and also for the introduction of biscuit for statuettes (*c.*1751–3). His *Mémoire historique sur la Manufacture Royale de porcelaine de France,* describing the early history of the factory, was published in 1878 (ed. G. Gouellan).

Lit: P. Verlet, *Sèvres,* Paris 1954.

Bachtiari or **Bakhtiari carpets,** *see* PERSIAN CARPETS.

Bacile amatori Italian term for maiolica plates decorated to serve as love gifts and suitably inscribed.

Back stool Early type of chair in the form of a four-legged stool to which a back has been added. A C16 term sometimes used in the C17–C18 for a chair without arms.

Baden-Baden pottery and porcelain factories The first factory founded by Zacharias Pfalzer in 1770 functioned until 1778 making useful wares in both porcelain and *faïence fine* decorated with flower paintings. It also produced porcelain statuettes and busts. A second factory making cream-coloured earthenware was established in 1793 and produced a wide variety of household wares including stoves. (For factory marks *see* p. 881.)

Lit: K. Hüseler, *Deutsche Fayencen,* Stuttgart 1956–8; H. Haug in *Archives Alsaciennes d'histoire de l'art*, I (1922) pp. 112ff.; O. Schmitz in *Oberrheinische Kunst* II (1925).

Badlam, Stephen (1751–1815). Leading American cabinet-maker of the Federal period. He served as a major in the Revolutionary Army but for reasons of health resigned his commission and set up as a cabinet-maker in Dorchester Lower Mills, Massachusetts. He was one of the few Americans to mark his furniture with a stamp, as on chairs in the Henry Francis du Pont Winterthur Museum and the Metropolitan Museum, New York. His masterpiece is the handsome chest of 1791 belonging to Yale University (with carved work by John and Simeon Skillin). His son, also called **Stephen** (1779–1847), worked as a cabinet-maker in Boston and, according to his label, kept up a 'constant supply of fashionable looking-glasses'.

Lit: M. M. Swan in *Antiques* LXV (1954), p. 380; Charles F. Montgomery, *American Furniture: The Federal Period in the Henry Francis Du Pont Winterthur Museum*, New York–London 1967.

Baerdt, Claes Fransen (*c.*1628/9–after 1691). He was born and spent his entire life at Bolsward in Friesland and apparently worked only for local patrons, yet he became one of the best Dutch silversmiths and a master of embossed work in what may be called the Floral Style. The high quality of his work is well displayed in a dish of 1681, now in the Fries Museum in Leeuwarden, which has a broad rim embossed with cornucopia spilling a rich hoard of flowers and fruits (grapes, hops, hazel nuts, wheat-ears and heads of Indian corn) with here and there a tiny insect. On other dishes the rim is decorated with flowers, especially daffodils, tulips and carnations. These naturalistic motives are rendered with the accuracy of a miniature painter, but without regard to scale.

Lit: J. W. Frederiks, *Dutch Silver*, The Hague 1952–61, vols I & IV.

Bahut A French medieval term for a shallow box with a hinged lid, attached to a chest, the whole being called a *coffre à bahut*. It was used for travelling, the bahut containing articles of immediate need. Later the term *bahut* was applied to any chest with an arched or convex lid.

Bail A hoop-handle, e.g. of a kettle, or a curving pull on a drawer.

Baillie Scott, Mackay Hugh (1865–1945). English architect and designer with a practice extending from England to Germany, Switzerland, Poland, Russia and the U.S.A. His masterpiece is the palace built for the Grand Duke of Hesse at Darmstadt (1898) with furniture made to his design by the Guild of Handicrafts. His furniture is simple, solid, rather cottagey (sometimes embarassingly 'cute') and decorated with a modicum of ART NOUVEAU motifs.

Lit: James D. Kornwolf, *M. H. Baillie Scott and the Arts and Crafts Movement*, Baltimore–London 1971.

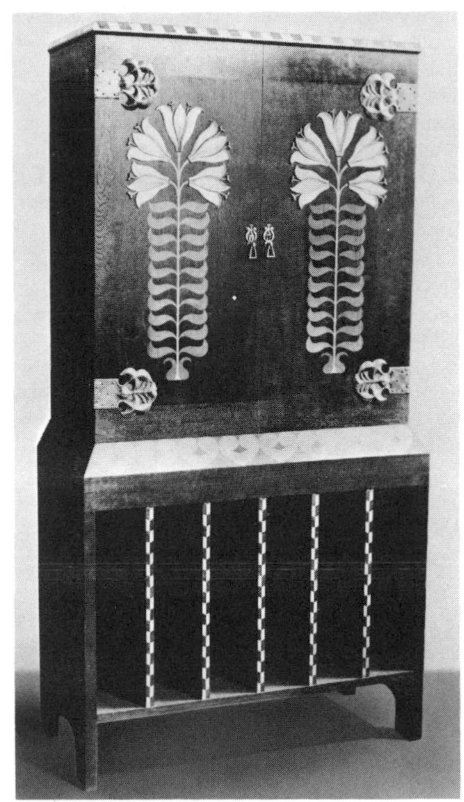

Baillie Scott: music cabinet designed for the palace at Darmstadt, c.1898 (Victoria & Albert Museum)

Baily, Edward Hodges (1788–1867). Sculptor and silver designer and modeller. He was a pupil of FLAXMAN and was very successful as a monumental sculptor, e.g. reliefs for the Marble Arch, London, and the Throne Room in Buckingham Palace, 1828. Like Flaxman he also worked for Philip RUNDELL as a modeller, beginning in 1815. After Rundell's death he joined Paul STORR for whom he designed and modelled elaborate presentation pieces as well as domestic plate.

Bain, Pierre, *see* LÉGARÉ, Gédéon.

Bakelite, *see* PLASTICS.

Bakewell, Robert (*fl.*1707–52). English ironsmith, a follower and possibly a pupil of TIJOU, he worked mainly in Derbyshire (chancel screen for All Souls', Derby, 1723–5, arbour in the garden of Melbourne Hall, 1707–11). His style is less luxuriant than Tijou's, distinctly Baroque rather than Rococo. He was particularly successful in combining and contrasting gently curving scrollwork with severe uprights.

Lit: J. Harris, *English Decorative Ironwork*, London 1960.

Bakewell's Glass Works The main Pittsburgh glass factory, founded by **Benjamin Bakewell** and **Benjamin Page** in 1808. Specialized in fine cut glass imitative of that made in England and Ireland. In 1825 began the production of pressed glass by a process patented by **John Palmer Bakewell,** a son of the founder. It closed in 1882.

Lit: G. S. & H. McKearin, *American Glass*, New York 1942; A. C. Revi, *American Pressed Glass and Figure Bottles*, New York 1964.

Bakhtiari carpets, *see* PERSIAN CARPETS.

Bakshis carpets, *see* PERSIAN CARPETS.

Baku carpets, *see* CAUCASIAN CARPETS.

Ball foot A round turned foot popular in late C17. *See also* CLAW AND BALL FOOT.

Ball, Tompkins & Black A prominent firm of New York silversmiths, directed by **Henry Ball, Erastus O. Tompkins** and **William Black** who in 1839 took over **Marquand and Co.,** a concern dating from 1801. It marketed presentation and other silver wares similar to those made for C. L. TIFFANY and some of the more notable pieces (e.g. Neo-Rococo tea-kettle in the Metropolitan Museum, New York) were made in the independent workshop of John Chandler MOORE who later worked for Tiffany. In 1851 Tompkins withdrew from the partnership. In 1876 the firm was restyled **Black, Starr and Frost** under which name it is still active.

Lit: *19th Century America: Furniture and Other Decorative Arts*, Exh. Cat., Metropolitan Museum, New York 1970.

Ball, William, *see* LIVERPOOL POTTERY AND PORCELAIN FACTORIES.

Ball, William, *see* SUNDERLAND POTTERIES.

Ball-and-bar thumbpiece Scottish type of thumbpiece used on pewter tankards in late C18 and early C19. The bar from the handle to the lid is straight and is surmounted with a ball at the handle end.

Ball-and-wedge thumbpiece Type of thumbpiece found on English C16 and C17 pewter tankards, a ball surmounting the thick end of the wedge.

Ballin, Claude I (*c.*1615–1678). He was one of the prominent goldsmiths employed by Louis XIV and was probably the most highly esteemed. He specialized in work on the grandest scale. Unfortunately all his secular work was destroyed in 1689 when the king ordered all silver objects to be sent to the mint and melted down. Only Ballin's ecclesiastical work survived this holocaust and it was destroyed a century later, during the Revolution. He became a *maître* in 1637. He was notable for his magnificent large pieces in a sumptuous Baroque style, such as *brancards* and silver tubs for orange trees. A few of his designs survive, but these are for pieces intended for private clients and probably give a very inadequate impression of the magnificence of his royal work at Versailles and elsewhere.

Lit: C. Hernmarck in *Gazette des Beaux Arts*, xli, 1953, pp. 103–8; Y. Bottineau & O. Lefuel, *Les Grands Orfèvres*, Paris 1965.

Claude Ballin I: design for a silver chandelier, (National Museum, Stockholm)

Ballin, Claude II (1661–1754). He was the nephew of **Claude Ballin I** and began his career as a silversmith under him, though he did not become a *maître* until 1688. Much of his work was destroyed in the second great melting down of royal plate in 1789, but a large Louis XIV style basin made for the Elector Maximilian Emanuel in 1712–13 survives in the Residenzmuseum, Munich, and a table-centre in the Hermitage Museum in Leningrad. He was perhaps rather *retardataire* in style, especially as compared with such contemporaries as GERMAIN. (For his mark *see* p. 893.)

Lit: Y. Bottineau & O. Lefuel. *Les Grands Orfèvres*, Paris 1965.

Ballin, Mogens (1871–1914). Danish painter and Art Nouveau metalworker. He went to Paris when young and associated as a painter with the Nabis, becoming a friend of GAUGUIN, but became a Catholic in 1893 and under the influence of the German Benedictine monastery at Beuren abandoned painting for metalwork. In Copenhagen he founded a studio (1899) where J. ROHDE and G. JENSEN worked for a time. He used silver and pewter for French-style Art Nouveau vases, lamps, jewellery, etc.

Lit: H. Selig (ed.), *Jugendstil*, Heidelberg–Munich, 1959.

Baltic chests A group of C16 chests, found mainly in England, the earlier with carvings of religious scenes (of a distinctly Protestant complexion), the later embellished with marquetry and called NONESUCH CHESTS. Both types were probably made on the Baltic coast (perhaps at Danzig) and imported, though they were at one time supposed to be of English make.

Lit: W. A. Thorpe in *Country Life Annual*, 1951, pp. 152–62.

Baluchistan rugs, *see* TURKMAN CARPETS.

Baluster or **Banister** A short post or pillar (e.g. a table leg) but usually one in a series supporting a rail or coping and thus forming a **Balustrade.** It is usually circular in section with an undulating profile: thus the name is applied to similarly shaped vases, drinking-glass stems, coffee-pots, etc.

Balustrade A series of BALUSTERS supporting a rail.

Balzac, Edmé-Pierre (*fl.* 1739–81). He and his brother **Jean-François** were prominent silversmiths in Paris, being received *maîtres* in 1739 and 1749 respectively. They both worked for the Crown. Examples by Edmé-Pierre Balzac are in the Louvre. (For his mark *see* p. 893.)

Bamboo furniture Strictly, furniture made from the wood of the *bambusa*. In the Far East bamboo was used only for very simple household furniture and hard woods were preferred for fine pieces. Bamboo was used in Europe from the C19 but again only for simple and generally rather ricketty furniture until very recently. The term is also applied loosely and incorrectly to late C18 and early C19 Chinoiserie furniture made of European woods carved (and usually painted) to simulate bamboo.

Banded Of a textile with parallel bands in the weft direction. If the bands are in the warp direction it is said to be striped.

Bandelwerk, *see* LAUB- UND BANDELWERK.

Banding A decorative inlaid border of contrasting woods, e.g. satinwood and mahogany. Straight-banding is cut along the length of the grain; cross-banding across the grain; feather-banding at an angle between the two.

Banquette A small bench, usually with an upholstered seat. In form it resembles a TABOURET lengthened and supported on six or more legs. In the Louis XIV period it was frequently upholstered with SAVONNERIE carpet. A *banquette croisée* is one made to stand in the embrasure of a window. The word *banquette* originally applied to a saddle for horses.

Bantam work A generally rather rough imitation of incised Coromandel lacquer made in late C17 England. In C17 and early C18 literature the term is occasionally applied to the genuine article as well.

Bapst, George-Michael, *see* STRAS(S), G.F.

Barbeaux French for cornflowers, sprigs of which became a common decorative motif on C18 and C19 French porcelain, especially that of the CHANTILLY, NIDERVILLER, PARIS and SÈVRES factories. It was said to have been introduced by **Hettlinger** at Sèvres in 1782 to please Marie Antoinette. In England it was sometimes known as the 'Angoulême sprig' from the Paris factory of the Duc d'Angoulême where it was commonly used. English porcelain decorators also used the same motif.

Barbedienne, Ferdinand (1810–92). He was a prominent Second Empire furniture manufacturer and the best known C19 Parisian bronze founder, working for Barye and other leading sculptors. From 1839 he worked in association with Achille Collas who had devised a method for making reductions of sculpture and by 1847 had established a factory for the production of bronzes in Paris. This was soon employing some 300 men and producing, in addition to bronzes, silver wares and reproduction furniture in a variety of styles, mainly neo-Renaissance though also some neo-Louis XVI Style pieces which rival those of his contemporaries BEURDELEY and GROHÉ. In 1850 he was commissioned to furnish the main reception rooms of the Hôtel de Ville in Paris. CARRIER-BELLEUSE and other fashionable artists worked for him and in the 1880s he produced Japonaiserie furniture and imitation Chinese and Japanese work in bronze. He exhibited at the Great Exhibition of 1851 in London a bookcase of ebony and bronze, with mounts modelled by Clesinger after Ghiberti and Michelangelo. At the 1862 International Exhibition he was represented by a large *champlevé* enamel bronze vase now in the Victoria & Albert Museum.

Lit: B. Mundt, *Historismus*, Catalogue of the Kunstgewerbemuseum, Berlin, vol. VII, Berlin 1973.

F. Barbedienne: gilt metal vase with champlevé enamelling, c.1862 (Victoria & Albert Museum)

Barberini tapestry factory Founded in Rome in 1627 by Cardinal Francesco Barberini, nephew of Pope Urban VIII, to weave tapestries for the Papal and Barberini palaces. Work began with a set depicting great European castles (1627–31) after cartoons painted by Pietro da Cortona to augment a set woven in PARIS after Rubens. Other products include a *Life of Christ* after P. da Cortona, G. F. Romanelli and others (1643–56) and a *Life of Urban VIII* (1663–83) which was the last to be woven before the factory closed.

Lit: D. Dubon, *Tapestries from the Samuel H. Kress Collection at the Philadelphia Museum of Art*, London 1964.

Barber's basin A shallow oval basin with the centre of one side cut out in a semi-circle so that it could be held close against a person's neck while being shaved by a barber. They were usually made of pottery, but also of pewter and sometimes of silver.

Barber's bowl, Toulouse faience, c18 (Musée Dupuy, Toulouse)

Barbizet, A. (*fl.*1850). French potter making from *c.*1850 elaborately modelled and coloured objects, especially imitations of the work of PALISSY. He seems to have specialized in large jardinières. Some of his products are marked with his initials.

Lit: A. Lesur & Tardy, *Les poteries et les faïences françaises*, Paris 1957–60.

Barbotine A type of SLIP first used at RHENISH POTTERIES before 300 A.D. to make small floral and other decorations on the rims of flat dishes. Later it replaced the earlier moulded decorations. It was applied by piping or trailing.

Barcheston tapestry factory, *see* SHELDON, William.

Bargello work or **Flame Stitch** or **Hungarian Stitch** Type of needlework in which each element of the pattern, usually pointed or flame-like, is worked in a single, graduated colour. Silk was generally used in Italy, crewel was more usual in England. It was used mainly for upholstery.

Barker, Benjamin, *see* PONTYPOOL JAPANNING FACTORY.

Barlach, Ernst, *see* SCHWARZBERG PORCELAIN FACTORY.

Barlow, Hannah, *see* DOULTON POTTERY AND PORCELAIN FACTORY.

Barnard, Edward, *see* EMES, John.

Barnsley, Sidney and **Ernest**, *see* GIMSON, Ernest William.

Barometers Scientific instruments for measuring atmospheric pressure by means of mercury in a long glass tube. They were invented in 1643 and began to appear in French and English houses by the late c17. For household use they were generally set in cases similar to, and sometimes made *en suite* with, clock-cases of roughly banjo-shape with tubes occupying the place of the pendulum and a dial to record the pressure. Usually they were made to hang on the wall but sometimes (especially in c18 France) they were free-standing. Until the c19 they appear to have been made more frequently in France and England than elsewhere. The invention of the aneroid barometer (1848) which has a small metal box instead of the glass tube, made it possible to reduce the size of the instrument. But until recently most aneroid barometers were put in banjo-shaped cases to make them look like the much more accurate mercury barometers.

Lit: N. Goodison, *English Barometers*, London 1969.

Baroque style Like MANNERISM this style originated in Italy. It is characterized by exuberant decoration, expansive curvaceous forms and an air of solemn, sometimes pompous grandeur. It was fully developed by *c.*1620 and quickly spread to N. Europe, especially the Low Countries, Germany and Austria, Spain and Portugal. A more classicizing version was developed in France under LOUIS XIV. It reached England late by way of Holland and France, *see* RESTORATION, WILLIAM AND MARY and QUEEN ANNE STYLES. The decorative arts were so strongly and directly influenced by the leading painters, sculptors and architects that relatively few craftsmen developed distinct artistic personalities. Architects took more interest than before in the furnishing of their buildings and some, like JUVARRA, designed furniture for them. But whether architect-designed or not, most Baroque

Baroque ivory tankard, with silver-gilt mounts, Augsburg, late c17 (Kunstgewerbemuseum, Berlin)

Baroque console table, gilt wood, probably Roman, c.1680 *(Palazzo Reale, Turin)*

Baroque pier-glass and table, carved and gilt wood, by Domenico Parodi, c.1690–1710 *(Palazzo Brignole, Genoa)*

furniture has an architectural character, e.g. Italian cabinets decorated with columns, mosaics and reliefs of *pietre dure*. The influence of sculptors, notably G. L. Bernini (1598–1680) was transmitted to ceramics, silver, ivory, etc., by SOLDANI, PETEL and others. The best Venetian Baroque furniture was carved by a sculptor, BRUSTOLON. And the massive Italian side-tables with boldly carved supports incorporating mermaids, tritons, eagles and the ubiquitous *putti* among thickly scrolling fronds of acanthus were

Baroque design for a bed, by Filippo Passarini, 1698

Baroque monstrance, silver partly gilt, by Franz Antoni Betle, Augsburg, c.1710–20 (Badisches Landesmuseum, Karlsruhe)

not only executed by sculptors but were intended as sculptural decorations for a gallery or hall rather than as useful objects. Similarly in silver, many Baroque designs, e.g. by G. GIARDINI, could as well be carried out in marble for a Baroque garden or fountain. As in earlier periods the influence of painters was felt mainly in tapestry design, e.g. Rubens's models for the BRUSSELS TAPESTRY FACTORY and Pietro da Cortona's cartoons for the BARBERINI TAPESTRY FACTORY. But maiolica, notably CASTELLI, was also influenced by contemporary painters. And Dutch silversmiths, such as BAERDT, BREGHTEL and de BRUYN, were indebted to Dutch still-life painters for inspiration. The most interesting Dutch C17 silver is in the AURICULAR STYLE which is also evident in carved decoration on some Dutch furniture of the period. The vogue for such fantastic decorations was probably connected with a desire for exoticism more generally answered by CHINOISERIE (e.g. DELFT POTTERY and JAPANNED FURNITURE by DAGLEY and

Schnell) which prepared the way for the freer, lighter and more elegant Rococo style. To draw a frontier between the Baroque and the Rococo is often very difficult and some, mainly German, artists and craftsmen have been associated with both styles, notably the porcelain modeller Kändler and the goldsmith Dinglinger. But furniture designs published as late as 1740 by Rumpp are still distinctly Baroque.

Barovier, Angelo (d.1460). One of the most famous makers of Venetian glass, praised by Filarete in *Trattato d'architettura* (1451–64). He was the great-grandson of **Jacobello** who was active at Murano in 1330. Two of his brothers owned glasshouses in Murano. Documents record his presence at Murano in 1424, 1434, 1435 and 1453. He is also known to have travelled to Milan in 1455 and Florence in 1459 when he was said to be 'most distinguished in the art of glass'; he may also have visited Naples and France. In 1457 he and another Murano glassmaker were officially given a privilege 'to work and have worked in their furnaces crystal glass during the time when it is not possible to work other glass'. This suggests that he was one of those responsible for the development of the *cristallo*, or crystal clear glass, for which Venice became famous in the later c15. But none of his products has been identified. The handsome late c15 marriage cup in the Museo Vetrario Murano, traditionally ascribed to him, seems to have been made after his death, probably in the 1470s, though it may possibly have been made by a member of the same family. In 1459 he passed the direction of his glasshouse to his son **Marino** (d.*c*.1490) succeeded by the brothers **Giovanni** and **Maria** who were running it in 1496 when an inventory of its products was drawn up showing that they included enamelled and coloured glass vessels of Lattimo and Calcedonia).

Lit: A. Gasparetto, *Il Vetro di Murano*, Venice 1958; L. Zecchin, *Nuovi appunti di storia vetraria muranese*, Venice 1958.

Barovier glasshouse A glass factory at Murano run by descendants of a family which had been connected with glass-making in Venice since the c13. **Giovanni Barovier** (1839–1908) and his brother **Antonio** (1822–96) worked for the Salviati glasshouse. The sons of the latter, **Benedetto** (1857–1930), **Benvenuto** (1855–1932) and **Giuseppe** (1863–1942), all began their careers in this concern but left it in 1878 to set up their own factory, 'Fratelli Barovier', making beads and a wide variety of vessels mainly in c16 styles. They showed their products at several of the international exhibitions, at Paris in 1889, London in 1891, etc. In 1936 the firm adopted the name 'Barovier & Toso' under which it still trades. It is now directed by Benvenuto's son **Ercole** (b.1889) with his son **Angelo** (b.1927), and produces glass in a frankly modern style. With the firm of Venini it is probably the most notable present-day producer of Venetian glass at Murano.

Marriage cup ascribed to Barovier, late c15 Venetian glass (Museo Vetrario, Murano)

Ercole Barovier: vase and bowl of Venetian glass designed for Barovier & Toro, Murano, c.1957 (Victoria & Albert Museum)

Lit: A. Gasparetto, *Vetri di Murano 1860–1960*, Verona 1960.

Barr, Martin, *see* WORCESTER PORCELAIN FACTORY.

Barry, Joseph B. (b.1757). Cabinet-maker, born in Dublin and trained in London, who settled before 1790 in Philadelphia where he soon became one of the leading furniture-makers. From 1804 he used a trade label incorporating designs from SHERATON's *Drawing Book*. By 1810 he was in partnership with his son advertising furniture 'finished in the rich Egyptian and Gothic style'. Surviving pieces are, however, in the Grecian EMPIRE style.

Lit: W. M. Horner, *Blue Book of Philadelphia Furniture*, Philadelphia 1935.

Bartmann jug, *see* BELLARMINE.

Basaltes ware or **Black Basaltes** The name given by WEDGWOOD to a very hard, fine-grained black stoneware made from Staffordshire clay, calcined ochre, ironstone slag and manganese dioxide, which he perfected before 1769. It was used for vases, busts (often large), medallions and useful wares. The vases were sometimes 'bronzed' with lightly fired metallic gold or painted by an encaustic process to resemble Attic red-figure wares (though the latter had been made by a reverse process of red clay glazed in black); useful wares were often decorated with engine-turned ornament. The ware was much imitated in STAFFORDSHIRE and elsewhere in England, also on the Continent (e.g. CREIL, KÖNIGSBERG, LA CHARITÉ-SUR-LOIRE, RENDSBURG, ULFSUNDA) but seldom with equal success.

Lit: M. H. Grant, *The Makers of Black Basaltes Ware*, Edinburgh–London 1910; W. Mankowitz, *Wedgwood*, London 1953.

Basile, Ernesto (1857–1932). A Sicilian architect, working mainly in Palermo, he was one of the more notable Italian exponents of ART NOUVEAU in the decorative arts as well as architecture. His father was professor of architecture at the university of Palermo. He began by working in various (mainly Sicilian) historical styles but in the 1890s developed an individual manner incorporating French-inspired Art Nouveau elements, as in the Hotel Villa Igea, Palermo (1898) and the furnishing of Caffè Ferraglia, Rome (1901). In collaboration with a Sicilian industrialist **Vittorio Ducrot** and a sculptor **Antonio Ugo** he designed some very elaborate, richly modelled, Art Nouveau furniture shown at the Turin exhibition of 1902 and the Venice Biennale of 1903.

Lit: M. Tafuri in *Dizionario biografico degli Italiani*, Rome 1965.

Baskerville, John (1706–75). Famous typographer and also the inventor of a new method of JAPANNING. The profits from his manufacture of japanned goods financed his work as a typographer. None of his japanned work can now be identified, the bulk of the surviving Birmingham japanned wares being of a later date.

Lit: J. Bennett, *John Baskerville*, Birmingham 1937–9.

Basketry The process of making containers out of a mesh of vegetable fibres by a technique similar to WEAVING. One of the most ancient of all crafts, it was brought to a high stage of development among Neolithic cultures. The earliest surviving specimens were made *c.*5000 B.C. in Iraq and are of types that have been produced consistently ever since. The earliest evidence of basketry in Europe is derived from a Swiss lake village of *c.*2500 B.C. and in America from finds in Peru of about the same date.

The most primitive form, coiled basketry – still produced in several parts of the world – is made by twisting a bundle of rushes, grass or fibres into a rope (or using a long natural growth such as rattan) and then coiling it spirally into the shape desired (generally spherical or ovoid), with each layer fastened to the one below with a sewing strip of similar material. Baskets were also made from prehistoric times onwards by plaiting fibres in long strips which were then coiled and sewn together with palm cord. A third type, probably the last in order of invention and now the commonest, is wickerwork or stake-frame basketry, made by weaving strands in and out of a wicker frame.

Basketry is closely allied to matting. The simplest form of mat was made by laying single bundles of rushes or flax side by side and joining them together by twining threads, either at intervals so that the rushes or flax bundles are clearly shown, or close together so that the twining threads form the surface and the rushes are merely a core. Mats were also made by interweaving rushes at right angles to one another by a process akin to weaving but executed entirely by hand and not necessitating the stretching of any members (a matting loom, when used, merely holds one set of fibres in place so that the cross fibres may more easily be passed in and out).

It is probable, though not proven, that basketry preceded both textile weaving and pottery. And there can be no doubt that the patterns most naturally produced by the various types of basket weave exerted a strong and lasting influence on the incised and painted decorations on pottery. There have been no developments in basketry technique since prehistoric times, though synthetic fibres are sometimes used.

Lit: Encyclopedia of World Art, New York–London 1960, vol. ii; H. Hodges, *Artifacts*, London 1964.

Bassano pottery, *see* NOVE POTTERIES.

Basse lisse, *see* LOW-WARP TAPESTRY.

Basse taille, *see* ENAMEL.

Basting spoon A long-handled spoon with a large oval bowl, especially of C18 date, so called because it is supposed to have been used for basting meat though probably intended for other use as well.

Bat printing, *see* TRANSFER PRINTING.

Bataille, Nicolas (*fl.* 1373–1400). Parisian manufacturer and vendor of tapestries who supplied two sets of hangings to the Duke of Savoy in 1376 and some two hundred and fifty pieces to the French Crown between 1387 and 1400. The only documented surviving product of his looms is the *Apocalypse* series at Angers (Musée de Tapisserie), designed by Jean de BONDOLF *c.* 1375. Five panels from a set of *Nine Heroes* (Metropolitan Museum, New York) of *c.* 1385 are sometimes attributed to him.

Lit: R.-A. Weigert, *French Tapestry*, London 1962.

Batavian ware A type of brown-glazed Kang-hsi porcelain exported from China by the Dutch through their trading station at Batavia. It is decorated with panels, often fan-shaped, painted in underglaze blue or *famille rose* colours. It was imitated at MEISSEN. LEEDS pearlware similarly coloured and decorated is also called Batavian ware.

Bateman, Hester (*fl.* 1761–93). She was a member of a family of London silversmiths and first recorded her maker's mark in 1761. She was probably the widow of a silversmith whose workshop she inherited, i.e. a workshop manager rather than a craftsman. The workshop produced much fine, simple household plate, especially in the 1780s. As one of the very few women silversmiths she has attracted a great deal of attention from collectors. (For her mark *see* p. 893.)

Lit: David S. Shure, *Hester Bateman*, London 1959.

Hester Bateman: silver cruet stand, London, 1788 (Victoria & Albert Museum)

Batik The Malayan name for a process of resist dyeing employed in the E. Indies for fabrics, and, by extension, for the type of bold exotic patterns used on fabrics dyed by this process. The process involved covering with melted wax the areas of cloth which were not to be dyed – the wax being removed later by immersion in boiling water. The process was introduced into Europe by the Dutch in the C16–C17 and used mainly for expensive materials such as velvet. From the C19 Batik patterns have been printed on cotton by other processes.

Lit: J. Irwin & V. Murphy, *Batiks* (in the) *Victoria & Albert Museum*, London 1969.

Battam, Thomas (*c.*1810–1864). English painter on pottery and porcelain. From 1833 he occasionally exhibited enamel paintings at the Royal Academy in London. In 1834 he began to work for the COPELAND PORCELAIN FACTORY. But he later established his own pottery and made careful reproductions of Greek vases. At the Great Exhibition of 1851 he showed a number of such pieces in a cave supposed to represent an Etruscan tomb.

Battersea enamel factory The most famous in England but very short lived, operating at York House, Battersea, only 1753–6. It specialized in

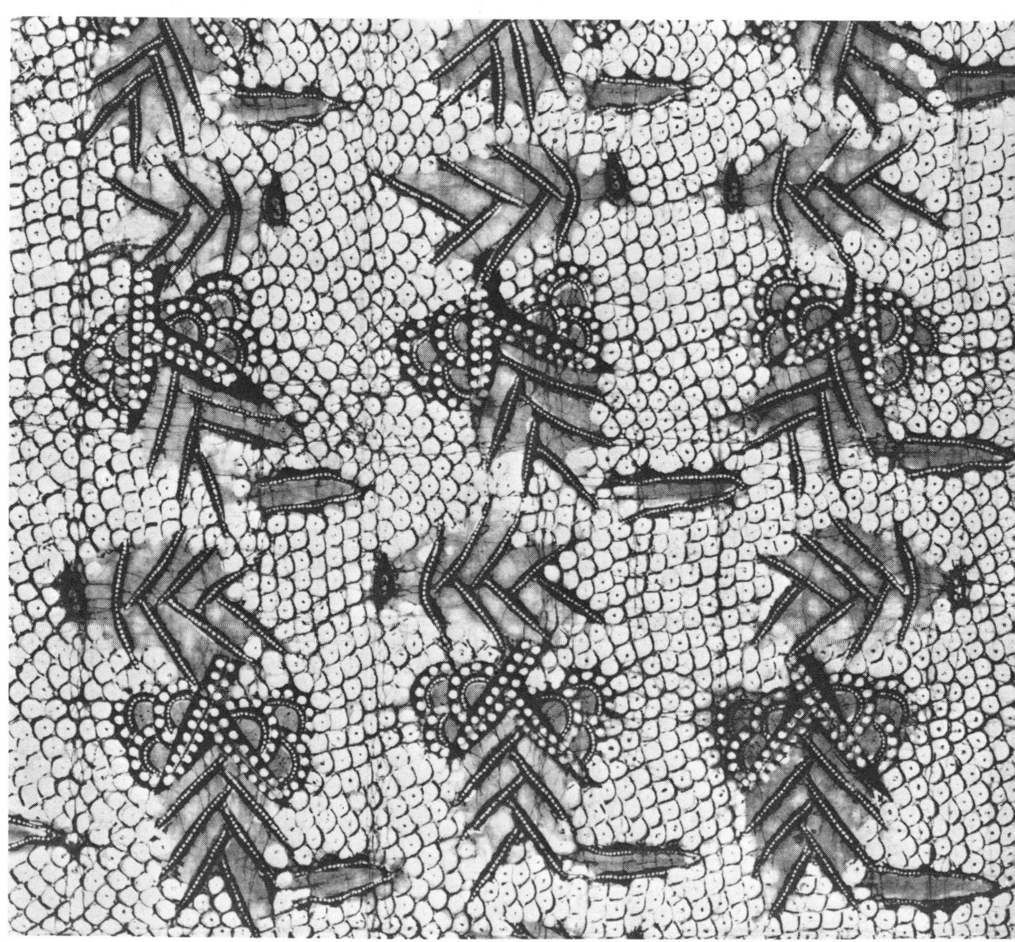

Batik: English or Dutch cotton fabric, hand painted and dyed; South Central Java, C19 (Victoria & Albert Museum)

Battersea enamel: plaque of George II by Simon François Ravenet, Battersea, c.1753–6 (Victoria & Albert Museum)

Rosewood armchair, probably by Charles A. Baudouine, New York, c.1850 (Metropolitan Museum of Art, gift of Mrs Charles Reginald Leonard)

small objects – snuff-boxes, étuis, plaques, etc. – enamelled in delicate colours and often with TRANSFER PRINTED decorations. John BROOKS, who probably invented the transfer-printing process, was the manager. But most of the objects commonly called Battersea enamel were in fact made at BILSTON or elsewhere in S. Staffordshire, or at Birmingham by BOULTON.

Lit: T. & B. Hughes, *English Painted Enamels*, London 1951; B. Watney & R. J. Charleston in *English Ceramic Circle Transactions*, VI, pt. 2, 1966; R. J. Charleston in *Victoria & Albert Museum Journal*, III (1967), pp. 1–12.

Baudekin A rich stuff, usually with a warp of gold thread and weft of silk. Later the word was applied generally to rich silk brocades. (Etymologically, the origin involves Baghdad, as with Baldachin.)

Baudouine, Charles A. (b.1808). Leading New York furniture-maker. He was of French descent, born in New York where he is known to have had a workshop in Pearl Street by 1830. He moved to Broadway in 1839–40. Shortly before he retired in 1855–6 he was employing some 200 hands, including 70 cabinet-makers. He made laminated rosewood furniture similar to that of BELTER but by a slightly different process to avoid infringement of Belter's patent (the backs of his chairs were composed of two pieces with a centre joint). Most of his furniture appears to have been in a rich neo-Rococo style. He also imported furniture, upholstery, etc. from France. He is said to have left a fortune of more than $4,000,000.

Lit: 19th Century America: Furniture and Other Decorative Arts, Exh. Cat., Metropolitan Museum, New York 1970.

Baudry, François (1791–1859). He was born at Nantes but settled in Paris by 1822 and became the leading furniture maker under Louis Philippe who appointed him *ébéniste du roi*. From 1827 onwards he exhibited regularly at the great Paris exhibitions, and a magnificent bed 'en nacelle' which was in the 1827 exhibition is now in the Musée des Arts Décoratifs, Paris. Latterly he specialized in dismountable pieces.

Lit: D. Ledoux-Lebard, *Les ébénistes parisiens (1795–1870)*, Paris 1965.

Bauer, Adam (*fl.* 1758–79). Court sculptor to the Duke of Würtemberg from 1761 (succeeding his master François Lejeune), he provided models for the LUDWIGSBURG PORCELAIN FACTORY until 1771 when he went to FRANKENTHAL as chief

Adam Bauer:
Nymph and Satyr in Ludwigsburg porcelain, c.1770
(Kunstgewerbemuseum, Berlin)

modeller. A number of figures and groups executed in the same style at these two factories are attributed to him. They include the Ludwigsburg group of an amorous nymph and satyr.

Lit: Alt-Ludwigsburger Porzellan, Exh. Cat., Schloss Ludwigsburg, 1959; M. Landenberger in *Keramos* 34 (1966), pp. 89–109 and P. W. Enders, *ibid* 45 (1969), pp. 18–38.

Bauhaus The most influential design school of the C20, the originator of a new method of teaching designers and a new approach to the problems of INDUSTRIAL DESIGN, reflecting contemporary notions of FUNCTIONALISM. It was born in 1919 when Walter Gropius (1883–1969) was appointed to succeed Henry VAN DE VELDE as director of the Art School and School of Arts and Crafts in Weimar which he united and renamed *Das Staatliche Bauhaus Weimar*. His declared aim was 'to co-ordinate all creative effort, to achieve in a new architecture the unification of all training in art and design. The ultimate, if distant, goal of the Bauhaus is the collective work of art – the Building – in which no barriers exist between the structural and decorative arts.' Students began with a preliminary course, under Johannes Itten, devoted to a detailed study of natural forms (vegetable, mineral, etc.), to plastic studies of composition with various materials and an analysis of Old Masters, aimed at releasing their creative powers, helping them to grasp the nature of different materials and processes and to understand the basic laws of design. They then proceeded to study theories of form and design and to work in the various workshops – in stone, wood, metal, clay, glass, textiles and paint. In his insistence on the importance of learning carpentry, metalwork, weaving, potting, etc. Gropius was indebted to the English ARTS AND CRAFTS MOVEMENT: in his conception of the machine as merely a mechanical development of the handcraftsman's tool he was barely a step ahead of it. This was to become most noticeable in the pottery and weaving departments and often justified WAGENFELD's later criticism of the Bauhaus that 'its designs were in reality craft products which through the use of geometrically clear basic shapes gave the appearance of industrial production'. However, Gropius appreciated that machine work could produce aesthetic qualities of its own and was probably correct in believing that the differences between industry and handicraft are due far less to the nature of the tools employed than to the subdivision of labour in one case and the individual control by a single craftsman in the other. His emphasis on the need for co-operative work on problems of industrial design and on the designer's creative responsibility to society reflected his left-wing political beliefs and produced an atmosphere very different from that prevailing at Taliesen in the U.S. where F. L. WRIGHT encouraged his pupils to become individualists. The aim of the Bauhaus was to produce prototypes for the mass production of things in daily use. In furniture their aim was fully realized in BREUER's epoch-making tubular steel chair – still the most characteristic piece of

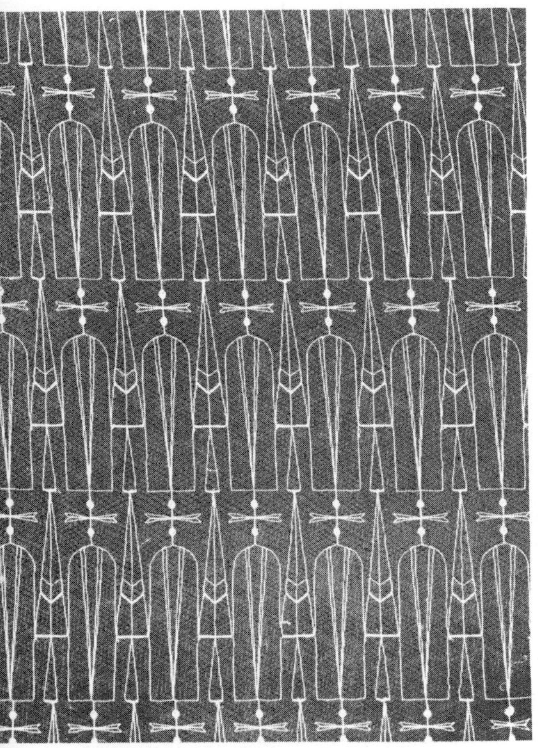
Bauhaus curtain fabric, machine-made cotton net with darned pattern, c.1920–25 (Courtesy of the Art Institute of Chicago)

c20 design. In 1925 the Bauhaus moved to Dessau where Gropius designed his well-known building to house it. He resigned in 1928 and was followed as director first by Hannes Meyer and then, in 1930, by MIES VAN DER ROHE. It moved to Berlin in 1932 and was closed down by the Nazis in 1933. The staff dispersed, carrying with them the Bauhaus ideals: Moholy-Nagy became director of the New Bauhaus – now the Chicago Institute of Design; Mies went to the Illinois Institute of Technology at Chicago; Kepes to the Massachusetts Institute of Technology; Albers

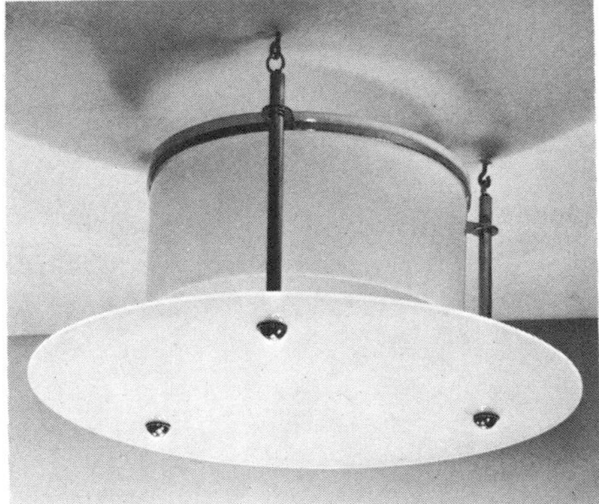
Bauhaus ceiling lamp, glass and chromium-plated by W. Gropius, c.1925 (Museum of Modern Art, New York, gift of Walter Gropius)

Bauhaus tea and coffee set in nickel silver, by W. Wagenfeld, c.1924 (Schlossmuseum, Weimar)

went to teach at Yale and Gropius finally settled at Harvard. Breuer also settled in the U.S. and in 1938 the Museum of Modern Art in New York published and exhibited the work of the Bauhaus. After the war Max BILL revived the Bauhaus programme at the very influential Design School at ULM in Germany and thus directly inspired some of the best mid-C20 industrial design in Europe, notably the products of BRAUN.

Lit: G. Naylor, *The Bauhaus*, London 1968; H. M. Wingler, *The Bauhaus*, Cambridge, Mass. 1969; W. Schedig, *Crafts of the Weimar Bauhaus*, London 1967.

Baumgarten tapestry factory The first American tapestry factory, founded in 1893 in Fifth Avenue, New York, by William Baumgarten with a master weaver and dyer from the English Royal Windsor Tapestry Manufactory. It soon moved to Williamsbridge, New York, and closed in 1912. Products included imitations of C18 tapestry panels and furniture covers.

Baumhauer, Joseph, *see* JOSEPH.

Bäuml, Albert, *see* NYMPHENBURG PORCELAIN FACTORY.

Baur, Matthias, *see* ANSBACH POTTERY & PORCELAIN FACTORY.

Baxter, Thomas (1782–1821). He was an outside porcelain painter working first in London, where his father followed the same profession, then from 1814 at Worcester where he decorated pieces for Flight and Barr. In 1816 he went to Swansea but returned to Worcester in 1819 and from then onwards seems to have worked for both factories. Examples of his work are in the Victoria & Albert Museum.

Bay State Glass Company Glasshouse in Cambridge, Massachusetts, founded in 1853 and closed *c.*1877. It produced plain, moulded, cut and engraved flint glass and mirrors.

Bayard, Charles, *see* BELLEVUE POTTERIES.

Bayer, J. C., *see* COPENHAGEN PORCELAIN FACTORY.

Bayeux tapestry, *see* APPLIQUÉ or APPLIED WORK.

Bay-leaf garland Classical decorative motif used to enrich TORUS mouldings, etc.

Bayreuth pottery A prolific faience factory probably founded in 1713–14 by Johann Caspar RIPP though not certainly active until 1719, taken over by the Margrave of Bayreuth 1724–8, but enjoying its period of greatest success between 1728 and 1744 under the ownership of a merchant **Johann Georg Knöller.** The earliest pieces are of white faience decorated in a rather misty blue characteristic of the factory, and brown-glazed wares with gilt decorations similar in appearance, though not in medium, to BÖTTGER's red stoneware. Both types were developed during the Knöller period when plates painted in blue with coats of arms surrounded by elaborate Baroque borders, and brown wares and yellow wares very delicately decorated with chinoiseries, scroll-work, etc. in gold and silver were produced. Several notable painters worked at the factory including G. F. GREBNER (from 1731), A. F. von LÖWENFINCK (1736–41) and J. P. DANNHOFER (1737–44), decorating pieces in their respective styles. Products included, in addition to the usual table-wares, candlesticks, butter-dishes in the form of fruit, logs, cows, birds and pug-dogs, and some peculiar jugs fashioned like top-boots. Standards declined sharply after 1744 though some later pieces were decorated by painters of ability. Cream-coloured earthenware was made as well as faience 1788–1806 and in its last years the factory made porcelain as well. It survived until 1852. (For factory mark *see* p. 881.)

Lit: F. H. Hofmann, *Geschichte der Bayreuther Fayencefabrik*, Augsburg 1928; K. Hüseler *Deutsche Fayencen*, Stuttgart 1956–8.

Bead and reel Classical decorative motif of alternate round beads and oblong reels.

Beadwork Coloured glass beads used for the decoration of textiles in conjunction with or instead of needlework in silks or wool. It was first practised by the Copts in Egypt. In Europe it became very popular in the late C16 and C17, especially in England, for the decoration of small domestic objects such as caskets, looking-glass frames, etc., and again in the C19 for chair-covers, pictures and especially for purses. In both periods the designs used were similar to those evolved for other forms of embroidery.

Beaker Drinking vessel without a handle and usually with a wide, lipped mouth; usually straight-sided but sometimes like an inverted bell.

Bear jug Pottery vessel in the form of a bear, sometimes hugging a dog, with a detachable head which could be used as a cup, made in brown stoneware at NOTTINGHAM and in Derbyshire, and in white salt-glazed stoneware in STAFFORDSHIRE in the C18.

Beatty & Sons, Alexander J. Glasshouse in Steubenville, Ohio, founded in *c.*1850 and making blown and pressed table-ware, notably goblets.

Beau Brummel An anachronistic American term for a Shaving Table. It is sometimes applied to a type of table made before Brummel was born, i.e. before 1778.

Beauvais carpets Smooth-faced tapestry floor carpets were made at the Beauvais Tapestry Factory from *c.*1780–90 and again from 1794 to *c.*1814. They were similar in design and style to SAVONNERIE carpets.

Beauvais tapestry factory Itinerant weavers in Beauvais produced five panels *The Kings of Gaul* (given to Beauvais Cathedral 1530) representing various mythical kings from the Flood to the Siege of Troy attired in François I costume. The royal factory was founded in 1664 by Colbert, subsidized and patronized by the Crown but run as a private enterprise (with disastrous results for a succession of directors). It began by producing VERDURES. Of greater interest is the series of Grotesques (after Jean I BERAIN *c.*1689) with *Commedia dell'Arte* figures beneath fantastic curtained canopies and surrounded by various classical and chinoiserie grotesque motifs, all in brilliant colours against a yellow ground called 'Spanish tobacco'. Numerous sets were woven with occasional variations until 1725 and imitations were made in BERLIN. Figurative tapestries were also woven: *The Conquests of Louis XIV* (*c.*1690), a set of four *Marine Triumphs* after Berain, a curious set of *Seaports* (1695), and a series of village scenes inspired by the paintings of Teniers. Under the directorship of the brothers **Filleul** (1711–22) the outstanding products were a set of fantastic chinoiserie scenes called *The Chinese Hangings* (after G.-L. Vernasal and J. B. Blain de Fontenay) though this set had been begun earlier. The best period began in 1726 when **J.-B. Oudry** was appointed chief designer and the factory became, in Voltaire's words, 'the kingdom of Oudry'. He insisted on higher technical standards and (as at the GOBELINS) greater fidelity to the painted cartoons. His own compositions abounded in flora and fauna – *The New Indian Hunts* (1727), *Country Pleasures* (1730) and *Fine Verdures* (1736). From Natoire he commissioned cartoons for *The Story of Don Quixote* (1735). But the main artist employed was François BOUCHER who designed forty-five tapestries for Beauvais including *Village Festivals* (1736), *The Story of Psyche* (1741), *Loves of the Gods* (1749), *Operatic Fragments* (1752), all in his peculiar brand of sensuous Rococo elegance.

Beauvais tapestry: fire-screen (Louvre)

Despite the Neo-Classical demand for tapestries with serious subject matter – answered by such sets as *The Iliad* (after J.-B. Deshays 1761) and *The Story of Alexander* (after Lavallé Poussin 1792) – the factory continued to specialize in bucolic or exotic scenes without any literary programme: *Russian Sports* (after J.-B. Le Prince 1769), *Country Pastimes* (after François Casanova 1772) and *Pastorals* (after J.-B. Huet 1780). Throughout the C18 furniture covers, often *en suite* with sets of hangings, were also woven. Smooth-faced tapestry floor carpets were woven 1780–91 (and again 1794–1814). The factory was closed in 1793 but re-opened in 1794 as a State-owned concern. In the C19 it specialized in furniture covers. It was finally amalgamated with the Gobelins factory in 1940.

Lit: H. Göbel, *Wandteppiche*, Leipzig 1923–34; R.-A. Weigert, *French Tapestry*, London 1962.

Beauvaisis potteries Literary references testify that the district around Beauvais was an important centre for pottery from the late C14 to the mid C16 when Rabelais mentioned its wares. And fragments recently found in Beauvais strengthen traditional attributions to this district of C15 lead-glazed lobed cups and C16 wares with a hard grey body, notably some richly modelled plates covered with a blue, green or brown glaze and also lead-glazed wares with handsome bold *sgraffiato* decorations (Musée National de Céramique, Sèvres). In the C17 and C18 peasant pottery was made at SAVIGNIES near Beauvais.

Lit: M. J. Ballot, *Bernard Palissy et les fabriques du XVIe siècle*, Paris 1924; E. Chami in *Cahiers de la céramique* 30(1963), pp. 79–116; *La céramique du Beauvaisis du moyen-âge au XVIIIe siècle*, Exh. Cat., Musée National de Céramique de Sèvres, 1973.

Becerril, Alonso, Francesco (d.1573) and **Cristobal** (d.1584). Spanish silversmiths famous for a huge and elaborate *custodia* made for the cathedral at Cuenca and destroyed in 1808.

Beckwith, Samuel, *see* FRANCE, William.

Bed A term signifying either the bedding (mattress and covers) or the bedstead or both. The use of a framework to raise the bedding above the ground became widespread in Europe only from the early C17. But bedsteads had, of course, been used occasionally since very early times. They were already in use in 1st-Dynasty Egypt (*c.*3000 B.C.) – rectangular frames, with straps to carry the

Italian Renaissance bed, probably late C15 (Palazzo Davanzati, Florence)

Built-in bed from Dordrecht, Holland, 1626 (Rijksmuseum, Amsterdam)

mattress, supported on short legs sometimes carved in the form of animal feet and generally higher at the head than the foot where there was an upright footboard. In later periods the framework and footboards were often elaborately carved and sometimes inlaid with precious materials. In Greece the framework on which the mattress rested was horizontal with a raised fulcrum or headrest at one end and sometimes a balancing ornamental fulcrum at the other. The legs were often carved and the sides of the fulcra decorated with carved or applied metal reliefs. Roman beds were similar in design and this type survived, with changes in decoration, through the Middle Ages to modern times. In the Middle Ages, however, it was more usual for the mattress to be laid on the floor or on a low wooden dais. In C15 Italy the bedding was sometimes set in the middle of a dais surrounded by long low chests which were also used for storage. Further developments affected the bed less than the

Four-poster bed upholstered with velvet, Dutch, c.1700 (Rijksmuseum, Amsterdam)

Lit à la Polonaise, *Louis XV period (Château de Versailles)*

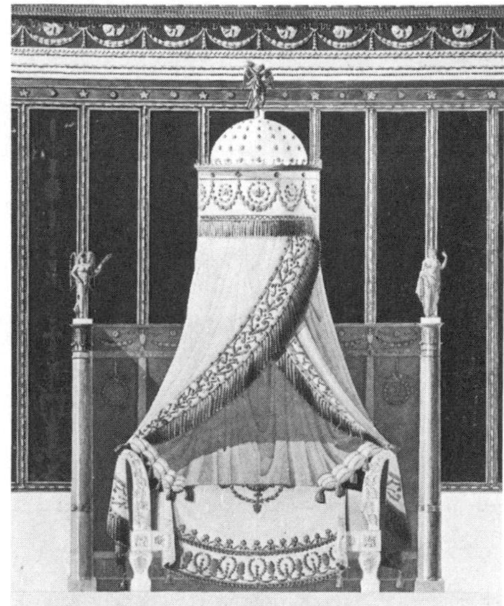

Empire style bed, by Arnoux
(École des Beaux Arts, Paris)

(Left) Lit à la Duchesse, *by J.-D. Dugourc,* c.1780
(École des Beaux Arts, Paris)

superstructure which became very elaborate in the richer houses during the Renaissance – a canopy or tester to protect the bed from dirt and insects falling from the ceiling and side curtains to exclude both draughts and prying eyes. The tester might be supported from the wall and/or ceiling or carried on corner posts of metal or wood in the form of columns, BALUSTERS or, more rarely, TERMS, CARYATIDS or TELAMONES. From the mid C17 greater attention was paid to the

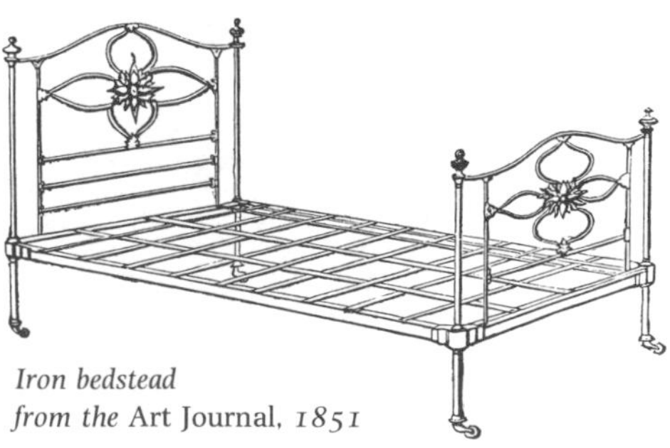

Iron bedstead
from the Art Journal, *1851*

Bedstead with marquetry decoration, by C. Herter, New York, 1880
(Metropolitan Museum of Art, gift of Paul Martini)

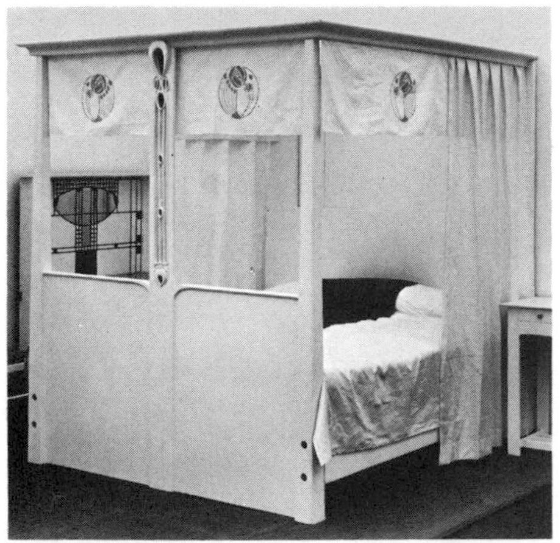

Bed designed by C. R. Mackintosh, Glasgow, c.1900 (University of Glasgow)

fabric hangings than to the woodwork. And in c18 France fanciful names were invented for different types of canopy – *lit à colonnes*, supported on four visible wooden columns, *à la polonaise* with curved iron supports forming a dome entirely swathed in curtains, *à la duchesse* attached at the back to the wall or ceiling. A *lit à l'anglaise* had a headboard and footboard of equal height joined by a similar member along one side and intended to stand in an alcove. In the Empire period the Greek form of bed was revived, but usually with a canopy of drapery attached to the wall above it. The c19 saw a gradual return to functional simplicity in the bedstead.

Angel bed. The English c18 name for a *lit à la duchesse*.

Four-poster bed. Any bed with a tester supported on posts at the corners.

Press bed. A bed that can be fitted into a cupboard or wardrobe when not in use. The cupboard is as high as the bed is long and the door may open downwards to carry the bedding or, in more elaborate examples, upwards to serve as a tester supported on poles at the foot. Such beds have been made in England since the c16.

Truckle bed. A low bedstead mounted on wheels so that it can be trundled under a standing bed when not in use. A piece of later medieval furniture which remained in use until the mid c18, especially for servants who slept in their masters' rooms.

Bedfordshire lace Lace made in the English County of Bedfordshire where émigré lace-makers from Flanders are known to have settled in the c16, though no specimens from this period are known to survive. From the early c17 pillow LACE is known to have been made at various places in Buckinghamshire and Northamptonshire as well, mainly in imitation of Flemish work. In the mid c18 Newport-Pagnell was probably the main centre of production.

Lit: B. Palliser, *History of Lace*, (rev. M. Jourdain & A. Dryden), London 1902.

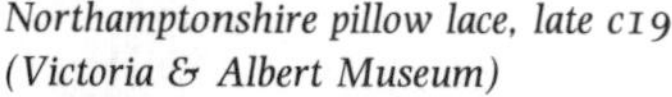

Northamptonshire pillow lace, late c19 (Victoria & Albert Museum)

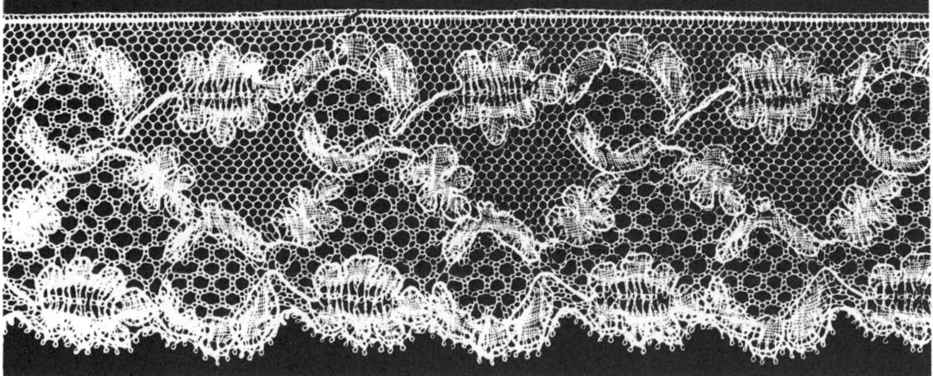

Bedstock The part of a bedstead supporting the mattress and the clothes.

Beechwood A straight-grained wood, light-brown to reddish-brown in colour, widely used in the C18 when it replaced walnut among country craftsmen in England, especially for seat-furniture. It was also used for 'STICK' FURNITURE, and for japanned (*see* JAPANNING) or gilded furniture.

Beefeater Flagon Modern name for a pewter flagon with a cover resembling the hats worn by the Yeoman of the Guard at the Tower of London.

Behrens, Peter (1868–1940). German architect and, with RIEMERSCHMID, the first industrial designer, i.e. the first to design for mass-production. He began as a painter, graphic artist and designer of slithery, curvilinear Art Nouveau furniture, glass, porcelain and jewellery. But by 1898 he was already designing prototype flasks for mass production in glass, notable for their plain and simple shapes. The following year he joined the *Die Sieben* group in Darmstadt whose aim was to integrate all the plastic arts, and the new style he began to evolve is seen in the house he built for himself in Darmstadt in 1901 and in a stark typeface of the same year, from which all trace of Art Nouveau fancy was banished. From 1907 he was architect and designer to A.E.G., the big German electrical combine, for which he built factories of a monumental simplicity, an unprecedented honesty of function and materials, and a certain grave beauty. The same qualities mark his designs for a wide range of industrial and domestic fittings from street-lamps to electric kettles, cookers, radiators, and also the firm's packaging, letter-heads, etc. All these relied for their effect solely on their simple shapes and proportions, and they successfully projected the brand image of a great industrial concern. They were widely imitated and probably contributed more than anything else to the introduction of high standards of design for machine-made goods. From 1922 Behrens taught architecture, first in Vienna, then in Berlin, numbering among his pupils LE CORBUSIER, GROPIUS and MIES VAN DER ROHE.

Lit: P. J. Cremers, *Peter Behrens*, Essen 1928; R. Banham, *Theory and Design in the First Machine Age*, London 1960; *Behrens*, Exh. Cat., Kaiserslauten 1966–7; H. Kreisel & G. Himmelheber, *Die Kunst des deutschen Möbels*, vol. III, Munich 1973.

Beilby, William (1740–1819). He was a glass enameller and worked with his sister **Mary** (1749–97) at Newcastle. They decorated numerous drinking glasses and decanters, generally in white with very delicate vignettes of rustic scenes, classical ruins or sprays of fruiting vine, and occasionally coats of arms in full heraldic colours. Thomas Bewick, the famous wood-engraver, was

Beilby: engraved decoration on a wineglass, c.1770 (Victoria & Albert Museum)

apprenticed to their brother **Ralph Beilby** (1743–1817), a silversmith and jeweller in Newcastle. William and Mary left Newcastle in 1778 to settle in Fife, Scotland.

Lit: J. Rush, *The Ingenious Beilbys*, London 1973.

Beinglas A type of semi-opaque white glass, similar in appearance to Venetian LATTIMO or LATTICINO, but made by adding the ash of calcined bones to the FRIT. Produced mainly at the BOHEMIAN GLASSHOUSES and in Thuringia *c.*1750–1850, and often decorated with enamels.

Bélanger, François-Joseph (1744–1818). French Neo-Classical architect and designer who, with his brother-in-law DUGOURC, played a leading role in the development of the *style étrusque* and late Louis XVI style. His early work owes something to ADAM (he visited England 1766/7). In 1777 he designed, built and furnished the Bagatelle in the Bois de Boulogne, Paris. It bears the same relation to the *style étrusque* as Ledoux's Pavillon de Louveciennes (1771) to the Louis XVI style.

Lit: J. Stern, *A l'ombre de S. Arnould: F.-J. Bélanger*, Paris 1930.

Belfast glasshouses A Bristol glass manufacturer, **Benjamin Edwards**, started a glasshouse in Belfast in 1781, producing enamelled, cut and plain glass, notably decanters with two or three triangular neck rings. The factory closed *c.*1829.

Bell and baluster turning A variation of the BALUSTER table leg, a bell-shaped section being above the baluster-shaped section. It was used in the late C17 onwards.

Bell flower motif American term for a conventional hanging flower bud of three or five petals used in repeated and diminishing pattern, similar to the HUSK MOTIF.

Bell metal An alloy of about four parts copper to one of tin, i.e. similar to BRONZE but with rather more tin. Though used mainly for bells, decorative objects were sometimes made from it, the most famous being the intricately cast Gloucester candlestick (English work of *c.*1110) in the Victoria and Albert Museum.

Bell, William, *see* HULL POTTERY.

Bellangé, Alexandre-Louis, *see* BELLANGÉ, P.-A.

Bellangé, Louis-François, *see* BELLANGÉ, P.-A.

Bellangé, Pierre-Antoine (1758–1837). He became a *maître ébéniste* in 1788 and was much patronized by Napoleon, but most of his recorded furniture dates from the Restauration period when he became official *ébéniste* to Louis XVIII and also held an official appointment under Charles X. He worked in a variety of styles ranging from the EMPIRE (e.g. desk in Musée Marmottan, Paris, and carved and gilt armchair in Museum für Kunsthandwerk, Frankfurt) to the TROUBADOUR. Among his patrons was President Monroe of the U.S.A. who ordered furniture from him for the White House in Washington. It is still there. His brother **Louis-François** (1759–1827) was also a furniture-maker, active since just before the Revolution. His work is less imposing and is often decorated with porcelain plaques which gives it an C18 air. He frequently used light-coloured woods. On his death his business was taken over by his nephew **Alexandre-Louis** (1799–1863), the son of Pierre-Antoine whose business he inherited the same year. Alexandre-Louis kept the two workshops separate and maintained the individual character of their products, that of his father's being mainly in mahogany and dark woods while that of his uncle increasingly concentrated on pieces decorated with porcelain and on BOULLE furniture. During the July Monarchy he became one of the principal furniture-makers. He also supplied furniture to George IV for Carlton House in London. In 1842 he became *ébéniste du roi* to Louis Philippe. His workshops were extremely productive and made a great deal of Louis XV reproduction furniture, thus anticipating a taste which was to become fashionable under Napoleon III. In 1855 he retired and his business was taken over by his son who does not, however, appear to have continued for many years.

Lit: D. Ledoux-Lebard, *Les ébénistes-parisiens (1795–1870)*, Paris 1965.

Bellarmine Important type of Rhenish stoneware jug with a moulded mask of a bearded man just below the neck and often with a coat of arms

Bellarmine: salt-glazed stoneware, Cologne, Maximinenstrasse workshop, c.1530 (Kunstmuseum, Düsseldorf)

below the mask. They were made from the C15 onwards and later named after Cardinal Roberto Bellarmino (1542–1621), who was hated in Protestant countries for his Counter-Reformation zeal. In Germany it is called a *Bartmannkrug*. Production of such jugs continued until the C19 in Germany and they were copied in England where they were also known as 'Greybeards' and 'd'Alva bottles'.

Lit: Gisela von Bock in *Keramos* 34 (1966), pp. 30–43; A. Thwaite in *The Connoisseur*, April 1973.

Belle Vue pottery, *see* HULL POTTERY.

Belleek porcelain factory Founded by **David McBirney** at Belleek in County Fermanagh, N. Ireland, in 1857 and producing a light, fragile, highly translucent feldspathic porcelain, similar to PARIAN WARE but with a lustrous pearly glaze, first put on show at the Dublin Exhibition of 1865. This type of porcelain, which is said to have been invented by William Goss of Stoke, Staffordshire, immediately won great popularity. It was much used for small vases and dishes, often in the form of shells, made to the design of a Dublin architect, W. R. Armstrong. Pieces were exhibited in the U.S.A. at the Centennial Exhibition of 1876. The American firm OTT & BREWER of Trenton began, with the assistance of William Bromley who had worked at Belleek, to produce similar wares in 1872. They were marked with the name 'Belleek'. Wares with a similar body were subsequently made by the LENOX COMPANY and,

Belleek porcelain: 'Dolium' shell, 1857–71 (Victoria & Albert Museum)

under the name of 'Lotus Ware' by KNOWLES, TAYLOR & KNOWLES. The products of these U.S. factories were much more richly modelled and decorated than the original Irish wares.

Lit: G. A. Godden (ed.), *Jewitt's The Ceramic Art of Great Britain, London* 1972.

Belleek ware, *see* BELLEEK PORCELAIN FACTORY.

Bellevue potteries. French faience factories near Toul (Meurthe-et-Moselle), the first of which was founded in 1755 and in 1771 passed to **Charles Bayard** and **François Boyer** who secured for it the title of a *Manufacture Royale*. It produced biscuit figures from models by CYFFLÉ, also large garden figures in painted terracotta. Table-wares were made in faience and cream-coloured earthenware, the latter painted with landscapes in black or brown. Potteries are still active at Bellevue. (Wares made at the HULL POTTERIES in England were sometimes marked 'Belle Vue' but there was no connection between the two factories.)

Lit: E.-J. Dardenne, *Essai sur Paul-Louis Cyfflé*, Brussels 1912.

Belli, Valerio (1468–1546). The most famous Italian Renaissance engraver of gems and, especially, rock crystal. He was born in Vicenza, probably trained in Venice and went in 1520 to Rome where he became friendly with both Michelangelo and Raphael. Pope Clement VII commissioned him to execute a cross and three medallions, all of rock crystal (now in the Vatican Library), apparently completed by 1524. In 1530 he returned to Vicenza where he completed in 1532 his most famous work – a casket composed of twenty panels of rock crystal engraved in the High Renaissance style with scenes from the life of Christ. This was also executed for Clement VII who gave it to François I (now in the Museo degli Argenti, Palazzo Pitti, Florence). He is known to have executed similar panels for a cross and pair of candlesticks, completed only shortly before his death, for Pope Paul III (the cross is possibly identical with one in the Victoria and Albert Museum, London). Documents record numerous other works which are lost. Casts were made from his rock-crystal carvings and reproduced as bronze plaquettes.

Lit: G. G. Zorzi in *L'Arte*, XXIII (1920), pp. 181–94.

Belli, Vincenzo (1710–87). He was the founder of a family of goldsmiths and silversmiths who made much of the best Roman domestic and ecclesiastical plate from the mid C18 to the mid C19. He was born in Turin, where he was trained, and settled in Rome by 1740, becoming a master of the guild the following year. His work ranges in style from a rather exuberant Rococo (ewer and basin of 1745–50, Museu de Arte Sagra, Lisbon) to a more solid and sober style reminiscent of contemporary English plate by such silversmiths as HEMING (e.g. ewer and basin of 1780 in Museo di Palazzo Venezia, Rome). He employed some 20 assistants. His son **Giovacchino** (b.1750) took over the workshop on his father's death and developed an Antique Revival style making sugar bowls in the form of Grecian urns, etc. He was succeeded by his son **Pietro** (1780–1828) and grandson **Vincenzo II** (d.1859).

Lit: C. G. Bulgari, *Argentari Gemmari e Orafi d'Italia*, vol. 1, Rome 1958.

Bellingham, John, *see* VAUXHALL GLASSHOUSES.

Bellosio, Eugenio (1847–1927). Milanese silversmith, he specialized in Neo-Mannerist work in which he emulated the costly virtuosity of CELLINI and GENTILI, e.g. his knives and forks with handles in the form of nymphs and satyrs *c.*1887 (Museo del Castello Sforzesco, Milan). He exhibited some spectacular examples of his technical skill at the Turin exhibition in 1898. He also made the silver altar in the parish church of S. Marta at Margreglio in the Brianza, north of Milan.

Lit: *Milan 70/70*, Exh. Cat., Milan 1970.

Belper pottery A Derbyshire factory active from *c.*1750 producing mugs, etc. in light brown stoneware until 1834. Similar wares were made nearby at DENBY.

Belter, John Henry (1804–63). He was a German furniture-maker who emigrated to America in 1844 and became extremely successful, replacing Duncan PHYFE as New York's best known cabinet-maker and eventually giving his name to a type of New York furniture. He specialized in Parlour Suites, made with elaborately carved, pierced and

J. H. Belter: rosewood table with marble top, 1856–61, labelled John Henry Belter (Museum of the City of New York)

J. H. Belter style sofa of 'parlor furniture' type, New York, c.1855 (Metropolitan Museum of Art, gift of Mrs Charles Reginald Leonard)

upholstered bentwood, and these became known as 'Belter Furniture'. Before going to America he had been apprenticed as a woodworker in Württemberg and had probably begun experimenting with bentwood. THONET exhibited examples of his bentwood chairs in Coblenz in 1841 and Belter may well have seen them. He may have known Thonet at this period. In New York he first took a shop in Broadway and in 1858 opened a large factory on Third Avenue where he is said to have employed some 40 apprentices. Rosewood was his favourite material for furniture but this dark heavily grained wood, which came mainly from Brazil and the West Indies, lacked sufficient strength for carved work and was difficult to use for veneering on curved surfaces. Belter invented a process by which rosewood could be used for the most voluptuously carved and intricately curved pieces, with elaborate perforated ornament. The process was patented by him at various times between 1847 and 1858. It was a plywood process, either entirely of rosewood or with the outer layers of rosewood. There could be as few as 3 and as many as 16 layers, usually there were between 6 and 8, to make a panel less than an inch thick. The grain of each layer was of course set at right angles to the next. The panel could be shaped in moulds by steam heat and later carved. It enabled him to replace the traditional rail and stile construction of chairs with moulded one-piece backs, carved and upholstered. Stylistically his furniture belongs to the heavily florid Neo-Rococo (the *zweites Rokoko*) which had begun to succeed the BIEDERMEIER style in Germany before he emigrated to America, and which is also found in Paris at the Court of Louis Philippe (1830–48). After settling in New York he probably used English and American pattern books, thus diluting his imported style. Contours are opulently rounded, legs bend into double-scrolled curves, there is much carved work, both in relief and in the round, of fruit and flowers and juicy leaves, with every now and then a bold symmetrical CARTOUCHE. It is redolent of its period, both in Europe and America, being as over-stuffed as it is over-decorated. After his death his firm continued under his brother-in-law **Springmeyer** until it went bankrupt in 1867.

It seems likely that at least two of Belter's competitors (Charles A. BAUDOUINE and Joseph MEEKS) infringed on his patents and manufactured very similar furniture. And other American furniture-makers, notably Alexander ROUX, worked in a similar Neo-Rococo style. It is therefore probable that some of the furniture attributed to Belter was not by him. Examples generally agreed to be by him are in the Metropolitan Museum, New York, the Museum of the City of New York, and the Brooklyn Museum.

Lit: J. Downs in *Antiques*, LIX, Sept 1948; E. H. Bjerkoe, *The Cabinet Makers of America*, New York 1957.

Benckgraff, Johann, *see* RINGLER, Joseph Jakob.

Benedetto, Maestro (*fl.*1510–20). Proprietor of the best maiolica factory in early C16 Siena. His wares are characterized by a fine, sometimes finicky, touch in the painting of religious (rarely mythological) scenes generally surrounded by white borders painted with arabesques and scrolls in blue – a type of ornament called by contemporaries *alla porcellana* and derived ultimately from China.

Lit: R. Langton Douglas in *Burlington Magazine*, LXXI (1937), p. 89.

Beneman (or **Benneman**), **Guillaume** (*fl.*1784–1811). He was a German furniture-maker who settled in Paris *c.*1784, became a *maître ébéniste* in 1785 and from then onwards superseded RIESENER in Court favour. His charges were moderate whereas Riesener's were excessive. He obtained nearly all the later royal commissions, except those of Marie Antoinette who remained faithful to Riesener. But his reputation as the leading exponent of the late Louis XVI style has recently been exploded by the discovery that a number of his finer pieces were in fact merely revisions or transformations of earlier work by other craftsmen, especially his fellow German Joseph STÖCKEL, and were often supervised by the sculptor HAURÉ, e.g. the magnificent commodes made *c.*1786 for Compiègne and now in the Louvre and at Fontainebleau. Stöckel's work was often neo-Roman in style but it became even more neo-Roman after Beneman's revisions, such as his table legs in the form of *fasces*. Beneman

G. Beneman: commode by G. J. Stöckel transformed by Beneman, c.1786 (Louvre)

survived the Terror to become one of the leading Directoire and Empire furniture-makers, often working to designs by PERCIER as in the commode and secretaire he made for Napoleon at Fontainebleau. His work is slightly heavy and Teutonic despite his long residence in France and his close collaboration with French craftsmen and designers. Examples of his furniture are in the Louvre in Paris and the Wallace Collection in London.

Lit: F. de Salverte, *Les ébénistés du XVIIIe siècle*, Paris 1962; F. J. B. Watson, *The Wrightsman Collection: Furniture*, New York 1966.

Bénitier French term for a vessel to hold Holy Water and be hung on a wall. It is usually made of faience or metal.

Bennett pottery A factory established in Baltimore in 1846 by two English brothers, **Edwin** and **William Bennett.** It was one of the first in the U.S. (along with the BENNINGTON POTTERY) to make jugs of a biscuit porcelain similar to PARIAN WARE with a coloured ground (blue or sage-green) and relief decorations in white. And it was the first in the U.S. to make industrial MAJOLICA, from 1853. Products included a wide range of useful wares and also some decorative pieces. William Bennett withdrew from the concern in 1856.

Lit: E. A. Barber, *The Pottery and Porcelain of the United States*, New York 1901.

Bennington pottery and porcelain factory One of the most important U.S. ceramic factories of the mid C19. An earthenware and brick manufactory established at Bennington, Vermont, in 1793 by **John Norton** began to produce stoneware by 1815. This concern was inherited in 1823 by the founder's sons **Luman** and **John** and survived until 1894. But in 1842–3 Luman's son, **Julius Norton** founded in partnership with **Christopher Webber Fenton** a factory making wares of higher quality and greater artistic pretensions. An English potter, John Harrison, who had worked at the COPELAND factory, was employed from 1846 and seems to have initiated the production of a type of biscuit porcelain similar to PARIAN WARE which was used both for figures and for jugs with relief decorations (usually in white on a coloured ground). In 1849 Fenton patented a 'flint enamel'

Bennington Pottery & Porcelain Co.: 'Niagara Falls' pitcher, Parian ware, c.1853 (Metropolitan Museum of Art, gift of Dr Charles W. Green)

glaze, mottled yellow, orange, blue and brown – an elaboration of the ordinary mottled brown 'Rockingham' glaze – applied to both useful wares and ornaments, especially to jugs with handles in the form of greyhounds. Most products were in the English styles of the time but specifically American motifs were sometimes incorporated in decorations – reliefs of waterfalls (called the Niagara Falls pattern) on Parian type wares. TOBY-JUGS representing U.S. notabilities were also made. The factory was styled the **United States Pottery** from 1853 until it closed in 1858.

Lit: R. C. Barrett, *Bennington Pottery and Porcelain*, New York 1958.

Benson, William Arthur Smith (1854–1924). Architect, designer and metalworker, he was associated with MORRIS who encouraged him to set up a workshop for turned metal on a commercial scale in 1880. A factory was built at Hammersmith and in 1887 a shop was opened in Bond Street, London. The firm continued until Benson retired in 1920. He also designed furniture and wallpapers for Morris & Co.

Lit: W. A. S. Benson, *Drawing, Its History and Uses*, Oxford 1925.

Bentwood Bentwood furniture is composed of PLYWOOD, usually in rod form but also in sheet form, bent under steam heat into curves. It was exploited in the early C19 in the U.S.A. by Samuel Gragg (1772–*c*.1855) who obtained a patent for an 'elastic chair' in 1808 in Boston. Contemporaneously BIEDERMEIER craftsmen in Germany and Austria used it for concave chair-backs. It then found its great master in THONET who used it in the form of rods. His contemporary BELTER used it mainly in sheet form, elaborately carved. In 1874, in New York, Isaac Cole patented a one-piece plywood chair which seems almost to anticipate the C20 when such notable furniture makers as AALTO and BREUER used bentwood and exploited its possibilities with imagination.

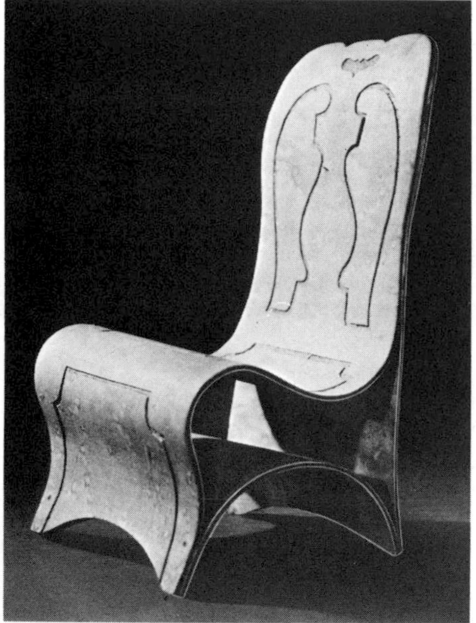

Bentwood chair patented by Isaac Cole, 1874 (Museum of Modern Art, New York)

Bérain, Jean (1637–1711). French architect and ornamental designer, he was one of the creators of the LOUIS XIV STYLE. He was the son of a Lorraine gunsmith and settled in Paris *c*.1644. He began by publishing designs for the decoration of small arms (1659) and locks (1662–3). From 1670 he was employed by the Crown as an engraver and in 1674 became *dessinateur de la Chambre et du Cabinet du Roi* with the duty of providing designs for royal festivities, ballets etc. When LE BRUN's star waned at Court Berain's rose and on Le Brun's death in 1690 he became chief designer with lodgings in the Louvre, alongside his relation BOULLE and his son-in-law Jacques Thuret, the royal clock-maker. His designs for furniture, chimney-pieces, boiseries, ceilings, etc., were engraved and published, many of them decorated with GROTESQUES of the type to which he gave his name – a light, elegant, whimsical style of decoration which hovers on the brink of the Rococo. Airy canopies held up by fantastic TERM figures and surrounded by springy coils of bandwork and acanthus foliage harbour graceful figures of classical gods, occasionally replaced by Chinamen with attendant monkeys in place of classical fauns. But despite Rococo premonitions they are never asymmetrical and always carefully fitted into their panels. The influence of his designs is apparent in much Louis XIV Style furniture, notably Boulle marquetry and carved picture frames, and also in tapestries, carpets and faience, especially that of MOUSTIERS. A collection of his engraved designs was published in 1711 in Paris as *Oeuvre de Jean Bérain, recueillies par les soins du sieur Thuret*. His son **Jean Bérain II**, 1678–1726, was also employed by the Crown as a

Bérain style decorations on a Moustiers faience plate, c.1730 (Musée Nationale de Céramique, Sèvres)

decorator and designer. His work is almost indistinguishable from his father's.

Lit: R. A. Weigert, *Jean I Bérain*, Paris 1937.

Bercka, Heinrich Wolf, *see* GABEL POTTERY.

Berettino or **Bianco sopra azzurro** An Italian form of ceramic decoration in opaque white on a light or dark blue tin-glaze. It was used on Faenza, Venice and other Italian maiolica wares from the early C16 onwards.

Bergama or **Bergamo carpets,** *see* TURKISH CARPETS.

Bergère, *see* CHAIR.

Berkey & Gay furniture, *see* GRAND RAPIDS FURNITURE.

Berlage, Hendrikus Petrus (1856–1934). Dutch architect and designer who was among the first to break away from C19 Historicism and to plead, in his writings, for logical construction and integrity of workmanship. These 'moral' qualities were in harmony with the social and political climate of the early C20 – when he began to win recognition from young opponents of the Art Nouveau movement which had passed him by –

H. P. Berlage: oak buffet, c.1909 (Gemeentemuseum, The Hague)

and are well expressed in his solid, chunky but very soundly made furniture, e.g. his oak buffet *c.*1900 (Gemeente Museum, The Hague) which is completely stripped of ornament and relies solely on its proportions and the bold use of structural members. Much of his furniture is technically of high quality and was made in the Amsterdam atelier known as 'Het Binnenhuis'. He also designed glass vessels of an austerely simple purity for the BACCARAT and PANTIN glasshouses. He was a propagandist for F. L. WRIGHT and was much admired by both RIETVELD and MIES VAN DER ROHE who was his pupil.

Lit: N. Pevsner, *Pioneers of Modern Design*, Harmondsworth 1960; R. Banham, *Theory and Design in the First Machine Age*, London 1960.

Berlin ironwork A wide range of decorative objects, from small statuary to jewellery, was produced by the **Royal Prussian Iron Foundry** from *c.*1800 until *c.*1840. Prominent Prussian artists of the early C19 provided designs – notably SCHINKEL – and the range was expanded to include many small household utensils, e.g. for smoking, writing, sewing and embroidery. The style varies from a bold Neo-Classical to a delicate Neo-Gothic. Berlin ironwork was much imitated in the 1930s. There were three foundries producing these wares in the early C19 – at Gleiwitz and Sayn outside Berlin and at Invalidenstrasse in Berlin. The Gleiwitz foundry, established in 1796, was producing architectural ornaments and small relief panels by 1800. The foundry in Berlin began in 1804 as a branch of the Gleiwitz foundry. In 1815 it absorbed the foundry at Sayn which had been started in 1769–70 by the Archbishop of Trier. The fashion for decorative objects in iron began to diminish in the 1830s and after 1845 the Gleiwitz foundry ceased production except 'to order'. The Berlin foundry was destroyed in 1848 but at Sayn production continued until 1865 when it was taken over by Krupp.

Lit: B. Mundt, *Historismus*, Catalogue of the Kunstgewerbemuseum, Berlin, vol. VII, Berlin 1973; A. Clifford, *Cut-Steel and Berlin Iron Jewellery*, Bath 1971.

Berlin porcelain factories The first was founded by **Wilhelm Kaspar Wegely** in 1752 and functioned for five years producing good though somewhat opaque hard paste porcelain table-wares decorated with landscapes, Watteau figures or naturalistic flowers, as well as some impressive vases with *putti* and flowers in relief, and statuettes generally deriving from MEISSEN or VINCENNES models but also including an original series of children with rather large heads and ungainly limbs dressed as members of various trades and professions. Craftsmen employed at this factory and at Meissen (notably Karl Just Christian Klipfel) joined a second factory founded in 1761 by a financier, **Johann Ernst Gotzkowsky** and managed by

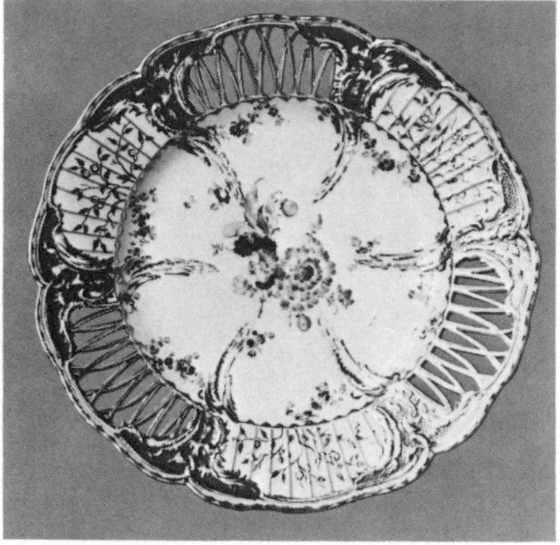

Berlin porcelain: dessert plate from the Potsdam Neue Palais service, 1765 (Museum für Kunst und Gerwerbe, Hamburg)

Johann Georg Grieniger with F. E. MEYER as *Modellmeister*. In 1763 Frederick the Great acquired this concern which has been run by the State ever since. The products of the first decade are among the most attractive of their period, made in porcelain of a creamy tone, modelled and painted with great delicacy in an eminently restrained Rococo style. They included outstanding table and tea and coffee wares made for the King, decorated with patterns in very low relief, paintings of flowers, landscapes, Watteau subjects, etc., and much use of *Mosaik* borders. Vases with Rococo scroll-work and flowers in relief are rather more elaborate but have similar painted decorations. Statuettes made after models by F. E. and W. C. Meyer are generally of rather elongated mythological figures and groups stylistically simi-

Berlin porcelain: coffee-pot and sugar-bowl, with Schwarzlot decorations, c.1768 *(Berlin-Porzellansammlung, Belvedere Charlottenburg, Berlin)*

(Left) Berlin porcelain: Venus, 1769–70, *modelled by W. C. Meyer (Berlin-Porzellansammlung, Belvedere Charlottenburg, Berlin)*

lar to French sculpture of the same period, but they also included numerous sets of children, animals and birds. The factory's most ambitious undertaking in this department was a huge table-centre with many figures and groups, made in 1770–72 as a diplomatic gift for Catherine the Great and now in the Hermitage Museum, Leningrad. Shortly after 1770 the adoption of a different type of *kaolin* led to the production of porcelain of a cold white tone and at about the same time the factory began to develop a severer style influenced by Neo-Classicism – forms were simplified, Rococo scroll-work was gradually abandoned and Antique decorative motifs began to appear. Under the patronage of Frederick William II, from 1786 onwards, this tendency was greatly accelerated. In the early C19 the Empire style, as developed at SÈVRES, was adopted, especially for table-wares, with much gilding and bands of solid colour. Notable products include vases and plates painted with views of buildings in and around Berlin (e.g. Schinkel's theatre). Statuettes and busts were made in biscuit porcelain sometimes

(Right) Berlin porcelain: plate, 1815–20 (Berlin-Porzellansammlung, Belvedere Charlottenburg, Berlin)

Berlin porcelain: teacup and saucer, 1832–7 (Berlin-Porzellansammlung, Belvedere Charlottenburg, Berlin)

after the marbles of J. G. Schadow (notably of his group of the two princesses Louise and Frederica). In 1818 Schadow modelled for the factory an elaborate table-centre presented to the Duke of Wellington (Apsley House, London). LITHOPHANIES made *c.*1830–50 are among the more interesting products of this period when a rather heavy 'Victorian' style was adopted for both table-wares and ornamental objects. The appointment of **Hermann Seger** (1839–93) as technical director in 1878 marks the beginning of a revival. He was the inventor of 'Seger-Porzellan' used for vases of simple Chinese shape with rich *flambé* glazes, in *sang de boeuf*, violet, green, yellow, etc. Early in the C20 the factory began to acquire models from a number of sculptors including Adolph AMBERG (1874–1913), author of a many figured 'marriage procession' table decoration, Josef WACKERLE, Paul Scheurich (1883–1945) and others. Hermann Hugo Hubatsch (1878–1940) worked for the factory from 1903 making several models of figures in modern dress, notably that of a lady of fashion seated in a Rococo chair. Under the artistic direction of **Theodor Hermann Schmuz-Baudiss** (1859–1942), from 1908 to 1926, good table wares with Art Nouveau decorations were also produced. In 1929 it began to produce very elegant and simple tea-services, designed by **Trude Petri-Raben** (b.1906), the prototypes for much plain white table-ware later produced in Europe and the U.S.

Berlin porcelain: teacup, designed by Trude Petri-Raben, c.1929 *(Museum of Modern Art, New York)*

The products of Wegely's first Berlin factory were marked with an impressed W in blue; those made at Gotzkowsky's factory 1761–3 were marked with a G in underglaze, though many of these pieces were decorated later. The best-known mark, a sceptre in underglaze blue, was used in various forms from 1763 onwards. The best collection of Berlin porcelain is in the Kunstgewerbemuseum, Berlin-Charlottenburg. (For factory marks *see* p. 881.)

Lit: E. Köllmann, *Berliner Porzellan 1763–1963*, Brunswick 1966; *Porzellan-Kunst: Sammlung Karl H. Brohan*, Exh. Cat., Schloss Charlottenburg, Berlin 1969.

Berlin potteries There were four faience factories of which the most important was founded by a Dutchman, **Cornelis Funcke**, in 1699. It flourished until *c.*1760. Notable for large and sometimes rather ungainly vases of Baroque shape with reeded bodies and chinoiserie decorations in blue and white. A few vases have ISNIK type sailing ships on a turquoise ground.

Lit: O. von Falke, *Alt-berliner Fayencen*, Berlin 1923; K. Hüseler, *Deutsche Fayencen*, Stuttgart 1956–8.

Berlin tapestry factory Founded in late C17 by Huguenot refugees from AUBUSSON. The finest product is the series *The History of the Great Elector* (1693). But the factory was engaged mainly in copying French tapestries, notably the BEAUVAIS *Grotesques* after BERAIN and *Chinese Hangings* after Vernasal and Blain de Fontenay.

Lit: H. Göbel, *Wandteppiche*, Leipzig 1923–34; D. Heinz, *Europäische Wandteppiche*, Brunswick 1963.

Berlin woolwork Needlework panels executed, usually by amateurs, in coloured wools (manufactured in Gotha and dyed in Berlin) on square-meshed canvas to floral or figurative (often religious) patterns. Numerous books of patterns were published, mainly in Berlin, from 1804; they were printed on a grid corresponding with the mesh of the canvas and could thus be copied exactly. Nowadays the design is often printed on the canvas. The panels are used for upholstery or sometimes framed as pictures.

Lit: B. Morris, *Victorian Embroidery*, London 1962; M. G. Proctor, *Victorian Canvas Work (Berlin Wool Work)*, London 1972.

Bernardi, Giovanni Desiderio (1496–1553). Italian engraver of hard stones, especially rock crystal. He was highly praised by Vasari. Born at Castlebolognese, the son of a goldsmith, he began his independent career by working for Alfonso I d'Este as an engraver and medallist. Before 1530 he settled in Rome where he enjoyed the patronage of Pope Clement VII and Cardinal Ippolito de' Medici for whom he executed two crystal carvings after designs by Michelangelo (lost but known from casts). He also made engravings after designs by PERINO DEL VAGA.

His most famous work is the series of engraved rock-crystal panels of the Cassetta Farnese set in silver by Bastiano Sbarri, 1548–61 (Museo di Capodimonte, Naples). Another series of his crystal panels was set in a cross and two candlesticks of silver by A. GENTILI (now in the treasury of St Peter's in Rome). Notable works by or generally attributed to him are in the Museo degli Argenti, Palazzo Pitti, Florence, in the National Museum, Copenhagen, in the Metropolitan Museum, New York, and in the Bibliothèque Nationale, Paris. Casts were taken from some of his carvings and reproduced in bronze plaquettes.

Lit: E. Kris, *Meister und Meisterwerke der Steinschneidekunst . . .*, Vienna 1929.

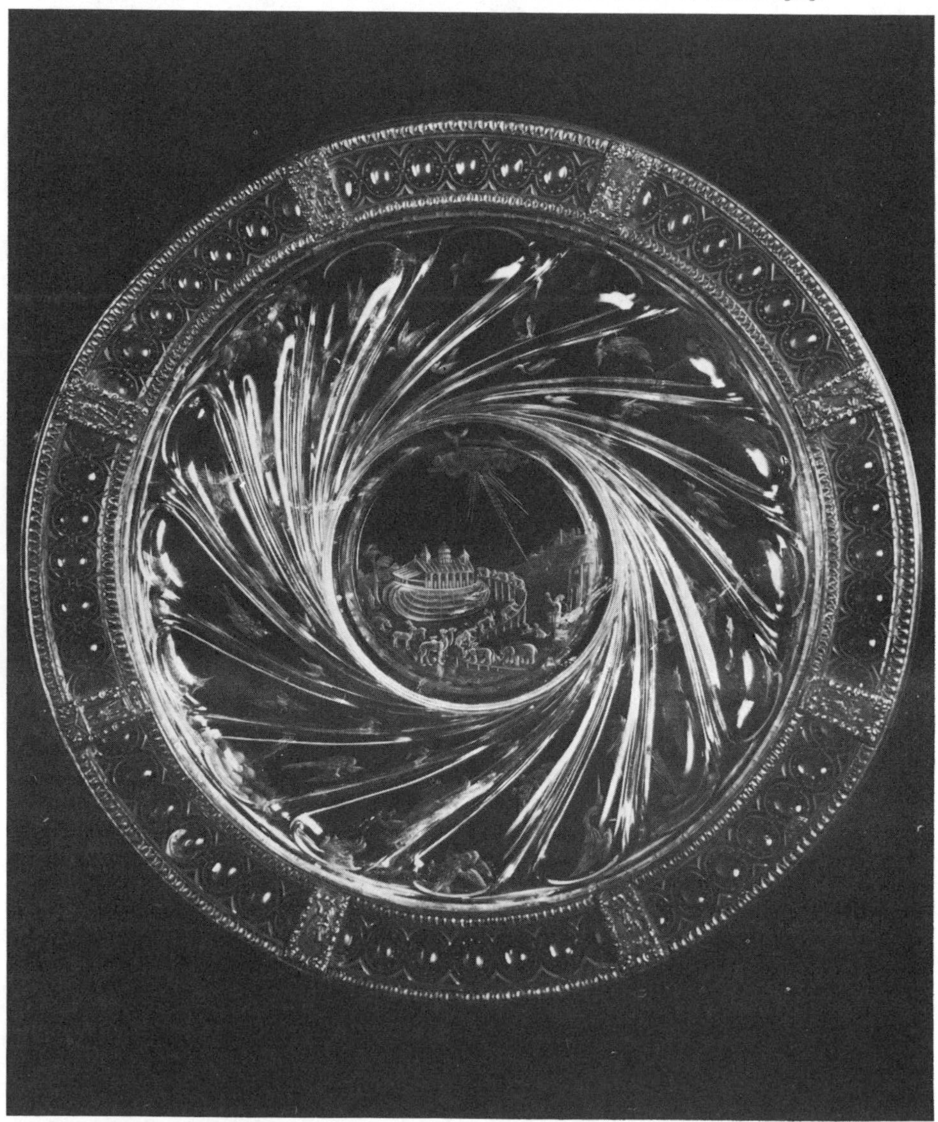

G. D. Bernardi: rock crystal dish engraved with scene from the story of Noah (Museo degli Argenti, Palazzo Pitti, Florence)

Bernward of Hildesheim, St (d.1022). The patron of the Hildesheim School of bronze-workers and credited with their finest products, though the extent of his participation (as designer, craftsman or patron) is uncertain. He became bishop in 993 and visited Rome in 989 and 1001. His most famous work is the pair of vast bronze doors (15ft high and each cast in one piece) intended for St Michael's church and now in the Cathedral at Hildesheim. They were commissioned by 1015. They comprise sixteen reliefs of Biblical scenes enacted by wonderfully lively figures, leaning out of the background with their large and very expressive heads in high relief. For this and for his silver Crucifix of 1007/8 (Hildesheim Cathedral Treasury) he derived inspiration from the early CAROLINGIAN period. For his bronze column candlestick of *c.*1000–1010 (Hildesheim Cathedral) decorated with scenes from the life of Christ in a continuous spiral, he was influenced by Roman Triumphal columns.

Lit: P. Lasko, *Ars Sacra 800–1200*, Pelican History of Art, Harmondsworth 1972.

Bernward of Hildesheim: silver candlestick, c.996–1000 (Hildesheim, Magdalenenkirche)

Berthevin, Pierre, *see* MOSBACH POTTERY.

Bertoia, Harry (b.1915). Sculptor and furniture-designer, born in Italy he settled in the U.S.A. in 1930 and designed his famous shell chair in 1952, now known internationally as the 'Bertoia chair' (manufactured by Knoll Associates Inc.). His furniture brilliantly exploits the sculptural possibilities of moulded wire and foam rubber as materials and he was among the few, with

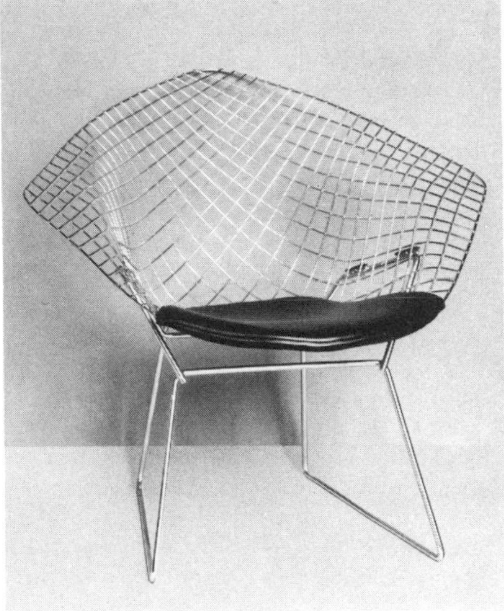

H. Bertoia: shell chair, 1951–2 (Musée des Arts Décoratifs, Paris)

EAMES and SAARINEN, to appreciate the new demands made by open-planning in architecture on the design for furniture and fittings. The Bertoia chair is a combination of frame and shell. The seat is suspended by side braces which allow great flexibility and automatic adjustment to two positions by means of an effortless shift of the sitter's body weight. The upper part is formed of a moulded mesh of chromium-plated steel wire.

Bertolucci, Giuseppe, *see* PESARO POTTERIES.

Besnier, Nicolas (*fl.*1714–54). Leading RÉGENCE silversmith; *maître* 1714, *Orfèvre du Roi* 1715. A toilet basin (Louvre) decorated simply with a Vitruvian scroll, delicate shells and heads of *putti* puffing out their cheeks is a characteristic performance. With OUDRY he was made administrator of the BEAUVAIS tapestry factory in 1734. (For his mark *see* p. 893.)

Lit: Y. Bottineau and O. Lefuel, *Les Grands Orfèvres*, Paris 1965.

Bethersden pottery, *see* SUSSEX POTTERIES.

Bettignies, Jean-Maximilian-Joseph de, *see* SAINT-AMAND-LES-EAUX POTTERIES and TOURNAI POTTERY AND PORCELAIN FACTORY.

Betts, Thomas (d.1767). Glass merchant in London producing cut glass and mirrors from 1740 onwards and, like his contemporary John AKERMAN, probably employing German or Bohemian glass-cutters as well as English craftsmen. He was succeeded by Jonathan Collet.

Beurdeley, Louis-Auguste-Alfred (1808–1882). He was the son of a Parisian furniture-maker whose business he greatly extended during the Second Empire. He specialized in C18 style furniture and bronzes (e.g. mounts for vases) which he sometimes interpreted in a personal manner. His son **Alfred-Emmanuel-Louis** (1847–1919) succeeded to his father's business and developed it even further, concentrating on reproduction C18 furniture, often of a very high quality. He liquidated the business in 1895.

Lit: D. Ledoux-Lebard, *Les ébénistes-parisiens (1795–1870)*, Paris 1965.

Bevan, Charles, *see* MARSH AND JONES.

Bevel A sloping edge, especially of a piece of glass or wood.

Beyer, Johann Christian Wilhelm (1725–1806). Architect, painter and sculptor who executed models for porcelain figures at the LUDWIGSBURG PORCELAIN FACTORY *c.*1761–7 and VIENNA 1768. He claimed to be a devotee of the Antique, but his porcelain models show no Neo-classical tendencies. They include elegantly *mouvementé* mythological groups, posturing musicians in contemporary dress, and – a masterpiece of delicate Rococo eroticism – a half-dressed fisher girl. He published two volumes of engravings of his work which include some of his porcelain models – *Österreiches Merkwürdigkeiten die Bild-*

J. C. W. Beyer: Fisher Girl, Ludwigsburg porcelain, c.1764 (Kunstgewerbemuseum, Berlin)

und Baukunst betreffend, Vienna, 1779 and *Die neue Muse oder der Nationalgarten*, Vienna, 1784.

Lit: Alt-Ludwigsburger Porzellan, Exh. Cat., Schloss Ludwigsburg 1959.

Beyerlé, Baron Jean-Louis de, *see* NIDERVILLER POTTERY & PORCELAIN FACTORY.

Bezel 1. The metal frame for a watch glass or the glass door in front of a clock-face.

2. The setting of a stone especially in a finger ring.

3. The inside rim of the cover or lid of an object.

4. An alternative form of BEVEL.

Bianco di Faenza Maiolica with a thick white glaze developed at Faenza in the 1540s and widely imitated elsewhere in Europe in the late c16 and c17, especially for useful wares. Painted decorations were usually applied rather sparingly.

Bianco di Faenza: dish painted in compendiario *style, late c16 (Victoria & Albert Museum)*

Bianco sopra azzurro, *see* BERETTINO.

Bianco sopra bianco Tin-glazed earthenware painted in opaque white on an off-white (generally bluish) ground. It was first used in c16 Italy but was later adopted in N. Europe as well.

Biarelle, Paul Amadeus (*fl.*1736–1752). He was a decorative designer, born at Liège, and worked with his brother **Johann Adolph** who executed designs by CUVILLIÉS at Schloss Falkenlust near Cologne. From 1737 they were both at Ansbach where they contributed to the decoration of the Residenz, one of the finest secular Rococo buildings in S. Germany. Here they began by working under the architect Paolo Retti. They also designed handsome console tables in collaboration with Johann Georg Worflein (*fl.*1736–1769).

Lit: H. Kreisel, *Die Kunst des deutschen Möbels*, vol. ii, Munich 1970.

Bibelot A personal trinket, e.g. a snuff-box, *étui*.

Bible-box A c17 box usually of oak and with a slanting top, used to hold a bible, books or writing materials. It stood on a table.

Bickley, Benjamin, *see* BILSTON ENAMEL FACTORIES.

Bideford pottery, *see* DEVONSHIRE POTTERIES.

Bidet A small bath on a low stand which can be bestridden, especially for washing the pudenda. First made in early c18 France, generally of walnut with a metal basin. Later the basins were sometimes of porcelain or silver and the stands of rare woods. Mme de Pompadour had one of marquetry with gilt bronze mounts. Double bidets for use by couples were occasionally made. Always more popular on the Continent than in England, though one was used by 'Fanny Hill'. *Illustrated next page.*

Biedermeier A decorative style popular in Germany and Austria (and to a lesser extent Scandinavia) from the 1820s to 1840s, when the furniture trade had recovered from the Napoleonic wars. It is named after a fictional character invented by Ludwig Eichrodt in 1855–7. Biedermeier symbolized the German bourgeoisie of the early c19 and his name was applied both to the period 1815–48 in general and also to that period's decorative style – mainly to the furniture,

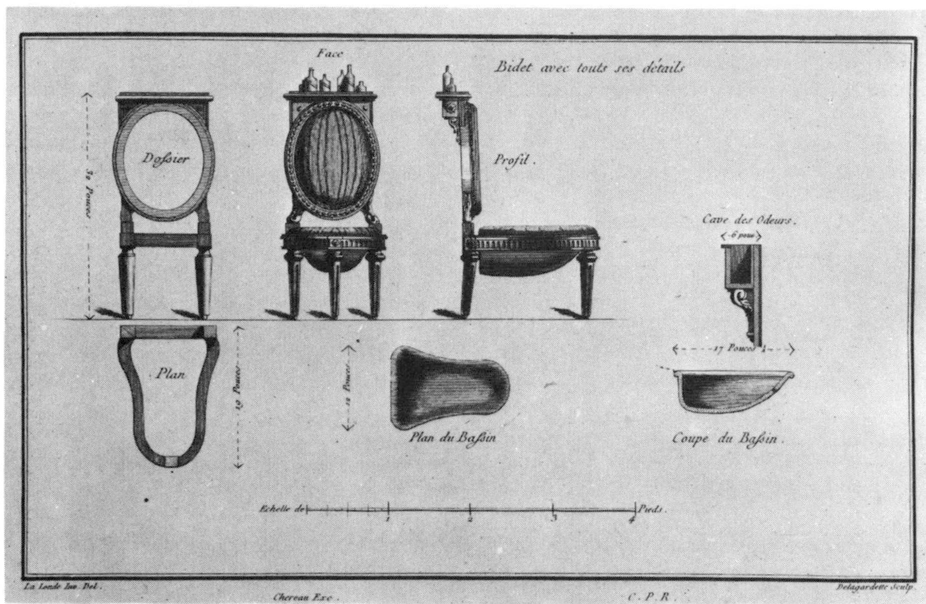

Bidet design by Lalonde, c.1780

though also to carpets, porcelain, glass, etc. Biedermeier furniture is solid, homely and comfortable-looking and has, at its best, great *gemütlich* charm and unpretentious elegance. Though it avoided all the pompous decorative motifs used on Empire furniture it in fact derived from French *bois clair* furniture of the Directoire and Empire periods, perhaps leavened slightly with English influence – it sometimes looks like ADAM furniture stripped of its ornamentation.

Biedermeier ice pails, Berlin porcelain, 1823–6 (Private Collection)

Simplicity and clean lines, combined with light-coloured woods (maple, cherry and apple) lend it a curiously modern appearance. Ornamentation is usually limited to pilasters, columns and palmettes, often applied in ebony to make a striking contrast against the background of light-coloured wood, and is all the more effective for being very sparingly used. The best Biedermeier furniture-maker was Joseph DANHAUSER of Vienna. He was much employed by the Archduke Charles and a large collection of his designs is in the Museum für angewandte Kunst, Vienna. See also Karl Friedrich SCHINKEL.

Lit: G. *Himmelheber, Biedermeier Furniture,* London 1974.

Biennais, Martin-Guillaume (1764–1843). His workshops produced much of the best Empire silver and gilt bronze though he himself, unlike his chief rivals Henri AUGUSTE and J. B. C. ODIOT, was an entrepreneur and dealer rather than a craftsman. Born at Lacochère (Orne), he had established himself in Paris *c.*1789 as a *tabletier* (i.e. a maker and vendor of such small articles as gaming-tables, cane handles of ivory, ebony, etc., and NÉCESSAIRES of which he later made a speciality). He began producing and dealing in silver and jewellery only after the suppression of the guilds in 1797. But he soon attracted the patronage of Napoleon and most of the 100,000 francs a year which Napoleon set aside for silver was spent with Biennais. He served Napoleon until the end of the Hundred Days, supplying the liturgical plate for his marriage with the Archduchess Marie-Louise and for other important occasions. He also supplied the Bavarian, Austrian and Russian Courts, as well as numerous private patrons. He developed a special type of dinner service, sold only to Imperial and Royal clients, with vessels of simple, elegant and neo-Grecian shape, very sparsely decorated with engraved and cast ornament alluding symbolically to the particular patron. His flair for combining elegance, neatness and utility is very evident in the *nécessaires* for which he became well known, e.g. that made for Napoleon in 1806 and now in the Louvre which contains 86 vessels and other pieces packed into a chest measuring 14 × 54 × 35 cm. In addition to silver and gilt bronze and jewellery his workshops also supplied furniture, especially transportable furniture and small pieces such as games tables and cabinets, e.g. the silver-inlaid Egyptiennerie coin cabinet of 1806, now in the Metropolitan Museum, New York, and various pieces at Malmaison. His furniture was sometimes to designs

M.-G. Biennais: silver-gilt tureen and plateau from the Borghese table service, 1794–1814, probably after a design by Percier and Fontaine (Metropolitan Museum)

by PERCIER and FONTAINE. He retired in 1819, leaving his silver and bronze business to his assistant Cahier. His furniture business was taken over by another former assistant, Birgkam. (For his mark *see* p. 893.)

Lit: S. Grandjean, *L'Ofèvrerie di XIXe siècle en Europe,* Paris 1962; D. Ledoux-Lebard, *Les ébénistes parisiens (1795–1870),* Paris 1965.

Biggin Strictly a cylindrical silver coffee-pot with a strainer, named after a man of this name who invented it; but the term, first recorded 1803, is sometimes applied to other types of coffee-pot.

Bigot, Alexandre (1862–1927). French ceramic artist who began as a student of mineralogy and turned to making pottery with crystalline and flambé glazes in the 1890s. By 1894 he was producing very handsome stoneware vases with mottled and speckled glazes. From *c.*1897 he developed stoneware for architectural decoration. He executed the frieze of animals to the model of

A. Bigot: stoneware vase, 1894 (Kunstgewerbemuseum, Berlin)

R. Jouve for the Porte Monumentale of the Paris 1900 exhibition. At this exhibition he won 6 prizes for his pottery. He was later concerned with the integration of ceramic decorations in reinforced concrete construction (e.g. façade of St Jean, Montmartre, Paris).

Lit: A. Lesur & Tardy, *Les poteries et les faïences françaises*, Paris 1957–60.

Bijar carpets, *see* PERSIAN CARPETS.

Bilbao American type of wall-mirror supposedly imported from Bilbao, late C18 and early C19. The frame is veneered with sheets of pink or variously coloured marble in the Classical style.

Bilivert or **Biliverti, Jacopo** *See* BYLIVELT, Jacques.

Bill, Max (b.1908). Swiss architect, painter, sculptor and designer, trained at the BAUHAUS and influential as a teacher and theorist of design. He invented the *Die Güte Form* programme for the Schweizerische Werkbund (1949), published *Form* in 1952 (dedicated to his revered master Henry VAN DE VELDE) and from 1951–6 was director of the ULM HOCHSCHULE FÜR GESTALTUNG for which he designed the buildings in a complex, open plan. Here the Bauhaus ideals of co-operative design were revived. Its aim is the 'humanizing of our increasingly mechanistic civilization'. The designs of BRAUN products owe much to it. Bill's own designs include the 'Patria' typewriter (ancestor of NIZZOLI's classic Olivetti *lettera* 22), triangular three-legged tables and chairs with heart-shaped backs and seats (1949–50), some ingenious nesting chairs of flat units (1950–51), an elegant sun-ray lamp (1951) and some beautifully detailed electric wall plugs (1958).

Lit: Max Bill: Oeuvre 1928–1969, Exh. Cat., Paris–Grenoble 1969–70.

Biller family One of the leading families of Augsburg silversmiths: they were Protestants and thus specialized in the production of secular plate. Five of them achieved prominence. **Albrecht** (1663–1720) was responsible for much work in a late Baroque style and published a volume of engraved ornament in 1703. Together with his brothers **Johann Ludwig the elder** (1656–1746) and **Lorenz** (d.1720 or 1726) he

Lorenz or Johann Biller: silver vase, late C17, Augsburg (Museo degli Argenti, Palazzo Pitti, Florence)

made a set of silver-gilt guéridons for the Court in Dresden (now in *Grünes Gewölbe*, Dresden). **Johann Jacob** (d.1723) was the author of two sets of engraved designs for goldsmiths' work. **Johannes** (1696–1746) was appointed in 1738 Royal Silversmith to the Prussian Court for which he had worked extensively. He was the son of Johann Ludwig the elder and brother of **Johann Ludwig the younger** (1692–1746). (For their marks *see* p. 893.)

Lit: S. Rathke-Köhl, *Geschichte der Augsburger Goldschmiedegewerkes vom Ende der 17 bis zum Ende der 18 Jhs.*, Augsburg 1964.

Billet Romanesque moulding composed of alternating blocks or cylinders. Also, in silver, the thumbpiece on a tankard, flagon, etc.

Billingsley, William (1758–1828). Leading English porcelain painter. Apprenticed at the DERBY factory 1775, left in 1796 and after working at various minor factories joined the WORCESTER factory in 1808. In 1813 he established a small porcelain factory at Nantgarw in Wales but this was a financial failure and in 1819 he sold it to COALPORT where he subsequently went to work. He excelled in naturalistic flower paintings for which he developed an individual mannerism – washing in the petals in full colour and then wiping out the highlights with a dry brush. He also painted landscapes, race-horses, etc.

Lit: W. D. John, *William Billingsley 1758–1828*, Newport, Mon. 1968.

Bilsted The wood of the *liquidambar styraciflua* tree, used in American cabinet-making as a substitute for mahogany, especially during the Revolutionary War.

Bilston enamel factories The source of most English painted C18 enamel boxes, scent-bottles, candlesticks, etc., commonly ascribed to BATTERSEA. The first was established before 1749 when it was acquired by **Benjamin Bickley** from whom it passed in 1776 to **Samuel Yardley** who transferred it to Wednesbury. There were several other factories at Bilston and Wednesbury and it is rarely possible to distinguish their products from one another or from those made by M. BOULTON. The best are among the most appealing English contributions to the Rococo style, painted with landscapes, bouquets of summer flowers, exotic birds, portraits, *fêtes champêtres* (often derived from prints after French and other masters) in a wide range of pastel colours with lovely tooled HONEY GILT scrollwork. The basic material was copper and various processes were employed – from 1776 the objects were dipped in baths of thick liquid white enamel to provide the ground colour, from the 1780s large areas of colour were applied over the white ground by spraying. Many wares were exported to the Continent (where they were in great demand, especially those with *rose Pompadour* grounds) until the 1790s when the factories began to decline: the last continued to function until the death of its owner Isaac Beckett in 1831.

Lit: B. Watney & R. J. Charleston in *English Ceramic Circle Transactions*, VI, pt. 2, 1966; R. J. Charleston in *Victoria & Albert Museum Journal*, III (1967), pp. 1–12.

Bilston japanning factories Established in Staffordshire in the 1690s, they were the first to make japanned tin-plated ironware, usually snuff-boxes and other small objects: *see* JAPANNING. They continued throughout the C18 and became very prosperous in the C19.

Bimann, Dominik (1800–57). The most distinguished Bohemian engraver of glass in the BIEDERMEIER STYLE. He was born in N. Bohemia and trained at the HARRACHOV GLASSHOUSE, also attending the art academy in Prague. He specialized in neat, clean-cut profile portraits engraved on glass vessels or, more usually, plaques, but also executed engravings of landscapes, allegories, genre scenes, and old master paintings (including the *Madonna della Sedia*). He obtained the glass which he engraved mainly from the Harrachov factory but worked at Prague and, in the summers, at the internationally frequented spa, Franzenbad (now Františkovy-Lázně). His brother **Vincenz** (d.1847/8) was also a notable glass engraver.

Lit: G. E. Pazaurek, *Gläser der Empire- und Biedermeierzeit*, Leipzig 1923; S. Pessatova in *Journal of Glass Studies*, VII (1965), p. 83ff.; F. A. Dreier in *Jahrbuch des Preussischer Kulturbesitz*, VI (1968), p. 210ff.

Bin label Large pottery label painted with the name of a wine or a number, made from the C17 and intended to hang beside a wine bin.

Binche lace A pillow lace similar to BRUSSELS LACE, made at Binche near Valenciennes in Hainault, from the C17 onwards (certainly before 1686). It is often fairly substantial and appears to have been used for bed-spreads, etc., as well as apparel. The old Flemish patterns were abandoned in the early C19 for machine-made net to which sprigs of pillow lace were applied.

Lit: B. Palliser, *History of Lace*, rev. M. Jourdain & A. Dryden, London 1902; L. W. van der Meulen-Nulle, *Lace*, London 1963.

Bindesbøll, Thorvald (1846–1908). Danish architect, graphic artist and designer. Worked for the **Copenhagen earthenware factory**, evolving (*c*.1893) a strongly personal style of abstract decoration (in a mixture of enamel and *sgraffiato* techniques) with splashes of colour and roughly drawn circles, which owes nothing to Art Nouveau and seems almost to anticipate the paintings of mid-C20 Abstract Expressionists.

Lit: V. Wanscher, *Gotlieb Bindesbøll 1800–1856*, Copenhagen 1932.

T. Bindesbøll: enamelled earthenware plate, 1901 (Musée des Arts Décoratifs, Paris)

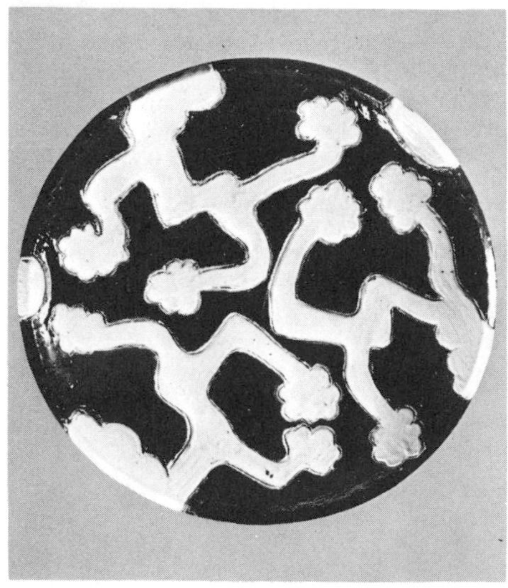

Bing & Grøndahl's Porcelain Factory Established in Copenhagen in 1853 by **M. H.** and **J. H. Bing** and **F. V. Grøndahl** but producing little of interest before 1885 when the painter **Pietro Krohn** (1840–1905) was appointed artistic director – a post he held until 1895. He was responsible for the Heron dinner service of 1888 in a kind of proto-ART NOUVEAU style. Products are rather like those of the Royal Danish Factory (see COPENHAGEN PORCELAIN FACTORY) and some artists worked for both concerns. Its most notable statuettes are those of women and children in contemporary costume after models by Ingeborg Plockross-Irminger (b.1872). Later Jean Gauguin (1881–1961) son of the painter, provided models. (For mark *see* p. 881.)

Bing & Grøndahl Porcelain Factory: coffee service designed by Kaj Bojesen, 1930–31 (Kunstindustrimuseet, Copenhagen)

Lit: Porzellan-Kunst: Sammlung Karl H. Bröhan, Exh. Cat., Berlin 1969.

Bing, Samuel (1838–1919). The *entrepreneur* of the ART NOUVEAU movement. He began as an art dealer in Hamburg, moved to Paris in 1871, visited the Far East in 1875 and opened a shop in Paris, *La Porte Chinoise*, for the sale of oriental, especially Japanese, objects, with a New York branch. In 1893 he went to the U.S. to report on architecture and design for the French government and returned much impressed by Sullivan and Richardson. In 1895 he opened a shop called *L'Art Nouveau* in rue de Provence, Paris, marketing the works of the leading Art Nouveau craftsmen and such painters as Bonnard, Toulouse-Lautrec, Vuillard and Munch.

Lit: R. A. Koch in *Gazette des Beaux Arts* LIII (1959), pp. 179–90; G. P. Weisberg in *The Connoisseur* CLXXII (1969), pp. 119–25, 294–9; S. Bing, *Artistic America*, (ed. R. Koch), Cambridge, Mass., and London 1970.

Bingham, Edward, *see* CASTLE HEDINGHAM POTTERY.

Binns, Charles Fergus (1857–1934). An English potter, he was appointed in 1900 the first director of the New York School of Clay Working at Alfred University which became the New York State College of Ceramics. He remained there until his death. He made high-fired stoneware vessels inspired by early Chinese pottery, but is important mainly for establishing the idea of the 'studio potter' in the U.S. and for his book, *The Potter's Craft*, 1922.

Bird-beaked jug or **Sparrow-beaked jug** A type of English – usually Bow, Worcester or Lowestoft – porcelain jug with a beak-shaped pouring lip. The body is usually pear-shaped, plain, though sometimes ribbed or fluted.

Birdcage support A type of hinge joining the top of a pedestal type table to the base, in such a way that the top can be revolved.

Bird's eye veneer A veneer of light wood, generally maple, with a marking of small spots thought to resemble birds' eyes.

Birmingham enamels, *see* BATTERSEA and BILSTON ENAMEL FACTORIES.

Biscuit Unglazed white porcelain with a texture similar to marble and used mainly for statuettes, busts, etc. Its potentialities as a medium for decorative objects seem to have been appreciated first by BACHELIER and examples were made at SÈVRES from 1753. In the later C18 most larger European porcelain factories produced biscuit objects. The substance proved particularly appropriate for reductions and imitations of antique sculpture as made in VIENNA, at the VOLPATO factory in Rome, etc., but in the C19 the cheaper PARIAN WARE became more usual for this purpose. The term *bisque* is incorrect.

Bishop-bowl A bowl in the form of a mitre and used for a type of punch called 'bishop', made of faience at various potteries in Denmark and Schleswig-Holstein in the later C18.

Bizarre silks Figured silks of a special type fashionable throughout Europe from *c.*1695 to *c.*1720, mainly as dress materials. Produced during a highly fashion-conscious period when weavers found it profitable to change their patterns every year, they were woven according to an extremely wide range of exotic designs composed mainly of curiously swaying and tropical-looking floral and foliage motifs, off-set by sharply jagged lines and rectangular architectural and other motifs. The dominant pattern is usually in gold or silver thread and is sometimes applied to a damask background designed in a contrary direction. Bizarre silks contrast sharply with the formally patterned Baroque silks of the C17 and the naturalistically patterned silks woven from *c.*1730 onwards. They were influenced by Oriental textiles and were at one time erroneously supposed to have been woven in India. They were in fact produced by many European factories, notably those of LYONS and SPITALFIELDS, and are among the earliest manifestations of a taste for asymmetry, characteristic of the Rococo.

Lit: P. Thornton, *Baroque and Rococo Silks*, London 1965.

Bizen potteries A group of potteries in or near the village of Imbe on the north shore of the Inland Sea of Japan described, with SETO, TOKONAME, etc., as one of the 'Six Ancient Kilns'. Pottery had been made in the district since prehistoric times but the term *Ko-Bizen* – or Bizen ware – is normally applied to pieces made in or after the Kamakura period (1185–1337). The earlier of these products are of stoneware with a hard grey body and with a reddish brown or slate blue surface either unglazed or covered with a kind of salt glaze (said to have been produced by throwing seaweed on the fire). Large grain jars, long-eared jars for the storage of leaf tea and other domestic vessels were the main products. TEA CEREMONY WARES – tea-jars, vases and water vessels but not bowls – made from the C15 onwards were greatly prized by generations of tea-masters. Figures of animals and birds with a dark brown glaze appear to have been made from the C15 though most surviving specimens date from 1760–1880. From the C16 the kilns were controlled by members of six families who enjoyed special privileges and whose descendants remained in charge until the early C20. Many pieces are marked with the names of their makers and some are dated.

Lit: Soame Jenyns, *Japanese Pottery*, London 1971.

Black basaltes, *see* BASALTES WARE.

Black Jack A tankard-shaped drinking vessel of moulded and sewn LEATHER or CUIR BOUILLI, lined with resin or pitch to make it water-tight and sometimes provided with a metal rim, in common use in Europe up to the C18.

Black metal or **Black pewter** An alloy of 60 parts tin and 40 parts lead, a cheap form of pewter used from the C14 for simple objects. The danger of lead-poisoning reduced its use for domestic wares.

Black Seto wares, *see* MINO POTTERIES.

Black, Starr & Frost, *see* BALL, TOMPKINS & BLACK.

Black-work Embroidery worked in black silk (sometimes with gold thread as well) on white linen, especially in Spain and Elizabethan England. Such embroidery was applied to costume and to such household objects as pillow covers.

Blanc-de-chine, *see* TÊ-HUA PORCELAIN.

Bleeding bowl A small shallow bowl, with a single flat projecting handle, used by barber surgeons when bleeding patients. They are of silver, pewter or pottery and date from the C17 to C18. The term is often applied erroneously to PORRINGERS.

Blénod, Barthélemy, *see* AVON POTTERY.

Bleu celeste A turquoise-blue ground colour used at SÈVRES from 1752, sometimes called *bleu turquin.*

Bleu de Deck, *see* DECK, Joseph-Théodore.

Bleu de roi A very rich bright lapis lazuli blue enamel ground colour originated at SÈVRES before 1760 and extensively imitated elsewhere, especially at WORCESTER and DERBY.

Bleu persan Faience painted in white or light colours on a dark blue ground, first made at NEVERS *c.*1670 and much imitated. The effect is often like a photographic negative of the normal blue on white scheme. In the C19 such wares were classed as 'Persian' – hence the name.

Blijk, J, van den, *see* STIPPLE ENGRAVING.

Blind Earl pattern A pattern of rose-leaves and buds in relief used on WORCESTER porcelain from *c.*1760 onwards and later named after an Earl of Coventry who went blind in 1780.

Blind tooling A decorative technique used in leather work, especially in BOOKBINDING. The design or lettering is stamped, embossed or otherwise impressed on the surface of the leather and left 'blind', i.e. without the addition of gold leaf or other colouring. If gold is applied it is called GOLD TOOLING. In bookbinding the technique of blind tooling is found from the very beginning, in Coptic bookbindings made in Egypt.

Blocked bindings In bookbinding, the trade term for STAMPED BINDINGS.

Blockfront or **Swell'd front** A uniquely American treatment of the front of case pieces, popular in C18 New England, especially with Newport cabinet-makers such as the GODDARDS and TOWNSENDS. It is rarely found in New York or Virginia. The centre of the front recedes in a flattened curve between convex sections of similar flattened curves. The central concave and flanking convex sections often terminate with carved shell ornaments.

Blonde lace A type of pillow lace made from the

1740s, of unbleached Chinese silk (later black and white silks), mainly at Arras, Lille and Chantilly.

Bloor, Robert, *see* DERBY PORCELAIN FACTORIES.

Bloor, Ott & Booth, *see* OTT & BREWER COMPANY.

Blue-dash chargers Modern name for certain C17–C18 tin-glazed earthenware dishes made at LAMBETH, Brislington and BRISTOL, painted in maiolica colours with borders of slanting dashes, and often with stylized portraits of Charles I and II, James II, William III, Adam and Eve, etc.

Bluejohn Highly decorative variety of fluorspar found in Derbyshire and known in France as *'bleu-jaune'*, hence the English name. It has a translucent appearance, with bands of colour ranging from dark purple and violet to light brown and yellow. Though known since Roman times it was not used extensively until after 1743 when the first large deposit of it was mined near Castleton. It immediately became very popular for ornaments, especially in France which imported large quantities. Later Matthew BOULTON used it extensively for candelabra with ormolu mounts.

Blue scale, *see* SCALE PATTERN.

Boarded chest A primitive type of chest with the front and back made of planks of wood hammered to vertical end-pieces or heavy corner stiles, generally reinforced with iron corner pieces, sometimes covered with leather or cloth. Distinct from the joined chest in which the sides are attached with mortice and tenon joints.

Bobbin lace, *see* Pillow LACE.

Boberg, Anna Katerina, *see* RÖRSTRAND POTTERY & PORCELAIN FACTORY.

Bocage Modelled leaves and flowers, generally in the form of a shrub or small tree forming the support for and background to a porcelain figure or group.

Boccaro or **Buccaro** The name, derived from Spanish and Portuguese – *bucaro* – originally given to a scented red earthenware made in Mexico, Chile and Peru, and imported into Europe by the Portuguese, but later applied to Chinese red and brown stoneware of YI-HSING and to the scented red earthenware of TALAVERA. It is not to be confused with *bucchero* ware, *see* ETRUSCAN POTTERY.

Boch, François and **Jean-François,** *see* VILLEROY & BOCH.

Boch, William, *see* UNION PORCELAIN COMPANY.

Boehm, Edward Marshall An American artist and potter famous for his naturalistically modelled and coloured birds made at his pottery at Trenton, New Jersey, *c.*1955–69. They are not unlike the porcelain models of birds made by **Dorothy Doughty** at the WORCESTER PORCELAIN FACTORY.

Boelen, Jacob (1657–1729). American silversmith of Dutch origin, working in New York. He made beakers, tankards (with coins set in the lid) and cups. His work, sometimes marked with a barred IB in a shield, shows Dutch influence.

Bogaert, Thomas (1597–1652/3). Utrecht silversmith, possibly trained under Adam van VIANEN whose AURICULAR STYLE he imitated on domestic silver. For church plate he adopted a normal Baroque style.

Lit: J. Fredericks, *Dutch Silver*, The Hague 1952–60.

Bohemian glasshouses A very large group of factories the first of which were established by the C15 and produced WALDGLAS. The crystal glass technique and the Venetian style were introduced in C16, and by the end of the C16 products began to include vessels of a slightly smoky pale topaz colour, distinctly German in shape (such as the HUMPEN) and decoration (rather crude genre scenes and elaborate heraldic achievements). In the late C17 some N. Bohemian factories began to make a new type of glass (including potash and a large proportion of chalk) of greater brilliance which was found a particularly good medium for elaborate engraved decorations. They produced a great quantity of finely engraved glass, though the best work was done by independent artists at the courts of various German princes. The main centre for such glass shifted *c.*1725 from Bohemia to Silesia where most of the best German Rococo engraved glass was produced. The Bohemian glass industry was revived shortly after 1815 and the factories turned out vast

Bohemian glass: vase, cut and wheel-engraved, stained yellow and pink and silvered, c.*1830–40 (Victoria & Albert Museum)*

(Right) Bohemian glass: goblet with engraved decoration by Vinzenz Bimann, c.*1840, Neuwelt, N. Bohemia (Kunstgewerbemuseum, Berlin)*

quantities of glass in the BIEDERMEIER style, specializing in flashed and cased pieces of brilliant colour. The term 'Bohemian glass' is often incorrectly applied to all manner of E. German glass.

Lit: Z. Pešatová, *Böhmische Glasgravuren*, Prague 1968; L. Urešová, *Victoria & Albert Museum. Bohemian Glass*, London 1965; A. von Saldern, *German Enamelled Glass*, Corning (N.Y.) 1965.

Böhm, August (1812–90). Notable Bohemian glass engraver who led a wandering life working first in his native land, then Stourbridge, London,

Hamburg and the U.S., returning to Bohemia shortly before his death. He executed engravings of portraits, religious subjects, battle scenes, horses, etc. on goblets and plaques.

Lit: G. E. Pazaurek, *Gläser der Empire und Biedermeierzeit,* Leipzig 1923; F. A. Dreier in *Jahrbuch Preussischer Kulturbesitz* VI (1969), p. 210 ff.

Bohme, Carl Wilhelm, *see* MEISSEN PORCELAIN FACTORY and BERLIN PORCELAIN FACTORY.

Bois de rapport Wood cut across the grain or end-cut to give a marked figure instead of a straight grain: used in marquetry and veneering.

Bois de rose, *see* TULIPWOOD.

Bois durci A substitute used to simulate ebony *c.*1850–1900 in France and England. It was patented in France by **F. C. Lepage** in 1855. Made from sawdust, water and blood, heated and then die-stamped into medallions, rosettes, etc.

Boiserie French for wood panelling, it is usually applied to C17 and C18 panelling elaborately decorated with shallow relief carvings of foliage, etc., notably by Rococo carvers such as Jacob VERBERCHT who specialized in *boiseries.* It was often painted, e.g. white with the carved ornament picked out in gold, or, in the mid C18, with brightly coloured VERNIS MARTIN in pinks, greens, yellows, blues, etc., as in the *petits appartements* at Versailles where fine examples survive.

Boissierer, *see* REPAIRER.

Boizot, Louis-Simon (1743–1809). French sculptor, he specialized in small-scale decorative pieces in marble and terracotta though he also worked on a large scale. He was trained under M.-A. SLODTZ and in Rome (1765–70). From 1773 to 1800 he was in charge of the sculpture section of the SÈVRES PORCELAIN FACTORY and modelled numerous figures and busts for reproduction in biscuit porcelain. The coronation group of Louis XVI and Marie-Antoinette is among the more notable and elaborate of his works. He also provided models for work in bronze, outstandingly the allegorical group (cast, chased and gilded by GOUTHIÈRE) for the 'Avignon' clock of 1771 (Wallace Collection, London) but also including furniture mounts for P.-P. THOMIRE. Stylistically he developed from a rather sweet classicizing Rococo style to a more solid and severe Neo-Classical manner. Surviving the Revolution, he executed several works on Republican and, in his last years, Napoleonic themes.

Lit: L. S. Lami, *Dictionnaire des sculpteurs de l'école française au dix-huitième siècle,* Paris 1910.

Bokhara carpets, *see* TURKMAN CARPETS.

Bolection moulding Moulding used to cover the joint between two members with different surface levels. It projects beyond both surfaces and is usually of S-section.

Bologna sgraffiato-ware dish, late C15 (Ashmolean Museum, Oxford)

Bologna potteries The source of the best C15 and early C16 SGRAFFIATO WARES. The earlier products are simply decorated and rather rough in comparison with maiolica. But in the late C15 one pottery (or perhaps a single potter) attempted to compete with the maiolica factories by producing much finer wares decorated with distinctly Renaissance *putti,* tightly breeched young musicians, etc., within borders of stylized leaves. The production of *sgraffiato* wares continued at Bologna into the C18. From *c.*1794 a factory run by **Carlo Aldrovrandi** produced cream-coloured earthenware. In the later C19 the factory of **Angelo Mingetti and Son** produced imitations of Renaissance maiolica.

Lit: W. B. Honey in *Burlington Magazine* XLVIII (1926), pp. 224 ff G. Morazzoni in *Cronache d'Arte* II (1925), pp. 235 ff; J. Chompret, *Répertoire de la majolique italienne*, Paris 1949.

Bombard A large jug made of moulded and sewn leather or CUIR BOUILLI, usually lined with resin or pitch to make it water-tight, in use from early times into the C18.

Bombé Literally 'blown-out': an exaggerated swelling shape given especially to the fronts of Rococo chests-of-drawers – a convex shape on two or more axes.

Bombé commode with Venetian lacca *decoration (Palazzo Rezzonico, Venice)*

Bonbonnière A small box for sweets, usually very fancifully decorated.

Bondolf (or **Bondol**), **Jean de,** also called **Jean** or **Hennequin de Bruges** (*fl.*1375). Flemish painter, manuscript illuminator and tapestry designer. He provided *c.*1375 the cartoons for one of the greatest masterpieces of French Gothic tapestry, *The Apocalypse* of Angers, a set of seven large hangings, each originally about 16ft 6ins by 80ft, which survives in mutilated condition (Musée de Tapisserie, Angers). It depicts scenes from the Apocalypse, derived from various C14 MS illuminations, and elaborate gothic baldachins sheltering meditative figures of uncertain and much discussed significance. Forms are simplified, colours are limited to about fifteen shades with blue, red and green predominating, and the technique is rather coarse with some five warp threads per cm. They were woven in the Parisian workshop of Nicolas BATAILLE.

Lit: R.-A. Weigert, *French Tapestry*, London 1962.

Bone china A type of porcelain made with the addition of bone ash which is pure white in colour. A patent for using bone ash was taken out by **Thomas Frye** of Bow in 1748 and this date marks its first known use, although the idea had been mooted a century earlier in Germany and it was familiar at least as early as the mid C18 as an ingredient of MILCHGLAS. It was later adopted at SÈVRES – some 6 or 7 years after Frye took out his patent. In England the manufacture of bone china quickly spread from Bow to other soft-paste factories, notably Lowestoft, Chelsea and Derby. Later a hybrid paste was adopted in England, containing china clay and stone. This, covered with a lead glaze, was introduced by SPODE at Stoke-on-Trent and by Barr at WORCESTER in the late C18 and became the standard English body during the C19 and is still being used. It gave England a distinctive place in the history of European ceramics. Bone china is softer than hard-paste, and more durable and less expensive to make than soft-paste. (Bone ash was also used as an ingredient of cream-coloured earthenware.)

Bonheur-du-jour A C18 French term for a lady's small writing-table with a cabinet of shelves, drawers or pigeon-holes, usually closed by a tambour shutter, along the rear edge of the table-top. Sometimes it has a cupboard or shelf underneath. It was often fitted for toilet purposes as well as for writing. It exists in a wide variety of shapes. First made in the mid C18 in France it is found soon afterwards in England also, often very richly decorated. Great ingenuity was applied to the fittings in order to compress the maximum number of compartments, holding different objects, into the minimum space. It is the most essentially feminine of all pieces of furniture. The origin of the name is obscure. It is first mentioned in 1770 which perhaps indicates the date of its rise to fashion.

Bonhomme, Henri and **Léonard,** *see* LIÈGE GLASSHOUSES.

Bonnefoy, Antonine, *see* MARSEILLES POTTERY.

Bonnet top A feature peculiar to American furniture of *c.*1730–85. The top of a piece of case furniture is formed by a broken pediment which runs from front to back, either in a solid block of wood or by side covers joining the front and back pediments.

Bonnin and Morris porcelain factory The source of the earliest known pieces of soft-paste porcelain made in America. A short-lived concern active only 1770–72, at Southwark, Philadelphia, it was founded by **Gouse Bonnin** from Antigua and **George Anthony Morris** (d.1773), a Philadelphia Quaker, and staffed mainly with English workmen. The paste was made of clay from White-Clay Creek, near Wilmington, Delaware, and bone ash. Products in the Brooklyn Museum, Philadelphia Museum of Art, Henry Francis Dupont Museum, Winterthur, etc, are marked with an underglaze blue P (for Philadelphia). They are decorated with flowers or chinoiseries in underglaze blue on a white ground and are similar in both material and form to those of the BOW PORCELAIN FACTORY.

Lit: G. Hood, *Bonnin and Morris of Philadelphia,* Chapel Hill 1972.

Bontemps, Georges (1799–1884). French glassmaker and director (1823–48) of the Choisy-le-Roi factory where he developed a process for making fine coloured glass on a large scale; he began producing *opaline* in 1827 and Venetian style filigree glass in 1839. He emigrated in 1848 and joined the firm of Chance Bros. at Smethwick near Birmingham. In 1868 he published *Guide du Verrier* which long remained the leading authority on the technique of glass-making.

Lit: E. O. Lami, *Dictionnaire de l'industrie,* vol. III, p. 358.

Bony, Jean-François (1760–1828). French painter, designer of silks and owner of a LYONS SILK FACTORY. He began as a pupil of LA SALLE but developed a somewhat severe Empire style which won him the patronage of the Empress Josephine for whom he designed silks for a coronation robe and furnishing fabrics for Malmaison. Some of his original designs and silks woven to them are in the Musée des Tissus, Lyons.

Lit: E. Dumonthier, *Étoffes d'ameublement de l'époque napoléonienne,* Mobilier National, Paris 1909.

Bonzanigo, Giuseppe Maria (1745–1820). He was the finest Italian C18 furniture-maker, working, like PIFFETTI, in Turin, mainly for the House of Savoy until the French invasion in 1796. He was primarily a sculptor and wood-carver, as was his

G. M. Bonzanigo: carved and gilt wood fire-screen, 1775 (Palazzo Reale, Turin)

father who specialized in elaborate cases for church organs. Born in Asti, he settled in Turin by 1773 and worked extensively for the royal palaces during the next twenty years. In 1787 he was appointed official wood-carver to the Crown. He continued in business after the French invasion and resumed work for the King after the restoration, his style remaining unchanged during these vicissitudes though he adjusted his iconography where necessary. He had the technical virtuosity of a miniaturist in ivory. Vases of flowers on stalks so fine that they seem to tremble, and decorative relief panels surrounded by leafy wreaths of papery flimsiness demonstrate his extraordinary dexterity. He also carved boiseries and large pieces of furniture – console tables, screens, commodes and bureaux – in an italianate version of the Louis XVI style, decorated with exquisitely carved urns and garlands of fruit and flowers. Examples survive in the Palazzo Reale in Turin and in the Casa di Caccia at Stupinigi.

Lit: V. Viale, *Mostra del Barocco Piemontese* catalogue, Turin 1963.

Bookbinding A cover made to protect and hold together the pages of a codex or printed book. The art of bookbinding originated in the Coptic monasteries of Egypt in the Early Christian period (probably C2) with the codex of papyrus sheets which superseded the scroll. These Coptic bindings consist of boards, made by sticking together several layer of papyrus, covered with leather and provided with thongs, thus forming a kind of parcel for the manuscript. The leatherwork was generally decorated with incised or stamped patterns (i.e. BLIND TOOLING). Fragments of such bindings survived from the C4 onwards. The technique of binding was developed in different ways by Islamic and by W. European craftsmen. The conception of a binding as a light-weight wallet for a manuscript was maintained in the East. Gatherings of sheets were lightly sewn to each other and glued to the inner spine of the cover which was of leather or pasteboard. Covers were often decorated with great delicacy, inside as well as outside (the inside of the 'boards' are often richer than the outside), with blind or gold tooled ornament, at first severely abstract but later with foliage and, from the C15 in Persia, figurative ornament. Some Persian leather bindings of the C15–C16 with inlaid work in several colours and exquisitely refined gold tooling are among the masterpieces of leatherwork and the bookbinders' art. Another type of Persian binding, particularly popular at Tabriz and Isfahan in the C16–C17 has boards of *papier maché* painted by miniaturists with picnic scenes, hunting scenes, etc. covered with transparent lacquer varnish. Persian styles of binding were imitated in both India and Turkey.

The vellum sheets on which the first European MSS. were written demanded stronger bindings to hold them together and to prevent the pages from buckling. Wooden boards hinged with leather at the spine and fastened by straps were used. The earliest examples – Gospels of St Cuthbert (Stonyhurst College, Lancashire) and three MSS. owned by St Boniface (Landesbibliothek, Fulda) – all of the C7, have sheets gathered and sewn in Coptic style. But by the C9 the practice of sewing the quires onto horizontal bands came into use. Very sumptuous decoration – of carved ivory, embossed or enamelled metal and sometimes precious stones – were provided for covers of Gospels and other liturgical books which were displayed on lecterns or altars. But the most usual material for bookbinding was leather, decorated with incised patterns (CUIR CISELÉ) or blind tooling. The widespread use of paper from the C14 made heavy bindings less necessary; and the invention of printing with movable type in the mid C15 greatly increased the number of bound books. The first printers generally maintained their own binderies or engaged special binders to work for them, and their books seem to have been sold to the public in simply bound form. But the demand for decoratively bound volumes increased and it became usual for printers to sell books in sheets. The process of stamping with small dies gave way to the use of large PANEL STAMPS and a handpress which made it possible to decorate the whole surface in a single operation. The cylindrical roll was used to impress repeating patterns from the late C15. At about the same time, the practice of GOLD TOOLING was introduced from the Islamic countries into Italy and was gradually taken up in N. Europe.

Distinctive styles of binding were developed in

Italy, notably the ALDINE and CAMEO styles. But Paris soon became the most important centre for bookbinding. Some of the finest work was executed in the studio of Claude de Picques (*c.*1510–75) – known as the *atelier au trèfle* from the frequent use of a trefoil tool – who was binder to Henri II and Catherine de Medici and was probably responsible also for some of the famous GROLIER and MAIOLI bindings. Other outstanding French bindings of the c16 are of the LYONESE and CENTRE AND CORNER types. Towards the end of the century a new and still more elaborate type

Cover of the Notger Gospels: late c10 ivory panel set in c12 Mosan enamels and c16 copper-gilt oval plaques (Musée Curtius, Liège)

Persian book cover, in two parts, papier mâché, coloured and gilded, C17 with modern restorations (Victoria & Albert Museum)

with much use of small tools all over the surface, later to be called FANFARE, was introduced probably by Nicolas and Clovis Eve who succeeded de Picques as royal binders. During this period BLIND TOOLED bindings were the rule in England, Germany and the Netherlands. In the C17 centre and corner bindings became popular in England. Bindings covered with embroidery in silk and gold and silver thread were also made though they can never have been very common. In the second half of the C17, especially after the Restoration, very handsome and elaborate bindings were produced in England, most notably the MEARNE BINDINGS named after the royal binder. But in France a much more severe style – that of the so-called JANSENIST BINDINGS – became fashionable. Work of very high quality was executed in nearly all parts of Europe in the C18. Tastes for ROCOCO ornament, CHINOISERIE and, in the later years, the ANTIQUE were all reflected in bookbindings. Outstanding binders included, in France DEROME, DU SEUIL, LE MONNIER and PADELOUP, in England James Bate who specialized in chinoiseries, EDWARDS OF HALIFAX and R. PAYNE. But work of very high quality was done by craftsmen whose names are less well known and a great many outstanding bindings remain anonymous. Styles of great delicacy were evolved in both Scotland and Ireland. In the C19 the GOTHIC REVIVAL found expression in CATHEDRAL STYLE bindings. But most fine binding of this period was imitative of earlier styles. It was not until the end of the century that binding was revived, especially by COBDEN SANDERSON under the influence of the ARTS AND CRAFTS movement. Soon afterwards ART NOUVEAU designs appeared, especially in French and German work. In the C20 French binding has been strongly influenced by Cubism and other contemporary styles.

From the C16 onwards printers normally issued books in sheets to be bound according to the taste of the buyer (or the intermediary bookseller). But in later C17 England printers began to have books bound in grey or blue boards with paper spines, a binding strong enough to hold them together and enable them to be read as soon as issued. Some such books never acquired more substantial bindings, a great number were very simply bound in leather with little if any ornament (generally confined to the spine) and only the minority were given fine bindings. A great change took place in the early C19, initiated in 1822 by the London publisher William Pickering who began to issue books in cloth bindings, known as trade bindings. Soon afterwards machines were introduced for glueing, instead of sewing, the pages together and to the cover. A small class of English books (mainly gift books) was provided with decorative EMBOSSED BINDINGS of leather: this was the first of several attempts to produce 'fine' looking bindings for a large public. Publishers' cloth bindings were also sometimes decorated in relief and all but the cheapest with gilt lettering and decorations on the spine. Technically these covers should be described as 'cases' rather than bindings as the pages are not bound to them by cord but merely attached by paper and glue.

Scottish book binding, c.1750 (Victoria & Albert Museum)

Lit: R. Devauchelle, *La reliure en France,* Paris 1959–61; E. P. Goldschmidt, *Gothic and Renaissance Bookbindings,* London 1928; C. Ramsden, *French Bookbinders 1789–1848,* London 1950; *Bookbinders of the United Kingdom (outside London) 1780–1840,* London 1954; *London Bookbinders 1780–1840,* London 1956; J. P. Harthan, *Bookbindings,* London 1961.

Book-rest A small lectern or stand with a slanting platform on which an open book may be supported, on an altar or a writing desk, sometimes built into the latter.

Boote, T. & R. Owners of a pottery established in 1842 at Burslem in Staffordshire notable mainly for the production of PARIAN WARE, earthenware with inlaid decoration, ironstone ware and tiles. At the Great Exhibition of 1851 they exhibited numerous products, notably a copy of the Portland Vase, a bust of Sir Robert Peel, vases, jugs and dinner services, several partly gilded and some partly coloured.

Booth, Enoch, *see* CREAM-COLOURED EARTHENWARE.

Bordeaux potteries A faience factory was founded in 1711 in Bordeaux, run by **Jacques Hustin** who was granted a privilege in 1714; on his death in 1749 it passed to his son **Jacques-Dennis-Ferdinand Hustin** (d.1778) whose widow directed it until 1783. Simply decorated plates and dishes were the staple products. For more elaborate pieces the decorations were derived first from MOUSTIERS, later from ROUEN and NEVERS. A few very large pieces were produced – vases more than a metre high and the face for the clock on the Bordeaux Bourse (1750). After the Hustins' last privilege expired in 1762 several other factories were founded. A porcelain factory producing wares similar to those of Paris operated 1781–90. A faience factory run by **David Johnston**

Bordeaux faience plate, attributed to J. Huston, c.1730 (Musée des Arts Décoratifs, Bordeaux)

1836–45 acquired more than local renown. Ceramics are still produced in and around Bordeaux.

Lit: Meaudre de Lapouyade, *Essai d'histoire des faïenceries de Bordeaux de XVIIIe siècle à nos jours*, Bordeaux 1926; J. Giacomotti, *French Faïence*, London 1963; M. Ernould-Gandouet, *La Céramique en France au XIX siècle*, Paris 1969; *David Johnston: Les débuts de la faïence fine à Bordeaux 1829–1845*, Exh. Cat., Musée des Beaux Arts, Bordeaux 1967.

Boreman, Zachariah (1738–1810). Porcelain painter who worked at the CHELSEA and, from *c.*1783, DERBY factories and from 1794 as an outside decorator in London. He specialized in delicate little monochrome (black or brown) landscapes, often of Derbyshire scenes.

Lit: J. Haslem, *The Old Derby China Factory*, London 1876.

Boselli, Giacomo (1744–1808). Notable Italian potter working at SAVONA. He was the son of a potter and admitted as a master to the potters' guild in Savona in 1768. His factory appears to have been extensive and made a very wide variety of wares – both tin-glazed and cream-coloured earthenware, decorated in high-temperature colours or enamel colours, as well as soft-paste porcelain statuettes. The most attractive are the plates painted in enamel colours with chinoiseries. But his masterpiece is a circular temple covered with maiolica panels which he erected in his garden in Savona (now the Giardino Pubblico) in 1786. Many of his products are signed with his name in a French form – **Jacques Boselly** – which occasioned a now discredited belief that he came from Marseilles.

Lit: A. Lane in *The Connoisseur* CXXXVI (1955), pp. 161–4; P. Torriti, *Giacomo Boselli e la ceramica savonese del suo tempo*, Genoa 1965.

Bosse, Abraham (1602–76). French draughtsman and engraver who was professor of perspective at the Académie in Paris from 1648 until 1665 when he was obliged to retire after a quarrel with LE BRUN. He is notable mainly for his representations of daily life but among the 1500 or so prints which he issued there are a number of designs for mirror frames in a bold Baroque style and several sheets of ornament.

Lit: A. Blum, *L'oeuvre gravé d'Abraham Bosse*, Paris 1924.

Bossi An Italian craftsman said to have worked in Dublin *c.*1785–98. He gave his name to marble inlaid with coloured compositions, especially chimneypieces and table tops, in the style of R. ADAM.

Boston and Sandwich Glass Company A glass-house at Sandwich, Cape Cod, Mass., founded by **Deming Jarves** who had withdrawn in 1823 from the NEW ENGLAND GLASS COMPANY. His new enterprise was first called the Sandwich Manufacturing Company but was renamed the following year. It began by making cut and blown glass but from *c.*1830 also produced pressed glass, coloured glass and, later, flashed glass in the usual range of styles. William E. Kern was employed as superintendent from the 1840s until 1867 (he subsequently worked at the PAIRPOINT MANUFACTURING COMPANY). The factory closed in 1888.

Lit: R. W. Lee, *Sandwich Glass*, rev. edn, Northborough, Mass., 1947.

Boston Rocker, *see* CHAIR: Rocking.

Botanical flowers Botanically exact representations of flowers painted on porcelain, rarely pottery, as distinct from the naturalistic though not strictly scientific DEUTSCHE BLUMEN as well as the fantastic stylized INDIANISCHE BLUMEN. They were copied from the illustrations in botanical books. The earliest are those known as Sir Hans Sloane's plants on CHELSEA porcelain. Such flowers occur on late c18 COPENHAGEN porcelain and products of the DERBY and SWANSEA factories.

Bott, Thomas (1829–70). English porcelain painter. He was the son of a carpenter and began by following his father's trade but taught himself to paint, worked at one of the STOURBRIDGE GLASSHOUSES, then as a portraitist and painter on porcelain in Birmingham. From 1852 he was employed by the WORCESTER PORCELAIN FACTORY where he developed a style of painting vessels in white glazed enamel on a dark blue ground. These pieces were called 'Limoges ware' from the similarity of the colour scheme to LIMOGES ENAMELS, though the forms of the pieces were often Grecian and the figurative decorations in the High Victorian Classical style, rather like those of SOLON's pâte-sur-pâte. His son **Thomas John Bott** (1854–1932) was also a porcelain painter. He began at the Worcester factory and was art director at Coalport 1890–1932.

Lit: G. A. Godden (ed.), *Jewitt's The Ceramic Art of Great Britain*, London 1972.

Bottengruber, Ignaz (*fl.*1720–36). He was a miniature and water-colour painter working in Breslau who became a leading HAUSMALER, decorating first MEISSEN and later VIENNA porcelain with Bacchic, hunting and military scenes framed by very rich scroll-work (e.g. cup and saucer of 1726 in the British Museum, bowl in Österreichisches Museum für angewandte Kunst, Vienna). He appears to have gone to Vienna in 1730, possibly because the Meissen factory had stopped the sale of white wares to Hausmaler, but was back in Breslau in 1736. His pupils included H. G. von Bressler and C. F. von Wolfsburg and he probably influenced Jacobus HELCHIS.

Lit: G. E. Pazaurek, *Deutsche Fayence- und Porzellan-Hausmaler*, Leipzig 1925.

Böttger, Johann Friedrich (1682–1719). The inventor of European hard-paste PORCELAIN. He began as an alchemist trying to make gold from base metals and searching for the Philosopher's Stone under the patronage of Frederick I of Prussia. In 1701 he moved to Dresden to work for Augustus the Strong, Elector of Saxony and King of Poland. There he continued his fruitless experiments in collaboration with the mathematician, scientist and court-official Ehrenfried Walther von Tschirnhausen (1651–1708) with whom he was set the easier task of making porcelain in 1707. By 1708 they succeeded in producing a porcellaneous red stoneware similar to that imported with consignments of tea from China and a translucent white porcelain body made of high-firing clay from Colditz (but without a homogeneous glaze). After Tschirnhausen's death he produced (in 1709) his first specimen of glazed white porcelain. He was appointed first director of the MEISSEN factory in 1710. Most of the wares produced under his direction were imitative of silver in both form and decoration. Though of interest mainly for their substance, some of the simpler pieces are also outstandingly handsome.

J. F. Böttger: red stoneware covered bowl, 1710–13 (Porzellansammlung, Dresden)

Lit: E. Zimmermann, *Die Erfindung und Frühzeit des Meissner Porzellan*, Berlin 1908; *Böttgersteinzeug Böttgerporzellan*, Exh. Cat., Dresden Staatliche Kunstsammlungen 1969.

Böttger lustre A purplish mother-of-pearl lustre made by J. F. BÖTTGER from gold at the Meissen factory and used in the 1720s by J. G. HEROLD for cartouches, etc.

Bottle glass Glass with a greenish or brownish tone from impurities in the silica, used for making bottles and occasionally other vessels.

Bottle vase A Chinese type of vase, pear-shaped with a flaring lip and narrow neck. It probably originated in the late T'ang dynasty.

Boucher, François (1703–70). The great French Rococo painter who epitomized the sensuous hedonism and nonchalant gaiety of mid-C18 courtly art. His direct connection with the decorative arts was limited to tapestry design: he was designer for the BEAUVAIS TAPESTRY FACTORY from 1734 and supervisor of the GOBELINS TAPESTRY FACTORY from 1755. But his paintings and drawings (and the numerous prints engraved from them) had a strong influence on the decorative arts throughout Europe. They were printed on textiles, reproduced in marquetry, painted on and modelled in porcelain (especially at SÈVRES). His son **Juste-François** (1736–81) worked in a pronounced Louis XVI style. He is notable mainly for some sixty-five *cahiers* of engraved designs for beds, chairs, commodes, book-cases, baths, screens, pedestals for sculpture, balconies, balustrades, etc., all in a rather heavy, rigid, eminently anti-Rococo style which he called 'à la moderne'. They appeared at intervals from *c.*1765 until the 1770s, covering a much wider range than the published designs of the other leading LOUIS XVI designer, J.-C. DELAFOSSE.

Lit: R.-A. Weigert, *French Tapestry*, London 1962; G. Zick in *Keramos* 29 (1965), pp. 3–47.

Boudeuse French term for a C19 type of sofa with a central back-rest, on either side of which people can sit.

Boudin, Léonard (b.1735). Although he worked for MIGÉON and became a *maître ébéniste* in 1761, he appears to have become mainly a furniture dealer. His own work is in a restrained Louis XV style, e.g. secretaire in the Cleveland Museum of Art. When, as is often the case, his stamp appears alongside that of another craftsman it seems likely that he was the dealer and merely stamped furniture that passed through his hands.

Lit: S. Eriksen, *Early Neo-Classicism in France*, London 1974.

Bouffioulx potteries The best known of a number of potteries in Flanders – others were at Châtelet, Namur, Bouvignies and Dinant – making from the late C16 onwards salt-glazed stoneware similar, though generally inferior, to that of the RHENISH POTTERIES, especially WESTERWALD.

Lit: D.-A. van Bastelaer, *Les Grès Wallons*, Mons and Brussels 1885.

Bough pot A vessel, usually of pottery or porcelain, for the display of branches of foliage or flowers. It usually has a perforated cover to hold and support the boughs or branches.

Bouillotte lamp A type of French table lamp, usually of brass or gilt-bronze, with a dish-shaped base supporting a shaft with two or three candle-brackets and a metal shade. The latter is usually painted dark green. The shaft often terminates in a finial. It is a late C18 type, named after the card-game *bouillotte*. *Illustrated opposite.*

Boulard, Jean Baptiste (*c.*1725–89). Leading LOUIS XVI STYLE *menuisier*, he was a contemporary of SENÉ with whom he appears to have sometimes collaborated. His work typifies the restrained taste of the last years of the *ancien régime*, e.g. frame for the screen made for the king's bedroom at Compiègne (now in the Louvre), the *lit à la Polonaise* made for the king in 1785 (now in the Petit Trianon, Versailles), the set of chairs made for the Salon de Jeu at Fontainebleau in 1786 (now divided between the Louvre, the Wallace Collection, London, and the Metropolitan Museum, New York). Though he became a *maître-menuisier* in 1754 he did not begin working for the Crown until 1777 – often under the supervision of HAURÉ. The carving of his chairs was executed by various *sculpteurs*, the gilding usually by Bardou. His son carried on the family business until 1832, receiving many commissions from Napoleon.

Lit: F. J. B. Watson, *The Wrightsman Collection: Furniture*, New York 1966.

Bouillotte lamp, Empire period (Château de Malmaison)

Boulle, André-Charles (1642–1732). He was the first great French *ébéniste* and the most celebrated of Louis XIV furniture-makers and designers. Before him the best furniture made for the French Court had been the work of foreigners such as the Dutchman Pierre GOLLE and the Italian Domenico CUCCI. Boulle perfectly expressed his period's taste for sumptuous and costly magnificence and gave his name to a type of furniture notable for its showy marquetry of tortoiseshell and brass, *see* BOULLE MARQUETRY. Born in Paris, the son of a carpenter, he was probably related to the Swiss cabinet-maker **Pierre Boulle** employed by Louis XIII. He began as a painter, being elected as such to the *Académie de Saint-Luc,* and was also, according to himself, an architect, mosaicist, engraver and bronze-worker. By 1664 he was well established. The following year Bernini made his famous visit to Paris and is said to have struck up a friendship with him, advising him on his designs. In 1672 he became *ébéniste du roi* on the recommendation of Colbert who described him to the king as the most skilful furniture-maker in Paris. From then onwards he worked continuously for the royal palaces, especially Versailles where his decoration of the Dauphin's *grand cabinet* (1681–3, now destroyed) was recognized as a masterpiece. But he continued to accept private commissions both from the French nobility and from wealthy commoners such as the financier and art collector Pierre Crozat, as well as from foreign royalty, e.g. Philip V of Spain and the Electors of Bavaria and Cologne. His furniture is distinguished by the nobility and monumentality of its architectural forms, by its unprecedentedly elaborate marquetry, by the outstanding quality of its gilt-bronze mounts (especially pictorial mounts depicting subjects from classical mythology) and by the sense of symmetry and rhythm produced by the use of 'first part' and 'counter part' marquetry on matching pairs of armoires, commodes, etc. He also designed some remarkable clock-cases, often surmounted by a sculptural group such as Apollo and his Chariot. His style seems to have changed very little throughout his long career though it probably became less heavy during the *Régence.* He collaborated with Le Brun, de Cotte and BÉRAIN, perhaps using the latter's designs for his marquetry. He was also a great collector, particularly of Old Master drawings from which he probably drew inspiration for his pictorial mounts. He published a series of engraved designs: *Nouveaux Desseins de Meubles et Ouvrages de Bronze et de Menuiserie inventés et gravés par A-C Boulle,* undated but probably published early in the C18 in Paris. In his day furniture-makers had not yet begun to stamp their work and the only documented pieces by him are a pair of commodes at Versailles made for the king's bedroom at the Grand Trianon in 1708/9. (The commode was a new type of furniture and Boulle may have played a part in its invention as he certainly did in its development.) Several other pieces of furniture

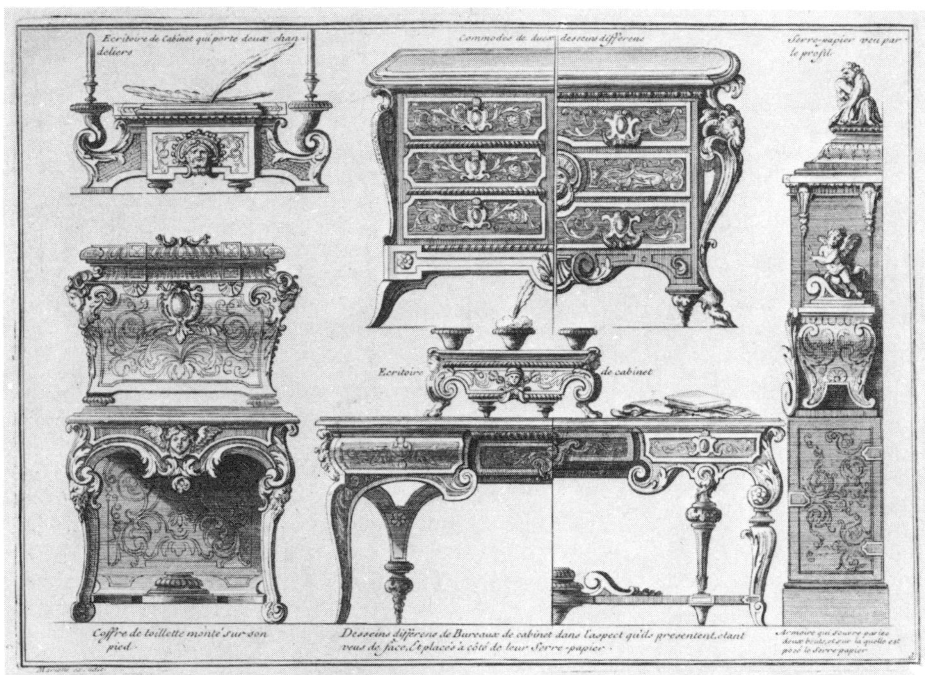

A.-C. Boulle: designs for furniture, early c18

A.-C. Boulle: Bureau de l'Electeur de Bavière, c.1723–5 *(Louvre)*

can be attributed to Boulle – in the Louvre, the Wallace Collection in London, the Metropolitan Museum in New York and the Hermitage in Leningrad. By 1718 he had retired but in 1720 his premises in Paris caught fire and his losses were so great that he is said to have returned to work and directed the *atelier* until his death. The output of his workshop is revealed by the account he drew up of his losses after the fire in 1720 when the number of pieces of furniture executed on commission and still on the premises amounted to 15 clock-cases, 5 bureaux and 8 commodes. After his death the workshop was carried on by his sons **André-Charles** (1685–1745) known as **Boulle-de-Sève** and **Charles-Joseph** (d.1754) through whom the Boulle tradition of high quality craftsmanship was transmitted to OEBEN (who joined the Boulle workshops in 1751) and thence to RIESENER though neither worked in Boulle's style. But Boulle style furniture continued to be made throughout the c18, e.g. by DUBOIS and LEVASSEUR in Paris and by many others less well known, and the tradition was carried on in the C19, especially during the Second Empire when WASSMUS FRÈRES and others specialized in imitation Boulle. Boulle style clock-cases also remained popular, being produced, for example, by Antoine Foulet (d.1775).

Lit: F. Comte de Salverte, *Les ébénistes du XVIIIe siècle*, Paris 1953; F. J. B. Watson, *Wallace Collection Catalogues: Furniture*, London 1956; H. Honour, *Cabinet-makers and Furniture Designers*, London & New York 1969.

Boulle marquetry Brass and tortoiseshell marquetry, a C10 Italian invention brought to France by Italian craftsmen imported by Marie de Médicis and then perfected by André-Charles BOULLE. It is prepared by glueing together sheets of brass and tortoiseshell, which are then cut according to the design required by a kind of fretwork technique. When cut, the layers can be combined to produce either a shell ground inlaid with brass (known as 'first-part') or a brass ground inlaid with shell (known as 'counter-part'). Pairs of wardrobes or commodes might thus be decorated, the one with first-part, the other with counter-part marquetry: or, alternatively, first-part and counter-part panels might be used for the outside and inside of a door. To obtain greater richness of effect the brass was often engraved. Those parts of the piece of furniture not decorated with Boulle marquetry were generally veneered in ebony. Boulle's followers and imitators sought more gaudy effects by painting the back of the shell or by veneering it over a coloured foil and by adding inlays of pewter or mother-of-pearl and horn stained a bright colour, usually blue, red or green. Boulle marquetry also became popular in mid-C17 Germany, e.g. furniture by **H. D. Sommer** of Kunzelnau (*fl.*1666–84) who had perhaps been a pupil of Boulle, and furniture by **Esser and Wolfhauer** of Augsburg. It remained fashionable in France throughout the C18 and in England, e.g. G. JENSEN and **Frederick Hintz** of London who advertised furniture inlaid with brass and mother-of-pearl in 1738. It was widely manufactured in the C19 both in France and England, e.g. Le Gaigneur's *Buhl Manufactory* off the Edgware Road, London, which was productive *c.*1815.

Boulle marquetry: detail for an armoire (Musée des Arts Décoratifs, Paris)

Boulton, Matthew (1728–1809). Hardware manufacturer, he is famous mainly for his partnership with James Watt whom he greatly assisted in the completion of the steam engine. But he is also notable for the high quality of the silver, Sheffield Plate, ormolu and other metalwork produced at his factory outside Birmingham. In 1759 he inherited his father's 'toy-making' business, i.e. manufacturing small metal objects such as buttons and buckles. He expanded this business to include the manufacture of steel jewellery, silver, ormolu, etc., and in 1762 began to erect at Soho, near Birmingham, a large factory which soon became the industrial showpiece of the district. He ran it in partnership with **John Fothergill** who died in 1782. He appears to have been the first to exploit Sheffield Plate for a wide range of domestic articles, diminishing the danger of the copper wearing through the silver coating by applying ribbons of solid silver along the edges and elsewhere. He also applied to the production of solid silver wares the system of divided labour he had developed for Sheffield Plate. The firm's large and profitable output of small articles such as buttons, watch-chains and buckles combined with the production of Sheffield Plate to help finance the finer products in wrought silver, such as candelabra, cassolets and *garnitures de cheminée* of bluejohn mounted in ormolu of exceptionally fine quality. Designs by Robert ADAM, William CHAMBERS and James WYATT were used but the firm also employed a staff of designers. Clients included George III and the Empress of Russia. Ormolu work was exported to France where it was much admired. But its production eventually proved unprofitable and it was stopped in 1775. Boulton was a friend of Josiah WEDGWOOD whom he resembled as a pioneer industrialist and similarly as a man of wide interests, a leading light of the Birmingham Lunar Society and, from 1785, a Fellow of the Royal Society. He retired in 1800 but his business was carried on by his son until 1846. Examples of Boulton's products can be seen in the Victoria & Albert Museum in London, the Birmingham City Museum and Art Gallery, and the Museum of Fine Arts in Boston.

Lit: H. W. Dickinson, *Matthew Boulton*, Cambridge 1937; E. Robinson in *The Economic History Review*, vol. xvi, 1963, pp. 39–60; R. Rowe, *Adam Silver, 1765–1795*, London 1965; N. Goodison, *Ormolu: The Work of Matthew Boulton*, London 1974.

M. Boulton: design for a tureen (Reference Library, Birmingham)

Bouquetière Form of glass bowl in late-C18 and early-C19 France, a revival of an early Venetian type with flared, wide mouth and wavy-edged brim, mounted on stem and foot and often decorated with mascarons and fluting.

Bourdalou(e) A C18 type of oval slipper-shaped urinal or chamber-pot intended mainly for the use of ladies when travelling, sometimes said to have been carried concealed in a muff. It is supposedly named after the famous French Jesuit preacher Louis Bourdaloue (1632–1704) whose sermons at Versailles were so popular that his congregations assembled hours in advance. But the earliest surviving examples date from *c.*1710 (made at DELFT) and the word – as *bourdalou* (m.) – is not recorded in print before it was defined in the *Dictionnaire de Trévoux* in 1771. Such chamber-pots were made throughout Europe, including England, and even in China and Japan (for export), usually of porcelain, more rarely of faience, silver or japanned metal. Those made at the Chantilly, Höchst, Meissen, Sèvres, Vienna and other notable porcelain factories are often very delicately decorated and are sometimes mistaken for sauce-boats.

Lit: A. Pecker in *Cahiers de la Céramique* II (1958), pp. 123–34; H. Newman in *The Connoisseur* CLXXV (1970), pp. 258–64, and CLXXVII (1971), pp. 22–31.

Bourg-la-Reine, *see* CHELSEA KERAMIC ART WORKS.

Bourg-la-Reine porcelain factory, *see* MENNECY PORCELAIN FACTORY.

Bourne & Son A family firm owning potteries at BELPER (1812–34), and DENBY to the present day. Earlier products included brown salt-glazed stoneware jugs with hunting scenes in relief and greyhound handles but most of their products were utilitarian.

Bovey Tracey pottery, *see* WEMYSS WARE.

Bow porcelain factory Bow shares with CHELSEA the distinction of being the first porcelain factory in England, but its early history is very obscure. Situated at Stratford Langthorne in the East End of London, it was founded by an Irish painter, Thomas FRYE, and a glass-merchant, Edward

Heylyn (1695–after 1758), who took out a patent in 1744 for making 'a certain material whereby a ware might be made of the same nature or kind, and equal to, if not exceeding in goodness and beauty, China or Porcelain ware imported from abroad'. The same document reveals that an important ingredient in this material was an imported china clay, presumably UNAKER which was just then being imported from Virginia by A. DUCHE. Soft-paste porcelain appears to have been made at the factory by 1748 when Frye took out a second patent, but few specimens have been identified. A number of pieces dated 1750 reveal that high standards

Bow porcelain figure of 'Kitty Clive', 1750 (Fitzwilliam Museum, Cambridge)

were soon reached – e.g. a plain white statuette of Kitty Clive (Fitzwilliam Museum, Cambridge) and two other figures, an ink-pot and bowl decorated in underglaze blue, and three enamelled ink-wells. The best period runs from 1750 to 1759 when Frye retired. Products included cups, mugs, ink-wells, and bowls decorated in underglaze blue, enamel colours (the Kakiemon quail pattern was much used) or with TRANSFER PRINTING (from 1754); some attractive white wares decorated in relief with shells or sprigs of plum blossom; and numerous pastoral and mythological figures, rather less well-modelled than those of Chelsea which they sometimes imitate, and generally unpainted. The paste is thick and heavy and subject to fire-cracking; the glaze soft and yellowish with a tendency to gather round the base. Stylistically products are in a muted, distinctly English, version of the Rococo. Wares produced after 1759 are rather more ambitious and rather less successful, some are richly enamelled probably by outside painters. A bewilderingly wide variety of marks (impressed, incised or painted in underglaze blue and/or red) were applied to products. In 1775 the factory was acquired by W. DUESBURY, owner of the DERBY PORCELAIN FACTORY, who removed the moulds and tools to Derby where they were joined by those of the Chelsea factory in 1786. (For factory marks *see* p. 881.)

Lit: Bow Porcelain, Exh. Cat., British Museum, London 1959–60; F. Hurlbutt, *Bow Porcelain*, London 1962.

Bowen, John (*fl.* 1734–61). He decorated BRISTOL pottery, usually in blue, with figures in landscapes, ships, etc. A signed dish dated 1761 is recorded.

Bowes, Sir Jerome, *see* VERZELINI, Jacopo.

Bow-front A convex curving front, usually on case furniture.

Box inkstand A rectangular inkstand incorporating one or two inkwells with a drawer or drawers beneath.

Boxwood A very hard yellowish or brownish wood with an extremely fine, close grain, from the box tree which is found commonly in Europe and elsewhere. It has been used for small ornamental carvings and also in furniture making, e.g. for fillets to frame a decorative motive.

Boyer, François, *see* BELLEVUE POTTERIES.

Boyvin, René, *see* ROSSO, Giovanni Battista.

Bracket A small ornamental shelf attached to a wall for the support of a CLOCK or decorative object, generally made of wood but sometimes of metal or ceramics.

Bracket foot Simple type of foot used on case furniture from *c.*1690 onwards, formed with two pieces of wood joined at the corner, the open side generally being cut in a simple pattern. The corner end may be straight or curved.

Bracquemond, Joseph Auguste, called **Félix** (1833–1914). French painter and print-maker who had made a considerable reputation in the artistic world of Paris before the 1860s when he turned his attention to the decoration of ceramics partly under the influence of the new vogue for Japanese art. He learned the technique of enamel painting from T. DECK in whose studio he worked for a while. A table service of CREIL faience, which he painted in the Japanese style with asymmetrically disposed birds, insects, beasts and foliage, was shown at the Paris Exhibition of 1867 and at the Vienna exhibition of 1873. He was employed by the SÈVRES factory in 1870 and then worked for ten years as director of the Paris design studio for the HAVILAND factory. His designs have a clean neatness and spare elegance which distinguish them from most contemporary essays in Japonaiseries. He also designed textiles, book-bindings, jewellery and table silver. And in 1902 he collaborated in designing furnishings for Baron Vitta's Villa Sapinière at Évian which were shown in the Paris Salon of 1902.

Lit: G. P. Weisberg in *The Art Bulletin*, September 1969, pp. 277–81.

J. A. Bracquemond: decoration on a Creil-Montereau earthenware plate, c.1880 (Musée des Arts Décoratifs, Paris)

Bradburn, John, *see* VILE, William, and FRANCE, William.

Bradbury, Thomas, *see* SHEFFIELD PLATE.

Bradley, Will (1868–1962). American book illustrator, poster designer and amateur architect. In 1901–2 he published in the *Ladies' Home Journal* a series of neat furniture designs, somewhat in the style of M. H. BAILLIE SCOTT with a sparse use of Art Nouveau decorative motifs. Although none appears to have been executed they exerted some influence on U.S. furniture design. Some of his designs for pianofortes were executed by Chickering and Sons of Boston, Mass.

Lit: R. Judson Clark (ed.), *The Arts and Crafts Movement in America 1876–1916*, Exh. Cat., Art Museum Princeton University, Art Institute of Chicago, etc., 1972–3.

Bradshaw, George Smith (*fl.*1756–93). He was a London cabinet-maker and upholsterer and seems also to have made tapestries. He was in partnership in 1756 (for one year) with **Paul Saunders,** a tapestry-weaver, and they supplied furniture and tapestries to Holkham Hall, Norfolk. Bradshaw alone was supplying furniture to Admiralty House in 1764–74. In 1756 a Mr Mayhew (presumably **John Mayhew,** later of INCE & MAYHEW) was working for him.

Bradwell Wood pottery, *see* ELERS, John Philip and David.

Braiding Embroidery executed in couched braid.

Brameld, John, *see* ROCKINGHAM POTTERY AND PORCELAIN FACTORY.

Brampton potteries A small group of Derbyshire factories active from the early C18 to the early C20 making ordinary brown stoneware household wares. In the C19, when the main factories were owned by **S. & H. Briddon** and **J. Oldfield,** products included chocolate-coloured wares with relief decorations and TOBY JUGS. Many C19 pieces have green-glazed interiors.

Lit: G. A. Godden (ed.), *Jewitt's The Ceramic Art of Great Britain,* London 1972.

Brancard A stand on which large vessels can be carried and displayed, found especially at Versailles under Louis XIV and made of silver, notably by BALLIN. None of these survives.

Brancas, Louis-Léon-Félicité, duc de (1733–1824). An amateur scientist who in his laboratory at the Château de Lassay made the first French hard-paste PORCELAIN, using *kaolin* from Alençon, 1763–8. He produced pieces on a limited scale and the few that survive (mostly in the Musée National de Céramique de Sèvres) have a grey imperfect body, e.g. biscuit reliefs of Henri IV and Louis XV.

Brandenburg porcelain, *see* PLAUE-ON-HAVEL POTTERY.

Brandiwijkom Dutch C17 and C18 silver, two-handled oval-shaped bowl, used for raisins in brandy.

Brandt, Marianne (b.1893). One of the most notable metal-workers at the BAUHAUS, which she joined as an instructress in 1923 after studying at the Weimar Kunsthochschule and travelling in Scandinavia and France. She was responsible for a number of vessels composed of pure geometrical forms 'cylinders and hemispheres' made out of nickel-silver – ash-trays, teapots, etc. (Schlossmuseum, Weimar). In 1949 she was appointed Professor of Industrial Form at the Hochschule für bildende Künste in Dresden but later settled in her native town, Karl Marx Stadt, formerly Chemnitz.

Marianne Brandt: nickel silver teapot made at the Bauhaus 1924 (Museum of Modern Art, New York)

Lit: W. Schedig, *Crafts of the Weimar Bauhaus,* London 1967.

Brandt, Reynier (1707–*c.*1784). He was a very productive Dutch silversmith working in a modified Louis XV style and did much to create an Amsterdam, as opposed to The Hague, type of Dutch silver. He specialized in baskets and trays and did not make table silver. His baskets are ogee-shaped with elaborate perforated sides forming an open tangle of engraved foliage. He also made some church plate.

Lit: J. W. Frederiks, *Dutch Silver,* vol. II, The Hague 1958.

Brangwyn, Sir Frank (1867–1956). English painter who acquired international renown as a designer of furniture, textiles and carpets. He began as a protégé of MACKMURDO, assisted William MORRIS (1882–4), then adopted the Art Nouveau style and worked for S. BING (1895–6). Later he took up industrial design exhibiting special 'cheap' furniture at Ghent (1913).

Bras de lumière French name for a wall-light or sconce. Some C17 examples were in the form of an arm with the hand clutching the candle-

Bras de lumière: gilt bronze, Louis XIV period

holder: hence the origin of the term, which was soon applied to all types of wall lights.

Brass Gold-coloured alloy of COPPER and ZINC (90% to 70% copper, a greater proportion of zinc produces a yellower metal) which is ductile, malleable and takes a high polish. It came into use in ancient times, though much later than BRONZE. In the Middle Ages it was often used for decorative and useful objects and the town of Dinant in Belgium became famous for such products which are often termed DINANDERIE. Subsequently it was much used throughout Europe for lighting fixtures – candlesticks, chandeliers, etc. – and furniture mounts, especially drawer handles.

Lit: L. Aitchison, *A History of Metals*, London 1960; G. Wills, *The Book of Copper and Brass*, Feltham 1969.

Bratina Russian type of loving-cup: globular, covered, and with a contracted lip (often decorated with a sententious inscription), usually of silver and sometimes richly enamelled and begemmed.

Brattishing Carved open-work cresting, as used on medieval screens, etc.

Braun Braun Aktiengesellschaft, a West German company making domestic electric appliances and scientific instruments. Founded in 1921 by **Max Braun** of Frankfurt, the company first produced a patented device for connecting driving belts. After a few years it moved into plastics components for radios and gramophones, then into production of whole sets. Household appliances and finally electric shavers, now the main line, were added to the range after the war. Max Braun died in 1951, leaving the business to his two sons **Artur** and **Erwin** who engaged Dr **Fritz Eichler** to direct the new design programme in close collaboration with the Hochschule für Gestaltung at Ulm. Beginning with the radio division, the whole programme was thoroughly overhauled. Braun later set up its own design department with **Dieter Rams** as chief designer. Almost all Braun appliances and their supporting publicity are now developed and designed within the company, with a resulting corporate image closely related to the character and appearance of the products. Braun has won awards in all the main design exhibitions and competitions, including the Italian Compasso d'Oro and the Interplas (London) award (twice), while thirty Braun appliances have been accepted for the permanent industrial design collection of the Museum of Modern Art, New York. It has become an archetype for consistency of design policy in industry.

Brazier A vessel in which charcoal may be burnt to heat a room, usually portable, made of metal (bronze, brass, occasionally silver in the C17) with a pierced cover. In use since ancient times in Europe – especially warmer countries where the houses had few fireplaces – and to this day in Spain and Italy, though superseded by the electric fire.

Break-front or **Broken front** A term applied to a book-case, commode or cabinet of which the central section projects slightly in front of the side sections.

Brede pottery, *see* SUSSEX POTTERIES.

Breghtel, Hans Coenraadt (1608–75). Born and trained in Nuremburg but in 1640 settled in The Hague where he became the leading silversmith. Began in a coarsened version of the AURICULAR STYLE which he abandoned in the 1650s for a rich Baroque manner with much floral decoration. His masterpiece is the gold coronation cup of Frederick III of Denmark (1653, Rosenborg Castle, Copenhagen) somewhat overwrought with *putti*, swans, crowns, etc.

Lit: J. W. Fredericks, *Dutch Silver*, The Hague 1952–61.

Bressler, H. G. von, *see* BOTTENGRUBER, Ignaz.

Bretby art pottery, *see* LINTHORPE POTTERY.

Breuer, Marcel Lajos (b.1902). Hungarian-born American architect, he is also one of the most influential C20 designers, especially of furniture. He introduced chromium-plated surfaces into the home, thus marking a total rejection of the Arts and Crafts tradition, and his tubular steel chairs and modular unit furniture for standardized mass-production revolutionized domestic and office furniture all over the world. He defines the task of the designer as that of 'civilizing technology'. He was trained at the BAUHAUS (1920 to 1925) and became head of the woodwork section there in 1925. In 1935 he left Germany for England and two years later settled in the U.S.A., at first in partnership with GROPIUS (until 1941) and later on his own. He now works mainly as an architect and industrial designer (e.g. his 1955 Rail Diesel Car for the Budd Co.). His important work as a furniture designer dates from before he went to the U.S.

His first chairs of 1921–2 were slightly more elegant versions of RIETVELD's celebrated armchair. The design is clearly articulated, with the weight-supporting framework expressed visually and the back and seat given a different character – softer, less cubistic and sharp edged. This extreme clarity of design was to mark all Breuer's work. His first tubular steel chair dates from 1925 and is said to have been inspired by the curved metal tubing of his bicycle handle-bars. Known as the 'Wassily' chair, it was chromium plated. The Bauhaus was furnished with it in 1926 and it probably inspired LE CORBUSIER's similar chair of 1929. It is still in commercial production. But it was, in conception, merely Rietveld's chair reworked in steel and fabric. The revolutionary conception of a cantilevered tubular steel chair, which Breuer was now to exploit so successfully, was Mart STAM's. (Tubular metal had of course been used earlier for furniture, e.g. by Winfield

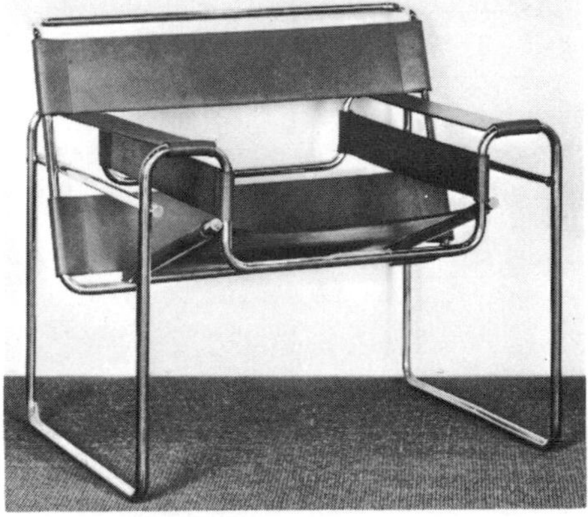

M. Breuer: the 'Wassily' chair in chromium-plated tubular steel and leather, 1925 (Musée des Arts Décoratifs, Paris)

M. Breuer: cantilever side-chair of chromium-plated steel tubing, wood and cane, 1928 (Victoria & Albert Museum)

of Birmingham, England, whose brass foundry produced tubular-brass bedsteads and, in 1851, a rocking chair to go with an Elizabethan four-poster, both in tubular brass. But the innovatory possibilities of this were not realized at the time.) Stam's chair, designed in 1924, was composed of an unbroken line of steel tubes but was un-resilient. In 1926 both he and MIES VAN DER ROHE produced cantilever chairs made out of single lengths of metal tubing and two years later Breuer produced his version, composed of a single unjoined loop of tube on to which panels of wood or caning are attached to form the back and seat. It is a classic design of the utmost simplicity and became the model for countless tubular steel chairs all over the world. It is still in commercial production. He also designed stools and tables with frames of tubular steel and, in 1933, some small tables made of aluminium rods. His influence spread rapidly and tubular steel soon became fashionable, especially in France (chairs by René Herbst 1927, Chareau 1930, Marcel Gascoin 1930, André Lurcat 1931, and of course Le Corbusier) and in the U.S.A. (chairs by Nathan George Howitt).

Breuer's later designs were less influential but equally brilliant. His aluminium strap furniture dates from 1933 and his bent plywood furniture from 1935–7 when Isokon Furniture Co. in England manufactured several now famous

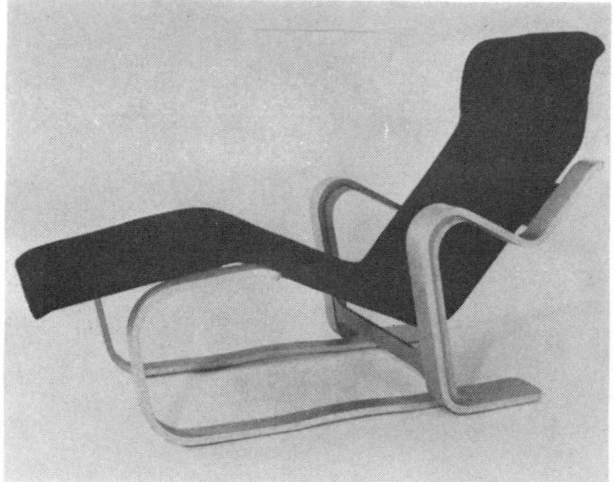

M. Breuer: laminated plywood chair, 1935–7, made by the Isokon Furniture Co., England

pieces from his designs, notably a reclining chair of elegant, form-fitting lines, some ingenious stacking tables and dining chairs of laminated wood frames and light, bent plywood seats, reminiscent of AALTO's furniture of a few years earlier. The table, made of a single moulded panel of plywood, is ingenious and original – probably the first to be made from a single piece of material. Breuer's later, especially post-war, furniture designs have been mainly experimental – usually concerned with the application of the resilient frame principle – but with his usual careful articulation and general clarity of design.

Lit: P. Blake, *M. Breuer Architect and Designer*, London 1949; M. Breuer, *Sun and Shadow*, 1956; A. Drexler & G. Daniel, *Introduction to Twentieth Century Design*, New York 1959; W. Schedig, *Crafts of the Weimar Bauhaus*, London 1967.

Brewster chair, *see* CHAIR.

Brian, Thomas, *see* CHELSEA & DERBY PORCELAIN FACTORIES.

Briand, Thomas, *see* CHELSEA PORCELAIN FACTORY.

Briati, Giuseppe, *see* VENETIAN GLASSHOUSES.

Brickard, Servatius (1676–1742). German cabinet-maker born in Brabant and working from 1705 in Bamberg for the Kurfürst Lothar Franz von Schönborn. He succeeded F. PLITZ-

S. Brickard: writing-desk, 1727 (Pommersfelden)

NER as chief cabinet-maker to the latter in 1724 and was officially appointed *Hofschreiner* (Court Cabinet-maker) in 1735. Several pieces of his furniture are at Pommersfelden, mainly stools and tables in a late Baroque style which is much more Germanic than that of Plitzner. His masterpiece is a writing-desk of 1727 with very fine marquetry (Pommersfelden). He was succeeded in the service of the Schönborn family by N. Baur.

Lit: H. Kreisel, *Die Kunst des deutschen Möbels*, vol. ii, Munich 1970.

Bride, *see* LACE.

Briggle, Artus van, *see* VAN BRIGGLE, Artus.

Bright cut decorations Sharply engraved designs, generally geometrical, on silver which have a glittering effect; popular mainly from the late C18.

Bright cut decoration: detail of silver spoon handle

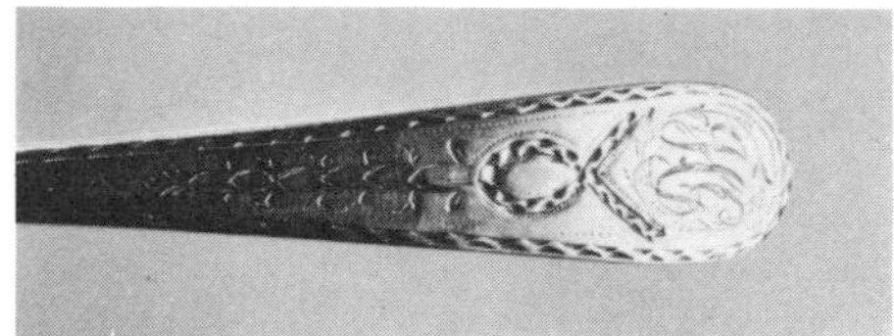

F. Briot: pewter ewer, c.1600 (Louvre)

Briot, François (*c.*1550–*c.*1616). French Mannerist metal-worker and the only artist of note to work in pewter. He was born at Damblain in Lorraine but, as a Huguenot, was forced to flee to Montbéliard in 1579. Here he worked as a pewterer making handsome ewers, basins, etc., very delicately ornamented with long-limbed figures and grotesque motifs in shallow relief (examples in the Louvre). In 1585 he was appointed engraver to the Montbéliard mint, being employed mainly in the production of coins and medals. His masterpiece is known as the *Temperantia Dish* (1585–90, Museum für Kunsthandwerk, Dresden). It made him almost as famous as CELLINI and was frequently copied – in pewter at Nuremberg by ENDERLEIN and others, in faience by PALISSY, and later in silver and other materials.

Lit: H. Demiani, *François Briot, Caspar Enderlein und das Edelzinn*, Leipzig 1897; H.-U. Haedeke, *Metalwork*, London 1970.

Briqueté ground A C18 Sèvres ground simulating brickwork. Early examples are in gold over dark blue.

Brislington pottery, *see* BRISTOL POTTERIES.

Bristol glasshouses Established in the 1740s and specializing in decanters, goblets, vases, etc. of a very fine blue usually decorated with gilding, notably by Lazarus and Isaac Jacobs, or an opaque white made in imitation of porcelain and often painted with flowers or chinoiseries by porcelain painters, notably by Michael EDKINS. Blue glass went out of production 1780–1820 when supplies of Silesian cobalt oxide needed to produce the colour were cut off. It is seldom possible to distinguish blue or white glass made at Bristol from that of NEWCASTLE or other English factories.

Lit: W. A. Thorpe, *A History of English and Irish Glass*, London 1929.

Bristol porcelain factories A soft-paste porcelain made with Cornish soapstone (steatite) was produced between 1749 and 1752 by **Benjamin Lund** in a factory in **Lowdin**'s glasshouse – formerly and misleadingly known as 'Lowdin's Bristol'. Lund had been granted a licence to mine soapstone at The Lizard, Cornwall, in *c.*1748 and W. COOKWORTHY was probably involved in devising the formula he used. Cream jugs, sauce boats, etc., sometimes with chinoiserie decorations in underglaze blue or polychrome enamel colours, were produced. But Lund's factory was taken over by the WORCESTER PORCELAIN FACTORY in 1752.

A hard-paste porcelain was produced at Bristol in Cookworthy's factory when it was transferred there from PLYMOUTH in 1770. In 1774 Cookworthy assigned his patent to Richard CHAMPION but after much litigation the factory closed in 1781–2 and the patent passed to the NEW HALL PORCELAIN FACTORY. Early hard-paste Bristol wares are hard to distinguish from those produced at Plymouth and such decorators as SAQUI and TEBO worked at both factories. Wares range from some elaborate and ambitious groups and figures imitative of SÈVRES to much simpler and often rather peasant style wares of great charm. (For factory marks *see* p. 882.)

Lit: F. A. Barret, *Worcester Porcelain and Lund's Bristol*, London 1966; F. Severne Mackenna, *Cookworthy's Plymouth and Bristol Porcelain*, Leigh-on-Sea, 1946; F. Severne Mackenna, *Champion's Bristol Porcelain*, Leigh-on-Sea 1947.

Bristol potteries A number of potteries in Bristol and nearby, at Brislington and WINCANTON, are notable for the production of TIN-GLAZED EARTHENWARE in the later C17 and C18. As no consistent system of marking was used products cannot be satisfactorily attributed to individual factories: it is also difficult to distinguish the earlier pieces from those made at LAMBETH and the later from those of LIVERPOOL. Late C17 wares generally assigned to Bristol and neighbourhood include 'BLUE-DASH chargers' splashily painted in maiolica colours with portraits of notable contemporaries (Charles II, William III, Duke of Marlborough) or bunches of flowers. From *c.*1720 chinoiseries in blue and white, similar to those of DELFT, became popular.

Bristol tin-glazed earthenware dish, late C17 (Victoria & Albert Museum)

Bristol tin-glazed earthenware dish, mid C18 (Victoria & Albert Museum)

Products included plates, punch bowls, posset-pots, tea caddies, etc. After 1755 the BIANCO SOPRA BIANCO technique was sometimes adopted for decorations of the borders of plates. From *c.*1775 production of tin-glazed wares gave way to that of cream-coloured earthenware made principally at a factory at Temple Back which survived until 1884.

Lit: F. H. Garner, *English Delftware*, London 1948.

Britannia metal An alloy of tin, antimony and copper, similar in appearance to pewter though lighter in weight and whiter in tone (hence its alternative name 'white metal'). It became a popular cheap substitute for pewter. Production costs were lower since Britannia metal could be rolled in the sheet and spun into thin-walled vessels over inexpensive wooden moulds. Neither bronze moulds nor hand finishing was needed. It appears to have been discovered in England shortly after the mid C18 when pewterers were beginning to suffer from competition by the makers of SHEFFIELD PLATE and also by the recently modernized potteries of Staffordshire. Large-scale manufacture did not begin until about 1780 and it was not until 1804 that James Dixon in Sheffield established the factory that became the leading producer. From 1816 onwards large quantities of Britannia wares were exported to America, notably by James DIXON & Sons Ltd. I. Babbitt and W. Crossman established a factory in Taunton, Mass., in 1824 for the production of Britannia metal wares. It was sometimes used as an alternative to nickel-silver for ELECTROPLATE from the 1840s.

Britannia standard, *see* SILVER.

Broad glass A flat piece of glass (as for a window) made by the 'broad' or 'Lorraine' process (introduced into England in the early C17) – i.e. by blowing a long bubble into a cylindrical mould, breaking the cylinder and reheating the glass to flatten it. It has a less brilliant 'fire-polish' than CROWN GLASS but is smoother. The process was much improved by **R. L. Chance** at the Spon Lane (Birmingham) Glasshouse *c.*1830.

Broadcloth An imprecise term used in England since the Middle Ages for various types of plain durable woollen textiles woven in wide strips and used for hangings or garments.

Brocade An imprecise term for a rich figured textile, especially one with a woven pattern in gold or silver thread (i.e. BROCART).

Brocade pattern, *see* IMARI PORCELAIN.

Brocard, Joseph (*fl.*1867–90). French glass-maker who revived the technique of enamelling as practised in Syria and executed some fine imitations of C13–C14 MOSQUE LAMPS, etc. He showed his work at exhibitions in Paris from 1867. In later years he executed original pieces in the Islamic style. He was much admired by and exerted an influence on E. GALLÉ.

Lit: A. Polak in *Annales du 4° congrès des 'Journées internationales du verre'*, Liège 1967, pp. 212–13.

Brocart French term for a textile with patterns in gold or silver thread.

Brocatelle 1. A LAMPAS-woven fabric with silk warps, characterized by the marked relief of the warp-faced weave.

2. A type of variegated marble, more correctly called *brocatello*, much used for table-tops in the C18.

Brodel, Vittorio, *see* TURIN POTTERIES and VINOVO PORCELAIN FACTORY.

Broderie Anglaise A type of all-white embroidery made in England and on the Continent from the late C18 onwards, mainly as dress material. Holes cut in the material are worked round in buttonhole stitch to form geometrical or formalized flower patterns.

Bromley, William, *see* OTT & BREWER COMPANY.

Broncit decoration Mainly geometrical decorations in matt black applied to glass designed by Josef HOFFMANN from *c.*1910 and made by LOBMEYR of Vienna; later became typical of the style of the WIENER WERKSTÄTTE.

Brongniart, Alexandre, *see* SÈVRES (or VINCENNES-SÈVRES) PORCELAIN FACTORY.

Bronze An alloy composed wholly or chiefly of copper and tin, used since the Bronze Age (*c*.2000–1800 B.C. in Europe, *c*.1000–500 B.C. in Britain). It is more fusible and thus more suitable for casting than pure copper: it is also harder and more durable. It was at first cast solid by pouring the molten metal into moulds of stone or baked clay. The solid casting process, with moulds in three or four pieces, was brought to a high level of technical skill by *c*.2500 B.C. at Ur, Iraq. But this method used up a great quantity of metal, much of which could be saved in a cored casting. In China of the Shang Yin dynasty (*c*.1766–1122 B.C.) the cored casting method with piece moulds was perfected. To produce such an object as a *tsun* or wine vessel, the lower part of the core was made of clay, thrown on a potter's wheel, dried and covered with wax of the thickness desired for the bronze, the upper part was then similarly modelled and covered with wax; the surface of the wax was carved in relief, successive layers of clay of increasing roughness were painted over it to the thickness of about 1 in. but with both vertical and horizontal divisions so that it could be removed in wedge-shaped sections to scrape the wax off the core and leave a free passage for the molten metal.

The CIRE-PERDUE process differs in that the mould around the wax and core cannot be opened up and the wax has to be driven out by heat. The piece-mould process leaves ridges on

Detail of bronze chia *type sacrificial vessel, Shang Dynasty,* 1200–1000 B.C. *(William Rockhill Nelson Gallery of Art, Kansas City)*

the surface of the bronze corresponding to the joins between the pieces but these are usually chiselled away in the process of finishing. In fact it is seldom easy to determine how a bronze object was cast. Both these processes were employed in Europe from the c4 B.C. onwards. Cores of compressed sand had been used since a very early period, but it was not until the c14 or c15 that the process of casting in moulds of sand was discovered – and it was used mainly for other metals.

After it has been cast the metal may be decorated by various techniques of 'cold' working. Thin panels or vessels may be decorated with repoussé work by hammering from the back. Linear decorations may be executed with a

Bronze Pien-Hu *with ornamentation characteristic of the late Huai style period. c3* B.C. *(Kunstindustrimuseet, Copenhagen)*

Bronze tripod from Pompeii (Museo Nazionale, Naples)

Bronze latchet, Irish, c2 A.D. *(National Museum of Ireland, Dublin)*

Bronze table designed by G. Valadier, 1789, the figures of Hercules cast from models by V. Pacetti (Vatican Library, Vatican City)

Bronze mortar, Flanders, c16 (Musée des Arts Décoratifs, Paris)

tracer, which produces a line hammered into the metal, or a graver which cuts away a piece of the metal. The texture of the surface may be varied by the use of punches. And the surface may be gilt wholly or in part (*see* ORMOLU).

Bronze has been extensively used as a medium for both sculpture and objects intended to be decorative as well as useful, e.g. andirons and aquamaniles. It was used with great accomplishment by ROMANESQUE craftsmen. Since the RENAISSANCE it has been used extensively for small scale sculpture and for decorations on furniture, also for whole pieces of furniture. In the c18 and c19 French craftsmen executed bronze work of outstanding quality for furniture mounts and such objects as clock-cases and candelabra (*see* GOUTHIÈRE, RAVRIO, THOMIRE, etc.).

Lit: L. Aitchison, *A History of Metals*, London 1960; H.-U. Haedeke, *Metalwork*, London 1970.

Bronzes d'ameublement Small independent bronze fittings and furnishings, e.g. clock-cases, fire-dogs, lamps and lighting appliances, key-hole

Furniture mount of gilt bronze in form of a siren-caryatid, probably by R. Dubois (Wallace Collection, London)

guards, etc. The term is not usually applied to bronze furniture mounts. Very high quality of design and execution was reached in C18 France when sculptors often provided the models, in terracotta, wood or wax. Casts were made by a *fondeur* either by the CIRE PERDUE process or from a mould of clay or sand, finished and chased by a *ciseleur* and usually gilded by a *doreur*, each separate process being, by guild regulations, the exclusive prerogative of a separate craftsman – *see* ORMOLU and FONDEUR-CISELEUR.

Brooks, Hervey Early C19 potter working at Goshen, Connecticut, from *c.*1820 onwards and making red earthenware domestic wares.

Brooks, John (*c.*1710–*c.*1756). He tried, unsuccessfully, to patent TRANSFER PRINTING for enamels and ceramics in Birmingham in 1751 and in London in 1753. He probably invented the process though John SADLER is known to have been employing it almost simultaneously. He was the manager of the BATTERSEA ENAMEL FACTORY until it closed in 1756.

Brooks, Thomas (1811–87). New York furniture-maker in partnership with Lorenzo Blackstone 1841–2 and with a warehouse in Fulton Street, Brooklyn, from 1850. The most notable of his productions is a cabinet made to hold a set of Audubon's *Birds of America* given by the New York firemen to Jenny Lind in 1850 (now in the Museum of the City of New York). Like his other known pieces it is in the richly wrought eclectic style known as 'Renaissance' in the mid C19, with much turned-work and figurative carving.

Lit: 19th Century America: Furniture and Other Decorative Arts, Exh. Cat., Metropolitan Museum, New York 1970.

Brosamer, Hans (*fl.*1535–50). Painter and engraver of Fulda and the author of *Ein* new *Kunstbuchlein* (probably *c.*1548), a series of designs for silver in the German Renaissance style decorated with plump *putti*, cherub heads, human figures (including a very amorous Adam and Eve), Jack-in-the-Green masks and bold acanthus ornament. Several vessels are of simple outline with a modicum of fluted or gadrooned and foliage decoration, and none presents much practical difficulty to the silversmith (unlike the designs of ROSSO, DU CERCEAU and others). The volume seems to have been widely used in N. Europe.

H. Brosamer: design for a ewer, from Ein *new* Kunstbüchlein, *Frankfurt, c.1548*

Brown ware, Northern and **Brown ware, Southern** Cautious modern terms for various types of Chinese brown glazed stoneware made from the SUNG period onwards, formerly ascribed to kilns in Honan (northern) and Fukien (southern) but now known to have been made over wider areas. Both wares are also called by the Japanese term **Temmoku.**

Brûle parfum A French term for a CASSOLETTE, in use from the later C19 onwards.

Brunello, Giovanni Battista, *see* ESTE POTTERY & PORCELAIN FACTORY.

Brunetto, T., *see* RATO POTTERY.

Brüning, Heinrich Christoph, *see* FÜRSTENBERG PORCELAIN FACTORY.

Brunswick potteries A small faience factory founded by Duke Anton Ulrich of Brunswick in 1707, leased out in 1710, bought by Duke Karl in 1756 and State-controlled until 1773 when leased to **J. B. E. Rabe** who bought it outright in 1776 and ran it until his death in 1803, finally closed in 1807. It began by producing blue-and-white wares in imitation of those of DELFT, but in the mid C18 also made handsome large ewers and vases with moulded Rococo decorations painted in high-temperature colours, for which it is mainly famed. Another faience factory in Brunswick of 1745–57, run by **Rudolph Anton Cheley** and his sons, produced vases with landscapes or chinoiseries within Baroque borders, figures of peasants, tureens in the shape of ducks and such unusual objects as a large barrel (1747, formerly Schlossmuseum, Berlin) and a bust of Duke Karl I of Brunswick. (For factory mark *see* p. 882.)

Lit: C. Scherer, *Braunschweiger Fayencen*, Brunswick 1929; G. Spies, *Braunschweiger Fayencen*, Brunswick 1971.

Bruschi, Gaspero, *see* DOCCIA PORCELAIN FACTORY.

Brussels carpet A type of carpet made at Brussels and elsewhere (e.g. at the KIDDERMINSTER CARPET FACTORIES) with a worsted warp brought to the surface in loops to form the pile. It has three sets of warp, a chain-warp which with a weft of fine linen or hemp forms the woven base, a stuffe-warp to give 'body' and the worsted pile warps (up to five or six). They were at first woven on draw-looms but in 1825 the JACQUARD mechanism was adapted to their manufacture at Kidderminster. They were first produced mechanically on the Brussels power-loom (invented by Erastus B. Bigelow of Massachusetts 1846–8, perfected by G. Collier of Halifax 1851) in general use in England by the 1860s. But this process used up a considerable quantity of expensive worsted warp and could reproduce patterns in no more than six colours. These disadvantages were overcome in the *tapestry-Brussels* or printed Brussels carpet for which the warp yarn forming the pile and pattern was dyed in stripes of the appropriate colours before weaving: it could thus be woven without the Jacquard mechanism for selecting yarns of different colours. In both types the loops of the pile were formed by the insertion of wires round which the yarn passed; if knife-ended wires were used the loops were cut, producing a type of carpet known as *tapestry-velvet*.

Brussels lace Many different types of LACE, both needlepoint and pillow lace, have been made in Brussels since the early C16 and some pieces are among the finest ever produced. The needlepoint lace, usually known as *point de gaze*, is very delicate, made in small pieces (patterns and ground worked simultaneously) with *cordonnet* stitched round the main elements of the pattern. The pillow laces include the types confusingly known as *point plat* and *point d'Angleterre*. Occasionally needlepoint and pillow lace techniques were combined for a single piece. Machine-made net was first produced at Brussels in 1768, and from the early C19 this was often used as a ground on which to apply decorative motifs, of needlepoint or pillow lace, called *Brussels appliqué*. *Illustrated opposite.*

Lit: B. Palliser, *History of Lace*, rev. M. Jourdain & A. Dryden, London 1902; L. W. van der Meulen-Nulle, *Lace*, London 1963; P. Wardle, *Victorian Lace*, London 1968.

Brussels pottery & porcelain factories There were several small C17 potteries at Brussels but products were indifferent until the C18 when **Corneille Mombaers** and **Thierry Witsenburg** founded a factory in 1705 which produced, from 1724 onwards, tureens and other vessels in natural forms (turkeys, ducks, cabbages, melons, fishes, etc.). They were unmarked but occasionally signed. The glaze has frequently run, giving a streaked or marbled effect. After 1766 this pottery was amalgamated with another, started in 1751 by **Jacques Antoisenet.** It produced faience figures, sometimes quite large, but closed in 1825. A third pottery was founded in 1802 by **van Bellinghen**

Brussels needlepoint lace:
detail of veil made for the Russian Imperial Family,
c.1810 *(Courtesy of the Art Institute of Chicago)*

and closed in 1866. Apart from the tureens in natural forms Brussels faience is generally similar to the commoner contemporary Delft and Northern French wares.

A porcelain factory was started by **J.-S. Vaume** in 1786 at Scharbeek. It was called *Manufacture de Monplaisir* and closed in 1790. Products are similar to contemporary Paris porcelain. Another factory was started at Etterbeek in *c.*1787 by **Chrétien Kuhne** and closed *c.*1803. Its products included *biscuit* figures and table-wares. A third factory, started by **Louis Cretté**, was in production *c.*1791–1803. Cretté usually signed his work. (For factory mark *see* p. 882.)

Lit: E. Hannover, *Pottery & Porcelain*, London 1924; J. Helbig, *La céramique Bruxelloise du bon temps*, Brussels 1946.

Brussels tapestry factories One of the most important groups of high and low warp tapestry looms in Europe. They first became prominent in the late C15 but products of this period are difficult to distinguish from those made elsewhere in Flanders or even France (the famous Brussels mark – a shield between two Bs – was not used until 1528). Early hangings generally assigned to Brussels include a *millefleurs* panel with the arms of Charles le Téméraire woven before 1476 (Musée Historique, Berne); the *Allegory of the Virgin as the Source of Living Water* of 1485 (Louvre), a rather over-crowded composition notable mainly for the nobility of the central figure; the very handsome *Virgin and Child with a Donor* of *c.*1600 (Musée des Tissus, Lyons) and the somewhat similar *History of the Virgin* (Patrimonio nacional, Madrid) both with much gold thread. The earliest surviving tapestry that was certainly woven at Brussels is the *History of Archamboult* of 1533 (Musées royaux d'Art et d'Histoire, Brussels), a symmetrical composition rather over-crowded with figures wearing long robes which sweep the ground, clearly influenced by the paintings of Hugo van der Goes (d.1482). The high technical quality of Brussels tapestries, unequalled elsewhere in Europe, led Pope Leo X to commission **Pieter van Aelst** to weave the *Acts of the Apostles* series after RAPHAEL's cartoons (1516–19). The weavers took some liberties – e.g. providing Christ with a flowered robe in place of the plain one intended by Raphael – but the set of hangings sent to Rome and hung on great occasions in the Sistine Chapel was a triumphant success and established Brussels as the leading tapestry centre for all Europe. The set was later copied, both at Brussels and elsewhere (e.g. MORTLAKE). This series marks the turning point in the history of tapestry weaving. Henceforth the designer of the cartoons, often a great painter, assumed greater importance while the weavers came to be regarded as no more than skilled executants. More Brussels tapestries were woven after Italian designs – Mantegna's *Triumphs of the Gods*, Giulio Romano's *Fructus Belli* and *Life of Scipio*. At about the same time the Italianate Bernard van Orly (*c.*1488–1541) emerged as the leading painter of cartoons for the Brussels weavers. His set of twelve *Hunts of Maximilian* 1525–40 (Louvre) and the *Battle of Pavia* woven for Charles V in 1531 (Museo di Capodimonte, Naples) initiated the custom of commemorating the deeds of rulers in tapestries. They are notable mainly for their boldly foreshortened running and staggering figures, their naturalistically rendered animals and their landscape backgrounds (the view of Pavia, still instantly recognizable, is particularly attractive). Other outstanding painters of cartoons included Van Orley's pupil Pieter Coecke (1502–50) author of the *Seven Deadly Sins* of 1540–50 (Patrimonio nacional, Madrid), and Jan Cornelisz. Vermeyan (1500–59). The early C17 revival of the Brussels tapestry factories was due largely to Rubens who provided the weavers with numerous cartoons. The finest of the Rubens tapestries is the *Apotheosis of the Eucharist* (first set in Monasterio de las Descalzas Reales, Madrid) woven at the factory of **Jean Raes** 1625–30 and frequently repeated – wonderfully bold Baroque compositions with figures larger than life set in architectural frames. Other series represented the histories of Constantine, Achilles and Decius Mus. After the death of Rubens, his pupil Jacob Jordaens provided further cartoons in much the same spirit. Once again, standards declined and when the GOBELINS factory was 'nationalized' by Colbert in 1662 (staffed with many of the best Flemish weavers) the main centre of tapestry production passed to Paris. The Brussels looms remained active, however, and produced numerous fine works in the late C17, notably the enormously popular genre scenes after paintings by David

Brussels tapestry: The Creation of Eve, *mid c16, after a design by Michiel Coxie (Palazzo Pitti, Florence)*

Teniers II. These continued to be produced throughout the c18 as well as a few new sets of distinction, such as the *Triumphs of the Gods* of 1717.

Lit: H. Göbel, *Wandteppiche*, Leipzig 1923–34; M. Crick-Kunziger in *Bruxelles au XVe siècle*, Brussels 1953; C. de Schoutheete de Tervarent, *La Tapisserie flamande aux XVIIe et XVIIIe siècles*, Brussels 1959; D. Heinz, *Europäische Wandteppiche*, Brunswick 1963.

Brustolon, Andrea (1662–1732). He was a Venetian sculptor who carved furniture of superb quality and of uniquely exuberant, sophisticated and fantastic design, though rather impractical. He was born at Belluno and was presumably brought up in the wood carving tradition of that alpine region, but at fifteen years of age he was apprenticed in Venice to thc Baroque sculptor Filippo Parodi. His earliest recorded work is a pair of angels for the Frari in Venice in 1684. His masterpiece is a set of furniture carved for the Venier family and now in Palazzo Rezzonico in Venice, including twelve chairs with boxwood arms in the form of gnarled tree branches, supported by statuettes of negro boys with ebony heads and arms and patches of ebony flesh glinting through their slashed boxwood breeches, GUERIDONS in the form of naked athletic negro slaves in ebony with boxwood chains around their necks, and a huge vase-stand incorporating figures of negroes, classical river gods, Charon, Cerberus and the Hydra. The latter piece is signed. The whole set was probably done before 1699 when Brustolon returned to Belluno. A similar set of furniture from the Villa Pisani at Stra is now in the Quirinale in Rome, with chairs and vase-stands carved with *putti*, fruit and

A. Brustolon: vase-stand, late c17 (Palazzo Rezzonico, Venice)

flowers. Many of his drawings, including designs for elaborate looking-glass frames, are in the Museo Civico, Belluno.

Lit: G. Biasuz & M. G. Buttignon, *A. Brustolon*, Padua 1969; H. Honour, *Cabinet Makers & Furniture Designers*, London & New York 1969.

Bruyn, Michiel de (1608–before 1670). Notable Utrecht silversmith who became a master craftsman 1630 and worked in England from 1657, in partnership with Christiaen van VIANEN 1661. Occasionally he adopted a tame version of the AURICULAR STYLE but was more successful in the normal Dutch Baroque idiom, as in boldly modelled sconces with tulip-shaped nozzles (1653, Rijksmuseum, Amsterdam) and many pieces of ecclesiastical plate.

Lit: J. W. Frederiks, *Dutch Silver*, The Hague 1952–61.

Bubble cup, *see* PALACE BOWL.

Buccaro, *see* BOCCARO.

Buch, Iver Winfeldt (1749–1811). Norwegian goldsmith who went as a youth to St Petersburg where he obtained an Imperial appointment. His earliest known work is a diamond-studded gold chalice of 1791 set with engraved gems and with relief ornament in the Louis XVI style (coll. Mrs Merryweather Post, Washington, D.C.). Most of his other works are massive with Antique Revival decorations, similar to, though often ante-dating, French Empire pieces. They include giant vases, tall candelabra and even large console tables entirely covered with silver, all in the Hermitage Museum, Leningrad.

Lit: A. Polak in *The Connoisseur*, CLXVIII (1968), pp. 20–23.

Buchwald, Abraham, *see* ECKERNFÖRDE POTTERY.

Buchwald, Johann, *see* KIEL POTTERIES.

Buckingham, Duke of, *see* VAUXHALL GLASS-HOUSES.

Buckinghamshire lace, *see* BEDFORDSHIRE LACE.

Buckwheat celadon A type of brown-spotted Lung-ch'üan CELADON much prized in Japan where it is called *Tobi-seiji*.

Bucrane (or **Bucranium**) An ox-skull, usually garlanded, often carved in the metopes of a Doric frieze. It was frequently used as an orna-

Bucranium: detail from gilt wood side-table (Osterley Park, Middx.)

mental motif for the decoration of furniture, porcelain, etc. in the late C18. Not to be confused with an AEGRICANES.

Buen Retiro porcelain factory Founded 1759 by Charles III on his accession to the Spanish throne and established in the park of Buen Retiro, Madrid. As the equipment, materials and, most important, the craftsmen were all transported from CAPODIMONTE its early products are almost indistinguishable from those of the Neapolitan factory. Its first major undertaking was a porcelain room for the royal palace at Aranjuez (1760–65) by GRICCI – an improvement on that which Gricci made at Capodimonte, having a ceiling as well as walls of porcelain and chinoiserie reliefs of greater fantasy, modelled with more assurance (possibly due to the influence of G. D. Tiepolo). Another porcelain room with reliefs of *putti*, urns and burgeoning vines was made for the Royal Palace, Madrid (1770–80). Independent figures and groups were also made, the best being rather large (about 1 ft) and representing characters from Tasso's *Gerusalemme liberata*. The soft paste used has a waxy texture and creamy tone. But the importation of Italian materials was abandoned in the 1770s and a rather unattractive yellowish paste was used until 1784 when a fine glassy white paste was produced. In the 1780s it produced some handsome Neo-Classical vases painted with groups of elegant Grecians rather in the WEDGWOOD manner. It made very few useful wares until 1804 when it was reorganized and lost all its character; it closed down in 1808. (For factory marks *see* p. 882.)

Buen Retiro porcelain: detail of the porcelain room, Royal Palace, Aranjuez, 1760–65

Lit: A. Lane, *Italian Porcelain with a note on Buen Retiro*, London 1954; A. W. Frothingham, *Capodimonte and Buen Retiro Porcelains: Period of Charles III*, New York 1955; B. Martinez-Caviro, *Porcelana del Buen Retiro Escultura*, Madrid 1973.

Buffet The name given, perhaps erroneously, to various types of C16 doorless, generally rather heavy, pieces of furniture constructed in two or more tiers and often used as sideboards. From the C18 onwards the term has become a synonym for a sideboard.

Bugatti, Carlo (1855–1940). One of the most remarkable Italian furniture designers of his day working in a highly original version of the ART NOUVEAU style. He was born in Milan, the son of a carver of architectural decorations, trained at the Brera and began as an architect. He turned to furniture-making before 1888 when at the Italian Exhibition in London he showed Turkish style smoking-room furniture and a screen in a very freely interpreted Japanese idiom. In the next few years he developed his highly original style with much use of metal and ivory inlays, interlaced cords and parchment with painted or pokerwork decoration. Occasionally there are echoes of Japanese, Middle-Eastern or even, in his use of circles and semi-circles, of Romanesque art, but the general effect is of almost strident novelty. He showed at the Turin exhibition of 1898, and at the Paris exhibition of 1900. And in 1900 he supplied furniture for the Khedive's palace in Istanbul. His triumph came in 1902 when at the Turin Exhibition he won a first prize with several rooms of furniture including an extraordinary suite of curvilinear pieces which seem to anticipate the organic forms of some mid-C20

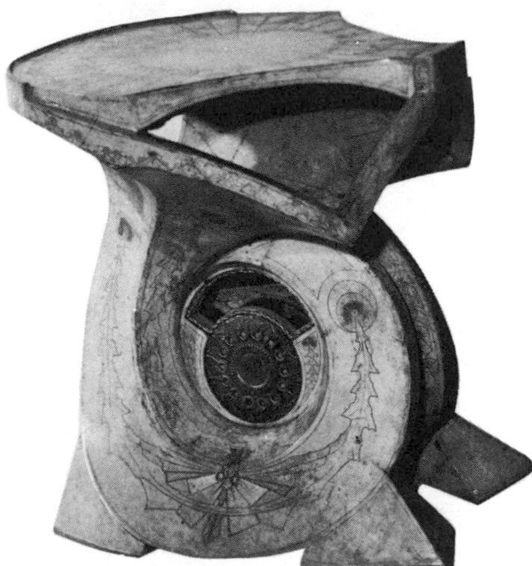

C. Bugatti: table, wood and parchment, 1902 (Private Collection)

designers – chairs with G-shaped supports, a table supported on a huge volute and a large vitrine which resembles a giant snail. In 1907 some of his pieces were included in the *Salon des peintres divisionistes* in Paris. Soon afterwards he left Milan – where his workshop was taken over by a firm named De Vecchi which continued to produce his simpler types of furniture – and settled in France at Pierrefonds where he eventually became mayor. Here he designed silverware for Hébrard but was engaged mainly in painting. One son, Ettore, became famous as a motor-car designer, another, Rembrandt, as an animal sculptor.

Lit: Milano 70/70, Exh. Cat., Museo Poldi Pezzoli, Milan, 1970; S. Jervis in *Arte Illustrata* 34–35–36 (1970), pp. 80–87.

Buhl, *see* BOULLE, André-Charles, and BOULLE MARQUETRY.

Bullet teapot An early C18 English type of silver teapot with a spherical, bullet-shaped body standing on a foot-ring. The lid is cut out of the upper part of the body. The form was revived by C19 silversmiths.

Bullock, George (d.1819). One of the most important English furniture-makers of the REGENCY period. He began his career as a sculptor in his native Liverpool where he was president of the newly founded Academy in 1810–11. But by 1805 he and a Mr Stokes had been in partnership as 'cabinet makers, general furnishers and marble workers'. He had moved to London by 1814, continued to work as a sculptor but also established what appears to have been an extensive furniture workshop and was, in addition, active as an antique dealer, supplying arms and armour to Sir Walter Scott whom he also provided with modern furniture. He specialized in rather massive pieces of furniture (even small tables were given a strong weighty appearance by him) with much marquetry and inlaid brass. Although his ornamental motifs have a Grecian look and he made frequent use of such classical motifs as the fret, palmette and anthemion, he also took pride in deriving others from British flora, the leaves of oak and ivy, harebells, pimpernels, etc. And he made a speciality of inlays composed of such British woods as bog-oak, elm, larch, etc. For this nationalism he was much praised by contemporaries. Several of his pieces of furniture were illustrated in Ackerman's *Repository of Arts*, 1816–24.

Lit: B. Reade, *Regency Antiques*, London 1953; A. Coleridge in *The Connoisseur*, CLVIII (1965), pp. 249–52, CLIX (1965) pp. 13–17.

Bumping glasses, *see* FIRING GLASSES.

Bun foot A flattened BALL FOOT, introduced late C17.

Bunzlau potteries Bunzlau in Silesia has been a pottery centre since the Middle Ages, specializing in stoneware with a fine grey-brown body covered with a wash of ferruginous material which gave it a rich lustrous coffee or rust-brown glaze. They were often decorated with applied reliefs in a yellowish-white clay. In the C18 and C19 the chief products were coffee pots and tankards in salt-glazed stoneware. In *c.*1810 Johann Gottlieb Altmann began making wares in a Neo-Grecian style, very unusual in stoneware, and these were copied by other potters at Bunzlau. Later, they produced wares in a Neo-Gothic style. Eventually, towards the end of the C19, the Bunzlau potteries were industrialized.

Lit: K. Strauss, *Alte deutsche Kunsttöpferein*,

Berlin 1923; G. Reineking von Bock, *Kunstgewerbemuseum der Stadt Köln: Steinzeug*, Cologne 1971; B. Mundt, *Historismus*, Catalogue of the Kunstgewerbemuseum, Berlin, vol. VII, Berlin 1973.

Buquoy, Georg Franz August Longueval, Count von, *see* HYALITH.

Bureau A term of French origin for a writing table or desk. The word is derived from *bure*, a type of coarse linen used in the Middle Ages especially to cover the tables and chests on which clerks wrote. A *bureau plat* is a flat-topped writing table, usually with a leather-covered top and with drawers in the frieze, very popular in France from the late C17 onwards. A small *bureau plat* is called a *table à écrire*. A *bureau à gradin* is a *bureau plat* with a set of drawers and/or pigeon holes along one side of the top. A *bureau à cylindre* (also called a

Bureau, mahogany, with gilt-bronze chinoiserie grilles, probably Brunswick, c.1750 (Kunstgewerbemuseum, Cologne)

(Below) Bureau plat by Bernard van Risenburgh II, wood marquetry with gilt-bronze mounts, c.1750 (Cleveland Museum of Art, Bequest of Mrs Frances F. Prentiss)

secrétaire à cylindre) is like a *bureau à gradin* with a roll-top which when closed covers both the pigeon holes and writing platform with a quarter-cylinder of slats of wood. A similar but much smaller desk with a sloping fall-front instead of the roll-top is called a *bureau en pente* (or *secrétaire en pente*). A *bureau-toilette* is a combined writing and toilet table. A *bureau Mazarin* is a C19 term for a BOULLE type marquetry desk on scroll legs with three drawers on each side and one drawer above a knee-hole recess which is closed by a cupboard.

The nomenclature of non-French types of bureau is less precise. The lean-to fall-front writing desk popular in England and America from the late C17 is usually called a bureau, and if it is surmounted by a bookcase a bureau-bookcase. In England the term bureau-table is applied to a type of late C17 flat-topped desk with drawers, the upper part of which is like a shallow box the lid of which may be raised and the front wall allowed to fall forward so that it may serve both for the storage of papers and as a writing platform. In the U.S. the term bureau-table signifies a dressing table with drawers on short legs with a knee-hole recess.

W. Burges: cabinet, with painted panels by E. J. Poynter, 1858 (Victoria & Albert Museum)

Burgau or **Burgandine** or **Burgos** A thick, iridescent, brightly coloured reddish-mauve mother-of-pearl, from a spiral shell found in the Near East. It was used in Europe for knife handles and for the decoration of small caskets, etc. In China it was occasionally inlaid in lacquer applied to porcelain, mainly of the CH'ING dynasty. Japanese lacquer workers also made use of it as an inlay on pieces called in Europe *lac burganté*.

Burges, William (1827–81). English architect and designer working in the richest Gothic Revival manner. He designed furniture mainly for his own use or as part of the vast schemes of interior rebuilding and decoration carried out for the Marquess of Bute at Cardiff Castle (1865) and Castle Coch (1875). His masterpiece of interior decoration is his own house, 9 Melbury Road, London (1875–81), which does not – as he claimed – look like 'a model residence of the 15th century', but which reveals a feeling for colour and fantasy, an almost childish delight in richness and grotesquerie, closer to the spirit of the Middle Ages than anything by his more staid and archaeologically 'correct' contemporaries. The Welsh castles are less effective mainly because the profusion of ornament becomes oppressive on their very much larger scale. A wash-stand of 1880 (Victoria and Albert Museum) provides a characteristic example of his furniture: in form it is almost severely simple and solid but fantasy breaks loose in its surface decorations, with garishly coloured paintings of birds and flowers, unnecessarily massive iron hinges to the small doors, inset quatrefoil and trefoil mirrors, a bowl of fine marble with a bronze tap in the form of a goat's head. Other pieces are adorned with paintings by artists as distinguished as E. J. Poynter and BURNE-JONES. He designed Gothic wallpapers for Jeffrey & Co. and some elaborately bizarre pieces of metalwork lavishly encrusted with precious and semi-precious stones.

Lit: C. Handley-Read in *Burlington Magazine*, CV (1963), pp. 496–509; C. Handley-Read in P. Ferriday, *Victorian Architecture*, London 1963.

Burgio potteries, *see* SICILIAN POTTERIES.

Burmese glass A type of late C19 American glass, pale greenish-yellow shading to pink in colour, first manufactured *c.*1885 by the Mount Washington Glass Company, New Bedford, Mass. It was used for table glass as well as for decorative pieces. It has either a dull or glossy finish. THOMAS WEBB & SONS of Stourbridge manufactured it in England from 1886 onwards, calling it 'Queen's Burmese'. The English variety is semi-opaque and salmon-pink shading to lemon yellow in colour.

Burne-Jones, Edward (1833–98). English painter and designer closely associated with William MORRIS for whom he designed tapestries and stained glass windows with Pre-Raphaelite Gothic figures of languid ladies and soulful knights. Also designed some furniture in a solid, simple version of the Gothic Revival style.

Lit: R. Watkinson, *Pre-Raphaelite Art and Design*, London 1970; M. Harrison & B. Watson, *Burne-Jones*, London 1973.

Burr An excrescence on the trunk or root of a tree which when cut is very decoratively marked and was therefore much used in oyster veneers, especially with walnut, elm or yew.

Burt, John (1690–1745). American silversmith working in Boston where he was probably apprenticed to John CONEY. Examples of his work belong to Harvard University, notably a pair of candlesticks marked 1724. His sons **Benjamin, Samuel** and **William** carried on their father's business, Benjamin being the best known. A tea-set by him is in the Museum of Fine Arts, Boston (M. and M. Karolik Collection).

Burton, William and **Joseph,** *see* PILKINGTON'S ROYAL LANCASTRIAN POTTERY.

Busch, August Otto Ernst von dem (1704–79). He was a Canon at Hildesheim and in about 1745 began to decorate porcelain by a technique borrowed from contemporary diamond-pointed engraving. He coloured the engraved lines by rubbing black pigment into them. Much of his work was done on Meissen porcelain, but he also used Fürstenburg wares. He did landscapes with ruins, floral sprays and birds, especially swans.

Lit: H. Dreyer, *Der Porzellanmaler August O. E. von dem Busch*, Hildesheim 1931.

Bustelli, Franz Anton (1723–63). The greatest Rococo porcelain modeller. Born in Switzerland (probably Locarno) and possibly trained as a sculptor in N. Italy, he was *Modellmeister* at the Bavarian Neudeck and NYMPHENBURG PORCELAIN FACTORY 1754–63. During this brief period he modelled a large number of statuettes of an elegant sophistication unequalled in the history of porcelain. Subjects include Chinamen, Turks, *putti*, the gods of Ovid's *Metamorphoses*, and groups of impassioned lovers philandering among ruins and great springing Rococo scrolls on which they rest. Finest of all is the series of sixteen *Commedia dell'Arte* actors – Pierrot, Pantaloon, The Captain, Leda, Lalage and the rest – elegantly mincing, posturing and gesticulating in attitudes of joy, surprise or coquettishness. Many of the figures are designed as pairs so that the Rococo curves of their poses complement one another, but although they are often affected they are never unnatural. They are represented in attitudes

F. Bustelli:
chinoiserie figure in Nymphenburg porcelain

which could not physically be held for more than a split second, caught in movement at the moment of supreme grace. No sculptor and, indeed, no medium less delicate than porcelain, has ever succeeded in catching the fleeting movements of the human figure with greater sensitivity. His only rival as a porcelain modeller is the much more prolific and longer lived KÄNDLER whose figures are rather less precious but also less elegant and less *mouvementé*. He brought the art of Rococo sculpture to its highest pitch of refinement just before it began to go out of fashion.

Lit: R. Rückert, *Franz Anton Bustelli*, Munich 1963.

Butler's tray A tray of wood, silver or japanned metal mounted on a folding stand or legs, very popular in C18 England.

Buttenmann, *see* TANZEMANN.

Bux, Johann Baptist, *see* SCHREZHAIM POTTERY.

B.V.R.B., *see* RISENBURGH, Bernard van.

Bylivelt, Jacques or Jacopo Bilivert (d.1603). He was a Mannerist goldsmith working at the Court of Francesco I Grand Duke of Tuscany. He was born in Holland at Delft or Maastricht but was working in Augsburg before 1573 when invited to Florence by Francesco de' Medici who appointed him director of his gallery. His most famous work was the Medici crown made 1577–83 but now known only from paintings and a drawing (Victoria and Albert Museum, London). The enamelled gold setting for a lapis lazuli vase (designed by Bernardo Buontalenti) of 1583, now in the Museo degli Argenti, Palazzo Pitti, Florence, appears to be the only documented work by him that survives. Several other pieces have been attributed to him, notably the Rospigliosi cup formerly ascribed to CELLINI (Metropolitan Museum, New York). On his death, his studio was taken over by his former assistant **Odoardo Vallet** (1542–1622), a goldsmith of French origin who had settled in Florence in 1589 and continued to work in the Mannerist style well into the C17 (e.g. enamelled gold mount for rock-crystal cup of 1618, Museo degli Argenti, Palazzo Pitti, Florence).

J. Bylivelt:
lapis lazuli vase with enamelled gold setting, 1583 (Museo degli Argenti, Palazzo Pitti, Florence)

Lit: K. Aschengreen Piacenti in *Mitteilungen des Kunsthistorisches Institut in Florenz* XIII (1965), pp. 107–24; Y. Hackenbroch in *The Connoisseur* CLXXII (1969), pp. 174–81; C. W. Fock in *Oud Holland* LXXXV (1970), pp. 197–209.

Byzantine style A term used to describe, at its narrowest, the predominant artistic style or styles developed in Constantinople between its establishment as Imperial capital in 330 and its fall in 1453. But it is often stretched to cover all the more sophisticated works of art produced under Christian patronage in W. Europe from the early C4 until the emergence of the ROMANESQUE STYLE and practically everything produced in E. Europe and Asia Minor under the influence of the Orthodox church. While the latter definition is too wide to be of much use, the former is too narrow to include c4 works produced in Milan, Ravenna, Alexandria, Antioch and Ephesus – artistic centres little less important than Constantinople at this date. By the early c6, however, Constantinople had emerged as the unquestioned artistic capital, occupying a position comparable with that of Paris in the Middle Ages or Rome in the Baroque period. In the decorative arts, as in architecture, painting and large scale sculpture, the Byzantine style developed out of late Imperial Roman art. It was however influenced also by the arts of the Middle East, but from at least the c6 onwards these classicizing and orientalizing trends were generally held in equilibrium. At its best it is characterized by a love of luxurious and bejewelled richness, extreme stylization in the treatment of figurative, floral or foliate motifs, a preference for flat rather than sculpturesque patterns and meticulous delicacy of craftsmanship.

So far as the decorative arts are concerned, the earliest works of importance are in silver. Some are predominantly late Antique in decoration, e.g. the Concesti amphora of late c4 with a battle of men and amazons in bold relief (Hermitage Museum, Leningrad) and this style survived into the c7 whenever pagan motifs were used, e.g. the mid-c6 fragment of a dish with a relief of Silenus (Dumbarton Oaks, Washington); the dish embossed with a very spirited Silenus and dancing Maenad of 610–29 (Hermitage Museum, Leningrad); or the bucket of the same date decorated with reliefs of gods and goddesses (Kunsthistorisches Museum, Vienna). A strikingly different style – ethereal, static and highly schematic – marks the silver dishes and patens which bear representations of the Emperors or religious scenes, either engraved or in very shallow relief, e.g. the mid-c4 Constantius II dish (Hermitage Museum, Leningrad), the dish with Theodosius I, Valentinian II and Arcadius, of 388 (Academia de la Historia, Madrid) or the Stuma and Riha patens of 565–78 (Archaeological Museum, Istanbul, and Dumbarton Oaks, Washington). A similar distinction can be drawn between secular and religious ivory carvings, though the CONSULAR DIPTYCHS carved in Rome are generally more realistic and classical than the Imperial and Consular diptychs carved in Constantinople. The classical style was, however, adopted for the Poet and

Detail of Byzantine silver dish, called the missorium of Theodosius, *388* A.D. *(Academia de la Historia, Madrid)*

Byzantine silk, c6 (Musée de Cluny, Paris)

the Muse diptych (Cathedral Treasury, Monza) probably carved in mid-c6 Constantinople. One of the most remarkable works in ivory of this period – and the only notable piece of Byzantine furniture to survive – is the throne of Maximian (Museo Arcivescovile, Ravenna) decorated with numerous rather overcrowded reliefs of religious subjects, probably executed in Constantinople in the mid-c6.

The Iconoclast controversy of the c8 brought the first great period of Byzantine art to a close. During the c8, however, some very notable silks were woven in Constantinople, one with a charioteer driving a quadriga as the main element in the pattern (Musée de Cluny, Paris), another with two emperors engaged in a lion hunt (Musée des Tissus, Lyons), both showing classical realism in the treatment of the animals but also much Persian influence. *See also* p. 736.

The second Byzantine golden age lasted from the mid-c9 to the Latin conquest of Constantinople in 1204, and numerous objects in a wide variety of media survive from it; the most outstanding are

Byzantine paten, alabaster and enamel, c10–11 (S. Marco, Venice)

perhaps the ENAMELS executed in the CLOISONNÉ technique, of exquisite workmanship and brilliant colour. On them the figures of saints and emperors as well as angels are rendered in the most highly stylized fashion, rather as symbols of ethereal essences than as human representations – notable examples include a book cover of 886–912 (Biblioteca Marciana, Venice), a reliquary of the True Cross of 964–5 (Cathedral Treasury, Limburg an der Lahn), the so-called Crown of Constantine IX Monomachos of 1042–50 (National Museum, Budapest) and parts of the Pala d'Oro from 1081–1118 (S. Marco, Venice). Some ivory carvings on the other hand, especially secular ones like the Veroli casket of the C10 (Victoria & Albert Museum, London), reveal a return to classicism especially in their rather fleshy treatment of the human figure. Similarly, classical figures appear on a glass bowl (the only important surviving example of Byzantine glass) probably made at Corinth in the C11 (Treasury, S. Marco, Venice). And some religious ivories, such

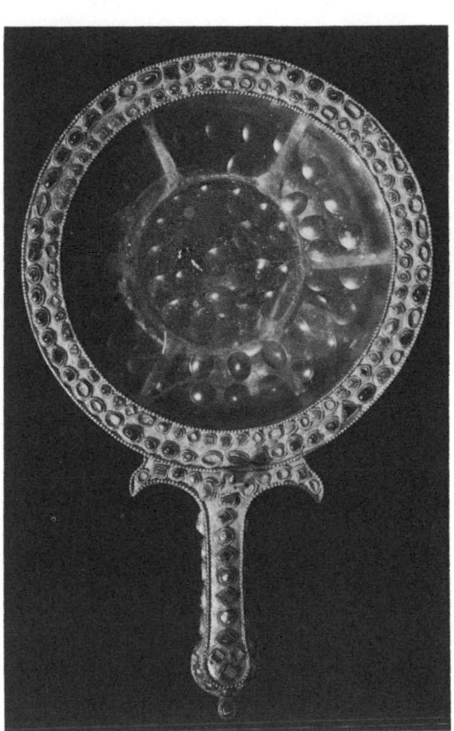

(Above left) Byzantine chalice, onyx and enamel panels, C11 (S. Marco, Venice)

(Above) Byzantine paten, rock crystal and silver-gilt mount, C11 (S. Marco, Venice)

(Left) Byzantine slip-ware dish, C12–13 (Archaeological Museum, Corinth)

as the triptych of *c.*1125–50 (Palazzo Venezia, Rome), also show a return to the more realistic standards of Antique art. This Antique revival coincided with an equally sophisticated cult of the exotic. Chinese phoenixes are carved at either end of a mid-C11 ivory casket (Cathedral Treasury, Troyes): some wonderful silks, woven in glowing colours, are decorated with stylized animals of obviously Persian derivation – lions (Cathedral Treasury, Cologne), eagles (Cathedral Treasury, Bressanone) and elephants (Cathedral Treasury, Aachen). It is however significant that an early C11 tapestry of a triumphant Emperor, perhaps Basil II, is in a style closer to mosaics and enamels – for representations of the Emperors formed part of religious art. Byzantine pottery was decorated in three predominant styles – religious, classicizing and exotic – the most interesting pieces being SGRAFFITO wares (e.g. in Staatliche Museum, Berlin and elsewhere).

After the Latin sack and occupation of Constantinople, the arts began to revive with the accession of Michael VIII Palaeologus to the Imperial throne in 1261. But the Empire was impoverished and although fine paintings were executed, the luxurious decorative arts of enamelling, ivory carving and silk weaving never recovered. However, the Orthodox church clung to the style evolved in the great Byzantine period and retained it for ritual vessels and vestments long after Constantinople had fallen to the Turks in 1453.

Engraved initial letter from Gerusalemme Liberata, *printed by Albrizzi, Venice, 1745 (enlarged)*

Cabaret A small, usually porcelain, tray with coffee cups to match: called a *tête-à-tête* if it has two cups and a *solitaire* if it has only one.

Cabinet A piece of case furniture consisting of a set of small drawers and/or pigeon holes, fronted by one or more doors, and intended for the storage and sometimes the display of small objects (especially precious objects). It is usually set on legs and sometimes on a stand from which it is detachable. It is distinct from the cupboard in that it has drawers and/or pigeon holes rather than simple shelves; and from the chest of drawers in that it has doors. The type originated in C16 Italy and was soon taken up in N. Europe, especially in the Netherlands where very handsome cabinets were made of ebony in the later C16 and in Germany where they were decorated with marquetry, especially at Augsburg. It became a very fashionable piece of furniture in the France of Louis XIV and in Restoration England. From the later C17 oriental lacquer cabinets (and European imitations of them) set on carved and gilt wood stands were very popular throughout N. Europe. Until the late C17 cabinets were generally the most elaborate pieces of furniture to be found in European houses, often made of rare woods and sometimes embellished with such materials as ivory and *pietre dure* – hence the term 'cabinet-maker' came to be applied to superior types of joiner from 1681 onwards.

Cabinet-on-stand, veneered in tortoiseshell and ebony with marble panels painted with Biblical scenes, Antwerp, c.1650 (Rijksmuseum, Amsterdam)

Cable moulding Medieval moulding like a twisted rope.

Cabochon An oval, convex gem; smooth and not cut into facets.

Cabochon ornament Carved ornament resembling a CABOCHON, often set in a floral surround, e.g. on the knee of a cabriole leg.

Cabriole leg Curved outwards at the knee and tapering inwards below, terminated by a club, hoof, bun, paw, claw-and-ball or scroll foot.

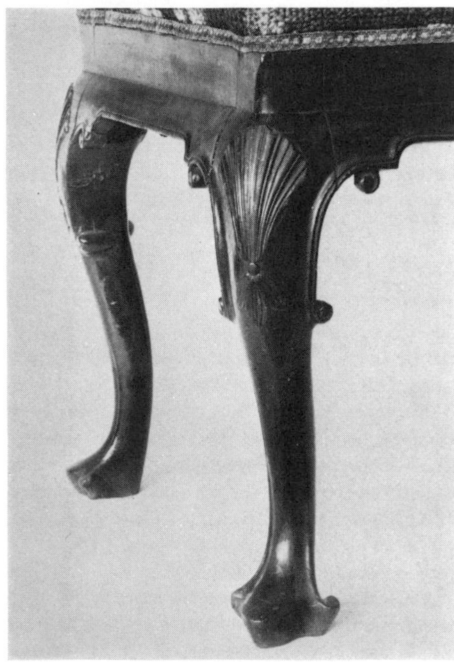

Cabriole legs on English walnut stool (Victoria & Albert Museum)

Popular during the first half of the C18 until superseded by the straight leg in Louis XVI and Empire furniture. The knee is usually decorated with a carved acanthus or cabochon ornament.

Cabriolet, *see* CHAIR, cabriole.

Cachemire A tall, reeded, octagonal covered vase, usually decorated in HIGH-TEMPERATURE COLOURS, a speciality of early C18 DELFT potteries but imitated elsewhere, especially in Germany.

Cache-pot An ornamental cover for a flower-pot, usually in pottery, porcelain or japanned metal. The term is C19 and many so-called *cache-pots* were in fact made as wine-coolers.

Caddy, *see* TEA-CADDY.

Caddy spoon A small and often fancifully shaped silver spoon for a TEA-CADDY.

Cadenas French name for a cadinet or casket, generally of gold or silver, made to contain spices and the personal cutlery of a high nobleman or member of the Royal Family and set on the dining table to mark his place. In form it is a small tray with compartments for condiments and cutlery at the back. It looks rather like a standish. Its function was similar to that of a NEF which it superseded in the C16. It remained in general use until the time of Louis XIV when it was reserved for the King and Queen, or for the royal princes and princesses when they dined without the King or Queen.

Cadinen pottery A factory founded in 1905 by Kaiser Wilhelm II near a source of clay on his private estate at Cadinen near Elbing. It began by producing imitations of Greek vases, Della Robbia reliefs, etc. But original glazed pottery reliefs and figures by such sculptors as A. AMBERG, Ludwig Manzel (1858–1936) and Emil Pottner (b.1872) were also made. It specialized in architectural ceramics, e.g. the Rococo-Revival Cadiner Saal in the Weinhaus Kempinski, Berlin (destroyed) and the Kaiser Friedrich Bad at Wiesbaden (1913). Other products included stoneware bowls, plates, etc. The factory remained active until 1945.

Lit: K. L. Graeupner in *Keramos* 44 (1969), pp. 43–54.

Cadinet English name for a CADENAS.

Cadogan teapot A teapot in the form of a Chinese peach-shaped wine pot, filled through a hole in

Cadogan teapot, Rockingham cream-coloured earthenware, early C19 (Victoria & Albert Museum)

the bottom. An Hon. Mrs Cadogan is said to have brought the original Chinese model to England, hence the name. It was adopted at the ROCKINGHAM PORCELAIN FACTORY in the early C19, and later by several STAFFORDSHIRE POTTERIES.

Cafaggiolo pottery One of the best Italian maiolica factories, at Cafaggiolo north of Florence. It was started under Medici patronage by two potters from MONTELUPO, Piero and Stefano di Filippo Schiavon (whose descendants were to take the surname FATTORINI in the C17). Some large jugs with rotund bodies and pinched lips very brightly painted with a peacock feather design are attributed to the early period of the factory (examples in the Victoria & Albert Museum, London). Outstandingly fine ISTORIATO wares were produced from *c.*1508–25. Some products reveal the influence of Florentine art – e.g., a dish painted with St George after Donatello's statue (Victoria & Albert Museum, London) and another with a Flora in the manner of Botticelli – but others appear to derive partly from Dürer's prints. A notable group of plates, clearly the work of a single hand, includes one signed by a certain Jacopo, generally identified as Jacopo FATTORINI. Another rather less gifted painter was responsible for several plates, one of which shows Pope Leo X carried in procession. The later wares, many of which are fully marked with the name of the factory, are of less interest, though including some fine pieces decorated in the Istoriato style or with grotesques similar to those on products of the URBINO POTTERIES. The last dated piece made at the factory is inscribed '1570' but the factory is known to have survived into the mid C18, probably making maiolica similar to that ascribed to the Montelupo potteries. Several different marks appear on wares ascribed to Cafaggiolo, including the name itself.

Lit: G. Ballardini, *La maiolica italiana*, Rome 1938; J. Chompret, *Répertoire de la majolique italienne*, Paris 1949; G. Cora, *Storia della maiolica di Firenze e del Contado, secoli XIV*^{e} *XV*, Florence 1973.

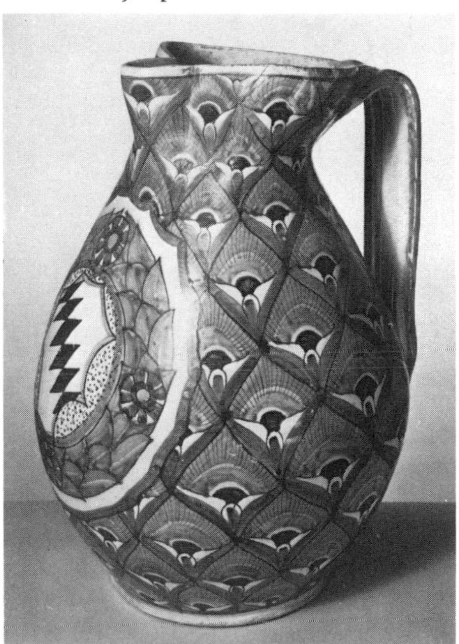

Cafaggiolo maiolica jug, 1480–90 (Victoria & Albert Museum)

Caffiéri, Jacques (1673–1755). He was the son of the sculptor Philippe Caffiéri (1634–1716) who had been brought from Italy to France by Mazarin. Jacques Caffiéri was trained as a sculptor and became the leading Louis XV FONDEUR-CISELEUR and one of the finest of all Rococo craftsmen in any medium. He became a *maître* shortly before 1715. From 1736 onwards he was constantly employed by the Crown, at Versailles, Fontainebleau, Choisy, Marly and other royal palaces.

J. Caffiéri: detail of gilt-bronze chandelier, c.1750 (Wallace Collection, London)

His masterpieces include two monumental chandeliers of gilt bronze (Wallace Collection, London) and a superb astronomical clock case, designed by C.-S. Passemant (Versailles). These date from between 1751 and 1753. He made many other magnificent *bronzes d'ameublement* and also furniture mounts of exceptional quality, collaborating with A.-R. GAUDREAU, e.g. the commode made for Louis XV's bedchamber at Versailles in 1739 (Wallace Coll., London). He was also a portrait sculptor of ability and his younger son, **Jacques** (1725–92) became *sculpteur du Roi* in 1783. His elder son **Philippe** (1714–74) assisted him, becoming a *maître* in 1756. Philippe's independent work developed away from the Rococo and towards Neo-Classical severity. Examples of their work are in the Louvre, Paris; the Wallace Collection, and Victoria & Albert Museum, London; the Residenz Museum, Munich; and the Cleveland Museum of Art, U.S.A.

Lit: J. Guiffrey, *Les Caffiéri*, Paris 1877; S. Eriksen, *Early Neo-Classicism in France*, London 1974.

Cahier, Jean-Charles (1772–after 1849). French silversmith who began as an assistant to BIENNAIS and set up on his own by 1806, specializing in ecclesiastical plate. His style was very similar to that of Biennais until after 1815 when he gradually veered towards the Neo-Gothic TROUBADOUR STYLE, reviving the use of enamel and filigree.

Lit: S. Grandjean, *L'Orfèvrerie du XIXe siècle en Europe*, Paris 1962.

Caillouté Pebbled – a type of gilded decoration used at SÈVRES, consisting of ovals interspersed with irregular smaller circles, outlined on a coloured background.

Cairene carpets, *see* TURKISH COURT CARPETS.

Cairene rugs, *see* MAMELUKE RUGS.

Cake basket A receptacle to hold cakes, bread or fruit at table, in use from the mid C18, of openwork silver (either pierced or basket-like), circular or oval with a swing handle. Keats's 'baskets bright of wreathed silver'.

Silver cake basket, by Richard Wills, London, 1771–2 (Victoria & Albert Museum)

Calamelli, Virgilotto (d.1570). Italian master potter who owned one of the best maiolica workshops in FAENZA, active from 1531 and carried on after his death by Leonardo Bettisi (d.*c*.1589). He produced ISTORIATO pieces but specialized in richly moulded BIANCO DI FAENZA wares, notably dishes and plates decorated with *putti* and other boldly sketched motifs in the COMPENDIARIO style, of which numerous examples are in the Museo Internazionale delle Ceramiche at Faenza.

Lit: G. Liverani in *The Connoisseur*, CXL (1957), pp. 160–63.

Calcedonia glass, *see* AGATE GLASS.

Caldas da Rainha pottery, *see* MAFRA POTTERY.

Caldwell, James, *see* WOOD, Ralph.

Caldwell, J. E., & Co. A firm of Philadelphia jewellers and silversmiths founded in 1839 and still active. In the mid C19 it made some handsome pieces of presentation plate similar to that made for TIFFANY in New York (e.g. pitcher in Philadelphia Museum of Art).

Lit: *19th Century America: Furniture and Other Decorative Arts*, Exh. Cat., Metropolitan Museum, New York 1970.

Calico A cotton fabric (so called because it was imported into England in the C16 from Calcutta then known as Calicut), especially the brightly painted fabrics which were very popular in C17 Europe.

Callegari (or **Caligari**), **Filippo Antonio,** *see* PESARO POTTERIES.

Callot figures Grotesque figures of dwarfs, very popular in the C18 as the subjects of statuettes made by goldsmiths (e.g. DINGLINGER) and in porcelain at MEISSEN, VIENNA and CHELSEA. They are so called from their similarity to figures in the series of engravings *Varie figure gobbi* (1622) by **Jacques Callot** (1592/3–1635). But most of them derive from prints after **Wilhelmus Koning** in *Il Calotto resuscitato oder Neu-eingerichtes Zwerchen Cabinett*, Amsterdam, 1716, several times reprinted.

Caltagirone potteries, *see* SICILIAN POTTERIES.

Camaieu, en Of monochrome painting in various tones on porcelain, pottery, enamel, etc. (also on canvas).

Cambrian pottery, *see* SWANSEA POTTERIES AND PORCELAIN FACTORY.

Cameo A gem, hardstone or shell having two layers of different colours, the upper of which can be carved in relief and the lower used as a ground. Sardonyx and agate were often used. The process is the reverse of INTAGLIO. It was much practised in the ancient world. Later specially prepared and coloured glass and paste were used.

Cameo glass, *see* CASED GLASS.

Cameo incrustation, *see* CRYSTALLO-CERAMIE.

Camlet Costly Eastern fabric made from Angora goat hair, or European substitutes made from C17 onwards, usually of wool, silk and hair (especially at Brussels) and variously figured, stamped, watered, etc. It was much used for bed hangings in C18.

Campani, Ferdinando Maria, *see* SIENA POTTERIES.

Canabas, Joseph Gegenbach, called (1712–97). A Parisian *ébéniste*, the son of a small craftsman from Baden, he settled in Paris in 1745 and became a *maître* in 1766. He specialized in multifunctional pieces and furniture that could be taken apart when travelling or campaigning, also in dining-room furniture. Most of his surviving pieces are in mahogany and of simple design without mounts or marquetry. But they are carefully designed, sober and eminently functional. Decoration is limited to fluting, brass fillets and recessed panels. His style is severe: domestic rather than decorative. His son **Pierre-Joseph** and two nephews, **François-Antoine** (*maître* 1779) and **François-Jean,** all seem to have worked with him. Examples of his furniture are in the Musée des Arts Décoratifs, Paris.

Lit: F. de Salverte, *Les ébénistés du XVIIIe siècle*, Paris 1962; F. J. B. Watson, *The Wrightsman Collection: Furniture*, New York 1966.

Canadella A Spanish type of glass ewer made in Catalonia. It has a long, wide cylindrical neck, a pear-shaped body, flat moulded base, a long slender spout and an equally long and slender handle. Examples date from as early as the C14.

Canapé French term covering the English terms SETTEE and SOFA, but sometimes distinguished from the SOPHA in that the wooden structure is not entirely concealed by upholstery. The word was first used in the late C17, and in the C18 numerous exotic names were given to various types, presumably by the *marchands* to attract customers. The significance of some C18 names (e.g. *paphose*) remains obscure. The term *canapé à confident* was applied to a straight-fronted sofa with triangular seats (sometimes detachable) outside the main arms (*see* CONFIDENT). But this term was also applied to a sofa made on a curved plan so that the two people seated on it would half face one another, also called a *causeuse* or a *tête à tête*. A *marquise* was a straight-fronted seat for two people; the *meridienne*, an Empire and Restauration type, had one end higher than the other; the *ottomane* (also called a *sultane* or *turquoise*) was built on an oval plan with one end higher than the other.

Candelabrum A standing candlestick with arms and nozzles for more than one candle.

Candelabrum: gilt bronze, by F. Ladatte, c.1770 (Palazzo Reale, Turin)

Candiana The name erroneously given to maiolica wares painted in the style of ISNIK, once supposed to have been made at Candiana near Padua but now known to have been produced at the PADUA POTTERIES.

Candle slide A small support for a candlestick often incorporated in C18 and early C19 desks, card-tables, work tables, etc., and generally made so that it can be slid into the body of the piece when not in use.

Candle stand, *see* TORCHÈRE.

Cane Ribs of split rattan (a type of palm) first imported into Europe from the Malay peninsula in the mid C17 and much used ever since for interwoven chair seats and backs.

Canephorus: gilt-bronze mount, attributed to Gouthière, on a work-table by Weisweiler, 1784 (Louvre)

Canephorus A sculptured female figure carrying a basket on her head: an architectural motif sometimes used on furniture, especially bronze mounts. *Illustrated previous column.*

Caneware or **Cane-coloured stoneware** A fine-textured buff-coloured stoneware, developed in the STAFFORDSHIRE POTTERIES in the 1770s. It superseded red stoneware and was much used by WEDGWOOD, SPODE and others.

Cannelé A silk fabric with horizontal ribbing, sometimes with gold and silver thread. It is similar to *côtelé* which has vertical ribbing.

Canopic vase An Ancient Egyptian type of vessel used for holding the entrails of embalmed bodies. It is egg-shaped, surmounted with a human head, and was copied by WEDGWOOD in his *rosso antico* ware with black decorations.

Cantagalli, Ulisse (d.1902). The founder, with his brother **Giuseppe,** of a pottery near Florence producing from 1878 onwards imitations and copies of Italian maiolica wares, including lustred wares, and also of PERSIAN and HISPANO-MORESQUE pottery and work in the Della ROBBIA style. Their lustred wares were admired by William DE MORGAN and some of his pottery was fired by Cantagalli. A number of pieces bear their joint signatures. The factory is still active.

Cantagalli earthenware vase, c.1900 *(Victoria & Albert Museum)*

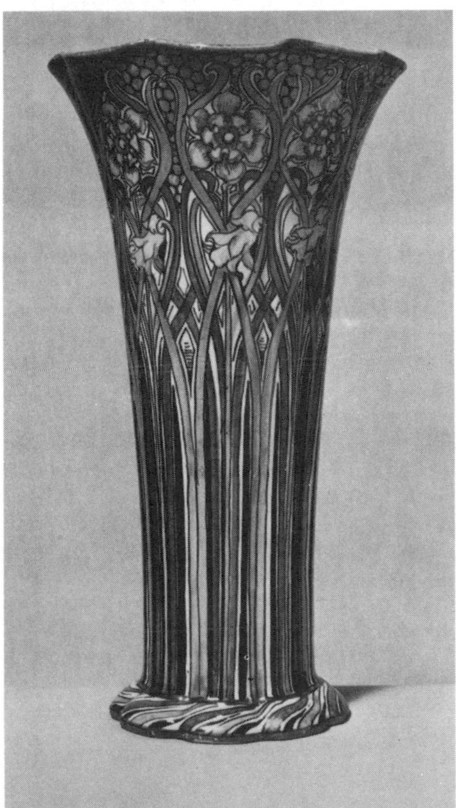

Cántaro A Spanish type of glass drinking vessel having two spouts rising from opposite sides of the shoulder. One spout is for filling, the other for drinking. The body is spherical or ovoid, resting on a spreading foot. A bail handle is attached crosswise between the spouts. Examples date from the C17. It is similar to the *càntir* which is an C18 type, also with two spouts but with a ring handle attached to the top of the body between the spouts.

Canted A chamfered or bevelled surface, i.e. obliquely faced.

Canterbury A small music stand or a plate and cutlery stand for supper parties without servants: in form a deep, partitioned tray on legs. According to Sheraton so called because a 'bishop of that See first gave orders for these pieces'.

Canton enamel A generic term for Chinese painted ENAMEL on copper. The technique was introduced from Europe in the C18 and has been used at Canton and probably elsewhere in China from then until the present day, mainly for export to Europe. Vases, cups, bowls, caskets, etc., were enamelled in the FAMILLE ROSE colour scheme in the C18; later the FAMILLE VERTE colour scheme became popular, especially in the C20 for ash-trays, matchbox-holders and suchlike. The decorations are usually floral but may include figure scenes which are sometimes derived from European prints.

Lit: R. C. Hobson in *Burlington Magazine,* XXII, 1912–13; M. Jourdain and R. S. Jenyns, *Chinese Export Art,* London 1950.

Cape Cod Glass Company Founded by Deming Jarves in 1858 when he broke with the BOSTON AND SANDWICH GLASS COMPANY. It produced many varieties of coloured and opaque glass –

Sandwich Alabaster, Peach-blow and Gold Ruby – but closed in 1869.

Capital The head or crowning feature of a column. *See* ORDERS.

Capodimonte porcelain factory Founded by Charles III King of Naples in 1743 in the grounds of the royal palace of Capodimonte. Its wares are of a fine, usually pure white, translucent soft paste which could be modelled with great delicacy and provided a good background for painting. Patterns for table-wares and ornamental vases were derived from MEISSEN and VIENNA but although some of the paintings on them are derived from prints after Watteau and other French artists, the rich bouquets of flowers, the fleshy mythological scenes and the landscapes, which are more usual, have a typically Neapolitan exuberance. The chief modeller, Giuseppe GRICCI, was responsible for some very lively groups of *Commedia dell'Arte* figures, Neapolitan *lazzaroni* and peasants. He also modelled the large reliefs of elegant gaily clad Chinamen for a chinoiserie room with walls entirely covered with interlocking panels of porcelain, made for the royal palace at Portici 1757–9 (now Museo di Capodimonte). When Charles III succeeded to the kingdom of Spain in 1759 the factory staff accompanied him to Madrid and worked at the BUEN RETIRO factory. (For factory mark *see* p. 882.) *See also:* NAPLES, ROYAL PORCELAIN FACTORY.

Lit: A. Lane, *Italian Porcelain*, London 1954; A. W. Frothingham, *Capodimonte and Buen Retiro Porcelains*, New York 1955; F. Stazzi, *L'Arte della ceramica Capodimonte*, Milan 1972.

Capodimonte porcelain cups, c.1745–50 *(Victoria & Albert Museum)*

Caquetoire, *see* CHAIR.

Carabin, François-Rupert (1862–1932). One of the strangest furniture-makers of his time. He was born in Alsace, trained first as a gem engraver, then went to Paris where he worked as a wood carver for a furniture factory in the Faubourg St Antoine. With Seurat, Signac and others he was a founder of the 'Société des artistes indépendants' in 1884. Though he worked in several media he was best known as a wood carver and in addition to executing purely decorative pieces he made tables and chairs incorporating the figures of buxom broad-hipped nude women – e.g. a writing table in the form of a gigantic book supported by four such figures dated 1890, and the chair dated 1893 (Musée des Beaux Arts, Strasbourg).

Lit: Y. Brunhammer & L. Merklen, *L'Oeuvre de Rupert Carabin 1862–1932*, Exh. Cat., Paris 1974.

Caradosso, Cristoforo Foppa, called (*c.*1452–1526/7). He was one of the most famous Renaissance goldsmiths but none of his works in gold or other precious metals is known to survive. He was a Milanese sculptor, medallist and goldsmith: Vasari called him 'an excellent goldsmith' and CELLINI said he was a 'most excellent craftsman' and particularly praised his small reliefs wrought from thin gold plates. He began by working for Lodovico il Moro in Milan, was active in various N. Italian cities in the 1490s, and in 1505 settled in Rome where he was employed by Pope Julius II, Leo X, Hadrian VI and Clement VII. His most famous work was the papal tiara made for Julius II in 1510, destroyed and now known only from a drawing of 1825 (British Museum). Several medals have been ascribed to him.

Carat, *see* GOLD.

Carcase The 'body' or main structure of a piece of furniture, to which the veneers are applied.

Card tray, *see* SALVER.

Card-cut ornament Lattice ornament carved in low relief.

Carder, Frederick (1864–1963). Anglo-American glass artist, born at Wordsley, Staffordshire. He began by working in his father's pottery but also studied science at Dudley and art at Stourbridge. He joined the glasshouse of STEVENS AND WILLIAMS as a designer in 1881. In 1903 he went to the U.S.A. as manager of the STEUBEN GLASS WORKS where he developed a type of iridescent glass called AURENE and initiated the production of cased-glass or cameo-glass like that of late C18 China. He also developed techniques of enamelling and etching on glass. He retired in 1933 but continued to work in his own laboratory perfecting a system of lost wax casting for the production of glass vases with decorations in high relief. He is generally regarded as the founder of the modern tradition in American art glass.

Lit: P. V. Gardner, *The Glass of Frederick Carder*, New York 1971.

Cardew, Michael (b.1901). One of the most notable English STUDIO POTTERS. After studying under B. LEACH at St Ives 1923–6 he set up

M. Cardew: slip-ware bowl, 1939 (Victoria & Albert Museum)

on his own at Winchcombe in the Cotswolds. He derived inspiration from English rather than Japanese pottery and specialized in the production of lead-glazed slipware, making vessels for everyday use, especially large and handsome cider jugs. In 1942 he went to West Africa where he took over the pottery school of Achimota College and then moved to Vumé on the Volta River where he produced stoneware.

Lit: M. Rose, *Artist Potters in England*, London 1955; M. Cardew, *Pioneer Pottery*, London 1969.

Carlin, Martin (d.1785). One of the most elegant and refined of Louis XVI period furniture makers.

M. Carlin: bureau à gradin *with Sèvres porcelain plaques, 1766 (Musée Nissim de Camondo, Paris)*

Despite his name he was of German birth, but he settled in Paris by 1759, probably joining OEBEN's workshop. He married Oeben's younger sister. He became a *maître-ébéniste* in 1766. He worked mainly for furniture-dealers or *marchands-merciers* such as Poirier and his successor Daguerre. He appears to have made little money. Most of his furniture is small in scale and is often decorated with SÈVRES plaques, usually set in wood lacquered black to imitate ebony. He used a distinctive design for his mounts, based on swags of tasselled drapery. The architect G.-P. Cauvet (1731–88) is said to have designed much of his furniture, and he may also have worked to designs by GONDOUIN and DUGOURC. Much of his furniture survives, e.g. in the Louvre and Musée Nissim de Camondo, Paris; the Wallace Collection, London, and Waddesdon Manor; the Metropolitan Museum and Frick Collection in New York.

Lit: F. de Salverte, *Les ébénistes du XVIIIe siècle*, Paris 1962; J. F. B. Watson, *The Wrightsman Collection: Furniture*, New York 1966.

Carlton House table, *see* TABLE.

Carolingian style The name given to objects made under Charlemagne (King from 768, Emperor 800–814) and his descendants until the C10 in those countries which formed part of his empire, notably France, Germany and the Low Countries. Charlemagne promoted a renaissance of Roman Christianity and attempted to re-establish the Roman Empire of the West. This is reflected in many objects, especially ivory carvings which are often difficult to distinguish from late Antique prototypes. Other objects are inspired by CELTIC art – and the great importance given to small movable objects made of precious materials seems also to have been inherited from the barbarian tribes of N. Europe. But the majority of surviving Carolingian objects reveal a fascinating combination of the Classical and the Celtic, of solid form and intricate surface decoration, often incorporating jewels of barbaric richness. Mediterranean models are transformed, charged with Northern emotion through the rhythmical patterns of curving lines. One of the few surviving pieces of Carolingian furniture, the early C9 'Throne of Dagobert' (Louvre) of

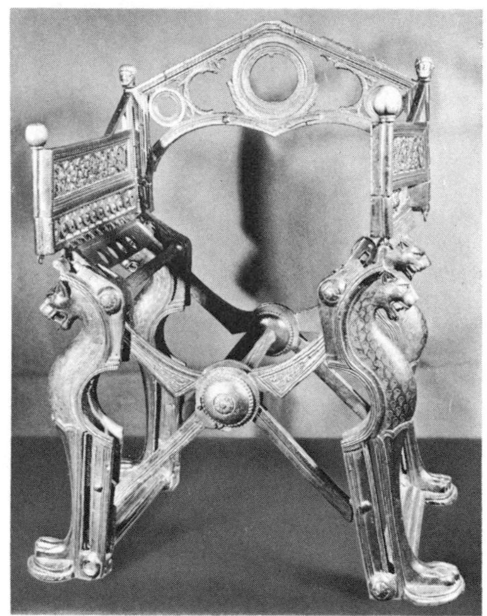

Carolingian: bronze Throne of Dagobert, early C9 (Louvre)

bronze, is based on a Roman currule chair with growling lion monopod legs but supplied with a back and arms pierced with Celtic-type decorations. Ivory carvings, generally intended as decorations for the bindings of manuscripts (e.g. Drogo Sacramentary of 826–55 and the Psalter of Charles the Bald of 860–70, both in Bibliothèque Nationale, Paris) are among the finest and most numerous objects to survive. They are also the closest in style to the late Antique. Golden reliquaries, book bindings, portable altars, etc., tend to be much more barbaric, though exquisitely worked with figurative reliefs, delicately scrolling tendrils of filigree, and enamels, set with cabochons. Occasionally Antique elements were incorporated, especially cameos and intaglios, and the famous reliquary statue of St Foy at Conques has a late Antique gold head (probably C5) set on a C9 body. Many of the finest objects appear to have been made in Rheims, e.g. the covers of the *Codex aureus* made for Charles the Bald *c.*870 (State Library, Munich), those of the Lindau Gospels *c.*870 (Pierpont Morgan Library, New York), and the wonderful portable altar of King Arnulf von Karnten *c.*890

Carolingian: engraved rock crystal, The Lothair Crystal, probably Lorraine, 855–69, in a c15 bronze mount (British Museum)

(Residenzmuseum, Munich) embossed in very low relief with dancing weightless figures in fluttering clothes strikingly similar to those found in manuscripts of the Rheims school. But it is seldom possible to assign objects to individual districts with any precision, partly because many of the craftsmen were itinerant. One of the great masterpieces of the period is the golden altar in S. Ambrogio, Milan, with gold reliefs of New Testament subjects surrounded by enamel frames set with cabochons and pearls, executed 824–59 by VUOLVINUS. The art of engraving on rock

Carolingian: Ciborium of King Arnulf von Karnten, gold, precious stones and pearls, probably made at Rheims, c.890 (Residenzemuseum, Munich)

crystal also flourished in this period, the most impressive example being the crystal of Lothair (British Museum), a small flat disk engraved with eight scenes from the story of Susanna. The Carolingian renaissance lost its momentum after the death of Charles the Bald in 877. The style was consciously revived in the Ottonian period (from 962) but soon merged into the ROMANESQUE of which it is often considered the earliest phase.

Carpet A thick fabric, usually of wool. The term was originally used to describe coverings to spread over tables, beds, etc., and only later, from the early C18 onwards, for floor coverings. The modern usage is imprecise, embracing all woven floor coverings and some other textiles (e.g. wall-hangings, furniture coverings, saddle bags, etc.) made in a similar way, that is, either with a knotted pile or woven like a tapestry. This apparent semantic confusion reflects a change in living conditions. The earliest form of floor covering was of rushes, matted by a process similar to BASKETRY, already in use in Mesopotamia *c.*5270–4630 B.C. and in the lake villages of central Europe *c.*2500 B.C. And in Europe such matting remained the normal type of floor covering until well into the C18. It was only when the use of woven fabrics for floor covering became general that the word carpet acquired its modern meaning. The old meaning is preserved in the term knotted carpet – a fabric made by a special technique irrespective of the purpose for which it was intended – the new in the terms tapestry carpet (a floor covering woven like a tapestry) and NEEDLEWORK CARPET.

Knotted carpets have been made in Central Asia since at least 2500 B.C., though the earliest extant date from the C5 B.C. (Hermitage Museum, Leningrad) and only a very few survive from before the C16. They are made by knotting short lengths of yarn to the warp threads of a plain woven fabric. The foundation material may be woven from wool, silk (as in early Persian carpets), hemp (especially in English carpets), cotton (recently) or jute (in modern factory-made carpets). The pile is of silk or wool tied to the foundation with knots (either the GHIORDES or PERSIAN KNOT). By using yarn of different colours elaborate patterns may be formed. The density of pile varies greatly – in the very finest there may be as many as 1000 knots per sq. in. When the carpet is ready to leave the loom, the pile is cut to an even surface, though the Chinese obtained relief effects by cutting it shorter in some places, usually round the outlines of the pattern.

Even now the process of knotting is more easily effected by hand than by machine (the first mechanism for knotting was developed in France in 1906): and knotted carpets should not be confused with machine-made 'Chenille' AXMINSTER CARPETS, BRUSSELS CARPETS and WILTON CARPETS which have a pile formed by the weave.

Tapestry or *smooth-faced carpets*, such as KILIMS, AUBUSSON carpets, etc., are woven in the same way as tapestries but with a bulkier weft. The earliest machine-made carpets were of this type, woven at Kidderminster on draw-looms from 1735 onwards and known as two-ply ingrain or DOUBLE CLOTH CARPETS.

Lit: K. Erdmann, *Oriental Carpets: An Account of their History*, London 1960; W. von Bode and E. Kühnel, *Antique Rugs from the Near East*, rev. ed., London 1970; C. E. C. Tattersall and S. Reed, *A History of British Carpets*, Leigh-on-Sea 1966; K. Erdmann, *Seven Hundred Years of Oriental Carpets*, London 1970.

Carr, Alwyn Charles Ellison, *see* RAMSDEN, Omar.

Carré, Jean, *see* CRUTCHED FRIARS GLASSHOUSE.

Carriage clock, *see* CLOCK.

Carrickmacross lace A type of appliqué work made in and near Carrickmacross in Ireland. It consists of pieces of fine cambric applied with needle stitches to a net ground and somewhat resembles CUTWORK though made in a completely different way. From *c.*1850 the cut-out pieces of cambric were attached to each other by needlepoint brides (*see* LACE): this type of work is called Carrickmacross guipure.

Lit: B. Palliser, *History of Lace*, rev. M. Jourdain and A. Dryden, London 1902; P. Wardle, *Victorian Lace*, London 1968.

Carrickmacross lace, with applied cutwork (Victoria & Albert Museum)

Carrier-Belleuse, Albert-Ernest (1824–87). French sculptor closely involved with the decorative arts. His sculpture seems to typify the hedonistic opulence and love of 'naughtiness' of the SECOND EMPIRE period. But he was initially out of sympathy with the régime and was obliged to leave the country after taking part in the abortive June revolution of 1849. He went to England where he was employed as a modeller at

A.-E. Carrier-Belleuse: tazza *with onyx bowl and gilt metal figures, made by Alphonse Pallu & Cie,* c.*1862 (Victoria & Albert Museum)*

MINTON'S POTTERY. In 1855 he returned to Paris and soon established himself as a fashionable portrait and decorative sculptor, specializing in such works as large bronze torchères supported by semi-nude female figures, particularly admired by Napoleon III who called him 'our Clodion'. From 1864 he employed the young Auguste Rodin (1840–1917) as an assistant mainly for the production of reliefs and figures executed in unglazed earthenware or, rarely, porcelain (e.g. Titan vase in Victoria & Albert Museum). He was artistic director of the SÈVRES PORCELAIN FACTORY from 1875 until his death, and during this period Rodin continued to work in ceramics (though only drawn or lightly modelled relief decorations) under his supervision. He also designed silver-ware (for CHRISTOFLE) and furniture.

Lit: R. Marx, *Rodin céramiste*, Paris 1907; H. W. Janson in *Art Bulletin* L (1968), pp. 278–80.

Carriès, Jean (1855–94). He was a French sculptor (mainly of bronze portrait busts). Under Japanese influence, he turned to studio pottery in the 1880s, working near sources of good clay at Cosne, St Amand-en-Puisaye and Montriveau in the Nivernais. He made vases and other vessels of good sturdy form decorated only with low-toned mottled or flambé matt glazes, and was largely responsible for establishing a vogue for hand-made wares of this type in France. He also executed, but with less success, figurative sculpture in stoneware. His pottery was inherited by G. HOENTSCHEL.

Lit: A. Alexandre, *Jean Carriès, imagier et potier*, Paris 1895; M. Ernould-Gandouet, *La Céramique en France au XIX*[e] *siècle*, Paris 1969.

Carron ironworks A foundry established near Falkirk in Scotland in 1759 and still active. In addition to heavier products (including cannons) it made household pieces such as fire-backs, andirons, etc., sometimes to designs by R. ADAM. The original moulds were preserved and casts from them have been made in recent years: these modern casts are marked, unlike those of the C18, with the name Carron.

Cartel, *see* CLOCK, CARTEL.

Cartlidge, Charles & Co, *see* UNION PORCELAIN WORKS.

Cartonnier or *Serre papier* A filing-cabinet, a piece of furniture fitted with pigeon-holes or compartments to hold papers. It could be either an independent piece of furniture or an accessory to some other piece, e.g. a writing table. In the C18 it usually stood either at or on the end of a writing table. The bottom section was often fitted as a cupboard and the upper part was sometimes surmounted with a clock. *See also* BUREAU PLAT.

Cartoon A full-scale preliminary design for a painting, tapestry, etc. For a LOW-WARP TAPESTRY it must show the composition in reverse, as in the famous RAPHAEL cartoons (Victoria & Albert Museum) where the figures all seem to be left-handed.

Cartouche Ornamental panel in the form of a scroll or sheet of paper with curling edges, usually bearing an inscription and sometimes ornately framed.

Cartouche by G.-M. Oppenordt, c.1730

Carver chair, *see* CHAIR.

Caryatid A sculptured female figure used as a column: an architectural motif sometimes used on furniture, especially as bronze mounts. *See also* CANEPHORUS.

Casa Pirota, *see* PIROTA, CASA.

Casali, Antonio, *see* PESARO POTTERIES.

Case furniture Furniture intended to contain

something, e.g. cupboard, bookcase, chest-of-drawers.

Cased glass A piece of glass covered with a thin layer of glass of a different colour (such as red or opaque white on a clear crystal base). In the Middle Ages the red and yellow panels in stained glass windows were of this type. The outer layer may be partly cut away to leave a pattern or a figurative or other design in colour against the ground – a process much adopted in Roman times (e.g. the Portland Vase) and again in the C19, notably by George WOODALL, when two or more casings were sometimes applied. It is also called **Cameo Glass** and **Verre Doublé.**

Lit: D. & H. Blount, *French Cameo Glass*, Des Moines 1968; G. W. Beard, *Nineteenth Century Cameo Glass*, Newport, Mon. 1956.

Cassapanca Italian type of wooden bench with a chest under the seat; often takes the form of a CASSONE with an upright back.

Cassel pottery & porcelain factories There were four factories at Cassel. (1) A faience factory founded in 1680, taken over by **Johann Christoph Gilze** in 1724 and by his son **Ludwig** in 1735. It produced blue-and-white wares in the DELFT and HANAU manner and, in the 1760s, some coloured wares. It closed in 1786–8. (2) A porcelain factory founded in 1766 by the Landgrave of Hesse, Frederick II, with the arcanist Nikolaus PAUL. It produced coffee and tea services in blue and white but is mainly notable for its figures for which a number of modellers were employed. It closed in 1788. (3) A faience factory founded in 1771 by the Court confectioner Simon Heinrich Steitz. It made glazed earthenware, especially vases and figures, sometimes imitating English agate wares and creamwares. It closed in 1862. (4) An earthenware factory founded in 1772 by Le Fort which closed in 1805. (For factory marks see p. 882.)

Lit: C. A. von Drach, 'Fayence- und Porzellanfabriken in Alt-Cassel' in *Bayerische Gewerbebezeitung*, 1891; G. E. Pazaurek, *Steingut: Formgebung und Geschichte*, Stuttgart 1927; W. B. Honey, *German Porcelain*, London 1947; S. Ducret, *Die landgräfliche Porzellan-manufaktur Kassel 1766–88*, Brunswick 1960.

Cassolette A term of French origin (in use in English from 1657) for a small brazier in which aromatic pastilles may be burned or liquid perfumes evaporated. It is generally shaped like a vase but in the later C18 the Antique tripod form, especially the ATHÉNIENNE, became highly fashionable. Cassolettes have been made from a very wide variety of materials including silver, copper, bronze, marble. Those made of more fragile materials, such as lacquer, porcelain or faience, were usually provided with metal linings. Cassolettes may be subdivided into essence vessels (for liquids) and perfume burners

Cassolette: red jasper bowl with chased and gilt-bronze tripod, by Gouthière, c.1772–82 (Wallace Collection)

(for solids). The term *brûle parfum* was used in France from the later C19.

Cassone Italian type of C15 and C16 chest, sometimes very richly decorated, e.g. with gesso friezes of *putti*, painted mythological or religious scenes, or TARSIA panels. It was frequently, though not necessarily, a dower chest.

in decline. Maiolica of inferior quality continued to be produced in the town until the mid C18.

Lit: J. Chompret, *Répertoire de la maiolique italienne*, Paris 1949; B. Rackham, *Italian Maiolica*, London 1952.

Castellana, Alla An imprecise term for a type of C16 and later Italian lead-glazed earthenware with SGRAFFIATO decorations, supposed to have been made at Città di Castello in Umbria but indistinguishable from similar wares known to have been made in other places.

Cassone, carved walnut, Rome or Florence, mid C16 (The Frick Collection, New York)

Castel Durante potteries Outstanding group of C16 Umbrian maiolica factories at Castel Durante (re-named Urbania in honour of Pope Urban VIII in 1635) where the art of ISTORIATO painting was brought to its summit by N. PELLIPARIO. Other notable painters were GIOVANNI MARIA and an anonymous artist, sometimes called Pseudo-Pellipario (whose plates are inscribed on the reverse *'Castel Durante'*, sometimes with the dates 1524, 1525 or 1526), working in an attractive and unusual palette of soft blues, greenish greys, pale orange and mulberry purple. Wares decorated with trophies and grotesques were also made. Very high technical standards were maintained and most wares are covered with a particularly clear and glossy outer glaze or *coperta* which enhances the colours of the pigments. Information about techniques and the range of products and manner of decoration in the mid C16 is provided by the book of C. PICCOLPASSO. But by this time the potteries were already

Castellani, Pio Fortunato (1793–1865). Notable Roman goldsmith and jeweller who discovered the secret of, and revived, the Etruscan technique of working in filigree with minute grains of gold. He specialized in making imitations of Greek and Etruscan jewellery highly praised by visitors to Rome. In 1852 the control of his workshop passed to his sons **Alessandro** (1822–83) and **Augusto** (1829–1914) who showed its products at several international exhibitions, and extended the range of styles to the Byzantine and Carolingian.

Castelli potteries The most interesting group of C17 and C18 Italian maiolica factories, near Teramo in the Kingdom of Naples. The earliest wares imitated BIANCO DI FAENZA. But *c.*1650 they began to revive the ISTORIATO style and continued to produce plates and large tiles painted in this manner until the late C18. In colour they are much cooler than most C16 Istoriato wares, with pale grey-blues, buffs, browns and olive greens predominating, and the compositions are usually derived from prints after Baroque artists (though Renaissance ones were also used). Subjects include landscapes as

Castelli maiolica roundel, 1730–40 (Victoria & Albert Museum)

well as religious and mythological scenes. *See also* F. A. GRUE.

Lit: B. Molajoli, *La mostra dell' antica maiolica abruzzese,* Faenza 1955; *Le antiche maioliche di Castelli d'Abruzzo,* Exh. Cat., Palazzo Venezia, Rome 1969.

Castle Hedingham pottery A factory at Castle Hedingham, Essex, founded in 1837 by **Edward Bingham** (d.1872). It began producing common earthenware for local use. The founder's son, also called **Edward** (b.1829), turned to the production of decorative wares beginning with trellis-work cache-pots in the early 1850s and producing more ambitious glazed wares from the 1870s. The firm was taken over in 1899 by **Edward William** (b.1857) who sold it in 1901 to the **Essex Art Pottery Company** though he remained as manager until 1905 when the factory closed down. Products are lead glazed with moulded reliefs or SGRAFFIATO decorations, often inspired by or copied from C16 and C17 (and very occasionally ancient Roman) wares and include tygs, mugs and candlesticks (sometimes with C17 dates incorporated in their decorations), miniature vessels which were a speciality, large vases and wall plaques, all of a distinctly rustic character. Some products have been mistaken for early English wares.

Lit: D. J. Bradley in *The Connoisseur* CLXVII (1968), pp. 77–83, 152–7, 210–16.

Castleford pottery A Yorkshire factory founded by **David Dunderdale** *c.*1790 and making CREAM-COLOURED EARTHENWARE in the style of the LEEDS POTTERIES. White stoneware decorated in bright blue and black basaltes were also produced. The factory used 'D. D. & Co/CASTLE-FORD' impressed as a mark.

Castor or **Caster** 1. A small vessel with a perforated top from which to cast ground pepper, sugar or other condiments: usually made of silver or pewter, from the C17 or earlier. They were often made in sets of three.

2. A small wheel or swivel attached to furniture to facilitate movement and used from at least the C16 onwards.

Castro, D. H. de, *see* STIPPLE ENGRAVING.

Castwork The parts of a silver object cast in moulds and soldered to the main body, especially handles, feet, finials, etc., as distinct from those hammered into relief.

Castwork handle on English silver ewer, London, 1705 (Victoria & Albert Museum)

Cat A rest for plates or dishes to be kept warm by the fireside, made of three rods joined X-wise in the centre.

Catalan glasshouses A number of factories, established in Catalonia in Roman times, survived the Dark Ages but produced little of interest before the late c15 when stirred to rival imports of Venetian glass. Crystal glass is generally yellowish, LATTICINO stripes are often of a greyish white and in the c16 forms are often even more fantastic than the Venetian. Enamel decorations, notably those executed in Barcelona, often incorporate Near Eastern motifs, symmetrical pairs of birds or stylized trees, running animals and arabesques. Little of importance was produced after the c16.

Lit: José Gudiol Ricart, *Los Vidrios Catalanes*, Barcelona 1941; Alice Wilson Frothingham, *Spanish Glass*, London 1964.

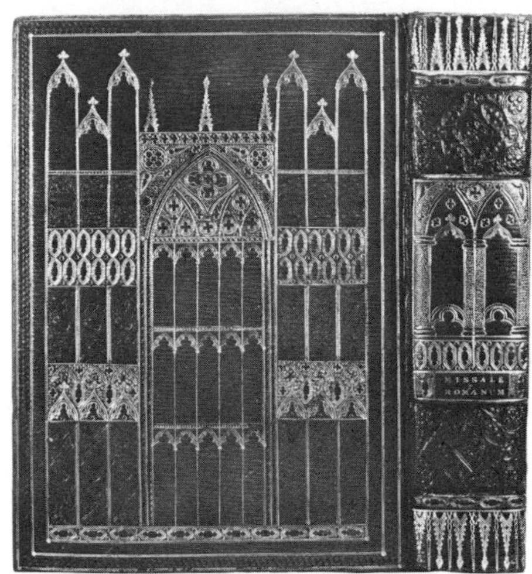

Cathedral style bookbinding, c.1830 (Victoria & Albert Museum)

Catalonian potteries Notable in the c15–c16 for tiles imitating those of VALENCIA with decorations in a violet-toned blue on white applied with the help of stencil-plates. Examples (in the Monastery of Santa Cruz, the Barcelona Archaeological Museum, the Victoria & Albert Museum, etc.) can be dated 1502–60. A group of c16–c17 lustre wares, similar to those of Valencia, are sometimes ascribed to Catalonia, also (with greater certainty) blue and white tin-glazed-earthenware drug jugs and plates painted in a rather peasanty style with animals and figures. In the c17–c18 polychrome wares (with a brownish orange and strong green predominating) decorated with figures of soldiers, ships, etc., appear to have been made in the region.

Lit: A. Lane, *Victoria & Albert Museum: Guide to the Collection of Tiles*, London 1939.

Cathedral style In bookbinding, a popular type of early c19 binding, simulating Gothic architecture, and executed either blind or with gold tooling. *Illustrated next column.*

Caucasian rug (Cherkessk) wool, late c18 or early c19 (Victoria & Albert Museum)

Caucasian carpets A wide variety of carpets made in the area between the Black Sea and the Caspian Sea, differing from group to group in technique (knotted pile, smooth-faced and embroidered) as well as design. The latch motif –

like a slanting angular letter J – recurs on most of them and is sometimes regarded as a distinguishing mark. Carpets have been made in this district over a very long period and although the oldest surviving specimens date from no earlier than the C16–C17 they incorporate motifs of stylized dragons and other creatures which recall the prehistoric Scythian animal style. Such motifs, sometimes combined with geometrical flower and leaf forms, generally executed in very bold colours, appear on both pile and smooth-faced carpets, notably the very large 'dragon carpets' (examples in the Metropolitan Museum of Art, New York). Another type is decorated with a trellis pattern of diagonal bars dividing the surface into lozenges filled with bold stylized flower and leaf motifs and sometimes stocky figures of human beings and animals in strongly contrasted colours. The carpets known as **Kubas** are somewhat similar but without the trellis: they have centralized designs springing from one or more rather inconspicuous points on the main axis. Other types of later origin are inspired by PERSIAN CARPETS, with central medallions, hunting scenes or garden designs, but worked out in a greatly simplified manner. Garden scenes and rather hard angular designs appear on the carpets called KAZAKS (a corruption of Cossacks) which have a very long pile: the earliest surviving examples date from the C18. Carpets woven by the nomadic **Chichi** (or Tchichi) are distinguished by heavy borders of star-rosettes, buds and stem-forms arranged in parallel bars, surrounding central patterns of stepped medallions. **Soumak** carpets, woven in and around Shemakha, are of the smooth-faced type (with many loose threads on the back) and are generally decorated with geometrical motifs. In the Shirvan district, the probable source of C17 dragon carpets, weavers produced fine though generally small medallion carpets as late as the early C20. Other places in the Caucasus where carpets were made include **Baku** (with a pile including camel hair and goat hair), in the **Daghestan** district and at **Derbend** (with much use of star motifs and diagonally striped borders), at **Kabistan** (with a cotton or mixed wool and cotton warp and weft and short pile), and in the **Karabagh** province. Carpets of good quality are still woven on traditional designs in the Causasus and exported by the Soviet trading organization.

Lit: K. Erdmann, *Oriental Carpets*, London 1960 and *700 Years of Oriental Carpets*, London 1970; U. Schurmann, *Caucasian Rugs* (1964), rev. edn 1974.

Caudle cup Alternative name for a PORRINGER, a vessel from which the warm spiced gruel called caudle or posset might be drunk.

Caughley pottery and porcelain factory A pottery was established at Caughley near Broseley in Shropshire soon after 1750. It began producing porcelain after it was taken over by **Thomas Turner** in 1772. In 1775 Robert HANCOCK formerly of the WORCESTER PORCELAIN FACTORY, joined the factory and introduced transfer-printing in blue underglaze and although the Caughley blue pigment is slightly brighter than that used at Worcester their products are difficult to distinguish. Worcester porcelain was deliberately imitated at Caughley. Gilding was also used on blue-and-white wares. Some polychrome wares appear to have been decorated by Humphrey & Robert CHAMBERLAIN. The factory was bought by John Rose in 1799 and amalgamated with the COALPORT PORCELAIN FACTORY. (For factory marks *see* p. 882.)

Lit: F. A. Barret, *Caughley and Coalport Porcelain*, Leigh-on-Sea, 1951; G. A. Godden, *Caughley and Worcester Porcelains 1775–1800*, London 1969.

Cauldon ware, *see* RIDGWAY, Job.

Cauliflower ware Green and yellow glazed earthenware vessels made from *c.*1750 by WHIELDON, WEDGWOOD and other STAFFORDSHIRE POTTERIES, in the form of cauliflowers, other vegetables, pineapples, etc.

Causeuse A French type of small CANAPÉ or large chair for two people, corresponding to the English small settee or love-seat. It is also called a *Marquise*. *Illustrated next page.*

Caussy, Paul, *see* ROUEN POTTERIES.

Caussy, Pierre-Paul, *see* QUIMPER POTTERY.

Cauvet, Gilles-Paul (1731–1788). Architect, sculptor and *ciseleur*, his work in silver was very distinguished (e.g., candlesticks dated 1783 in the

Causeuse by Cruchet, upholstered with Beauvais tapestry, made 1858 for the Grand Salon at St Cloud (Mobilier Nationale, Paris)

Celadon box with incised decoration and brownish glaze, Northern Celadon type, Sung Dynasty, c11–c12. (Percival David Foundation of Chinese Art, London)

Louvre) and he was an outstanding designer. A number of engravings after his designs were issued in 1777 for wall panelling, arabesque decorations, furniture, vases, etc., in the Louis XVI style.

Lit: D. Guilmard, *Les Maîtres Ornemantistes*, Paris 1880.

Cavetto A quarter-round concave moulding.

Cedar A hard durable wood, usually of a reddish colour, from the trees of the cedar family. It is pleasantly aromatic and unattractive to insects, hence its wide use by furniture-makers, especially for storage chests.

Celadon A European name (probably derived from the character Céladon, who wore soft grey-green ribbons, in Honoré d'Urfé's early c17 pastoral *L'Astrée*) for a type of Chinese stoneware or porcelain of a grey to brownish body with an olive green glaze derived from iron oxide. It is usually classified in two types: Northern Celadon and Southern or Lung-ch'üan Celadon, with YÜEH WARE as the prototype. Northern Celadon was made during the Sung Dynasty but not after the capital moved south to Hang-chou in 1127. Southern or Lung-ch'üan Celadon (made in Chekiang) was made throughout the Sung Dynasty and later. Northern Celadon does not seem to have been exported whereas Lung-ch'üan was widely exported. It was later imitated in Korea and Japan. Decorations are sparse, generally limited to relief decorations – flowers, birds, fishes, etc. – under the glaze, at first carved with a knife, later impressed with stamps. In c18 France pieces were often mounted in ormolu.

Lit: G. St. G. M. Gompertz, *Celadon Wares*, London 1968.

Cellaret Chest, usually of wood and of ornamental design, to hold bottles of wine in a dining-room.

Cellini, Benvenuto (1500–1571). He was a highly accomplished Mannerist sculptor and the most famous goldsmith of all time. Born and trained as a goldsmith in Florence, he moved in 1519 to Rome where he spent the next twenty years working mainly as a medallist and goldsmith, until he went to France in 1540. He was employed at Fontainebleau by François I for whom he executed his first large-scale sculpture. He returned to Florence in 1545 and remained there until his death. In his celebrated *Autobiography*, which presents the most intimate self-portrait of any c16 artist, he describes in detail the numerous works he executed in gold. But the only one which survives is his famous salt-cellar modelled in Rome for Ippolito d'Este in 1540 and completed in France for François I (now in the Kunsthistorisches Museum, Vienna). Oval in form and about 10 inches high, it consists of nude male and female statuettes (representing Neptune and the Earth) reclining amongst sea-horses and dolphins with a little ship to hold the salt and a triumphal arch (which he described as an Ionic temple) to hold the pepper; the base is wrought with reliefs of recumbent figures derived from Michelangelo's Medici tombs. The brilliance of the gold is offset by a sparing use of bright enamels. The figures, placed in elegant Mannerist postures, are of an extraordinary sensuous voluptuousness and the whole work is modelled with an exquisite sensibility rare among makers of bronze statuettes and unique among goldsmiths. A gold jewel-studded morse which he made for Pope Clement in 1530–31 was destroyed in 1797 but is recorded in a C18 drawing (British Museum, London). Several outstanding works in gold and silver and hardstones have been attributed to him without justification, including works signed by other artists, e.g., the cross and candlesticks in St Peter's Rome signed by Antonio GENTILI. One work, the Rospigliosi Cup in the Metropolitan Museum in New York, is still widely though probably mistakenly ascribed to him, simply because it is of outstandingly high quality. It has recently been attributed to Jacques BYLIVELT.

Lit: E. Plon, *Benvenuto Cellini*, Paris 1883; J. Pope-Hennessy (ed.), *The Life of Benvenuto Cellini Written by Himself* (trans. J. Addington Symonds), London 1949; E. Camesasca, *Tutta l'opera del Cellini*, Milan 1955.

Celtic style The Celts were the indigenous peoples of West Central Europe – an area comprising E. France, the Low Countries, W. Germany and Austria – who gradually expanded across the Continent to the Iberian peninsula, N. Italy and the Black Sea and invaded the British Isles. Their liking for curvilinear surface ornamentation is already apparent in the metalwork and pottery of the Iron-Age Hallstatt and La Tène cultures. Though influenced by artifacts from the Mediterranean and Oriental metalwork (transmitted by the Scythians) the art of the Celts shows, from the C5 B.C., a remarkable homogeneity. It is marked by a love of entangled curvilinear ornament covering the whole surface of cups, swords, articles of personal adornment, etc., and a tendency to reject naturalism in favour of stylization. Classical heads on Hellenistic coins were taken over and transformed by Celtic artists into almost abstract patterns; they similarly transformed naturalistic Greek motifs into arrangements of lozenges and spirals. Such mid-C4 B.C. works as a helmet found at Amfreville (Louvre) and a flagon of bronze set with pieces of coral found at Basse-Yutz (British Museum) reveal their accomplishment as metalworkers. From the C3 they made use of enamel for the embellishment of metal.

Celtic tribes invaded England *c.*250 B.C. and their art seems to have lived on there despite the subsequent Roman invasion and occupation. They also established themselves in Ireland. Such objects as the Birdlip mirror and Battersea shield

Celtic style bronze mirror from Birdlip, C1 A.D. (Gloucester City Museum)

(British Museum) display the very high standard of metalwork reached in C1 A.D. England. They are decorated with motifs which recur in later

Irish and English art. The Germanic invasions of the c5 strengthened Celtic influence in England. But the great period of Hiberno–Saxon Celtic art begins in the c7. The gold jewellery buried at Sutton Hoo in 654–5 (including some pieces of earlier date) is of extraordinary technical accomplishment and decorative richness, with much use of animal motifs, interlace and close geometrical patterning worked out in garnets and coloured glass. No work of comparable quality is known to have been executed in Ireland, possibly because the Irish were Christians and did not bury precious objects with the dead. And the extent to which Hiberno–Saxon art is 'Irish' or 'English' is the subject of unresolved dispute. But there can be no doubt that the Irish Christian Mission which arrived in Northumbria in 635 fostered artistic development. The outstanding achievements of Hiberno–Saxon art are the manuscript illuminations executed in Northumbria and Ireland from the c7. Metalwork was decorated in a manner similar to the manuscripts, with close complex patterns of interlaced ribbons or long-bodied sinuous animals and human beings. The metal is wrought with great skill, sometimes embellished with enamels or set with stones. Outstanding pieces include the c8 Tara brooch and the Ardagh chalice (both in the National Museum of Ireland, Dublin). The style was exported to the Continent. The cover of the Book of Lindau (Pierpont Morgan Library, New York), probably made near St Gall, and the Tassilio chalice of 777 (Kremsmünster Abbey) made in Bavaria, are two of the more notable objects which reveal its influence. Celtic art also contributed to the formation of the CAROLINGIAN STYLE. One of its last notable manifestations is the c11–12 Shrine of St Patrick's bell (National Museum of Ireland, Dublin). But specifically Celtic elements gradually disappear from English art of the later c9 and the figures on the embroidered stole of St Cuthbert of 909–916 (Durham Cathedral) have already acquired a classical monumentality.

The decorative motifs of Celtic art were revived in the late c19–early c20, especially by artists and craftsmen of the GLASGOW SCHOOL.

Lit: N. K. Sandars, *Prehistoric Art in Europe*, Pelican History of Art, Harmondsworth 1968; M. & L. De Paor, *Early Christian Ireland*, London 1960.

The Shrine of St Patrick's bell, silver, gilt-bronze and precious stones, Irish, 1091–1105 (National Museum of Ireland, Dublin)

Censer A portable incense burner or thurible, for ecclesiastical use. The incense is sprinkled over burning charcoal. It usually takes the form of a spherical bowl with a perforated lid, suspended on three chains with a fourth chain for the lid.

Centre and corner bindings A late c16 style of book-binding with sunken panels.

Century guild, *see* MACKMURDO, Arthur Heygate.

Ceramic Art Company, *see* LENOX COMPANY.

Ceramics A c19 term covering both PORCELAIN and all types of POTTERY.

Cerasoli, Gregorio, *see* ROME POTTERY & PORCELAIN FACTORY.

Certosina: Italian cassone, c.1500 *(Rijksmuseum, Amsterdam)*

Certosina Type of C15 Italian marquetry of INTARSIA, made with polygonal tesserae of wood, bone, metal and mother-of-pearl arranged in geometrical patterns. Especially popular in Lombardy and Venetia.

Chaffers, Richard, *see* LIVERPOOL POTTERY AND PORCELAIN FACTORIES.

Chafing dish A portable grate to hold burning charcoal for heating food in a dining-room, usually of silver or silvered copper.

Chair A seat for one person with a back and/or arms (as distinct from the STOOL which has neither). In form it derives from the throne which was generally immovable and had a symbolical significance as the seat of a ruler. Elaborate thrones were made in Assyria and Babylon. But the chair seems to have been an Egyptian invention of about the 4th Dynasty (*c.*2610). It appears to have been relatively common in the Middle Kingdom (*c.*2050–1785): surviving examples are of carved wood, sup-

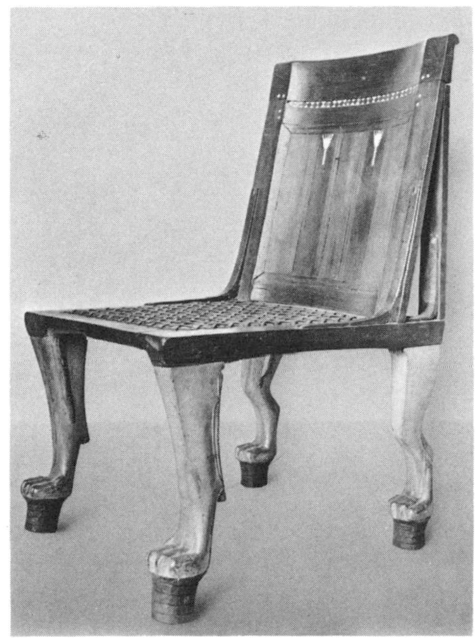

Ancient Egyptian chair (Louvre)

ported on four lion-footed legs with high backs and sometimes arms, and seats of woven cord. The Greeks devised a more comfortable type of chair, the *klismos*, supported on four sabre legs with curving supports rising from the seat (generally as a continuation of the back legs) and carrying at shoulder height a curved backboard. A tub-shaped type of chair was developed by the Etruscans and later used by the Romans who also adopted the *klismos*. In the Dark Ages the chair became a rarity and it was not until the Renaissance that it reappeared as a normal piece of furniture in all richer houses (though the stool remained the most usual type of seat until the C17 and later in more backward districts). From this

Venetian C16 walnut chair (Victoria & Albert Museum)

time onwards increasing attention was given to the design of chairs with regard both to comfort and appearance. The history of the upholstered easy chair, thickly padded at every possible point of contact with the body, begins in early-C18 France, though it was not until the C19 that they became common outside the houses of the rich. The main tendency in C20 chair design has been towards structural clarity and simplicity, the saving of space and provision for the support of the body in various postures determined by a careful study of anatomy (*see* ERGONOMICS). The only revolutionary innovation in form is the result of the application of the cantilever principle to chair design (*see* STAM and MIES VAN DER ROHE).

Banister back chair. Early C18 American type of chair with turned members and back of split balusters.

Barcelona chair, see MIES VAN DER ROHE.

Bergère. French name for an upholstered arm chair with a rounded back and wide seat, differing from other armchairs in being upholstered between the arms and seat. First made in France *c*.1725 and soon after in other European countries.

Boston chair. C18 American type of chair made in and exported in quantity from Boston. It has a leather upholstered seat and a back with a broad central splat gracefully curved, probably in imitation of Chinese chairs.

Brewster chair. The most elaborate type of STICK FURNITURE made in C17 British America, named after an elder of the Massachusetts colony. It has a framework of turned members with vertically placed turned spindles filling the back, the space between the arms and seat, and the seat and stretchers. Usually made of ash or maple with a rush seat.

Cabriole chair. Mid-C18 name for a chair with a padded back, from the French *chaise en cabriolet* which has a back slightly coved to fit the human back.

Cane chair. A chair with a seat and often back of tightly woven cane.

Caquetoire. C16 French type of chair, rather small and low, so called from its popularity with women who wished to sit and chatter (*caqueter*).

Carver chair. C17 American type of chair named after the governor of the Massachusetts Bay

Chair designs by P. Vredeman de Vries, 1630

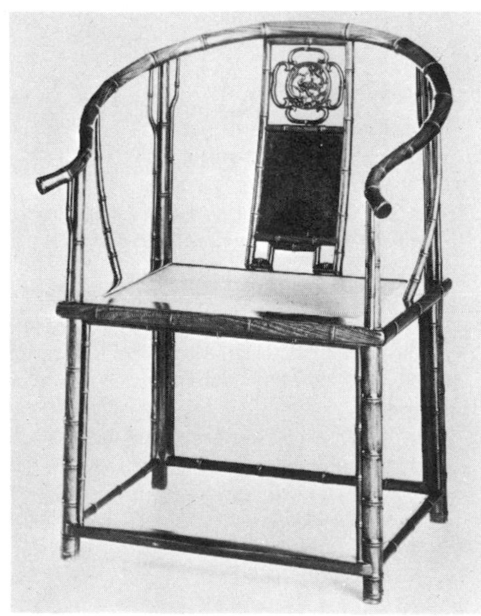

Chinese chair of Huang Hua-li, wood, Ming dynasty, late c16-early c17
(William Rockhill Nelson Gallery of Art, Kansas City)

Colony, a simpler version of the *Brewster chair* with stretchers but no spindles beneath the arms and seat.

Caxton chair. The simple cane-seated chair with turned front legs and stretchers, made at High Wycombe in England from the mid c19 especially, for churches, schools, village halls, etc.

Chair-table. An armchair with a large back which is hinged so that it can be swung forwards to rest on the arms, converting the piece into a table. Chairs of this type were made from the Middle Ages to the late c17 in Europe and until rather later in America.

Chaise à la Reine. c18 French term for an upholstered chair with a flat back, i.e. not a concave back like a *chaise en cabriolet.*

Chaise en cabriolet. An upholstered chair slightly curved at the back to fit the human figure and thus more comfortable than one *à la Reine.*

Crapaud. c19 French term for a type of heavily upholstered low armchair.

Bergère, by L. Delanois (Louvre)

Chaise à la Reine, French, c.1790 *(Rijksmuseum, Amsterdam)*

Chair-table, oak, English, c17 (Victoria & Albert Museum)

Curricle chair. Early c19 English type of chair with a rounded or tub-shaped back.

Curule chair. A seat with arms but no back on which the 'curule' or magistrates of ancient Rome sat. The medieval *X-chair* is derived from it.

Dantesca chair. A nineteenth-century term for an Italian *X-chair.*

Derbyshire chair. Mid-c17 English type of oak chair with the back in the form of an arcade or with broad hooped rails. Also called a Yorkshire chair and apparently commonest in the N. of England.

Farthingale chair. Modern name for a type of Elizabethan upholstered chair with a wide but not very deep seat, low back and no arms.

Fauteuil en Gondole. c18 French term for an armchair with a deep rounded back which first appeared *c.*1760. The term *en gondole* was also applied to *ottomans.*

Fauteuil, upholstered with Beauvais tapestry (Louvre)

Crapaud, French, mid c19 (Château de Compiègne)

Glastonbury chair. Collectors' term for a c16 English chair of curule type with a flat back similar to that associated with the last Abbot of Glastonbury in Wells Cathedral. The type has been extensively faked in modern times.

Hall chair. English type of chair made from the early c18 until the mid c19, usually of mahogany with a solid seat and back, often painted with a coat of arms in the centre and sometimes elaborately carved, used in halls and corridors.

Hardoy chair. An inexpensive easy chair developed from the folding chair of wood and canvas used by the Italian army in North Africa 1942–3. It was developed by three Argentinians: Antonio Bonet, Juan Kurchan and Jorge Ferrari-Hardoy. It is non-folding and constructed of a continuous metal frame from which a leather seat is suspended from the corners on pockets.

Hitchcock chair. American type of chair named after the chair-maker Lambert Hitchcock (1795–1852) of Hitchcockville, Connecticut, but also made by others and elsewhere in the Eastern U.S. It is derived from a late Sheraton pattern, of light construction with turned legs, a shaped or rush seat and a back made of spindles crowned by an oval turned top-rail, generally painted black or green with stencilled decorations in gilt.

Hogarth chair. A Queen Anne type of chair with a splat-back. It is characterized by curving lines and cabriole legs and appears in paintings by William Hogarth, hence the name (used since the mid c19).

Ladder back chair. Modern name for a chair with several horizontal rails or slats (often cut in curving lines) across the back.

Library or *reading chair.* c18 English type of arm-chair with a padded leather-covered saddle-shaped seat and an adjustable platform to hold a book projecting from the back – designed so that the occupant may either sit on it in the normal

Library chair, or reading chair, mahogany, English, c.1720 (Victoria & Albert Museum)

way or straddle the seat facing the back. Often incorrectly called a cock-fighting chair.

Lolling chair. Late C18 American name for an armchair with upholstered seat and back, the seat generally low and shallow, the back high with serpentine cresting. Also known as a Martha Washington chair, though this name was little used in the C18.

Martha Washington chair, see Lolling chair.

Mendlesham chair. A type of Windsor chair of stick construction with a solid elm seat and turned legs, said to have been first made by Daniel Day of Mendlesham, Suffolk.

Morris chair. A mid-C19 English type of armchair with upholstered arms and cushioned back and seat. The back is adjustable, on a hinge at its base.

Perroquet. Late-C17 French type of chair, like a PLIANT with a back.

Porter's or *page's chair.* English type of upholstered armchair with wings and an arched top making a niche to screen the occupant from draughts; made from the mid C18 onwards.

Rocking chair. A chair mounted on pieces of wood with curved undersides so that the occupant may rock it backwards and forwards. THONET

Porter's chair

Steel tube chair and bed, by R. W. Winfield, Cambridge Steel Works, Birmingham, 1851

designed one of the most elegant types, but the rocking chair was less popular in Europe than the U.S. where two C19 types were named, both derived from the *Windsor chair* – the **Boston Rocker** and the **Salem Rocker** which has a lower back.

Siège courant. In French C18 interiors, a chair that stood in the centre of a room and could be moved, as distinct from the *siège meublant* which remained always by the wall. Their use was governed by strict protocol and *sièges meublants* were usually not sat on but were purely decorative.

Slat back chair. A simple late-C17 type of chair with horizontal slats across the back – the *ladder back chair* which may be more elaborate is derived from it.

Sleeping chair. An upholstered armchair with a winged back which by means of a ratchet can be adjusted to any desired angle, first made in the Restoration period. (For illustration *see* p. 657.)

Spoon back chair. Popular American term for a chair with a back shaped to fit the human form, especially one of early C18 design.

Thrown chair. English name for a C16–C17 type of armchair with a frame of knobbly turned members and a triangular seat.

Voyeuse. C18 French term for a rather low-seated chair with a padded top to the back on which the occupant may rest his elbows when sitting astride the seat while watching card-playing or other games of chance. A special *voyeuse à genoux* was invented for women to kneel on, it being inelegant for women to sit astride. First made in France *c.*1740 and later in England where it was called a *'conversation chair'*.

Wainscot chair. Modern term for a C16–C17 chair with a panelled back.

Windsor chair. Traditional type of English chair with a shaped solid wood seat into which the legs, the bow and spindles of the back are dowelled: the stretchers are dowelled into the legs. Made since the C17, notably at High Wycombe, Bucks., where they have been produced on an industrial scale since the early C19; also made extensively in the U.S. On early examples the seat is generally of elm, the bow of ash or yew and the

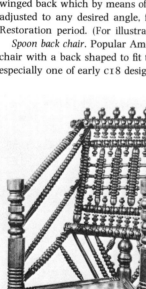

Thrown chair, ash and oak, English, c.1620 (Victoria & Albert Museum)

Windsor chair, painted wood, English, c.1760 (Victoria & Albert Museum)

Windsor settee, painted wood, American, 1750–70 (Metropolitan Museum)

X chair (called a Savonarola chair)

legs of beech. Originally they were used by the upper classes out of doors and by others both indoors and out, but from the late C18 have been regarded mainly as a type of rustic furniture.

Wing chair. An upholstered chair with padded arms and a high back terminating in wings which come forward to protect the occupant's head from draughts. First made in late-C17 England, it remained fashionable until the mid C18 and continued to be made throughout the C18 and

Chaise longue, duchesse brisée *by L. Delanois (Louvre)*

C19. The basic design has been revived and modernized in the C20, e.g. by Arne JACOBSEN.

X-chair. A medieval type of chair supported on an X-shaped frame, sometimes called a Savonarola chair. *See also* SILLON DE CADERAS.

Yorkshire chair, see Derbyshire chair.

Lit: J. Gloag, *The Englishman's Chair,* London 1964; G. Frey, *The Modern Chair: 1850 to today,* 1970.

Chaise longue, couch, day bed A long lounge chair, extended frontally so that a single person can recline upon it, either upholstered or supplied with cushions. In French a *chaise longue* with a rounded back is called a *duchesse;* if the foot is surrounded on three sides by a low curving back it is called a *duchesse en batteau,* and if it is made in two or three parts each of which may be used separately as a seat it is called a *duchesse brisée. Illustrated opposite below.*

Chaise percée, *see* CLOSE STOOL.

Chalice Wine cup used at Mass; called a 'Communion Cup' in English reformed churches.

Chalkware American term for figures and ornaments made in Plaster of Paris in imitation of pottery and porcelain. They were originally imported from Europe, then made in America though often by itinerant Italian 'image-sellers' from moulds brought over from Italy. **Henry Christian Geyer** of Boston advertised chalkware 'of this Country Produce' in 1768. Staffordshire pottery ornaments were popular when imitated in chalkware. Chalkware was never glazed. Early pieces were sized and decorated with oil paint, later pieces were decorated with water colours.

Chamber candlestick A small portable candlestick set on a plate-shaped base with a scroll or ring handle generally provided with an extinguisher which fits into a slot in the handle, and sometimes snuffers, made from the late C17.

Chamberlain, Robert (b.1735). An English porcelain decorator who, after working at Dr Wall's WORCESTER PORCELAIN FACTORY, founded in the same city in 1783 a rival concern which began by decorating products of the CAUGHLEY, COALPORT and possibly NEW HALL factories. From 1800 this factory produced porcelain on a large scale specializing in richly decorated table-wares. It was amalgamated with the older firm in 1840. Two other members of the Chamberlain family were associated with the same concern: Robert's brother, **Humphrey** (d.1824) and **Walter,** a painter, who was a proprietor of the Worcester factory in 1848.

Lit: F. A. Barrett, *Worcester Porcelain,* London 1953.

Chambers, Sir William (1723–96). One of the most important architects in late-C18 England. He was of Scottish parentage, born in Sweden but educated in England. At sixteen he joined the Swedish East India Company and in the next nine years made three voyages to the Far East, going twice to Canton. This experience made him better acquainted than most of his contemporaries with Chinese architecture and decorative arts and he put his knowledge to good effect in his first book *Designs for Chinese Buildings,* London 1757, illustrating several pieces of furniture as well as buildings. Though apparently drawn from memory rather than (as he stated) derived from sketches made in the East, these designs are in a more authentic Chinese style than the CHINOISERIES fashionable in the mid C18 and for this reason, perhaps, had relatively little influence. In the meantime, however, he had left the East India Co. in 1749 and had begun to study architecture, first under J.-F. Blondel in Paris and then in Rome, before settling in 1755 in London where he immediately secured royal patronage. As an architect he developed a scholarly, somewhat academic, style based in English Palladianism and refined by the Neo-Classicism of Soufflot and his contemporaries whom he had known in Paris. Unlike his great rival Robert ADAM, he was more concerned with official commissions for the Office of Works (of which he was Comptroller 1769–82 and Surveyor-General and Comptroller 1782–96) than with the building and decorating of private houses and thus less involved in the design of furniture and furnishings. In 1759, however, he designed the furniture for the 'great room' of the Society of Arts in London (only the President's chair survives) and furniture was made to his designs for Blenheim Palace and Charlemont

House (destroyed). He also designed an astronomical clock for the King (still in the Royal Collection) with columns and a dome like a miniature of one of his buildings. And he clearly influenced the importation of the early Louis XVI style into England.

Lit: J. Harris, *Sir William Chambers*, London 1970.

Chambrette, Jacques, *see* LUNEVILLE and SAINT-CLÉMENT POTTERIES.

Champfer Surface produced by bevelling off an angle.

Champion, Richard (1743–91). He was closely involved in the discovery and early development of porcelain in England. He knew William COOKWORTHY from 1764 onwards and had probably reached a business understanding with him by 1770, when the PLYMOUTH PORCELAIN FACTORY was moved to Bristol. In 1774 Cookworthy assigned his patent to Champion who petitioned the House of Commons for an extension of 14 years but was challenged by WEDGWOOD and various Staffordshire potters. The cost of litigation was too much for Champion who tried to sell his patent to a group of Staffordshire potters who later started the NEW HALL PORCELAIN FACTORY. Champion became Deputy Paymaster-General of the Forces until 1784 when he emigrated to South Carolina where he died.

Lit: F. Severne Mackenna, *Champion's Bristol Porcelain*, Leigh-on-Sea 1947.

Champlevé, *see* ENAMEL.

Chance Bros. glasshouse, *see* BROAD GLASS.

Chance, William and **Robert Lucas,** *see* NAILSEA GLASSHOUSE.

Chandelier Originally the French term for a candlestick but later used also for a wall light or sconce and, up to the mid C18, for a hanging light-fixture suspended from the ceiling. After the mid C18 the latter has been known in France as a LUSTRE. In England the term chandelier has continued to be used for a hanging light-fixture suspended from the ceiling.

Channon, John (*fl.*1733–83). A member of an Exeter cabinet-making family, he settled in London between 1733 and 1737 by which time he had started a furniture-making business in St Martin's Lane. He lived there until 1783. A bookcase at Powderham Castle, near Exeter, is signed 'J. Channon 1740' and this has enabled a group of very fine and important brass-inlaid furniture, lavishly mounted in ormolu, to be attributed to him. Examples are in the Victoria & Albert Museum, London; The Fitzwilliam Museum, Cambridge; Temple Newsam House, Leeds; Kenwood House, Hampstead and the City Art Gallery, Bristol.

Lit: J. Hayward in *Victoria & Albert Museum Bulletin*, April 1966.

Chantilly lace Pillow lace was made at Chantilly from the early C17. The type for which the town is best known is a very fine black (less frequently white) silk lace with a hexagonal *fond*, onto which the pattern is worked. Each element of the pattern is outlined with a thicker strand of flat untwisted silk instead of the more usual *cordonnet*. Such lace was exported to Spain for mantillas. From the mid C19 machine-made lace was also produced at Chantilly.

Lit: B. Palliser, *History of Lace*, rev. M. Jourdain & A. Dryden, London 1902; L. W. van der Meulen Nulle, *Lace*, London 1963.

Chantilly porcelain factory Founded in *c.*1725 under the patronage of Louis-Henri de Bourbon,

Chantilly soft-paste porcelain pot pourri, c.1725–40 (Musée Condé, Chantilly)

Prince de Condé, an impassioned collector of Japanese ARITA porcelain, and managed by **Ciquaire Cirou** until his death in 1751. Only soft-paste porcelain was made, covered until *c.*1735 (and sometimes later though much less frequently after 1751) with an opaque tin glaze, like that used for faience, which provides a beautifully lustrous background for painted decorations in enamel colours. Products include amusingly grotesque figures of Chinamen, sometimes squatting beside vases to serve as perfume burners. Useful wares include very delicately modelled tea-pots, jugs, tureens, *bourdaloues* and numerous plates. Decorations were at first in the Japanese Kakiemon style but sometimes derived at second-hand from those on MEISSEN porcelain. After Cirou's death the factory was run by a succession of managers the last of whom was an Englishman, C. POTTER. In the 1750s wares were decorated with naturalistic flowers of the Meissen type (freely interpreted), but the factory thereafter came under the stronger influence of Vincennes-SÈVRES. Soft-paste of good quality with a normal slightly yellow lead-glaze was now employed. Wares were generally white rather sparsely decorated in underglaze blue – notably plates with formal borders surrounding rather small central motifs (a posy of flowers or a bird perched on a Rococo scroll). Enamel colours were also used for similarly sparse decorations. The 'Chantilly sprig', like a cornflower in profile, a motif invented at the factory and often used on later wares, was much copied elsewhere. The factory set into a decline in the early 1780s was bought by Christopher POTTER in 1792 and closed in 1800. Its mark was a hunting horn. The products of the factory have been extensively faked since the C19. (For factory mark *see* p. 882.)

Lit: X. de Chavagnac & A. de Grollier, *Histoire des manufactures françaises de porcelaine,* Paris 1906; W. B. Honey, *French Porcelain of the 18th Century,* London 1950.

Chantourné A French type of headboard characterized by Baroque C-scrolls and found on Louis XIV period beds.

Chapelle, Jacques, *see* SCEAUX POTTERY AND PORCELAIN FACTORY.

Chapin, Eliphelet (1741–1807). Connecticut furniture-maker born at Somers and working at East Windsor. Cherrywood highboys in the mid-C18 American version of the Chippendale style have been attributed to him but no documented works are known. At East Windsor he worked in partnership with **Aaron Chapin** (d.1838) from 1774 to 1783 when the latter moved to Hartford. Aaron (often confused with Eliphelet) was a practitioner of the Federal style derived from Hepplewhite (e.g. documented mahogany sideboard in Wadsworth Atheneum, Hartford). From *c.*1807 Aaron worked with his son **Laertes** (d.1847).

Lit: H. P. Maynard in *The Connoisseur,* CLXX (1969), pp. 126–9.

Chaplet, Ernest (1835–1909). French studio potter. After serving his apprenticeship at the SÈVRES factory he began working in various historical styles, first Hispano-Moresque, then Renaissance. In the late 1870s he turned for inspiration to Normandy peasant kitchen crockery and began to produce gaily coloured stoneware of attractive simplicity (Musée de Sèvres; Kunstindustri Museum, Copenhagen). In 1885 he started a pottery workshop in Paris for HAVILAND and in 1887 a porcelain factory at Choisy-le-Roi where he specialized in Chinese-shape vases with flambé glazes, which were much admired at the time. He was friendly with and fired all the pottery made by GAUGUIN.

Lit: R. Marx in *Art et Décoration 1910,* I, pp. 89–98; M. Bodelsen, *Gauguin's Ceramics,* London 1964; M. Ernould-Gandouet, *La Céramique en France au XIX siècle,* Paris 1969.

Chareau, Pierre (1883–1950). French architect and designer notable for some finely finished furniture and interior decoration in a *de luxe*

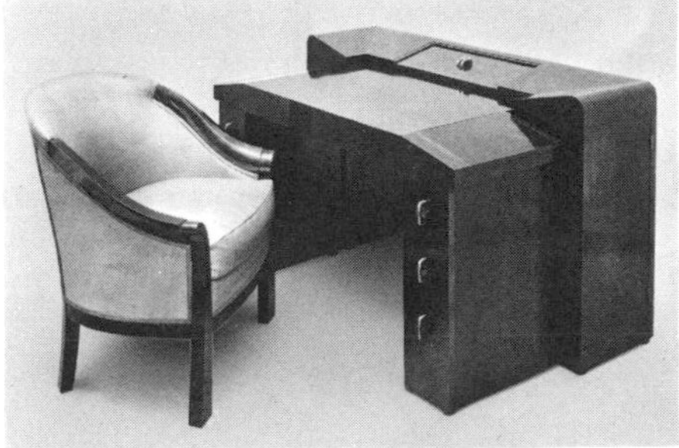

P. Chareau: desk and chair of ebony, 1925 (Musée des Arts Décoratifs, Paris)

version of the International Modern style, e.g. his *bureau d'une Ambassade* of 1925 (Musée d'Art Moderne, Paris). In 1930 he designed an ingenious tubular steel chair, derived from BREUER's famous chair of 1928, though not on the cantilever principle. But it was formed out of one continuous piece of metal tubing. His later work is less interesting, veering dangerously near to the superficial modernity of the Odeon Cinema style.

Charger A large, usually wooden, plate or dish on which a joint of meat was served and cut. The cut meat was served on similar but smaller wooden plates or dishes called *trenchers*.

Charka Russian type of small cup with a single handle, usually of silver and sometimes enamelled.

Charles X style, *see* RESTAURATION STYLE.

Charpentier, Alexandre (1856–1909). French sculptor and Art Nouveau furniture designer. Began by designing rectilinear furniture inspired by the English ARTS AND CRAFTS movement, but *c.*1900 he adopted a sinuous Art Nouveau style, with frequent use of reliefs of serpentine female nudes. *Illustrated next column.*

Chasing The tooling or surface modelling of metal either to remove blemishes (e.g. roughnesses left by CIRE-PERDUE casting) or to raise patterns in relief with hammer or punch (e.g. in decorations on silver).

Chasuble A sleeveless vestment covering the body and shoulders, worn by a Christian priest over the alb and stole when celebrating the Eucharist. It is roughly oval in shape with a central hole for the head.

Chatônes A Spanish type of ornamental nailhead much used for decorating furniture.

Checker or **Chequerwork** A pattern of squares resembling that of a chess-board. A favourite motif with C16 and C17 cabinet-makers for inlay decoration.

Cheley, Rudolph Anton, *see* BRUNSWICK POTTERIES.

A. Charpentier: reading stand, 1901 (Musée des Arts Décoratifs, Paris)

Chelsea Keramic Art Works A pottery established at Chelsea, Massachusetts, in 1866 by **Alexander Robertson** but producing nothing out of the ordinary run until 1872 when he was joined by his brother **Hugh C. Robertson** (1845–1908) who initiated the production of art pottery. Copies of Greek vases were among the first decorative wares to be made (example of 1876 in Boston Museum of Fine Arts). Plaques and vases decorated with paintings after G. Doré and Hans Makart were also produced. From 1876 the factory made wares imitative of those of LIMOGES with underglaze decorations, and marketed them under the trade name *Bourg-la-Reine*. But the influence of Chinese ceramics, especially vases with monochrome or flambé glazes, became increasingly strong, especially after 1884 when Hugh Robertson obtained control of the firm. Wares with blue-green, yellow-green, green-brown or *sang de boeuf* glazes were made. But in 1888 the concern was obliged to close for want of capital. It was rescued in 1891 by a group of Bostonians who employed Hugh Robertson as manager. Soon afterwards it began to produce wares with a crackled glaze which proved very popular and became its main speciality. In 1896 the factory was moved to Dedham, Massachusetts and renamed the **Dedham Pottery.** At the St Louis World's Fair of 1904 its products received one of the highest awards. After Hugh Robertson's death, the factory was run by his son **William** but thenceforth made little but table-wares. It closed in 1943.

Lit: L. Hawes, *Dedham Pottery and the Earlier Robertson's Chelsea Potteries*, Dedham, Mass. 1968.

Chelsea porcelain factory Probably the first and in many ways the best in England. (The BOW PORCELAIN FACTORY obtained its patent in 1744 but no products can be dated earlier than 1748 whereas there are surviving Chelsea wares dated 1745, see below.) The factory's early history is very obscure: but it may have acquired the secret of porcelain manufacture from Thomas Briand who demonstrated a fine white porcelain to the Royal Society in 1742. The earliest known products are small cream-jugs in the form of two reclining goats marked with the date 1745, the word 'Chelsea' and an incised triangle from which the name of the first phase of production – 'triangle period' – is derived. They are in a very soft translucent paste similar to white glass. The most notable products of the period are salt-cellars in the form of crayfish resting on rocks, clearly derived from a silver prototype. Some unmarked pieces of similar substance, notably a statuette GIRL IN A SWING are sometimes attributed to Chelsea though they may be products of another workshop of the same period. The first manager of the concern, **Charles Gouyn,** left in 1749 and was succeeded by Nicolas SPRIMONT, a silversmith by training who may have been associated with the concern since its foundation, under the ownership of Sir Everard Fawkener, secretary to the Duke of Cumberland.

During the first two years under the new management, known as the 'raised anchor period' (from an anchor in relief applied as a mark), some products still reveal the influence of metalwork, especially dishes and other useful wares. An advertisement of 1750 states that a wide variety of tea, coffee and other table-wares as well as ornaments were being made. Many pieces were based closely on MEISSEN prototypes. From an artistic point of view the finest products are those of the following 'red anchor period' *c.*1752–8 when an anchor in underglaze red was used as a mark. Some are imitative of

Chelsea porcelain plate, red anchor period, c.1753 (Victoria & Albert Museum)

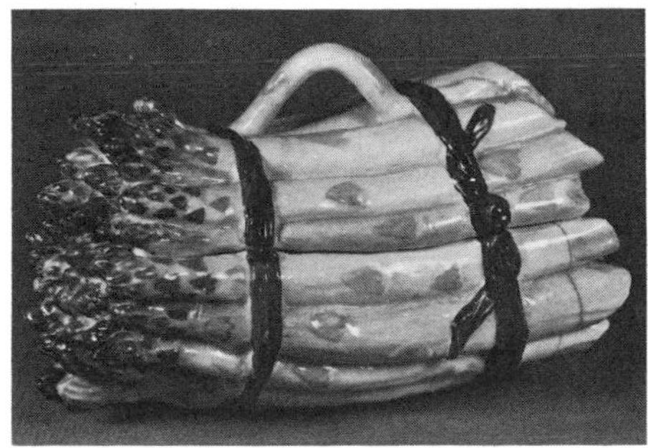

Chelsea porcelain tureen, red anchor period, c.1756 (Victoria & Albert Museum)

Chelsea porcelain, Foundling Vases, c.1762–3 *(Victoria & Albert Museum)*

Meissen (e.g. of Kandler's *Commedia dell'Arte* figures) but with a slight rusticity that takes the edge off the brittle sophistication of the originals and gives them an appealing spring-like freshness. But some are original, including a wide range of allegorical and peasant figures from models by J. WILLEMS (who appears to have been employed since 1750), a pot-pourri in the form of a dovecote and plates painted *c.*1755 with nicely reproduced botanical specimen flowers (known as Sir Hans Sloane's plants). The factory closed for about a year in 1757–8 while Sprimont was ill. When it reopened a gold anchor was used as the mark. The original paste had been abandoned *c.*1755 when bone-ash was first used as an ingredient: from 1758 the body was more opaque, the glaze thicker with a tendency to coagulate and craze. The source of artistic influence now shifted from Germany to France. Even so, the products continued to be unmistakably English. Vases imitated from SÈVRES in both form and colour lose their Parisian *hauteur*, a print from Boucher is charmingly anglicized in a group of a shepherd-boy teaching a young hoyden to play the pipe in front of a luxuriant hawthorn *bocage*. A slightly countrified version of the Rococo style – evident in table-wares, figures and such 'toys' as scent-bottles and *étuis* – brightly painted and lavishly gilded remained dominant until 1769 when the factory was sold to **William Duesbury** of DERBY. Wares produced between 1770 and 1784, when it finally closed, are indistinguishable from Derby products of the same period and are usually called 'Chelsea-Derby'. (For factory marks *see* p. 882.)

Lit: W. King, *Chelsea Porcelain*, London 1922; F. Severne Mackenna, *Chelsea Porcelain: The Red Anchor Wares*, Leigh-on-Sea 1951; F. Severne Mackenna, *Chelsea Porcelain: The Gold Anchor Wares*, Leigh-on-Sea 1952; J. V. G. Mallet in R. J. Charleston (ed.), *English Porcelain 1745–1850*, London 1965.

Chelsea porcelain group of 'The Music Lesson', c.1765 (Victoria & Albert Museum)

Chenet The French term for an ANDIRON or fire-dog.

Ch'êng-hua porcelain Chinese porcelain made in the reign of the MING Emperor Ch'êng-hua (1465–87). The finest are decorated with ENAMEL COLOURS, sometimes applied to the *biscuit* and not over the glaze. On these wares the decorations are rather more sparse than on those of the HSÜAN-TÊ period. The reign mark was often forged in later periods.

Lit: S. Jenyns, *Ming Pottery and Porcelain*, London 1953.

Chenille A cord with short threads of silk or wool set at right angles to it, forming a velvety thread. Used mainly for needlework trimmings. The term is also applied loosely to various C19 and later types of imitation velvet.

Chenille Axminster, *see* AXMINSTER CARPET.

Chéret, Joseph (1838–94). French sculptor and ceramic artist, brother of the painter, poster-designer and lithographer Jules Chéret (1836–1930). He was a pupil of CARRIER-BELLEUSE, began at a porcelain factory at Boulogne-sur-Mer and worked for CHRISTOFLE and other concerns,

J. Chéret: tray in stoneware, c.1900 (Kunstgewerbemuseum, Berlin)

eventually becoming director of the Pallemberg firm at Cologne. From 1877 he provided designs for BACCARAT glass. He made models for the SÈVRES PORCELAIN FACTORY of which he was briefly artistic director, 1886–7. His later work is in a fluid Art Nouveau style (e.g. stoneware dish with dragonflies and a female nude half submerged in water, 1894, Kunstgewerbemuseum, Berlin).

Lit: W. Scheffler, *Kunstgewerbemuseum, Berlin: Werke um 1900*, Berlin 1966.

Cherokee clay, *see* UNAKER.

Chest A large wooden box with a hinged lid used for storing clothes, valuables, etc., made in all parts of the world (China and the Far East as well as Europe) from very early times. Examples from ancient Egypt survive. In Europe it was the most important type of case furniture from the Middle Ages to the late C17 when it began to be superseded by the CHEST OF DRAWERS. Chests were often painted and/or carved with decorative devices or, more rarely, figure subjects. The Italian word for a chest, CASSONE, is generally reserved for those of Italian origin though sometimes applied to those made under Italian influence in N. Europe especially in the C16–C17. After the end of the C17 the chest was generally regarded as a purely utilitarian piece of furniture and was little, if at all, decorated.

Chest of drawers From the mid C16 chests and travelling coffers were occasionally fitted with small drawers in the base, under the large compartment which was accessible only from the top. The chest of drawers gradually assumed its modern form in the course of the C17 and had superseded the chest by the early C18. A few types have acquired special names, e.g. BUREAU, CHIFFONIER, CHIFFONNIÈRE, HIGHBOY, LOWBOY, TALLBOY.

Chesterfield A large, well-stuffed sofa with no woodwork showing.

Chesterfield potteries A small group of Derbyshire factories active mid C18 to mid C19 making

Chest: German Renaissance, oak carved and painted with the story of Tobias, Lüneberg, 1545 (Museum für Kunst and Gewerbe, Hamburg)

rather coarse brown stoneware sometimes decorated with reliefs of hunting scenes or drinking bouts.

Lit: G. A. Godden (ed.), *Jewitt's The Ceramic Art of Great Britain*, London 1972.

Cheval glass Upright, full-length mirror swung on a four-legged frame or horse. Especially popular during the Empire period when known as a Psyche.

Cheveret An English C18 type of small table. It has an oblong top, a shallow drawer below, and is supported on four slender tapering legs joined with a shelf. It was often made in satinwood.

Chia and **Chiao**, *see* CHÜEH.

Chia Ching porcelain Chinese porcelain made in the reign of the MING Emperor Chia Ching (1522–66). The best wares are blue and white, with a blue of peculiar intensity. On polychrome pieces a new iron-red enamel was used overglaze. During this period the export trade in porcelain was much increased both to the Middle East and Europe.

Lit: H. Garner, *Oriental Blue and White*, London 1954.

Chia-Ch'ing porcelain Chinese porcelain made in the reign of the CH'ING Emperor Chia-Ch'ing (1796–1821) and, unless marked, very difficult to distinguish from the wares made in the latter part of the CH'IEN LUNG period.

Lit: Soame Jenyns, *Later Chinese Porcelain: The Ch'ing Dynasty (1644–1912)*, London, rev. ed., 1971.

Chicaneau, Pierre, *see* SAINT-CLOUD POTTERY AND PORCELAIN FACTORY.

Chichi carpets, *see* CAUCASIAN CARPETS.

Chicken ware A delicate type of Chinese porcelain first made during the Ch'êng-hua period (1465–87), decorated with cocks, hens and chickens with a peony, in *tou-ts'ai* colours. It was much imitated in C18 China.

Chien ware A type of Chinese stoneware made in the southern Fukien province from the SUNG period. The most notable pieces are tea bowls, with a rather coarse body and very thick brown glaze sometimes streaked with grey or blue (called hare's fur) or spotted with blue, many of which were exported to Japan where they were adopted as TEA CEREMONY WARES, and referred to as *Temmoku*. The ware was imitated at Chi-chou in Kiangsi and also in Japan.

Lit: B. Gray, *Early Chinese Pottery and Porcelain*, London 1953.

Ch'ien Lung porcelain Chinese porcelain made in the reign of the CH'ING Emperor Ch'ien Lung (1736–95). Imitations of earlier, especially SUNG, wares were produced: and on some of those in the Imperial collection the Emperor himself engraved inscriptions recording his admiration. Both blue-and-white and polychrome wares (notably *famille rose*, as well as *famille verte*, *noire* and *jaune*) were produced in quantity but the decorations on them grew increasingly busy and towards the end of the period the technical quality began to fall off as well. In fact the period was one of steady decline.

Lit: S. Jenyns, *Later Chinese Porcelain: The Ch'ing Dynasty (1644–1912)*, rev. ed., London 1971.

Chiffonier Anglicized name for the French CHIFFONNIÈRE (made in England by Chippendale from the 1760s). Also an English C19 type of dining-room furniture, consisting of a small cupboard with a top forming a sideboard.

Chiffonnière A C18 French term for a piece of furniture for the storage of stuffs (*chiffons*) and small articles of clothing. It is usually, but not necessarily, a small, low chest-of-drawers (narrower than the normal COMMODE). *See also* TABLE EN CHIFFONNIÈRE.

Chimney board A board which may be fitted into a fireplace when it is out of use to prevent draughts and soot from coming down the chimney and entering the room. They were used mainly in France and Italy from the C18 onwards and were usually painted with a vase of flowers or still life, sometimes by a notable artist, e.g. Chardin.

China clay, *see* KAOLIN.

China stand An ornamental wooden stand for a porcelain vase. Various types were made from the late C17 when the vogue for large Chinese bowls and vases became widespread, ranging from those like four-legged stools or low tables to those like candle-stands.

China stone The English name for PETUNTSE.

China trade porcelain, *see* CHINESE EXPORT PORCELAIN.

Chinese carpets Knotted carpets were made in China from very early times but only a few fragments survive from before the C15. Later carpets have a pile of either silk or wool, usually rather coarsely knotted. Yellow, blue and white predominate in the colour schemes. Designs are partly floral but generally symbolical, with the motifs much more widely spaced than on Middle Eastern carpets; sometimes the centre is filled with a single human figure. Some long strips have patterns which join up when they are folded round cylindrical pillars. Often the surface of the pile is cut so that it is much shorter round the outlines of the figures, giving a relief effect peculiar to Chinese carpets. The Chinese also made imitations of PERSIAN CARPETS.

Lit: Exposition de tapisseries et tapis de la Chine, Paris, Manufacture nationale des Gobelins, 1936; A. V. Dilley & M. S. Dimand, *Oriental Rugs and Carpets*, New York 1960; H. A. Lorentz, *Chinesische Teppiche*, Munich 1975.

Chinese Chippendale A type of CHINOISERIE furniture illustrated in CHIPPENDALE's *Director* (1754), hence its name. But it may not have been invented by Chippendale. It was certainly current before 1754. It is confined to seat furniture, small cabinets, etc., on which lattice-work can be given prominence. Ornament is sparingly used and it is square and angular in outline – in fact closer to Chinese furniture than is most Chinoiserie furniture.

Lit: H. Honour, *Chinoiserie* (1961), London 1974.

Chinese export porcelain Porcelain made in China for export to Europe and, from the late C18, the U.S. (that made for Persia in the Yüan and Ming periods is not generally classified under this heading). From the late C15 blue-and-white ware were occasionally made for Europeans and decorated with their armorial devices (heraldically peccable). By the late C16, towards the end of the Ming period, several provincial factories seem to have begun to specialize in making blue-and-white wares for Europe – similar in shape and decoration to those made for the home market but generally of inferior quality. Under the CH'ING dynasty the export trade increased steadily and quantities of YI-HSING stoneware, CELADON, white TE-HUA porcelain (called *blanc-de-chine* in Europe) as well as blue-and-white and polychrome porcelain (especially FAMILLE JAUNE, ROSE and VERTE) were sent each year to Europe. Certain concessions were made to European habits and tastes – plates were made with wide flat rims, saucers were supplied with teacups, vases were made in sets of three or five to form *garnitures de cheminée* – but otherwise wares were similar in form to those made for the Chinese market. The decorations tended to be much more crowded and without much symbolical significance (Europeans naturally preferred picturesque mixtures of dragons and men and flowers to symbols of the Eight Precious Things). Occasionally European wares were copied, sometimes decorations were derived from European prints, and patterns were occasionally sent out from Europe (*see* C. PRECHT). In the late C17 or early C18 the CHING-TÊ-CHÊN factory began to produce armorial dinner services commissioned by Europeans who sent out drawings or prints of their coats of arms to be enamelled in the centre of every plate and tureen and surrounded by pretty borders of Chinese flowers. These proved enormously popular, especially in England, throughout the C18. From the late C18 similar wares were made for the U.S., but more often decorated with monograms, representations of the American Eagle and Stars and Stripes, or little ships flying the American flag, than with heraldry. All the export wares of the C18 have great charm even if they are inferior to the more sensitively and more chastely decorated wares made for the home market. But in the C19, as European interest in China declined, the Chinese began to cater for increasingly lower strata of European society and standards fell off sharply. The best products of this period are probably the unpretentious blue-and-white 'Nanking' plates produced in great quantity. The Chinese were, however, extremely prompt to cater for the late C19 and early C20 European interest in earlier Chinese ceramics and by 1912 they were already faking T'ANG tomb figures for export to Europe – only three years after the first genuine T'ang figure had reached Europe from China! – though such products are not, of course, 'export porcelain'. Chinese Export Porcelain is often called 'East India Company Porcelain' or 'Compagnie des Indes' after the companies which shipped the wares to England and France: in the U.S. it is often known as China Trade Porcelain or occasionally Oriental Lowestoft, or even Jesuit china.

Lit: M. Jourdain & R. Soame Jenyns, *Chinese Export Art in the Eighteenth Century*, London 1950; D. F. Lusingh Scheurleer, *Chinese Export Porcelain, Chine de Commande*, London 1974; M. Beurdeley, *Porcelaine de la Compagnie des Indes*, Fribourg 1974; D. S. Howard, *Chinese Armorial Porcelain*, London 1974.

Chinese wallpaper Hand-painted paper hangings made in China for the European market since the mid C17. (Chinese houses had either painted silk hangings or plain coloured paper hangings.) They were executed in gouache, very occasionally over designs printed in black. There are three main categories: those with tall flowering trees and gaily plumaged birds perching in their branches; town scenes with numerous figures of Chinamen engaged in potting, weaving, trading, etc.; and a combination of the two with flowering trees in the upper part and scenes from Chinese life below (these are said to date from after *c.*1775). The best papers were produced *c.*1740–90 and exported mainly to London and Paris whence they found their way all over Europe and to N. America. They were and still are imitated in Europe. *Illustrated next column.*

Lit: C. Oman, *Catalogue of Wallpapers*, Victoria & Albert Museum, London 1929.

Chinese C18 wallpaper (Victoria & Albert Museum)

Ch'ing The Manchu dynasty which succeeded the MING and ruled over China from 1644 to 1912, a period of almost continuous economic, political and, from the mid C18, cultural decline.

The tendency towards elaboration which had become marked in the preceding MING period was aggravated. And at the same time the conservative classicistic outlook of Chinese artists and patrons prevented the introduction of any new ideas to enliven a repertory of tired ornament which grew increasingly stale. The handsome forms of MING and earlier furniture remained unchanged but they were gradually overgrown by rank carved decoration. The same could be said of bronzes and of textiles (though carpets are an exception until the early C19). Fine jade carvings were produced until the mid C18 but here again a desire for elaborate decorations within a traditional framework eventually led to the production of monstrosities. Fortunately, however, the art of the potter suffered least and very beautiful porcelain was made until the early C19 (*see* K'ANG HSI PORCELAIN, YUNG-CHÊNG PORCELAIN and CH'IEN-LUNG PORCELAIN). During this period the export trade increased considerably and a distinction should be made between objects produced for home consumption and those intended for Europe: CHINESE EXPORT PORCELAIN, CHINESE WALLPAPERS, CANTON ENAMELS, COROMANDEL and other lacquer, etc., which are sometimes handsome but more frequently badly designed and shoddily made.

Lit: Soame Jenyns, *Later Chinese Porcelain: The Ch'ing Dynasty (1644–1912)*, London, rev. ed., 1971.

Ch'ing-pai wares A large class of Chinese porcelain with a pale blue glaze (the word *ch'ing-pai* means bluish white) made during the SUNG and YÜAN periods in the Ching-tê-chên district of Kiangsi province and probably at many other places in Southern China. Vessels are often elaborately modelled (vases with fluted bodies, lobed bowls with foliate rims), and those of the Yüan period sometimes have applied panels of relief decoration. The ware was not very highly regarded in China but extensively exported to Persia and even Europe.

Lit: B. Gray, *Early Chinese Pottery and Porcelain*, London 1953.

Ching-tê-chên A town near Nanking in Kiangsi province which became a centre of the Chinese porcelain industry in the SUNG period and was named after the Sung Emperor Ching-tê. The Imperial porcelain factory founded here in 1369, destroyed 1675 and reconstructed 1683, produced nearly all the finest Chinese porcelain from the MING period onwards (the only notable exceptions being the white porcelain of TÊ-HUA and the red stoneware of YI-HSING). From the early C18 mass-production methods were adopted for making all but the very finest products.

Chinkinbori Literally 'sunk gold engraving', a Japanese term for lacquer decorated with incised designs into which gold has been rubbed.

Chinoiserie Western imitations or evocations of Chinese art, seldom accurate and always rendered with some deference to the European stylistic ideals of the time. In the C14 Chinese silks were imitated at the LUCCA SILK FACTORIES and in the late C16 Chinese blue-and-white porcelain decorations at the MEDICI PORCELAIN FACTORY. But the term Chinoiserie is generally reserved for

Chinoiserie bed, lacquered and gilt wood, attributed to W. Linnel, c.1750 (Victoria & Albert Museum)

Chinoiserie design by Paul Decker, Nuremberg, post 1705

objects made in the C17 and C18. The most notable of the C17 include pottery made at

Chinoiserie panel of Lyons silk, probably after design by Pillement, c.1760–70 (Kunstgewerbemuseum, Berlin)

DELFT, NEVERS and SOUTHWARK, French and English embroideries, JAPANNED furniture produced in Holland and England (where STALKER AND PARKER published in 1688 a volume of appropriate decorations for it), English silver of the 1680s engraved with wispy oriental figures, and SOHO TAPESTRIES. With the exception of pottery vases, all these objects are of normal European form: only their decorations are exotic and these are usually combined with or toned down by European motifs (e.g. japanned cabinets on carved baroque stands). This subdued exoticism developed in the early C18 under ROCOCO influence into a style more whimsically elegant and wilfully fantastic than anything produced in China: but the asymmetricality of Chinese art may have influenced the Rococo. Dragons, strange birds and queerly dressed Chinamen were modelled in porcelain, carved in wood on the supports of console tables and the frames of looking-glasses, cast in bronze, embossed in silver, while fantastic Chinese landscapes with pagodas and stunted trees were painted on walls, on porcelain or pottery plates

(Left) Chinoiserie design by J. Pillement, c.1750

and vases, woven in silks and tapestries, painted or inlaid on furniture. Whole rooms were decorated in the Chinese taste, the most spectacular being those at Capodimonte in Italy and Aranjuez in Spain which were lined throughout with porcelain (see CAPODIMONTE and BUEN RETIRO PORCELAIN FACTORIES). Often Chinoiserie objects were displayed with CHINESE WALLPAPERS and CHINESE EXPORT PORCELAIN. The English developed CHINESE CHIPPENDALE furniture, the Germans concentrated on statuettes (notably those made at the MEISSEN, NYMPHENBURG and HÖCHST PORCELAIN FACTORIES), and the French specialized in elaborate bedragonned ormolu mounts for Chinese or European porcelain vases. But apart from such national preferences, the style developed as a species of the international Rococo in the C18. And the designs of such French artists as BOUCHER, HUET, PILLEMENT and WATTEAU were widely used all over Europe, especially in England and Germany. With the Neo-Classical reaction against the Rococo, the fashion for Chinoiserie declined but it did not die out. Subdued Chinoiserie motifs survived, especially on furniture, textiles and porcelain, until after the end of the C18. And one of the finest and richest Chinoiserie interiors – the Royal Pavilion, Brighton – was created between 1802 and 1821. The mid-C19 Rococo Revival brought Chinoiserie back to fashion but it was quickly superseded by JAPONAISERIE.

Lit: H. Honour, *Chinoiserie* (1961), London 1974; *China und Europa*, Exh. Cat., Berlin 1973.

Worcester porcelain sauce-boat with chinoiserie decorations, c.1760 (Victoria & Albert Museum)

Chinoiserie silver tea-caddy, by Pierre Gillois, 1766–7 (Victoria & Albert Museum)

Chintz, c19 English (Victoria & Albert Museum)

Chintz An English variation of a Sanskrit word (meaning variegated) applied in c16 and c17 to imported Indian calico and later to European printed COTTON fabrics. In England chintz had become so popular by the early c18 that in 1722 Parliament legislated against both importation and manufacture of calicos. This was rescinded in 1774 as regards manufacture, but not as regards importation. In the c19 chintz was superseded by the stronger CRETONNE.

Lit: J. Irwin & K. B. Brett, *Origins of Chintz*, London 1970.

Chip carving A primitive type of carved decoration found on much N. European oak furniture of the later Middle Ages and c16, executed with a chisel and gouge, generally in roundels. *Illustrated next column.*

Chip carving: decoration on English c13 oak chest (Victoria & Albert Museum)

Chipchase, Robert (*fl.* 1767–1810). London furniture-maker first recorded in partnership with a **Mr Lambert** of Beak Street, Golden Square, and from 1790 with his son **Henry**. He was employed by the 3rd and 4th Dukes of Atholl and several pieces of furniture by him survive at Blair Castle, notably chairs and settees in the style associated with HEPPLEWHITE.

Lit: A. Coleridge in *The Connoisseur*, CLXI (1966), pp. 96–101.

Chippendale, Thomas (1718–79). He is the best-known English furniture-maker and the author of the first comprehensive book of furniture designs: *The Gentleman & Cabinet Maker's Director* (1754, 2nd edn, 1755, 3rd edn, 1762). He was born in Yorkshire, the son of a carpenter, and was established in London by 1748 when he married. From 1754 onwards he had a shop, workshops and timberyard in St Martin's Lane, London, and for much of his career he was occupied mainly in running his very extensive business rather than in cabinet-making himself. (He is even known to have been importing unfinished French furniture in 1769.) His firm undertook the complete furnishing and decoration of large houses. He was in partnership first with **James Rannie** (d.1766) and later with **Thomas Haig** who survived him and carried on the business with his son **Thomas Chippendale** (1749–1822). The *Director* made Chippendale's name a household word. Nothing on such a scale had ever been published before, either in England or elsewhere. Almost every type of domestic furniture was illustrated in it. The designs are predominantly Rococo in style, including Neo-Gothic and Chinoiserie, some of the latter being of the type known as CHINESE CHIPPENDALE. Several of the designs are so elaborate and fantastic as to be impractical, at any rate in carved mahogany or other hardwood. It has been suggested that he employed Matthias LOCK, H. COPLAND and perhaps others to 'ghost' designs for him but there is no proof of this. He specifically claims in the preface to have made most of the designs himself and it seems likely that he did so, especially for the case pieces. But whoever made the designs helped himself freely to both English and continental pattern books. Several of the designs border on plagiarism and none is of great originality. Nor does Chippendale's supremacy among English furniture makers, as opposed to furniture designers, rest on the furniture he made in the Rococo (or *Director*) style. William VILE, Pierre LANGLOIS and others worked in this style with equal skill. Chippendale's finest furniture is in the Neo-Classical style introduced by Robert ADAM and is therefore very different from that commonly associated with his name. It dates from *c.*1765 onwards and was made largely for houses recently built or decorated by Adam, e.g. Nostell Priory or Harewood House. However, none of Chippendale's furniture appears to have been designed by Adam. It has been suggested that this Neo-Classical Chippendale furniture was designed by Thomas Chippendale the younger, who published *Sketches for Ornament* in 1779, and this seems not unlikely. Some of this furniture is extremely simple and plain, but some is of great elaboration, notably large commodes,

Chippendale design for a sofa, 1760

Chippendale design for a chest of drawers from The Gentleman & Cabinet Maker's Director

Chippendale library table supplied to Harewood House, c.1770 (Temple Newsam House, Leeds)

library tables, etc., with extremely delicate marquetry decoration, occasionally with ivory inlays and often with ormolu mounts in an anglicized version of the LOUIS XVI STYLE.

None of Chippendale's furniture was stamped and authenticity can therefore be established only by bills or other documentation. Furniture after designs in the *Director* is not necessarily by him or his firm though there is a presumption that it came from him if it is of high quality and was made for a house whose owner subscribed to the *Director*.

After his death the firm of Chippendale and Haig was carried on by his son Thomas. His partner Thomas Haig retired in 1796 and in 1804 he went bankrupt. But he appears to have recovered quickly and resumed business. He maintained the firm's high level of craftsmanship and his furniture is among the best in the REGENCY STYLE, e.g. the furniture he made for Stourhead.

Lit: A. Coleridge, *Chippendale Furniture*, London 1968; D. Fitz-Gerald in *Journal of the Furniture History Society*, IV, 1968; H. Honour, *Cabinet Makers & Furniture Designers*, London & New York 1969.

Chiu, *see* KUEI.

Choisy-le-Roi glasshouse, *see* BONTEMPS, George.

Choisy-le-Roi pottery Founded in 1804, it only rose to prominence after it came under the direction of Hippolyte Boulenger in *c.*1863. In 1867 it had 300 employees and its products included industrial, architectural and ornamental pottery. The latter was shown at all the big C19 exhibitions – notably in the Crystal Palace in 1851 – and it exploited all the historical styles from *Henri Deux* to the Baroque. A variety of pastes was also developed, from a so-called 'maiolica' to *pâte-sur-pâte* and marbled wares. The factory changed hands in 1878 and was enlarged, but it concentrated increasingly on industrial and utilitarian (especially sanitary) wares. It closed in 1934.

Lit: M. Ernould-Gandouet, *Le céramique en France au 19ᵉ siècle*, Paris 1969.

Chou The Chinese dynasty which succeeded the SHANG-YIN and flourished from 1027 B.C. to 221 B.C. It was similarly notable for its bronze ritual vessels. Forms tend to be slightly more attenuated than in Shang-yin bronzes and square-shaped vessels are much less frequent. Decora-

Chou dynasty: bronze ting, *Warring States period, 481–221* B.C. *(William Rockhill Nelson Gallery of Art, Kansas City)*

(*Left*) *Chou dynasty: table leg, bronze inlaid into gold and silver,* 1027–256 B.C. *(William Rockhill Nelson Gallery of Art, Kansas City)*

Chou dynasty: bronze Fang-i *with cover, Early Western Chou,* c.1000–722 B.C. *(William Rockhill Nelson Gallery of Art, Kansas City)*

tions are likewise less rich and are usually abstract rather than zoomorphic.

Chrismatory A vessel to contain the Chrism or consecrated oil, also the case or container of ivory, silver, pewter, etc., to hold such vessels.

Christofle, Charles (1805–63). He founded the largest firm of silver and ELECTROPLATE manufacturers in France, becoming the equivalent of G. R. ELKINGTON in England and H. G. REED in the U.S.A. The firm still produces a large proportion of the table-wares in daily use in France. Though he was not nearly so highly thought of by the connoisseurs as was F. D. FROMENT-MEURICE, he played a more important role in the history of the decorative arts. He began as a jeweller but had turned to the manufacture of silver and household plate by the late 1830s. In 1842 he bought the French rights in Elkington's patent and obtained the monopoly of making electroplate in France. By 1847 his annual turnover exceeded two million francs. He made table-wares and other goods in a variety of historical styles, at first mainly in the Louis XV and Louis XVI styles and was much patronized

Christofle electroplated knives for Napoleon III, designed by Froment-Meurice, 1853 *(Musée des Arts Décoratifs, Paris)*

by Napoleon III who commissioned a large dinner service from him in 1853 (pieces now in the Musée des Arts Décoratifs, Paris, and at the Musée du Château de Compiègne). The firm also produced some furniture, e.g. a bronze table designed by CARRIER-BELLEUSE (Musée des Arts Décoratifs, Paris) and fine quality bronze mounts in the Louis XVI style for Second Empire reproduction furniture. On Charles Christofle's death the firm passed to his son **Paul** and his nephew **Henri Bouilhet** who continued to develop the business. (On Paul's death in 1907 they had some 1500 employees, mainly at the Saint-Denis factory, and they had branches by then at Karlsruhe, Vienna and Brussels.) At the 1900 Paris exhibition they introduced a new type of plated ware called 'Gallia Metal' which was heavier and more sonorous when struck than Electroplate. They produced Art Nouveau wares in Gallia Metal and later some Art Deco products. Their table-wares for the Atlantic liner *Normandie* in 1935 were distinguished. Since the Second World War they have employed such well-known designers as Gio PONTI and Tapio WIRKKALA.

Lit: H. Bouilhet, *L'Orfèvrerie Française aux XVIIIe et XIXe siècles*, Paris 1910.

Chüeh A type of Chinese Bronze Age wine vessel made during the Shang-Yin and Early Chou dynasties (*c.*1500–*c.*1000 B.C.). It has an ovoid body, a gouge-shaped spout balanced by a triangular-shaped flange, a loop handle, and it rests on three triangular slightly spreading legs. Two short capped columns, of unknown purpose or significance, appear at the bottom of the spout. The *Chia* and *Chiao* are related types. The *Chia* has a wide circular or rectangular mouth instead of the spout and flange, and its body is larger, sometimes carried on four instead of three legs. The *Chiao* has two flanges instead of a spout and flange and it lacks the Chüeh's curious capped columns. For illustration *see* SHANG-YIN.

Chün ware A type of glazed stoneware made in Central Honan province (especially in the Lin-ju and Yü districts) and probably elsewhere in Northern China from the time of the SUNG dynasty onwards, continuing well into the Ming dynasty. It is rather thickly potted with a very thick blue glaze varying in tone from the palest lavender to a rich purple, sometimes mottled, or splashed with crimson (from copper), and occasionally crazed. The wares include bowls, jars, bottles and incense burners.

Lit: B. Gray, *Early Chinese Pottery and Porcelain*, London 1953.

Chün ware dish of plum blossom form, with crackled lavender glaze, Sung Period, (Percival David Foundation of Chinese Art, London)

Cialli, Antonio and **Lorenzo,** *see* ROME POTTERIES & PORCELAIN FACTORIES.

Ciborium The receptacle used for the reservation of the Eucharist, usually of silver. Gothic examples often have a spire-shaped cover above a cylindrical or occasionally polygonal, font-shaped bowl. Flatter covers were introduced in the Renaissance.

Cimarre French term for a ceremonial vessel (especially for wine) with two handles – an ordinary bail handle for pouring and a swing handle for carrying – sometimes spouted, generally made of pewter. Alternatively called a *cymaise*, *cymarre* or *semaise*.

Cire-perdue Bronze-casting technique. The model is made of wax round a core of burnt clay and enclosed within an envelope of clay mixed with plaster. The whole is baked and the molten wax run off through a vent. Molten bronze is then run in to take the place of the wax. The clay envelope can then be cut away and the core broken up inside and shaken out through a hole left for the purpose. The result is a hollow bronze exactly reproducing the original wax model. The surface is usually chased and patinated. The technique has the advantages of giving a fine finish; of allowing a cast in the round to be taken as a whole and not, as in other methods, e.g. sand-casting, by means of two or more separate casts; and of requiring the minimum of bronze. But it has the disadvantage of allowing only one cast to be taken. Further bronzes can only be obtained by taking a cast of the first but something of the directness of the original is naturally lost with each repetition or *surmoulage*.

Cirou, Ciquaire, *see* CHANTILLY PORCELAIN FACTORY.

Ciselure The finishing process given to bronzes by tooling and chasing.

Cist A small receptacle for toilet articles or ceremonial objects. The term is generally reserved for those of Greek and, especially, Etruscan origin: the latter are generally oval, made of bronze and elaborately decorated with engraved ornament.

Cistercian ware Late medieval English red pottery, rather thin and fired to stoneware hardness, with a dark brown or black glaze and decorations in applied white clay or trailed slip. So called because the only specimens found were on sites of Cistercian abbeys and appear to date from before their dissolution in 1540.

Lit: B. Rackham, *Medieval English Pottery*, London 1948.

Clair de lune A very pale moonlight blue glaze, sometimes rather lavender blue, without crackle, first found in K'ANG HSI PORCELAIN but perfected in YUNG CHÊNG PORCELAIN. It is a C19 term, introduced by Jacquemart.

Clantha ware, *see* LINTHORPE POTTERY.

Clarke, William, *see* LILLE POTTERIES AND PORCELAIN FACTORIES.

Claw and ball feet
on an English mahogany side-table, c.1740
(Victoria & Albert Museum)

Claw and ball foot Popular C18 termination for furniture legs: said to be oriental in origin (e.g. Chinese bronzes), the original dragon's claw being replaced in Europe by an eagle's claw. It superseded the club foot in England.

Clay, Henry, *see* PAPIER MACHÉ.

Cleffius, Lambert (d.1691). Owner of a DELFT POTTERY producing both blue-and-white wares and red earthenware teapots. He is first recorded in 1678. His factory, *De Metale Pot*, was taken over by L. EENHORN in 1691.

Clerici, Felice, *see* MILAN POTTERIES.

Clérissy, Pierre I (*c.*1651–1728). French potter who initiated the production of faience at MOUSTIERS. He was the son of **Antoine I** (d.1679) who made only earthenware at Moustiers, the brother of **Joseph** (*c.*1649–84) who went to work at MARSEILLES, and the father of **Antoine II** (1673–1743). From 1710 he was in partnership with Antoine II who ran the factory from Pierre I's death until 1736 when he retired and handed it over to his son **Pierre II** (1704–94). The latter became *seigneur de Trévans* in 1736, an official of the Parlement of Aix in 1747 and was created Baron de Roumoules in 1774. He took little part in running the factory after 1757 and sold it in 1783.

Clermont-Ferrand potteries Of the several factories established here only one was of importance. It was founded in 1732 and appears to have survived for less than a decade, producing blue-and-white faience similar in style to that of MOUSTIERS and little inferior in quality. Examples are in the Musée de Cluny, Paris, and in the Musée National de Céramique de Sèvres at Sèvres.

Lit: J. Chompret *et al., Répertoire de la faïence française,* Paris 1933–5.

Clews, James and **Ralph** (*fl.*1817–36). Owners of one of the STAFFORDSHIRE POTTERIES at Cobridge which produced transfer-printed earthenware for export to the U.S.A., often decorated with American subjects. The factory closed in 1834 and James Clews started a pottery at Troy, Indiana, but failed and returned to England in 1836.

Cleyn, Francis, *see* MORTLAKE TAPESTRY FACTORY.

Clichy glasshouse Founded at Billancourt, Paris, 1837; moved to Clichy-la-Garenne 1844 and closed down 1885. Specialized in cheap table glass for export but also produced some fine *opaline*, cased glass, *millefiore* paper-weights and engraved cups which were much praised when shown at the international exhibitions in London, 1851 and 1862.

Lit: Paul Hollister, jr., *The Encyclopedia of Glass Paperweights,* New York 1969.

Clifton Art Pottery, *see* LONHUDA POTTERY.

Clobbered wares Oriental porcelain with underglaze decorations over-painted in Europe with lacquer or other colours which do not need to be fired. Also European earthenware decorated by the same process.

Clocks

Act of Parliament clock. Popular name for an English type of clock made to hang on a wall, with a very large face and usually a short trunk enclosing the weights and pendulum, generally made for inns, from the mid c18. The name derives from an Act of Parliament of 1797 which imposed a duty on clocks and watches but was repealed in 1798. It was erroneously supposed that such clocks were put up in inns for the benefit of those unwilling or unable to pay the tax.

Annular. A clock with a horizontal ring-shaped dial; the most familiar kind is urn-shaped with the dial as a frieze round the top of the urn. A pointer may move round the dial but often the pointer is fixed and the band of the dial revolves – as on a famous late c18 French clock in the Wallace Collection where a cupid's arrow serves as pointer and two bands numbered for minutes and hours move round the equator of a globe.

Balloon. A late c18 type of bracket clock vaguely resembling an early ascension balloon in form. It was very popular in England though it may have originated in France. The convex or flat dial is enamelled or silvered and the trunk is

Bracket clock: early c18 English, mechanism by George Graham (Private Collection)

Cartel clock, chased and gilt cast bronze, c.1740–50, mechanism signed 'Baltazar/Paris' (Kunstindustrimuseet, Copenhagen)

Lantern clock, English, by David Bouquet (d.1665) (Victoria & Albert Museum)

gracefully waisted and rests on a rectangular base with small bracket feet. It is often made of mahogany inlaid with exotic fruit woods in the Sheraton style.

Banjo. An American type of wall clock, invented by Simon Willard (1753–1848) who patented it in 1802. In form it somewhat resembles an inverted banjo. The shaft and pendulum door are often decorated with églomisé panels, views of Mt Vernon and Perry's victory on Lake Erie being popular subjects. Barometers were also made in a similar form, with the resonator downwards. The term is not contemporary for either clocks or barometers.

Bracket. A clock designed to stand on a bracket which may be attached to a wall. The clock case and bracket were made *en suite*.

Carriage. A small travelling clock with a brass-framed glass case which enables the works to be seen on all sides. It was supplied with a leather case which opens to show the face. Popular in France and England in the mid and late C19.

Cartel. A clock made to hang on a wall, so called from the *cartel* or point at the bottom of the case. It should not be confused with a BRACKET clock which must be supported on a bracket. The case is usually very elaborate, especially in the Rococo period when such clocks were very

Longcase clock with marquetry case, English, c.1680 (Victoria & Albert Museum)

Pedestal clock, French, late c18 (Louvre)

popular in France, some of the finest being made by C. CRESSENT.

Lantern. An English type of bracket clock, in form a cube surmounted by a hemispherical dome. It was first made in the early C17 and remained popular into the C18. It was widely imitated from the mid C19 onwards.

Longcase. The correct name for the Grandfather or Grandmother clock. The tall narrow case was devised *c.*1670 to house the long pendulum and weights of the anchor escapement clock invented by the English clock-maker William Clement. It has remained popular ever since. Cases have been decorated according to prevailing styles. In the C18 the dial was normally flanked by columns and crowned by a pediment, the lower part being left fairly plain.

Pedestal clock. One made to stand on a pedestal designed *en suite* with its case. Not to be confused with a LONGCASE clock which it sometimes resembles in appearance.

Skeleton clock. A clock with all its mechanism visible, usually protected by a glass dome. C19 interest in science made such clocks very popular and many were shown at the Great Exhibition.

Cloisonné, *see* ENAMEL.

Close stool Movable C15 latrine, usually a box containing a pot and often richly upholstered with velvet and silk, studded with gilt nails. In the C18 it was often veneered, but was rapidly superseded by the pot-cupboard or night-table. *Illustrated next column.*

Closter Veilsdorf, *see* KLOSTER VEILSDORF.

Club foot Popular C18 terminal in the form of a club: used with either a cabriole or straight leg until the late C18.

Cluny lace Various generally rather coarse types of LACE made in the late C19 mainly at Mirecourt in Lorraine and Le Puy. It is called Cluny lace because some of the patterns were derived from examples of old lace in the Musée de Cluny in Paris.

Lit: B. Palliser, *History of Lace,* rev. M. Jourdain & A. Dryden, London 1902; L. W. van der Meulon-Nulle, *Lace,* London 1963.

Close stool, made in Toulouse, C.1750 *(Musée P. Dupuy, Toulouse)*

Coalport and Coalbrookdale porcelain factory Founded by **John Rose** (d.1841) who after training at the Caughley (Shropshire) porcelain factory set up a pottery nearby at Jackfield in 1780, moved it to Coalport shortly afterwards, bought the Caughley factory in 1799 and the Nantgarw factory in 1819, securing the services of W. BILLINGSLEY as painter. It began by specializing in table-wares, often decorated from 1801 with the 'Indian Tree Pattern', an attractive design, more chinoiserie than Indian, which was first used here. In 1820 a leadless feldspathic glaze was introduced. From the 1830s wares were decorated with faint transfer-printed outlines subsequently coloured by hand: this process enabled the factory to keep pace with growing demands and yet retain some of the qualities of hand-decorated porcelain. Mid-C19 products included table services finely painted with flowers or fruit on coloured grounds, reproductions of MEISSEN and SÈVRES wares (sometimes correspondingly marked) and very elaborate long vases encrusted with applied flowers. From *c.*1890 an extensive export business was carried on with the U.S.A. and Canada. Thomas John BOTT was art director 1890–1932. After changing hands and premises the factory survives at Stoke-on-

Coalport porcelain teapot, c.*1820 (Victoria & Albert Museum)*

Coalbrookdale epergne, sugar tureen and lotus vase, exhibited at the Crystal Palace 1851

Trent and continues to produce good porcelain. (For factory marks *see* p. 882.)

Lit: Geoffrey A. Godden, *Coalport & Coalbrookdale Porcelains,* London 1970; B. H. Tripp, *Grand Alliance. A Chapter of Industrial History,* London 1951.

Coaster A tray or trolley for circulating food or bottles round a dining-table. Usually a low, round decanter stand of silver with a wooden base with baize to slide on, but it sometimes took other, more fanciful, forms, e.g. a wooden cannon on wheels. Also called a slide or beer-wagon.

Cobb, John (*c.*1710–1778). The partner of William VILE with whom he ran one of the most successful firms of furniture-makers and upholsterers in mid-C18 London. Until Vile retired in 1765, he appears to have been in charge of the upholstery side of the business: they undertook work of interior decorating as well as supplying furniture. He was employed as an upholsterer by George III. But his firm continued to produce furniture, notably some outstandingly fine mar-

J. Cobb: commode, 1771 (Corsham Court, Wilts.)

quetry pieces with Adamesque decorations supplied in 1772 to Corsham Court and still there. He is said to have popularized a type of artists' and architects' drawing table with a movable top. A contemporary records that he was 'perhaps one of the proudest men in England; and always appeared in full dress of the most superb and costly kind, in which state he would strut through his workshops, giving orders to his men'. An entrepreneur rather than a craftsman, he made a considerable fortune.

Lit: R. Edwards & M. Jourdain, *Georgian Cabinet Makers*, London 1955; A. Coleridge, *Chippendale Furniture*, London 1968.

Cobden-Sanderson, Thomas James (1840–1922). Leading English bookbinder and printer. Began as a barrister but under the influence of William MORRIS he forsook the law for handicrafts and opened a bindery in 1884, specializing in limp parchment covers discreetly decorated in gold with Art Nouveauish patterns. He continued to make fine bindings after 1900 for the Doves Press which he founded with Sir Emery Walker.

Lit: F. B. Adams (ed.), *Bookbindings by T. J. Cobden-Sanderson*, Exh. Cat., New York 1968.

Cochius, P. M., *see* LEERDAM GLASSHOUSE.

Cockbead or **Cock beading** A small moulding of semi-circular section applied to the edges of drawer-fronts on mid- and late-C18 English furniture.

Cockpit Hill pottery A factory at Derby owned by **W. Butts, John Heath** and others 1751–79, making wares of Staffordshire type including cream-coloured earthenware which is rarely marked. The DERBY PORCELAIN FACTORY was started in 1756 by John HEATH (in association with William DUESBURY and André Planché) and it seems likely that the early Derby figures of *c.*1750 were made by Planché at the Cockpit Hill factory. Thomas RADFORD worked there.

Cock's head hinge An H hinge with cock's head terminations.

Coconut cup A type of decorative standing cup, the body being a coconut shell, richly mounted in silver and supported on a silver stem with a flared foot and base. It was popular in the C15 and C16 in Europe.

Coconut cup, probably English, C16 (Victoria & Albert Museum)

Codman, William, *see* GORHAM COMPANY.

Codnor Park pottery A Derbyshire factory making stoneware bottles 1821–32. In 1833 it was acquired by BOURNE & SON who ran it until 1861 when the workmen were transferred to DENBY.

Lit: G. A. Godden (ed.), *Jewitt's, The Ceramic Art of Great Britain*, London 1972.

Coffee, William John (*fl.*1790–1846). An English sculptor who began his career in Coade's artificial stone factory in London, then went *c.*1792 to the DERBY PORCELAIN FACTORY where he modelled a number of figures. He appears to have been connected with other porcelain factories before returning to work as a sculptor in terracotta. In 1816 he emigrated to the U.S.

Lit: G. A. Godden, *Jewitt's, The Ceramic Art of Britain*, London 1972.

Coffer A chest or strong-box, especially one covered with leather or other material and banded with metal. A trussing coffer is fitted with rings or handles to facilitate transport.

Cogswell, John (*fl.*1769–82). Leading American furniture-maker working in Boston and notable for his bombé pieces with finely carved detail in the American Chippendale style, similar to the best Philadelphia furniture of the period by AFFLECK or RANDOLPH.

Lit: Joseph Downs, *American Furniture: Queen Anne and Chippendale Periods in the Henry Francis Du Pont Winterthur Museum*, New York 1952.

Coiffeuse French term for a dressing table, *see* TOILETTE.

Coin glass A drinking glass with a coin of money in a knop forming part of the stem. The earliest recorded examples date from the early C18. The glass is not, of course, necessarily as old as the coin embedded in it.

Cold colours or **Cold painting** A form of ceramic or glass decoration by means of unfired colours, usually oil colours or lacquer colours. Very few examples survive since 'cold' colours quickly wear off due to use and cleaning, etc. But some Meissen red stoneware appears to have been 'cold' painted by Martin SCHNELL with lacquer colours and some early BOW PORCELAIN may have been decorated with oil colours.

Cold stamping A decorative technique used in leather work, especially bookbinding. The design is made by stamping, by hand, small metal dies on the dampened leather. It was, with CUIR CISELÉ, the earliest decorative technique used in European bookbinding. The introduction of PANEL STAMPS *c.*1400 led to its being superseded by the much less laborious technique of STAMPED BINDINGS. Both techniques were executed in 'blind', i.e. without gilding.

Cold-working In metalwork, objects hammered out without heating.

Cole, Sir Henry (1808–82). English industrial designer and writer on the decorative arts. Founded 'Summerly's Art Manufactures' (1847–50) to 'promote public taste' by designing himself and commissioning painters and sculptors (notably John Linnell, Richard Redgrave and John Bell) to design household objects, especially pottery, for the larger manufacturers. The products are self-consciously 'artistic' and generally fussy. But this was the first of many attempts to improve industrial design. He was much

Minton porcelain vase designed by R. Redgrave for Summerly's Art Manufactures, 1847 (Victoria & Albert Museum)

involved with (and disillusioned by) the Great Exhibition of 1851 and became the first director of the South Kensington (now Victoria & Albert) Museum.

Lit: A. Bøe, *From Gothic Revival to Functional Form*, Oslo–Oxford 1957; N. Pevsner, *Some Architectural Writers of the Nineteenth Century*, Oxford 1972.

Silver christening cup, designed by R. Redgrave for Summerly's Art Manufactures, 1847 (Victoria & Albert Museum)

Coleman, William Stephen (*c.*1830–1904). English painter and ceramic decorator. He was the son of a doctor and began as a medical student but took up painting in both oils and watercolours. In the later 1860s he turned to the decoration of ceramics working first for the COPELAND factory then for MINTON. He designed for the latter a very attractive table service, transfer-printed in colour with botanically accurate specimens of flora. He also executed 'unique' plaques and plates painted with figure scenes rather in the manner of W. CRANE. In 1871 he was put in charge of the short-lived 'Art-Pottery Studio' which Minton's set up in Kensington to exploit the vogue for amateur ceramic painting.

Colenbrander, Theodorus (1841–1930). Dutch pottery and textile designer. He began as an architect but turned to pottery in the 1880s, evolving a new decorative style with abstract plant-like forms painted in very bold colours, derived from Javanese Batik wares. He was director of the Rozenburg pottery from 1885 onwards and in 1895 became director of the Amersfoot wallpaper and textile factory.

T. Colenbrander: earthenware vase designed for the Rozenburg Pottery, The Hague, 1885 (Hessisches Landesmuseum, Darmstadt)

Lit: R. Schmutzler, *Art Nouveau*, London 1964.

Collcutt, Thomas Edward (1840–1924). He was best known as an architect (Imperial Institute,

London, 1887–93, now destroyed), but was also an influential furniture designer. He began with very simple Neo-Gothic pieces in oak, then developed a Neo-Renaissance manner and, simultaneously, the very personal style displayed in his once-famous ebonized cabinet made by Collinson & Lock and exhibited at the South Kensington International Exhibition of 1871. This piece typifies his style, with its painted and carved panels, bevelled glass and turned supports, with a profusion of shelves and other divisions. He was responsible, anonymously, for most of the designs in Collinson & Lock's 1872 catalogue and supplied designs to them for many years as well as to Gillow's and to Maple & Co. The sturdy dining-chair with turned legs and stretcher and turned balusters at the back which he designed for Collinson & Lock became an almost standard pattern in late Victorian England.

Lit: Elisabeth Aslin, *19th Century English Furniture*, London 1962.

Collesano potteries, *see* SICILIAN POTTERIES.

Collinot, E. (*fl.*1859–62). French potter and designer, published with Adalbert de Beaumont a set of 217 engravings entitled *Recueil de dessins pour l'Art et l'Industrie*, Paris 1859. In 1862 he established at Boulogne-sur-Seine a pottery specializing in wares of Persian or Isnik inspiration. One of his assistants here was Léon Parvillé (d.1885), an imitator of Eastern styles and techniques of enamel painting.

Cologne potteries Began to operate in the early Middle Ages making hard-fired unglazed earthenware. They achieved artistic distinction *c.*1520–1600 when they produced handsome salt-glazed stonewares of a grey body washed with ferruginous clay to give a speckled surface of browns and dull yellows (aptly called tiger-wares in England where they were prized and often mounted in silver). BELLARMINES were a speciality, generally decorated only with a small panel (often a coat of arms) beneath the bearded head. Other wares include large globular jugs decorated in applied relief with Gothic traceries of oak leaves or vine leaves, and much rarer jugs in the form of owls or dogs. As a result of a dispute between the potters and the Cologne city authorities, the kilns

Cologne stoneware jug, c.1525–50 *(Victoria & Albert Museum)*

appear to have been transferred at the end of the C16 to Frechen where bellarmines continued to be made even into the C18. Of the several faience factories at Cologne only one is of interest: that established by E. Cremer in the last years of the C18 and producing tankards and dishes painted in high-temperature colours usually with religious subjects.

Lit: O. von Falke, *Das rheinische Steinzeug*, Berlin 1908; G. Reineking von Bock, *Kunstgewerbemuseum der Stadt Köln, Steinzeug*, Cologne 1971.

Colombini, Gino (b.1915). Italian designer specializing in mass-produced domestic equipment in PLASTIC. He made his name internationally in 1948 at the Low Cost Furniture Competition, New York, for storage units designed with Franco ALBINI. The following year he became head of the technical office of Kartell Samco, Milan, which began by manufacturing motor-car accessories in plastics and then, from 1951 onwards, household equipment in plastics, especially polyethylene and polystirol. These products are designed with great clarity and feeling for the material and manufacturing process, resulting in a clean, cool look similar to that of BRAUN products though softer and more organic-looking.

Colombo, Joe Cesare (1930–71). Italian architect-designer working in Milan. In the early 1950s he helped found the *avant-garde* group *Art Concret* and later took part in numerous exhibitions both in Europe and the U.S.A. After 1962 he was much concerned both with interior and product design; the two came together in the all-plastic kitchen, which won a silver medal at the 1966 Triennale di Milano. He was best known for his furniture, which is extremely versatile and dynamic. Interchangeable and moving parts allow his pieces to

J. Colombo: chair of plastic with interchangeable legs, 1965 (Victoria & Albert Museum)

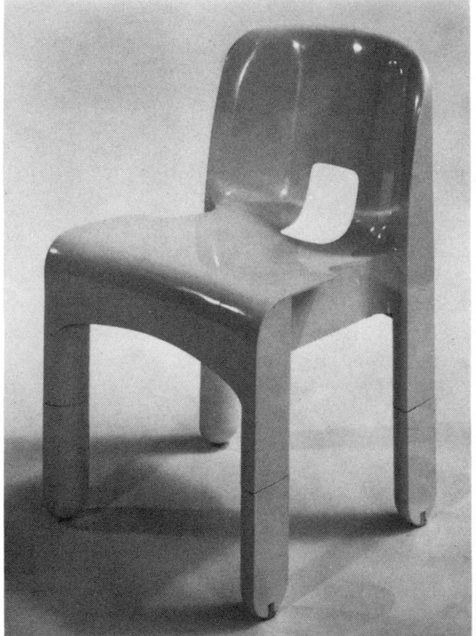

be moved easily about the room. His plastic armchair, made by Kartell of Milan, is in the collection of the Museum of Modern Art, New York.

Colonna, Edward (1862–after 1936). Born near Cologne, trained as an architect in Brussels, he emigrated to the U.S.A. in 1882. He worked with TIFFANY and the Associated Artists in New York and then went West, settling at Dayton, Ohio, where he designed parlour- and sleeping-cars for the Barney & Smith Manufacturing Co. He published in 1887 at Dayton an *Essay on Broom-Corn* which was far in advance of its time and foreshadowed the Art Nouveau of Horta. Unfortunately all but two copies were destroyed in a warehouse fire. In 1898–1903 he designed jewellery, furniture and household accessories for Bing's *L'Art Nouveau* in Paris. He returned to the U.S. in 1905.

Lit: M. Eidelberg, 'Edward Colonna's Essay on Broom-Corn' in *The Connoisseur*, 1971, vol. 176, no. 708.

Columbine cup Elaborate German type of silver cup of complicated form sometimes made by

Columbine cup, silver, Nuremberg, mid c16 (Victoria & Albert Museum)

candidates for admission to goldsmiths' guilds. The form probably became defined in C16 Nuremberg.

Comans, Marc de, *see* PARIS TAPESTRY FACTORIES.

Combe, Joseph, *see* LYONS POTTERIES.

Combed ware Pottery covered with slips of two or more colours combed or brushed into feathered patterns like those of the marbled papers used by bookbinders. This method of decoration has been widely used from an early period, especially on peasant pottery.

Commode, with lacquer panels, by Demoulin and Caffiéri (Musée de Tours)

Commedia dell'Arte figures Characters or 'masks', as they were called, from the Italian *Commedia dell'Arte* – Pantaloon, Harlequin, Scapino, Pulchinello (or Punch) and Capitano Zerbino, etc. They appeared in painted decorations since the C16 and became particularly popular in the C18 throughout Europe, being painted on Venetian glass, modelled in blown glass and incorporated in marquetry decoration on furniture, as well as in pottery and porcelain for which they provided the models for innumerable statuettes, sometimes forming whole series, and also groups. They appear in BÖTTGER's red stoneware *c.*1715 and in 1736 KÄNDLER began his great series for Meissen. These provided prototypes which were widely used – at Mennecy, Chelsea, Bow and Longton Hall, at Höchst, Fulda, Kloster-Veilsdorf, and at Capodimonte and Doccia. BUSTELLI, at Nymphenburg, made another great series though this seems to have seldom been directly imitated.

Lit: H. Tait, 'The Commedia dell'Arte in Glass and Porcelain' in *Apollo*, October 1963.

Commode French name for a CHEST OF DRAWERS, used in English for one of French pattern and especially for one of decorative appearance rather than a utilitarian bedroom piece. It was so called because it was a more convenient piece of storage furniture than the chest. As a piece of decorative furniture it became more popular than the tall cabinet as its height corresponded with the dado and thus it did not interfere with the decoration

Commode à encoignures, *by J. F. Leleu, 1772 (Wallace Collection, London)*

of tapestried, mirrored or painted walls above. It may have been invented by the French royal *ébéniste* Guillemard or by BOULLE who played an important part in its development. The earliest type, which appeared *c.*1700, stood on high legs and had only two drawers. A type with short legs and three or more tiers of drawers was made during the Régence and soon called a *commode à la Régence*. The divisions between the drawers which determined the design of these early types were abolished during the Louis XVI period when the front was treated as a single decorative unit and the drawers were supported on runners inside the case rather than on shelves. Names were provided for various types: *commode en console* with rather long legs and only one shallow drawer, intended to stand beneath a looking-glass; *commode à encoignures* with shelves or cupboards on either side of a single tier of drawers; *commode à vantaux* with doors in front of the drawers; *demi-commode* small and narrow and intended to stand under a looking-glass; *petite commode*, small late C18 type, with several tiers of drawers usually on tall legs. *See also* CHIFFONNIÈRE. In England commodes are classified according to the form of their front, e.g. BOMBÉ, BREAK-FRONT, SERPENTINE. From the mid C19 the term was also used in England for a CLOSE STOOL.

Commode à vantaux, *by G. Benneman, c.1786 (Château de Fontainebleau)*

Communion cup The vessel which took the place of the CHALICE in the Anglican Communion

Service. Intended for congregational communion, it is generally larger than the Roman Catholic chalice from which only the priest drinks, and in the early days of the Reformation several chalices were sometimes melted down to make a single communion cup. The standard form evolved in the late 1560s has a beaker-shaped bowl, a knopped stem and a circular foot: it usually has a cover which can be removed and used as a paten. This remained the basic pattern (though sometimes the bowl was more bell-shaped) until the C19 when the chalice form, which had been briefly brought back under Archbishop Laud in the C17, became more usual in all but the most severely evangelical Anglican churches.

Lit: C. Oman, *English Church Plate 597–1830*, London 1957.

Compagnie des Arts Français, *see* SÜE, Louis.

Compagnie des Indes, *see* CHINESE EXPORT PORCELAIN.

Compendiario style or **Stile compendiario** The original name for a style of decorating BIANCO DI FAENZA wares with boldly sketched figures in blue and orange-yellow. It originated at the FAENZA POTTERIES in the mid C16, was subsequently taken up elsewhere and remained popular until the early C18. The figures usually occupy only a small part of the surface of the piece and thus serve to set off and enhance the beauty of the thick white tin glaze.

Lit: G. Liverani in *The Connoisseur*, CXL (1957), pp. 160–63.

Comport A glass stand for SYLLABUB GLASSES. It usually had a round top on a heavy stem mounted on a flared foot. In C18 England it was of cut flint-glass, in the C19 of pressed glass, sometimes silvered.

Composition or **Compo** A mixture of whiting, resin and size used from the C18 onwards for moulded ornaments: usually fixed to furniture by glue or panel pins.

Compound twist stem The stem of a drinking glass with two AIR TWISTS or enamel twists (or one of each) encircling one another, popular in the second half of the C18.

Coney, John (1655–1722). He was the most prolific early New England silversmith and was almost certainly apprenticed to either John HALL or Jeremiah DUMMER whose sister-in-law he was eventually to marry. In 1676 a covered cup by him was presented to the church of the First Parish in Concord, where it may still be seen. Many fine pieces of Coney's silver survive, mostly drinking vessels and usually of a solid, squat

J. Coney: silver sugar box (Currier Gallery of Art, Manchester, New Hampshire)

tankard type. His finest surviving work is the Stoughton Cup given to Harvard University in 1701. Stylistically his work derives from England, e.g. the sugar or sweetmeat boxes by him and now in the Boston Museum and the Currier Gallery of Art, Manchester, New Hampshire, which are very close to one made in London in 1676. Like his contemporaries in the provincial cities in England, Coney copied the silver made in the capital. He was also skilled and well known as an engraver and probably engraved the plates from which the first American bank-notes were printed. He certainly engraved those issued in 1702. Among his apprentices was the father of Paul REVERE.

Lit: H. F. Clarke, *John Coney Silversmith*, Boston, Mass., 1932; H. J. Gourley III, *The New England Silversmith*, Exh. Cat., Providence, Rhode Island, 1965.

Confident or **Canapé à confident** French term applied to two different types of sofa: (1) with the ends curving forward so that two people sitting on it would be half-facing each other; or (2) with small triangular seats outside the arms at either end. Both originated in mid-C18 France, but HEPPLEWHITE illustrated the latter type in 1788, terming it a *confidante* and saying that it could be made so that the seats at either end were detachable.

Connecticut chest C17 American type of oak chest, also called a 'Sunflower' or 'Hartford' chest, probably developed by N. DISBROWE. The front is decorated with panels carved with sunflowers and the stiles with applied bosses and spindles painted black.

Conrade, Courrade or **Corrado, Domenico, Baptiste** and **Augustin,** *see* NEVERS POTTERIES.

Console (1) A carved ornamental bracket with a compound curve and usually of greater height than projection.

(2) A side-table with a marble top supported on a carved substructure of two or more legs of a bracket of console form, usually linked by a stretcher. Such pieces of furniture were often placed beneath a wall mirror and supported a vase or piece of small sculpture.

Design for a console, by Hoppenhaupt

Constitution mirror Modern term for an American C18 type of mirror with a carved gilt eagle surmounting the frame.

Consular diptych Two small oblong panels of ivory hinged like the pages of a book and carved in low relief with portraits of a Roman Consul on the outside of the leaves (the inner sides being hollowed out to receive a thin layer of wax on which a message could be written with a stylus). A law of 384 A.D. granted the Consuls in office the exclusive privilege of sending 'their names and portraits, engraved on gilt tablets of ivory, as presents to the provinces, the cities, the magistrates, the senate and the people'. The practice of sending them continued until 541 when the anachronistic office of Consul was merged in that of the Emperor. Some fifty examples survive, the earliest being that of Probus (406) in the museum at Aosta. They vary in size and richness according to the rank of their recipients. In style they range from late Roman to Byzantine. The most elaborate have full-length portraits showing the consul seated on the curule chair, holding in his right hand the *mappa circensis* – the handkerchief thrown down as a signal for the games in the arena to begin – and, beneath his feet, a carving of some incident in the arena or a symbolical arrangement of money bags as a promise of generosity. Simpler examples are carved with medallion portrait heads or inscriptions in foliated frames. Closely associated with the Consular diptyches are the religious diptychs, carved on the outer sides of the two panels with religious scenes while the inner sides were inscribed with the names of the living and dead for whom prayers were said during the Eucharist.

Lit: R. Delbrueck, *Die Consulardiptychen . . . ,* Berlin 1926–9.

Cookworthy, William (1705–80). He was the first maker of true porcelain in England, probably learning the secret from Andrew DUCHÉ who reached England from the U.S.A. in 1743. Cookworthy (a Quaker apothecary of Plymouth) discovered *kaolin* on the estate of Lord Camelford in Cornwall in 1745 and soon afterwards an equivalent of *petuntse*; by 1765 his experiments had so far advanced that trial firings of true porcelain appear to have been made at Bristol. In 1768 he applied for a patent and opened the PLYMOUTH PORCELAIN FACTORY. This was transferred to Bristol in 1770 and in 1772 Cookworthy retired, assigning his patent to CHAMPION in 1774. It is also likely that the use of Cornish soapstone at Bristol and later at Worcester was due to Cookworthy. There is a Cookworthy Museum at Kingsbridge, Devon.

Lit: John Prideaux, *Relics of William Cookworthy*, London 1853; [G. Harrison], *Memoir of William Cookworthy, by his grandson*, London 1854; F. S. Mackenna, *Cookworthy's Plymouth and Bristol Porcelain*, Leigh on Sea 1946.

Cooper, James, & Sons, *see* DRESSER, Christopher.

Cope An ecclesiastical vestment worn by Christian priests in procession. It is a semi-circular piece of cloth, worn over the shoulders like a cloak.

Copeland porcelain factory, *see* SPODE POTTERY AND PORCELAIN FACTORY.

Copenhagen porcelain factory Several attempts were made to produce porcelain in or near Copenhagen in the mid c18: but it was not until 1774 that **Frantz Heinrich Müller** founded a private company (with the Queen as principal shareholder) which was granted a privilege in 1775, taken over by the King of Denmark in 1779 and styled the **Royal Danish Porcelain Factory.**

Copenhagen porcelain plate 'Flora Danica' service, 1790–1802 (Royal Collection, Rosenberg Castle, Copenhagen)

Its wares were of a fine hard paste: the earlier pieces owe much to the influence of SÈVRES and BERLIN. The outstanding c18 product is the famous *Flora Danica* table service of 1602 pieces, each painted with botanically accurate rendering of a Danish wild plant by J. C. Bayer after J. C. Oeder's book on Danish flora. It was begun in 1790 for the Empress Catherine II of Russia but not completed until 1802 (after her death) and is now in Rosenborg Castle, Copenhagen. A smaller service made in 1781 and decorated with birds is hardly inferior (Kunstindustrimuseet, Copenhagen). The factory produced much blue-and-white table-ware and specialized in very elegant breakfast services each of 10 or 14 pieces (for 2 or 4 people), sold in silk-lined mahogany boxes. Figures are mostly derivative from German and French factories but include a wholly original set of Norwegian Peasants and some attractive Miners. Very large vases, mirror frames and columns were made *c.*1800. Early in the c19 the factory fell on hard times but was revived by **Gustav Friedrich Hetsch,** director 1828–57. The best products of these years were miniature reproductions of sculpture by Thorvaldsen, issued from 1835. Another bad period followed: the concern was sold by the Crown in 1868 and

Copenhagen porcelain puppy, model by Erik Nielsen, 1900 (Karl H. Bröhan Collection, Berlin)

merged with the Alumina pottery in 1882 though without losing its original name. The great revival which now took place was largely due to the architect and painter **Arnold Krug** (1856–1931) who was appointed artistic director in 1885 and attracted several artists to the factory besides executing painted decorations and models. He specialized in underglaze painting in a palette of slightly smoky blues and greys which henceforth became typical of Copenhagen porcelain. Products of this period were decorated either with Japanese motifs or in an accomplished ART NOUVEAU style, but some vases of simple Chinese form rely for their effect on the abstract patterning provided by crystalline glazes. Numerous statuettes were also made, peasant figures after models by Christian Thomsen (1860–1921), birds, animals and fish, which were a speciality, from models by K. C. T. Kyhn (b.1880), T. C. Madsen (1880–1965) and others. Similar statuettes are still made, together with simple modern table-wares and the works of artist potters employed at the factory which is among the most notable in Europe today. Throughout its history it has used as a mark the motif of three waves in underglaze blue. *See also* BING & GRØNDAHL'S PORCELAIN FACTORY. (For factory mark *see* p. 882.)

Lit: E. Hannover, *Pottery and Porcelain*, London 1924, vol. iii; V. P. Christiensen, *Den Kgl. Danske Porselaine Fabrik*, Copenhagen 1938; *Porzellan-Kunst: Sammlung Karl H. Bröhan*, Exh. Cat., Berlin 1969.

Copenhagen potteries There were three notable C18 faience factories. The first, with premises in the Store Kogensgade, Copenhagen, was founded and granted privileges in 1722. It produced during its best period, under the direction of **Jöhann Ernst Pfau** (1727–49), good blue-and-white (rarely polychrome) wares similar to those of DELFT in texture as well as design. An exuberant version of the Rococo style was adopted for decorations after 1750 when **Christian Gierløf** took over the ownership and direction of the concern which was closed *c.*1770. In 1755 a faience factory was established at **Kastrup** on the island of Amager by the Danish Court Architect **Jacob Fortling** employing a painter from STRASBOURG. It began by making gaily coloured wares in the Strasbourg style, but after 1772 turned to the production of industrial stoneware and, later, English style cream-coloured earthenware, finally closing *c.*1814. A third factory was established at **Østerbro** in 1763, staffed by workmen from the other two factories, but was forced to close in 1769: its products are difficult to identify.

Lit: E. Hannover, *Pottery and Porcelain*, London 1924.

Coperta A clear lead-glaze applied to and fired with tin-enamel on Italian maiolica in the C16 and later. It was described by PICCOLPASSO. It corresponds to KWAART on Delft earthenware.

Copier, Andries Dirk (b.1901). Leading modern Netherlandish glass designer who joined the staff of the Royal Netherlands Glassworks at LEERDAM in 1917, soon became its artistic director and has been largely responsible for its development. His work, which is austere to the point of severity, is divided into two groups named Serica and Unica, the former comprising pieces executed in limited numbers, the latter far more expensive pieces each of which is unique. He has been concerned with the techniques of glass-making as well as design.

Lit: Glasschool Leerdam, Exh. Cat., Stedelijk Museum, Amsterdam, 1947.

Copland, H. (*fl.*1738–68). Georgian furniture-designer and engraver who played an important part in developing the ROCOCO style in England. He was practising it as early as 1738, published some very free Rococo designs in 1746 as *A New Book of Ornaments*, collaborated with M. LOCK on a volume with the same title in 1752 and provided plates for Robert Manwaring's *Chair Makers' Guide* in 1766.

Lit: P. Ward-Jackson, *English Furniture Designs*, London 1958.

Copper The first metal to be used by man, it occasionally occurs in a relatively pure state (like gold) in nuggets which can be worked without smelting. From an early stage, however, it was also extracted from ores by smelting. It does not cast satisfactorily in a pure state but sheets of it can be fashioned into vessels and other objects by cold hammering. Articles have been made from it since the Bronze Age. But as it is easily corroded vessels intended for the storage or preparation of food have normally been lined with another material, usually tin. In the more advanced cultures it has generally been regarded as an inferior metal suitable only for utilitarian wares. Most copper vessels are thus undecorated. But copper sheet coated with silver is the material from which SHEFFIELD PLATE is made. And copper was also used extensively as the ground for ENAMEL painting.

Copper is a component in the alloys from which the finer base metal wares are made: it is alloyed with tin to make BRONZE, with zinc to make BRASS, with lead, tin and other metals to make PEWTER and with nickel and zinc for the nickel-silver used for ELECTROPLATE. It may also be alloyed with GOLD. *See also* HERRENGRUND CUP and ISERLOHM BOXES.

Lit: L. Aitchison, *A History of Metals*, London 1960; G. Wills, *The Book of Copper and Brass*, Feltham 1969; H. H. Haedeke, *Metalwork*, London 1970.

Coptic style The Copts were Christian Egyptians who broke away from the Church after the Council of Chalcedon in 451 A.D. They established their own hierarchy in the c6 and in the c7 sided with the Arabs against the Byzantine Emperor, thus preserving their independent existence both as a church and people, which has survived until the present day. They early developed an artistic style which, though derived initially from Hellenistic and Byzantine art, and later influenced by Islamic art, is nevertheless unique and individual. A large number of examples survive from very early times, including buildings, illuminated manuscripts, bookbindings, bronzes, glass, pottery, etc. In the decorative arts the most interesting are the textiles, woven in linen, silk or wool with embroidered or painted decorations, and ranging in size from large tapestries (e.g. wool tapestry of c5–c6 in Dumbarton Oaks Collection, Washington, D.C.) to small rectangular panels of linen or silk, apparently made for application to vestments or secular garments (at elbows and knees). Surviving examples can rarely be dated precisely though the presence of Pagan figures derived from Hellenistic art probably indicates an early date. The most notable textiles appear to have been made in the c5 and c6. They exploit a bold simplicity and limited range of colours in emphatic designs incorporating human and animal figures.

Coptic textile, Vulcan, Mars and Venus, c3–c4 (Victoria & Albert Museum)

Lit: P. de Bourget, *Coptic Art*, London 1971.

Coquillage Carved Rococo ornament of shell form.

Corbel A bracket, projecting horizontally to support something above.

Cordial Glass A type of English drinking glass introduced *c.*1700. It is usually 6 to 8 inches high, with a small flute-shaped bowl tapering gently to form the stem and resting on a spreading foot. An alternative type has a small cup-shaped bowl on a moulded or plain stem on a spreading foot.

Cordonnet, *see* LACE.

Cordova leather or **Cordovan** An old English term for high quality LEATHER and especially for large panels of embossed leather, usually painted and gilded, for hanging on walls as an alternative to tapestry. Leather had the advantage of being more draught-proof and damp-proof than tapestry and was also little affected by insects. Such hangings were made in Cordova from the c9 but from the c14 the main centre of production was in the Low Countries and they were also made elsewhere until the fashion for them declined in the early C18 with the rise in popularity of wallpapers and chintz. In Spain, however, such hangings which are made from sheepskin were called *guadameci* (from the Libyan town of Ghâdames) and the term *córdobane* was reserved for tanned goatskin. What was popularly called Cordova leather in England was generally Dutch calfskin. (The English word 'cordwainer' also derives from the name Cordova.)

Lit: J. W. Waterer, *Spanish Leather*, London 1971.

Corinthian order, *see* ORDERS.

Cork glasshouses Three of the best Irish glass factories were established at Cork. **The Cork Glasshouse,** 1793–1818, began by specializing in blown-moulded wares and later produced fine hand-cut vessels, those made after 1812 often bearing an impressed mark: Cork Glass Co. **The Cork Terrace Glasshouse,** 1819–41, produced fine cut-glass table-wares and lustres. The most famous, **The Waterloo Glasshouse Company,** 1815–35, specialized in large cut-glass table services, many of which were supplied to military messes. It also made blown-moulded decanters, jugs, etc., and such curiosities as glass trumpets.

Lit: Phelps Warren, *Irish Glass*, London 1970.

Cornelius & Co. Metalwork factory in Philadelphia, founded in 1812 by Christian Cornelius who began as a silversmith but soon turned to cast bronze work and specialized in making Argand lamps (a type of oil lamp) of which he became the main producer in the U.S. by 1845. The factory remained active until the end of the C19. It also made cast bronze stands for candelabra, mounts for porcelain, etc., often in the Neo-Rococo style.

Lit: 19th Century America: Furniture and Other Decorative Arts, Exh. Cat., Metropolitan Museum, New York 1970.

Cornice The top projecting member of an ENTABLATURE or, more loosely, any projecting ornamental moulding.

Corning Glass Works One of the largest glasshouses in the world, founded in 1851 at Somerville, Massachusetts, and moved to Corning, New York, in 1868. It began by specializing in glass for industrial and scientific use, providing the first electric light bulbs for Thomas A. Edison. But it also produced (and continues to make) household wares, notably from 1908 wares in heat-resistant glass later called PYREX. In 1918 it absorbed the STEUBEN GLASS WORKS whose manager F. CARDER became art director of the whole concern. In 1933 under the direction of a French-trained American sculptor Sidney Waugh (1904–63) a department was established for the production of pieces of engraved crystal glass called 'Steuben Glass'. The Corning Corporation supports a museum exclusively devoted to ancient and modern glass, at Corning, N.Y.

Coromandel lacquer A type of lacquer with incised decorations, originally very brightly coloured though now usually faded, made in central and northern China from the C17 onwards, mainly for export to Europe. The name is derived from the English East India Company's trading posts on the Coromandel coast of India. The most impressive examples are large screens made from the late C17 to the early C18, composed of up to a dozen tall panels decorated with lush flowery landscapes. (Much smaller screens, more sparsely decorated with birds and flowers, were made for the Chinese home market.) The panels of such screens were also used occasionally in Europe to line whole rooms in the early C18 (e.g. Schloss Eremitage, Bayreuth). Smaller panels were used to decorate cabinets, looking-glass frames, etc. English imitations, called BANTAM WORK, were never very successful. *Illustrated opposite.*

Lit: M. Jourdain and R. S. Jenyns, *Chinese Export Art*, London 1950.

Coromandel wood, *see* EBONY.

Corona A form of hanging light consisting of one or more hoops, usually of metal, to which oil lamps or nozzles for candles are attached.

Costrel A bottle with one or more ears or handles through which a cord may be passed so that it can be suspended from the waist of a traveller, especially a pilgrim (as mentioned by Chaucer).

Cotterill, Edmund, *see* GARRARD, Robert.

Coromandel lacquer screen, c18 (Victoria & Albert Museum)

Cotton A fabric made from the fibres which clothe the seeds of the cotton plant (Gossypium). It is of fine texture, reasonably durable and provides an excellent basis for printed or painted decorations. Cotton fibres have been spun into threads and woven into textiles since very early times, probably *c.*3000 B.C. in India where cotton was cultivated by *c.*1000 B.C. Cotton wrappings found in Peru show that it was in use there by *c.*2000 B.C. It was not, however, grown in the Mediterranean area until the C5 B.C. In Roman times a cotton industry was established on Malta, but Indian cotton was still preferred for its superior quality and whiteness. From the C2 A.D. a mixed linen and cotton fabric – FUSTIAN – was made in Egypt. Cotton was also grown in Syria whence much of the best quality was imported into Europe in the Middle Ages. But in the C8 its culture was introduced into Spain by the Moors and an important industry was established which spread by the C12 to Italy and France, by the C13 to Flanders, by the C14 to Germany and by the C15 to England. Northern weavers worked with imported cotton, preferring that of Syria and Egypt which was much superior in quality to any grown in S. Europe. But in the early C19 the U.S.A. became the major producer of cotton.

Painted cotton was imported into Europe from India in the C16 and in greater quantities in the C17, *see* CHINTZ. The first successful attempts to imitate these fabrics were made almost simultaneously in France, Holland and England in the 1670s and decorated by means of block-printing (see COTTON, BLOCK-PRINTED). Despite severe restrictions to protect the wool and silk industries

Block-printed cotton, English, second half of the C18 (Victoria & Albert Museum)

in England and France the industry prospered (in England it was illegal from 1720–74 to use pure cotton for dress or domestic purposes though a fabric with a linen warp and cotton weft was permitted). In the early 1750s a new process of decorating by means of copper-plates was invented and soon became very popular (*see* COTTON, PLATE-PRINTED). A third method of decoration by means of engraved rollers was developed *c.*1815 (*see* COTTON, ROLLER-PRINTED).

As a result of the development of mechanized processes of preparing and weaving the thread, Manchester became the main centre of the cotton industry early in the C19.

Lit: M. Dreger, *Künstlerische Entwicklung der Weberei und Stickerei*, Vienna 1904; H. Clouzot, *Painted and Printed Fabrics* (with notes on English and American cotton printing by F. Morris), New York 1927; G. Turnbull, *A History of the Calico-Printing Industry of Great Britain*, Altrincham 1951.

Cotton, block-printed A cotton fabric decorated by means of engraved wood blocks, similar to those used for printing woodcut book illustrations. The process originated in India and was introduced into Europe in the 1670s. At first colour schemes were limited to the black, reds, purples and browns obtainable from madder but by the 1750s indigo-blues and weld-yellows were also employed, sometimes on the block but often added later by brush. The first designs were free adaptations of the lush Indian floral patterns on imported wares, and exotic flower patterns have always remained popular for printed cotton. Naturalistic European flowers begin to make their appearance in the 1750s and were also destined to enjoy a long success, up to the present day. New dyes which became available in the late C18 increased the printers' palette and enabled them to compete successfully with the producers of plate-printed cottons. Among the best products are those of early-C19 English, especially Lancashire, factories – boldly designed, richly coloured and, when used for curtains or chair covers, giving an impression of snug comfort. But standards fell off drastically in the 1830s.

Lit: F. M. Montgomery, *Printed Textiles, English & American Cottons & Linens, 1700–1850. . .*, London 1970.

Cotton, plate-printed Cotton fabric decorated by means of engraved copper plates. This process was first used successfully in 1752 by Francis Nixon at the Drumcondra printworks near Dublin. It was introduced into England by 1756 and to France in the late 1770s by OBERKAMPF who set up a factory at Jouy which has given its name to all such wares – *toiles de Jouy*. The decorations are in monochrome – usually rich purple, red or sepia or a rich indigo-blue which was almost an English monopoly in the C18, on a white ground – though additional colours were very occasionally added by block-printing or by hand. Designs were obtained from a wide range of sources – flower and bird prints, chinoiseries after Jean PILLEMENT, pastoral scenes in the style of BOUCHER, and sometimes prints of contemporary events. The effect is cool, neat and distinctly feminine. The technique was outmoded by the invention of roller printing.

Lit: Victoria & Albert Museum: European Printed Textiles, London 1949; F. M. Montgomery, *Printed Textiles, English & American Cottons & Linens, 1700–1850, . . . ,* London 1970.

Cotton, roller-printed Cotton fabric decorated by means of engraved metal cylinders. The process was invented and patented in 1783 by a Scotsman, Thomas Bell, and used by factories in the Preston area, mainly for the production of cheap dress materials. An improved technique developed *c.*1810 soon began to affect the whole cotton-printing industry in England and to drive plate-printing out of use. The first designs are in monochrome and similar to plate-printed cottons in appearance, though they have a horizontal emphasis dictated by the rollers. But soon appreciation of the potentialities of the new process, especially the possibility of reproducing crisper and more delicate draughtsmanship, led to a new style which also affected the producers of block-printed cotton. Designs included Gothic, Chinoiserie and sporting scenes, occasional celebrations of the modern age in views of railway stations, etc., but the majority are floral. The development of numerous new dyes made possible the production of multi-coloured fabrics. Unfortunately the new colours began to go to the printers' heads by the 1830s when painful combinations of pink, violet, orange and green were much used. Matters were made still worse by the discovery of aniline dyestuffs in 1856. Harmony was restored in England by William MORRIS and the ARTS AND CRAFTS Movement

Plate-printed cotton, English, c.1770 (Victoria & Albert Museum)

Roller-printed cotton, English, 1824 (Victoria & Albert Museum)

and on the continent by practitioners of a much-needed ART NOUVEAU.

Lit: F. M. Montgomery, *Printed Textiles, English & American Cottons & Linens, 1700–1850, . . . ,* London 1970.

Couch, *see* CHAISE LONGUE.

Couched work Embroidery in which the thread is laid on the ground material and held down by stitching.

Counter Originally a small table or chest with the top marked for counting money, sometimes with a cupboard below, in use in England from the Middle Ages to the C16. The word was later applied to the large piece of furniture which the shopkeeper uses for the display of wares and as a barrier between him and his customers.

Counterchange pattern A pattern composed of interlocking parts of identical shape, distinguished from one another by differences of colour or texture.

Courant, *see* CHAIR, *siège courant.*

Court cupboard A fairly low cupboard (*court* meaning short) of a type made in late-C16 and C17 England and C17 America for the display of plate and as a service table. It was constructed in two stages above a base supported by balusters usually of the cup and cover column type at the front corners and plain posts at the back: sometimes a drawer was fitted between the two stages; if the upper stage is partly or wholly enclosed by doors it should be called a hall or parlour cupboard.

Court cupboard, oak, English, early C17 (Victoria & Albert Museum)

Court, Jean de (*fl.*1541–64). Painter of LIMOGES ENAMELS, he used unusually bright colours on a black ground for panels sometimes derived from prints by Etienne Delaune and other artists. Another artist of the same surname, presumably a relation, **Suzanne** (*fl.*1600) was among the last Limoges enamellers of importance: she decorated plates, caskets, ewers, etc. with Mannerist figure subjects in brilliant colours.

Lit: E. Rupin, *L'Oeuvre de Limoges,* Paris 1890; P. Verdier, *The Walters Art Gallery: Catalogue of the Painted Enamels of the Renaissance,* Baltimore 1967.

Courtauld, Augustus (*c.*1686–1751) and **Samuel** (1720–65). English silversmiths of French extraction. Augustus was apprenticed to the Huguenot silversmith S. PANTIN in 1701. His best known work – odd rather than beautiful – is the Sword-bearer's Salt in the Mansion House, London. His son Samuel was apprenticed to his father but set up on his own and made a wide range of domestic wares in a Rococo style. After Samuel's death the business was carried on by his widow **Louisa** – in partnership with **George Cowles** (1768–77) and then with her son **Samuel.** He closed the business in 1780 and emigrated to America. (For his mark *see* p. 893.)

Lit: J. F. Hayward, *The Courtauld Silver . . .,* New York 1975.

Courting mirror Primitive early C19 type of American mirror framed with strips of painted glass in metal mouldings. Their origin is unknown.

Courtois or **Courteys, Pierre** (*c.*1520–*c.*1586). Notable LIMOGES ENAMEL painter, probably a pupil of Pierre REYMOND and working in a similar style (e.g. plates in Musée de Cluny, Paris: retable in the Louvre). His son **Martial** and another relation **Jean Courtois** signed enamels derived in style from the School of Fontainebleau.

Lit: E. Rupin, *L'Oeuvre de Limoges*, Paris 1890; P. Verdier, *The Walters Art Gallery: Catalogue of the Painted Enamels of the Renaissance*, Baltimore 1967.

Cousinet, Henri-Nicolas (*fl.*1724–68). Leading Parisian Rococo silversmith: *maître* 1724. His masterpiece is the elaborate silver-gilt *Nécessaire* of Marie Leczinska (1729–30, Louvre) in which every object is delicately chased and engraved with flower and shell motifs and many are embellished with endearing dolphins emerging from clumps of bulrushes to serve as feet, handles and spouts. His brother **Ambroise-Nicolas** (*fl.*1745–58) was also a silversmith, responsible for a group of sixteen silver-gilt statuettes of lively couples from different countries of the world (Museu Nacional de Arte Antiga, Lisbon). (For his mark *see* p. 893.)

H.-N. Cousinet: silver chocolate pot (Louvre)

Lit: Y. Bottineau & O. Lefuel, *Les Grands Orfèrves*, Paris 1965.

Cow milk jug A small milk jug in the form of a cow whose tail serves as a handle and mouth as a spout; it is filled from a hole in the back. Sometimes made in silver from the mid C18, more usually in pottery or porcelain, Holland and England.

Cox, James (*fl.*1757–91). Leading English maker of AUTOMATA. In 1757 when he is first recorded he was already working in London where in 1772–5 he maintained an open room known as Cox's Museum. He was much employed by the East India Company which presented his works to oriental potentates – one, given to the Emperor of China in 1766, was a gem-encrusted golden chariot drawn along by a coolie and bearing a seated lady who fanned herself with one hand while holding in the other a fluttering singing bird. He also worked directly for the Chinese and Russian courts from the 1770s. His studio was large and his assistants were probably responsible for making the smaller and simpler objects. In 1781 his son, **John Henry Cox**, opened a workshop in Canton, importing watch mechanisms from Switzerland to animate the automata, but left before 1796.

Lit: C. Le Corbeiller in *Burlington Magazine*, CXII (1970), pp. 351–6.

Coxon, Jonathan, *see* LENNOX COMPANY.

Cozzi porcelain factory Founded in Venice by **Geminiano Cozzi** 1764 and granted a monopoly for making porcelain in the Venetian states 1765. Produced table-wares and vases of a hard greyish paste with a glistening glaze painted in bright, sometimes clashing, colours and thick gilding with sprightly Venetian carnival scenes as well as the usual C18 repertory of mythological, chinoiserie and floral designs. Some plates were decorated with copies of paintings by Veronese and later Venetian masters. Statuettes include COMMEDIA DELL'ARTE actors, grotesque pagods, dwarfs, an allegory of the Venetian Republic (repeated many times) and, from the 1780s, miniature copies of antique busts. Closed down 1812.

Lit: A. Lane, *Italian Porcelain*, London 1954.

Crabstock Handles and spouts of ceramic teapots and other vessels were made in the form of crab-stock, i.e. the knotted, gnarled branches of a young crab-apple tree. They are found mainly on English wares (notably on those produced by the Staffordshire, Leeds, Liverpool and Derby potteries) but also sometimes elsewhere, such as Vincennes-Sèvres cream jugs.

Crace, John C. (1754–1819). He was the founder of one of the most important firms of c19 London furniture-makers and interior decorators. In 1788 he began to work for the Prince of Wales at the Brighton Pavilion on which he was to be employed intermittently for the rest of his life. He supplied much Chinese furniture, porcelain, and such objects as banners and model junks, between 1802 and 1804, but it was his son **Frederick** (1779–1859) who played a leading part in the interior decoration of the Royal Pavilion between 1815 and 1822, designing and executing, with a large staff of assistants, the exotic decorations of the main rooms for which he received nearly £31,000. (Many of the designs are now in the Cooper-Hewitt Museum, New York.) Under Frederick's son, **John Gregory Crace**, the firm became notable for its Gothic style furniture. From 1843 he worked in close collaboration with A. W. N. PUGIN, producing furniture, textiles and wallpapers to Pugin's designs for various private houses, for the Houses of Parliament and, in 1851, for the Medieval Court at the Great Exhibition. Egyptian style furniture designed by W. Holman Hunt was also made. The head of the firm in the next generation was **John Diblee Crace** (b.1838). He began by designing furniture in Pugin's Gothic manner but specialized in decorations in the Italian Renaissance style, with an occasional excursion into the Pompeiian. At the very end of the century the firm executed restorations and redecorations at the Brighton Pavilion.

Lit: C. Musgrave, *Royal Pavilion*, London 1959; P. Stanton, *Pugin*, London 1971.

J. G. Crace: wardrobe designed by Pugin and exhibited at the 1851 Exhibition (Victoria & Albert Museum)

Crackle, *see* CRAZING.

Crailsheim pottery Founded *c.*1715 by **Georg Veit Weiss** and run by his son and grandson and the latter's widow until *c.*1810. Wares included tankards decorated in both high-temperature and enamel colours with stag-hunting and boar-hunting scenes, coats-of-arms, flowers, etc. A yolk-of-egg yellow is distinctive. No regular mark was used but examples inscribed with the name of the factory survive, e.g. in Würzburg Museum.
Lit: H. Gretsch, *Die Fayencefabrik in Crailsheim*, Stuttgart 1928; K. Hüseler, *Deutsche Fayencen* I, Stuttgart 1956.

Crane, Walter (1845–1915). English painter, designer and book illustrator, a follower of William MORRIS and the main propagandist of the ARTS AND CRAFTS MOVEMENT. He was best as a designer of textiles and wallpapers, especially those intended for nurseries, in a pale-coloured rather wispy version of the Morris style, tinged with enough ART NOUVEAU influence to win him European renown. He also designed pottery.
Lit: W. Crane, *An Artist's Reminiscences*, London 1907; E. Aslin, *The Aesthetic Movement*, London 1969.

Crapaud French term (literally: toad) for a mid-C19 type of heavily upholstered low armchair.

Craquelure, *see* CRAZING.

Crazing, also termed 'crackle' or 'craquelure'. The crackling of the glaze on ceramics as a result of differences in expansion and contraction of the body and glaze in firing. It was at first an accidental defect but was soon turned to decorative effect in China and it is difficult to determine whether its appearance in early SUNG period wares was intentional. By the late Sung period it was clearly intentional, being both contrived and controlled. And from the later C19 the decorative effects attained by the Chinese with crazing were being imitated by Western (especially studio) potters.

Cream-coloured earthenware or **cream ware.** A type of hard lead-glazed pottery with a cream-coloured body containing flint. The process of manufacture was not so much an invention as a gradual development of other techniques, especially that of T. ASTBURY who had made use of ground flint (silica) in the body. It was first made in STAFFORDSHIRE by **Enoch Booth** of Tunstall, but an improved type was made in 1765 by WEDGWOOD who called it 'Queen's ware' in honour of Queen Charlotte. It was durable, relatively cheap to produce, of light weight, as thin as porcelain, could be used for openwork decorations, and provided an excellent basis for TRANSFER PRINTING or painted decorations. It was soon copied at other English potteries (notably LEEDS) and much was exported to the Continent where further imitations were made in nearly every country, driving TIN-GLAZED EARTHENWARE factories out of business and threatening the porcelain factories. A Wedgwood potter John Bartlam established a factory for making the ware in S. Carolina in 1770 and it was subsequently produced by many other N. American potteries. A porcellaneous version is called PEARL WARE.
Lit: D. C. Towner, *English Cream-Coloured Earthenware*, London 1957.

Credence Obsolete term for a sideboard or side-table: it is now used only for the small table or shelf near the altar in a church, used for the eucharistic elements before consecration.

Credenza Italian term for a sideboard or serving-table as well as a CREDENCE.

Creepers A pair of simple fire-dogs intended for use and placed behind or between more elaborate ANDIRONS intended for decoration.

Creil pottery The first French factory to produce printed earthenware in imitation of and to compete with SPODE and other English factories that were flooding the Continent with inexpensive table-wares in the early C19. It was founded in 1795 at Creil (Oise) by **Saint-Cricq-Cazaux** who went into partnership with an Englishman, **Bagnall,** in 1803. Success was immediate. The wares were white or yellow, printed in black, sepia or reddish brown with a wide variety of landscapes, views of buildings, hunting scenes (often English) and topical scenes (portraits of the Bonaparte family under the Empire). Another factory which had been making cream-coloured earthenware at Montereau was united with Creil

1818–25 and from 1840 until closure in 1895. Late C19 wares are often decorated with satirical prints. The name Creil is popularly used for all French earthenware of this type though much was made elsewhere, notably in two potteries at Sèvres. The name of the factory impressed was used as a mark.

Lit: M. Aries, *La Manufacture de Creil, 1795–1894*, Paris 1974.

Creil pottery plate, c.*1810,*
with portrait of Joseph Bonaparte, King of Spain
(Musée de l'Île de France, Sceaux)

Cremer, E., *see* COLOGNE POTTERIES.

Crespin, Paul (1694–1770). English silversmith of French extraction, his parents having settled in England *c.*1687 as Huguenot refugees. He produced domestic silver in a Rococo style, working with Nicholas SPRIMONT. In 1734 he made part of the large service for the Empress Catherine of Russia, most of which was subsequently melted down but a cup and cover by Crespin survives in the Hermitage, Leningrad. He retired in *c.*1759. (For his mark *see* p. 893.)

Cressent, Charles (1685–1758). Sculptor and leading French furniture-maker in the Régence and early Rococo styles. He holds a position parallel to that of Oppenord in architecture and Watteau in painting, both of whom influenced his work. He was one of the very few *ébénistes* whose name was well enough known to be mentioned in C18 sale catalogues. But since *ébénistes* were not obliged to stamp their furniture until 1751 not a single piece known is stamped by him and, as a result, a large amount of furniture has been attributed to him, sometimes on flimsy evidence. Several high-quality commodes were for long attributed to him but are now known to be by

C. Cressent:
cartel clock in gilt-bronze case, c.*1747*
(William Rockhill Nelson Gallery of Art, Kansas City)

GAUDREAU. But very fine Régence and Louis XV style furniture in the Gulbenkian Collection, the Wallace Collection, at Waddesdon Manor and at the Residenz in Munich is convincingly attributed to him. A number of fine *cartel* CLOCKS can also be attributed to him.

He began as a sculptor in Amiens where he was probably apprenticed to both his grandfather (an *ébéniste*) and his father (a sculptor). In 1714 he was elected to the Academie de Saint Luc in Paris as a sculptor. But in 1719 he married the widow of the *ébéniste* Joseph Poitou, a rival of BOULLE and *ébéniste* to the Regent, and from that time onwards seems to have largely abandoned sculpture for furniture-making, though he continued to make occasional busts. He took over Poitou's furniture-making workshop and succeeded him as *ébéniste de duc d'Orleans*, the Regent. His patrons included the King of Portugal and the Elector of Bavaria. His early and best furniture is characterized by opulent forms, plain wood veneers and elaborate bronze mounts which he modelled, cast and gilded himself. This was contrary to Guild regulations and he was prosecuted for it on several occasions. But he was always protected by the duc d'Orleans. His mounts have a sculptor's boldness and vigour of modelling, such motifs as *putti*, birds, dragons and ESPAGNOLETTES being characteristic. They are purely decorative, almost anti-functional, unlike those of his great predecessor Boulle, and can best be seen on his commodes where they often completely disguise the divisions of the drawers, e.g. the famous 'dragon commode' in the Wallace Collection, London, and the 'commode aux enfants musiciens' in the Residenz at Munich. He or Gaudreau probably created the Louis XV type of commode with its high legs, serpentine front and non-functional mounts. He also made some superb clock-cases in gilt bronze, notably a cartel-clock with figures symbolizing *Love triumphing over Time* of which several versions exist (Louvre, Paris, and Wallace Collection, London). He accumulated a large and valuable art collection which eventually brought him into financial difficulties. By 1748 he was nearly bankrupt. At about this date he changed his style, perhaps in order to reduce costs and increase production. His former elaborate bronze mounts and plain veneers were abandoned and floral marquetry was used instead in his later work.

Lit: F. J. B. Watson, *Wallace Collection Catalogue: Furniture*, London 1956; and *The Wrightsman Collection: Furniture*, New York 1966; T. Dell in *Burlington Magazine*, April 1967.

Cresset A fire bracket, usually of iron.

Cresson, Louis (1706–61). The most important member of a notable family of Louis XV *menuisiers*, he became a *maître* in 1738 and was patronized by the Crown. His chairs and other upholstered furniture are very elegant and refined, more so than those by his brother **Michel** (1709–*c*.1773) or his relation **Jean Baptiste** (d.1780).

At least ten furniture-makers named Cresson are recorded in C18 Paris and the exact relationship between them has not yet been established. They include **Louis II Cresson**, a *maître* in 1772 and still active in 1779. **Jacques-Louis Cresson**

J.-L. Cresson: chair (siège à la Reine) *(Bibliothèque Nationale, Paris)*

(1743–95) became a *maître* when only sixteen in 1759 and was engaged in chair-making though he became primarily a furniture dealer. He was actively involved in the Revolution and was guillotined after the fall of Robespierre.

Lit: F. J. B. Watson, *The Wrightsman Collection: Furniture,* New York 1966.

Crest and **Cresting** A medieval ornamental finish, usually foliate and regular, along the top of a horizontal member.

Cretonne A French term of uncertain origin for a strong fabric of hempen warp and linen weft first made near Lisieux in Normandy. It is stronger than CHINTZ which it is said to have largely replaced by 1860 in France. In England the term is used for a strong unglazed cotton cloth decorated with a printed design in colours and used for hangings, upholstery, etc. It began to be manufactured in England in about 1860–70.

Cretonne appliqué Elements of pattern (flowers, leaves, birds, etc.) cut out of a piece of printed cotton and applied to a plain, often black, ground with buttonhole stitch and often worked over with embroidery in coloured silks. Also called *broderie perse.*

Cretté, Louis, *see* BRUSSELS POTTERY & PORCELAIN FACTORIES.

Creussen pottery, *see* KREUSSEN POTTERY.

Crewel work A type of needlework executed in gaily coloured wools on white or beige linen grounds generally in bold floral designs derived from Indian printed cottons. Made mainly for bed hangings or curtains in late C17 and early C18 England. The designs tend to be closer and robuster on the earlier examples: the later are usually sprinkled with widely spaced floral sprays. *Illustrated opposite.*

Criaerd, Mathieu (1689–1776). A Parisian *ébéniste* of Flemish origin, he became a *maître* in 1738. He specialized in LOUIS XV STYLE furniture embellished with floral and geometrical marquetry, or with Oriental or pseudo-Oriental lacquer framed with Rococo mounts. The high quality of his work is evidenced by the fact that he supplied furniture to OEBEN the *ébéniste du Roi.* His younger son **Sébastien-Mathieu** carried on the business after he retired in 1767, using his stamp. His elder son **Antoine-Mathieu** (b.1724) became a *maître* in 1747 and worked independently. His furniture is mostly in the LOUIS XVI STYLE.

Lit: F. J. B. Watson, *The Wrightsman Collection: Furniture,* New York 1966.

Crich ware A brown stoneware, similar to NOTTINGHAM stoneware, made at Crich (or Critch) in Derbyshire 1750–1800. It is not to be confused with CROUCH WARE.

Crinoline group Modern term for a porcelain group including a woman dressed in a wide-spreading hooped skirt usually accompanied by a fashionably dressed man. (The crinoline is a mid-C19 garment.) Such groups were first modelled by KÄNDLER at the MEISSEN PORCELAIN FACTORY in 1737 and soon imitated elsewhere, at NYMPHENBURG, VIENNA, etc.

Cripps, William (*fl.*1730–67). English silversmith, apprenticed to D. WILLAUME the younger 1730–31. He made mainly domestic silver.

Criseby pottery, *see* ECKERNFÖRDE POTTERY.

Criselling A fine network of cracks on the surface of glass caused by the progressive degeneration to which old glass is subject. The apparent immediate cause is condensation on the surface and dissolution of some of the silicates in the glass. The Glass Sellers Company in London made a report in 1676 on criselling, with reference to its occurrence in glass by George RAVENSCROFT.

Cristobal de Augusta, *see* AUGUSTA, Cristobal de.

Crochet work A knitted textile made with hooked needles, the finest being Irish, notably that made in early C19 by poor children in the schools of the Ursuline Convent at Blackrock, County Cork.

Croft A small writing table with a dozen small drawers in the support and a flat top with drop leaves, of a type invented in late-C18 England by the **Rev. Sir Herbert Croft.**

Crewel work: by Abigail Pett, late c17 (Victoria & Albert Museum)

Cros, Henri (César-Isidore-Henri) (1840–1907). French sculptor whose interest in polychromy led him by way of reliefs in coloured wax to work in glass. In 1884 he developed a technique for imitating antique carved gems in PÂTE DE VERRE and in 1889 began exhibiting reliefs in this substance. From 1893 he had a studio at the SÈVRES PORCELAIN FACTORY. His works were influenced by contemporary painters and were much admired by Rodin. At the Paris international exhibition of 1900 he won a gold medal for his glass relief *L'Histoire du feu* (Musée des Arts Décoratifs, Paris). Though he occasionally made vases of *pâte de verre* he used the substance mainly as a medium for sculpture. Its potentialities were further developed by A. DAMMOUSE and F.-E. DÉCORCHEMONT.

Lit: R. Jean, *Les arts de la terre*, Paris 1911; A.-M. Belfort in *Cahiers de la céramique*, 39 (1967), pp. 176–87.

Cross One of the most ancient symbolical and ornamental devices. For the main types *see illustrations.*

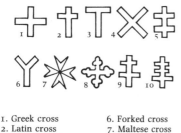

1. Greek cross	6. Forked cross
2. Latin cross	7. Maltese cross
3. St Anthony's cross	8. Clover-leaf cross
4. St Andrew's cross	9. Cross of Lorraine
5. Double cross	10. Papal cross

Cross banding Decoration on furniture or panelling by means of thin strips of veneer, cut across the grain. *See* STRAIGHT BANDING.

Cross hatched ware, *see* PERSIAN POTTERY.

Cross stitch An embroidery stitch formed by two threads crossing at right angles. It is used for *gros point* embroidery.

Crouch ware A brown salt-glazed stoneware, sometimes called 'critch ware' but not to be confused with Derbyshire CRICH WARE. It was made principally in Staffordshire *c.*1740–60 from local clays mixed with sand and given a ferruginous wash before firing in a salt-glaze oven.

Crown glass A flat piece of glass (as for a window) made by spreading a blown bubble into a flat sheet by rapid rotation of the rod. The centre is marked with a bull's eye at the point where the rod was attached. This type of glass was superseded by BROAD GLASS.

Cruet A small bottle or vial usually with a stopper. In domestic use, one to contain oil or vinegar for the dining-table. Ecclesiastically, one for the wine or water used in the celebration of the Eucharist. The term is now more loosely used, domestically, for a stand for condiments at table.

Crunden, John (1740–*c.*1828). He was a London architect and designer, probably a pupil and assistant to Henry Holland the elder. He published *The Joiner's and Cabinet Maker's Darling, or Pocket Director* in 1770 which contains a number of Chinoiserie designs used by furniture-makers. In the same year he published *The Carpenter's Companion for Chinese Railing and Gates . . . from the original designs of J. H. Morris, carpenter, and J. Crunden.*

Crutched Friars glasshouse London glasshouse founded *c.*1570 by **Jean Carré** (d.1572) to produce Venetian style glass. He employed first Lorraine and later Venetian craftsmen. In 1572 the factory was taken over by VERZELINI and produced goblets of soda-lime glass, sometimes engraved by A. de Lysle, as well as domestic wares before it was burnt down in 1575.

Crystal, *see* ROCK CRYSTAL.

Crystal glass Clear colourless glass made by a technique – manganese is added to the FRIT as a decolouring agent – employed by the Romans and rediscovered in the C15 VENETIAN GLASSHOUSES where it was called *vetro di cristallo* from its similarity to rock crystal. The process was transmitted by Venetians, like VERZELINI, to England, the BOHEMIAN GLASSHOUSES, HALL-IN-THE-TYROL, LIÈGE, etc.

Crystalline glaze A matt pottery or porcelain GLAZE marked with large crystals of zinc or calcium produced by allowing the kiln in which the ware has been fired to cool very slowly. Such effects were probably obtained accidentally at first – like the flecks which occur when a glaze has been overloaded with a colourant. But they were exploited as a method of abstract decoration, especially in Europe from the late C19, by potters and ceramic chemists, notably H. Seger at the BERLIN PORCELAIN FACTORY.

Crystallo-céramie French term for moulded porcelain reliefs set within a piece of clear crystal glass, often a paper-weight, first made in early C19 France and taken up by A. PELLATT in England. Also called cameo incrustation.

Cucci, Domenico (*c.*1635–1704/5). Cabinet-maker and sculptor born at Todi in Italy, he settled in Paris *c.*1660 (probably brought from Italy by the luxury-loving Cardinal Mazarin), was naturalized French in 1664, and became the leading Louis XIV *ébéniste* alongside BOULLE. He worked at the GOBELINS factory as head of a workshop and contributed greatly to the luxurious grandeur of Versailles and other royal palaces with his ostentatiously sumptuous cabinets of ebony encrusted and inlaid with lapis lazuli, jasper and other hard stones, silver, pewter, tortoiseshell, gilt bronze, etc. He established a new conception of regal magnificence and the highest standards of craftsmanship. Though fully employed by the Crown until 1683, when LE BRUN was disgraced and work at the Gobelins began to decline, he seems later to have been ready to execute occasional private commissions. Most of his royal furniture was sold in the C18 and broken up for the value of the materials, some of which were probably re-used (e.g. by

Cuerda seca tiles, C15 (Victoria & Albert Museum)

WEISWEILER and other furniture makers). The only known surviving examples of his work are a pair of ebony cabinets, inlaid with *pietre dure* and richly ornamented with gilt bronze mounts, which were made for Versailles in 1681–3 and are now at Alnwick Castle, Northumberland.

Lit: P. Verlet, *French Royal Furniture*, London 1963; R. A. Weigart & C. Hernmarch, *Les relations artistiques entre la France et la Suède 1693–1718*, Stockholm 1964; H. Honour, *Cabinet Makers and Furniture Designers*, London–New York 1969.

Cuccumos, Filippo, *see* ROME POTTERY AND PORCELAIN FACTORIES.

Cuenca (Spanish *cell*). Technique of decorating pottery tiles, practised in Spain from the mid C16. The pattern is impressed into the clay of the tile in such a way that little walls of clay mark the outlines and prevent the different coloured glazes from intermingling.

Cuenca carpets From the C15 onwards Cuenca was, with ALCARAZ, the main centre for SPANISH CARPETS and in the C17 and C18 became one of the most productive in Europe. C15–C17 carpets resemble those of Alcaraz. But from the mid C17 the Turkish or GHIORDES KNOT was used for woollen pile carpets on goats' hair foundations, with undyed warp and dyed woof. In the C18 and C19 it became a Royal Factory. English and French carpets superseded Turkish as models and excellent copies of SAVONNERIE and AUBUSSON carpets were made.

Cuerda seca Technique of decorating pottery tiles and occasionally dishes: originated in the Near East and much used in Spain from *c.*1500. Outlines of the decorative pattern are drawn in a mixture of manganese and grease to prevent the coloured glazes from intermingling. *Illustrated previous page.*

Cuir Bouilli Leather moulded in various forms to make jugs, drinking vessels, cases for silver objects, etc. The basic process of moulding leather by softening it with water, manipulating it over a core of stone, wood, etc., to the shape desired, and drying it in moderate heat until

Cuir Bouilli leather case for the 'Luck of Edenhall', English, C15, with cut and punched decorations (Victoria & Albert Museum)

hardened, was discovered in Neolithic times. The moulded leather sets both more quickly and harder if it is dipped in very hot water – hence the term *cuir bouilli* which came into use in France and England in the C14. Leather moulded in this way was either impregnated with wax or (in the case of jugs, bottles, etc.) lined with pitch or resin. The surface might be decorated by incising, blind stamping or gold tooling.

Cuir ciselé Leather decorated by cutting (not stamping or tooling) a design on the surface. The incised lines were usually deepened and widened with a bone or wooden point. The technique was mainly used in book-binding and was, with cold-stamping, the earliest used in Europe.

Cul de lampe A carved corbel, shaped like the bracket, supporting an ecclesiastical lantern, often used by French C18 cabinet-makers on the label or apron. Also used by printers as a tail-piece.

Cup and cover column A baluster of a type found on late Elizabethan furniture, shaped like a deep-bowled Communion cup with a domed lid.

Cupboard Originally, in medieval England, an open structure of shelves on which cups, especially of silver, might be placed for storage or display. From the later C15 doors were sometimes placed in front of a part of the shelves. But cupboards entirely closed by doors did not become common until the C17 when they were usually called presses. Nowadays cupboards are often 'built in' when the room is designed or remodelled.

Curfew A hood-like metal cover for covering wood embers in a fireplace, not to put them out but to keep them alight.

Custine, Adam-Philibert, Comte de, *see* NIDERVILLER POTTERY & PORCELAIN FACTORY.

Custodia A Spanish type of portable tabernacle. Although portable it is often extremely large and heavy. Magnificent and very elaborate examples were made by Enrique de ARFE and his family.

Cut card work A method of decorating silver by soldering foliate patterns, cut from flat sheets of silver, to the surface of a vessel. Popular in late-C17 and early-C18 France and England.

Cut card work decoration

Cut glass Fairly thick glass decorated with geometrical patterns deeply incised by a lapidary's wheel. The process is derived from that used (since Antique times) for the decorations of rock crystal and was first applied to glass by Caspar LEHMANN in late-C16 Prague. LEAD GLASS with its light-dispersing quality was found particularly suitable for this type of decoration which was adopted mainly in England and Germany. C18 English examples are simply sliced and facetted; those of the C19 are much more elaborately cut to convert the surface into a series of sparkling prisms. English cut glass won great popularity on the continent where it was much imitated until the late C19 when GALLÉ began to lead fashion away from this type of decoration which absurdly came to be regarded as a negation of the essential quality of glass. Glass incised with figurative patterns by the same process is generally called 'engraved glass'.

Cutwork A decorative openwork fabric made from linen of which portions are cut away to leave a pattern and then filled with geometrical ornament worked with needle and thread in buttonhole stitch, etc. It was made in Italy from the C15, called *punto tagliato*, and was one of the precursors of true LACE. Several books of designs for such work were published in the C16, notably that by M. PAGANO.

Cuvilliés, François (1695–1768). Leading German Rococo architect and designer. Born in Flanders, he began as Court Dwarf to the Elector Max Emanuel of Bavaria, studied architecture under J.-F. Blondel in Paris 1720–24 and became Court Architect in Munich in 1725. His interiors in the Residenz, Munich (1729–37, partly destroyed) and the Amalienburg in the Park of Nymphenburg near Munich (1734–9) have a sparkling gossamer delicacy hardly to be equalled elsewhere. From 1738 until his death he published a series of engraved designs for ornament, *boiseries* and furniture even lighter and more fantastic than those of his French contemporaries. A few pieces of furniture after his designs are known (e.g. side-table in Kunstgewerbemuseum, Cologne). By the time of his death the Rococo style was so *vieux jeu* that his son never completed the publication of his designs.

Lit: F. Wolf in *Oberbayerisches Archiv*, LXXXIX, 1967; H. Kreisel, *Die Kunst des deutschen Möbels*, vol. ii, Munich 1970.

Cyfflé, Paul-Louis (1724–1806). Sculptor and porcelain modeller. Born in Bruges, he began as a painter and took up sculpture when he settled at Lunéville 1746. In addition to executing large scale works he modelled figures for the LUNÉVILLE FAIENCE FACTORY (1752), then for the factories at SAINT-CLEMENT (1758), OTTWEILER (1765) and NIDERVILLIER (1772–80). He also ran his own factory for making figures in *terre de Lorraine* (unglazed pipe-clay similar in appearance to *biscuit*) at Lunéville (1768–77) and at Hastières Lavaux (1785–*c.*1790). He specialized in rather sentimental rustic figures – dreamy young gardeners, children weeping over a dead bird, a cobbler whistling to a caged bird, a woman mending stockings, etc.

Lit: E.-J. Dardenne, *Essai sur Paul-Louis Cyfflé*, Brussels 1912.

Cyma recta A double curved moulding, concave above and convex below: also called an ogee moulding.

Cyma reversa A double curved moulding, convex above and concave below: also called a reverse ogee moulding.

Cymric style, *see* LIBERTY, Sir Arthur Lazenby.

From Giambattista Bodoni's
Manuale Tipografico, *Parma, 1818*

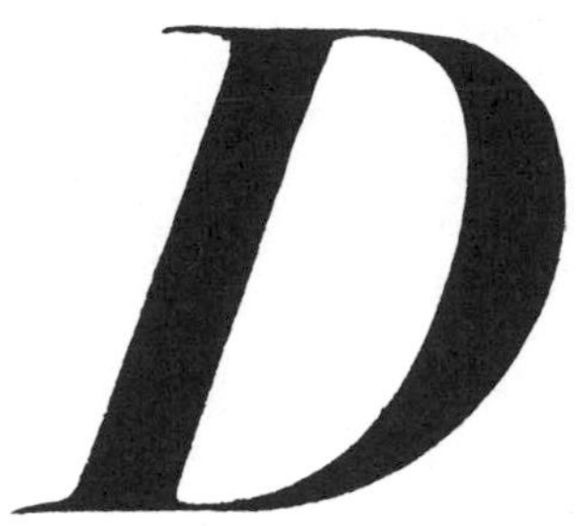

Daghestan carpets, *see* CAUCASIAN CARPETS.

Dagly, Gerhard (*fl.* 1687–1714). He was born, probably in the 1650s, at Spa, which had long been one of the main centres for the production of European lacquer or JAPANNING (*see also* SPA JAPANNING WORKSHOPS). He became the leading master of the art. In 1687 he was appointed *Kammerkünstler* to Friedrich Wilhelm, the 'Great Elector' of Brandenburg, and became *Directeur des Ornaments* the following year. He remained in Berlin until 1713 when he was dismissed from his position. He decorated both furniture and panelling and appears to have worked not only in the traditional black and gold colour scheme but also painted figures in bright reds, greens and blues on a creamy white ground, giving the appearance of porcelain. No signed or documented works by Dagly are known but several pieces of *Japanned* furniture have been attributed to him (notably in Schloss Charlottenburg, Berlin, and in the museums of Cassel and Brunswick). His most famous pupil, Martin SCHNELL, settled in Dresden after 1713. His brother **Jacques** (1655–1728) settled in Paris where he obtained a patent for a varnish factory and is said to have brought new life to the *manufacture des oeuvres de chine*.

Lit: W. Holzhausen, *Lackkunst in Europa*, Brunswick 1959; H. Huth, *Lacquer in the West*, Chicago–London 1971; H. Kreisel, *Die Kunst des deutschen Möbels*, vol. II, Munich 1970.

Dalmatic An ecclesiastical garment with wide sleeves and decorated with two stripes running up the front over the shoulders and down the back. It is worn mainly by the deacons assisting a priest at a High Mass.

D'Alva bottle Alternative (but less usual) name for a BELLARMINE, called after Fernando Alvarez de Toledo, Duke of Alva, active in persecuting Protestants in the Netherlands 1567–73.

Damascening Strictly a process of giving a watered pattern to steel, mainly sword blades, practised at Damascus and elsewhere. Wrought iron was broken up, mixed with charcoal, heated for a long period at a high temperature and allowed to cool slowly, producing a brittle high-carbon steel. By re-heating the steel in a current of air with intermittent forging, some of the absorbed carbon was removed and the bar of metal ready for its final forging. The term damascening is commonly applied to the process of decorating steel with gold or silver beaten into undercut grooves, more correctly termed inlaying, *see* STEEL. *Illustrated next page.*

Damask (1) A reversible figured white or monochrome textile in which the pattern is formed by two faces of the same weave. Damask weaves include areas of satin and sateen (or reverse satin) i.e. areas in which the floating threads are in the warp (satin) and areas in which they are in the weft (sateen), often forming elaborate patterns, which are revealed in the surface sheen (as in the table linen which was very popular in the C19).

(2) A term loosely applied to any silk fabric with a rich raised, usually floral, pattern.

Dammouse, Albert-Louis (1848–1926). French sculptor, glass-maker and potter. He was the son of Pierre-Adolphe Dammouse (1817–*c.*1880) who was a modeller at the SÈVRES PORCELAIN FACTORY. Trained as a sculptor in Paris, he also

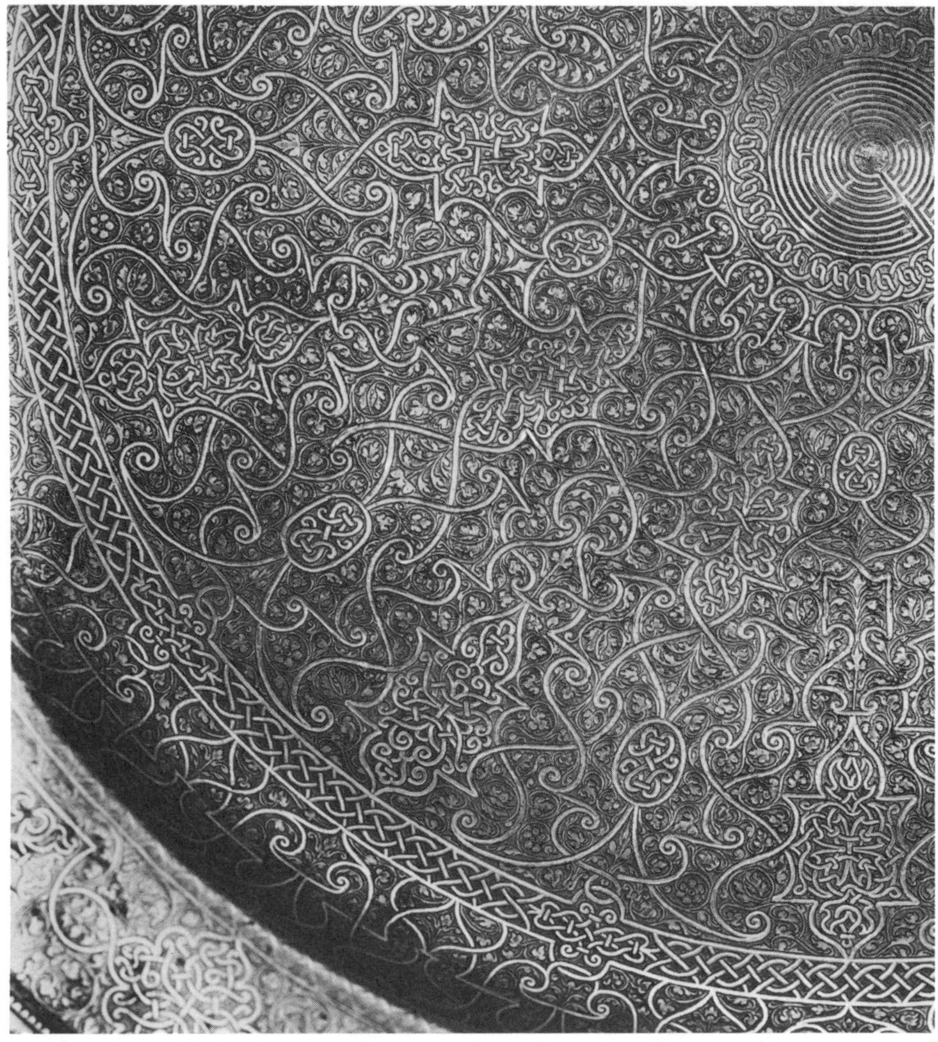

Damascened brass dish, detail, Venetian-Saracenic, early c16 (Victoria & Albert Museum)

worked in the studio of M.-L. SOLON from whom he learned the *pâte-sur-pâte* technique of ceramic decoration which he began to employ in a small studio at Sèvres after Solon left for England. His first products were pastiches of Italian maiolica for which he was awarded prizes at exhibitions from 1874. From 1878 he worked for the factory of Poynat et Dubreuil of Limoges decorating wares shown in the Paris exhibition of the same year, notably a huge enamelled panel 3 × 2 metres. From 1882, however, he was mainly occupied in the production of stoneware influenced by Japanese pottery and with artfully rough-textured surfaces, in his own studio at Sèvres, though continuing to work for various porcelain factories, notably HAVILAND. From 1898 he was also engaged in making glass (*pâte de verre*) of a distinctly ART NOUVEAU type. He attained considerable renown and his works were described in detail in contemporary art magazines.

Lit: A. Polak, *Modern Glass*, London 1962; R. and L. Grover, *Carved and Decorated European Art Glass*, Rutland, Vermont, 1970; M. Ernould-Gandouet, *La Céramique en France au XIX siècle*, Paris 1969.

Danhauser, Joseph (d.1830). The owner of the most important furniture factory in Vienna from 1804 until his death. He had many royal and noble patrons including Archduke Karl and Duke Albert von Sachsen-Teschen (founder of the Albertina) for whom he produced furniture in the EMPIRE STYLE. But he was mainly engaged in making pieces for middle-class homes and became one of the creators of the Austrian BIEDERMEIER style. A collection of some 2,500 designs from his factory is now in the Österreichisches Museum für angewandte Kunst, Vienna. The factory was inherited by his son **Joseph** (1805–45) who was a painter and closed it down in 1838.

Lit: R. Feuchtmueller and W. Mrazek, *Biedermeier in Österreich*, Vienna 1963; G. Himmelheber, *Biedermeier Furniture*, London 1974.

Dannecker, Johann Heinrich von, *see* LUDWIGSBURG POTTERY AND PORCELAIN FACTORY.

Dannhäuser, Leopold, *see* VIENNA PORCELAIN FACTORY.

Dannhöfer, J. P., *see* BAYREUTH POTTERY and VIENNA PORCELAIN FACTORY.

Dantesca chair, *see* CHAIR.

Dantesque style Mid-C19 Italian decorative style corresponding to the Victorian GOTHIC REVIVAL in England and the TROUBADOUR STYLE in France, but strongly nationalistic and inspired by Renaissance as well as Medieval art. Knobbly walnut sideboards carved with tightly packed Renaissance motifs, ponderous *cassoni*, tables on supports bulging with harpies and grotesque heads, X CHAIRS upholstered in dark red cut velvet (the favourite material for upholstery) are characteristic.

Darley, Matthias (*fl.* 1741–80). Engraver and designer, he engraved most of the plates for CHIPPENDALE's *Director*. In 1751 he published his first book of designs: *A New Book of Chinese, Gothic and Modern Chairs*. In 1754 he published, in collaboration with Edwards, *A New Book of Chinese Designs*. Both books were influential in spreading the taste for CHINOISERIE in England. In 1770 appeared his *The Ornamental Architect or Young Artist's Instructor*.

Lit: P. Ward-Jackson, *English Furniture Designs*, London 1958.

Darmstadt Grand-Ducal ceramic factory Founded in 1905 by the Art-Nouveau-loving Grand Duke Ernst Ludwig von Hessen, with J. J. SCHARVOGEL as director from 1906 until 1913 when it closed. It specialized in stoneware of simple, yet distinctly Art Nouveau shapes with speckled decoration.

Lit: O. Pelka, *Keramik der Neuzeit*, Leipzig 1924.

Darned netting A rather loose network of threads, knotted at their points of intersection, onto which a figurative, floral or other pattern is darned. It is one of the precursors of true LACE.

Darned netting, late C17
(Victoria & Albert Museum)

Dasson, Pierre and **Henri** They were the principals of a mid-C19 firm of Parisian reproduction-furniture makers of exceptionally high quality. A copy made by Dasson of the OEBEN-RIESENER *bureau du roi Louis XV* is in the Wallace Collection, London.

Daum, Auguste (1853–1909) and **Antonin** (1864–1930). Art Nouveau glass makers who directed a factory at Nancy which from 1889 produced vessels in a slightly less extravagant and much less refined version of the style of E. GALLÉ. (For additional illustration *see* JAPONAISERIE.)

Lit: A. Polak, *Modern Glass*, London 1962; R. & L. Grover, *Carved & Decorated European Art Glass*, Rutland, Vermont 1970.

Daum glass vase, c.1905 (Kunstgewerbemuseum, Berlin)

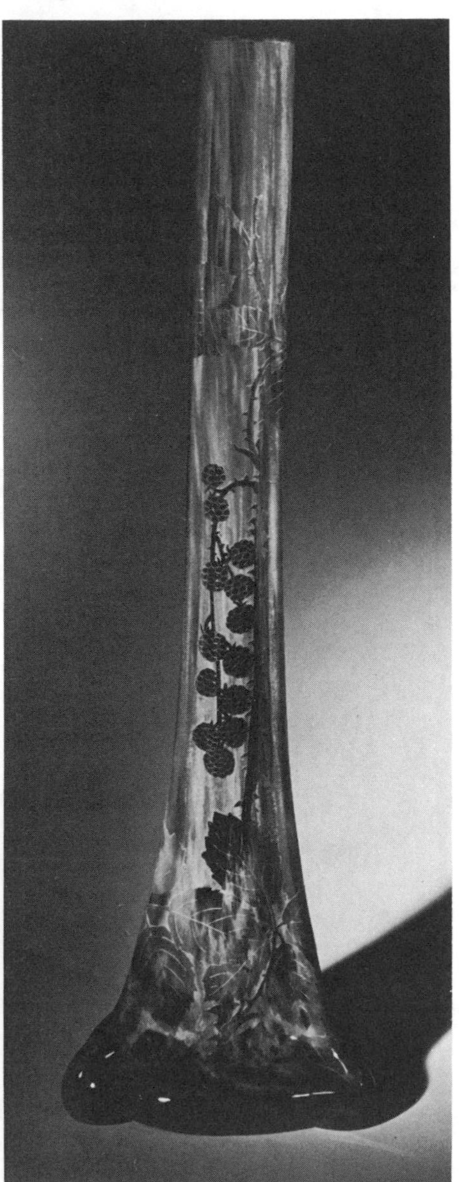

Davenport A small writing desk with a sloping top above a case of drawers, first made in late C18 England by GILLOW for a certain Capt. Davenport and very popular in the early C19.

Davenport, from Designs and Catalogue by C. & R. Light, *London 1880*

Davenport pottery and porcelain factories A factory making cream-coloured and blue-printed earthenware was started by **John Davenport** at Longport, Staffordshire, in *c.*1793 and a porcelain factory was added in *c.*1820. The porcelain imitated DERBY PORCELAIN in its decoration, and more than one of the painters employed at Derby also worked for the Davenport factory (notably Thomas Steele). Tea and dessert services seem to have been a staple product. The factory closed in 1887. *Illustrated next column.* (For factory mark *see* p. 882.)

Lit: G. A. Godden, *An Illustrated Encyclopaedia of British Pottery and Porcelain*, London 1966; T. A. Lockett, *Davenport Pottery and Porcelain 1794–1887*, Newton Abbot 1972.

Davenport pottery: printed earthenware plate, c.1845 (Victoria & Albert Museum)

David, Jacques-Louis (1748–1825). The greatest French painter of his time and leader of the NEO-CLASSICAL movement. He was also one of the first to design furniture (notably chairs) imitated directly from Antique prototypes, made in the 1780s for his own use and also for his patron the Comte d'Artois, by G. JACOB.

Davis, Alexander Jackson (1803–92). He was a leading C19 architect in the U.S.A., designed several Greek Revival State Capitols but also worked in a Neo-Gothic style. He also designed Neo-Gothic furniture, among the best produced in the U.S. in the 1830s and 1840s.

Lit: E. Donnell, *A. J. Davis and the Gothic Revival*, New York 1936; K. M. McClinton in *The Connoisseur*, CLXX (1969), pp. 54–61, 179–87.

Davis, William, *see* WORCESTER PORCELAIN FACTORY.

Day bed, *see* CHAISE LONGUE.

Day, Lewis Foreman (1845–1910). English designer involved in the ARTS AND CRAFTS MOVEMENT but working mainly for industry. It was 'practically settled by the public that they want machine-work', he wrote, 'we may protest that they have chosen unwisely but they will not pay much heed to us.' From 1870 he designed furniture, textiles, wallpapers, ceramics and metalwork, generally in a rather thin version of the MORRIS style.

De Morgan, William Frend (1839–1917). Leading English pottery designer, a formative influence on the ARTS AND CRAFTS MOVEMENT and to some extent on ART NOUVEAU. After training at the Royal Academy Schools he fell in with MORRIS, BURNE JONES and Rossetti in the early 1860s. He began to produce tiles and pottery in London in 1869, moved (1882) to Morris's Merton Abbey, then set up a factory at Fulham (1888). From 1892 onwards he spent the winters in Florence and worked with CANTAGALLI. Reacting against the Victorian fashion for C18 style vases decorated with naturalistic flowers, imitations of Chinese porcelain and knobbly Gothic Revival wares, he sought inspiration from HISPANO-MORESQUE, Persian and occasionally Greek pottery. His decorative plates, tiles (of which he made a speciality) and vases are painted either in LUSTRE (the technique of which he revived) or in so-called 'Persian' colours with green, black and turquoise predominating. Although he derived his motifs from a wide variety of sources,

W. De Morgan: lustre painted earthenware dish, 1882–8 (Victoria & Albert Museum)

including Greece and (after 1899) Crete, his wares have unmistakable individuality. A master of carefully integrated flat patterns, he did for pottery what Morris had done for wallpapers and textiles. Individual motifs – leaves, animals, fishes, birds, Grecian ships – are stylized but drawn with great liveliness and are perfectly related to the shapes of the vessels or tiles on which they are painted. The general effect is as richly luxuriant as a Morris wallpaper. His designs were generally applied to the pottery by assistants. He retired in 1905.

Lit: W. Gaunt & M. D. E. Clayton-Stamm, *William De Morgan*, London 1971.

De Stijl, *see* RIETVELD, Gerrit.

Deal Fir or pine wood, imported in quantity from the Baltic into England where it largely replaced oak for panelling and was much used for the carcases of furniture veneered in walnut or mahogany from the C17 onwards. Baltic pine is soft, white and straight-grained.

Debschitz, Wilhelm von (1871–1948). German painter and designer, also an influential teacher of the decorative arts. He began in the Prussian Kadettenkorps but left in order to become a (self-taught) painter inspired by such late Romantics as Moritz von Schwind, Ludwig Richter, etc., soon coming under the influence of W. MORRIS and W. CRANE. In 1891 he settled in Munich. Here in 1902 he founded, in partnership with H. OBRIST, a school for training artists and craftsmen, the *Lehr- und Versuchsateliers für angewandte und freie Kunst*, generally known as the *Debschitzschule* after Obrist left in 1904, one of the first organizations of its kind to be based on up-to-date psychological theories of education and artistic expression. The products of this school won a gold medal at the Bavarian Jubilee exhibition in Nuremberg in 1906. It included a metalwork shop and later a textile workshop (from 1906) and a pottery (from 1907). In 1906 he also founded, in collaboration with H. Lochner, a commercial workshop for the applied arts – *Ateliers und Werkstätten für angewandte Kunst*. His own designs were composed of bold abstract forms (e.g. bronze inkwell now in the Landesmuseum at Stuttgart). After the war he was appointed director of the state Handwerker- und Kunstgewerbeschule in Hanover.

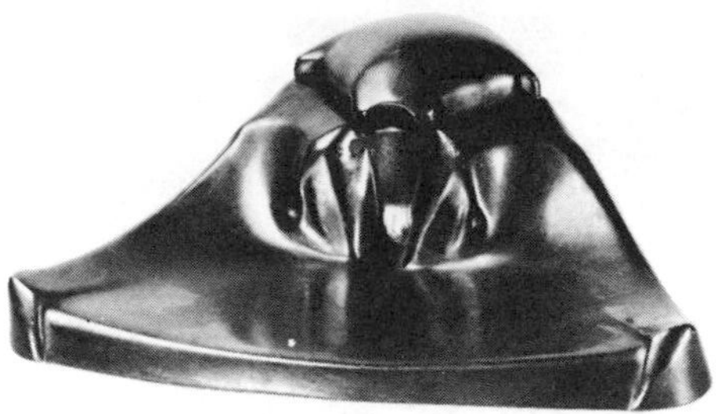

W. von Debschitz: bronze inkwell, 1906 (Württembergisches Landesmuseum, Stuttgart)

Lit: W. Scheffler, *Kunstgewerbemuseum Berlin: Werke um 1900*, Berlin 1966.

Decalomania An American late C18 technique for decorating furniture with prints – i.e. an American version of LACCA CONTRAFATTA.

Decanter A bottle with a stopper, usually of cut glass, in which decanted wine is served at table.

Deck, Joseph-Théodore (1823–91). One of the best French ceramic artists of his day and the founder of the artist-potter tradition. He was born in Ober-Elsass, began his career in a stove factory in Strasbourg, and after working in several European countries set up a pottery in Paris in 1856. He experimented with glazes and in 1861 produced his celebrated turquoise blue, later called after him *bleu de Deck*. Some of his early earthenware plates were decorated by painter friends, notably Harpignies, Félix Bracquemond and Eléonore Escallier. He also produced imitations of SAINT-PORCHAIRE wares, Persian and ISNIK pottery and Italian maiolica. This changed in the 1870s when he became one of the pioneers of the JAPONAISERIE cult. He favoured wares painted with naturalistic decorations in bright colours and from 1878 began to produce plates, vases, etc., with gold backgrounds, which were very popular. In about 1880 he began to make porcelain with fine flambé glazes. He became administrator of the SÈVRES PORCELAIN FACTORY in 1887, leaving his brother **Xavier** in charge of his Paris factory. Appropriately his grave in the Montparnasse cemetery in Paris is marked by a large ceramic monument designed by his brother.

Lit: E. Gerspech, *Deck, faïencier et porcelainer*, Paris 1883; M. Ernould-Gandouet, *La Céramique en France au XIX siècle*, Paris 1969.

Deckelpokal German for a covered cup of metal or glass.

Decker, Paul (1677–1713). German architect and ornamental designer, he was born in Nuremberg and worked in Berlin from 1699 to 1705. His ornamental designs for goldsmiths' work, glass engraving, lacquer, etc., published in Nuremberg during the last years of his life, include attractive chinoiseries and grotesques, influenced by J. BERAIN.

Lit: H. Kreisel, *Die Kunst des deutschen Möbels*, Vol. II, Munich 1970.

Décor bois *Trompe l'oeil* decorations applied to c18 porcelain and faience (especially NIDERVILLIER) simulating strongly grained wood to which prints, slightly curving at the edges, have been applied.

Décor bois *teapot, Tournai faience, c19 (Musée des Arts Décoratifs, Paris)*

Décorchemont, François-Émile (1880–1971). A French painter who began exhibiting landscapes in Paris in 1898 but soon turned his attention to and became well known for his work in glass. From 1900 he made vessels, generally of a rather massive character, by the recently developed PÂTE DE VERRE technique. At first they were almost opaque but from 1904 he discovered methods of colouring the glass with metallic oxides to produce pieces of a cloudy translucency similar to hard stones. The early works tend to be rather richly decorated in the ART NOUVEAU style; later pieces, especially those of the 1920s, are much simpler, with incised ornament and bold reliefs. His work is well represented in the Musée des Arts Décoratifs, Paris.

Lit: R. Chavance in *Art et Decoration*, XLIX (1926), p. 75ff; F. Duret-Robert in *Connaissance des Arts* 256 (June 1973), pp. 131–40.

Dedham pottery, *see* CHELSEA KERAMIC ART WORKS.

Delafosse, Jean-Charles (1734–91). French architect, he is best known for his ornamental designs for furniture, metalwork, trophies, vases, cartouches, etc. They were influential and contributed

J.-C. Delafosse: design from Nouvelle iconologie historique, *Paris 1771*

to the dissemination of the *goût antique* at a time when the Louis XVI style was coming into fashion. Among his vast output of decorative engravings which began to appear in 1768 as *Nouvelle Iconologie Historique*, expanded in 1773, 1776 and 1785, with additional sets of plates, amongst which there is a set of furniture designs in a rather heavy *à la grecque* style with much use of laurel pendents and thick, ropey swags and Greek-key frets but with occasional lingering echoes of the Rococo in chair-feet with scrolled-up toes.

Lit: D. Guilmard, *Les maîtres ornemantistes*, Paris 1880; S. Eriksen, *Early Neo-Classicism in France*, London 1974.

Delaherche, Auguste (1857–1940). One of the most important French ceramic artists of his time. He attended the École des Arts Décoratifs in Paris from 1877 to 1883, then worked for the ceramic factory of **Ludovic Pilleux**, 'L'Italienne' near Beauvais, making tiles and other architectural ornaments until 1886 when he was appointed director of the galvanoplastic section of the CHRISTOFLE electroplate factories. In 1887 he took over the HAVILAND pottery studio of E. CHAPLET in Paris, where he made handsome stoneware vases decorated with different glazes and, occasionally, stylized flower and leaf motifs. From 1890 he had a studio at Héricourt, near Beauvais, where he worked in the summer, and in 1894 he moved definitively to Armentières where he made porcelain as well as stoneware. Here he more or less abandoned all figurative decorations, producing wares of very simple form which rely for their effect on the colour, texture and fortuitous patterns of their crystalline, flambé or aventurine glazes. From 1904 he made only unique pieces. He was very highly regarded, won a medal at the Paris International Exhibition of 1889 and a Grand Prix at that of 1900; in 1907 a retrospective exhibition of more than 400 of his works was held in Paris at the Musée des Arts Décoratifs. Acquired by museums and collectors on both sides of the Atlantic, his finely executed wares exerted considerable influence on studio potters of the early C20. *Illustrated next column.*

Lit: Exposition Delaherche, Musée des Arts Décoratifs, Paris 1907; M. Ernould-Gandouet, *La Céramique en France au XIX siècle*, Paris 1969.

L. Delaherche: stoneware bottle, 1889 (Victoria & Albert Museum)

Delamain, Henry (d.1757). A potter working in Dublin, better known as one of the partners in the BATTERSEA ENAMEL FACTORY.

Delanois, Louis (1731–92). Leading Parisian chair-maker working mainly in the LOUIS XV STYLE. He became a *maître* in 1761. Between 1768 and 1770 he supplied much furniture for Mme du Barry's apartment at Versailles and Pavillon de Louveciennes including some chairs in the LOUIS XVI STYLE which seem, however, to be somewhat exceptional in his *oeuvre*. An account book reveals that between 1761 and 1777 he included among his clients Stanislas II Poniatowski, King of Poland, the Prince de Condé, the Comte d'Artois, the Duc de Chartres and the Duc de Choiseul. But in 1777 he sold his stock and rented his workshop to Martin Julien and thenceforth devoted himself to timber dealing and speculation in real estate – with disastrous financial consequences. He went bankrupt in 1790. (For illustration *see* p. 168.)

Lit: S. Eriksen, *Louis Delanois, menuisier en sièges (1731–1792)*, Paris 1968.

Delaunay, Nicolas (*c*.1655–1727). French silversmith and medallist who became director of the Monnaie in Paris and began to make the *vaiselle d'or* or royal dinner service for Louis XV in 1724. It was carried on after his death by Thomas GERMAIN and eventually completed by ROETTIERS in 1749. Nothing of it survives, so far as is known. Delaunay played a dominant role in the development of Rococo silver and was very influential, e.g. on Nicolas BESNIER.

Lit: P. Verlet in *La Revue de l'art*, 1956.

Delaune, Etienne (1518/9–83). French engraver and the author of some very influential ornamental designs for silversmiths, jewellers, enamellers, cabinet-makers and armourers. He was a draughtsman of great delicacy and an ornamentalist of rare ability despite his characteristically Mannerist *horror vacui* which induced him to cram his compositions with squirming human figures, sea monsters, flowers, fruit and bands of strapwork. Most of his designs are for ornament but a few are for ewers, *tazze*, etc. Of the several pieces based on them one of the best is a large silver-gilt basin of 1563 in the Louvre.

Lit: D. Guilmard, *Les maîtres ornemantistes*, Paris 1880.

Delft Dutch town which became in the mid-C17 the most important centre for good quality tin-glazed earthenware. Its name is sometimes applied to similar tin-glazed wares produced elsewhere in N. Europe, especially Germany (FRANKFURT and HAMBURG) and England (BRISTOL, LAMBETH and SOUTHWARK), and to save confusion wares made at Delft are often called Dutch Delft. Tin-glazed earthenware inspired by Italian maiolica was made in the C16 in various Low Country towns, first at Antwerp (1508), then Amsterdam, Rotterdam, Haarlem and, in 1584, Delft. Early in the C17 these potteries began to abandon the hot maiolica colours for a blue-and-white scheme made fashionable by the vogue for

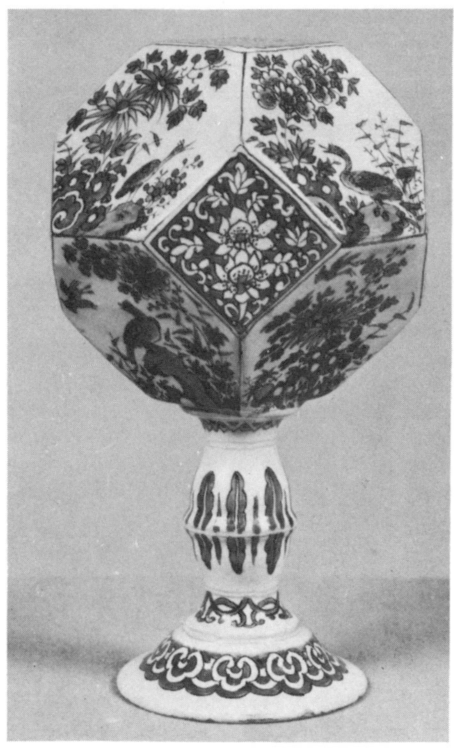

Delft wig-stand (AK monogram), tin-glazed earthenware, late C17 (Victoria & Albert Museum)

Chinese porcelain (imported in quantity by the Dutch East India Company founded in 1609) and already used at NEVERS, FRANKFURT and SOUTHWARK. Delft emerged as the most important centre for such wares shortly after 1650. New factories were established in disused breweries (forced out of trade by competition from England) whose names they maintained – The Moor's Head, the Rose, the Greek A, and several others. By 1675 the Delft factories were among the most productive and among the best in Europe, turning out a great quantity of useful and ornamental wares – tiles, table services, vases (often very large), *tulipières*, etc., generally decorated in blue and white, though sometimes and less successfully in high-temperature colours, usually with exotic flowers or chinoiseries but occasionally, and again less happily, with Italian religious or mythological scenes. Some of the masterpieces of these potteries are, however, to be found among pieces departing from the blue-and-white chinoiserie norm, notably the panels of polychrome tiles depicting huge vases of flowers, and the vases, plates, tiles, etc. painted with Dutch landscapes, notably those by Frederick van FRYTOM, or genre scenes reminiscent of and sometimes copied from the work of contemporary easel painters. Technically they are very fine but decorations tend to be overcrowded (especially on polychrome wares) and forms tend to be rather ponderous when not copied from Chinese porcelain. The most notable factories were those of L. van EENHORN, S. van EENHORN, R. HOPPESTYN and A. KOCX. Another group of factories specialized in the imitation of the Chinese red stoneware of YI-HSING, making handsomely formed simply decorated teapots which influenced the wares of DWIGHT and ELERS in England. Neither potters nor painters at Delft were able to compete with French and German craftsmen of the C18 and

Delft (Greek A Factory): tin-glazed earthenware jar, late C17 (Kunstindustrimuseet, Copenhagen)

Delft tulipière, tin-glazed earthenware, c.1700 (Rijksmuseum, Amsterdam)

standards began to fall off *c.*1725. Some factories fell back on wares popular in the C17, others applied themselves to the fabrication of such ceramic nightmares as vases in the form of fiddles, shoes or sledges, fussily decorated with landscapes in blue and white. Several potteries survived by producing cheap blue-and-white table-wares until they were driven out of fashion by English salt-glazed stoneware and CREAM-COLOURED EARTHENWARE. By the C19 only two tin-glazed earthenware factories survived at Delft. The industry was revived in 1876 when new mass-production methods were introduced, but the modern factories never succeeded in escaping from their C17 past. (For various factory marks *see* pp. 882–3.)

Lit: D. Korf, *Dutch Tiles*, London 1963; C. H. de Jonge, *Delft Ceramics*, London 1970.

Delftfield pottery, *see* GLASGOW POTTERY.

Delftware, English The name given to TIN-GLAZED EARTHENWARE made in England. It was first made at a pottery established in 1571 in Aldgate, London, by **Jacob Janson** (d.1593). Later it was made at the SOUTHWARK, LAMBETH and BRISTOL potteries.

Lit: A. Ray, *English Delftware Pottery*, London 1968; F. H. Garner & M. Archer, *English Delftware*, London 1972.

Della Robbia, Luca, *see* ROBBIA, Luca della.

Della Robbia pottery A short-lived concern called the Della Robbia Company of Birkenhead, Cheshire, was started in 1894 by Harold Rathbone and made tiles, plaques, vases, etc. with maiolica-like glazes though the decoration was usually Art Nouveau in style. It closed *c.*1906.

Delorme, Jean Louis Faizelot (*fl.*1763–80). He is the best known member of a large family of Parisian furniture-makers. His father **François Faizelot Delorme** (1691–1768) specialized in lacquer furniture and became a *maître ébéniste*. His brothers **Adrien** and **Alexis** also became *maîtres ébénistes*, in 1748 and 1772 respectively. Adrien was known for his marquetry. Examples of J. L. F. Delorme's work are in the Wallace Collection, London.

Demay, Jean-Baptiste-Bernard (1759–1848). A Parisian *menuisier*, he became a *maître* in 1784. He worked for the Crown and was responsible for the well-known and much-copied chairs with the Queen's monogram flanked by arrows in the pierced back. He also seems to have designed the *Montgolfier* chair with a splat in the shape of a hot-air balloon, made to celebrate Montgolfier's pioneer flight in 1784. Most of his work is in the LOUIS XVI STYLE – in plain mahogany, with inlays – but he went on working after the Revolution, in later manners. Examples of his furniture are in the Musée des Arts Décoratifs and Carnavalet in Paris.

Lit: F. J. B. Watson, *The Wrightsman Collection: Furniture*, New York 1966.

Demerdji carpets, *see* TURKISH CARPETS.

Denby pottery Founded in the Derbyshire village of Denby in 1809, it began by producing undistinguished Staffordshire type stoneware. It now specializes in very simply designed but handsome fireproof kitchen wares.

Dennis, Thomas (*fl.*1660–1700). A 'joyner' working in Ipswich, Massachusetts, and one of the very few early American furniture-makers to be identified. The best early New England furniture is sometimes attributed to him.

Dentil Small rectangular block of which a series is arranged like teeth under a cornice.

Derbend carpets, *see* CAUCASIAN CARPETS.

Derby porcelain factories The first was functioning in an experimental way by 1750 – the date of some undistinguished white cream jugs one of which is marked 'Derby' and another, in the Victoria & Albert Museum, 'D.1750' – and had possibly been started by **Thomas Briand** of the CHELSEA factory *c.*1745 with **James Marchand.** Some figures, now known as DRY-EDGE FIGURES because of a glaze retraction at the base leaving an edge of white biscuit visible, also date from this early period as well as domestic and other wares. In 1756 William DUESBURY from Chelsea joined a banker John Heath who had an interest in the COCKPIT HILL POTTERY and **André Planché,** a 'china-

Derby porcelain vase, c.1755–8
(Victoria & Albert Museum)

Derby biscuit porcelain of George III, c.1773
(Royal Collection, reproduction by gracious permission of H.M. the Queen)

maker of Derby', in an agreement to start a factory and this presumably became the first Derby Porcelain Factory. From 1756 it was advertised as a 'second Dresden'. No regular mark was used until 1770 (apart from an occasional forgery of the CHELSEA anchor) but many pieces are securely attributed to this period. They have a light-weight somewhat glassy body, the earlier specimens are decorated in pale almost translucent enamel, and are generally imitative of Chelsea and MEISSEN (probably by way of Chelsea). The best are statuettes, especially pastoral figures disporting in front of leafy *bocages*. Table-wares, rather simpler than those of Chelsea, were also made. A new period, known as the Chelsea–Derby period, began in 1770, when Duesbury acquired the Chelsea factory, and lasted until he closed it in 1784. During these years the products of both factories bore the same mark – an anchor and the letter D. In these years SÈVRES provided the main source of inspiration for figures and Louis XVI style vases and useful wares. The production of BISCUIT figures (the first in England) also began: the finest is a set of three groups of members of the Royal Family after a painting by Zoffany. The 'Crown Derby' period began in 1784 when the factory adopted a crowned D as its mark; Duesbury died two years later and was succeeded by his son. Many of the earlier types continued to be made. Other products included simply decorated table-wares, distinctly Neo-Classical in shape and sometimes painted with fresh naturalistic flowers by W. BILLINGSLEY and others. Notable statuettes were produced after models by J. J. Spängler (a Swiss) and Pierre Stephan. In 1811 the factory was acquired by **Robert Bloor** who, though he went mad in 1826, gave his name to the final period, until closure in 1848. It was a period of steady decline in which the factory lost all individuality. Several other porcelain factories were established in Derby in the C19, some of them making imitations of C18 wares (with C18 Derby marks). The most notable was the 'Crown Derby' firm, founded in 1877, styled the 'Royal Crown

Derby Porcelain Company' from 1890, which began by specializing in table-wares decorated with very richly gilded and painted Japanese patterns. It still flourishes. (For factory marks *see* p. 883.)

Lit: F. B. Gilhespy, *Derby Porcelain*, London 1961; Franklin A. Barrett & Arthur L. Thorpe, *Derby Porcelain, 1750–1848*, London 1971.

Derbyshire potteries A number of factories, the earliest at TICKENHALL, others active from the C18 at BELPER, BRAMPTON, CHESTERFIELD, COCKPIT HILL (in Derby), CODNOR PARK and DENBY, much less successful than those in the adjoining county of STAFFORDSHIRE, but producing similar wares.

Derome, Jacques-Antoine (1696–1760). French bookbinder, father of **Nicolas-Denis** (1731–88). Both father and son specialized in elegant inlay bindings with much very fine gold tooling. Notable examples of their work are in the Bibliothèque de l'Arsenal, Paris. Many other members of the family were bookbinders.

Deruta potteries An important group of Italian potteries in Umbria which began to make maiolica in the late C15, possibly under the patronage of Cesare Borgia. Early wares appear to have been similar to those of FAENZA: some outstanding jars (examples in the Victoria & Albert Museum and elsewhere) painted with friezes of classicizing palmette ornament are generally attributed to 'Deruta or Faenza' and a notable painter known as the St Veronica Master appears to have worked in both places. Lustred wares were made from the beginning of the C16 (e.g. a spouted drug vase dated 1501 in the British Museum) but similar pieces are assigned to GUBBIO. A group of plates of *c.*1500–1520, known as 'petal back' plates (from the monochrome petal-like decorations on their backs) and generally assigned to Deruta, is distinguished for paintings in a pure orange-yellow, a soft lemon, a dark and a greyish blue, delicate green and purple-brown sometimes with the addition of lustre. Subjects range from boldly rendered grotesques to a copy after Raphael's Madonna da Foligno and hunting scenes. The best known products date from the 1520s and

Deruta maiolica dish, c.1520 (Victoria & Albert Museum)

(Left) Deruta maiolica drug vase, c.1505 (Victoria & Albert Museum)

later – often very large dishes painted in golden lustre and blue with busts of young men and women, allegories, figures after Perugino's frescoes of Heroes, saints, or religious devices set within large boldly rendered borders of formalized flower and leaf motifs. The ISTORIATO style appears in plates by a painter who signed himself **El Frate** dated 1541–5. In the later C16 the grotesque style of URBINO was imitated. C17 and C18 products included votive plaques of an appealing naïveté, such as those with which the walls and columns of the pilgrimage church of the Madonna di Bagno (just outside Deruta) are panelled. Pottery is still made at Deruta.

Lit: L. de Mauri, *Le maioliche di Deruta*, Milan 1924; J. Chompret, *Répertoire de la maiolique italienne*, Paris 1949; B. Rackham, *Italian Maiolica*, London 1952.

Desk An English term of medieval origin, with no precise equivalent in other languages, for various types of furniture for the use of readers or writers, covering the lectern or reading desk as well as the BUREAU and SECRETAIRE. In the Middle Ages and until late in the C16 the writing desk generally took the form of a small portable box in which papers and writing equipment could be stored, with a sloping lid which could serve both as the support for an open book and a writing surface. From the later C16 such boxes were often mounted on stands. The lid was originally hinged at the top; when it was hinged at the bottom so that it could be brought forward and supported in some way to provide a writing platform this early type was transformed into an escritoire, and later developed into the fall-front desk or bureau. For types of desk see: BONHEUR DU JOUR, BUREAU, CARLTON HOUSE TABLE, CROFT, DAVENPORT, ESCRITOIRE, SCRUTOIRE, SECRETAIRE, SECRETARY.

Dessert Italian name for a table centre, especially one of the late C18 or early C19 composed of plateaux, numerous statuettes in bronze or porcelain and sometimes little models of buildings. *Illustrated below.*

Deutsche Blumen A type of floral decoration on ceramics introduced at Vienna *c.*1725 and at MEISSEN *c.*1740 by J. G. HÖROLDT. The flowers are rendered naturalistically and were often based on such botanical prints as those illustrating the works of J. W. Weidmann. It was very popular and quickly supplanted the more formalized types of INDIANISCHE BLUMEN or Oriental flower decoration. It was adopted especially by the factories at HÖCHST, VINCENNES, CHELSEA, WORCESTER and DERBY.

Deutscher Werkbund A German association of *avant-garde* manufacturers and a few architects, artists and writers, inspired by MUTHESIUS and guided by similar ideas to those held by the DEUTSCHE WERKSTÄTTEN. It was founded in 1907 in Munich with the aim of 'selecting the best representatives of art, industry, crafts and trades, of combining all efforts towards high quality in industrial work, and of forming a rallying-point for all those who are able and willing to work for high quality'. It played a leading role in creating a new and eminently serious standard for

Dessert in biscuit porcelain, by Volpato, Rome (Palazzo Pallavicini, Rome)

INDUSTRIAL DESIGN and the acceptance of the machine. And it also inspired the foundation of similar organizations in other countries – Austria (1910), Switzerland (1913), Sweden (1910–17), and England (Design & Industries Association 1915). Its ideals were later taken over by Gropius for the BAUHAUS.

Lit: H. Eckstein, *50 Jahre Deutscher Werkbund*, Frankfurt-am-Main 1958.

Deutsche Werkstätten In 1898 the designer and furniture-maker Karl Schmidt (1891–1948) started the Dresdener Werkstätten für Handwerkkunst, inspired by the Münchener Vereinigte Werkstätten für Kunst in Handwerk started the previous year by Hermann OBRIST, Bernhard PANKOK, Bruno PAUL and Richard RIEMERSCHMID. The aim was to create a national art without any stylistic imitation, based on sound construction through the cooperation of artisan and artist or architect. In 1906 the Deutsche Werkstätten in Dresden produced its first machine-made furniture, designed by some of the leading German architects. They were among the first to work for INDUSTRIAL DESIGN. Their most important contribution to modern design was in pioneering the production of furniture made of standardized parts, later called unit furniture. Their first unit furniture, designed by BRUNO PAUL, was exhibited in 1910 as *Typenmöbel*.

Devant de cheminée, *see* CHIMNEY BOARD.

Devonia lace, *see* HONITON LACE.

Devonshire potteries A number of small factories in N. Devonshire, notably at Barnstaple, Bideford and Fremington, making slipware from the C17 to the present day. Apart from some large jugs decorated with such nautical motifs as mariners' compasses and ships, made at Bideford, products are generally similar to other English slipwares.

Diamond point engraving A technique for decorating glass. It seems to have started in Venice in the C16 (e.g. Giacomo VERZELINI) and culminated in central and north Europe during the C17 and C18 especially at HALL-IN-THE-TYROL GLASSHOUSE and in various Bohemian and Dutch glasshouses. It is a process of scratching or stippling the surface of the glass. The same technique was applied to porcelain, less successfully, by A. O. E. von dem BUSCH.

Diaper A textile with a repetitive pattern limited to a simple arrangement of rectangles or lozenges formed by the contrast of the warp face and the weft face of the same weave. By extension, any similar chequerwork pattern on any material.

Diasprum The medieval name for a silk weave showing the pattern and ground in the same colour but different texture. The ground is woven in a simple cloth weave with fine wefts: for the pattern a heavy weft is taken over two ground warps and one binder warp and under one binder warp, giving a chiselled relief effect. It was a speciality of Byzantine and SICILIAN SILK FACTORIES.

Diatreton, *see* VASA DIATRETA.

Dickhut, J. K., *see* PROSKAU POTTERY.

Dietrich, Christian Wilhelm Ernst, *see* MEISSEN PORCELAIN FACTORY.

Dietterlin, Wendel (1550–99). German architect and engraver important mainly for his publication *Architectura und Ausstheilung der V. Seuln* (1593/4) with plates which represent the northern Mannerist conception of architectural decoration at its most bizarrely extravagant and nightmarishly ingenious – abounding in frantically interlaced strapwork, wildly misapplied classical motifs and figures which range from a squirming eroticism to a tortured agony of sinister implication. A second edition published in Nuremburg (1598–9) has many additional plates which are sober by comparison with the earlier ones. Both books were extensively used not only by architects but also by decorative artists and designers, most of whom were far less sophisticated than Dietterlin whose designs they reduced to banality. His son, **Wendel Dietterlin** the younger, was a goldsmith who was working at Lyons in 1614 and published some engraved designs for grotesque decorations.

Lit: H. Kreisel, *Die Kunst des deutschen Möbels*, Munich 1968.

Dillwyn, Lewis Llewellyn, *see* SWANSEA POTTERIES & PORCELAIN FACTORY.

Dimity A stout cotton cloth, woven with raised stripes and figures. Originally Italian but manufactured in England since the early C17: used especially for bedhangings.

Dinanderie Brassware made since the early Middle Ages in and around Dinant, near Liége, especially fairly simple small household objects such as cooking utensils, candlesticks, etc. The term is also sometimes used to describe the products of MOSAN METALWORKERS and, more loosely, for brassware made in other places, including the Levant and India.

Lit: J. Tavernour Perry, *Dinanderie*, London 1910.

Dinglinger, Johann Melchior (1664–1731). He was one of the greatest European goldsmiths, and more fortunate than CELLINI and JAMNITZER in that all his major works survive (in the Grünes Gewölbe or Green Vaults in Dresden). He was the last to work successfully and on a large scale in the tradition established by Cellini and Jamnitzer, and although he is usually called a Baroque craftsman his works are closer in feeling to those of the Mannerists. He was born near Ulm and apprenticed there before he settled in Dresden by 1693 where he spent the rest of his life working for the Elector, Augustus the Strong. He was appointed Court jeweller in 1698. He specialized in very elaborate enamelled and bejewelled ornaments, usually of an exotic nature, such as aigrettes with tossing plumes of diamonds, rich sword hilts, etc. His first major work for Augustus was 'the golden coffee set' of 1701. This was followed by *The Grand Mogul's Birthday*, a fantastic decorative group of some 132 exquisitely modelled figures of men and animals, the *Dianabad* of 1704 which consists of a chalcedony bowl set in a mesh of enamelled gold and silver and precious stones and supported on the curving horns of a stag's head; and this was followed by the *Obeliscus Augustalis* in 1722, one of his finest productions. His last work was in many ways the most extraordinary of all, the *Apis Altar*, which is one of the masterpieces of C18 EGYPTIENNERIE.

Lit: E. von Watzdorf, *Johann Melchior Dinglinger*, Berlin 1962.

Diphros Greek name for a STOOL.

Directoire style A severely simplified and rather self-consciously classicizing version of the LOUIS XVI STYLE which began before the Revolution, reached its peak during the Directoire, 1795–9,

J. H. Dinglinger: detail from the Apis Altar, 1730 (Grünes Gewölbe, Dresden)

Directoire design for furnishings by J.-B.-P. Moitte, 1794–5 (École des Beaux Arts, Paris)

and persisted into the Empire period, e.g. chairs by JACOB with few bronze enrichments and little if any inlaid decoration. Its austerity was probably due as much to economic necessity as to aesthetic preference. In a country bankrupted by revolution and war costly materials could no longer be imported from abroad nor could gold be lavished on furniture mounts. Republican symbols – the fasces, the cap of liberty, etc. – were used on furniture, faience, wallpapers and especially on cottons printed at OBERKAMPF'S factory. The ex-royal GOBELINS TAPESTRY FACTORY, the SAVONNERIE CARPET FACTORY and the SÈVRES PORCELAIN FACTORY had almost ceased work during the Revolution but began production again during the Directoire.

Directoire armchair, by Jacob frères, 1796–1803 (Musée des Arts Décoratifs, Paris)

Disbrowe, Nicholas One of the very few early American furniture-makers to be identified. Born in England *c.*1612, he settled in Hartford, Connecticut, by 1639. The 'Hartford' or 'Sunflower' chests were probably developed by him or his successors.

Discharge printing A method of decorating textiles, especially COTTON, by dyeing the piece a solid colour and then printing the design with a chemical which bleaches – or discharges – the colour to produce a white pattern on a coloured ground, first used *c.*1806.

Dish cross A framework of silver or Sheffield plate made to support a dish at table; in the form of two arms hinged crosswise with a centrally placed spirit lamp. Made in later C18 England.

Dish ring A support for a bowl, usually made of silver in the form of a ring about 3 ins. high and 8 ins. in diameter, pierced with Rococo ornament. They were an Irish C18 speciality but also made in England. Also called a potato ring.

Dish ring, silver, Dublin, c.*1770 (The City Museum, Leeds)*

Dixon, Austen & Co., *see* SUNDERLAND POTTERIES.

Dixon, James, & Sons Ltd A firm of English silversmiths which was established in Sheffield in 1806 and became the leading maker of Britannia metal and E.P.N.S. wares exported to the U.S.A. in the mid c19. At the Great Exhibition in 1851 they showed both plated and solid silver wares, notably some pieces derived from plant forms including a coffee and tea service based on the *Nepenthes* (pitcher plant) with a salver modelled on a leaf of the *Victoria Regina* water-lily. In the 1880s they produced plated wares designed by C. DRESSER including an angular toast-rack and a semi-spherical kettle.

Lit: S. Bury, *Victorian Electroplate*, London 1971.

Doat, Taxile (b.1851). French ceramic artist, born at Albi and trained at Limoges and in Paris. He was employed by the SÈVRES PORCELAIN FACTORY from 1877 to 1905 but also had his studio from 1892 in Paris and from 1898 at Sèvres. He worked mainly in porcelain (seldom in stoneware), using high-temperature colours and showing a preference for relief decorations in white on a coloured ground. He is credited with more than two thousand pieces. His book *Grand-feu Ceramics* was first published in an English translation at Syracuse, New York, in 1905. In 1909 he was appointed director of a newly founded ceramic school of the University of St Louis, U.S.A.

Doccia porcelain factory Founded near Florence by **Marchese Carlo Ginori** (1701–57) who in 1735 initiated experiments to make porcelain with Italian clays. He engaged J. K. W. ANREITER VON ZIRNFELD of Vienna to head the painting workshop and the Florentine sculptor Gaspero Bruschi as chief modeller. Work began in 1737: by 1740 specimens were sent to Vienna enabling Ginori to obtain a privilege for making porcelain in the (Austrian) Grand Duchy of Tuscany. A greyish, slightly rough-textured hybrid hard paste was used, covered with a glaze that tends to lack brilliance and have a smeary look. The defects of the medium are most notable in small figures and the earlier table-wares. The most successful products are on a fairly large scale. Ginori obtained the models, originally intended for bronze statuettes, from the sculptor Massimiliano SOLDANI, and the porcelain groups derived from them, notably a *Deposition*, are of a grandeur which makes the figures of most other c18 factories look *petite* and trifling. These majestic Baroque groups were repeated from time to time until the 1790s. Reductions of Antique marbles were also made. Among the table-wares the best are those boldly painted with

Doccia porcelain, deposition group after a model by Massimiliano Soldani (1742). mid c18 (Corsini Collection, Florence)

Doccia porcelain plate with tin-enamel glaze, 1770–90 (National Museum of Wales, Cardiff)

coats of arms or with a unique FLEURS DES INDES pattern called *a tulipano* (though it includes no tulips and the central motif is a stylized peony). On the death of the founder the factory was inherited by his three sons. From 1765 a new body was introduced and used in conjunction with a glaze containing tin oxide to give opacity and whiteness. At about the same time the SÈVRES Louis XVI style was not very successfully adopted. In the C19 the factory reverted to its C18 patterns and after 1868 some products were fraudulently marked with the crowned N of the NAPLES ROYAL PORCELAIN FACTORY. It remained under the control of the Ginori family until 1896 when it was incorporated with the Società Richard of Milan under the name of **Richard-Ginori.** Handsome and often very large ART NOUVEAU pieces were made in the 1890s and early C20. Gio PONTI was employed as a designer between 1923 and 1938. Giovanni Garibaldi (b.1908), who has been artistic director since 1947, has introduced excellent modern designs, e.g. a table service of 1954 which stacks vertically into a column. The firm produces most of the best quality porcelain in Italy today. It also runs the Museo di Doccia at Sesto Fiorentino where examples of all phases of the factory's activity are displayed. (For factory mark *see* p. 883.)

Lit: A. Lane, *Italian Porcelain*, London 1954; Leonardo Ginori-Lisci, *La porcellana di Doccia*, Milan 1963; G. Liverani, *Il Museo delle porcellane di Doccia*, 1967.

Don pottery A factory at Swinton in Yorkshire, near the better known ROCKINGHAM factory, founded *c.*1790, acquired by **John Green** of the LEEDS POTTERY *c.*1800, taken over by **Samuel Barker** of Mexborough in the late 1830s and closed in 1893. It specialized in cream-coloured earthenware, sometimes transfer-printed, and also produced black stoneware. 'DON POTTERY' impressed was used as a mark.

Lit: G. A. Godden (ed.) *Jewitt's, The Ceramic Art of Great Britain*, London 1972.

Donaldson, John (1737–1801). English enameller and portrait miniaturist who is said to have worked at the CHELSEA PORCELAIN FACTORY (perhaps decorating large gold anchor vases *c.*1760–65) and is known to have decorated WORCESTER vases with mythological subjects. His works are signed with a monogram.

Lit: R. L. Hobson, *Worcester Porcelain*, London 1910.

Dopskal A Swedish type of small drinking bowl, usually of silver, with one or two handles and with or without a cover.

Doreurs, Corporation des The Parisian guild of craftsmen specializing in gilding the bronze objects made by the Corporation des FONDEURS with which it was amalgamated in 1776. It was dissolved in 1791.

Dorez, Barthélémy, *see* LILLE POTTERY & PORCELAIN FACTORY.

Dorez, N. A., *see* SAINT-AMAND-LES-EAUX POTTERY AND PORCELAIN FACTORY.

Dorflinger, Christian (1828–1915). He was a very successful glass manufacturer in the U.S.A., known internationally for the high quality of his cut glass and engraved glass. Born in Alsace, he emigrated to the U.S.A. in 1846. In 1860 he established the **Greenpoint Glass Works** in Brooklyn. In 1865 he established his glasshouse at White Mills, Pennsylvania, renaming it the **Wayne County Glass Works** in 1873. In 1881 it became **C. Dorflinger and Sons.** He employed several skilled and well-known craftsmen, e.g. Nicholas Lutz.

Lit: J. F. Newton in *Antiques*, XLV (1944), pp. 27–9.

Dorotheenthal pottery A faience factory was founded at Dorotheenthal near Arnstadt in Thuringia by a daughter of the Duke of Brunswick *c.*1716. Its best products, made before *c.*1750, were plates and vessels painted with LAUB UND BANDELWERK ornament – somewhat similar to those of ABTSBESSINGEN – and pictorial panels especially of religious subjects. Other products included figures, jugs, etc., painted in very bright high-temperature colours. It closed shortly before 1806.

Lit: M. Sauerlandt in *Der Cicerone*, II (1910), p. 639ff, IV (1912), p. 201ff; K. Hüseler, *Deutsche Fayencen*, Stuttgart 1956–8.

Dortu, Jacob, *see* NYON PORCELAIN FACTORY.

Douai pottery factory A factory making *faïence fine* was started at Douai in 1781 by two Englishmen, **Charles** and **James Leigh.** It closed in 1820. It was known as **Houzé de l'Aulnoit & Cie** and produced cream-coloured earthenware similar to that of the LEEDS POTTERY FACTORY. Other potteries at Douai made similar wares.

Lit: A. Houzé de l'Aulnoit, *Essai sur les faïences de Douai dites grès anglais,* Lille 1882.

Double cloth carpets Floor coverings made from two sets of worsted warp and two sets of woollen weft, woven on the draw loom in such a way that the same pattern appears on back and front but in reversed colours. It is the earliest type of machine-made carpet, first produced at the KIDDERMINSTER CARPET FACTORIES and often called Kidderminster carpet. It is also a multiple-cloth carpet, though this term covers also the Scotch carpet – a three-ply or triple-cloth carpet of a type that was perfected at Kilmarnock in 1824. A slightly different type of double-cloth carpet known as 'tapestry ingrain' resembled the dearer three-ply carpet and was first produced in England in 1841 but developed mainly in the U.S. (by A. Smith of New York) from 1850.

Double cup A pair of cups which may be fitted together at the rims so that one forms the cover to the other. Silver cups of this type were popular mainly in c16 Germany. *Illustrated next column.*

Double cup in silver by Hans Petzolt, Nuremberg, late c16 (Rijksmuseum, Amsterdam)

Doublure A term used in bookbinding for the inside face of the covers, especially when lined with leather and decorated.

Doughty, Dorothy, *see* WORCESTER PORCELAIN FACTORY.

Doulton Pottery and Porcelain Company The pottery was established by **John Doulton** (1793–1873) at Lambeth, South London, in 1815 as 'Doulton & Watts' and was known as such until 1858. It specialized in stoneware sanitary, laboratory and other useful articles. In about 1860 it began to revive earlier types of stoneware, notably copies of c18 brown stoneware vessels, and from 1862 onwards it produced the well-known salt-glazed wares with blue decorations. From 1866 the pottery was closely associated with the Lambeth School of Art then directed by the progressive John Sparkes under whom the MARTIN brothers and George TINWORTH were trained. Tinworth joined Doulton and many jugs, tankards and reliefs were made from his models – even some large-scale fountains, etc. The Martin brothers also worked for Doulton but never joined the firm. In 1870 the French painter J.-C. Cazin joined Doulton and introduced *sgraffiato* techniques which were taken up by **Hannah Barlow** (1851–1916) and her sister **Florence** (d.1909) who worked for Doulton from the 1870s onwards decorating wares with animal and other scenes. They became very popular, being known as **'Barlow ware'.** By the early 1870s Continental collectors and even museums had begun buying Doulton's 'artistic' products and the extraordinary and rapid success of these is reflected in the steep increase in the number of 'art potters' employed – six in 1873, forty-four in 1875, three hundred and forty-five in 1890. The range of wares similarly increased – earthenware decorated with enamel colours from 1873, 'silicon' ware (1879) and 'marquetry' ware (1887). In 1884 a porcelain factory was opened at Burslem, Staffordshire. Some remarkable tile panels were made by W. J. NEATBY *c.*1900. From 1914 C. J. NOKE was art director.

Lit: D. Eyles, *Royal Doulton 1815–1965*, London 1965; R. Dennis, *Catalogue of the Exhibition of Doulton Stoneware and Terracotta 1870–1925*, London 1971.

Dovetailing A carpenter's technique of joining two pieces of wood at right angles by means of wedge-shaped tenons and mortices, carved out of each piece. A refinement introduced *c.*1700 and called lap or stop dovetailing enabled the ends of the tenons of one piece to be concealed.

Dowel pin Headless wooden peg used in furniture for fastening together two members or pieces of wood.

Drawn work or **Drawn thread work** A type of openwork fabric made from at least 1460; the immediate forerunner of LACE. It is made from a panel of linen from which some threads are drawn out and the rest grouped and whipped together to form geometrical and other patterns. *Illustrated next page.*

Dredger A vessel with a perforated lid through which a powder or granulated substance (e.g. pepper, salt, sand, sugar) may be sprinkled, sometimes called a caster.

Dreihausen pottery The name generally given to a small group of German C15 stoneware vessels of imposing form decorated with stamped ornament (rather like basket-work) and applied bearded masks or figures in high relief. Only a

Dreihausen type of stoneware jug, called the 'Daun Cup of Welcome', early C15 (Staal.Kunstsammlungen, Kassel)

Drawn work, Italian, c.1540
(Victoria & Albert Museum)

few pieces are known, in the Cathedral of Limbourg-am-Lahn; Historisches Museum, Frankfurt-am-Main; National Museum, Copenhagen; etc. Late C15 or early C16 salt-glazed stoneware jugs and cups, with widely flared mouths and ring handles, of a grey body coloured reddish brown on the surface are sometimes associated with them. The place of origin of all these pieces remains obscure and it is no longer believed that any were made at Dreihausen.

Lit: J. Horschik in *Keramos*, 53–4 (1971), pp. 11–33.

Drentwett family A large and important family of Augsburg silversmiths several of whom bore the same Christian name. **Abraham** (d.1666) was responsible for the outstandingly fine auricular style silver gilt hilt dated 1653 on the *Pfälzer Schwert* now in the Residenzmuseum, Munich. Another **Abraham** (*c*.1647–1727) is known chiefly for his engraved designs for goldsmiths' work of an exuberantly Baroque cast, with much figurative ornament, but he also produced some handsome pieces of silver. He worked as a wax modeller as well. A number of very large pieces of Rococo silver bear the marks of members of this family, e.g. a set of four guerdons of 1740 by **Philip Jacob Drentwett** (1694–1754) in collaboration with Bernard Heinrich Weyhe (1701–82) in Rosenborg Castle, Copenhagen.

A. Drentwett: designs for silver and furniture, c.1710

Lit: S. Rathke-Köhl, *Geschichte der Augsburger Goldschmiedergewerbes vom Ende der 17 bis zum Ende der 18 Jhs*, Augsburg 1964; H. Kreisel, *Die Kunst des deutschen Möbels*, Vol. II, Munich 1970.

Dresden faience factory Founded by J. F. BÖTTGER in 1708 a year before he discovered porcelain and the subsequent foundation of the MEISSEN factory. **Peter Eggerbrecht** (d.1738) who had been working at the BERLIN faience factory, became manager in 1710 and leased the factory in 1712. Apart from a period in Russia, 1718–21, he remained there until his death. The only important Dresden faience dates from his time – egg-shaped drug-pots for the Court pharmacy, *Commedia dell'Arte* figures and some very large club-shaped chinoiserie vases. After Eggerbrecht's death the factory was carried on by his widow and, from 1756, by his daughter **Christiane Le Lonay.** It closed in 1784. (For factory mark *see* p. 883.)

Lit: K. Hüseler, *Deutsche Fayencen*, Stuttgart 1956.

Dresden lace, *see* LACE.

Dresden porcelain, *see* MEISSEN PORCELAIN FACTORY.

Dresser, *see* CUPBOARD.

Dresser, Christopher (1834–1904). English designer and influential writer on the decorative arts who, unlike RUSKIN and MORRIS, fully accepted the implications of mechanized production and stressed the importance of design rather than craftsmanship. After studying at the government School of Design in London he began his career as a botanical draughtsman and first made his name as a botanist with a particular interest in the geometry of plant structure. He published several books and articles on botany, being awarded a doctorate by the University of Jena in 1860, but he failed, the same year, to obtain the chair of botany at University College, London, and thereupon seems to have turned his attention back again to the decorative arts. He was strongly influenced by Owen JONES. In 1857–8 he had published a series of articles on *Botany as adapted to the Arts and Art Manufactures* in the widely diffused *Art Journal* and in 1862 he published *The Art of Decorative Design* and also *The Development of Ornamental Art,* a critical guide to the International Exhibiton of that year and, in 1871–2, *Principles of Design.* The exhibition fired him, like so many of his contemporaries, with an admiration for the arts of Japan with which he then became deeply involved. In 1877 he went to Japan in a semi-official capacity and collected Japanese objects on behalf of TIFFANY of New York. In 1879 he formed a partnership with Charles Holmes of Bradford for the importation of Japanese and other oriental wares into England. He published a long account of the arts of Japan in 1882. In the meantime, before 1867, he had begun to work as a designer of carpets for Messrs Brinton & Lewis and also to advise other English firms on design. He became art manager of the Art Furnishers' Alliance 1880–83. A fast worker, he produced an enormous quantity of designs for all kinds of household objects – wallpapers, furniture, metalwork, pottery, glass, textiles, etc. As art director of the LINTHORPE POTTERY (near Middlesbrough) 1879–82 he was responsible for the design of numerous vessels, some derived from Japan, others, more surprisingly, from Peruvian pottery. For James Cooper & Sons of Glasgow he designed glass vessels distantly based on historical prototypes or plant forms, but generally of a distinctly Art Nouveau cast. His

C. Dresser: *design for a teapot with rivets, for Elkington & Co.,* c.1898

most interesting designs were for silver and especially E.P.N.S. (for several manufacturers such as ELKINGTON 1875–88, Hukin & Heath *c.*1878, James DIXON 1879–82), many of which reveal a concern for function, an austere liking for undecorated simple geometrical forms and an almost brutalist penchant for exposed rivets, far in advance of the time and sometimes even seeming to anticipate BAUHAUS design.

Lit: N. Pevsner in *Architectural Review,* LXXXII (1937), pp. 183–6; S. Bury in *Apollo,* LXXVI, 1962; R. Dennis & J. Jesse, *Christopher Dresser,* Exh. Cat., Fine Art Society, London 1972.

Dressing-table A table usually fitted with a looking-glass and with drawers to hold such articles for the toilet as brushes, combs, pomade pots, scent bottles, etc. In England tables seem to have been made expressly for this purpose in the early C18 (at about the time when the TOILETTE

Dressing-table, mahogany with marquetry decoration, English, c.1770 *(Victoria & Albert Museum)*

came into use in France), but the name indicates function rather than form.

Dreste, Caspar, *see* WIESBADEN POTTERY.

Dreyfuss, Henry (1904–72). Leading American industrial designer and, with N. Bell Geddes, Raymond LOEWY and W. D. TEAGUE, one of the founders of the profession. He was born in New York, began as a stage designer on Broadway 1921 and opened an industrial design office in

1929. His first important design was a table telephone for Bell in 1930. His final 1950 version of this design (model '500') is his masterpiece and a modern classic from which telephones in use all over the world are derived (e.g. the English G.P.O. 1958 model) though it remains by far the best, easier to use and read and visually more robust and satisfying. He also designed excellent alarm clocks for Ingraham Co., vacuum-cleaners, flat irons and washing machines for Hoover (from 1934 onwards), lavatory basins for Crane Co. (from 1935), television sets and air-conditioners for R.C.A. (from 1946), not to mention motor cars, farm machinery (e.g. the John Deere '720' Tractor of 1956), aircraft interiors (e.g. the 1951 Super G. Constellation for Lockheed Aircraft Corp.). He was a pioneer believer and experimenter in ERGONOMICS, the author of one of the best popular accounts of the subject, *Designing for People* (1955) and of numerous technical charts published as *The Measure of Man* (1960). He also published *Industrial Design: A Pictorial Record* (1957). He had offices in South Pasadena and New York.

Drinking horn A C14 or earlier type of drinking vessel made from the horn of an ox or buffalo or the tusk of an elephant, and mounted usually in silver. Occasionally the whole vessel is of silver, the natural form of the horn being preserved. The type continued to be made until the C16.

Drinking horn, mounted in copper gilt, Danish, C15 (British Museum)

Drissel, John, *see* PENNSYLVANIA DUTCH STYLE.

Drop or **Pear drop** or **Tear drop handle** A metal, usually brass, pear-shaped pendant handle attached to a drawer by pins and a flat plate of the same material. It was very popular in the late C17 and early C18 but was also used on furniture of later periods.

Drop-in seat Upholstered or caned seat for a chair, supported on but detachable from the frame of the chair, first made *c.*1710.

Drug pot, *see* ALBARELLO and PHARMACY VASES.

Dry-edge figures A term for early DERBY PORCELAIN figures made before William Duesbury became co-partner in 1756, perhaps at the COCKPIT HILL POTTERY using **Thomas Briand**'s formula. The dry-edge occurs where the glaze has stopped short of the base, leaving a few millimetres of white biscuit body showing (though this peculiarity is found elsewhere, e.g. on Longton Hall pieces). Domestic and other useful wares seem to have been produced at Derby contemporaneously with these early figures.

Lit: B. Watney, 'Pre-1756 Derby Domestic Wares, Contemporary with "Dry-Edge Figures"' in *The Burlington Magazine*, January 1967, pp. 16–20.

Du Cerceau, Jacques Androuet the elder (*c.*1520–*c.*1584). French architect and designer who published some very influential engraved designs for furniture, silver and textiles. Georges d'Armagnac, Bishop of Rodez (who introduced Serlio to François I) is said to have enabled him to visit Rome in the 1540s. He was back in France by 1549 when he published his first book *Arcs* in Orléans. His *Livre Contenant Cinquante Bastimens* appeared in Paris in 1559. This made his name though his best-known books, the two-volume *Plus excellents Bastiments de France*, did not appear until 1576 and 1579. He was an unashamed plagiarist and began by helping himself to the inventions of various Renaissance designers in Italy (POLIDORO, VICO, Agostino VENEZIANO) and Germany (BROSAMER). Later he adopted many motifs and ideas from the work of Italian Mannerists. He issued *c.*1550 a set of engraved furni-

J. A. Du Cerceau: designs for cabinets, c.1550

ture designs which is the earliest known after that by the MASTER H. S., for a coherent group of household furniture. His designs are ponderously architectural in form. The STRAPWORK and other relief ornamentation is rather thin and flat but the carved elements are boldly sculptural and often very fantastic, e.g. a bed supported at one end on a writhing snake and on an elephant's foot at the other. A few surviving pieces of furniture seem to show his direct influence (e.g. a walnut cabinet in the Frick Collection in New York) but only one example executed (in part) after a design by him is known – a table at Hardwick Hall, England. His designs for silver include vases and ewers in the form of the human body (after PERINO DEL VAGA) and a series of designs for the insides and undersides of the bowls of *tazze* with mermaids, tritons, etc., in bold relief. The latter were used by silversmiths in Paris (e.g. bowl in the Fitzwilliam Museum, Cambridge) and the Netherlands. A younger member of the large Du Cerceau family, **Paul Androuet** (1630–1710), was a draughtsman, engraver and goldsmith and published designs for arabesques, grotesques, etc.

Lit: E. Bonaffé, *Le meuble en France au XVI siècle*, Paris 1887; H. de Geymuller, *Les Du Cerceau*, Paris 1887; S. Jervis, *Printed Furniture Designs before 1650*, London 1974.

Du Paquier, Claudius Innocentius, *see* VIENNA PORCELAIN FACTORY.

Dublin potteries At least one Delftware factory was operating in Dublin from *c.*1730–*c.*1771. **John Crisp & Co** is recorded in 1747 and was probably the factory taken over in 1752 by **Henry Delamain** (d.1757) and continued by his widow and others until *c.*1771. Wares are decorated chiefly with landscapes and narrow scroll borders, in bright blue or deep manganese purple. Most wares are unmarked but some are marked 'Dublin' or with a harp. (For factory mark *see* p. 883.)

Dubois, Abraham (*c.*1777–1807). An American silversmith, he worked at Philadelphia producing domestic silver in an elegant Federal style. A tea-service of *c.*1785–95 is in the Yale University Art Gallery.

Dubois, Jacques (*c.*1693–1763). He was a Parisian furniture-maker, and became a *maître-ébéniste* in 1742. He was a master of the Rococo style, working sometimes to designs by PINEAU, and using both oriental lacquer and *vernis Martin*. His son **René** was to become even better known.

Dubois, René (1737–99). He was the son of JACQUES DUBOIS and the most important member of a distinguished family of Parisian furniture makers. He was trained under his father, became a *maître-ébéniste* in 1754 and in 1779 was officially recognized as *ébéniste de la Reine*. He was one of the pioneers of the Louis XVI Style, making *c.*1765 the very handsome table and filing cabinet which the king gave to Catherine II of Russia (now in the Wallace Collection, London) – the former, known as the Tilsit Table, is adorned with carved wood figures, probably by his brother **Louis** (1732–*c.*1790) who was also a sculptor. They both showed a marked preference for classically inspired ornament. Another of his masterpieces is the chest of drawers incorrectly known as the marriage coffer of

R. Dubois: chest of drawers (known as the marriage coffer of Queen Marie Antoinette), c.1770 *(Wallace Collection, London)*

Marie Antoinette (Wallace Collection, London), set with Japanese lacquer and gilt-bronze mounts –mermaids at the corners, a pair of amorous doves billing against a Japanese landscape background, and very tidy festoons of flowers along the base. He specialized in the use of oriental lacquer set in rectangular (but occasionally irregular chinoiserie) frames and adorned with gilt-bronze garlands. He also worked in the BOULLE technique, on one occasion at least making use of A. C. Boulle's designs. He retired in 1779.

Lit: F. J. B. Watson, *Louis XVI Furniture*, London 1960.

Dubois, Robert, *see* TOURNAI POTTERY AND PORCELAIN FACTORY.

Duché, Andrew (1709–78). American potter of Huguenot origin whose father had settled in Philadelphia. In 1736 he went to live at Savannah in Georgia and within two years discovered the equivalent for Chinese *kaolin* and feldspathic rock for making porcelain. In 1743 he went to England to sell or exploit his discovery, taking a load of the clay with him. He appears to have gone first to Bow to see Thomas FRYE whose patent for porcelain taken out in 1744 refers to the use of a clay 'the produce of the Chirokee nation in America, called by the natives unaker'. He also saw William COOKWORTHY. Little is known of his activities after his return to America but he made a considerable fortune partly, perhaps, from the export of clay to England. The *Bristol Journal* of November 1764 reported the arrival of 'porcelain' from Georgia, presumably manufactured by Duché. Pieces have been attributed to him but no certain examples of his porcelain have been identified.

Lit: R. P. Hommel in *The Chronicle of Early American Industries* I (1934–5); *Bow Porcelain 1744–1776*, Exh. Cat., British Museum, London 1959–60; G. Hood in *Art Quarterly*, XXXI (1968), pp. 168–84.

Duchesse, *see* CHAISE LONGUE.

Duck foot The American name for the three-toed foot of a CABRIOLE LEG.

Ducoin, Pierre, *see* MONTPELLIER POTTERY.

Duesbury, William (1725–86). Notable English porcelain painter and factory owner. Born at Longton in Staffordshire, he established *c.*1750 a studio in London for painting porcelain from BOW, CHELSEA, DERBY and LONGTON HALL. He returned to the Midlands in 1756 and acquired an interest in the Derby factory; he bought the Chelsea factory in 1770 and the Bow factory in 1775. He appears never to have signed his work.

Lit: Mrs D. A. MacAlister, *William Duesbury's London Account Book 1751–1753*, London 1931; Franklin A. Barrett & Arthur L. Thorpe, *Derby Porcelain 1750–1848*, London 1971.

Dufour, Joseph (*fl.*1805–36). The leading French maker of SCENIC WALLPAPER during the Empire and Restoration periods. He began at Mâcon where *c.*1805 he produced a very handsome paper, *Les Sauvages du Mer du Sud*, composed of twenty rolls and representing the adventures and death of Captain Cook against the exotic landscape of the South Pacific. He moved to Paris in 1807. His many papers, several of which remained in production until 1860 (the firm was styled **Dufour et Leroy** from 1820), printed in bright clear colours are among the most decorative productions of their period. They include views of Paris, Venice, London, Constantinople and the Bay of Naples (all with buildings arranged according to fancy); *Les Français en Egypte* (1814), *Les Campagnes Françaises en Italie* (1814); groups of antique sculpture in grisaille, and some illustrations of literature, notably *The Lady of the Lake*, *Don Quixote* and *El Cid*. From 1825 he also produced papers with religious subjects. He worked extensively for export to England and America after 1815. *Illustrated next column.*

Lit: E. A. Entwistle, *A Literary History of Wall Paper*, London 1960; E. A. Entwistle, *French Scenic Wallpapers, 1810–50*, London 1971.

Dufour & Leroy wallpaper,
Télemaque dans l'île de Calypso, *1825*
(Musée des Arts Décoratifs, Paris)

Dufrène, Maurice (1876–1955). Leading Parisian designer of furniture, textiles, metalwork, glass, ceramics and whole interiors, especially in the ART DECO style of which he was a creator. He began to exhibit designs while still a pupil at the École des Arts Décoratifs in Paris. From 1903 he

M. Dufrène: porcelain sugar bowl, 1903 (Karl H. Bröhan Collection, Berlin)

manifested a reaction against ART NOUVEAU and sought to create a style equally free from historical elements but less mannered in form and decoration. As a professor at the École Boulle in Paris from 1912 to 1923 and as a writer in the periodical *Art et décoration* he exerted considerable influence on the younger generation. From 1921 he directed the studio 'La Maîtrise' of the Parisian store Galeries Lafayette, designing inexpensive mass-produced furniture, and also some expensive and expensive-looking custom-built pieces. Generally his designs were basically traditional with the addition of modernistic elements, but sometimes he worked in an enriched version of H. VAN DE VELDE's style.

Dugourc, Jean-Démosthène (1749–1825). Leading French furniture designer. After studying in Rome he became a pupil and assistant of BÉLANGER whose elder sister he married in 1776. In 1780 he was appointed *dessinateur de la Chambre et du Cabinet de Monsieur* and in 1784 *dessinateur du Garde-Meuble de la Couronne*. With Bélanger and Georges JACOB he was largely responsible for the late LOUIS XVI style (as Bélanger declared) and especially the *style étrusque*. Drawings reveal that he was an excellent if somewhat archaeologizing designer. BOULARD, CARLIN and SENÉ and other leading furniture-makers worked to his designs. In 1799 he went to Madrid as architect to the Spanish Court but returned to France in 1814 and quickly became the leading RESTAURATION

J.-D. Dugourc: Lyons silk panel, c.1815–25 (Courtesy of the Art Institute of Chicago)

designer, notable mainly for rich classically inspired designs for LYONS silks and BEAUVAIS tapestries.

Lit: D. Guilmard, *Les maîtres ornemantistes*, Paris 1880.

Dumb waiter A stand of, usually, three tiers of revolving circular trays, placed near a dining-table for self-service. An English invention of *c.*1740 not adopted elsewhere until the late C18.

Dumb waiter, English, late C18 (Victoria & Albert Museum)

Dummer, Jeremiah (1645–1718). The earliest known American-born silversmith. Apprenticed to John HULL (1624–83), an English silversmith who had emigrated to Boston, and who worked mainly in a severe version of the late C17 English style. Examples of Dummer's work are in the Worcester Art Museum, Yale University Art Gallery and the Museum of Fine Arts, Boston.

Lit: H. F. Clarke & H. W. Foote, *Jeremiah Dummer*, Boston, Mass. 1935.

Dummy board figures Representations of men, women or children painted on a thin panel of wood (rarely canvas) and cut out to give a life-like effect. They probably originated in the Low Countries and were also used in late-C17 England as fire screens, and became very popular as decorations (usually placed near a wall so as to cast a shadow) in the mid C18. Maids with brooms, seated ladies, elegantly dressed men and pedlars were among the favourite subjects. Many imitations were made in mid-C19 England and again *c.*1920–39.

Dunand, Jean (1877–1942). He was born at Lancy in Switzerland, studied at the school of decorative arts in Geneva, then went to Paris where he worked under Jean Dampt (1854–1946). He began as a sculptor but after 1902 turned to the decorative arts, working mainly in metal and lacquer. At first his designs were naturalistic but after the war he adopted a geometrical ART DECO style. His most notable products are vases made of base metals and encrusted with geometrical patterns in gold, silver, enamel, etc. In 1921 he began exhibiting with Jean GOULDEN. *Illustrated opposite.*

Lit: Les années '25', Exh. Cat., Musée des Arts Décoratifs, Paris 1966.

Dunderdale, David, *see* CASTLEFORD POTTERY.

Dunlap, John (1746–1792). American furniture-maker born at Chester, New Hampshire, and working from 1768 at Goffstown. He served in the militia and rose to the rank of major. In 1773 he was joined by his brother **Samuel** (1752–1830). They made furniture, ranging from handsome highboys to very simple chairs and tables, much of which survives in New Hampshire. Major John Dunlap's account books also survive and provide a unique record of the practice of an American furniture-maker of this period.

Jean Dunand: Games table and chairs, lacquered wood and leather, c.1929 (Private Collection)

Lit: The Dunlaps and their Furniture, Exh. Cat., The Currier Gallery of Art, Manchester, New Hampshire, 1970.

Duplessis, Jean-Claude (d.1774). Italian goldsmith, sculptor, *fondeur-ciseleur* and designer, whose original name was Ciamberlano, he was born in Turin. He was working for the House of Savoy in 1733 but had settled in Paris by 1742 when he was commissioned to make a pair of bronze braziers for Louis XV to give to the Sultan's ambassador. His style is more restrained than that of his compatriot MEISSONNIER (who may have persuaded him to go to France); his ornamental designs depend chiefly on acanthus leaves and figural motifs, and some of them appear to be related to those of Pierre GERMAIN as engraved in the latter's *Modèles et éléments d'orfèvrerie* (1748). He specialized in designing bronze or silver Rococo style mounts for porcelain and in 1747 joined the Vincennes porcelain factory, moving with it to SÈVRES and remaining on the staff until his death, though he continued to work on his own account as well (he supplied mounts for porcelain to the *marchand-mercier* Lazare Duvaux). He gave his name to a type of Sèvres vase with a flared scalloped rim and curious outcurving handles and is credited with the invention of several other models, e.g. the *vaisseau à mat,* elephant candelabra, etc. In 1758 he was appointed *orfèvre du Roi.* He also made mounts for furniture, notably for the celebrated *bureau du Roi Louis XV* by OEBEN and RIESENER 1760–69 (Louvre).

Lit: G. Levallet in *La Renaissance de l'art français,* V (1922), pp. 60–67.

Dupont, Pierre, *see* SAVONNERIE CARPET FACTORY.

Duranti, Pietro, *see* NAPLES TAPESTRY FACTORY.

Durantino, Guido, *see* FONTANA FACTORY.

Dürer, Albrecht (1471–1528). The greatest German painter and engraver, Dürer began his

A. Dürer: drawing of five cups, inscribed 'Tomorrow I shall do more' (Landesmuseum, Dresden)

career as a goldsmith in Nuremberg, working under his father **Albrecht the elder** (1427–1502). Though concerned mainly with the figurative arts he made, from time to time throughout his career, a number of drawings for metalwork either as designs for craftsmen or as studies for details in his own paintings and prints – including richly embossed covered cups either of the 'columbine' type or based on such natural forms as the gourd. Cups ascribed to L. KRUG (whose father was an associate of Dürer's father) sometimes show similarities with these drawings. And the style of metalwork was revived in late-c16 Nuremberg by H. PETZOLT and others, possibly as an expression of a 'Dürer revival'.

Lit: H. Kohlhausen, *Nürnberger Goldschmiedkunst des Mittelalters und der Dürerzeit*, Berlin 1968.

Durham China Company, *see* TYNESIDE POTTERIES.

Durlach pottery A faience factory founded at Durlach (Baden) by J. H. WACHENFELD 1723, it continued to function until 1847. Its best period runs from 1762 to 1818, under the management of **C. F.** and **J. A. Benckieser** when a speciality was made of pear-shaped jugs and coffee pots painted in a late Rococo style with figures of rural workmen with inscriptions and dates. Cream-coloured earthenware was also made. No factory mark was used but the painters sometimes marked their work. After *c.*1818 cream-coloured earthenware was marked 'Durlach' impressed.

Lit: O. Hanger, *Durlacher Fayencen*, Karlsruhe 1951; K. Hüseler, *Deutsche Fayencen* I, Stuttgart 1956; E. Petrasch, *Durlacher Fayencen 1723–1847*, Exh. Cat., Karlsruhe 1975.

Duseuil, Augustin (1673–1746). Leading Parisian bookbinder, he worked for the Duc de Berry from 1714 and was bookbinder to Louis XV from 1717. He specialized in very elaborate work. His reputation extended to England and Alexander Pope remarked (*Moral Essays* IV) of the books in Timon's 'library': 'These Aldus printed, those Du Seuil has bound.'

Duvivier, Claude (*fl.*1720–35). Parisian silversmith known for a Rococo candelabra with roses emerging from an asymmetrical swirl of silver (1734, Musée des Arts Décoratifs, Paris) which follows exactly a design by MEISSONNIER.

C. Duvivier: silver candlestick after a design by Meissonnier, 1734–5 (Musée des Arts Décoratifs, Paris)

Duvivier, Henri-Joseph, *see* TOURNAI POTTERY AND PORCELAIN FACTORY.

Dwight, John (*c.*1635–1703). A figure of outstanding importance in the development of English pottery. He began as an ecclesiastical lawyer but in 1671 took out a patent for 'Transparent Earthenware, Commonly knowne by the Names of Porcelain of China and Persian Ware, as also the Misterie of the Stone Ware vulgarly called Cologne Ware'. Establishing a pottery at Fulham he produced BELLARMINES similar to but coarser than those of RHENISH STONEWARE, and in 1676 and 1677 contracted to supply stoneware bottles to the Glass Sellers' Company. He also made red stoneware similar to that of YI-HSING, especially pots for tea which was becoming a fashionable drink. To protect his patents he took legal action against other potters including J. P. and D. ELERS who had been among his employees. These wares mark the beginning of the line of development which leads to WEDGWOOD and the establishment of Staffordshire as an international centre for the production of pottery. But from an artistic point of view his most notable products were salt-glazed stoneware figures which rank among the best examples of English sculpture of their period, ranging from small statuettes of ancient gods and the very

J. Dwight: life-size stoneware bust of Prince Rupert, c.1675 (British Museum)

beautiful portrait of his dead daughter Lydia (Victoria & Albert Museum) to a life-size and very life-like bust of Prince Rupert (British Museum).

Lit: F. H. Garner in *Transactions of the English Ceramic Circle*, V (1937), pp. 30 ff., and K. A. Esdail, *idem* VI (1939), pp. 40 ff.

Dyes Colouring matters, generally applied in solution and used for tingeing textiles, paper, leather, ivory, linoleum, plastics, etc. They differ from pigments in that they combine, often chemically, with the material treated. To 'fix' them, i.e. make them insoluble after application, MORDANTS are used though they may still remain unfast to light, washing and alkali. Until the mid C19 dyes were natural (i.e. organic), mostly of vegetable or insect origin. The majority had been in use since prehistoric or at least very early times. The only important additions before 1800 were some American wood and insect dyes e.g. brazil wood. The original colour range was very limited.

Blues: Woad and indigo, vegetable dyes, the former known in Egypt and Mesopotamia since *c.*3000 B.C., the latter in Egypt since *c.*2500 B.C., though not in common use until *c.*500 B.C.

Reds: Madder, a vegetable dye, known in antiquity and perhaps earlier (pieces of 3rd millennium B.C. cotton from the Indus valley are said to be dyed with it). Kermes and cochineal, insect dyes – from the dead bodies of female scale insects parasitic on certain plants – the former a native of the Old World and known in antiquity, the latter from the New World.

Purples: Purpura and murex, animal dyes from whelk-like molluscs found especially in the E. Mediterranean between Tyre and Sidon and used for the Roman 'Imperial Purple' the secret of which was lost with the fall of Byzantium. The purple or violet cudber dye, prepared from lichens, was discovered in the C18 by Dr Cuthbert Gordon.

Yellows: Weld, saffron, sunflower and annetto vegetable dyes, known since prehistoric times as was fustic, a wood dye.

Other colours could be obtained by combinations, e.g. greens from indigo and weld. Black was obtained by superimposing dark shades or by adding extract of oak-gall to iron sulphate.

Though E. Buncroft distinguished substantive and adjective dyes (see below) in 1794, no scientific advance was made in the dyeing industry until the introduction of Prussian blue and the revolutionary discovery of the first synthetic dyestuffs in the mid C19. **Sir William Henry Perkin** (1838–1907) discovered the first accidentally when trying to prepare quinine from allyltolmidine in 1856. He produced the first aniline dye – from nitro-benzene derived from coal tar – patented it and began commercial production in 1857. It dyed silk a brilliant violet: cotton had to be mordanted with tannic acid. Popularity was immediate and it was known in France as *mauve*. Queen Victoria wore a dress of this colour at the Great Exhibition of 1862, and it was also used to dye penny postage stamps. Further aniline dyes soon followed – magenta (1859), sulphonated blue (1859) and black (1863). A second group of synthetic dyes – the Azo dyes – were developed in the 1860s, notably Bismack brown and induline.

Two further important synthetic dyes resulted from Kekule's benzene formula of 1865; alizarin which was discovered by **Heinrich Caro** and Perkins independently in 1869 and quickly superseded madder; ingotin, discovered by **A. von Baeyer** *c.*1880, though not manufactured commercially until 1897, superseded indigo. Sulphur dyes (green and black) were discovered by **Croissent** and **Bretonnière** in 1873. Methylene blue, discovered by Caro in 1876, was followed by its derivative methylene green. In 1884 **Böttger** discovered Congo red, the first synthetic dye that would dye cotton directly.

Dyers classify dyes according to the processes of applying them:

Vat dyes: These are insoluble in water and have to be converted into a soluble derivative, such as leuco-indigotin, before they can be absorbed by the fibres of a fabric. After being impregnated with the leuco form, the dye is re-converted to its original form, usually by oxidization.

Substantive dyes: These dye a fabric directly and are easy to use but apt to wash out.

Adjective dyes: These are mordant dyes which have to be fixed.

Sulphur dyes: These are direct dyes for cotton and are usually applied from a solution containing soda and sodium sulphate.

Ingrain dyes: These are insoluble Azo dyes which are produced on the fabric itself by soaking it in a solution of some compound capable of reacting with a diaz-salt to form an insoluble body. On dipping the fabric in a bath of this diaz-salt the dye is precipitated on the fibres.

Dyes may be applied to fibres in the hank (i.e. before the thread is woven into a fabric) or in the cloth (after weaving). Pattern dyeing involves various techniques, by painting with a brush, by stencilling, or by wax resist (or BATIK) in which areas are reserved by a coating of wax, the material dip-dyed, washed and boiled to remove the wax. In a cruder form of resist dyeing, called tie-dyeing, areas of the fabric are tied off or bound with wax-impregnated cord to protect them from the dye. Dyes thickened with gum may also be applied by means of printing blocks, copper plates, etc. (*see* COTTON, BLOCK-PRINTED, etc.).

Lit: E. Mairet, *Vegetable Dyes*, London, 1939; S. Robinson, *A History of Dyed Textiles*, London 1969.

Dyottville Glass Works An American glasshouse at Kensington, Pennsylvania. It was established in 1771 as the **Kensington Glass Works** but changed its name in 1831 when it was bought by **Dr T. W. Dyott.** It produced flint-glass table-wares as well as vials and bottles but is known especially for its pictorial and historical flasks. Dyott went bankrupt in 1838 but the glasshouse continued in production, adding coloured glass to its range in the 1840s.

Dyson Perrins, Charles William, *see* WORCESTER PORCELAIN FACTORY.

Dyzes or **D'Yses, Jean,** *see* SAMADET POTTERY.

Wood-cut letter from Opera *of Boethius, printed by Luc Antonio Giunta, Venice, 1536*

Eames, Charles (b.1907). American architect and designer, he is one of the most influential furniture designers in the mid C20. His plastic shell chairs have been copied all over the world, revolutionizing domestic and office furniture as widely as did BREUER's tubular steel chair in the 1920s. He was trained as an architect and worked in Eliel Saarinen's office 1939–40. He and Eero SAARINEN were the first to appreciate and exploit the artistic possibilities of the new mid-C20 materials and process techniques, notably PLASTICS, which enable a chair seat, for example, to be manufactured in much the same way as a motor-car body is stamped out in a die-press. And he and Saarinen were also among the first to appreciate that a new type of furniture was demanded by modern architecture with its glass walls and open-planning which forces furniture away from the walls and out into the centre of a room where it is seen in the round like free-standing sculpture. The famous house he designed for himself in Santa Monica, California, in 1949 is a steel frame building made with standard prefabricated parts, reminiscent of Japanese architecture in its lightness and open-planning. He was also the first to use airplane plastics for furniture and his and Saarinen's designs have been strongly influenced by airplane 'aesthetics'. Their chairs often have an airborne look. In general Eames's furniture epitomizes the mid-C20 trend away from geometrical austerity and angularity towards more organic and sculptural forms.

His first notable design came in 1940, in collaboration with Saarinen, for a chair in moulded plywood and aluminium. The plywood seat was moulded into a multi-curved shell which anticipated the forms taken by plastics after the

(Below and opposite above) C. Eames and E. Saarinen: design for an armchair, 1940, one of the winning designs submitted for the exhibition 'Organic Design in Home Furnishing' (Museum of Modern Art, New York)

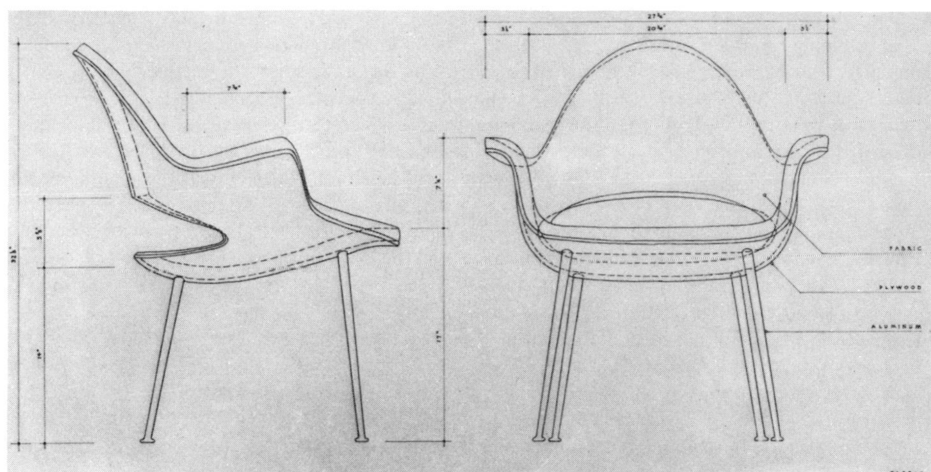

war. The design was awarded a prize by the Museum of Modern Art in New York in 1941 but wartime shortages and difficulties prevented the execution of the chair according to the design. It was not until after the war that Eames could embark on his career in which he pioneered the use of stamped plastic in furniture. (At first he used steel coated with neoprane but later polyester reinforced with fibreglass which is virtually indestructible, withstands stains and marks, and quickly absorbs room temperatures.) For chairs a single sheet of plastic was stamped out to form the seat, back and arms, usually set on a conventional metal rod or wire support to give the maximum visual contrast with the moulded shell. In 1948 he designed his classic model, mounted on a delicate metal rod support.

C. Eames: lounge chair and footstool of laminated rosewood and anodized aluminium with down- or foam-filled cushions, 1957

The so-called 'Eames Chair' is of a different type, a dining-chair consisting of two pads of moulded body-curved plywood attached to a metal rod frame with rubber cushions as connectors. It was designed in 1946 for Herman Miller Inc., who manufacture it. His other notable and influential designs include a plastic-seated upright chair supported on a cage of metal rods (1951), and a much admired and plagiarized armchair and footstool in laminated rosewood and anodized aluminium, with feather-stuffed Naugahyde cushions, was designed in 1957. In 1963 he designed some excellent polished aluminium tandem seating for O'Hare Airport, Chicago.

Eames has not confined his attention to chairs. He has designed fine collapsible tables on slender metal rod supports, a remarkably elegant screen composed of undulating panels of ash plywood, radio cabinets, etc. With Eero Saarinen in 1940 he made designs for standardized storage units, based on an 18-inch module and so devised that the shelved cabinets stand on bench-like supports which may alternatively be used as seats or tables. Following this up in 1950 he devised a series of storage units in which the wood of drawers and shelves is contrasted with the polished aluminium of the frame. All the components of these units were taken from readily available industrial products – continuous angle-pieces, with rods as tracers, for the frame, and regularly shaped plywood panels for the woodwork.

Eames Furniture is marketed by Herman Miller Inc., and is made under licence in England by Hille.

Lit: A. Drexler, *Charles Eames – Furniture*, New York 1973.

Earthenware, *see* POTTERY.

East Indian Company porcelain, *see* CHINESE EXPORT PORCELAIN.

Eastlake, Charles Lock (1836–1906). English architect and writer on art, architecture and interior decoration. He was the nephew of Sir Charles Lock Eastlake, P.R.A. (1793–1865). He is remembered mainly for his *History of the Gothic Revival* (1872) but was famous in his own day for his *Hints on Household Taste in Furniture, Upholstery and other Details* (1868) which was very influential and helped to drive the crowded, fussy, over-stuffed furniture and furnishings of the Early Victorian period out of fashion. He set out to combine 'a sense of the picturesque . . . with modern comfort and convenience' and emphasized simplicity, rectangularity and honest craftsmanship. His prolific designs included wallpapers, textiles, ceramic tiles, wrought-ironwork, etc., as well as furniture. They were all 'austerely picturesque' and he aimed not at the 'absolute forms' but the 'spirit and principles of early manufacture'. Between 1860 and 1900 Eastlake furniture became first fashionable, then commonplace. He was as well or even better known in America where his book was published in 1872 and where his name became a household word. Furnishings in an 'improved' taste were said, in America, to be 'Eastlaked'. But much of the so-called 'Eastlake Style' furniture produced in the U.S. was of a rather shoddy type of Gothic Revival which seldom answered his demands for simplicity, solidity and sound craftsmanship.

C. E. Eastlake: bedroom chest-of-drawers from Hints on Household Taste, *1869*

Lit: R. W. Symonds & B. B. Whinneray, *Victorian Furniture*, London 1962; Charles L. Eastlake, *A History of the Gothic Revival* (1872), ed. J. Mordaunt Crook, Leicester 1970; M. J. Smith

Madigan, *Eastlake-influenced American Furniture 1870–1890*, Hudson River Museum, New York 1974.

Ébéniste A French cabinet-maker, as distinct from a MENUISIER or joiner. The *ébéniste* specialized in veneered furniture or *ébénisterie* (from ebony which was used in the earliest veneered furniture); the *menuisier* specialized in carved pieces in plain woods, especially chairs, beds, etc. Although a *maître* in the furniture-makers' guild (*corporation des menuisiers-ébénistes*) was allowed to practise both techniques, this rarely happened and the distinction between *ébéniste* and *menuisier* was maintained down to the Revolution. Similar specialization did not occur in other countries.

The art of veneering or *ébénisterie* appears to have been introduced into France from Germany and the Low Countries in the early C17 by the furniture-maker Jean Macé who was employed by Marie de Medici. The word *ébéniste* first appears in official documents in France in 1657. The distinction between *ébéniste* and *menuisier* was not formally recognized until 1745, in the revised statutes of the Corporation des Menuisiers.

Eberlein, Johann Friedrich (1693/6–1749). Sculptor, born in Dresden, who, after working for the Saxon Court and in England, became in 1735 the principal assistant of J. J. KÄNDLER at MEISSEN where he was involved in the design and execution of several major works, e.g. the Neptune Fountain (destroyed) and Swan Service. Though an assistant to Kändler he had more experience as a sculptor and may have exerted some influence on him.

Lit: E. Zimmermann, *Meissner Porzellan*, Leipzig 1926.

Ebonized Stained or otherwise coloured to look like EBONY. Woods were so treated from the Renaissance onwards, quite commonly for furniture in the English Regency and American Empire Styles.

Ebony A very heavy, hard wood, fine-grained and jet black in colour, sometimes streaked with yellow or brown. It comes from the *Diospyros Ebenum* or other species of the large *Ebenaceae* family of trees found in tropical climates. That used by French *ébénistes* came mostly from Madagascar. A variety with pronounced light-coloured strips from the Coromandel Coast is known as **Zebra Wood** or **Coromandel Wood.**

Echinus A quarter-round or ovolo moulding, often enriched with EGG AND DART pattern. Strictly, the curved moulding below the abacus of a Greek Doric capital.

Echizen potteries One of the 'Six Ancient Kilns' of Japan, but much less productive than the SETO, TOKONAME and other potteries thus described. They were situated near Takefu in the Fukui prefecture and appear to have been active from the C12. The most notable early products are big water jars, up to 1 m. in diameter, of globular form with natural wood-ash glazes.

Lit: S. Jenyns, *Japanese Pottery*, London 1971.

Eckernförde pottery A faience factory founded at Criseby in Schleswig in 1759, moved to Eckernförde in 1765, and closed down in 1785. During its best period, when **Johann Buchwald** was working there as modeller, from 1761–8 (with his son-in-law A. LEIHAMER as painter from 1764), it produced boldly modelled and decorated Rococo table-centres, tureens and vases painted with flowers in brilliant colours. Products also included large trays and table tops. (For factory mark *see* p. 883.)

Lit: K. Hüseler, *Geschichte der Schleswig–Holsteinischen Fayence-Manufacturen im 18 Jahrhundert*, Breslau 1929.

Eckmann, Otto (1865–1902). German graphic artist and Art Nouveau designer. He began as a landscape painter but in 1894 burned all his canvases and took up the decorative arts, working in Munich. His main achievement was the creation of a semi-italic Art Nouveau type-face. A debilitated world weariness, expressed in wilting flowers and drooping curves, marks his work, which included designs for metalwork and tapestries – though his furniture could be simple and bold, with a suggestion of the rustic. *Illustrated next page.*

Lit: H. Selig (ed.), *Jugendstil*, Heidelberg–Munich 1959; R. Schmutzler, *Art Nouveau*, London 1964.

O. Eckmann: cupboard, c.1900 (Hessisches Landesmuseum, Darmstadt)

Écuelle A shallow bowl, usually of silver but sometimes of porcelain or faience, with two handles and a cover. It was used for individual service of soup, etc., and was very popular in late-C17 and C18 France, less common in England, Germany and Italy.

Edinburgh weavers Formed in 1934 as a subsidiary of **Morton Sundour Fabrics** to manufacture high-quality furnishing fabrics. Under the direction of **Alastair Morton** (d.1963), the firm commissioned designs by such artists as Marino Marini, William Scott, Hans Tisdall, Jo Tilson, Keith Vaughan and Victor Vasarely. Prints were included, but the best work was in finely executed, large-scale woven fabrics whose subtlety of pattern and colour marked them out from their competitors. Now controlled by Courtaulds, the firm still produces work of distinction.

Edkins, Michael (1734–1811). English decorator of ceramics and, more notably, glass, working in Bristol. His ledger (Bristol Museum) reveals that he worked for several different glass-makers, presumably on a free-lance basis, 1762–87. Opaque glass vessels painted with flowers and butterflies similar to those which appear on porcelain of the same period are often attributed to him. But no documented works by him are recorded. *See also* BRISTOL GLASSHOUSES.

Edwards, John (1671–1746). He was an American silversmith, working in Boston where he had probably been apprenticed to Jeremiah DUMMER. He was in partnership with **John Allen.** He made both domestic and church plate and examples are in the Worcester Art Museum and the Yale University Art Gallery. His joint mark with Allen is an IE and IA in quatrefoil. His sons **Samuel** (1705–62) and **Thomas** (1701–55) and his grandson **Joseph** were all silversmiths in Boston.

Edwards of Halifax An C18 bindery founded by **William Edwards** and continued by his sons. Several innovations in decorative bindings were due to them: concealed fore-edge painting under gold (visible only when the leaves are splayed out); a technique, patented by Edwards in 1785, for underpainting transparent vellum in colour or monochrome; and the so-called 'Etruscan bindings' in calf stained to imitate the terracotta colours of Greek and Etruscan vases.

Eenhorn, Lambertus van (1651–1721). He succeeded L. CLEFFIUS owner of a very prolific DELFT pottery, *De metale Pot*, 1691–1721, producing wares painted in high-temperature colours, notably plates and vases decorated in yellow on a black ground, and red stoneware, in addition to the usual blue-and-white chinoiserie pieces.

Lit: C. H. de Jonge, *Delft Ceramics*, London 1970.

Eenhorn, Samuel van (d.1685). Brother of **Lambertus van Eenhorn** and son of **Wouter van Eenhorn** from whom he took over in 1675 one of the best DELFT faience factories, *De Griekische A* (the Greek A), which he ran until 1685. He specialized in vases, large ornamental plates and such curiosities as wig-stands decorated in blue and white with rather closely packed chinoiseries. Figures are outlined in purple or black TREK, the blues vary attractively in density and the glaze tends to be bluish. On his death the factory passed to A. KOCX.

Lit: C. H. de Jonge, *Delft Ceramics*, London 1970.

Egell, Paul (1691–1752). Leading German Rococo sculptor, he was Court Sculptor to the Elector at Mannheim from 1721. He is known mainly for his figurative works but also executed console tables and other pieces of carved furniture in an elegant and rather smooth Rococo style for the Schloss at Mannheim and the Thurn and Taxis Palace at Ratisbon.

Lit: H. Kreisel, *Die Kunst des deutschen Möbels*, vol. II, Munich 1970.

Egeri, Karl von (d.1562). Glass stainer working in Zurich and specializing in small panels of the type made as presents in Switzerland. The influence of HOLBEIN is evident in his use of Renaissance detail, but he had an individual taste for rank vegetation, burgeoning garlands and flamboyant plumed head-dresses (e.g. a panel of 1551 in the Victoria & Albert Museum, London).

Egermann, Friedrich (1777–1864). Notable Bohemian glass manufacturer, the inventor of Lithyalin (1828), a type of coloured glass simulating various precious stones. He also produced vessels of stained ruby and amber glass.

Lit: R. & L. Grover, *Carved and Decorated European Art Glass*, Rutland, Vermont, 1970.

Egg and dart or **egg and tongue** Repeating pattern of alternate eggs and arrow-heads, usually applied to an ovolo (quarter-round) moulding or an astragal (half-round).

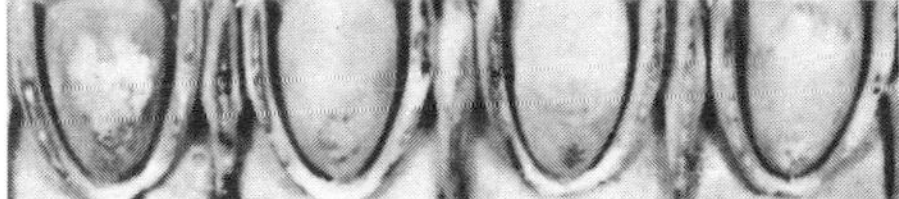

Egg and dart

Eggerbrecht, Peter, *see* DRESDEN FAIENCE FACTORY.

Eggshell porcelain Popular name for very thin porcelain, scarcely thicker than the shell of a hen's egg, especially that made in China from the MING period onwards.

Eglomisé, *see* VERRE EGLOMISÉ.

Egyptian taste or **Egyptiennerie** The fashion for decorative motifs derived from ancient Egyptian symbols, hieroglyphics and architectural ornament. Sphinxes, pyramids and obelisks made occasional appearances in Renaissance art but not until the C18 was the full range of motifs employed. One of the earliest full-blooded manifestations is the fantastic gem-encrusted Apis Altar, incorporating bird-headed men and topped by an obelisk decorated with (meaningless) hieroglyphics, made by J. M. DINGLINGER in 1731 (Grünes Gewölbe, Dresden). Egyptian art was treated with greater respect by G. B. PIRANESI who designed (1769) seriously solid chimney-pieces in the style and also a frescoed Egyptian room for the English Coffee House in Rome (which probably inspired James Playfair's Egyptian billiard room of 1792 at Cairness House, Scotland). The discovery of numerous Roman C3 A.D. artifacts incorporating Egyptian motifs (connected with the cult of Osiris) led Neo-classical designers to draw on Egypt in much the same way that Rococo designers had drawn on China. Winged disks, Egyptian caryatids, slaves holding lotus

Egyptian taste: table designed by Agostino Fantastici, c.1820, made in Siena (Collection: R. Bianchi-Bandinelli)

flowers, began to make their European *début* on furniture, silver and ceramics, especially in England, France and Italy of the 1780s and 1790s. A new boost was given to the fashion in France by Napoleon's North African campaign of 1798 and the subsequent publication of books containing accurate illustrations of Egyptian buildings and their decorations, notably V. Denon's *Voyage dans la Basse et la Haute Egypte* 1802 (published during the Peace of Amiens and thus available in England as well as France). Acquiring a Napoleonic significance, Egyptian motifs proliferated on furniture, silver and ceramics of the Empire. BIENNAIS made a coin cabinet modelled on the pylon at Ghoos; SÈVRES sugar bowls accurately reproduced the form of Egyptian funerary urns. In England Thomas HOPE led the fashion for archaeologically correct *Egyptienneries* which affected the design of furniture, silver and – to a lesser extent – ceramics. It lingered on in England and on the Continent until the 1830s.

Lit: N. Pevsner, *Studies in Art, Architecture & Design*, vol. I, London 1968.

Egyptian taste: sugar bowl from the Sèvres 'Egyptian Service' (Collection: Duke of Wellington)

Ehrenfeld glasshouse A factory near Cologne producing pressed and Bohemian-style glass in the mid C19. Under the direction of Oskar Rauter from 1872 it also produced handmade pieces, freely imitated from old German and Venetian prototypes (especially FLÜGELGLÄSER), which were first put on the market in 1880 and won prizes at several international exhibitions, Nuremberg 1881, Antwerp 1885, Paris 1900. Other products included elegantly simple tablewares and, around 1900, glasses tinged with Art Nouveau influence.

Lit: Kunstgewerbemuseum Köln: Glas, Cologne 1963.

Ehrenreich, Johan Ludwig Eberhard, *see* MARIEBERG, STRALSUND and KÖNIGSBERG POTTERIES.

Eilbertus of Cologne (*c.*1130–40). A portable altar decorated with champlevé enamel is inscribed *Eilbertus Coloniensis me fecit* (Berlin, Staatliche Museen). Nothing else is known about Eilbertus but he has been associated with the *'zeichnerische Stil'* or 'sketchy style' of the early C12 in Germany and a number of works have been attributed to him, e.g. a portable altar of *c.*1150–60 with the Cardinal Virtues (Berlin, Staatliche Museen) and six large enamelled plaques of *c.*1150 (Hildesheim Cathedral Treasury).

Lit: P. Lasko, *Ars Sacra 800–1200*, Pelican History of Art, Harmondsworth 1972; M.-M. Gauthier, *Émaux du moyen âge occidental*, Fribourg 1972.

Ekberg, Josef, *see* GUSTAVSBERG POTTERY.

Electroplate Wares made of metal, usually nickel and therefore commonly called E.P.N.S. though sometimes of copper, and coated with silver by electrolysis. The process was patented by G. R. ELKINGTON in 1840, anticipating by a few months the patenting in France of a similar process by *Ruolz*. Elkington revolutionized the silver trade and Electroplate quickly superseded SHEFFIELD PLATE as a cheap substitute for solid silver. By 1852 there was only one metal workshop in Sheffield still making Sheffield Plate. The great advantage of Electroplate is that worn articles can be replated cheaply and easily. Apart from Elkington in England the chief makers of Electroplate were REED & BARTON in the U.S.A. and Elkington's licensee in France CHRISTOFLE.

Elkington began experiments in 1830 to discover a method of gilding less dangerous than the mercury process. The first of his many patents, taken out in 1839, was for an improved method of 'gilding copper, brass and other metals or alloys of metals' by a process which in fact involved electrolysis though it is doubtful if he was aware of its physio-chemical niceties. In March 1840 he took out a patent for plating by means of a galvanic current.

His process was the culmination of a series of experiments carried out by scientists in different parts of Europe. Alessandro Volta had discovered that a current of electricity may be generated by bringing two or more metals into contact with a suitable fluid. It was then found that an electric current passed through a conducting liquid would decompose its ingredients and set their elements free at the immersed poles. In 1801 Dr William Hyde Wollaston succeeded in coating a piece of silver with copper and in 1805 L. V. Brugnatelli gilded two silver medals by electrolysis. In 1815 Paul STORR gilded a goblet by electrolysis, and it seems likely that RUNDELL, BRIDGE & RUNDELL produced other similar wares.

But the process would have had little practical value had it not been discovered that the alloy known variously as German silver or Nickel Silver – an alloy of about forty parts copper, twenty spelter and twenty nickel (first discovered in the C18) – provided the best base on which to deposit silver by electrolysis, though BRITANNIA METAL was also used (known as E.P.B.M.). It was then discovered by the Elkingtons (with a metallurgist Alexander Parkes and a surgeon John Wright) that thick, even and durable deposits of silver could be obtained by the addition of cyanides of silver to the liquid. This left a film of frosty white silver that had to be burnished. It was not until 1847 that it was discovered, by two of Elkington's employees, that the addition of bisulphide of carbon would cure this defect.

Lit: W. Blum & G. B. Hobaboom, *Principles of Electroplating and Electroforming*, London & New York 1949; P. Wardle, *Victorian Silver and Silver Plate*, London 1963; S. Bury, *Victorian Electroplate*, London 1971.

Electrotype A metal reproduction made by a process developed in the 1830s and related to that of the ELECTROPLATE. Instead of depositing by electrolysis a skin of silver or gold or other metal on a finished base metal article, as in electroplating, the whole article was made in the plating vat. It is an electrical equivalent of casting. Electrotypes are known on the continent as Galvanoplastic copies. The process may have originated with W. de la Rue in 1836 but it was being developed almost simultaneously in *c.*1839 by Professor H. H. van Jacobi of St Petersburg, by Thomas Spencer of London and C. J. Jordan of London. In the 1840s ELKINGTON patented a series of improvements evolved by his metallurgist Alexander Parkes and subsequently dominated the English trade in electrotypes. At first electrotypes were made of copper from wax moulds of the object being reproduced – which might be a piece of Italian Renaissance silver, a contemporary piece of metalwork or a natural object – but later metal moulds were made from a cast. Eventually, several skilled designers and craftsmen made objects specifically with a view to their reproduction as electrotypes, e.g. Antoine VECHTE's National Medallion of 1856 and L. Morel-Ladeuil's Milton Shield of 1867, both now in the Victoria & Albert Museum.

Lit: S. Bury, *Victorian Electroplate*, London 1971.

Electrum A natural alloy of silver and gold used from very early times for metalwork (e.g. in Persia) but more usually as a source for both gold and silver. It now yields about 15 per cent of the world's supply of silver.

Elephant foot A pattern of octagons arranged in rows and columns on Middle Eastern (especially TURKMAN) carpets. Various symbolical meanings have been attributed to it in the West.

Elers, David and John Philip (*fl.*1686–1700). They were brothers who began their careers as silversmiths in Holland, settled in England *c.*1686 and worked as assistants to John DWIGHT in his pottery at Fulham from 1690 to 1693 when they set up on their own at Bradwell Wood in Staffordshire making brown mugs and red stoneware teapots, thus infringing on Dwight's patent. David Elers appears to have been a merchant and John Philip Elers the chemist and potter. The relatively few pieces that may be attributed to them comprise small mugs, teapots, tea-canisters and tea-cups of thin fine red stoneware, which sometimes seems to have been turned on a lathe after throwing, generally decorated with reliefs (from delicately cut metal stamps) of sprays of prunus or chinoiserie birds and occasionally gilt or enamelled. They closed their workshop in 1698 and John Philip had established himself as a dealer in Dublin by 1700 (he was the ancestor of the novelist Maria Edgeworth). But their wares were much imitated and set a new standard for pottery in STAFFORDSHIRE.

Lit: W. B. Honey in *Transactions of the English Ceramic Circle*, II (1934), pp. 7 ff.

Elizabethan silver bell-salt, 1594–5 (Victoria & Albert Museum)

(Left) Elizabethan stained-glass from Preston Hall, Suffolk, c.1600 *(Victoria & Albert Museum)*

(Opposite) Elizabethan petit point table cover, c.1600 *(Victoria & Albert Museum)*

Elizabethan style A term of little stylistic meaning since it is applied to objects made in England during the reign of Elizabeth I (1558–1603), which are often difficult to distinguish from those made under Henry VIII (1509–47), Edward VI

(1547–53) and Mary I (1553–8). The major change in English decorative arts had begun under Henry VIII with the introduction of the RENAISSANCE STYLE by HOLBEIN and various immigrant Italian craftsmen. Under Elizabeth this Italian influence was maintained by the Venetian VERZELINI in glass but otherwise Germany, France and the Low Countries became much more influential. Flemish and German pattern books like those of BROSAMER, Virgil SOLIS and Hans COLLAERT were imported. There was also an influx of Protestant refugee craftsmen from various N. European countries. Elizabethan woodwork, metalwork and textiles may be decorated with a variety of ornamental motifs – some inherited from the native Gothic past, others derived from Italy direct and still more of Italian origin transmitted (and distorted) by Germany and the Low Countries. Different types of craftsmen were susceptible to influences from different directions. The only characteristic common to all the finer objects is richness of surface decoration: 'Costly apparel, tents and canopies Fine linen, Turkey cushions boss'd with pearl, Valance of Venice gold in needle work' and so on.

Furniture tended to be massive, squat and richly carved with a mixture of Gothic and Renaissance motifs. Sturdy balusters of cup-and-cover form were popular for the legs of tables, the supports of shelves of court-cupboards, etc. Marquetry representing fantastic buildings was occasionally used on the finer pieces, notably the so-called Nonsuch chests. Pottery was very simple and probably used at table only in the humbler houses, though Chinese porcelain, Isnik pottery and German stone-glazed wares were imported and set in elaborate silver mounts for the rich. In glass there is a similar distinction between the coarse green Weald glass for common use and imported Venetian crystal glass or English imitations made by immigrant Italians like Verzelini. Textiles show perhaps the strongest links with the Gothic past, especially the cushion covers and table covers embroidered with delicate arabesque patterns of flowers, foliage and coiling tendrils. Most tapestry hangings were imported, though William SHELDON's factories wove a number with figures of Flemish origin interpreted with an attractive homely naïveté. The finest Elizabethan objects, both for craftsmanship and design, are in silver. They range from the Protestant severity of Communion cups to the elaboration of salts and ceremonial cups and flagons. But here again foreign influences were strong, patterns were often derived from Flemish or German sources, and most of the engraved work seems to have been carried out by foreign craftsmen who had settled in London.

Elkington, George Richards (1801–65). A Birmingham metalwork manufacturer who revolutionized the silver trade by developing an electroplating process which he patented in 1840, anticipating by a few months a similar patent taken out in France by **Ruolz.** He was born in Birmingham and inherited a gilt toy and spectacle factory which he ran in partnership with his cousin **Henry Elkington** (*c.*1810–52). His first experiments were directed towards a method of gilding less dangerous than the mercury process. His electroplating process was not perfected for a few years after 1840. In 1842 a wealthy pen manufacturer, Josiah Mason, was taken into partnership and the firm became **Elkington, Mason & Co.** The electroplating patent was licensed out to various silversmiths (e.g. CHRISTOFLE in France in 1842, JAMES DIXON & SONS in Birmingham in 1848) but by 1847 Elkington's own factory was producing large quantities of electroplated table-wares for hotels, clubs, steamship companies, etc., as well as for private customers. From that time onwards ELECTROPLATE rapidly superseded SHEFFIELD PLATE as a cheap substitute for solid silver. One of its great advantages – that articles could be cheaply and easily replated – was quickly

Elkington's 1847 catalogue, promoting his electroplating process.

recognized and exploited. Elkingtons prospered mainly from the mass-production of useful wares, especially for hotels and restaurants. But the firm also produced decorative pieces in a great variety of styles from the Moorish (e.g. vase in Museum für angewandte Kunst, Vienna) to the Italian Renaissance, including reproductions made by the related process of ELECTROTYPES for which Elkington also took out patents. Examples of their electrotypes are in the Victoria and Albert Museum. They also competed with such firms as GARRARD, and STORR's successors Hunt & Roskill, in the production of massive solid silver presentation and exhibition pieces. Several, mainly French, artists were employed as designers for the more ornamental pieces, notably Albert Wilms (who had previously worked for Christofle and for FROMENT-MEURICE in Paris), Benjamin Schlick (who was much admired by the Prince Consort), Pierre-Émile Jeannest (who had previously worked for MINTON's pottery and porcelain factory) and **Léonard Morel-Ladeuil** (*c.*1820–88) who had been a pupil of Antoine VECHTE. Morel-Ladeuil was employed by Elkington from 1859 until his death and was responsible for such intricate and, at the time, greatly admired works as the Inventions Vase of 1863 and the Milton Shield for which he won a gold medal at the Paris Exhibition of 1867 (both in the Victoria & Albert Museum). G. R. Elkington made a fortune and at the time of his death the staff of the firm numbered more than a thousand men and women. And it continued to prosper and grow. In the 1880s some severely functional pieces of electroplate were made to designs by C. DRESSER, but these appear to have been exceptions to the generally more traditional rule of their products. The firm still flourishes – as part of British Silverware Ltd since 1963.

G. R. Elkington: the 'Inventions Vase', designed by L. Morel-Ladeuil, silver, Birmingham 1863 (Victoria & Albert Museum)

Lit: P. Wardle, *Victorian Silver and Silver Plate*, London 1963; H. Honour, *Goldsmiths and Silversmiths*, London and New York 1971; S. Bury, *Victorian Electroplate*, London 1971.

Elliott, Charles (*fl.*1783–1810). London cabinet-maker specializing in very elegant satin-wood furniture often decorated with delicately discreet inlays. He was much patronized by the Royal Family whom he also served as an upholsterer from *c.*1784.

Lit: R. Edwards & M. Jourdain, *Georgian Cabinetmakers*, London 1955.

Elliott, John (1713–91). Born in England, he emigrated to Philadelphia in 1753 and became well known as a maker of mirrors, especially fret-work mirrors but also carved and gilded mirrors in the Chippendale style. He retired in 1776 but his business was carried on by his descendants until 1809. They also dealt in mirrors, sconces, etc., imported from London.

Lit: J. Downs, *American Furniture, Queen Anne and Chippendale Periods, in the Henry Francis du Pont Winterthur Museum*, New York 1952.

Elmslie, George Grant (1871–1952). Architect and designer of furniture, textiles, glass, metalwork, etc. He was born in Scotland, emigrated to the U.S.A. with his parents in 1884 and in 1887 began to work alongside F. L. WRIGHT and G. Maker in the Chicago office of the architect J. L. Silsbee. From 1889 he worked under Louis H. Sullivan and acted as his chief designer from 1895 to 1909 when he went into partnership with two other architects. He designed complete sets of household furnishings, including carpets, usually ornamented with prickly stylized plant motifs similar to those found on buildings by Sullivan.

Lit: R. Judson Clark (ed.), *The Arts and Crafts Movement in America, 1876–1916*, Exh. Cat., Art Museum Princeton University, Art Institute of Chicago, etc., 1972–3.

Elsinore tapestries A group of Danish tapestry panels of which fourteen survive (National Museum, Copenhagen and Kronborg Castle), woven at Elsinore 1581–4 to cartoons by a

Elsinore tapestry, 1581–4 (National Museum, Copenhagen)

Flemish painter, **Hans Knieper,** for the Kronborg Castle. They represent the succession of (mostly legendary) Danish Kings standing against landscape backgrounds which occasionally include scenes of war and hunting.

Lit: H. Göbel, *Wandteppiche*, Leipzig 1923–34; M. Mackeprang & S. F. Christensen, *Kronborg Tapeterne*, Copenhagen 1950.

Elton, Sir Edmund Harry (1846–1920). English art potter who in 1883 succeeded to a baronetcy and inherited Clevedon Court in Somerset where, with the aid of an assistant potter, **G. Masters,** he made earthenware vessels decorated with flower patterns in coloured slips (blue, red or green). His products, known as 'Elton ware', were shown at the Arts and Crafts Exhibition Society of which he was a member.

Elward, Marsh and Tatham, *see* MARSH, William.

Émail brun Despite its name this is not a type of ENAMEL, though it was used together with champlevé enamel in the Middle Ages. Parts of a copper sheet are covered with linseed oil, set off by gilding; the mercury of the gilding and linseed oil are then burnt away so that the copper is left a rich brown colour in contrast to the gold. It first appears on the front cover of Bernward's 'Precious Gospels' of *c.*1000–1010 (Hildesheim Cathedral Treasury) and was much used in the C12.

Émail ombrant A technique of decorating pottery by applying a coloured (usually green) glaze over impressed (i.e. intaglio) motifs so that the colour is darkest where the intaglio is deepest. First employed in the 1840s.

Embossed bindings A C19 type of bookbinding which developed from the early C19 revival of STAMPED BINDINGS. A die, instead of a panel stamp, is used and the leather is embossed before, not after, binding. The origin and date of introduction of embossed bindings are not known. In England they appeared soon after 1820 and by the mid C19 were very popular. There were three main types: cathedral, arabesque and engine-turned (i.e. with designs composed of very fine lines produced from dies, engine-turned with the Rose Machine).

Embossed binding, English, c.1840 (Victoria & Albert Museum)

Lit: E. Jamieson, *English Embossed Bindings 1825–1850*, Cambridge Bibliographical Society, Cambridge 1972.

Embossed work A generic term for relief decoration on metals, whether cast, CHASED or REPOUSSÉ and whether executed by hand or machine. In the C16 the term was also used for carved decorations on wood.

Embriachi, Baldassare degli (*fl.c.*1400). Founder and most important member of a N. Italian (probably Venetian) school of carvers in bone and, more rarely, ivory. His works range from small caskets to large altar-pieces composed of long narrow slightly curved bone panels carved with religious figures in a heavy late Gothic style. *Illustrated next page.*

Embroidery A textile embellished by hand with stitched patterns of threads, usually of silk or wool. The craft is very old and has been practised in all parts of the world. For types of embroidery see: APPLIQUÉ, BARGELLO WORK, BERLIN WOOLWORK,

Embriachi style casket, N. Italian, c15 (Victoria & Albert Museum)

BRODERIE ANGLAISE, CREWEL WORK, DRAWN WORK, OPUS ANGLICANUM, PATCH-WORK, PETIT POINT, QUILT, SAINT-CYR EMBROIDERIES, STUMP-WORK. For notable designers see: M. MACDONALD, J. B. MONNOYER, A. del POLLAJUOLO, P. RANSON, R. SHORLEYKER.

Lit: M. Schnette and S. Müller-Christensen, *The Art of Embroidery*, London 1964.

Emens, Jan, *see* MENNICKEN, Jan Emens.

Emes, John (d.1808). English silversmith who worked in London in partnership with **Henry Chawnor** from 1796 until 1798 when he registered his own mark. Chawnor probably retired in 1798. On Emes's death, his widow **Rebecca** continued the firm in partnership with his former chief journeyman **Edward Barnard** (as Emes & Barnard) who on her death in 1828 traded under the name of Barnard & Sons. The firm produced attractive domestic plate in the Regency style and, latterly, some fine presentation pieces, e.g. the Weymouth Regatta Cup of 1827–8 in the Victoria & Albert Museum. (For his mark *see* p. 893.)

Emperor carpets, *see* PERSIAN CARPETS.

Empire style The French late Neo-Classical style, closely associated with the tastes of Napoleon I who became first Consul in 1799, Emperor in 1804 and was finally banished in 1815. Despite the upheavals of the Revolution the transition from the LOUIS XVI STYLE to the Empire style was remarkably smooth (with a rather ambiguous intervening DIRECTOIRE STYLE). All the leading craftsmen had been trained in the previous period, many of them were already famous and had executed royal commissions, notably BENNEMAN, JACOB, MOLITOR, THOMIRE, WEISWEILER. Ornamental designs published in the reign of Louis XVI by CAUVET, DELAFOSSE, NEUFFORGE, SALEMBIER and others were used and imitated. The main changes were in emphasis rather than style and were due to designers rather than craftsmen. Under the Consulate P.-F.-L. FONTAINE and Charles Percier emerged as the leading designers. Working first for Josephine Bonaparte and then for Napoleon himself they created a specifically Empire style by a judicious mixture of antique forms and ornaments with such Napoleonic motifs as bees, giant Ns in laurel wreaths and eagles, together with *Egyptiennerie* devices

Empire style: plaque 'La Bataille d'Eylau', Sèvres porcelain, 1807

which acquired a new symbolic significance after Napoleon's Egyptian campaign. They provided Jacob and his son JACOB-DESMALTER with furniture designs and their influence is apparent

Empire style: bed made for the Empress Josephine, probably to a design by Percier & Fontaine, in the workshops of Jacob-Desmalter et Cie, 1810 (Château de Malmaison)

on the silver made by BIENNAIS and ODIOT, silks woven at LYONS (where BONY was the leading designer), the bronzes of Thomire, etc. Their most important innovation was in the lavish use of draperies for interior decoration, probably the result of orders to prepare opulent-looking apartments for the Emperor and Imperial family at short notice. Plain or simply patterned silks and velvets were looped in great sweeps over pelmets and on the framework of beds, sometimes small rooms were given a tent-like appearance by fabrics draped on the walls (not stretched as hitherto) and suspended from the ceiling. This tented style became very popular and soon JACQUEMART AND BÉNARD and ZUBER were producing wallpapers which imitated the effect. Wall-paintings were almost entirely replaced by patterned wallpapers and SCENIC PAPERS, especially by DUFOUR. In furniture design, geometrical simplicity of form (often adapted from the Antique, e.g. sabre legs, currule-like stools, etc.) and unity of material

(Below) Empire style: designs from Percier & Fontaine's Recueil de décorations intérieurs, *Paris 1812*

Empire style: chair by Jacob-Desmalter et Cie (Château de Malmaison)

Empire style: clock, celebrating marriage of Napoleon and Marie Louise in 1810 (Château de Compiègne)

(usually mahogany with a sparing use of gilt-bronze enrichments) became the rule. This facilitated production on an industrial scale, and it is significant that the most celebrated furniture-maker of the period, Jacob-Desmalter, was a factory owner and director rather than a craftsman making individual pieces for each patron. The same could be said of the silversmith Biennais and the bronze worker Thomire. After its reorganization in 1800 the SÈVRES PORCELAIN FACTORY began to function on more efficient lines, the freedom of the individual modellers and painters being severely curtailed as a result.

The style spread in the wake of Napoleon's armies, and under the patronage of his relations, to Holland and to Germany, Scandinavia, Italy and Spain. It was popularized partly by means of La Mésangère's pattern book *Meubles et objets de goût* 1802, as well as the numerous illustrations he published in fashionable magazines. Various porcelain factories, like that at NAPLES, began to imitate the Empire style wares produced at Sèvres. Numerous furniture-makers followed the patterns set by Jacob-Desmalter and others in Paris, e.g. the Florentine Giovanni SOCCI. The style was also taken up by cabinet-makers in the U.S.A., notably by LANNUIER and, more freely, by Duncan PHYFE. It persisted both in France and elsewhere long after Napoleon's final defeat. The contemporary English REGENCY STYLE might also be considered a variant of the Empire style.

Lit: S. Grandjean, *Empire Furniture 1800–1825*, London 1966.

Empire style, Second, *see* SECOND EMPIRE STYLE.

Enamel A vitreous substance, usually lead-soda or lead-potash glass with or without colourants and opacifiers, fused to a metal surface under heat (usually about 800°C.). A similar vitreous substance applied to pottery or other materials is called a GLAZE. Enamel should be distinguished from vitreous substances which do not fuse with a metal backing. It has been used for the decoration of metal since very early times. The main types are as follows:

Basse taille with translucent enamel applied over reliefs of gold or silver so that the colour of the enamel is strongest where the relief is most deeply cut. This process, a refinement on *champlevé*, was first perfected in the PARIS ENAMELS of the early C14. An almost identical process was developed contemporaneously and probably quite independently in Italy where it is known as *lavoro di basso rilievo* (see below).

Champlevé with enamels poured into grooves engraved on the surface of the silver, bronze or copper object to be decorated and then polished down to the same level as the surrounding metal. This process was used by the Romans, Celts and medieval enamellers, being perfected in MOSAN ENAMELS of the C12. It was more extensively used for LIMOGES ENAMELS of the C12–C14. It is also called *en taille d'épargne*.

Cloisonné with the enamel poured into *cloisons* or compartments formed by a network of metal bands on the surface of the object: the tops of the bands remain exposed dividing one area of colour from another. This is one of the most ancient processes and is probably Near Eastern in origin. It was very successfully employed by BYZANTINE and CELTIC craftsmen. The Pala d'Oro in St Mark's, Venice, is a masterpiece in this technique. From Byzantium the technique was transmitted to China in the C14 and thence throughout the Orient.

En résille sur verre with powdered enamel packed into gold-lined incisions engraved on a medallion of blue or green glass with which it fuses when fired. This difficult process was adopted only in France during the second quarter of the C17, mainly for miniature cases.

En ronde bosse with opaque enamel covering figures or decorative devices modelled in the round.

Champlevé enamel, detail of crucifix base, after Godefroid de Huy, c12 (Hôtel Sandelin, St Omer)

Cloisonné enamel eagle, Merovingian (the enamel is missing from most of the cloisons) (Musée de Cluny, Paris)

Cloisonné enamel, detail of the Pala d'Oro, c12 *(S. Marco, Venice)*

Enamel en ronde bosse, *with diamonds, rubies, emeralds and gold and silver, St George, Munich,* c.1590 *(Residenzmuseum, Munich)*

Lavoro di basso rilievo, with translucent enamel applied over reliefs of gold or silver: a process almost identical with *basse taille.* It was developed in Italy contemporaneously with *basse taille* and probably quite independently. The earliest dated example is a chalice signed by **Guccio di Mannaia** and made between 1288 and 1292 (S. Francesco, Assisi).

Painted enamels with the coloured enamels painted onto the surface. The plaque or object of copper was first covered with a layer of white enamel and fired, and the design was then applied in different colours over this with repeated firings. This process was invented at Limoges in the late c15. From the mid c16 enamels were often painted on a black, instead of a white, ground which formed the basis for *grisaille* painting. If colours were used on a black ground, layers of gold or silver foil were inserted between coats of enamel to provide a warm or cold tonality. A distinct technique of painting on an enamelled ground with powdered enamel mixed with oil, supposedly invented by **Jean Toutin** (1578–1644) was much used in the c18 especially for portrait miniatures and the decoration of such small objects as snuff-boxes and watch-cases. (*See* Battersea enamels, Bilston enamels, Canton enamels, Geneva enamels, Venetian enamels.)

Plique à jour like *cloisonné* but without a metal backing so that the light can shine through the

Cup decorated with painted enamel on copper, by Elias Adam, Augsburg, early c18 *(Victoria & Albert Museum)*

Champlevé enamel decorations on gold cup attributed to Hans Karl, c.1600 (Residenzmuseum, Munich)

Limoges enamel dish, copper painted with enamel decoration by Limousin after Raphael, mid c16 (Musée P. du Puy, Toulouse)

translucent enamel giving a stained glass window effect.

Surrey enamelling with the enamel applied to brass objects, especially andirons, candlesticks, horse harness and sword hilts, cast with recessions to hold the paste. A cheap form of enamel-ware in various parts of Europe in the C17.

An object is said to be decorated with *en plein* enamelling if the enamel has been applied to its surface and not to plaques attached to the surface.

Lit: O. Untracht, *Enamelling on Metal,* New York 1957; E. Steingräber in *Reallexikon zur deutschen Kunstgeschichte* Vol. V (Émail), Stuttgart 1967; H. Garner, *Chinese & Japanese Cloisonné Enamels,* London 1970; M.-M. Gauthier, *Émaux du moyen âge occidental,* Fribourg 1972.

Enamel colours Pigments used for the decoration of metal, glass, and especially PORCELAIN and TIN-GLAZED EARTHENWARE, first developed in SUNG Dynasty China (C10–C13) and used in Persia in the C13 on both pottery and glass. In the C15 they were taken up by glass-makers in Venice whence they passed to Germany. Their first appearance on European pottery is *c.*1622 at KREUSSEN, though they were not used extensively and the full palette of colours was not developed until the late C17. They were in use throughout Europe by the mid C18. They include a vermilion, crimson and pink outside the range of HIGH-TEMPERATURE COLOURS to which European ceramic artists had previously been limited. Composed of metallic oxides (usually of copper, iron and manganese) mixed with powdered glass, they fuse at a temperature of about 750°C. and as they cannot stand greater heat they must be applied to porcelain after it has had its initial firing and to tin-glazed earthenware after it has had its second firing. The objects to which they have been applied must therefore be given a further firing in a low-temperature or muffle kiln. As they need not be applied at a porcelain factory they were commonly used by HAUSMALER as well as on factory-decorated pieces, e.g. at MEISSEN. They were also used for the decoration of metal objects of the BATTERSEA ENAMEL type.

Enamel twist decoration Spiral patterns of threads of opaque (usually white) glass (like AIR TWIST DECORATION) within the stems of C18 and later wine-glasses, especially English.

Encaustic brick or **tile** A clay brick or tile inlaid with patterns in a different coloured clay, popular in the Middle Ages and again in the C19. Strictly, the word 'encaustic' refers to the process of firing or burning and not to the decorative technique.

Encoignure A corner cupboard, generally referred to in the C18 as an *armoire d'encoignure.* It was sometimes made without a door, open in the front to reveal shelves. It sometimes had a tapering tier of shelves above (an *étagère*). Commodes were sometimes made with two matching *encoignures.* If these formed part of the commode itself it was called a *commode en encoignure.* Other pieces of furniture besides cupboards were made *en encoignure,* e.g. chairs, tables, stools.

End boards Solid boards, generally carved in profile, used as the ends of chests or the supports of stools or benches. They were common in the Middle Ages and provided the normal supports for stools until the early C17 when legs became more usual.

Endell, August (1871–1925). German architect and Art Nouveau designer influenced by OBRIST in Munich. Designed textiles, furniture and jewellery, gradually refining his style from the lushest Art Nouveau to one in which curves become functional and decorations minimal. He also wrote and pontificated on the theory of the decorative arts.

Lit: H. Selig (ed.), *Jugendstil,* Heidelberg-Munich 1959; H. Kreisel–G. Himmelheber, *Die Kunst des deutschen Möbels,* Munich 1973.

Enderlein, Caspar (1560–1633). He was the leading Nuremberg maker of display pewter (i.e. relief-decorated pewter). Born and trained in Basle he settled in Nuremberg in 1583 and made his reputation with a copy of BRIOT's Temperantia Dish for which he cut two different moulds of stone. He made tankards, dishes, jugs, etc., sometimes in collaboration with **Jacob Koch II** (d.1619). None of the surviving pieces cast from Enderlein's moulds is signed with his stamp, but his models continued to be used for a hundred years or more after his death.

Lit: H. Demiani, *François Briot, Caspar Enderlein und das Edelzinn,* Leipzig 1897; H.-U. Haedeke, *Metalwork,* London 1970.

Enghalskrug Literally 'narrow-necked jug', German term for a C17–C18 long-necked jug, usually of faience. It generally has a globular body, sometimes a plaited rope-like handle and is occasionally mounted in pewter. Such jugs were made at ANSBACH, FRANKFURT, HANAU, etc.

Engine turned decorations A type of regular hatched decoration (chequers and diapers) applied to metals and ceramics by turning on a lathe.

Engobe French term for a coating of SLIP applied all over a piece of pottery to cover its natural colour: it also provides a ground through which SGRAFFIATO decorations may be incised or on to which glazes or painted ornament may be applied.

Engraving The process of decorating a metal surface with inscribed lines and, by extension, a print made from an engraved copper or steel plate. Many engravers worked both as decorators of silver and other metals and as print-makers.

Entablature The upper part of an ORDER, consisting of architrave, frieze and cornice.

Entre-fenêtre French term for a narrow tapestry panel, generally intended to hang between windows, woven *en suite* with the *alentours* of a set of larger figurative panels. The term is probably C19.

E.P.B.M., Electro-Plated Britannia Metal, *see* BRITANNIA METAL, ELECTROPLATE.

Epergne A TABLE-CENTRE, usually of silver – an English (not French) term of uncertain origin and date.

Epergne, silver, Thomas Pitts, London, 1764 (formerly Ionides Collection, Buxted Park)

E.P.N.S., Electro-Plated Nickel Silver, *see* ELECTROPLATE.

Erfurt pottery A faience factory functioning from 1717 to *c.*1792 and notable mainly for handsome cylindrical tankards painted with animals, landscapes, chinoiseries or flowers in HIGH-TEMPERATURE COLOURS, a strong blue, light red and yellow predominating. During its best period, from 1734, it was owned by a family of pewter manufacturers and many of the tankards are mounted in pewter. Dishes, jugs and figures were also made. (For factory mark *see* p. 883.)

Lit: A. von Przychowski in *Das Erfurter Kunsthandwerk* (ed. H. Kunze), Erfurt 1929; K. Hüseler, *Deutsche Fayencen,* Stuttgart 1956–8.

Ergonomics Literally the habits or laws of work, a recently coined word for the study of the human being in relation to machines, utensils, furniture, etc. Linking the study of functional anatomy (as practised by KLINT and others since the early C20) with experimental psychology in reference to industrial design, it first rose to prominence in the 1939–45 war in connection with military equipment. Since then it has been applied to the design of machine tools, motor-cars, aircraft and also furniture, e.g. chairs, by determining averages and ranges of body sizes, length of reach and force that can be applied by limbs in varying positions, etc. Ergonomics was taken up in a big way by Henry DREYFUSS in the U.S. where it is termed less pretentiously, but rather ambiguously, human engineering. In England the Ergonomics Research Society was founded in 1949 and publishes a learned journal. But ergonomics has had, as yet, relatively little influence on the decorative arts since most designers prefer the old rule of thumb approach and many manufacturers regard it with as much suspicion as market research and other expensive statistical studies.

Ersari carpets, *see* TURKMAN CARPETS.

Escritoire Old name for a writing desk, especially of the small portable type made since the C16 and consisting of a nest of drawers enclosed in a box with a sloping front that is hinged along the bottom edge and may be let down to provide a writing platform. From the late C17 onwards the term *escritoire* or *scrutoire* was applied to such fall-front desks mounted on a stand or more usually a chest of drawers. Nowadays this is also called a secretary. In the U.S. these terms are applied to a desk with a bookcase above, such as would in England be called a bureau bookcase.

Escutcheon (1) A shield bearing a coat of arms or any similar shield-shaped ornament.

(2) A metal plate protecting a keyhole in a piece of furniture.

Escutcheon: gilt-bronze keyhole guard

Espagnolette (1) A decorative motif popularized by Watteau and Audran and widely used by furniture designers of the Régence and early Louis XV periods, e.g. in CRESSENT's furniture. It consists of a female head backed by a large stiff upright lace collar of a vaguely Spanish type. *Illustrated opposite above left.*

(2) The elongated and hinged fastening used on double French doors and windows. Despite the name, it appears to have been of French, not Spanish, origin and to have come into use in the early C17. *Illustrated opposite above right.*

Essence vase, *see* CASSOLETTE.

Espagnolette: gilt-bronze mount on chest-of-drawers by C. Cressent, c.1750 (Wallace Collection)

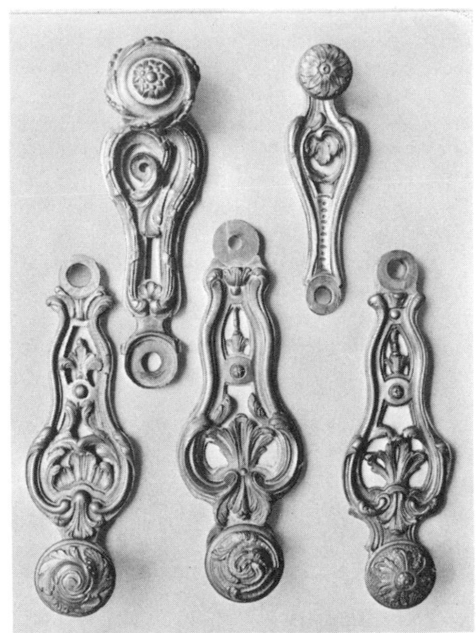

Espagnolettes, gilt-bronze, Louis XV period (Musée des Arts Décoratifs, Paris)

Estampille The maker's mark stamped on French furniture and bearing the name, initials or monogram of the maker. It was struck with an iron stamp (not branded) and the name appears in intaglio, usually on some inconspicuous part of the piece. On small fragile pieces of furniture the name might be written. Members of the Paris Corporation des MENUISIERS-ÉBÉNISTES were obliged by law to stamp all the furniture they made for sale after the 1751 revision of the Corporation statutes until their suppression in 1791, though there were exceptions. Royal craftsmen were exempt: and all furniture made for the Crown was exempt. The widows of *maîtres* were allowed to use their husband's *estampille* to sign furniture produced by the workshop during her lifetime.

Estampille on a corner cupboard door (Victoria & Albert Museum)

Este pottery and porcelain factories The first factory at Este (in the Veneto S.W. of Venice) was founded in 1758 by **Giovan Battista Brunello** (*c.*1718–78) but little is known of its products. Another establishment was started by **Girolamo Franchini** (1728–1808) shortly before 1780 in association with a Frenchman **Giovanni Pietro Varion** (1737–81) who had formerly worked for Brunello and initiated the making of porcelain at Este. The products of the Franchini factory included statuettes and useful wares in both porcelain and cream-coloured earthenware. Decorative pieces include some very ambitious table-centres including numerous figures, in one case derived from the early C18 sculptor Francesco Bertos. Both factories remained active throughout the C19. They were allied for a short while from 1830 onwards and were united definitively in 1893. The concern is still active under the title **Este Ceramiche e Porcellane.**

Lit: G. Barioli, *Mostra dell'antica ceramica di Este*, Este 1960.

Estevé, Pierre and **Jean,** *see* MONTPELLIER POTTERY.

Étagère A set of shelves, either free-standing or forming part of another piece of furniture, e.g. an ENCOIGNURE. In C19 England it was called a WHATNOT.

Etching The process of decorating metal with patterns bitten into the surface by acid. It was originally used for the decoration of armour in the late C15 and of various small objects in brass, copper, iron and (rarely) silver in the C16, especially in Germany. From the C16 it was developed mainly as a process of print-making.

Étiolles porcelain factory A small factory near Paris, established in 1768 by J.-B. Monier and E.-D. PELLEVÉ producing hard-paste wares similar to those of the PARIS factories. Its date of closing is not known. (For factory mark *see* p. 883.)

Lit: X. de Chavagnac & A. de Grollier, *Histoire des manufactures françaises de porcelaine*, Paris 1906.

Etna Glass Works, *see* AMELUNG, J. F.

Etruscan bindings, *see* EDWARDS OF HALIFAX.

Etruscan pottery Dates from *c*.700 B.C. to *c*.100 B.C. Most Etruscan vases imitate GREEK POTTERY and, later, HELLENISTIC POTTERY but a distinctive type called *bucchero* was also produced. This developed from the earlier pre-Etruscan *impasto* ware of the Villanovan culture which succeeded the Terremare Bronze Age civilization in Italy. *Impasto* ware was primitive, being roughly shaped by hand and then finished on a wheel. It was unglazed but given a sheen by burnishing. Decorations, mostly geometrical and sometimes Orientalizing, were incised and sometimes reinforced with red ochre. The Etruscan *bucchero* ware was a refinement on this *impasto* ware, the colour being black throughout, obtained by complete instead of partial reduction in the firing. Early examples are wheel thrown, with thin walls. Later, i.e. *c*.600 B.C., wares are heavier with decoration mostly in relief and not incised.

Lit: A. D. Trendall, *South Italian Vase Painting*, Oxford 1967.

Etruscan style A subspecies of NEO-CLASSICISM, so called because its ornamental motifs – palm-

Étui: Bilston enamel, late C18 (Victoria & Albert Museum)

ettes, anthemion, figurative scenes in light colours on a dark ground – and predominantly black, terracotta and white colour scheme were derived from GREEK POTTERY vases supposed in the late c18 to be Etruscan. It was invented *c.*1774 by Robert ADAM and the best surviving example of its application to walls and furniture is the Etruscan room at Osterley Park (1775). A variant was developed in France by BÉLANGER and DUGOURC shortly afterwards.

Lit: E. Harris, *The Furniture of Robert Adam*, London 1963.

Étui Small box or case for personal, female, articles such as bodkins, needles, scissors, thimbles. It was designed to be carried in a pocket or hung on a *châtelaine*. Popular mainly in the c18, it was often elaborately decorated, usually in enamel. *Illustrated previous column.*

Eulenkrug A German type of jug in the form of an owl, found among the earliest examples of tin-glazed earthenware in Germany *c.*1540–60. The design has been attributed to Augustin HIRSCHVOGEL. *Illustrated next column.*

Exeter carpet factory, *see* PASSAVANT, Claude.

Eulenkrug, tin-glazed earthenware, Bressanone (?), mid c16 (Kunstgewerbemuseum, Berlin)

Typographic ornaments used by Pierre Simon Fournier le jeune in Modèles des Caractères, *Paris, 1742*

Fabeltiere decoration Type of ceramic decoration introduced by A. F. von LÖWENFINCK *c.*1730 at MEISSEN depicting fabulous beasts. It is not to be confused with animal subjects from Aesop's fables which were also used by pottery and porcelain decorators, e.g. at CHELSEA.

Faber, Johann Ludwig (*fl.*1678–93). He was a Nuremberg glass and faience painter (or *Hausmaler*) and was probably a pupil of Johann SCHAPER. He used *Schwarzlot* or black enamel colour and his subjects were usually landscapes, figures or flowers. His style was neater and sharper than Schaper's.

Lit: G. E. Pazaurek, *Deutsche Fayence- und Porzellan-Hausmaler,* Leipzig 1925.

Fabergé, Peter Carl (1846–1920). Russian goldsmith and jeweller of Huguenot extraction, born in St Petersburg where his father, Gustav, had settled and opened a jewellery and silver shop in 1842. He was trained in St Petersburg, travelled in Western Europe and in 1870 took over the family concern which soon became the leading firm of jewellers in the city, receiving the Imperial appointment in 1881. In 1882 he was joined by his younger brother **Agathon** who had been brought up in Dresden and was thus familiar with the work of DINGLINGER which seems to have influenced the 'works of fantasy' subsequently produced by the firm. Branches were opened in Moscow (1887), Kiev (1905) and London (1906). At the height of its activity it employed more than five hundred assistants, designers, modellers, gem cutters, goldsmiths and enamellers. Fabergé himself seems to have directed artistic and commercial policy, designing only the most important pieces such as the elaborately wrought and ingeniously contrived Easter eggs which Alexander III gave annually to his Empress and Nicholas II to his mother and Empress. Made of a wide variety of precious and semi-precious materials, each of these eggs consisted of a shell which could be opened to reveal the 'surprise' – a statuette, a basket of hard-stone flowers, a series of enamel portraits, etc. Very much smaller and less expensive Easter eggs were made for the ordinary market. Fabergé's fame was diffused in Western Europe by the decorative objects which the Romanovs gave to their royal relations, notably Queen Alexandra of England. He was also much patronized by the richer members of Edwardian society. The range of the workshops was wide, including dinner services and tea services, cigarette cases, pen rests, frames for

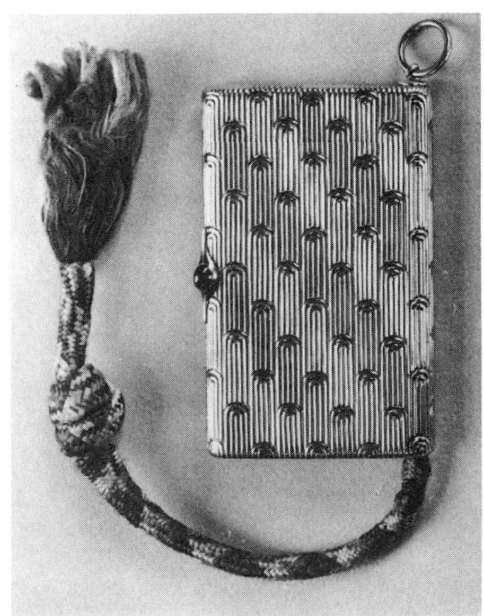

Fabergé cigarette case of red and yellow gold, 1912–15 (Musée des Arts Décoratifs, Paris)

miniature portraits, cigar lighters, etc., as well as such ornaments as hard-stone statuettes of animals and Russian peasants and sprays of flowers with gold stalks and jewelled petals standing in rock crystal vases. Decorative motifs were usually inspired by French C18 models or, much less frequently, by the traditional arts of Russia, though some later products reveal the influence of Art Nouveau. The concern was nationalized after the 1918 Revolution, the staff disbanded and the stock sold. Fabergé died in exile in Lausanne.

Lit: A. K. Snowman, *The Art of Carl Fabergé*, London 1953; M. C. Ross, *The Art of Karl Fabergé and his Contemporaries*, Norman, Oklahoma 1965.

Façon de Venise The term used to describe glass made in the Venetian style by non-Venetian glasshouses.

Faenza potteries A group of Italian potteries in existence as early as 1142 but of no importance before the mid C15 when they began to make maiolica for which they soon won international renown (the word 'faience' is derived from Faenza). The earliest dated product is a circular plaque of 1475 boldly painted with the sacred monogram within a border of formalized flower and leaf motifs (Musée de Cluny, Paris). In the last quarter of the C15 they were producing the best maiolica in Italy – large dishes, wall tablets of religious subjects, drug-pots, etc., characterized by powerful colour schemes with dark blue, deep purple and orange predominating and touches of lemon yellow and greenish turquoise. Figures and ornamental motifs are drawn with the sinewy vigour of contemporary Ferrarese painters, as on a plaque of the Virgin and Child dated 1489 (Victoria & Albert Museum). Notable products of the period include a magnificent set of plates made for or in memory of Matthias Corvinus, King of Hungary (d.1490), each decorated with an allegorical scene within an elaborate border incorporating the arms of the king and his wife (Victoria & Albert Museum). Reliefs of religious subjects were also executed. Many notable pieces of maiolica of this period can, however, be ascribed either to Faenza or DERUTA where similar work seems to have been executed. Soon after 1500 the bold early patterns were rejected

Cage of bianca a trafora *maiolica, Faenza, late C16 (Museo Internazionale delle Ceramiche, Faenza)*

Faenza maiolica basin, C15 (Victoria & Albert Museum)

in favour of more softly coloured and delicately drawn motifs and, in the 1520s, grotesques derived from Raphael's Vatican Loggie. Though some artists continued to work in the Faenza tradition, painting scenes within wide borders, the ISTORIATO style was adopted, notably by one of the leading factories, the CASA PIROTTA. Most of the wares dating from 1500–1530 have been ascribed to one or other of some eight painters, notably the painter of a dish with *Christ among the Doctors* signed by *Mo. iero da Forli'* (Victoria & Albert Museum), the artist signing with the monogram F.R. (e.g. the plate depicting *The Building of Solomon's Temple* in the British Museum), another working in a style similar to that of GIOVANNI MARIA, the painter of a dish with the Death of the Virgin meticulously copied after Martin Schongauer, the painter of the Coriolanus panel (Victoria & Albert Museum), Maestro BENEDETTO of Siena and B. MANARA. The last notable painter appears to have been Virgilotto Calamelli (d. before 1570). As the Istoriato style began to go out of fashion the potteries turned their attention to the production of *Bianco di Faenza* wares covered with a newly developed hard, thick white glaze. Such wares are often richly modelled and include very handsome openwork baskets, boldly gadrooned bowls and dishes, ewers and vases with dolphin handles, drug-pots on lion feet, etc., sparsely decorated with softly coloured, freely drawn motifs at first in the Mannerist, later in the Baroque style. The potteries have remained active until the present day (following trends of fashion from the c16 onwards) and the city boasts an important ceramic museum. Numerous marks were used, both monograms and devices, and some of them have been attributed to individual potters working at Faenza.

Lit: G. Ballardini, *Le ceramiche di Faenza*, Rome 1933; J. Chompret, *Répertoire de la maiolique italienne*, Paris 1949; G. Liverani (on *Bianco di Faenza*) in *The Connoisseur*, CXL (1957), pp. 160–63; G. Liverani, *Five Centuries of Italian Majolica*, New York–London 1960.

Fahlström, Anders, *see* RÖRSTRAND POTTERY & PORCELAIN FACTORY.

Fa-Hua, *see* SAN-TS'AI.

Faïence (1) The French name for TIN-GLAZED EARTHENWARE, called after BIANCO DI FAENZA wares which became popular in c16 France. Also applied to German, Scandinavian and Spanish tin-glazed wares. The main factories were at: ALBISSOLA, ALCORA, ANSBACH, ARNHEM, BAYREUTH, BERLIN, FRANKFURT, FULDA, HAMBURG, HANAU, HÖCHST, KÜNERSBERG, LUNEVILLE, LYONS, MARIEBERG, MARSEILLES, MOUSTIERS, NIDERVILLER, NEVERS, ROUEN, SAVONA, STRASBOURG.

(2) An archaeologist's term for ancient Egyptian wares made of glazed powdered quartz.

Faïence d'Oiron, *see* SAINT-PORCHAIRE POTTERY.

Faïence fine French name for lead-glazed white pottery or CREAM-COLOURED EARTHENWARE.

Faïence japonnée French c18 term for faience decorated in enamel-colours in an oriental style.

Faïence parlante French term for faience wares with inscriptions in their decorations as made at NEVERS and elsewhere.

Lit: F. Girard, *Les faïences parlantes du XVIIIe siècle*, Bourg-en-Bresse 1938.

Faïence patriotique French term for faience wares decorated with patriotic, especially Revolutionary, emblems and inscriptions.

Lit: Champfleury, *Histoire des faïences patriotiques sous la Révolution*, Paris 1867 and 1875.

Faïence patriotique, probably Ancy-le-Franc, 1791 (Musée Carnavalet, Paris)

Fair Hebe jugs, *see* VOYEZ, John.

Fairings A type of small German C19 to early C20 porcelain ornament, either of figures or in the form of a small box, usually depicting indelicate subjects and mass-produced for sale at fairs, bazaars, sea-side stalls, etc. They were made mainly by **Conta & Böhm** of Pössnach in Saxony and perhaps by **Springer** at Elbogen in Czechoslovakia. They are now being reproduced.

Lit: W. S. Bristowe, *Victorian China Fairings*, London 1971.

Falcon glasshouse, *see* PELLATT, Apsley.

Falconet, Etienne-Maurice (1716–91). Leading French sculptor working in a gently classicizing style and excelling in elegantly slender and delicately seductive nude nymphs. His famous group of Venus chastising Cupid with a bunch of roses is characteristic. As chief modeller at SÈVRES 1757–66 he provided numerous models for biscuit statuettes of tender charm (sometimes reductions of his own larger marble statues), the most notable being a group of children engaged in various activities called the *Enfants Falconet* (1757), *La Lanterne magique* (1757), *Baigneuse* (1758), *Louis XV en armure* (1760), *Psyche* (1761), *Maître d'école* and *Maîtresse d'école*, after Boucher (1762), *Pygmalion* (1763), *Jupiter and Leda* after Boucher (1764), *Le Baiser donné* and *Le Baiser rendu* after Boucher (1765). He also modelled elaborate table-centres and salts executed in silver by AUGUSTE and GERMAIN. Bronze furniture mounts have been attributed to him but it is unlikely that he either made or produced models for them. His style was widely imitated.

Lit: L. Réau, *Etienne-Maurice Falconet*, Paris 1922.

Faldistorium or **Faldistory** An armless chair used by a bishop or other prelate when not occupying his throne, e.g. placed in the chancel of a church in which he is officiating. It is generally a type of *Curule* CHAIR with metal supports and a leather seat stretched between the side rails.

Faldstool English term for various distinct types of ecclesiastical furniture including the FALDISTORIUM and also a movable folding stool at which worshippers kneel (especially that used by an English monarch at his or her coronation) and a small desk at which litany is said or sung.

Falize, Lucien (1838–97). He is famous as the last and most skilful of all goldsmiths practising in historical styles – Medieval, Renaissance, Rococo, etc. He spent fifteen years studying and experimenting in order to revive the technique of *basse taille* or translucent enamel painting. And he went on working in historical styles long after others had abandoned all such revivalism and had gone in search of a contemporary style or

L. Falize: enamelled gold cup, 1896 (Musée des Art Décoratifs, Paris)

Art Nouveau. He was the son of a Parisian jeweller whose business he took over in 1880, going into partnership with the silversmith and historian of silver, **Germain Bapst.** Falize concentrated on showpieces, many of which were illustrated and described at length in the art periodicals of his day, e.g. the Neo-Rococo toilet table and service he made in 1888 for presentation to Princess Laetitia Bonaparte. His masterpiece is perhaps an enamelled gold 'hanap' or cup in the Renaissance style, completed in 1896 and now in the Musée des Arts Décoratifs in Paris.

Lit: O. Massin, *Lucien Falize, Orfèvre Jouillier* . . . , Paris 1897; H. Honour, *Goldsmiths and Silversmiths*, London 1971.

Fall front The door of a cabinet or desk hinged along the bottom so that it opens by falling forwards and may be supported on struts to provide a horizontal platform. It is also called a **'drop-front'.**

Famille jaune, noire, rose and verte porcelain A showy type of Chinese porcelain, made mainly for export to Europe, decorated in ENAMEL COLOURS. In *famille verte* a brilliant apple green and a strong iron red predominate amongst yellow, aubergine purple and violet blue. This colour scheme was adopted in the K'ANG HSI period and replaced the earlier MING five-colour scheme in which blue was rendered in underglaze and not in enamel. *Famille jaune*, with a dominant yellow background, was made from the same period. The designs (usually floral) are rendered in patches of flat colour – a technique copied by European ceramic painters for FLEURS DES INDES. A third type, *famille rose*, was introduced in the YUNG CHEN period: in addition to the enamels formerly in use it has a prominent rose pink introduced from Europe where it was known

Famille rose plate, Chinese, early c18 (Victoria & Albert Museum)

Famille noire vase (Victoria & Albert Museum)

as PURPLE OF CASSIUS. The style of painting is freer and decorations often include figure subjects as well as flowers and fruit. A fourth type, *famille noire*, with a black ground of a brownish-black pigment from cobalt and manganese overlaid by a thin greenish enamel, is now thought to have been of mid-C19 origin. The *famille* terminology is C19 French, based on a classification of Chinese porcelain by Albert Jacquemart.

Lit: Soame Jenyns, *Later Chinese Porcelain: The Ch'ing Dynasty (1644–1912)*, London, rev. ed., 1971.

Fan style In bookbinding, a variant of the C16 CENTRE-AND-CORNER pattern. It was an Italian innovation and appeared soon after 1600. The corners of a rectangular panel are filled with half-opened fans and two fans, placed back to back, form a circular or wheel ornament for the centre. It was little used by French bookbinders but was popular in Italy, Germany, Spain and Sweden throughout the C17 and survived in Scotland until the C18 becoming almost the national style.

Fanfare bindings A late-C16 to mid-C17 French style of bookbinding. It developed from the strap-

Fanfare bookbinding, Paris, c.1570 (Kunstindustrimuseet, Copenhagen)

work designs used on GROLIER and C16 Italian bindings, but the tooling is more delicate and the strapwork is reduced to a complicated all-over pattern of oval and circular compartments usually based on the figure 8. The intervals are tooled with sprays of olive, bay or laurel leaves, as well as fleurons, etc. In the middle a space was left blank for a coat of arms. The back was often decorated with a continuous spray of foliage. About 1635 tooling began to be executed *au pointillé* and in general the designs became more delicate, achieving an almost filigree effect. Fanfare bindings are often attributed to Nicolas and Clovis Eve who were Royal Binders in Paris from 1579 to 1634. The term 'fanfare' is not contemporary. It dates from 1829 when the binder Thouvenin revived the style for the decoration of a book entitled *Fanfares et corvés abbadesques* (published in 1613).

Lit: G. D. Hobson, *Les relieures à la fanfare*, London 1935.

Fangi-i A type of Chinese Bronze Age (Shang and Early Chou) vessel of casket shape with a cover resembling a hipped roof surmounted by a similarly shaped knob. A semicircular notch appears in the centre of the lower edges. It was probably used for storing grain though it has been suggested that it was used for wine. It is usually very lavishly decorated.

Faris, William (1728–1804). He began as a clockmaker in Philadelphia and later in Annapolis. After 1760 he became a silversmith but he was probably a merchant rather than a craftsman. Only a few very simple pieces made in his shop are known, e.g. three pieces made by his son **Charles** in 1790 and now in the Metropolitan Museum, New York. He is remembered mainly on account of his diaries and accounts (published by Lockwood Barr) which provide a unique and most valuable record of a small-town American silversmith at this period.

Lit: Lockwood Barr in *Maryland Historical Magazine*, 1941, vol. xxxvi, and 1942, vol. xxxvii.

Fasces A bundle of rods bound up with an axe in the middle, its blade projecting. It became an ensign of authority in ancient Rome. Later it was used purely ornamentally.

Fattorini, Jacopo (*fl.* 1508–20). A member of a family of potters who were working at CAFAGGIOLO from the late C15 and adopted the surname Fattorini in the C17. A group of outstandingly fine maiolica plates and dishes made at this factory and painted by the same hand include some which are signed 'Jacopo' and are generally ascribed to him. The earliest appears to be a plate painted with a satyr's family, after Dürer, dated 1508. Another shows a maiolica painter at work (British Museum). The most notable are a series of large dishes dated 1514 (Fitzwilliam Museum, Cambridge; Victoria & Albert Museum) depicting a classical triumph of the type so loved by Florentine artists, with an abundance of muscular

J. Fattorini: maiolica dish, Cafaggiolo, 1514 (Fitzwilliam Museum, Cambridge)

nudes, fashionably dressed musicians, horses and unicorns – like a Botticelli in pottery. This artist has been identified with either **Jacopo,** son of **Stefano Fattorini,** or **Jacopo di Giovanni** known as **Jacopone** (d.1553); but some authorities more cautiously refer to him simply as 'Jacopo'.

Lit: G. Guasti, *Di Cafaggiolo e d'altre fabbriche di ceramiche in Toscana,* Florence 1902; J. Chompret, *Répertoire de la maiolique italienne,* Paris 1949.

Fauchier, Joseph, *see* MARSEILLES POTTERY.

Fauconnier, Jacques-Henri (1776–1839). French silversmith who began under ODIOT, became his *chef d'atelier* but set up on his own by 1823. Under the protection of Louis Philippe's sister he established a school for goldsmiths in Paris in 1830. He initiated the Renaissance revival in French metalwork. In the early C19 the sculptor Barye was in his workshop. His business was carried on by his nephews and pupils, **Auguste** and **Joseph Fannière.**

Lit: S. Grandjean, *L'Orfèvrerie du XIXe siècle en Europe,* Paris 1962.

Fauquez, Pierre-Joseph, *see* SAINT-AMAND-LES-EAUX and TOURNAI POTTERY AND PORCELAIN FACTORY.

Fauteuil French for an armchair. For *fauteuil en gondole,* a specific type, *see* CHAIR.

Favrile glass The name given by L. C. TIFFANY to his hand-made iridescent glass wares.

Fay, J.-B. (*fl.* 1780–90). Ornamentalist working in Paris where he published some attractive designs in the late Louis XVI style, notably a *Cahier de vases,* which includes cylindrical coffee-cups painted with tidy festoons of flowers, and a *Cahier de bijouteries dans le goût moderne.* He also engraved furniture designs by LALONDE.

Lit: P. Jessen, *Der Klassizismus im Ornementstich,* Berlin 1924.

Fazackerley colours, *see* LIVERPOOL POTTERIES AND PORCELAIN FACTORY.

Feather banding or **Herringbone inlay,** *see* BANDING.

Feathered or **Feather-edged ornament** A border of chased fluted decoration applied to the handles of silver spoons and forks especially in the second half of the C18 in England and America.

Featherwork Decorative panels made with birds' feathers, produced mainly by amateurs in C18 England, when they were often quite large and used as hangings; and in the C19, when they were worked into realistic pictures of birds and framed.

Federal style A chronological rather than strictly

stylistic term applied to American arts of the period from the establishment of the Federal Government in 1789 to *c*.1830. It therefore covers the later silver of P. REVERE and the furniture of M. ALLISON, S. BADLAM, C.-H. LANNUIER, S. MCINTIRE, D. PHYFE, J. SEYMOUR, etc. Immediately after the War of Independence American craftsmen took up the most recent English styles: furniture-makers used the engraved designs of ADAM, HEPPLEWHITE and SHERATON. Despite the arrival of such French immigrant craftsmen as Lannuier who introduced the French EMPIRE STYLE, English influence remained dominant throughout the period. The terms American Directoire and American Empire are sometimes used to distinguish furniture influenced by French models.

Lit: C. F. Montgomery, *American Furniture, The Federal Period, in the Henry Francis du Pont Winterthur Museum*, New York 1966.

Feilner, Simon, *see* FÜRSTENBERG PORCELAIN FACTORY and HÖCHST POTTERY AND PORCELAIN FACTORY.

Feldspathic glaze A translucent glaze made from powdered feldspar mixed with various other ingredients, e.g. lime, potash, sand or quartz, which must be fired at a very high temperature. It may be coloured by the addition of various metals – oxide of cobalt for blue, iron for greens (CELADON) and browns, and copper for reds and lavender blues. These types of glaze were developed in China and used in Europe from the C18, though more extensively from the C19, on hard-paste porcelain.

Fell, Isaac (1758–1818). Furniture-maker who was born at Lancaster, emigrated to America and settled at Savannah, Georgia, *c*.1744. In the War of Independence he was taken prisoner and sent to England but soon returned to Savannah. He made simple furniture in the English mid-C18 style and advertised his mahogany pieces in the *Georgia Gazette* in 1789.

Lit: Mrs C. M. Theus, *Savannah Furniture 1735–1825*, Savannah 1967; and in *The Connoisseur*, CLXIX (1968), pp. 124–32.

Fell, Thomas, *see* TYNESIDE POTTERIES.

Felletin tapestry factories, *see* AUBUSSON TAPESTRY FACTORIES.

Felt An unwoven woollen fabric of a type made since very early times. By one process cut wool is laid on a mat, sprinkled with oil, rolled and unrolled until it coheres, washed, stretched and allowed to dry. By a slightly more complex process (which remains the basis of industrial production), the wool is cut, washed, laid out and hammered with clubs (or fulled), then steamed by damping down and heating – the fulling and steaming being repeated several times.

Fender A low metal screen placed in front of a fire to prevent brands or coals from rolling into the room, in use since the C17.

Fenton, Christopher Webber, *see* BENNINGTON POTTERY AND PORCELAIN FACTORY.

Feraghan carpets, *see* PERSIAN CARPETS.

Férand, Jean-Gaspard, *see* MOUSTIERS POTTERIES.

Ferat, Jean-Baptiste, *see* MOUSTIERS POTTERIES.

Fernández, Juan, *see* TALAVERA DE LA REINA POTTERIES.

Fernandino style Spanish furnishing style of the reign of Ferdinando VII (1820–33), roughly equivalent to French RESTAURATION and English late REGENCY though rather more solid and practical. It is predominantly rectangular in form, with plain finely grained wood veneers and mounts of gilt wood (rarely bronze).

Ferner, F. J. (*fl.c.*1750). A HAUSMALER who signed numerous pieces of MEISSEN porcelain rather crudely decorated with enamelled and gilt flowers, figure subjects, animals, etc., which have been added to the underglaze blue decorations executed in the factory. He was a prolific rather than a notable artist and a very shadowy figure: his place of activity and dates are unknown.

Lit: G. E. Pazaurek, *Deutsche Fayence- und Porzellan-Hausmaler*, Leipzig 1925.

Ferrara potteries Although contemporary documents reveal that maiolica was made at Ferrara from the mid C15 no products have been securely identified.

Ferrara tapestry factory Established by Ercole II d'Este in 1536 with Flemish master weavers **Jan** and **Nicholaus Karcher** and **Jan Rost** from Brussels. The earliest tapestries woven include a set of *Metamorphoses* after cartoons by Battista Dossi. In 1539 Nicholaus Karcher left for Mantua and in 1546 Rost left for Florence. Thereafter the factory continued under Jan Karcher and his son Luigi until it closed in 1580.

Ferretti, D., *see* LUDWIGSBURG POTTERY AND PORCELAIN FACTORY.

Ferronerie French wrought-iron work, also decorative scrolled patterns derived from it for painted decorations, especially on faience.

Festoon Ornament in the form of a garland of fruit and flowers, tied with ribbons and suspended at both ends in a loop.

Festoon, from an engraving by Francesco Piranesi, 1780

Feuillâtre, Eugène (1870–1916). French goldsmith and enameller who began by working for LALIQUE but established himself independently by 1900. He exhibited at the Paris International Exhibition in that year. He worked in the Art Nouveau style in glass, silver and translucent enamel. *Illustrated next column.*

E. Feuillâtre: enamelled silver and glass pot, 1900 (Kunstgewerbemuseum, Berlin)

Fibreglass A material made out of the basic components of GLASS but of fibrous form, much used for domestic fabrics since 1951, especially in the U.S. A panel of the material sealed between sheets of glass has heat-conserving properties. It may also be moulded for garden urns, chimney-pieces, architectural ornaments, etc.

Fiddle pattern A C19 English pattern for spoons and forks – with a shaped stem, broad top and notched shoulders at the base just above the bowl. It is either plain or with threaded edges sometimes stamped with a shell at the top.

Fielded panel A panel with bevelled edges and a flat central field.

Fife pottery, *see* WEMYSS WARE.

Figured Of a textile woven with a pattern of figures, flowers, fruit, etc., as distinct from plain, striped, chequered or diapered patterns.

Filigree Openwork decorations made out of very slender threads and usually minute balls of gold or silver (rarely other metals), used for jewellery since Classical times. It became very popular in the Carolingian and Romanesque periods and adorns the Ottonian Imperial crown and orb of

Filigree silver salver, Spanish, c17 (Victoria & Albert Museum)

c.962 (Schatzkammer, Vienna) and various reliquaries, bookbindings, etc. In the later Middle Ages the main centres of production were Siedenburgen and Venice where it was used with very good effect for mounting rock crystal cups. A more widespread fashion for this type of work began in the c17 when small decorative objects like caskets, handles for spoons and forks, miniature pieces of furniture, etc. were made entirely of filigree (which had hitherto been regarded as a type of applied decoration). Excellent work was produced until late in the c18, especially in northern Spain, and at Genoa, Augsburg and Bergen. In 1814 Fortunato Pio Castellani opened a workshop in Rome for the production of Etruscan style filigree jewellery which proved very popular and was widely imitated. It slipped out of fashion towards the end of the c19 but is still made, especially in Italy, though mainly as tourist souvenirs.

Lit: Thah Riisøen & Alf Bøe, *Om filigran*, Oslo 1959; A. Bøe in *Concise Encyclopaedia of Antiques*, vol. III, London 1961.

Filigree glass An improved and elaborated form of RETICELLO GLASS, decorated with interweaved spirals of opaque white, coloured and gold threads beneath the surface. First made at Murano in c16 and popular ever since, especially in c19 France.

Fillet (1) A narrow, flat band, e.g. between two mouldings.

(2) A wheel tool used in leatherwork, especially in bookbinding, for impressing a straight line or parallel straight lines. The term is also used for the line produced by the tool.

Filleul Brothers, *see* BEAUVAIS TAPESTRY FACTORY.

Finch, Alfred William (1854–1930). A potter of English parentage, born and educated in Belgium, where he came into contact with H. VAN DE VELDE, then in Paris where he began to paint under the influence of Seurat. In 1897 he settled in Finland where he was invited by L. Sparre (b.1863) to take charge of the ceramic department of the short-lived Iris workshop at Porvoo (closed 1902). His pottery was simple, sometimes almost rustic in quality, rather sparsely decorated with Art Nouveau motifs. He also taught at the school of industrial art in Helsinki and exerted considerable influence on the development of the crafts in Finland.

Fine figure Good grain or natural markings in wood, making a decorative pattern.

Finial A decorative knob, generally in the form of an acorn or urn but often much more elaborate, applied to furniture or the covers of vessels made in silver, pottery, porcelain, glass, etc. A flame finial is in the form of an urn with flames rising from the top.

Finiguerra, Maso (1426–64). Florentine goldsmith, draughtsman and engraver, notable mainly for his works in NIELLO, most of which are known only from sulphur casts. He was strongly influenced by Filippo Lippi and Ghiberti and by Antonio Pollaiuolo with whom he collaborated 1456–64. His most important work in *niello* is a silver pax (1452–5) in the Museo Nazionale, Florence.

Lit: J. G. Phillips, *Early Florentine Designers and Engravers*, Cambridge, Mass., 1955.

Finnish rugs, *see* RYIJY RUGS.

Fire-back A thick panel of cast iron placed at the back of a hearth to protect the wall from the fire and reflect the heat into the room. They have been made since the c16 and decorated in low relief with heraldry, Biblical or mythological scenes or ornamental motifs.

Firing glasses English type of c18 drinking glasses with short stems and thickened feet to withstand hammering on the table, similar to TOASTMASTERS' GLASSES but without thickening of the bowls.

Fischer, Christian, *see* PIRKENHAMMER PORCELAIN FACTORY.

Fischer, Moritz, *see* HEREND POTTERY AND PORCELAIN FACTORY.

Fisher, Alexander (1864–1936). English goldsmith, painter and sculptor. He was trained as a painter at the South Kensington Schools 1881–4. Fired with an interest in enamelling by Dalpayrat, he went to Paris to study its technique. On his return to London in 1887 he set up a studio and soon became well known for his jewellery and decorative objects with enamelled figures in a late Pre-Raphaelite style. He took charge of the enamelling section of the L.C.C. Central School of Arts and Crafts in 1896 and established his own school in Kensington in 1896. He wrote for such periodicals as the *Art Journal* and *Studio* in which his own works were frequently illustrated (a series of articles on *The Art of the Enameller* was re-issued as a book). His works were shown at many international exhibitions. The most notable included a large triptych overmantel in the Byzantine style for the 1st Earl of Balfour, a table centre incorporating a ship, mermaids and electric lights, for Lord Carmichael, and a triptych *Life of St Patrick* with an entangled Celtic frame in the National Museum of Ireland, Dublin. But his workshop also produced small pieces of domestic and ecclesiastical plate.

Lit: Victorian Church Art, Exh. Cat., Victoria & Albert Museum, London 1971–2.

Five-colour ware, *see* WU-TS'AI.

Flagon Originally a sacramental vessel, it was later adapted for secular use, especially for beer, being then called a 'tankard'. It is of elongated shape with either a flat or domed lid and a thumbpiece for raising it. It was made in silver, pewter, stoneware, faience and porcelain.

Flagon, English silver, c.1660

Flambé glaze A lustrous rich red glaze with streaks and splashes of blue colours on porcelain or stoneware, produced by firing a copper GLAZE in a reducing atmosphere. It was first developed in the CH'IEN LUNG period in China and much taken up in Europe from the late C19, especially by H. Seger at the BERLIN PORCELAIN FACTORY (from 1880), E. CHAPLET in France and Bernard Moore in England.

Flame stitch, *see* BARGELLO WORK.

Flashed glass Similar to CASED GLASS but made by a different process and with a much thinner outer layer, or flashing.

Flat chasing A metal decoration technique for linear ornament executed with punch and hammer. It is a substitute for engraving and is used for decorating SHEFFIELD PLATE which cannot be engraved.

Flat-back figures Earthenware ornamental figures intended to be seen from the front only, made from the mid C19 in Staffordshire potteries and elsewhere, including Scotland. They were usually press-moulded. Used largely for mantelpiece ornaments.

Lit: R. G. Hagger, *Staffordshire Chimney Ornaments,* London 1955.

Flaxman, John (1755–1826). Leading English Neo-Classical sculptor. His father was a caster of plaster models which he supplied to the WEDGWOOD POTTERY for which John began to work as a modeller in 1775. He modelled friezes of such classical scenes as the Muses (1777), the Sacrifice to Cupid (1782) or Hercules in the Garden of the Hesperides (1787), also relief portraits of many contemporary notabilities. Financed by Wedgwood he went to Rome in 1787 and stayed there until 1794 but continued to provide Wedgwood with designs. Thereafter he was engaged mainly as a marble sculptor. His reliefs, which were reproduced in great quantity in JASPER WARE and black BASALTES WARE, are very elegant, very correctly classical but sometimes rather dry. He also provided models for silver executed by Paul STORR.

Lit: W. G. Constable, *John Flaxman,* London 1927.

Fleischmann, C. W., *see* RAEREN POTTERIES.

Flemish scroll A double scroll, the form taken by the front legs and stretchers connecting them on many late-C17 English chairs.

Fletcher & Gardiner A firm of U.S. silversmiths run by **Thomas Fletcher** in partnership with **Sidney Gardiner.** They began at Boston, Mass., in 1809 and moved in 1811 to Philadelphia where they specialized in making large and handsome pieces of presentation plate, often urn-shaped with rich relief decorations somewhat in the manner of Paul STORR. Fletcher was the leading partner, provided the designs and also made buying trips to Europe; and after Gardiner withdrew in 1827 he continued on his own until the late 1830s. Tea services were also included among their products.

Lit: K. M. McClinton in *The Connoisseur*, CLXXIII (1970), pp. 211–20.

Flettner, Peter, *see* FLÖTNER, Peter.

Fleurat, Pierre, *see* ANGOULÊME POTTERY.

Fleurs des Indes, *see* INDIANISCHE BLUMEN.

Fleurs fines, *see* DEUTSCHE BLUMEN.

Flight, Thomas, *see* WORCESTER PORCELAIN COMPANY.

Flint enamel ware, *see* BENNINGTON POTTERY AND PORCELAIN FACTORY.

Flint glass Originally a type of glass made in C17 England by George RAVENSCROFT with silica derived from English flints rather than imported Venetian pebbles. The term is loosely applied to English LEAD GLASS (for which the silica is derived from sand rather than flints).

Lit: W. A. Thorpe, *A History of English and Irish Glass*, London 1929.

Flintporslin, *see* RÖRSTRAND POTTERY & PORCELAIN FACTORY.

Float In a textile, a thread not bound into the weave by alternate threads in the other direction, e.g. a weft which passes over two or more warps before passing under another.

Flock wallpaper A paper (or sometimes cloth) printed, painted or stencilled with a design in slow drying adhesive to which powdered wool is applied so that the pattern shows in velvety relief. First used in early-C17 France and England as a cheap substitute for cut velvet hangings and very popular in the C18. It has recently returned to fashion.

Florence porcelain factories, *see* DOCCIA, MEDICI PORCELAIN FACTORY.

Florence potteries A group of factories in and around Florence (mainly at Bacchereto, CAFAGGIOLO, Beccamorto, MONTELUPO Pistoia, Prato, Puntormo, San Gimignano) and sometimes described as the Tuscan potteries, produced the best Italian maiolica from the late C14 until *c.*1475 when FAENZA took the lead. Maiolica was made in Florence from *c.*1300. Techniques and decorative devices were initially derived from HISPANO-MORESQUE POTTERY imported into Italy in fairly large quantities, and some pieces are direct imitations, though without the use of lustre. But the potteries gradually developed characteristic forms and styles of decoration especially for jugs, ALBARELLI and OAK LEAF JARS. Obviously Italianate human figures and animals begin to appear amid formalized foliage before the mid C15, especially on tiles and large dishes. Although they are of outstanding beauty most wares seem to have been made for use rather than decoration. But strongly modelled busts also appear to have been made before the end of the C15, notably St John the Baptist (Ashmolean Museum, Oxford) and a negress (Musée de Cluny, Paris). The potteries in Florence seem to have closed after 1530. For later ceramics made in the region of Florence see: DOCCIA PORCELAIN FACTORY, MEDICI PORCELAIN FACTORY.

Lit: G. Cora, *Storia della maiolica di Firenze e del Contado, Secoli XIVe XV*, Florence 1973.

Florence tapestry factory Established by the Grand Duke Cosimo I in 1546 with Flemish master weavers **Nicholaus Karcher** and **Jan Rost** or **Rostel** (d.1560). The earliest set of tapestries woven represents the story of Joseph, after cartoons by Bronzino and Pontormo. Bachiacca provided designs for several tapestries including a set of panels decorated with very elegant grotesques which are perhaps the most attractive ever produced by the factory and were much imitated in N. Europe, especially at BRUSSELS. Francesco Salviati and Alessandro Allori were among the other notable painters employed as designers. The factory remained active until 1744, outstanding among its later products being those designed by G. C. Sagrestani (1660–1731). *Illustrated opposite.*

Lit: M. Viale-Ferrero, *Arazzi italiani*, Milan 1961.

Florentine mosaic The English name for *Comesso di*

Florentine tapestry, after a cartoon by Bronzino and assistants, 1549 (Palazzo Vecchio, Florence)

Florentine mosaic panel by Baccio Cappelli, 1709 (Victoria & Albert Museum)

Pietre Dure or decorative panels made of a mosaic of irregularly shaped laminae of PIETRE DURE, i.e. semi-precious hard stones such as chalcedony, agate, jasper, lapis lazuli. Though long practised elsewhere the art was brought to its height of technical and artistic excellence in Florence where a workshop was founded by Francesco de'Medici in 1588. It still flourishes. Products include table-tops, caskets, pictures and cabinets decorated either with geometrical designs or, more usually, with flowers and fruits (sometimes in relief), landscapes, portraits, religious scenes, etc. The best are so exquisitely made that they may at first sight appear to have been painted. They were very popular in the C18 when many pieces were bought by the richer visitors to Florence and used to decorate furniture made in Paris or London. The more expensive Louis XVI furniture-makers, notably BENNEMAN, CARLIN and WEISWEILER, seem to have particularly favoured its use. Florentine mosaic panels were also made at the BUEN RETIRO PORCELAIN FACTORY, mainly for use as table tops.

Lit: L. Bartoli & E. A. Maser, *Il Museo dell'Opificio delle Pietre Dure*, Florence 1953.

Floris, Jan or **Flores, Juan** (*fl.*1524–66). Flemish potter, brother of the designer Cornelis Floris (see GROTESQUE). He went to Spain and was working in Plasencia in 1562 when Philip II, wishing to improve the design of tiles made at TALAVERA, appointed him royal tile-maker. He provided designs for Alcázar, Madrid and the palaces of El Pardo and Segovia. A very fine large wall-panel representing the Crucifixion set in a surround of Flemish Mannerist architectural ornament, in the sacristy of S. Vicente, Plasencia, and three altar frontals from the Convento of S. Domingo el Real, Madrid (now in the Museo Arqueológico, Madrid) were probably made under his guidance.

Lit: A. W. Frothingham, *Tile Panels of Spain*, New York 1969.

Florsheim pottery Faience factory established near Frankfurt-am-Main in 1765 producing mainly fairly simple wares decorated either in blue or in HIGH-TEMPERATURE COLOURS in a peasanty style, but also some more ambitious pieces decorated in enamel colours in the style of STRASBOURG and a very elaborate table centre (Museum für Kunst und Gewerbe, Hamburg). From the 1780s it produced CREAM-COLOURED EARTHENWARE. The factory still exists. (For factory mark *see* p. 883.)

Lit: L. Dehé, *Florsheimer Fayencen*, Hamburg 1924.

Flötner, Peter (*c.*1485–1546). Influential German Renaissance ornamental designer and engraver working in Nuremberg from 1522 onwards. He was probably trained in Augsburg. He published prints for metalwork and furniture decorated with classical architectural motifs, *putti*, grotesques and arabesques, e.g. a design for a four-poster bed supported on Ionic columns, with bucrania on the frieze, etc. There are several surviving examples of German Renaissance furniture after his designs, e.g. oak and ash cupboard dated 1541 in the Germanisches Nationalmuseum, Nuremberg.

P. Flötner: decorative design, 1533

Lit: E. F. Bange, *Peter Flötner*, Leipzig 1926; *Peter Flötner und die Renaissance in Deutschland*, Exh. Cat., Nuremberg 1947; S. Jervis, *Printed Furniture Designs before 1650*, London 1974.

Flower, Bernard (d.1517). Glass stainer born in Germany or the Netherlands. He settled in England in or before 1496, became King's Glazier by 1505 and executed windows for the Henry VIII Chapel in Westminster Abbey (now destroyed). In 1515 he began the wonderful series of windows in King's College Chapel, Cambridge, still Gothic for the most part but with Renaissance details: the series was completed by Galyon HONE and others.

Lit: H. G. Wayment, *The Windows of King's College Chapel, Cambridge* (in *Corpus Vitrearum Medii Aevi, Great Britain*, Suppl. Vol. I), London 1972.

Flügelglas German name for a type of goblet with the stem composed of scrolls of glass somewhat resembling wings, as of a fantastic butterfly. The type originated in C16 Venice, was imitated in N. Europe and revived in the late C19.

Fluting Shallow, rounded parallel grooves running vertically on the shaft of a column, pilaster or other surface.

Fogelberg, Andrew (*c.*1732–93). Silversmith, probably to be identified with Anders Fogelberg who was apprenticed to Berent Halck of Halmsted. He was established in London in the 1770s and from 1780–93 was in partnership with **Stephen Gilbert** and made some of the best English Neo-Classical silver. He seems to have introduced the practice of decorating plate with silver medallions copied from TASSIE's casts. Paul STORR was apprenticed to him 1785–93.

Lit: R. Rowe, *Adam Silver,* London 1965.

Foggini, Giovanni Battista (1652–1755). Florentine sculptor, architect and designer, he was employed by the Medici from 1687 onwards and was from 1695 in control of the Court workshops for which he produced designs and models. Fine examples of Florentine craftsmanship designed by him survive, notably the Reliquary of St Daniel in ebony, gilt-bronze, silver, *pietre dure* and rock crystal, 1705 (Medici Chapel, S. Lorenzo, Florence) and the Elector's Cabinet of ebony with *pietre dure* inlay, gilt-bronze mounts and mother-of-pearl appliqué tracery, 1707–9 (Palazzo Pitti, Florence). He also designed the remarkable silver altar frontal executed by the Lubeck goldsmith **H. Brunick** for SS. Annunziata, Florence, 1680–82, and the equally remarkable frontal executed by **Cosimo Merlini** and **B. Holzman** for the Chiesa Collegiata di S. Maria, Impruneta, 1711–14. For illustrations *see* BAROQUE and PIETRE DURE.

Lit: K. Aschengreen Piacenti & A. Gonzalez Palacios in *The Twilight of the Medici,* Exh. Cat., Detroit/Florence 1974.

Foil (1) A lobe or leaf-shaped curve formed by the cusping of a circle or an arch. An arrangement of three lobes is called a trefoil, four lobes a quatrefoil, etc.

(2) A thin slip of gold, silver or other metal.

Foillet, J., *see* LACE.

Folded foot The reinforced foot of a drinking glass made by folding the edge of the base disc underneath.

Foliot, Nicolas-Quinibert (1706–76). He was a Louis XVI period chair-maker and a rival of BOULARD and SENÉ. He was one of the creators of the LOUIS XVI STYLE chair – more sober and restrained and often more delicate and refined than its Rococo predecessor. He supplied a great quantity of chairs, beds and other upholstered furniture to Versailles, including the throne (1767). His brother **François I** (d.1761) and nephew **François II** (b.1748) were also *menuisiers*, the latter supplying the Crown up to his retirement in 1786, e.g. Louis XVI's bed (now lost) for Versailles to designs by GONDOUIN. A set of his chairs survives at Versailles. His most famous set of furniture, known as the 'Mobilier des Dieux' after the tapestry with which it was upholstered, was probably made for Marie Antoinette's use at Choisy *c.*1770 and is now partly in the Louvre. His work is generally very difficult to identify as it is seldom stamped, having been made for the Crown and thus exempt. The *sculpteur* Babel carved some of his chair frames and he is also known to have collaborated on occasion with the *sculpteur* Guillaume Dupré. Bordon gilded some of his chairs and Chatard did those of the 'Mobilier des Dieux' suite.

Lit: F. J. B. Watson, *The Wrightsman Collection: Furniture,* New York 1966.

Follot, Paul (1877–1941). Parisian designer of interiors, furniture, textiles and table-wares and one of the creators of the ART DECO style. He was a pupil of the painter and designer Eugène Grasset (1841–1917) whom he succeeded as professor of the *Cours superieur d'art décoratif de la Ville de Paris.* He began to work as an independent decorator in 1904 and soon developed a personal variant of ART NOUVEAU, simple in form but rich in materials and decoration. Believing that art was the 'privilege of an élite', he endowed his interiors and individual pieces of furniture with an appearance of opulent comfort. He exhibited regularly at the *Salon des Artistes décorateurs* and at the *Salon d'automne* and provided interiors for the *Exposition internationale* of 1925. From 1923 he was director of the design studio of the Parisian store *Bon Marché,* providing furnishings for a large upper-middle-class public which demanded ostentatiously fine craftsmanship and novelty of design but abhorred eccentricity and the more overt manifestations of 'modernity'. *Illustrated next page.*

Lit: Les années '25', Exh. Cat., Musée des arts décoratifs, Paris 1966.

P. Follot: chair of sycamore, ebony and amaranth, c.1913 (Musée des Arts Décoratifs, Paris)

Fond, *see* LACE.

Fondeur-ciseleur A metal-worker and member of a guild of metal-casters *(fondeurs)* who specialized in finishing the surface by chasing before gilding. *Ciselure* or chasing was brought to a high degree of elaboration and refinement in C18 France; burnished, matt and delicately or coarsely pounced surfaces were produced to give vitality to bronzes. Much of the finest such work went into furniture mounts which French furniture-makers were forbidden to make (by their Guild regulations) and who therefore had to employ *fondeurs-ciseleurs* outside their workshops. The most famous *fondeurs-ciseleurs* were J. CAFFIÉRI, J. C. DUPLESSIS, P. GOUTHIÈRE and P. P. THOMIRE.

Fondeurs, Corporation des The Parisian guild of metal-workers specializing in casting and chasing bronze for sculpture, furniture and porcelain mounts and such decorative objects as clock-cases, *chenets*, candelabra, etc. It was run on lines similar to those of the Corporation des MENUISIER-ÉBÉNISTES. In 1776 it was combined with the guilds of engravers on metal and gilders on metal (called the Corporation des Fondeurs-Ciseleurs) and finally dissolved in 1791.

Fondporzellan Porcelain with an under-glaze coloured ground and reserved panels in white for decorations painted with enamel colours. It was first used at MEISSEN *c.*1722 when a rich brown colour (*Kapuzinerbraun* or *Kaffeebraun*) was used. A yellow ground was introduced at Meissen in 1727. Green, crimson-purples and other colours were also used. At Sèvres the dark *gros bleu* colour was introduced in 1749, *bleu celeste* and *jaune jonquil* in 1752, *rose Pompadour* and other colours in 1756. Similar ground colours were used by English and other porcelain factories.

Fontaine, Pierre-François-Léonard (1762–1853). French architect, interior decorator and designer who, with his friend and close collaborator **Charles Percier** (1764–1838), was mainly responsible for creating the EMPIRE style. Both men were trained in Paris under the architect A.-F. Peyre and studied in Rome both Classical and Renaissance architecture though they were more attracted to the latter. They returned to France in 1791, provided designs for the Assemblé National (not executed) and designed furniture to be executed by Georges JACOB in a severe 'style républicaine' for the Convention Nationale. In 1792 Fontaine went to London but soon returned to Paris to work with Percier, now scenic designer to the Opera. In 1798 they designed ANTIQUE Style furniture, once again to be made by Jacob, for the Council of Five Hundred. In 1799 they were introduced, by the painters J.-L. David and Isabey, to Joséphine Bonaparte who commissioned them to transform Malmaison, where they first showed their full abilities. Subsequently Napoleon began to employ them to create an appropriate visual background to his life. Their *Recueil des décorations intérieurs* (1801, re-issued 1812) not only used the term 'interior decoration' for the first time but showed that they had already created an Empire style which needed only the addition of a few motifs – giant Ns in laurel wreaths, eagles and bees – to make it fully Napoleonic. It includes designs for canopied beds, throne-like armchairs flanked by winged lions and such preposterous fantasies as a huge jardinière cum goldfish-bowl and bird-cage, supported by sphinxes with flower-pots on their heads and crowned by a statue of Hebe. Their furniture is always of simple form lavishly decorated with Antique motifs. It is all very elegant but somewhat stagey. Napoleon kept them fully employed until 1814 as architects (Arc du Carrousel, Rue de Rivoli, designs for the palace of the King of Rome, etc.), as pageant masters (Coronation, marriage with Marie Louise), as interior decorators (Malmaison, Tuileries, Louvre, Saint-Cloud, Versailles) and as designers of furniture, silver, textiles, etc. They were equally adept at providing settings for the grandeur of the Emperor (Tuileries throne-room) and the simplicity of the General (the tent-like council chamber at Malmaison), for the nobility of Art (galleries for antique statues in the Louvre) or the coquetry of Women (Joséphine's bedroom). Many of their decorative schemes had to be completed quickly – hence, perhaps, their addiction to lavish draperies on walls and over beds, thrones and windows. Apart from the rooms at Malmaison very few of their decorative schemes survive.

Despite their fidelity to Napoleon they continued to enjoy official patronage after the Restoration. Working in partnership less frequently, though still on terms of the closest intimacy, Percier devoted most of his time to his pupils while Fontaine practised as an architect (e.g. restorations at Palais Royal 1814–31 and the progressive glass-vaulted Galeries d'Orléans) and retained until 1848 the post of architect to the Tuileries and the Louvre. They were buried in the same tomb with a third friend from their student days in Rome, all three claiming to have remained true to their youthful vows of amity and celibacy.

Lit: M. L. Bivier, *Pierre Fontaine*, Paris 1964; S. Grandjean, *Empire Furniture 1800–1825*, London 1966.

Fontainebleau porcelain factory, *see* PETIT, Jacob, and AVON POTTERY AND PORCELAIN FACTORY.

Fontainebleau tapestry factory A temporary workshop set up by Francis I *c.*1540 to weave a

A. Fontana: engraved rock crystal panels set in casket made for Duke Albrecht of Bavaria, c.1565–70 (Residenzmuseum, Munich)

magnificent set of hangings (Kunsthistorisches Museum, Vienna) which reproduces the sophisticated Mannerist wall decorations by Rosso and Primaticcio in the Galerie François I, Fontainebleau.

Lit: R. H. Göbel, *Wandteppiche*, Leipzig 1923–34; R.-A. Weigert, *French Tapestry*, London 1962.

Fontana, Annibale (*c.*1540–87). Italian hardstone carver, bronze worker and sculptor of Milanese origin but probably trained in Rome. He appears to have begun as an engraver on rock crystal, executing *c.*1560–70 the outstandingly fine panels for the casket of Duke Albrecht of Bavaria (Schatzkammer in Residenzmuseum, Munich) described by Raffaello Borghini in 1584. Later he worked mainly as a sculptor in marble and bronze, executing in 1580 four large candlesticks for the Certosa, Pavia, which are among the masterpieces of Mannerist bronze work. *Illustrated on previous page.*

Lit: E. Kris, *Die Meister und Meisterwerke der Steinschneidekunst . . .*, Vienna 1929.

Fontana factory The most notable maiolica factory in URBINO founded *c.*1520 by N. PELLIPARIO's son, Guido, who took the name of Fontana, and carried on by his son, Orazio (*c.*1510–71). Began by producing ISTORIATO wares but is better known for works in the BIANCO DI FAENZA technique adopted in the 1550s. Specialized in elaborately modelled and often very large vessels – wine coolers with lion monopod supports and handles, great pilgrim bottles, vases with writhing snake or dolphin handles, fountains, etc. – painted in delicate colours with grotesques (inspired by Raphael) on a white ground. Smaller objects are still more sculpturesque – an inkstand adorned with a statuette of a drunkenly reclining Silenus, another in the form of a man seated at an organ, a sauce-boat fashioned like a dolphin lying on its back. The factory remained active in the C17.

Lit: J. Chompret, *Répertoire de la maiolique italienne*, Paris 1949; G. Dorfles, *Le ceramiche di Fontana*, Florence 1949; B. Rackham, *Italian Maiolica*, London 1952.

Fontebasso, Giuseppe and **Andrea,** *see* TREVISO POTTERY & PORCELAIN FACTORIES.

Footman A late-C18 English type of TRIVET standing on four legs, made of iron or brass. The word is recorded in this sense from 1767.

Footman, English (Derbyshire), c18 (Victoria & Albert Museum)

Forestier, Pierre-Auguste (1755–1835). A Parisian *fondeur-ciseleur* who, with his brother **Étienne-Jean,** carried on a notable bronze-working business started by their father **Étienne** (*c.*1712–68). Étienne supplied bronzes to A.-C. BOULLE, G. JOUBERT and J.-F. OEBEN for whom he made some of the bronze mounts for the *bureau du Roi*. Étienne-Jean became a *maître* in 1764. With Pierre-Auguste he worked extensively for the Crown during the last few years of Louis XVI's reign and they collaborated with such furniture-makers as BENEMAN, supplying bronze mounts. After the Revolution Pierre-Auguste set up a shop for furniture mounts, vases, candelabra, etc. He sometimes worked to designs by Percier & FONTAINE and became one of the best *bronziers* of the Napoleonic and Restauration periods.

Lit: S. Grandjean, *Empire Furniture 1800–1825*, London 1966.

Fork The eating fork was first used in the Middle Ages, apparently only for sweet foods (fruit in

Fork and folding spoon, silver-gilt, Flemish, c16 (British Museum)

syrup, etc.), mainly in S. Europe though northern examples are known. This type of fork, often made *en suite* with a spoon and sometimes combined with a spoon and tooth-pick, was a personal object rather than one provided by a host for his guests. The practice of using a fork, with a knife, to eat meats appears to have been established in c16 Italy and gradually to have spread north, reaching England in the early c17 though it was by no means widespread until after the Restoration. This necessitated forks that were simpler, stronger and larger than those only suitable for sweets, now called SUCKET FORKS. The first meat forks had two or three prongs but a four-pronged type was developed before the end of the c17. From the c17 handles have been similar to those of spoons.

Forlì pottery Maiolica was made in Forlì from the early c16 (if not before) but only a few documented pieces are known (e.g. examples in Louvre and Victoria & Albert Museum), ranging in date from 1542 to 1564, and very similar to those made in the nearby town of FAENZA. A maiolica factory was functioning in Forlì as late as 1661, but none of its products has been identified.

Lit: C. Grigioni in *Faenza*, XXXII (1946), pp. 35ff.

Formica A rigid laminated PLASTIC material which was invented in 1913 in the U.S.A. and now manufactured by Formica Ltd. The surface sheet is usually a urea/formaldehyde resin bonded by a urea/formaldehyde adhesive to a plastic body made from either a phenolic or a urea type resin. This in turn may be backed with plywood. The surface is waterproof, resistant to heat and more or less scratchproof. It is much in demand for durable and decorative finishes for kitchen furniture, etc.

Fortling, Jacob, *see* COPENHAGEN POTTERIES.

Forty, Jean-François (*fl.*1772–90). French ornamental designer, engraver and bronze worker, probably born in Marseilles though he worked in Paris. He designed the ironwork for the staircase and entrance hall of the École Militaire, Paris (*c.*1755), and the grille closing the entrance court of the Palais Royal, Paris. But he is best known for his many engraved designs in the early LOUIS XVI STYLE, *Oeuvres de sculpture en bronze contenant Girandoles, Flambeaux, Feux de Cheminées, Pendules, Bras, Cartels, Baromètres* . . . issued in eight parts, *Oeuvres d'orfévrerie à l'usage des églises*, issued in three parts and including designs for monstrances, candlesticks, etc., *Projet de deux toilettes* and *Oeuvres de serrureries*. He made much use of such Antique ornaments as acanthus leaves, trophies and the Vitruvian scroll. His designs for chandeliers often have sockets for the candles fashioned like flowers.

Lit: D. Guilmard, *Les maîtres ornemantistes*, Paris 1880.

Fothergill, John, *see* BOULTON, Matthew.

Foullet, Antoine (*c.*1710–1775). He was a Parisian furniture-maker and became a *maître* in 1749. He appears to have specialized in clock cases, of which there were forty in his stock when he died. Some of them were wholly of bronze. His furniture is LOUIS XV in style. His son **Pierre-Antoine,** who became a *maître* in 1765, worked with him until he went bankrupt in 1769. He was in prison for debt when his father died: however, surviving pieces by him appear to have been made later, e.g. bureau in the Wallace Collection, London.

Lit: S. Eriksen, *Early Neo-Classicism in France*, London 1974.

Fouquay, Nicolas, *see* POTERAT, Edmé, and ROUEN POTTERIES.

Fournier, Louis-Antoine (*c.*1720–86). French sculptor, porcelain modeller and arcanist. He was employed at VINCENNES 1746–9 and possibly responsible for a figure of a naiad (example in Victoria and Albert Museum). He then worked at Chantilly 1752–9. But he is notable mainly for his period in Copenhagen, 1759–66, where he helped to establish a porcelain factory and provided some 20 different models for pretty potpourri with applied flowers, plates with ozier pattern borders, elegant little jugs and cylindrical coffee-cups with simulated twig handles (some 170 surviving pieces are recorded). He also modelled a bust and some portrait reliefs. After returning to France in 1766 he appears to have forsaken porcelain modelling.

Lit: B. L. Grandjean in *Det danske Kunstindustrimuseum: Virksomhed 1964–9*, Copenhagen 1969, pp. 79–128.

Frampton, Sir George James (1860–1928). He was a prominent English sculptor, (R.A. 1902, knighted 1908), and from 1888 he was also involved in the decorative arts both as a craftsman (metalwork and ivory), and as designer and supporter of the ARTS AND CRAFTS Movement. He designed and made pieces of presentation plate in the Arts and Crafts style slightly tinged with Art Nouveau influence.

G. J. Frampton:
silver cigar box made by Gilbert Marks, 1897
(Victoria & Albert Museum)

France, Charles William Fearnley (b.1898). Manufacturer of handsome simple mass-produced furniture. Born at Dewsbury, he settled in Denmark in 1936 and took over a mattress factory. After the war his firm, C. W. France & Co., pioneered the export boom in Danish furniture. His main innovation was the use of interior spring cushions for framed chairs, which he began to produce in 1948.

France, Edward (*fl.*1767–1803), *see* FRANCE, William.

France, William (*fl.*1764–7). He was a notable English cabinet-maker in partnership with the royal cabinet-maker **John Bradburn** who was assistant and successor to William VILE. He is best known for the work he carried out for John Chute of The Vyne and for the tables made to Robert ADAM's design for Sir Lawrence Dundas. On his death in 1767 he was succeeded by **Edward France,** possibly his son, who provided (1768–70) much furniture which is still *in situ* at Kenwood House. Some of it was designed by Adam while other pieces are in a style associated with CHIPPENDALE. Edward France went into partnership with **Samuel Beckwith** before 1791, and under the name of France and Beckwith they supplied furniture to the Crown and private patrons until 1803.

Lit: A. Coleridge, *Chippendale Furniture*, London 1968.

Francesco di Pieragnolo, *see* VENICE POTTERIES.

Francesco Durantino (*fl.*1544–53). Maiolica painter working in the ISTORIATO style and known by two signed pieces, a saucer dish dated 1544 (British Museum) and a very handsome wine cistern of 1553 made at 'Monte Bagnolo' near Perugia (Art Institute, Chicago). A few other pieces have been attributed to him. He may be identical with a **Francesco di Pieragnolo** of Castel Durante who, with his father-in-law, ran a pottery in Venice 1545–50. *Illustrated below.*

Lit: V. J. Scheidemantel in *Museum Studies* (Chicago) III (1968), pp. 42–62.

Franchini, Girolamo, *see* ESTE POTTERY & PORCELAIN FACTORY.

Franck, Kaj (b.1911). Finnish industrial designer whose influence on glass and ceramic design is comparable to that of AALTO on furniture. He is mainly responsible for the high standards of

Francesco Durantino: maiolica wine cistern, 1553 (Courtesy of the Art Institute of Chicago)

everyday utility wares, both for table and kitchen, produced in post-war Finland. He combines originality and imagination in design with great practical ability, especially as regards industrial mass-production. His cups, tumblers, etc., are always well-balanced, the lips are always drip-proof. He has designed excellent drinking glasses for the Nostijo glasshouse, porcelain and earthenware crockery for the ARABIA POTTERY (notably the 'Kilta' series) and enamelled metal bowls, etc. – all unpretentious and inexpensive, practical yet elegant. He prefers pure cylindrical forms and bright glazes of gay plain colours. His sense of fantasy is most evident in glass, generally to good effect (e.g. his 'Soap Bubble' vases) but sometimes declining into rather embarrassing whimsicality.

Frankenthal porcelain factory One of the most distinguished in C18 Germany, it was founded in 1755 by P. A. HANNONG, who had been obliged to leave STRASBOURG, and was run by his sons until 1762 when it was acquired by the Elector Palatine Karl Theodor. The best products are those of the first 20 years when a rather unusual type of hard paste with a glaze which absorbs the enamel colours – rather in the manner of soft paste – was used. Useful wares of the 1750s are in the Strasbourg style. But attractive if rather stiff statuettes of rustic, allegorical, chinoiserie, *Commedia dell'Arte*, etc. figures were made after models by J. W. Lanz who also came from the Strasbourg factory. Such figures soon became a speciality and the factory is known to have produced some 800 different subjects after the work of a number of different modellers whose identity and relationship to one another are sometimes difficult to establish. Outstanding among them are the *Music Lesson* (after Boucher; *see* page 672), a *Commedia dell'Arte* series, a large number of Chinese figures and an enchanting little chinoiserie summer house attributed to J. F. von LÜCK; a series of allegorical figures in poses of exaggerated elegance, groups of *Apollo and Daphne* (after Bernini) and *Atalanta and Meleager*, and a large *Apotheosis of Karl Theodor* by Konrad LINCK (1732–93); and, in a very playful vein, *Hawkers, Dancers and Beggars* by Karl Gottlieb LÜCK (d.1775). A severer style was introduced by J. P. MELCHIOR who was model master 1779–93. Other notable products include clock cases, mirror frames, chandeliers with extravagant Rococo mouldings. Table-wares tend to be imitative first of MEISSEN then of SÈVRES but are often painted with great delicacy. The factory's history was troubled after the French invasion 1794–5 and it closed in 1799. The moulds were taken to GRÜNSTADT where they were used in the C19 (for both pottery and porcelain) and some went to MANNHEIM, KAISERLAUTERN and NYMPHENBURG. (For factory mark *see* p. 883.)

Frankenthal porcelain chinoiserie group 1765–70 (Antique Porcelain Company, New York)

Lit: L. W. Böhm, *Frankenthaler Porzellan*, Mannheim 1960; J. Terrasson, *Les Hannong et leurs manufactures Strasbourg, Frankenthal*, Paris–Lausanne 1971.

Frankfurt-am-Main pottery One of the first German faience factories, founded in 1666 by a French potter (**Johann Simonet**) who had been previously employed at HANAU. Until 1723 it was producing wares which technically and artistically rival the best DELFT pottery, for which they have often been mistaken since no regular system of marking was used. Posset bowls, pear-shaped jugs, gourd-shaped vases, candlesticks, large decorative plates and monumental vases a metre high were among the objects made. As on Delftwares the tin-enamel was covered with a lead glaze which gives the surface a white porcelain brilliance. Usually products are decorated in blue,

Frankfurt tin-glazed earthenware plate, c.1680 *(Museum für Kunst und Gewerbe, Hamburg)*

or blue and manganese, with exotic plant motifs or chinoiseries of an engagingly wayward fantasy – frisky little Chinamen and jungles of flora, notably those painted by Johann Caspar Ripp (1681–1726) who worked at Frankfurt from 1702 to 1708. But Biblical scenes and other figurative subjects also appear on large dishes. Some pieces were decorated by HAUSMALER. The factory declined after 1723 and closed in the 1770s. Wares are usually unmarked but an 'F' with a date is sometimes found.

Lit: A. Feulner, *Frankfurter Fayencen*, Berlin 1935; K. Hüseler, *Deutsche Fayencen*, Stuttgart 1956–8.

Frederick Augustus I, Elector of Saxony and King of Poland (1670–1733). The founder of the MEISSEN PORCELAIN FACTORY, he succeeded as Elector of Saxony in 1694 and was elected king of Poland 1697–1703 and 1709–1733. The 'Augustus Rex' mark on some pieces of Meissen – a monogram of the letters AR in underglaze blue – indicated that they were intended (if not always adopted) for royal palaces or royal gifts. It appears mainly on pieces made 1725–30 but was also used during the reign of his successor Frederick Augustus II (d.1763).

Freiberg pottery A late-C17 Saxon stoneware factory producing handsome jugs decorated with bands or panels of carved geometrical or formalized flower ornament enamelled in white, black, red or light blue. These jugs are often mounted in pewter.

Lit: K. Hüseler, *Deutsche Fayencen*, Stuttgart 1956–8.

Fret A geometrical ornament of intersecting horizontal and vertical straight lines repeated to form a band, e.g. a key pattern.

Fret

Fretwork Carved geometrical patterns of intersecting lines either pierced (as on the galleries of tables in the CHINESE CHIPPENDALE style) or in relief. In the later C19 the term was applied also to openwork patterns carved out of thin pieces of wood with a fret-saw.

Friedberg pottery, *see* GÖGGINGEN POTTERY.

Frieze An architectural term for the middle division of an entablature between the architrave and cornice, but also applied to the band below the cornice on a piece of furniture or, more loosely, to any decorated band. A 'cushion frieze' is of convex profile.

Frigger Colloquial glassmakers' term for a decorative glass object – e.g. walking-stick, drum-stick, top-hat, model ship or figure of an animal – made in a craftsman's spare time, often from left-over material. It is rarely possible to establish the place of origin of such objects.

Frijtom, Frederik van (*fl.*1632–1702). Dutch painter who specialized in decorating DELFT plates and plaques with very delicate blue-and-white landscapes in the manner of Antoine Waterloo.

Lit: A. Vecht, *Frederik van Frijtom, 1632–1702; Life and Work of a Delft Pottery-Decorator*, Amsterdam 1968.

Frit (1) The mixture of calcined sand and other materials which becomes GLASS after firing.

(2) The vitreous composition from which soft-paste PORCELAIN is made.

(3) Ground-up glass used in the glazing of POTTERY.

(4) An archaeologist's term for a substance made from materials similar to glass and used for amulets, seals, etc. in the ancient Middle East, especially Egypt.

Fromageau, Jean-Baptiste (*c.*1726–after 1781). A Parisian *ébéniste, menuisier* and furniture dealer, he became a *maître* in 1755. He was unusual in being both *ébéniste* and *menuisier*, producing very fine commodes, tables, and *secrétaires* as well as small, elaborately fitted pieces. In style his work ranges from the RÉGENCE to the early LOUIS XVI style, often with elaborate floral marquetry.

Lit: F. J. B. Watson, *The Wrightsman Collection: Furniture*, New York 1966.

Froment-Meurice, François-Désiré (1802–55). The son of a goldsmith, he became the most famous silversmith and jeweller in Paris in his day, patronized by the fashionable and aristocratic, eulogized in print by such famous writers as Balzac, Gautier and Victor Hugo. He leapt to fame at the Paris Industrial Exhibition of 1839, when he was made *argentier de la ville de Paris*. His work at the 1844 exhibition established him as the leading silversmith in France. He aimed at a revival of Mannerist virtuosity, a typical example of his work being the dressing-table and toilette service given by the ladies of France to the Duchess of Parma in 1845. It is mainly in the Gothic style though with some C18 Rococo features and very elaborately decorated. Very few of his works can now be traced. A massive silver bracelet of 1841 is in the Musée des Arts Décoratifs, Paris. On his death his business was taken over by his son **Émile** (1837–1913) who continued to produce work in much the same style until late in the century when Art Nouveau came into fashion.

F.-D. Froment-Meurice: carved ivory tankard exhibited at the Great Exhibition, 1851

Lit: H. Bouilhet, *L'Orfèvrerie Française aux XVIIIe et XIXe siècles*, Paris 1910; F. Dumont in *Connaissance des Arts*, November 1956.

Fromery, Alex An early-C18 Berlin enameller who worked on copper and used raised gilding. The Meissen painter C. F. HEROLD worked with him *c.*1740–50.

Frothingham, Benjamin (1734–1809). He was born in Boston, the son of a cabinet-maker by whom, presumably, he was trained. He had set himself up on his own at Charlestown, Massachusetts, before 1756. In 1759 he took part in the expedition to capture Quebec and in 1775 he was made first lieutenant and served throughout the Revolution until 1782, being wounded at Bethlehem and becoming a friend of George Washington. He was afterwards known always as Major Benjamin Frothingham. Only eight pieces of furniture bearing his label are known but many others have by analogy been attributed to him. (A mahogany card-table in the Du Pont Museum at Winterthur is labelled.) The majority are in the so-called American Chippendale style – not unlike those made by John GODDARD and the TOWNSENDS in Newport, but a presumably post-1782 example is in the Hepplewhite style. His eldest son, **Benjamin III** (d.1832) was also a cabinet-maker.

Lit: E. H. Bjerkoe, *The Cabinet Makers of America*, New York 1957.

Frullini, Luigi (1839–97). He was a Florentine sculptor who turned to furniture-making of an elaborate, delicately carved and very expensive kind. And the Neo-Quattrocento or Neo-Early-Renaissance style he developed was well calculated to appeal to mid-C19 taste. He carved frames, candelabra, clocks, bookbindings, etc., as well as cabinets, chests, cassone and other substantial pieces which provided space for the display of his virtuosity as a sculptor in wood. Examples of his work were exhibited at the World Exhibitions in London in 1862 and in Paris in 1867 and he found clients on both sides of the Atlantic.

Frye, Thomas (1710–62). A painter and mezzotint engraver who was born near Dublin and went *c.*1730 to London where in 1744 and 1748 he took out patents for making porcelain. He was the inventor of bone-china, co-founder and until 1759 manager of the BOW PORCELAIN FACTORY. After retiring from Bow, on account of ill-health, he resumed his career as a print-maker and painter.

Lit: Bow Porcelain 1774–1776, Exh. Cat., British Museum, London 1959–60.

Frytom, Frederik van, *see* FRIJTOM, Frederik van.

Fu A type of Chinese Bronze Age food vessel introduced during the middle of the CHOU dynasty, i.e. *c.*700 B.C. It is rectangular with four feet and a cover. The cover is identical, except for two loop handles, so that it can be reversed and used as another dish.

Fuddling-cup An English, specifically West-Country, drinking vessel consisting of three or more cups interconnected at the base and with entwined handles. A speciality of two Somerset potteries – **Crock Street** and **Donyat** – where they were made of *sgraffiato* slipware from the mid C17 to late C18. Also made in tin-glazed earthenware at BRISTOL.

Fuhrlohg (or **Fürloh**), **Christopher** (*fl.*1759–87). Cabinet-maker notable especially for his excellent work in marquetry. He was born in Stockholm, the son of a cabinet-maker, **Johan Hugo Fürloh** (d.1745), and completed his apprenticeship in 1759. In 1762 he left Sweden travelling with G. HAUPT to Amsterdam and Paris where he arrived in 1764, and appears to have worked for an *ébéniste*, possibly Simon Oeben (brother of J.-F. OEBEN). But he soon crossed over to England where he executed a very fine marquetry commode which he signed and dated 1767 (Castle Howard, Yorkshire). He may have been working for J. LINNEL at this date but appears to have set up on his own before 1772 when he signed another commode (private coll.) decorated with a central figurative panel after a design by Angelica Kauffman. A strikingly similar commode probably made *en suite* but unsigned is in the Lady Lever Art Gallery, Port Sunlight. These three pieces display his mastery of the early LOUIS XVI STYLE. He must have been one of the most accomplished cabinet-makers working in London at the time. A number of other pieces have been attributed to him on stylistic grounds. He was assisted 1769–76 by his half-brother **Johann Christian Linning.** On a trade card issued *c.*1772 he described himself as '*Ébéniste*' to the Prince of Wales but no work executed for the Prince has been traced. He is last recorded in 1787 when he moved out of premises in Gerrard Street North but is thought to have remained active until after the close of the century.

Lit: J. Hayward in *Burlington Magazine*, CXIV (1972), pp. 704–11.

Fulcrum Latin word for the raised portion at the

Fulcrum from a Roman bed, bronze inlaid with silver, probably C1 A.D. *(Museo dei Conservatori, Rome)*

end of a bed or couch, serving either as a head-rest or foot-board. On Greek and Roman beds the sides of the fulcra were often decorated with reliefs, either carved or applied in bronze or silver.

Fulda pottery and porcelain factory A faience factory founded in 1741 under the patronage of the Prince Bishop of Fulda and functioning until 1758, it was among the best of its time in Germany. Plates, vases, tureens, etc. were decorated in muffle colours and gold (less frequently in HIGH-TEMPERATURE COLOURS) on an unusually pure white enamel ground. Exceptional products include a pair of candlesticks 81 cm high (Landesmuseum, Cassel). But it is best known for wares painted by A. F. von LOWENFINCK who worked here 1741–4 and by Maria Schick whom he later married. The porcelain factory was founded in 1764, again under the patronage of the Prince Bishop, and after a difficult start continued until 1790. It is distinguished mainly for its statuettes of great delicacy, probably the work of a single modeller who has not been identified. They include figures of male and female gardeners, shepherds and shepherdesses and a group of a Mozartian flautist and two female musicians playing in an intricate Rococo arbour. Tablewares were also made and became the staple products from 1775 until 1790 when the factory closed. (For factory mark *see* p. 883.)

Lit: H. H. Josten, *Fulda Porzellanfiguren*, Berlin 1929; K. Hüseler, *Deutsche Fayencen*, Stuttgart 1954; E. Kramer in *Keramos*, 13 (1961), pp. 8–18.

Fulham carpet and tapestry factory A short-lived concern set up in London by a French emigré **Pierre Parisot** (1697–1769) from the SAVONNERIE factory, first in Westminster in 1750, then in Paddington and finally in Fulham in 1753. It quickly expanded with numerous ex-SAVONNERIE workers but exorbitant prices forced closure in 1755 and the stock was auctioned. The sale catalogue reveals that it specialized in small pieces of tapestry for chairs, pole screens, etc., and also in Savonnerie type carpets. Claude PASSAVANT bought the factory.

Lit: H. Göbel, *Wandteppiche*, Leipzig 1923–34; W. G. Thomson, *A History of Tapestry*, London 1930.

Fulham pottery, *see* DWIGHT, John.

Fulper pottery A factory established in 1805 at Flemington, New Jersey. Throughout the C19 it produced only utilitarian wares, but *c.*1910 began to exploit the vogue for art pottery, making very handsome simply shaped vessels decorated with crystalline glazes marketed under the trade name *Vasekraft*. Their most original products were table lamps shaped like toadstools made of pottery with irregular glazes and panels of glass set in the top.

Lit: R. Judson Clark (ed.): *The Arts and Crafts Movement in America 1876–1916*, Exh. Cat., Art Museum, Princeton University, Art Institute of Chicago, etc. 1972–3.

Fumed oak Oak furniture exposed to the fumes of strong ammonia (or painted with ammonia) which gives it a powdery-grey surface. It was immensely popular in the 1920s and 1930s when much modern furniture was treated (and a certain amount of old furniture was ruined) in this way.

Functionalism Strictly, the theory that buildings or products which function well and use materials with the maximum economy are necessarily beautiful and, conversely, that those which do not function well and use materials extravagantly cannot be beautiful. A pure functionalist, if such existed, would design entirely without any aesthetic intention. The concept owes something to theories about 'beauty and fitness for purpose' propounded in the C18 by English empiricists and later elaborated by Kant, also to the Neo-Classical rejection of superfluous ornament. But it was not until the later C19 that the Chicago architect Louis Sullivan declared that 'form follows function', and Otto Wagner, in his inaugural lecture as professor at the Vienna Academy in 1894, that 'Nothing that is not practical can be beautiful'. In 1904 Paul Souriau stated that 'there can be no conflict between the beautiful and the useful' and in 1908 the rabidly anti-ornament theorist and propagandist Adolf Loos published his famous and influential *Ornament and Crime*. These ideas were quickly taken up and spread rapidly, exerting great influence on INDUSTRIAL DESIGN, especially, after the First World War, at the BAUHAUS. The term Functionalism was, however, increasingly misunderstood and abused and became eventually almost synonymous with the International Modern Style in architecture and the similar 'style' in design developed around the Bauhaus.

Functionalism, as understood in a strictly utilitarian and materialistic sense, suffered from its inherent tendency towards extreme austerity and puritanism. Its exponents discounted the less rational aspects of the relationship between man and the man-made environment. Most designers would still agree today that a designed object should operate efficiently before anything else, but this can hardly be called Functionalism. Nowadays, it is generally accepted that the aesthetic component in a designed product is only partly related to its material utility. In other words, Functionalism is acquiring psychological overtones and another order of priorities is beginning to emerge among young designers, many of whom feel that technology can be left to cope with efficient operation and that it is the designer's job to create objects to which people can respond emotionally and sensually.

Funk, Mathäus (1697–1783). Leading Swiss furniture-maker. He was the son of **Johann Lorenz,** who was probably of Swiss origin but who went from Frankfurt to Switzerland in 1695 and settled at Berne in 1706. One of his brothers, **Johann Friedrich** (1706–75) was a sculptor, another **Daniel Beat Ludwig** (1726–87) was a clockmaker. His most notable work is a bracket clock (with movement by Daniel Beat Ludwig Funk) in the style of CRESSENT. He had what was probably the most important cabinet-making workshop in Switzerland, employing journeymen from Germany and Sweden. Johann Friedrich made some pieces of carved furniture, e.g. pier-table and pier-glass frame in Hôtel de Musique, Berne (1769).

Lit: H. Kreisel, *Die Kunst des deutschen Möbels,* vol. ii, Munich 1970.

Fürstenberg porcelain factory Founded in Brunswick by Duke Carl I of Brunswick in 1747 though it did not begin to produce porcelain until 1753

Fürstenburg porcelain jug, painted in enamel colours, c.1760 (Museum für Kunst und Gewerbe, Hamburg)

after three men from HÖCHST had been taken on – the arcanist **Johann Benckgraff** (1708–53), the model-master **Simon Feilner** (d.1798) and the painter **Johannes Zeschinger** (b.1723). Early vases and table-wares are notable mainly for their rich relief decorations of Rococo scrollwork often picked out in gold or colours. Handsome and vigorous if rather stocky statuettes after models by Feilner include a large series of *Commedia dell'Arte* figures (1754) and a set of Miners (1757). The best period runs from *c.*1768 to 1790. At its start something of a speciality was made of painted panels often in the form of pictures with elaborate Rococo frames. Vases and table-wares were made and often painted with landscapes, figure subjects, birds, etc., of great delicacy. The Rococo style was abandoned soon after 1770 when the factory came increasingly under the influence of BERLIN and SÈVRES. The most interesting decorative pieces of the following years are in biscuit – medallions and busts of ancient poets and philosophers and contemporary notabilities, from models by Johann Christoph Rombrich (d.1794), equestrian statues of Frederick the Great and the Emperor Joseph II. Others were less solemn – the figure of a woman looking for a flea and a group of a woman seated at a table between her husband and her lover. From *c.*1790 the Neo-Classical influence became steadily more pronounced. Under the management of L. V. GERVEROT between 1795 and 1814 inspiration was derived first from WEDGWOOD (for whom he had worked) and then from the Empire style products of Sèvres. **Heinrich Christian Brüning** (1779–1855), a painter employed at the factory from 1797 until his death, decorated a large number of C19 pieces with landscapes and figure subjects in a rich easel-painter's style which was very popular. The factory was transferred to private hands in 1859. It still flourishes and produces good modern wares. (For factory mark *see* p. 883.)

Lit: C. Scherer, *Das Fürstenberger Porzellan*, Berlin 1909; *Fürstenberg Porzellan aus 3 Jahrhunderts*, Exh. Cat., Kestner Museum, Hannover 1956; S. Ducret, *Fürstenberger Porzellan*, Brunswick 1965.

Fustian A coarse cloth with a LINEN warp and COTTON weft first made in Egypt in the C2 A.D. and named after Fostat, a suburb of Cairo. In England it was made extensively between 1720 and 1774 when the use of pure cotton materials was prohibited. Later the name was applied to a thick twilled cotton cloth with a short pile, generally dyed a dark colour.

Engraved initial letter from Latin edition of Caesar, published by Jacob Tonson, London, 1712 (reduced)

Gabel pottery A factory founded *c.*1630 by **Heinrich Wolf Bercka** on his estate at Gabel in Bohemia, producing wares stamped with seals similar to those of STRIEGAU. Products included jugs, round and octagonal plates, cups and saucers of white or red earthenware often with moulded reliefs of flowers and figures (oriental or European) and sometimes cold enamel painting (most of which has flaked off). It appears to have been more productive than the Striegau factory to which all such pieces were formerly ascribed.

Lit: J. Horschik in *Keramos* 33 (1966), pp. 3–55.

Gadrooning Convex curves or inverted fluting, usually applied as an edging.

Gadrooning on English silver salt, late c17

Gaillard, Eugene (1862–1933). French Art Nouveau furniture designer employed by S. BING. His works are generally simpler than those of the School of NANCY but he made a similar use of whip-lash curves and very low relief carvings which have a moulded appearance.

E. Gaillard: settee (Stadtmuseum, Cologne)

Gaitán, Alonso de Figueroa, *see* TALAVERA DE LA REINA POTTERY.

Gallé, Émile (1846–1904). Leading French glass-maker: an outstanding exponent of ART NOUVEAU and the founder of the SCHOOL OF NANCY. He was liberally educated at Nancy and Weimar (where he studied mineralogy) and apprenticed to the Meisenthal glasshouse 1866–7. At first he worked under his father who had a studio for decorating faience and glass in Nancy, but he also travelled to England, where he studied Oriental glass at South Kensington (1871), and to Italy (1877). In 1878 he began to exhibit under his own name pastiches of Venetian and Islamic

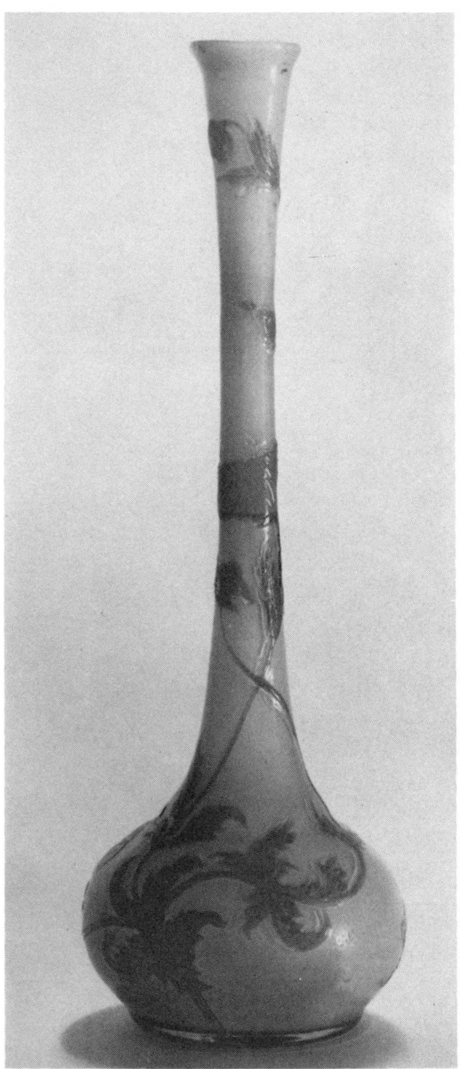

E. Gallé: opaque cased glass vase, c.1900 *(Kunstgewerbemuseum, Zurich)*

enamelled glass which revealed his technical mastery of glass-making and decoration. In 1884 he began to develop a more personal, Art Nouveau, style, quickly achieved European and American renown and by 1890 was running a large factory turning out a stream of glass vessels no two of which were identical though many were similar. Many of these were sold by S. BING'S Parisian shop, *L'Art Nouveau*. Reacting against the mid-C19 fashions for heavy cut crystal glass and *opaline*, he emphasized the ductility and translucency of his medium. Employing practically every technique known to the glass-maker (apart from diamond cutting) he was probably most successful with cased glass vessels in two or more colours (grey and amethyst were among his favourites) which take on subtly different tones from the qualities of light they transmit. He skilfully exploited imperfections, e.g. crazings, air bubbles and cloudings. For decorations he favoured rather willowy flowers and foliage, insects (particularly dragonflies) and such marine creatures as octopuses and sea-anemones (influenced by Japanese art). His vases are occasionally inscribed with a few lines of poetry, by Baudelaire

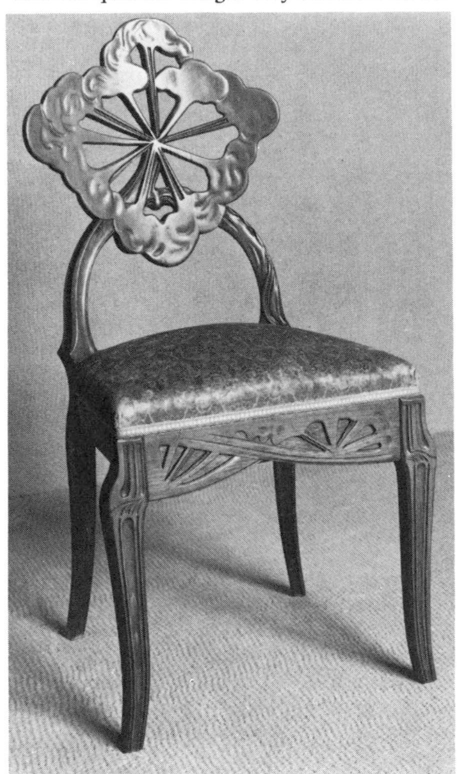

E. Gallé: chair, 1902 *(Musée des Arts Décoratifs, Paris)*

or Verlaine. Straight lines and simple geometric shapes are never employed for the decorations or forms of his vessels which have an easy fluidity and well-balanced poise. Though often elongated, they are seldom as wilfully attenuated, top-heavy and *outré* as those of his many imitators (though excellent work in a somewhat similar style was executed in Nancy by DAUM FRÈRES). From the 1880s he also designed and produced furniture of the lushest Art Nouveau variety with much very delicately executed marquetry decoration especially of rambling plant forms – a table like a vast water-lily (1900, Musée des Arts Décoratifs, Paris), a *lit papillon* inlaid with an enormous mother-of-pearl moth (1904, Musée de l'École de Nancy). After his death his factory, then employing three hundred workmen, was carried on by V. PROUVÉ and continued to produce glass and furniture in his style (and often after his designs) until it closed in 1914, meticulously marking every piece with a star beside the name *Gallé* to distinguish these later products from those made in his life-time.

Lit: A. Polak, *Modern Glass*, London 1962; R. & L. Grover, *Art Glass Nouveau*, and *Carved and Decorated European Art Glass*, Rutland, Vermont 1967 and 1970; H. Hilschenz, *Das Glas des Jugendstils*, Munich 1973.

Gallia metal, *see* CHRISTOFLE, Charles.

Gallipot A small glazed pot of a type used by apothecaries. Originally the term indicated that the pot had been brought in a galley from the Mediterranean or elsewhere.

Galloon (1) A narrow close-woven ribbon or braid, of gold, silver or silk thread, used as a trimming.

(2) The plain ribbon-like outer border of a panel of tapestry, sometimes woven with the mark of the factory or weaver.

Galvanoplastic copy An ELECTROTYPE.

Gambin or **Gambini, Giulio,** *see* NEVERS POTTERIES.

Games table A table with a top marked as a board for chess or other games, made from the Middle Ages but more frequently from the early C18.

Gaming table A table made for card-playing. The term is usually applied to a type made in England from the early C18 with a hinged two-leaf top which, when open and supported on a swing-leg, provides a large square baize-covered platform, often with recesses at the corners for candlesticks and shallow wells for counters.

Garde meuble de la couronne The French Royal furniture store (there was one attached to every palace). It was administered by a central department in charge of furnishing the palaces of the kings of France, established in 1663.

Garden pattern carpets, *see* PERSIAN CARPETS.

Gardner's porcelain factory Founded at Verbilki near Moscow *c.*1758–65 by an Englishman, **Francis Gardner,** whose descendants ran it until 1891. Its best products are statuettes of Russian peasants made in the early and mid C19, like those of the ST PETERSBURG IMPERIAL PORCELAIN FACTORY but rather more richly coloured. (They were rivalled by those of the GORBUNOVO PORCELAIN FACTORY.) Late products included tea-services painted with roses in white medallions on strong blue, red or green grounds, sometimes made for export to Turkey or Central Asia and appropriately marked in Arabic characters. (For factory mark *see* p. 883.)

Lit: D. Roche and I. Issaievitch, *Exposition de céramique russes anciennes*, Sèvres 1929; M. C. Ross, *Russian Porcelains*, Norman (Oklahoma) 1968.

Garlic vase A type of Chinese vase, bottle-shaped with a swelling at the mouth like a garlic bulb, sometimes ribbed.

Garnier, Pierre (died *c.*1800). He was the son of a cabinet-maker **François Garnier** and became a *maître ébéniste* in 1742. His work develops in style from the Rococo to the Directoire and he was patronized by such fashionable and influential patrons as the Marquis de Marigny who employed him to furnish his Parisian *hôtel* in 1778. Examples of his work are in the Wallace Collection and the Victoria & Albert Museum.

Garnish A set of vessels, usually of pewter, for table use.

Garniture de cheminée A set of ornaments for a chimney-piece. In the C17 it usually consisted of two or three small porcelain or pottery vases. Later it became more elaborate and was sometimes of silver though porcelain remained more popular. In the late C18 the combination of a clock with two flanking and matching candlesticks was usual. Various other types were known, notably those composed of Chinese Export Porcelain which usually came in sets of five, two trumpet-shaped beakers and three covered vases of baluster shape.

Garrard, Robert (1793–1881). He was the son of **Robert Garrard the elder** (d.1818), a partner in an old-established silversmith business in London (established in 1735 by **G. Wickes** who was goldsmith to Frederick, Prince of Wales, son of George II. He was joined in 1747 by **Edward Wakelin** (d.1784) and in *c.*1759 **J. Parker** joined the firm which became Parker & Wakelin. In 1776 Edward Wakelin's son **John** became a partner and ran the firm with **William Taylor** until 1792 when Parker and Taylor retired. Wakelin then took **Robert Garrard the elder** into partnership and the firm became Wakelin & Garrard until 1802 when Wakelin died or retired). On the death of the latter his three elder sons inherited this concern and Robert took immediate command, rapidly developing it into one of the most prosperous in Europe. He succeeded RUNDELL as royal goldsmith in 1830 and became Crown jeweller in 1843. The firm's success depended mainly on their useful wares, for the dining-table, tea-table and study, all very showy but also very solid, and Garrard tureens and dishes still have great appeal. But they have always been best known for their more elaborate and fanciful pieces, with which they became, with HUNT & ROSKELL, the leading makers of presentation silver. Their racing cups and trophies and commemorative table-centres are remarkable, e.g. the table-centre made in 1842 to a design by the Prince Consort which included portraits of four of Queen Victoria's dogs (Royal Collection on loan to the Victoria & Albert Museum, London). For these pieces Garrard employed a sculptor Edmund Cotterill from 1833 until his death in 1860 when he was succeeded by W. F. Spencer. The firm survived until 1952 when it was amalgamated with the Goldsmiths' and Silversmiths' Company of Regent Street, London.

R. Garrard: Moorish table-centre in silver, designed by Edmund Cotterill after a sketch by the Prince Consort (Royal Collection, reproduced by gracious permission of H.M. the Queen)

Lit: A. G. Grimwade in *The Proceedings of the Society of Silver Collectors*, 1961; H. Honour, *Goldsmiths and Silversmiths*, London 1971.

Garrett, Thomas, *see* SPODE POTTERY AND PORCELAIN FACTORY.

Garthorne, Francis (*fl.*1690–1713) and **George** (*fl.*1681–1700). Brothers and two of the best and most prolific English silversmiths of their day, working in the style of the HUGUENOT refugees and excelling in massive pieces of plate. Much employed by William and Mary for whom they made a very handsome Baroque ewer (at Windsor Castle) and a magnificent twelve-branch chandelier (at Hampton Court).

Lit: J. F. Hayward, *Huguenot Silver in England 1688–1727*, London 1959.

Gate, Simon, *see* ORREFORS GLASSHOUSE.

Gate-leg table, *see* TABLE.

Gaudí y Cornet, Antonio (1852–1926). Outstanding Spanish architect working in Barcelona who designed some furniture in a version of the Art Nouveau style no less strongly personal than that of his buildings (e.g. church of the Sagrada Familia 1883 onwards, Palacio Güell 1885–9, Casa Batlló and Casa Milá both begun 1905). His chairs, cabinets, etc., composed of thick juicy eddying scrolls merging into one another with a bold defiance of symmetry, make even the most elaborate products of such French designers as GALLÉ and MAJORELLE look timidly inhibited. He appears to have designed furniture exclusively for the buildings of which he was architect. The largest collection of such pieces belongs to the society Amigos de Gaudí, Barcelona.

A. Gaudí: cabinet, c.*1900*
(Courtesy of Ediciones Poligrafos, 1900 in Barcelona)

Lit: G. Collins, *Antonio Gaudí*, New York, 1960; J. J. Sweeny & J. L. Sert, *Antonio Gaudí*, New York and London 1960.

Gaudreau or **Gaudreaux, Antoine Robert** (*c.*1680–1751). A leading French Rococo furniture-maker, Gaudreau was the contemporary and rival of CRESSENT. Very little is known about him and since his work is unstamped it is now difficult to identify – unstamped either because it was made before the use of an *estampille* became obligatory or because it was made for the Crown and therefore exempt. From 1726 he worked extensively for Louis XV, notably on the interior decoration of the Bibliothèque Royale and the Tuileries in Paris. He was also patronized by Mme de Pompadour. He specialized in sumptuous pieces, with very elaborate sculptural mounts. His masterpieces are a medal-cabinet, made in 1738 for the King's private apartments at Versailles and now in the Bibliothèque Nationale in Paris, and a commode made in the following year for the King's bedroom at Versailles and now in the Wallace Collection in London. Both were designed by or in collaboration with the SLODTZ brothers and the latter has mounts by CAFFIÉRI. In a more restrained style he made a low cupboard bookcase for the King's Cabinet d'Angle at Versailles (delivered in 1744 but later altered by RIESENER and now in the Cabinet des Médailles of the Bibliothèque Nationale) and a *commode à la Régence* for the Dauphin's apartment at Fontainebleau in 1745.

A.-R. Gaudreau: commode with gilt-bronze mounts by Caffiéri, 1739
(Wallace Collection, London)

Lit: F. J. B. Watson, *The Wrightsman Collection: Furniture*, New York 1966.

Gaudy Dutch Gaily decorated STAFFORDSHIRE pottery produced for the American market *c.*1810–30, specifically to please a regional taste, *see* PENNSYLVANIA DUTCH. Usually cottage wares, they are painted in underglaze blue with bright thick overglaze enamels, often imitating Imari patterned wares produced at Derby and Worcester *c.*1780–1820.

Gauffered Of a textile, other than velvet, decorated with an embossed pattern. Velvet decorated in this way is said to be stamped.

Gauffering In bookbinding, the decoration of the gilded edges of a book with heated finishing tools.

Gauguin, Paul (1848–1903). The great French Post-Impressionist painter who also worked as a potter. In collaboration with E. CHAPLET he began to make stoneware in the autumn of 1886 in the (unhappily forlorn) hope of augmenting the scanty income he derived from painting. His jugs, vases, jardinières, etc., were modelled by hand (not thrown on a wheel) and decorated with paintings or reliefs, often of Breton women similar to those in his paintings of the Pont Aven period. Forms are richly sculptural, usually asymmetrical, the colours brilliant with a telling use of white among oranges, blues and browns. After his return from Martinique in 1887 he made a series of jugs and vases decorated with beautifully modelled human heads, sometimes in the form of busts, others with female nudes. Early in 1889 he modelled a few more ceramics, notably a jug in the form of a self-portrait (Kunstindustri Museum, Copenhagen), some rather similar portrait vases and a few statuettes. He returned to pottery for the last time during his final stay in France 1893–5 – statuettes and vases strongly influenced by the primitive arts of Tahiti. Only fifty-seven examples of his work in pottery are known to survive. His son **Jean** (1881–1961) became modeller and chief designer to the BING & GRØNDAHL porcelain factory in Copenhagen.

Lit: M. Bodelsen, *Gauguin's Ceramics*, London 1964.

P. Gauguin: vase in burnt clay with Hina talking to Tefatou, the Spirit of the Earth: unsigned, 1893–5 (Kunstindustrimuseet, Copenhagen)

Gauron, Nicolas-François (*fl.*1753–88). Porcelain modeller working at MENNECY in 1753 (where he modelled the figure of a *Naiad*) and possibly at VINCENNES in 1754. In 1758 he became chief modeller at TOURNAI where his main work was an allegorical group of Charles d'Oultremont, Prince-Bishop of Liège (1764). After working in Brussels, he joined the WEESP PORCELAIN FACTORY then started a faience manufactory at Liège which he sold *c.*1770. He was employed by the CHELSEA factory in 1773 and is last recorded working at the Monplaisir porcelain factory in Brussels in 1787–8.

Lit: H. Nicaise in *Revue Belge d'archéologie et d'histoire de l'art*, 1935.

Gegenbach, Joseph, *see* CANABAS.

Genoa lace Genoa is known to have been one of the first places where LACE was made but few if any documented early examples survive. Both needlepoint and pillow lace were made. Some of the pieces of pillow lace were very large and made with some 700 bobbins manipulated by four workers. Metal, gold and silver lace trimming was also a speciality of the city and was much prized in the c18.

Genoa potteries Maiolica is known to have been made at Genoa in the c16. No fully documented examples have been identified but handsome pictorial panels of tiles in Genoese churches may well have been made in the city (e.g. St John the Baptist and St George in the Botto chapel in S. Maria in Castello, *c.*1524). Later wares appear to be indistinguishable from those of ALBISSOLA and SAVONA. A mark in the form of a lighthouse which appears on many late-c17 and early-c18 wares has sometimes been thought to be that of a Genoese pottery. Certain marks have been attributed to Genoa but have also been claimed for other Ligurian potteries.

Lit: Mostra del'antica maiolica ligure dal secolo XIV al secolo XVIII, Exh. Cat., Palazzo Reale, Genoa, 1939; G. Morazzoni, *La maiolica antica ligure,* Milan 1951.

Genoa silk factories First established in the Middle Ages but of international importance only from *c.*1670 to *c.*1750 when they were producing the finest silk damasks and velvets made in Europe both for clothing and furnishing fabrics. The figured velvets had bold pomegranate type designs and a wonderfully rich appearance. Imitations woven at LYONS, TOURS and SPITALFIELDS were reckoned inferior by contemporaries but are now difficult to distinguish from those of Genoa. Numerous examples of the thick, rich, usually black or red Genoa velvets are to be found in the church treasuries of the city.

Lit: Exh. Cat., *Mostra delle Antiche Stoffe Genovesi dal Secolo XV al Secolo XIX,* Genoa 1941.

Genre pittoresque, *see* RÉGENCE STYLE.

Gentili, Antonio (1519–1609). The son of a goldsmith, he was born in Faenza and went to Rome *c.*1550 and was accepted as a master craftsman there in 1552. He was assayer to the papal mint from 1584 to 1602 when he resigned in favour of his son **Pietro.** He is known to have executed numerous pieces of ecclesiastical silver but the only documented works which survive are a silver gilt altar cross and two candlesticks presented by Cardinal Alessandro Farnese to St Peter's in 1582 and the silver binding of the *Farnese Hours* (P. Morgan Library, New York) commissioned after 1589 by Cardinal Odoardo Farnese. A knife, fork and spoon with figurative handles and also a drawing for a similar spoon (Metropolitan Museum, New York) have been ascribed to him.

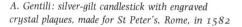

A. Gentili: silver-gilt candlestick with engraved crystal plaques, made for St Peter's, Rome, in 1582

Lit: E. Kris in *Dedalo* IX (1928–9), pp. 97–111; C. G. Bulgari, *Argentari Gemmari e Orafi d'Italia*, Rome 1958.

George, Jean (d.1765). Parisian goldsmith who became a *maître* in 1752 and specialized in elegant enamelled boxes for snuff, bonbons, etc. Such boxes were sometimes called *Georgettes* after him. The enamelled decorations which form their main charm were executed by a variety of other hands. On his death his firm was taken over by his pupil **Pierre-François Matteis de Beaulieu** under whom it survived until after 1791.

Lit: A. K. Snowman, *Eighteenth Century Gold Boxes of Europe*, London 1966.

Georgian silver sauce-boat by Paul de Lamerie, London, 1736 (Private Collection)

Georgian An umbrella term for the wide variety of decorative styles popular in England during the reigns of George I, II and III until the beginning of the REGENCY (i.e. during the period 1714–1811) but sometimes including the Regency and reign of George IV as well (1811–30). It covers the English versions of the late BAROQUE, ROCOCO and NEO-CLASSICAL styles, including the CHINOISERIE and GOTHIC REVIVAL variations on them, as well as numerous rustic products (e.g. STAFFORDSHIRE POTTERY and WINDSOR CHAIRS) which were hardly affected by international stylistic currents. In architecture the first half of the period was dominated by the Palladian revival. Although this mainly affected exteriors it left its mark on furniture design, e.g. book-cases with pedimented tops, echoing the Palladian façade. Italian-inspired and sponsored by noblemen who had been on the Grand Tour, the movement was also instrumental in introducing the Italian late-Baroque style in furniture, notable mainly in marble-topped side-tables on richly carved supports incorporating eagles, Hercules masks, shells, sphinxes or *putti* (e.g. those designed by William KENT) and pedestals in the form of term figures (e.g. those by Benjamin GOODISON). Other popular types, such as fall-front bureaux, chairs and small tables on cabriole legs, and pier tables with gesso tops, were merely more elaborate versions of QUEEN ANNE types. Rococo influence

Georgian side-table, c.1726 (Temple Newsam House, Leeds)

Georgian silver-gilt beaker by Aymé Videau, London, 1743 (Private Collection)

Georgian silver candlestick by John Carter, London, 1771–2 (Victoria & Albert Museum)

came in from France, first in silver by Paul de LAMERIE (mid-1730s) and furniture designs by Matthias LOCK, Thomas JOHNSON and Thomas CHIPPENDALE. The French Rococo also influenced the design of silks woven at SPITALFIELDS. German Rococo influence appears only in porcelain produced at the BOW, CHELSEA and DERBY factories. Generally, however, the English seem to have been less attracted by the pure Rococo of the continental designers than by Chinoiserie Rococo. They developed a uniquely English form of Chinoiserie furniture, popularly known as CHINESE CHIPPENDALE. The reaction against the Rococo gathered momentum after 1750 as two new styles gained popularity, the English Gothic Revival as sponsored by Horace Walpole and his friends, and the Neo-Classical introduced by James STUART and Robert ADAM (the latter parallel to the French LOUIS XVI STYLE). Adam's influence was pervasive, affecting furniture, silver, textiles (notably carpets by Thomas MOORE) and domestic metalwork. SÈVRES, rather than MEISSEN as hitherto, began to provide the fashionable models for the porcelain factories. In the 1760s, however, the WEDGWOOD POTTERY gradually gained predominance with its very elegant Neo-Classical wares; and before the end of the century it was leading European fashion. In furniture design, a tendency towards greater lightness and simplicity became apparent from the later 1780s as the styles associated with HEPPLEWHITE and SHERATON came into vogue, and the more insistently classical decorative motifs went out of favour (only to return with a vengeance in the Regency period).

Gera pottery and porcelain factory A faience factory founded in 1752 and functioning until 1780; it produced vases, tankards, etc., painted with flowers in HIGH-TEMPERATURE COLOURS on a fine white enamel ground. The porcelain factory began in 1779 imitated MEISSEN (and its mark) but also produced attractive small pieces decorated with views of Gera, portrait medallions, etc. sometimes on coloured grounds but more usually on DÉCOR BOIS.

Lit: R. Graul & A. Kurzwelly, *Altthüringer Porzellan*, Leipzig 1909; K. Hüseler, *Deutsche Fayencen*, Stuttgart 1956–8.

Germain, Pierre II (1720–83). French Rococo silversmith (no relation to Thomas GERMAIN), born in Avignon, trained in Paris under Thomas Germain, later under ROETTIERS and BESNIER and made a master craftsman in 1744. Important mainly as the author of *Eléments d'Orfèvrerie* (Paris, 1748) an influential series of patterns for silver in a restrained Rococo style. (For his mark *see* p. 893.)

Lit: A. Marcel, 'L'orfèvre Pierre Germain dit le Romain' in *Mémoire de l'Academie de Vaucluse*, 1916, pp. 229–60.

Germain, Thomas (1673–1748). He was the best French Rococo silversmith and was one of the creators of the Rococo style. He successfully adapted the exuberant conceits of the *ornementistes* to the medium of silver. He was celebrated by Voltaire in his poem *Les Vous et les Tu* and won European renown with patrons in England, Portugal and Russia as well as France. He was the son of **Pierre Germain** (1645–84) a silversmith prominent under Louis XIV but none of whose works survive. Thomas Germain began as a painter, went to Rome (1687–1702) and there began working as a goldsmith and may have been influenced by Giovanni GIARDINI. He was employed on the altar for the chapel of St Ignatius in the Gesù perhaps chasing and finishing the bronze ornaments. Nothing else is known about his years in Rome, except that he was active as an independent silversmith by 1697. His only surviving work of these years are two silver reliefs in Sens cathedral of 1700. But his first-hand experience of Roman Baroque was as important for his subsequent development as it was for G.-M. OPPENORDT's, who was also in Rome at this period. He returned to France by 1706 and appears to have specialized at first in ecclesiastical silver (e.g. silver-gilt monstrance and gilt copper altar set for Notre Dame in Paris). In 1720 he became a *maître* and in 1723 *orfèvre du Roi* along with Nicolas BESNIER and Claude II BALLIN. From then onwards he was continually employed on royal commissions, though he was able to work for private patrons as well. His most spectacular work is a table-centre decorated with greyhounds, hunting horns and *putti*, made in 1730 for a Portuguese patron (Museu Nacional de Arte Antiga, Lisbon). His ability as a craftsman and his originality as a designer is no less apparent on several smaller pieces such as a pair of wine-coolers fashioned like irregular tree-trunks with snails and vine-leaves attached to them (1727–8, in the Louvre, Paris) or a pair of salts decorated with very realistically modelled turtles and crustaceans (1734–6, the Louvre, Paris). He also made simple *écuelles* and tureens of elegantly bulging Rococo shape with artichoke or pomegranate knobs and salvers surrounded by tendrils of boldly modelled foliage. In 1741 he began to build to his own design and at his own expense a small church in Paris, dedicated to St Louis du Louvre (demolished in 1810). On his death control of his workshops passed to his fourth son **François-Thomas** (1726–91) who also succeeded to his royal appointment. He continued work on major commissions which his father had left unfinished (e.g. the elaborate lamp for St Geneviève, Paris, of 1744–54). His independent work is in a similar style to that of his father but he allowed his fantasy freer rein and made, in addition to some exquisitely modelled Rococo cutlery, tureens, etc., such curiosities as salt-cellars supported by Red Indian children in feathered head-dresses and a biscuit box in the form of a ship. The latter was made for the King of Portugal (now in the Museu Nacional de Arte Antiga, Lisbon). He is said to have employed between 60 and 80 workmen and his output was very large. He also made bronzes d'ameublements, e.g. firedogs dated 1757, in the Louvre. But he went bankrupt in 1764 and was dismissed from his royal appointment. He never recovered from this reverse. (For their marks *see* p. 893.)

T. Germain: silver wine cooler, 1727–8 (Louvre)

Lit: G. Bapst, *Les Germains*, Paris 1887; H. Honour, *Goldsmiths & Silversmiths*, London and New York 1971.

German silver, *see* NICKEL SILVER.

Gerrits, Jarich, *see* LELY, Johannes van der.

Gerverot, Louis-Victor (1747–1829). One of the more interesting of the later-C18 porcelain arcanists and painters who travelled from place to place. He began as a porcelain painter at SÈVRES, then moved to NIDERVILLER, FULDA, LUDWIGSBURG, ANSBACH, HÖCHST, FRANKENTHAL, OFFENBACH, WEESP (1771), SCHREZHEIM (1773–5) and OUDE LOOSDRECHT (*c.*1777–8). Then he went to England, worked for WEDGWOOD in 1786 and J. TURNER immediately afterwards. Returning to the Continent, he established an 'English-earthenware' factory at Cologne 1788–92. In 1795 he was appointed director of the FÜRSTENBURG PORCELAIN FACTORY. Here he made use of the discoveries he had learnt on his travels, especially in England. He kept the factory going through the Napoleonic wars but was dismissed in 1814 for having collaborated with the French. He then went to work as manager of the Wrisbergholzen pottery in Hanover.

Lit: S. G. Davis in *Burlington Magazine* LI (1929), pp. 227ff.

Gessner, Salomon, *see* ZURICH POTTERY & PORCELAIN FACTORY.

Gesso A composition of gypsum (plaster of Paris) and size and sometimes other materials (linseed oil and glue), used mainly by sculptors (for casts) but also used for the decoration of furniture from the Middle Ages onwards. When applied in several layers, often with the addition of other materials (linseed oil and glue), to the surface of furniture it provides an excellent medium for carved ornament and gilding. It was used for the decoration of *cassoni* in C15–C16 Italy and also smaller pieces, *see* PASTIGLIA. In late-C17 and early-C18 England it became very popular for the decoration of chairs, mirror-frames and, especially, pier tables which are decorated on the legs and top with intricate reliefs of band work modelled in such a way that when gilded the raised portions are brightly burnished and the ground is matt. James MOORE so used it. In England parchment shavings were added to the composition. Gesso has also been used in place of wood for delicate relief work on furniture (especially for exuberant Rococo curlicues which may more easily be modelled on a wire base than carved in wood) and also cast for picture frames, etc., though COMPOSITION or COMPO is more usual for these purposes.

Geyger, Johann Caspar, *see* WÜRZBURG PORCELAIN FACTORY.

Ghiordes carpets, *see* TURKISH CARPETS.

Ghiordes knot, also called **Turkish knot.** The knot used for the pile of nearly all Turkish, Caucasian, English and some Persian carpets. It is tied in a symmetrical manner on two adjacent warp threads. It cannot be used for very fine close pile carpets.

Gianantonio da Pesaro, *see* VENICE POTTERIES.

Giardini, Giovanni (1646–1721). He was the leading Roman goldsmith of his day but few of his works survive, the majority having been destroyed during the Napoleonic wars. As a designer he ranks among the masters of late Baroque art and probably exerted an important formative influence on such Rococo silversmiths as Thomas GERMAIN who trained in Rome. He became a master silversmith in 1675 and in the

G. Giardini: design for candelabra, 1714

following year he and a partner took over the workshop of **Marco Gamberucci** who supplied plate to the Vatican. He dissolved this partnership in 1680 and was joined by his brother **Alessandro** (b.1655). In 1698 he was appointed bronze founder to the papal government. His surviving works are mostly ecclesiastical: a magnificent papal mace of *c.*1696 in the Victoria & Albert Museum, London; a tabernacle of porphyry, silver, gilt-copper and crystal of 1711 in the Kunsthistorisches Museum, Vienna; a crucifix in San Francesco, Matelica. A holy-water stoup of silver, gilt-bronze and lapis lazuli in the Minneapolis Institute of Art is attributed to him. In 1714 one hundred of his designs, both secular and ecclesiastic, were engraved and published in Prague as *Disegni diversi . . .*, reissued 1750 in Rome as *Promptuarium Artis Argentaria . . . .* (For his mark *see* p. 893.)

Lit: C. G. Bulgari, *Argentari, Gemmari e Orafi d'Italia*, Rome 1958, vol. I; H. Honour, *Goldsmiths & Silversmiths*, London & New York 1971.

Gibbons, Grinling (1648–1721). Leading English Baroque sculptor famous mainly for his decorative carvings in wood though he worked as much, if not more, in marble, stone and bronze. He is now known especially for his extremely delicately carved limewood festoons of accurately rendered flowers, leaves and fruit, executed as ornament for panelled interiors, picture frames, overmantels, etc. Despite his almost obsessive attention to detail, they have a boldly Baroque fluency of design and rank among the best decorative carvings of their period in all Europe. Documented examples are at Luton Hoo (formerly at Cassiobury House, 1676–7), Windsor Castle (1677 onwards), Burghley House (1682), Kensington Palace (1691–3), Hampton Court Palace (1691–6 and 1699–1710), Petworth Place (1692), Trinity College Chapel, Oxford (1693–4) and the choir stalls and screen of St Paul's Cathedral, London (1696–7). Similar wood carvings were executed by several of his contemporaries in England, and some are of good quality, e.g. staircase from Cassiobury House probably by **Edward Pearce**, now in the Metropolitan Museum, New York.

Lit: D. Green, *Grinling Gibbons*, London 1964.

Gierløf, Christian, *see* COPENHAGEN POTTERIES.

Giese, Johann Ulrich, *see* STRALSUND POTTERY.

Gilding Decorating with gold; *see* HONEY-GILDING, LACQUER GILDING, MERCURY GILDING, ORMOLU, SIZE GILDING, SILVER GILT and SILVER PARTY GILT.

Giles, James (1718–80). English outside decorator of porcelain and glass. He was the son of a 'China painter' of the same name and was born in London, apprenticed to a jeweller and is recorded from 1749 as a 'Chinaman' (i.e. vendor of porcelain) and from 1763 as an independent 'China and enamel painter'. In his London studio he decorated pieces of white porcelain made at the WORCESTER and probably at the BOW, LONGTON HALL and other factories. In 1770 he sold by auction a stock of porcelain he had decorated, and in 1774 a stock of glass (apparently opaque white and blue glass decorated in gilt). He seems to have gone bankrupt in 1776. Although he did not sign his works, a number of pieces are generally attributed to him, notably porcelain and glass vessels very delicately painted in gold or enamels, often *en camieu*, of flowers or Antique Revival motifs (bucrania, paterae, etc.).

Lit: R. J. Charleston in *The Connoisseur* CLXII (1966), pp. 96–101.

Gillinder, James, & Sons A Philadelphia glasshouse established in 1860 by an English glass-worker, **William Gillinder**, who had emigrated to the U.S. in 1854. It produced high quality cut and pressed glass and became famous for its frosted glass, especially its Westward Ho pattern in frosted glass. Gillinder glass was prominent at the Philadelphia Centennial Exposition in 1876. The firm was originally called the Franklin Flint Glass Company and became first 'Gillinder and Bennet' and later Gillinder and Sons. In 1912 **William T. Gillinder** and his brother **James** purchased the Bronx and Ryal glasshouse at Port Jervis and produced glass there under the name of Gillinder Brothers. The Philadelphia glasshouse closed in the 1930s.

Lit: J. Hollister, *The Encyclopedia of Glass Paperweights*, New York 1969.

Gillingham, James (b.1736). He was a Philadelphia furniture-maker, active 1765–70 in the CHIPPENDALE style.

Gillis, Antoine, *see* TOURNAI POTTERY AND PORCELAIN FACTORY.

Gillows The leading firm of English C18–C19 cabinet-makers outside London. It was founded by a joiner **Robert Gillow** (1703–73) in or shortly after 1727 when he became a freeman of the Borough of Lancaster. He took his eldest son **Richard** into partnership in 1757; another son, **Robert,** went to London in 1776 to run a show-room and warehouse which had been built *c.*1765 on the site occupied by their successors, **Waring & Gillow** in Oxford Street until 1974 (though no member of the family has been connected with the firm since 1817). Their main factory remained in Lancaster and they were much patronized by northern and Scottish gentry, e.g. Duke of Atholl, Earls of Strafford and Derby. They were Roman Catholics and were patronized by their co-religionists. But they undertook extensive commissions in the south, e.g. furnishing Mrs Piozzi's house at Streatham in 1784. And they carried on a lively export trade to the Baltic and the West Indies. In the 1760s they began to stamp some pieces of their case furniture, being the first English firm to adopt this practice. They are best known for handsome, well-made but relatively simple furniture in the late GEORGIAN and REGENCY styles. In the C19 they employed several of the leading designers, e.g. T. E. COLLCUTT and B. J. TALBERT. They absorbed Collinson & Lock in 1897 and amalgamated with S. J. Waring & Son shortly afterwards. In the 1930s they employed Serge Chermayeff and P. FOLLOT as designers.

Lit: A. Coleridge, *Chippendale Furniture*, London 1968.

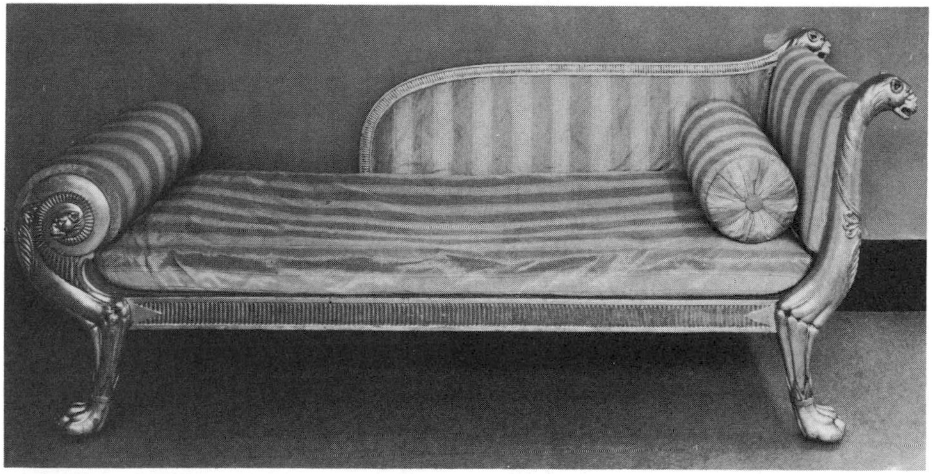

Gillows: sofa of carved and gilt beechwood, 1805 (Victoria & Albert Museum)

Gillows: armchair, c.1815, from Eaton Hall, Cheshire

Gilze, Johann Christoph & Ludwig, *see* CASSEL POTTERY & PORCELAIN FACTORY.

Gimson, Ernest William (1864–1919). English architect and designer prominent in the ARTS AND CRAFTS movement (he came under William MORRIS's influence in 1884). He learned to make turned ash chairs but is more important as a designer. With a group of skilled craftsmen including Sidney and Ernest Barnsley (1865–1926, 1863–1926), he set up a workshop in the Cotswolds in 1895. His furniture reveals an intimate appreciation of materials and techniques (e.g. wood treated to make the most of its grain); it is elegant, clean-lined, sometimes rather spindly, often decorated with inlays and anything but cottagey.

Lit: Exh. Cat., *Ernest Gimson*, Leicester 1969; B. G. Burrough in *The Connoisseur* CLXXI (1969), pp. 228–32, CLXXII (1969), pp. 8–14.

E. W. Gimson: cabinet and stand, ebony inlaid with mother-of-pearl, c.1910 (Leicester Museum and Art Gallery)

Ginger jar A Chinese type of porcelain jar with a wide covered mouth and ovoid body slightly tapering towards the base, often decorated with Prunus blossom. They are said to have been filled with sweetmeats, ginger and tea as a Chinese New Year gift and returned when empty.

Ginori porcelain, *see* DOCCIA PORCELAIN FACTORY.

Gioannetti, Vittorio Amadeo, *see* VINOVO PORCELAIN FACTORY.

Giot, Richard, *see* SCEAUX POTTERY & PORCELAIN FACTORY.

Giovanni Maria (*fl.c.*1490–1515). Outstanding maiolica painter working at CASTEL DURANTE (and possibly FAENZA as well). The earliest signed specimen of his work is a plate with the arms of Pope Julius II, dated 1508, but late C15 pieces have been attributed to him. He appears to have begun by painting plates with rather small figure subjects or busts in the centre and borders of foliage. Later he specialized in fantastic or allegorical subjects on plates with very handsome elaborate grotesque borders in a distinctive palette with much use of rich amber yellow, clear green and dark blue. The figure of a bound blindfold Cupid recurs in his work.

Lit: B. Rackham in *Pantheon* II (1928), p. 435; III (1929), p. 88.

Giovanni Maria: maiolica plate, Castle Durante, c.1510 (Victoria & Albert Museum)

Girandole A candelabrum. The name derives from the Italian *girandola*, a type of firework. In the late C17 the name was applied to an elaborate type of candelabrum with pendants of cut crystal or glass, forming a pyramid of light. In the C18 the name was applied to all candelabra as well as chandeliers or lustres, with or without crystal pendants. In England in the C18 the word was used especially for large carved and gilt wood sconces in the Rococo style. The term is also used for a wall bracket, often with a mirror back. In the late C18 the mirror was often made circular and convex, and was sometimes used alone.

Designs for girandoles by T. Johnson, 1757

'Girl in a swing' porcelain Two white soft-paste porcelain figures of a girl in a swing (Victoria & Albert Museum and Museum of Fine Arts, Boston) probably made 1749–54 and a few allied pieces of a similar body to the triangle wares of the CHELSEA PORCELAIN FACTORY, but with a higher proportion of lead oxide in their composition, are generally thought to be the products of another factory in Chelsea. **Charles Gouyn**, a partner of

'Girl in a Swing', soft-paste porcelain, probably Chelsea, 1749–54 (Victoria & Albert Museum)

SPRIMONT at Chelsea until 1749, may have been the director of this concern.

Lit: A. Lane and R. J. Charleston in *Transactions of the English Ceramic Circle* V (1962), pp. 111–14.

Giulio Romano (Giulio Giannuzzi) (1492–1546). The great Italian Mannerist painter and architect who also designed tapestries, goldsmith's work, and indeed every kind of decorative art, especially for members of the Gonzaga family at Mantua. His designs include a sweetmeat box in the form of a Roman sarcophagus, elaborate urns and a dolphin-shaped ewer which curiously anticipates the style of the Van VIANENS. They had wide influcnce but no objects based directly on them are known to survive.

Lit: F. Hartt, *Giulio Romano*, New Haven 1958.

Giustiniani pottery and porcelain factory Founded in Naples by **Nicola Giustiniani** from Cerreto *c*.1760, it produced at first cream-coloured earthenware and tin-glazed earthenware decorated in enamel colours and also attractive maiolica tiles (e.g. the floor tiles in Cappella S. Maria dei Miracoli in the Chiesa di Gesù delle Monache, Naples). It enjoyed its most successful period under the direction of **Biagio Giustiniani**, grandson of the founder, in the early C19 (especially after the closure of the NAPLES ROYAL PORCELAIN FACTORY in 1821). Products included attractive household wares, statuettes of figures in contemporary dress, life-size busts, garden statues, flower pots, etc. It also produced biscuit reproductions of antique statues. But it is best known for its faithful copies of antique vases and adaptations of their forms and ornament as in the large 'Etruscan' dinner service, Museo Duca di Martino alla Floridiana, Naples. From 1829 a type of porcelain was made. In 1848, shortly after Biagio's death, the concern failed and its stock was sold up but two sons continued to work on a small scale. **Michele Giustiniani**, a great-grandson of the founder, built the concern up again first in partnership with an uncle but from 1870 on his own. Under his direction it produced a wide range of decorative and useful objects, including imitations of Renaissance maiolica. Its products won prizes at international exhibitions. But it failed commercially as a result of over-expansion and closed down shortly after 1885. 'GIUSTINIANI' impressed was the main factory mark.

Lit: L. Mosca, *Napoli e l'arte ceramica*, rev. ed., Naples 1963; M. Rotili, *La manifattura Giustiniani*, Benevento 1967.

Glamorgan pottery, *see* SWANSEA POTTERIES & PORCELAIN FACTORY.

Glasgow potteries A faience factory named **Delftfield** was founded in 1748 and made wares decorated with Chinese-style flowers in soft manganese, lime-yellow, grey-blue, bluish-green and dark violet-blue, on a rather grey-white ground. But very few products have been identified. From 1770 it turned to the production of CREAM-COLOURED EARTHENWARE. It closed in 1810. Another pottery in Glasgow, established by **John** and **Matthew P. Bell** in 1842 made PARIAN ware and a wide range of earthenware. It closed in 1940.

Lit: J. A. Fleming, *Scottish Pottery*, Glasgow 1923; M. Archer in *The Connoisseur* CLXIII (1966), pp. 16–22.

Glasgow school A group of architects and designers associated with the Glasgow School of Art, notably C. R. MACKINTOSH, Margaret and Frances MACDONALD and George WALTON, who evolved a distinctly Scottish and sometimes rather strait-laced version of ART NOUVEAU, with much use of CELTIC ornament. Exhibiting at Liège (1895), Venice (1899), Vienna (1900), Turin (1902), they acquired international acclaim and exerted a vital influence on the pioneers of industrial design, especially in Germany and Austria.

Glass A hard, usually translucent and often transparent, material made by the fusion at high temperature of silica (in the form of sand, flint or quartz) with the aid of an alkaline flux (potash or soda) and various other substances such as limestone, or potash of lead. When it is in a molten state the 'metal', as it is technically called, is ductile and can be drawn out into very long threads or blown into bubbles which can be shaped with shears and tongs or made to take the form of moulds. It can be coloured by the addition of metallic oxides to the frit (i.e. the basic materials before they are fused). When it has cooled it may be decorated in a variety of ways: the surface may be painted either with ENAMEL COLOURS which are fixed by a second firing in a muffle kiln, or with much less durable oil colours which need no firing. It may alternatively be engraved with a diamond point, with a lapidary's wheel or by sand blasting, or it may be etched with acid (a mixture of potassium fluoride and hydrochloric acid).

Glass appears to have been invented in the Eastern Mediterranean, probably Egypt, where solid glass objects were made *c.*2500 B.C. and extensively from *c.*1500 B.C. Glass vessels of these periods were cast with a core of compressed sand. Sometimes molten rods or 'canes' of glass of different colours were wound round a core of sand or clay, attached to the end of an iron bar, and tooled or combed into feathered patterns often similar to the markings on semi-precious hard stones. In this early period – as until relatively recent times in the Far East – glass was regarded as a substitute for precious or semi-precious stones. But the discovery of the process of glass-blowing early in the CI B.C. in Syria soon transformed it into one of the most popular media for useful and decorative domestic objects especially containers for fluids, drinking vessels, etc. From this time most glass vessels made in the Near East and Europe were blown – and until the C19 by human lungs, as many still are today. Nearly all the basic methods of decorating blown

Glass jar, Syria, c2 (Kunstgewerbemuseum, Zurich)

glass by colouring or cutting were developed before the c4 A.D., mainly in Syria and Egypt, and many pieces of CASED GLASS, especially those of the VASA DIATRETA type reveal the astonishingly high level of technical accomplishment attained in this early period. Glass decorated in gold leaf, now called VERRE ÉGLOMISÉ, was also made in Roman times, e.g. the triple portrait medallion in the Brescia Museum. The art of glass-making continued to flourish in the E. Mediterranean after the fall of the Roman Empire in the West and its contraction in the East. The art of enamelling on glass was brought to an unsurpassed pitch of excellence under Islamic rule in the c13–c14 and the large MOSQUE LAMPS made from the early c14 are among the major masterpieces of the glass-maker's art.

The technique of making glass vessels for common use was introduced into Italy, Gaul and the Rhineland under Roman Imperial rule, and survived the fall of the Empire. The quality of the material declined from the c4, however, and the majority of vessels made from this period onwards were technically imperfect, of greenish or brownish colour, with bubbles and streaks in the body. But some of the c5–c8 pieces described as TEUTONIC GLASS have considerable aesthetic merits. RÜSSELBECHER – drinking vessels with strange hollow projections sometimes likened to elephants' trunks – are the most remarkable and reveal the technical skill of the glassworkers. Utilitarian green glass, made throughout Europe until the present day and known as WALDGLAS, WEALD GLASS or *verre de fougère*, springs from the traditions established by makers of Teutonic glass. But from the c12 in N. Europe the making of glass vessels took second place to the production of window glass. More attention appears to have been devoted to the production of finely coloured panels for use in STAINED GLASS windows than to the making of vessels which were used mainly by the poorer classes (the rich drank out of cups of precious metals).

In the c14 the VENETIAN GLASSHOUSES began to emerge as the most notable in W. Europe and

Glass goblet and cover, Venice, late c15 (Victoria & Albert Museum)

in the C15 were producing enamelled coloured vessels of very high quality. It was here that the art of making clear crystal glass was discovered in the early C16 and immediately raised the status of glass vessels. An important glass industry was

Glass goblet in the Venetian style, C17 (Victoria & Albert Museum)

Glass goblet and cover, Kungsholm Glasshouse, C18 (National Museum, Stockholm)

also established at ALTARE near Genoa. Craftsmen from Venice (e.g. VERZELINI) and Altare soon diffused the art of making crystal glass throughout N. Europe. As the materials available varied slightly from place to place, so the glass made in them differed in hardness, brilliance, clarity, etc., and influenced methods of decoration. A hard crystal glass made in Germany provided an excellent medium for engraved decorations by such artists as K. LEHMANN, G. SCHWANHARDT, GONDELACH, the HESS FAMILY, SCHWINGER, etc. Significantly it was in Germany, especially at POTSDAM, that the HOCHSCHNITT process of engraving glass was developed, though it was in the Netherlands that the art of engraving on glass was brought to one of its highest points by such artists as M. T. R. VISSCHER, F. GREENWOOD and D. WOLFF who has given his name to a whole class of engraved glasses. These Dutch artists worked with a diamond point sometimes on thin-walled vessels of English make. In England a type of lead-glass, discovered by G. RAVENSCROFT *c*.1675, became very popular and provided an excellent medium for delicately formed wine-glasses, jelly-glasses, candlesticks, etc. A new method of decorating glass, not with figurative or floral ornament, but with sliced facets which catch the light (i.e. CUT GLASS) was developed in England in the mid C18 and soon became very popular. Similar glass was also made in Ireland, at CORK, WATERFORD and elsewhere. This Anglo-Irish glass was widely imitated in Europe and the U.S.A. throughout the C19. The BOHEMIAN GLASSHOUSES and those in Silesia became prominent in the C19 and produced much coloured cut-glass and FLASHED GLASS.

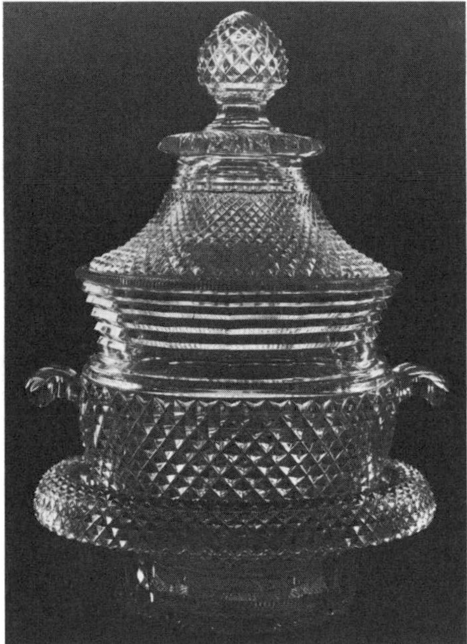

Cut-glass wine-cooler, English, c.1825 (Victoria & Albert Museum)

The first great technical development in glass since the C1 BC invention of blowing was the process of making PRESSED GLASS by pouring the molten metal into a mould, which determines the outer shape, and then thrusting in a plunger of the desired inner shape. This was introduced in 1825 in the U.S. and soon taken up elsewhere. A process of mechanically blowing bottles into moulds was developed at Castleford in Yorkshire in 1887 – a somewhat different method was invented by M. J. Owens in the U.S. in 1898. In the C20 the most important technical development has been the creation of various types of heat-resistant glass, the best known being PYREX.

The C19 mechanization of the glass industry and the cheapening of the product was accompanied by the revival of manual techniques for the making and decoration of very expensive ornamental pieces. At STOURBRIDGE various artists, notably T. and G. WOODALL, revived the technique of carving cased glass, inspired by Romano-Syrian work. Slightly later E. GALLÉ and DAUM in France and L. C. TIFFANY in the U.S. developed CASED GLASS and other techniques for the production of vessels, electric-light fittings, etc. in the ART NOUVEAU style. Though PLASTICS,

Glass vases exhibited by W. Hofmann & Meyr, Austria, at the Great Exhibition, 1851

which are less easily broken, have begun to replace glass for daily use, ornamental glass remains popular and has attracted the attention of notable contemporary designers. *See also:* BROAD GLASS, CROWN GLASS, CRYSTALLOCERAMIE, FIBREGLASS, LOOKING GLASS, PÂTE DE VERRE.

Lit: W. B. Honey, *Glass: A Handbook*, London 1946; F. Neuberg, *Ancient Glass*, London 1962; F. Rademacher, *Die deutschen Gläser des Mittelalters*, Berlin 1963; A. von Saldern, *German Enamelled Glass*, Corning (N.Y.) 1965; D. Harden et al., *Masterpieces of Glass*, London 1968.

Glass tankard, Orrefors Glasshouse, c.1920 (Kunstgewerbemuseum, Zurich)

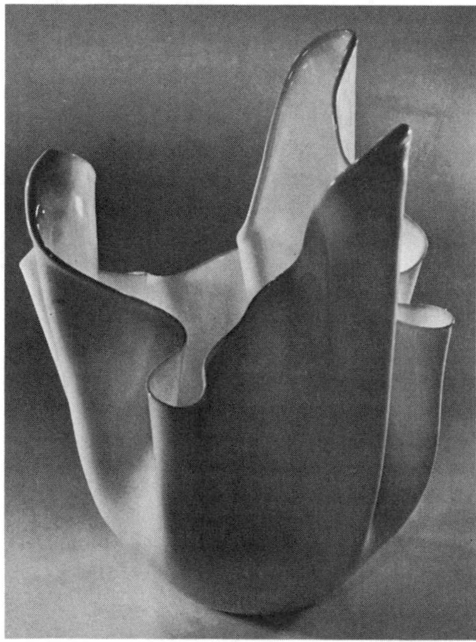

Glass vase by Paolo Venini, 1949, hand-blown opaque white glass (Museum of Modern Art, New York)

Glass ash-tray, designed by F. C. Carder, before 1934, Corning Glass Works, Steuben Division (Museum of Modern Art, New York)

Glass bowl by Tapio Wirkkala, 1953, translucent crystal glass, Iittala glasshouse, Finland (Museum of Modern Art, New York)

Glaze A vitreous coating applied to POTTERY to make vessels watertight and also as a form of decoration (not to be confused with the non-vitreous GLOSS on Greek and Roman pottery). The glaze is made from silica which is present in most clays used for pottery. But as the melting-point of silica is 1,710°C. – far above that of any ceramic body – some other substance must be used as a flux to lower it, e.g. oxides of sodium, potassium, lead, calcium, barium, magnesium, zinc or aluminium. The names of glazes are derived from the fluxes used. In ancient Egypt soda-lime glazes were applied to objects made from quartz or steatite (known very misleadingly as 'Egyptian faience') but not to pottery. The art of glazing pottery seems to derive from China where both lead glazes and alkaline glazes were used at an early period.

LEAD GLAZE was first developed in China, probably in the C3 BC and introduced into Europe by the Romans. One of the easiest to use, lead glaze is applied by powdering the formed clay vessel or object with lead oxide, white lead or galena and firing at a temperature of, or slightly above, 750°C. It is transparent but may be stained yellow or brown with iron (often in the form of ferruginous clay), green with copper, blue with cobalt, and purple or brown with manganese. It may also be opacified with tin to produce a TIN GLAZE (i.e. that found on MAIOLICA). Tin-glaze was probably invented in Persia in the C9 and transmitted to Europe by way of Spain. As lead volatizes at about 1,150°C. pottery which needs to be fired at a higher temperature must be given a preliminary 'biscuit' firing, and then fired a second time for glazing.

Alkaline glazes can be applied only to pottery which matures at a high temperature. Wood ash contains the essential ingredients for such a glaze which seems first to have been produced accidentally (in China and Japan) as a result of wood ash in the kiln coming into contact with the clay and producing a lustrous green glaze running down the sides of a vessel. This is called a 'natural glaze' if it covers only part of the body and appears to have been formed accidentally (though apparently accidental wood ash glazes were produced intentionally in Japan, especially for TEA CEREMONY WARES). A wood ash glaze may be produced by dusting the surface of a pot with ash before firing. A SALT GLAZE is applied by throwing salt into the kiln fire so that it vaporizes and reacts with the steam from the fuel to form a glaze with the silica in the body of the pottery. But it can be used only on bodies which mature at about 1,250°C. e.g. STONEWARE. FELDSPATHIC GLAZES (made from pulverized feldspar) fuse at a still higher temperature (1,550° C.) and are those found on hard-paste PORCELAIN: they were developed at an early period in China but not adopted in the West until the C18.

Slip glazes form a distinct category and are made from a coating of ferruginous clay SLIP applied to a more refractory body after it has been 'biscuit' fired. In C19 Europe, especially England, experiments were directed to producing leadless glazes for low-fired earthenware in order to avoid the poisonous effects of lead. Alternative fluxes such as borax were used.

As a result of impurities in materials or variations of temperature in the kiln, glazes (especially feldspathic glazes) may crackle or craze in firing. CRAZING was both contrived and controlled as a method of decoration in China in the C12 and in Japan slightly later. Similarly, monochrome glazes may develop streaks and splashes of other colours, and this tendency was exploited to produce *sang de boeuf* and other FLAMBÉ GLAZES. Both crazed and flambé glazes were much imitated in Europe and the U.S. from the late C19. At the same period Western potters also experimented with CRYSTALLINE GLAZES which create abstract patterns on the surface of a piece of pottery or porcelain..

Lit: D. Rhodes, *Clay and Glazes for the Potter*, London 1958; F. Singer and W. L. German, *Ceramic Glazes*, London 1960; H. Hodges, *Artifacts*, London 1964.

Glier, Hans, *see* WALDENBURG POTTERIES.

Glomy, J.-B., *see* VERRE ÉGLOMISÉ.

Gloss A pottery surface distinct from a GLAZE which it superficially resembles, produced by covering the pot in a slip of very fine clay containing the mineral illite and firing in an oxidizing fire. Greek 'black gloss' and Roman 'red gloss' (e.g. ARRETINE WARES and TERRA SIGILLATA) pottery has this type of surface.

Gmunden pottery A factory founded at Gmunden near Salzburg in 1863 but producing nothing of interest until 1908 when the owner's son, **Franz Schleiss** (b.1884) who had been trained at the Kunstgewerbeschule in Vienna, set up an art pottery department called the Künstlerische Werkstätte Franz und Emilie Schleiss. In 1910 this workshop was amalgamated with that established in Vienna by M. POWOLNY. Under the title of Vereinigte Wiener und Gmundener Keramik G.m.b.H., it showed products in an attractive Viennese version of Art Nouveau at many international exhibitions.

Lit: F. Lipp in *Keramos* 24 (1964), pp. 20–29.

Gobelins, Manufacture des The name commonly given to the *Manufacture royale des meubles de la Couronne*, a factory established in Paris in 1663 on behalf of Louis XIV by Colbert who declared that the age of private patronage had passed and only a king could stimulate the artistic life of the realm. To provide furnishings of regal magnificence for the several royal residences some 250 craftsmen – tapestry weavers, painters, bronze workers, furniture makers (notably D. CUCCI), lapidaries, goldsmiths and silversmiths – were employed under the direction of Charles LE BRUN who supplied numerous preliminary designs for every type of work. It was also intended to serve as a school for the decorative arts and apprentices were given instruction in drawing before they began to specialize in particular crafts. Few products survive apart from a pair of cabinets by Cucci, some panels of PIETRE DURE mosaic, and tapestries (*see* GOBELINS TAPESTRY FACTORY), one of which depicts a visit from the King to the factory in 1667 and shows the range of its products: massive silver vases, tables topped with pietre dure mosaics, an ebony cabinet encrusted with bronze and lapis lazuli, a carpet and, of course, tapestries, all in the opulently classicizing LOUIS XIV STYLE. Production of such rich furnishings fell off after Le Brun's disgrace in 1683 and ceased altogether in 1694 when the factory was closed because of the King's financial difficulties. After it was re-opened in 1699 it was devoted solely to tapestries.

Lit: H. Jouin, *Charles Le Brun et les Arts sous Louis XIV*, Paris 1889; J. J. Guiffrey, *Comptes des bâtiments du roi sous la règne de Louis XIV*, Paris 1881–1901; R. A. Weigert, *Le style Louis XIV*, Paris 1945.

Gobelins tapestry factory The most important tapestry factory of the late C17 and C18 when it was producing panels of a technical perfection never equalled. It derives its name from a family which set up *c.*1440 a scarlet dyeing workshop on the outskirts of Paris in a village subsequently called Gobelins. These premises were converted into a tapestry factory before 1607 and in 1662 were taken over on behalf of the Crown by Colbert who installed there Charles LE BRUN and his staff of weavers from MAINCY. It had one LOW-WARP and three HIGH-WARP workshops. The premises included houses with little gardens for the weavers and their families. Although it worked mainly for the King who supplied the basic materials, it was free to accept orders from private patrons. Le Brun supervised the work very closely, providing finished CARTOONS in oils (not tempera as hitherto) and insisting that they be reproduced with great fidelity, apart from slight variations in colour. After finishing work which had been begun at Maincy, the factory next produced sets of *Elements*, *Seasons* and *The Story of Alexander*, of which the latter was so popular that it was rewoven eight times and copied elsewhere. The most interesting tapestries of this period are those celebrating the magnificence of Louis XIV – *The Story of the King* in fourteen large panels and a set of twelve *Months* each of which shows a different royal residence. The designs, in Le Brun's rather pompous classical Baroque style, are rendered with an attention to detail, chiaroscuro and modelling which could hardly be bettered in oil paint. Le Brun's autocratic powers were curtailed in 1683 and although his cartoons remained in use most of the new tapestries were derived from paintings by old masters, notably Raphael, Giulio Romano and Poussin. An exotically luxuriant *Indies* series was based on paintings by the Dutch artists Albert Eckhout and F. Post. As a result of financial difficulties precipitated by the War of the League of Augsburg, the factory was closed in 1694.

It was reopened in 1699 under the control of the Superintendent of Buildings with an artistic director in charge of design – Robert de Cotte (1699–1735), Jean-Baptiste Oudry (1735–55)

Gobelins tapestry, 'Louis XIV visiting the Gobelins factory', designed by Charles Le Brun, c.1667 (Château de Versailles)

and François BOUCHER (1755–70). Work began with a set of eight *portières* designed by Claude III AUDRAN in a style verging on the Rococo – each with a classical god posturing beneath a fantastic airy canopy garlanded with flowers, set about with bric-à-brac and enlivened by cats and parrots. With *The Story of Don Quixote* (1714, after Charles-Antoine Coypel) it initiated the production of tapestries in which the figurative scenes occupy less space than the elaborate ALENTOURS. The finest of this type is the set of *Gods* by Boucher (1758 onwards) with alentours by the flower painter Maurice Jacques (*c.*1712–84) which appealed particularly to English patrons for whom chair covers were woven *en suite* (Osterley Park, Middlesex; Newby Hall, Yorkshire; Metropolitan Museum, New York). Numerous figure subjects with simulated carved gilt wood frames were also woven, notably the very opulent *Story of Esther* (after Jean-François de Troy, 1737–40) which was repeated fifteen times (Compiègne; Fontainebleau; Windsor Castle; Uffizi, Florence; etc.). The King was celebrated in a series of *Hunts of Louis XV* (after Oudry, 1734–45). Other sets answered the vogue for exoticism – the strange *Turkish Embassy* (after Charles Parrocel, 1731–4) and *The New Indies* (after François Desportes, 1737–41) with semi-naked and truly noble savages posed against tropical backgrounds. Nearly all the leading French painters were employed to provide cartoons and tapestries came to be regarded as a very expensive alternative to oil painting. Indeed, small panels of portrait and sentimental genre scenes were made the size of easel paintings and exhibited annually at the Salons from 1763. To reproduce the subtleties of oil colour in silk stimulated the invention of new dyes (many of which have proved impermanent) especially when the Scottish master-weaver **Jacques Neilson** (*c.*1718–88) was in charge of the dye-works between 1768 and 1784. Neilson was head of the low-warp factory from 1750 onwards and introduced various technical improvements to obtain higher quality and fidelity of reproduction

Gobelins tapestry 'Loves of the Gods', 1775–6, by Boucher and Neilson (Osterley Park, Middx.)

without increase in cost. Under him the low-warp factory approached the high-warp factory in quality, and remained very much cheaper.

In the 1770s the factory adapted its productions somewhat uneasily to Neo-Classicism. Under the direction of **Pierre-François Cozette** (1714–1801), who had been trained as a painter, the high-warp workshop produced a series of *Loves of the Gods* including panels made from cartoons by Jean-Baptiste Pierre and Joseph-Marie Vien (with borders woven at BEAUVAIS). After the Revolution, in 1794, a jury that considered 321 subjects recently in production condemned 120 as reactionary and 136 as frivolous. The factory was revived under Napoleon and some panels woven immediately before the

Revolution (e.g. a set of *Four Seasons* after Antoine Callet) were repeated. *Portières* with Napoleonic devices were also produced. And a set of small panels for a screen was derived from designs by J.-L. David. Restauration and later-C19 products include copies of old tapestries and some religious subjects. **Chevreul,** the director of the laboratory 1824–89, composed a palette of 14,400 shades of silk which made possible the weaving of faithful copies after paintings by old masters and such contemporaries as Ingres and Horace Vernet. Natural dyes were abandoned for synthetic dyes in 1911 thus providing a still wider range of colours in which Monet's *Nymphéas* and decorations by Odillon Redon and Jules Chéret were copied. The factory is still active but now works only for the State.

Lit: M. Fenaille, *État Général des tapisseries de la Manufacture des Gobelins,* Paris 1903–25; R. A. Weigert, *French Tapestry,* London 1962.

J. Goddard: mahogany knee-hole dressing-table, c.*1760–70 (Rhode Island School of Design)*

Goblet A drinking vessel with a bowl supported on a stem, as distinct from a beaker or tumbler.

Go-cart A light framework on casters inside which a child can learn to walk, also called a baby-cage.

Goddard, John (1723–85). Born at Dartmouth, Massachusetts, where his father was a 'housewright', **John Goddard** settled with his family at Newport, Rhode Island, in the 1740s. He and his younger brother **James** were apprenticed to Job TOWNSHEND whose daughter he married. By the 1760s John Goddard had established himself as the leading cabinet-maker in Newport. He is associated with the development of BLOCKFRONT pieces decorated with shallow shell relief carvings which are a kind of hallmark of Newport furniture though, like the blockfront, they can be found elsewhere. Stylistically his furniture derives from England but it has a distinctively American character, being as sensible, well-made and unpretentious as the prose of Benjamin Franklin. Examples can be seen in the Metropolitan Museum, New York, the Du Pont Museum at Winterthur, Delaware, and the Rhode Island School of Design, Providence, R.I.

As a Quaker he took no part in the Revolution and was listed as a suspect sympathizer of the English in 1776. The Revolution ruined him and he died bankrupt but his business was carried on by his sons **Stephen** (1764–1804) and **Thomas** (1765–1858) until Stephen's death in 1804. A card-table bearing their label shows that they had begun to work in the HEPPLEWHITE style. Stephen Goddard's son, **John II,** also worked as a cabinet-maker, dying in 1843.

Lit: E. H. Bjerkoe, *The Cabinet Makers of America,* New York 1957.

Godefroid de Huy, also known as **Godefroid de Claire** (*c.*1145–73). A certain Godefroid, canon of the monastery of Neufmoûtier near Huy, is recorded *c.*1240 to have been unequalled as a goldsmith and to have made many shrines in many places and objects for kings. Two shrines, now lost, for Notre Dame de Huy are recorded in 1274 to have been made by Godefroid in 1173, and he has been identified with the goldsmith 'G' to whom Abbot Wibald of Stavelot wrote in 1148 concerning the famous Remaclus retable of which only fragments of Mosan enamel survive (Frankfurt, Museum für Kunsthandwerk). He is also recorded by Jean d'Outremeuse (1338–1400) in his *Chronique en bref.* A number of important works have been attributed to Godefroid – e.g. the head-reliquary of Alexander of 1145 (Brussels, Musée Cinquantenaire) and the shrine of St

Crucifix base, after Godefroid de Huy, champlevé enamel, c12 (Hotel Sandelin, St Omer)

E. W. Godwin: ebonized wood sideboard made by William Wall, c.1867 (Victoria & Albert Museum)

Heribert (St Heribert, Deutz-Cologne) – but no work certainly by him has survived.

Lit: P. Lasko, *Ars Sacra 800–1200*, Harmondsworth 1973; M.-M. Gauthier, *Émaux du moyen âge occidental*, Fribourg 1972.

Godet French and English late medieval term for a cup, now generally reserved for a type of shallow handled cup of that period.

Godwin, Edward William (1833–86). Architect, designer and advocate of dress reform, he was called 'the greatest aesthete of them all' by Oscar Wilde. He numbered Wilde and Whistler among his patrons and was largely responsible for two important late-c19 innovations in design – the so-called QUEEN ANNE STYLE of interior decoration and 'Anglo-Japanese furniture'. He began as an architect working mainly in a Neo-Gothic style but also designing some notable warehouses. He was a friend of BURGES though much less exuberant a Gothic revivalist. In 1862 he came under the influence of Japanese art, admiring especially the bold asymmetrical compositions, the clarity of line and colour, and the lightness and airiness of Japanese prints. He decorated his own house in Bristol in what he thought to be a Japanese style – bare floors sparsely covered with rugs, white walls hung with Japanese prints and a few pieces of simple early-c18 (Queen Anne) furniture. The effect must have been strikingly fresh and clean. From 1868 onwards he was less active as an architect than as a designer of furniture, wallpapers, carpets, textiles and other furnishings. By 1870 he was one of the leading figures in the Aesthetic Movement, designing and building the White House in Chelsea for Whistler (1877–8) and designing with Whistler the 'Butterfly suite' of furniture for the 1878 Paris Exhibition. In 1884 Oscar Wilde commissioned him to redecorate his house in Tite Street, Chelsea.

Godwin's designs mark a break with c19 Historical Revivalism. His furniture is Anglo-Japanese in name only, being wholly unlike anything made in Japan. Nor had he any interest in the revival of craftsmanship (in contrast to MORRIS and his friends). In design he aimed at effects 'by the mere grouping of solid and void and by more or less broken outline'. His favourite material was ebonized wood, usually in square-section lathes of machine-made regularity. His furniture was thus very suitable for factory production, and it was widely imitated. Its chief merits are its simplicity and lightness, its well adjusted proportions and the subtlety of contrast between solids and voids. Examples are in the Victoria & Albert Museum, London.

Lit: D. Habron, *The Conscious Stone*, London 1949; Alf Bøe, *From Gothic Revival to Functional Form*, Oxford 1957; E. Aslin, *Nineteenth Century English Furniture*, London 1962 and *The Aesthetic Movement*, London 1969.

Göggingen pottery A faience factory near Augsburg, functioning 1748–52 and producing a wide variety of decorative and useful wares (notably narrow-necked jugs) decorated with Rococo designs in blue or HIGH-TEMPERATURE COLOURS. On its closure unfinished wares were bought by the manager **Joseph Hackhl** who started another factory nearby at Friedberg where similar wares were made until *c.*1768.

Lit: K. Hüseler, *Deutsche Fayencen*, Stuttgart 1956–8.

Gold Regarded since very early times as the most precious of metals. It is found in various parts of the world, either as veins in several different types of rock, or alloyed with silver in ELECTRUM, or as flakes, dust or nuggets. It is of unique ductility (a single grain may be drawn into a wire 500 ft long), malleability (it may be beaten into a leaf four-millionths of an inch thick) and permanence (it will not melt below 1,065 °C. and even then retains its properties). These qualities, combined with rarity, account for the value placed on it and for the mystical properties at one time attributed to it – in Europe gold was regarded as a metal peculiarly suitable for liturgical objects, while the Aztecs called it by a name which means 'the excrement of the Gods'. In its pure state it is much too soft and rather too heavy for use in metalwork, so it is alloyed with other metals in various proportions (pure gold is of 24 carats, a half-and-half alloy is of 12 carats: the finest alloys commonly in use are of 18 or 22 carats). The colour of the gold is varied by the type and quantity of metal used in the alloy: copper gives a reddish, silver a pale greenish, tinge; a mixture of copper and silver makes it much yellower than the pure metal, platinum makes it silvery (a 25 per cent platinum 75 per cent gold alloy produces 18 carat white gold). These variations in colour have been put to good aesthetic use by goldsmiths, sometimes by combining gold of different alloys in a single piece, e.g. C18 French snuff-boxes. Like silver, gold may be moulded, or decorated by ENGRAVING, EMBOSSING or ENAMELLING. Though occasionally used for liturgical vessels and pieces of secular plate (e.g. the salt-cellar by B. CELLINI), gold has been used more frequently in modern times for jewellery, small boxes, etc. On larger scale objects it appears most frequently as GILDING applied to metal, wood or porcelain.

Lit: L. Aitchison, *A History of Metals*, London 1960; C. H. V. Sutherland, *Gold. Its beauty, power and allure*, London 1959; H. Pohl, *Gold*, Stuttgart 1958.

Gold tooling A decorative technique used in leather work, especially for bookbinding. The design or lettering is stamped, embossed or otherwise impressed on the surface and gold leaf is then applied with heated tools. (If gold is not applied the technique is called BLIND TOOLING). Gold tooling was introduced in Italy in the C15. It was not a European invention but an importation from the Moslem world. It was used in Morocco as early as 1256 and in Persia by the mid C14. (The gilding of stamped leather by painting with liquid gold is a different technique and had long been practised in Persia and North Africa.) Gold tooling reached Europe through Venice shortly after 1450 and through Naples *c.*1475. Middle Eastern Islamic influence was strong in Venice whereas Moorish and North African Islamic influence was more felt in Naples. The earliest European gold-tooled leather bookbinding so far identified is on a manuscript of Strabo's 'Geographia' (now in the Bibliothèque Rochegude at Albi) written at Padua in 1459 for presentation to King René of Anjou.

Golle, Pierre (*fl.*1670–90). He was a leading Louis XIV period cabinet-maker and was brought to France from Holland by the luxury-loving Cardinal Mazarin for whom he made two large ebony cabinets. He was established at the Gobelins and, like his contemporaries BOULLE and CUCCI, specialized in sumptuous, costly furniture with a lavish use of inlay and carving, often inlaid with floral marquetry or with pewter and with marble columns and gilded legs. His younger brother **Adrian Golle,** also a cabinet-maker, worked in Holland, for Princess Mary wife of William of Orange later William III of England. Daniel MAROT was their nephew. Adrian Golle was, like his brother, a refugee after the Revocation of the Edict of Nantes.

Lit: P. Verlet, *French Royal Furniture,* London 1963.

Gombron (or **Gombroon**) **ware** C17–C18 English name for Oriental porcelain named after the port of Gombron (modern Bandar Abbas) on the Persian Gulf where the East India Company had a trading station and whence both Chinese and Persian wares were sent to England. The term is now used more specifically for a type of C16–C17 Persian pottery (precise origin unknown) with a very hard, white and thin, almost translucent body. Decorations are incised under the glaze, sometimes being combined with RICE GRAIN DECORATION and sometimes with blue and black painting. Jars, ewers, bowls and plates were among the wares made.

Gomme, Donald (b.1916). English furniture and industrial designer, responsible for the well-known 'G-plan furniture' of 1953. This is a set of simple, well-designed and inexpensive modular furniture and is produced by his firm of furniture-makers in High Wycombe, founded by his father **Ebenezer Gomme** in 1898. The popular Gomme chair of 1962 is an adaptation of the Victorian armchair inspired by the famous EAMES chair-and-footstool of 1957.

Gondelach, Franz (1663–1717). Leading German Baroque glass engraver working at the Court of the Landgrave of Hesse-Cassel, 1695–1716. A master of the HOCHSCHNITT process, he engraved goblets with portraits or elaborate patterns of *putti,* bacchantes, etc. sporting amongst shells and luxuriant acanthus foliage. *Illustrated next column.*

Lit: G. E. Pazaurek, *Franz Gondelach,* Berlin 1927.

Franz Gondelach:
glass flask with engraved decorations, c.1715
(Stattl.Kunstsammlungen, Kassel)

Goodison, Benjamin (d.1767). One of the best English cabinet-makers of the early Georgian period though less fashionable than William HALLETT. From 1727 he had premises in Long Acre, London. He specialized in PARCEL-GILT mahogany furniture, boldly designed, often in the manner of William KENT, with rather heavy but effective ornament. A favourite motif was opposed acanthus scrolls centring on a shell, crown or plume of feathers. He supplied furniture to the royal palaces from 1727 and examples still survive at Hampton Court and Windsor Castle. He also made furniture – tables, cupboards, chandeliers and probably chairs – for the 1st Earl of Leicester at Holkham, Norfolk. Other patrons included Sarah, Duchess of Marlborough, the Earl of Cardigan and Viscount Folkestone. After his death his workshop was carried on until 1783 by **Benjamin Parran.**

Lit: A. Coleridge, *Chippendale Furniture*, London 1968; R. Edwards and M. Jourdain, *Georgian Cabinet-Makers*, rev. edn., London 1955.

Gorbunovo porcelain factory A Russian factory founded near Moscow *c.*1800–1806 by an Englishman named **Charles Milly** but later owned by **A. Popoff.** It continued until 1872. Its best period was 1812–25 when its products rivalled GARDNER's in excellence. They also followed Gardner's in style, notably in their small figures of Russian peasants.

Gorevan carpets, *see* PERSIAN CARPETS.

Gorham Company One of the largest firms of silversmiths in the U.S.A., founded in 1818 by **Jabez Gorham** (b.1792) in Providence, Rhode Island. Its expansion dates from *c.*1841 when it introduced mechanical methods for the manufacture of wares in solid silver. Thomas J. Pairpoint, an English sculptor formerly employed by the London firm of silversmiths, Lambert and Rawlings, was taken on as chief designer in 1868. In the same year the Company began to make wares of sterling silver standard and to employ trade and date marks. Most of the designs were derived from C18 prototypes. But after the appointment of another Englishman, William Codman, as chief designer shortly before 1900, individual hand-wrought pieces in a restrained version of ART NOUVEAU were produced and marketed under the trade name of 'Martelé'. At the St Louis International Exposition of 1904 the company won the Grand Prize for a display which included a remarkable desk and chair of ebony, ivory, mother-of-pearl and silver (Rhode Island School of Design Museum). The company continues to make silverwares of fine quality.

Gorham Company: silver and ebony dressing-table and chair, 1903 (Rhode Island School of Design, Museum of Art, gift of Mr and Mrs F. Thurber)

Lit: K. M. McClinton, *Collecting American 19th Century Silver*, New York 1968.

Goss porcelain factory Founded in 1858 by **William H. Goss** (b.1833) in Hanley, Stoke-on-Trent, it was known as the **'Falcon Works'** after the goshawk used as the mark. Products included jugs, tobacco jars, etc., and also ornamental pieces in Jewelled Ware for which Goss invented an improved process. PARIAN WARE and an egg-shell porcelain (later developed at BELLEEK) were also produced. But the factory's great success from 1880 onwards was due to its heraldic porcelain, i.e. marked with the coats-of-arms of cities, towns, etc., the pieces themselves often being miniature models of local objects of interest such as the font in which Shakespeare was baptised. They were bought in large quantities as mementoes and keepsakes and were also collected. By 1912 the 'League of Goss Collectors' numbered over a thousand members. In addition to heraldic porcelain, miniature models of houses, dolls' tea-sets, etc., and, during the First World War, miniature models of British tanks, bombs and shells were also made. In 1929 the factory was sold by the Goss family and it closed in 1940. (After 1929 wares were marked 'England' below the name 'W. H. Goss').

Lit: M. J. W. Willis-Fear, *The History of the Pottery Firm of W. H. Goss at Stoke-on-Trent*, Newcastle 1965; N. Emery, *William Henry Goss and Goss Heraldic China*, Stoke-on-Trent 1969; D. Rees and M. G. Cawley, *A Pictorial Encyclopedia of Goss China*, London 1970.

Gostelowe, Jonathan (1744–95). American cabinet-maker noted for pieces in the Philadelphia Chippendale style.

Gotha porcelain factory Founded in 1757 and

distinguished mainly for the very delicate decorations on its wares, first in the Rococo style but more frequently in a classicizing manner. Forms tended to be imitative mainly of FÜRSTENBERG PORCELAIN. Small coffee sets were a speciality. The factory continued into the C19. Other porcelain factories were established in the same town in the later C19. (For factory mark *see* p. 884.)

Lit: R. Graul and A. Kurzwelly, *Altthüringer Porzellan*, Leipzig 1909.

Gothic In architecture the style of the pointed arch, the rib vault and the flying buttress – a style which first appeared complete in Saint Denis Abbey 1140–44. Soon afterwards, sculpture became less robust and more elegant; painting became increasingly intricate in composition and jewel-like in colour. The decorative arts followed this transition from the monumental, solid and severe ROMANESQUE to a style, or series of styles, of which lightness, transparency and intricacy are the key-notes. It is no coincidence that many of the finest achievements of Gothic art are in STAINED GLASS. A comparison between church-shaped reliquaries of the Romanesque and Gothic periods illustrates the contrast between the styles: the former have an architectural solidity which suggests that their makers would have been equally capable of building a cathedral whereas the latter have a toy-like quality and echo somewhat playfully the great conceptions of the master builders of Amiens and Chartres. Architectural motifs – the traceried arch either open or blind, pinnacles, crockets, pendants – were extensively used for the decoration of metalwork and woodwork, following architectural development from the relative simplicity of C12–C13 early Gothic to the elaboration of C14–C15 Flamboyant Gothic. Similarly, figures painted in enamel or modelled in relief follow the development of large-scale sculpture and painting. The division between the artist (architect, sculptor or painter) and the craftsman (metalworker, ivory or wood carver, tapestry weaver, etc.) became increasingly marked, not in quality of work but in the ability to initiate stylistic development. No Gothic craftsman occupies a place comparable historically to that of GODEFROID DE HUY in the Romanesque period.

Many of the finest surviving examples of the Gothic style in the decorative arts are in metalwork. A vast quantity of ecclesiastical silver survives – reliquaries, monstrances, chalices, patens, cruets, etc., very richly fashioned and often decorated with enamels. In the earlier part of the period the *champlevé* enamelling technique was still used at LIMOGES and elsewhere but in the C14 translucent enamels became more popular (some of the finest on the reliquary by UGOLINO DI VIERI at Orvieto Cathedral). Domestic metalwork was rarer (though contemporary inventories

Reliquary of the Holy Thorn, gold enamelled and set with jewellery, French, late C14 (British Museum)

The Studley Bowl, silver gilt, English, late c14 (Victoria & Albert Museum)

testify to a profusion in the houses of the great): surviving pieces, such as French NEFS and English salts, appear to have been preserved mainly because their value lay in the artistry of their elaborate forms rather than their weight of precious metal. Similarly with furniture, most of the surviving pieces are elaborate and ceremonial,

Gothic silver-gilt throne of King Martin of Aragon, c.1400 (Barcelona Cathedral)

Gothic ostensory from Voghera, silver-gilt and enamelled, 1456 (Castello Sforzesco, Milan)

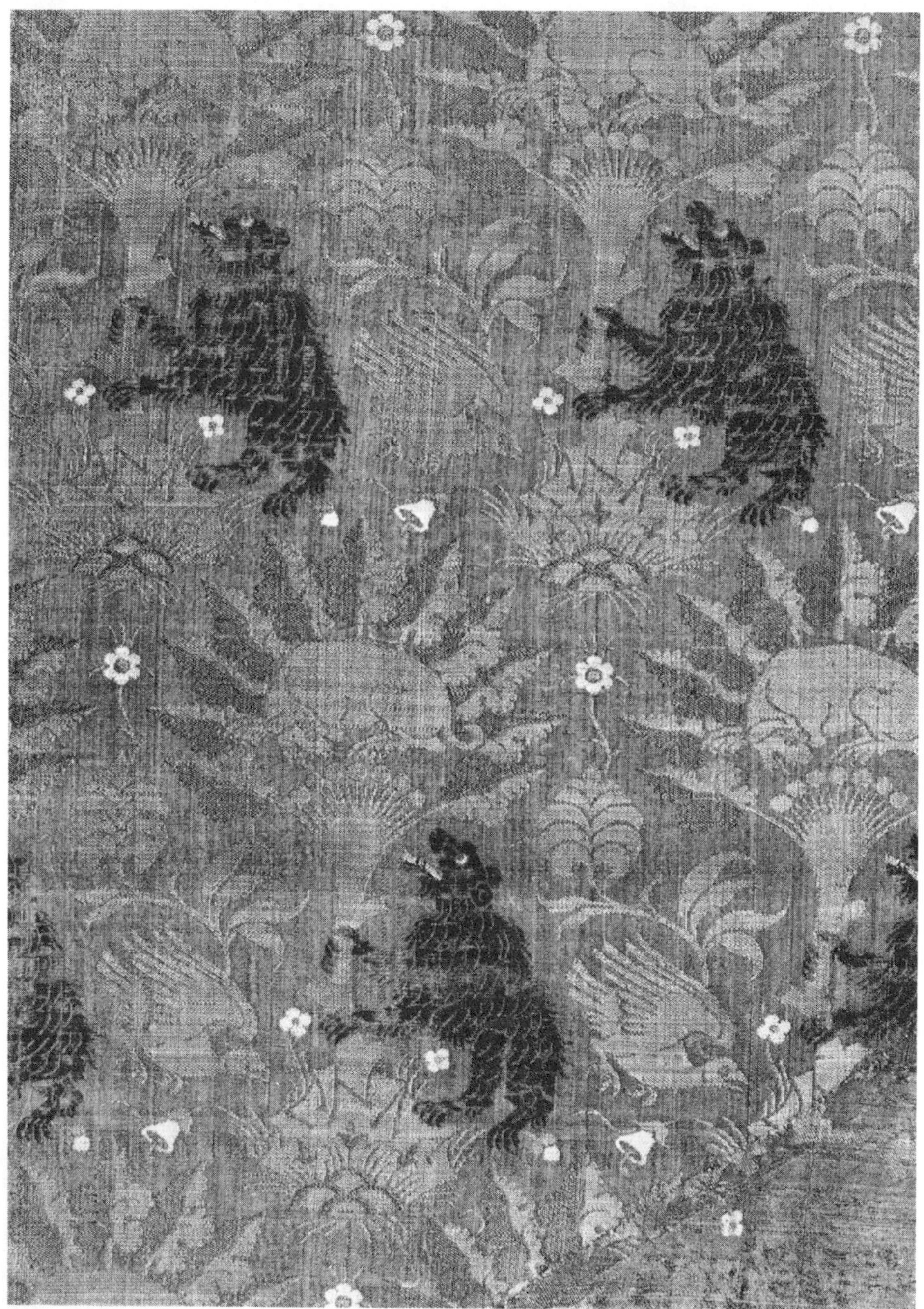

Gothic silk from the Convent of Lün, Italian, late c14 (Museum für Kunst und Gewerbe, Hamburg)

(Right) *Gothic livery cupboard in oak, English, c15–16 (Victoria & Albert Museum)*

Gothic writing-table, carved walnut, from Wettingen monastery, late c15 (Schweiz Landesmuseum, Zürich)

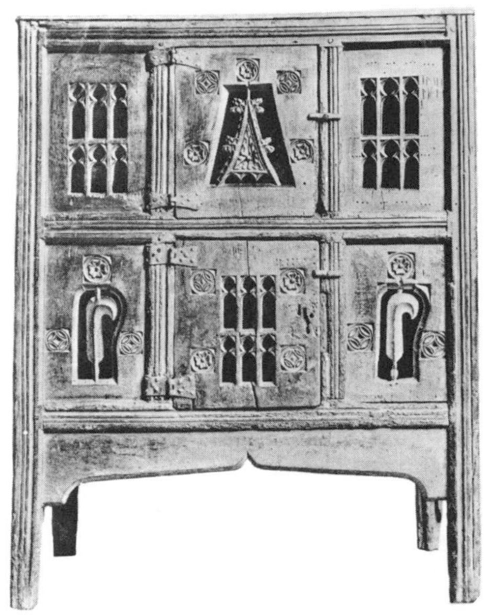

e.g. the wildly traceried and crocketted mid-c14 silver throne of King Martin of Aragon (Barcelona Cathedral), the English Coronation Chair (Westminster Abbey) and the so-called throne of Alfonso V of 1470 (Museu Nacional de Arte Antiga, Lisbon). Of the much simpler but hardly less rigidly uncomfortable furniture which appears in c14–c15 paintings, very few examples survive (and as taste in furniture changed very slowly those few may well be much later in date). The Gothic palace or rich merchant's house owed its splendour not to its wooden furniture but to the rich fabrics used to cover it and the massive silver plate displayed in it. Coffers carved with reliefs of armed knights standing beneath Gothic arches (e.g. that in the Musée de Cluny, Paris) or jousting knights (Victoria & Albert Museum) must always have been rarities. Smaller domestic objects, especially ivory caskets, mirror frames and even combs were frequently carved with courtly themes, either real (fashionably dressed couples playing chess or hawking) or allegorical (the storming of the Castle of Love). But the vast majority of Gothic IVORY carvings are of religious subjects.

The art of tapestry weaving reached its height in the Gothic period in France, the main centres being PARIS, TOURNAI and ARRAS. Subject matter was religious (the Angers *Apocalypse*), courtly, or elaborately and now perplexingly allegorical (The *Dame au Licorne* series in the Musée de Cluny, Paris). For silk textiles the main centres were in Italy: the finest products display a curious mixture of European heraldic and Oriental motifs and are generally assigned, on very flimsy

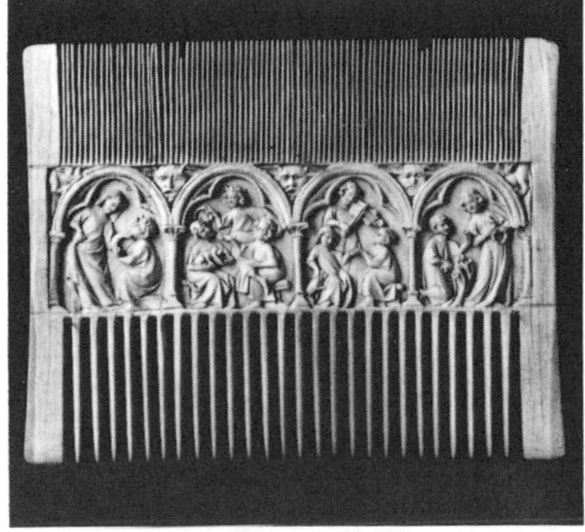

Gothic ivory comb, French, c14 (Museo Nazionale, Florence)

evidence, to LUCCA and VENICE. In embroidery England led Europe, producing OPUS ANGLICANUM vestments which were renowned throughout the continent.

In the decorative arts, as in architecture, painting and sculpture, the Gothic style began to give way to the Renaissance in C15 Italy. It lasted much longer in N. Europe, growing even richer and more sophisticated, more intricately convoluted and refined. It survived, especially for church plate, well into the C16.

Gothic Revival The earliest manifestations of the Gothic Revival in the decorative arts are the various chalices of C15 pattern made under the influence of such High Churchmen as Lancelot Andrewes from *c.*1615–40 in England. Their purpose was eminently serious – to suggest the Apostolic Succession of the Anglican Church – and they played a minor role in a large programme. The Gothic style was revived again in England in the C18, but for decorative and superficially sentimental reasons. The revival began with architecture, chiefly garden buildings of a very

The 'extravagant style of Modern Gothic Furniture and Decoration', from Pugin's The True Principles of Pointed or Christian Architecture, *1841*

Gothic Revival armchair, English, c.*1760 (Private Collection)*

Gothic Revival bookbinding, French, c.*1830 (Musée des Arts Décoratifs, Paris)*

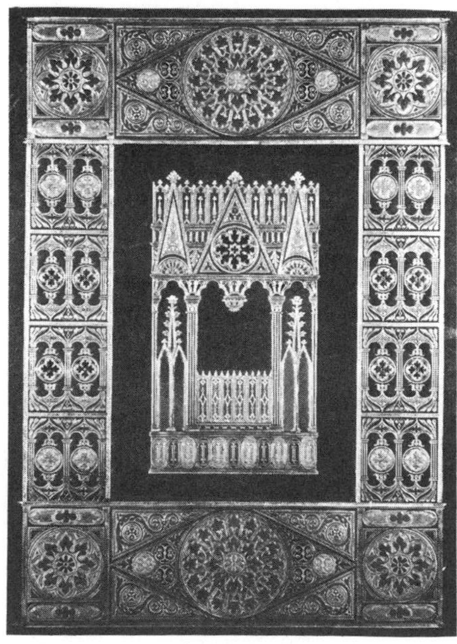

flimsy kind, sometimes mock-ruins. Batty LANGLEY published in 1742 a notorious set of very un-medieval designs entitled *Gothic Architecture Improved* and in 1750 W. and J. HALFPENNY began to produce their little builders' pattern books with designs for summer houses in the Gothic and Chinese styles and sometimes a mixture of both. The first Gothic Revival furniture was probably intended for such buildings. The seal of fashion was stamped on the revival by Horace Walpole at Strawberry Hill (1750–70) where a slightly more archaeologizing approach was shown, e.g. an Archbishop's tomb provided a design for a chimney-piece, a rose window for a plaster ceiling. Gothic tracery was printed on wall-papers, an octagonal chapter house was reduced to the scale of a parlour. In the 1760s Robert ADAM, T. CHIPPENDALE and others applied Gothic window-tracery, pinnacles and crockets to chairs, cabinets, bookcases, etc., of otherwise normal Georgian form. Silver candlesticks were likewise adorned with Gothic motifs. On the continent there were few manifestations of the Gothic Revival before the end of the C18, apart from a well-known room frescoed by G. D. Tiepolo in the Villa Valmarana, Vicenza, *c.*1757, and a number of garden buildings in Germany and France. Early in the C19 France developed a national variant in the TROUBADOUR STYLE, and Italy in the DANTESQUE STYLE. Furniture and metalwork decorated with Gothic motifs – often 'correct' in detail but invariably misapplied – were made in most European countries until the 1860s. But a reaction against this type of Neo-Gothic was initiated in the 1830s in England by A. W. N. PUGIN who protested against the misuse of architectural detail and designed furniture, church plate and jewellery based strictly on medieval precedents. He was followed in England by the more fanciful W. BURGES and the more purist W. MORRIS and his associates. In France VIOLLET LE DUC took a similar line in theory, but this did not prevent him from designing C15 Gothic interiors for railway carriages.

Gotzkowsky, Johann Ernst, *see* BERLIN PORCELAIN FACTORY.

Gouge work Decorations scooped out with a gouge as on much C17 English oak furniture.

Gourd cup C16–C17 type of cup with an irregularly ovoid bowl and cover reminiscent of a gourd, often mounted on a stem like the gnarled trunk of a tree, popular in N. Europe including England. Designs for such cups were published by H. BROSAMER and Virgil SOLIS.

Gout stool A footstool with a padded top which may be adjusted to support a gouty foot at the least uncomfortable angle, made mainly in C18 England.

Gouthière, Pierre (1732–1812/14). Outstanding Louis XVI *fondeur-doreur*, specializing in the most elaborately chased and gilded *bronzes d'ameublement* and mounts for furniture of the ultra-refined floral or foliated type found on RIESENER furniture. He perfected (perhaps invented) a variation of the MERCURY GILDING process whereby parts of a gilt bronze could be given a matt finish to contrast with the burnished parts and thus greatly enrich the total effect. He became a *maître-doreur* in 1758 but did not make his name until 1770 with his work for Madame du Barry's Pavillon de Louveciennes. His patrons were bad payers and in 1788 he went bankrupt. The Revolution completed his financial ruin and he died in poverty. He seldom signed his bronzes and

P. Gouthière, the 'Avignon' clock, gilt-bronze, designed by L.-S. Boizot, 1771. The movement is by J.-P. Delunésy. (Wallace Collection)

most Gouthière signatures are on fakes. Authentic examples are rare, e.g. the 'Avignon' clock, Marie Antoinette's Fontainebleau wall-lights, the duc d'Aumont's perfume-burner in the Wallace Coll., London. He probably worked less for furniture-makers than has been supposed and there is no proof that he ever collaborated with Riesener, though it is almost certain that he collaborated with WEISWEILER.

Lit: J. Robiquet, *Gouthière, Sa Vie – Son Oeuvre*, Paris 1912.

Gouyn, Charles, *see* CHELSEA PORCELAIN FACTORY and 'GIRL IN A SWING' PORCELAIN.

Goyer, Jean (b.*c.*1725–30). He was the son of a Parisian cabinet-maker **François Goyer** (d.1763) and was trained as a bronze founder though he became a *maître-ébéniste* in 1760. He appears to have specialized in clock cases and to have employed (illegally) bronze founders in his furniture workshops. His most remarkable work is a very large and extraordinary secretaire, made with DUBOIS, now at Waddesdon Manor, England.

Lit: S. Eriksen, *Early Neo-Classicism in France*, London 1974.

Grainger, Lee & Co., *see* WORCESTER PORCELAIN FACTORY.

Grainger, William (*fl.*1616). English pewterer famous because he signed a pewter relief cast candlestick known as the 'Grainger candlestick' with his full name and the date 1616 (Victoria & Albert Museum). He was Master of the Pewterer's Company in London. A pewter bowl mounted on a high pedestal in St Mary's Church, West Sheffield, Berkshire, has been attributed to him.

Graining *Trompe l'oeil* painting on furniture or panelling or other woodwork, imitating the appearance of another wood, usually a finer and more expensive wood. It was practised in England from at least as early as the C16.

Grand feu colours The French name for HIGH-TEMPERATURE COLOURS.

Grand Rapids furniture Furniture manufactured by a number of independent companies at Grand Rapids, Michigan, the main centre for furniture production in late-C19 and early-C20 U.S.A. The first workshop was opened by **William Haldane** in 1836. Mechanization was introduced *c.*1850. The

Grand Rapids furniture: sideboard by Pullman, c.1856 (Grand Rapids Public Museum)

Grand Rapids furniture: table, probably by Berkey & Gay, c.1870–88 (Grand Rapids Public Museum)

expansion of the industry was due mainly to **Julius Berkey** who opened a small workshop in partnership with **Alphonso Hamm** in 1860, with **Elias Matter** in 1862 and with his brothers in 1865. In 1867 he was joined by **George M. Gay** and their factory soon became the largest in the area. From 1873 it was known as Berkey and Gay Furniture and it remained active until 1948. The Grand Rapids group of factories won national renown when they showed their products at the Philadelphia Centennial Exhibition in 1876. Several new factories were opened soon afterwards and in 1878 a permanent exhibition of furniture made in the town was opened. At this date they specialized in Neo-Renaissance pieces with much mechanical carved work. Simple MISSION STYLE pieces were made later. By 1908 there were 49 furniture factories in the district. They prospered until the Depression of the 1920s when many were closed. But the industry began to revive *c.*1938 with the introduction of modern designs for mass-produced furniture.

Lit: M. Sironen, *A History of American Furniture*, East Stroudsburg, Penna., 1936.

Grandfather clock A clock with a tall clockcase, standing 6 ft or more from the ground. The name is said to derive from a popular song of *c.*1880.

Granite ware The name of two diverse C19 English types of pottery. (1) Earthenware sprayed with lead glaze in blue or gray to resemble granite and produced by WEDGWOOD and several STAFFORDSHIRE POTTERIES. (2) A strong, hard, white earthenware made for rough use, e.g. on board ship, and for export. It was produced by the DAVENPORT POTTERY and others from the 1850s onwards.

Grassi, Anton, *see* VIENNA PORCELAIN FACTORY.

Gray, Eileen (b.1878). Architect, furniture designer and lacquer painter. She was born in Ireland, trained as a painter at the Slade School of Art in London and then worked as a restorer of old lacquer. In 1907 she settled in Paris where she worked for a while with a Japanese lacquer painter, Sagawara. She began by making only unique pieces, but those shown at the Union des Artistes Modernes in Paris in 1922 had a success which encouraged her to establish a workshop producing pieces made to her design. And at 217 rue du Faubourg Saint Honoré in Paris she opened a shop with a front (of her own design) which is a remarkably precocious example of the International Modern style. Her products, mainly in the ART DECO style, included tables supported on simulated lotus flowers, screens, sometimes with figurative designs sometimes composed of many rectangles of wood lacquered in a single colour, etc. From 1927 she designed buildings and furniture in a very elegant, very simple modern style influenced by LE CORBUSIER – notably a villa at Roquebrune with its chairs, tables, etc., 1927–9. She showed an ambitious project for a holiday centre in Le Corbusier's Pavillon des Temps Nouveaux at the Paris International Exhibition in 1937.

Lit: J. Rykwert in *Domus*, 469 (December 1968), p. 33; P. Garner, 'The Lacquer Work of Eileen Gray and Jean Dunand' in *The Connoisseur*, May 1973.

Eileen Gray: occasional table, c.1929 *(Private Collection)*

Grease pan The small dish beneath the nozzle of a candlestick.

Greatbach, William (1735–1813). Potter who began as an apprentice of WHIELDON, set up on his own at Lane Delph making cream-coloured wares with transfer-printed decorations (teapots with a print of the Prodigal Son are the best known) and also table-wares shaped like fruit which he sent to WEDGWOOD for glazing. He was financially ruined 1770, worked for the TURNERS of Lane End and ended up at Wedgwood's 1788–1807 who gave him a pension.

Grebner, Georg Friedrich (*fl.*1718–41). Painter, possibly a HAUSMALER, who decorated wares of several German faience factories notably NUREMBERG (1720–30), BAYREUTH (1731–3), OETTINGEN–SCHRATTENHOFEN (1738–40) and Donauwörth (1741). He painted landscapes, floral motifs, coats of arms, etc, mainly in blue at Nuremberg, in polychrome elsewhere. Many of his decorations are signed and dated to the day.

Lit: G. E. Pazaurek, *Deutsche Fayence- und Porzellan-Hausmaler*, Leipzig 1925.

Greek pottery The art of throwing POTTERY on the wheel was introduced into the Greek world by *c.*1800 B.C. and very ably practised, sometimes on a large scale, by Minoan and Mycenaean craftsmen. These wares were sometimes decorated with paintings of freely rendered plants and sea creatures. During the Greek dark ages the use of such motifs was discontinued and in the c10–c9 B.C. abstract geometrical decorations of concentric circles and bands, zig-zags, triangles, chequerwork patterns, etc. were the only ornaments used, painted in lustrous brown slip on the light-coloured surface of the clay. At this time the basic vase forms were also developed. Centres of production were widely dispersed, each with distinctive wares, in Asia Minor, Rhodes, Chios, Cyprus and other islands and, of course, Athens. In the c8 highly stylized figures of men, birds, fish and animals began to make their appearance in the decorations. By the c7 figures were given prominence on vases in the so-called Orientalizing style. At Corinth potters made something of a speciality in bottles and jugs fashioned in the shape of birds and beasts. Attica began to emerge as the main centre for the production of pottery in the c6 (exporting wares to other parts of the Mediterranean) and from the early c5 Athens exerted a dominant influence on styles.

The earlier Attic wares are decorated in the black figure technique, i.e. with the decorations applied to the pale surface of the clay in a thin slip which changed colour from red to black or dark brown in the firing. Figures painted in this manner were articulated with incised lines and a limited use of white and red colouring. A revolution in the technique of vase painting occurred *c.*530 B.C. with the adoption of the more naturalistic red figure style, i.e. with the figures reserved in the colour of the clay and contours and inner lines drawn in slip, against a black slip background. This style became steadily more popular though black figure was still used, especially for the Panathenaic vases. A third, white ground, technique was also employed from the c6 onwards – the whole or part of the surface was covered with a chalky white slip over which the figures were painted with incised details. In the latter part of the c5 this technique was much used for funerary *lekythoi* which were often further decorated in tempera colours, most of which have perished.

The names of several outstanding pottery painters are known from signed works; others, isolated stylistically, have been given anonyms. Notable black figure painters include the Nessos Painter, the Gorgon Painter, Sophilos, Kleitias, all of the first half of the c6, Lydos (*fl.c.*560–540), the Amasis Painter (*fl.c.*560), Exekias (*fl.c.*550–520). Red figure painters include Epiktetos (*fl.c.*520–490), Euphronios (*fl.c.*515–500), Euthymides (*fl.c.*520–500), the Kleophrades Painter (*fl.c.*500–480), Makron (*fl.c.*495–480), the Brygos Painter (*fl.c.*500–480), Douris (*fl.c.*500–470), the Berlin Painter (*fl.c.*500–470), the Pan Painter (*fl.c.*480–450), the Penthesilea Painter (*fl.c.*460–440), the Niobid Painter (*fl.c.*465–450), the Achilles Painter (*fl.c.*460–430), Polygnotos (*fl.c.*445–430), the Meidias Painter (*fl.c.*420–400).

The range of shapes adopted by Greek potters is relatively limited. The *hydria* was intended for carrying water, the *amphora, pelike* and *stamnos* for wine or other liquids. The various *krater* (*volute-, calyx-, column-*, and *bell-krater*) were used for mixing wine and water. The *lebes* which had to be supported on a stand was a wine vessel. The *psykter* was used for cooling wine. The *kylix*, *kantharos* and *skyphos* served as drinking cups. The *oinochoe* was a wine jug, the *lekythos* an oil jug. The *alabastron* held ointment or oil for the body.

Lit: J. D. Beazley, *Attic Red Figure Vase Painters*, Oxford 1942, *Attic Black Figure Vase Painters*, Oxford 1956, *Paralipomena*, 1971; A. Lane, *Greek Pottery*, London 1963.

Green, John, *see* WROTHAM POTTERY.

Greene, Charles Sumner (1868–1957). American architect practising at Pasadena, California, in partnership with his brother **Henry Mather Greene** (1870–1954) from 1893, shortly after they both graduated from the Massachusetts Institute of Technology School of Architecture. They built numerous private houses, some of them quite large, at first in an undistinguished Neo-Georgian style but from 1901 (after the elder brother's visit to England) in a manner which owes something to Philip WEBB and something to F. L. WRIGHT but was gradually developed in a wholly original way. One of the most notable, the Gamble House of 1907–9, Pasadena, is now a museum of their work. For the houses of their more affluent clients they designed every detail of furniture and decoration with an emphasis on fine woodwork. Their furniture designs often reveal Oriental (Chinese as well as Japanese) influence, and sometimes there is a touch of chinoiserie in their decorations. Though sometimes reminiscent of the products of the English ARTS AND CRAFTS movement, their furniture is more elegant, more obviously costly and generally rather better made – e.g. mahogany pieces with ebony pegs and splines in place of the oak with dowel pins of the same wood used by Philip Webb. It is also much more sophisticated than U.S. MISSION FURNITURE. To those of their clients who were not prepared to pay for very expensive custom-built pieces they recommended the furniture of Gustav STICKLEY. (And their work was highly praised in Stickley's periodical *The Craftsman*.) Some decorative elements in their houses, such as panels of glass and lamps, were supplied by the TIFFANY studios. Rugs were specially made to their design in England. Their most important buildings and furnishings were all executed before 1910. The brothers drifted apart after 1916 when Charles settled at Carmel, California. Though both continued to practise as architects neither seems to have designed any more furnishings.

Lit: R. L. Makinson in *The Prairie School Review* V (1968), pp. 5–26; R. Judson Clark (ed.), *The Arts and Crafts Movement in America 1876–1916*, Exh. Cat., Art Museum, Princeton University, Art Institute of Chicago, etc., 1972–3.

Greene, John (*fl.* 1667–73). An English importer and vendor of glass, active in London in partnership with **Micheal Measey.** His correspondence

Frans Greenwood: diamond engraved figures after Callot on wineglass, 1720 (Victoria & Albert Museum)

with a Venetian glass manufacturer, Alessio Morelli, now in the British Museum (Sloane MSS. 857), dating 1667–73, includes drawings of many types of glass vessels made in Venice at this time. Vessels similar to these designs are sometimes called 'Greene glasses'; they include drinking glasses with conical bowls and short knopped stems, glasses similar to German *Römer*, tumblers and a few more elaborate winged glasses.

Lit: W. B. Honey, *Glass: A Handbook*, London 1946; J. E. Barrington Haynes, *Glass Through the Ages*, Harmondsworth, rev. edn, 1959.

Greenwood, Frans (1680–1762). Notable amateur glass engraver of English origin working in Holland. Inspired by mezzotints or dotted engravings, he developed a technique of stippling designs on glass with a diamond point. He executed landscapes, genre, mythological and amorous scenes, generally derived from prints. *Illustrated previous page.*

Lit: W. Buckley, *Notes on Frans Greenwood*, London 1930.

Grégoire, Gaspard (1751–1846). A notable silk-painter, born at Aix-en-Provence, the son of a silk merchant. He painted on various types of silk and is best known for his small portraits after Old Masters on panels of velvet (Musée des Tissus, Lyons).

Greiner, Gotthelf, *see* LIMBACH PORCELAIN FACTORY and WALLENDORF PORCELAIN FACTORY.

Greiner, Johann Georg, Johann Friedrich and **Christian Daniel,** *see* RAUENSTEIN PORCELAIN FACTORY.

Grendey, Giles (1693–1780). He was a prominent London furniture-maker, the son of a Gloucestershire farmer. Apprenticed in London in 1709 he became a Liveryman of the Joiners' Company in 1729 and Master in 1766. He appears to have had a flourishing export business. A magnificent suite of red lacquer furniture made by him was, until 1935, in the Castle of Lazcano in Spain

G. Grendey: beechwood day-bed japanned in gold and silver on a scarlet ground, 1730 (Victoria & Albert Museum)

(some pieces now in the Victoria & Albert Museum, London, and the Metropolitan Museum, New York). £1,000 worth of furniture 'packed for exportation' was lost when his premises in Clerkenwell were burnt in 1731. For the home market he seems to have made sound, good quality furniture and also some high quality pieces in mahogany, often with double serpentine scrolled panels. But he also made some quite simple furniture for country clients. His work is sometimes labelled. He retired in 1779. His daughter married John COBB.

Lit: A. Coleridge, *Chippendale Furniture*, London 1968; S. Jervis in *Country Life*, 6 June 1974.

Grenier, Pasquier (d.1496). Leading TOURNAI tapestry contractor and weaver much patronized from 1459 by Philip the Good, Duke of Burgundy, for whom he provided a particularly splendid series of *The Story of Alexander* woven in gold and silver thread as well as wool (two panels survive in Palazzo Doria Pamphili, Rome). Other works include *Esther and Ahasuerus* (Louvre; Musée Lorraine, Nancy), *The Knight of the Swan* (Museum für angewandte Kunst, Vienna; St Catherine's Church, Cracow) and a panel with woodcutters at work in the forest (Musée des Arts Décoratifs, Paris). The compositions are crowded with richly dressed figures of a characteristically late Gothic elegance. His sons, notably **Jean** (d.1519), inherited his cartoons and carried on the business.

Lit: R.-A. Weigert, *French Tapestry*, London 1962.

Grès, *see* STONEWARE.

Grès de Flandres Old name for RHENISH STONEWARE, especially from RAEREN.

Greybeard Alternative but more recent (1788) term for a BELLARMINE, possibly derived from a combination of *grès* with the bearded face on such vessels.

Greyhound jug A pottery jug with a handle in the form of a greyhound, made in several C19 factories in England and the U.S.A. where they are known as hound-handled pitchers.

Gribelin, Simon (1661–1731). He was a French Huguenot designer, the son of a watchmaker at Blois, who settled in London *c.*1680. He became a member of the Clockmakers' Company in 1686. His designs were published as *A Book of Several Ornaments*, London 1682, and *Livre D'Estampes de Sim. Gribelin*, London 1722. Although many of his designs were invented for watches and clocks, they were very influential among Huguenot silversmiths in London – notably de LAMERIE and Samuel COURTAULD – and many pieces were decorated with engraved ornament in his style and sometimes directly after his designs.

Lit: C. Oman in *Apollo*, 1957 pp. 218–221; Y. Hackenbroch in *The Connoisseur*, June 1968.

Gricc (or **Gricci**), **Giuseppe** (d.1770). One of the most gifted and original porcelain modellers of his time. He was model master at CAPODIMONTE from the factory's foundation in 1743 and moved with it to BUEN RETIRO in 1760. His two masterpieces are the porcelain rooms at Capodimonte and Aranjuez with their many reliefs of chinoiserie figures and fantastic chandeliers. But he also provided models for *Commedia dell'Arte* figures of great vitality and an elegance much less affected than those of his contemporaries in Germany – also of street-hawkers, fishermen and even some religious subjects, notably an impressive large Pietà group (Villa Floridiana, Naples and Museo Municipal, Madrid). His sons **Carlos** (d.1795) and **Felipe** (d.1803) succeeded him at Buen Retiro.

Lit: A. Lane, *Italian Porcelain*, London 1950; A. W. Frothingham, *Capodimonte and Buen Retiro Porcelain*, New York 1955; F. Stazzi, *L'arte della ceramica Capodimonte*, Milan 1972.

Grieniger, Johann Georg, *see* BERLIN PORCELAIN FACTORY.

Griffen, Smith and Hill pottery A factory at Phoenixville, Pennsylvania, active 1879–90 and specializing in industrial MAJOLICA with thick richly coloured glazes covering rather lush ornament in relief – maple-leaves, cauliflowers, shells and seaweed, etc.

Griffin A mythological creature with a lion's body and an eagle's head and wings, of classical origin and used as a decorative motif for furniture from the Renaissance onwards.

Gripper Axminster, *see* AXMINSTER CARPET.

Grisaille Painting in various tones of grey, usually for *trompe l'oeil* reliefs, etc.

Groff, Wilhelm or **Guillielmus de** (*c.*1680–1742). Sculptor and furniture designer, he was born in Antwerp, went to Paris *c.*1700 and began to work for the Crown *c.*1708. In 1714 he executed in Paris a bronze statuette of Max Emanuel, Elector of Bavaria, who called him to Munich next year and appointed him Court Sculptor. He executed much decorative sculpture for the interiors and gardens of the Electoral palaces. He also designed furniture, entirely in the French RÉGENCE STYLE, e.g. *bureau-plat* in Wittelsbach Collection, Schloss Berchtesgaden. Some pieces were made to his design by **Johann Michael Höcker.**

Lit: H. Kreisel, *Die Kunst des deutschen Möbels*, vol. ii, Munich 1970.

Grohé, Guillaume (1808–1885). A German furniture maker, he became the leading Second Empire reproduction-furniture maker in Paris. He and his brother **Jean-Michel Grohé** were settled in Paris by 1827 and began by dealing in works of art generally. Guillaume Grohé gradually transformed the business into a furniture workshop. They exhibited furniture at the 1834 exhibition – it was described as being Neo-Gothic and Neo-Egyptian – but after 1861 Guillaume exhibited alone, his brother presumably having retired. He specialized in reproduction C18 furniture and he achieved very high quality, employing such skilled craftsmen as Liénard for marquetry, and Fannières for bronze mounts. In 1884 his work was compared favourably to BOULLE, RIESENER and GOUTHIÈRE in an article in *Le Figaro*. He supplied furniture to Louis Philippe, Napoleon III and the Empress Eugènie who patronized him especially for his reproduction Louis XVI furniture. In 1862 he began supplying furniture to Queen Victoria also. Examples of his furniture are at Fontainebleau, Compiègne and the Musée Carnavalet, Paris.

Lit: D. Ledoux-Lebard, *Les ébénistes-parisiens (1795–1870)*, Paris 1965.

Grolier bindings French C16 bookbindings made for **Jean Grolier,** Vicomte d'Agnisy (1479–1565) who was Treasurer of the Duchy of Milan in 1510 and Treasurer General of France from 1547 to 1565. They mostly date from 1520–40 though some are later, *c.*1555. They were supplied by Parisian binders such as the *atelier au trefle*. In design they develop from simple geometrical strapwork patterns to elaborate curvilinear interlacing patterns combined with arabesques. They were often enclosed within Roll borders. The strapwork was often coloured, usually black or red. Later Grolier bindings anticipate the style of FANFARE BINDINGS of the later C16 though they were generally more restrained than the contemporary MAIOLI BINDINGS.

Lit: H. M. Nixon, *Bookbindings from the Library of Jean Grolier*, London 1965.

Groove and tongue ornament Carved decoration on furniture, like fluting sunk in a surface and partially filled with convex mouldings resembling tongues.

Gros bleu, *see* FONDPORZELLAN.

Gros point Canvas embroidered in CROSS STITCH.

Grosso, Niccolò (*fl.c.*1500). One of the few identifiable Renaissance ironsmiths. A Florentine, he was nicknamed Caparra (payment in advance) and, according to Vasari, was the best of his profession. His masterpieces are on the exterior of Palazzo Strozzi, Florence – an hexagonal lantern in the form of a classical temple, link-holders and stands for flag-poles incorporating exquisitely wrought sphinx-like creatures. Many other pieces of Florentine ironwork have been attributed to him. *Illustrated next column.*

Lit: E. Baccheschi & S. Levy, *Ferri battuti italiani*, Milan 1966.

Grotesque A fanciful type of decoration composed of small, loosely connected motifs, not unlike ARABESQUES but including human figures, monkeys, sphinxes, etc. It was described by Peacham in his *Graphice* (1612) as 'an unnatural or unorderly composition for delight's sake, of men, beasts, birds, fishes, flowers, etc. without (as we say) Rime or Reason.' It derived from ancient Roman decorations, either painted or in low

N. Grosso: wrought iron lantern, c.1500 (Palazzo Strozzi, Florence)

Grotesque decoration designed by Raphael in the Vatican Loggia, from an engraving by G. Savorelli and P. Camporesi

relief, which came to light in the Renaissance, e.g. in Nero's Golden House on the Esquiline. These decorations had been buried for centuries and the subterranean ruins in which they were discovered were popularly known in Italy as 'grotte', hence the name 'grotesques'. Many early Renaissance artists (e.g. Filippino Lippi, Signorelli, Pinturicchio, Perugino) used individual motifs from these recently discovered 'grotesques' but it was not until 1516 that they were revived as complete decorative schemes, by RAPHAEL in Cardinal Bibbiena's *stufetta* in the Vatican. They became famous when Raphael used them throughout the Vatican Loggie (1518–19). These were largely executed by his assistant Giovanni da Udine who later decorated the Villa Madama,

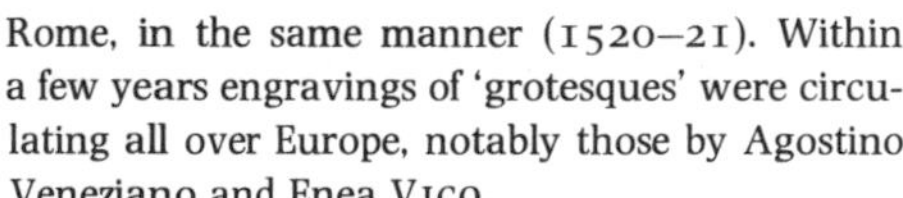

Grotesque design by Cornelis Floris, 1554

Grotesque design by Claude Gillot, from his Livre de portière, *early c18*

Rome, in the same manner (1520–21). Within a few years engravings of 'grotesques' were circulating all over Europe, notably those by Agostino Veneziano and Enea VICO.

Ancient Roman decorations *alla grotesca* were usually composed of tablets or medallions filled with painted scenes or cameos. Ceilings were found with such decorations arranged in compartments in an interlocking pattern and Giovanni da Udine revived this style in the ceilings at the Villa Madama. But for wall decorations the style was developed in the form of narrow panels, as devised by Raphael for the Vatican Loggie. This had the advantage that the somewhat loose structure of grotesque decorations could be strengthened by arranging the ornamentation symmetrically on either side of a firm vertical axis. STRAPWORK was later introduced for the same reason and gradually spread from the surrounding frame to penetrate into the design itself, thus providing a stiff framework around which the fanciful ornamentation might be arranged, as is shown in engraved grotesques by DU CERCEAU, Cornelis du Bos and Cornelis FLORIS.

After *c.*1530 the influence of ARABESQUES was increasingly felt in grotesques – e.g. in the engraved grotesques by Adrien Collaert, Luas Kilian and BERAIN – where the movement of the linear pattern recalls that of arabesques, especially in the ogival patterns which the lines form when intersecting and in the tendency of the bands to fall into polygonal patterns within the design.

By the mid C16 grotesques had spread from Rome and Italy to the rest of Europe and during the next three hundred years they were applied to almost every medium, to Urbino maiolica, Beauvais tapestries, painted ceilings by William Kent and, of course, in innumerable engravings. During the C18, however, the strapwork bands became increasingly slender and sinuous and Rococo grotesques by such designers as GILLOT and SALEMBIER almost dispense with strapwork or any other internal structure so that the ornamentation swirls free and the artist's fancy is unconstrained.

Lit: F. Piel, *Die Ornament-Grotteske in der italienischer Renaissance*, Berlin 1962; P. Ward-Jackson, 'Some main streams and tributaries in European ornament from 1500 to 1750', pts I & II, in *Victoria & Albert Museum Bulletin*, April and July, 1967; N. Dacos, *La découverte de la Domus Aurea et la formation des grotesques à la Renaissance*, London–Leiden 1971.

Groult, André (1884–1967). French designer of furniture, metalwork, etc., who began to exhibit in 1910 at the Salon d'Automne and the shows of the Artistes Décorateurs in Paris. Reacting against ART NOUVEAU he developed a personal style influenced by the furniture of the Restauration and Louis-Philippe periods, with much use of light-coloured woods, ample curves and plump upholstery. He contributed to several pavilions at the Exposition of 1925 and from about that date worked in the more expensive and expansive ART DECO manner.

Lit: Les années '25', Exh. Cat., Musée des Arts Décoratifs, Paris 1966.

A. Groult: armchair, c.1925
(Musée des Arts Décoratifs, Paris)

Ground colours, *see* FONDPORZELLAN.

Grue, Francesco Antonio (1618–73). The founder of a family of maiolica painters working in the revived ISTORIATO style at CASTELLI. His works include large shields and altar frontals as well as the usual decorative and useful wares. His son, **Carlantonio** (1655–1723), is notable mainly for painted tiles and plates inspired by the Carracci and Pietro da Cortona. **Saverio Grue** (1731–99) excelled as a painter of landscapes and worked from 1771 at the NAPLES ROYAL PORCELAIN FACTORY.

Lit: G. Minghetti, *Ceramisti*, Milan 1939; L. Moccia in *Faenza* XLVI (1960), pp. 59–64, XLVII (1961), pp. 87–9, LIII (1967), pp. 55–7; R. Paparella Treccia in *Faenza* LXI (1975), pp. 13–19.

Grueby, William H. (1867–1925). Outstanding U.S. art potter. He began at the **J. and J. G. Low Art Tile Works** in Chelsea, Massachusetts, then went into partnership with a **Mr Atwood** making tiles and other architectural decorations. He set up on his own in 1894 forming the **Grueby Faience Company** producing tiles and plaques in a variety of styles – Moorish, Chinese and Italian Renaissance. But in 1898 he began to produce the wares for which he is best known – vases of boldly sculptural form decorated with matt glazes with very subtle textures and colours, usually various shades of green but also yellows, browns, blues and, rarely, red. He was concerned mainly with the glazes while **George P. Kendrick** designed the forms, both under the influence of DELAHERCHE and CHAPLET whose wares had been exhibited in the U.S. Most of their vases are decorated with modelled leaf-forms which seem to cling to the surface. Tiles have similar glazes but are more often polychromatic and decorated with stylized landscapes, flowers, etc. At the Buffalo Pan-American Exposition of 1901 he exhibited with Gustav STICKLEY in whose periodical, *The Craftsman*, his wares were highly praised. Vases were commissioned from him by TIFFANY as lamp bases to be covered with glass shades. But the factory was never financially prosperous and went bankrupt in 1908. A new concern, named the **Grueby Faience and Tile Company**, was established mainly for the produc-

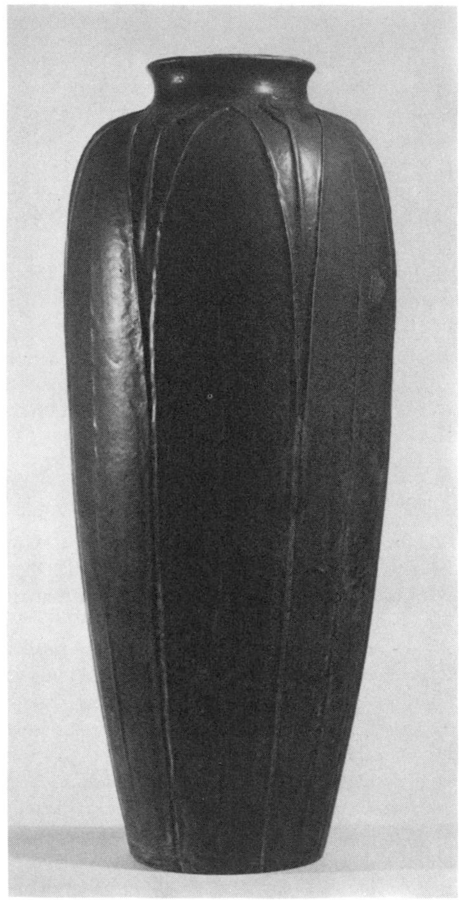

Grueby Faience Co.: vase, 1903
(The Art Museum of Princeton University)

tion of tiles (few if any vases were made after 1911). The firm was bought in 1919 by the **C. Pardee Works** of Perth Amboy, New Jersey, which continued to make tiles in Grueby's manner until the late 1920s.

Lit: R. Judson Clark (ed.), *The Arts and Crafts Movement in America 1876–1916*, Exh. Cat., Art Museum, Princeton University, Art Institute of Chicago, etc., 1972–3.

Grünstadt pottery A Rhineland factory established in 1801 with materials and forms from FRANKENTHAL, making initially rather yellowish white earthenware (partly moulded after Frankenthal models) but later specializing in printed wares like those of SPODE and other English factories. It is still flourishing. The name or the initials 'GBG' usually appear in the marks.

Guadamaci A Spanish term for leather finely tooled with elaborate designs brightly coloured and gilded. The name derives from Gadames in Tripolitania.

Gubbio potteries Although pottery was made in the Umbrian town of Gubbio from the C14 onwards no painted maiolica appears to have been produced before *c.*1498 when G. ANDREOLI and his brother **Salimbene** established their factory producing wares decorated in the LUSTRE technique for which it is famous. This factory was continued under G. Andreoli's son, **Vincenzo**, until *c.*1576 and is the only one recorded in the town. Wares made at URBINO and elsewhere were occasionally sent here to be lustred, especially *c.*1535–55. The art of lustre decoration was revived in Gubbio in the mid C19 by **Giovanni Spinacci** (*fl.*1853–76) who won prizes for his imitations of Renaissance maiolica at several international exhibitions.

Lit: E. Giovanoli, *Gubbio nella storia e nell'arte*, Città di Castello 1932; J. Chompret, *Répertoire de la maiolique italienne*, Paris 1949; B. Rackham, *Italian Maiolica*, London 1952.

Gudenberg, Baron von, *see* ROZENBURG POTTERY & PORCELAIN FACTORY.

Guéridon A candlestand or small, usually circular, table suitable for holding a candelabrum. It generally takes the form of a pedestal or column supported on feet and surmounted by a tray. Louis XIV *guéridons* were often carved to resemble a negro carrying a tray and a celebrated Moorish slave of that period and famed in Provençal popular songs, called *Guéridon*, is said to have given his name to this type of table. *Illustrated next column.*

Guibert, Honoré (*c.*1720–91). Born at Avignon, he settled in Paris by 1760. In 1763 he became a *maître sculpteur*, specializing in carved picture frames and *boiseries*. He carved the *boiseries* in the salon de compagnie in the Petit Trianon (1766–67) and in the Opéra in Versailles (1768–9) where he worked to designs by Gabriel, as he also did elsewhere.

Lit: S. Eriksen, *Early Neo-Classicism in France*, London 1974.

Guichard, Johann Philipp, *see* MAGDEBURG POTTERIES.

Guillibaud, Jean-Baptiste, *see* ROUEN POTTERIES.

Guilloche A continuous scroll pattern formed by two or more bands twisted one within the other to form a plait: the interstices are usually filled with rosettes or semispheres. It was originally used as a frieze enrichment in classical architecture and revived for furniture and metalwork from the mid C16.

Guimard, Hector (1867–1942). French architect and furniture designer, a leader of the ART NOUVEAU movement which was sometimes called the 'style Guimard' (by his friends) or the 'style bouche de Métro' (by others) after the Parisian Métro stations which he designed *c.*1900. All his works, whether buildings, metal screens, LINCRUSTA panels or furniture, seem to be wrought out of a confluence of slithery carved

Guéridon of box-wood, partly lacquered, c.1690–99. *by A. Brustolon (Palazzo Rezzonico, Venice)*

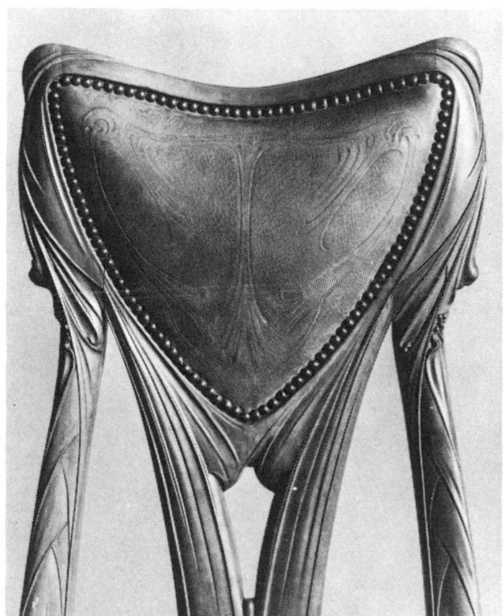

H. Guimard: detail of chairback, c.1900 *(Musée des Arts Décoratifs, Paris)*

forms, often of a seaweedy appearance, though the furniture he designed for his own house (*c.*1902–12 and now largely in the Museum of Modern Art in New York) includes some remarkably forward-looking pieces, notably an asymmetrical desk which not only employs 'free-form' shapes but foreshadows the 'L-plan desk'. His designs always have originality and distinction but they were those most frequently and disastrously imitated by commercializers of Art Nouveau.

Lit: Exh. Cat., *Hector Guimard*, Museum of Modern Art, New York 1970.

Guipure An inexact term applied to both needlepoint and pillow lace without grounds, supported by BRIDES.

Gumley, John (*fl.*1694–1729). He was an extremely successful furniture-maker, specializing in mirrors, but was perhaps an *entrepreneur* rather than a craftsman or designer. He is first heard of in 1694 when he advertized 'all sorts of cabinet work, as Japan Cabinets, India and English, with Looking Glasses, Tables, Stands, Chests of Drawers, Screutores, writing Tables, and dressing suits of all sorts'. In 1712 his business was puffed by Richard Steele in *The Spectator*. His fortune appears to have been made mainly from glass. In 1703 he supplied Chatsworth with magnificent 12 ft high mirrors with engraved heraldic devices and applied ornaments of sapphire blue glass (still at Chatsworth). In 1705 he opened a glasshouse in Lambeth. But he seems to have continued to supply furniture of all kinds for in 1715 he and James MOORE succeeded Gerrit JENSEN as royal cabinet-makers. In 1714 his daughter married the future Earl of Bath. After his death his business was carried on by his son **James** (d.1734) who was appointed chair- and cabinet-maker to Frederick Prince of Wales in 1732. *Illustrated next column.*

Lit: R. Edwards & M. Jourdain, *Georgian Cabinet Makers*, London 1955; H. Honour, *Cabinet Makers & Furniture Designers*, London & New York 1969.

J. Gumley: looking-glass in carved and gilt wood frame, c.1715 (Hampton Court Palace)

Gustavsberg pottery A factory founded in 1827 on the island of Värmdö near Stockholm producing a variety of useful and ornamental wares. From the early 1860s it manufactured bone-china of English type, PARIAN WARE figures and colour-glazed 'majolica'. Later in the century stoneware with flambé glazes was also produced. The painter **Gunnar Gunnarsson Wennerberg** (1863–1914) who had studied at SÈVRES, was artistic director from 1897 to 1908 and began by producing imitations of WEDGWOOD Jasper ware with up-dated decorations; later he designed table-wares in a simplified Art Nouveau style and developed a technique of *sgraffiato* decoration, especially for large vases and urns. His pupil **Josef Ekberg** (1877–1945) provided the factory with designs from 1897 until 1945 at first in a leafy Art Nouveau manner. From 1917 onwards designs were also obtained from **Wilhelm Kåge** (b.1889) who became artistic director – notably the very simple 'soft forms' table service of 1940. He, Stig Lindberg (b.1916) and others have also produced studio pottery at the factory. It is now one of the largest producers of useful and decorative wares in Sweden. (For factory mark *see* p. 884.)

Lit: O. Pelka, *Keramik der Neuzeit*, Leipzig 1924; *Porzellan-Kunst, Sammlung Karl H. Bröhan*, Exh. Cat., Schloss Charlottenburg, Berlin 1969, pp. 132–4.

Gutta-percha A medium for moulded decorations on furniture, walls, etc., made from the sap of an E. Indian tree, *Dichopsis gutta*, and much used in Europe in the later C19.

Gyles, Henry (1645–1709). Glass stainer working in York where he provided windows for the Minster and Guildhall (the latter now in the Victoria & Albert Museum, London). He worked mainly in black enamel and silver-yellow stain on clear glass and is at his best in heraldic panels.

Lit: J. A. Knowles, *Essays in the History of the York School of Glass Painting*, London 1936.

From Specimen of Printing Types and Ornaments, *Johnson & Smith, Philadelphia, 1834*

Habaner ware A term of doubtful derivation used to describe a type of peasant maiolica made in Moravia and Hungary from the late C16, initially, it is supposed, by Anabaptist immigrants from Germany. The earlier specimens have openwork borders in an Italian style, the later C17–C18 pieces are gaily and splashily decorated with flowers, figures, animals, etc.

Lit: K. Layer, *Oberungarische Habaner Fayencen,* Berlin 1928; E. Meyer Heisig, *Deutsche Bauerntöpferei,* Munich 1955; B. Kristinkovitch, *Haban Pottery,* Budapest 1962.

Habermann, Franz Xaver (1721–96). Leading German ornamental designer and sculptor working in Augsburg. He published more than five hundred engraved designs for furniture, silver, ironwork, etc., both ecclesiastical and domestic, also for carriages, organs, altars. Highly susceptible to changes in taste, he began in the ROCOCO STYLE and ended up with a Germanic version of the LOUIS XVI STYLE. *Illustrated next column.*

Lit: H. Kreisel, *Die Kunst des deutschen Möbels,* vol. II, Munich 1970.

Hackhl, Joseph, *see* GÖGGINGEN POTTERY.

Hackwood, William (d.1839). The principal WEDGWOOD modeller 1769–1832, responsible mainly for adapting antique busts and reliefs for reproduction in basaltes and jasper wares, but also the author of a few large reliefs (e.g. *Aesculapius and Hygieia* 1791) and several portrait medallions including one of Josiah Wedgwood.

Hadley chest An American type of chest, rectangular with a hinged top, the front having three sunken panels with one, two or three long

F. X. Haberman: decorative design, c.1770

drawers below. It stands on short legs formed by continuations of the stiles. The carved decorations are usually of tulip-patterns with vines and leaves. The name derives from Hadley, Massachusetts, where a number of such chests happened to be located.

Hadley, James, *see* WORCESTER PORCELAIN FACTORY.

Hafner ware Lead-glazed pottery, usually tiles but also vessels, made by the Hafner (stove-makers) of Germany, Austria and Switzerland from the C14 onwards. The tiles are moulded in relief and covered with a green glaze, though after *c.*1500 brown, yellow and other colours were used as well. Decorations are generally of Biblical subjects with distinctly rustic, heavy-limbed figures. Paul PREUNING produced wares of very much finer quality. Silesian Hafner ware is the name given to some elaborate tin-glazed dishes of *c.*1550 with designs (portraits or coats of arms) made up of areas of colour separated from one another by deeply cut lines.

Lit: E. Meyer Heisig, *Deutsche Bauerntöpferei*, Munich 1955; R. Franz, *Der Kachelofen*, Graz 1969.

Hagi pottery A small Japanese factory near Hagi, the chief town of Yamaguchi, possibly functioning from the early C16. It owes its fame to the arrival of a Korean potter **Li Kyong** (later called **Koraizaemon**), immediately after the Korean war of 1596, who made imitations of Korean wares and also tea-bowls with a cloudy salmon pink glaze. The factory seems to have specialized in rather light coloured TEA CEREMONY WARES. It remained active until the late C19.

Lit: S. Jenyns, *Japanese Pottery*, London 1971.

Hague, The, porcelain factory, *see* THE HAGUE PORCELAIN FACTORY.

Haguenau pottery and porcelain factory, *see* STRASBOURG POTTERY AND PORCELAIN FACTORY.

Haig, Thomas, *see* CHIPPENDALE, Thomas.

Haircord carpet A type of BRUSSELS CARPET woven with haircord.

Halb-fayence German term for earthenware covered with a clear lead glaze over a white slip, *see also* MEZZA-MAIOLICA.

Hald, Edward, *see* ORREFORS GLASSHOUSE and RÖRSTRAND POTTERY & PORCELAIN COMPANY.

Hall, John (*fl.*1840). The author of America's first furniture pattern book *The Cabinet Maker's Assistant* (Baltimore 1840) which codified American Empire furniture. It was widely used by U.S. cabinet-makers.

Hallett, William (*fl.*1732–1770). He was a well-known London cabinet-maker but his work is now difficult to identify. Only one signed piece by him is known – a mahogany cabinet in a private collection. He is recorded as having supplied furniture to Longford Castle, Wilton House, Holkham Hall and other grand houses. He appears to have had connections with VILE and COBB and it seems likely that his furniture was similar to theirs in style.

Lit: A. Coleridge, *Chippendale Furniture*, London 1968.

Hall-in-the-Tyrol Glasshouse Founded 1534 and flourishing into the C17, producing Venetian style coloured and crystal glass decorated with diamond-engraving and unfired lacquer painting and gilding. Examples are in the Hofmuseum, Vienna, and in the Bayerisches National Museum, Munich.

Lit: H. Heimer, *Die Glashütte zu Hall in Tirol*, Munich 1959.

Hall-mark The official mark applied to a piece of gold or silver as a guarantee of its standard of purity. Sometimes the mark of the assay office or guild is supplemented by other marks indicating the degree of fineness of the metal (i.e. the quantity of base metal in the alloy), the year in which it was assayed, and the name of the maker – the last as a means of identifying anyone culpable of malpractice. The marks were applied by means of stamps and are not to be confused with inscriptions or ASSAY GROOVES made when a piece of metal was removed for testing. (The latter sometimes resembles a letter N or Z but no significance can be attached to its form). In ancient Roman times ingots of gold or silver were sometimes marked with official stamps guaranteeing purity and in the Eastern Empire marks were applied also to wrought metal from the late C5. In N. Europe the practice of hall-marking began to be established in most countries in the early C14.

An English law of 1300 established a standard for silver as an alloy of 925 parts silver and 75 of base metals. When it had been tested in the assay office in London a piece of silver of this standard was marked with a stamp of a leopard's head which has remained the London mark to the present day (originally the head was crowned but from 1820 uncrowned). From 1363 a mark indicating the maker was added, at first a device, later (from 1697) his initials. From 1478 a letter of the alphabet was added to indicate the year, changed each May (at first on the 19th, later on the 29th). From 1544 a lion passant was also included as a national mark. By this time assay offices had also been established in the provinces, but they generally employed less elaborate systems of marking than that in London until the C18. Special marks were adopted in place of the leopard's head by Chester (the arms of the city from 1686), Exeter (an X in the C16–C17, a three-towered castle from 1701), Newcastle (three Xs or three castles from the mid-C17) and York (half-leopard's head, half fleur-de-lys probably from 1411, a cross charged with five lions passant from 1700). Later offices were established in 1773 at Birmingham (an anchor) and Sheffield (a crown). There were also offices with individual marks at Dublin, Edinburgh and Glasgow. A new standard of silver – with 41 parts base metal to 959 silver – established by Act of Parliament in 1697 was maintained until 1719 and during these years the figure of Britannia replaced the lion passant and the form of the leopard's head was changed. The old marks were restored with the return to the sterling standard. From 1784 a stamp of the sovereign's head was added to indicate that a tax on wrought plate had been paid: the use of this stamp was discontinued in 1890 except for two years, 1935 to mark the jubilee of George V and 1953 for the Coronation of Queen Elizabeth II.

In France gold objects were hall-marked from 1313 and by 1400 there were 186 French cities authorized to mark wrought gold and silver. At first objects were stamped only with the maker's mark surmounted by a fleur-de-lys and the mark of the guild. Date letters were introduced later. C18 pieces were also marked with the stamp of the *fermier* to whom the tax on plate was paid. Those of silver-gilt were stamped with the word *argent* from 1765 to the Revolution when, for a brief period, 1789–97, no marks were used.

In the Netherlands hall-marks were introduced in the C14. Different marks were used in 31 towns until 1814 when a national system of marking was introduced. Nuremberg goldsmiths marked their wares from the C14 but no consistent system of marks was employed until 1550. In Augsburg, the other great German centre for work in precious metals a city mark was used from 1529. Similarly in other European countries hall-marks were employed by the guilds in most cities where gold and silver were wrought, generally with makers' marks and marks to indicate date. Regulations controlling hall-marks were imposed with varying degrees of strictness but tended to be more generally observed in the later centuries and the larger cities (especially Paris and London). For marks *see* pp. 890–92.

The U.S. is the only Western country where hall-marks have never been used. But many U.S. silversmiths have used makers' marks and some have indicated the standard of the alloy of which the piece of plate is made.

Lit: For all Europe, *see* M. Rosenberg: *Der Goldschmiede Merkzeichen*, Frankfurt am Main 1922–8, 4 vols; E. Beuque, *Dictionnaire de Poinçons officiels français et étrangers, de leur création (XIV*[e] *siècle) à nos jours*, 2 vols., Paris 1925–8. For Great Britain, *see* C. J. Jackson, *English Goldsmiths and their Marks*, London 1921, reprinted 1948. For the Byzantine Empire, *see* E. C. Dodd, *Byzantine Silver Stamps*, Washington, D.C. 1961. For the Netherlands, *see* bibl. in M. H. Gans & Th. M. Duyvené de Wit-Klinkhamer, *Dutch Silver*, London 1961. For Italy, *see* C. G. Bulgari, *Argentieri gemmare orafi d'Italia*, Rome 1958 (in course of publication).

Hamadan carpets, *see* PERSIAN CARPETS.

Hamburg potteries A group of handsome pieces of faience bearing dates ranging from 1624 to 1668 and including several decorated with the arms of the city of Hamburg (or of local families) are generally thought to have been made there, though there is no other evidence for the existence of a factory in the city. They include large jugs with unusual pear-shaped bodies and dishes with scalloped edges decorated with a mixture of heraldic and Chinese motifs in a strong blue and, occasionally, with touches of yellow, green or red, on a white ground which is often crazed. A pottery founded in the 1720s specialized in the production of stoves which are among the best of their time, first made up of blue and white tiles in the Dutch manner but subsequently provided with moulded framework.

Lit: K. Hüseler, *Deutsche Fayencen*, Stuttgart 1955.

Hammann, Johann Wolfgang, *see* WALLENDORF PORCELAIN FACTORY.

Han The Chinese dynasty which flourished from 206 B.C. to 220 A.D., following the turbulent period of the Ch'in emperors (221–206 B.C.) which marked the most violent break in the history of Chinese art and civilization. Though little was produced as aesthetically satisfying as the bronzes of the SHANG-YIN and CHOU dynasties (to which Han artists appear to have looked back with reverent nostalgia) and although the whole period was politically disturbed, firm foundations were laid for the subsequent development of Chinese art. The most remarkable products of the period are carved reliefs. In the decorative arts – and the European distinction between them and the 'major' arts does not obtain in China – great advances were made in the art of lacquer, textile weaving and ceramics. Lacquer boxes, bowls and table tops decorated with foliate scrolls of an exquisite delicacy and animals which combine an extraordinary elegance with vitality, reveal that the art of lacquer painting had already reached perfection. Polychrome silks were woven by complex techniques in an astonishingly wide range of patterns, both abstract and figured. Bronze and pottery vessels tend to be of similar rather simple squat shapes. The best pottery was made in the Yüeh district of Chekiang and includes some of the first perfect examples of high-fired lead glazed stoneware, ranging in colour from buff-yellow to dark green. Tomb figures and models of buildings were also made of this pottery.

Han Dynasty pottery tower with iridescent green glaze, 200 B.C.–220 A.D. (William Rockhill Nelson Gallery of Art, Kansas City)

Hanap A large standing-cup and cover of silver, sometimes an ostrich egg or coconut shell mounted in silver. It was used at the dining-table from the C16 to the early C17.

Hanau pottery One of the first and most productive of German faience factories, established near Frankfurt-am-Main by two Dutchmen in 1661 and functioning until 1806. Early wares are rather coarse imitations of DELFT pottery with similar blue and white designs but lacking the glossy Delft *Kwaart* or overglaze. Manganese and other high-temperature colours were occasionally used and a few pieces are painted over in enamel colours and gold, notably by Johann Caspar RIPP between 1708 and 1710. The white ground is often sprinkled with blue dots, a decorative peculiarity of the pottery which was often maintained after *c.*1725 when Dutch style chinoiseries, landscapes and figure subjects were replaced by European floral motifs. Large stoves with moulded Rococo scrollwork were also made in the C18.

Lit: E. Zehr, *Hanauer Fayencen*, Marburg 1913; K. Hüseler, *Deutsche Fayencen*, Stuttgart 1956.

Hancock, Joseph, *see* SHEFFIELD PLATE.

Hancock, Robert (1730–1817). Engraver and mezzotinter important mainly for his engravings used for TRANSFER PRINTING on enamelled metalwares and porcelain. He was born at Burslem in Staffordshire. He appears to have worked at the BATTERSEA ENAMEL FACTORY until it closed in 1756, then at the BOW PORCELAIN FACTORY. In 1757 he began supplying prints (of Frederick the Great) to the WORCESTER PORCELAIN FACTORY of which he was a shareholder 1772–4. In 1775 he was supplying prints to the CAUGHLEY PORCELAIN FACTORY and from this time onwards seems to have worked on a free-lance basis. His prints of rustic scenes are in the manner of mid-C18 English genre painters and have great charm.

Lit: C. Cook, *The Life and Work of Robert Hancock*, London 1948 and *Supplement* 1955.

Hancock, William (b.1794). A leading cabinet-maker in Boston, Mass., from 1820 to 1849, producing well-made furniture in the English REGENCY style. A handsome sofa with cylindrical arms which enclose drawers (Metropolitan Museum, New York) is among the few pieces which bear his label. His brother **Henry Kellam Hancock** was also a cabinet-maker.

Lit: 19th Century America: Furniture and Other Decorative Arts, Exh. Cat., Metropolitan Museum, New York 1970.

Hand cooler An egg-shaped piece of marble, crystal, hard stone, glass or other material held by C18 French ladies to keep the hand cool before offering it to be kissed. Made also in England from the late C18.

Hand warmer A small object with a receptacle for embers or hot water, made in such a way that it could warm without scorching the hand that held it. The commonest type, made in the later Middle Ages in France, Germany and Italy (notably Venice), has the container for the hot substance surrounded by a sphere of pierced and sometimes elaborately decorated metal. In C15 France hand warmers were often made to resemble books and their surfaces were engraved with inscriptions.

Handel Company glasshouse It was started at Meriden, Connecticut, in 1885 by **Philip J. Handel** and by 1900 had a branch factory in New York City as well. A wide variety of decorative glass was

Haniwa terracotta figure, Japan, c.300–600 A.D. *(Musée Guimet, Paris)*

produced, mainly ART NOUVEAU in style, but shades for gas and electric lamps became the staple product. They were similar to but cheaper than TIFFANY lamps. The factory closed in the 1930s.

Haniwa Terracotta cylinders made in Japan, *c.*300–600 A.D., for the external adornment of tombs. The most interesting are surmounted by human heads or whole-length human figures modelled with an astonishing vitality of expression. They appear to represent the warriors, dancers, etc. who took part in funeral ceremonies. *Illustrated previous column.*

Lit: S. Jenyns, *Japanese Pottery*, London 1971; Fumio Miki, *Haniwa*, New York and Tokyo 1974.

Hannong, Charles-François (1669–1739). The founder of an important family of faience and porcelain factory managers and owners. He was of Spanish extraction, born in Maastricht in Holland, began his career as a pipe-maker and in 1721 started the STRASBOURG and Haguenau faience and porcelain factories. He was succeeded at both places by his son **Paul-Antoine** (1700–60) who became proprietor of the FRANKENTHAL PORCELAIN FACTORY from 1755 until 1759. Paul-Antoine's son, **Pierre-Antoine** (1739–after 1794) began as manager at Strasbourg (1760–62), established porcelain factories at VINCENNES (1765), in the Faubourg Saint Denis in PARIS (1771) and at VINOVO (1776). Returning to Alsace he attempted to revive the production of porcelain at Haguenau (1783–4), tried to pay his debts by holding a lottery of porcelain, then established an unsuccessful manufactory of CREAM-COLOURED EARTHENWARE at Verneuil (1786) and ended up as director at SÈVRES in 1794. (For factory mark *see* Strasbourg, p. 888; for illustrations *see* STRASBOURG POTTERY.)

Lit: H. Haug, *Les faïences et porcelaines de Strasbourg*, Strasbourg 1922; J. Terrasson, *Les Hannong et leurs manufactures Strasbourg, Frankenthal*, Paris and Lausanne 1971; *L'oeuvre de Hannong, Faïence de Strasbourg et Haguenau*, Exh. Cat., Strasbourg 1975.

Hanoverian pattern A modern term referring to English table-silver made *c.*1710–75 and characterized by the slightly upturned ends of the stems and the tapering ribs running down the front of the stems.

Hanseatic bowls A C12 and C13 German type of chased and engraved metal (usually bronze) bowl for use with a ewer. They were made in northern Germany from the Lower Rhine to the Baltic, mainly in the Meuse valley, Lorraine and Lower Saxony. But they were not necessarily decorated in the same places as they were made. In form they are round and of varying depth with a narrow but pronounced horizontal rim and without feet. The decoration is confined to the inside which bears engraved scenes from either classical mythology, the Bible or legends of the Saints, or from allegories of Virtues and Vices.

Harache, Pierre (d.1700). One of the first and best of the Huguenot refugee silversmiths who sought asylum from religious persecution in England. He was a native of Rouen and was admitted to the Goldsmiths' Company, London, in 1682. After 1688 he was patronized by William III whose monogram appears on a handsome gold salver by Harache formerly in the English Royal Collection and now belonging to the Duke of Brunswick. He worked in the French style with much use of figurative ornament and cut-card work – e.g. wine-cooler of 1697 belonging to the Barber–Surgeons' Company, London; helmet-shaped ewer of the same year owned by the Vintners' Company; and a pair of exceptionally handsome

P. Harache: two-handled silver cup and cover, 1691 (Temple Newsam House, Leeds)

wine-bottles of 1699 at Eton College. (For his mark *see* p. 893.)

Lit: J. F. Hayward, *Huguenot Silver in England*, London 1959; J. Banister in *Country Life*, 10 June, 1965.

Hardman, John (1811–67). Director of a metal workshop in Birmingham, notable mainly for his collaboration with A. W. N. PUGIN whom he first met in 1837. He came of a Roman Catholic family and was the son of **John Hardman** (d.1844) owner of a button-making factory which he later inherited. In 1837 he, his father and their partner, another button-manufacturer, and the firm of ELKINGTON formed a consortium to exploit the process of electro-gilding. Next year he set up the firm of **John Hardman & Co.** as 'medieval metal-workers' making ecclesiastical and domestic plate to designs by Pugin, advertising a wide range of objects including crucifixes, processional candlesticks, and morses for copes as well as chalices, patens, etc. These were made in a rich Gothic style, either of silver or E.P.N.S., the former often decorated with enamels, gemstones, etc. In this concern his partner was **William Powell** whose son **John Hardman Powell** (1827–95) was Pugin's only pupil. From the 1840s they executed other types of church furnishing including brass work (chandeliers and monuments), embroideries, and stained glass, and carried out wall decorations. They were also employed at the Houses of Parliament. After Pugin's death in 1852 John Hardman Powell succeeded him as chief designer. Gothic Revival metalwork was also made to the designs of other architects, notably W. BURGES. In the later C19 the firm gradually ceased to execute anything but stained glass which it still produces under the name of 'John Hardman Studios'.

John Hardman & Co.: silver teapot designed by John Hardman Powell, Birmingham, 1861–2 (Victoria & Albert Museum)

Lit: S. Bury in *The Connoisseur* CLXV (1967), pp. 29–35; *Victorian Church Art*, Exh. Cat., Victoria & Albert Museum, London 1971.

Hardoy chair, *see* CHAIR.

Hard-paste porcelain, *see* PORCELAIN.

Harewood A veneer of SYCAMORE WOOD dyed a brownish-grey colour, much used for the decoration of English furniture in the late C18.

Harleian bindings A dignified type of English C18 bookbinding in the manner of those made for the library of Robert and Edward Harley (1661–1724 and 1689–1741), the first and second Earls of Oxford, by various binders including **Thomas Elliott** and **Christopher Chapman.** Harleian bindings are usually of red Morocco decorated with broad ROLL borders or borders with a repeat pattern made with single tools, and usually with a large central ornament, often of lozenge shape.

Harrachov glasshouse One of the most important Bohemian glass factories. It was founded in 1712 at Nový Svět (Neuwelt) and gradually grew in size: by 1803 it was employing a staff which included 100 cutters. From 1808 it was run by **Johan Pohl** (1769–1850) who increased its size and improved the quality of products, making it a leading producer of the most fashionable types of glass in the BIEDERMEIER style. In 1887 it was acquired by **Josef Riedl** who already owned a flourishing glasshouse at Polubný which had specialized in making glass to be decorated elsewhere. Under his rule it was further expanded and soon became one of the leading producers of luxury glass in Europe.

Harrison, John, *see* BENNINGTON POTTERY & PORCELAIN FACTORY.

Hartley, William, *see* LEEDS POTTERY.

Hash-dish A type of c18–c19 English silver or plated tureen, circular with straight sides and a close-fitting cover, sometimes set on a frame which incorporates a spirit lamp.

Hasp A contrivance usually of leather or metal for fastening the door of a cupboard, the lid of a chest, the boards of a bound book, etc.

Hauer or **Hoyer, Bonaventura Gottlieb** (1710–82). He decorated porcelain at MEISSEN from 1724 onwards.

Haufenbecher or **setzbecher** Late c16 and early c17 German type of beaker that could be fitted into another like a picnic cup: usually of silver: popularized by Virgil SOLIS.

Haupt, Georg (1741–84). Swedish furniture-maker born in Stockholm, the son of a Nuremberg carpenter. Until 1763 he was apprenticed in Germany. Later he worked in Holland and then in Paris for several years, perhaps for Simon OEBEN. A writing desk at the Institut Géographique in Paris is inscribed as having been made by him in 1767. He then went to London and is recorded as having executed a table to a design by Sir William Chambers in 1769. He returned to Stockholm the same year. In 1770 he made a magnificent LOUIS XVI STYLE desk for Gustav III, now in the Royal Palace, Stockholm. He also made (1773–4) a splendid cabinet for a mineralogical collection, given by Gustav III to the Prince de Condé and now in the Musée Condé at Chantilly.

Lit: M. Lagerquist, *Georg Haupt, ébéniste du Roi*, Stockholm 1952; M. Lagerquist & M. Jarry in *Revue de l'Art Français*, 1953; R. de Broglie in *Gazette des Beaux-Arts*, 1963, pp. 2–16.

G. Haupt: cabinet for mineralogical specimens, 1774 (Musée Condé, Chantilly)

Hauré, Jean (*fl.*1774–96). French sculptor, pupil of Jean-Baptiste II Lemoyne and *entrepreneur des Meubles de la Couronne*, he supervised much of the best furniture made for the Crown from 1784 until the Revolution, notably that by BENEMAN and SENÉ. He also provided designs and models for royal furniture, e.g. Louis XVI's bed at St Cloud. His wax model for a bed for Thierry de Ville d'Avray's apartment at the Paris Garde Meuble is now in the Museum of Fine Arts, Boston.

Lit: F. J. B. Watson, *The Wrightsman Collection: Furniture*, New York 1966.

Hausmaler (German: home painter). A free-lance artist decorating faience or porcelain independent of factory supervision and in his own studio – but limiting himself, necessarily, to work in ENAMEL COLOURS and gilt. A few pieces of NUREMBERG faience were painted by such artists in the later c17. In the early c18 Augsburg became an important centre for this work, sometimes executed by silversmiths skilled in enamelling. From *c.*1725 faience was normally factory-decorated and the *Hausmaler* worked only on porcelain. The factories occasionally attempted to discourage the *Hausmaler* by refusing to sell undecorated wares or by releasing only imperfect or outmoded pieces. But some of the finest decorations on German c18 ceramics are the work of *Hausmaler*, notably J. K. W. ANREITER VON ZIRNFELD, J. AUFENWERTH, I. BOTTENGRUBER, A. O. E. VON DEM BUSCH, F. J. FERNER, G. F. GREBNER, J. HEEL, J. G. HEINTZE, J. HELCHIS,

F. F. MAYER, J. F. METZSCH, D. PREISSLER, W. RÖSSLER, J. SCHAPER, B. SEUTER, F. A. SIEBEL, C. F. VON WOLFSBURG. Some independent Dutch enamellers decorated MEISSEN, Chinese and Japanese porcelain and even STAFFORDSHIRE stoneware. Such decorations seem to have been little executed in France. In England there were several porcelain-decorating studios of the German type, notably those of W. ABSOLON, T. BAXTER, W. DUESBURY, J. GILES and J. RANDALL.

Lit: G. E. Pazaurek, *Deutsche Fayence- und Porzellan-Hausmaler*, Leipzig 1925.

Haute lisse, *see* HIGH-WARP TAPESTRY.

Haviland porcelain factories Two prominent Franco-American concerns producing household wares. **David Haviland** (1814–79) began as a retailer in New York in 1839 and in 1842 went to France where he founded, at LIMOGES, the factory of Haviland et Cie., making porcelain mainly for export to the U.S.A., including large dinner services for the White House in 1861 and 1880. Most products were in the usual range of C19 styles. In 1873 the firm set up a design and decorating studio at Auteuil near Paris. In 1881 it moved to Paris. BRACQUEMOND, DAMMOUSE and CHAPLET were employed, the latter from 1875. Chaplet's designs were much influenced by Japanese ceramics. The *atelier Haviland* produced some of the best French art pottery of the time. **Charles Field Haviland** (b.1842), the son of David's elder brother **Robert** (b.1803, founder of the firm of R. B. Haviland & Company in Augusta, Georgia), was taken to Limoges as a child, began working in his uncle's factory, married into the Alluaud family of Limoges and took over their large factory. In 1870 he founded the firm of Charles Field Haviland in New York.

Lit: Hans-Jorgen Heuser in *Keramos* 62 (1973), pp. 3–33; *Céramique impressioniste, l'atelier Haviland de Paris-Auteuil 1873–1882*, Exh. Cat., Bibliothèque Forney, Paris 1974–5.

Hawthorn vase An obsolete name for a large *famille noir* or *famille verte* vase decorated with prunus branches.

Haystack An Irish pewter tavern measure of conical form sometimes called a haycock.

Heal, Sir Ambrose (1872–1959). English furniture designer. He transformed his father's furniture business in London into one of the most progressive in England, issuing his first catalogue of Heal's Plain Oak Furniture in 1898. His simple, solid

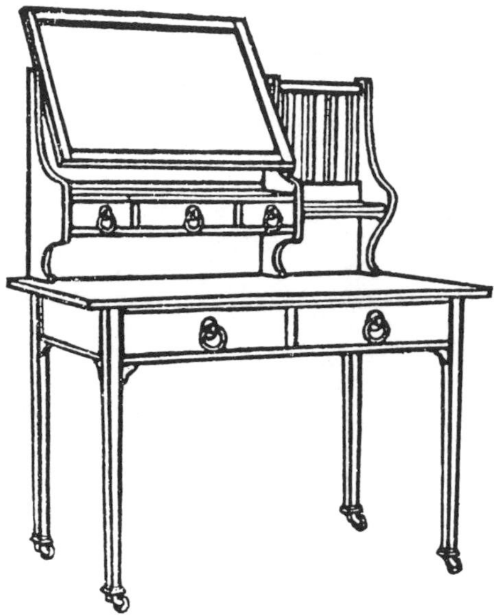

Heal & Son: dressing-table from their Simple Bedroom Furniture, *London 1899*

furniture, usually of lightly fumed and waxed oak and sometimes adorned with inset panels of pewter or ebony, has an attractively fresh quality reminiscent of VOYSEY. He also designed, from *c.*1900 onwards, much well-mannered if seldom very exciting oak furniture which provided middle-class homes with an inexpensive alternative to flimsy Reproduction Furniture and costly Arts and Crafts pieces. More recently the firm of Heal's has become one of the leading London importers and retailers of the best modern furniture and domestic fittings. Heal's Fabrics have produced a wide range of well-designed prints at exceptionally low prices.

Lit: David Joel, *Furniture Design Set Free*, London 1969.

Heath, John He and his brother **Christopher** were among the owners of the COCKPIT HILL POTTERY and he was later in partnership with William

DUESBURY at Derby (from 1756) and Chelsea (from 1770). He went bankrupt in 1780.

Heaton, Clement J. (1861–1940). English designer of stained glass and also a metal-worker and enameller. He was the son of **Clement Heaton** (1824–82) co-founder of the firm of stained glass manufacturers and general decorators called **Heaton, Butler & Bayne** which carried out many important ecclesiastical commissions, often in collaboration with the architect Sir Arthur Blomfield (e.g. in the chapel of Trinity College, Cambridge, and in Sandringham Paris Church, Norfolk). After beginning in his father's firm, he branched out on his own, working in metals (bronze decorations for the Law Courts at Victoria, Australia) and acquiring the technique of *cloisonné* enamelling (he was the only Englishman of his day to do so). He was closely associated with A. MACKMURDO who provided him with designs for enamel, and with the Century Guild for whom he provided designs. And he established his own firm, **Heaton's Cloisonné Mosaics Ltd.**, producing plaques, book-covers, lamps, etc. In 1893 he emigrated to Switzerland, settling at Neuchâtel where he executed elaborate *cloisonné* mosaics, to the design of Paul Robert, to decorate the monumental staircase of the Musée des Beaux Arts. Other works in Switzerland include glass mosaics for the façade of the historical museum, Berne, decorations in the Law Courts in Lausanne, stained glass windows for churches in Neuchâtel and Chaux-les-Fonds, etc. He also designed embossed wallpapers made by a process which he patented. In 1912 he settled in the U.S. where he was mainly engaged in the design of stained glass windows for churches, latterly in collaboration with his son **Maurice** (b.1900), who was responsible for windows in the Rockefeller Center, New York, and the Court Rooms of the Bay County Building in Bay City. Maurice Heaton developed a new technique for enamelling on glass in 1947.

Lit: C. H. Walker in *American Architect*, September 1929; *Craft Horizons* XIV, May 1954, pp. 10–14.

Hedwig glasses A famous group of C11–C12 Egyptian glass beaker-shaped vessels boldly cut in cameo relief of which only 12 are known (British Museum, Rijksmuseum Amsterdam, etc.). Most of them were preserved in cathedral treasuries as reliquaries, some having C13 metal mounts. The type piece, in the Breslau Museum, is decorated with a Tree of Life design and is traditionally said to have belonged to St Hedwig who died in 1243.

Lit: R. Schmidt in *Jahrbuch des Schlesischen Museums für Kunstgewerbe und Altertümer*, N.F. VI (1912), p. 53ff.

Heel, Johann (1637–1709). Goldsmith, enameller, glass engraver, ornamentalist and HAUSMALER born and trained in Augsburg and working from 1668 in Nuremberg. His ornamental designs (e.g. a series entitled *Johann Heels Goldschmidts-Büchlein* n.d.) are in a rich Baroque style. Somewhat similar engravings of birds and fruit on ruby glass vessels and paintings on faience signed with the initials I.H. are generally attributed to him.

Lit: W. B. Honey in *Burlington Magazine* LX (1932), p. 139.

Heemskerk, William Jacobsz van (1613–92). Cloth-merchant, dramatist and poet of Leiden who was also a proficient amateur glass engraver. He decorated several bottles and other pieces of glass with inscriptions and elaborate calligraphic scrolls from 1648. Examples of his work are in the 'De Lakenhal' museum, Leiden, British Museum and the Victoria & Albert Museum.

Lit: J. G. van Gelder in *Oud Holland* LVII (1940), pp. 181–91.

Heider, Maximilian von (b.1839). German chemist and potter who established in the late C19 at Schongau am Lech the firm of **Max von Heider & Söhne**, the sons being **Hans** (1867–1952), **Fritz** (b.1868) and **Rudolph** (b.1870). The pottery specialized in stoneware sometimes with the heads of birds or masks in relief, covered with lustre or free-flowing coloured glazes. Faience tiles, wall fountains and chimney-pieces were also made. Products were shown at several international exhibitions – Paris 1900, Dresden 1901, Turin 1902, St Louis 1904, etc. From 1907 he taught at the Kunstgewerbeschule in Magdeburg. Of the sons, Rudolph was also a sculptor and the other two painters and all three of them taught in art schools.

Lit: R. Borrmann, *Moderne Keramik*, Leipzig 1902.

Heinrici, Johann Martin (1711–86). German painter and leading master of PIQUÉ work. He began as a porcelain painter at MEISSEN (1741–56), went to FRANKENTHAL during the Seven Years War, and decorated numerous snuff-boxes with elegant Rococo motifs in gold and mother-of-pearl inlay. He returned to Dresden as court painter in 1763 and was also engaged as a colour and porcelain chemist at MEISSEN from 1764.

Lit: G. E. Pazaurek, *Deutsche Fayence- und Porzellan-Hausmaler*, Leipzig 1925.

Heintze, Johann Georg (b.*c.*1707). He was a porcelain painter at Meissen where he trained under J. G. HEROLD from 1720 onwards, becoming a journeyman in 1725 and receiving a fixed monthly salary from 1733 onwards. In 1745 he retired and in 1748 was imprisoned on suspicion of being a HAUSMALER. In 1749 he escaped, was recaptured at Prague, but escaped again and reached Vienna and eventually Berlin. His decorations include landscapes, harbour scenes, battle scenes, etc. They are sometimes confused with those of C. F. HEROLD.

Lit: G. E. Pazaurek, *Deutsche Fayence- und Porzellan-Hausmaler*, Leipzig 1925.

Helchis, Jacobus (*fl.*1730–49). Porcelain decorator, possibly a HAUSMALER, decorating products of VIENNA PORCELAIN FACTORY with great delicacy in an unusual black monochrome style occasionally relieved with touches of yellow and pink. His masterpiece is a bowl and cover painted on the sides with a rocky landscape (British Museum). He also decorated a large table service (dispersed) each piece of which is painted with a landscape. He may also have worked in polychrome. He was employed as an arcanist at a very short-lived porcelain factory at Neudock in Bavaria in 1747–9.

Lit: Apollo XLVIII (October 1948), pp. 79–82.

Hellenistic pottery (*c.*300–*c.*100 B.C.) is notable for its relief decoration which gradually superseded the painted decoration usual in GREEK POTTERY. This relief work is imitated from embossed metalwares and in some cases (e.g. Calene bowls) the same moulds seem to have been used. The reliefs were moulded either with the vase itself or separately and afterwards attached to a wheel-thrown vase. The latter method was used in so-called Pergamene ware of *c.*200–100 B.C., the former in so-called Megarian ware of *c.*100 B.C. The Megarian bowls were not pressed or poured in moulds but combined wheel-work with moulding. A mould with impressed decorations on its inner side was fitted on a jigger (i.e. a wheel with a revolving head on which a mould could be fitted) and inside the clay was spun to form the bowl. When completed the decorations were produced on the exterior of the bowl by pressing the fingers into the hollows of the mould and then smoothing over when the bowl was again revolving. Finishing touches could be given after removal from the mould. The surface was covered with a glaze which became black in a reducing fire.

Lit: Schaefer, *Hellenistische Keramik aus Pergamon*, Berlin 1968.

Hellot, Jean, *see* SÈVRES (or VINCENNES-SÈVRES) PORCELAIN FACTORY.

Helmet ewer A type of ewer popular from the early C16 to the early C18 with an ovoid body on a low stem, a scrolled handle and mouth reminiscent of an inverted Roman helmet, made in metalwork at Nuremberg and elsewhere and also in faience at Rouen and elsewhere. A later type omitted the ovoid body and perhaps more closely resembles an upturned Roman helmet.

Helmhack, Abraham (1654–1724). German HAUSMALER, glass painter, enameller and engraver born in Ratisbon. He executed *Schwarzlot* decorations on glass. Four large glass discs painted around their edges with a sequence of religious scenes in unfired oil colours, to serve as magic lantern slides, are in the Victoria and Albert Museum. But he is best known for his paintings, usually of religious subjects in a Baroque style, on tin-glazed earthenware, e.g. an *Eghalskrug* of *c.*1690 in Germansiches Museum, Nuremberg.

Lit: K. Pilz in *Keramos* 2 (1958), pp. 23–33.

Heming, Thomas (*fl.*1745–82). Although famous in his own day, Heming is now a shadowy figure. He is first recorded in 1745 when he registered his mark at Goldsmiths' Hall, London. In 1760 he became royal goldsmith to George III. His ecclesiastical plate is very plain (communion vessels for royal chapel at Windsor Castle; Trinity Church, New York; Christchurch, Williamsburg, Virginia). More characteristic are his Rococo silver-gilt toilet sets with elegantly modelled and chased floral, shell and wave ornament on each piece, notably that made for Princess Caroline Matilda in 1766 (Kunstindustrimuseum, Copenhagen). From 1773 to 1781 **George Heming,** presumably his son, was working at Thomas Heming's Bond Street shop in partnership with **William Chawner.** In 1775 they received a commission from Catherine the Great for two dinner services and two dessert services. They are said to have employed some 400 craftsmen on this commission. (The vast Orloff service had just been completed for Catherine the Great by ROETTIERS). Thirty-eight candelabra by Thomas Heming are also recorded to have been in the Russian Imperial collection. (For his mark *see* p. 893.)

Lit: A. G. Grimwade in *The Connoisseur* 1956, vol. cxxxvii, pp. 175–8.

T. Heming, silver vine-wreathed cup, 1753 (David H. H. Felix Collection, Philadelphia)

Hennell, David (1712–85). London silversmith and the founder of a dynasty which still survives trading under the name of **Robert George Hennell.** David Hennell registered his first mark in 1736 and his son **Robert** (1741–1811) registered a joint mark with him in 1763. David, who retired in 1772, made good, simple domestic plate, sometimes with discreet Rococo ornament. Robert made handsome Adam style pieces. His sons **David** (b.1767) and **Samuel** (1778–1837) worked together, using joint marks, until 1802 when David retired leaving his father and Samuel in partnership. After his father's death Samuel took **John Terry** into partnership for two years, 1814–16. (For David I's mark *see* p. 894.)

David Hennell I's grandson **Robert** (b.1769) went into partnership with **H. Nutting** in 1809 but this broke up after a year and in 1809 Robert registered his own mark. He retired in 1833 and was succeeded by his son **Robert** (1794–1868) and eventually by his grandson **Robert** (*c.*1826–92).

Lit: P. Hennell, 'The Hennells Identified' in *The Connoisseur*, December 1955, pp. 260–66.

Henningsen, Poul (b.1894). Danish industrial designer, architect and writer. As editor of *Kritisk Revy* (1926–8) he launched an attack against the meretricious artiness of the Danish ceramic and furniture industries, exhorting their designers: 'Think a little and consider your obligations to make things for the delight of your fellow men in their daily life! Throw away your artists' berets and bow-ties and get into overalls. Down with artistic pretentiousness! Simply make things which are fit for use: that is enough to keep you busy, and you will sell vast quantities and make lots of money.' This is similar in tone to BAUHAUS propaganda but he and his fellow Danes (e.g. KLINT), unlike the Germans, believed in retaining traditional forms whenever possible, i.e. whenever functional: hence their immediate and considerable commercial success. Henningsen's best designs have been for light fittings (made by Poulsen & Co. Copenhagen), beginning with the 'PH Shade' for a table lamp of 1924 and followed by several similar shades for table and hanging lamps, still in commercial production. Basically his shades all consist of three or more concentrically arranged transparent and opaque saucer-shaped members, designed to transmit, diffuse and reflect the beam of light. Elegant and functional, they are among the best examples of industrial design.

Henri Deux ware Pottery produced at SAINT-PORCHAIRE in the C16 and extensively imitated and faked in the C19, when this name was applied to it.

Hentschel, Julius Konrad, *see* MEISSEN PORCELAIN FACTORY.

Hepplewhite, George (d.1786). Hepplewhite became famous two years after his death with the publication of his book of designs, *The Cabinet-maker and Upholsterer's Guide* (1788, revised 1789 and again in 1794). During his lifetime he seems to have been less successful and well-known as a cabinet-maker than many of his contemporaries. He began as an apprentice to GILLOWS in Lancaster, settling in London by about 1760. He may never have had a workshop of his own. Not a single piece of furniture by him has been identified. But his posthumous book epitomized the Neo-Classical style of 1780–85 and his name soon became a household word, as famous as that of SHERATON with which it is often bracketed. The *Guide* contains some three hundred designs, covering all types of furniture, and illustrates admirably the application of ADAM's principle of uniting elegance and utility. It was very widely used as a trade catalogue, especially by 'countrymen and artizans' for whom it was particularly intended. As a result much Hepplewhite furniture is of country origin and was probably made some years after the style had gone out of fashion in London. Hepplewhite also contributed designs to the *Cabinet-makers' Book of Prices* (1788) most of which is by THOMAS SHEARER.

The Hepplewhite style was not an original invention. The *Guide* merely codified the various types of furniture in fashion during the last decade of Hepplewhite's life, slightly modifying and strengthening them to suit the technical abilities and requirements of ordinary cabinet-makers. Hepplewhite furniture is eminently simple, rational and yet extremely elegant and refined. It is lightly but strongly constructed, often in satinwood inlaid with other exotic woods. Characteristic of the style are bow- and serpentine-fronted chests of drawers and oval, heart-shaped and, above all, shield-back chairs, usually with straight and tapered legs. (Hepplewhite did not, as is sometimes said, invent the shield-back chair.) Also typical of the style are the Prince of Wales feathers and wheat-ears with which the central splat of shield-back and other chairs are decorated.

Lit: C. Musgrave, *Adam and Hepplewhite Furniture,* London 1966.

A. Hepplewhite: design for a worktable from The Cabinet-maker and Upholsterer's Guide, *London 1789*

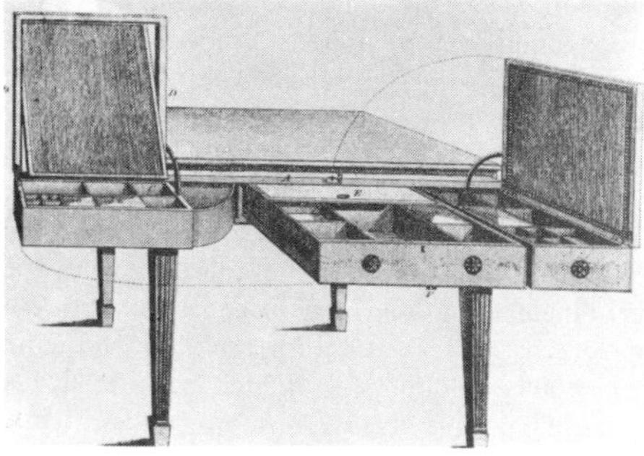

Herat carpets, *see* PERSIAN CARPETS.

Herculaneum pottery, *see* LIVERPOOL POTTERIES AND PORCELAIN FACTORIES.

Hereke carpets, *see* TURKISH CARPETS.

Herend pottery and porcelain factory A Hungarian factory founded in 1838 by **Moritz Fischer** (d.1880), it produced domestic and ornamental wares in all the European historical styles as well as the oriental. They were very showy and elaborate, eminently suitable for presentation and for royal gifts for which the factory was much patronized. It continues to flourish as a State concern.

Lit: K. Csany, *Geschichte der ungarischen Keramik, der Porzellane und ihre Marken,* Budapest 1954.

Herez carpets, *see* PERSIAN CARPETS.

Herm A three-quarter length figure on a pedestal,

an architectural device used on furniture and metalwork mainly in the Renaissance and Baroque periods.

Herman Miller, Inc. Furniture makers in Zeeland, Michigan. Its current emphasis on well-designed modern furniture stems largely from **George Nelson,** the Director of Design. Nelson introduced EAMES who, acting as a consultant, designed several types of chairs for the firm, including the now-famous stacking chair in moulded plastic, as well as an upholstered lounge chair with a moulded plywood shell. Among the more recent products of the company is the 'Action Office', a suite of elegant, compactly designed desks, cabinet units, message centres and conference tables in combinations of wood and plastic with die-cast polished aluminium legs. The designs were executed by the Nelson Office in collaboration with the staff of the Miller organization. A later development of the concept is a series of library furnishings – reading desks and tables, individual carrels – which incorporate many of the features of the Action Office.

Herold (or **Heroldt**), **Christian Friedrich** (*c.*1700–*c.*1779). German porcelain painter. He seems to have begun by working in Berlin for Alexander Fromery, a maker of enamel boxes. From 1725 to 1777 he was employed as a painter at the MEISSEN PORCELAIN FACTORY though he continued to decorate enamel boxes for Fromery and in 1763 was prosecuted for working as a HAUSMALER. A few signed paintings, possibly among those executed on his own account, are recorded (e.g. cup and saucer dated 1750 in the British Museum) and many others have been attributed to him on stylistic grounds. At the Meissen factory he worked first as a painter of chinoiseries and was probably responsible for those painted in black or red outline and washed with colour. But he is known mainly for his harbour scenes with rather dark foreground figures which enhance the atmospheric effect. His relationship to J. G. HEROLD has not been established but they were possibly cousins.

Lit: G. E. Pazaurek, *Meissener Porzellanmalerei des 18 Jahrhunderts,* Stuttgart 1929; M. Hornig-Sutter in *Keramos* 57 (1972), pp. 11–25.

Herold (or **Höroldt**), **Johann Gregor** (1696–1775). Outstanding German porcelain painter largely responsible for the early success of the MEISSEN factory (especially vases and table wares) which he joined as chief painter in 1720 after spending a year in Vienna where he learned the enamel technique. He was hired, and specially praised, for his ability to produce blue, red and other colours that acquired a faultless surface texture during firing. In 1723 he was named Court painter and from 1731 *Hofkommissar* with a fixed salary. He developed a distinctive style for chinoiserie subjects with fantastic spidery figures and no less fantastic buildings and trees. He also seems to have introduced other new types of decoration, European landscapes (*c.*1722), harbour scenes (*c.*1730), European flowers and birds in a naturalistic style (*c.*1737). He signed few pieces but many have been attributed to him from their similarity with etchings which he

C. F. Herold: decoration on a Meissen porcelain cup and saucer, signed and dated 1750 (British Museum)

J. G. Herold (or Höroldt): decoration on a Meissen porcelain vase, signed and dated 1726 (Porzellansammlung, Dresden)

signed. It is probable that he was less frequently engaged in painting than in providing designs and supervising the painting studios. Significantly, perhaps, a vase formerly in the Royal Palace at Dresden (destroyed in World War II) was inscribed: *Johann Gregorius Höroldt inven.* without the usual *fecit.* With the growing influence of J. J. KÄNDLER at Meissen, his authority declined and at the beginning of the Seven Years War, in 1756, he fled to Frankfurt-am-Main, returning in 1763 and retiring in 1765.

Lit: A. Schönberger, *Meissner Porzellan mit Höroldt Malerei,* Munich 1955; A. Klein in *Keramos* 50 (1970), pp. 63–70.

Heron, Robert Methven, *see* WEMYSS WARE.

Herrebøe pottery The most important faience factory in Norway, founded near Friedrichshald in 1757 but not functioning on a large scale until 1762. It is notable mainly for its blue-and-white (rarely polychrome) table-wares decorated in the Rococo style either with figures or (more successfully) abstract motifs of exuberant vitality and unabashed asymmetricality. Some of the best are signed with the initials HF, probably for **Heinrich Christian Friedrich Hosenfeller** (1722–1801) a painter who is known to have worked here. The production of faience seems to have ceased in 1772 and the factory closed in 1778. (For factory mark *see* p. 884.)

Lit: I. Opstad, *Herrebøe Fajance Fabrique,* Borregaard 1959; L. Opstad in *Keramos* 58 (1972), pp. 3–14.

Herrengrund cup A type of C16 and especially C17 copper vessel made as a show-piece, usually decorated with chased, engraved or enamelled ornament or set with precious stones. Sometimes little moulded figures were also added, and curious inscriptions, which led to various legends as to the origin of Herrengrund cups and to the erroneous idea that they were made of iron or sheet-iron transformed into copper or coated with copper by the secret powers of Herrengrund water. They were in fact made from cupriferous ore of which there are deposits at Herrengrund, Ligethen and Neusohl in Hungary.

Lit: G. Alexander, *Herrengrunder Kupfergefässe,* Vienna 1927; F. Kirnbauer and R. Steiskal-Paur, *Herrengrunder Kupfergegenstände,* Vienna 1959.

Herter, Christian (1840–1883). Leading member of the New York firm of furniture-makers and interior decorators, **Herter Brothers.** He was born in Stuttgart, and son of a furniture-maker. He went to New York *c.*1860 to join his elder half-brother **Gustav** who had been there since 1848. He worked as a silver designer for TIFFANY, and in 1851 set up a cabinet-making workshop in Mercer Street, New York. The brothers were in partnership by 1866. But in 1868 Christian went back to Europe to study under the decorator Pierre Victor Galland (1822–92) in Paris. Returning to New York in 1870, Christian bought out Gustav who then went back to Germany. He was one of the first U.S. furniture-makers to abandon the usual run of historical styles and produce pieces rather similar to those made contemporaneously in England, with a discreet use of oriental motifs. Marquetry furniture like that made for the rail-

C. Herter: bedroom furniture,
New York, c.1865–80
(Metropolitan Museum of Art, gift of Paul Martini)

road magnate Jay Gould in 1877–82 (now in the Metropolitan Museum, New York) is strongly reminiscent, in its bold simple outlines, of the best English ARTS AND CRAFTS pieces. He employed a large staff of craftsmen and designers, the latter including the architect Charles B. Atwood (1849–95).

Lit: *19th Century America: Furniture and Other Decorative Arts,* Exh. Cat., Metropolitan Museum, New York 1970.

Hess family A family of glass and gem engravers of Bohemian origin, the eldest of whom, **Johann,** fled to Frankfurt-am-Main during the Thirty Years War. His son **Johann Benedikt I** (*c.*1636–74) and grandsons **Sebastian** (d.1731) and **Johann Benedikt II** (1672–1736) decorated glasses rather in the style of such Nuremberg engravers as H. SCHWINGER and G. F. KILLINGER. **Peter** (1709–82), the son of Johann Benedikt II, worked in Cassel from 1746 for the Landgraves of Hesse, executing hard-stone mosaics.

Lit: G. E. Pazaurek in *Der Kunstwanderer,* 1927, p. 95.

Hetsch, Gustav Friedrich, *see* COPENHAGEN PORCELAIN FACTORY.

Hetzendörfer, Simon, *see* AMBERG POTTERY.

Heubach porcelain factory Established in 1822 at Lichte near WALLENDORF in Thuringia and owned by members of the Heubach family. It produced little of interest before the early C20 when the Heubach brothers who then owned it began to produce decorative objects somewhat in the style of those produced by the COPENHAGEN factory. Models were obtained from a number of sculptors – birds and animals from William Krieger (1877–1945), Otto Pech (1882–1950), Sigismund Wernekinck (1877–1921) and Paul Zeiller (1880–1915) and a very coy Pierrette from Wera von Bartels (b.1886).

Lit: O. Pelka, *Keramik der Neuzeit,* Leipzig 1924.

Heurtaut, Nicolas (b.1720). He was a Parisian chair-maker, a contemporary of DELANOIS, and became a *maître* in 1755. He was still active in 1771. His chairs are richly carved and often covered with Gobelins tapestry. Examples survive in the Louvre in Paris and the Metropolitan Museum and Frick Collection in New York.

Lit: S. Eriksen, *Early Neo-Classicism in France,* London 1974.

Hewelke porcelain factory A small concern founded and directed by a porcelain merchant, **Nathaniel Friedrich Hewelke** and his wife **Maria Dorothea,** who after the occupation of Dresden by Prussian troops fled to Italy and settled in Udine in 1757. They obtained from the Venetian government in 1758 a monopoly of porcelain-making for twenty years. They began production at Udine, moved their factory to Venice in 1761 but appear to have closed it and returned to Dresden shortly after 1763. (In 1764 the privileges they enjoyed were granted to the COZZI PORCELAIN FACTORY.) The few products that have been identified are of a hard porcelain, yellowish in tone and covered by a rather matt uneven glaze: they include tea-table wares, prettily painted, and a handsome relief portrait (British Museum).

Lit: A. Lane, *Italian Porcelain*, London 1954.

Hewson, John (1744–1821). English calico printer who, with the encouragement of Benjamin Franklin, emigrated to America and founded a factory at Philadelphia before 1774. He sided with the Colonials in the War of Independence and his factory was burnt down, but he re-established it in partnership with an English designer and engraver, **William Lang**, in 1779. Products included handkerchiefs with George Washington on horseback as the central decorative motif and some very elegant chintz counterpanes with Indian style floral motifs. (Philadelphia Museum.)

Lit: F. M. Montgomery, *Printed Textiles, English & American Cottons & Linens, 1700–1850, ...* London 1970.

Heylyn, Edward, *see* BOW PORCELAIN FACTORY.

Highboy A uniquely American variant of the English TALLBOY, introduced *c.*1700 and especially popular in Philadelphia. It is a chest-of-drawers on either a low stand or a table-like base fitted with drawers. The latter was also made separately and known as a 'lowboy'. Highboys were produced throughout the C18, the finer examples having cabriole legs, broken pediments and finials. The term 'highboy' is C19. *Illustrated next column.*

Highboy, Philadelphia, c18 (William Rockhill Nelson Gallery of Art, Kansas City)

High-temperature colours Pigments which, when applied to earthenware, withstand the high temperature necessary to unite them with a tin-glaze and fuse it to the surface of the clay. They are limited to shades of green, derived from copper oxide, blue from cobalt, purple from manganese, yellow from antimony, and orange from iron. Most TIN-GLAZED EARTHENWARE was decorated with these colours until the C18 when *petit feu* or ENAMEL COLOURS came into general use.

High-warp tapestry (*Haute Lisse*). A tapestry woven on a loom with the warp threads wound on rollers arranged vertically one above the other. The weaver transfers the main outlines of the CARTOON to the warp threads, referring to it for details of design and colour as the work proceeds with the weft. The method is slower and much more expensive than that used for LOW-WARP TAPESTRY but usually produces a higher quality textile.

Hill jar A curious type of Chinese jar, made in both bronze and pottery during the Han dynasty, surmounted with a conical cover moulded to resemble hills, sometimes with animals and hunting scenes also. Bronze hill jars have perforated covers for use as censers. Similar jars were made in Europe by Mannerist goldsmiths.

Hill, John, *see* WATERFORD GLASSHOUSE.

Hillebrand, Friedrich (d.1608). He was the most prominent of a family of goldsmiths and engravers at Nuremberg. He became a *Meister* in 1580. He specialized in vessels in the form of birds (swans, parrots, etc.) decorated with mother-of-pearl inlay

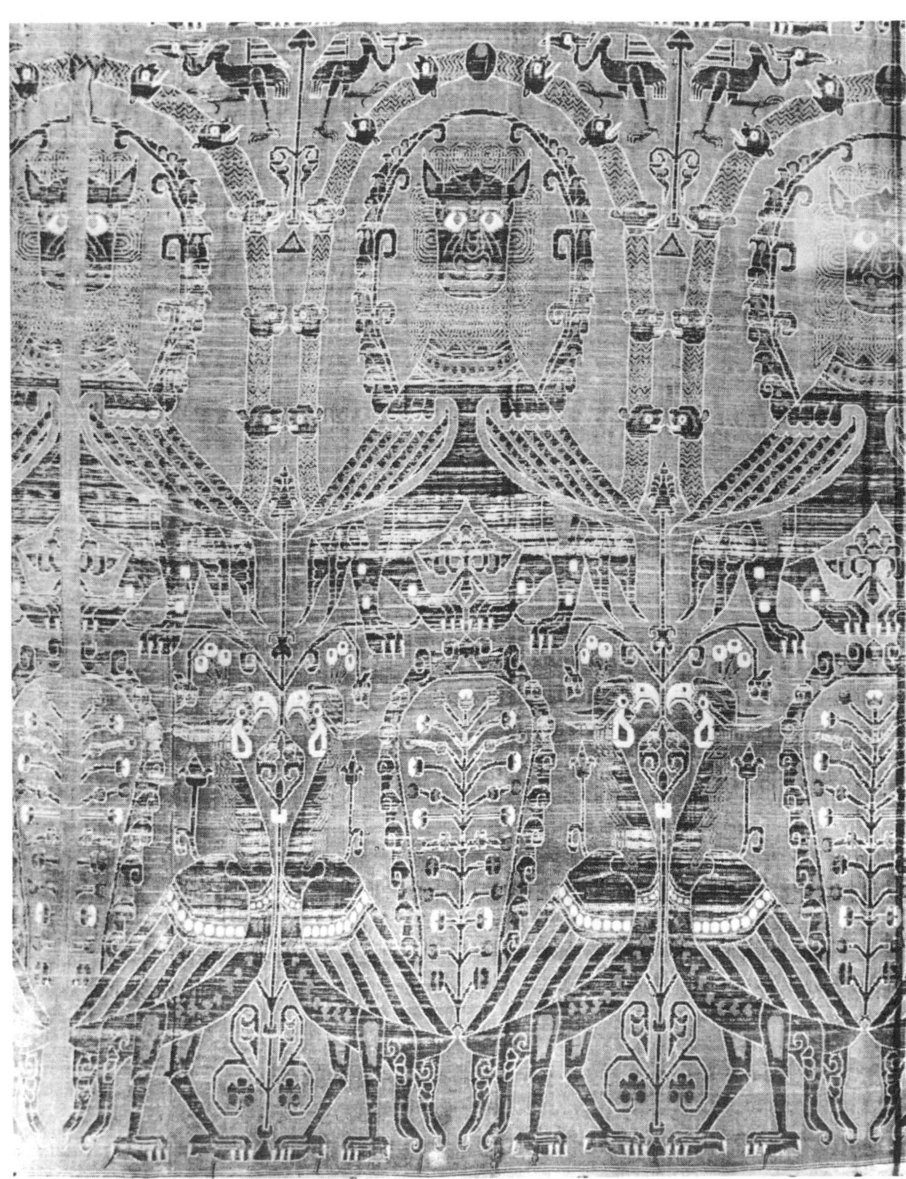

Hispano-Moresque silk, c12 (Museo, Arqueológico, Vich)

and often incorporating nautilus shells. Examples are in the Grünes Gewolbe at Dresden.

Hipped knee A type of CABRIOLE chair-leg with carved ornament which extends from the knee to the seat rail. It is found from the early C18 onwards.

Hirado wares A type of Japanese porcelain made at Mikawachi near ARITA from the mid C17 and exported to Europe from the port of Hirado. It is similar to the blue-and-white ware of Arita. In the early C19 a distinctive purplish blue was adopted for the underglaze decorations which often represent children at play. The best date from 1750–1830.

Lit: S. Jenyns, *Japanese Porcelain*, London 1965.

Hiramé Japanese lacquer decorated with evenly but widely spaced pieces of gold or silver leaf.

Hirschvogel, Augustin (1503–53). Versatile Nuremberg craftsman who was painting Italianate tin-glazed earthenware 1531–6 and also practised as an engraver, glasspainter, medallist and cartographer. The design of jugs shaped like owls, EULENKRUG, has been attributed to him.

Lit: K. Schwartz, *Augustin Hirschvogel*, Berlin 1917; W. B. Honey in *Burlington Magazine* LXIX (1936), pp. 111–119.

Hispano-Moresque silks Sericulture and the art of silk weaving were introduced into Spain by the Arabs in the early c8 and soon raw silk and woven fabrics were being exported in quantity, even to the E. Mediterranean. By the C10 the most important centre of production was Almeria, but silks were also woven at Malaga, Murcia, Seville, Granada and Saragossa. Very little is known for certain of their appearance. A group of silk textiles of jewel-like colour and with geometrical or arabesque patterns (sometimes animals or birds, rarely human figures, and Kufic inscriptions) has been assigned to Spain but it is difficult to distinguish such textiles from those woven contemporaneously at Baghdad. The C12 burial robe of Robert of Anjou, King of Naples (St Sernin, Toulouse) has been assigned to both Spain and Sicily (see SICILIAN SILKS). It has rows of confronted peacocks and little gazelles, separated by arabesque trees. C15 Spanish silks in the Mudejar style show an individual and very attractive combination of Islamic and Gothic motifs. *Illustrated previous page.*

Lit: O. von Falke, *Kunstgeschichte der Seidenweberei*, Berlin 1913; F. L. May, *Silk Textiles of Spain*, New York 1957.

Hispano-Moresque ware Lustre pottery produced in S. Spain, especially MALAGA and PATERNA from the C13–C15 and VALENCIA from the C15 onwards. The first ceramics of artistic merit to be made in Europe since classical times, they enjoyed wide fame and sparked off the development of Italian MAIOLICA. Vessels included the ALBARELLO. The LUSTRE technique was derived from Persia: decorations include European and Islamic motifs and often Kufic inscriptions (which C16 and later Spanish painters imitated in a meaningless pattern of lines). The various places in which pottery was made are mentioned in numerous contemporary documents and most surviving pieces have been assigned to them.

Lit: M. G. Martí, *Ceramica del Levante español: siglos medievales*, 3 vols., Barcelona 1944–52; A. W. Frothingham, *Lustreware of Spain*, New York 1951; R. Ettinghausen, 'Notes on the Lustre ware of Spain' in *Ars Orientalis* I (1954).

Hispano Moresque lustre ware dish, probably Valencia, C15 (Louvre)

Hitchcock, Lambert (1795–1852). Chairmaker who was born at Cheshire, Connecticut, and set up a factory near Barkhamstead at a place soon named Hitchcockville after him. He produced from *c.*1826 large quantities of chairs marked with the label 'L. Hitchcock, Hitchcockville, Ct' and from 1829 **'Hitchcock, Alford and Company,** Hitchcockville, Conn.' The standard type, called a 'Hitchcock chair' has round turned front legs, square section rear legs continued upwards as the stiles of the back, a turned top-rail with enlarged centre part, a wide slat across the centre of the back and a rush, caned or wooden seat: it was generally painted black and decorated on the top rail and slat across the back with painted or stencilled flowers, fruit, etc., in colours or gilt.

Ho A type of Chinese Bronze Age wine kettle. It may have either three or four legs, a handle decorated with an animal's head, a straight spout and a cover attached by a chain. The HUAI STYLE introduced a variation – cabriole legs, and S-curved spout ending in a beak and an arched handle over the cover.

Hobbs, Brockunier & Company A glasshouse at Wheeling, West Virginia, established under this name in 1863 (previously known as Hobbs, Burnes & Company) producing pressed glass table-wares on a very large scale. In the late 1880s it began to make ornamental vessels of cased glass termed 'peachblow' with a milk-white body covered with a layer of reddish-yellow glass (either glossy or matt) emulating the 'peach bloom' colour found in Chinese K'ANG HSI porcelain.

Lit: A. C. Revi, *Nineteenth Century Glass*, New York 1959.

Hochschnitt The technique of engraving glass in cameo (rather than intaglio) so that the decoration is in relief. A very tricky process first employed in the Middle East and later in C17–C18 Germany, notably by Franz GONDELACH. *Illustrated next column.*

Höchst pottery and porcelain factory Founded near Mainz in 1746 by the porcelain painter A. F. von LÖWENFINCK who left in 1749 and was succeeded by **J. C. Göltz** and **J. F. Clarus.** Faience

Hochschnitt engraved glass goblet, Silesia, late C17 (Victoria & Albert Museum)

wares painted in bright ENAMEL COLOURS included a wide range of useful wares, notably elaborately modelled small tureens and sauce-boats frothing with asymmetrical curves, and large tureens in the form of pug-dogs, turkeys, capercailzies, boars' heads, cabbages, etc. Pear-shaped vases and dishes with thickly scrolled edges moulded with a feather pattern were other specialities. The painting was always of high quality and some particularly fine pieces are signed by **Johannes Zeschinger** (b.1723) who was employed here from *c.*1750 until 1753 when he went to the FÜRSTENBURG PORCELAIN FACTORY. The production of porcelain began in 1750 and faience was abandoned in 1758. Table-wares were initially Rococo in form and decoration – modelled and painted with much scroll-work – gently classicizing from *c.*1765 and more whole-heartedly so from *c.*1780. As on the faience, the standard of painting was high: subjects included genre pieces after prints by Chodowiecki and a series of scenes from a contemporary play (large service of *c.*1772 in Kunstgewerbemuseum, Frankfurt-am-Main). But the most distinguished porcelain products are probably the statuettes. A set of *Commedia dell'Arte* figures from models made by **Simon Feilner** before he left for the Fürstenberg Factory in 1753 are among the earlier pieces. A large centre-piece, 'The Chinese Emperor', with many subsidiary figures of Chinamen are probably the work of **Laurentius Russinger** (chief modeller 1762–6) who was also responsible for several attractive French style figures and groups. Under J. P. MELCHIOR (chief modeller 1767–79) numerous delicately sentimental pastoral figures, some mythological figures (rather in the style of FALCONET) and many biscuit portrait reliefs (including one of Goethe) were produced. After Melchior's departure in 1779 antique style busts and figures were made but the factory concentrated mainly on table-wares until it closed in 1796. Some of the models were later acquired by **Daniel Ernst Müller** of Damm who reproduced them in earthenware from *c.*1830. (For factory mark *see* p. 884.)

Lit: K. Roeder & M. Oppenheim, *Das Höchster Porzellan*, Mainz 1930; H. Jedding in *Keramos* 7 (1960), pp. 1–12; Ludwig Baron Döry, *Höchster Porzellan*, Exh. Cat., Historische Museum, Frankfurt-am-Main 1963.

Höcker, Johann Michael, *see* GROFF, Wilhelm.

Hodgetts, William, *see* STEVENS AND WILLIAMS.

Hoentschel, Georges (1855–1915). French architect, interior decorator and potter. After the death of his close friend J. CARRIÈS in 1894 he carried on his pottery studio making similar wares with matt glazes, but was rather less dependent on Oriental forms. In 1900 he designed the pavilion of the Union Centrale des Arts Décoratifs for the Paris Universal Exhibition of 1900.

Hoffmann, Josef (1870–1956). Austrian architect and designer, a founder of the Vienna SECESSION (1899) and one of the pioneers of functional design. Starting from an Art Nouveau belief in the need for unity between architecture,

Höchst porcelain figures of dancers, perhaps modelled by J. F. von Lück, 1757–8 (Kunstgewerbemuseum, Berlin)

J. Hoffmann: chair, 1903–6
(Musée des Arts Décoratifs, Paris)

decoration and furniture, he developed, partly under the influence of C. R. MACKINTOSH, a stark, functional and distinctly un-Art Nouveau style. He designed furniture, sometimes made by THONET, mainly for his own buildings, notably Palais Stoclet in Brussels (1905–11), but he designed attractively simple metalwork and jewellery to be executed by the WIENER WERKSTÄTTE of which he was a founder in 1903, also some excellent glass, for manufacture by J. & L. Lobmeyr of Vienna. The latter includes some exquisitely fragile tulip-shaped wine and champagne glasses designed in 1920. They are among the most elegant table glasses ever made.

Lit: L. Kleiner, *Josef Hoffmann*, Berlin 1927; *Die Wiener Werkstätte*, Exh. Cat., Österreichisches Museum für angewandte Kunst, Vienna 1967.

Hoffmann, W., *see* LACE.

Hogarth chair, *see* CHAIR.

Holbein, Hans the younger (1497/8–1543). The great German painter, also a notable designer. He designed much goldsmiths' work for Henry VIII in England from 1533 onwards. His designs, of which several survive, were in an elaborate RENAISSANCE STYLE with acanthus leaves, arabesques, human heads, *putti* and a lavish use

H. Holbein the younger: design for a cup
to be given by Henry VIII to Jane Seymour, c.1536
(Ashmolean Museum, Oxford)

of pendant pearls and incrustations of precious stones. The only surviving piece made to his design is a very rich rock-crystal bowl, mounted in enamelled gold and set with pearls and precious stones, of outstandingly elegant form despite its intricacy of ornament (Residenzmuseum, Munich). Still more elaborate was the cup he designed for Henry VIII to give to Jane Seymour, set with thirty sizable diamonds, broken up in 1629 but known from two drawings (British Museum: Ashmolean Museum, Oxford). He also designed stained glass. Ten of his goldsmiths' designs were engraved by Hollar.

Lit: P. Ganz, *Die Handzeichnungen Hans Holbiens d. J.*, Berlin 1937; J. F. Hayward in *Burlington Magazine* C (1958), pp. 120–24; J. F. Hayward in *The Connoisseur* CLIX (1965), pp. 80–84.

Holbein rug, *see* TURKISH CARPETS.

Holitsch pottery A faience factory started in 1743 at Holitsch in Hungary at the request of Francis of Lorraine, consort of Maria Theresa. It continued under Imperial protection until 1827. Wares imitate Strasbourg with ENAMEL COLOUR decorations or imitate CASTELLI WARES with HIGH-TEMPERATURE COLOURS. After 1786 they began producing lead-glazed cream-coloured earthenware. (For factory mark *see* p. 884.)

Lit: J. Kybalorva, *Holitscher Fayence*, Munich 1970.

Hölke, Friedrich, *see* PIRKENHAMMER PORCELAIN FACTORY.

Holland, Henry (1745–1806). English architect employed by the Prince of Wales (later George IV) to enlarge and alter Carlton House, London (1783–5), and to build the original Marine Pavilion at Brighton (1786–7). In this capacity he commissioned, and sometimes designed, much furniture from the leading English and French cabinet-makers, e.g. WEISWEILER. Apart from some elaborate essays in Chinoiserie (Brighton Pavilion) he worked in an enriched, and sometimes rather overweighted, version of the ADAM style which prepared the way for the opulence of the REGENCY style. His influence was considerable, partly through the publication of his designs by SHERATON.

Lit: D. Stroud, *Henry Holland*, London 1968.

Hollins, Samuel (1748–1820). The proprietor of a pottery on the Caulden Canal, Vale Pleasant, Shelton, Staffordshire, making good unglazed dark green and dark red stonewares. He appears to have made this over to his son-in-law **Matthew Mare** *c.*1815. He was also one of the partners in the NEW HALL PORCELAIN FACTORY, from 1782.

Hollow ware Ceramic vases, cups, jugs, etc., as distinct from flat ware (plates and plaques).

Hone, Galyon (*fl.*1492–1526). Glass stainer, who became a master of the Antwerp guild in 1492 and moved to England where he was appointed King's glazier and executed much of the stained glass for King's College Chapel, Cambridge, where he succeeded Bernard FLOWER. The great East window is his, to cartoons by Dirick VELLERT.

Lit: H. G. Wayment, *The Windows of King's College Chapel* (in *Corpus Vitrearum Medii Aeri: Great Britain*, Supplementary vol. I), London 1972.

Honey gilding The main C18 method of applying gilt decorations to ceramics, especially PORCELAIN, much employed at SÈVRES. Gold leaf is ground up in honey, applied with a brush and secured by a light firing. It is durable in use, soft in tone and could be laid on thick enough to permit tooling and chasing. It is superior to size-gilding and lacquer-gilding since it is 'fired'. This technique was one of Europe's first ceramic contributions to the East.

Honiton lace The earliest and best English lace, made *c.*1620–*c.*1725. It is very delicate pillow-

Honiton lace, machine-made net veil, late C19 (Victoria & Albert Museum)

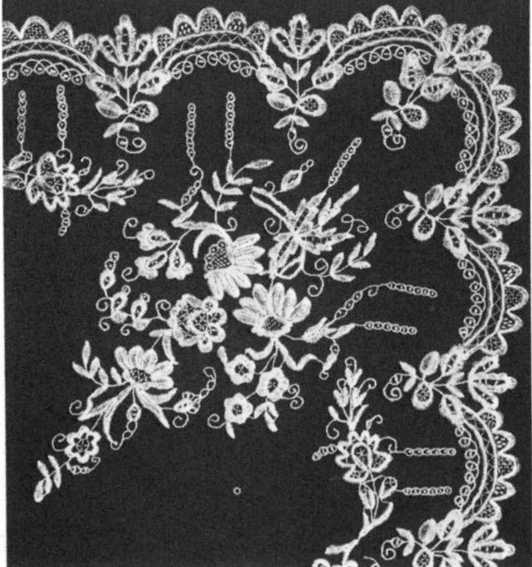

lace made of Antwerp thread on attractive floral designs. Machine-made lace was produced at Honiton from the mid C19 and a little later the craft of hand-made lace was revived. A late-C19 speciality was Devonia lace worked in floral designs in such a manner that the petals are raised in relief by the tension of the threads.

Lit: B. Palliser, *History of Lace*, rev. M. Jourdain & A. Dryden, London 1902; P. Wardle, *Victorian Lace*, London 1968.

Hoof foot A terminal for chair legs in the form of an animal's foot, first used by the ancient Egyptians. It was popular in C17 and C18 Europe. The French term is *pied de biche*.

Hooked rugs A type of floor and bed covering made in N. America in the C18 and C19. The background material is homespun linen, later factory-woven cotton or burlap, and the pile is formed of narrow strips of woollen (later cotton) rags drawn up from the back of the ground fabric in loops and sometimes cut. Relief effects could be obtained by varying the lengths of the loops. The range of patterns is wide, from simple geometrical designs to much more ambitious landscapes, seascapes, animals or vases of flowers. Most surviving examples date from *c.*1840–1900. The term is loosely applied to two types of N. American rugs of the same period: yarn-sewn rugs with a pile of several strands of two-ply yarn sewn through a linen or two-ground fabric; and patched rugs of linen, tow, woollen cloth or cotton sacking on to which scraps of woollen fabric are sewn.

Lit: E. H. Ries, *American Rugs*, New York 1950.

Hoolaart, G. H. (*c.*1716–72). Dutch glass-engraver, possibly related to F. GREENWOOD whose wife bore the same name. He used a stippling technique (*see* STIPPLE ENGRAVING) and left areas of plain glass to represent shadows.

Hope, Thomas (1769–1831). Born in Holland, the son of a rich banking family of Scottish origin, he settled in England *c.*1796 and became an influential patron of the arts, the *arbiter elegantiarum* of Regency England and a highly original furniture designer. He had spent 8 years travelling in Greece and the Eastern Mediterranean where he acquired a passion for Greek art and architecture, and he continued to travel widely after he settled in England, keeping abreast of artistic developments in Rome and Paris. He began to design furniture in order to provide himself with a suitable background for his collection of classical and neo-classical statuary and *objects d'art*. His archaeological inclinations led him to copy ancient furniture more closely than had been attempted before by anyone except J.-L. David and N. ABILDGAARD – both, significantly, painters who designed furniture mainly for their own use. Hope's Grecian chairs, with sabre legs and tilted backs, are copied direct from Greek vase paintings. Though he seems to have known PERCIER and FONTAINE personally he would probably have thought their furniture designs too archaeologically incorrect and was therefore little influenced by them, despite their similarity. Hope is best known for his work in the Egyptian taste, inspired by V. Denon's *Voyage dans la basse et la haute Egypte* (1802). Hope published his designs as *Household Furniture and Decoration* (1807),

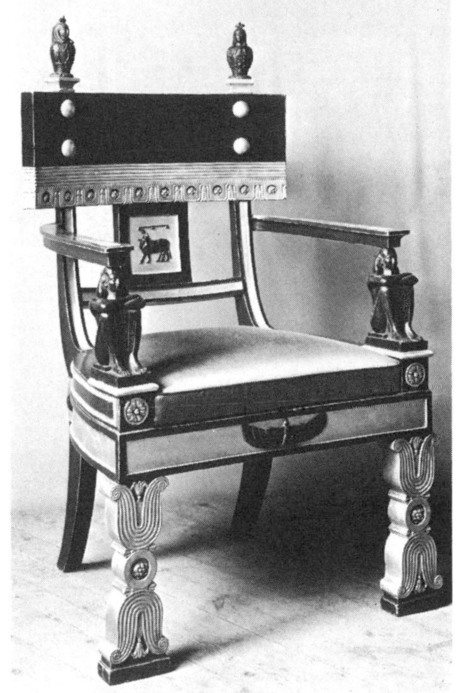

T. Hope: painted wood chair in the Egyptian taste, c.1805 (Faringdon Collection, Buscot Park, Berks.)

and thereby exerted considerable influence on furniture design in England. His shapes are square and solid and the decoration is purer and more consistent than that of most French EMPIRE furniture, i.e. it is either classical, with lion monopods, stiffly curling Ionic volutes and bold anthemion ornaments, or Egyptian with hieroglyphics, winged disks, crouching lions, etc. Numerous English cabinet-makers adapted these designs though the furniture they produced is generally rather less pedantically correct and archaeologically uncomfortable. Hope's own furniture seems to have been executed by refugee craftsmen, usually French *émigrés* of whom two are known by name, Decaix and Bogaert. Examples are in Lord Faringdon's collection at Buscot Park.

Lit: J. Harris, *Regency Furniture Designs*, London 1961; D. Watkin, *Thomas Hope and the Neo-Classical Idea*, London 1968.

Hoppenhaupt, Johann Michael (1709–1769). German Rococo decorator and furniture-designer. He was born at Merseburg, the son of a sculptor and architect **Johann Michael Hoppenhaupt** (1685–1751), trained in Dresden and Vienna and appears to have led a wandering life until he settled in Berlin in 1740, the year Frederick the Great succeeded to the Prussian throne. He was employed as *Kabinettsbildhauer* at the Berlin Schloss under Frederick's architect and decorator, Knobelsdorff and J. A. NAHL. His younger brother, with whom he is often confused, **Johann Christian Hoppenhaupt** (1719–1786), also went to Berlin in 1740 and was appointed Directeur des Ornements in 1746, in succession to Nahl, thus becoming responsible for interior decorations at the Berlin Schloss (now destroyed), at Sans Souci where his major work was the music room, at the Potsdam Stadtschloss (now destroyed) and later at the Neues Palais, Potsdam. Johann Michael Hoppenhaupt published between 1751 and 1755 numerous ornamental and other designs, engraved by J. W. Miel, for chimney-pieces, sedan chairs, boiseries covered with eddying waves of Rococo curlicues, rather corpulent *bombé* commodes and some fantastically elaborate, wilfully impractical console tables with musicians or Chinamen perching insecurely on the tossing scrolls of their supports. They may derive from the published designs by CUVILLIÉS but they are further removed from French Rococo. It may be doubted whether any furniture was executed precisely according to his designs. But the designs themselves exerted some influence, notably on HABERMAN of Augsburg and, perhaps, on Thomas JOHNSON in England.

Lit: E. Hempel, *Baroque Art and Architecture in Central Europe*, Pelican History of Art, Harmondsworth 1965; H. Kreisel, *Die Kunst des deutschen Möbels*, vol. ii, Munich 1970.

Hoppesteyn, Rochus Jacobsz (d.1692). He was a DELFT potter, the son of **Jacob Wemmertsz Hoppesteyn** (d.1671), and owner of *Het Moriaenshooft* (the Moor's Head) faience factory, producing vases painted with Italianate mythological scenes as well as the usual Delft chinoiseries, adopting a clear bright red colour and gilding as well as the usual blue-and-white colour scheme.

R. J. Hoppesteyn:
Delft tin-glazed earthenware vase, 1680–90
(Kunstgewerbemuseum, Berlin)

Lit: E. Neurdenberg in *Feestbundel Dr Abraham Bredius*, Amsterdam 1915; J. N. Bastert in *Bulletin Museum Boymans* (Rotterdam) VI, 1955, pp. 33–6.

Horchhaimer, Nicholas (d.1583). The first master pewterer in Nuremberg to make large PEWTER bowls with figure decoration cast in low relief. His technique differed from that used by Lyons pewterers. Instead of engraving the decoration on the copper or brass moulds, Horchhaimer etched them in the metal or stone moulds in the same way that armourers decorate their work, but in *intaglio*. The effect was a rather flat relief reminiscent of woodcuts and was later known as 'the wood-cutting style'. His colleague Albrecht PREISSENSIN used the same technique and large bowls made by them are rarer than relief-cast pewter. The decorations are either abstract, e.g. arabesques, or scenes from the Passion or classical mythology.

Lit: H.-U. Haedeke, *Metalwork*, London 1970.

Horn, drinking, *see* DRINKING HORN.

Horn furniture Antlers were used from the Middle Ages to the C16 for hanging lamps, notably those of the *Kronleuchter* and *Leuchterweibchen* types. Furniture made from antlers became popular in the mid C19 when H. F. C. Rampendahl of Hamburg specialized in it. Frankfurt is thought to have been the main centre for such furniture. Messrs Yetley and Messrs Silber & Fleming of London also made it. In the U.S.A. buffalo horns were similarly used for chairs, sofas, etc. in the late C19 and later.

Lit: S. Jervis in *Victoria & Albert Museum Yearbook*, no. 3, 1972.

Hornick, Erasmus (d.1583). He was a Flemish goldsmith and designer of the most extravagantly MANNERIST kind. He was probably working in Antwerp between *c.*1540 and 1550 but is first recorded in Augsburg in 1555 when he married. In 1559 he settled in Nuremberg where he was associated with JAMNITZER and **Jacopo da Strada** to whom some of his designs have been attributed. He was admitted to the Nuremberg goldsmiths' guild in 1563 but left there in 1566. In 1582 he became *Kammergoldschmied* to the great Mannerist patron the Emperor Rudolph II in Prague. His designs, of which he published several books, survive in great numbers both as engravings and drawings. Many are for jewellery, medallions, etc., but his rich vein of fantasy emerges in those for vases and other vessels for execution in hardstone, rock-crystal, exotic shells and precious metals.

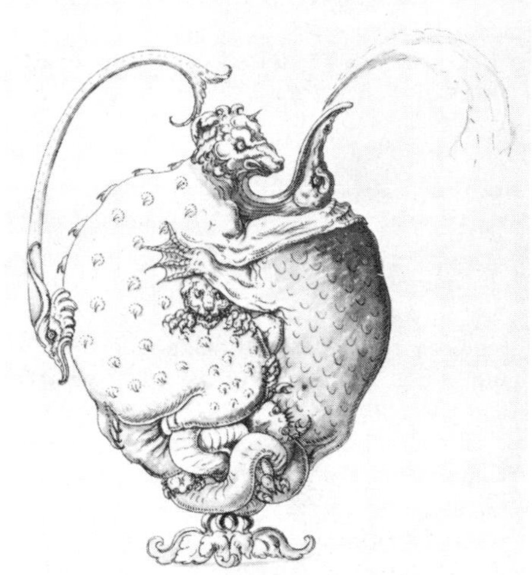

E. Hornick: drawing of ewer, c.1560 (Victoria & Albert Museum)

Lit: John Hayward, 'The drawings and engraved ornament of Erasmus Hornick' in *The Burlington Magazine*, July 1968, pp. 383–9.

Höroldt, Johann Gregor, *see* HEROLD, Johann Gregor.

Horsehair A cloth made of horsehair with a linen or cotton warp. Stiff and harsh but very smooth, shiny and durable, it was much used for upholstery in England from the late C18 onwards. It is usually plain black in colour, but can be striped or chequered.

Horta, Victor (1861–1947). Belgian architect and designer; one of the originators of ART NOUVEAU. He designed furniture for the houses he built in Brussels. Characteristic of his style are electric light fixtures in the form of flowers with long upright or nodding stems terminating in sprays of metal or glass petals which hold conspicuous naked bulbs. Details of his work were widely imitated by commercializers of the Art Nouveau style which he himself abandoned *c.*1905. The rest of his career was devoted to teaching architecture.

Lit: Pioneers du XXe siècle, Exh. Cat., Paris 1971; F. Borsi & P. Portoghesi, *Victor Horta,* Brussels 1970.

Hosenfeller, Heinrich Christian Friedrich, *see* HERREBØE POTTERY.

Hot-water plate An early C19 invention. Made of silver or, more usually, of Sheffield Plate it is a circular or oblong-shaped shallow pan with two handles and a hinged trap for filling with hot water or, alternatively, a hot iron bar. It was placed under dishes to keep them warm and was usually made *en suite* with entrée dishes.

Hsüan-Chi A type of Chinese ritual jade resembling a P'I but with a serrated edge. It is thought to have been used in connection with astronomical observations.

Hsüan-tê porcelain Chinese porcelain made in the reign of the Emperor Hsüan-tê (1426–35). The blue-and-white wares are the best of the MING period and were much imitated later. The paste is of fine quality, the glaze is thick and decorations are of great vitality. Wares with underglaze decorations in copper red were also produced. And some were decorated in the *wu ts'ai* five-colour scheme of underglaze blue with iron-red, yellow, green and turquoise blue enamels.

Lit: S. Jenyns, *Ming Pottery and Porcelain,* London 1953.

Hu A Chinese Bronze Age wine storage vessel which continued to be made in the HAN and later periods. There are various types, e.g. gourd-shaped, square-shaped and flat or moon-shaped. The latter is called a *Pien-hu.* For illustration *see* BRONZE.

Huai style The late Chinese Bronze Age style current from *c.*600 B.C. onwards to the end of the Bronze Age. The term derives from the Huai river near where the first examples were discovered. The style is more complex and intricate in ornamentation than that of SHANG-YIN and Early CHOU dynasties which precede it.

Huan A type of Chinese ritual jade resembling a flat disk with a circular hole in the centre considerably larger than that of a P'I. Its significance is unknown.

Huaud, Pierre (*c.*1612–80). A French enamel painter who settled in Geneva in 1630 and helped to establish the Geneva school of enamellers. He had three sons who practised the same craft, **Pierre II** called **Huaud l'aîné** (1647–1700) who worked for some years for the Elector of Brandenburg, **Jean-Pierre** called **Huaud le Puiné** (1655–1723) and **Ami** (1657–1724). They all specialized in watch-cases delicately painted with landscapes, mythological scenes, etc.

Lit: H. Clouzot, *Dictionnaire des Miniaturistes sur Émail,* Paris 1924.

Hubatsch, Herrmann Hugo, *see* BERLIN PORCELAIN FACTORY.

Hubbard, Elbert (1856–1915). U.S. writer who, after retiring with a fortune from the Larkin Soap Company in 1893, founded a community of craftsmen, the **Roycrofters,** at East Aurora, New York. This was based on the principles of W. MORRIS (whom he had met on a visit to England in 1894) and incorporated a very successful printing press and workshops for the production of metalwork, leatherwork and simple oak benches, tables, chairs, etc. of the type known as MISSION FURNITURE. Of the craftsmen who worked here the most notable were **Dard Hunter** (1883–1966), **Karl Kipp** and **Frederick Kranz.** Hunter designed furniture, metalwork and books influenced by the Viennese SECESSION style after he visited Vienna in 1908; but he left the Roycrofters in 1910. This Viennese influence was passed on to Kipp, a former banker who settled at East Aurora in 1908 and directed a fairly large metal workshop (with up to 35 assistants) producing hammered copper vases, trays, candlesticks, etc. Kranz was a German who, after working in Philadelphia, settled in East Aurora *c.*1909 and ran the leather shop which produced cases, waste-paper baskets, frames, etc. decorated with Art Nouveau motifs. Members of the community also made portrait busts of their heroes, Morris, Whitman and Hubbard himself who was venerated as a sage. Hubbard was an

E. Hubbard: 'Roycrofter' oak chair, c.1905–12 (The Art Museum of Princeton University, Mr and Mrs R. W. Blasberg Collection)

apostle of aestheticism, of long hair and flowing ties, editor of *The Philistine*, author of the *Message to Garcia* and other 'philosophical' works. His teaching and his idea of a community may have had some influence on F. L. WRIGHT. He and his wife went down on the *Lusitania* in 1915 but the Roycroft workshops survived until 1938.

Lit: F. Champney, *Art and Glory: The Story of Elbert Hubbard*, New York 1968; R. Judson Clark, *The Arts and Crafts Movement in America 1876–1916*, Exh. Cat., Art Museum, Princeton University, Art Institute of Chicago, etc., 1972–3.

Hubble, Nicholas, *see* WROTHAM POTTERIES.

Hubertusburg pottery A Saxon faience factory founded in 1770 by J. S. F. TÄNNICH, producing attractive vases and table-wares decorated in muffle colours in a late Rococo style, few of which are known. It suffered from competition from MEISSEN, was given to the Elector of Saxony and came under the direction of Graf Marcolini who initiated the production of CREAM-COLOURED EARTHENWARE imitative of that being imported in quantity from England (pieces were sometimes marked WEDGWOOD). It was run by the Saxon government from 1814 to 1835 when it was sold to a merchant of Leipzig; it finally closed in 1848. Wares of the Tännich period are sometimes marked 'HUBERTUSBURG T' or 'H.T.'. The usual C19 marks included the initials 'K.S.ST.F.' impressed. The initials 'W & M' impressed indicate a date after 1840.

Lit: K. Berling, *Die Fayence- und Steingutfabrik Hubertusberg*, Dresden 1909; K. Hüseler, *Deutsche Fayencen*, Stuttgart 1956.

Huet, Christophe (d.1759). French Rococo painter, engraver and designer. He painted the enchanting *singerie* wall decorations in the Château de Chantilly and the no less elegant *chinoiserie* ones in the Château des Champs. His engravings, including a series of *singeries*, were widely used both for marquetry decoration on furniture and painted decoration on porcelain.

Huet, Jean-Baptiste (1745–1811). French painter and textile designer, nephew of Christophe HUET. He designed wallpaper for RÉVEILLON and in 1783 became chief designer of plate-printed cottons for OBERKAMPF at the Jouy factory. His first work there represented the process of cotton manufacture in series of vignettes printed in a single colour on a white ground. Other early designs show groups of fashionably dressed figures ambling round the bridges, fountains, columns and other delights of a *jardin anglais* and beautifully recapture the artificially rustic atmosphere of a *ferme ornée* like that of Marie Antoinette. In a more serious mood he designed *The Apotheosis of Louis XVI* and, surprised by political events, was able to transform it into *Louis XVI Restorer of Liberty* (printed in 1789). More openly Revolutionary sympathies (he was Captain of the Sèvres company of the National Guard) became apparent in *La Fédération* (*c*.1793) which shows *citoyennes* elegantly dancing among the ruins of the Bastille. In 1802 he designed the very popular *Paul and Virginia* but soon abandoned the scattered vignette type of design so intimately associated with the Jouy factory for all-over compositions of classical architectural motifs and figure subjects framed in octagons, vesicas, etc., e.g. *Leda* and *Cupid and Psyche*.

Lit: Musée des Arts Décoratifs, Paris, *Les Nouvelles collections de J.-B. Huet*, Paris 1906; H. Clouzot, *Histoire de la manufacture de Jouy . . .*, Paris 1928.

Huguenot silver Silver by or in the style of Huguenot refugees who settled in England after the revocation of the Edict of Nantes (1685) and in greater numbers after 1688. Their style gradually replaced the Dutch style popular in the RESTORATION period and by 1700 dominated English silver. Solemn and monumental, their work is marked by bold decorations, especially straps and formalized leaves in CUT CARD WORK, and use of cast ornament with handles, knobs and supports often in the form of human or animal figures. The Huguenots were influenced by the engraved designs of P. DU CERCEAU, Jean BÉRAIN and Jean LE PAUTRE but either because they were more usually of provincial than Parisian origin or to satisfy the taste of stolid English patrons, they worked in an austerer style than the leading Louis XIV silversmiths. They introduced into England several new types of vessel, notably the helmet-shaped ewer with basin *en suite*, the pilgrim bottle, the soup tureen and the ÉCUELLE. The leading craftsmen were Pierre HARACHE, Paul de LAMERIE, Simon PANTIN, Pierre PLATEL, Philip ROLLOS, D. TANQUERAY and D. WILLAUME; their English imitators included G. and F. GARTHORNE, Anthony NELME and Benjamin PYNE.

Lit: J. F. Hayward, *Huguenot Silver in England 1688–1727*, London 1959.

Hull, John (1624–83). English-born silversmith whose family emigrated to Boston in 1634. He was appointed, in 1652, to coin new money – shillings and sixpences. As a silversmith he worked in partnership with **Robert Sanderson** (1608–1693) and in 1659 J. DUMMER was apprenticed to him. Two caudle cups in the Museum of Fine Arts, Boston, are among the few surviving examples of his work.

Lit: H. F. Clarke, *John Hull: a Builder of the Bay Colony*, Portland, Maine 1940.

Hull pottery A pottery at Kingston-upon-Hull was founded in 1802 (by Job RIDGWAY and others) apparently without much success. After it had closed for some years it was bought in 1825 by **William Bell** who named it the **Belle Vue Pottery** and ran it until 1840, producing large quantities of cream-coloured earthenware, often painted or transfer-printed. He had a depot in Hamburg and carried on a brisk export trade to Germany. After 1825 wares were often marked 'BELLEVUE POTTERY HULL' surrounding one or two bells.

Lit: A. Hurst, *Catalogue of the Boynton Collection of Yorkshire Pottery*, York 1922.

Humble, Hartley, Greens & Co., *see* LEEDS POTTERY.

Humpen A German type of drinking glass of cylindrical form sometimes decorated with enamels or engraving, made from the C16 onwards.

Hund(t), Ferdinand (*c*.1704–1758). German Rococo carver and furniture-maker. He settled in

F. Hund: fire-screen, 1736 (Residenz Würzburg)

Würzburg in 1735 and in the next year began working in the South wing of the Residenz under the architect Balthasar Neumann who described him as the best ornamental carver. He was responsible for the frothy Rococo woodwork in the Parade-Audienzzimmer, 1742. He also made much carved furniture for the Residenz, console tables, fire-screens, gueridons (a pair are now in the Bayerisches Nationalmuseum, Munich). In 1751 he entered the service of the Prince Bishop of Speyer at Bruchsal where he worked on decorations and furnishings for the Schloss. All his work at Bruchsal and much of that at Würzburg was destroyed in the Second World War, but a number of pieces of furniture have been attributed to him.

Lit: H. Kreisel, *Die Kunst des deutschen Möbels*, vol. ii, Munich 1970.

Hungarian stitch, *see* BARGELLO WORK.

Hunger, Christoph Conrad (*fl.*1715–45). Somewhat disreputable porcelain ARCANIST errant who began as a goldsmith, then worked at MEISSEN, moved to VIENNA in 1719 and helped to found the VEZZI PORCELAIN FACTORY in Venice in 1720. He unsuccessfully offered his services to the Danish government in 1737 but helped to establish the ST PETERSBURG IMPERIAL PORCELAIN FACTORY in 1745. He was probably something of a charlatan, knowing less of porcelain-making than he claimed but nevertheless helping to transmit some part of the secret discovered at Meissen. But a few signed pieces of porcelain with enamel painting and raised gilding demonstrate that he was an able decorator.

Lit: G. E. Pazaurek, *Deutsche Fayence- und Porzellan-Hausmaler*, Leipzig 1925.

Hunslet Hall pottery, *see* LEEDS POTTERY.

Hunt & Roskell, *see* STORR, Paul.

Hunter, Dard, *see* HUBBARD, Elbert.

Hunting carpets, *see* PERSIAN CARPETS.

Hunzinger, George (*fl.*1861–80). New York furniture-maker of German origin who specialized in the production of chairs, often of novel and

G. Hunzinger: side-chair, New York, 1869 (Metropolitan Museum of Art, gift of Mrs Florence Weyman)

sometimes of fantastic form, in various types of wood and simulated bamboo. He took out a patent for a reclining chair in 1861. From 1866 to the 1880s he is recorded in the New York directories as a chair manufacturer. Several of his products are illustrated in KIMBALL'S *Book of Designs* of 1876.

Lit: *19th Century America: Furniture and Other Decorative Arts*, Exh. Cat., Metropolitan Museum, New York 1970.

Huquier, Jacques-Gabriel (1695–1772). French engraver and ornamental designer. His *Livre de differents fragments à l'usage de la serurerie (sic)* c.1740 includes designs for elaborately fluid Rococo wrought iron stair rails and some rather more restrained candelabras, lanterns, etc. He also published engravings of fantastic floral motifs, similar to those of PILLEMENT.

Lit: D. Guilmard, *Les maîtres ornemantistes*, Paris 1880.

Hurd, Jacob (1703–58). Silversmith working in Boston, Mass., in a simplified and sometimes monumentally solid version of the English mid-C18 style. Many pieces of his domestic plate survive (Museum of Fine Arts, Boston). His sons **Nathaniel** (1729–77) and **Benjamin** carried on their father's business.

Lit: H. French, *Jacob Hurd and his Sons, Nathaniel and Benjamin, Silversmiths*, Cambridge, Mass., 1939.

Hurdals Werk Norwegian glasshouse producing fine lead glass goblets, decanters, candlesticks, etc., generally in the English style, 1777–1809. Staffed originally by craftsmen from NÖSTETANGEN. It later specialized in dark blue glass vessels, especially potpourri urns, sugar casters, salt-cellars, etc.

Lit: A. Polak in *Concise Encyclopaedia of Antiques*, vol. IV, London 1958.

Husk motif A wheat-ear, much used as a decorative motif on furniture and metalwork of the Neo-Classical period, especially in England and the U.S.A.

Hustin, Jacques and Jacques-Dennis-Ferdinand, *see* BORDEAUX POTTERIES.

Hutch Anglicized name for the French *huche* – a chest for the storage of food or clothes, sometimes of very rough construction but occasionally decorated with carving and mounted on legs. To judge from inventories and wills, one of the commonest articles of furniture in medieval and C16 houses.

Hvidt, Peter (b.1916). Danish furniture designer who, with **Osla Mölgaard-Nielsen** (b.1907), pioneered industrial methods and the use of metal and plastics in furniture making in Denmark, notably in his 'Ax' series of tables and chairs in 1950 for Fritz Hansen Ltd. Previously Danish furniture had been based on hand craftsmanship and the use of wood. Hvidt uses wood as well as metal and plastics, but with steam-bending and other pressure-moulding techniques. His designs are elegant and smooth.

Hyalith A dark sealing-wax red and sometimes dense black BOHEMIAN glass made from 1820 onwards at several glasshouses in southern Bohemia near Gratzen owned by **Georg Franz August Lengueval, Count von Buquoy.** They may have been produced to imitate Wedgwood's *rosso antico* and *black basaltes* wares.

Hyckes, William, *see* SHELDON, William.

Hydria, *see* GREEK POTTERY.

From Historyes of Troy,
designed by William Morris, London, 1892

Ifield, Henry, *see* WROTHAM POTTERY.

Iga potteries A group of Japanese potteries in the Iga Province (now Mie prefecture) which, like the nearby SHIGARAKI POTTERIES, began by making wares for local farmers. From the late c16 or early c17 they produced TEA CEREMONY WARES especially flower vases with a grey body covered with a persimmon-brown glaze splashed with green. They are often cracked or split and nearly always curiously distorted in ways that particularly appeal to Japanese teamasters.

Lit: S. Jenyns, *Japanese Pottery*, London 1971.

Igel A c16 German type of small squat tumbler or club-shaped vessel of glass, usually green glass, covered with prunts or glass studs.

Ikat An Indonesian term now used to describe the process by which a pattern is resist-dyed on the warp and/or weft before weaving; also a woven textile made by this process.

Ilmenau porcelain factory Founded near Weimar in 1777, producing wares which Goethe declared to be worse than any in the neighbourhood, it was taken over by the Duke of Saxe-Weimar 1782. Its most attractive products are imitations of WEDGWOOD blue jasper-ware medallions (mainly portraits) made from 1792 when the factory was leased to **Christian Nonne** who bought it in 1808. Under the name of **Nonne and Roesch** the factory survived until after 1871. Other porcelain factories were established at Ilmenau in the late c19 and early c20. (For factory mark *see* p. 884.)

Lit: R. Graul and A. Kurzwelly, *Altthüringer Porzellan*, Leipzig 1909; K. Hüseler, *Deutsche Fayencen*, Stuttgart 1956–8.

Image toys The c18 name for rustic pottery statuettes, especially those of STAFFORDSHIRE.

Imari porcelain The European name for a type of JAPANESE PORCELAIN made for export at ARITA and shipped from the port of Imari from the late

Imari porcelain bottle, c.1700
(Musée Guimet, Paris)

C17 onwards. It is very richly decorated with flowers, figures, ships, etc., in dark under-glaze blue, red enamels and gold, sometimes with touches of turquoise, green, aubergine and yellow. The name 'Brocaded Imari' is applied to pieces with an overall floral decoration reminiscent of a rich silk textile. They were much imitated in C18 and C19 England at the DERBY, MINTON, SPODE and WORCESTER PORCELAIN FACTORIES.

Lit: S. Jenyns, *Japanese Porcelain*, London 1965.

Imperial porcelain factory, *see* ST PETERSBURG IMPERIAL PORCELAIN FACTORY.

Imperial yellow A rich golden yellow glaze derived from iron with a small addition of antimony, which has become a collectors' term for yellow monochrome wares from the Ch'eng hua period onwards. The finest examples are from the K'ang Hsi and Ch'ing periods.

Ince, William (*fl.*1758–1802) and **Mayhew, John** (d.1811). London cabinet-makers and upholsterers who first established themselves with their book, *The Universal System of Household Furniture* (published serially 1759–62), modelled on CHIPPENDALE's *Director*, and containing designs for furniture and metalwork in a rather heavy-handed Rococo style. (Mayhew began *c.*1758 in partnership with Samuel NORMAN but left him the following year to join Ince.) A cabinet made by them in the 1760s (Kunstindustrimuseet, Copenhagen) shows a not very happy combination of classical form with fiddly gothicky tracery. Moving with the times, they adopted a square no-nonsense Classical style in the 1790s and later a more elegant Regency manner.

Lit: P. Ward-Jackson, *English Furniture Design*, London 1958; R. Edwards, ed., *W. Ince, The Universal System of Household Furniture*, London 1960.

W. Ince & J. Mayhew: design from The Universal System of Household Furniture, 1759–62

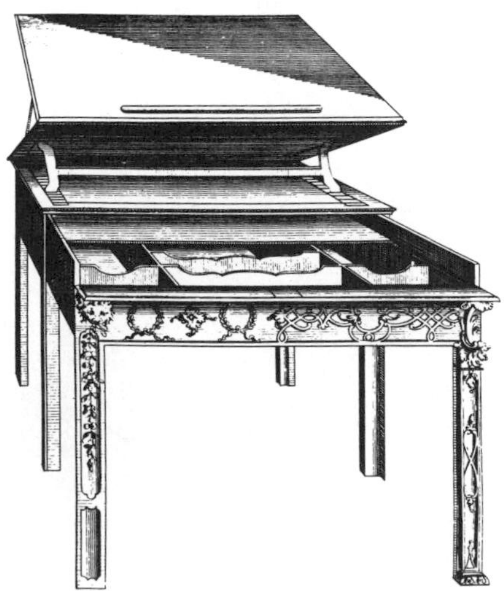

Indian mask A decorative motif consisting of a mask with a feathered head-dress, popular in Europe especially for the decoration of furniture in the late C17 and early C18.

Indianische Blumen Literally Indian flowers, the German name for the highly formalized, botanically fanciful, flower motifs derived from Oriental porcelain (especially FAMILLE VERTE and Japanese KAKIEMON style wares) which made their appearance on MEISSEN porcelain from *c.*1725 and were soon taken up by painters of porcelain in France, Italy and England as well as Germany. In France they were called *Fleurs des Indes*. Each motif consists of petals firmly outlined and filled in with simply graded colours. At Meissen they were superseded *c.*1740 by naturalistic DEUTSCHE BLUMEN (German flowers) which are botanically recognizable, much more freely painted and subtly coloured and without hard outlines. But Indianische Blumen remained popular elsewhere, even as late as the 1770s at DERBY.

Indiscret A settee formed of three linked armchairs, lavishly upholstered and with buxom curves, it was fashionable during the SECOND EMPIRE of which style it is very typical. *Illustrated opposite page.*

Industrial design There is no accepted definition of the term Industrial Design. At its narrowest it is used as a synonym for 'product design' or the design of objects for MASS PRODUCTION by industrial methods, but it is also used more loosely for graphic and other types of design connected with mass production and for the styling of, for example, machine tools and locomotives which are not produced in quantity. However, a definition based simply on the distinction between

Indiscret, Second Empire period (Ministère des Finances, Paris)

industrial and handicraft production – i.e. between the serial production of copies, each identical with the next, and the unique craft product each dependent on the individual maker's hand – is inadequate. For such a definition would necessarily embrace the designers for early industrialized concerns, e.g. WEDGWOOD, OBERKAMPF or THONET, who were certainly not Industrial Designers in the modern sense of the term. In fact the Industrial Designer did not emerge until after production systems were fully mechanized and had advanced to the assembly-line or conveyor-belt stage. At this point the designer became all-important since the possibility of modification during production was eliminated. And he became closely involved in the production process itself. His task was to create a model or standard which could be multiplied indefinitely by a machine. To conform to the standard, the industrial product must be designed and planned as complete at the end of the production line. It must not undergo any further manipulation. The design must therefore be adapted specifically to the system of production. By this definition, most if not all modern furniture would be excluded from Industrial Design since it is only partly produced to a standard model, some finishing and hand-polishing being done later.

Industrial Design has its theoretical basis in FUNCTIONALISM. As a profession it has its origins in the late C19 and early C20 when dissatisfaction with the products of industry turned from outright condemnation to a recognition that the machine could be used to produce good work in its own right, *see* William MORRIS, VICTORIAN STYLE, ARTS AND CRAFTS MOVEMENT. Industrial design was born in a reforming climate of opinion and its inherent puritanism is only now being replaced by a gayer, more relaxed approach. Whereas beauty and utility were regarded as indivisible and inseparable it is now accepted that the artistic component in an industrial product is only partly related to its material utility. Form should not only express function but should embody a psychological and emotional expressiveness as well.

Though it was in England that the aesthetic values inherent in standardized production and industrialization were first explicitly discussed and appreciated it was in Germany that they were first fully realized in practice. Peter BEHRENS, Richard RIEMERSCHMIDT and Bruno PAUL may claim to have been the first Industrial Designers in our sense of the term. Behrens was designing prototype flasks for mass production in 1898 and in 1907 became designer to AEG, the big German electrical combine. Riemerschmidt and Paul designed furniture for mass production by the DEUTSCHE WERKSTÄTTEN in 1905 and 1906 respectively, Paul's being called *Typenmöbel* – one of the earliest examples of standardized production. In 1907 the DEUTSCHE WERKBUND, inspired by MUTHESIUS, was founded to promote high quality in industrial design and it was shortly followed by the founding of similar organizations in other countries – Austria (1910), Switzerland (1913), Sweden (1910–17) and England (1915). But it was only after the First World War that Industrial Design was first accepted and taught – at the BAUHAUS. The Bauhaus marked the full acceptance of the machine in design and many of the early classics of Industrial Design were achieved there. Most of the staff emigrated to England and the U.S. in 1933 but the Bauhaus ideals were revived after the Second World War at ULM (Hochschule für Gestaltung) by the former Bauhaus student Max BILL. More recently, in 1951, the Rat für Formbegung was established at Darmstadt as the official West German Council of Industrial Design.

In Britain, the Design and Industries Association was formed in 1915 to promote good design standards, but it was not until 1930 that the Society of Industrial Artists (now the Society of Industrial Artists and Designers) was founded and designers obtained a proper professional body. No Industrial Design school existed and until the reorganization of the Royal College of Art in 1948 the majority of British industrial designers were trained as architects. The foundation of the Council of Industrial Design in 1944 marked a decisive turning point in state patronage. In 1957 the International Council of Societies of Industrial Design was founded in London.

In the U.S. there was little change in design for industry until the late 1920s despite Frank Lloyd WRIGHT's pioneering efforts and despite the fact that advanced mass-production methods had first been exploited there on a big scale, even as early as the 1790s (e.g. Eli Whitney's arms factory and the endless-belt production line at Olive Evan's flour mills). Such early examples of mass production as the Singer sewing-machine were exhibited at the 1851 Exhibition in London, illustrating the American ambition, as stated in the catalogue, to increase 'the number and quality of articles suited to the wants of the whole people'. But it was not until the 1930s that industrial design was securely established as a profession – *see* DREYFUSS, LOEWY and TEAGUE. In 1938 the Museum of Modern Art, New York, began its stimulating and very influential annual surveys of good design, and in the same year it exhibited and published the work of the Bauhaus. By then all the leading Bauhaus staff were in America where the Bauhaus ideals were quickly absorbed through their work as teachers – Gropius at Harvard, Moholy-Nagy at the Chicago Institute of Design, Kepes at the Massachusetts Institute of Technology, MIES VAN DER ROHE at the Illinois Institute of Technology, Chicago, and Albers at Yale. In 1944 the Society of Industrial Designers (later called the American Society of Industrial Designers) was formed with W. D. Teague as first president. In 1948 the National Association of Schools of Design was founded and in 1957 the Industrial Design Educational Association.

Ingman, Elias Magnus, *see* RÖRSTRAND POTTERY & PORCELAIN FACTORY.

Ingrain carpet, *see* DOUBLE CLOTH CARPET.

Inlay Decorative technique used on furniture until replaced by MARQUETRY in the C17. A pattern composed of differently coloured woods or other materials, notably ivory or horn, is inset into the

Inro: Japanese lacquer by Shu-osai, early c19 (Victoria & Albert Museum)

Intarsia panel by Fra Giovanni da Verona, c.1476 (Monte Oliveto Maggiore, Siena)

solid wood of the carcase, most of which remains undecorated.

Innsbruck glasshouse A small factory established near Innsbruck by the Archduke Ferdinand (son of the Emperor Ferdinand and younger brother of Maxmilian II) shortly after he became regent of the Tyrol in 1567. It was devoted mainly to making vessels and window glass for the Archduke, though some products were made for sale to the general public. Staffed by a succession of Venetian glassblowers and other craftsmen it specialized in clear *cristallo* vessels in the Venetian style several of which passed from the Archducal collection in Schloss Ambras to the Kunsthistorisches Museum, Vienna – including a beaker said to have been blown by the Archduke himself and set in an elaborate gem-studded silver mount.

Lit: E. Egg, *Die Glashütten zu Hall und Innsbruck im 16 Jahrhundert*, Innsbruck 1962.

Inro A small lacquer box divided into compartments for seals, medicines or other objects, attached to a cord and worn by the Japanese whose clothes had no pockets. Great ingenuity was applied to the lacquer decorations, especially in the C18 and C19. *Illustrated previous page.*

Intaglio Incised relief carving, the opposite of cameo, especially on gems, hard-stones or glass.

Intarsia An Italian type of marquetry or inlaid panelling used for the decoration of choir-stalls, etc. Designs were linear until *c.*1450 when representational motifs began to appear, notably architectural perspectives and still-life groups of regular solids which lent themselves to simplification into geometrical patterns. Lutes, faceted cups, astrolabes and various instruments of precision became popular as subjects for the latter. Such great artists as Ucello and Piero della Francesca are known to have designed *intarsia* panels. The famous sculptors and architects **Giuliano** and **Benedetto da Maiano** executed *intarsia* panels in 1465 to designs by the painter Baldovinetti for Florence cathedral (now in the Museo dell'Opera del Duomo, Florence). **Baccio Pontelli** (d.1492) carried out the well-known panelling in the *studiolo*, Palazzo Ducale, Urbino. **Lorenzo da Lendinara** (d.1477) and **Cristoforo da Lendinara** (d.1491) were famous practitioners of whose work examples survive in Modena Cathedral (dated 1477) and in the Pinacoteca at Lucca. **Fra Giovanni da Verona** (d.1525) executed the choir-stall panels at Monte Oliveto Maggiore which are technical *tours de force*. *Illustrated previous page.*

Lit: F. Arcangeli, *Tarsie*, Rome 1942; E. Carli, *L'Abbazia di Monteoliveto*, Milan 1961; A. Chastel in *Revue des Arts*, III (1953), pp. 141–54.

International Silver Company, *see* MERIDEN BRITANNIA COMPANY.

Ionic Order, *see* ORDERS.

Ireson, Nathaniel, *see* WINCANTON POTTERY.

Iribe, Paul (1883–1935). French caricaturist, interior decorator and designer of furniture, wallpaper, textiles and jewellery. As a designer he began in the Art Nouveau style but soon evolved an independent manner which was to influence the later development of ART DECO. His most notable pieces are comfortable well-upholstered chairs of simple fluid form with finely carved or inlaid woodwork. From 1908 he employed P. LEGRAIN. In 1914 he went to America where he worked for the theatre and cinema, designing for Cecil B. de Mille among others. After returning to France in 1930 he was mainly engaged in designing jewellery for Coco Chanel.

Lit: Les Années '25' Exh. Cat., Musée des Arts Décoratifs, Paris 1966.

Irish glass, *see* BELFAST, CORK and WATERFORD GLASSHOUSES.

Iron A metallic chemical element extracted from ores by smelting and used in Europe since the 5th millennium, first for weapons and utensils, later for decorative objects as well. The pure metal was rarely used and most of the objects commonly said to be of 'wrought iron' would by a metallurgist be correctly termed low-carbon steel (that is, an alloy with less than 0.5 per cent carbon). Wrought

Ironwork designs by G. Huquier, c.1750

iron – the name can be applied to the material both before and after it has been fashioned by a smith – is ductile and durable and may be worked into very elaborate shapes. It has been much used for making gates, grilles, balconies, stair-rails, lanterns, door hinges and sometimes furniture. Largely superseded by cast iron in the early C19, it returned to favour with the ARTS AND CRAFTS movement in England and similar craft revivals on the Continent in the 1890s. Cast iron or grey iron has a much higher percentage of carbon in the alloy (up to 5 per cent) and is of low ductility. It has usually been cast in moulds of compressed sand. First used in China for making bronze moulds, it has been extensively used in Europe since the C14 and America since the C17 for making pots, pans, etc. Since the late C15 it has also be used for making fire-dogs, fire-backs, etc., and from the early C19 for furniture and railings. For some of the leading masters of iron-work see: R. BAKEWELL, N. GROSSO, J. LAMOUR, G. B. MALAGODI, J. TIJOU.

Lit: L. Aitchison, *A History of Metals*, London 1960; *Made of Iron*, Exh. Cat., University of St Thomas, Houston, Texas, 1960; O. Höver, *Wrought Iron*, London 1962; E. Baccheschi & S. Levy, *Ferri battuti italiani*, Milan 1966.

Ironstone china A very tough porcellaneous substance made by adding glassy ironstone slag to the usual hard porcelain constituents, patented by **Charles James Mason** in 1813 and made exclusively by his Staffordshire factory until 1827; later produced by several English and U.S. factories. It was found suitable for table-wares and also very large objects including chimney-pieces and vast 'vestibule vases' 5 ft high.

Lit: G. A. Godden, *Illustrated Guide: Mason's Patent Ironstone China and Related Ware*, London 1971.

Isabellino style Spanish furnishing style which succeeded the FERDINANDINO STYLE. It corresponds to English VICTORIAN and French SECOND EMPIRE. It is named after Queen Isabella who reigned 1833–68, but it persisted until the end of the century. The emphasis is on well upholstered comfort. Decorations are profuse, generally of somewhat tired Rococo curlicues though sometimes of Neo-Gothic arcades, crockets, etc.

Iserlohn boxes Copper, or sometimes brass, boxes for snuff or tobacco with engraved, chased or embossed lids depicting allegorical or rustic scenes or, quite often, an idealized portrait of Frederick the Great. They were made in the mid C18 at Iserlohn in Westphalia and also elsewhere, notably in Holland.

Isfahan carpets, *see* PERSIAN CARPETS.

Islamic pottery The glazed earthenware produced in the Middle East under Islamic rule, of outstanding importance in the history of ceramics not only for its own sake but also for its influence on Europe. The wares of the best period C9–C13 are now known from examples that survived underground in the ruined cities of Raqqa (Syria), Fostat (old Cairo) and Samarra (near Baghdad). Most of the earlier examples show strong Chinese (TANG) influence in their decorations. And it was probably in an attempt to produce ware of a Chinese whiteness and glossiness that TIN-GLAZED EARTHENWARE was first developed in about the C9 at Baghdad. This technique was later transmitted to Europe and greatly influenced the subsequent development of European pottery. An independent school of Islamic potters flourished under the Samanids (874–999) in E. Persia and Turkestan, producing very handsome wares of a pink or buff body decorated in thickly coloured clay slip under a transparent lead glaze usually with Kufic inscriptions in purplish black on a white ground, occasionally stylized birds and animals, very rarely human figures. Pottery was affected by the change which came over all Islamic arts under the Seljuk Turks (from mid-C11) bringing livelier designs and more sensitive detail. Chinese (SUNG) influence encouraged the production of a soft-paste porcelain made mainly at Rayy and Kashan – monochrome bowls and cups in white, cobalt blue, aubergine or, most popular of all, turquoise, decorated like CELADON WARES with underglaze incised decorations. Very thin translucent wares were sometimes pierced with holes filled with transparent alkaline glaze. The technique of LUSTRE painting, introduced in the C9, was later developed at Kashan whence it was transmitted to Spain for the decoration of HISPANO-MORESQUE POTTERY. Underglaze painting in cobalt blue and overglaze painting in

Islamic lead-glazed earthenware dish, from Nishapur, E. Persia, c9–10 (Victoria & Albert Museum)

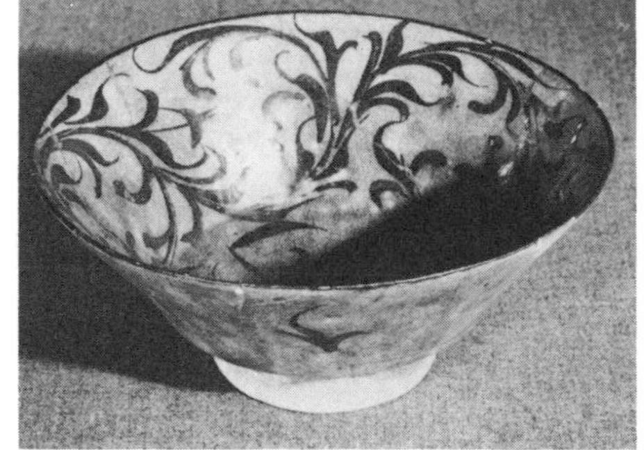

(Right) Islamic earthenware bowl decorated in black under a turquoise blue glaze, Kashan, Persia, early c13 (Victoria & Albert Museum)

enamel were also practised in Persia. Decorations were usually of formalized flower or leaf motifs with occasional animals and birds and sometimes human figures. After the Mongol invasion of Persia which began in 1219 only

Kashan continued to flourish as a centre for pottery. Another wave of Chinese (YUAN) influence soon came in bringing much richer foliage, floral and figurative decoration. The richest wares were decorated in a combination of overglaze and underglaze by a technique described in a treatise written at Tabriz in 1301. Little is known of the Islamic pottery made in the C14 and C15 though a Chinese-inspired vogue for blue-and-white wares seems to have developed in Syria and Persia. In the early C16 ISNIK emerged as the most important centre for pottery in the Middle East. For later pottery made in Persia, *see* PERSIAN POTTERY.

Lit: A. Lane, *Early Islamic Pottery*, and *Later Islamic Pottery*, London 1957; G. Fehērvāti, *Islamic Pottery*, London 1973.

Islamic style The religion of Islam, based on the teaching of the Arab prophet Mohammed (570–632), inspired the creation of an ornamental style applied to all manner of objects, large and small, intended for secular as well as religious use – buildings, textiles, metalwork, ceramics, carvings in ivory, wood, hard-stone, etc. The Koran which regulated every detail of the lives of the Faithful provided few precise rules for the arts apart from a ban on the production of cult images. But although the prohibition on representations of the Prophet, his predecessors and other holy men was invariably observed, opinions differed as to whether this also implied the proscription of all representations of the human form. Some Muslims held that any naturalistic painting or carving, even of leaves and flowers, constituted a blasphemous trespass on the prerogative of the Creator. Others permitted the representation of animals and human beings, though generally without shadows. The main tendency of Islamic art was, however, towards stylizations and flat pattern, and much use of inscriptions in fine calligraphy, even in Persia where the Koranic prohibition was most lightly interpreted.

Islamic metalwork, the so-called Baptismal Bowl of St Louis, by Muhammad ibn az-Zayn, c13 (Louvre)

This artistic style developed as Islam spread from the Arabian peninsula to Syria (the Caliphate was transferred from Medina to Damascus in 661), to Egypt, along the N. African coast to Spain and eventually through Anatolia to

Byzantium. The origin of the basic arabesque pattern appears to lie in late antique carvings of vine leaves and acanthus fronds which were gradually stylized into flat patterns. Other elements seem to have been derived from the indigenous arts of the countries which were overrun (e.g. Coptic motifs from Egypt and Visigothic from Spain). A general stylistic unity was, however, maintained until the C16. The outstanding Islamic artifacts seem to have been made for the luxury-loving rich of the main capital cities, from Samarkand, Baghdad, Damascus and Cairo to Granada and Cordova. But as even the finest types of objects were sometimes transported from one end of the Islamic world to the other, and the craftsmen who made them also moved about, it is often difficult to determine the place of origin or date of particular pieces. Metalwork of the highest quality – brass bowls, ewers, candlesticks, etc., delicately inlaid with silver and sometimes gold – though generally ascribed to MOSUL was also made in Persia and elsewhere. (Islamic metalworkers also settled in Venice – *see* VENETIAN-SARACENIC METALWORK.)

Perfect integration of form and flat pattern distinguishes the best Islamic metalwork and also glass MOSQUE LAMPS, the ivory caskets carved in S. Spain in the C10–C11, rock-crystal vessels carved in Persia and Egypt, and several distinct types of ceramics, notably PERSIAN POTTERY, HISPANO-MORESQUE WARE and ISNIK POTTERY. In textiles the outstanding achievements of Islamic craftsmen include Persian silks, HISPANO-MORESQUE SILKS and of course PERSIAN CARPETS and TURKISH CARPETS.

Lit: M. S. Dimand, *A Handbook of Muhammedan Art*, New York 1947; O. Grabar, *The Formation of Islamic Art*, New Haven and London 1973.

Isleworth pottery A Middlesex earthenware factory established *c.*1760 by **Joseph Shore** with **Richard** and **William Goulding** (hence the mark: *S & G*) making until *c.*1825 various useful wares of STAFFORDSHIRE type including combed slipware. German C19 wares made at Bodenbach in Bohemia and at Aschach in Bavaria, and marked *S & G*, have sometimes been ascribed erroneously to Isleworth.

Lit: H. Clay in *Burlington Magazine* XLIX (1926), pp. 83ff.

Isnik potteries A group of factories at Isnik (ancient Nicaea) some 60 miles S.E. of Istanbul, which produced the most beautiful post-medieval Islamic wares. Production began *c.*1490 with dishes, jugs, ewers, and mosque lamps, robustly made in a mixture of white clay and glassy matter decorated with elaborate arabesques of leaves and flowers in blue on a white ground under a brilliant colourless glaze. From *c.*1525 the range of colours was gradually expanded to include turquoise, sage green and manganese purple, the painting became much freer, and arabesques were almost abandoned for compositions of stylized

Isnik painted earthenware dish, c16 (Musée de Cluny, Paris)

tulips, carnations, roses and other flowers, all springing from a single point, with arching stems making an asymmetrical but nicely balanced pattern. Products included tiles, mainly for the decoration of mosques in Istanbul, which were made in great quantities until *c.*1620. Both for tiles and plates, ewers, etc. a new colour scheme was developed *c.*1555, with a new bright copper green, in place of sage green, and a strong sealing-wax red which stands up in relief from the surface. The most numerous wares are large dishes with flat rims painted with loose bunches of flowers, occasionally figure scenes and, from *c.*1600, three-masted ships in buoyant full sail. Straight-sided tankards, ewers and vases were also made. In the C17 standards gradually fell off and the paintings became increasingly stiff and lifeless. Close imitations of Isnik wares were made at PADUA *c.*1630. Imitations were made in France and elsewhere from the later C19. Until recently the earlier Isnik wares were incorrectly attributed to Kutahya, those of the middle period to Damascus, and those with the red pigment to the island of Rhodes and these labels are still sometimes used.

Lit: A. Lane, *Later Islamic Pottery*, London 1957.

Istoriato Maiolica wares decorated with historical, mythical, Biblical or genre scenes over their entire surface, intended less for use than for decoration.

Ivory Strictly the tusk of an elephant but also, more loosely, any similar hard, white or cream-coloured substance, e.g. the tusks of narwhals, walruses (morse ivory), hippopotamuses, fossil mammoths and the horn of rhinoceros. Ivory has a fine grain and lends itself to displays of technical dexterity. This quality has been much exploited in the Orient, e.g. Chinese filigree carvings, balls within balls, Japanese NETSUKE, etc. It also takes on a high polish and is translucent in thin sheets. It has been used as a medium for carving since the palaeolithic age. Some of the finest ivory carvings date from the Early Christian or Late Antique period (from the late C4), notably CONSULAR DIPTYCHS and other diptychs carved with pagan and Christian subjects, also caskets and pyxes. Such carvings were frequently imitated in the CAROLINGIAN period,

Ivory casket, Cordoba, 964 A.D.
(Museo Arqueologico Nacional, Madrid)

Ivory panel, Madura, Madras, c18
(Victoria & Albert Museum)

Ivory comb, known as the comb of St Heribert, late c9 (Schnütgenmuseum, Cologne)

mainly on caskets and as decorations for the bindings of manuscripts. Some very beautiful ecclesiastical carvings were executed in Anglo-Saxon England c10–c11, e.g. a crozier in the Victoria & Albert Museum. The GOTHIC style began to influence ivory carvers shortly after 1250. Statuettes, some of which rank among the masterpieces of Gothic sculpture (e.g. *The Coronation of the Virgin* and the *Deposition* in the Louvre), diptychs and triptychs of religious subjects were produced in large quantities in France and elsewhere (it is seldom possible to determine their precise place of origin). Ivory was also used for secular objects, notably caskets and small hand mirrors, often carved with courtly or chivalric themes in low relief. The art of ivory carving set into a decline shortly before the mid C15 and received little stimulus from the Renaissance. In the C16 it was used less for sculpture than for domestic articles such as seals, rosaries, mirror-

Ivory salt cellar by Georg Petel, early C17 (Royal Collection, Stockholm)

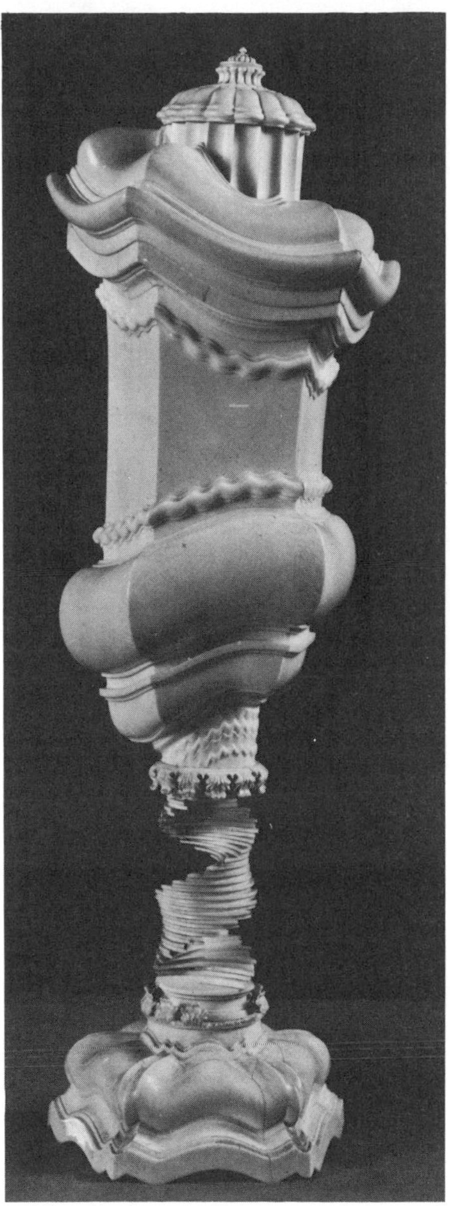

(Right) Ivory cup and cover, Florentine, 1681 (Victoria & Albert Museum)

cases, memorandum tablets, hunting horns, powder flasks, the handles of daggers and table-knives, the pommels of swords and the decorative parts of saddles. It has been used for such purposes ever since, also occasionally as an inlay for furniture. Figurative ivory carving was revived in the Baroque period, especially in Germany and the Low Countries: the leading carvers included Francois Duquesnoy, Gerard van Opstal, Lucas Faid'herbe, Georg Patel, Christof Harrich, Christof ANGERMAIR, J. M. MAUCHER, and Balthazar STOCKAMER. In the early c18 the Norwegian Magnus Berg, the Frenchman Jean Cavalier and David Le Marchand and, later, the Tyrolean Simon Troger, executed some very fine work, sometimes of extreme virtuosity. Vast quantities of ivory carvings were produced in the c19 – reproductions, fakes and innumerable original works which tend to emphasize, with minute undercut decorations, the less pleasing qualities of the medium – its slithery surface and translucency.

Ivory urn, attributed to J. Maucher, late c17 (Victoria & Albert Museum)

Ivory chess-man with balls-within-balls base, Chinese, c19 (Victoria & Albert Museum)

Lit: L. Grodechi, *Ivoires français*, Paris 1947; G. C. Williamson, *The Book of Ivory*, London 1938; H. W. Hegerman, *Elfenbein*, Hanau 1966.

Engraved initial letter from edition of Sallust, printed by Joachin Ibarra, Madrid, 1772

Jack, George (1855–1932). Architect and furniture designer, born in the U.S.A., studied architecture in Glasgow and entered the London office of Philip WEBB *c.*1880. He became chief furniture designer to **Morris & Co.** *c.*1890. Strongly influenced by the QUEEN ANNE REVIVAL he designed rather rich furniture, often with Morrissey foliage patterns in marquetry.

Jackfield pottery A Shropshire factory directed by **Maurice Thursfield** *c.*1750–75, making, especially, black glazed red earthenware decorated with oil gilding and unfired painting (which has usually worn off), often with Jacobite inscriptions. Black milk-jugs in the form of cows are often ascribed to Jackfield though they are known to have been made in STAFFORDSHIRE as well.

Jackfield ware Black lead-glazed earthenware made in Staffordshire, often with applied decorations such as vine leaves and grapes picked out with oil-gilding. They were not made at the JACKFIELD POTTERY as is sometimes erroneously thought, and may well antedate it.

Jackson, John Baptist (*c.*1701–*c.*1780). Leading English print-maker and wallpaper designer. He began as an engraver, went to Paris *c.*1726 where he met PAPILLON, and developed a new process of making *chiaroscuro* prints. He moved to Rome and Venice where he executed numerous *chiaroscuro* prints after paintings by Titian, Veronese, Jacopo Bassano, etc. He returned to England in 1746 and quickly adapted the *chiaroscuro* process to wallpapers, setting up a factory in Battersea. In a book published in 1754 he attacked the current vogue for Chinese wallpapers and advocated papers decorated with prints after paintings by Claude, Gaspar Poussin, Salvator Rosa and other landscape painters, or with *trompe l'oeil* prints of antique vases and statues. But he failed to wean the English public from Chinese papers and seems to have had little success with the more sober wares he offered. Only a few fragments of his wallpapers survive – panels of Italianate landscapes printed from several wood blocks in at least eight shades of colour (Victoria & Albert Museum, London). He also designed paper decorated with attractive naturalistic flowers.

Lit: J. Kainer, *John Baptist Jackson . . . ,* Washington 1962.

Jacob, Georges (1739–1814). He was a figure of considerable importance in the history of French furniture, being one of the last of the C18 *menuisiers* and among the first C19 furniture manufacturers. His work forms a bridge between the LOUIS XVI and EMPIRE styles. Of Burgundian peasant origin, he went to Paris as a youth and is said to have served his apprenticeship under DELANOIS, a successful *menuisier* who clung obstinately to the Rococo Louis XV style. He became a *maître menuisier* in 1765 and began by working in a predominantly Rococo manner. But he soon adopted the more fashionable Louis XVI style and by the early 1780s he had established himself as one of the leading chair-makers in Paris. The general form of the Louis XVI chair – its rectangular outline and richly carved floral and classical ornament – owes much to him. He was also among the first in France to use ungilded wood – mahogany – for chairs. Characteristic features of his early chairs are triangular foliated motifs at the junction of arm and back, of his later chairs, square-framed rosettes at the top of the legs. To gain lightness without loss of strength he began, *c.*1780, to plane away the inner angle of the frame beneath the seat. He introduced the sabre leg and shortly before the Revolution began making lyre-backed chairs, presumably inspired by English models as was also his use of mahogany. He also made beds and, unlike other *menuisiers*, occasionally produced tables. Sometimes his ornament is over-weighted, as on his famous bed of 1782 in the Residenz, Munich, heavily enriched with carved cornucopias and princely insignia and originally incorporating a marble group of *Cupid and Psyche* by the sculptor M.-C. Monnot (who may have been responsible for the whole design). He worked for several foreign clients, supplying chairs through the *marchand-mercier* Daguerre for Carlton House, London, and Woburn Abbey. Though employed by Marie Antoinette, the Comte d'Artois and the King's cousin, the Duc de Chartres, he worked relatively little for the Court who preferred SENÉ, BOULARD and FOLIOT as chair-makers.

The most interesting of his works for the Crown is a set of chairs made for Marie Antoinette's dairy at Rambouillet and now at Versailles. These were designed by the painter Hubert Robert in the so-called Etruscan Style, i.e. decorated with a profusion of palmettes and other antique ornaments. More remarkable are the chairs and day-bed made for and to the design of the Neo-Classical painter J.-L. David shortly before 1788, for these were among the first pieces of useful household furniture made in direct imitation of Greek and Roman prototypes; they were upholstered in red wool decorated with black palmettes. Also to David's design he made a mahogany bed decorated with gilt bronzes for the Duc de Chartres (son of Philippe Égalité and later Louis-Philippe). The pieces themselves have vanished but some idea of their appearance can be gained from David's paintings, *Paris and Helen* and *Brutus* (Louvre), both of which were completed in 1789.

Jacob was almost ruined by the Revolution (the Comte d'Artois alone owed him 85,000 *livres*) but David protected him and introduced him to PERCIER and FONTAINE who designed furniture he made for the *Comité du salut publique* under the Terror. He retired in 1796, handing over his business to his sons **Georges II** and **François-Honoré-Georges** (later to call himself JACOB-DESMALTER). But in 1800 he returned to help in the large task of furnishing the consular apartments in the Tuileries, and on the death of Georges II Jacob went into partnership with his other son, working under the business name of *Jacob-Desmalter et Cie*. They provided much of the finest furniture for the Napoleonic palaces, often working to the designs of Percier and Fontaine in a style of truly imperial opulence – chairs with sphinxes supporting their arms, X-stools with lion-heads, commodes adorned with gilt-bronze antique ornaments, richly draped beds with carved cornucopias, swans and much juicy antique leaf ornament, etc. Some of their best pieces were made for Josephine and are still at Malmaison. The workshop grew to an industrial size and (since the *corporations* with their restrictive rules had been abolished during the Revolu-

G. Jacob: armchair, designed by Hubert Robert for the dairy at Rambouillet, 1787 (Château de Versailles)

tion) could now produce both *ébénisterie* and *menuiserie*. Georges Jacob finally retired in 1813 and died in the following year. His cousin **Henri Jacob** (1753–1824) who became a *maître-menuisier* in 1779, imitated his style and profited from his name though his work is much inferior. His furniture is stamped 'H. Jacob'. *For additional illustrations see* DIRECTOIRE STYLE.

Lit: H. Lefuel, *Georges Jacob*, Paris 1923; F. J. B. Watson, *Louis XVI Furniture*, London 1960; D. Ledoux-Lebard in *Apollo*, Sept. 1964, pp. 199–205.

Jacob-Desmalter, François-Honoré-Georges (1770–1841). The son of Georges JACOB under whom he trained. He and his brother **Georges II Jacob** (1768–1803) took over their father's business in 1796, stamping their products *Jacob frères*. In 1803 he assumed the name Jacob-Desmalter and went into partnership with his father under the name *Jacob-Desmalter et Cie*, and produced some of the best Empire furniture. Neither his father's death nor the Restoration made much difference to his style. In 1825 his son **Georges-Alphonse** (1799–1870) took over the business and continued to produce furniture in the Jacob manner, though of increasing heaviness, until 1847 when he retired and sold the concern to JEANSELME. *For additional illustrations see* EMPIRE STYLE.

Lit: H. Lefuel, *François-Honoré-Georges Jacob-Desmalter*, Paris 1925; S. Grandjean, *Empire Furniture 1800–1825*, London 1966.

Jacobite glass Wineglasses made after 1688 (and in greater quantity after 1745) and engraved with portraits of the Old or Young Pretender or, more usually, Jacobite symbols (the rose, the oak, etc.). Extensively faked.

Jacobs, Lazarus and **Isaac,** *see* BRISTOL GLASS-HOUSES.

Jacobsen, Arne (1902–71). Danish architect and designer who worked with great elegance and refinement in the International Modern style. During the 1950s he designed some excellent cutlery and furniture, notably a very graceful and economic little stacking chair with a moulded plywood seat supported on a tripod steel rod or laminated wood base (1953, later modified and produced wholly of moulded plywood, 1957), an

F. H. Jacob-Desmalter: cradle of the King of Rome, with ormolu mounts by Thomire, 1811 (Louvre)

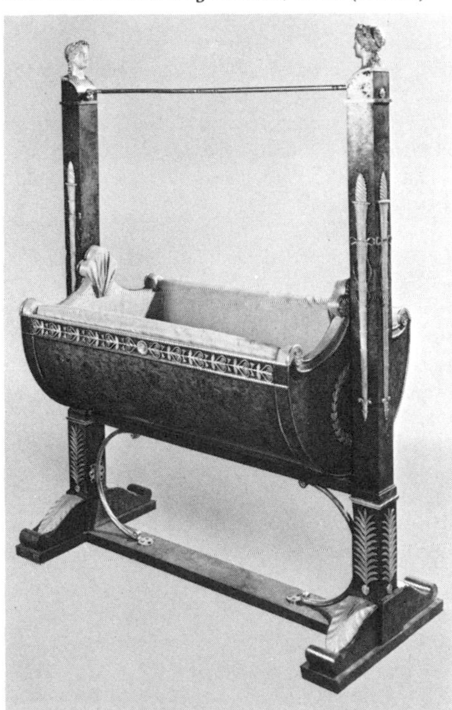

A. Jacobsen: Swan chair, 1958 (Musée des Arts Décoratifs, Paris)

elegant and now famous upholstered fibre-glass chair on a chromium-plated steel swivel base, known as the Egg ('Aegget') chair, and the similarly suave 'Swan' chair and sofa (designed for the S.A.S. Hotel in Copenhagen in 1958). More recently his furniture had become rather mannered, e.g. the high-backed chairs designed for St Catherine's College, Oxford, in 1963. He had also designed abstract patterned carpeting and floral patterned cottons.

Lit: T. Faber, *Arne Jacobsen*, Milan 1964.

Jacomo da Pesaro, *see* VENICE POTTERIES.

Jacopo Maiolica painter at Cafaggiolo. *See* FATTORINI, Jacopo.

Jacquard loom A hand loom capable of weaving very complicated patterns and needing only one man to operate it. It was invented *c.*1805 by **Joseph-Marie Jacquard** (1752–1834) of Lyons but first came into use in France *c.*1815, revolutionizing the textile industry. It culminated the work of other inventors, combining the needles and hooks of **Bouchier** (1725) and the chain of cards of **Falcon** (1728), and replaced the cylinder of **Vancauson** (1745) by a prism and lantern wheel.

Jacquemart and Bénard Leading firm of wallpaper producers in Paris during the French Revolution. Established in 1791 as the successor to RÉVEILLON, producing papers in the same style, especially the Pompeiian manner. But topical motifs were soon introduced. HUET designed a Pompeiian paper with the 'Altar of Liberty' as the main motif; other papers had caps of liberty, fasces and scales of Justice surrounded by tricolour ribbons. Under the Empire they produced at least one SCENIC WALLPAPER (*La Chasse à Courre*) but generally specialized in designs similar to those for textiles or *trompe-l'oeil* imitations of scalloped silk hangings or knotted draperies held together by cords and tassels. During the Restoration period they took up the new topical motifs and issued one paper (1825) decorated with the Bourbon Order of Saint Esprit. The elder Jacquemart died in 1804 and was succeeded by his son who ran the firm with great success until 1840.

Lit: H. Clouzot & C. Follot, *Le Papier peint en France*, Paris 1935.

Jacques, Charles-Symphorien, *see* SCEAUX POTTERY AND PORCELAIN FACTORY and MENNECY PORCELAIN FACTORY.

Jade A mineralogically imprecise term for various kinds of hard stone, notably nephrite (a calcium-magnesium silicate) and the superficially similar but structurally different dark green or emerald-coloured jadeite (a sodium-aluminium silicate). Nephrite has been prized in the areas where it is found (notably Chinese Turkestan and Central America) and worked into amulets, ceremonial implements, etc., since prehistoric times. It is ice-cold to the touch, so hard that it cannot be scratched by steel, translucent, gives a musical note when struck, takes a high, oily polish, and ranges in colour from white (the most highly prized in China known as Mutton Fat Jade (*yang-chih-yü*) because of its greasy, lard-like appearance) to various shades of brown and green of which that known as Spinach Jade (*po-ts'ai-yü*) from Siberia is notable. Chinese carvers have striven to make the most of all its properties. The earliest examples are ritual implements dating from the Neolithic period and the art of jade carving was perfected by the SHANG YIN period. Jade carvings are exceptionally difficult to date but a tendency towards elaboration, displays of virtuosity in undercutting, etc., are apparent after the SUNG period. Jadeite was not worked in China before the C18 and then used mainly for articles of jewellery. *Illustrated opposite.*

Lit: S. H. Hansford, *Chinese Carved Jades*, London 1968.

Jalousie A Venetian blind or shutter with slats arranged in a similar manner.

Jamnitzer, Wenzel (1508–85). He was the greatest German Mannerist goldsmith. A member of a large family of goldsmiths and silversmiths, he was born in Vienna but moved with his father **Hans** (died *c.*1549) and his brother **Albrecht** (died 1555) to Nuremberg sometime before 1534 when he became a *Bürger* of the city and a master of the Goldsmiths' guild. In 1543 he was appointed coin and seal die-cutter to the city; in

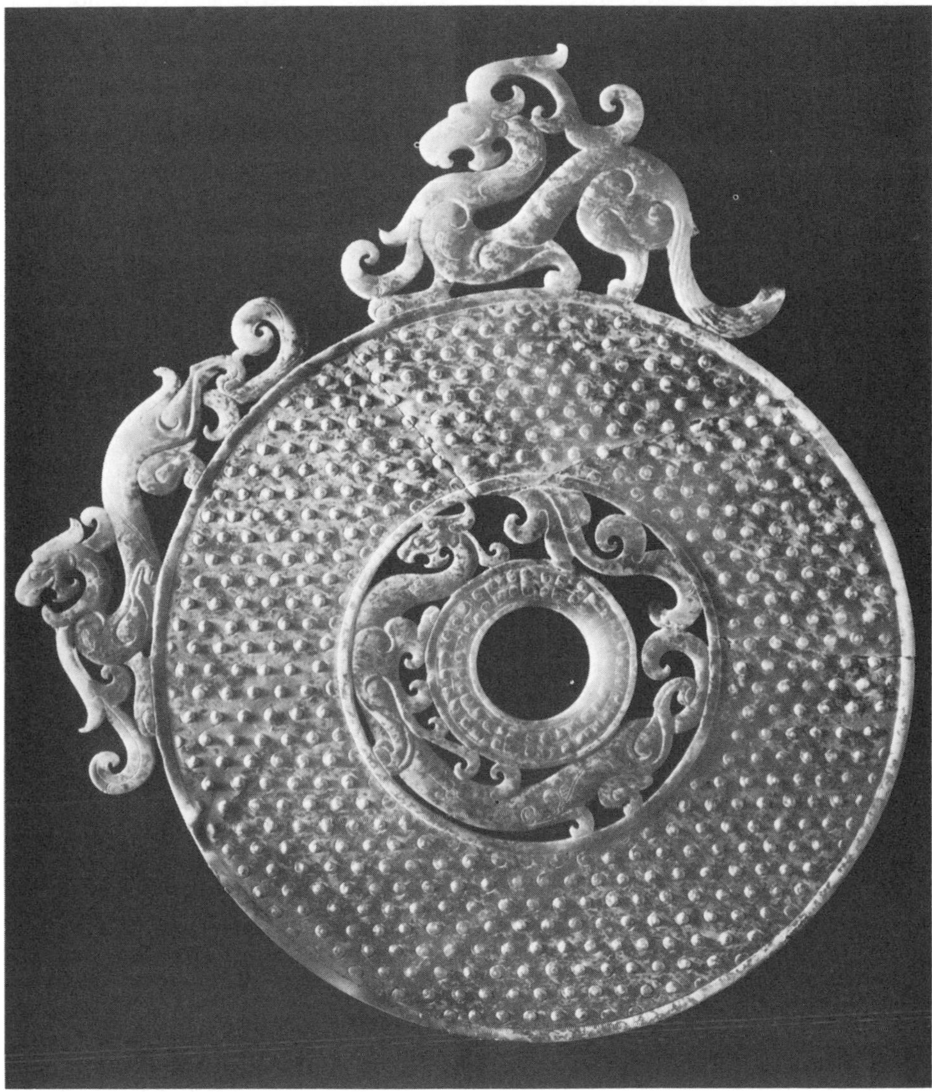

Jade: Chinese disk or Pi, *Warring States period, 481–221* B.C. *(William Rockhill Nelson Gallery of Art, Kansas City)*

1552 he became master of the city mint and was thus recognized as the leader of the Nuremberg goldsmiths. In 1556 he became a member of the *Grosse Rat* or great council of the city and thereafter held increasingly prominent appointments in the city council. As *Kaiserlicher Hofgoldschmied* he served four Hapsburg Emperors. His earliest surviving work is the 'Merckelsche' table-centre in the Rijksmuseum in Amsterdam. It was completed by 1549 and is named after a Nuremberg merchant who saved it from the melting-pot in 1809. It is almost a compendium of the goldsmiths' art and displays Jamnitzer's consummate mastery in modelling, embossing, engraving and enamelling, besides his peculiarity of using casts of insects, reptiles and grasses. In 1556 he made an even larger table-centre for the Emperor Maximilian II of Austria, completed for the Emperor Rudolf II, but of this only the four gilt-bronze caryatids survive (Kunsthistorisches Museum, Vienna). Among his assistants at this time was Matthias ZUNDT. The *Kaiserpokal* or Imperial Cup which Jamnitzer made in 1564 still survives (Kunstgewerbemuseum, West Berlin) but it is less complex than his table-centres and follows a standard C16 pattern. His Mannerist tendencies were to find full expression in the jewel casket of *c*.1560 and nautilus-shell cup of *c*.1570, both in the Residenzmuseum in Munich, and in a delicately embossed mirror frame in the Metropolitan Museum in New York. He is best known, however, for his fantastic and minutely realistic ornament of insects, shells and creeping reptiles – silver counterparts of the pottery of Bernard PALISSY – such as his silver box in the Kunsthistorisches Museum in Vienna and the extraordinary basin in the Louvre in Paris and the equally strange ewer in the treasury of Ragusa cathedral in Sicily. His son **Hans II** (*c*.1538–1603) became a master of the Nuremberg Goldsmiths' guild in 1563 and to him (as well as to his father) has been attributed a handbell seething with reptiles, locusts and other insects in the British Museum in London. Albrecht's son, **Bartel** (*c*.1548–96) became a master in 1575 and is known by several fine pieces of silver, notably a pair of nautilus shell cups supported by a mermaid and a triton in the Kassel Museum. To the next generation belonged the son of Hans II, **Christoph** (1563–1618, master 1592). Much of his work is simple but his more elaborate pieces, executed in a transitional Mannerist-Baroque style, reveal that he was very nearly as good a craftsman as his grandfather, e.g., a cup fashioned like an angel with spread wings (1595, Armoury Museum, Moscow), a fantastically over-

W. Jamnitzer: casket of silver gilt set with precious stones, Nuremberg, c.1560 *(Residenzmuseum, Munich)*

C. Jamnitzer: silver ewer, Nuremberg, c.1600 (Kunsthistorisches Museum, Vienna)

wrought ewer and basin (Kunsthistorisches Museum, Vienna) and an endearing table fountain in the form of an elephant (Kunstgewerbemuseum, West Berlin).

Lit: M. Rosenberg, *Jamnitzer*, Frankfurt-am-Main 1920; J. Hayward in *The Connoisseur*, 1957, clxiv, pp. 148–54; K. Pechstein in *Jahrbuch des Berliner Museums*, VIII (1966), pp. 237–85.

Jansenist bindings Late C17 French type of bookbinding, very plain and austere with little ornamentation or gilding except in the doublures. They became the fashion at the Court of Louis XIV, being much favoured by Mme de Maintenon. They contrast sharply with the ornate and sumptuous Louis XIV Style in general.

Japanese pottery and porcelain Pottery has been made in Japan since the Neolithic period but the potter's wheel was not introduced until *c.*200 B.C. Wares of the Nara and Heian periods (645–1185) show strong Chinese influence and this influence persisted throughout the history of Japanese ceramics. But the best and most interesting Japanese wares are those furthest from the Chinese. Their most individual characteristic is their completely free decoration – often no more than a flower or a leaf or a calligraph splashed in far off-centre. Most of the pottery is ornamental rather than utilitarian since ordinary household wares were usually made of lacquered wood. But the jars, bowls, trays, incense burners, scent-boxes, etc., made for the Zen Buddhist Tea Ceremony were always of pottery (not porcelain) and form the main category of Japanese ceramics. They were of the most austere simplicity, rather heavy, with an artfully rough finish and quite unlike anything made by the smooth-porcelain-loving Chinese. The main centre of production was at Seto and the term *Seto-mono* became colloquially equivalent to pottery itself. The most famous types of Seto pottery are the white Shino ware and bluish-green Oribe ware (late C16 to early C17). But *see also* KARATSU WARES, RAKU WARES and OGATA KENZAN. Since their first appearance in the West in the late C19, Japanese TEA CEREMONY WARES have exerted a strong influence on European STUDIO POTTERS. Porcelain was made in Japan from 1616 (when a source of china clay was discovered) at ARITA and later at Mikawachi and Kutani. Increasingly large quantities were produced for export to Europe where those decorated in the KAKIEMON style became very popular in the C18. The arrival of Americans and Europeans in Japan in the mid C19 confirmed the Japanese belief that Western taste was execrable and many of the most hideous of all ceramic nightmares were created for export to Europe and America in the last decades of the century, those made at SATSUMA being notorious. But they continued to produce exquisitely sensitive Tea Ceremony pottery for their own use.

Lit: S. Jenyns, *Japanese Pottery*, London 1971; S. Jenyns, *Japanese Porcelain*, New York 1965.

Japanning The name given to various methods of imitating oriental LACQUER in Europe and North America. The essential ingredient of true lacquer, the resin of the *rhus vernicifera*, was not available in Europe. European imitations were made of gum-lac, seed-lac or shell-lac, different preparations of the substance deposited on trees by an insect (*coccus lacca*), dissolved in spirits of wine. For the decoration of wooden objects – furniture, small boxes, brush handles, trays, etc. – numerous coats were applied, various colours being used, mainly black, dark green, sealing-wax red (an English speciality) and occasionally late C17 and later at PONTYPOOL. It was practised extensively in C18 and C19 Europe and from *c.*1740 onwards in N. America where it is called Toleware or Tolerware. Such wares were generally decorated either with chinoiseries or with bunches of gaily coloured flowers and could never be mistaken for oriental lacquer.

Lit: H. Huth, *Lacquer of the West*, Chicago and London 1971.

yellow. Decorations were outlined in gold size, built up with a composition made of gum arabic and sawdust and then coloured, polished and gilded with metal dust. The whole surface was burnished. The finest examples are difficult to distinguish from true lacquer though the decorations, which are usually (but not invariably) chinoiseries, give them away. Another type of japanning was applied to metal wares – canisters, trays, teapots, etc. The basic material was tinplated sheet iron (*tôle* in French) covered with a black asphaltum varnish, heat dried and then decorated in gold and colours. This process was first developed at BILSTON in Staffordshire in the

Japonaiserie An exotic style practised in C19 Europe, derived from but seldom directly imitative of Japanese works of art. Although Japanese porcelain and lacquer had been imported since the C17 and decorative motifs from them had been used by European craftsmen and designers, no Japanese cult comparable with CHINOISERIE arose. The opening of Japan to the West in the 1850s (the crucial trading agreement was signed in 1858) precipitated a flood of laudatory literature on the country. The first European exhibitions of Japanese art were held in London in 1854 and 1862. Imports rapidly increased, of wood-block prints, lacquer INRO, NETSUKE and some ex-

(Opposite page) Japanned commode in green and gold, Venice, c.1740 (Palazzo Rezzonico, Venice)

Japanned clock-case (movement by Thomas Windmills) (Moniz Galvaos Collection, Lisbon)

amples of furniture and rough lead-glazed JAPANESE POTTERY as well as objects made expressly for the European market. Several French potters, e.g. DAMMOUSE and DECK, abandoned European styles for free essays in Japonaiserie and a great deal of furniture in this style was also made, much of it gimcrack. But in England E. W. GODWIN designed some pleasantly fresh, clean-lined tables and cabinets which were inspired by rather than imitative of Japanese furniture and pointed the way towards the simplicity of C20 industrial design. *Illustrated next column.*

Lit: H. Honour, *Chinoiserie*, London 1961; *Japonisme. Japanese influence on French Art 1854–1910*, Exh. Cat., Cleveland Museum of Art, 1975.

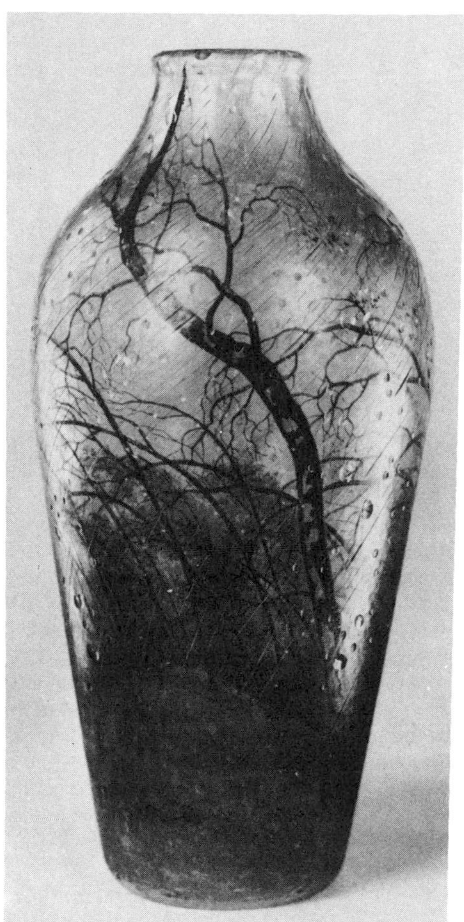

Japonaiserie: glass vase by Daum, c.1885 (Musée des Arts Décoratifs, Paris)

Jardinière A stand for flower pots, usually in metal but sometimes in wood.

Jarry, Jacques, *see* APREY POTTERY FACTORY and SCEAUX POTTERY AND PORCELAIN FACTORY.

Jarves, Deming, *see* BOSTON AND SANDWICH GLASS COMPANY.

Jasper ware Fine-grained, hard, slightly translucent stoneware made by adding sulphate of barium to the usual clay, perfected by WEDGWOOD in 1775. It is pure white but can be stained to a wide variety of colours, the most famous being the Wedgwood blue. For the earliest pieces the colour was mixed with the body (called 'solid jasper') but after 1777 it was applied to the surface in washes (called 'jasper dip') leaving moulded relief ornament white.

Lit: R. Reilly, *Wedgwood Jasper*, London 1972.

Jaune jonquille, *see* FONDPORZELLAN and SÈVRES (or VINCENNES-SÈVRES) PORCELAIN FACTORY.

Jeannest, Pierre Émile, *see* ELKINGTON, George Richard, and MINTON'S POTTERY AND PORCELAIN FACTORY.

Jeanselme, Charles-Joseph-Marie (1827–after 1871). He was the son of **Joseph-Pierre-François Jeanselme** (d.1860) who acquired in 1847 the JACOB-DESMALTER concern and built up one of the largest cabinet-making workshops in mid-C19 Paris. They supplied the royal and imperial residences with a great quantity of furniture ranging from reproduction Boulle to Louis XVI in style. In 1863 Charles Jeanselme took into partnership the *ébéniste* **Godin,** who took over the business when Jeanselme retired in 1871. In 1880 his son **Charles-Joseph-Henri** joined the business as a partner. In 1893 they absorbed LEMARCHAND'S business. A **Pierre-Antoine Jeanselme,** called **Jeanselme Jeune,** does not appear to have been related to Charles-Joseph-Marie Jeanselme but was active in Paris as a furniture-maker in the 1850s.

Lit: D. Ledoux-Lebard, *Les ébénistes-parisiens (1795–1870)*, Paris 1965.

Jelliff, John (1813–93). American furniture maker working at Newark, New Jersey, from 1836 until 1890 when he retired. His furniture is well made, usually in walnut or rosewood and in Neo-Gothic, Neo-Rococo or Neo-Louis XVI styles.

Lit: M. E. White in *Antiques* LXXIV (1958), pp. 322–5.

Jelly glass A glass, sometimes with one or two handles, made in the C18 to hold a single portion of jelly, custard, syllabub, etc. No specific form seems to have been evolved, but the name is usually reserved for glasses with tall vase-shaped bowls on very low stems.

Jenaer Glaswerk German glasshouse founded in 1884 at Mainz making glass for industry, optical glass, and household wares, etc. Its most notable products include table wares made to the design of W. WAGENFELD in the 1920s and kitchen wares designed by Heinz Loffelhardt in the 1950s and 60s.

C.-J.-M. Jeanselme: chair,
(Victoria & Albert Museum)

Jenaer Glaswerk: jugs, c.1950
(Kunstgewerbemuseum, Zurich)

Jennens & Bettridge A notable English firm of PAPIER MÂCHÉ manufacturers who took over the Birmingham factory of **H. Clay** in 1816, had showrooms in London, at 6 Hallam Street West, Belgrave Square, and remained active until 1864. One of their employees, G. NEVILLE, discovered a technique of painting on black papier mâché in 1831 but left them in 1846. In 1847 they patented a type of inlaid decoration with coloured glass, tortoiseshell, mother-of-pearl, ivory and sometimes gem stones. At the Great Exhibition of 1851 they showed a number of products ranging from small boxes and trays to an elaborately modelled easy chair, a pianoforte, and a child's cot with much symbolical decoration designed by the sculptor John Bell.

Lit: G. B. Hughes in *Concise Encyclopaedia of Antiques*, vol. IV, London 1959.

Jensen, Georg (1866–1935). A Danish silversmith, he originated the 'Jensen style' which has been much imitated in Europe and the U.S.A. After training as a goldsmith in Copenhagen he is said to have joined Mogens BALLIN's pewter and silver workshop for a time. In 1900 he travelled in France and Italy. On returning to Denmark he started a small porcelain factory which failed. He then turned to jewellery and silver. In 1905 he exhibited successfully at The Hague and in 1907 began his long and fruitful association with the painter **Johan Rohde** with whom he evolved a personal style of striking simplicity which was to make his name famous. His jewellery and some of his early silver is Art Nouveau in style. Later, his flat-ware and teapots, coffee-pots and other domestic wares are distinguished by their clean outlines, sense of balance and solidity. His knives have shorter blades, his forks shorter and more widely spaced prongs than was usual. His vessels often have the famous Jensen satiny surface produced by annealing the piece, immersing it in sulphuric acid and then buffing it in such a way as to allow slight oxidization to remain. The firm he founded in Copenhagen still survives and maintains its reputation for good, solid, sensible silverware. His son **Soren Georg Jensen** (b.1917) is now the chief designer and the firm has branches all over the world, notably in New York and London. Examples of Jensen's earlier pre-Second World War silver are in the Kunstindustrimuseum, Copenhagen, Victoria & Albert Museum, London and the Busch-Reisinger Museum, Harvard University, Cambridge, Mass.

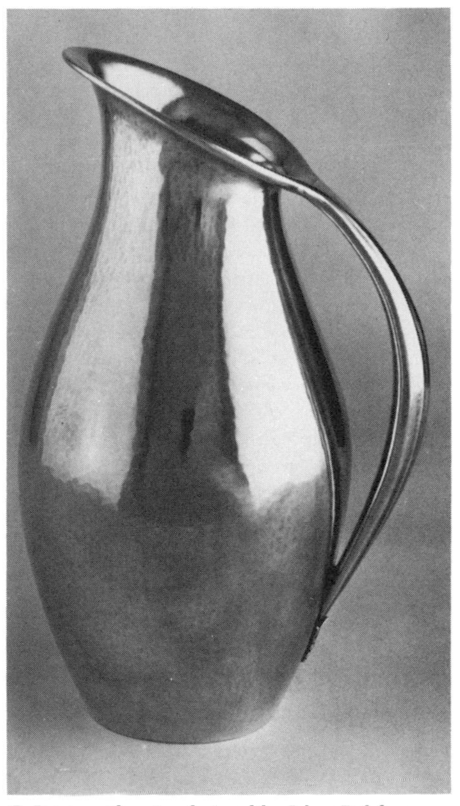

G. Jensen: silver jug designed by Johan Rohde, 1925 (Kunstindustrimuseet, Copenhagen)

Lit: I. M. Olsen, *Solvsmeden Georg Jensen*, Copenhagen 1937; W. Schwartz, *Georg Jensen*, Copenhagen 1958.

Jensen, Gerreit or **Gerrit** (*fl.c.*1680–1715). His name was sometimes anglicized to Johnson. He was the most accomplished of the Anglo-Dutch cabinet-makers who had such an enormous influence on William and Mary furniture. Presumably Flemish or Dutch by birth, he had settled in London by 1680. After the 1688 Revolution he was much employed by the Crown – in fact he was cabinet-maker to the royal household during four reigns, from Charles II to Queen Anne. In 1693 he took premises in St Martin's Lane in London. He retired in 1715. He appears to have been the first cabinet-maker in England to achieve individual distinction, although he was totally forgotten for some two centuries after his death. The furniture he made for Charles II has vanished, but several pieces he made for William and Mary survive at Windsor Castle and Hampton Court. His work is Dutch pseudo-Louis XIV in style and notable for its 'fine' or arabesque marquetry with metal inlays similar to BOULLE MARQUETRY: indeed he might be called the English Boulle though his work is, of course, very much more modest. He is known to have had direct contact with French cabinet-makers, notably Pierre GOLLE. He also specialized in mirrors and in japanning. In his later work marquetry gave way to japanning.

Lit: R. Edwards & M. Jourdain, *Georgian Cabinet Makers*, London 1955.

Jesuit porcelain Chinese mid-C18 porcelain decorated, usually in monochrome, with religious subjects copied from European prints, generally supposed to have been decorated to the order of Jesuit missionaries for export to Europe, though there is no evidence for this.

Jever pottery A central German faience factory (near Zerbst) founded in 1760 by J. F. S. TÄNNICH and producing handsome tablewares (notably tureens in the form of swans), figures and openwork baskets painted in high temperature colours (without red). But quality declined after Tännich left for the KIEL factory and it closed in 1776. The name 'JEVER' was sometimes used as a mark.

Lit: O. Riesebieter, *Die deutschen Fayencen des 17 und 18 Jahrhunderts*, Leipzig 1921.

Jewel ornament C17 type of relief ornament composed of ovals, pyramids and other simple forms arranged geometrically, especially in carved woodwork.

Jewelled decoration A type of ceramic decoration invented *c.*1781 at SÈVRES by **Cotteau.** Drops of coloured enamel were applied and fused over gold or silver foil. A similar process seems to have been in use earlier at St-Cloud and in Germany. It was revived in the mid C19 at WORCESTER and the GOSS PORCELAIN FACTORY.

Johnson, Thomas (1714–*c.*1778). English Rococo furniture maker and designer, he was born in London and had established himself as an independent craftsman by the later 1740s. He issued his first collection of designs, *Twelve Gerandoles*, in 1755 and a further set in monthly parts 1756–7 and then in volume form in 1758 (reissued with one extra plate as *One Hundred and Fifty New Designs*, 1761). In 1760 he published *A New Book of Ornaments*, from which only one plate survives though others are known from C19 reproductions. All the furnishings for which

T. Johnson:
design for a kettle stand, 1757

Johnson published designs are of a type known at the time as 'carvers' pieces'. They include no case-furniture or seat-furniture. They are limited to such objects as girandoles, mirror frames, side- or console-tables, candle-stands, etc., all pieces which are decorative rather than useful and allow scope for the display of the carver's fantasy. Stylistically they owe much to France. Because of their intricacy it has been doubted whether any of the designs could have been realized in wood. But a number of pieces of furniture have been discovered which correspond quite closely with Johnson's engraved designs, e.g. candle-stand in the Victoria & Albert Museum, London. It is not known whether such pieces were made by Johnson or in his workshops.

Lit: H. Hayward, *Thomas Johnson and the English Rococo*, London 1964.

Johnston, David (*fl.*1836–45). English potter who in 1836 acquired a pottery factory on the quai de Bacalan, Bordeaux, which he ran with **M. J. Viellard,** employing 400 workmen by 1839 and specializing in blue printed wares of English type (examples in Musée nationale de céramique de Sèvres). He also attempted to make porcelain but this ruined him and the firm went into liquidation in 1845. *See also* BORDEAUX POTTERIES.

Johnston, Thomas (*fl.*1732–67). He was an American japanner and engraver working in Boston. Nearly all American japanned furniture of the early C18 was made in Boston where cabinet-makers were specializing in it in 1712.

Joined (or **Joint**) **stool** Early term for a wooden stool of which the component parts are fitted together with mortice and tenon joints or made by a joiner – as opposed to a piece of STICK FURNITURE.

Jomon pottery A very early group of Japanese ceramics, made in the course of some 7,000 years until about C3 B.C. in Central and S. Japan, but rather later in the North. Vessels were made without a wheel, by coiling strips of clay, and baked over open fires. The body is rough and unrefined but many pieces are elaborately decorated in relief or with incised ornament. The most impressive are large urns up to 60 cm. high.

Lit: J. E. Kidder, *Prehistoric Japanese Arts: Jomon Pottery*, Tokyo 1968.

Jones, Owen (1809–74). English designer, writer and architect. Toured the Middle East (1833) and Spain (1834) acquiring a love of Islamic and Hispano-Moresque arts which he helped to popularize in his *The Grammar of Ornament* (1856). This included not only the 'historical' styles much used by Victorian architects and designers but also oriental and even some primitive ornament. He insisted, like Ruskin, on honesty to materials and sound craftsmanship. He anticipated MORRIS by advocating formalized patterns (rather than naturalistic bouquets of flowers) for the decoration of wallpapers and textiles, and the Art Nouveau movement by suggesting that historical styles should be used less as material for imitation than as a source of inspiration. But the designs (for furniture, metalwork, carpets, textiles and wallpapers) in which he expressed his ideas are sometimes curiously arid. *Illustrated next page.*

Lit: A. Bøe, *From Gothic Revival to Functional Form*, Oslo and Oxford 1957.

Joseph or **Joseph Baumhauer** (d.1772). A German furniture-maker who settled in Paris, he became a *maître* in 1767 by special *brevet du Roi*. Highly skilled as a craftsman, his work is nevertheless slightly heavy and Teutonic in manner. His best furniture is in the Louis XV style though he also worked in the Louis XVI style, as well as in the Boulle technique and with PIETRE DURE panels. Examples of his work are in the Musée des Arts Décoratifs, Paris, the Wallace Collection, London, and the National Gallery, Washington, D.C.

Lit: F. J. B. Watson, *The Wrightsman Collection: Furniture*, New York 1966.

Joshaghan carpets, *see* PERSIAN CARPETS.

Joubert, François (*fl.*1749–93). French Rococo silversmith working in Paris where he became a *maître* in 1749. Madame de Pompadour was among his patrons. A magnificent tureen of 1761–2, with naturalistic Rococo ornament comparable in its refinement to that of Thomas GERMAIN, is in the Louvre. (For his mark *see* p. 894.)

O. Jones: wallpaper, 1874
(Victoria & Albert Museum)

Joubert, Gilles (1689–1775). One of Louis XV's chief furniture-makers, he was a contemporary and rival of GAUDREAU and CRESSENT. Though highly accomplished he was unoriginal and his style changed very little. He was continuously employed by the crown from 1748 onwards, having married a cousin of Mme de Pompadour's favourite *ébéniste* P. MIGEON. In 1758 he was appointed *ébéniste ordinaire du Garde-Meuble de la Couronne*, but he did not become *ébéniste du roi* until he was aged 74 – on OEBEN's death in 1763. He very rarely stamped his work and probably farmed out many of his royal commissions to CRIAERD, LACROIX and others. His conservative style is best seen in the two corner-cupboards he made in 1755 for the king's private apartments at Versailles to go *en suite* with Gaudreau's medal-cabinet of 1738. They are his masterpieces and are now in the Bibliothéque Nationale, Paris. On the accession of Louis XVI in 1774 he was replaced by RIESENER as *ébéniste du roi* and retired. His works are difficult to identify as many pieces mentioned in documents were made before the use of the *Estampille* was obligatory and his later work, being for the Crown, was exempt from stamping. But examples may be seen in the Wallace Collection, London, the Louvre, Paris, the Frick Collection, New York and the J. Paul Getty Museum, Los Angeles.

Lit: P. Verlet, *Le mobilier royal français*, Paris 1955; F. J. B. Watson, *The Wrightsman Collection: Furniture*, New York 1966.

Jourdain, Francis (1876–1958). Leading French designer of the inter-war period. He was the son of the Belgian-born **Frantz Jourdain** (1847–1935), architect of the iron-frame building for the well-known Paris store *La Samaritaine*. He was also a writer on aesthetics and a member of the Parisian literary world. After beginning his career as a painter he became, from 1911, more closely involved with the decorative arts, as a designer of furniture, textiles, wallpaper and ceramics. At the 1925 Exposition he was in charge of the smoking room and gymnasium of the *Ambassade Française*. But he generally worked in a very simple recti-linear style and designed furniture for inexpensive mass-production.

Lit: L. Moussinac, *Francis Jourdain*, Geneva 1955.

Ju ware (Ju-Yao) The rarest and finest type of Chinese stoneware, made at Ju Chou in central Honan for SUNG imperial use during a short period in the early C12 before the capital moved south in 1128. It has a buff body covered with a very fine regular light bluish glaze (lavender to green) with apparently intentional crazing. Forms – mainly bowls, bottles and brushwashers – are of the utmost delicacy and simplicity. There are

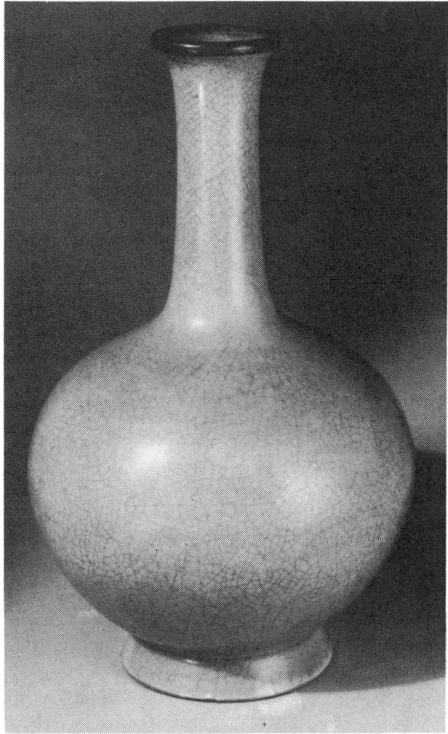

Ju ware bottle with copper-bound rim, Sung Dynasty (Percival David Foundation of Chinese Art, London)

fine examples in the Percival David Foundation of Chinese Art in London.

Lit: B. Gray, *Early Chinese Pottery and Porcelain*, London 1953.

Jugendstil, *see* ART NOUVEAU.

Juhl, Finn (b.1912). Danish architect and furniture designer who, with Arne JACOBSEN, Paul

Kjaerholm and Hans Wegner, has dominated the Danish furniture industry since the late 1940s. Though restrained, his work breaks with the severely functional and anonymous style established in Denmark by Kaare Klint. He regards furniture almost as a branch of sculpture, making much play with free forms and the abstract linear patterns created by diagonal bracings, etc. The exquisite simplicity and subtlety of his work demands fine woods and impeccable craftsmanship.

Jungfrauenbecher: silver double-cup by P. Christiensen Beyer, Norway, 1794 (Victoria & Albert Museum)

Jullien, Joseph, *see* Sceaux pottery and porcelain factory and Mennecy porcelain factory.

Jungfrauenbecher Late-c16 and c17 German type of wager cup in the form of a girl with a wide-spreading skirt holding a bowl above her head. The bowl is pivotted so that when the figure is inverted the skirt forms an upper cup and the bowl a lower one. Made especially in Nuremberg. *Illustrated previous column.*

Juvarra, Filippo (1678–1736). The greatest Italian architect of his period and one of the few recorded designers of Italian Baroque furniture. As court architect in Turin 1714–35 he directed a team of craftsmen, e.g. Piffetti and probably designed most of their furniture. Some of his drawings for console tables with human or animal figures emerging from elegant scroll work are preserved (Biblioteca Reale, Turin).

Lit: V. Viale, *Mostra del Barocco Piemontese*, Cat., Turin 1963.

F. Juvarra: design for a console table, c.1730 (Royal Library, Turin)

Wood-cut letter designed by Albrecht Dürer, 1525

Kabistan carpets, *see* CAUCASIAN CARPETS.

Kaendler, Johann Joachim, *see* KÄNDLER, Johann Joachim.

Kåge, Wilhelm, *see* GUSTAVSBERG POTTERY.

Kähler, Hermann August (1846–1917). Danish potter who, after working in the studio of the sculptor H. V. Biesen and in ceramic factories in Berlin and Zurich, took over his father's pottery at Naestved in 1872. Here he began by making faience and ceramic decorations for buildings but was soon experimenting with colours, glazes and especially the technique of lustre decoration. His most notable products were earthenware vases decorated in high-temperature colours, ranging from a coppery brown to deep violet-blue and a rich red lustre, either mottled or painted in an Art Nouveau manner. A number of notable artists including T. BINDESBØLL provided him with designs. He also executed Art Nouveau work to the design of O. ECKMANN. Karl Hansen Reistrup (1863–1929) provided models for figurative work, especially heads of animals. Kähler's contribution to numerous international exhibitions (e.g., Paris 1889, Chicago 1893, Munich Sezesion 1899) were highly praised in the art magazines of the time. He exerted considerable influence on art pottery in Scandinavia and elsewhere.

Kaisin, Johann Jakob, *see* WIESBADEN POTTERY.

Kakiemon, Sakaida (1596–1666). One of the most famous Japanese porcelain makers and painters, credited with the introduction into Japan, in 1644, of the process of painting in overglaze enamel colours and a style of decoration which is named after him. (He was the son of a potter **Ensai** (1574–1651), who had established kilns near ARITA with the help of Korean assistants.) His products cannot be distinguished from pieces made by his two sons (**Kakiemon II** and **III**) as none of them is marked but it seems unlikely that either the quality of material or decorative style associated with his name were fully developed before 1670, i.e. until after his death. The wares are of a highly refined, very smooth milk-white porcelain with a flawless glaze over which decorations, mainly flower and figure motifs, are overpainted in orange-red, green, lilac-blue, sometimes with a discreet use of yellow, turquoise and gold (and occasionally underglaze blue as well). The elements are painted asymmetrically and rather sparsely, enhancing the prominent white ground. The famous 'quail pattern' is characteristic: two quails rather off-centre, surrounded by slender asymmetrically arranged branches of stylized flowering plants. In the early C18 the quality of this ware set a standard for European porcelain factories, and the manner of decoration was much imitated, especially by the BOW, CHANTILLY, CHELSEA, MEISSEN, MENNECY and WORCESTER factories. The Kakiemon family still survives.

Lit: S. Jenyns, *Japanese Porcelain*, London 1965.

Kalb, Johann, *see* WESTERWALD POTTERIES.

Kaltemail A German term (literally cold enamel) for a kind of lacquer applied in the C16 and C17 in place of true enamel to metal, wood and ceramics which could not be fired – because they were either so delicate as to be liable to damage or too big to put in a kiln.

Kambli, Johann Melchior (1718–1783). He was one of the outstanding Rococo decorators and furniture-makers in Germany. Born in Zurich (the son of a clockmaker), he worked for Frederick the Great at Potsdam and Berlin from 1746 onwards. The first piece he is known to have made at Potsdam is a cartonnier for Sans Souci very much in the French manner. But he soon developed a more personal style, with much use of very finely executed gilt-bronze mounts, and was largely responsible for the creation of a distinct Potsdam Rococo style in furniture. In 1752 he established an independent workshop for bronzes at Potsdam. He executed decorations and bronze console tables to the designs of J. A. NAHL for the *bronzezimmer* in the Berlin Palace (1754–5, destroyed). From 1764 he made bronze mounts often of great opulence and fantasy for marquetry furniture by J. F. and H. W. SPINDLER.

Lit: H. Kreisel, *Die Kunst des deutschen Möbels*, vol. ii, Munich 1970.

Kanara Long narrow strips of carpet woven in pairs to go along the sides of a Persian room, often called runners.

C. F. Kandler: silver coffee jug, London, 1739 (Kunstgewerbemuseum, Berlin)

Kandler, Charles (*fl.*1725–50). The best and most exuberant Rococo silversmith in England after de LAMERIE. His masterpiece is a vast wine cistern of 1734 (Hermitage, Leningrad) based on a model by the sculptor Michael Rysbrack – a weighty Dionysian fantasy more than 5 ft across, with reliefs of *putti* and much vine ornament on the basin, resting on chained panthers and with handles in the form of bibulous Maenad and Bassarid term figures. Smaller works, like the tea-kettle of 1727–37 (Victoria & Albert Museum) liberally adorned with cast and embossed tritons, mermaids, shells, etc., reveal the influence of French and German Rococo silversmiths.

Kandler, Charles Frederick (*fl.*1735–78). German silversmith working in London, possibly the son of Charles KANDLER whose Britannia standard silver mark he adopted in 1735. He made much domestic silver in Rococo and Neo-Classical styles. *Illustrated previous column.* (For his mark *see* p. 894.)

Kändler, Johann Friedrich, *see* ANSBACH POTTERY & PORCELAIN FACTORY.

Kändler, Johann Joachim (1706–75). The greatest German porcelain modeller, responsible for much of the success of the MEISSEN PORCELAIN FACTORY and the author of works which were imitated throughout Europe. Trained as a sculptor in Dresden under B. Thomae (a pupil of Balthasar Permoser) he joined the Meissen factory in 1731 and was chief modeller there from 1733 to 1775 directing the other sculptors employed at the factory as well as making models himself. He began with a series of large, wonderfully spirited birds and animals (some more than a metre high) for the Japanese Palace in Dresden. (They were mostly based on sketches he made of the exotic birds and other animals in the Moritzburg zoo, hence their unprecedented naturalism and sense of movement.) Other large-scale works include a *Martyrdom of St Francis Xavier* (1738–40), a Crucifixion Group (1743), a series of Apostles (each one metre high) and a candlestick with angels for the Pope (1772–3). Such works were naturally too expensive for general production, and he was obliged to abandon his most extravagant project – a monument to Augustus

III of Saxony with a life-size equestrian figure surrounded by allegorical figures, all in porcelain – though parts of it were made. He designed some of the more elaborate vases made at the factory and also played a part in the design of table-wares, notably the Swan Service for Count Brühl (1737–41). But he was mainly engaged in modelling small figures, from 1736 onwards, quickly developing from the Baroque to the Rococo style which he adopted whole-heartedly after a visit to Paris in 1747. His output was enormous – more

J. J. Kändler: Punchinello and Pantaloon, Meissen porcelain, c.1740 (Private Collection)

than a thousand different subjects in all – *Commedia dell'Arte* actors, Turks, Chinamen, huntsmen, shepherds, miners, courtiers, gods and goddesses, tinkers, freemasons, monkey musicians, parakeets, pug dogs, etc. Though executed on a small scale they were never conceived as miniatures and avoid any suggestion of daintiness. Nor is there any touch of the mawkish about his fashionable courtly lovers and no less elegant shepherds and shepherdesses – they laugh with an uninhibited *joie de vivre* which animates all his figures (and which his imitators signally failed to catch). Many are derived from engravings (especially after Boucher) but he treated his sources with independence and originality, using them as no more than aids to his prodigal invention. His prestige waned after 1764 when he was made subordinate to C. W. E. DIETRICH.

Lit: H. Gröger, *Johann Joachim Kaendler: der Meister des Porzellans, zur zweihundertfunfzigsten Wiederkehr seines Geburtsjahres,* Dresden 1956; W. B. Honey, *Dresden China,* London 1954.

K'ang Hsi porcelain Chinese porcelain made in the reign of the CH'ING Emperor K'ang Hsi (1662–1722). Blue-and-white wares were improved technically so that the ground is of a pure white and the decorations of a brilliant sapphire blue. Polychrome wares of the type known in Europe as FAMILLE VERTE and *famille jaune* were produced in quantity both for the home market and for export. Decorations tend to be rather over-crowded, especially on the export wares and perhaps the most beautiful ceramic products of

K'ang Hsi porcelain sang de boeuf *bowl, c.1700 (Percival David Foundation of Chinese Art, London)*

K'ang Hsi porcelain dish decorated in famille verte *colours, late c17 (Percival David Foundation of Chinese Art, London)*

the period are the monochrome vases of SANG DE BOEUF, Peach Bloom red, various blues, CELADON and MIRROR BLACK.

Lit: S. Jenyns, *Later Chinese Porcelain*, London 1965.

Kantharos, *see* GREEK POTTERY.

Kaolin or **China clay** The essential ingredient in hard-paste PORCELAIN of which it forms about 40–50 per cent of the body. It is a white clay produced by the action of water on the feldspar of granite. It was known in China in the c7 or c8. A French Jesuit missionary, François Xavier d'Entrecolles, brought the first samples to Europe in 1712. The first deposits to be found in Europe were at Aue (used at MEISSEN), at Passau (used at VIENNA, LUDWIGSBURG, etc), at St Yrieix (used at SÈVRES), and at St Austell, Cornwall (used at PLYMOUTH). The first to be found in the U.S. was in Virginia and North Carolina, *see* UNAKER.

Kapuzinerbraun or **'Capuchin Brown',** *see* FOND-PORZELLAN.

Kara Dagh carpets, *see* PERSIAN CARPETS.

Karabagh carpets, *see* CAUCASIAN CARPETS.

Karaman carpets, *see* TURKISH CARPETS.

Karatsu potteries More than 200 kilns distributed over a wide area on Kyushu, by the straits of Tsushima dividing Japan from Korea, and for a short while among the most prolific in all Japan. Though sometimes said to have been founded much earlier they are not recorded as active before the late c16. They were established by Koreans – both voluntary immigrants and prisoners taken in the wars of 1592–1614 – who introduced techniques new to Japan, notably the use of the foot-kicked wheel, as well as Chinese and Korean types of ware. Their products are of rather coarse texture, covered with wood-ash, opaque white, or iron-brown glazes, generally undecorated but sometimes freely painted with landscapes, pine-trees or bamboos. Most of them were intended for ordinary household use but some were acquired by tea-masters and a few kilns seem to have specialized in TEA CEREMONY WARES. Production fell off in the mid c17 when many kilns were abandoned and others turned to the production of porcelain.

Lit: S. Jenyns, *Japanese Pottery*, London 1971.

Karcher, Nicholaus, *see* FERRARA TAPESTRY FACTORY and FLORENCE TAPESTRY FACTORY.

Kärner, Theodor, *see* NYMPHENBURG PORCELAIN FACTORY.

Kas American version of the c17 Netherlands *kast* or large wardrobe. It was made by Dutch settlers in the Hudson and Delaware valleys *c.*1675–1750 and more widely until the early c19. It is heavy, with panelled doors, an overhanging cornice and ball-feet: sometimes decorated all over with *grisaille* panels of enormous swags of fruit.

Kashaki carpets, *see* PERSIAN CARPETS.

Kashan carpets, *see* PERSIAN CARPETS.

Kashan pottery, *see* ISLAMIC POTTERY.

Kashgar carpets, *see* TURKMAN CARPETS.

Kashi Enamelled Islamic tiles produced in Persia and India in the c16 and c17.

Kaskai carpets, *see* PERSIAN CARPETS.

Kassel pottery and porcelain, *see* CASSEL POTTERY AND PORCELAIN.

Kastrup, *see* COPENHAGEN POTTERIES.

Katchlie-Bokhara carpets, *see* TURKMAN CARPETS.

Kayser, Engelbert (1840–1911). Proprietor of the most notable late c19 German firm of pewterers with a design office in Cologne and factory at Bockum near Krefeld, producing wares in a highly developed version of the Art Nouveau style from 1896 onwards. He won prizes at various international exhibitions – Paris 1900, Düsseldorf 1902, St Louis 1904. His products are among the best examples of mass-produced

E. Kayser, pewter tray, Cologne, c.1898 (Kunstgewerbemuseum, Berlin)

Art Nouveau wares. (For additional illustration *see* p. 606; for his mark *see* p. 894.)

Lit: H. U. Haedeke, *Zinn*, Brunswick 1963.

Kazak carpets, *see* CAUCASIAN CARPETS.

Keiser (or **Keizer**), **Aelbregt Cornelisz de** (d.1667). The owner of one of the DELFT POTTERIES and a member of the Delft guild of St Luke from 1642. He is credited with fine polychrome wares with elaborate chinoiserie decorations, but as the mark ascribed to him (A K in monogram) has also been attributed to **Adriaenus Koeks** and was certainly imitated by other potters, his products have not been successfully identified. His son **Cornelis** (d.1684) was also a potter and member of the guild of St Luke; and two of his daughters married the brothers **Adriaen** and **Jacobus Pijnacker** who were also notable potters.

Lit: C. H. J. de Jonge, *Delft Ceramics*, New York 1970.

Keller, Sebastian, *see* LUNÉVILLE POTTERY.

Kellinghusen potteries Deposits of good clay in the neighbourhood of Kellinghusen in Holstein encouraged several potters to establish faience factories in the later C18: five are recorded, the first founded in 1763, several survived into the C19 and one was functioning until 1860. They made good peasant wares decorated in high temperature colours usually with flowers. Figures were also made. (For factory mark *see* p. 884.)

Lit: K. Hüseler, *Die deutsche Fayencen*, Stuttgart 1956.

Kelsterbach pottery and porcelain factories A faience factory founded at Königstädten near Kelsterbach (Hesse Darmstadt) in 1758, moved to Kelsterbach in 1760 and was taken over by the Landgrave Ludwig VIII of Hesse Darmstadt in 1761. It made good, generally blue-and-white, household wares. Porcelain was also made 1761–8 (notably figures after models by P. A. Seefried who had worked at NYMPHENBURG and was strongly influenced by BUSTELLI) and 1789–1802 (mainly copies of figures from other factories). From 1802 cream-coloured earthenware became the staple product until the factory closed after 1823. (For factory mark *see* p. 884.)

Lit: K. Roder, *Das Kelsterbacher Porzellan*, Darmstadt 1931; K. Hüseler, *Die deutsche Fayencen*, Stuttgart 1956.

Kempe, Samuel, *see* PLAUE-ON-HAVEL POTTERY.

Kendrick, George P., *see* GRUEBY, William H.

Kent, William (1684–1748). English architect, interior decorator and furniture designer. He began as a painter but turned to architecture *c.*1730 under the influence of his patron Lord Burlington. His interiors are rich in stucco-work, painted decorations, carved and gilt wood, vast marble chimney-pieces, etc., producing a sumptuous effect in striking contrast to the Palladian severity of their exteriors. He derived much in the way of designs for doorcases and chimney-pieces from Inigo Jones, and a volume published by John Vardy (1744) is titled *Some Designs of Mr Inigo Jones and Mr William Kent*. For furniture designs he looked to Italy where he spent ten years. All are massively solid – side-tables on thick scrolled supports with festoons, stiffly curling foliage, classical masks and *putti*, chairs with richly carved legs and arms, a bed with a gigantic shell (a favourite device with Kent) surmounting the head, and pedestals with gilt swags and acanthus leaf ornament. His influence was great. The best of his furniture is at Kensington Palace, London, Houghton Hall, and Chatsworth.

Lit: M. Jourdain, *The Work of William Kent*, London 1948.

Kenzan, Ogata Shinsei, called (1663–1743). One of the most famous Japanese potters, also a calligrapher, poet, painter and lacquerer. He was the son of a rich merchant of Kyoto and was given a good education. His first instructor in pottery was a grandson of KOETSU, Honami Koho (1603–84); he is also said to have taken lessons from NINSEI and was certainly associated with Ninsei's son Seiemon. He set up his first kiln in 1687/8, but he seems usually to have employed others to throw his pots, confining his activities to their decoration and, especially in his later years, sometimes painting both pottery and porcelain vessels made outside his own studio. His style was initially influenced by his elder brother **Korin** (d.1716) a celebrated painter, with whom he sometimes collaborated in decorating pottery in a very bold manner (usually buff stoneware painted in monochrome brown with great economy of brushstrokes). The greater part of his wares are of low-fired earthenware painted in soft browns, blacks and blues and a special white slip which he developed. The decorations usually depict snow-covered landscapes, pines and bamboos with snowflakes clinging to them, flowers and grasses. But he also executed some much richer decorations with flowers in enamel colours. In his last years he wrote a book on pottery-making *Edo Densho* which has been translated into English by Bernard LEACH. The name of Kenzan passed (like those of other notable Japanese potters) from master to favourite pupil, and thus Bernard Leach, who studied under **Kenzan VI,** has the title of **Kenzan VII.**

Lit: B. Leach, *Kenzan and His Tradition*, London 1966; S. Jenyns, *Japanese Pottery*, London 1971.

Kermanshah carpets, *see* PERSIAN CARPETS.

Kerr, W. H., *see* WORCESTER PORCELAIN FACTORY.

Kettle stand A small table to support a hot-water kettle or urn, sometimes with a galleried top, sometimes with a metal-lined box-shaped top with an opening for the kettle spout, and generally with a slide which can be pulled out to support a teapot. Such tables were made in England throughout the C18, and some very fantastic designs for them were published.

Key pattern, *see* FRET.

Khilim A Middle-Eastern tapestry-woven rug, as distinct from a pile rug. Colours tend to be gaudy and the patterns very bold (partly due to the visual effect of the smooth-surface technique), producing a pleasantly barbaric appearance. SOUMAK CARPETS are similar but made by a slightly more complicated technique.

Khiva carpets, *see* TURKMAN CARPETS.

Khorassan carpets, *see* PERSIAN CARPETS.

Khotan carpets, *see* TURKMAN CARPETS.

Kian ware A generally discredited name for a type of Chinese BROWN WARE made at Chi-chou in Kiangsi and various places in Fukien, similar to but much coarser than CHIEN WARE.

Kidderminster carpet, *see* DOUBLE CLOTH CARPETS.

Kidderminster carpet factories The earliest carpet-factories of importance in England. They were founded early in the C17, if not earlier, and specialized in tough, simple, inexpensive rugs and carpets. From 1735 the factory of Pearsall and Brown produced DOUBLE-CLOTH carpets. The production of BRUSSELS CARPET began in 1749, in competition with the WILTON CARPET FACTORY. JACQUARD LOOMS were introduced in 1825 and the industry expanded rapidly between 1807, when one thousand looms were in operation, and 1838 when there were over two thousand. But products remained utilitarian and stylistically unadventurous. 'Spool' AXMINSTER type carpet was produced from 1878.

Lit: C. E. C. Tattersall and S. Reed, *A History of British Carpets*, Leigh-on-Sea 1966.

Kiel pottery A notable faience factory established in 1763, owned by the Duke of Holstein until 1766, and directed by **J. S. F. Tännich** from STRASBOURG until 1768–9, then by **Johann Buchwald** from ECKERNFÖRDE until 1771–2. It produced fine white wares decorated in enamel (rarely high-temperature) colours in the Rococo style – plates and dishes (sometimes with pierced basketwork or wavy rims), bishop bowls, elaborate pot-pourri vases, flower pots, wall fountains, etc. Occasionally direct imitations of Strasbourg tureens were made. Many pieces are distinguished by the high quality of their painted decorations, notably those by Johann and A. LEIHAMER. Although the factory continued until 1788, the finer types of wares do not appear to have been made after 1772. (For factory mark *see* p. 884.)

Lit: K. Hüseler, *Die Kieler Fayence-Manufacturen*, Flensburg 1923; R. J. Charleston in *Faenza* L (1964), pp. 84–93.

Kilim, *see* KHILIM.

Killinger, Georg Friedrich (d.1726). Nuremberg glass engraver, first recorded in 1694. He decorated the bowls of numerous goblets with very delicately executed landscapes, hunting scenes and heraldic achievements, often signing his work (notable examples in British Museum and Victoria and Albert Museum, London).

Lit: R. Schmidt, *Das Glas*, Berlin and Leipzig 1922; W. B. Honey, *Glass: A Handbook*, London 1946; E. Meyer-Heisig, *Der Nürnberger Glasschnitt des 17 Jahrhunderts*, Nuremberg 1963.

Kimball The publisher of a retailer's catalogue of furniture entitled *Book of Designs*, New York 1876, illustrating pieces manufactured by such New York and other U.S. furniture-makers as G. HUNTZINGER, Kilian Brothers, etc.

King's pattern An early C19 English pattern for spoons and forks – with a shaped stem, decorated with a shell at the base, and a waisted top also decorated with a shell motif. The Queen's pattern is slightly simpler without a shell at the base of the stem and no decorations on the back.

Kingwood, *see* ROSEWOOD.

Kipp, Karl, *see* HUBBARD, Elbert.

Kirchner, Johann Gottlob (b.*c.*1706). Modeller employed at the MEISSEN PORCELAIN FACTORY 1727–8 and, as chief modeller, 1730–33. He is said to have left on account of a quarrel with J. J. KÄNDLER who succeeded him as chief modeller. During his first period he modelled a table fountain (Metropolitan Museum, New York) and began the series of large animals for the Japanese Palace (continued by Kändler). In his second period he executed some figures of Saints, a clock case and statuettes of beggars. A large *St Peter* intended for the chapel of the Japanese Palace may be by him, though it has also been attributed to Kändler who appears to have worked on some of his models. After leaving Meissen he appears to have worked as a sculptor and painter in Berlin.

Lit: C. Albiker, *Die Meissner Porzellantiere in 18. Jahrhunderts*, Berlin 1959; J. Handt and H. Rakebrand, *Meissner Porzellan des 18 Jahrhunderts*, Dresden 1956.

Kirk & Son Inc. The oldest surviving U.S. firm of silversmiths, established by **Samuel Kirk** (b.1793) in Baltimore in 1815. From 1828 it specialized in making vessels with very rich repoussé decorations: hence the name 'Baltimore silver' which is sometimes applied to such wares though similar work was executed contemporaneously elsewhere.

Kirkcaldy pottery, *see* WEMYSS WARE.

Kirman carpets, *see* PERSIAN CARPETS.

Kir-sehr carpets, *see* TURKISH CARPETS.

Kjaerholm, Poul (b.1929). Leading Danish furniture designer of the 1950s and 60s, he works

P. Kjaerholm: chair in steel and wicker-work, 1957 (Kunstindustrimuseet, Copenhagen)

exclusively for industrial production. He uses metal frames, generally rectangular section steel rods, combined with natural materials – woven cane, canvas, leather, wood, slate, rope. Although opposed to the handicraft tradition of modern Danish furniture his work is distinguished mainly by its refinement and impeccable detailing which gives it almost a handmade look.

Klinger, Johann Gottfried (1711–81). Porcelain painter working 1726–46 at MEISSEN where he is said to have introduced the practice of adding shadows beside flowers or insects to give a *trompe l'oeil* effect. In 1746 he went to work at the VIENNA PORCELAIN FACTORY where he was appointed chief painter in 1750 and remained for the rest of his career. He was also concerned with the techniques of porcelain making.

Klint, Kaare (1888–1954). Danish furniture designer and theorist, he was the son of the well-known architect, **P. V. Jensen Klint,** and began himself as an architect, working under Carl Petersen. But he soon turned to furniture design and by 1916 was designing storage furniture of a radical new type. He pioneered the use of natural, unvarnished wood, undyed leather, natural colour textiles, etc., and preached simplicity, economy and the importance of systematic function studies in furniture design, i.e., ERGONOMICS. In 1924 he founded and was first professor of the furniture department at the Danish Academy of Arts. As a teacher and theorist, as well as a designer, he more than anyone was responsible for the boom in Scandinavian furniture in the 1920s and 30s.

He had no desire to be modern for the sake of modernity and studied and encouraged his students to study the furniture of the past in the belief that 'the ancients were more modern than we', and that the best types evolved in the past, if stripped of their period ornament, would be suitable models for contemporary designers. His approach was analytical, seeking the essential characteristics of form and construction in good furniture of the past – especially in that of ancient Egypt and Greece, C18 England (notably the simpler works of Chippendale) and in the wonderfully simple and elegant chairs and tables made by the Shakers in America and, probably, in the eminently neat and practical chests-of-drawers made for ships throughout the C19. He was also open to C20 influence and his teak chair of 1933 is derived from LE CORBUSIER'S cowboy *chaise longue* of 1929.

K. Klint: teak deck-chair, designed 1933

His concern for ergonomics is illustrated by his sideboard, perhaps his most distinguished design, for which he worked out the average dimensions of the crockery and cutlery used in a Danish home and created a case that would contain in the smallest possible space the maximum amount needed by a single household. He was also aware how much appearance contributes to comfort – how, for example, most people demand that a chair should look, as well as be, capable of supporting the human body.

The clean beauty of his furniture depends to a large extent on the texture of the waxed and polished but unvarnished wood and the excellence of the construction (his designs were realized by the firm of Rudolf Rasmussens Snedkerier of Copenhagen). It was not cheap and its market was limited to the middle class. His best designs are all eminently simple and sensible and unpretentious – almost to the point of anonymity – which is their outstanding merit. Later Scandinavian designers have tended to elaborate on his style, making much greater use of complex curves and indulging in virtuoso performances of intricate joinery.

Lit: Ulf Hard af Segerstad, *Modern Scandinavian Furniture*, London 1964.

Klipfel, Karl Jacob Christian, *see* BERLIN PORCELAIN FACTORY.

Klismos A Greek type of chair, used also in Rome and revived in the late C18 and early C19. *See* CHAIR.

Kloster-Veilsdorf porcelain factory Leading Thuringian factory founded in 1760 by Prince Friedrich Wilhelm Eugen von Hildburghausen. Products included table wares imitative of MEISSEN but often very well painted with naturalistic flowers, landscapes framed by curtains, birds, genre scenes of the Teniers type and pastorals à la Watteau. Figures of *Commedia dell'Arte* actors (similar to those of FÜRSTENBERG), gods and goddesses were also made. After the founder's death in 1797 the factory was sold: it has been run as a private concern ever since. (For factory mark see p. 884.)

Lit: R. Graul and A. Kurzwelly, *Altthüringer Porzellan*, Leipzig 1910; E. Kramer in *Keramos* 20 (1963), pp. 3–30; 53–4 (1971), pp. 77–96.

Knife box A decorative case fitted internally with slots in which knives could be stored blade down. In early- and mid-C18 England it was normally box-shaped with a slanting top of fine wood or covered with shagreen; in the later C18 often urn-shaped. The latter type was favoured by R. ADAM who made decorative use of it in the design of dining-room furniture.

Knock-down furniture, *see* PACKAGE FURNITURE.

Knole settee A settee with a high back and hinged arms which may be held upright or sloped out from the seat: named after a unique early-C17 specimen at Knole Park, Kent. It was immensely popular for rich suburban furnishing in England in the 1920s and 30s.

Knoll Associates American furniture and interior design firm, founded in 1938 by a German immigrant, **Hans Knoll** (1914–55). It now has subsidiary companies all over the world, which operate under the name **Knoll International.** Hans Knoll wanted to create 'a unified classic-contemporary style' appropriate to modern architecture, by marketing the work of leading designers and architects. In 1943 he married **Florence Schust,** who was born in Switzerland, brought up with Eero SAARINEN and trained in architecture under MIES VAN DER ROHE at the Illinois Institute of Technology. She persuaded Mies, Saarinen and Harry BERTOIA to contribute designs.

Florence Knoll (who took over the direction of the firm on the death of its founder in 1955) exercised close supervision over all aspects of the business, designed many individual pieces herself and in 1945 branched into interior design. She began by furnishing the Manhattan offices of the Rockefeller family, and many other commissions followed – from the U.S. Government and large corporations in America and Europe.

The first subsidiary company was established in Germany in 1951. Furniture designs circulate among the Knoll International companies and are manufactured locally. Any company may initiate a design, subject to approval from New York.

Knowles, Taylor & Knowles: 'Lotusware' porcelain with raised jewelled decoration, c.1895 (The Smithsonian Institution, Washington, D.C.)

Knöller, Johann George, *see* BAYREUTH POTTERY.

Knop The decorative swelling on the stem of a cup: usually half way up the stem.

Knotted lace An early type of lace made in C16 Italy with short lengths of thread before the introduction of bobbins enabled lace-makers to work with long threads.

Knowles, Taylor & Knowles Company A porcelain factory established in 1872 at East Liverpool, Ohio, producing both useful and decorative wares but specializing in, and best known for, very fine BELLEEK porcelain. Its kilns were destroyed by fire in 1889 and subsequently it produced a translucent bone china marketed as 'Lotusware', specimens of which were shown at the Columbian Exposition of 1893 in Chicago. The decorative products were often enriched with jewelled decoration. *Illustrated previous page.*

Lit: 19th Century America: Furniture and other Decorative Arts, Exh. Cat., Metropolitan Museum, New York 1970.

Knulling A type of GADROONING of irregular outline used for the decoration of silver wares, especially borders, in mid-C18 England.

Knütgen, Anno (d.*c.*1590). One of the most prominent members of a family of potters which had been active in SIEGBURG from 1425. Though no pieces are signed, some of the best Siegburg stoneware made in the mid and late C16 is attributed to his pottery, including some large waisted vases with sockets for candles, pilgrim bottles and ring-flasks as well as the usual range of wares (*Schnellen, Schnabelkännen,* etc.). He is thought to have employed the modeller F. TRACK. In *c.*1590 he moved with his sons **Bertram** and **Rütger** to Höhr near WESTERWALD but is said to have been very old at this date and died soon afterwards. Among his kinsmen **Peter Knütgen** signed some wares (mainly tankards) in the 1560s and **Christian** signed a number of handsome pieces (notably *Schnabelkännen*) dated between 1568 and 1605. *Illustrated next column.*

Lit: O. von Falke, *Das rheinische Steinzeug,* Berlin 1908; K. Strauss, *Alte deutsche Kunsttöpfereien,* 1923.

C. Knütgen: salt-glazed stoneware Schnabelkanne, *Siegburg, 1591 (Kunstgewerbemuseum, Cologne)*

Ko ware A type of Chinese stoneware made for the Southern SUNG imperial court at Kang-chou C12–C13, described in the earlier Chinese ceramic literature, but difficult to distinguish from what is generally called KUAN WARE. The term has recently been applied to a very rare class of ware with a dark body much thinner than the several 'coats' of glaze with which it is covered.

Kocx (or **Koeks**), **Adrianus** (d.1701). Succeeded Samuel van EENHORN as owner of the *Greek A* pottery at DELFT, 1686–1701. Produced many of the most ambitious pieces of Delftware including tall pagoda-shaped *tulipières* decorated with chinoiseries in blue and white. Chinese decorative motifs were often imitated closely but as often applied to vases of European form. His factory mark, AK in monogram, was copied by contemporary potteries in Delft and even in China and much applied to fakes in the C19.

Lib: C. H. de Jonghe, *Delft Ceramics,* London 1970.

Koetsu, Honami (1558–1637). Japanese potter, the most notable maker of RAKU apart from members of the Raku 'family', also a painter, calligrapher, lacquerer, swordsmith, iron-worker and wood-carver. He came of a *samurai* family of hereditary sword-sharpeners. With the painter **Soatsu** he collaborated on several paintings, most notably the deer scroll in Hakone Museum. A few pieces of lacquer are attributed to him, including a writing-case in the Imperial Museum, Tokyo. Iron tea-kettles and bamboo vases are also ascribed to him. But he is best known for his *raku* tea-bowls one of which, called *Fujisan*, is said to be the most famous in Japan (Coll. Count Sakai). These bowls were highly prized by tea-masters and imitated in later periods. In 1615 he retired to an estate at Takagamine where he established a kind of colony of craftsmen devoted to the various branches of the arts with which he was concerned.

Lit: S. Jenyns, *Japanese Pottery*, London 1971.

Kok, J. Jurian, *see* ROZENBURG POTTERY & PORCELAIN FACTORY.

König, Alfred Otto, *see* MEISSEN PORCELAIN FACTORY.

Königsberg potteries A faience factory was established in 1772 at Königsberg in East Prussia by **Johann Eberhard Ludwig Ehrenreich** (1722–1803) producing wares in the Rococo style similar to those of MARIEBERG and STRALSUND (though more often blue-and-white than polychrome) where he had previously worked. After Ehrenreich retired in 1788, it turned to the production of lead-glazed earthenware coloured either pale yellow or bluish-purple, and survived until 1811. Another pottery which flourished 1775–85 made imitations of WEDGWOOD wares including black basalte medallions (a portrait of Kant is the most notable piece) and also stoneware with marbled, agate or dark brown glazes. Faience was marked with an 'Æ' impressed, with the date added. Lead-glazed earthenwares were marked with a 'K' impressed, sometimes more than once on each piece and sometimes with a date. Wares of the second factory were sometimes marked *'frères Collin à Königsberg'*.

Lit: G. E. Pazaurek, *Steingut, Formgebung und Geschichte*, Stuttgart 1927.

K. Köpping: glass goblet, Wiesbaden, c.1896 (Kunstgewerbemuseum, Berlin)

Köpping, Karl (1848–1914). German artist who began by studying chemistry and then turned to painting and etching. After some years in Paris he joined the staff of the Berlin Akademie in 1890. Shortly afterwards he began to concern himself with glass, designing very thinly blown vessels of great elegance and fragility made by **Friedrich Zitzmann** at Wiesbaden. Study of the glazes on Japanese ceramics enabled him to achieve unusual combinations of colours in translucent vessels. He was a member of the editorial board of the German Art Nouveau magazine *Pan* from 1896.

Lit: G. E. Pazaurek, *Kunstgläser der Gegenwart*, Leipzig 1925.

Kordenbusch, Georg Friedrich, *see* NUREMBERG POTTERIES.

Korean pottery and porcelain Though strongly influenced by Chinese wares, the ceramics produced in the Korean peninsula are seldom without a distinct national character. The earliest, which have been found in tombs dating from the period of the Silla kingdom (*c.*57 B.C.–935 A.D.) are of hard grey stoneware and include both vessels and naturalistic figurines. Under the Koryo dynasty (918–1392) porcellaneous wares similar to those of contemporary China, especially CELADON, were made. Those of the C12 were often of outstanding quality. Some have a distinctive 'kingfisher colour' glaze, sometimes with underglaze painting in brown, and the most elaborate are enriched with moulded and pierced work. The most celebrated type is that with *mishima* decorations – little stars and flowers, occasionally representations of trees, birds, etc., in black or white slip inlaid in the surface of the vessel, rubbed smooth and covered with a celadon glaze. White porcelain was also produced on a limited scale, and brown glaze wares were also made. The production of the finer types of ware seems to have been abandoned under the Yi dynasty (1392–1910). But the somewhat rustic brown glazed wares attracted the attention of Japanese tea-masters who used them as TEA CEREMONY WARES. Other products of this period include porcelain vigorously painted in underglaze blue or, more notably, iron brown and copper red.

Lit: G. St G. M. Gompertz, *Korean celadon and other wares of the Koryo period*, London 1963, and *Korean pottery and porcelain of the Yi period*, London 1968.

Korean celadon vase, C12
(Temple Newsam House, Leeds)

Kosta glasbruk Glasshouse founded in 1742 at Kosta in Småland, Sweden. Apart from some attractive late-C18 drinking glasses, it produced little of interest until the C20 when it became one of the most important factories for table glasses in Sweden (with ORREFORS). **Elis Bergh** (b.1881), **Ewald Dahlskog** (b.1894) and **Edvin Ollers** (b.1888) have all been employed as designers.

Kothgasser, Anton (1769–1851). Leading Austrian glass enameller: began at the VIENNA PORCELAIN FACTORY and also worked as a window-glass painter. He painted numerous

A. Kothgasser, glass beaker
painted in enamel colours, Vienna, c.1830
(Victoria & Albert Museum)

tumblers and beakers in transparent enamel colours with very delicate romantic landscapes.

Lit: G. Pazaurek, *Gläser der Empire und Biedermeierzeit*, Leipzig 1923.

Kovsh Russian type of boat-shaped vessel with a single handle, used for ladling out drinks. Usually of silver but sometimes made of hard wood like a mazer, it was popular until the mid c18.

Kovsh, silver, Russian, c.*1740*

Kraak porcelain A type of Chinese blue-and-white porcelain of the late Ming (Wan-Li) and early Ch'ing dynasties, decorated in panels of repeating or partly repeating designs. 'Kraak' is Dutch for a 'carrack' or Portuguese galleon trading with the East Indies, one of which was captured in 1603 while carrying porcelain of this type. Kraak porcelain was the first Chinese porcelain to reach Europe in quantity and was later imitated in Delft pottery.

Kranz, Frederick, *see* HUBBARD, Elbert.

Krater, *see* GREEK POTTERY.

Krautstrunk German name for a glass tumbler covered with prunts supposedly like the stem of a cabbage, made of green glass, from the c15.

Kreussen potteries The production of fine stoneware of a light brownish-grey body covered with a brown salt glaze developed in the late c16 out of the HAFNER industry established nearly a century earlier at Kreussen, near Bayreuth, under the direction of various members of families named **Vest** and SPECKNER. Dated pieces range from 1614 (tankard in Germanisches Nationalmuseum, Nuremberg), and all the best appear to have been made in the first quarter of the c17, though stone-

Kreussen salt-glazed stoneware tankard, 1628 (Museum für Kunst und Gewerbe, Hamburg)

ware continued to be made there until the 1730s. They include vessels of various shapes, notably four-sided flasks with metal screw stoppers and rather squat tankards decorated with figure subjects or heraldry in applied reliefs (as on RHENISH STONEWARE) and sometimes bright opaque enamel colours. The enamelled pieces are the first ceramics to be decorated by this technique in Europe and are probably the work of glass enamellers. From 1618 tin-glazed wares were also made by L. Speckner – flasks (of the same form as those in stoneware), cups, drug vases, plates and dishes generally painted with formalized flower motifs, sometimes with coats of arms, rarely with figures, in light blue on a pure white ground. Several pieces are dated, the last being of 1668 (Danske Folkemuseum, Copenhagen). (For factory marks see p. 884.)

Lit: H. Eber, *Creussner Töpferkunst*, Munich 1913; H. Kohlhaussen, *Geschichte des deutschen Kunsthandwerks*, Munich 1955; G. Reineking von Bock, *Kunstgewerbemuseum der Stadt Köln, Steinzeug*, Cologne 1971.

Krohn, Pietro, *see* BING & GRØNDAHL'S PORCELAIN FACTORY.

Krug, Arnold, *see* COPENHAGEN PORCELAIN FACTORY.

Krug, Ludwig (*c.*1488/90–1532). Leading Nuremberg goldsmith and the son of a goldsmith who on one occasion worked in collaboration with DÜRER's father. He became a master craftsman in 1484 and was master of the Nuremberg mint 1494–1509. Apart from a stone relief (State Museum, West Berlin) his only documented work is an elaborate covered cup known from a drawing in an inventory of the treasury at Halle (Hofbibliothek, Aschaffenburg). On the basis of this drawing a number of early C16 vessels of outstandingly high quality have been attributed to him – a cup set with shell-cameos (Museum of Decorative Arts, Budapest), a cup formerly in the Moscow Kremlin, an egg-shaped cup in the Kunstgewerbemuseum, West Berlin, a cup crowned by the figure of a woman at a well in the Kunsthistorisches Museum, Vienna, and nefs in the treasury of S. Antonio, Padua, and the Germanisches Nationalmuseum, Nuremberg.

L. Krug: design for a cup, c.1526 *(Hofbibliothek, Aschaffenburg)*

Lit: H. Kohlhausen, *Nürnberger Goldschmiedkunst des Mittelalters und der Dürerzeit*, Berlin 1968.

Ku A type of Chinese Bronze Age vessel (probably a drinking vessel), tall, slender and extremely elegant. It resembles a long beaker, with a

Ku, Shang Dynasty, bronze (The St Louis Art Museum)

narrow, tight-waisted body which flares out into a trumpet mouth much wider than the base. It was made during the SHANG-YIN and early CHOU dynasties only, *c.*1500–1000 B.C.

Kuan ware A type of very fine Chinese stoneware of the Southern SUNG period (1128–1279) made in or near the imperial capital Hang-chou. The word *kuan* means official and should strictly be applied only to wares made for the Imperial Court. But the term is generally applied to all fine wares, of southern Sung date, with a rather dark body and crazed glaze ranging in colour from ash-grey to lavender. The wares include bowls, bottles, vases, dishes, etc., always of very simple 'classic' form. The dark body tends to show through the glaze at the rim and foot of a vessel. The relationship of the ware to KO WARE is somewhat obscure.

Lit: B. Gray, *Early Chinese Pottery and Porcelain*, London 1953.

Kuang-tung ware Stoneware with a thick blue glaze, usually streaked and mottled with greyish green, white or brown, made near Canton. Imitation CHUN and YI-HSING wares were also produced there.

Kuba carpets, *see* CAUCASIAN CARPETS.

Kubachi ware A type of C16 PERSIAN POTTERY, named after the small town in the Caucasus where most of it was discovered. Its origin is unknown. Surviving pieces are mostly large dishes and plates decorated in polychrome colours (dark red, brown, green, white, yellow and black) under a clear colourless crackled glaze. Both human figures and animals appear in the decorations, sometimes portraits with elaborate floral or scroll borders.

Kuei (1) A type of Chinese Bronze Age food vessel made both in bronze and pottery during the SHANG-YIN, CHOU and CH'IN dynasties though rarely after *c.*600 B.C. In form a deep circular bowl with spreading lip and foot-ring, it usually has two handles, sometimes four and occasionally none. Middle Chou period vessels usually have three small feet, and sometimes have covers. They are often called *Chiu. Illustrated next page.*

(2) A type of Chinese sceptre made of jade. In form it can be either a long flat tablet with a point at one end or it may divide at the tip into two arcs. They were probably made as emblems of office or badges of rank.

Kulah carpets, *see* TURKISH CARPETS.

Kunckel, Johann (1630–1703). The leading German glass technologist and maker of his day. He was born at Rendsburg, the son of a glass-house master whose craft he learned. But he began his career as a chemist in the service of Duke Franz Carl von Lauenburg and after a period of travelling, during which he visited Holland, turned his attention to alchemy, and was employed in the secret laboratory of the Elector of Saxony in the 1670s. In 1677 he published *Chymische Anmerkung*, a treatise which is mainly scientific though it reveals his belief in the

Kuei, Chou Dynasty, bronze (William Rockhill Nelson Gallery of Art, Kansas City)

possibility of making gold from base materials. After a brief period lecturing at Wittenberg he was invited to Prussia by the 'great' Elector Friedrich Wilhelm and put in charge of the POTSDAM GLASSHOUSE in 1678. Next year he published a treatise on glassmaking, *Ars Vitraria Experimentalis,* which includes a translation of A. NERI's *L'Arte Vetraria* with the comments on it published in England by Christopher Merrett, but also contains a great deal of practical information derived from personal experience. He put his knowledge to good effect at Potsdam where he made, after initial difficulties, a fine clear crystal glass. He also invented and produced a ruby glass from which vases, drinking vessels, etc. could be made (earlier types of ruby glass could be used only for imitation jewellery). He was confronted with financial and other difficulties after the death of the Elector in 1688. In 1693 he went to Stockholm to give advice on mining to the King of Sweden who ennobled him. But he returned to Germany after five months, and devoted the rest of his life to chemistry, writing an analysis of urine (1696) and preparing other studies which were posthumously published as *Laboratorium chymicum,* 1716.

Lit: H. Maurach, *Johann Kunckel,* Berlin 1933.

Künersberg pottery Faience factory established near Memmingen in 1745 by a successful financier, **Jakob Küner** (1692–1764), producing a wide range of useful and decorative wares (including figures) in the Rococo style painted in high-temperature colours or (more notably) enamel colours with gilding. Products included tankards, slender narrow-necked jugs, plates with wavy edges, elaborately modelled vases and plaques. The painted decorations are often of high quality, especially birds, insects and sprays of naturalistic flowers. The factory seems to have closed *c.*1767. (For factory mark *see* p. 884.)

Lit: J. Miedel, *Künersberg und seine Fayencefabrik*, Memmingen 1929; K. Hüseler, *Deutsche Fayencen*, Stuttgart 1956.

Kungsholm Glasbruk: covered goblet, c18 (National Museum, Stockholm)

Kungsholm glasbruk The first Swedish glasshouse of importance, founded in Stockholm 1676 by an Italian who proved to be an imposter and fled to England, 1678; thereafter administered by Swedish noblemen. Early products show Venetian influence and include some very handsome large goblets with stems intricately wrought in the form of the royal monogram and crown. Baroque patterns remained popular until the factory closed down in 1815. Imitations were made at the **Skanska Glasbruket**, 1691–1762. *Illustrated previous column.*

Lit: A. Pollak in *Concise Encyclopaedia of Antiques* IV, London 1959.

Kurdistan or **Kurdish carpets**, *see* PERSIAN CARPETS.

Kutani porcelain factory A small private Japanese factory at Kutani Mura, West Honshu, founded by and working exclusively for the Maeda family of hereditary feudatories in the late C17. Products are painted with very bold designs of plants, animals, landscapes or textile diapers in a rich palette of yellow, green, dark purple and blue enamels. Some pieces are decorated in yellow and purple on a blue-green ground. Red enamel was also used and, rarely, underglaze blue. Designs show the influence of both Chinese porcelain and the products of the ARITA PORCELAIN FACTORIES, which subsequently imitated Kutani wares. The original factory seems to have been active only in the 1670s and 1680s. The porcelain industry was, however, re-established at Kutani in 1823 by Iidaya-Hachiroemon who for a few years ran a factory producing imitations of the earlier wares, also pieces with decorations in gold on a solidly applied red enamel ground.

Lit: S. Jenyns, *Japanese Porcelain*, London 1965.

Kuttrolf A type of German WALDGLAS vessel with a curious curved neck composed of several intertwining tubes which merge at the mouth.

Kuznetsoff family The owners of a large number of Russian potteries and porcelain factories established early in the C19 and responsible by the end for about two-thirds of the whole Russian ceramic industry. These factories made the full range of C19 commercial wares, mainly in imitation of W. European prototypes, but also including attractive figures of Russian peasants like those made at the GARDNER factory which was absorbed by the Kuznetsoff empire in 1891.

Kwaart A clear lead-glaze applied to and fired with tin-enamel on earthenware made at DELFT and (more rarely) elsewhere in the C17 and C18 to give greater glossiness. It is the equivalent of COPERTA on Italian maiolica.

Kwabornament, *see* AURICULAR STYLE.

Kyhn, K. C. T., *see* COPENHAGEN PORCELAIN FACTORY.

Kylix, *see* GREEK POTTERY.

Kyoto potteries The most important group of Japanese potteries of the Edo period (1615–1867), situated round the Imperial capital and patronized by the Emperor and his Court. The main centre was at AWATA where the two most famous decorators NINSEI and KENZAN and their followers worked. The term 'Kyomizu wares' is applied to the products of kilns – small scale studios rather than factories – in the districts of Kyoto called Kyomizuzaka and Gojo-zaka, some of which made porcelain, generally in imitation of Chinese MING dynasty wares, as well as painted earthenware in the Japanese tradition. Many of these wares are marked: they include work by **Okuda Eisen** (1753–1811), who specialized in imitating Chinese pieces, **Mokubei** (1767–1833), also a skilful imitator of Chinese wares, and **Ninami Dohachi** (1783–1856), notable for TEA CEREMONY WARES painted in colours. Other distinguished potters include the several members of the Rokubei family – the founder **Rokubei I** (1737–99), maker of Korean style tea pieces and unglazed wares, his son **Rokubei Seisa** (d.1860) who specialized in imitations of Chinese blue-and-white porcelain, and his son **Rokubei Shoun** (d.1883) who was famed for his teapots decorated with crabs. RAKU wares were also made in the Kyoto district. Potteries are still active around Kyoto.

Lit: S. Jenyns, *Japanese Pottery*, London 1971.

Initial letter from Hypnerotomachia Poliphili, *printed by Aldus Manutius, Venice, 1499*

La Chapelle-des-Pots potteries Earthenware has been made at La Chapelle-des-Pots near Brizambourg (Charente-Inférieur) from the C14 to the present day. The most interesting products date from the C16 and in technique herald the work of B. PALISSY, a native of the district – boldly modelled wares of a pale hard body covered with a green glaze marked with flecks of yellow and touched with brown. They are known from fragments, dug up by excavators, which permit the attribution to La Chapelle-des-Pots of some very handsome C16 pieces, e.g., pilgrim bottle with lion masks and the arms of Anne de Montmorency, Constable of France, in the Louvre. These potteries are not to be confused with those at La Chapelle-aux-Pots near BEAUVAIS where somewhat similar wares appear to have been made in the C16.

Lit: M. J. Ballot, *Bernard Palissy et les fabriques du XVIe siècle*, Paris 1924.

La Farge, John (1835–1910). American glass painter born in New York, the son of a fresco and glass painter under whom he was trained, though he also studied in Paris in the studio of T. Couture (1856). His earliest works were wall paintings and stained glass windows for churches in a style influenced by the Pre-Raphaelites. In the 1870s he began to produce at his studio in West 10th Street, New York, panels of opaline iridescent glass – which he called American glass – with flowers, leaves and abstract ornament arranged as flat patterns without perspective (influenced by the theories and works of W. MORRIS). Such panels could be used either for windows or screens. They were commissioned from him by several leading architects, notably H. H. Richardson who was a personal friend, and decorated the homes of the Vanderbilts, Whitneys and other millionaire families. He was also a writer on art and exerted considerable influence on the development of taste in the U.S.

Lit: R. Cortissoz, *John La Farge*, Boston 1911; J. G. Lloyd, *Stained Glass in America*, Jenkintown, Penna, 1963.

La Granja glasshouse Established under royal patronage by a Catalan, Buenaventura Sit, near the Royal Palace of La Granja de San Ildefonso in 1728. Began by specializing in mirrors but also produced vessels in the Catalan version of the Venetian style. From 1740 a succession of French, Swedish and German craftsmen directed the production of hollow wares which are generally imitative and rarely show any Spanish features. It passed into private hands in 1829 and thereafter made only common glass.

Lit: Alice Wilson Frothingham, *Spanish Glass*, London 1964.

La Granja: glass tumblers, c18 (Museo Artes Decorativas, Barcelona)

La Rochelle potteries Of several C18 faience factories only one was of importance, functioning from 1749 to 1789 and producing attractive wares decorated with birds, sprays of flowers, insects, etc. in strong HIGH-TEMPERATURE COLOURS with blue and yellow predominating, rather in the style of NEVERS (though the decorations of ROUEN, MOUSTIERS and STRASBOURG were also adapted). Some vases have flowers or shells applied in relief. No factory mark is known but the name and various initials and monograms were sometimes used.

La Rochelle faience tureen (Musée d'Orbigny, La Rochelle)

Lit: G. Musset, *Les faience rochelaises*, La Rochelle 1888.

Labhardt, Christoph (*c.*1641–95). Swiss-born engraver of hard-stones and glass who worked at the court of the Landgraf Carl of Hesse in Cassel. Using a water-driven cutting mill he executed very bold Baroque relief work in rock crystal and glass, sometimes carving figures in the round. He was a virtuoso craftsman capable of work of great boldness or minute delicacy. A casket in Schloss Rosenborg, Copenhagen, is a notable example of his work. Several other members of his family worked in Cassel as gem engravers, notably his posthumously born son **Johann Christoph** (1695–1742) and grandson **Johann Christoph II** (1741–1814) who was also active in London.

Lit: R. Hallo in *Altes Kunsthandwerk* I (1927), pp. 181–204.

Lacca contrafatta An Italian imitation of oriental LACQUER in which the relief decorations are formed by cut-out prints stuck to the surface and varnished. It was made mainly in the Venetian states in the C18 and has an attractive though distinctly rustic appearance. The Italian word 'lacca' is used loosely for any painted or varnished decoration applied to furniture, including true oriental lacquer and JAPANNING.

Lace A decorative openwork fabric usually of linen but also of silk or gold or silver thread, first made in the late C15 in Italy and Flanders. It has been used on or for apparel, liturgical vestments and cloths for church and home. Pictorial panels have also been made. There are two main types: **needlepoint** which is earlier and **pillow lace** (also called bobbin lace). Needlepoint is essentially a type of embroidery. It is a development of CUT WORK, DARNED NETTING, DRAWN WORK and RETICELLA; but whereas they are made from woven textiles (and embroidery is supported on a textile or other substance), needlepoint is made from a single thread and a needle making embroidery stitches. The maker of needlepoint lace usually followed a design drawn on parchment or paper which was cut away when the work was finished. The earliest type of needlepoint, PUNTO IN ARIA, though an entirely free lace, generally maintains the geometrical patterning of cut work, etc. But from the early C17 laces were made to free designs. Pillow lace, which sometimes has a similar appearance, is made from numerous threads (wound on bobbins) plaited and twisted together in a variety of ways – for the simpler types like that of HONITON some 30 threads were used but for the more elaborate types made at CHANTILLY, MECHLIN, VALENCIENNES, etc. more than a hundred threads were needed. Sometimes the coarser lace is called 'bobbin lace' and the finer 'bone lace', possibly because the threads for the latter were wound on small bones. Technically, pillow lace is a development of MACRAMÉ. It may have originated in Italy but was perfected in northern Europe, especially Flanders. Machinery for lace-making was invented in 1808–9 by **John Heathcote** (1783–1861) and came into widespread use in the 1840s though much of the finest work was (and some still is) hand made.

The terminology of lace is confused: e.g. a point is a needle stitch, *point de Venise* is thus a needlepoint lace made in Venice or elsewhere in the same style; but *point d'Angleterre* is a pillow (not needlepoint) lace made in Brussels and else-

Lace: Point de Venise *(Musée de Cluny, Paris)*

Lace: Point d'Angleterre *(Musée de Cluny, Paris)*

where in Flanders. Technical terms can be divided into two categories referring to (a) the structure of a panel of lace and (b) technical and stylistic groups generally associated with places of production.

(a) In a piece of lace the main elements of the design (generally flower or leaf motifs but sometimes human figures, animals, urns, columns, etc.) are composed of numerous threads stitched together and sometimes outlined by a *cordonnet* or little cord of several threads whipped or buttonholed together. These elements are joined by *brides* (slender threads or groups of threads), either plain or *picotées* (decorated with *picots* or tiny loops), or by a regular mesh or net called the *fond* or *réseau*. Ornamental devices known as *modes* or fillings may be used between the main elements of the pattern replacing the *fond* or *réseau* in some areas.

(b) Various types of lace are called after the towns or countries in which they are thought to have originated, but as lace-makers moved from one place to another these names do not necessarily indicate the place of origin of a particular piece (e.g. Mechlin lace was made at Bruges, Antwerp, Louvain and Ghent as well as Mechlin). There are the several Venetian types, all of needlepoint – *gros point de Venise* with bold main elements in very high relief giving the effect of carved

Lace: Gros point de Venise
(Musée de Cluny, Paris)

ivory, *plat point de Venise* with rather bold flower and leaf motifs similar to the above but without relief work, *point de Venise à réseau* with similar elements connected by the *réseau* and not by *brides*, *point de Venise à Rose*, a miniature version of *gros point de Venise*. Laces of these types made in France are called *point de Colbert*, those made in Spain, *punto España*. But a distinct variation was evolved in France, *point de France*. Other notable types of needlepoint lace include: *point d'Alençon* with a uniform *fond* and many *modes*. The main types of pillow lace are: *Binche*, a lace of very fine thread and close texture with complex but often inconspicuous patterns and with a wavy edge following the line of the pattern; *Mechlin*, a straight-edged lace with the pattern outlined with a shiny thread; *Milanese* with rather bold sometimes figurative patterns made either *à brides* or *à réseau*; *point d'Angleterre* with *cordonnet* outlining the pattern and a generally hexagonal mesh *fond* worked after the pattern had been made; *Valenciennes* a straight edged lace with a diamond mesh *fond* (*vrai réseau de Valenciennes*) worked with a pattern which usually consists of scrolls and flowers without *cordonnet*. *Point de Dresde* or Dresden lace is not a true lace but drawn work on muslin. Of the many places where lace and similar textiles were made the most important included ALENÇON, ANTWERP, BEDFORDSHIRE, BINCHE, BRUSSELS, CARRICKMACROSS, CHANTILLY, GENOA, HONITON, MALTA, NOTTINGHAM, VALENCIENNES, VENICE and YOUGHAL. The present-day production of machine-made lace is very widely diffused, one of the main centres being St Gall in Switzerland.

For designs, lace makers generally followed contemporary fashions in needlework. Numerous pattern books for various types of openwork fabrics were published in the C16 and early C17, the first being those of M. PAGANO (from 1542). Other notable early pattern-books include: Pellicciolo, *Fontana de gli esempli*, Venice *c.*1545; G. B. and M. Sessa, *Le pompe*, Venice 1557 (5th edition 1559) and pt. II 1560 (2nd edition 1562); Giovanni Andrea Valvassori, *Ornamento delle belle et virtuose donne*, Venice after 1567; Federigo de Vinciolo, *Les singuliers et nouveaux pourtraicts et ouvrages de lingerie*, Paris 1587 (13th edition 1612, also published in Turin, Lyon, Strasbourg, Basel, Montbéliard); Cesare Vecellio, *Corona delle nobili et virtuose donne*, Venice 1591 (17th edition 1625), *Studio delle virtuose dame*, Rome 1597, *Fiori d'ogni virtu*, Rome 1610 (6th edition under different title 1636), *Gemma pretiosa delle virtuose donne*, Rome 1615; Jacques Foillet, *Nouveau pourtraicts de point coupé*, Montbéliard 1598, *Muster von Klöppelspitzen*, Montbéliard *c.*1600; Wilhelm Hoffmann, *Neues vollkommenes Modelbuch*, Frankfurt 1604 (expanded edition with 600 designs 1607); and the works of H. SIBMACHER and I. C. PARASOLE.

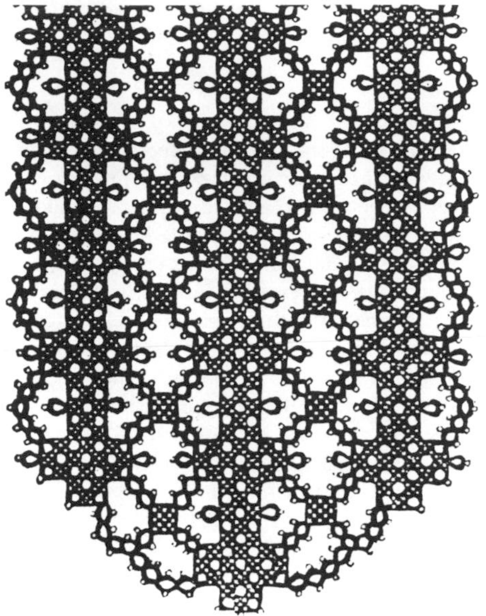

Lace: design by Sessa, from Le Pompe, 1557

Lace: design by Vinciolo (drawn netting), from his Les singuliers et nouveaux pourtraicts, 1587

Lit: B. Palliser, *History of Lace*, rev. M. Jourdain & A. Dryden, London 1902; M. Dreger, *Entwicklungsgeschichte der Spitze*, Vienna 1902; A. Lotz, *Bibliographie der Modelbücher*, Leipzig 1933; L. W. van der Meulen-Nulle, *Lace*, New York 1964.

Lace bindings A C18 French style of bookbinding in which the C17 lace or *dentelle* borders were expanded to fill most of the cover, leaving only a central space for a coat-of-arms. The edges were tooled in a wavy pattern to give a lacy effect also. DEROME and Dubuisson worked in this style.

Lace box A box with small interior compartments to hold pieces of lace. The name is popularly given to wide and shallow boxes made in late-C17 England and often decorated with marquetry, though they were not necessarily intended to hold lace.

Lace pattern silks A large group of figured silk materials woven *c.*1685 to 1730, mainly in France. The pattern consists of a central formalized floral motif surrounded by a frame of diaper pattern which sometimes resembles lace. At one time these silks were erroneously supposed to date from the Louis XIII period.

Lit: P. Thornton, *Baroque & Rococo Silks*, London 1965.

Lacework A type of porcelain decoration introduced at MEISSEN *c.*1764 by M.-V. ACIER (or possibly at STRASBOURG by J. A. HANNONG 1766–81). Lace was dipped in slip and fired which burnt the lace away and left a simulacrum in porcelain. It was used very sparingly and delicately until the C19 when figures were produced with elaborate flounced skirts, etc. by this technique.

Lachenal, Edmond (b.1855). French potter who began as an employee of DECK, rose to be chief of his design department, and in 1880 founded his own factory at Châtillon-sous-Bagneux. He began by making Japanese-inspired stoneware for which he won prizes at the international

Lachenal: stoneware dish, c.1914 *(Musée des Arts Décoratifs, Paris)*

exhibitions. He also produced porcelain and earthenware painted with birds, flowers, etc. in the ART NOUVEAU style, also statuettes some of which were executed in collaboration with Rodin. His son **Raoul** (b.1885) was also a potter, specializing in stoneware with flambé glazes.

Lit: A. Lesur and Tardy, *Les poteries et les faïences françaises*, Paris 1957–60.

Lacis French name for DARNED NETTING.

Lacquer A waterproof varnish of oriental origin. There are two distinct types and authorities differ as to which should be termed 'true' lacquer. The finer, which probably came into use first, is made from the sap of the *rhus vernicifera* tree (indigenous to China but later introduced into Japan), a grey syrupy juice which changes its molecular form on exposure to air – it polymerizes and may thus be termed the first plastic known to man. Once the liquid has been strained and superfluous moisture removed from it by heating, it may be applied with or without the addition of a colouring agent to wood, fabric, leather or other materials. It is applied in numerous coats, each of which is allowed to dry before the next is added, forming a crust so hard that it can be carved in relief. Lacquers of two or more colours may be combined, sometimes in strata so that one is revealed by carving through that on top of it. The technique of making small lacquer objects was perfected in China by the beginning

Red lacquer throne of the Emperor Ch'ien Lung, (Victoria & Albert Museum)

Japanese lacquer vase with gilt-bronze mounts, Paris, 1745–9 (Louvre)

of the C4 B.C. and later transmitted to Japan. Cups, vases, boxes and large chests and screens were extensively imported into Europe from the C16. At this time the higher quality wares came from Japan and generally had gilt decorations on a black ground. The Chinese also produced incised Coromandel lacquer (so called because it was sent to Europe by way of trading stations on the Coromandel coast).

Another type of lacquer, also insoluble in water, is made from the secretion of the lac insect *Coccus lacca* which is indigenous to India. When extracted, by immersing the larvae of the insect in boiling water, it is concentrated by evaporation and stretched into sheets which set hard on cooling and may be dissolved in alcohol

Japanese lacquer panel mounted on a chest-of-drawers by R. Dubois, c.1765 (Wallace Collection, London)

Chinese lacquer panel, with imitation lacquer by Pietro Messa, 1737 (Palazzo Reale, Turin)

F. Ladatte: gilt-bronze cartel clock, 1775 (Palazzo Reale, Turin)

to serve as a varnish with or without a colouring agent. This substance, called shellac, is an important ingredient in many European imitations of lacquer made from the early C17 and on a very large scale during the C18. These imitations have few of the properties of lacquer (e.g. they are not perfectly waterproof) and are more properly called 'japan' (*see* JAPANNING). The finest type originated in France and is called *vernis Martin* after G. MARTIN and his brothers who developed it. An imitation still further removed from the oriental originals was made in C18 Italy and is called LACCA CONTRAFATTA.

Lit: O. Mänchen-Helfen in *Wiener Beiträge zur Kunst- und Kultur-Geschichte Asiens*, vol. xi (1937), pp. 32–64; Matunosuke Kanda, *Japanese Lacquer*, Tokyo 1941; W. Willetts, *Chinese Art*, Harmondsworth 1958; W. Holzhausen, *Lackkunst in Europa*, Brunswick 1959; H. Huth, *Lacquer in the West*, Chicago and London 1971.

Lacquer gilding A method of applying gilt decorations to ceramics (much used on BÖTTGER's wares) by grinding up gold leaf with lacquer varnish and applying the mixture with a brush. It is more permanent than the earlier method of SIZE-GILDING.

Lacroix, Roger, *see* VANDERCRUSE, Roger.

Lacy glass American term for pressed glass with relief patterns of bead-work, foliage, arabesques, etc. covering the surface, made mainly *c.*1830–50. Not to be confused with *lace glass* a term sometimes used to describe VETRO DA TRINA.

Ladatte (Ladetti or Ladetto), Francesco (1706–87). Piedmontese sculptor who executed small decorative works and furniture mounts as well as large scale statues and reliefs. He was born in Turin and in 1718 when still a child went to Paris where he was trained and won the first prize for sculpture at the Academy in 1729. He then went to Rome but in 1732 returned to Turin where he worked for the Court executing bronze mounts of great elegance for furniture by PIFFETTI. He went back to Paris (1737–43) became a member of the Academy and exhibited at the Salon. In 1744 he returned to Turin where he was appointed sculptor in bronze to the King in 1745 and spent the rest of his life. His later works include candelabra and girandoles (Palazzo Reale, Turin), a magnificent gilt-bronze inkstand (Coll. Fila, Biella) and a very elaborate cartel clock (1775, Palazzo Reale, Turin) all in the delicate French Rococo style in which he had been trained and to which he remained faithful long after it had been superseded in France. *Illustrated previous column.*

Lit: J. Fleming in *The Connoisseur*, CXLII (1958), pp. 152–3; L. Mallé in *Essays in the History of Art Presented to Rudolf Wittkower*, London 1967, pp. 242–54.

Ladder-back A chair-back of horizontal slats. Medieval in origin, it was used continuously thereafter, principally for simple, country furniture.

Ladik rugs, *see* TURKISH CARPETS.

Laeuger, Max (1864–1952). German potter, interior decorator and architect, trained at the Kunstgewerbe-Schule in Karlsruhe where he was later (1885–98) a teacher. As a potter he was notable mainly for vases of simplified oriental form decorated in a limited range of colours (black and white on green; yellow and green on blue) with stylized flowers, especially long-stemmed tulips, which were much admired when shown at the Paris International Exhibition of 1900. He also produced elaborate ceramic tiles and other wall decorations for churches and especially interiors of his own design. From 1921 he was employed at the Karlsruhe Majolika-Manufaktur. Much of his work from the following years is figurative and sculptural, e.g., large wall fountain of 1925 with nude female figures in blue and white for the Stadthalle in Mulheim-am-Ruhr, plaque of 1930 with female nude in high relief (Badisches Landesmuseum, Karlsruhe). He also wrote on the art of pottery and exerted considerable influence on the development of studio pottery in Germany.

M. Laeuger:
glazed earthenware plaque, 1930
(Badisches Landesmuseum, Karlsruhe)

Lit: Max Laeuger, Exh. Cat., Mannheim 1964–65.

Lajoue, Jacques de (1686–1761). French painter and ornamental designer, one of the outstanding exponents of the Rococo style. Prints after his drawings (often engraved by HUQUIER), incorporating numerous fountains, fantastic colonnades, balustrades and wide staircases sweeping up and down in graceful curves, had great influence on the designers of printed cotton, marquetry, etc.

Lit: D. Guilmard, *Les maîtres ornementistes*, Paris 1880–81.

Lakes Colouring matters to be distinguished from pigments and dyes. They are produced in the dyeing process when a MORDANT is used to fix a DYE. A 'lake' or complex of dye and mordant is formed within the fibres of the fabric and since this 'lake' is insoluble the dye is fixed. The same dye will produce different-coloured lakes if different mordants are used.

Lalique, René (1860–1945). Leading French Art Nouveau jeweller and glass-maker. Established a workshop in Paris (1885) and later supplied jewellery for S. BING's shop, *L'Art Nouveau*. Reacting against the C19 fashion for large cut stones he designed bracelets, necklaces, buckles, combs, etc. in which the stones (often only semi-precious) are of no greater importance than the settings; he favoured asymmetrical patterns and adopted all the favourite motifs of the Art Nouveau artist – dragon-flies, beetles, peacocks, sinuous female nudes, limp flowers, etc. After 1902 he designed much glass: first scent bottles, then vases, clocks, light-fixtures, statuettes, screens and panels for furniture – of clear crystal glass engraved with frosted patterns of flowers, animals or figures. He established his own glasshouse at Combes-la-Ville in 1909 and another at Wingen-sur-Möder in 1921.

Lit: R. & L. Grover, *Carved and Decorated European Art Glass*, Rutland, Vermont 1970.

R. Lalique: glass vase, 1900–1910 (Musée des Arts Décoratifs, Paris)

Lalonde, Richard de (*fl.* 1780–90). French ornamental designer who published *c.*1780 *Cahiers d'Ameublement* with numerous designs for chairs, commodes, doorcases, tables, chimney-pieces, etc. in a highly refined and rather feminine version of the Louis XVI style though sometimes in a more severe Neo-Classical style with a liberal use of Roman fasces, helmets, etc., as ornamentation. (A commode by STÖCKEL at Fontainebleau is based on one of the latter type.) As it was intended for practical use in the cabinet-maker's shop, he included plans, sections of mouldings and details of carved decoration. A volume entitled *Différentes Grilles pour les Châteaux, les Choeurs et les Chapelles de Communion*, with attractive designs for ironwork in a Neo-Classical style with occasional restrained Rococo flourishes, appeared in 1789, too late to be of any practical use. His *Cahier d'Orfèvrerie* (1789) is more in tune with the times and includes designs for household plate of almost austere classicism.

R. de Lalonde: design for a confident, *c.1780*

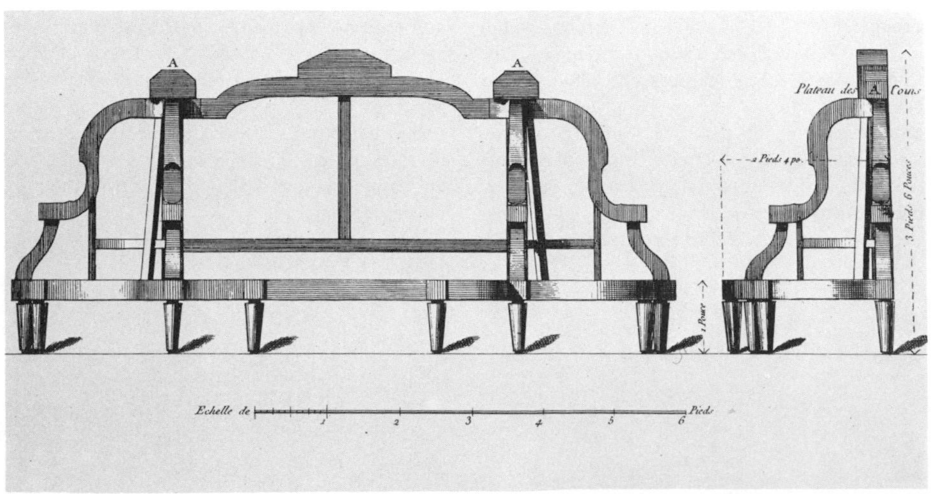

Lambert & Rawlings A mid-c19 firm of London silversmiths, founded by **Francis Lambert** (d.*c.*1841) and **William Rawlings** (d.*c.*1862). In 1842 the firm probably took over part of Rundell, Bridge & Rundell's business. They produced a wide range of both ecclesiastical and domestic plate, examples of which were shown at the Great Exhibition in 1861 (e.g. a wine flagon now in the Victoria & Albert Museum). The firm survived into the c20 as **Harman & Lambert.**

Lambeth potteries Established in London *c.*1665 and producing tin-glazed earthenware (i.e. Delft ware) at first similar to that previously made at SOUTHWARK and contemporaneously at BRISTOL. In the c18 they made some very attractive blue-and-white wares decorated with chinoiseries. Southwark wares have often been ascribed erroneously to Lambeth.

Lit: F. H. Garner, *English Delftware*, London 1948; A. Ray, *English Delftware Pottery*, London 1968.

Lambrequin Originally the scarf worn across a knight's helmet and its stylized representation in heraldry, later any deeply scalloped piece of drapery and, by extension, a fringe-like ornament painted on ceramics, carved on furniture, etc. Such ornaments were very popular during the Louis XIV and Régence periods.

Lambrequin ornament

Lamé A textile with a weft of metallic yarn.

Lamellé A type of leather decoration. Slits are cut in patterns, usually geometrical, and slender silver or other metal strips are passed through them.

Lamerie, Paul de (1688–1751). He was the best known English silversmith of his day and some of the finest pieces of English Rococo silver were made in his workshop. But he was very prolific and some of the pieces bearing his mark are in no way superior to those produced by some of his contemporaries. He was born at 's Hertogenbosch in Holland of Huguenot refugee parents who took him to London where they were settled by 1691. He was apprenticed to a Huguenot silversmith, Pierre Platel, in London in 1703. He began independent work in 1712 when he was made free of the Goldsmiths' Company and opened a shop in Windmill Street. In 1716 he was appointed goldsmith to the King. He began by working in two styles popular in early-c18 England – the starkly unornamented Queen Anne style and the Huguenot style with much gadrooning, cut-card ornament and heavy cast work. His most impressive piece of this early period is probably the wine-cistern made in 1719 and now in the Minneapolis Institute of Arts. A similar piece, dated 1726, is in the Hermitage Museum in Leningrad. The simpler pieces of plate made in his workshops throughout his career conform to designs established early in the c18 – tankards, teapots, coffee-pots, salvers, communion vessels – often decorated with engravings. One of his salvers is thought to have been engraved by Hogarth (Victoria & Albert Museum). By the 1730s he was producing cast and embossed plate in an individual version of the Rococo style, e.g., his covered cup of 1737 in the Fishmongers' Company, London, which combines Rococo ornament with naturalistic features reminiscent of c16 work and other features possibly derived from AURICULAR silver. In the period 1739–42 he produced some very richly decorated pieces which are close to French Rococo silver, e.g., the ewer and dish in the collection of Viscountess Galway. Most of his work in the later 1740s is decorated with Rococo motifs, though rather sparsely. The tea-kettle and bread basket of 1745, now in the Metropolitan Museum, New York, are good examples of his work at this time. *Illustrated next page.* (For his mark *see* p. 894.)

Lit: P. A. S. Phillips, *Paul de Lamerie*, London 1935; J. F. Hayward, *Huguenot Silver in England 1688–1727*, London 1959.

Lamour, Jean (1698–1771). The leading French master of Rococo wrought iron and one of the finest metal-workers of any country or period.

P. de Lamerie: silver wine cistern, 1719 (Minneapolis Institute of Arts)

P. de Lamerie: toilette service in silver (Ashmolean Museum, Oxford)

Born in Nancy where he succeeded his father as *Serrurier de la Ville* in 1720, he owed his great opportunity to Stanislas Lecksinski who succeeded to the Duchy of Lorraine in 1738 and gave him all his important commissions: banisters for the château de Chanteheux, balconies and banisters for the Seminary; grilles, balconies and banisters for the Hôtel de Ville; and, his great masterpiece, the gates and railings in Place Stanislas (1751–9). His work has an elegant intricacy unmatched by any other iron-worker and an astonishing imaginative fecundity. He seldom repeated a motif yet his railings, banisters, etc. have an apparently spontaneous homogeneity of gaily rippling patterns. He was of course assisted by numerous craftsmen, some of whom are known by name. After the death of Stanislas in 1766 he seems to have retired with a handsome fortune to live among the collection of pictures he had acquired.

Lit: C. Cournault, *Jean Lamour*, Paris 1903; O. Höver, *Wrought Iron*, London 1962.

Lampas A figured textile with a pattern composed of weft floats (segments of threads crossing at least two yarns between points of binding) bound by a binding warp and added to a ground fabric (of tabby, twill, damask, etc.) formed by a main warp and a main weft. It is similar to DAMASK in appearance but heavier. It is the correct name for most of the textiles popularly but imprecisely called 'brocade', but may also be called a tissued fabric. Much of the best C18 upholstery was executed in silk lampas.

Lamp-blown glass Toys, figures, ornamental groups and other small articles made from rods and tubes of a readily fusible glass heated in the flame of a lamp and blown, pincered, drawn out or otherwise manipulated by hand. They are sometimes extremely elaborate and delicate, e.g. a glass ship with rigging in finely drawn glass threads (Victoria & Albert Museum). The place of origin is seldom known. They were made and sold at country fairs all over Europe in the C19.

Lampe bouillotte, *see* BOUILLOTTE LAMP.

Lancaster glassworks A glasshouse founded in New York in 1849 making jugs and bowls with LILY PAD DECORATION as well as druggists' wares, etc. It closed *c.*1900.

Lancastrian pottery, *see* PILKINGTON'S ROYAL LANCASTRIAN POTTERY.

Landberg, Nils, *see* ORREFORS GLASSHOUSE.

Lanfrey, Claude-François, *see* NIDERVILLER POTTERY & PORCELAIN FACTORY.

Lange lyzen, *see* LONG ELIZAS.

Langevin, Louis, *see* NANTES COTTON PRINTING FACTORY.

Langley, Batty (1696–1751). English ornamental designer and the author of numerous practical guides for builders, carpenters, gardeners, etc., often produced in collaboration with his younger brother **Thomas** (b.1702) who was a draughtsman and engraver. His *The City and Country Builder's and Workman's Treasury of Designs*, London 1740 (reissued with additional plates 1741, 1750, 1756), includes designs for furniture, iron gates, and such church furnishings as pulpits, altar-pieces and fonts, as well as architectural details. Most of the furniture designs are in a plain PALLADIAN style but a few are copied without acknowledgement from Continental pattern books – a dressing table from J. J. SCHÜBLER, a clock from Johann Friedrich Lauch (*fl.*1720–60) and six elegant Rococo tables from N. PINEAU'S *Nouveaux Desseins de Pieds de Tables*. Greater originality was displayed in *Ancient Architecture restored and improved* . . . , 1742, reissued and better known as *Gothic Architecture improved by rules and proportions in many grand designs of columns, doors, windows* . . . , 1747. This book formalized Neo-Gothic decorations into a series of 'orders' and seems to have been used as a source of designs by makers of bookcases, chairs, etc. in a pretty, flimsy, wildly inaccurate 'Gothick taste', with an abundance of crockets, ogee arches and rosettes.

Lit: P. Ward-Jackson, *English Furniture Designs of the Eighteenth Century*, London 1958.

Langlois, Pierre or **Peter** (*fl.*1760). A French cabinet-maker, he had established himself in

London by 1759–60 and became the finest exponent of the Louis XV and Louis XVI styles in furniture outside France. His commodes with marquetry decoration and gilt-bronze mounts are of a quality little below the best Parisian work of the period and the equal of the best furniture being made in London, e.g., by VILE AND COBB. Examples, dating from the 1760s, are at Woburn Abbey, in the Fitzwilliam Museum, Cambridge, and in the Metropolitan Museum, New York. Very different in style to these commodes are a pair of carved and gilded folding card-tables at Syon House and some painted and gilt pier tables formerly at Audley End, which have been attributed to Langlois. They are in an Adamesque style.

Lit: A. Coleridge, *Chippendale Furniture*, London 1968; P. Thornton & W. Rieder, *The Connoisseur* Dec. 1971, pp. 283–8; Feb. 1972, pp. 105–12.

Languet In ornament, a U- or tongue-shaped element, usually repeated to form a frieze or band called a band of languets or a tongue pattern.

Lang-yao, *see* SANG DE BOEUF.

Lannuier, Charles-Honoré (1779–1819). A French cabinet-maker, he emigrated to America in 1803 and became the leading furniture-maker in New York in rivalry with Duncan PHYFE and Michael ALLISON. He was trained in France in the Louis XVI style, probably under his elder brother **Nicolas** who became a *maître ébéniste* in 1783. (A commode by Nicolas Lannuier is in the Musée des Arts Décoratifs in Paris.) He advertised himself in the New York Evening Post in 1803 as a maker of 'all kinds of furniture . . . in the newest and latest French Fashion', and his work always remained recognizably French in origin though he succeeded in creating what might be termed a New York Empire Style. It is considerably lighter and more delicate than the Directoire, Consulate and Empire styles from which it is derived. His work is of consistently high quality and is remarkable for its combination of rich materials (rosewood, white marble and ormolu) and for the excellence of its detailing, especially the die-cast brass banding, lion's paw feet and ormolu mounts. He seems to have imported the latter from France. He worked mainly for clients in New York and the Hudson valley and a surprisingly large number of signed or labelled pieces by him have survived, for his production must have been considerably smaller than that of Duncan Phyfe. Examples are in the Metropolitan Museum of Art in New York.

Lit: Berry B. Tracy in *The Metropolitan Museum of Art Bulletin*, April 1967, pp. 283–291; Charles F. Montgomery, *American Furniture: The Federal Period in the Henry Francis du Pont Winterthur Museum*, New York–London 1967.

Lanz or **Lanze, Johann Wilhelm,** *see* STRASBOURG POTTERY AND PORCELAIN FACTORY and FRANKENTHAL PORCELAIN FACTORY.

Laodicea carpets, *see* TURKISH CARPETS.

Lapierre, Arnaud, *see* MONTAUBAN POTTERY.

Lapis lazuli A semi-precious stone, deep ultramarine blue in colour, mainly composed of lazulite flecked with golden pyrite. It is very slightly translucent. It was used by Renaissance and Mannerist craftsmen for ornamental vases, etc. (notably by BYLIVELT), also in PIETRE DURE inlays and occasionally on furniture, etc.

Lapping The process used for covering exposed copper in SHEFFIELD PLATE, usually along rims and edges. Various methods were developed, notably by Thomas Boulton and Samuel Roberts. The standard method became that of applying U-shaped silver wire along the edges.

Laqabi ware A type of C12 ISLAMIC POTTERY, attributed to Rayy and Kashan, distinguished by the technique – polychrome glazes separated by raised or incised lines. The glazes are applied directly on to the white ground. The designs often include birds, especially peacocks, surrounded by plant designs or cable patterns or, more rarely, inscriptions against a scroll background.

Lasalle, Philippe de (1723–1805). Leading Lyons silk designer and manufacturer. He was trained in Paris as a painter under BOUCHER and evolved an extremely attractive ornamental style which retained all the delicacy and elegance of the Rococo yet harmonised perfectly with the early LOUIS XVI STYLE furniture it accompanied.

P. de Lasalle: silk panels for a screen, c.1780 (Château de Fontainebleau)

His designs usually incorporate naturalistic birds and bunches of flowers with a discreet use of bows, swags and occasional vases, in colour-schemes of a May morning freshness. The supplier of numerous furnishing silks for Versailles and Fontainebleau, he was ennobled by Louis XVI. He also worked for the Russian and Spanish Courts. He was ruined by the Revolution.

Lit: E. Pariset, *Histoire de la fabrique Lyonnaise*, Lyon 1901; P. Thornton, *Baroque and Rococo Silks*, London 1965.

Latten Base yellow alloy, similar to or the same as brass.

Lattice work An openwork FRET much used in CHINESE CHIPPENDALE FURNITURE.

Latticino, Latticinio or **Lattimo glass** A translucent milky white glass made with lead, first produced at Murano in the C16 – the ancestor of OPALINE. Whole vessels could be made of it, in imitation of porcelain, but it was developed in Venice especially for the decoration of clear glass and gave its name to this type of decoration. Threads of *latticino* are embedded in the substance of clear glass in simple or complicated, interlacing patterns. Glass decorated with the more intricate patterns of this kind is known as

Vetro da trina or lace glass. Glass decorated with *latticino* came into use by *c.*1535 and is described in Biringuccio's *De la Pirotechnica* (1540). It remained in fashion into the C18 when **Giuseppe Briati** (d.1772) specialized in it, and was revived in the C19.

Latz, Jean-Pierre (*c.*1691–1754). One of the best though – because he rarely marked his work – less known Louis XV *ébénistes*. He was born in Germany, went to Paris in or before 1719, soon set up on his own and was well established before 1741 when he was appointed an *Ébéniste privilégié du Roy*. In 1749 he was prosecuted for casting and finishing metal mounts for furniture on his premises. At that time his stock included 236 clock cases in various stages of production. An inventory drawn up on his death refers to 170 clocks besides other types of furniture. Two outstandingly fine long-case clock cases signed by him are known, one dated 1744 with BOULLE style *première partie* marquetry and exuberant Rococo gilt-bronze mounts (Cleveland Museum of Art), the other with wood marquetry and gilt-bronze mounts (Waddesdon Manor, Bucks.). He clearly specialized in clock cases and also made bracket clocks. A few commodes, corner cupboards and desks marked by him are known and a number of others have been attributed to him.

Lit: H. Hawley in *The Bulletin of the Cleveland Museum of Art* LVII (1970), pp. 203–59.

Laub und bandelwerk (Foliage and scroll-work). A German term for a late Baroque framing motif consisting of formalized leaves and strapwork, much used for the decoration of glass, leather, textiles and especially ceramics in the earlier C18. At MEISSEN it was used on BÖTTGER stoneware and as a border for chinoiseries during the H. G. HEROLD period.

Laurel chain A Greek ornamental band composed of forms resembling bay leaves.

Laurence Vitrearius The first recorded English glassmaker. He came from Normandy and settled at Dyers Cross, Pickhurst, near Chiddingfold in the Surrey-Sussex Weald in *c.*1226. In *c.*1240 he was making stained glass for Westminster Abbey.

Law, Thomas, *see* SHEFFIELD PLATE.

Lay, Philipp Friedrich, *see* OFFENBACH POTTERY.

Lay-metal Obsolete term for PEWTER.

Lazulite A blue tinted PARIAN WARE.

Lazy Susan American term for a type of revolvable stand for condiments placed in the centre of a dining table.

Le Brun, Charles (1619–90). French painter and designer, the virtual creator of the LOUIS XIV STYLE. Trained as a painter under Simon Vouet, he studied in Rome 1642–6, acquiring from Nicolas Poussin and Pietro da Cortona a classicizing high Baroque style. He helped to found the *Académie Royale* in 1648 and soon took Vouet's place as the leading French painter. In 1658 he was put in charge of the MAINCY TAPESTRY FACTORY and in 1663 appointed the first director of the Manufacture des GOBELINS. At the Gobelins he not only painted cartoons for tapestries but also provided designs for, and supervised the work of, the goldsmiths, *ébénistes*, bronze-workers, etc., insisting on the highest possible standards of craftsmanship. These objects, which provide a fitting background to the pomps of the *grand siècle* and made Versailles the cynosure of regal taste for all Europe, reveal his love of opulence tempered by a certain well-bred classical restraint which eschewed the gaudy, the intricate, the bizarre and the merely ingenious. On the death of his protector, Colbert, in 1683 he fell from royal favour.

Lit: Charles Le Brun, Exh. Cat., Versailles 1963.

Le Corbusier, Charles-Edouard Jeanneret, called, (1887–1965). The most brilliant and original of modern architects, he also designed furniture in the 1920s – in collaboration with **Charlotte Perriand** and his brother **Pierre Jeanneret** – and exerted a profound influence on the development of modern furniture. He was influenced by MUTHESIUS whose ideas on design he picked up as a student in Germany under Peter BEHRENS in 1910. With his belief that the house is a *machine à habiter*, he had no time for the self-consciously 'artistic' furniture of the post-war period. And at the now famous Paris 1925 Exhibition where so many such pieces were shown, his contribution was the *Pavillon de l'Esprit Nouveau* furnished with the simplest THONET bent-wood chairs. In 1925 he also published *L'art décoratif d'aujourd'hui* in which he explained that industrialization had made 'decorative art', in the commonly accepted sense of the term, impossible and said that its contemporary equivalent should be sought in standard industrial products. 'Decorative art is equipment, beautiful equipment', he wrote. Next year, with Charlotte Perriand, he began to design chairs, tables and built-in cupboards suitable for the modern apartment. A number of these pieces were exhibited in a room designed for the *Salon d'Automne* in 1929. The chairs had tubular steel framework with leather upholstery and included a revolving desk chair, the *grand confort* armchair, and *basculant* with a pivoting backrest and taut leather straps for arms, and the well-known *chaise longue* called the 'cowboy chair'. Even after fifty years this *chaise longue* is still the most successful of modern reclining chairs, carefully adapted to the comfort of the human body in a variety of positions, and of great elegance in the interplay of gentle curves and straight lines.

Le Corbusier: armchair known as the siège grand confort, *1926* *(Musée des Arts Décoratifs, Paris)*

Le Corbusier: chaise longue *known as the cowboy chair, 1927* *(Musée des Arts Décoratifs, Paris)*

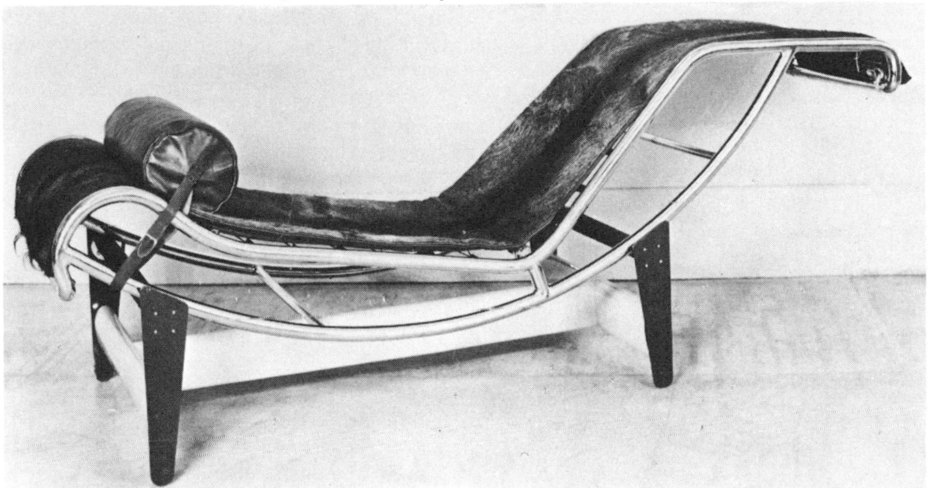

In his view the furniture, or 'interior equipment', of a house could be reduced to three categories: cases for storage, tables and seats for work or leisure. It was with Le Corbusier that case furniture began to be swept off the floor-space and returned to its medieval position in the wall, or sometimes to form the wall. According to Charlotte Perriand, he was activated by a desire to 'standardize and industrialize equipment and make it available to the general public'. He was among the first to appreciate that mass-produced objects could have merits not equal but superior to those of hand-made ones, in beauty as well as utility – hence his admiration for Thonet furniture and such factory-made products as laboratory jars and simple café glassware. But he was a traditionalist as well as a revolutionary. His *siège grand confort*, with bulky rectangular cushions in a tubular steel frame, derives from the English leather-covered club armchairs. He reduced the prototype to its essential components – rigid framework and soft cushions – re-composed it and redesigned it for factory production in large numbers. His *chaise longue* owes a similar debt to Thonet's rocking-chairs and reveals a like process of extracting and then rendering back. In his use of tubular steel he was indebted to Mart STAM and BREUER, but his furniture is rather more human and displays a greater concern for comfort, both visual and physical.

He gave most of the credit for his furniture designs to Charlotte Perriand, his collaborator, but it is difficult to determine exactly what share she had in them. Attention to the contrast of materials – calf-skin and chromium-plated steel – and a sense of elegance suggests feminine sensibility. Her independent work of the 1930s is, however, much less original and displays a taste for rustic crafts and peasant furnishings very much at variance with Le Corbusier's admiration for factory-made products. And the furniture she designed after leaving his studio is not without a touch of the arty-crafty. Yet Le Corbusier produced no furniture designs of importance after she left his office. It seems that the furniture first exhibited in 1929 was the fruit of a perfectly integrated partnership. Several of these pieces came back into production in the 1950s and are still being made.

Lit: S. Giedion, *Mechanization Takes Command*, New York 1948; J. L. Sert and C. Perriand in *Aujourd'hui*, March 1956; C. Jencks, *Le Corbusier and the Tragic View of Architecture*, London 1973.

Le Creusot glasshouse, *see* VERRERIE DE LA REINE.

Le Febvre (or **Le Febure**), **François** (*fl.*1635–57). Parisian goldsmith who published two small but influential books on designs for engraved or repoussé work on silver – *Livre de fleurs et de feuilles pour servir de l'art d'orfèvrerie* (1635) of 6 sheets, and *Livre de feuilles et de fleurs utiles aux orfèvres etc.* (1657) of 10 sheets.

Lit: D. Guilmard, *Les Maîtres ornementistes*, Paris 1880.

Le Gaigneur, Louis Constantin (*fl.*1815–6). Somewhat mysterious French cabinet-maker who settled in London (probably after the Revolution) where in 1815 he owned the *Buhl Manufactory* at 19 Queen Street, Edgware Road. A handsome kneehole writing-table with *contre-parties* marquetry in the style of A.-C. BOULLE (Wallace Collection, London) was supposed to date from the Louis XIV period until his signature was noted on the marquetry of a pair of similar tables at Windsor Castle. He is also known to have supplied inkstands in the same style for Carlton House.

Lit: F. J. B. Watson, *The Wallace Collection Catalogues: Furniture*, London 1956.

Le Pautre, Jean (1618–82). French Baroque designer, brother of the architect Antoine Le Pautre (1621–91) and father of the early Rococo designer **Pierre Le Pautre** (*c.*1648–1716). He was one of the creators of the LOUIS XIV STYLE, sharing to the full his master LE BRUN's taste for sober magnificence and solemn splendour. His engraved designs, of which over two thousand are known, provide a uniquely comprehensive survey of the style, from grotesques and term figures to massive sculptural chimney-pieces, carved and gilt furniture, heavily canopied beds and elaborate ceilings. He replaced the thin, flat ornament of his Mannerist predecessors, e.g. DU CERCEAU, with boldly monumental human and animal motifs, often rather oppressively heavy but expressive and rhythmical. His urns, for example, are derived from classical prototypes but transformed by his Baroque sense of fantasy, encrusted with nymphs and satyrs, burgeoning with fruits, flowers and foliage of a swampy luxuriance and depicted in such a dramatic way that they seem to dwarf the human figures and even the buildings in the background. His later work is lighter and more graceful, foreshadowing that of his successor BERAIN. Few, if any, of his designs can have been executed exactly but they became a source of inspiration for many furniture-makers and other craftsmen. His son **Pierre Le Pautre** worked as a draughtsman and designer at Versailles and the other royal palaces under J. Hardouin Mansart from 1699 until his death. He played an important part in the creation of the ROCOCO STYLE, being among the first to break through the rigidity and symmetricality of Louis XIV design.

Lit: D. Guilmard, *Les Maîtres ornementistes*, Paris 1880; P. Jessen, *Des Barock in Ornamentstich*, Leipzig 1926.

Leach, Bernard Howell (b.1887). Leading English studio potter. Born in Hong Kong of British parents, he began as a painter and etcher in England, went to Japan in 1909 and studied pottery under Ogata Kenzan VI (last of the line founded by Ogata KENZAN). In 1920 he returned to England and founded the Leach pottery at St Ives with his Japanese pupil **Shoji Hamada** who later went back to Japan where he became the leading potter of his day. Although owing something to medieval and C17 English pottery (especially slipware), Leach has derived inspiration mainly from Japanese RAKU wares. His works include both table-wares and handsome flower vases of simple, sturdy form relying for their decorative effect on the subtlety of their glazes and occasional boldly splashed or incised motifs. He believes that

B. H. Leach: bowl, c.1924 (Victoria & Albert Museum)

'Pots, like all forms of art, are human expressions'. By his works and writings (notably *A Potter's Book*, 1940) he has been largely responsible for establishing in Europe the Japanese concept of the potter as an 'Artist' and not a mere craftsman, together with the notion that a hand-thrown pot with an irregular surface texture is in some way 'superior' to more highly finished wares, whether of pottery or porcelain, made by hand or machine, Greek, C18 or modern. Though he turned his back on INDUSTRIAL DESIGN, his works have had some influence on industrial designers.

Lit: M. Rose, *Artist Potters in England*, London 1955; B. Leach, *A Potter's Work*, Bath 1967.

Lead glass A type of glass containing oxides of lead which enhance its brilliance, used from early times for PÂTE DE VERRE and for vessels by George RAVENSCROFT (1675) and later English glassmakers.

Lead glaze A transparent glaze composed of silicaceous sand, salt and alkali such as potash and sometimes a mineral to colour it, fused with the acid of natural sulphide of lead (galena) or lead oxide, applied to pottery that has already been fired and united to the surface by a subsequent firing at a lower temperature. It was widely used in the Middle Ages when it was generally coloured brown or green (by the addition of copper). If lead glazes of more than one colour are applied to a pot they must be separated from one another (by a ridge of clay or a greased band) so that they do not intermingle in the firing. An almost colourless lead glaze (known in Italy as *coperta*, in Holland as *Kwaart*) was applied to the best TIN-GLAZED EARTHENWARE after it had been painted and before it received its second firing, to enhance the sheen of the surface. The fumes of the lead proved injurious to workmen and lead glazes have seldom been used since the early C19 when a transparent FELDSPATHIC GLAZE was developed.

Leather An animal tissue rendered flexible and durable by oil dressing, tawing or tanning. The unprepared skin which is both stiff and perishable, consists of three layers, the epidermis with fur or hair growing out of it, the corium which can be made into leather, and a tissue of fat or flesh beneath. Skins were used for clothing in Palaeolithic times and the process of making leather from them appears to have been developed in the Neolithic Age. Leather was certainly in use in Pre-Dynastic Egypt (i.e. before 5000 B.C.) for clothing, sandals, bags and bottles. It was much used in both Greece and Rome and throughout the Roman Empire. Fragments of Coptic leather BOOKBINDINGS survive from the C4 A.D. At an early date the Libyan town, Ghadâmes, became the leading centre for the production of leather made from tawed goatskin. (The name of this town is preserved in the Spanish word *guadameci* though this came to indicate sheepskin rather than goatskin). In the C8 Cordova (whence the English word cordwainer) became famous for the production of very fine leather, at first white or dyed red, but sometimes covered with gold or silver foil. By the C14 techniques of decorating the material with hand punches or painting were perfected here. But by 1305 Moorish craftsmen from Spain had migrated to the Low Countries which, by the end of the C16, became the main centre for the production of fine leather embossed in relief, coloured and used for large wall-hangings, table-covers, etc., as well as for small objects. Most of the so-called 'Spanish leather' is in fact Netherlandish. The production of leather for wall-hangings declined in the early C18. The basic techniques of leather preparation which had been established in Spain in the C11 remained little altered until the C19.

Leather casket, Basel, late C14 (Kunstgewerbemuseum, Berlin)

(Right) Detail of leather scabbard for Cesare Borgia, Italian, c.1500 (Victoria & Albert Museum)

Processes. There are three basic preparatory processes: chamoising, by which the skin is treated with oil or fats (the connection with the chamois is obscure); tawing, by which it is treated with alum; and, the latest in historical sequence,

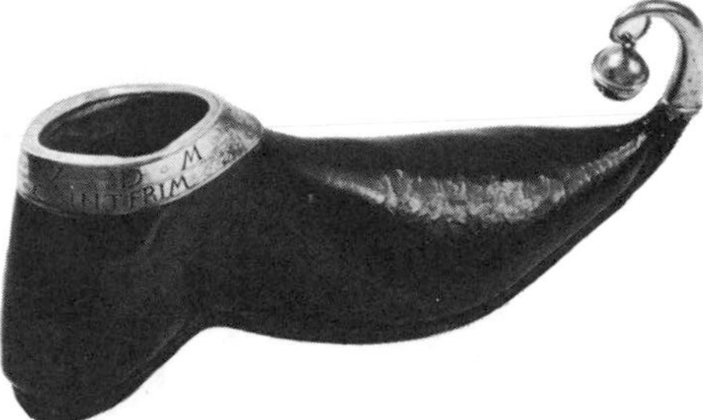

Leather drinking vessel with silver mounts, N. German, c.1548 (Kunstgewerbemuseum, Berlin)

Detail of leather hanging, stamped and gilded, Spain or the Netherlands, c17 (Victoria & Albert Museum)

tanning, by which it is immersed in a tannic solution originally obtained from oak galls or oak bark, later from the sumach plant. Skins of different types of animal – usually goat, sheep or calf – yield leather of varying qualities and call for different methods of processing, two of which are sometimes combined e.g. tawing and oil dressing.

After it had been prepared the leather might be dyed. It could then be stretched over a frame of wood or other material and sewn or rivetted into the form of containers (bottles, jugs, pails, etc.). Alternatively, it could be moulded by the CUIR BOUILLI process or by laminating thin layers stretched over a solid core (generally used for light-weight articles such as sheaths). Surface patterns were obtained by punching, incising, carving or by bruising the panel over a relief of carved wood. Ornamental motifs could be applied to the surface with metal stamps (BLIND TOOLING). Gold tooling, introduced into Europe from the East in the C16, is effected by impressing gold leaf with a hot iron into blind stamped tooling: it is applied both to bookbindings and to small boxes, etc.

Lit: G. A. Bravo & J. Trupke, *10,000 Jahre Leder*, Basel and Stuttgart 1970; J. W. Waterer, *Spanish Leather*, London 1971.

Leaver, Gabriel (1757–95). Furniture-maker who was born in London, emigrated to America in the 1770s and settled at Savannah, Georgia, where *c.*1782 he married the sister-in-law of the furniture-maker Isaac FELL. Handsome mahogany pieces in the Chippendale style are attributed to him.

Lit: Mrs C. M. Theus, *Savannah Furniture 1735–1825*, Savannah 1967; and in *The Connoisseur* CLXIX (1968), pp. 124–32.

Lecreux, Nicolas, *see* TOURNAI POTTERY AND PORCELAIN FACTORY.

Leeds pottery A factory was established near Leeds in the 1750s, producing in the following decade a wide range of wares mainly imitative of those of WHIELDON, sometimes decorated in enamel by the studio of Robinson and D. RHODES. From 1776 **William Hartley** became the dominant figure in the concern then called Humble, Green & Co. (from 1781 to 1820 Hartley, Greens & Co.), which soon began to produce the cream-coloured earthenware for which it is famous – similar to that of WEDGWOOD but with a less even glaze, which generally shows a primrose yellow or pale green tinge where it runs thick, and with a much more frequent use of moulded decorations and, especially, pierced work. From the late 1780s PEARL WARE with a slightly bluish glaze was also made. Decorations were executed in enamel colours or with transfer printing in red or black. Products include a very wide range of useful and decorative wares, which vary in form and decoration between the cottagey and the elegantly Neo-classical, rather lumpy statuettes and very handsome, largish (up to 45 cm high) horses

Leeds pearlware horse, early c19 (Temple Newsam House, Leeds)

Leeds creamware epergne, late c18 (Temple Newsam House, Leeds)

made to stand in the windows of saddlers and corn chandlers. An extensive export trade with the Continent was carried on until the Revolutionary Wars. (Many wares were decorated in enamel in Holland.) The original concern went bankrupt in 1820 but production continued fitfully under a succession of proprietors until 1878. From 1888 **Slee's Modern Pottery** reproduced c18 wares, especially the elaborately pierced vases, sometimes from the original moulds and patterns, but in a material slightly lighter in weight and with a rather more lustrous and even glaze. Genuine old Leeds pottery is rarely marked, but the name (sometimes with Hartley Greens & Co. added) was sometimes impressed, the letters being much more evenly set in modern wares than in old ones. Wares of the **Hunslet Hall** pottery, the chief local rival of Hartley, Greens & Co. (operating from before 1792 by Petty and Rainforth) are impressed 'Rainforth & Co.'.

Lit: D. Towner, *The Leeds Pottery*, London 1963.

Leerdam glasshouse The Royal Netherlands Glassworks which after the appointment of **P. M. Cochius** as director in 1915 became notable for the production of decorative pieces of very high quality and good modern table-wares. It has employed a number of notable designers including the architect Karel Petrus Cornelis de Bazel (1869–1923), Christiaan Johannes Lanooy (1881–1948), Joris Johannes Christiaan Lebeau (1878–1945), Cornelis de Lorm (1875–1942) and A. D. COPIER who has been largely responsible for artistic direction since he joined the staff as a designer in 1917. Younger designers include

Sybren Valkema (b.1916) whose work is strongly influenced by non-representational sculpture, Floris Meydam (b.1919), Willem Heesen (b.1925), Gerard Jacobus Thomassen (b.1926) who specialises in table-wares, Jacobus Franciscus Linssen (b.1936) and Brigette Altenburger (b.1942). A glass school is attached to the factory which also maintains a museum of glass.

Lit: Glasschool Leerdam Exh. Cat., Stedelijk Museum, Amsterdam 1947.

Légaré, Gédéon (*c.*1615–76). Parisian goldsmith with a workshop in the Louvre which he shared with his brother-in-law **Pierre Bain**, an enameller. Engravings of several of his designs were published under the title *Livre de Feuilles d'Orfèvrerie* n.d. His kinsman **Gilles** (b.*c.*1610), who also had a workshop in the Louvre, published a *Livre des ouvrages d'Orfèvrerie*, probably in 1663, which included designs for seals, rings, necklaces and other pieces of jewellery. He was a Huguenot and left France after the revocation of the Edict of Nantes, but another set of his designs of which only the title page is known, *Nouveau livre d'ornements*, was published in 1692.

Lit: D. Guilmard, *Les maîtres ornemantistes*, Paris 1880.

Legrain, Pierre (1889–1929). A leading Parisian furniture designer and interior decorator and one of the creators of the ART DECO style. After training at the École des Arts Appliqués, Germain Pilon, he joined the studio of Paul IRIBE with whom he worked 1908–14 collaborating on the apartment of Jacques Doucet. From 1917 he designed bookbindings for Doucet who, in 1925, put him in charge of the interior decoration of his famous studio at Neuilly. He designed a good deal of furniture in the 1920s, showing a marked preference for rich or unusual materials with a sparse use of geometrical decorations. Many of his pieces – especially stools with curved seats resting on central supports – are strongly influenced by primitive African furnishings. He also designed a grand piano with a glass case.

P. Legrain: chaise longue, c.1925 (Musée des Arts Décoratifs, Paris)

Lit: M. Dormoy *et al., Pierre Legrain, relieur*, Paris 1965; L. Thornton in *The Connoisseur* CLXXIX (1972), pp. 166–9.

Lehman, Benjamin He was a cabinet-maker and chair-maker in Philadelphia and published a price-list of his work in 1786. Nothing more is known about him.

Lehmann, Kaspar (*c.*1565–1622). German engraver of hard-stones and glass. He was born at Ülzen in N. Germany, began his career by working for Duke Wilhelm V of Bavaria and from 1588 was employed in Prague by the Emperor Rudolf II who ennobled him in 1595 (as Kaspar Lehmann von Löwenwald). Apart from a brief period (1606–8) in Dresden working for the Elector of Saxony, he spent the rest of his life in Prague. In 1610 Rudolf II appointed him official precious-stone and glass engraver – *Kaiserlicher Kammer-Edelgestein und Glasschneider*. He was also given the monopoly of glass engraving in the Hapsburg lands. Although he was not, as is sometimes said, the first artist to execute wheel engraving on glass (he stated himself that he learned the art of engraving glass in his youth), he played a part of considerable importance in developing the technique of engraving precious and semi-precious stones with a lapidary's wheel for the decoration of crystal clear glass. None of his hard-stone carvings has been identified and only one signed example of his work on glass is known (armorial beaker in Schwarzenberg Collection, Vienna). But several very finely engraved panels of glass are generally ascribed to him, three of them in the Victoria & Albert Museum. His privileges were inherited by G. SCHWANHARDT.

Lit: R. Schmidt, *Das Glas*, Berlin and Leipzig 1922; W. B. Honey, *Glass: A Handbook*, London 1946.

Lehn ware, *see* PENNSYLVANIA DUTCH STYLE.

Lei A Chinese Bronze Age wine or water vessel made during the SHANG-YIN and Early CHOU dynasties. It can be either circular or rectangular in section, with wide sloping shoulders, ring handles and a hollow foot. For illustration *see* SHANG-YIN.

Leihamer, Abraham (1745–74). North German faience painter who worked at the KIEL, STOCKELSDORF, ECKERNFORDE, RÖRSTRAND and MARIEBERG factories, specializing in very delicate little landscapes and feathery chinoiseries in the manner of PILLEMENT (e.g. stove of 1773 in Museum für Kunst und Gewerbe, Hamburg).

Lekythos, *see* GREEK POTTERY.

Lelarge, Jean Baptiste (1743–1802). The son and grandson of *menuisiers*, he became a *maître-menuisier* in 1775 and one of the best Louis XVI chair-makers. He continued in business during the Revolutionary and Directoire periods, though his work remained rather conservative in style. Chairs by him may be seen in the Louvre in Paris, the Wallace Collection in London, the Metropolitan Museum in New York, and the Museum für Kunst und Gewerbe, Hamburg.

Lit: F. J. B. Watson, *The Wrightsman Collection: Furniture*, New York 1966.

Leleu, Jean-François (1729–1807). Born in Paris, he was one of the few great Louis XVI furniture-makers who were French, most of the others being German. He began in OEBEN's workshop and hoped to gain control of it on Oeben's death but was ousted by his rival RIESENER. He became a *maître-ébéniste* in 1764. His chief patron was the Prince de Condé though he also worked for the Court, especially Mme du Barry and Marie Antoinette. Though versatile he lacked Riesener's originality in design and inventiveness in technique. But his furniture is outstanding. In design it is always dignified and often monumental, while the craftsmanship is impeccable. Most of his pieces are veneered with patterned marquetry but he also made use of Sèvres porcelain plaques and panels of lacquer. In 1780 his son-in-law **Charles-Antoine Stadler** joined him as a partner and carried on the business until 1811. Leleu retired *c.*1792. He seems to have survived the Revolution with his fortune intact. Examples of his furniture are to be seen in the Louvre and Musée des Arts Décoratifs, Paris, in the Wallace Collection and Victoria & Albert Museum in London, at Waddesdon Manor, Bucks., and in the Frick Collection in New York.

Lit: F. J. B. Watson, *The Wrightsman Collection: Furniture*, New York 1966.

Lely, Johannes van der (*fl.*1683–1749). Leading Dutch silversmith at Leeuwarden, the grandson, son and father of notable silversmiths. Worked in a rich version of the Louis XIV style, probably under the influence of MAROT, with much use of crisply modelled floral reliefs and acanthus leaf ornament as on the Reliquary of St Ignatius (Frisian Museum, Leeuwarden).

Lit: J. W. Fredericks, *Dutch Silver*, The Hague 1952.

Lemarchand, Charles-Joseph, *see* LEMARCHAND, Louis-Edouard.

Lemarchand, Louis-Edouard (1795–1872). He was one of the best RESTAURATION furniture-makers. His father **Charles-Joseph Lemarchand** (1759–1826) was one of the last *ébénistes* of the

C.-J. Lemarchand: writing and toilet table, c.1810 (Musée des Arts Décoratifs, Paris)

ancien régime (he became a *maître* in 1789 and worked at Saint Cloud) but he continued successfully under the Empire, making simply designed furniture rather sparingly decorated with bronze mounts. He retired in 1817. Louis-Edouard began as an architect, then turned soldier and did not join his father until 1815. He took over his father's business in 1817. He was much employed by Charles X and Louis Philippe for whom he made furniture in a rather ponderous version of the Empire style. He also made imitation BOULLE furniture (an example is at Versailles) and also imitation C18 lacquer furniture. His best-known piece was the ebony coffin in which Napoleon's remains were taken from St Helena to the Invalides in 1840. In 1846 he was joined by **André Lemoyne** who took over his business when he retired in 1864. It eventually passed to JEANSELME in 1893.

Lit: D. Ledoux-Lebard, *Les ébénistes-parisiens 1795–1870*), Paris 1965.

Lemire, Charles-Gabriel Sauvage, called (1741–1827). Pottery and porcelain modeller, born at Lunéville and working from 1759 at NIDERVILLER. He began with figures in the style of CYFFLÉ but soon adopted a more severely classicizing style, e.g., nude figures of ancient deities. His masterpiece is an allegorical group commemorating Marie Antoinette's stay in Strasbourg in 1770 on her marriage journey (Musée d'Unterlinden, Colmar). But he also executed religious subjects, e.g., large Virgin and Child of 1784 in the Musée nationale de Céramique, Sèvres. In 1781 he established a drawing and modelling school in Niderviller and in 1800 moved to Paris where he worked mainly as a sculptor of large-scale works in marble.

C. Lencker: silver-gilt dish, Augsburg, late c16 (Kunsthistorisches Museum, Vienna)

Lemonnier, Louis-François (*fl.*1737–76). Notable Parisian bookbinder who, with his son **Jean-Charles-Henri** (*fl.*1757–72), was responsible for some of the finest of French inlaid bindings. Several of their works are decorated with chinoiserie ornament of delicate fantasy. They worked for the Duc de Lavallière, one of the most prominent book collectors of the time. Examples of their work are in the Bibliothèque Municipale, Versailles, and the Bibliothèque Sainte-Geneviève in Paris.

Lencker, Christoph (d.1613). He was a member of a distinguished family of goldsmiths in Augsburg. His masterpiece is a magnificent silver-gilt dish elaborately embossed and chased in the Mannerist style with scenes from the story of Europa (Kunsthistorisches Museum, Vienna). He was assisted by his son **Zacharias** (d.1612), author of a relief of the Christ child and angels (Kunsthistorisches Museum, Vienna). Another member of the family, **Johannes** (*c.*1573–1637) was probably trained under Christoph. *Illustrated previous page.* (For Christoph Lencker's mark *see* p. 894.)

Lit: E. Kris, *Goldschmiedearbeiten des Mittelalters, der Renaissance, und des Barock*, Vienna 1932.

Lenox Company A large porcelain factory established at Trenton, New Jersey, in 1889 by **Jonathan Coxon** and **Walter Scott Lenox** who had previously been artistic director of OTT & BREWER Company where he had learned the secret of making BELLEEK porcelain. First called the Ceramic Art Company, it was re-named Lenox Company in 1906 and is still active. Throughout its history it has specialized in tablewares and decorative objects of very thin porcelain.

Lenticle In the door of a long-case CLOCK, the glass panel through which the movement of the pendulum bob may be seen.

Lenzburg potteries Two Swiss potteries flourished at Lenzburg in the C18. One, started by **Marcus Hünerwadel** in 1762, produced tablewares decorated with hunting scenes and flowers, derivative in style from KÜNERSBERG and STRASBOURG. It closed in 1767. A second pottery was started in 1774 by **Hans Jacob Frey** (1745–1817). It specialized in faience stoves decorated with landscapes in Rococo or Louis XVI surrounds. They are among the best of their kind. It also produced tablewares, decorated with flowers in a style reminiscent of Strasbourg. But it failed and closed in 1796. (For factory mark *see* p. 884.)

Lit: S. Ducret, *Die Lenzburger Fayencen und Öfen des 18 u. 19 Jahrhunderts*, Aarau 1950.

Leonardo di Ser Giovanni (*fl.*1358–71). He was the leading Florentine goldsmith of his day and one of the most distinguished artists, worthy to stand alongside his great contemporaries in painting, Lippo Vanni, Agnolo Gaddi and Spinello Aretino. In 1361 he was put in charge of the chasing and gilding of the silver relief panels depicting Biblical scenes on the Epistle or left-hand side of the great silver altar in Pistoia cathedral. These reliefs were probably designed by Pietro di Leonardo *c.*1357. (The front of the altar was completed in that year.) In 1366 Leonardo di Ser Giovanni and Betto di Geri were commissioned to make a dorsal later incorporated in the altar of St John the Baptist for the Baptistery, Florence (now in the Museo dell'Opera del Duomo). In 1367 he was commissioned to make the Gospel side of the Pistoia silver altar. He presumably designed as well as made the 9 relief panels depicting scenes from the story of St James which form this side of the altar completed in 1371. *Illustrated opposite.*

Lit: E. Steingräber in *The Connoisseur*, CXXXVIII, 1956, pp. 148–54.

Leopold, Johann Gottlieb, *see* PROSKAU POTTERY.

Leroy, Louis, *see* MARSEILLES POTTERY.

Les Islettes pottery A faience factory established at Bois d'Épense (Meuse), near Lunéville, in 1785 which began by producing wares rather coarsely imitative of STRASBOURG with brightly coloured paintings of hens, flowers, chinoiseries, etc., also a few figures imitative of LUNÉVILLE. Under the Revolution and Empire it turned to making FAIENCE PATRIOTIQUE. It survived until the mid C19. No factory mark is known but wares were sometimes inscribed.

Lit: E. Tilmans, *Faïence de France*, Paris 1954; M. Ernould-Gandouet, *La Céramique en France au XIX siècle*, Paris 1969.

Leonardo di Ser Giovanni: detail of silver altar of St John, c.1370 (Museo dell'Opera del Duomo, Florence)

Lessore, Émile Aubert (1805–76). French painter and lithographer (a pupil of Ingres) who turned to the decoration of pottery and porcelain. He is known to have worked for the Laurin factory at Bourg-la-Reine near Paris, at SÈVRES and, in England, at the MINTON factory. But he was most closely associated with the WEDGWOOD POTTERY for which he worked from the later 1850s, first in England and then at his own studio at Fontainebleau (the factory shipped cases of undecorated wares to him from England). He painted plates and dishes rather as if they were canvases, in a free style with nymphs, cupids, etc.

Lestrade, David, *see* MONTAUBAN POTTERY.

Lesum pottery A faience factory established at Lesum, near Bremen, in 1755 by **Johann Christoph Vielstich** (1722–1800) produced a wide range of useful wares decorated in high-temperature colours. Tureens in the form of birds and beasts, open-work baskets, cylindrical tankards and stove tiles seem to have been specialities. The production of faience ceased in 1800. (For factory mark *see* p. 884.)

Lit: W. Gerhold in *Jahrbuch der bremischen Sammlungen*, 1911; K. Hüseler, *Deutsche Fayencen*, Stuttgart 1956–8.

Lethaby, William Richard (1857–1931). English architect, designer and writer. Trained as an architect under Norman Shaw but also influenced by William MORRIS and Philip WEBB. He designed furniture, some in a modified Chippendale style, the rest in a more rustic manner decorated with rather coarse floral marquetry in unstained woods, also pottery (for WEDGWOOD), metalwork and embroideries. Important mainly as an influence on others, especially the ARTS AND CRAFTS movement, and as Professor of Design at the Royal College of Art, London, (from 1900), where he preached the message of William MORRIS.

Lit: *W. R. Lethaby*, Exh. Cat., Tate Gallery, London, 1932; B. G. Burrough in *The Connoisseur* CLXXIII (1970), pp. 33–7.

Levasseur, Étienne (1721–98). Parisian furniture-maker who was trained in the BOULLE workshop and became a *maître* in 1767. He specialized in repairing and copying Boulle furniture and also made pieces in the same style. He was also one of the first French *ébénistes* to use mahogany, often with inlays of brass, working in a manner which sometimes seems to anticipate the Empire style. Examples of his work are in the Louvre, Paris, Wallace Collection, London, etc. His workshop was carried on by his son, **Pierre-Étienne,** and his grandson, known as **Levasseur jeune,** into the Louis Philippe period.

Lit: D. S. MacColl in *Burlington Magazine* XLI (1922), p. 265ff.; F. de Salverte, *Les ébénistes du XVIIIe siècle*, Paris, rev. ed., 1964.

Levavasseur, Jacques-Nicolas and **Marie-Thomas-Philémon,** *see* ROUEN POTTERIES.

Li A Chinese Bronze Age vessel for holding food, made during the SHANG-YIN and Early CHOU dynasties and perhaps later. In form – which is peculiar to China and perhaps derives from Neolithic pottery – it is composed of three conical vessels merged together at the top. The form is very practical for heating.

Libbey Glass Company, *see* NEW ENGLAND GLASS COMPANY.

Liberty, Sir Arthur Lasenby (1843–1917). A leading figure in the ART NOUVEAU movement, he was the English counterpart and forerunner of S. BING. He began as an assistant at the shop of Farmer and Rogers in Regent's Street, London, managing, from 1862, a department dealing in Oriental objects. When this firm closed in 1874 he opened his own shop in Regent's Street in 1875, 'East India House', specializing in orientalia and JAPONAISERIE but also offering furniture, fabrics, ornaments, etc., in the Moorish and a variety of European historical styles. Soon the products of the ARTS AND CRAFTS MOVEMENT were also stocked. From 1884 he had the advice of E. W. GODWIN who encouraged him to join the crusade for dress reform which led him to produce new types of fabrics. He also employed C. F. A. VOYSEY as a fabric designer. In 1889 he opened a Parisian branch which helped to diffuse the English Art Nouveau style throughout Europe (it is still known as STILE LIBERTY in Italy). From 1894 he produced silver in an Art Nouveau version of the Celtic style which he termed 'Cymric' and from 1903 a new type of pewter, with a high proportion of silver in the alloy, which he called 'Tudric'. Metalwork enriched with complicated Celtic ornament and adorned with blue or turquoise enamel, fabrics with flower motifs (tulips, irises, poppies, waterlilies) attenuated and woven into almost abstract patterns, and furniture with tapering outlines and elaborate large metal hinges and handles are the most notable of the objects he commissioned and sold, though they formed only a part of his stock in trade which included objects in a variety of Revivalist styles. His professed aim was to produce 'useful *and* beautiful objects at prices within the reach of all classes', and in this way he forms a link between MORRIS and HEAL, though he was not, like them, a designer. He was knighted in 1913. The firm still flourishes and has recently revived many of its Art Nouveau fabrics.

Lit: J. Laver, *The Liberty Story*, London 1959; S. Bury in *Architectural Review*, CXXXIII (1963); A. Adburgham, *Liberty's: A Biography of a Shop*, London 1975.

Liberty style, *see* ART NOUVEAU.

Library steps A ladder from which the upper shelves of a bookcase may be reached, often fitted into a chair, stool, table or other piece of furniture, sometimes so contrived that it can fit into a pole.

Liège glasshouses Several factories were established in and around Liège in the late C16 – early C17, but the first of importance was that founded in 1638 by the brothers **Henri** and **Léonard Bonhomme,** entrepreneurs (not craftsmen) who more or less monopolized the production of glass in the Low Countries. In addition to making expensive pieces in the fashionable Venetian style, their factories also turned out quantities of utilitarian ware in the Waldglas tradition but generally of improved quality. Liège remained one of the more important centres for glassmaking to the present day. The famous VAL SAINT LAMBERT GLASSHOUSE is in the suburbs of the city.

Lit: F. Pholien, *La verrerie au pays de Liège*, Liège 1889; H. van Heule in *Annales du 1° congrès des 'Journées internationales du verre'*, Liège 1958, pp. 133–43.

Lien A Chinese Bronze Age cylindrical vessel made in the HUAI period and perhaps later. It is sometimes decorated with inlaid gold and other metals.

Lieutaud, Balthazar (d.1780). The best French clock-case maker, he specialized in *Régulateurs* of the most sumptuous and monumental type, often with movements by Berthoud or Robin. He became a *maître-ébéniste* in 1749. His early clock-cases are Rococo in style, usually with a violin-shaped central section. More typical are his later, Louis XVI style, cases which are usually tall and tapering, with heavy Neo-Classical mounts after DELAFOSSE and often surmounted by some imposing sculptural group in gilt-bronze by such sculptors as CAFFIERI, e.g., his ebony *régulateur* at Versailles surmounted by Apollo and his chariot. He often repeated his more successful clock-cases with only slight variations. His widow carried on his business until 1784 or later. Sometimes he worked together with François DUHAMEL (1723–1801), as on a famous *régulateur* clock-case in the Conservatoire Nationale des Arts et Métiers, Paris. *Illustrated next column.*

Lit: F. de Salverte, *Les ébénistes du XVIIIe siècle*, rev. ed., Paris 1962.

Lignum vitae A very hard, heavy wood, greenish-brown or greenish-black in colour with a peculiar acid aromatic scent. It comes from the *Guaiacum officinale* tree in South America and was much used in the C17 especially by Dutch furniture-makers.

Lille potteries and porcelain factories Several different faience factories were active in Lille in

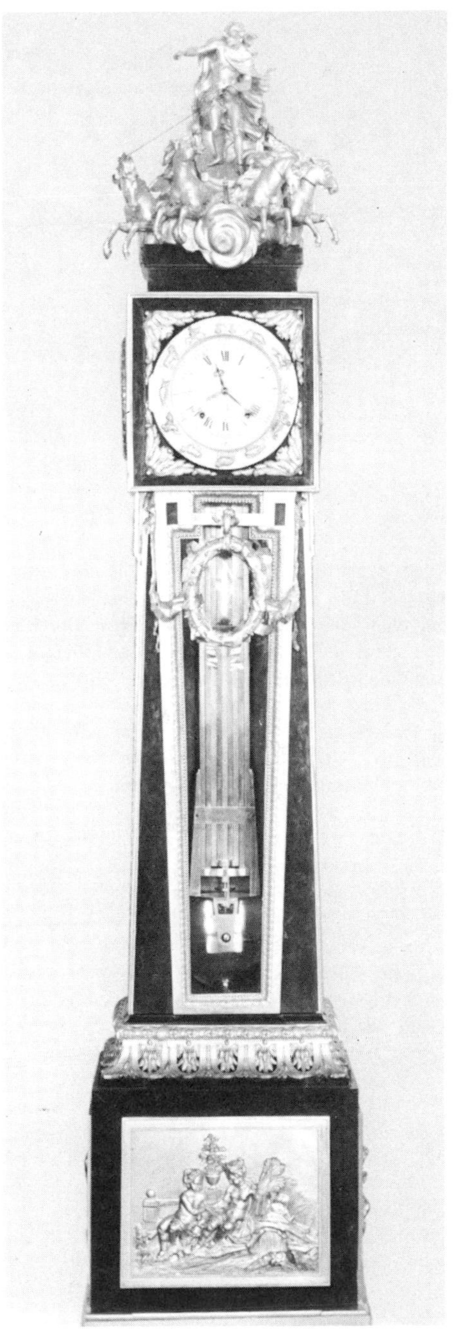

B. Lieutaud: régulateur, c.1770 *(Château de Versailles)*

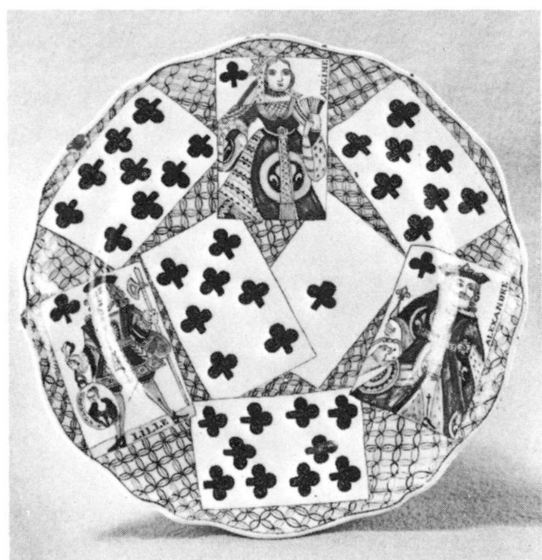

Lille faience plate with trompe l'oeil *decoration, late c18 (Musée des Beaux Arts, Lille)*

the c18: the earliest began in 1696 and ran until 1802, another (which also made soft-paste porcelain) was founded by **Barthélémy Dorez** in 1711 and functioned until *c.*1820, and there was one which specialized in tiles (1740–after 1772). Few wares were marked but pieces generally attributed to Lille include blue-and-white and polychrome table-wares in the *style rayonnant* of ROUEN or imitative of DELFT, some curious jugs in the form of women (rather like TOBY JUGS) and a notable portable altar painted with the Crucifixion (Musée nationale de céramique de Sèvres). A cream-coloured-earthenware factory was established in 1773 by **William Clarke** of Newcastle who moved to Montereau two years later and became a partner in a factory eventually united with the CREIL POTTERY. A factory making hard-paste porcelain rather like that of PARIS was begun under the protection of the Dauphin in 1784 and continued until 1817, marking its products with a sketchy dolphin. (A mark, *Lille 1767* under a crown, copied from a genuine Lille plate in the Museum at Sèvres, was extensively used on modern forgeries of uncertain origin). No factory mark was used for faience, though sometimes wares were inscribed with the name of the town. Other supposed marks are unreliable. No mark has been identified with certainty for soft-paste porcelain, but hard-paste porcelain wares were usually marked with a dolphin, often so roughly painted as to be almost unrecognizable.

Lit: J. Houdoy, *Histoire de la céramique lilloise*, Paris 1869; W. B. Honey, *French Porcelain of the 18th Century*, London 1950.

Lily pad decoration Applied decoration found on c19 American glass, especially of South Jersey type. It is often found on jugs. A thick layer of glass is attached to the bottom of the bowl of the vessel and drawn up and tooled into stem-like forms ending in variously shaped small pads.

Limbach porcelain factory Founded by **Gotthelf Greiner** in 1772 and producing in the following two decades table-wares imitative of MEISSEN (the Meissen mark was also imitated until 1787) and rather stiff little statuettes of figures with pretty flower-painted clothes. In 1792 the founder passed the concern on to his five sons. (For factory mark *see* p. 884.)

Lit: R. Graul and A. Kurzwelly, *Altthüringer Porzellan*, Leipzig 1909.

Lime glass Although carbonate of lime (chalk) was used in glass-making in Bohemia and Silesia from the late c17, the term lime glass is generally applied to the light-weight substitute for lead glass invented in 1864 by William Leighton at a glasshouse at Wheeling, West Virginia, and used especially for bottles.

Limehouse porcelain factory A very short-lived concern in London which advertized its wares in 1747 but appears to have closed in or very shortly after 1748. No products have been identified.

Limoges enamels The first school of Limoges enamel painters began in the mid c12 under the influence of MOSAN ENAMELS, examples of which were given by Abbot Wibald of Stavelot to the Abbey of Solignac near Limoges in 1134. It flourished until the c14, at first in monastic and then in lay workshops. A large export trade was carried on in candlesticks, reliquaries, crucifixes, ostensories, etc., now to be found in church treasuries throughout Europe and in museums all over the world. The CHAMPLEVÉ technique was adopted and colour schemes were similar to those of the Mosan school, i.e., blue, yellowish green and white, but with rather more red. The rendering of figures is much less violently expressive than in Mosan enamels. Limoges was the most productive centre for ecclesiastical enamels (little or no secular work was done) and the general artistic level was high though it boasted no artists of the calibre of GODEFROID DE HUY and NICOLAS DE VERDUN. After a brief pause Limoges emerged as the main centre for the production of PAINTED ENAMELS in the late C15 and held the lead throughout the C16. The outstanding enamellers were the 'MONVAERNI', N. and J. PENICAUD, L. LIMOSIN, P. REYMOND, J. COURT, P. COURTOIS, H. Poncet and Colin Noylier. They were engaged mainly in secular work, the most interesting being in the Mannerist style. Enamels of both early and later Limoges types were extensively faked in the C19, especially in France, and deceptively accurate imitations were made by SAMSON.

Lit: E. Rupin, *L'Oeuvre de Limoges*, Paris 1890; *Cahiers de la céramique* 13 (1959), 35 (1964); P. Verdier, *The Walters Art Gallery: Catalogue of the Painted Enamels of the Renaissance*, Baltimore 1967; M.-M. Gauthier, *Émaux du moyen âge occidental*, Fribourg 1972.

Limoges pottery and porcelain factories A faience factory was established at Limoges in 1736 and ran for a few years making run-of-the-mill household wares. The main source of kaolin and petuntse in France is at Saint-Yrieix, near Limoges, where materials used at SÈVRES were quarried from 1768 onwards. This probably encouraged the establishment of a hard-paste porcelain factory under the patronage of the Comte d'Artois (brother of Louis XVI) in 1771. It was acquired by the King in 1784 as a *Manufacture Royale* – the idea being that it should provide plain white wares for decoration at Sèvres (though this does not seem to have worked out very satisfactorily in practice). Its products resemble the simpler types of Sèvres and the work of the PARIS factories. After the Revolution a number of factories (*see* HAVILAND PORCELAIN FACTORIES) were established at Limoges which soon became (and still remains) the main centre for the production of porcelain in France, specializing in ordinary table-wares. (For factory mark *see* p. 884.)

Lit: La porcelaine française de 1673 à 1914; La porcelaine contemporaine de Limoges, Exh. Cat., Musée des Arts Décoratifs, Paris 1929; G. Fontaine, *La céramique française*, Paris 1946; M. Ernould-Gandouet, *La Céramique en France au XIX siècle*, Paris 1969.

Limoges ware, *see* WORCESTER PORCELAIN FACTORY.

Limosin (or **Limousin**), **Léonard** (*c.*1515–*c.*1576). The best and most original of the LIMOGES ENAMEL painters, and the only one to leave Limoges and go to Court. François I patronized him and Henri II made him *valet de chambre* and *émailleur peintre du Roi* (1548). He began under the influence of DÜRER (18 Passion scenes of 1532, Musée de Cluny, Paris) but soon acquired the courtly Mannerist style of the School of Fontainebleau. He excelled in portraits, painting several of François I, executed some fine ecclesiastical work, notably the Crucifixion altarpiece for the Sainte Chapelle, Paris (1553, now in the Louvre), and also painted secular objects such as goblets and tazzas. A relation, **Jean Limousin** (d. after 1646) worked in Limoges, enamelling plates, cups, mirrors and even spoons with Mannerist figure scenes in brilliant colours and often with metallic foil, on a black ground (British Museum, Louvre, etc.). *Illustrated next page.*

Lit: E. Rupin, *L'Oeuvre de Limoges*, Paris 1890; P. Verdier, *The Walters Art Gallery: Catalogue of the Painted Enamels of the Renaissance*, Baltimore 1967.

Linck, Franz Konrad (1730–1793). Sculptor who was chief modeller at the FRANKENTHAL PORCELAIN FACTORY 1762–6, where he continued to provide models and designs until 1775. He specialized in mythological and allegorical figures and groups of a suave Rococo elegance, e.g., *Apotheosis of the Elector Karl Theodor* (Musée de Cluny, Paris), allegories of months, seasons and continents, figures of *Oceanus* and *Thetis*.

Lit: M. Sauerlandt, *Deutsche Porzellanfiguren*, Cologne 1923.

Lincrusta Patent name for a wall-covering made

L. Limosin: painted enamel panel from the altarpiece for the Sainte Chapelle, Paris, 1553 *(Louvre)*

by the LINOLEUM manufacturer **F. Walton** from 1877. Like linoleum it is composed mainly of oxidized linseed oil which is stamped in embossed panels. It was used to imitate linenfold and other types of wood panelling, stamped leather, or shallow stucco-work. The most interesting products, dating from *c.*1900, are abstract reliefs in the ART NOUVEAU style by GUIMARD.

Lindberg, Stig, *see* GUSTAVSBERG POTTERY.

Lindenast, Sebastian (*c.*1460–1526). He belonged to a prominent family of Nuremberg craftsmen who had the monopoly of gilded and silvered copperwares made in the city from the mid C15 to the mid C16. He was a contemporary and lifelong friend of the sculptors Peter Vischer and Adam Kraft. His most famous work is the Männleinlaufen, a clock on the exterior of the Liebfrauenkirche in Nuremberg, with animated figures. Among the works of outstanding quality attributed to Lindenast are a copper silvered and gilt statuette of St James the Greater and a silvered copper bowl with a statuette of a hart in the centre (Germanisches Nationalmuseum, Nuremberg), and a castle cup, copper gilt and enamelled (Victoria & Albert Museum, London).

S. Lindenast: copper-gilt and enamelled cup, Nuremberg, c.1500 *(Victoria & Albert Museum)*

Lit: H. Kolkhausen, *Nürmberger Goldschmiedkunst des Mittelalters und der Dürerzeit,* Berlin 1968.

Lindslee, Thomas, *see* WINCANTON POTTERY.

Lindstrand, Viktor, *see* ORREFORS GLASSHOUSE.

Lindström, Karl and **Nils Erik,** *see* RÖRSTRAND POTTERY & PORCELAIN FACTORY.

Linen A textile woven from thread made from the bast fibres of the flax plant (*Linum usitalissimum*), which can easily be separated from the rest of the stem and are both strong and durable. First known to have been woven in Neolithic Egypt (*see* WEAVING) where fabrics of remarkably fine quality were produced. The Greeks made little use of it. Romans imported their best linen from Egypt though flax was cultivated in N. Italy. The plant flourishes on damp soil and was also cultivated in Roman times in Spain, Gaul and the Low Countries and, by the Middle Ages, throughout Europe. But Egyptian linen remained the best until *c.*1300. The quality of linen depends to a great extent on its treatment after weaving, notably the process of bleaching which improves its texture as well as its whiteness. It was for this reason that Dutch linen (produced mainly at Haarlem) was the most highly esteemed in the C18. Since linen yarn lacks the elasticity of cotton and wool and is thus inclined to break under the strain it cannot easily be woven on a power-operated loom. It was largely bypassed by the Industrial Revolution and hand-woven until the introduction of the linen power-loom in the 1850s by which time it had ceased to be the most important textile woven from vegetable fibres. For whereas, until the late C18, cotton had been a luxury product and linen a common one their relationship was reversed by the industrialization of textile production.

A textile woven with a linen warp and cotton weft is called FUSTIAN, one with a linen warp and worsted weft is called Linsey-woolsey (though both these names are sometimes given to other mixtures of yarn).

Linen press A cupboard, for the storage of linen, which began to replace the chest in the C17. Also a frame with two boards and a wooden screw for pressing linen.

Linenfold A conventional representation of a piece of linen laid in vertical folds, of C15 Flemish origin and much used by Tudor woodcarvers for the decoration of panelling and furniture (mainly chests and the doors of wardrobes).

Ling A small Chinese Bronze Age bell, elliptical in section, with a handle. It is similar to a Swiss cowbell.

Lining papers Sheets of paper printed with designs – usually in black on a colour – and intended for lining boxes, drawers, etc. The designs tend to be smaller and closer than those on WALLPAPER which was also put to this use.

Linnel, John (d.1796). He was an accomplished and highly fashion-conscious furniture designer and cabinet-maker. His father **William Linnel** (d.1763) had begun as a carver and eventually built up a large and prosperous cabinet-making and upholstery business with premises in Berkeley Square, London. William Linnel's most interesting work anticipates (*c*.1752) the so-called Chinese Chippendale style, the most spectacular example of which it seems almost certain he made to designs by his son John (the bed, now in the Victoria & Albert Museum, and bedroom furniture from Badminton House, Glos.). Later John Linnel passed through three stylistic phases – Kentian Baroque, as at Kedleston House where his sculptural furniture survives, notably a sofa with gilt merman supports; Adamesque, as at Shardeloes, Bucks., and Osterley Park, Middx.; and finally Regency, as at Woburn, Beds. and Uxbridge House in London. During this last phase he was closely connected with the architect Holland.

Lit: P. A. Kirkham in *Journal of the Furniture History Society*, 1967, pp. 29–44; H. Hayward, *op. cit.*, 1969, pp. 1–115, and in *Apollo*, Sept. 1969.

Linoleum Originally the trade name for a type of floorcloth patented by **Frederick Walton** in England in 1860, but applied loosely to any floorcloth with a jute canvas foundation coated with solidified oil or similar material. Floorcloths of canvas covered with layers of oil paint were first made in early C17 England. In 1754 one Nathan Smith began to manufacture at Knightsbridge a more resistant material made of canvas with a surface composed of a mixture of rosin, pitch, beeswax, linseed oil, etc. This was superseded in 1844 by a mixture of indiarubber and cork dust rolled on to canvas sheets. Walton's linoleum was much cheaper to produce and had a rubbery surface composed of solidified linseed oil, rosin and kauri gum. Much modern linoleum is made in the same way, though synthetic materials have begun to replace the linseed oil. The cheaper types are decorated with patterns printed in oil colours, which tend to wear off: the more expensive are inlaid and much more durable. Their surface is composed of materials mixed with different colours and applied through stencils to the canvas backing, or of a mosaic of squares and oblongs of linoleum cut from sheets of various colours, making parquetry or tile patterns.

Lit: Walton, *The Infancy and Development of Linoleum Floor Cloth*, London 1925.

Linthorpe pottery A factory founded near Middlesbrough, Yorkshire, in 1879 by a local landowner, **John Harrison**, with **Henry Tooth** as manager and C. DRESSER as art director. Wares were made from local clay with thick variable coloured glazes. During the first years the designs were provided by Dresser, some original, others inspired by Japanese and pre-Columbian Peruvian pottery. The factory continued to make such wares, also simple handsome teapots, etc., until the end of the century though both Dresser and Tooth left in 1882. Similar pieces were made, also to Dresser's designs, at the **Bretby Art Pottery** run by Tooth and William Ault 1882–7, and at the **Ault Pottery**, Swadlincote, run by Ault from 1887 until the early C20. A large collection of Linthorpe wares is in the Memorial Museum, Middlesbrough.

Lit: J. R. A. Le Vine, *Linthorpe Pottery*, Middlesbrough 1970; C. Bracegirdle in *Country Life* CXLIX, 1971, pp. 1022–5; R. Dennis & J. Jesse, *Christopher Dresser*, Exh. Cat., Fine Arts Society, London 1972.

Lion Cachet, Carel Adolph (1864–1945). Dutch Art Nouveau wood engraver and furniture designer working (from 1897) at Vreeland, near Utrecht. Adopted a rich version of the Art Nouveau style employing a wide variety of rare materials (palisander wood, coromandel, etc.) for individual pieces of furniture and whole interiors, especially for steamships.

Lion's paw foot Decorative termination to the leg of a piece of furniture (generally a chair) used in the late C17 to early C18 and again in the early C19.

Lipper, Wilhelm Ferdinand (before 1742–1800). German architect and furniture designer who succeeded Johann Conrad Schlaun in charge of the interior decoration of the Residenzschloss at Münster. He worked in both a modified Rococo style and in the ZOPFSTIL. Several of his drawings for furniture are in the Landesmuseum, Münster. His younger brother **Clemens Lipper** (1742–1813), a canon of St Johann, Osnabruck, was an amateur architect and designer of ecclesiastical furniture in the *Zopfstil*.

Lit: K. Bussmann, *Wilhelm Ferdinand Lipper*, Münster 1972.

Lippincott and Margulies One of the largest industrial design companies in the U.S.A., founded in 1946 by **Gordon Lippincott** (b.1909) and **Walter P. Margulies** (b.1914). A separate European company was established in 1962, with its headquarters in Bermuda, main offices in London and Toronto, and subsidiary offices in Paris and Madrid. The main United States company has five divisions which together provide a highly professional service in both the creative and economic aspects of design. Clients include Eastern Airlines, Chrysler, Borg Warner, Esso Service Stations, Decca Radar, U.S. Rubber and Phillips.

Lisieux pottery A mid-C17 faience factory making tiles known as *carreaux de Lisieux* decorated with patterns of formal flowers, foliage, fleurs-de-lis, etc. in white, various blues and yellow. The outline of each pattern was deeply incised (probably by a metal stamp) to prevent the variously coloured glazes from intermingling. Lead-glazed wares, including the roof finials used on buildings in Normandy, were also made at Lisieux from the C16.

Lit: E. Deville, *La céramique du pays d'Auge*, Paris 1927.

List, J. G., *see* PIRKENHAMMER PORCELAIN FACTORY.

List, Johann Georg Friedrich, *see* DURLACH & MOSBACH POTTERY.

Lithophanies Porcelain panels moulded in intaglio with pictorial subjects, often after famous paintings by old masters, which appear in light and shade when viewed by transmitted light. They are said to have been invented by the **Baron de Bourgoing** in 1827 and were made at MEISSEN from 1828 and at the BERLIN PORCELAIN FACTORY *c.*1827–50. But they were also made at GOTHA and PLAUE in Germany, by the MINTON and COPELAND factories in England and also at WORCESTER where **Grainger Lee & Co.** were granted a licence to manufacture them in 1829. There is a museum devoted to them at Toledo, Ohio, U.S.A. – The Blair Museum of Lithophanies.

Lithyalin, *see* EGERMANN, Friedrich.

Littler, William (1724–84). Staffordshire potter and porcelain manufacturer, in partnership with **Aaron Wedgwood** at Brownhills, making salt-glazed stoneware, then owner and manager of the LONGTON HALL PORCELAIN FACTORY from *c.*1750 until it closed in 1760. Later he became manager of the **Baddeley & Fletcher** pottery at Shelton.

Littler's blue A deep blue glaze sometimes found on salt-glazed stoneware and named after William LITTLER though it was used by many other English C18 potters.

Liverpool potteries and porcelain factories A tin-glazed earthenware factory was established in the early C18 (first dated specimen 1716) making blue-and-white wares like those of BRISTOL and LAMBETH and there were twelve such factories by 1760, apparently engaged largely in export trade to the Colonies. A speciality was made of punch bowls, sometimes very large and often painted with ships on the interiors and naval

Liverpool tin-glazed earthenware punch bowl, 1766 (Victoria & Albert Museum)

trophies outside. Some wares were decorated in enamel colours of an unusual range (dark and light purple, green, russet red, bright blue and yellow) named 'Fazackerley colours' after a **Mr and Mrs Thomas Fazackerley** whose names appear on a couple of mugs painted with them. From at least 1756 many wares were decorated with TRANSFER PRINTED designs, notably in the establishment of J. SADLER and Green. Among the potteries those of the Penningtons were notable (**James Pennington** made cream-coloured earthenware and Delftware from 1769 onwards and is said to have operated the **Copperas Hill** factory in 1773–4, being succeeded by his brother **John** (d.1786). Their brother **Seth** was a partner in a pottery at **Shaw's Brow** from *c.*1776–99 and became sole owner until 1805 when he retired). **Zacharias Barnes** (1743–1820) supplied tiles to J. SADLER for transfer-printing and also made Delftware. He also made porcelain, heavily-potted with a flecked glaze and a yellowish body.

There were several small porcelain factories flourishing in Liverpool after the mid 1750s, e.g. that of **William Ball** who is credited with porcelain made from *c.*1755 in Ranleigh Street, Liverpool, transfer-printed with enamel overpainting. But the best known is that of **Richard Chaffers** (d.1765) which produced wares similar but generally inferior to WORCESTER in both design and body (which included soaprock, as did that of William Ball). In 1796 a factory founded in 1794 by **Richard Abbey** (formerly an employee of Sadler & Green) was taken over by **Worthington Humble and Holland** and named **Herculaneum.** It was staffed mainly with men from Staffordshire and flourished until 1841, producing cream-coloured earthenware, basaltes ware and lustred earthenware, generally imitative of WEDGWOOD and other STAFFORDSHIRE potteries. Herculaneum wares were marked with the name impressed, or painted (usually in red) after 1833.

Lit: F. H. Garner, *English Delftware,* London 1948; A. Smith, *An Illustrated Guide to Liverpool Herculaneum Pottery,* London 1970.

Livery cupboard An English type of C15–C16 cupboard for storing food. Ventilation was usually provided by pierced decoration or by spindled doors. It does not seem to have been made after the Restoration. The word 'livery' is derived from *livrée,* delivery or dispensing of food, etc.

Lobate Style, *see* AURICULAR STYLE.

Lobing, *see* GADROONING.

Lobmeyr, J. & L. Outstanding Viennese firm of glass decorators founded by **Josef Lobmeyr** (1792–1855), a glazier from Grieskirchen near Linz, in 1822 and still flourishing. It became internationally famous under the direction of the founder's sons **Josef** (1828–64) and **Ludwig** (1829–1917). The latter seems to have played the leading part in the firm's development, designing models and also commissioning designs from leading artists in Vienna, including the architect Theophil von Hansen (1813–91). He was closely associated with the *Österreichisches Museum für angewandte Kunst* founded in 1864, and was also something of a social figure. Most of their glass was made at the Meyrs Neffe glasshouse in S. Bohemia, owned by **Wilhelm von Kralik** who married a daughter of Josef Lobmeyr. Products included many very elaborate pieces in the current Bohemian styles (and revivals of historical styles). But the most interesting are the drinking glasses, decanters, etc., of an elegant, sometimes austere, simplicity. Ludwig Lobmeyr retired in 1902 and the direction of the firm passed to his nephew **Stephan Rath** (1876–1960) who associated with and obtained designs from the artists of the Wiener SECESSION, notably J. HOFFMANN who became co-director in 1910.

Lit: S. Rath, *Lobmeyr*, Vienna 1962; M. Despot in *Journal of Glass Studies*, IV (1962), pp. 103–7; *150 Jahre österreichisches Glaskunst: Lobmeyr 1823–1973*, Exh. Cat., Vienna 1973.

Lock, Matthias, or **Matthew** (*fl.c.*1724–69). Furniture designer who played a leading part in introducing the French Rococo style into England.

M. Lock and Copland: illustration from A New Book of Ornaments, *1752*

He appears to have been apprenticed in 1724 to a London carver named Richard Goldsaddle. He published in 1740 *A New Drawing Book of Ornaments*, one of the first collections of *rocaille* motifs to appear in England. His many published furniture designs – notably *Six Sconces* (1744), *Six Tables* (1746) and *A New Book of Ornaments* . . . (with H. Copland, 1752, reissued with some differences 1768) – freely interpreted the Rococo in a distinctly English manner with a profusion of 'C' scrolls, masks, birds, winged dragons and even cascades of water. Numerous drawings (Victoria & Albert Museum, and Metropolitan Museum) reveal that he also worked occasionally in the Neo-Palladian and Adam styles. He was probably employed by CHIPPENDALE as a designer and/or furniture-maker from *c.*1752. A few pieces of furniture can be assigned to him – notably those formerly at Hinton House, Somerset, now in the Victoria & Albert Museum, – but they lack the gay elegance and lightness of touch which distinguish his designs.

Lit: P. Ward-Jackson, *English Furniture Designs of the Eighteenth Century*, London 1958; J. F. Hayward in *The Connoisseur* CXLVI (1960), pp. 284–6; A. Coleridge, *Chippendale Furniture*, London 1968.

Locke, Joseph (1846–1936). Glass maker born at Worcester and apprenticed from 1858 at the WORCESTER PORCELAIN FACTORY. He left in 1865 to join the glass-decorating firm of Guest Brothers in Stourbridge, then he moved to the glasshouse of Hodgetts and Richardson. He executed a cased glass replica of the Portland Vase which was exhibited by Hodgetts and Richardson in an incomplete state at the Paris Exhibition of 1878. After working at two other glasshouses in Stourbridge he went to the U.S.A. in 1883 and joined the NEW ENGLAND GLASS COMPANY where he developed various types of coloured glass, notably Amberina. After an unsuccessful attempt to start a business of his own in Pittsburgh, he joined the United States Glass Company as chief designer.

Lit: G. W. Beard, *Nineteenth Century Cameo Glass*, Newport, Mon. 1956.

Lodi potteries Several tin-glazed-earthenware factories were active in the C18 producing wares decorated in blue and white, sometimes polychrome, imitative of those of ROUEN, MOUSTIERS and STRASBOURG, as well as plain white household wares. Plaques painted with religious subjects in a distinctly Italian style were also made.

Lit: G. Russo Perez, *La maiolica antica de Lodi,* Milan 1932; Countess Terni di Gregory in *The Connoisseur* XCIII, 1934, pp. 158ff.

Lodovico, Maestro, *see* VENICE POTTERIES.

Loetz, Witwe A glasshouse at Klostermühle in Southern Bohemia, trading under the name of the widow of **Johann Loetz,** and one of the best of the late C19. It won prizes at the Brussels Exhibition of 1888 and the Paris International Exhibition of 1889. Shortly before 1900 it began to produce very handsome though sometimes extraordinarily shaped iridescent glass vessels similar to, and probably inspired by, TIFFANY'S 'favrile' glass. They are decorated in the Art Nouveau style with feathery combed motifs or an erratic network of trailed lines. Later products, of *c.*1915, included vessels decorated in the style of the WIENER WERKSTÄTTE, designed by H. Bolek, M. POWOLNY and others.

Lit: Glas aus der Sammlung des Kunstgewerbesmuseum Zürich, Zurich 1969.

W. Loetz: glass vase, c.1900 *(Kunstgewerbemuseum, Zurich)*

Loewy, Raymond (b.1893). Parisian born, a graduate of Paris University and École de Lanneau (Engineering), Loewy began his career as a fashion illustrator in New York in 1919. In 1926 he styled the Hupmobile for General Motors and in 1929 was appointed Art Director for Westinghouse Electric Company. In the same year he started his own industrial design office, partly as a result of a commission to design the casing of a duplicating machine for a British firm, Gestetner. His design for a Sears Roebuck refrigerator, the Coldspot (1932), was one of the principal early examples of the marketing advantages of industrial design applied to consumer products.

The Loewy firm, probably the largest of its kind in the U.S., was renamed Raymond Loewy/William Snaith Inc. in 1961 when William Snaith, a former managing partner, was made President and Loewy became Chairman. A European affiliate, **Compagnie de l'Esthetique Industrielle,** is located in Paris.

Loewy has published *The Locomotive: Its Esthetics* (1937) and *Never Leave Well Enough Alone* (1951).

Lohr-am-Main glasshouse German factory founded in 1688 by **Johannes Wenzel** (d.1696) making table-wares and chandeliers. In 1698 it was taken over by the Kurfürst Lothar von Schönborn who had it transformed into a mirror factory making looking-glass of high quality, much of which survives in the Schloss at Pommersfelden.

Lit: H. Kreisel, *Die Kunst des deutschen Möbels,* vol. ii, Munich 1970.

Loir, Alexis (1640–1713). Prominent LOUIS XIV STYLE goldsmith and designer (*maître* 1669). None of his metalwork survives: his engraved designs for such varied objects as carriages, wheel-chairs, fans, gueridons, braziers, etc., are all in the classical Baroque style of LE BRUN.

Long Elizas English corruption of the Dutch name –lange Lyzen – for the attenuated figures of women painted on C18 Chinese porcelain and imitated at the WORCESTER factory in the 1760s.

Long-case clock, *see* CLOCK.

Longton Hall porcelain factory The first porcelain factory in Staffordshire, it was run by a salt-glaze potter, William LITTLER, from *c.*1750 to 1760 and produced both decorative and useful wares in a rather heavy soft paste similar to that of CHELSEA. Dishes, sauce-boats, teapots and small tureens composed of simulated overlapping leaves were a speciality. The earliest figures (known as 'Snowmen' figures and sometimes attributed to DERBY until their true origin was discovered) are rather clumsy and covered with a thick semi-transparent glaze. Later figures were derived from a wide variety of sources – salt-glaze statuettes, MEISSEN porcelain and even Italian bronzes – though some models were original, e.g., a *Britannia*, a market woman selling butter, and an actor. Useful wares were occasionally decorated with topographical painting derived from French prints or with transfer printing, sometimes executed by J. SADLER and Green in Liverpool. Some of the workmen left in 1758 to join the Derby factory and it is often supposed that W. DUESBURY acquired stock and machinery for Derby when the Longton Hall factory closed in 1760. (For factory mark *see* p. 885.)

Lit: B. Watney, *Longton Hall Porcelain,* London 1957.

Longton Hall porcelain, Europe, *c.1758–60 (Temple Newsam House, Leeds)*

Longueval, Georg Franz August, Count von Buquoy, *see* HYALITH.

Lonhuda pottery A factory established in 1892 at Steubenville, Ohio, by Messrs **W. A. Long, Hunter and Day** and producing 'art pottery' decorated with painting in coloured slips under the glaze. The most interesting wares are those modelled on American-Indian pots with decorations in the Japanese style. In 1905 Long founded the **Clifton Art Pottery** at Newark, New Jersey, where he produced wares imitative of Pueblo-Indian pots in decoration as well as form.

Looking-glasses or **Mirrors** The earliest were of highly polished metal. The Romans occasionally made them of glass backed by lead or other metal and some medieval mirrors are also of this type. In the Gothic period they were generally small (whether of metal or glass) and often set in ivory frames decorated with attractive reliefs of chivalrous subjects. Glass convex mirrors were being made at Nuremberg and elsewhere in S. Germany by the C15 (their shape determined by the bubble of glass from which they were blown). The VENETIAN glassmakers *c.*1500 discovered the art of making flat mirrors by the 'broad' process (blowing the glass into a cylindrical form which is then cut longitudinally and placed in a heated chamber where it is flattened under heat with a wooden tool and backing it with an amalgam

Looking-glass, with carved and gilt wood frame, by Michel Herman, c.1785 (Musée Curtius, Liège)

of mercury and tin). By the mid C16 Venetian glass mirrors had become popular throughout Europe and drove metal ones out of fashion. The Venetians retained a virtual monopoly of looking-glasses until the late C17 when the process of making them of plate glass was developed in France at the SAINT GOBAIN GLASSHOUSE (the molten glass was poured on to iron tables covered with sand where it was rolled and finally ground and polished with abrasives to a perfectly flat surface). The Saint Gobain process made possible the production of looking-glasses of much greater size and evenness of surface and it subsequently became widespread. Mirrors have usually been enclosed in frames of varying shapes determined by changes in artistic styles. From the C18 they have occasionally been decorated with engraved patterns. The size and shape of toilet mirrors made to stand on dressing-tables has been influenced by the size and shape of wigs and coiffures.

Lit: G. F. Hartlaub, *Zauber des Spiegels*, Munich 1951; G. Wills, *English Looking Glasses*, London 1965; H. Comstock, *The Looking Glass in America*, New York 1968.

Looping A method of decorating glass by applying coloured threads of glass to the body of a vessel while it is being blown, dragging them upwards with a tool and embedding them in the surface. It has been used since ancient times.

Loos, Adolf (1870–1933). Leading Austrian architect and very influential figure in the development of INDUSTRIAL DESIGN. He was born at Brno in Moravia, studied at Dresden and then spent three years in the U.S. 1893–6. On returning to Europe he settled in Vienna where he came under the influence of the architect Otto Wagner (1841–1918) and began writing for various periodicals, *Das Kunstblatt*, *Die Zeit*, *Die Wage*, etc. He designed some very simple functional furniture, glass and other household objects, but is of greater importance for the writings in which he denounced the use of ornament and even of curves – his most famous article, of 1908, was entitled *Ornament und Verbrechen* (ornament and crime) and widely translated. He was naturally opposed to J. HOFFMANN and the WIENER WERKSTÄTTEN. But he was less severe in practice than in theory and had a fondness for rich materials.

A. Loos: drinking glasses made by Lobmeyr, c.1930 (Kunstgewerbemuseum, Zurich)

Lit: N. Pevsner, *Pioneers of Modern Design*, Harmondsworth, rev. ed. 1960; L. Münz & G. Künstler, *Adolf Loos*, London 1966.

Losanti ware, *see* McLaughlin, Mary Louise.

Lotto carpets, *see* Turkish carpets.

Lotus ware, *see* Belleek porcelain factory and Knowles, Taylor & Knowles Company.

Loudon, John Claudius (1783–1843). Primarily a landscape gardener and horticulturist, he also wrote the *Encyclopedia of Cottage, Farm and Villa Architecture and Furniture . . . ,* in 1833 which went through eleven editions by 1867. The furniture designs are scattered through the book and they cover all types from fashionable 'period' pieces to cheap utility furniture, including such hitherto seldom or never illustrated types as invalid furniture and mechanical furniture. Loudon was also interested in vernacular styles and his book provides the most comprehensive survey published in England in the C19.

Louis, Jean-Jacob, *see* Ludwigsburg pottery and porcelain factory.

Louis XIV style Many styles have been named after monarchs, but none is more closely associated with the personality of the ruler than that of Louis XIV. Its origins may be traced to the refined tastes of the luxury-loving Cardinal Mazarin, the all-powerful First Minister during most of the king's minority, who patronized French industries and encouraged outstanding foreign craftsmen to settle in France, e.g. Golle and Cucci. From 1661, when he began his personal rule, Louis XIV took a close personal interest in the furnishing and decoration of his various royal residences, notably Versailles, on which enormous sums were lavished. They were transformed into elaborate symbolical backgrounds to the glory of his reign, celebrating and displaying his wealth and power. Never before had the decorative arts been used so extensively and so effectively for propaganda purposes. The king was ably assisted by his minister Colbert who was largely responsible for founding the Manufacture Royale des Gobelins which, under the direction of Le Brun, was devoted exclusively to providing rich furnishings for the Crown. Colbert's protectionist financial policy also helped to encourage other branches of French industry

Louis XIV style: gilt-bronze chandelier (Musée des Arts Décoratifs, Paris)

Louis XIV style: silver-gilt ewer, by Nicolas Delaunay, Paris, 1697 (Poitiers Cathedral)

– ceramics, glass manufacture, silk weaving, etc. – thus making France artistically self-sufficient and eventually the leader of European fashion. In glass, for example, an order for large mirrors to furnish Versailles led to the foundation of the SAINT GOBAIN GLASSHOUSE where a new process was exploited for large plate-glass mirrors which gradually drove Venetian blown-glass mirrors out of fashion not only in France but all over Europe.

The Louis XIV style is one of great richness tempered by classical restraint: forms are heavy; colours tend to be sombre. The whole reflects perfectly the grandeur and solemn formality of Louis XIV's court. The costliest materials were naturally favoured at Versailles – rare woods, *pietre dure*, tortoiseshell, Japanese lacquer, gold and silver (the latter especially for furniture). But much of the exuberance and flamboyance of the BAROQUE style was ironed out. A change

Louis XIV style: cabinet with Boulle marquetry and gilt-bronze mounts (Louvre)

became apparent in 1683 when Le Brun lost control of the Gobelins factory. His successor, Jean BERAIN, introduced a rather lighter, less pompous style which foreshadowed the RÉGENCE or early ROCOCO STYLE. As a result of a financial crisis precipitated by the wars in Europe, the use of precious materials on furniture declined after 1693: the massive silver furniture made for Versailles was melted down and much of it replaced by Oriental lacquer imported, at very little cost to the Crown, by the Compagnie des Indes. A. C. BOULLE, the best *ébéniste* of the period, produced extremely sumptuous furniture veneered with tortoiseshell and brass which, because of the superb craftsmanship, was hardly less magnificent and expensive-looking than that made in solid silver. A sumptuary edict against the use of silver plate in 1709 gave a fillip to the potteries of ROUEN and NEVERS and also encouraged the use of pewter.

Objects designed for royal use were usually decorated with symbolic motifs associated with the king – the LL monogram, Apollo's head in a sunburst, etc. Classical architectural motifs were popular for the decoration of furniture and silver. The best pottery was decorated either with chinoiserie or in the STYLE RAYONNANTE or, as at MOUSTIERS, with arabesques in the manner of Berain. Later the vogue for BIZARRE SILKS grew ever stronger.

It was during this period that France took the lead in decorative design in Europe. French-made furniture, silks, silver and tapestries were sent to London, Stockholm and various German courts. But the influence of the Louis XIV style might never have spread as rapidly through N. Europe had not the Revocation of the Edict of Nantes in 1685 driven Protestant craftsmen and designers into exile. MAROT went to Holland and thence to England. Numerous HUGUENOT SILVERSMITHS and silk weavers found asylum in London. Tapestry weavers went to Holland and Germany.

A reaction against the formality of the Louis XIV style began to make itself felt in France *c.*1700 in the work of LE PAUTRE and other designers and many of the decorative objects made before the King's death in 1715 are in the RÉGENCE STYLE.

Louis XV style The French version of the ROCOCO STYLE. It began to emerge *c.*1700, reached its height of popularity *c.*1720–50 and fell out of fashion well before the King's death in 1774. The King, who succeeded as a minor in 1715 and

Louis XV style: commode, probably by C. Cressent, c.1730, *after a design by Pineau (Wallace Collection, London)*

began to rule in 1723 (*see* RÉGENCE STYLE) exerted little direct influence on it though Mme de Pompadour patronized the best furniture-makers, silversmiths, porcelain factories (*see* SÈVRES), etc. The style reflects to some extent the increasing predominance of women in social life, the taste for smaller and more intimate rooms, for informality and spontaneity in manners. The style appears at its best in MEISSONIER's and PINEAU's wilfully asymmetrical *genre pittoresque* – all eddying scrolls and scattered flowers – at its most accomplished in GOBELINS tapestries after BOUCHER, at its freshest in the paintings of flowers on MARSEILLES and STRASBOURG FAIENCE, at its most opulently refined in the bronze-mounted furniture of CRESSENT, OEBEN, B. II van RISENBURGH or the silver of T. GERMAIN, at its most whimsically fantastic in PILLEMENT's chinoiseries. All these works share an unclassical but none the less well-bred elegance of poise, a delight in sparkling surface effects, a predominance of gentle S curves over straight lines and an exquisite sensitivity to subtle colours and textures. The most characteristic type of Louis XV furniture is the commode, as developed by CRESSENT, with high legs and serpentine front embellished with non-

Louis XV style: tapestry, from the Psyche series after designs by Boucher, Beauvais, 1741 (Quirinal Palace, Rome)

Louis XV style: gilt-bronze mount on a commode, attributed to C. Cressent (Wallace Collection, London)

functional ormolu mounts curling like the tendrils of an exotic creeper over the surface and often concealing the division of the drawers. Notable *ébénistes* of the period include GAUDREAU, MIGEON (who specialized in small and very exquisite pieces), OEBEN (who made much use of elaborate

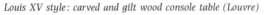

Louis XV style: carved and gilt wood console table (Louvre)

marquetry), B. II van RISENBURGH, JOUBERT and LIEUTAUD. The leading maker of gilt-bronze mounts for furniture was CAFFIERI. Chairs became both more comfortable and more elegant and were delicately carved with floral or shell motifs by such *menuisiers* as CRESSON and TILLIARD. Various new types of seat furniture were invented and appropriately named – e.g., the *causeuse* and *marquise* (*see* CANAPÉ), the *bergère* and *chaise en cabriolet* (*see* CHAIR) and the *duchesse* (*see* CHAISE LONGUE).

The silversmiths of the period were no less accomplished than the furniture-makers though few examples of their work survive. COUSINET was the most accomplished though he lacked T. Germain's exuberant invention. Porcelain factories at CHANTILLY, MENNECY and SÈVRES produced delightful soft-paste table-wares and statuettes as well as bidets and bourdaloues of Rococo form decorated with sprigs of freely painted flowers. Similar naturalistically rendered flowers appear on the silks woven at LYONS to the designs of REVEL and others. Many of the finest GOBELINS tapestries date from this period when OUDRY and Boucher were the chief designers. Pompous historical scenes went out of fashion and were largely replaced by landscapes or mythological scenes set in elaborate alentours. A change in taste became apparent *c.*1750 as a reaction against the excesses of the Rococo (and perhaps also as a nostalgic return to the grandeurs and glories of the Louis XIV style in a period of military defeat and financial depression). The stylistic transition was, however, a gradual one

Louis XV style: inkstand, Mennecy soft-paste porcelain, c.*1755 (Victoria & Albert Museum)*

and several notable craftsmen (e.g. the *ébéniste* VANDERCRUSE and the silversmith ROETTIERS) appear to have been able to work equally well in either the Louis XV or the Louis XVI style, according to the wishes of their patrons.

Louis XVI style The style current during Louis XVI's reign emerged in the 1750s and was fully developed by the time of Louis XVI's accession in 1774. It began as a reaction against Rococo licence and frivolity and may have been partly prompted by a nostalgic yearning for the glories and grandeurs of the Louis XIV period. (It is significant that BOULLE MARQUETRY and the use of *pietre dure* and figurative bronze mounts returned to favour on furniture.) But it also reflected a need for stability and accepted standards, for what BACHELIER called a style 'less susceptible to changes of fashion'. Under this new style – calm, restrained and sometimes a little pedantic – neat geometrical forms were preferred to freehand flourishes, bombé fronts were flattened, curves were ironed out of the legs of chairs and even the handles of spoons and forks; twisting, twirling tendrils of leaves and flowers gave way to ornaments derived from classical architecture, e.g. the Vitruvian scroll, the Greek fret, the palmette, anthemion and bucranium. Yet the form, as opposed to the ornamentation, of Greek and Roman furniture was rarely copied. The earliest known pieces of Louis XVI style furniture (made for Lalive de Jully *c.*1757, Musée Condé, Chantilly) are very austere, but in general the style developed gradually and many furniture-makers who had worked in the Louis XV manner adapted themselves to the new style or worked happily either in the old or new style though the latter grew increasingly severe in the 1770s and 1780s. In the 1770s BELANGER, DUGOURC and JACOB began to evolve the more self-consciously 'antique' ETRUSCAN STYLE which eventually developed into the DIRECTOIRE or first phase of the EMPIRE STYLE. A similar process is apparent in the other decorative arts, though Rococo features were slower in disappearing, e.g., silks woven at LYONS to the designs of LASALLE. At the GOBELINS TAPESTRY FACTORY hangings with elaborate alentours, e.g. Boucher's *Loves of the Gods*, gave place to large figurative scenes depicting more solemn occasions. SÈVRES PORCELAIN

Louis XVI style: silver tureen, by J. N. Roettiers, 1770–75, from the Orloff service (Metropolitan Museum of Art)

Louis XVI style: gilt-bronze wall-light (Musée des Arts Décoratifs, Paris)

vases gradually assumed more austere shapes. In porcelain and terracotta statuettes the early phase of the style is exemplified by FALCONET's models for Sèvres and those of sentimental subjects by CYFFLÉ, as well as the delicately sensuous terracottas of Clodion and Marin. A severer

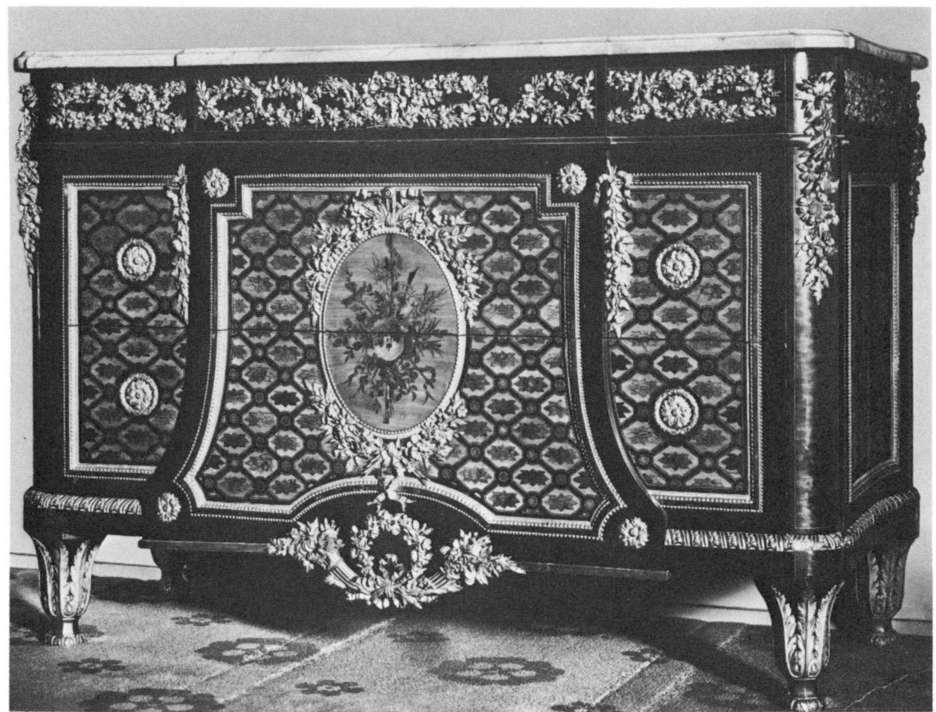

Louis XVI style: commode, by J. H. Riesener, 1782 (Louvre)

and more self-consciously classical style of the 1770s and 1780s marked the models of BOIZOT. Falconet also designed silver for AUGUSTE and the younger GERMAIN. Cottons printed after the designs of HUET and others at OBERKAMPF'S factory and wallpapers produced at REVEILLON'S are less often classical than sentimental.

The Louis XVI period was the golden age of French cabinet-making: never before or since has so much money been spent on furniture. Most of the leading Parisian *ébénistes* were German or of German origin, e.g., BENNEMAN, CARLIN, OEBEN, RIESENER, SCHWERDFEGER and WEISWEILER. ROENTGEN never even worked in France though he joined the Paris guild. But there were several excellent French-born furniture-makers as well, e.g. DUBOIS, LELEU, TOPINO and VANDERCRUSE (the latter two of foreign origin): and the leading *menuisiers* were also French, e.g. BOULARD, FOLIOT, JACOB, LELARGE and SENÉ. The outstanding bronze worker was GOUTHIÈRE. The furniture designer assumed much greater importance in this period and it is significant that much of the conspicuously classicizing furniture was designed by painters or architects such as Louis-Joseph Le Lorrain and J.-L. David. The latter provided designs for Jacob. Never before had so many engraved designs for furniture been published: the earliest by NEUFFORGE, others by Dugourc, Boucher the younger, ROUBO and DELAFOSSE. Designs for silver were published by FORTY and for embroideries by RANSON, while SALEMBIER provided designs for antique style ornament suitable for every medium. This profusion of engraved designs naturally helped to spread the style throughout Europe. The French also carried on an extensive export trade in furniture, porcelain, textiles, silver, etc., with other European countries: and some French-trained craftsmen emigrated – e.g. LANGLOIS to England.

Louis XVI style: clock, gilt-bronze and Sèvres porcelain, perhaps by Thomire & Robin, 1788 (Musée des Arts Décoratifs, Paris)

Louis Philippe style The style current in France during the reign of Louis-Philippe, 1830–48. It was a continuation of the RESTAURATION STYLE, heavier, gaudier and distinctly more bourgeois. At the beginning of the period the TROUBADOUR STYLE was still popular but gradually went out of fashion in favour of more accurate imitations of Gothic and Renaissance furniture. The leading furniture-makers were JACOB-DESMALTER and LEMARCHAND both of whom maintained a rather ponderous version of the EMPIRE STYLE. The best silversmiths were FAUCONNIER and FROMENT-MEURICE. This period also saw a return to mid-C18 fashions, e.g., *damas Pompadour* which was on sale in 1835 and lace-hung dressing-tables called *toilettes Pompadour*. *Illustrated next column and next page.*

Lourdet, Simon, *see* SAVONNERIE CARPET FACTORY.

Louis Philippe style: textile design by Chenavard and Stark, c.1830 (Musée des Arts Décoratifs, Paris)

Louis Philippe style: bureau
(Château de Chantilly, chambre du duc d'Aumale)

Louvre carpet workshops, *see* SAVONNERIE CARPET FACTORY.

Louvre tapestry workshops, *see* PARIS TAPESTRY FACTORY.

Love-bird thumbpiece A popular type of thumbpiece on pewter tankards, representing two birds joined at their beaks.

Love seat Modern name for a type of early C18 English settee only just wide enough to seat two people. *See also* CAUSEUSE.

Love spoons Wooden spoons with large handles, usually with openwork decoration of pierced hearts. Common in Wales, they are also found in Scandinavia and Switzerland.

Loving cup A large cup, generally of silver and with two handles, passed round at the end of a banquet for each person to drink from in turn. The term denotes function rather than form but is sometimes applied loosely to any two-handled drinking cup.

Lowboy An American C18 type of dressing table or low chest of drawers of one or two tiers on tall legs, similar to the lower stage of a HIGHBOY which it was often made to match.

Lowdin, William, *see* BRISTOL PORCELAIN FACTORY.

Löwenfinck, Adam Friedrich von (1714–54). One of the most famous of German porcelain and faience painters. He began as an apprentice at MEISSEN (1726) initially as a flower painter, later as a painter of chinoiseries; in 1736 he went to the BAYREUTH factory and is sometimes said to have gone from there to CHANTILLY (to escape Saxon officials demanding his return to Meissen) but was working at ANSBACH by 1740. In 1741 he went to FULDA where he was appointed Court enamel painter, but in 1745 he was at WEISSENAU. He founded the HÖCHST PORCELAIN FACTORY in 1746 but left to start a factory at Coblenz (unsuccessfully) in 1749 and ended as director of the Hagenau branch of the STRASBOURG factory in 1750–4. He is said to have specialized in painting naturalistic flowers at Meissen and may have been responsible for their diffusion on German faience. Signed drawings in the Meissen archives reveal that he also developed an individual style of chinoiserie decoration, quite distinct from that of J. G. HEROLD and influenced by Japan rather more than by China. But the chinoiserie decorations attributed to him have been the subject of much controversy. He may also have devised the tureens in the forms of birds and also certain Rococo table-wares made at Höchst and Strasbourg and later imitated by many other factories. Two of his brothers, **Christian Wilhelm** (d.1753) and **Karl Heinrich** (1718–54) were also porcelain and faience painters. So also was his wife, **Maria Seraphina Suzanna Magdalena Schick** (1728–1805) whom he married in 1747. She succeeded him at Hagenau, married again, was widowed again and managed the LUDWIGSBURG FAIENCE FACTORY c. 1763–95.

Lit: O. Seitler in *Keramos* 11 (1961), pp. 22–9; L. L. Lewin in *Keramos* 13 (1961), pp. 57–80; 15 (1962), pp. 18–20; 16 (1962), pp. 36–44; A. Klein & R. H. Wark in *Keramos* 38 (1967) pp. 3–21.

Löwenick, Peter, *see* SIEGBURG POTTERIES.

Lowestoft porcelain factory It was founded in 1757 and produced soft-paste porcelain similar in quality to Bow – and similarly made with bone ash – specializing in table-wares of simple form decorated in underglaze blue (painted or transfer printed) generally with chinoiseries similar to those on WORCESTER porcelain. After 1770 some pieces were decorated in enamel colours. Many pieces bear inscriptions – such as 'A trifle from Lowestoft' or the name of the owner – and some tablets were painted with the name and birth-date of a child. Figures of children and animals were also made. The factory closed *c.*1800 but its manager, **Robert Allen,** continued to work as a porcelain painter, maintaining a muffle kiln. A Chinese teapot he decorated and signed appears to have given rise to the legend that a large quantity of armorial CHINESE EXPORT PORCELAIN (still miscalled 'Oriental Lowestoft' occasionally, especially in the U.S.) was made in Lowestoft.

Lowestoft porcelain jug, c.1765
(Victoria & Albert Museum)

Lit: G. A. Godden, *The Illustrated Guide to Lowestoft Porcelain,* London 1969.

Low-temperature colours, *see* ENAMEL COLOURS.

Low-warp tapestry (*Basse lisse*). A tapestry woven on a loom with the warp threads wound on rollers arranged horizontally and moved by treadles. It is produced by a quicker and therefore cheaper method than HIGH-WARP TAPESTRY and is usually of lower quality though great technical improvements were introduced by Neilson at the low-warp factory of the GOBELINS TAPESTRY FACTORY in the mid C18. The CARTOON is placed underneath the warp so that the weaver can follow it easily and faithfully, but as he works from the back of the tapestry he reproduces it in reverse.

Loyal, Charles, *see* SAINT-CLÉMENT POTTERY.

Lübbers, Georg Nicolaus, *see* STOCKELSDORF POTTERY.

Lucas, John Robert, *see* NAILSEA GLASSHOUSE.

Lucca silk factories Lucca was famous since Roman times for the production of woollen cloth. In the C13 it became a notable centre for silk weaving and may have benefited from an influx of S. Italian weavers who had left Naples after the fall of the House of Hohenstaufen in 1266. In the C14 Lucchese silks were famous throughout Europe but little is known of their appearance. A large group of C14 silks, incorporating such Chinese motifs as swooping phoenixes, is usually assigned to Lucca (though none is certainly known to have been made there). The designs are much freer than on any earlier European textiles and each pattern consists of at least three motifs which are repeated diagonally and not, as hitherto, vertically. Some very similar silks with rather more tightly composed patterns and rather chunkier motifs, are generally assigned to the VENETIAN SILK FACTORIES. The production of orphreys woven from edge to edge with religious scenes incorporating several figures – notably the Annunciation, Resurrection and Assumption – repeated one above the other, was begun in the early C15 at Lucca and also at Florence and Siena. Velvets were also woven and by 1421 this branch of the industry had grown to such a size that different guilds were formed for the weavers of plain and patterned velvet. The patterned velvets of the later C15 and C16 appear to have been similar to those woven elsewhere in Italy, with bold formal motifs of pomegranates, etc. Lucca remained a notable centre for silk production until the late C18 and carried on a considerable trade in plain, watered and flowered silks.

Lit: C. G. E. Bunt, *Sicilian & Lucchese Fabrics*, Leigh on Sea 1961.

Luce, Jean (b.1895). French designer of ceramics and glass who first made his name at the Paris

Italian silk, C15, possibly from Lucca (Musée des Arts Décoratifs, Paris)

J. Luce: plate, c.1925 (Musée des Arts Décoratifs, Paris)

exhibition of 1925 where he showed pottery and porcelain discreetly decorated in the ART DECO style. He owned a shop in Paris selling high quality glass, porcelain and faience.

Lück (or **Lücke**), **Johann Christoph Ludwig von** (*c.*1703–1780). German sculptor, ivory carver, porcelain modeller and arcanist first recorded in 1728–9 as chief modeller at the MEISSEN PORCELAIN FACTORY where he was responsible for a statuette of Augustus the Strong in armour and other small pieces. In 1750–51 he was employed at the VIENNA PORCELAIN FACTORY where he made models for statuettes of children as allegories of the seasons. Then he went to FÜRSTENBERG as an arcanist. In 1754–5 he founded the SCHLESWIG faience factory. Thereafter he seems to have worked mainly as an ivory carver. Two other porcelain modellers of the same name are recorded and were probably relatives. **Karl Gottlieb von Lück** (d.1775), probably a son of J. C. L. von Lück, worked at FRANKENTHAL as a modeller from 1766 to 1775 and was responsible for some of the factory's best statuettes, notably hunting figures, family groups and especially a little Chinese summer-house with attendant Chinamen. **Johann Friedrich von Lück** (d.1797), who may have been a son or nephew of J. C. L. von Lück, worked at Meissen as a repairer, possibly at HÖCHST, and, from 1758 to 1764, at Frankenthal as a modeller. He returned to Meissen as chief of the staff of repairers. No certain works by him are known though several statuettes are attributed to him. For illustration *see* ROCOCO STYLE.

Lit: M. Sauerlandt, *Deutsche Porzellan-Figuren*, Cologne 1923.

Ludwigsburg pottery and porcelain factory The porcelain factory was founded in 1756 and taken over in 1758 by Duke Carl Eugen of Württemburg as 'a necessary attribute of the glory and dignity' of a prince. It began production in 1759 under the arcanist J. J. RINGLER who was director until 1799. The quality of the paste was at first poor and never pure white and thus more suitable for figures than vases and table-wares. The latter are undistinguished imitations of the productions of other factories though sometimes attractively painted. Figures, which rank among the best of

Ludwigsburg: porcelain figure, 1765 (Württenbergisches Landesmuseum, Stuttgart)

their time, were the outstanding products of the factory executed under the general artistic direction of the chief painter G. F. RIEDEL. Some models in a restrained Rococo style were provided by the Court sculptors, notably Domenico Ferretti and J. C. BEYER who was overseer of the modelling workshop *c.*1764–7. Jean-Jacob Louis (1703–72), who was chief repairer from 1762, executed some large birds, groups of animals, gardeners, hunters, a lady at a spinet, a charming group satirizing the fashion for high coiffures (*Die hohe Friseur*) and, perhaps most notably, a series of tiny fairground scenes with booths and their attendant showmen, etc. From the early 1770s figures more sentimental and classicizing were produced. And in the 1790s models were provided by the distinguished Neo-Classical sculptor Johann Heinrich Dannecker (1758–1841). But by this time the factory had set into a decline. There was a brief revival in 1806–16 when both workmen and the Empire style were imported from France. But the factory finally closed in 1824. A faience factory had been established at the same time as the porcelain factory but was run as a separate concern though taken over in 1763 by the Duke of Württemberg who put the widow of A. F. von LÖWENFINCK in charge. It functioned on a fairly small scale producing table-wares attractively painted with flowers (a large white bust of Duke Carl Eugen is exceptional). It was united with the porcelain factory in 1795. A manufactory of cream-coloured earthenware began as part of the faience factory in 1776 but was run as a separate concern from 1784. (For factory mark *see* p. 885.)

Lit: H. Christ, *Ludwigsburger Porzellanfiguren*, Stuttgart 1921; *Alt. Ludwigsburger Porzellan*, Exh. Cat., Schloss Ludwigsburg 1959.

Lumello, Giovanni, *see* VINOVO PORCELAIN FACTORY.

Lund, Benjamin, *see* BRISTOL PORCELAIN FACTORIES.

Lunette A semi-circle, sometimes filled with figurative or abstract ornament.

Lunéville pottery A faience factory, founded by **Jacques Chambrette** in 1731, it produced table-wares similar to those of STRASBOURG, NIDERVILLER and SCEAUX, as boldly Rococo in form and decoration but generally with a tin-glaze less purely white, rather hotter and stronger colours and less delicately executed painting. Such wares are indistinguishable from those made at the SAINT CLÉMENT POTTERY, also owned by Chambrette. The most notable and individual products were figures – large faience lions and dogs intended to stand in doorways or gardens and small figures in *terre de pipe* after models provided by P.-L. CYFFLÉ from *c*.1752 until 1766 when he established his own factory, also in Lunéville. Chambrette died in 1758 leaving the factory to his son and son-in-law who obtained for it the title of a *Manufacture Royale* and initiated the production of English style cream-coloured earthenware but ran into financial difficulties. They were obliged to sell it in 1788 to Sebastian Keller and his partner whose descendants ran it throughout the C19, occasionally repeating early models (notably the large lions and dogs). The factory name, impressed, was the usual mark, often with initials added.

Lit: A. Lane, *French Faience*, London 1948; M. Ernould-Gandouet, *La Céramique en France au XIX siècle*, Paris 1969.

Lurçat, Jean (1892–1965). French painter and tapestry designer. Trained at Nancy under Victor PROUVÉ he began in an Art Nouveau style (book bindings) and settled in Paris in 1912 as a painter. His tapestry designs date from the 1930s onwards, beginning with *Les Illusions d'Icare* in 1936 for the GOBELINS and a long series for AUBUSSON, notably the *Garden of Cocks*, *Harvest* (1939), *Winter* (1940), *Liberty* (1942), *Man* (1945), *The Four Elements* (1946). Inspired partly by the C14 work of the PARIS TAPESTRY FACTORIES, notably the *Apocalypse of Angers*, and partly by Pre-Columbian textiles, he led a movement back to first principles in tapestry weaving, adopting coarse materials and drastically reducing the colour range, even allowing the weavers some scope in the choice of shades.

Lustre 1. An iridescent metallic surface used for the decoration of ceramics, especially ISLAMIC POTTERY, HISPANO-MORESQUE POTTERY and MAIOLICA. The pigments were made from metallic oxides – silver to produce a pale brassy yellow and copper for a rich ruby red – mixed with fine ochre and applied to the already glazed surface of pottery which was then re-fired at a fairly low temperature (about 800°C.) under reducing conditions in a muffle kiln. A thick film of this pigment made the vessel look like a piece of burnished copper, thinner films produced subtler iridescent effects. Generally, however, lustre was combined with underglaze colours. The technique of lustre painting appears to have been invented by the glass painters of Egypt in the C7 or C8 A.D., to have been taken up by pottery painters and perfected at Baghdad in the C9. At the end of the C10 the best potters from Baghdad appear to have moved to the Fatamid court at Cairo whence the technique of lustre painting was transmitted to Spain (notably MÁLAGA) by the C13 and on to Italy (where the main centres for such work were DERUTA and GUBBIO) in the late C15 or early C16. But lustred wares seem to have slipped out of fashion in the late C16 except in Spain where they have been made fairly consistently, though in a rather crude manner, from the C17. The ancient technique was revived in the C19, notably by W. DE MORGAN in England and U. CANTAGALLI in Italy. The technique is a very tricky one and the C16 writer on pottery PICCOLPASSO stated that only 6 per cent of the pieces fired were satisfactory. Pottery was, however, given a metallic appearance much harder and less subtle by a process developed mainly in England by WEDGWOOD and other STAFFORDSHIRE POTTERIES, also adopted by the LEEDS, SUNDERLAND, SWANSEA and TYNESIDE POTTERIES. A silver surface was obtained from platinum salts; a gilt, coppery, pink or purple lustre from gold. A nacreous lustre used to decorate WORCESTER and BELLEEK wares in the mid C19 was obtained from nitrate of bismuth. Resist lustre was developed in early-C19 England, notably at the DAVENPORT POTTERY where a stencil technique of waxing and then brushing with lustre was patented. Designs were also painted on the glaze in a resist (honey, glycerine or varnish) which could be either washed off or burnt off in the kiln.

Lustre, detail of an English cut-glass chandelier, c.1815, (Victoria & Albert Museum)

Lit: A. W. Frothingham, *Lustreware of Spain*, New York 1951; R. Ettinghausen, 'Notes on the lustre ware of Spain' in *Ars Orientalis* I (1954); J. Bedford, *Old English Lustreware*, London 1965.

2. French name for a CHANDELIER. In the C16 the more elaborate types of French chandelier were decorated with rock-crystal drops and in the C17 with many-faceted pieces of crystal which reflect the light of the candles: they were called *chandeliers de cristal*. Expensive crystal was often replaced by cut glass from the late C17 when the term *lustre* began to be applied (as it still is) to all chandeliers whether or not they incorporate pieces of crystal or glass.

3. A C19 English name for a vase with cut glass drops hung from the rim.

Lutestring or **Lustring** An imprecise term, in use from the C14 to the late C18, for a glossy silk fabric. It was latterly applied to a *taffeta lustré* – a taffeta which had been stretched and while under tension smeared with a syrupy gum which gave it a glossy sheen, a process said to have been invented in 1656 at LYONS where much of this material was produced in the C18.

Luting The process of joining separate pieces of clay together with liquid SLIP, e.g. when applying clay decoration to a vessel.

Lutma, Johannes (*c.*1585–1669). Dutch silversmith working from 1621 in Amsterdam. He was probably a pupil of Adam van VIANEN whose AURICULAR style he imitated and developed, using similar fluid, fishy forms in his decorations but with greater attention to symmetry and an even greater softness in the modelling. A curious little dish with a monster (lobster body and tortoise head) emerging out of the eddying scrolls of the rim and a ewer with a dolphin turning a somersault as a handle (1641 and 1647, both Rijksmuseum, Amsterdam) are characteristic works. He was also a medallist. *Illustrated next page*. (For his mark *see* p. 894.)

Lit: J. W. Fredericks, *Dutch Silver*, The Hague, 1952.

Lutz, Nicholas (*fl.*1869–90). French glassmaker who emigrated to the U.S.A. in 1869 and worked

J. Lutma: silver ewer, Amsterdam, 1647 (Rijksmuseum, Amsterdam)

for the BOSTON AND SANDWICH GLASS COMPANY specializing in striped glass and paper-weights enclosing small simulated fruit and leaves. In 1888 he joined the MOUNT WASHINGTON GLASS COMPANY and later moved on to the UNION GLASS COMPANY.

Lyncker, Antor, *see* THE HAGUE PORCELAIN FACTORY.

Lynn glasses The name given to a group of late-C17 to early-C18 English glass vessels with horizontal ribbing, at one time supposed to have been made in Norwich but now attributed to glass-houses in or near Kings Lynn, Norfolk.

Lyonese A late C16 French style of book-binding, so called because it was used to bind many books printed in Lyons. The decoration is polychrome, with strapwork panels either painted, lacquered or enamelled. English Elizabethan bindings are often in this style, with heavy centre and corner-pieces.

Lyons potteries Several Italian craftsmen are recorded as making faience in Lyons from *c.*1510 onwards. Although no marked or otherwise documented products are known, a fairly large group of late C16 dishes and ewers decorated in the ISTORIATO style with rather gaudily coloured and not very well drawn Mannerist compositions (sometimes derived from books published in Lyons) is generally ascribed to the city. The production of painted faience was revived *c.*1733 when **Joseph Combe** and **Jacques-Marie Ravier** started a factory, with the privilege of a *Manufacture Royale*, making attractive wares similar to those of MOUSTIERS. But there were several other C18 factories in the city and their products can rarely be differentiated. A speciality seems to have been made of wares decorated with pictures of saints and inscriptions (e.g. the name and birth of the owner whose patron saint is depicted) called *faiences patronymiques*.

Lit: C. Damiron, *La faïence de Lyon*, Paris 1926.

Lyons silk factories The most famous and the best in Europe from the early C18 onwards. They led European taste in silks and their patterns were copied all over the continent. Lyons was one of the main centres for trade in Italian silks before 1466 when Louis XI set up his own silk industry there. But because of the hostility of the Franco-Italian merchants the industry was transferred to TOURS. A new start was made at Lyons in 1536 and quantities of plain and very simply patterned materials were soon being produced. The production of rich figured silks began in the early C17. By 1660 more than three thousand master weavers were at work in Lyons which took the lead from Tours for French silk production. Protective measures imposed by Colbert (ban on importation of foreign silk 1667) helped the industry. At this period Baroque patterns similar to those woven in Italy seem to have been used. The fashion for BIZARRE SILKS may have originated in Lyons. But it was Jean REVEL who finally established the city as the leader of fashion in silks *c.*1730 when flat patterns gave way to naturalistically shaded designs of fruit and flowers. He was succeeded as leading designer by Philippe de LASALLE who worked for the Pernon factory which supplied not only the French Court but the Empress of Russia and the Sultan of Turkey with furnishing fabrics of the most exquisite quality ever made (hitherto Lyons had concentrated on dress materials). At the outbreak of the Revolution twenty thousand craftsmen were employed in the Lyons silk industry: by 1799 there were only two thousand. But under the lavish patronage of Napoleon the industry revived and the factories, which now began to use the JACQUARD loom, produced vast quantities of Empire style silks (the best designed by Jean BONY) for the various Imperial residences. Many were still unfinished in 1815 and with slightly modified designs (eliminating Napoleonic devices) were used by the restored Bourbons. In the mid C19 the factories were engaged mainly in producing opulent flowered silks and repetitions of C18 patterns woven in the pale colours to which the originals had by then faded. In the 1920s the Bianchini-Férier factory began to employ **Raoul Dufy** (1877–1953) to design silks and their example of commissioning work from leading contemporary painters was followed by several other factories. The industry has recently adapted itself to the use of nylon and other synthetic materials but is still famous mainly for silk and produces much of the best woven in Europe.

Lit: E. Pariset, *Histoire de la fabrique lyonnaise,* Lyons 1901; P. Thornton, *Baroque & Rococo Silks,* London 1965.

Wood-cut initial letter from Cosmographicall Glasse *by William Cunningham, printed by John Day, London,* 1559 *(reduced)*

MacCarthy, Daniel, *see* WEESP PORCELAIN FACTORY.

Macdonald, Margaret (1865–1933). Designer, metal-worker and embroideress, trained at the Glasgow School of Art. Worked in a style similar to C. R. MACKINTOSH whom she married in 1900 and assisted. Also collaborated with her sister **Frances** (1874–1921) a metal-worker who married, 1899, another member of the Glasgow School, the furniture designer **J. Henry McNair.**

Lit: Charles Rennie Mackintosh, Margaret Macdonald Mackintosh Memorial Exhibition, Exh. Cat., McLellan Galleries, Glasgow 1933; T. Howarth, *Charles Rennie Mackintosh and the Modern Movement*, London 1952.

Macheleid, Georg Heinrich, *see* VOLKSTEDT PORCELAIN FACTORY.

McIntire, Samuel (1757–1811). Architect, sculptor and decorative carver of Salem, Massachusetts, he was the son of a joiner and became the outstanding example of the early American craftsman-builder tradition. Most of his work dates from after the Revolutionary War in 1782, when Salem superseded Boston as a centre of fine craftsmanship. He began with a number of plain, square three-storey houses notable mainly for their carved wood decoration. In 1795 he began his most important commission, Derby Mansion (destroyed) for which the architect Charles Bullfinch provided designs though McIntire was alone

Mahogany sofa from Salem, Massachusetts, with carving probably by McIntire (The Henry Francis du Pont Winterthur Museum, Winterthur, Delaware)

responsible for the carved detailing. He appears to have carved not only chimney-pieces (now in the Metropolitan Museum, New York) and door-cases but also furniture for Derby Mansion. But both here and in other instances where he is recorded to have worked on furniture, he seems to have provided the carved work only, e.g. the Lemon chest-of-drawers of 1796 (now in Museum of Fine Arts, Boston). He is also recorded to have carved decorations, especially baskets of flowers, for the top rail of sofas, and several such have been attributed to him. These and the furniture from the Derby Mansion are in a light, up-to-date style derived from HEPPLEWHITE's pattern book of 1782. In his door-cases and chimney-pieces he was influenced by ADAM. His son **Samuel Field MacIntire** carried on the business after his death.

Lit: E. H. Bjerkoe, *The Cabinet Makers of America*, New York 1957; C. F. Montgomery, *American Furniture of the Federal Period in the Henry Francis du Pont Winterthur Museum*, New York/London 1967.

Mackintosh, Charles Rennie (1868–1928). Outstanding Scottish architect and designer, he was the leader of the GLASGOW SCHOOL and a prominent figure in the international ART NOUVEAU movement. He was born and educated in Glasgow where he qualified as an architect in 1889 and joined the firm of John Honeyman and Keppie, becoming a partner and working with Keppie until 1914. He designed and furnished the revolutionary Glasgow School of Art (1897), a number of tea-rooms in Glasgow for Miss Cranston (1897–1910) and several private houses (notably Windyhill and Hill House, both near Glasgow). He began to design furniture for his own use *c.*1890 and soon afterwards provided designs for the Glasgow firm of furniture-makers Guthrie and Wells. But the greater and more important part of his decorative work, which ranged from furniture to cutlery, was intended for the buildings and interior schemes he designed. As a furniture-designer he was influenced by GODWIN and probably, for his colour schemes, by the paintings of Whistler. He reacted against the MORRIS tradition and the ARTS AND CRAFTS movement (whose members found his work distasteful), showing little interest in the details of craftsmanship and less in the natural beauty of wood. He favoured white painted woodwork very sparsely decorated in gem-like colours (sometimes incorporating pieces of amethyst glass) with intricate flat flower patterns which look like Japanese motifs elaborated and entwined by a Celtic manuscript illuminator. Designs are based on combinations of straight lines and very gentle curves, the former predominating: chairs

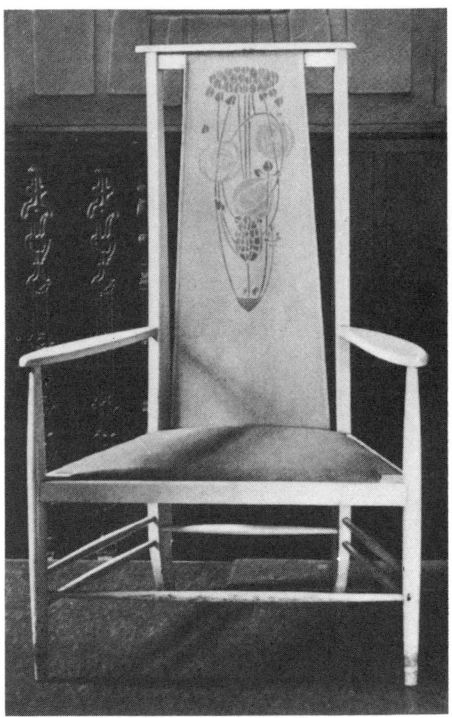

C. R. Mackintosh: armchair of painted wood with stencilled canvas back, 1901–2 (University of Glasgow, Mackintosh Collection)

have tall attenuated backs, tables have spindly supports, cupboards are topped by wide projecting cornices. In complete rooms he emphasized the subtlety of special effects by rather scanty furnishing, striving to create a poetic atmosphere. Meier-Graefe called them *'chambres garnies pour belles âmes'*. His furniture has a curiously virginal quality differentiating it from the robust masculinity of Arts and Crafts work and also from the lush opulence and almost debauched sensuality of French *Art Nouveau*. It won little popularity in

England and Scotland, but on the Continent (he exhibited at Venice 1899, Vienna 1900, Turin 1902) it appeared as something refreshingly new and exerted considerable influence especially in Austria and Germany.

He left Glasgow in 1914 and spent the rest of his life in London. In 1916 he altered and furnished a house in Northampton, in a rather unsuccessful version of the style of Josef HOFFMANN. He designed printed textiles for W. Foxton (1919) and built a studio in Chelsea for Harold Squire (1920). His last years, complicated by financial difficulties and ill-health, were devoted mainly to painting. A memorial exhibition held in Glasgow in 1933 stimulated some interest in him and Nikolaus Pevsner's writing (from 1936 onwards) gave him the recognition he merited. But it was not until the general revival of Art Nouveau in the 1950s that his furniture began to exert any influence on designers.

Lit: N. Pevsner, *Pioneers of the Modern Movement*, London 1936 (rev. ed. as *Pioneers of Modern Design*, London 1960); T. Howarth, *Charles Rennie Mackintosh and the Modern Movement*, London 1952; F. Alison, *Charles Rennie Mackintosh as a designer of chairs*, London 1974.

Mackmurdo, Arthur Heygate (1851–1942). English architect and designer, one of the originators of ART NOUVEAU. He began as an architect, travelled to Italy with Ruskin (1874) and became a friend of William MORRIS. In 1882 he founded the **Century Guild,** a group of artists and craftsmen whose aim was 'to render all branches of art the sphere no longer of the tradesman but of the artist. It would restore building, decoration, glass-painting and sculpture'. As the organ of the Guild he started a periodical called *The Hobby Horse* (1884). Meanwhile, he had published a book on *Wren's City Churches* (1883) with a revolutionary title-page which is the earliest example of ART NOUVEAU design. He designed textiles in a similar manner, all whiplash curves, wind-swept flowers and wilting leaves; he also designed furniture, rather more in the Morris style. After 1904 he devoted himself exclusively to plans for social and currency reform.

Lit: N. Pevsner, *Studies in Art, Architecture and Design*, vol. II, London 1968.

McLaughlin, Mary Louise (1847–1939). American art potter. The daughter of an architect in Cincinnati, she began to take an interest in ceramic decoration in 1872 partly under the influence of the writings of William MORRIS. In 1879 she founded the Women's Pottery Club, a group of amateurs who executed underglaze decorations on pottery (thrown and fired at the ROOKWOOD POTTERY 1880–83) and enamel painting on porcelain. She began to make porcelain in 1898 and after a number of experiments produced vases which she called **Losanti Ware** (after L'Osantiville, the early name for Cincinnati) and exhibited in Buffalo in 1901, Turin 1902, and at the St Louis World's Fair in 1904. An aunt by marriage of Edward COLONNA who was working in Paris, she was *au fait* with recent developments in French decorative arts and her vases have characteristically ART NOUVEAU decorations of carved flower and leaf forms. She was also a painter, embroiderer, lace-maker and writer.

Lit: American Ceramic Society Bulletin XVII (1938), pp. 217–25; R. Judson Clark (ed.), *The Arts and Crafts Movement in America 1876–1916*, Exh. Cat., Art Museum, Princeton University, Art Institute of Chicago, etc. 1972–3.

Macramé A fringe of knotted thread or cord,

Macramé fringe, Italian, late c16 (Victoria & Albert Museum)

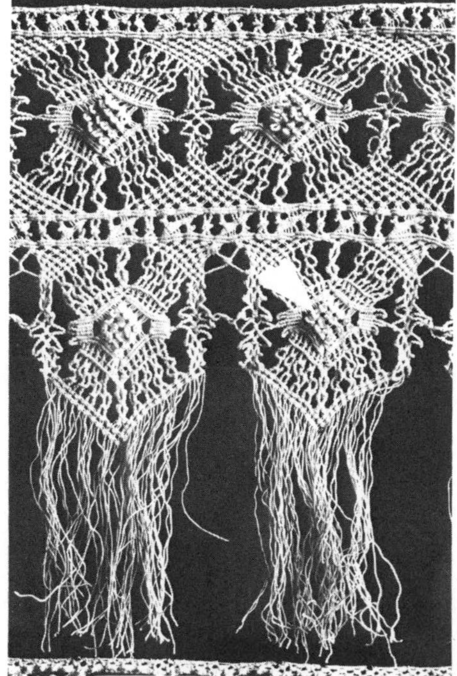

similar to the very elaborate type at the end of a Turkish towel (the Turkish for towel being *macrama*).

Lit: D. Z. Meilach, *Macramé. Creative Design in Knotting*, London 1971.

Madeley porcelain factory, *see* RANDALL, John.

Madrid tapestry factory Founded in 1720 by Jakob van der Goten of Antwerp in premises near the church of Santa Barbara. The first products were VERDURES, followed by a Don Quixote series (*c.*1735), a *Story of Cyrus* (*c.*1745) and a series of rustic Flemish scenes after Teniers (*c.*1750). Works of higher quality were produced from *c.*1765 when an Old Testament series was woven to cartoons by the Italian painter Corrado Giaquinto. But the fame of the factory rests mainly on the tapestries woven after cartoons by **Goya** between 1774 and 1791. Of these the first eight (1774/5) represent scenes of hunting, fishing and shooting. The rest are of 'costumes and diversions of the time', i.e. scenes from contemporary life (mainly rustic) – a drunken brawl outside a tavern, curious groups of gawky, large-headed children, an enormous scene with men in long cloaks and women in high mantillas which has a peculiarly sinister atmosphere, a group of youths, a Mephistophelean doctor of medicine, etc. Though they may lack the full force of Goya's scathing indigation (as manifested in the *Caprichos*) these works are strongly marked by his peculiar blend of misanthropy and humanism, his social satire and 'sick' humour which gives them a unique place in the history of the otherwise strictly courtly art of the tapestry. The factory closed in 1835.

Lit: H. Göbel, *Wandteppiche*, Leipzig 1923–34; E. Lafuente Ferrari, *La tapiceriá en España*, 1943.

Madsen, T. C., *see* COPENHAGEN PORCELAIN FACTORY.

Mafra pottery A factory established at Caldas de Rainha in Portugal in 1854 and known mainly for its sometimes almost deceptively faithful imitations of the work of B. PALISSY.

Magdeburg potteries Three factories at Magdeburg in Hanover. The first was founded in 1754 by **Johann Philipp Guichard** (1726–98) and began by making faience table-wares with basketwork borders similar to those of MÜNDEN but from 1786 specialized in English style cream-coloured earthenware of which it became one of the main producers in Germany. It closed in 1839. A factory founded by **Johann Heinrich Wagener** in 1791 made stoves in the classical style. In 1799 a cream-coloured earthenware factory was founded by **Elias Karl Rousset** in partnership with **Georg Schuchard** who took it over in 1806 and whose family ran it until 1865.

Lit: G. E. Pazaurek, *Steingut: Formgebung und Geschichte*, Stuttgart 1927.

Maggiolini, Giuseppe (1738–1814). He was the most notable cabinet-maker of his period in Italy, but was essentially a craftsman rather than a designer, and his work is notable mainly for its marquetry decoration. His name has been applied rather indiscriminately to late-C18 Italian marquetry furniture, but several signed pieces by him survive. He began as a carpenter in the Cistercian monastery of S. Ambrogio della Vittoria at Parabiago near Milan. From 1771 onwards he was working in Milan or for Milanese patrons, being employed by the Austrian Governor General, the Archduke Ferdinand, and later by the Napoleonic viceroy, Eugène Beauharnais. Such artists as Appiani and Levati provided him with drawings of trophies of musical instruments, cornucopia-like scrolls of acanthus leaves, ruffled ribbons, tendrils of ivy and bunches of flowers as well as more strictly antique architectural ornaments for his marquetry panels. He may also have used Giocondo ALBERTOLLI's engraved designs. Examples of his furniture are in the Palazzo Reale, Milan and the Museo Civico, Milan. *Illustrated next page.*

Lit: G. Morazzoni, *Giuseppe Maggiolini*, Milan 1953.

Magot French word, originally signifying a grotesque tailless monkey, denoting in the C18 a grotesque oriental figure, especially in porcelain. Later the word was used as a contemptuous term for C19 export porcelain generally.

Mahmud El-Kurdi, *see* VENETIAN-SARACENIC METALWORK.

G. Maggiolini: commode inlaid with palisander, ebony, mahogany and other woods, 1790 (Castello Sforzesco, Milan)

Mahogany The dark, hard, close-grained wood of the *Swietenia mahogani* tree which is indigenous to Central America and the West Indies. Its qualities were first recognized by the carpenter on Sir Walter Raleigh's ship in 1595 but it was not until the early C18 that it was imported in quantity to Europe (mainly from Jamaica) as a material for furniture-making. It remained an English speciality until the late C18 when its use spread to France and then, with the Empire style, to the rest of Europe. It varies in colour from red to dark brown and is rarely strongly marked (but *see* ACAJOU MOUCHETÉ or fiddle-back mahogany). It is very hard and unattractive to woodworm.

Maidenhead spoon Similar to an APOSTLE SPOON but with a female bust, said to represent the Virgin Mary, as a finial.

Maigelein A C15 type of cylindrical WALDGLAS beaker, moulded with network in low relief and with a high projecting 'kick' inside. The term was not very strictly applied and is used for several different types of cup in glass or metal.

Maincy tapestry factory Established in 1658 by the French Surintendant des Finances, Nicolas Fouquet, to weave tapestries for his own Château Vaux-le-Vicomte, under the artistic direction of Charles LE BRUN. Only a few PORTIÈRES had been woven by 1661 when the factory closed on Fouquet's fall from power. But Le Brun and the staff of weavers were taken over by Colbert to form the nucleus of the GOBELINS TAPESTRY FACTORY.

Lit: R.-A. Weigert, *French Tapestry*, London 1962.

Maioli bindings French C16 bookbindings made *c.*1550–60 for Thomas Mahieu, secretary to Catherine de Medici. His name was latinised as *Maiolus.* Though possibly made by the *'atelier au trèfle'* which supplied GROLIER, the decoration of Maioli bindings is generally richer, with punched and gilded backgrounds and areas of speckled dots setting off the coloured interlacings.

Lit: G. D. Hobson, *Maioli, Canevari and others,* London 1926.

Maiolica Italian name for TIN-GLAZED EARTHENWARE, derived from a corruption of Majorca whence HISPANO-MORESQUE WARES were imported into Italy in the C15. It is sometimes applied to all European tin-glazed earthenware but is more properly used only for Italian wares and direct imitations of them. The main factories were at BOLOGNA, CAFAGGIOLO, CASTEL DURANTE, CASTELLI, DERUTA, FAENZA, FLORENCE, GUBBIO, MONTELUPO, PADUA, TURIN, URBINO, VENICE.

Lit: G. Ballardini, *Corpus della maiolica italiana,* Rome 1933–8; J. Chompret, *Répertoire de la maiolique italienne,* Paris 1949; B. Rackham, *Italian Maiolica,* London 1952; G. Liverani, *Five Centuries of Italian Maiolica,* London 1960.

Majolica or **Industrial majolica** A corrupt form of the word *maiolica* applied in the C19 to a type of earthenware very richly modelled and covered with thick almost aspic-like coloured glazes (usually lead glazes). It was originated by MINTON, first shown at the Great Exhibition of 1851, and became very popular especially for such large objects as jardinières and umbrella stands. Fountains and large figures were also made of it. Similar wares were soon made elsewhere in England, in the U.S. by E. & W. BENNETT of Baltimore (from 1853) and in Sweden at the RÖRSTRAND and GUSTAVUSBERG factories (from the 1860s).

Majorelle, Louis (1859–1926). He was the son of a cabinet-maker, **Auguste Majorelle,** who worked in Nancy and specialized in reproduction C18 furniture. He was trained as a painter (under Millet in Paris) but gave up painting and returned to Nancy to run the family workshops when his father died in 1879. Until 1890 he continued to work, like his father, in C18 styles for furniture. In the 1880s GALLÉ's first Art Nouveau pieces of furniture were made (in Nancy), and by 1900 Majorelle had so successfully turned over to the new style that he had become the main producer of Art Nouveau furniture in France and perhaps in Europe. He mechanized his workshops which were said to have been 'organized in the manner of a big industrial concern': and although his factory produced nothing that could not have been made as well, if not better, by the techniques

'Majolica' ewer and plateau, by Thomas Allen for Minton & Co., c.1862 (Victoria & Albert Museum)

L. Majorelle: mahogany and gilt-bronze occasional table, Nancy, 1902 (Musée des Arts Décoratifs, Paris)

of hand-craftsmanship, it was able to produce luxury furniture at a price within the range of the middle-class.

Though not an innovator in design, Majorelle was rather more than a highly competent popularizer. If his furniture lacks the fantasy of Gallé's it possesses other notable qualities. The forms are always well devised and the carved decorations seem naturally to grow out of them. Some pieces, like his water-lily table, have a graceful elegance hard to parallel outside French Rococo furniture.

His factory was a First World War casualty, being largely burnt down in 1916. He returned to Nancy in 1918 and began the work of reconstruction, abandoning the by then out-of-fashion Art Nouveau in favour of a style which was to emerge at the Paris 1925 exhibition, on whose jury he served. Waving lines and irregular forms were replaced by straight lines, circles and squares but despite this vogue for severity he contrived to give his furniture an air of opulence which, once again, made it attractive to a middle-class clientèle. Examples of his furniture are in the Musée de l'École de Nancy, Nancy, and in the Musée des Arts Décoratifs, Paris.

Lit: P. Juyot, *Louis Majorelle, Artiste décorateur maître ébéniste,* Nancy 1927; Y. Rambosson in *Mobilier et décoration,* July, 1933.

Makkum potteries A tin-glazed-earthenware factory at Makkum in Friesland making household wares similar to, but coarser than, those of DELFT and specializing in tiles. It was founded in 1675 by **Freerk Jans Tichelaar** and is still run by his descendants. Another factory making only tiles, directed by members of the **Kingma** family, functioned from the mid C17 to 1835. Examples are in the Rijksmuseum, Amsterdam.

Lit: N. Ottema, *Friesche Majolica,* Leeuwarden 1920.

Malachite A bright, very showy, expensive-looking, copper-green stone, usually with prominent black veinings. It is found mainly in Russia and was used frequently by FABERGÉ. Large pieces are rare but table-tops and ornamental columns have been made of it. It is usually opaque but when thinly cut and highly polished sometimes becomes slightly translucent.

Málaga potteries The earliest notable centre for the production of lustred HISPANO-MORESQUE WARE. It has been suggested that they were producing such wares as early as the C12, but fragments of this date found in the Málaga district were probably of E. Mediterranean origin. They were possibly established by potters of Persian origin. They were certainly active by the mid C13 and, soon afterwards, carrying on an extensive export trade with Egypt, Sicily and (from 1303) England. Although there are numerous contemporary references to the potteries none of their wares has been securely identified. A bowl in the Islamisches Abteilung, Staatliche Museen,

Málaga (?) lustred earthenware 'Alhambra' vase, C13 (Museo Nazionale, Palermo)

Berlin, has a symbol painted on its base which some (but not all) students have read as the Arabic word for Málaga. But it is widely believed that as Málaga was the most famous centre for the production of lustred wares in the C13 the finest surviving specimens of that date must have been made there – a number of tiles still in their original setting in the entrance to the Cuarto Real de Santo Domingo, Granada, and five large (more than 1 metre high) vases with wing-shaped handles (Museo Arqueológico Nacional, Madrid; Istituto de Valencia de Don Juan, Madrid; the Alhambra, Granada; Museo Nazionale, Palermo; Hermitage Museum, Leningrad). The vases are normally called 'Alhambra vases' from their similarity of shape to one which has never left the precincts of the Alhambra though it is probably later in date (generally assigned to the late C14, together with a very similar vase in the National Museum, Stockholm). Sometimes these vases are attributed to a pottery in Granada, but without documentation. They are among the finest of all European ceramics, potted with complete mastery of the medium and very beautifully decorated with foliage, Islamic arabesques and Kufic inscriptions in gilt lustre and dark blue. The Málaga potteries seem to have ceased producing lustre wares in the early C15. They still made tin-glazed earthenware until the mid C16 but after the city fell to the Christian Kings in 1487 the more skilled potters probably emigrated to PATERNA.

Lit: A. W. Frothingham, *Lustreware of Spain*, New York 1951.

Malagodi, Giovanni Battista (1729–97). One of the few named Italian smiths. He was born and worked in Modena where he executed many exceptionally fine iron gates, grilles, balconies, etc. in an elegant Rococo style with lively scroll-work and foliage, e.g., Civico Ospedale, Palazzo dell'Università, Palazzo Montellari, Palazzo Sabatini, etc.

Malériat, Leopold, *see* SINCENY POTTERY.

Maling, C. T., *see* TYNESIDE POTTERIES.

Mallard, Prudent (1809–79). Cabinet-maker born and trained in France who went to the U.S.A. and worked in New York from 1829 to 1838 when he moved to New Orleans where he had a workshop in Royal Street. After the departure of the much older F. SEIGNOURET in 1853 he became the leading maker of furniture in New Orleans, executing pieces in rich versions of the Renaissance and Neo-Rococo styles.

Mallet vase A type of Chinese vase resembling a mallet, with flattened shoulders and narrow neck on which there are sometimes two handles in the form of fish or dragons.

Mallet-Stevens, Robert (1886–1945). He was one of the most fashionable French architects of the inter-war period. He was trained at the École d'Architecture in Paris but reacted against its Beaux-Arts classicism and developed a self-consciously modern style influenced by Josef HOFFMANN. At the 1925 Exposition Internationale des Arts Décoratifs he designed several interiors which provided appropriately expensive and modernistic settings for furniture by CHAREAU and objects designed by F. JOURDAIN. In 1930 he became the first president of the Union des Artistes Modernes. Although he did not design household or decorative objects, he played a part of great importance in the creation of the ART DECO style and his utterly unfunctional modernism had a great appeal for many who wished to be up to date but fought shy of the clear stark rationalism of LE CORBUSIER.

Lit: A. Sartoris, *R. Mallet-Stevens*, Milan 1930.

Malling jugs English tin-glazed-earthenware jugs speckled blue, purple and brown in imitation of RHENISH STONEWARE, sometimes set in silver mounts, named after an example formerly in the Kentish church of West Malling but of unknown origin. They were possibly made in London.

Malmsten, Carl (b.1888). Swedish furniture designer, teacher and the founder of three schools of handicrafts. In 1916 he won the first prize for furniture for Stockholm Town Hall on which he was employed until 1923. He then fitted out the Stockholm concert hall, 1924–5. A bitter opponent of functionalism, he advocates simple craftsman-made furniture and his own best work has an attractively wholesome farmhouse quality, though he has also made expensive and distinctly upper-bourgeois marquetry cabinets and cosily upholstered chairs.

Maltese lace A silk pillow lace made from 1833, originally by members of the Ciglia family, on the island of Malta. Both black and white pieces were made and early specimens are often of very fine quality. The Maltese cross was often worked into designs: but lace was made to similar patterns elsewhere, in France, England and Ireland.

Mameluke rugs Cut pile carpets woven in Egypt, probably in Cairo itself, and also called Cairene rugs (the former term is used to differentiate them from carpets made after the overthrow of the Mamelukes in 1811). They are related technically to the carpets made by the Copts before the Arab conquest. But the earliest surviving examples date from the C16 or C17 and the majority are C18. Designs are close and geometrical with much use of sprays and bands of flower and leaf motifs.

Lit: E. Kühnel and L. Bellinger, *Catalogue of Cairene Rugs and Others Technically Related*, Washington 1955.

Manara, Baldassare (*fl.*1532–6). Notable maiolica painter of Faenza who signed several fine ISTORIATO plates, e.g., *Triumph of Time* (Ashmolean Museum, Oxford), and a dish painted with a battle scene (British Museum). He was influenced by the wares of URBINO.

Lit: J. Chompret, *Répertoire de la maiolique italienne*, Paris 1939.

Mandarin porcelain An obsolete term for a type of CHINESE EXPORT PORCELAIN decorated at Canton, generally with overcrowded patterns of figures and flowers in ENAMEL COLOURS on a white ground.

Manganese A purple colour used on ceramics by applying manganese oxide, generally beneath the glaze.

Manheim glasshouse, *see* STIEGEL, Henry William.

Manicus, Frederick (1740–85). Dutch silversmith, he worked in Amsterdam and is known mainly for his elegant Neo-Classical pieces – e.g. tall, slender Corinthian column candlesticks. They are as elegant and refined as contemporary French or English silver though subtly different in style.

Lit: J. H. Fredericks, *Dutch Silver*, vol. II, The Hague 1960.

Manisses pottery, *see* VALENCIA POTTERIES.

Man-made fibres A term of wider meaning than Synthetic Fibres. It comprises all fibres that are not of natural origin, such as WOOL, COTTON, SILK. They fall into two main groups: the regenerated fibres, derived from natural raw materials, and the synthetic fibres. The same method of production is common to both: the raw materials are chemically treated and the resulting thick viscous spinning liquid or polymer is extruded through small holes in a spinneret and solidifies in cool air to form a continuous filament. The continuous filament yarns are woven or knitted into fabrics; alternatively, they may be cut into short lengths, known as staples, or spun. Fabrics produced from these yarns are thicker, softer and warmer to the touch. Processes have also been developed for the production of textured, bulked or crimp yarns. The leading manufacturers – e.g. in Britain, I.C.I., Courtaulds, British Enkalon and Chemstrand – all market several types of fabric with widely differing characteristics.

Of regenerated fibres, the first to be developed and the best known is viscose rayon (1910), which is similar to cotton in structure, but more versatile, and is widely employed for furnishing fabrics and carpets. Sarille is a crimp fibre used to produce fabrics with wool-like characteristics: Durafil has great strength and resistance to abrasion, and is used for added toughness in many different types of fabric. Cellulose acetates have similar properties to rayon fibres, though their chemical structure is quite different. One of the best known is Tricel. Protein fibres, produced from natural proteins found in milk and fish, are known under the generic name of azlon and are blended with other fibres in carpets and felts.

Synthetic fibres are made from polymers and the first group to be made by the process of chemical synthesis were the polyamide fibres, now known as nylon. Nylon is strong, light, elastic and resistant to abrasion, and different varieties are widely employed for clothing and furnishing textiles, bedding and carpets. Terylene is a polyester fibre, and is used both by itself and in blends, being resilient and shrink-resistant. Crimplene is a bulked polyester, mainly employed for knitted fabrics.

Other synthetics include the acrylic fibres, such as Acrilan and Courtelle, which are soft yet hard-wearing and are used for household textiles and carpets; glass fibres, made principally from sand, silica and limestone, which are fireproof and moisture-resistant, and are used extensively for furnishing fabrics; metallic fibres, like Lurex, which do not tarnish and can be washed or dry-cleaned.

The growth of man-made fibres has been spectacular – like PLASTICS they have superseded traditional fibres for many specialized applications and new compounds are constantly being developed.

Lit: D. C. Hague, *The Economics of Man-Made Fibres*, London 1957; R. W. Moncrieff, *Man-made Fibres*, London 1963.

Mannerist style A highly sophisticated mutation of the RENAISSANCE style, which first appeared in paintings executed in Florence and Rome in the 1520s, rapidly affected the decorative arts and spread to N. Europe. It is characterized by a love of sinuous and elegantly contorted forms, a delight in precious and semi-precious materials and rather sharp acid colours, coupled with a taste for ingenious and bizarre, complex and ambivalent compositions and all forms of visual wit. It is pre-eminently and exclusively a Court style. Human figures, attenuated to an almost preposterous elegance, usually nude (the females with complex coiffures to emphasize the nakedness of their bodies) and shown in twisted postures suggestive of sexual ecstasy, proliferate as never before or since on household objects – carved furniture, silver cups and ewers and even the handles of spoons and forks, bronze andirons, painted maiolica plates, tapestries, etc. – while the fashion for bronze statuettes reached a new height with the small-scale masterpieces of Giovanni Bologna and A. de Vries. Silver or hardstone cups were occasionally supported by human figures locked in sexual intercourse. Figures play a prominent part in GROTESQUE decorations and are often combined with STRAPWORK which is one of the hallmarks of the style, especially in N. Europe. At once sensuous and cerebral, the style appealed mainly (as it still does) to the cultivated hedonist and it flourished in all the leading C16 Courts – those of Rome, Florence (Medici), Mantua (Gonzaga), of Fontainebleau and Paris (Francis I) and of Prague (Rudolph II). Its extremely rapid diffusion was due partly to artists moving continually from one Court to another and partly to the increased production and circulation of engraved designs. Numerous designs for silver were made by painters, including GIULIO ROMANO, PERINO DEL VAGA, POLIDORO DA CARAVAGGIO, G. B. ROSSO and Francesco SALVIATI, himself a silversmith. The architects DIETTERLIN, A. DU CERCEAU and H. V. de VRIES published designs for furniture and ornaments which might be applied to a wide range of objects. Designs for silver were also published by Enea VICO and several Germans, notably Georg Wechter (*fl.*1574) and Jonas Silber (*fl.*1570–90).

Most of the leading Mannerist painters provided designs for tapestries woven at BRUSSELS, FLORENCE, FONTAINEBLEAU and PARIS. They also exerted a strong influence on the LIMOGES ENAMEL painters, notably COURT, COURTOIS, LIMOSIN and REYMOND and the maiolica painters of FAENZA, LYONS and URBINO (where the FONTANA and PATANAZZI factories specialized in vessels, often extravagantly shaped, decorated with elegant *grotesque* ornament). Furniture, usually with much figurative decoration in low

Mannerist style: walnut cabinet, mid C16 (The Frick Collection, New York)

relief, naturally shows the influence of Mannerist sculptors and one of the best French furniture-makers was a sculptor, H. SAMBIN. Carved furniture of ungilt and unpainted wood is typical of the style. Cabinets of architectural form with a pedimented top were a Mannerist introduction: and there was a revival of a type of ancient Roman table standing on two or three wood or marble supports richly carved with figures and foliage (e.g., Farnese Table in Metropolitan Museum, New York).

But it was in metalwork that Mannerism found its most notable expression in the decorative arts. One of the best c16 sculptors, Benvenuto CELLINI, was primarily a goldsmith and the salt cellar he made for Francis I epitomizes the ideals of his patrons in its exquisite craftsmanship, 'learned' symbolism, and in the sensuous appeal of the materials and decoration (nude figures). The most characteristic type of Mannerist plate is the ewer with an oviform body richly embossed, a fantastically flared lip and a handle in the form of twisting snakes or an acrobatic nude. Such vessels were also executed in pewter, notably by BRIOT, and in tin-glazed earthenware. But much of the most exquisite Mannerist goldsmiths' work is to be found in the elaborate enamelled mounts devised for cups and basins of semi-precious hardstones like lapis lazuli, chalcedony, agate and rock crystal (e.g. those made for Rudolph II and now in the Kunsthistorisches Museum, Vienna).

Mannerist style: covered cup by A. Schweinberger, 1602–3 (Kunsthistorisches Museum, Vienna)

The Mannerist delight in the bizarre – associated with the cult of the *frisson* and the passion for grottoes – gave rise to a fashion for objects seething with slithery reptiles, notably the pottery of Bernard PALISSY and silver by the JAMNITZER. It was from the latter, and from Italian ornamental prints, that P. van VIANEN developed at Prague the AURICULAR STYLE which forms a link between Mannerism and the Baroque.

Mannlich or **Männlich, Jacob** (*fl.*1625–46). He was the first of a notable family of German goldsmiths working mainly in Augsburg and Troppau. His son **Heinrich I** (*c.*1625–98) became a master in Augsburg in 1658 and made both domestic and ecclesiastical plate. Another member of the family, **Daniel** (1625–1701) settled in Berlin in 1650 and was appointed Court Goldsmith in 1665, being succeeded by his son **Otto** on his death. Heinrich's son **Johann Heinrich** (1660–1718) worked in Augsburg and examples of his work are in the Brunswick Museum and the Grünes Gewolbe in Dresden. His son **Heinrich II** is said to have worked in England for George II. (For their marks *see* p. 894.)

Lit: Augsburger Barock, Exh. Cat., Rathaus, Augsburg 1968.

Mantelpiece The ornamental structure above and around a fireplace, especially the c19 type with shelves which can be draped (called mantelboards or mantelshelves).

Manufacture Royale des Meubles de la Couronne, *see* GOBELINS, MANUFACTURE DES.

Manwaring, Robert (*fl.*1760–70). He was a London cabinet-maker who published several books of designs, especially for chairs: *The Carpenter's Compleat Guide to . . . Gothic Railing*, London 1765; *The Cabinet and Chair-Maker's Real Friend and Companion . . .*, London 1765; *The Chair-Maker's Guide*, London 1766. Chairs have been attributed to him or his workshop by analogy with his published designs, e.g. a picturesque rustic chair in the Victoria & Albert Museum, London; and a chinoiserie chair in the Metropolitan Museum, New York.

Lit: A. Coleridge, *Chippendale Furniture*, London 1968.

Manzana-Pissarro, Georges (1871–1961). French painter, the son of Camille Pissarro, under whom he was trained. He is most notable for such decorative works as paintings on glass and tapestries, often of exotic scenes.

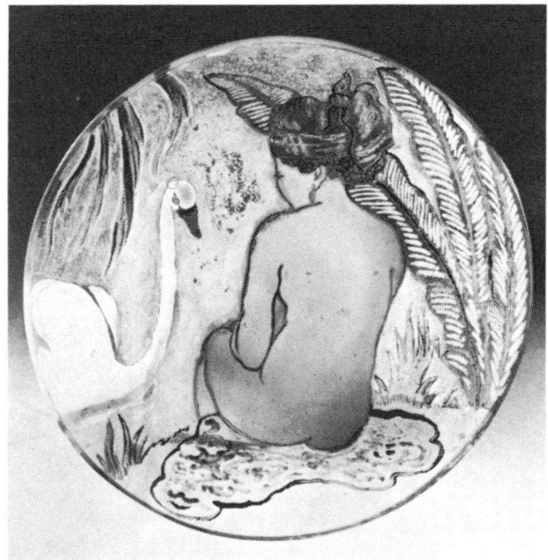

G. Manzana-Pissarro: painted glass plate c.1913 (Musée des Arts Décoratifs, Paris)

Maple A fine, close-grained and fairly hard wood varying in colour from reddish-brown to yellowish-white. It is found in Europe and in the U.S.A., especially in New England. The very decorative Burr Maple is obtained from wood cut near the root to show the pronounced curly marking of the grain. Bird's Eye Maple has dark spots in the lines of the grain. Maple was used for furniture especially in the C18 in Central Europe and in the early C19 in France.

Marbled ware Pottery resembling heavily veined, coloured marble, made either by combining clays of different colours or by covering the surface with slip of two or more colours or by colouring the glaze by the use of different metallic oxides.

Marblehead pottery An art pottery studio at Marblehead, Massachusetts, founded in 1905 as part of Dr Herbert J. Hall's sanatorium, and intended to provide 'quiet manual work' for 'nervously worn out patients', but soon transformed into an independent concern. It produced vases and jars as sober in form as in colour, decorated with incised and painted geometrical patterns, stylized flowers, dragonflies, etc. under speckled matt glazes.

Lit: R. Judson Clark (ed.), *The Arts and Crafts Movement in America, 1876–1916*, Exh. Cat., Art Museum, Princeton University, Art Institute of Chicago, etc., 1972–3.

Marc, André, *see* SÜE, Louis.

Marchand, James, *see* CHELSEA and DERBY PORCELAIN FACTORIES.

Marchand-mercier A *marchand-mercier* belonged to a sub-division of one of the great Parisian guilds and dealt in furniture and works of art of various kinds. He combined the modern roles of antique dealer and interior decorator, and exercised great influence on taste and fashion through his control over the designers and craftsmen he patronized. (The guild regulations forbade *marchands-merciers* from having their own workshops: they had to patronize outside, independent craftsmen.) Such fashions as that of decorating furniture with Sèvres plaques, for instance, was almost certainly due to the *marchands-merciers* and not to the craftsmen, designers or patrons. The leading C18 *marchands-merciers* in Paris were concentrated in the Saint-Honoré quarter, as are many of their present-day counterparts. Among the best known were **Lazare Duvaux,** whose *Livre Journal* of 1748–1758 has been published, **Simon-Philippe Poirier** (d.1785) and his successor **Dominique Daguerre.**

Lit: P. Verlet, 'Le commerce des objets d'art et les marchands merciers à Paris au XVIIIe siècle' in *Annales*, January–March 1958; F. J. B. Watson in *L'Oeil*, Sept. 1967, pp. 12–21.

Marcion, Pierre-Benoit (1769–1840). He was second only to JACOB as an Empire furniture-maker. From 1798 onwards he was making high quality pieces in mahogany richly decorated with gilt bronze mounts. His premises in Paris were called 'Aux Egyptiens'. In 1809 he collaborated with JACOB-DESMALTER and Benoit in refurnishing the Grand Trianon at Versailes for Napoleon. Furniture by him is still at the Grand Trianon. Other pieces are in the Château de Malmaison. After 1815 he found himself in financial difficulties due to his not having obtained payment for work carried out under Napoleon and in 1817 he gave up furniture-making.

Lit: D. Ledoux-Lebard, *Les ébénistes-parisiens (1795–1870)*, Paris 1965.

Marcolini, Count Camillo (1736–1814). He was director of the MEISSEN PORCELAIN FACTORY from 1774 to 1813 when the factory was in steady decline. Despite his innovations, such as *biscuit* figures and imitation Jasper Ware the factory was in debt by 1799. He was eventually dismissed in 1813. Wares produced while he was director have a star between the hilts of the crossed swords of the usual Meissen mark.

Marcotte, Leon (*fl.*1848–*c.*1880). Prominent New York furniture-maker. He was French, began his career as an architect and married the daughter of **Auguste Émile Ringuet Le Prince,** owner of a firm of Parisian furniture-makers (of 9 rue Caumartin) which exhibited at several exhibitions including the Great Exhibition, London, 1851, and exported to the U.S.A. He opened a New York branch of the firm, styled Ringuet Le Prince and Marcotte, in 1849. Ringuet Le Prince retired in 1861 and Marcotte continued in his own name from that date. This concern sold both furniture imported from France and pieces made in its New York workshop. It specialized in Louis XVI style furniture of dark woods with a sparing use of delicately wrought ormolu mounts.

L. Marcotte: sofa, c.1860
(Metropolitan Museum of Art)

Lit: 19th Century America: Furniture and Other Decorative Arts, Exh. Cat., Metropolitan Museum, New York 1970.

Mare, André, *see* SÜE, Louis.

Marieberg pottery Leading Swedish faience factory established by Johann Ludwig Eberhard Ehrenreich (1722–1803) on an island near Stockholm in 1758 producing exuberantly Rococo wares gaily decorated with scrolls and flowers in enamel colours (occasionally underglaze blue but seldom if ever in other high-temperature colours). One of its most appealing products (apparently made nowhere else) is a table centre in the form of a covered vase set on a spiral staircase which a little Chinaman ascends. Designs for tureens, etc. were provided by C. PRECHT 1761–5. A type of veined marbled decoration, usually in black, grey and white but occasionally including red, yellow and other colours, made by mixing oxides with the tin glaze, was peculiar to the factory. Ehrenreich left in 1766 for STRALSUND. Transfer printed decorations were used from 1766 and more

Marieberg faience tureen decorated by Per Akermark, c.1765 (Victoria & Albert Museum)

extensively after 1769 when simpler and more classical forms were adopted. Soft-paste porcelain wares (especially reeded custard cups) similar to those of MENNECY were made 1766–9, a startlingly white opaque glazed hybrid porcelain 1769–77 and hard-paste from 1777. Cream-coloured earthenware was also made. The factory was bought by RÖRSTRAND in 1782 and closed in 1788. (For factory mark *see* p. 885.)

Lit: G. H. Strale, *Mariebergs historia och tillverkningar 1758–1788,* Stockholm 1880; E. Hannover, *Pottery and Porcelain,* London 1924.

Marinot, Maurice (1882–1962). French glassmaker. He began as a painter associated with the Fauves but began to work in glass in 1911 at Troyes. His works are ornamental rather than practical and consist mainly of bowls and flasks, modelled with a feeling for solid sculptural form, either clear or coloured (he had a trick of sandwiching a core of coloured glass between two transparent layers), sometimes enamelled but more often, and more satisfactorily, etched with

M. Marinot: vase of clear crystal glass with impressed decoration, 1934 (Victoria & Albert Museum)

freely drawn figures. He made much decorative use of such 'imperfections' as air bubbles and crackling. Ill health forced him to give up glassmaking in 1937.

Lit: R. J. Charleston in *The Victoria & Albert Museum Bulletin,* Vol. I, no. 3, 1965.

Marks on pottery and porcelain A wide variety of marks – impressed, modelled, painted or printed – have been and still are applied to ceramics for a number of different purposes. Chinese porcelain-makers habitually marked their wares with four or six characters signifying the name of an Emperor and indicating either the period in which the piece was produced, or (just as frequently from the C17 onwards) the style or quality of the earlier ware it was intended to resemble. In Europe some Greek pottery-painters and, more rarely, potters signed their work. Roman makers of red SAMIAN WARE or *terra sigillata* often marked their products by pressing a seal into the unfired clay (hence the latter name). But subsequently no marks appear to have been applied to ceramics in Europe until the C16 when some, generally very fine, pieces of Italian maiolica were inscribed with the name of the painter or, more frequently, with a symbol or monogram the precise significance of which is seldom clear. In the late C16 the MEDICI PORCELAIN FACTORY initiated the practice of marking its products with a factory mark in underglaze blue. Later marks fall into three groups signifying: (1) the factory of origin; (2) the name of the individual painter, modeller or other craftsman in some way responsible for the piece; (3) ownership. (For illustrations of a selection of the more notable factory marks *see* pp. 881–9.)

1. Some C17 tin-glazed-earthenware factories (notably those of DELFT) marked their products with symbols or monograms which were occasionally imitated by rival concerns. In 1680 an unsuccessful attempt was made to register the marks used on red-stoneware teapots made at Delft and it was not until 1764 (when the industry was already in decline) that Delft potters agreed to put registered marks on all their wares. The systematic use of factory marks began in 1724 at MEISSEN where the crossed swords from the Saxon coat-of-arms was applied to nearly all products. Most other notable continental porcelain factories followed suit, each selecting a device of special significance (often taken from the patron's coat of arms) though some adopted marks intentionally similar to that of Meissen. In England the CHELSEA factory adopted first an incised triangle then an anchor for its products; but other English porcelain factories used no regular marks (apart from imitations of those on Meissen and Chelsea) until the 1760s. In 1766 French porcelain manufacturers were legally required to use marks registered with the police, though not all of them did so. The leading German and some French faience factories followed the lead of the porcelain factories and marked their wares. But in England the practice of marking all types of wares seems to have been initiated by J. WEDGWOOD. Marks proliferated in the C19 when the practice of imitating those of contemporary factories declined with the development of copyright laws, but there began, contemporaneously, the practice of forging the marks on old wares of interest to collectors. The factory mark was, and still is, used to protect a manufacturer's market and name from the competition of others producing wares of similar appearance but of lower price and inferior quality.

2. With the exception of the signatures of HAUSMALER (which are like those of any other painters), most of the other marks found on porcelain and faience seem to relate to the craftsmen responsible for making or decorating individual pieces: they are generally cryptic symbols intended only for administrative purposes in the factory (e.g. as a means of discovering a craftsman responsible for faulty work). It is rarely possible to discover their precise significance. The commonest on C18 porcelain figures seem to be those of REPAIRERS. At the SÈVRES PORCELAIN FACTORY, however, painters and gilders normally marked their work with initials or devices.

3. Marks of ownership – apart from painted inscriptions on the more popular types of ware – are comparatively uncommon. They include the 'Château marks' on some Sèvres of the Restauration period and, more notably, the Johanneum inventory marks engraved by wheel on the bases of pieces of Meissen and Oriental porcelain from the Johanneum, Dresden, many of which were sold 1919–20. The AR – Augustus Rex – mark also found on Meissen porcelain appears to indicate that the piece in question was ear-marked for the king before it was fired.

Lit: W. Chaffers, *Marks and Monograms on Pottery and Porcelain*, London 1968 (15th ed); W. B. Honey, *European Ceramic Art*, London 1952.

Marlborough leg English term of uncertain origin for a straight square leg, sometimes tapering and sometimes with a plinth foot, used on furniture from the mid C18 onwards, especially in the U.S.A. The inside edge is sometimes chamfered.

Marot, Daniel (1663–1752). Architect and designer, he was born in Paris but spent most of his life in Holland and England. He published many engraved designs for furniture and interior decoration and created an individual variant of the LOUIS XIV STYLE. His father was the architect **Jean Marot** (*c.*1619–79) who published *L'Architecture française* in two volumes which are generally known as 'le grand Marot' and 'le petit Marot'. His uncle was Pierre GOLLE. Marot is said to have worked in BOULLE's *atelier* before he fled to Holland in 1685 as a Huguenot refugee. He became 'designer general', as it were, to William of Orange and was largely responsible for the interior decoration of the royal palace at Het Loo. He followed William to England in 1694 and was employed at Hampton Court. In so far as Continental Baroque influenced the William and Mary Style it was mainly due to Marot. He returned to Holland in 1698 and died there. His *Oeuvres* were published in 1702, with a second enlarged edition in 1712. He does not appear to have worked as an architect proper until 1715 when he built Schuylenberg House in The Hague.

Lit: M. D. Ozinga, *Daniel Marot*, Amsterdam 1938; H. Honour, *Cabinet Makers and Furniture Designers*, London and New York 1969.

D. Marot: designs for chairs, stools and pelmets, c.1690–1702

Marquand & Co., *see* BALL, TOMPKINS & BLACK.

Marquetry A decorative VENEER applied to the carcase of furniture and composed of shaped pieces of wood or other suitable material (e.g. bone or ivory) forming a mosaic. It may be of a

Marquetry: detail from a writing table by J. F. S. Spindler, c.1767 *(Sanssouci, Potsdam)*

floral, arabesque or other pattern, or a figurative scene. If the pattern is geometrical it is called PARQUETRY. Marquetry was first practised in Germany and the Low Countries. It was introduced from there to France in the early C17 (*see* ÉBÉNISTE) and to England *c.*1675. It should not be confused with INLAY.

Lit: W. A. Lincoln, *The Art and Practice of Marquetry*, London 1971.

Marquise, *see* CHAIR.

Marrow spoon A long-bowled spoon for extracting marrow from a bone, it is normally double-ended either with a normal bowl at one end or with marrow scoops of different widths. Spoons of this type were made from the early C18 onwards.

Marseillemuster A border pattern for plates and dishes used at MEISSEN and consisting of oblong panels framed by raised Rococo scrolls, alternating with dotted trellis-work. It was introduced *c.*1743 by J. J. KÄNDLER.

Marseilles potteries One of the best groups of C18 French faience factories. The earliest of importance was at Saint-Jean-du-Désert, 1679–1733, producing wares barely distinguishable from MOUSTIERS. A potter from this factory, **Joseph Fauchier,** took charge of a factory in Marseilles itself in 1710, making richly decorated plates, statuettes and crucifixes and, with particular success, such large objects as wall fountains boldly modelled with applied figures of *putti* and deities. After his death in 1751 the factory was directed by a nephew of the same name. Other notable factories were those directed by La Veuve PERRIN (active 1748–93), **Louis Leroy** (1749–78), **Joseph-Gaspard Robert** (*c.*1750–93), and **Antonine Bonnefoy** (1762–1815). Their wares, which are difficult to tell apart when unmarked, are modelled in a restrained version of the Rococo style in which the springing curves are softened by a slight provincial burr. They are notable mainly for their very distinctive painted decorations in ENAMEL COLOURS – groups of juicy fish and crustaceans, freshly coloured and loosely bunched sprigs of flowers (drawn from nature and not from prints), little landscapes, seascapes and rustic idylls, and frail spidery chinoiseries derived from PILLEMENT. All are characterized by an air of happy, easy-going Mediterranean informality which distinguishes them from the more rigidly modelled and tightly painted wares of northern faience factories. All the charm vanishes when, after the 1770s, the motifs are imprisoned in regularly shaped frames. No factory mark is known but various initials are found, e.g. 'V.P.' for La Veuve Perrin and 'R' for Robert.

Lit: H. J. Reymond, *Faïences anciennes de Marseille XVII et XVIII siècles*, Berne 1964; E. Fabre, *Die französischen Fayencen des Mittelmeergebietes*, Cologne 1965.

Marseilles faience plate, St-Jean-du-Désert, late C17 (Musée nationale du céramique, Sèvres)

Marsh and Jones A firm of Victorian furniture-makers in Leeds and London. It may have been established (in Leeds) as early as *c.*1760 by an employee of GILLOWS but it did not become prominent until after 1864 when it was bought from Thomas Kendell by **John Marsh** and **Edward Jones.** They worked in the Gothic Revival and other historical styles, often after designs by Bruce TALBERT and others, notably Charles Bevan who was one of the early 'reformers' in furniture design. (A piano designed by Bevan for Marsh & Jones is at Temple Newsam House, Leeds.) In the 1880s and 90s they were making rosewood furniture after designs by W. R. LETHABY. They also adopted the Art Nouveau style and in 1907 Edwin Lutyens was designing for them. Later, they furnished the liner *Saturnia.*

Their furniture is usually labelled with the name of the craftsman as well as that of the firm.

Lit: L. O. J. Boynton in *Journal of the Furniture History Society*, 1967.

Marsh, William (*fl.*1775–1810). He was a prominent Regency cabinet-maker in London and supplied furniture to the Prince of Wales for the Brighton Pavilion and to the Whitbreads for Southill. From 1790 he was in partnership with a certain **Elward** and in 1795 **Thomas Tatham** (1763–1818), the elder brother of Charles Heathcote TATHAM, joined the firm which was known as Elward, Marsh & Tatham, later as Marsh & Tatham and eventually as Tatham & Bailey.

Lit: R. Edwards & M. Jourdain, *Georgian Cabinet-Makers*, London, 1955.

Martelé, *see* GORHAM COMPANY.

Martha Gunn A female version of the TOBY JUG depicting a celebrated C18 Brighton bathing woman.

Martha Washington chair, *see* CHAIR.

Martin, Guillaume (d.1749). One of four brothers who perfected the finest type of European JAPANNING, named *vernis Martin* after them: the other brothers were named **Étienne-Simon** (d.1770), **Julian** (d.1783) and **Robert** (1706–66). Guillaume and Étienne-Simon Martin were granted a monopoly for making imitations of Chinese and Japanese lacquer in relief in 1730 (renewed 1744). But they are best known for their monochrome or gold-dusted *vernis Martin*, a term soon applied to all French lacquer of this type. *Vernis Martin* was developed from a varnish called *cipolin* (containing garlic). It is remarkably lustrous and of a peculiarly fine texture, ranging in colour from pearl grey, lilac, pale green to a strong Prussian blue, sometimes sparkling with gold dust beneath the surface. It was applied in as many as forty coats each of which was polished before the next was added. Panelling, carriages, sedan chairs, commodes, tables, chairs, etc., and a wide range of smaller objects, including fans, snuff-boxes, *etuis*, etc., were decorated with it. The surviving documented works of the Martin brothers include the panelling of the apartments of the Dauphine at Versailles (1749). Smaller objects can rarely be attributed to them rather than to other craftsmen using the same process. Robert's son **Jean-Alexandre** (1739– after 1791) worked for Frederick the Great at Sanssouci and Potsdam and was appointed *vernisseur du roi* there in 1760.

Lit: H. Racinais, *Un Versailles inconnu, les petits appartements des Rois Louis XV et Louis XVI au Château de Versailles*, Paris 1950, pp. 41ff.

Martin, Robert Wallace (1843–1923). He and his brothers were notable English studio potters – **Charles Douglas** (1846–1910), **Walter Frazer** (1859–1912) and **Edwin Bruce** (1860–1915). Robert Wallace Martin was trained at the Lambeth School of Art under John Sparkes and, like his fellow student and life-long friend George TINWORTH, began by working for the DOULTON POTTERY though neither he nor any of his brothers joined the firm. He also trained as a sculptor, under J. B. Philip of the Albert Memorial and under Pugin's assistant at the Houses of Parliament, and this confirmed his taste in pottery for the Neo-Gothic and grotesque. In 1873 he set up a studio for the production of salt-glazed stoneware in Fulham. In 1877 he moved to larger premises at Norwood Green, Southall, Middx. The brothers worked in close collaboration and produced objects of a truly medieval virility,

Martin Brothers: salt-glazed stoneware vase, c.1886 (Victoria & Albert Museum)

never repeating a pattern – jugs influenced by c16 German stone-ware or in the form of grinning human faces, tobacco jars fashioned like owls, grotesque chessmen, etc. From the 1890s painted decorations of flowers and birds show some Art Nouveau influence. The concern closed down in 1914.

Lit: G. A. Godden (ed.), *Jewitt's Ceramic Art of Great Britain 1800–1900*, London 1972; C. R. Beard, *A Catalogue of the Collection of Martinware formed by Mr J. F. Nettlefold together with a short history of the firm . . .*, London 1936.

Maser, John, *see* PENNSYLVANIA DUTCH STYLE.

Mason, Charles James (1791–1856). English potter, he was the son of Miles Mason (d.1822) who ran a factory at Lane Delph, STAFFORDSHIRE, making wares similar to those of NEW HALL. From 1813 he produced at Fenton his patented IRONSTONE CHINA wares, ranging from

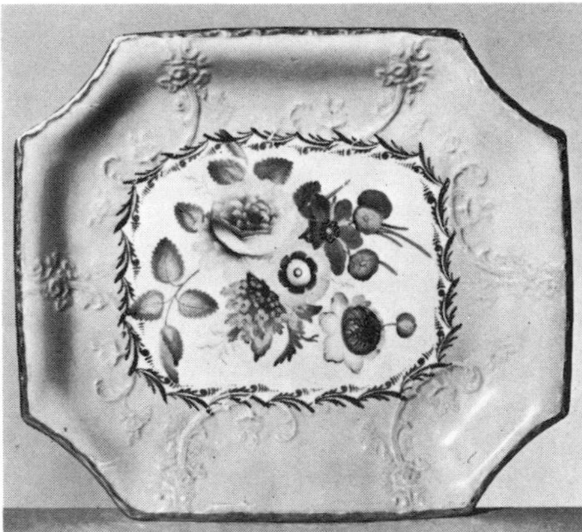

Mason's ironstone: fruit dish, early c19 (Victoria & Albert Museum)

dinner plates and moulded jugs decorated with transfer printing in underglaze blue to large vases and even chimney-pieces, usually decorated with Japanese motifs in very rich bright colours. Until 1829 he was in partnership with his brother **George Miles Mason** (1789–1859) trading as G. M. & C. J. Mason, then as C. J. Mason & Co. The firm failed in 1848. His factory was bought by Francis Morley in 1851. The name 'MASON' or 'MASON'S PATENT IRONSTONE CHINA' or 'MASON'S CAMBRIAN ARGIL', impressed or painted in blue, were used as marks.

Lit: R. Haggar; *The Masons of Lane Delph*, London 1952.

Mass production The making of identical products by machine in very large numbers. The development of mass production methods has been the most important single factor in determining the character of design since the Industrial Revolution, *see* INDUSTRIAL DESIGN. Its techniques call for a rigid plan of manufacture and subdivision of labour. Each aspect of a piece of work has to be specialized but, at the same time, products have to be acceptable to many thousands of people, often with differing social and cultural backgrounds. Making objects in this way marks a complete break with the methods of hand-craftsmanship. Mass production has decisively overthrown the slowly developed traditions of centuries, and subdivision of labour has led directly to the development of the professional Industrial Designer to take over one of the individual craftsman's roles. The industrial designer emerged when production systems reached the fully mechanized and assembly-line stage. For at this point all possibility of modification during production was eliminated and the designer therefore became all-important. He created the model or standard which could be multiplied indefinitely by machine and which would be complete at the end of the production line, without any further manipulation.

In the c19 mass production led to the use of machines to reproduce in large numbers products and decorative motifs that had previously been made by hand, and little effort was made to discover qualities inherent in machine workmanship. Many aestheticians were opposed to the use of the machine and mass production, in spite of the fact that the rapidly developing urban economy could not exist without the backing of industry. The return to rurality and handwork implicit in the thinking of reformers like William MORRIS was foredoomed and at the beginning of the c20 designers and architects (notably Frank Lloyd WRIGHT in his essay *The Art and Craft of the Machine*, 1902) began to come to terms with mass production. In 1907 Theodor Fischer told the newly created DEUTSCHE WERKBUND, 'There is no fixed boundary line between tool and machine . . . It is not mass production and subdivision of labour that is fatal, but the fact that industry has lost sight of its aims of producing work of the highest quality . . .'

Today industrial designers accept the problems of mass production and find in its economic and technical constraints a stimulating challenge. It is also a social challenge, because mass production leads to the paradox of a wealthy community in which many products are standardized. Although mass production has broadened the choices open to the majority it has done so at a price.

Massier, Clément (*c.*1845–1917). French potter, the son of a potter at Vallauris. He had a studio at Golfe-Juan near Cannes where he made wares decorated with lustre glazes.

Masters, G., *see* ELTON, Sir Edmund Harry.

Mathews, Arthur Frank (1860–1945). American painter, architect, interior decorator and furniture designer, the creator of a Californian variant of Art Nouveau. He was trained as an architectural draughtsman and painter in Oakland, California, where his parents had settled in 1867. From 1885 he studied in Paris, exhibiting paintings in the Salon from 1887 to 1889 when he returned to California. In 1890 he became director of the California School of Design and in 1894 married a pupil, Lucia Kleinhaus (1870–1955) with whom he worked in close collaboration for the rest of his life. He began to execute mural decorations and paintings on furniture in the later '90s and after the earthquake of 1906 was mainly occupied in such work for San Francisco houses and public buildings. From 1906 to 1920 he ran 'The Furniture Shop', employing some fifty craftsmen, to carry out whole schemes of interior decoration and also to make and market individual pieces of furniture, tapestries, stained glass windows, picture frames, ornamental boxes, etc., decorated with freshly coloured flowers – especially California poppies – influenced by Japanese art and, despite his expressed disapproval of it, European Art Nouveau. Much of his work is in the Oakland Museum.

Lit: H. L. Jones, *Mathews: Masterpieces of the California Decorative Style*, Exh. Cat., The Oakland Museum, 1972.

Mathsson, Karl Bruno (b.1907). Leading Swedish designer who exploited bentwood for mass-produced furniture in the 1930s, following AALTO. Though less well-known internationally than Aalto, his furniture is equally elegant and lithe.

Matting A mat surface or the production of a mat surface, especially on silver, by means of small dots punched with a matt-tool or small circles punched closely over the surface.

Matusch or **Matouche, Johann** (*fl.*1701–31). He was a cabinet-maker of Bohemian origin working in Ansbach from 1701 onwards. He was appointed the Margrave's *Hofschreinerei-Inspektor* in 1715. He trained two of the most talented German furniture-makers of the day, F. PLITZNER and M. SCHUMACHER who succeeded him as Court cabinet-maker (*Hofebenist*) in 1737. His only fully documented work is the Boulle-type marquetry writing desk which Plitzner began in 1723 and he finished in 1725. But many pieces have been attributed to him, notably some very fine marquetry games-boards.

Lit: H. Kreisel, *Die Kunst des deutschen Möbels*, vol. ii, Munich 1970.

Maucher, Johann Michael (1645–1700). Notable German Baroque ivory carver who specialized in carving very elaborate cups and urns exuberantly decorated with figures of men and monsters in high relief.

Lit: W. Klein, *Die Elfenbeinschmutzer-Familie Maucher* . . . , Gmünd 1933.

Mayer, Elijah He was a Staffordshire potter working at Hanley from *c.*1784 and making fine quality stonewares, notably cream-coloured stoneware and black basaltes, often with engine-turned decorations. From 1820 his firm was known as E. Mayer & Son. Wares are often impressed with the name 'E. Mayer'.

Mayer, Franz Ferdinand (*fl.*1745–70). Notable HAUSMALER working at Pressnitz in Bohemia, probably the head of a small studio, decorating (often defective) pieces of MEISSEN porcelain with pastoral, hunting or genre scenes sometimes copied after engravings. He often decorated the borders of plates with four loose bunches of flowers. Several signed pieces are known (Victoria & Albert Museum) and many others have been attributed to him.

Lit: G. E. Pazaurek, *Deutsche Fayence- und Porzellan-Hausmaler*, Leipzig 1925.

Mayhew, John, *see* INCE, William.

Mazarin blue or **Mazareen blue** A dark blue enamel ground colour used on CHELSEA 1758–69 and DERBY porcelain in imitation of Sèvres *gros bleu* – a full dark uneven colour applied under the glaze and taken up by it. It is an English term and appears in contemporary advertisements for Chelsea wares. The connection with Cardinal Mazarin is obscure. In France the term *bleu Mazarin* refers to a blue (sometimes mottled) glaze found on CH'ING dynasty porcelain.

Mazarine A flat pierced plate, fitting into a larger dish so that the liquid could be strained from boiled fish placed on it.

Mazer or **Mazer bowl** A drinking vessel or large bowl made of a close-grained wood, especially spotted maple but sometimes walnut or beech, usually mounted in silver with a rim and a base. Vessels of this type were very popular in the Middle Ages, mainly in Northern Europe, and survived in use until the early C16. The mounts were sometimes richly ornamented.

Mazzucotelli, Alessandro (1865–1938). Italian master of ART NOUVEAU wrought iron. Born in Lodi, he began by studying architecture but poverty obliged him to become an iron-smith like his father. He set up his own workshop in Milan in 1895 and was well established by 1902 when he took part in founding the Istituto Superiore di Arti Decorative at Monza. In the same year he won a diploma at the Turin exhibition, the first of the many such prizes he was awarded. A visit to Paris, London and the Low Countries in 1903 brought him into closer contact with N. European Art Nouveau which subsequently influenced his style. He made grilles, balconies, banisters and lighting fixtures of great complexity with much floral work and sometimes nightmarish butterflies and dragonflies. Much of his best work was for buildings by the architect Giuseppe Sommaruga, notably for the masterpiece of the *floreale* style (the Italianate version of Art Nouveau), Palazzo Castiglioni, Milan (1901–3) for which QUARTI made the furniture. After the war he worked in a style analogous to ART DECO. Many of his pupils set up their own workshops under his guidance.

Lit: R. Bussaglia, *Mazzucotelli: The Italian art nouveau artist of Wrought Iron*, Milan 1971.

Meander An ornamental pattern of winding lines (e.g., VITRUVIAN SCROLL) or crossing rectangular lines (e.g., GREEK KEY or FRET).

Mearne bindings A type of English bookbinding, in a sumptuous Restoration style, named after **Samuel Mearne** (d.1683), Royal Binder to Charles II. Mearne was trained as a binder under Jeremy Arnold but became a publisher, printer and bookseller as well as bookbinder and it seems likely that he did no more than supervise his bindery. None of the elaborate bindings named after him has in fact been identified as his work.

Measey, Michael, *see* GREENE, John.

Mechlin lace The town of Mechlin was reputedly the best centre for the production of Flemish lace in the C17 but no certain examples survive. The term is usually applied to a type of pillow lace made from the 1720s, often to attractive Rococo patterns which are outlined in a flat thread heavier than that used for the rest of the fabric. The pattern and ground – generally an hexagonal mesh – were made together. This type of lace became very popular and was much copied elsewhere.

Lit: P. G. Trendell, *Victoria & Albert Museum, Guide to the Collection of Lace*, London 1930; B. Palliser, *History of Lace*, rev. M. Jourdain & A. Dryden, London 1902.

Medallion Literally a large medal, the term is also used to describe prominent circular, oval or elliptical motifs in ornament, especially those framing figurative subjects. In descriptions of

Persian carpets the term is used for bold central motifs of whatever shape.

Medici porcelain factory The first European factory to produce soft-paste porcelain of which examples have survived. Bernardo BUONTALENTI, architect, sculptor and designer, tried to make porcelain in Florence before 1568, but the Medici factory, founded by the Grand Duke Francesco I de 'Medici, is known to have produced soft-paste porcelain only between 1575 and 1587. This was a soft translucent paste composed of white clay from Vicenza, white sand, powdered rock crystal, calcined lead and tin, coated with a creamy thick lead glaze which was applied after pieces had been painted and biscuit-fired. In substance it resembles opaque glass rather than true porcelain. It is of a greyish or yellowish white generally decorated in blue (sometimes bright, otherwise rather grey), sometimes with manganese outlines, though one piece with green and yellow as well is recorded. Occasionally pieces went awry in the firing and few are without some slight flaws. The shapes of vessels were derived from MAIOLICA or silver. A few are decorated with classical grotesques, as on the maiolica of URBINO, but most are painted with trees, animals, birds and human figures of unmistakably oriental origin and are among the very first examples of chinoiserie. Only fifty-nine pieces of Medici porcelain survive, the majority marked with the six balls of the Medici coat of arms or, more usually, a drawing of the dome of Florence Cathedral, in underglaze blue. (For factory mark *see* p. 885.)

Medici porcelain bottle, 1575–87 (Louvre)

Lit: G. Liverani, *Catalogo delle porcellane dei Medici*, Faenza 1936; A. Lane, *Italian Porcelain*, London 1954.

Meeks, Joseph, & Sons A leading firm of New York furniture-makers active from 1797 to 1868. In 1833 they issued an advertisement illustrating 41 pieces of furniture, mostly in a heavy but generally simplified version of the English Regency style – pier tables with dumpy columns and lion-paw feet, dining tables with central supports, etc. – some of them adapted from the pattern book of G. SMITH. In the 1840s they were making pieces in the Gothic Revival style, including a set of walnut chairs for the White House in Washington (1846–7). Later they turned to the Neo-Rococo and produced laminated rosewood furniture similar to that of G. BELTER. From 1835 they had an agency in New Orleans and they are said to have supplied furniture to all parts of the U.S.A.

Lit: J. & L. W. Pearce in *Antiques* LXXXV, (1964), pp. 414–20 and XC, (1966), pp. 69–73.

Mege, Antoine, *see* APREY PORCELAIN FACTORY. He also worked at the MOUSTIERS POTTERY.

Mei p'ing (lit. '*prunus branch*'). One of the classic Chinese vase shapes, of baluster form with broad shoulders and a very narrow neck, named after and intended to hold a branch of flowering prunus. *Illustrated next page.*

Meigh pottery A firm established *c.*1780 by **Job Meigh** who took over the Old Hall factory at Hanley, Staffordshire, which had previously produced white salt-glazed wares. He later went into partnership with his sons **Job** and **Charles.** In 1822 the younger Job was awarded a medal by the Society of Arts for a new type of glaze for the interior of cheap cooking vessels to replace the ordinary lead glaze which was liable to dissolve on contact with vinegar and other substances and could poison food. From 1843 the

(Left) Mei-p'ing shape porcelain vase with mirror black glaze, Ch'ing Dynasty, late c17 (Percival David Foundation of Chinese Art, London)

C. Meigh, stoneware 'Minster Jug', 1842 (Victoria & Albert Museum)

factory belonged to Charles Meigh (*fl.*1842–51) who was among the first to exploit the popular taste for the Gothic Revival, registering in 1842 his 'Minster jug' of stoneware – surrounded with reliefs of figures in Gothic niches – which proved very popular. But he was no less successful with Neo-Renaissance pieces and was awarded a medal by the Society of Arts for his Bacchic mug of 1847. At the Great Exhibition of 1851 he showed a large number of products in porcelain, Parian ware and stoneware and won a medal for a pair of 1 m. high vases of stoneware gilt and painted with views of the Crystal Palace and portraits of the Queen and Prince Consort (Victoria & Albert Museum, London). *(Illustrated next column.)*

Meillonas pottery A French faience factory founded in 1759 by **Hugues de Marron,** *seigneur* de Meillonas, in his château near Bourg-en-Bresse. It began by producing wares decorated in high-temperature colours in the Rococo style (some painted by Protais Pidoux who had formerly worked at APREY) but later returned to imitations of MOUSTIERS. The founder was guillotined in 1794 but the factory survived, producing useful wares, until 1830. No factory marks were used.

Lit: E. Milliet, *Notice sur les faïences artistiques de Meillonas,* Bourg-en-Bresse 1877.

Meissen porcelain factory The first and for half a century the best in Europe. It set a high standard which was emulated everywhere, even in China. Founded in 1710 as the Royal Saxon Porcelain Manufacture by Augustus the Strong, Elector of Saxony and King of Poland, at Meissen, near

Dresden, its first products were in the director BÖTTGER's fine and extremely hard red stoneware. In form they followed Baroque silver and were decorated with relief ornament (acanthus leaves, lion masks, etc.) with engraved designs, or painting in lacquer or (not very satisfactorily)

Meissen vase, Böttger's red stoneware (Porzellansammlung, Dresden)

enamel colours. But some, perhaps the most attractive, pieces are either polished or cut in facets (the German term is *gemuschelt*) on a glass-engraver's wheel – a process which accentuates the hard-stone like beauty of the material. Stoneware was gradually superseded by the white hard-paste porcelain of which Böttger had discovered the secret in 1708 though he did not announce it until 1709. The first white wares – put on the market in 1713 – were generally similar in form and decoration to the stoneware but also included vases with pierced openwork, teapots and cups with sprigs of prunus in relief, statuettes of dwarfs (after prints by Callot) and saints, and copies of a Chinese *blanc de Chine* figure of Kuan-yin (also executed in stoneware) and of grimacing oriental pagods. The Böttger period is of importance mainly as one of experiment and technical development.

From an artistic point of view the factory's great period began in 1720 with the appointment of J. G. HEROLD as chief painter. He perfected the enamelling process, evolving a much larger palette than had previously been available for the decoration of ceramics, and initiated the production of wares with plain surfaces to be decorated with paintings. For some 15 years the factory was dominated by and owed its success to the artists in the painting studio who decorated its wares with an astonishing variety of chinoiseries, landscapes with feathery trees, minutely rendered port scenes, and a whole fantastic flora of brightly painted exotics. Statuettes were also made, in greater quantities than before, notably some handsome Baroque figures of saints and some animals and birds by J. G. KIRCHNER. But it was not until after the appointment of J. J. KÄNDLER as chief modeller in 1733 that the work of the modellers began to assume greater importance than that of the painters. By the late 1730s Kändler seems to have obtained virtual control of the artistic policy of the factory. With several assistants, notably Johann Friedrich EBERLEIN and Peter REINICKE, he produced a multitude of large and small statuettes of men and animals and birds. He was mainly responsible for the design of the famous swan dinner service made (1737–41) for the factory's director Count Brühl, every plate of which is decorated in relief with swans and reeds and rushes and other watery motifs, while the tureens are composed of a riot of curves from which swans, dolphins, nereids and mermaids wantonly emerge. But his influ-

Meissen porcelain stork with fish, modelled by J. J. Kändler, 1732 (Porzellansammlung, Dresden)

Meissen porcelain tankard, with silver mounts, decorated by J. G. Herold, 1726 (Kunstgewerbemuseum, Berlin)

Meissen porcelain teapot, modelled by J. J. Kändler, 1739 (Irwin Untermyer Collection, New York)

ence, if not his hand, may also be traced in many vases and table-wares more sculptural than those previously produced at the factory. During his ascendency the style of painted decorations underwent a change as the rather tight *Indianische Blumen* derived from oriental porcelain gave way to the more freely rendered naturalistic flowers (*Deutsche Blumen*) more suitable for the decoration of irregular surfaces.

Meissen porcelain group by J. J. Kändler, 1739–43 (Porzellansammlung, Dresden)

The factory's great period coincided with the height of the Rococo which found a perfect expression in the crisp fragility of Meissen porcelain. Table-wares and ornaments were exported to all parts of Europe and even beyond: the factory had agents in Paris, Amsterdam and Warsaw besides 32 German cities. And its products were very widely imitated. But the occupation of Dresden by Frederick the Great in 1756 slowed down production and eventually brought its era of great prosperity to an end. Taste was changing, the Rococo going out of fashion (Winckelmann's great history of ancient art, published in Leipzig in 1764, includes a sharp attack on the frivolity of contemporary porcelain figures). A complete re-organization of the factory began in 1763; next year **C. W. E. Dietrich** (1712–74), professor of painting at the Dresden Academy, was made artistic director. Herold left in 1765 and a French sculptor V.-M. ACIER was appointed to work as a chief modeller beside Kändler. Vain attempts were made to rival SÈVRES by producing pieces in the early 'Louis XVI' style. Curves and scrolls were ironed out of

Meissen dish with Deutsche Blumen decoration, 1745–50 (Victoria & Albert Museum)

table-wares, statuettes began to lose their vitality and often declined into simpering coyness. The French style was more successfully assimilated under the direction of Count C. MARCOLINI from 1774 with **Johann Elias Zeissig** known as **Schönau** (b.1737), who had studied in Paris under the influence of Greuze, as artistic director. Products included table-wares painted with landscapes, portraits or sentimental genre scenes (on one service each piece was painted with an incident from Goethe's *Sorrows of Werther*) within neat frames, and biscuit figures of allegories and classical deities. But the factory survived the Napoleonic wars with difficulty. The Rococo style was revived 1833–70 when innumerable vapid shepherdesses covered with lace-work and applied flowers were produced. In the 1870s some amusing statuettes of contemporary figures were made – abundantly clad bathing belles, soldiers in boots and spiked helmets. The ART NOUVEAU style was flirted with from the late 1890s: notable products included the Crocus breakfast service of 1896 designed by Julius Konrad Hentschel (1872–1907) who also made some lively figures; delicate plates in white and gold by H. VAN DE VELDE (1904); animals and birds from models by Clemens Paul Walther (1876–1933) and others; figures of winter-sportswomen by Alfred Otto König (b.1871) and of dancers and musicians by P. SCHEURICH. Copies of C18 figures and other wares from the original models, have been in constant production from the C19 to the present day. Since 1945 the factory has been styled VEB Staatliche Porzellan-Manufacktur Meissen, but it continues to use the famous crossed-swords mark in underglaze blue first adopted in 1724. No mark has been more frequently copied by other factories. Other marks found on Meissen porcelain include impressed numerals which are mould numbers (according to an inventory begun in 1763); initials in underglaze blue, probably of painters; incised symbols probably of REPAIRERS; the letters AR in monogram in underglaze blue for Augustus Rex, apparently indicating pieces earmarked for the royal collection; numbers and letters engraved by wheel on pieces once in the royal collection at the Johanneum (partly dispersed 1919–20). (For factory marks *see* p. 885.)

Lit: E. Zimmermann, *Meissner Porzellan*, Leipzig 1926; C. Albiker, *Die Meissner Porzellantiere im 18 Jahrhundert*, Berlin 1959; S. Ducret, *German Porcelain and Faience*, New York 1962; R. Rückert, *Meissner Porzellan 1710–1820*, Munich 1966; G. Reinheckel in *Keramos* 41/2 (1968); O. Walcha, *Meissner Porzellan*, Güterloh 1975.

Meissonnier, Juste-Aurèle (*c.*1693–1750). He was one of the leading Rococo designers and, with PINEAU, the creator of the *genre pittoresque*, the second and more fanciful and anti-classical phase of the Rococo in France. He was also an architect, painter and silversmith. Very little of his work survives, apart from engraved designs (dated between 1723 and 1735). As a personality he was said to be *'présomptueux et mégalomane'* and his difficult character as much as the extreme nature of his version of the Rococo probably accounts for the fact that he was less patronized by Frenchmen than by foreigners. Nevertheless, he seems to have prospered for he had a valuable collection of fine furniture and pictures.

He was born in Turin where his father, of Provençal origin, was a goldsmith and sculptor, probably employed by the Court under the direction of JUVARRA. He left Turin for Paris in 1720, perhaps with Juvarra who went to Lisbon, London and Paris in 1719–20. He established himself in Paris very quickly, succeeding BERAIN in 1725 as *architecte-dessinateur de la Chambre et*

J.-A. Meissonnier: design for a candlestick, 1728

du Cabinet du Roi. He practised as a silversmith until *c.*1735 but very few of his works survive. Only one of his buildings still stands: a house in Bayonne, now the Chambre de Commerce. None of the interiors he designed for patrons in Poland and Portugal survives. His fame therefore rests on the series of 120 engraved designs for architecture, interior decoration, furniture, silver and bronze. A bold asymmetry is the key-note of all these designs. The best are for silver and bronze, notably candelabra composed of richly curving scrolls, scattered with flowers, which look in the engravings as if they had been twisted out of puff-pastry by a cook of genius. They are always strongly three-dimensional in conception so that it was necessary to show a candlestick, for example, from three different points of view in his engraved designs in order to make its form comprehensible. One of his designs for a candlestick was followed by CLAUDE DUVIVIER (1734, Musée des Arts Décoratifs, Paris); another was used at MEISSEN for the famous Swan Service. His furniture designs suggest that he was too much inclined to regard wood as a substitute for metal, viscous and malleable, so that he twisted the supports of tables and chairs into thick, treacly curves. His designs for interiors are sometimes overcharged. They inspired few direct imitations but provided the point of departure for many Rococo artists and craftsmen who reworked them with an addition of light and frivolous elegance which made them more widely popular. Though the taste for Rococo was beginning to wane by 1745 Meissonier was blamed, in his obituaries, for having abandoned symmetry and led the craze for novelty.

Lit: F. Kimball, *The Creation of the Rococo*, Philadelphia 1943; D. Nyberg (ed.), *Oeuvre de Juste-Aurèle Meissonier*, New York 1969.

Mekeren, Jan van (*c.*1690–*c.*1735). Leading Dutch furniture-maker, he specialized in cabinets and other pieces with floral and still-life marquetry panels, more realistic and painterly than those of his great French contemporary A. C. BOULLE. The designs of his marquetry derive from Dutch still-life painting and are executed with such technical virtuosity that they sometimes have an almost *trompe l'oeil* effect.

Trompe l'oeil marquetry cabinet, attributed to J. van Mekeren, c.1700 (Rijksmuseum, Amsterdam)

Melchior, Johann Peter (1742–1825). He was a German sculptor best known as a porcelain modeller at Höchst (1767–79), Frankenthal (1779–93) and Nymphenburg (1797–1822). At Nymphenburg he was joint *Modellmeister* with Auliczek. He began in a style similar to Falconet but most of his works are much more sentimental, especially his numerous figures of children. He is best known for his pastoral figures made at Höchst, but he also excelled in relief portraits (the most notable being that of Goethe, who was a personal friend) which were reproduced in biscuit. His later works are Neo-Classical in style.

Lit: F. H. Hofmann, *Johann Peter Melchior 1742–1825*, Munich 1921; O. M. Oppenheim, *Johann Peter Melchior als Modellmeister in Höchst*, Frankfurt 1957; E. Kramer in *Keramos* 56 (1972), pp. 3–68.

Meles carpets, *see* Turkish carpets.

Melort, A., *see* stipple engraving.

Mengaroni, Ferruccio, *see* Pesaro potteries.

Mennecy porcelain factory Founded 1734 in Paris, it was transferred to Mennecy in 1748 and to Bourg-la-Reine in 1773. After 1753 it was much restricted by laws imposed to protect the Vincennes factory (e.g., gilding was prohibited). Only soft-paste porcelain was made, of fine quality ranging in colour from dark ivory to milky white, brilliantly painted in enamel colours amongst which a purple rose is prominent. Inspiration came first from Saint Cloud, then from Vincennes. Tea services, coffee-pots, custard cups, small vases, knife handles and little boxes were the most usual products, elegantly modelled in a restrained Rococo style, painted at first with Kakiemon style motifs, later with naturalistic flowers. They are sometimes adorned with rather prickly flowers in relief. Statuettes include a very handsome white River God from a model by Nicolas-François Gauron, young men in open-necked shirts and some elegant posturing *Commedia dell'Arte* actors. It seems doubtful if any porcelain was made after *c.*1780 when the factory turned to producing cream-coloured earthenware in imitation of Wedgwood. The factory closed in 1806. (For factory mark *see* p. 885.)

Lit: G. Fontaine, *La céramique française*, Paris 1946; W. B. Honey, *French Porcelain of the 18th Century*, London 1950.

Mennecy soft-paste porcelain spittoon, c.1750 (Musée des Arts Décoratifs, Paris)

Mennicken, Jan Emens (*fl.*1566–94). The most distinguished of a family of potters working at

J. E. Mennicken: stoneware jug marked 'I.E.' (for Jan Emens), Raeren, late c16 (Landesmuseum, Düsseldorf)

RAEREN making handsome large stoneware jugs decorated with reliefs of classical (later religious) subjects. In signing pieces he frequently dropped his surname, inscribing himself simply *Jan Emens*; other members of his family, presumably close relatives, **Peter** and **Wilhelm** or **Wynant** did the same. **Baldem Mennicken** (*fl.*1575–84) and his son **Jan Baldems** were also makers of fine stoneware. **Johann Mennicken** is known to have moved *c.*1595 from Raeren to Westerwald where two other Raeren potters of the same surname, **Leonhard** and **Wilhelm**, are known to have been working *c.*1615.

Menuisier A French joiner, as distinct from a cabinet-maker or ÉBÉNISTE. The *menuisier* specialized in small (*menus*) objects, such as chairs and other pieces constructed with plain wood and carved, *ébénistes* in veneered furniture. Although a *maître* in the furniture-makers' guild (*corporation des menuisiers-ébénistes*) was allowed to practise both techniques, this very rarely happened and the distinction between *menuisier* and *ébéniste*, originally begun in the mid C17, was maintained down to the Revolution when the guilds were abolished. Similar specialization did not occur in other countries. To what extent the *menuisier* was in fact the 'maker' of the chairs, etc. he produced is uncertain. An C18 French chair was usually the work of four different craftsmen, each with his own establishment – the *menuisier* who made the frame, the *sculpteur* who carved the ornaments on it, the *doreur* who gilded it and the *tapissier* who upholstered it.

Mercury gilding A process of applying gilt to metals used from the C17 onwards and later used for ceramics as well. It is still used occasionally. An amalgam of gold and mercury is applied to the object which is then fired in a low-temperature oven so that the mercury is driven off, leaving a thin film of gold. The process is usually repeated several times until the layer of gold is thick enough to be burnished to a hard brilliance. A variation of the process, known as Matt Gilding, was invented towards the end of the C18, probably by GOUTHIÈRE.

The process can only be practised under severely restricted conditions today because of the harmful effects on the craftsmen. The mercurous oxide fumes driven off in the process are highly noxious and in the C18 very many workers and craftsmen perished from 'fossy jaw', a disease caused by mercury gilding. Many large prizes were offered for the invention of a process which would avoid or mitigate this, but none was discovered. RAVRIO left 3,000 francs to the person who could find some way of protecting gilding craftsmen from the harmful vapours.

Mercury twist stem The stem of a drinking glass with one or more unusually large AIR TWISTS, made in mid-C18 England.

Merese knop A sharp-edged, button-like knop between the bowl and the base of a stemless drinking glass, otherwise between the stem and the base.

Meriden Britannia Company A factory at Meriden, Connecticut, founded by **H. C. Wilcox** in 1852 to make Britannia metal wares but producing electroplated wares by 1855 and, later, solid silver. It gradually absorbed other firms of silversmiths and electroplate manufacturers (notably those of the ROGERS brothers) and from 1898 has traded under the name of the **International Silver Company** which is now one of the largest manufacturers of silver wares in the world.

Meridienne, *see* CANAPÉ.

Merrymen plates Tin-glazed earthenware plates decorated in sets of six, each one painted with a line from a jingle: 'What is a mery man/Let him doe all what he kan/To entertayne his gess/With wyne and mery jest/But if his wife doth frown/All meryment goos downe'. Sets are dated between 1684 and 1742. They were probably made in London and the earliest may be the work of an immigrant Dutch potter. Of somewhat similar sets of plates, one (dated 1697) is painted with a six-line grace, another (of 1711), known as the servant series, with lines referring to the plates themselves and ending: 'My grate fault is I can't be mended'.

Lit: F. H. Garner, *English Delftware*, London 1948.

Meshed carpets, *see* PERSIAN CARPETS.

Meso-American pottery Utilitarian pottery seems to have been made in Mexico from *c.*1500 B.C. Early dishes and storage jars were sometimes decorated with incised ornament or slip. Modelled figurines (usually female) were also produced from an early stage, probably for use in fertility rites. With the rise of higher cultures (Zapotec, Mixtec, Olmec, etc.) a wide variety of ceramic forms and styles of decoration was evolved. Fine wares were produced around Teotihuacán before the C7 A.D., notably vessels decorated after firing with stylized patterns in coloured stucco in shades of blue, green and pink and applied like cloisonné. The Totonac of the Gulf region made very lively figures of dancers with laughing faces (rare in the art of Meso-America), also a variety of vessels decorated with animal or geometrical patterns in white, brown or black slip on an orange body. Mixtec wares are distinguished for the quality of their painted decorations which are similar to those on Mixtec codices. Thin and well fired pottery was made by the Aztecs, usually painted with ritual motifs including skulls, ranging from biconical drinking cups and oval dishes to huge braziers and life-sized human figures. Maya wares are also adorned with religious symbols and scenes, outlined in black and brightly coloured red and occasionally turquoise on a buff ground. The Maya also made moulded whistle figures sometimes in the form of ball-game players. Their later wares (*c.*1100–1200) include two distinctive types, one known as 'fine orange', a high-fired ware with a lustrous vitrified surface, and the so-called 'plumbate' ware with a dull glaze sometimes mottled with orange and olive green. Of the later Meso-American wares, those made *c.*1300–1500 at Coclé in Panama are outstanding: they include a diversity of dishes, bottles, jars and other vessels covered in a whitish slip on which stylized representations of crocodiles, snakes, crabs, birds, etc. are boldly painted in black, red, purple, blue and green. Effigy jars were also made here in the form of animals, fish or humans.

Lit: G. H. S. Bushnell, *Ancient Arts of the Americas*, London 1965.

Methey (or **Metthey**), **André** (1871–1920). French studio potter. He began as a sculptor but on receiving Garnier's *Traité de céramique* as a prize for drawing he decided to turn to pottery. Despite great physical and financial difficulties (similar to those of PALISSY long before), he built his own kiln. At the *Salon des indépendants* in 1901 he exhibited a collection of ceramics decorated in the manner of the Fauve painters with whom he was friendly. He then persuaded a number of prominent contemporary painters – Renoir, Bonnard, Denis, Valtat, Derain, Rouault, Vlaminck, Van Dongen – to paint on his plates which he exhibited at the *Salon d'Automne* 1907. Thereafter he painted his ceramics himself, first in lead glaze and then, from 1908, in enamel. Forms are simple, colours bright, designs strong, distantly inspired by early Italian maiolica, Isnik, Persian and C18 French rustic pottery. He worked at Asnieres from 1903 until his death from tuberculosis.

A. Methey: stoneware vase, c.*1910 (Musée nationale de Céramique, Sèvres)*

Lit: H. Clouzot, *André Methey 1871–1920*, Paris 1922.

Metropolitan slipware A class of slipware which was probably made in London where many pieces have been found. They are of red earthenware rather roughly decorated with stylized flowers in trailed slip with dates (1638–59) and inscriptions sometimes of a Puritan cast, and include bowls, mugs, jugs and chamber-pots one of which (Hanley Museum) bears the legend: 'Earth I am et tes most tru disdan me not for so are you'.

Lit: B. Rackham and H. Read, *English Pottery*, London 1924.

Metzsch or **Metsch, Johann Friedrich** (d.1766). German HAUSMALER first recorded in 1731 when he purchased unpainted porcelain from the MEISSEN factory. He worked in Bayreuth, where he seems to have run a small studio from 1735, painting porcelain cups and bowls, occasionally with continuous landscapes running right round the exterior, more usually baskets of flowers within scrolled borders, chinoiseries or mythological subjects. The figure scenes are generally in red, purple or black monochrome surrounded by frames of polychrome flowers. After 1751 he was employed at the FÜRSTENBERG PORCELAIN FACTORY, but it is not known what he did there.

Lit: G. E. Pazaurek, *Deutsche Fayence- und Porzellan-Hausmaler*, Leipzig 1925.

Meublant, *see* CHAIR, *Siège courant.*

Meure, Peter, *see* ARCHAMBO, Pcter.

Meyer, Christoffel Jansz He was a C17 Dutch glass engraver, working at The Hague and specializing in allegorical subjects on tall glasses usually with much hatching.

Meyer, Friedrich Elias (1723–85). German sculptor employed as a modeller under KÄNDLER at MEISSEN, then as chief modeller at the BERLIN PORCELAIN FACTORY until his death. Little is known of his work at Meissen though several statuettes are attributed to him. In Berlin he was responsible for the design of table-wares as well as statuettes, the latter including some very handsome rather large Chinamen and many lithe mythologies and allegorical figures. He was assisted from 1766 to 1772 by his brother **Wilhelm Christian** (1726–86).

Lit: M. Sauerlandt, *Deutsche Porzellanfiguren*, Cologne 1923.

Mezza-maiolica The name formerly given to lead-glazed and other Italian pottery which preceded the true tin-glazed maiolica. (The distinction is in fact a false one since tin was present in the white glaze of many earlier wares.)

Mezzarisa, Francesco di Antonio (d.*c.*1575). The owner of a notable FAENZA maiolica factory active from 1527 and carried on after his death until 1587. He began by making wares in the ISTORIATO style; but in 1540 he employed an assistant to make 'white ware' (i.e. BIANCO DI FAENZA) and by 1545 he was exporting such products to Genoa. His workshop was one of the first to exploit the fashion for *bianco di Faenza* decorated in a version of the COMPENDIARIO style rather more florid (and much less successful) than that of V. CALAMELLI.

Lit: C. Liverani in *The Connoisseur* CXL (1957), pp. 160–63.

Midband American term for a moulded band slightly below the centre of a silver tankard or cup, both for strengthening and decoration.

Mies van der Rohe, Ludwig (1886–1969). German-born architect and designer, the last and greatest exponent of the International Modern Style in architecture and the creator of some of the best pieces of modern furniture. He succeeded GROPIUS as director of the BAUHAUS in 1936 but emigrated to the U.S.A. in 1938 and became

Mies van der Rohe: cantilever tubular steel chair, 1926 (Victoria & Albert Museum)

professor at the Illinois Institute of Technology, Chicago. His important contributions to furniture design date from the 1920s. In 1926 he designed a tubular steel cantilever chair, and although this was not the first – Mart STAM had introduced the resilient cantilever principle in his chair design of 1924 – it is the simplest and purest statement of this design concept and was to be very influential (*see* BREUER). In 1930 he produced an equally elegant armchair version known as the 'Brno chair', made of chromium-plated steel bars. But his most famous piece of furniture is the 'Barcelona chair' designed for the German pavilion at the 1929 International Exhibition in Barcelona. It is constructed of delicately curved chromium-plated steel strips with leather straps supporting two rectangular black leather cushions. With the same precision of detail and immaculate finish, poise and elegance as his great buildings, it has rightly become a modern classic and is still in commercial production (by Knoll Associates). However, it demands careful hand-finishing to produce the desired 'machine-made' look and – despite its apparent modernity, it is basically a Roman currule chair or medieval X-chair turned sideways. In 1947 he designed a one-piece chair for manufacture in a single operation but this has never been made.

Lit: P. Johnson, *Mies van der Rohe*, New York 1947; L. Hilbersheimer, *Mies van der Rohe*, Chicago 1956; A. Drexler, *Mies van der Rohe*, Milan 1960.

Mies van der Rohe: Barcelona chair and stool, 1929 (Musée des Arts Décoratifs, Paris)

Migeon, Pierre II (1701–58). The most important member of a dynasty of French furniture-makers beginning with his father **Pierre I** (born *c.*1670). Pierre II took over the family business in 1739. He does not appear to have become a *maître*, probably because he was a Calvinist and could not join the Corporation without special dispensation. He specialized in small pieces and ingenious convertible furniture, often using 'mirror veneers' in plain kingwood or tulipwood. Occasionally he used lacquer and was among the first *ébénistes* to decorate his furniture with veneers of mahogany. From 1740 he worked extensively for the Court, especially for Mme de Pompadour of whom he became a favourite. According to d'Argenson she gave him a pension of three thousand francs for making her a particularly pretty *chaise-percée* (*see* CLOSE STOOL). He was also a furniture-dealer and stocked work by such makers as CRIAEARD, LACROIX and DUBOIS. Notable examples of his own furniture are in the Louvre and Musée des Arts Décoratifs in Paris. His son **Pierre III** (1733–75) became a *maître* in 1761 but seems to have been more of a dealer than a furniture-maker. His not very individual style hovers between the Rococo and the Neo-classical.

Lit: F. J. B. Watson, *The Wrightsman Collection: Furniture*, New York 1966.

Mihrab A prayer niche, usually with a pointed arch, facing Mecca in a mosque. A conventionalized representation of it is used as the central motif of the design on PRAYER RUGS; and it is also used in Islamic tile decorations.

Milan potteries There were three notable C18 faience factories in Milan. That run by **Felice Clerici** (1745–88) produced wares decorated in blue, red and gold on a very fine white ground, usually inspired by Japanese (IMARI) and Chinese porcelain. **Pasquale Rubati**, a painter formerly employed by Clerici, opened a rival concern in 1756 (continued by his widow and son until *c.*1830) imitating MEISSEN patterns often with paintings in reserved panels on a bright blue ground. A factory in the suburb of Santa Cristina *c.*1775–82 is known by a few pieces painted with chinoiseries or flowers. (For factory mark *see* p. 885.)

Lit: C. Baroni, *Saggio sulle antiche ceramiche di Milano*, Milan 1931; *Maioliche di Lodi, Milano e Pavia*, Exh. Cat., Museo Poldi-Pezzoli, Milan 1964.

Milchglas Opaque glass made with oxide of tin for opacity. It is white and translucent, like milk, and was first made in Venice in the C15 contemporaneously with the introduction of MAIOLICA glaze. Attempts were made at Venice and perhaps elsewhere at this date to develop *milchglas* as a substitute for porcelain. At Potsdam and Basdorf in the early and mid C18 *milchglas* was produced as an imitation porcelain. It was called *porzellanglas* at Potsdam. And similar wares were produced in Bohemia and Holland and at the Bristol glasshouses.

Milde, Arij de (*fl.*1680–1706). Owner of the best red STONEWARE pottery in Delft, specializing in teapots very delicately decorated in relief with sprigs of prunus and other Chinese motifs reminiscent of YI-HSING red stoneware. He was associated with Samuel van EENHORN.

Lit: C. H. J. de Jonge, *Delft Ceramics*, New York 1970.

Mildner glass A type of German decorated glass, usually slightly conical cylindrical tumblers, with one or two inset medallions on the sides. The medallions are engraved with gold decoration on the outside and silver decoration on the inside on red backgrounds. The outside medallions usually depict religious subjects or portraits, those inside usually bear inscriptions. The medallions are fitted into the sides of the glass from which pieces of identical shape have been cut. The name derives from **Johann Mildner** (1764–1808) of Gutenbrunn, Austria, who used this type of decoration and usually signed his work.

Lit: G. Pazaurek, *Gläser der Empire- und Biedermeierzeit*, Leipzig 1923; I. Schlosser, *Das Alte Glas*, Brunswick 1965.

Milès, *see* SOLON, Marc-Louis-Emanuel.

Millefiore glass, or **Mosaic glass** or *vetri murrini*. Glass decorated within the body with brightly coloured discs composed of sections of *canna vitrea*.

Millefiore glass, bowl, Alexandria, c2–1 B.C. *(Kunstgewerbemuseum, Zurich)*

This technique, used by the Romans, was rediscovered at Murano in C16 and has remained popular ever since, especially for decorative paperweights in C19 France.

Mille-fleurs tapestries A large group of tapestries depicting exquisitely dressed figures against backgrounds of numerous freshly coloured flowering plants and occasional small animals and birds. Little is known of their origin except that they were woven in late-C15 and early-C16 France: they have been claimed for the TOURNAI TAPESTRY FACTORIES but are probably the work of itinerant weavers in the Loire region. The most beautiful, and the most famous, is the *Dame au Licorne* series (Musée de Cluny, Paris), an allegory of uncertain significance depicting a finely dressed lady, a white unicorn (symbol of chastity) and a very tame lion with numerous very lively and endearing rabbits, dogs, foxes and other creatures scampering among the myriad flowers star-scattered over each panel. None of the others has quite the enigmatic fascination of this work, but many are of fine quality, e.g., the *Noble Pastoral* with fashionable courtiers spinning and sheep-shearing (Louvre), *Courtly Life* (Musée de Cluny, Paris), *The Departure for the Hunt* (Art Institute, Chicago), *The Hunt of the Unicorn* (Metropolitan Museum, New York), and a few religious subjects notably *Angels Carrying the Instruments of the Passion* (Musée des Tapisseries, Angers).

Lit: R.-A. Weigert, *French Tapestry*, London 1962.

Mina'i ware A type of overglaze-painted ISLAMIC POTTERY made in Seljuk, Iran, in the C12 and early C13, the finest at **Rayy** before the Mongol invasion of 1224 though it was also made at **Kashan** and **Sava.** *Mina'i* means enamel and the ware so called is decorated with blue, green, brown, black, dull red, white and gold painted over an opaque white or sometimes turquoise glaze and fixed by a second firing. The decorations often depict Court scenes or Persian legends or hunting scenes, similar to those depicted by Persian miniature painters some of whom may perhaps have decorated *mina'i* wares. A less sophisticated, slightly later but related ware is called *lavjardina* after its cobalt blue glaze. It was made in the Sultanabad area in the late C13 and C14 and the decorations are usually non-figurative.

Ming The nationalistic dynasty which ruled China from 1368 until 1644, succeeding the Mongol YÜAN dynasty. Despite the most rigid isolationism in politics, a few artistic techniques were introduced from the West (notably *cloisonné* ENAMEL) and in the later C15 the foundations were laid for the ever increasing trade in CHINESE EXPORT PORCELAIN and lacquer made expressly for the European market. The general tendency in the arts was towards increasing elaboration and this led eventually to an almost Victorian fussiness in metalwork, textiles and lacquer inlaid with mother-of-pearl. Porcelain ousted pottery in Mandarin houses. The finest dates from the earlier part of the period and includes some very beautiful and refined blue-and-white wares. The later years are marked by the introduction of additional colours, the use of enamel over the glaze and, again, effects of increased richness and elaboration. (*See:* HSÜAN-TÊ PORCELAIN, CH'ÊNG-HUA PORCELAIN, CHIA-CH'ING PORCELAIN, WAN LI PORCELAIN). In contrast, the furniture is of an aloof simplicity and sobriety.

Lit: A. M. Joseph, *Ming Porcelain*, London 1971.

Ming Dynasty rosewood bed (Philadelphia Museum of Art)

Ming Dynasty porcelain jar decorated in tou-ts'ai enamels, Ch'eng-hua period, 1465–87 (Percival David Foundation of Chinese Art, London)

Minghetti, Angelo, *see* BOLOGNA POTTERIES.

Minneteppich German term for a C15 tapestry representing a scene of courtly love.

Mino potteries A group of Japanese potteries, situated N. of Nagaya, founded by potters from SETO in the late C16 or early C17 and from the start making TEA CEREMONY WARES. They were the source of the wares confusingly known as **Yellow Seto** (vessels with incised plant motifs covered with a pale buff or yellow glaze splashed with green), **Black Seto** (mainly tea-bowls with an intense black glossy glaze), **Shino** (rather crudely potted pieces with a reddish body covered with thick crackled grey or white slip and boldly painted with a few strokes generally suggesting leaves, in brown or blue) and **Oribe** (the most colourful of such wares, with bizarre decorations in brown and glazes of several colours on a salmon-pink ground, named after a tea-master Oribe-no-Sho Shigenari, 1544–1615). It was once supposed that these four types of ware were made in succession, but more than one type appears to have been made contemporaneously in the same kilns. The best wares date from the beginning: but handsome pottery – especially bottles with brown or black glazes, often miscalled **Old Seto** ware – was made in the later C17 and C18. The production of blue-and-white porcelain was introduced in the early C19, and the district now provides the bulk of porcelain exported from Japan.

Lit: S. Jenyns, *Japanese Pottery*, London 1971.

Minton's pottery and porcelain factory Founded at Stoke-on-Trent, Staffordshire, in 1796 by **Thomas Minton** (1765–1836), the reputed inventor of the WILLOW PATTERN. Began by making earthenware, with soft-paste porcelain 1798 *c.*1811 and hard-paste porcelain from 1821. Early wares are decorated either with patterns like those of DERBY or with simple sprigs of flowers but after the appointment of a French potter, **Léon Arnoux** (1816–1902), as artistic director, they became much richer. Works in a very wide range of historical styles and techniques were produced – HENRI DEUX WARE, Italian C16 maiolica, Louis XVI style SÈVRES – scrupulously marked and intended to show the

Minton blue-printed porcelain Passion Flower Plate, 1850 (Victoria & Albert Museum)

factory's proficiency rather than to deceive. Other products included MAJOLICA, PÂTE-SUR-PÂTE vases and plaques by M. L. SOLON, elaborate

Minton porcelain table-centre with figures in Parian ware, exhibited at the Great Exhibition 1851

Minton vase with 'Watteau' figures, c.1862 (Victoria & Albert Museum)

PARIAN WARE figures and table-centres, a few ceramic nightmares (monstrous fountains 30 ft high and a complete staircase), and vast quantities of richly decorated, rather self-consciously 'artistic' table wares. Pierre Émile Jeannest (1813–57) worked as a modeller from *c.*1845 onwards, and from 1854 the chief modeller was CARRIER-BELLEUSE who later became director at SÈVRES. The ART NOUVEAU style was successfully adopted in the 1890s. The factory still flourishes, producing porcelain of high quality. (For factory mark *see* p. 885.)

Lit: G. A. Godden, *Minton Pottery and Porcelain of the First Period*, London 1968.

Miotti, Vincenzo (*fl.*1711–47). He was a Murano glassworker who specialized in enamelling opaque white glass (i.e. MILCHGLAS), often in imitation of porcelain. Dated examples survive from 1731–47. The Miotti glasshouse (called **Al Gesu**) began in the early C17 but flourished especially under Vincenzo Miotti and his sons in the C18.

Lit: A. Gasparetto, *Il vetro di Murano*, Venice 1958.

Mirror black A lustrous black glaze applied to Chinese porcelain, sometimes with the addition of gilding, from the K'ANG-HSI period onwards: it is known in China as *wu chin*. It is to be distinguished from the black ground colour used on *famille noire* porcelain.

Mirrors, *see* LOOKING-GLASSES.

Miseroni family One of the most notable groups of carvers and engravers of precious and semi-precious hard-stones of the late C16 to C17. They were of Milanese origin but worked mainly in northern Europe, especially in Prague for the Imperial Court. The eldest was **Girolamo** (b.*c.*1520–30) and his brother **Gasparo** who worked for Cosimo I de'Medici in Florence. Three sons of Girolamo were distinguished craftsmen – **Giulio** (1559–93) who worked in Spain from 1582, **Ottavio** (d.1624) who worked at Prague for Rudolf II from 1588 and was appointed precious stone carver to the Court, and **Giovanni Ambrogio** who also worked for Rudolf II from 1598. Ottavio's son **Dionysio** (d.1661), who was employed by the Imperial Court from 1623, was responsible for some of the finest hard-stone carvings now in the Kunsthistorisches Museum in Vienna, including an oil vessel carved out of an emerald 10 cm high and the large 115 cm-high rock crystal pyramid made for the Emperor Ferdinand III in 1653. Dionysio was appointed official hard-stone carver to the Imperial Court and custodian of the treasures. His son **Ferdinand Eusebius** (d.1684) inherited these posts. A portrait group by K. Skreta (Rudolphinum, Prague) shows members of the family with some of their works.

Lit: H. Klapsia in *Jahrbuch der Kunsthistorisches Sammlungen in Wien*, N.F.XIII (1944).

Mishima, *see* KOREAN POTTERY AND PORCELAIN.

Mission furniture Very simple, generally oak, furniture made in the U.S. especially by G. STICKLEY and E. HUBBARD in the first decade of the C20, inspired by and somewhat similar to that of the ARTS AND CRAFTS movement in England. The term is said to derive from the functionalist beliefs of the designers who declared that furniture has a mission – to be used. But it may also be associated with the simple architecture of the early Franciscan mission stations in California.

Mitre cutting A type of CUT GLASS decoration executed with a V-shaped grinding wheel at an angle of about 60° to the surface.

Mocha pottery A type of earthenware made to resemble Mocha stone (moss agate) – a milky-coloured stone with moss-like markings in green and reddish-brown. First produced in England in the 1780s and made throughout the C19 also in France and the U.S. mainly for taverns and humble homes. The wares were decorated with coloured bands of specially prepared slip and the effects of moss were obtained by letting fall on the wet pottery drops of 'mocha tea' (an infusion of tobacco juice in stale urine and turpentine) which instantly ramified into moss, fern, tree- or feather-like shapes.

Modes The fancy openwork stitches between the main elements of the pattern in a piece of bobbin or needlepoint LACE, also called fillings or *jours*.

Modillion A small bracket or console, especially one of the type used to support the upper member of a Corinthian or Composite cornice.

Mogensen, Børge (b.1914). Danish furniture designer, a pupil and faithful follower of Kaare KLINT. His work is always based on meticulous function studies and often has a pleasantly nautical trimness. It combines functionalism with handicraft quality. He thinks 'furniture should become more beautiful with use, like well-worn sports equipment.' His best known work to date is the demountable and very adaptable 'BB' cabinet made to meet the storage needs of a small apartment.

Mogul, *see* MUGHAL.

Mohn, Samuel (1761–1815). German porcelain and glass painter born near Merseburg, working at Weissenfels, Halle (1802), Berlin (1803 and 1806), Leipzig and Stettin (1804) and Dresden (from 1809). He began as a HAUSMALER painting silhouette portraits on a white or pink ground of cups and saucers, usually of BERLIN porcelain. From 1806 he worked mainly on glass, painting drinking glasses with views of towns (notably Dresden), landscapes, etc. in transparent enamels. He was assisted by his son **Gottlob Samuel** (1789–1825) who began by working in the same style and painting delicate bunches of naturalistic flowers on glass beakers, but went in 1811 to Vienna where he was much employed, by the Emperor and Imperial family, painting glass window panels. (He gave up painting glass vessels in 1820.) Gottlob Samuel Mohn's most notable works are stained glass portraits with Neo-Gothic architectural surrounds, executed for the Neo-Gothic Franzensburg at Laxenburg (an Imperial summer residence) near Vienna, where he spent his last years.

Lit: G. E. Pazaurek, *Gläser der Empire- und Biedermeierzeit*, Leipzig 1923; F. Novotny (ed.), *Romantische Glasmalerei in Laxenburg*, Vienna 1962.

S. Mohn: enamel painted glass, c.*1811–12 (Victoria & Albert Museum)*

Moiré Textiles in which a watered or rippled effect is produced by pressing certain warp rib fabrics (usually heavily ribbed taffetas) in such a way as to flatten parts of the ribs and leave the rest in relief so that the flattened and unflattened parts reflect the light differently.

Moiré wallpaper A wallpaper painted or printed in imitation of MOIRÉ silk.

Mokubei, Aoki (1767–1833). He was the most famous Japanese ceramic artist of his day and his work was extremely highly valued. He began as a founder but after reading a Chinese work on ceramics, the *T'ao-hsuo of Chu Yen*, he turned in 1801 to making pottery in Kyoto. By 1807 he had a pottery in Kanazawa employing a hundred workers and producing imitation Chinese wares. In 1809 he returned to Kyoto where he worked for the rest of his life. His Chinese-style wares include celadon and enamelled porcelain but also pottery, notably tea ceremony wares. Mokubei was also a painter.

Mokume Japanese term (literally: wood aspect) for lacquer or metalwork with the appearance of wood graining.

Mola, Gaspare (1567–1640). North Italian metal-worker – goldsmith, medallist, die-cutter and maker of arms and armour – born at Coldrè near Como and trained in Milan. He worked in Florence and Modena before settling in Rome. In 1625 he was appointed engraver at the Papal Mint. His surviving works, all in a late Mannerist style, include a sword in the Musée de l'Armée, Paris, a silver shield and helmet in the Museo Nazionale, Florence, and a very handsome plaque of silver-gilt inlaid with red jasper (Cini Collection, Venice) made shortly after 1601 to celebrate the institution of the Gregorian calendar. Though latterly known mainly as a medallist he appears to have been engaged in goldsmiths' work until his death. He was also an art dealer.

Lit: Z. Giunta di Roccagiovanni in *Antichità Viva*, January, 1963.

Molitor, Bernard (d.1833). Of German origin, he settled in Paris in 1773 with his brother **Michel** (1734–1810) and became one of the best Directoire and Empire furniture-makers. He launched himself in Paris by advertising a secret remedy for furniture bugs and also a new type of footwarmer, called a *chauffrette à la Comtesse*, in the form of a pile of books, suitable for use in church or in the theatre. He became a *maître* in 1787 and received several royal commissions. After the Revolution he was employed by the Napoleonic regime, though not very widely: and although his best work dates from this period it does not seem to have been greatly appreciated at the time. He seldom stamped his work and authentic pieces are difficult to identify. Though he was perhaps influenced by WEISWEILER his best work is more typically Empire in style, e.g., his chairs with griffin heads in the Musée Marmottan, Paris.

Lit: D. Ledoux-Lebard, *Les ébénistes-parisiens (1795–1870)*, Paris 1965.

Mombaers, Corneille, *see* BRUSSELS POTTERY & PORCELAIN FACTORIES.

Monier, J.-B., *see* ÉTIOLLES PORCELAIN FACTORY.

Monnoyer, Jean-Baptiste (1635–92). French painter who published two volumes of floral ornaments for the use of decorative artists: *Livre de Fleurs Propre Pour Peintres et Brodeurs* with naturalistic flowers arranged in garlands; and *Livre de Plusieurs Corbeilles de Fleurs* with them placed in baskets. Their influence is apparent in many late-C17 French embroideries.

Monopod or **Monopodium** A classical (Roman) type of chair or table support revived by Neo-Classical furniture designers. It is in the form of an animal's head and body with a single leg and foot.

Monstrance A vessel in which the Host may be displayed, either on an altar or in processions. It is usually made of silver or gold and often embellished with precious stones, enamels, etc. From the Baroque period onwards it has been customary to surround the receptacle for the Host with a sunburst.

Montauban potteries Several faience factories were active in Montauban in the C18, producing wares similar to those of other southern French potteries of the same time, e.g., MOUSTIERS. The most notable were those established by **David Lestrade** in 1761 and **Arnaud Lapierre** in 1770: the former closed in 1811, the latter in 1820. Examples are almost impossible to identify with certainty. No factory mark is known though one piece is recorded as being inscribed 'Montauban en Quercy 1799'.

Lit: E. Forestié, *Les anciennes faïences de Montauban, Ardus, etc.*, Montauban, rev. edn., 1929.

Monteith A wine-glass cooler in the form of a bowl, generally of silver or glass, with a notched rim which could hold the feet of wine glasses while their bowls were suspended in the water which it contained. It is first recorded in 1683 by Anthony à Wood who said that it was named after a Scotsman called Monteith who wore a cloak with its bottom scalloped.

Montelupo potteries A group of potteries established between Florence and Pisa in the C14 in close association with the FLORENCE POTTERIES and making handsome maiolica. From the C17 they specialized in peasant wares splashily decorated in vivid colours (yellow ochre predominating) with animals, swaggering soldiers, etc. The town is still the centre of a rustic pottery industry. (For factory mark see p. 885.)

Montelupo maiolica dish, c.1625 (Victoria & Albert Museum)

Lit: G. Cora, *Storia della maiolica di Firenze e del contado, secoli XIVe XV*, Florence 1973; *Ceramiche antiche di Montelupo*, Exh. Cat., Villa Guiccardini, Sesto Fiorentino 1973.

Montpellier potteries A faience factory established by **Pierre Estevé** in 1590 (continued from 1596 by his son **Jean** in partnership with **Pierre Ducoin**) appears to have produced handsome BIANCO DI FAENZA drug jars. In the early C17 other factories in the town were making drug jars attractively decorated with flowers and fruit for two local hospitals. By the C18 several faience factories were active, the most notable being that of **Jacques Olivier** which was styled a *Manufacture royale* from 1725, but their products are unmarked and difficult to distinguish from those of other S. French potteries e.g. MOUSTIERS and MARSEILLES. Manganese purple predominates in the colouring of wares attributed to Montpellier. The production of faience continued into the C19.

Lit: J. Thuile, *La céramique à Montpellier au XVIe et XVIIe siècles*, Paris 1943; J. Thuile in *Cahiers de la céramique* 32 (1963), pp. 232–51; E. Fabre in *Keramos* 25 (1964), pp. 39–61.

Monvaërni workshop (late C15). The name formerly given to a number of artists who were mainly responsible for reviving the art of enamelling in LIMOGES in the late C15. About forty examples of their work are known (Musée des Arts Décoratifs and Louvre, Paris, and elsewhere). They are of PAINTED ENAMEL, and usually derived from prints by SCHÖNGAUER, Dürer and others (sometimes elements from several prints being combined on the same piece) and rather primitive in comparison with the works of such later masters as PENICAUD, LIMOSIN and REYMOND. There is no evidence that they come from a single workshop.

Lit: E. Rupin, *L'Oeuvre de Limoges*, Paris 1890; P. Verdier, *The Walters Art Gallery: Catalogue of the Painted Enamels of the Renaissance*, Baltimore 1967.

Mooleyser, Willem (*fl.*1666–97). Notable Dutch glass engraver working in Rotterdam. He signed several diamond-engraved drinking glasses finely decorated with flowers, figure subjects and inscriptions, one of which (Victoria & Albert

Museum, London) commemorates the coronation of William and Mary as sovereigns of England.

Lit: F. W. Hudig in *Oud Holland* XLIII (1926), p. 221; H. E. van Gelder, *Glas en ceramiek*, Utrecht 1955.

Moore, Bernard, *see* FLAMBÉ GLAZE.

Moore, James (d.1726). He was the leading English furniture-maker of his day together with John GUMLEY with whom he was in partnership from 1714. They succeeded Gerrit JENSEN as royal cabinet-makers in 1715. Gumley was probably an *entrepreneur* rather than a craftsman or designer. Moore specialized in richly carved and gilt gesso pieces and he supplied high quality furniture of this palatial type, sometimes to designs by William KENT, to many of the great houses of his time, e.g., Kensington Palace, Cannons and Blenheim. He is first heard of in 1708 and by 1714 he was furnishing Blenheim Palace for Sarah, Duchess of Marlborough, who appointed him Clerk of the Works in 1716 in succession to Vanbrugh and Hawksmoor. He usually incised his name on his gilt gesso pieces.

Lit: R. Edwards and M. Jourdain, *Georgian Cabinet Makers*, London 1955; H. Honour, *Cabinet Makers & Furniture Designers*, London and New York 1969.

Moore, John Chandler (*fl.*1832–51). New York silversmith who set up his own workshop in 1839 making wares mainly for BALL, TOMPKINS & BLACK. He specialized in rather elaborate Neo-Rococo pieces made as presentation plate. His son **Edward** took over the workshop in 1851, worked exclusively for TIFFANY and in 1868 was absorbed by Tiffany & Co.

Lit: *19th Century America: Furniture and Other Decorative Arts*, Exh. Cat., Metropolitan Museum, New York 1970.

Moore, Thomas (*fl.*1756–78). English carpet manufacturer, first mentioned in 1756 when he won a prize from the Royal Society of Arts for a hand-knotted carpet. His factory, in Chiswell Street, Moorfields, London, specialized in making carpets of very high quality, considered by contemporaries to be rather expensive. Some are said to have been designed on Persian patterns but all those now known were executed to designs by Robert ADAM (Syon House, Middx., 1769; Osterley Park, Middx., 1775 and 1778; Saltram House, Devon; Harewood House, Yorks., etc.). The colours are brilliant, the designs Neo-Classical with much use of palmettes, Greek frets, garlands, etc., echoing without exactly reproducing the patterns of the ceilings below which they were placed.

Lit: C. E. C. Tattersall and S. Reed, *A History of British Carpets*, Leigh-on-Sea 1966.

Moorfields carpet factory, *see* MOORE, Thomas.

Moquette A textile woven in the same manner as VELVET (with cut or uncut pile) in coarse wool and linen materials, usually for upholstery or carpeting. It was made from the Middle Ages onwards in many parts of Europe, notably the Low Countries. The term covers both BRUSSELS CARPET and WILTON CARPET.

Mordants Substances applied to fabrics in order to bite or hold a DYE which would not otherwise be fast. The action is chemical and mordants were usually acidic or basic, e.g., tannin, alum. The mordant and dye forms a solid complex, known as a LAKE, which is insoluble and thus fixes the dye. Different mordants will produce different-coloured lakes with the same dye. In the Middle Ages the commonest mordants were aluminium sulphate, potassium or ammonium alum. The preparation of pure alum was important since the admixture of any iron salts produced a darker shade. The chief source of alum in Europe was at Tolfa, Italy. In the C16 a solution of pewter in *acqua fortis* (nitric acid) was introduced and become popular with the discovery by the Kuffler brothers that it turned red cochineal dye a bright scarlet. The Kufflers founded a company to commercialize their discovery in *c.*1635 at Bow in England and at Leiden and near Arnhem in Holland. By 1670 it was in use at the GOBELINS factory in France. In the C19 lead acetate, iron acetate and aluminium acetate were introduced as mordants.

Moreen A cheap imitation in wool or in wool and cotton of *moiré*, much used for curtains and upholstery in the C18.

Morel-Ladeuil, Léonard, *see* ELKINGTON, George Richard.

Morelli, Alessio, *see* GREENE, John.

Morgan, William De, *see* DE MORGAN, William.

Morley, James, *see* NOTTINGHAM POTTERIES.

Morocco Originally a goatskin leather from Morocco but later the term often signifies imitations made in sheepskin or lambskin. Morocco was frequently used in bookbinding from the early C17 onwards, at first usually coloured brown or green, later red, black or blue. By the C17 red Morocco had largely superseded brown calf in bookbinding.

Morratxa, *see* ALMORRATXA.

Morris, George Anthony, *see* BONNIN AND MORRIS PORCELAIN FACTORY.

Morris, Joshua (*fl.*1720–30). English tapestry weaver and the proprietor of a workshop in Soho, London, which produced *c.*1720–30 some very appealing silk and wool tapestries depicting huge Rococo vases overflowing with full-blown naturalistic flowers, after designs by the French flower-painter, **Adrien de Clermont.** He also produced some chinoiserie hangings and commissioned Hogarth to make a tapestry design which provoked a lawsuit.

Lit: H. C. Mariller, *English Tapestries of the Eighteenth Century*, London 1930.

Morris, William (1834–96). English designer, craftsman, poet and political (socialist) theorist, the leading figure in late Victorian decorative arts. After a good middle-class education (Marlborough and Oxford) he began as an architect in the office of G. E. Street where he met Philip WEBB, but took up painting, 1856. Attempts to furnish the house he shared with BURNE-JONES in London (1857–9) and The Red House which Webb built for him (1860) revealed that 'all the minor arts were in a state of complete degradation', as he later wrote, 'and accordingly in 1861 with the conceited courage of a young man I set myself to reforming all that and started a sort of firm for producing decorative articles'. This firm was **Morris, Marshall, Faulkner & Co.** which proved an immediate financial success, moved from modest to large workshops in London, was reorganized as **Morris & Co.** in 1875 and moved out to Merton Abbey in 1881. It survived until 1940. He began with embroideries (which he sometimes executed himself), then turned to wallpapers (1862), stained glass, printed and woven textiles, carpets, rugs, tapestries and furniture. The wallpapers were printed by Jeffrey & Co. and the earliest designs for textiles by various firms, but he established a workshop at Hammersmith for hand-knotted carpets in 1880: at Merton Abbey he set up looms for tapestries and woven textiles in 1881 and produced printed textiles from 1883. His final venture was the **Kelmscot Press** founded in 1890 for the production of exquisitely printed books. In each field he mastered the technique of production, studying such matters as the use of vegetable dyes, before proceeding to design. With a genius for flat pattern, a rare understanding of natural forms – the curl of a leaf, the relationship between a flower and its stalk – and an inexhaustible fecundity of imagination, he evolved

W. Morris: trellis pattern wallpaper, 1862 (Whitworth Art Gallery, Manchester)

numerous floral and foliage patterns which seem none the less natural for being carefully balanced and closely integrated. After his first essays with lightly coloured airy designs in the 1860s he gradually adopted the much richer, denser style of his maturity. On papers and fabrics and the backgrounds of tapestries (designed with Burne-Jones) dark paeonies, roses, pimpernels and fritillaries of a midsummer luxuriance are intertwined with branches of willow and tendrils of honeysuckle. He was inspired to some extent by C16 and C17 fabrics, just as he turned to oriental models for his carpet designs, but he impressed the stamp of his forceful personality on everything he touched, with the result that his works are never aridly imitative of natural forms

W. Morris: Compton wallpaper, 1896 (Whitworth Gallery of Art, Manchester)

or of historical styles. He designed no furniture apart from a few pieces for his own use, though his influence may be felt in that designed for Morris & Co. by Webb and George JACK. His influence also marks the pottery of William DE MORGAN.

In much of his theory he was a prophet of the C20, rather like Ruskin to whom he was indebted. Preaching the gospel of art for the masses, he asked, 'What business have we with art at all unless all can share it?' It was largely due to his teaching that greater care was given to the design of ordinary houses and their contents. But his hostility to machinery combined with the belief that 'real art' can only be made 'by the people and for the people as a happiness for the maker and user' led him to an untenable position. The beautiful handmade products of his firm were far too expensive for ordinary people and inevitably went to satisfy 'the swinish luxury of the rich'. To resolve the conflict he retreated into poetic dreams of a future in which machinery would be abandoned and the medieval guild system restored. To this unreal haven he was followed by the members of the ARTS AND CRAFTS movement. But the essentials of his message were taken up on the Continent, notably by VAN DE VELDE through whom he exerted a vital influence on the early development of C20 INDUSTRIAL DESIGN.

Lit: Morris and Company 1861–1940, Exh. Cat., Arts Council, London 1961; P. Thompson, *The Work of William Morris*, London 1967; A. C. Sewter, *The Stained Glass of William Morris*, New Haven and London 1974.

Morse The metal clasp for fastening a COPE at the neck, often richly wrought and jewelled.

Morse ivory Walrus horn, used in North Europe as a medium for small decorative and devotional carvings. It is similar to ivory in texture and colour.

Mortar A vessel in which ingredients can be pounded with a pestle, hence it is usually cup-shaped and of a hard material such as marble or bronze or bell-metal. Mortars were in common use throughout Europe until the C18 – notably by chemists and apothecaries.

Mortimer & Hunt, *see* STORR, Paul.

Mortise and tenon joint A means of joining two pieces of wood by a tenon or projection (usually rectangular) carved out of the end of one to fit exactly into the mortise or cavity hollowed out of the other. It has been used since the C16.

Mortlake tapestry factory The most important in England, founded in 1619 and staffed with Flemish weavers. The first products were a set of nine panels representing *The Story of Venus and Vulcan*, 1620–22 after C16 designs. In 1623 Prince (later King) Charles I acquired for the factory RAPHAEL's cartoons for *The Acts of the Apostles* from which numerous copies were woven, with borders designed by the artistic director **Francis Cleyn** (d.1658). Other sets produced at this period included two sets of *Months* and *The Story of Hero and Leander*. In quality these tapestries rival those woven in France and Flanders at the same period. But standards began to decline as Royal patronage slackened in the years immediately before the Civil War. Under the Protectorate a set of *The Triumph of Caesar* based on Mantegna's paintings (now at Hampton Court) was begun. The factory continued to produce tapestries after the pre-war cartoons during the Restoration period, adding one new set of Italianate *Playing Children*. These works are of poorer quality than those woven before the Civil War and are characterized by their very simple borders. In the 1670s the weavers dispersed, some joining the SOHO factory, others, notably Francis Poyntz and Stephen Demag, working on their own. However, the Mortlake mark – a white shield bearing a red cross – continued in use until the factory finally closed in 1703.

Lit: H. C. Mariller, *English Tapestries of the Eighteenth Century*, London 1930; H. Göbel, *Wandteppiche*, Leipzig 1923–34.

Mosaic bindings Bookbindings with polychrome decoration either painted, inlaid or, more usually, onlaid. The onlay technique, by which very thinly pared leathers of different colours are laid on top of the leather binding, was used with sumptuous effect by such French binders as PADELOUP and LE MONNIER. With onlaid panels of citron-yellow leather or bright green or red leathers, Baroque book-binders obtained exuberant effects which contrast with the delicacy and intricacy of the contemporary LACE BINDINGS.

Mosaic glass, *see* MILLEFIORE GLASS.

Mosäik German name for a type of enamelled SCALE-PATTERN decoration applied to porcelain from the mid C18 at MEISSEN, BERLIN, etc., and imitated at WORCESTER in England.

Mosan enamels and metalwork The first great school of West European enamel painters flourished in the Meuse valley in the C12. They used the CHAMPLEVÉ technique derived from Byzantium, probably as a result of the Crusades. The

Mosan enamel panel from the Alton Towers triptych, C12 (Victoria & Albert Museum)

main centres of production were Liège and Huy, the main artists GODEFROID OF HUY and NICOLAS OF VERDUN, the main patrons Abbot Suger of S. Denis and Abbot Wibald of Stavelot who gave Mosan enamels to the Abbey of Solignac, near Limoges, in 1134, and a portable altar to his own abbey in 1165 (now in the Musée des Beaux Arts, Brussels). Objects ranged in size from small discs to a large ambo and included reliquaries, caskets, portable altars, etc. The favoured colour scheme was of blues and yellowish-greens with a great deal of white. Compositions tend to be simplified into decorative patterns of colour, but the figures are often very expressive, more so than those on BYZANTINE or LIMOGES enamels. Sometimes Mosan enamels are combined with figure sculpture of the type for which Mosan craftsmen were famous, e.g., a crucifix base of 1170–80 in the Musée de Ville, Saint Omer. The Mosan style of enamel painting was imitated at Troyes and elsewhere and inspired the Limoges school.

The Meuse valley was also a notable centre for the production of plain bronze liturgical and domestic objects in the C12 – crucifixes, aquamaniles, candlesticks, etc. The outstanding masterpiece is the font made by **Rainer of Huy** 1107–18 (St Barthélemy, Liège). Smaller objects are usually very similar to those produced contemporaneously in the Rhine valley, so much so that it is seldom possible to ascertain their origin.

Lit: S. Collon-Gevaert *et al., Art Roman dans la Vallée de la Meuse*, Brussels 1962; G. Swarzenski, *Monuments of Romanesque Art*, London n.d.; *Rhein und Maas Kunst und Kultur 800–1400*, Exh. Cat., Cologne and Brussels 1972; M.-M. Gauthier, *Émaux du moyen âge occidental*, Fribourg 1972.

Mosbach pottery A faience factory in Baden founded under the protection of the Elector Palatine by **Pierre Berthevin** (from MARIEBERG), run by J. S. F. TÄNNICH (1774–81) and by **Johann Georg Friedrich List** from the DURLACH POTTERY (1781–7). Products included the usual household wares, the earlier in the style of STRASBOURG, the later in that of Durlach. In the last years of the C18 the factory abandoned faience in favour of cream-coloured earthenware which seems to have been the staple product until it closed in 1836. (For factory mark *see* p. 885.)

Lit: K. Hüseler, *Deutsche Fayencen*, Stuttgart 1956; *Mosbacher Fayencen 1770–1836*, Exh. Cat., Reiss Museum, Mannheim 1971.

Moscow porcelain, *see* GARDNER'S PORCELAIN FACTORY.

Moser, Kolo (Koloman) (1868–1918). Austrian Art Nouveau painter and designer, he was a founder of the Vienna SECESSION (1897) and, with Joseph HOFFMANN, of the WIENER WERKSTÄTTE (1903). He was trained at the Vienna Akademie (1886–92) and at the Kunstgewerbeschule (1892–5) where he became a professor in 1899. Important mainly as a painter and book illustrator, he also designed jewellery, glass, textiles and furniture. His textiles, with interlocking patterns of foliage, birds, etc., are similar to those of MACKMURDO. His furniture is rectilinear in form, not unlike that of Hoffmann, e.g., sideboard made to his design by Portois and Fix of Vienna, 1900 (Museum für angewandte Kunst, Vienna).

Lit: R. Weissenberger, *Die Wiener Secession*, Vienna, 1900 (Museum für angewandte Kunst, Vienna 1971.

Mosque lamp A glass vessel of vase shape with a wide flaring neck, bulbous body and a flat base or trumpet-shaped stem, intended to be hung in a mosque. On the shoulder of the body there are, generally three or six, ears from which it may be suspended on chains. Strictly speaking it is not a lamp but an ornamental shade for an oil lamp which is placed inside it. The form seems to have been developed in the late C13 (a specimen in the Metropolitan Museum, New York, was made shortly after 1286) and most of the finest examples were made in Syria during the C14 and C15 (later specimens some of which may have been made in Egypt tend to be coarser). The glass is of a brownish or greenish tone often clouded with bubbles and decorated in coloured enamels with flower and leaf motifs, 'heraldic' devices, and very bold inscriptions. Many examples bear a quotation from the Koran which indicates their symbolical significance: 'God is the light of the Heavens and the Earth: His light is as a niche in which is a lamp, the lamp in a glass, the glass as it were a glittering star.' The best mosque lamps are among the greatest masterpieces of the glass-

Mosque lamp, enamelled glass, c14 (Louvre)

Mosul brass candlestick inlaid with silver and gold, early c14 (William Rockhill Nelson Gallery of Art, Kansas City)

maker's, and especially the enameller's, art and many attempts were made to rival their excellence in the c19. The most notable collection outside Egypt is in the Victoria & Albert Museum, London.

Lit: G. Wiet, *Lampes et bouteilles en verre émaillé*, Cairo 1929; C. J. Lamm, *Mittelalterliche Gläser und Steinschnittarbeiten aus dem Nahen Osten*, Berlin 1929–30; W. B. Honey, *Glass: A Handbook*, London 1946.

Mosul carpets, *see* PERSIAN CARPETS.

Mosul metalwork The city of Mosul (now in N. Iraq) was a renowned centre for the production of finely engraved and inlaid brass from the time of the Seljuks. The Spanish traveller Ibn Sa'id praised its products in the c13 and work of fine quality seems to have been executed there until the late c15. The earliest certain piece is a ewer made before 1220 by Ibrahim ibn Mawaliyà (Louvre). Decorative motifs include human figures, birds and beasts as well as the more strictly Islamic types of ornament. A seated figure holding a crescent moon which appears on many pieces of Islamic metalwork was at one time supposed erroneously to be the emblem of the city of Mosul and a kind of hall-mark. The city's fame for metalwork was such that craftsmen probably working elsewhere signed their products as 'citizens' of Mosul. Documented examples of work done in Mosul are rare (fine pieces in British Museum, and Staatliches Museum für Völkerkunde, Munich).

Lit: M. S. Dimand, *A Handbook of Muhammadan Art*, New York 1947; D. Barrett, *Islamic Metalwork in the British Museum*, London 1949.

Mother-of-pearl The pearly substance which lines the shells of many different types of mollusc. It has been used since early times for the decoration of metalwork and jewellery, especially during the Renaissance and later. Since the c17 it has been used as an inlay for furniture, especially during the c19 on *papier-mâché* furniture.

Lit: G. E. Pazaurek, *Perlmutter*, Berlin 1937.

Mould-blown or **moulded glass** A glass vessel blown into a mould from which it takes its form. This technique of glass-making was adopted in Roman times. It was extensively used industrially from the early C19. In 1802 Charles Chubsee of STOURBRIDGE invented a type of two-piece mould in which vessels similar to those of cut glass could be made: a three-piece mould with one fixed and two hinged sections was used from *c.*1830.

Moulded pedestal stem A stem with a pronounced shoulder, of a drinking glass, sweetmeat dish, candlestick, etc., particularly popular in the C18.

Moulin, César, *see* APT POTTERY.

Moulins potteries Several faience factories were active at Moulins in the C18, producing wares inspired by those of the nearby NEVERS POTTERIES but also influenced by ROUEN and SINCENY. Few pieces are marked but those generally ascribed to Moulins include wares decorated with attractive though distinctly rustic chinoiseries in high-temperature colours dating from the 1750s. Plain white pieces and popular wares decorated with inscriptions and pictures of saints appear to have been the staple products from *c.*1760 until the end of the C18. Some wares are marked in red 'à moulins'.

Lit: R. de Quirielle, *Les faïences de Moulins,* Moulins 1922.

Mount Mellick embroidery A type of whitework executed in white knitting cotton on stout satin jean, usually fruit, flower and foliage patterns, first made *c.*1830 at Mountmellick in Queen's County, Ireland, and revived as a local industry in the 1880s by a Mrs Millner.

Mount Vernon Glass Works Founded in 1810 in New York State, it was taken over in 1833 by the **Granger family** and in 1844 moved to Mount Pleasant near Saratoga. It produced flint-glass table-ware, bottles, etc.

Mount Washington Glass Company Founded in 1837 at New Bedford, Massachusetts, it was later active in South Boston also. It produced blown, cut and pressed glass, but is famous mainly for its ART GLASS, especially PEACHBLOW and AMBERINA. In 1885 it took out a patent for BURMESE GLASS which shaded from rose-pink to yellow and

Mount Washington Glass Co.: amberina glass sugar-bowl and creamer, c.*1885, with New England Glass Co. cracker jar (Metropolitan Museum of Art, gift of Mrs Emily Winthrop Miles)*

was produced for both table-glass and decorative wares. Burmese glass was made under licence in England by Thomas Webb & Sons of Stourbridge who called it 'Queen's Burmese'.

Lit: K. M. Wilson in *VII International Congress on Glass: Comptes rendus,* Brussels 1965, ii.

Moustache cup A drinking cup of porcelain or pottery with an arrangement to keep the drinker's moustache out of the liquid, first made in the mid C19 by **Harvey Adams & Co.** of Longton, Staffordshire.

Moustiers potteries One of the most important and influential groups of French faience factories, producing wares which were imitated in Spain and Italy as well as France. The town, some 60 miles N.E. of Marseilles, is in a district where there are rich deposits of clay. The most notable factory was founded by Antoine CLÉRISSY (d.1679) and began with earthenware but his son Pierre (d.1728) initiated the production of faience which was continued under the direction of his son Antoine II and grandson Pierre II who sold the concern in 1783 to Joseph Fouque (1714–1800) whose descendants ran it until 1852. The earliest faience wares (*c.*1680–1710) are of handsome simple forms (rather like those of ROUEN and NEVERS) decorated in underglaze blue with figurative subjects – often after the engravings of Antonio Tempesta (1555–1630), more rarely after Frans Floris (1518–70) – surrounded by delicately painted *lambrequins* and *ferroneries*. Some of the best of these pieces were painted by Gaspard VIRY. Products included large dishes, drug-jars and rectangular panels. But the most notable wares are those made *c*.1710–40 comprising a wide variety of objects – dishes large and small, octagonal, wavy-edged or round, helmet-shaped ewers, *écuelles*, coffee-pots, large wall fountains and even a chimney-piece – decorated in soft blue on a very smooth, milky-white or sometimes slightly pinkish-white ground with grotesques and arabesque ornament inspired

Moustiers faience ewer, early c18 (Musée des Arts Décoratifs, Paris)

by the engraved designs of Jean BÉRAIN. In 1738 another factory was founded by J. OLERYS who had worked at ALCORA where he learned the art of painting in high-temperature colours (though not including red) which he introduced to Moustiers. Some of the products of this factory (e.g. wall plaques) are directly imitated from Alcora and most of them incorporate motifs derived from the same source (e.g. a stylized solanum or potato flower). The most interesting and original are large plates decorated with paintings of fantastic figures and beasts isolated from one another and arranged in an informal, almost haphazard, way. In the 1770s the factory of Jean-Baptiste Ferrat (which had been founded in 1718) began to produce wares decorated in enamel colours in the style of the STRASBOURG and MARSEILLES factories. Another factory established by Jean-Gaspard Féraud in 1779 began by producing wares decorated with figure subjects and naturalistic flowers in an unusually soft range of high-temperature colours. This factory survived until 1874. Faience is still made in large quantities at Moustiers. (For factory mark *see* p. 885.)

Lit: H. J. Reynaud, *Faïences anciennes de Moustiers*, Berne 1961; A.-J. Held in *Cahiers de la céramique* 18 (1960), pp. 90–119; E. Fabre in *Keramos* 22 (1963), pp. 15–25, 23 (1964), pp. 23–39, 24 (1964), pp. 30–45, 25 (1964), pp. 57–61.

Mucha, Alfonso Maria (1869–1939). Art Nouveau graphic artist and designer, born in Czechoslavakia and trained in Munich, Vienna and Paris where most of his best work was done. In 1894 he became associated with Sarah Bernhardt whom he advised on theatrical productions, clothes and jewellery. He designed a jewellery shop for Georges Fouquet in Paris (1901, demolished) and some very elaborate jewellery, notably a bracelet in the form of a disquietingly realistic snake. Some tables and chairs made to his design are in the form of naturalistic tree-trunks. He also designed some elaborate figurative wallpaper panels printed in twelve colours, similar in style to the posters for which he was famous. After 1903 he devoted himself mainly to painting.

Lit: B. Reade, *Art Nouveau and Alphonse Mucha*, London 1963.

Mudéjar A Spanish decorative style evolved by Moslems in Christian Spain or by Christians working within the Spanish Moslem tradition. (Literally, the term refers to Moslems who remained in Christian Spain after the re-conquest.) The style is best known in architecture, e.g. the C14 Alcázar in Seville, but the term is also applied to Hispano-Moresque ceramics, carpets and furniture with similar ornamentation.

Muffineer A small caster with a perforated top, originally one for sprinkling salt or sugar on muffins. Also a dish for muffins.

Muffle kiln colours, *see* ENAMEL COLOURS.

Mughal The art of the Courts of the Muslim rulers of India. The first, Babur, who reigned 1526–30, was succeeded by Humayun who spent some years (1540–54) as an exile at the Court of Shah Tahmasp in Tabriz where he appears to have developed a taste for Persian art which he introduced into the Indian peninsula on his return in 1554. Under his son Akbar (1556–1605) the arts, especially textile weaving, jade carving and metalwork, flourished and a style derived from both Hindu and Persian arts was developed. Persian carpets were imported in quantity but weavers evolved a distinctly Mughal style with patterns incorporating realistically rendered flower and leaf motifs. Under Shah Jehan (1628–57), builder of the Taj Mahal, a more emphatically Islamic art came into being. Its most notable manifestations are in architecture and miniature painting but much work of exquisite quality was executed in enamelled and nielloed metalwork, in gold, ivory carvings and especially hard-stone carvings. On a more popular level there are the textiles painted by the wax-resist technique and extensively exported to Europe. The influence of European decorative arts, introduced by merchants and missionaries, became increasingly strong and the quality of the products of the Court workshops seems to have declined during the reign of Awrangzib (1658–1707). But the Mughal tradition survived in the Rajput states, notably Jaipur, where fine silks and carpets were made until the C19.

Mule chest An English, mainly C17, type of chest with a drawer or drawers side by side in the plinth under the main compartment which is opened from the top. It was the forerunner of the chest of drawers.

Mull Scottish term for a snuff-box (originally one incorporating a mill for grinding the snuff), generally one made of a natural horn and provided with a decorative lid intended to stand on a table. A large 'sneeshing mull', as it was sometimes called, might be provided with spoons and other implements attached to it by chains.

Müller, Daniel Ernst, *see* HÖCHST PORCELAIN FACTORY.

Müller, Ferdinand, *see* NYON PORCELAIN FACTORY.

Müller, Frantz Heinrich, *see* COPENHAGEN PORCELAIN FACTORY.

Müller, Karl, *see* UNION PORCELAIN WORKS.

Muller, Michael (d.1682). Glass stainer working at Zug in Switzerland, he specialized in small pictorial roundels (usually of religious scenes) executed in transparent enamel colours on panes of clear glass – a technique of which he was one of the first masters. He was influenced stylistically by Northern Baroque painters.

Multiple cloth carpet, *see* DOUBLE CLOTH CARPET.

Münden pottery A faience factory outside Münden in Hanover was founded by **Carl Friedrich von Hanstein** in or before 1737. Its most notable products were vases with pierced double walls and plates with open basket-work rims, decorated in rather pale high-temperature colours. Tureens, tankards and figures were also made. From about 1775 (when the founder was succeeded by his son) it began to make English style cream-coloured earthenware which was the staple product from 1793 until 1854 when it closed. Wares of the von Hanstein period are marked with three crescents, sometimes with the painter's initials added below.

Lit: O. Riesebieter, *Die deutschen Fayencen des 17 und 18 Jahrhunderts,* Leipzig 1921.

Munich tapestry factory The first was established by a Flemish weaver, **J. van der Biest,** in 1604 to produce tapestries for the Elector's *Residenz.* In the late C17 Flemish Protestants established a second factory which survived until 1803, though its products were never of very high quality.

Muntin The central vertical member of the framework of a piece of furniture, the outside members being STILES.

Murano glasshouses, *see* VENETIAN GLASSHOUSES.

Murer, Christoph (1558–1614) and **Josias Murer** (1564–1630). Brothers and prolific glass stainers working in Zurich and specializing in small heraldic and allegorical panels. They were virtuoso craftsmen, equally able to execute tiny landscapes with an exquisite delicacy and to render coats of arms and their mantlings with a superbly pompous flamboyance.

Murray, Keith (b.1892). English architect and industrial designer. In the 1930s he was employed by WEDGWOOD to design table-wares of a somewhat austere elegance. He also designed vases and table glass for Messrs Stevens & Williams of Brierley Hill, Stourbridge.

Music plates Dessert plates painted with the words and music of a song to be sung at the end of a meal, first made at DELFT in the late C17, subsequently at MOUSTIERS, NEVERS, ROUEN, etc., and extensively faked in the C19.

Lit: O. E. Ris-Paquot, *La céramique musicale et instrumentale,* Paris 1889.

Muthesius, Hermann (1861–1927). German propagandist for the modern style in architecture and industrial design. While attached to the German Embassy in London for research on English housing he was much impressed by recent developments in architecture and design (notably the work of such men as VOYSEY). Back in Berlin he was appointed Superintendent of the Prussian Board of Trade for Schools of Arts and Crafts, and in this capacity gave in 1907 an outspoken lecture condemning the Historicism of German crafts and industries. It raised a storm of indignation but led to the formation of the DEUTSCHER WERKBUND. His aim was to create a true machine-age style by applying English principles of design (derived originally from MORRIS) to industry.

Lit: N. Pevsner, *Pioneers of Modern Design,* Harmondsworth 1960.

Mutz, Richard (1872–1931). German potter who in 1896 took over a pottery established by his father, (a marine painter, **Herman Mutz,** 1845–1913), at Altona just outside Hamburg, producing stoneware inspired by Japanese ceramics. He specialized in wares with free-flowing richly coloured glazes. In 1904 he moved to Berlin where he established a pottery studio and shop (first in Berlin, in 1908 at Charlottenburg, and later at Gildenhall), where shortly after 1906 he produced stoneware statuettes after models of Russian peasants made by E. Barlach, as well as vessels similar to those he had made at Altona.

Myers, Myer (1723–95). The leading silversmith of his day in New York. Began working in a chastened Rococo style, strongly influenced by English patterns, but later adopted the Neo-Classical.

Lit: J. W. Rosenbaum, *Myer Myers Goldsmith,* New York 1954.

Hand-drawn initial letter from Les Ecritures Financière, et Italienne-Bastarde *by Louis Barbedor, Paris, 1647 (courtesy of the Trustees of the British Library)*

Nabeshima ware, *see* ARITA PORCELAIN FACTORIES.

Nacre French for MOTHER-OF-PEARL.

Nahl, Johann August (1710–85). German designer, carver and furniture-maker, famous mainly for the effervescent Rococo decoration he executed 1741–6 for Frederick the Great at Berlin and Potsdam. His style is more vivacious and has greater fantasy than that of any French Rococo designer. His masterpieces were the Music Room at Potsdam and the Golden Gallery in the Charlottenburg palace. He was succeeded as designer at Potsdam by HOPPENHAUPT. His furniture is sculptural and rather heavy in comparison to his stucco decorations.

Lit: F. Bleibaum, *Johann August Nahl . . . ,* Leipzig 1933; H. Kreisel, *Die Kunst des deutschen Möbels,* vol. ii, Munich 1970.

Nail head decoration Carved decoration consisting of small pyramids, found on furniture from the Middle Ages to the C16.

Nailsea glasshouse Founded by **John Robert Lucas,** a partner in the Limekiln bottleworks in Bristol, who, in 1788, built kilns and 19 cottages for employees at Nailsea some 8 miles W. of Bristol. In 1793 he went into partnership with his brother-in-law **Edward Homer** and **William Chance** whose son **Robert Lucas Chance** ran it for a while. The factory began by making crown window glass, though a subsidiary factory owned by the partnership at Stanton Wick made black bottles until it closed in 1815. Sheet window glass was made from 1844 and rolled plate glass from the 1860s. No flint glass was ever made here. As a side-line the factory produced jugs, vases, bottles, rolling pins, etc., of black bottle glass flecked, striped or splashed in white; or, from 1844, of crown or sheet glass with coloured decorations. The employees probably made FRIGGERS. But as these products were unmarked they cannot be distinguished from those made at many other glasshouses in England and the U.S.A. The glasshouse closed in 1873.

Lit: H. Chance in *The Connoisseur* CLXV (1967), pp. 168–72; K. Vincent, *Nailsea Glass,* Newton Abbot 1974.

Nancy, School of A group of designers dominated by E. GALLÉ and including the DAUM brothers, Louis MAJORELLE and V. PROUVÉ, producing most of the best French ART NOUVEAU glass and furniture from the 1880s until Gallé's death in 1904. Though highly original they were far from being revolutionary and it is in their work that the affinities between Art Nouveau and ROCOCO are most obvious. They excelled in lush, rather over-blown floral and figurative decorations, and completely rejected the machine and the functional theories of the more sober-minded and forward-looking Art Nouveau designers. Thus their work stands at the end of the C19 whereas that of MACKINTOSH, VAN DER VELDE, HOFFMANN and others marks the beginning of the C20.

Lit: R. Schmutzler, *Art Nouveau,* London 1964.

Nankeen ware (or **Nanking china**) An obsolete English and American C19 term for various types of Chinese porcelain, especially the cruder blue-and-white wares and the richly enamelled wares which were being imported in quantity. Nanking was never a notable centre for the production of ceramics.

Nantes cotton printing factories The first, founded by **Louis Langevin** in 1758, lasted less than twenty years. Another, founded by **Aristide Petitpierre** *c.*1760, lasted for nearly a century producing printed cottons of the type for which OBERKAMPF's Jouy factory was famous, decorated with such subjects as *Panurge dans l'île des lanternes, Le mouton cheri, Les Bergers Écossais,* and Robinson Crusoe.

Lit: B. Roy, *Une capital de l'indiennage: Nantes,* Nantes 1948.

Nantgarw porcelain factory Founded in South Wales by W. BILLINGSLEY in 1813, making a glassy translucent artificial porcelain with a thick soft glaze. Some products were painted in decorating studios in London and may have been made for them (since supplies of Continental porcelain could not be obtained at this period). The factory was moved to SWANSEA in October 1814 but in 1817 Billingsley and his partner William Weston Young returned to Nantgarw where the former worked until 1819 and the latter until 1822, probably as decorators rather than makers of porcelain. The factory mark is 'NANT-GARW' with 'C.W.' below, impressed. The C.W. stands for 'China Works'. Forgeries often have the mark painted in red.

Lit: E. Morton Nance, *The Pottery and Porcelain of Swansea and Nantgarw,* London 1942; W. D. John, *Nantgarw Porcelain,* Newport 1948.

Naples (Giustiniani) pottery and porcelain factory, *see* GIUSTINIANI POTTERY AND PORCELAIN FACTORY.

Naples Royal porcelain factory Founded 1771 by Ferdinand IV of Naples. It used a translucent glassy white paste similar to that previously used at CAPODIMONTE. Early products are in a rather feeble Rococo style abandoned in the 1780s for the Neo-Classical. Large dinner services were made for diplomatic gifts, notably the 282-piece Etruscan Service presented to George III in 1787 (now at Windsor Castle), with soup-dishes, tureens and jam pots imitating Greek vases and plates and decorated with paintings of Greek and Etruscan vases. Other tablewares were painted with views of Naples and its surroundings, groups of peasants, etc. In 1781 **Filippo Tagliolini** (*c.*1746–1812) was summoned from Vienna to become chief modeller. His masterpiece is a biscuit group of *Jupiter striking down the Titans* (Museo di Capodimonte), a 5-ft high mountain of tumbling figures in various stylized attitudes of despair and

Naples Royal Porcelain Factory: plate, late c18 (Earl Spencer Collection)

Naples Royal Porcelain Factory: cruet from the Etruscan service, 1785–7 (Royal Collection, by gracious permission of H.M. the Queen)

pain. He also modelled miniatures of antique statues and some very charming figures in late c18 costume. Under Napoleonic rule the factory was acquired by a French firm, 1807, and produced Empire style tables-wares, some fine busts of the Murat family and further copies of antique marbles. It finally closed down 1821. The mark used 1771–1807, a crowned N, was fraudulently applied to some DOCCIA porcelain in the mid c19. (For factory mark *see* p. 885.)

Lit: A. Lane, *Italian Porcelain*, London 1954.

Naples tapestry factory It was founded in 1737 by Charles III, King of Naples (also founder of the CAPODIMONTE PORCELAIN FACTORY) with weavers from the FLORENCE TAPESTRY FACTORY directed by **Domenico De Rosso** and **Giovanni Francesco Pieri** who left Florence after the death of the last Medici Grand Duke. Its first product was a portrait of the founder completed in 1739 (Capodimonte). The first of a set of large panels representing the Elements were completed in 1743. Its major work was a series of panels illustrating *Don Quixote*, woven to augment the set of 12 panels woven at the GOBELINS and given by Louis XV to the Neapolitan ambassador who presented them to Charles III. Under the direction of **Pietro Duranti** (who had worked in Rome before moving to Naples where he set up a private high-warp workshop) 13 Don Quixote panels and four overdoors to cartoons by Giuseppe Bonito, faithfully imitating the *alentours* of the Gobelins set, were completed by 1762 (Palazzo del Quirinale, Rome). A further set of at least 28 panels with overdoors and narrow *entre-fenêtres* was woven to cartoons by various Neapolitan artists 1767–79. Other series include a set of Elements (1763), the story of Cupid and Psyche (1783–6) and the life of Henry IV of France (1791). The factory closed in 1799.

Lit: N. Spinosa, *L'Arazzeria Napoletana*, Naples 1971.

Nara pottery Japanese ceramics of the Nara period, A.D. 672–780 during the latter part of which, after 710, the capital was established at Nara, south of Kyoto. In this period the Court was in close contact with, and strongly influenced by the civilization of T'ANG China. And there has been much discussion as to whether certain wares found in Japan (especially those with a mottled 'three-colour' glaze, *see* SAN-TS'AI) are Japanese or Chinese. It is now generally believed that they are Japanese. The outstanding group of these wares is that placed in the Shosoin at Nara in 756 by the Dowager Empress Komyo who dedicated the personal possessions of her late husband, the Emperor Shomu, to the Great Buddha – they are possibly the earliest ceramics to survive intact above the ground. They include some of the earliest fully glazed wares made in Japan, notably begging bowls and covered jars of great simplicity and refinement.

Lit: S. Jenyns, *Japanese Pottery*, London 1971.

Nautilus shell cup, set in silver-gilt mount, with precious stones, German, c16 (Kunstgewerbemuseum, Berlin)

Nashiji Japanese term (literally: pear ground) for gold or silver sprinkled lacquer supposedly resembling the skin of a pear. If the gold or silver is sprinkled irregularly it is called *muranashiji*.

Nautilus shell cup A cup made with a nautilus shell (large, nacreous shell from the Indian Ocean) elaborately mounted in gold or silver. Intended for display rather than use. The finest were made in late C16 and early C17 Germany. *Illustrated previous column.*

Navaho Rugs Boldly patterned rugs woven by the Navaho Indians of New Mexico, Arizona and Utah. In the mid C19 white traders, noting the skill of Navaho women as weavers of blankets (originally learnt from the Spaniards), encouraged them to make rugs for sale. The first were strongly influenced by European designs and the wool from which they were made was often coloured with synthetic dyes provided by the traders. But with the increase in interest in indigenous crafts in the C20 the Navaho have been persuaded to weave traditional Indian designs and use only local vegetable dyes with much undyed black, brown and white wool.

Lit: H. P. Mera, *Navajo Textile Arts*, New York 1975.

Neatby, William James (1860–1910). English Art Nouveau designer born in Leeds where he began his career in an architect's office, then joined the staff of Burmantoft's pottery. In the 1890s he went to London where he became director of the architectural department of DOULTON'S POTTERY in Lambeth, and designed elaborate tiled panels for the exteriors and interiors of buildings in an Art Nouveau style with strong Pre-Raphaelite echoes – the Winter Gardens at Blackpool (1896), the Everard Building, Bristol (completed 1901) – with William Morris and Gutenburg staring at one another through the wings of an angel – and, his masterpiece, the meat hall in Harrod's Department Store in South Kensington (1901–5).

Lit: J. Barnard in *The Connoisseur* CLXXV (1970), pp. 165–71.

Nécessaire A portable case for personal articles needed at the same time, as when travelling, and usually including toilet necessities, sewing instruments, toothpicks, cutlery, and even, sometimes, cooking utensils. The earliest were small and pocket-sized, often elaborately decorated, e.g., in shagreen mounted with silver. Larger ones were sometimes in the form of caskets or trunks.

Needlepoint lace, *see* LACE.

Needlework carpet A carpet with a canvas ground decorated in cross-stitch or tent-stitch with wool or, rarely, silk. Needlework carpets were usually made by amateurs. In the C16 and C17 designs

The Burghley Nef: nautilus shell mounted in silver partly gilt, by Pierre le Flamand, Paris, 1482–3 (Victoria & Albert Museum)

were based on TURKISH CARPETS but in the C18 floral patterns were more usual.

Nef Vessel shaped like a ship, usually of silver: used in the later Middle Ages for the lord's napkin, knife and spoon. By the C16 they were used as table ornaments, especially in Germany and Switzerland, and many were very elaborate and accurate models of fully rigged ships, richly enamelled and peopled with little figures of sailors. *Illustrated previous page.*

Lit: C. Oman, *Medieval Silver Nefs,* London 1963.

Nehou, Louis-Lucas de, *see* PERROT, Bernard, and SAINT-GOBAIN GLASSHOUSE.

Nehracher, Matthias, *see* ZURICH POTTERY AND PORCELAIN FACTORY.

Neilson, James or **Jacques,** *see* GOBELINS TAPESTRY FACTORY.

Nekola, Karl and **Joseph,** *see* WEMYSS WARE.

Nelme, Anthony (*fl.*1672–1722). A large number of pieces of silver survive bearing the mark of Anthony Nelme and all are of high quality. Otherwise nothing is known of him except that he was apprenticed in 1672 to Richard Rowley, obtained the freedom of the Goldsmiths' Company in 1679, becoming fourth Warden in 1717 and second Warden 5 years later. He set up his shop at Amen Corner in London in 1685 and opened another shop in 1691 in Foster Lane. He was clearly one of the leading London silversmiths of his day and probably had a large workshop. His early work was in the Restoration style of the 1660s, e.g. sugar caster of 1683 (Manchester City Art Gallery). He made a pair of large silver-gilt altar candles for St George's Chapel, Windsor Castle, in 1694 (*see* p. 862). They are elaborate and very splendid. The designer is unknown but since Grinling GIBBONS was royal sculptor in wood at this date he may have been involved. Much of Nelme's later work is stylistically close to HUGUENOT SILVER, e.g. his Pilgrim bottles of 1715 at Chatsworth (*see* p. 611). But the most appealing of Nelme's works are those made during the last 15 years of his life in the stark and simple QUEEN ANNE STYLE. Few silversmiths answered the demand for plate of sterling solidity and simplicity, truth and lack of pretentiousness better than Nelme. His many teapots, hot-water jugs, inkstands, and even such larger objects as looking-glasses, have an easy elegance of form and beautiful smooth coherence which more than compensates for a want of applied decoration. The national qualities of British silver are seen at their best in such pieces. (For his mark *see* p. 894.)

A. Nelme: silver inkstand, London, 1717 (City Art Gallery, Manchester)

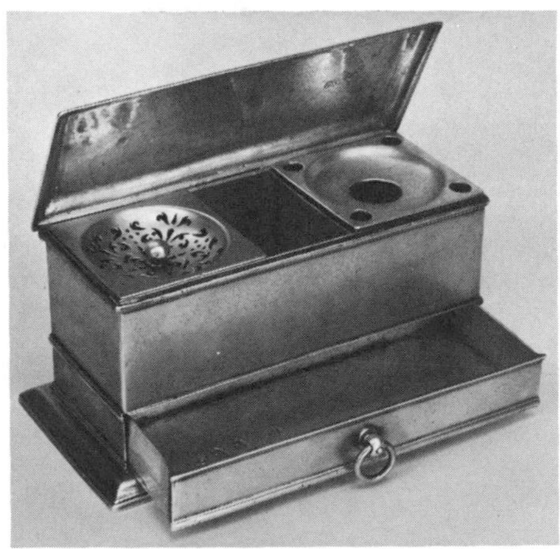

Lit: J. F. Hayward, *Huguenot Silver in England 1688–1727,* London 1959.

Nelme, Francis (*fl.*1719–59). He was the son of Anthony NELME who took him into partnership in 1721. He carried on his father's business and used his father's patterns but is known for his more fancy pieces, e.g. an enamelled gold cup of 1731 (in the Louvre). Its decoration was added later.

Nelson, George, *see* HERMAN MILLER, INC.

Neo-classicism The anti-ROCOCO style which began to emerge in the 1750s and was well established in most of Europe by the 1770s. Dignified, restrained and sometimes rather chilly, it is characterized in the decorative arts by the fondness for simple geometrical forms, the sparing use of Greek and Roman architectural ornament,

Neo-classical mahogany stool designed by Hubert Robert, made by G. Jacob in 1787 (Château de Versailles)

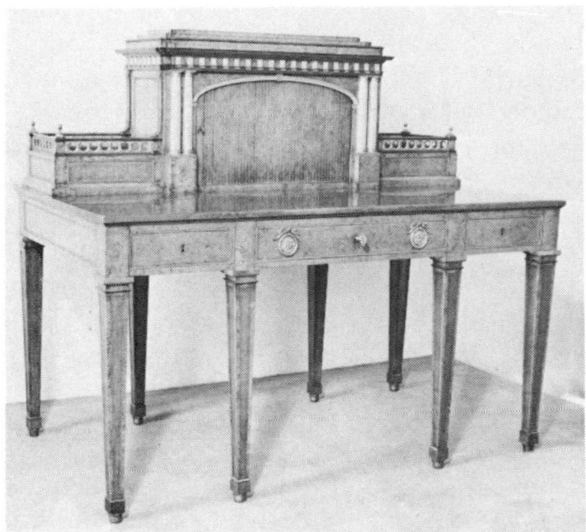

Neo-classical writing-table by D. Roentgen, c.1780–90 (Badisches Landesmuseum, Karlsruhe)

sobriety of colour and a preference for linear and flat, rather than richly sculptural decoration. Classical antiquity was imitated as a means to create a style more rational and noble than the Rococo rather than as an end in itself. Though many examples of Greek and Roman furniture were known – from vase paintings, wall paintings and carvings as well as pieces of Roman furniture excavated at Pompeii – direct copies were remarkably rare before the last decade of the C18 (e.g., pieces designed by J.-L. DAVID in the later 1780s and by ABILDGAARD *c.*1800). The same may be said of metalwork and ceramics (apart from WEDGWOOD's imitations of Greek vases), though silversmiths sometimes adapted designs from antique pottery and porcelain-makers frequently copied antique sculpture. The style originated at about the same time, but apparently independently, in France and England and most of its more notable manifestations in the decorative arts were created in these two countries (see LOUIS XVI STYLE and GEORGIAN STYLE) or under their influence. American furniture-makers like BADLAM and silversmiths like REVERE were directly inspired by English models and pattern books. The influence of R. ADAM spread through the architect Cameron to St Petersburg and even to the TULA IRONWORKS. French influence on furniture design was predominant in Germany (most of the leading Parisian *ébénistes* were, in

Neo-classical tureen, Wedgwood Pearl Ware, late C18 (Victoria & Albert Museum)

Neo-classical silver lamp by Benjamin Smith and Digby Scott, London, 1806–7 (Victoria & Albert Museum)

fact, Germans) and Italy and is evident even in the richly decorated work of BONZANIGO. French engraved designs by DELAFOSSE, LALONDE, NEUFFORGE and others were widely diffused. SÈVRES dominated the German and Austrian porcelain factories. But from the 1770s these and other European ceramic factories – from Spain to Russia and including France itself – were strongly influenced by the elegantly simple table-wares and decorative pieces of the Wedgwood pottery. In Rome a somewhat independent version of Neo-classicism, much bolder than that of either England or France, began to emerge in the later 1760s. Here the presiding genius was PIRANESI – through his famous engraved views of ancient Rome as well as his furniture designs – and the outstanding craftsman was the silversmith VALADIER. This enriched variant of the style was adopted by the Milanese ALBERTOLLI who published prints of juicy classical ornament, and by the leading Italian marquetry worker MAGGIOLINI. Piranesi was also largely responsible for the international vogue for EGYPTIENNERIE which was to Neo-Classicism what Chinoiserie had been to the Rococo style. But in early-C19 France Egyptian motifs were adopted by decorative artists for their Napoleonic significance *(Retour de l'Egypte)*, a symptom of the attitude which quickly transformed the Neo-classical into the EMPIRE STYLE.

Lit: H. Honour, *Neo-classicism*, Harmondsworth 1968; *The Age of Neo-Classicism*, Exh. Cat., Burlington House and Victoria & Albert Museum, London 1972.

Neo-Gothic, *see* GOTHIC REVIVAL.

Neri, Antonio (1576–1614). Florentine priest who from 1602 worked as an experimental glass-maker under the patronage of Don Antonio de' Medici to whom he dedicated a book on glass-making *L'Arte Vetraria* in 1612. He began by making glass imitations of precious and semi-precious stones in Florence and Pisa. In 1604 he went to Amsterdam to visit the scientist Emmanuele Ximines and worked in a glasshouse there. His book, largely based on the results of his own practical experiments in glass-making remained a standard work on the subject until the C19 and was translated into Latin, English, German, French and Spanish: annotated editions were published by Christopher Merrett in England (1662) and KUNCKEL in Germany.

Lit: W. E. S. Turner in *Additional Papers of the VI International Congress on Glass*, Washington, D.C., 1962.

Nesstfell, Johann Georg (1694–1762). German cabinet-maker, born at Alsfeld in Hesse and working in 1717 as a journeyman at Schloss Wiesentheid for Rudolf Franz Erwein von Schön-

J. G. Nesstfell: reading stand, 1724 (Schloss Wiesenthied)

J.-F. Neufforge:
designs from Recueil élémentaire . . . , *1756–80*

born (nephew of the Kurfürst Lothar Franz) who made him his *Hofschreiner* or Court Cabinet-maker in 1724–5. He was a master of marquetry in an elegant late Baroque style. Notable works by him include bookcases of 1725 and a reading stand *c.*1730 at Schloss Pommersfelden. He executed woodwork for churches, e.g. his remarkable Rococo choirstalls of 1743–50, in walnut inlaid with ebony, ivory, horn, mother-of-pearl, silver and pewter, in the upper choir of the abbey church at Banz. He also made astronomical instruments.

Lit: H. Kreisel, *Die Kunst des deutschen Möbels*, vol. ii, Munich 1870.

Neuber, Johann Christian (1735–1808). Saxon gem-engraver and goldsmith who settled in Dresden in 1762, worked for the Court from 1767, and was appointed Court jeweller in 1780. Although he made such large objects as table-tops, pedestals and a chimney-piece (Grünes Gewölbe, Dresden), he is best known for his exquisite small boxes composed of various hard-stones set in gold, sometimes provided with little books identifying the types of stone and their provenance. These little boxes are known as *Neuberdose.*

Neufforge, Jean-François (1714–91). Flemish designer born at Liège, settled in Paris in 1738 and published there his *Recueil élémentaire d'Architecture* (8 vols, 1756–80). The volumes issued in 1765 and 1768 contain the first Neo-classical furniture designs to be published in France – solid, heavy, rectilinear, with bold classical (sometimes Egyptian) motifs, though with occasional backward glances to BOULLE. His tables and chests-of-drawers tend to be unusually long and low and his chairs have very stout squat legs. He influenced the development of the LOUIS XVI STYLE, inspiring J.-F. BOUCHER, J.-C. DELAFOSSE, J.-D. DUGOURC and R. LALONDE. *Illustrated above.*

Lit: S. Eriksen, *Early Neo-Classicism in France*, London 1974.

Nevers glasshouse Established after 1566 (when Lodovico Gonzaga became Duke of Nevers) by Italian craftsmen whose descendants seem to have run it until the C18. It specialized from 1595 in little glass figures and 'toys', fashioned in a wide variety of elegant and grotesque forms from glass rods or tubes softened at the flame of a lamp, blown or manipulated with pincers and often fastened to a wire armature. Religious figures and groups, animals, very elaborate landscapes with trees and flowers and human figures, all fashioned from glass rods, made by this process, are commonly called *verre de Nevers*, though it is seldom possible to distinguish the Nevers products from those made in Rouen, Bordeaux, Marseilles, Venice, Germany, Spain and England.

Lit: J. Barrelet, *La Verrerie en France*, Paris 1954; A.-J. Held in *Cahiers de la céramique* 20 (1960), pp. 294–310.

Nevers potteries One of the most important groups of French faience factories. The first was founded in 1588 by the brothers **Conrade** from ALBISSOLA in partnership with **Jules Gambin** (or **Giulio Gambini**), an Italian potter who had worked in Lyons. This concern was encouraged by Lodovico Gonzaga, an Italian soldier of fortune who had acquired the Duchy of Nevers. Its products are strongly Italianate including handsome ISTORIATO dishes, ewers, pilgrim bottles, etc. Though still run mainly by Italians or men of Italian extraction the potteries adopted more characteristically French styles in the mid C17 and designs for *Istoriato* wares were inspired by (sometimes copied from) such artists as Poussin and Vouet. But a more potent influence came from the East: the forms of Chinese vases were carefully copied (as early as 1644) and gay chinoiseries frequently used for decoration both on them and on Baroque-shaped ewers and vases. Colour schemes are subdued, with misty blues, soft orange, olive green and pale yellow predominant. But after the

Nevers faience ewer with painted decoration after Michel Dorigny, c.1650–60 (Louvre)

Nevers Bleu Persan *faience flower-pot, c.1670 (Victoria & Albert Museum)*

(Right) Nevers style glass, 'Judgement of Paris', 1777 (Musée des Arts Décoratifs, Paris)

mid C17 the oriental blue-and-white scheme became increasingly popular, and in the 1670s BLEU PERSAN wares were produced. The standard of painting was exceptionally high and the groups of elegant Orientals loitering through exotic landscapes on many pieces are among the best C17 chinoiseries. By the end of the C17 the factories had lost the lead in fashion to ROUEN and MOUSTIERS and became imitative though they remained highly productive. The most interesting of the later pieces are crudely but sometimes vivaciously painted table-wares decorated with pictures of saints or other popular subjects which gave way to Revolutionary symbols and legends at the end of the C18 when Nevers became one of the main sources for FAIENCE PATRIOTIQUE. The number of factories in the town declined sharply after the C18. In the mid C19 that of **Ristori** was producing imitations of C17 Nevers wares. Pottery is still made in the town. No factory mark was ever used at Nevers though various initials and inscriptions are found.

Lit: M. J. Ballot, *La céramique française: Nevers, Rouen . . . ,* Paris 1925; A. Lane in *Faenza* XXXII (1946), pp. 43ff. and in *Burlington Magazine* LXXXIX (1947), pp. 37ff., H.-P. Fourest in *Cahiers de la céramique* 9 (1958), pp. 10–24.

Neville, George An employee of the Birmingham firm of JENNENS & BETTRIDGE who in 1831 discovered the technique of painting on black PAPIER MÂCHÉ. He is said to have 'signed' his works with a convolvulus flower with one petal turned down and painted in a contrasting colour. He set up as a *papier mâché* producer in 1846 in partnership with a Mr Alsager and prospered.

Lit: G. B. Hughes in *Concise Encyclopaedia of Antiques,* vol. IV, London 1959.

New Bremen Glasshouse, *see* AMELUNG, Johann Friedrich.

New England Glass Company One of the best and largest U.S. glasshouses, it was founded by **Deming Jarves** and associates in 1817 at Cambridge, Mass. (Jarves withdrew in 1823 to found the BOSTON AND SANDWICH GLASS COMPANY). The New England Glass Company began by making clear lead glass, deeply cut in the English manner, and it also made vessels of blown glass and pressed glass. In the 1850s it became notable for ornamental pieces of flashed or overlay glass in the style of that made in Bohemia. Millefiori paperweights were also produced. An engraver of German origin, **Louis Vaupel,** was employed from 1856 to 1885 decorating individual pieces by the wheel-engraving process, generally with hunting-scenes. Another employee, **Joseph Locke,** developed types of coloured glass which were patented – *Amberina,* pale amber merging into ruby (1883)

New England Glass Co.: amberina glass bowl, c.1885 (Mr and Mrs Samuel B. Feld Collection, New York)

and *Pomona,* pale amber with etched decorations and sometimes motifs stained pale blue (1885). A distinct PEACHBLOW glass – white flushing to red – and AGATA were also made. The company was acquired in 1878 by **William T. Libbey** whose son **Edward Libbey** moved it in 1888 to Toledo, Ohio, where it still operates under the name of the **Libbey Glass Company.**

Lit: Libbey Glass, Exh. Cat., Toledo Museum of Art, Toledo, Ohio, 1968; L. W. Watkins in *Journal of Glass Studies* XII (1970), pp. 149–64.

New Geneva Glass Works Founded in 1797 in Pennsylvania by a Swiss, **Albert Galletin,** and others who had been employed by J. F. AMELUNG at the New Bremen Glass Manufactory. Apart from window glass and bottles, it produced free-blown and pattern-moulded table-ware, mainly green and yellow.

New Hall porcelain factory Established in Staffordshire in 1781 and producing hard-paste porcelain at first in imitation of Chinese export wares with very elaborate groups of mandarins in exotic landscapes. From 1791 much simpler patterns were adopted – usually isolated sprigs of flowers in *famille rose* colours – which remained popular well into the C19. But from *c.*1812 the factory made a form of bone porcelain rather than true hard-paste. (For factory mark *see* p. 886.)

New Hall porcelain teapot, c.1810 *(Victoria & Albert Museum)*

Lit: D. Holgate, *New Hall and its Imitators,* London 1971.

Newbery, Jessie R. (1864–19). Scottish embroiderer and textile designer, neé Rowat (daughter of a shawl manufacturer at Paisley), who married in 1889 **Francis H. Newbery,** principal of the Glasgow School of Art where she taught 1894–1908. As a practitioner and teacher she played an important part in developing the style of textile decoration associated with the GLASGOW SCHOOL.

Newcastle glasshouses Tyneside became a glassmaking centre in the C17 when immigrant craftsmen established themselves there, notably the **Tysack** and **Henzell** or **Henzey** families from Lorraine and the **Dagnia** family from Italy. Later, a brilliant flint-glass was made there and was much favoured by Dutch glass engravers such as David WOLFF. These and the glasses enamelled by the BEILBYS in Newcastle provide some indication of the types of glass made in the Newcastle area. The tall knopped and air-beaded stem and certain types of domed and terraced foot and straight enamel- and air-twist stems recur in authentic Newcastle glasses. Production declined in quality in the C19 and Newcastle was noted later mainly for pressed-glass imitations of cut glass.

Newcastle-on-Tyne potteries, *see* TYNESIDE POTTERIES.

Newcomb College pottery An art pottery workshop established in 1895 at Newcomb College (the women's division of Tulane University), New Orleans, in emulation of the ROOKWOOD POTTERY. It was directed by **Ellsworth Woodward** (1861–1939) with a skilled ceramic decorator **Mary G. Sheerer** as design instructress. The products, mainly vases, were thrown by master potters and only decorated by the students. Although originally intended as a teaching

Newcomb College Pottery: vase, decorated by Mary G. Sheerer (Cincinatti Art Museum)

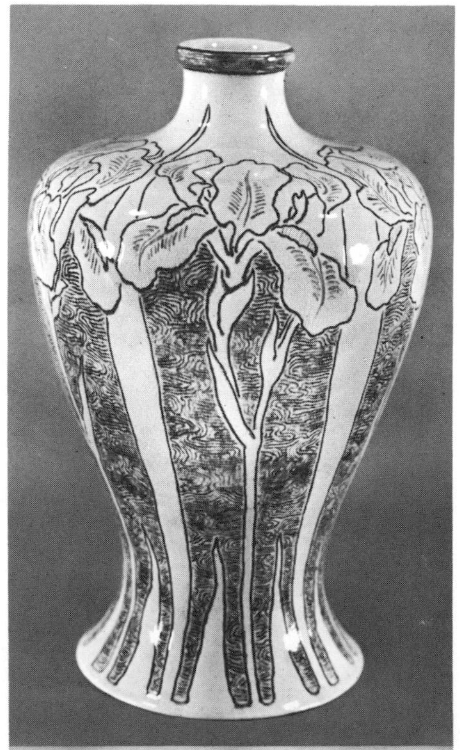

establishment, it began to market its wares in 1897 and secured international notice when it was awarded a bronze medal at the Paris Exposition of 1900. Forms were derived from Oriental ceramics or peasant pottery. Decorative motifs – limited to the flora and fauna of the southern States – were at first incised and coloured in tones of blue and green. From 1910 a wider range of coloured matt glazes was used. Products vary greatly in quality but the best are among the more notable examples of Art Nouveau art pottery. They all bore a label declaring that 'designs are not duplicated'. The pottery closed in 1930.

Lit: R. W. Blasberg in *Antiques* XCIV (1968), pp. 73–; R. Judson Clark (ed.), *The Arts and Crafts Movement in America 1876–1916*, Exh. Cat., Art Museum, Princeton University, Art Institute of Chicago, etc., 1972–3.

Nickel silver, or **German Silver** An alloy – 50 per cent copper, 25 per cent zinc, 25 per cent nickel – resembling silver though slightly more grey in colour. It was developed between 1840 and 1847 by ELKINGTON and it forms the base of EPNS or Electroplate. It has been used in other ways also. The Chinese PAKTONG is similar though yellowish and of slightly different proportions of copper, zinc and nickel. Paktong was in use in China at least as early as the C18.

Nicolas of Verdun (*fl.* 1181–1205). Goldsmith and enameller of the MOSAN School, he was one of the greatest craftsmen of the Middle Ages and as important an artist as any of the painters or sculptors. He was 'in the van of the development of the early Gothic style' (Panofsky). He was presumably a generation younger than GODEFROID DE HUY, being first recorded in 1181 when he inscribed (presumably on finishing) his great series of enamels at Klosterneuberg near Vienna. It is assumed that he was born by 1150. His masterpiece at Klosterneuberg was made for an ambo but later, *c.*1330, reduced to a large retable (5 metres long by 1.10 high) of fifty-one panels of CHAMPLEVE enamels on copper. It is the most important surviving example of medieval enamel painting and is still *in situ*. The colours are bright – red, blue, turquoise, green and white – and the figures rank with the finest Romanesque manuscript paintings. There can be little doubt that he is identical with the 'Nicolaus de Verdun' named on the so-called reliquary of the Virgin in Tournai cathedral in 1205 (restored in the C19) on which prominence is given to the figures in relief and enamel is used only for the frames. Of the several unsigned works attributed to him the most readily acceptable is the gold reliquary of the Magi in Cologne cathedral, begun in the early 1180s. Badly damaged reliquaries of St Annone at Sieberg and St Pantaleone at Cologne (finished in 1186) and a little enamelled plaque of Bishop Bruno of Cologne (Art Institute of Chicago) show affinities with his work, but may equally well be by a follower. On the other hand the Trivulzio candlestick in Milan cathedral, often ascribed to him, clearly derives from another tradition.

Nicolas of Verdun, enamel panel from altarpiece, 1181 (Klosterneuberg, near Vienna)

Lit: O. Demus in *Encyclopaedia of World Art*, New York and London 1959, vol. ix; E. Castelnuovo, *Nicolaus di Verdun*, Milan 1966; P. Lasko, *Ars Sacra 800–1200*, Harmondsworth 1972; M.-M. Gauthier, *Émaux du moyen âge occidental*, Fribourg 1972.

Niculoso, Francisco (d.1529). Italian potter, probably born in Pisa and possibly trained at Faenza, who settled by 1498 at Triana, a suburb of Seville, where he introduced the Italian Renaissance style for large pictorial panels of maiolica tiles. His earliest dated work is a tomb slab of 1503 in the church of S. Anna, Triana. In 1504 he executed two altarpieces for chapels in the Alcazar, Seville (that of the Visitation in the chapel of the Catholic Kings survives) and glazed reliefs, in the della Robbia manner (by Pedro Millán), for the doorway of S. Paola, Seville. In 1509 he was commissioned to execute *frontale* for all the altars in Seville Cathedral (destroyed). His masterpiece (though sadly damaged) is a large altarpiece of 1518 in the monastery of S. María de Tentudía in the Sierra Morena. There is a handsome signed tiled panel of the Visitation by him in the Rijksmuseum, Amsterdam. He appears to have derived his designs from contemporary prints, making especial use of the engravings of Zoan Andrea, Giovanni Antonio da Brescia and Nicoletto Rosex da Modena for the grotesque decorations which he used abundantly as frames for religious scenes.

Lit: A. W. Frothingham, *Tile Panels of Spain*, New York 1969.

Niderviller pottery and porcelain factory Founded by Baron Jean-Louis de Beyerlé in 1754 near Sarrebourg in Lorraine with workmen from the STRASBOURG factory whose Rococo style it adopted. The first products were of faience of an ivory tone delicately painted with flowers and figures in a somewhat softer palette than that used at Strasbourg, with a rose pink and dark purple predominating. Products included dishes and plates with pierced basket-work rims, tureens topped with modelled vegetables and *pot-pourris* with fragile openwork covers – all modelled with an abundance of eddying Rococo scrolls. Porcelain was made from 1765 but not on a large scale until 1768. In 1770–71 the factory was sold to Adam-Philibert, Comte de Custine. At about this date the production of faience with DECORS BOIS, for which the factory is famous, appears to have begun. Statuettes made in both faience and

Niderviller faience, décor bois *with* trompe l'oeil *print,* 1773 *(Palais Rohan, Strasbourg)*

porcelain from models by LEMIRE and, after 1780, CYFFLÉ, rival those of SÈVRES. For both decorative and useful wares the Louis XVI style was adopted in the 1770s. When the Comte de Custine was guillotined in 1793 his manager, Claude-François Lanfrey, acquired the concern which he ran until his death in 1827 making mainly cream-coloured earthenware and common faience. In the later C19 it produced copies of C18 wares from the original moulds. It is still active. (For factory mark *see* p. 886.)

Lit: A. Lane, *French Faience*, London 1948.

Niederer, Roberto (b.1928). Glass-maker born in Naples but of Swiss nationality with workshops in Zurich and Calabria. He specializes in blown glass produced by traditional methods, generally rather thick and sometimes with intentional surface irregularities – e.g., a set of decanters with a grained surface taken from the wooden moulds in which they were blown.

Niedermayer, Johann Josef and **Mathias,** *see* VIENNA PORCELAIN FACTORY.

Niello A black substance composed of powdered silver, lead, copper, sulphur and often borax, used as a filling for incised decorations on silver and fixed by the application of heat; also, a silver plaquette decorated with niello. Niello work reached its height of technical and artistic excellence during the early Renaissance in Italy, especially in Florence. It was much practised also in C19 Russia where it is known as **Tula-work.**

Nieuwenhuis, Theodore (1866–1951). Dutch Art Nouveau designer, pupil of the architect P. J. H. Cuypers, working in Amsterdam where he designed many domestic interiors and became (1908) director of the main applied arts workshop. He had the usual fondness for curved lines, coiled snakes, peacock feathers, etc. but used them with restraint and his works are on the sober side. Also designed pottery for the De Distel factory, Amsterdam.

Niglett, John (*fl.*1714–33). He was a free-lance pottery painter working in Bristol where he was apprenticed in 1714. A dish in the Bristol Museum dated 1733 bears initials believed to be those of Niglett and his wife. Other pieces decorated by the same hand are known – often with vigorously stylized Chinese figures derived from K'ANG HSI porcelain decorations.

Nimes pottery, *see* SIGALON, Antoine.

Ninsei, Nonomura Seibei called **Ninsei** (*fl.*1649–57). A potter and pottery decorator working near Kyoto in the C17 and generally regarded by the Japanese as the greatest of their ceramic artists. His dates of birth and death are unknown (though various authorities record the latter as early as 1658 and as late as 1705) but four signed and dated works range from 1649 to 1657. He was probably the first potter to apply to earthenware the technique of painting in enamels formerly reserved for porcelain and was certainly the first to use them for decorations in an entirely Japanese (rather than Chinese) manner. He was in fact the founder of the Edo-period (1615–1867) school of Japanese ceramic artists. He made storage vases for tea *(chatsubo)*, incense burners in the form of shells or birds, and numerous tea bowls, often painted in colours and gold on a black ground. These wares have a thin body covered with an evenly crackled glaze and are painted in rich soft colours. He appears to have invented a metallic black-green glaze and also a pearl-white glaze with a pink flush. The decorations are generally elaborate and reveal the influence of contemporary lacquer. His works were very highly prized from the beginning and they were extensively imitated and faked. He had four sons and several pupils, possibly including Ogata KENZAN who was certainly associated with Ninsei's son.

Lit: S. Jenyns, *Japanese Pottery*, London 1971.

Nipt diamond waies A form of glass decoration, mentioned in G. RAVENSCROFT's price-list of 1677, consisting of glass threads trailed vertically on a vessel and pincered together at regular intervals to make a lozengey network.

Niris carpets, *see* PERSIAN CARPETS.

Nizzoli, Marcello (b.1895). Italian painter, sculptor, scenographer and industrial designer. He is the creator of two mid-C20 classics of industrial design, the Olivetti typewriter *Lettera 22* (1954) and the Necchi sewing-machine (1956). The *Lettera 22* typewriter is the culmination of a long line of excellent Olivetti designs by Nizzoli, combining the virtues of the Hermes *Baby* and Max BILL's *Patria* typewriter. His other notable recent designs include the Olivetti 'Tetractys' automatic printing computor (1957) and the Necchi 'Supernova Julia' automatic sewing-machine (1960).

Noguchi, Isamu (b.1904). Japanese-American artist and designer, born in Los Angeles. He spent his childhood in Japan, returned to the U.S. in 1918 and studied medicine, went to Paris 1927–8 where he knew the sculptors Brancusi, Calder and Giacometti. Between 1929 and 1931 he was making pottery in Kyoto but then returned to Europe and eventually to the U.S. where he made some of the most advanced free-form furniture of an extremely organic type in the early 1940s. But he is best known for his wire-framed, white-paper standing lamp-shades in a wide variety of shapes – spherical, tubular, barley-sugar twists, etc.

Noke, Charles John (1858–1941). A pottery painter and modeller trained at the WORCESTER PORCELAIN FACTORY and working from 1889 for the DOULTON POTTERY AND PORCELAIN COMPANY of which he was Art Director 1914–36. He developed two types of heavy earthenware named Holbein ware (1895) and Rembrandt ware (*c.*1898) and made use of flambé glazes. He was also responsible for the design of small articles decorated with figures from the Bayeux 'tapestry', scenes from Shakespeare's plays and R. H. Barham's poem *The Jackdaw of Rheims.* He was succeeded as Art director at Doulton's by his son **Cecil Jack Noke** (d.1954).

Nonesuch chests A group of C16 chests found in England, richly decorated in marquetry with fantastic architecture. Sometimes supposed to be of English make but more probably made in Danzig and imported. The name has no reference to Nonsuch Palace but simply means unequalled. *Illustrated below.*

Nonne, Christian, *see* ILMENAU PORCELAIN FACTORY and VOLKSTEDT PORCELAIN FACTORY.

Nonesuch chest (Lady Lever Collection on loan to the City of Birmingham Museum & Art Gallery)

Norman, Samuel (*fl.*1746–67). London furniture-maker who set up on his own after serving an apprenticeship to a carver and gilder Thomas Woodin 1746–53. In 1755 he married the daughter of and went into partnership with an established furniture-maker, **James Whittle.** The concern was extended to upholstery and cabinet-making in 1758 and for a while J. INCE was a third partner. On Whittle's death in 1759 Norman took charge of the firm but the premises were burnt down later that year and he lost all his stock. In 1760 he took over the firm of **Paul Saunders,** who specialized in tapestry work for furniture, was employed by the Crown and held the title of Yeoman Arrasworker. In 1762 Norman was appointed Master Carver in Wood to the Office of Works and supplied gilt frames for Windsor Castle: he was also patronized by several of the wealthier families and appears to have been one of the more prominent London furniture-makers of his time. But in 1767 he went bankrupt. Few of the products of his workshops have as yet been traced: the most notable being a bed with fine Rococo carved work at Hopetoun House, Scotland, and some pier-glass frames at Woburn Abbey, Beds. But various girandoles including one 'with Sheep in China Taste' are recorded. He is also known to have worked under the direction of R. ADAM at Moor Park, Herts., in 1764.

Lit: P. A. Kirkham in *Burlington Magazine*, CXI (1969), pp. 501–13.

Northamptonship lace, *see* BEDFORDSHIRE LACE.

Northwood, John (1836–1902). Glass decorator mainly responsible for the revival of cased (or Cameo) glass carving in England. He was born at Wordsley in Staffordshire and apprenticed to a local glasshouse belonging to the Richardson family. He established his own workshop *c.*1860. His first notable work, the Elgin vase completed 1873 (Birmingham City Art Gallery), was of clear flint glass engraved in shallow relief with horsemen from the Panathenaic frieze of the Parthenon. In 1873–6 he executed a copy of the Portland Vase, the first to be made in the same medium as the original. He made a number of other carved cased glass pieces, e.g., Pegasus vase completed 1882 (Smithsonian Institute, Washington), in addition to carrying on a general glass manufacturing concern in partnership with his brother **Joseph** (1839–1915). His son **John** (b.1870) was a carver of cased glass and for many years director and technical manager of STEVENS & WILLIAMS. His nephew **William Northwood** (1858–1937) was also a carver of cased glass.

Lit: G. W. Beard, *Nineteenth Century Cameo Glass*, Newport, Mon., 1956.

J. Northwood: the Pegasus Vase, carved cased-glass, 1882 (The Smithsonian Institution, Washington D.C.)

Norton, John, Luman and **Julius,** *see* BENNINGTON POTTERY & PORCELAIN FACTORY.

Norwegian tapestry factories Tapestries were woven in Norway from the C9 and a few fragments of this period and the C11 survive. The earliest

Norwegian tapestry of The Wise and Foolish Virgins, *late c17* *(Kunstindustrimuseet, Oslo)*

surviving piece of importance is of *c.*1180 and is woven in wool on a linen warp (Kunstindustrimuseet, Oslo). It represents the months of April and May (the latter in the guise of a svelte young knight on horseback) and was made for the Baldishol Church, Hedmark: its simplified figures have the vitality of Romanesque enamels, and the colours are hardly less brilliant. The arrival of weavers from N. Germany and Denmark gave new impetus to the tapestry industry in the C16 when numerous small workshops with high-warp looms were set up. The best products date from the C17 – fairly large panels of Biblical scenes naively rendered in bright clear colours without any attempt at modelling or shading and surprisingly uninfluenced by Baroque paintings but wonderfully vital and decorative. One of the finest depicts the *Wise and Foolish Virgins*, stocky peasant girls in geometrically patterned dresses, the former brandishing their burning lamps, the latter holding handkerchiefs, all tightly packed inside a zig-zag frame which owes something to Persian carpet design (Kunstindustrimuseet, Oslo).

Lit: H. Göbel, *Wandteppiche*, Leipzig 1923–34.

Nøstetangen glasshouse The most important Norwegian glass factory, founded 1741 at Nøstetangen near Drammen by Christian VI of Denmark and Norway. At first patronized mainly by the Court at Copenhagen and staffed by craftsmen from Thuringia, early products were imitated from German patterns. The factory was reorganized 1753 and in 1755 lead glass was introduced by English craftsmen. During its best period, 1760–70, the factory made two types of wares: vessels of soda-lime glass of a pinkish-purple colour, roughly made with frequent imperfections and generally based on German patterns for everyday use; and high-quality lead glass decanters, goblets, etc., in the English style with Venetian undertones, often well engraved in the Rococo manner. It also made attractive chandeliers of an individual type, hung about with a variety of coloured and crystal blown-glass ornaments which give them an insubstantial bubbly appearance (set of three in Kongsberg church, 1759–66). The factory closed down in 1777 and most of the craftsmen moved to HURDALS VERK.

Lit: A. Polak, *Nøstetangen*, Oslo 1966.

Nottingham lace Machine-made LACE much, but by no means all, of which was made from the mid C19 at Nottingham in imitation of various types of hand-made lace. It was inexpensive and much used for curtains, etc. in late Victorian England.

Nottingham potteries Established at least as early as the C13, they produced green and brown lead-glazed earthenware. In the C16 and C17 tygs with many handles were made. But the potteries owe their fame to the production of salt-glazed stoneware from *c.*1690. James Morley of Nottingham, who was among the potters sued in 1693 by J. DWIGHT for infringement of his stoneware patent, issued an advertisement illustrating such wares in the last decade of the C17. But the earliest known dated piece of Nottingham stoneware is of 1700 (private collection. There is a jug dated 1703 in the Victoria & Albert Museum). Early C18 pieces are thinly potted, light in weight, and have a grey body covered with a wash of ferruginous clay which gives a warm brown tone and an unusually smooth salt glaze. Products include posset pots, cylindrical mugs, large and small jugs, teapots and bell-shaped cups, decorated with incised designs and occasionally formalized flowers painted in slip. Decorations seem to have become more profuse, and less satisfactory, towards the mid C18. Jugs in the form of bears with detachable heads to serve as cups were made in the mid C18 as in Staffordshire. The potteries declined steadily in the later C18 and are said to have closed in 1803.

Lit: A. Parker in *Transactions of the Thornton Society of Nottinghamshire* XXXVI (1932), pp. 79ff.

Nove pottery and porcelain factories The first of several faience and porcelain factories was established at Nove near Bassano (W. of Venice and N. of Vicenza) in 1728 by **Giovanni Battista Antonibon** whose descendants ran it until late in the C19. Earlier and mid-C18 wares include attractive maiolica dishes, tureens, etc., modelled in a slightly rustic Rococo style and decorated in high-temperature colours. Tureens in the form of fishes were also made. The production of porcelain of a hybrid paste began in the 1750s (certainly before 1762): teapots, cups, etc. are of delicate simple form and often prettily painted, sometimes with characteristically Venetian masquerade figures. Statuettes are generally in a late Rococo style but also, in the late c18–early c19, include figures after statues by Canova. Similar statuettes were made from the later c18 in cream-coloured earthenware which was also used for household wares. The best of the latter are decorated by **Giovanni Maria Baccin** with Watteauesque scenes. He leased the Antonibon factory from 1773–1803 (impressed mark: G M over B with a star painted in red enamel). From the c19 many other factories were established at Nove which is now one of the main centres for ceramic production in Italy. (For factory mark *see* p. 886.)

Nove cream-coloured earthenware group, Antonibon-Pasolin factory, 1782–1802 (Museo Civico, Bassano del Grappa)

Lit: G. Lorenzetti, *Maioliche venete del Settecento*, Venice 1936.

Nuppen German term for rather large drops of glass applied to the surface of a vessel and drawn out to points: hence the *Nuppenbecher*, a drinking glass thus ornamented, made from the c15.

Nuremberg glasshouses Founded in mid c16 and producing Venetian style vessels. The city was of greater importance as a centre for glass engravers and painters in the c17 and c18 – notably Johann SCHAPER.

Lit: R. Schmidt, *Das Glas*, Berlin 1922; E. Meyer-Heisig, *Der Nürnberger Glasschnitt des 17-Jhr.*, Nuremberg 1963.

Nuremberg potteries In the c16 Nuremberg was an important centre for the production of stoves made of moulded green or black lead-glazed tiles. The HAFNER ware of PREUNING and others was also made there. And between 1530 and 1536 HIRSCHVOGEL appears to have been making faience in the city, although none of his works is marked or can be securely identified. But a number of fine pieces of German c16 faience can be reasonably ascribed to Nuremberg (mainly in the Germanisches Museum, Nuremberg, including a plate with the Virgin and Child in blue dated 1530). Later-c16 and early-c17 pieces are also ascribed to the city. Faience was again made in Nuremberg in the c18. A factory founded by two merchants in 1712 produced a wide variety of wares but especially narrow-necked jugs, cylindrical tankards and dishes, decorated in blue (often on a pale blue or grey ground) and sometimes with high-temperature green, yellow, manganese and red. Many of the more elaborately decorated pieces are inscribed with the names of their painters, notably Georg Friedrich Kordenhusch (d.1763) who was possibly a partner in the factory. Subjects include vases of flowers, local landscapes, Biblical and mythological scenes. But the products of the factory were also decorated by HAUSMALER several of whom lived in Nuremberg. The fortunes of the factory and the quality of its wares declined sharply after *c.*1770 though it survived until *c.*1840. (For factory mark *see* p. 886.)

Lit: W. Stengel in *Mitteilungen aus dem Germanischen Museum*, 1908, 1911; O. Riesebieter,

Die deutschen Fayencen des 17. und 18. Jahrhunderts, Leipzig 1921.

Nylon, *see* MAN-MADE FIBRES.

Nymphenburg porcelain factory One of the most important in C18 Germany, founded under the patronage of the Elector of Bavaria at Neudeck near Munich in 1747 though it produced little until after 1753 when J. J. RINGLER was taken on as arcanist. In 1761 it moved to a new building near the Electoral summer palace, Nymphenburg, where it has remained ever since. The earliest products were in a not very satisfactory hard paste, but from 1757 a porcelain body of exceptional fineness and whiteness was adopted. The most notable products are the statuettes which benefit much from the high quality of the material. Outstanding among them are the exquisite Rococo figures modelled by F. A. BUSTELLI who was chief modeller 1754–63. During this period the factory also made a speciality of cane handles and small boxes, and employed goldsmiths to mount them. Table-wares and *veilleuses* of the same date are attractive and often very prettily painted, but show less originality and are often imitative of those of other factories. Unlike MEISSEN, the factory profited from the Seven Years' War when it carried on an extensive export trade. But from the mid 1760s it began to run into financial difficulties (the staff was reduced from 200 to about 80 in 1767) and the quality of products declined. Bustelli was succeeded in 1764 by D. AULICZEK who introduced a somewhat stiff version of the Louis XVI style for figures. A revival was effected under J. P. MELCHIOR who was chief modeller and overseer 1797–1810. Portrait reliefs and busts and classical figures were the most notable products of these years. Table-wares show the influence of the SÈVRES Empire style. In the early C19 figures were made after models by the leading Bavarian sculptors, Franz and Ludwig Schwanthaler. The most distinguished product of this period was the 'Onyx table service' made for Ludwig I from 1835 and decorated with paintings of antique statues in the Munich collection. In 1862 State support for the factory ended and it was leased to Ferdinand Scotzniovsky who produced only utilitarian wares. A revival began in 1888 under the direction of Albert Bäuml. In the early C20 good Art Nouveau table-wares, some spirited birds and animals after models by Theodor Kärner (b.1885) who was employed at the

Nymphenburg porcelain ice-pot, c.1755–60 (Victoria & Albert Museum)

Nymphenburg porcelain Pekinese dog, modelled by T. Kärner, 1912 (Karl H. Bröhan Collection, Berlin)

factory 1905–18, and figures in contemporary costume after models by P. SCHEURICH and J. WACKERLE. The factory still survives, producing decorative and useful wares of high quality and also reproductions of C18 wares. (For factory mark *see* p. 886.)

Lit: F. H. Hofmann, *Geschichte der bayerischen Porzellan Manufaktur Nymphenburg*, Leipzig 1922.

Nyon porcelain factory After ZÜRICH, the best in Switzerland. It was founded *c.*1780 by **Ferdinand Müller** in partnership from 1781 with **Jacob Dortu** (1749–1819) who had worked at BERLIN, MARSEILLES and MARIEBERG and who became director 1809–13. Products are in a technically flawless hard paste decorated attractively but simply, usually in imitation of PARIS wares. The most attractive are cups, coffee-pots, etc., painted with butterflies or sprigs of flowers. In the last years of Dortu's management the factory was engaged mainly in the production of cream-coloured earthenware and imitations of WEDGWOOD's stonewares. It survived until 1860. (For factory mark *see* p. 886.)

Lit: A. de Molin in *Gazette des Beaux Arts* XXXIII (1905), pp. 210ff.; E. Pelichet in *Faenza* XXXIV (1948), pp. 35–7; E. Pelichet, *Merveilleuse porcelaine de Nyon*, Paris 1974.

Wood-cut initial letter used by Michel Vascosan, Paris, 1556

Oak Wood from various trees of the *quercus* genus used for furniture-making from very early times. It is hard, close-grained and generally of a pale colour though some dark forms are known (the nearly black bog-oak comes from trunks of dead trees found immersed in peat bogs). In N. Europe it was the wood mainly used for fine furniture throughout the Middle Ages, giving way to walnut in France in the late C16 and in England in the late C17: simpler furniture has been made from it to the present day. The heads of pollarded oak-trees yield a richly coloured, densely grained wood sometimes used as a veneer in the early C19.

Oak-leaf jars Maiolica drug pots with rounded bellies, short necks and two strap-shaped handles, decorated (usually in purple and green or blue on white) with birds, beasts, heraldic motifs or human figures amidst an irregular diaper of stylized leaves rather like those of the oak. Made especially in C15 FLORENCE.

Oak-leaf jar, probably Florentine, C15 (Louvre)

Lit: H. Wallis, *Oak-leaf Jars*, London 1963.

Oberg, Thure, *see* ARABIA POTTERY.

Oberkampf, Christophe-Philippe (1738–1815). Textile designer and pioneer industrialist, the founder of the factory at Jouy which gave its name to *toiles de Jouy*. He was born at Weisenbach, the son of a dyer who discovered in the 1740s a new process for printing in blue on white COTTON. At this date the production and printing of cotton was strictly illegal in France but after a roaming apprenticeship he joined the staff of a protected Paris cotton-printer. A financier, hearing in 1758 that the restrictions on cotton manufacture were soon to be lifted, set him and his brother **Frédéric** up in a factory at Jouy en Josas where the first Oberkampf-designed engraved printed and dyed cotton was run off in March 1760. The concern was an immediate success: in 1764 a new and larger factory was begun at Jouy and a saleroom opened in Paris. The factory was created a *Manufacture royale* in 1783 and Oberkampf, who had been naturalized in 1770, was ennobled in 1787, bought out his partners and made a fortune. By prudent subscription to patriotic funds and no less prudent adoption of Republican devices to decorate his cottons, he survived the Revolution to make an even larger fortune under the Consulate and Empire. His success was due to various factors – the proximity of the factory to Versailles whence the courtiers made a practice of visiting it, a keen eye for changes in taste, an insistence on high-quality materials (he began by importing the best cotton from India by way of England), a readiness to adopt new techniques (plate printing shortly before 1770 and roller printing *c.*1805), industrial methods of production, and also good personal relations. He also profited greatly from the excellence of his chief designer J.-B. HUET. Most of the cottons he produced were flowered dress materials. In 1775 he began to produce elaborate furnishing textiles for the royal palaces, some of them printed from as many as eight blocks and in 1781 furnishing fabrics of the type with which his name is most closely associated – little vignetted scenes of such

C.-P. Oberkampf: toile de Jouy, *decorated with scenes by J.-B. Huet illustrating the manufacture of* toiles de Jouy, *1783*
(Musée des Arts Décoratifs, Paris)

subjects as *The Delights of the Four Seasons* or *The Pleasures of the Farm,* printed in blue or red on a white ground. After his death the vast concern was inherited by his relations who sold it in 1820: it then passed through several hands and was finally bankrupt and wound up in 1843

Lit: H. Clouzot, *Histoire de la manufacture de Jouy . . . ,* Paris 1928.

Obrisset (or **O'Brisset**), **John** (*fl.*1705–28). A French craftsman who settled in London where he became well known as a maker of small boxes of pressed horn or tortoise-shell decorated with portraits in relief.

Lit: P. A. S. Phillips, *John Obrisset, Huguenot, Carver, Medallist,* London 1931.

Obrist, Hermann (1863–1927). Swiss sculptor and Art Nouveau designer. After studying natural history at Heidelberg he worked at the Karlsruhe Kunstgewerbeschule (from 1888). He founded an embroidery workshop in Florence, 1892, moved to Munich 1894 and helped to establish the Munich *Vereinigten Werkstätten für Kunst im Handwerk,* 1897, of which he later became director. He designed some furniture but is important mainly for his embroidery designs based on plant forms, notably one of a cyclamen with roots and stalks arranged in an intricate pattern of curves called by a contemporary 'the whiplash'.

Lit: R. Schmutzler, *Art Nouveau,* London 1964; *Hermann Obrist . . . ,* Exh. Cat., Berne 1967.

Odiot, Jean-Baptiste-Claude (1763–1850). French Empire silversmith, he was the head of a workshop which rivalled that of BIENNAIS with whom he occasionally collaborated. He produced wares in a similar style though the best tend to be more massive and more self-consciously inspired by the Antique. Unlike Biennais he came from a family of silversmiths, was trained in the craft, and was received as a master by the Paris Corporation in 1785, when he took over his father's workshop. In 1792 he served in the Republican army and thus escaped the Terror. Under the Empire he worked much for Napoleon, became official *orfèvre* to Mme Mère, and collaborated with THOMIRE on the cradle for the King of Rome, 1811 (Kunsthistorisches Museum, Vienna). In 1814 he rejoined the army with the rank of colonel. But after the *Restauration* he became *orfèvre* to Louis XVIII, who gave him the Legion d'Honneur, continuing to work in the Empire Style. He retired in 1827 when his firm was taken over by his son **Charles** whose son **Jean-Baptiste** (1828–

J.-B.-C. Odiot: silver-gilt tureen, 1815–25 (Odiot Collection, Paris)

1912) succeeded to it in 1868. (For his mark *see* p. 894.)

Lit: H. Bouilhet, *L'Orfèvrerie française aux 18e et 19e siècles,* Paris 1910; S. Grandjean, *L'Orfèvrier du XIXe siècle en Europe,* Paris 1962.

Oeben, Jean-François (*c.*1721–63). He was the best French furniture-maker of the mid C18, i.e. of the transitional period between the Louis XV and Louis XVI styles. A skilled mechanic and metal worker, he specialized in *meubles à secrets* and *meubles à surprises,* compact, elaborately fitted, multi-purpose pieces, usually concealing a number of accessories, which came into demand after 1750 along with the fashion for smaller and more intimate rooms such as boudoirs, etc. German by birth, Oeben settled in Paris sometime between 1741 and 1749 when he married the niece of Roger LACROIX. In 1751 he began working for Charles-Joseph Boulle (grandson of A.-C. BOULLE). Largely due to the patronage of Mme de Pompadour he became *ébéniste du roi* in 1754. He did not become a *maître ébéniste* until 1761. His assistants included RIESENER and LELEU. Despite his success he died bankrupt. His widow carried on his business and used his stamp until 1767 when she married Riesener who had been in effective control of the workshop since Oeben's death. (Since Oeben did not become a *maître* until shortly before his death, most of the pieces of furniture marked with his *estampille* are probably partly if not wholly the work of Riesener.)

Apart from its mechanical ingenuity, Oeben's furniture is characterized by its elaborate marquetry – boldly pictorial marquetry especially of realistically rendered baskets of flowers framed with interlaced ribbons, sometimes of such extreme virtuosity as to give an almost *trompe l'oeil* effect, e.g., his small tables in the Residenzmuseum, Munich, and in the Rijksmuseum, Amsterdam. Towards the end of his life he adopted geometrical, usually multiple cube, marquetry, e.g., his secretaire in the Louvre. His masterpiece, which made his name famous and marked a decisive stage in the evolution of the BUREAU, is the large cylinder-top desk, known as the *Bureau du Roi Louis XV,* now at Versailles. It was commissioned in 1760. He was responsible for the complicated mechanism as well as the design of this extraordinarily elaborate and sumptuous piece, though it was completed after his death by Riesener whose signature it bears.

His younger brother **Simon François Oeben** (d.1786) was also an *ébéniste du roi* and his sister married Martin CARLIN. One of his daughters was the mother of Eugéne Delacroix (though whether her husband Charles Delacroix was the painter's father remains something of a mystery).

Illustrated next page and p. 664.

Lit: A. Boutemy in *Bulletin de la Société de l'Histoire de l'Art Francais* 1962 and in *Gazette des Beaux-Arts* April 1964; R. Stratman, *Der Ebenist Jean-François Oeben,* Heidelberg 1971; R. Stratman, 'Der ebenist Simon Oeben' in *Aachner Kunstblätter* XLII (1972), pp. 262–81.

Oeil de perdrix (partridge eye) A type of porcelain decoration used first and mainly at SÈVRES consisting of a repetitive pattern of dots in gold or enamel colour encircled by smaller dots, used

Oeil de perdrix *decoration on Sèvres porcelain, 1766 (Victoria & Albert Museum)*

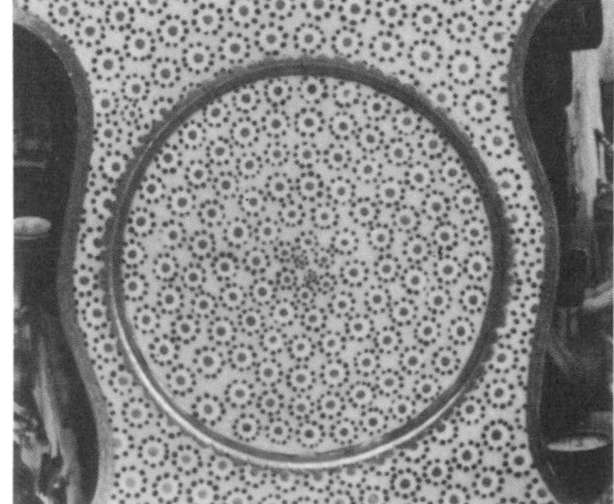

J.-F. Oeben: marquetry sécretaire en abattant, *c.1760 (Schloss Nymphenburg, Munich)*

as an alternative to plain, trellised, etc. grounds. The same term is applied to various types of lace ground with prominent dots in the meshes.

Oettingen–Schrattenhofen pottery Bavarian faience factory established at Oettingen in 1735 and moved to the park of Prince Albrecht Ernst of Oettingen-Oettingen at Schrattenhofen in 1737. The most notable products are tankards painted in high-temperature colours in an exuberant Rococo style. Brown ware like that of ANSBACH and BAYREUTH was also made. From the later C18 into the C19 cream-coloured earthenware was the staple product. (For factory mark *see* p. 886.)

Lit: K. Hüseler, *Deutsche Fayencen*, Stuttgart 1956; A. Boyer in *Keramos* 19 (1963), pp. 3–21.

Offenbach pottery A faience factory at Offenbach near Frankfurt-am-Main founded in 1739 by **Philipp Friedrich Lay** who had previously worked at HANAU. Its products were mainly table-wares painted in high-temperature colours with flowers, birds or figure subjects in a somewhat rustic style. It remained active until the early C19. (For factory mark *see* p. 886.)

Lit: K. Hüseler, *Deutsche Fayencen*, Stuttgart 1956.

Ogee An S-shaped moulding, i.e., CYMA RECTA or CYMA REVERSA.

Oinoche, *see* GREEK POTTERY.

Okawachi porcelain factory, *see* ARITA PORCELAIN FACTORIES.

Olbrich, Joseph Maria (1867–1908). He was an Austrian architect (trained under Otto Wagner) and Art Nouveau designer, one of the founders of the Vienna SECESSION for which he designed premises (1898), his first and most famous building. In 1899 the Grand Duke of Hesse called him to Darmstadt where he was establishing a colony of artists. Olbrich designed the Ernst Ludwig Haus which was to serve as the communal studio and most of the houses for the artists. He spent the rest of his life at Darmstadt. He also designed, mainly for the artists' colony, furniture, table-silver, lamps, metal-work and various household fitting and furnishings. In 1906 he designed carriage-work for Opel automobiles. In his designs he reacted against naturalism in favour of abstract patterns of flowing lines and irregular rounded shapes. In his furniture and silver he relied on clear-cut forms rather than surface detail. And he probably exerted some influence on modern design through his friends Peter BEHRENS and Josef HOFFMAN. Examples of his furniture and furnishings are in the Hessisches Landesmuseum, Darmstadt.

Lit: N. Pevsner, *Pioneers of Modern Design*, Harmondsworth 1960; *Joseph M. Olbrich*, Exh. Cat., Darmstadt 1967; H. Kreisel & G. Himmelheber, *Die Kunst des deutschen Möbels*, Vol. III, Munich 1973.

Old English pattern English type of spoon or fork with a plain flat stem spreading slightly towards the end of the handle which is gently curved back, made from the mid C18.

Old Seto wares, *see* MĪNO POTTERIES.

Olerys, Joseph (1697–1749). A notable S. French potter who was born in Marseilles and was probably trained as a painter in the Clérissy factory at MOUSTIERS. He is said to have run a small faience factory in Marseilles 1723–6. In 1726–7 he joined the staff of the ALCORA factory and in 1737 returned to France and set up a factory in partnership with his brother-in-law **Jean-Baptiste Laugier** (1688–1765) at Moustiers making use of the techniques he had learned in Spain (notably high-temperature colours).

Oliphant An obsolete form of the word 'elephant' now retained only for a medieval ivory cup carved from the entire tusk of an elephant. Such cups were often very elaborately carved.

Olivier, Jacques, *see* MONTPELLIER POTTERIES.

Ollivier, François, *see* APREY PORCELAIN FACTORY.

Omega workshops A short-lived concern founded in London in 1913 by the art critic **Roger Fry**, with the twin aims of improving the standard of decorative design in England and encouraging such gifted young artists as Duncan Grant,

Omega Workshops: woollen pile rug, 1914 (Victoria & Albert Museum)

Vanessa Bell, Wyndham Lewis and Henri Gaudier-Brezska. In many ways it was inspired by William MORRIS and Fry declared that the artists were 'working with the object of allowing free play to the delight in creation in the making of objects for common life'. But Fry lacked Morris's business sense and set ridiculously low prices on Omega products. He also unwisely insisted on anonymity which offended some of the artists who seceded after three months. And he failed to appreciate the importance attached to sound craftsmanship by English buyers. The affair struggled through the war years only to close down in 1920. Products included furniture, textiles and ceramics. Although some pieces are robust most of the furniture tends to be ricketty and of interest only for its gaily painted decorations. Some of the pottery made by Fry himself is handsome in its simplicity of design and decoration. But the best things were the carpets (made at WILTON) and the furnishing fabrics (printed in France) with excellent flat patterns worked out in bright colours. They represent the first attempts to apply the principles of Fauve and Cubist painting to the decorative arts in England. It was a brave experiment which foreshadowed, though it failed to influence directly, the development of English industrial design in the later 1920s and 1930s.

Lit: Furniture, textiles and pottery made at the Omega Workshops, Exh. Cat., Arts Council, Lewes 1946.

O'Neale, Geoffrey (or **Jeffrey**) **Hamet** He was a porcelain painter who worked on CHELSEA, WORCESTER and Chinese porcelain. Signed examples of his work on Worcester pieces are in the British Museum. *Aesop's Fables* provided many of his subjects which usually depict a horse or other animals or figures in a landscape. He may have worked for James GILES who ran a porcelain decorating shop in London and he may be identical with a Mr O'Neil, a painter at the Chelsea factory between 1770 and 1773.

Lit: W. B. Honey in *Antiques,* March 1932 p. 127.

Onslow pattern English mid-C18 type of spoon or fork decorated on the upper part of the stem with radiating fluting and with a top which curls round in a volute.

Opaline Modern name for translucent coloured glass of a slightly milky appearance, especially that made in C19 France and called by its makers *opale* or *en couleurs opale.*

Opaque twist stem The stem of a drinking glass enclosing one or more spirals of opaque white or coloured threads made by the same process as in Venetian LATTICINO GLASS. This type of stem was popular in England and Holland from the mid C18.

Oppenheim, Mayer (*fl.*1755–89). Glassmaker

known for his ruby glass for which he took out a patent in London in 1755 and in Birmingham in 1764. He founded a glasshouse in Birmingham *c.*1760. Later he appears to have settled in France where he took out a patent in 1789 for an improved method of glassmaking.

Oppenordt, Gilles-Marie (1672–1742). Leading RÉGENCE ornamentalist, a facile and prolific draughtsman whose designs were widely influential. Born in Paris, the son of an *ébéniste* of Dutch origin, he went to the French Academy 1692–9 and developed a High Baroque style, picked up from Bernini and Borromini. But this won him little favour in France, except for ecclesiastical work. Gradually succumbing to the influence of Pierre LE PAUTRE he adopted an early Rococo style and began to design domestic interiors in 1714. He was much patronized by the Regent to whom he was the accredited architect from 1715. But he never ventured into the more advanced Rococo of MEISSONNIER and PINEAU. In his own time he was known mainly as a draughtsman and after his death HUQUIER published three collections of his designs for decorative panels, cartouches, mouldings, consoles, clock-cases, chandeliers, chimney-pieces, etc., familiarly known as the Petit, Moyen and Grand Oppenordt (1748).

Lit: D. Guilmard, *Les maîtres ornemantistes*, Paris 1880; Fiske Kimball, *The creation of the Rococo*, Philadelphia 1943; E. Berckenhagen, *Die französischen Zeichnungen der Kunstbibliothek Berlin*, Berlin 1970.

Opus anglicanum English medieval ecclesiastical embroidery, especially that of the C13 and C14 which was the finest produced anywhere in Europe at the time and constitutes the greatest English contribution to the art of textiles. Its outstanding merits seem to have been 'discovered' in 1246 by Pope Innocent IV who was so impressed by the vestments of English bishops visiting Rome that he ordered gold embroideries for his copes and chasubles from the London merchants who dealt in such wares (they were by that date more usually the work of independent craftsmen than of monks and nuns). Several later Popes commissioned elaborate vestments from the English embroiderers (like that of 1288 in the Museo Communale, Ascoli Piceno, Italy; or those given in 1309 by Pope Clement V to the cathedral of S. Bertrand de Comminges) and their examples were followed by numerous patrons, especially in France and Spain. Opus Anglicanum differs from contemporary Continental work (which was sometimes executed in imitation of it) in quality and style rather than in technique. The ground material might be of silk or satin, and COUCHED gold thread was generally used for backgrounds with figures worked in silks in a fine split-stitch which was varied in direction to give an illusion of modelling (e.g., white silk stitches in concentric circles to suggest the modelling of a cheek). Every detail was executed with an astonishing miniscule perfection. Stylistically the embroideries are closely related to contemporary English manuscript illuminations and in some instances the designs were provided by manuscript illuminators. Decorative motifs, such as columns and arcades, were adopted from contemporaneous Early English and, more usually, Decorated architectural styles. The few C13 examples are rather on the severe side with elongated ascetic-looking figures set in delicate patterns of scroll-work (e.g. the Clare Chasuble in the Victoria & Albert Museum, London; the Ascoli cope in the Museo Communale, Ascoli Piceno, is much richer and was probably based on a design provided by the Pope who ordered it). With the C14 a much more elaborate style was developed: figures are more numerous and crowded and the overall patterns are more closely integrated. On the Syon Cope (Victoria & Albert Museum) fifteen linked quatrefoils contain New Testament scenes and figures of saints while the interstices are filled with feathered seraphim. A slightly later cope (Museo Civico, Bologna), perhaps the finest of all, is embroidered with the Martyrdom of St Thomas à Becket and numerous New Testament scenes, each shown under a Decorated Gothic arch the spandrels of which are filled with figures of angels holding censers or playing musical instruments. Towards the mid C14 the decoration grew so profuse that it began to dominate the figures which peep out of a thicket of vine and ivy tendrils. At about the same time the quality of English embroidery began to decline though it still enjoyed favour on the Continent and compares well with contemporary Continental work. In the C15 the motifs used for decorating copes

Opus Anglicanum: detail of The Syon Cope, *coloured silk and silver and gold threads on linen, English, late c13 (Victoria & Albert Museum)*

and chasubles were standardized – lilies, crowns, stars and seraphim with feathered tights and spiky wings balancing on wheels – and they were generally cut out and applied to a plain velvet ground. Figure subjects, much more coarsely embroidered than hitherto, were reserved for orphreys; the figures themselves were often 'loaded' (padded to give a relief effect) and the backgrounds heavily worked with gold thread. The art of ecclesiastical embroidery in England more or less died with the Reformation.

Lit: Opus Anglicanum, Exh. Cat., Victoria & Albert Museum, London 1963; A. G. I. Christie, *English Medieval Embroidery,* London 1938.

Orders In classical architecture, a column with base (usually), shaft, capital and entablature decorated and proportioned according to one of the accepted modes – Doric, Tuscan, Ionic, Corinthian or Composite – which were first codified by Sebastiano Serlio in 1540. They were applied to furniture and some small objects (e.g. caskets shaped like temples, columnar candlesticks) from the Renaissance onwards but seldom proportioned and decorated correctly before the late C18.

Oribe ware, *see* MINO POTTERIES.

Oribe-no-Sho Shigenari, *see* MINO POTTERIES.

Oriental Lowestoft A name formerly applied to CHINESE EXPORT PORCELAIN which was at one time erroneously supposed to have been made at LOWESTOFT.

Orléans potteries and porcelain factories A faience factory was active at Orleans in the later C17 but few of its products are known. A factory founded in 1753 and described in 1767 as *Manufacture Royale de porceleyne de Orléans* made both soft- and hard-paste porcelain (little of which has been identified) e.g. MENNECY type porcelain figures and earthenware in the English style – notably 'agate' and marbled table-wares. Various other factories are known to have been active at Orleans in the late C18 and early C19. (For factory mark *see* p. 886.)

Lit: G. Fontaine, *La céramique française,* Paris 1946.

Ormolu Decorative objects, especially mounts for furniture, of bronze, cast, chased and fire-gilt. The term is generally reserved for C18 and later objects, gilded by the MERCURY GILDING process. The finest work was executed in France, notably by GOUTHIÈRE; in England the best was produced at the factory of Matthew BOULTON. Ormolu should be distinguished from the much larger class of gilt-bronze objects which were dipped in acid and lacquered.

Orphrey A strip or cross-shaped piece of embroidery, often worked very richly with gold thread, applied to such ecclesiastical vestments as CHASUBLES and COPES.

Orrefors glasshouse Swedish glass factory founded near Kalmar in 1898 and producing decorative wares from 1915 with **Simon Gate** (from 1916) and **Edward Hald** (from 1917) as artistic directors joined by **Viktor Lindstrand** in 1929. Hald had studied painting under Matisse and during his directorship (1933–44) the factory produced some of the best decorative glass made in Europe – bold thick vases sometimes of bubbled or tinted glass with deeply engraved designs.

Orrefors glass vase, engraved by K. Rössler, designed by Edward Hald, c.1930 (Victoria & Albert Museum)

Table-wares were made at a subsidiary factory at Sandvik, generally of simple facet-cut form and of dusky-green or smoky-brown colour. After the war **Sven Palmquist** developed a new technique,

'Ravenna' glass – heavy, often tinted, into which simple non-figurative patterns are inlaid: and **Nils Landberg** (b.1907) has designed some excellent drinking glasses, light-fittings and also decorative glass, notably bowls of steel-blue potash crystal of extreme bubble-like thinness.

Lit: G. Janneau, *Modern Glass*, London 1931; A. Polak, *Modern Glass*, London 1962; C. Hernmarck, *Orrefors*, Orrefors 1951.

Orvieto potteries The source of some of the earliest (C13–C15) Italian maiolica vessels (mainly bowls, dishes and jugs) rather roughly potted and sometimes clumsy in form, decorated in manganese purple and green over a rather thin tin-enamel glaze, with distinctly Gothic, often very spirited, formalized foliage, animals or figures. Crowned figures and crowned heads drawn in outline, and strongly cross-hatched grounds in dark purple appear to have been local peculiarities of decoration. Otherwise the wares are similar to those of the same period made in other parts of Italy. The term 'Orvieto ware' is sometimes applied incorrectly and indiscriminately to all pieces of early maiolica.

Lit: G. Liverani in *Faenza* XXV (1937), pp. 3ff; G. Liverani, *Five Centuries of Italian Majolica*, New York & London 1960.

Osmond, Robert (d.1789). A bronze founder, he became a *maître-fondeur* in Paris in 1746 and appears to have specialized in clock cases, especially *cartel* CLOCKS, of which examples survive in the Musée Nissim de Camondo in Paris, the National Museum in Stockholm and elsewhere. His relationship to **Louis-Charles Osmond** and **Jean-Baptiste Osmond**, who became *maîtres-fondeurs* in 1757 and 1764 respectively, is uncertain but the former may have been his son.

Lit: S. Eriksen, *Early Neo-Classicism in France*, London 1974.

Østerbro, *see* COPENHAGEN POTTERIES.

Ostrich-egg cup A type of cup consisting of an ostrich-egg, the surface of which is sometimes painted, serving as the bowl set in a generally elaborate silver mount. Such cups were made from the C15 (a French example of *c*.1410–20 is in the Schatzkammer of the Residenz in Munich)

Ostrich-egg cup, with silver mounts by H. Petzolt, Nuremburg, 1594 (Minneapolis Institute of Arts)

and most extensively in the C16. They were intended for decoration rather than use.

Ott and Brewer Company The most important of the several porcelain factories at Trenton, New Jersey. It was established in 1863 under the name of **Bloor, Ott & Booth**, producing mainly earthenware, and was reconstituted as Ott & Brewer in 1871. With the assistance of William Bromley who had worked at the BELLEEK factory in Ireland it was the first American factory to make the Belleek ware which became very popular. It also produced PARIAN WARE. For a short while the Canadian sculptor Isaac Broome (b.1835) was employed as modeller for products shown at the Philadelphia Centennial Exhibition in 1876 – notably a Parian ware bust of Cleopatra with much gilding and a cup supported by three baseball players (New Jersey State Museum, Trenton). Another notable employee was W. S. LENOX who left in 1896 to found his own factory.

Lit: *19th Century America: Furniture and other Decorative Arts*, Exh. Cat., Metropolitan Museum, New York 1970.

Ottoman Late-C18 English name for a long, low, upholstered sofa, also called a **Turkey Sofa.** The term is still less precise than the French *ottomane* (see CANAPÉ).

Ottoman carpets, *see* TURKISH COURT CARPETS.

Ottweiler pottery and porcelain factory A Rhenish factory founded in 1763 under the patronage of Prince Wilhelm Heinrich of Nassau by E.-D. PELLEVÉ who left in 1767 and was followed by a succession of French and German directors. Both faience (little of which has been identified) and porcelain were made in the early years. Products included table-wares often very attractively painted in enamel colours with Rococo style mythological and *Commedia dell'Arte* scenes often after prints by J. E. Nilson. Figures were also made but few have been identified. Glazed earthenware in the English style became the staple product from 1784 until 1794 when the factory closed and its materials and models were taken to SARREGUEMINES. Earthenware is unmarked. Porcelain is sometimes marked 'N.S.' (for Nassau Saarbrucken) with or without a date.

Lit: K. Lohmeyer in *Der Cicerone* XVI (1924), pp. 540 ff; K. Hüseler, *Deutsche Fayencen*, Stuttgart 1956.

Oude Loosdrecht porcelain factory, *see* WEESP PORCELAIN FACTORY.

Oudenarde tapestry factories Oudenarde became a centre for tapestry weaving in the C15 and in the C16 was very productive though it was not until the C17 that it began almost to rival the BRUSSELS factories. It excelled in furniture tapestries but also produced landscapes, *verdures* and figure subjects from cartoons by D. Teniers and other Flemish artists. In the late C17 many of the weavers emigrated to France and the factories never really recovered though the last did not finally close until 1787.

Oudry, Jean-Baptiste (1686–1755). The greatest French animal painter of his time. He became painter to the BEAUVAIS TAPESTRY FACTORY in 1726 and its director in 1734, providing the designs for such tapestries as *The New Hunts* (1727), *Country Passtimes* (1730), *Comedies of Molière* (1732), *Metamorphoses of Ovid* (1734), *Fines Verdures* (1735) and *Fables of La Fontaine*

J.-B. Oudry: Gobelins tapestry from the 'Hunts of Louis XV' series, 1733–46 (Uffizi, Florence)

(1736). He also designed the delightful *Hunts of Louis XV* (1733–46) woven at the GOBELINS. Although he worked so much for the tapestry factories he remained essentially a painter in oils and insisted, perhaps too forcefully, that the weavers should try to copy every nuance of his colours.

Oushak carpets, *see* TURKISH CARPETS.

Outrebon, Nicolas I (*fl.*1703–15), **Nicolas II** (d.1779), **Jean-Louis-Dieudonné** (*fl.*1772–91). A prominent family of Parisian silversmiths. Nicolas I became a *maître* in 1703; his son Nicolas II became a *maître* in 1735 and worked for François-Thomas GERMAIN. Nicolas II's son Jean-Louis-Dieudonné registered his *poinçon* in 1772. Examples of the work of all three Outrebons are in the Louvre. (For mark *see* p. 894.)

Outside decorators on ceramics, *see* HAUSMALER.

Over-glaze decorations Painted or printed decorations applied to ceramics after they have been glazed, e.g., paintings in ENAMEL COLOURS on porcelain or faience.

Overstuffed seat The seat of a chair with the upholstery carried over and secured beneath the seat-rail.

Ovolo A wide convex moulding, sometimes called a quarter-round.

Oxbow front American term for the undulating front of a chest of drawers or other piece of case furniture with a concave flanked by two convex curves, i.e., the opposite of a SERPENTINE FRONT.

Oystershell veneer Laminae of wood cut transversely from the smaller branches of walnut, olive, kingwood, *lignum vitae*, and laid together as a parquetry veneer in association with lighter-coloured woods. A Dutch C17 technique, but also practised elsewhere, mainly for cabinet doors and drawer fronts.

Ozier patterns Repetitive relief ornaments simulating basket-work, used for the decoration of porcelain at MEISSEN and subsequently copied by many other European factories. The earliest was apparently devised by J. G. HEROLD *c.*1735 and used on the Sulkowsky table service; it is called *Ordinair-ozier* or Sulkowsky pattern, has mouldings in sets of four divided by radial ribs at intervals, and was confined to the rims of plates. *Altozierrand* of about the same date, similarly used on the rims of plates, is a regular basketwork pattern with radial ribs. The *Altbrandsteinmuster* used from about 1740 has panels divided into sets of three with curved ribs. The *Neuozierrand* of 1742 has a plain inner border and basketwork outer border with four sets of spiralling ribs. The *Brühlisches Allerlei-Dessin* is a combination of basketwork with flowers, shells, etc.

Ozier pattern: plate from the Sulkowsky service, Meissen, pre-1737

Constructed letter by Albrecht Dürer, from Unterweisung mit dem Zirkel und Richtscheit (Instruction with Compass and Ruler), *published by Hieronymous Formschneider, Nuremberg,* 1538

Package furniture Furniture sold in units which can be packed flat and easily assembled with a screwdriver. First made in Sweden and Denmark in the 1940s and now throughout the Western World. Also called **Knock-down furniture.**

Pad foot A CLUB FOOT resting on a disk, often used as a terminal for a cabriole leg from the early C18 onwards.

Padeloup, Antoine-Michel (1685–1758). One of the most famous French bookbinders of the C18. He was bookbinder to Louis XV from 1733. He developed a type of inlaid binding with large pieces of red, green and lemon-yellow leather in scroll and floral patterns. Notable examples of his work are in the Bibliothèque Municipale, Dijon, and the Bibliothèque Nationale in Paris.

Padouk or **Padauk wood** A well-marked red wood, a kind of rosewood from the Burmese leguminous tree *Pterocarpus macrocarpus.* It was occasionally used by English C18 furniture-makers.

Padua potteries In the C15 and C16 the source of an unusual type of SGRAFFIATO WARE with large areas of the slip cut away to provide a background to the (usually foliated) design, thus producing a relief effect similar to Chinese SUNG dynasty pottery. A later factory produced *c.*1630 some curious maiolica imitations of Turkish (ISNIK) wares – plates painted with loose bunches of carnations, tulips and reedy leaves surrounded by borders of formalized waves. Wares are sometimes marked with a cross, date and '*a padoa*'.

Lit: B. Rackham in *Burlington Magazine* LXVIII (1936), pp. 113–114; G. Liverani, *Five Centuries of Italian Maiolica,* London 1960.

Pagano, Matio (*fl.*1530–59). The author of some of the earliest pattern books for CUTWORK, RETICELLA and LACE, all published in Venice: *Giardinetto nuovo di punti tagliati,* 1542 (8th edition 1558); *Ornamento de le belle et virtudiose donne,* 1543 (5th edition 1554); *Il specchio di pensieri delle belle et virtudiose donne,* 1544 (4th edition 1550); *Lhonesto essempio,* 1553 (2nd edition 1556) *Specchio di virtu,* 1554; *La gloria e l'honore de punti tagliati et punti in aere* (5th edition 1563); *Trionfo di virtu,* 1559 (3rd edition 1568). The designs are abstract or floral and maintain the geometrical grid imposed by the fabric in cutwork, though, as the titles indicate, the later volumes were intended for makers of PUNTO IN ARIA lace, as well as the earlier types of openwork fabric.

Design for lace by Pagano, from Gloria de punti tagliati, 1554

Lit: A. Lotz, *Bibliographie der Modelbücher,* Leipzig 1933.

Pagod or **Pagoda figure** Originally an oriental idol: from the C18 a chinoiserie parody of such a figure, generally large-bellied, squatting and grinning.

Pagoda motif A representation of a Chinese pagoda tower much employed in CHINOISERIE decorations.

Paillons French word for spangles, applied to those of gold, silver or colours cut in simple geometrical shapes and set in translucent enamel on boxes, étuis, etc.

Painted enamel, *see* ENAMEL.

Pairpoint Manufacturing Company An electroplate factory established at New Bedford, Mass., in 1880. In 1894 it absorbed the MOUNT WASHINGTON GLASS COMPANY. Products included flashed glass vessels of colours (notably an emerald) developed by **William E. Kern** (formerly of the BOSTON AND SANDWICH GLASS COMPANY). From 1900 it was known as the Pairpoint Corporation.

Lit: *19th Century American Furniture and Other Decorative Arts,* Exh. Cat., Metropolitan Museum of Art, New York 1970.

Pairpoint, Thomas J., *see* GORHAM COMPANY.

Paiva, José Francisco de (1744–1824). Portuguese architect and furniture designer working in Oporto. Many of his designs for furniture – chairs, clock cases, bookcases, cabinets, etc. – survive, some influenced by French prototypes but the majority inspired by or directly copied from the published designs of CHIPPENDALE and HEPPLEWHITE. Surviving furniture made after his designs includes some magnificent chests of drawers in the Carmelite church in Oporto and a tall, pedimented cupboard in the church of S. Martinho do Lordelo de Ouro, Oporto.

Lit: M. H. Mendes Pinto, *José Francisco de Paiva,* Lisbon 1973.

Paktong An alloy of copper, zinc and nickel resembling silver but slightly tinged with yellow. The European equivalent (of slightly different proportions of copper, zinc and nickel) is called NICKEL SILVER or German Silver. It is similar to the Indian alloy TUTENAG. Paktong is first recorded in the early C18 but was probably in use much earlier. It seems to have originated in Yunnan province. It was frequently used by Chinese furniture-makers for hinges, etc.

Lit: W. D. John, *Paktong,* Newport, Mon. 1970; A. Bonnin, *Tutenag and Paktong,* Oxford 1924.

Palace bowl A type of small Chinese cup or bowl with high well-rounded sides turning in slightly at the rim. It is found mainly in Chün ware and Lung-ch'üan celadon. It is sometimes called a **Bubble Cup.**

Palagi, Pelagio (1775–1860). Painter, sculptor, architect and designer, he was trained in Rome where he worked on the redecoration of the Quirinal Palace for Napoleon, but settled in Milan in 1818 and later, in 1832, in Turin. In Turin he was put in charge of the decoration of the royal palaces and was also made director of a school of design. The furniture he designed between 1836 and 1840 for the Palazzo Reale in Turin is very

P. Palagi: armchair, 1836–40 (Palazzo Reale, Turin)

showy and magnificent, and of high quality. The woodwork is thickly gilded and he made great play with robustly carved human or mythological figures. Especially fine is the gilt-bronze table which he designed for the Council Chamber and which was cast in Milan in 1836. His furniture is still in the palace in Turin.

Lit: H. Honour, *Cabinet Makers and Furniture Designers*, London and New York 1969.

Palampore A type of PINTADO or painted cloth imported into England from Masulipatam in the C17.

Palermo potteries, *see* SICILIAN POTTERIES.

Palissandre, *see* ROSEWOOD.

Palissy, Bernard (*c.*1510–*c.*1590). He was an outstanding French potter and one of the most colourful figures in the history of ceramics. He was also a naturalist, particularly fond of reptiles, and developed a type of pottery which could reproduce their slithery forms and muddy colours with extraordinary fidelity. He was born at Agen, apprenticed to a glass painter and travelled round France before settling at Saintes where *c.*1539 he began a series of experiments to make an improved type of pottery, with a kiln in his own house. According to his own account he soon exhausted his purse and was reduced to using the floors and furniture to fire his pots (to the fury of his wife). By 1548 he began to produce his so-called 'rustic-wares' – dishes shaped like little ponds with realistically modelled snakes, lizards, snails and insects in and around them, all coloured with glazes with rather slimy greens, greys, browns and blues predominating. Like his German contemporary, the goldsmith W. JAMNITZER, he made casts of dead reptiles for use in modelling. He also made wares known as *terres jaspées* – dishes, ewers, vases, etc., decorated in relief with Biblical or mythological scenes covered with variously coloured glazes. He was patronized by the Constable de Montmorency who commissioned him in 1555 to execute a grotto of pottery for his château at Écouen. By this time he had become a Huguenot and as such was imprisoned in Bordeaux in 1562 but released by the Constable. Created *inventeur des rustiques figulines du roi* he was protected from religious persecution for a while. In 1563–4 he moved to La Rochelle where he published his *Recepte Veritable par laquelle tous les hommes de France pourront apprendre à multiplier leurs thrésors* and prepared the plan for a grotto which he presented to Catherine de Medici who, in 1566, summoned him to carry it out at the Palace of the Tuileries in Paris. He fled from Paris to Sedan at the time of the massacre of St Bartholomew's Day but returned *c.*1576, and published his *Discours admirable de la nature des eaux et fontaines* in which he described at length his activities as a potter. In 1586 he was prosecuted for heresy and spent the rest of his life as a prisoner in the Bastille de Bucy. The only surviving ceramics known to have been made by Palissy are fragments of his Tuileries grotto (excavated in 1878 and now in the Louvre). His rustic wares and other works appear to have been widely imitated in his own time and probably into the C17. The basis for the attribution of individual pieces to him is normally qualitative, though two groups differentiated on technical grounds are certainly to be ascribed to his followers. Imitations and fakes, especially of the rustic wares, were made on a large scale in the C19 – the most notable of the former being by Charles AVISSEAU and the Landais family of Tours, Georges Pull of Paris and the MAFRA POTTERY.

B. Palissy style dish, lead-glazed earthenware, late C16 (Louvre)

Lit: L. Audiot, *Bernard Palissy*, Paris 1868 (repr. Geneva 1969); M. J. Ballot, *La céramique française: Bernard Palissy et les fabriques du XVIe siècle*, Paris 1924; G. de Rothschild & G. Grandjean, *Bernard Palissy et son école . . .*, Paris 1952.

Pall A rich, generally embroidered, cloth, especially one of black, purple or white velvet used to cover a coffin, hearse or tomb.

Palladian style The architectural style inspired by

the works and especially the publications of **Andrea Palladio** (1508–80), introduced into England by Inigo Jones (1573–1652) and revived in the early C18 by Lord Burlington (1694–1753) and Colen Campbell (1673–1729). Palladio is not known to have designed any furniture. But in early-C18 England furniture was made in a style thought suitable for the interior of a Neo-Palladian house – rather massive with much use of pediments, cornices, lion masks and paws, acanthus leaves, swags, etc., derived from architectural ornament or antique sculpture. It sometimes shows the influence of Italian Baroque furniture but is generally more rigid and restrained. Lord Burlington's protégé William KENT was probably the most notable of the designers. Another architect, and an associate of Kent, John Vardy (d.1765) designed furniture in a similar style (drawings in the Victoria & Albert Museum) and published the influential book *Some Designs of Mr Inigo Jones and of Mr William Kent*, London 1744. William Jones (d.1757) included designs for pedimented looking-glass frames in the manner of Kent in *The Gentleman's or Builders' Companion*, London 1739. And the classical designs published by B. LANGLEY are similar. Cabinet-makers who executed furniture in this style include B. GOODISON, G. GRENDY and W. VILE.

Lit: P. Ward-Jackson, *English Furniture Designs of the Eighteenth Century*, London 1958.

Palmer, Humphrey (*fl.*1760–78). The owner of the **Church Works pottery** at Hanley, Staffordshire producing from 1760 wares in a style similar to, and often imitated from, those of WEDGWOOD (including black basaltes from 1769). For a period he employed J. VOYEZ who had previously worked for Wedgwood. But he was financially unsuccessful. In 1778 he went into partnership with **J. Neale** who soon took the pottery over. It survived into the C19 when it was acquired by the RIDGWAY family.

Lit: G. A. Godden (ed.), *Jewitt's The Ceramic Art of Great Britain*, London 1972.

Palmette A fan-shaped decorative motif resembling a palmated leaf or a panicle of flowers. One type of Greek palmette resembles honeysuckle flowers, another is more like a palm-leaf. Both

Palmette

were used in bands of ANTHEMION ornament especially on Ionic buildings (e.g., the Erechtheum, Athens) and the former type is sometimes incorrectly termed an anthemion. They were also used as painted motifs on pottery. Greek types of palmette were revived during the Renaissance and extensively used thereafter in the decoration of ceramics, metalwork, furniture, etc., especially in the late C18. The same term is applied to many other formalized palmate motifs including those occurring in Celtic ornament, on Oriental carpets, etc.

Palmquist, Sven (b.1906). Swedish glass engraver and designer trained at the school attached to the ORREFORS GLASSHOUSE where he was employed from 1928. He is responsible for two of the types of coloured glass made at Orrefors, named *Kraka* and *Ravenna*, generally rather thick heavy pieces with non-representational patterns inlaid in bright colours.

Lit: Venini-Murano, Orrefors Glas, Exh. Cat., Kestnermuseum, Hanover 1957.

Panache French name for a bunch of feathers, often used to crown each corner of the canopy of a bed in the C18.

Panel stamps Metal blocks cut or engraved with a pictorial or decorative device, stamped on a book cover by means of a press. They enabled the decoration of a book to be completed in one operation at the binder's press. *See* STAMPED BINDINGS.

Panelled chest A C16 or early-C17 English chest constructed with a framework of rails, stiles and muntins held together by mortice and tenon joints, the work of a joiner, as distinct from a BOARDED CHEST which was the work of a carpenter.

Pankok, Bernhard (1872–1943). German Art Nouveau designer and graphic artist. Worked in Munich 1892–1902, contributing to the magazine *Jugend*, assisting in the foundation of an arts and crafts studio (Vereinigten Werkstätte für Kunst im Handwerk), and designing furniture in an unusually heavy version of the Art Nouveau style. He moved to Stuttgart in 1902 where he was director of the Staatliche Kunstgewerbeschule 1913–17.

Lit: S. Günther, *Interieurs um 1900. B. Pankok, B. Paul u. R. Riemerschmid als Mitarbeiter d. Vereinigten Werkstätten f. Kunst im Handwerk*, Munich 1971; H. Selig (ed.), *Jugendstil*, Heidelberg & Munich 1959; *Bernard Pankok 1872–1943*, Exh. Cat., Stuttgart 1973.

B. Pankok: vitrine of mahogany and cherry wood, 1901 (Kunstgewerbemuseum, Berlin)

Pantin, Cristalleries de French glasshouse founded in 1851. Its most distinguished products were very handsome, elegantly simple decanters and drinking glasses made *c.*1900 to designs by H. P. BERLAGE.

Pantin, Simon (d.1731). One of the best Huguenot refugee silversmiths working in London where he registered his mark at Goldsmiths' Hall in 1701 and set up a workshop at the Sign of the Peacock in St Martin's Lane. His maker's mark – a peacock with his initials – is found on many pieces of domestic plate in the simple Queen Anne style with only a modicum of Huguenot type decoration (e.g., teapot of 1705 in the Victoria & Albert Museum; jug at Jesus College, Oxford). A handsome tureen which he contributed to a large dinner service for the Empress Catherine of Russia 1725–6 survives in the Hermitage Museum, Leningrad. His workshop was taken over in 1731 by his son **Simon Pantin** (d.1733) whose widow ran it until 1739 when **Lewis Pantin** took control. (For his mark *see* p. 894.)

Lit: J. F. Hayward, *Huguenot Silver in England*, London 1959.

Papal rose A vase containing the simulated branch of a flowering rose made of gold and given by the Pope on Rose Sunday (the fourth in Lent) to a ruler who had rendered notable services to the church. One of the earliest to survive is that given by Clement V to the Prince-Bishop of Bâle in the early C14 (Musée de Cluny, Paris); another outstanding early example is that given by Pius II to the City of Siena in 1459 (Palazzo Communale, Siena). Later examples include that sent by Pius VII to the Empress of Austria (now in the

Papal rose, gold, early c14, given by Pope Clement V to the Prince-Bishop of Bâle (Musée de Cluny, Paris)

Schatzkammer, Vienna) and that given by Pius X in 1856 to the Empress Eugénie (now in St Michael's Abbey, Farnborough).

Pap-boat A small boat-shaped vessel, usually of silver or pottery, used for feeding infants, mainly in the c18.

Paper-weight Any small object intended to be laid on loose papers. The most interesting are those of glass made at the BACCARAT and CLICHY factories in early-c19 France.

Papier mâché A material made from pulped or otherwise prepared paper, glue, chalk and sometimes sand. It hardens after moulding and baking and will take a high polish after painting or JAPANNING. Perhaps of oriental origin, it first appeared in Europe in the c17 in France and was introduced into England by 1672. In 1772

Papier mâché *chair, early c19 (Victoria & Albert Museum)*

Henry Clay (d.1812) of Birmingham patented a method of glueing together sheets of specially prepared paper under heat to form strong, heat-resistant panels which provided an excellent surface for japanning and painting and were made into tea-trays, etc. This substance was at first called 'paper ware', but the name *papier mâché* was given to it from 1816 by the Birmingham firm, **Jennens and Bettridge**. In *c.*1830 an improved form was patented by Charles Bielefeld. These and other, less durable, forms of the material became very popular in C19 England and, to a lesser extent, the U.S.A. (notably at Litchfield, Connecticut, where much was produced). It was often embellished with inlays of mother-of-pearl and used for small household objects and light furniture, especially tables and chairs.

Lit: S. P. De Voc, *English papier mâché of the Georgian & Victorian Periods*, London 1971.

Papier peint The name given to printed patterned WALLPAPER in late-C17 France to distinguish it from the plain papers previously used. PAPILLON used the more accurate term 'papiers de tapisseries imprimés'.

Papillon, Jean (1661–1723). Leading Parisian wallpaper-maker. He began to produce in 1688 *papiers de tapisserie* printed in sheets which form a consecutive design when pasted on a wall (a technique first developed in early-C15 England). His papers were printed from very large wood blocks and coloured by brush and stencil. He also made a very impermanent lustre paper by a process similar to that of FLOCK PAPER. But his main achievement was to raise the status of wallpaper from a material used only by the poor, as a cheap substitute for wall-hangings, to one which was found in the wealthiest French houses. After his death his son **Jean Baptiste Michel** (1696–1776) ran the factory until *c.*1740 and published in 1766 the *Traité Historique et Pratique de la Gravure en Bois* which includes a long and not very accurate history of wallpaper-making in France. Both father and son made papers with stripe and diaper patterns, flowing designs of foliage, others incorporating framed pictures and some bearing large pictorial compositions intended to fill a whole wall. But they are known from the son's engravings rather than from extant specimens which (despite various optimistic attributions) are very few and fragmentary.

Lit: H. Clouzot & C. Follot, *Histoire du Papier Peint en France*, Paris 1935.

Parasole, Isabetta Catanea (fl. 1595–1616). The authoress of several influential and very popular books of designs for LACE, all published in Rome: *Specchio delle virtuose donne*, 1595 (3rd edition 1598); *Studio delle virtuose dame*, Rome 1597; *Fiori d'ogni virtu*, Rome 1610 (6th edition under different title 1636); *Gemma pretiosa delle virtuose donne*, Rome 1615 (2nd edition 1625).

Parcel gilt Silver gilded in parts, or furniture gilded in parts.

Pardoe, Thomas (1770–1823). English porcelain decorator, mainly a painter of flowers (sometimes copied from plates in Curtis's *Botanical Magazine*) who worked at the DERBY, WORCESTER, and, from 1797, SWANSEA factories. In 1809 he settled in Bristol as an outside decorator enamelling COALPORT and other wares. In 1821 he went to NANTGARW. He often signed his work.

Lit: E. M. Nance, *The Pottery and Porcelain of Swansea and Nantgarw*, London 1942.

Parian ware A type of white porcelain with a slightly granular surface resembling pure white statuary marble. It was used mainly for busts and figures, occasionally for decorative dishes and vases and sometimes for shirt-studs and jewellery (the latter being much patronized by Queen Victoria). It was first produced at the COPELAND factory in 1844. Next year the Art Union of London, in an effort to improve both industrial arts and public taste, commissioned Copeland to make a number of figures after the works of leading contemporary sculptors. Other factories, notably MINTON, WEDGWOOD and WORCESTER, followed this lead and produced similar pieces. At the Great Exhibition of 1851 several manufacturers exhibited Parian ware pieces, also known as 'Statuary porcelain', some of them very large (life-size figures were moulded in parts). Similar wares were produced on the Continent and in the U.S.A. by the BENNINGTON POTTERY, etc.

Lit: C. & D. Shinn, *The Illustrated Guide to Victorian Parian China*, London 1971.

Paris enamels A term used to describe a group of C14 enamels executed in Paris and, probably, N. France and Flanders. They include some of the earliest examples of BASSE-TAILLE enamelling (e.g., the portable altar-piece in the Poldi-Pezzoli Museum, Milan, in which it is combined with *champlevé* enamel). With the exception of a magnificent silver ewer in the National Museum,

Paris enamel decoration on a silver ewer, c.1330–40 (National Museum, Copenhagen)

Copenhagen, of *c.*1330–40 – perhaps the finest surviving piece of medieval domestic silver – all the known Paris enamels are ecclesiastical. They include a paten of 1333 (National Museum, Copenhagen), a folding portable altar-piece (Kunsthistorisches Museum, Vienna), a triptych (Namur Cathedral), a crucifix (Carrand collection, Museo Nazionale, Florence), a crozier (Cologne Cathedral) and the Royal Gold Cup of *c.*1380 (British Museum). The silver reliefs to which the enamels are applied are sometimes so high that the flesh areas of the figures or even the whole figures are left raised and uncoloured. The drawing is of great elegance and precision, strongly influenced by Parisian book illuminations of the early C14. In the late C14 to early C15 some very fine examples of *rond bosse* enamelling were executed in the Parisian workshops, notably the reliquary of the Holy Thorn, with its little enamelled figures of God the Father, the Saints and the trumpeting angels supported on a castellated Gothic base (British Museum), the *Goldene Rössel* of 1403 at Altötting, the reliquary of Sixtus V at Montalto and the reliquary from the chapel of the Order of the Saint Esprit (Louvre).

Lit: U. Middeldorf in *Gazette des Beaux Arts*, 6th ed LV (1960), pp. 231–44; M.-M. Gauthier, *Emaux du moyen âge occidental*, Fribourg 1972.

Paris potteries and porcelain factories There were faience factories in Paris from the mid C17, increasing in number during the C18 (there were 14 in 1789). None appears to have developed an individual style. The most interesting was probably the **Ollivier factory** in the rue de la Roquette which specialized in stoves painted in enamel colours shortly before and during the Revolution (a stove in the form of the Bastille presented to the Convention in 1790 is now in the Musée National de Céramique de Sèvres).

None of the porcelain factories began production before the late C18. But a large number were then established, making hard-paste wares generally imitative of SÈVRES, as a result of the relaxation of the laws protecting the monopoly of Sèvres in 1766 and 1770. The most productive appears to have been the **La Courtille factory** in the rue Fontaine-au-Roy, founded in 1771 by **Jean-Baptiste Locré de Roissy** who had worked at Leipzig, and managed from 1774 by **Laurentius Russinger** from HÖCHST. Although its products were known as *porcelaine allemande* only the first seem to have been German in style. Others were decorated in the Louis XVI style and the factory is said to have pirated BOIZOT's biscuit figures modelled for Sèvres. This factory survived until *c.*1840. Most of the other notable Paris factories were under the protection of members of the Royal Family or other notabilities. Their products are often attractive – especially late-C18 table-wares with sprigged decorations – but rarely original. They include that at **Clignacourt** founded in 1771 under the protection of the Comte de Provence (later Louis XVIII) and active until 1798; that in **faubourg Saint Denis** founded by P.-A. HANNONG in 1771, under the protection of the Comte d'Artois from 1779, and surviving until 1828;

that in **rue Thiroux** founded *c.*1775 under the protection of Marie Antoinette and despite many changes of hands active until after 1869; that at **Pont au Choux** which had made cream-coloured earthenware in the English style from *c.*1765 and began to produce porcelain in 1777; that in the **rue de Bindy** founded in 1780 under the protection of the Duc d'Angoulême (originating the cornflower sprig pattern known as the 'Angoulême sprig') which, after several moves, closed in 1829; that in **rue Popincourt** which was

Paris porcelain (rue Popincourt factory) jug in basin, c.*1790 (Victoria & Albert Museum)*

founded in 1782, which rose to some importance in the Directoire and Empire periods and survived until 1835; that in the **rue Amelot,** founded in 1784 and under the protection of the duc d'Orléans from 1786, active until after 1798; that in the **petite rue Saint-Gilles** founded in 1785 under the patronage of the Duchesse d'Angoulême, later run in collaboration with other establishments and surviving until 1867; that in the **rue de Crussol** founded in 1789 by an Englishman **Christopher Potter**; and that in the **rue des Récollets** conducted from *c.*1793 to 1825 by **Desprez** who had formerly worked at Sèvres and specialized in porcelain cameos in imitation of WEDGWOOD's jasper wares. (For factory marks *see* p. 886.)

Lit: X. de Chavagnac & A. de Grollier, *Histoire des manufactures françaises de porcelaine,* Paris 1906; Regine de Plinval de Guillebon, *Paris Porcelain 1770–1850,* London 1972.

Paris tapestry factories First established in the mid C13. The earliest surviving works are the late C14 panels of the *Apocalypse of Angers,* woven to cartoons by Jean de BONDOLF in the factory of Nicolas BATAILLE. The successive disasters of the Battle of Agincourt in 1415, the plague of 1418 and the occupation of Paris by the English in 1420 brought this luxury industry to a halt. Looms were functioning again by 1460 but now they took second place to ARRAS and TOURNAI. In the mid C16 some works of high quality were produced, notably *The Story of St Mamas* (Langres Cathedral: Louvre) woven between 1543 and 1545 by **Pierre Blasse** to cartoons of a truly Mannerist *horror vacui* with abundance of elegant contorted figures and fantastic architectural backgrounds by Jean Cousin the Elder. Henri IV encouraged a revival of the industry from 1598 by enticing Flemish weavers to settle in Paris, establishing sericulture in Provence and (1601) banning the importation of VERDURES. Looms were set up in the Faubourg Saint-Antoine, the Faubourg Saint-Germain and the Louvre. In 1607 **François de la Planche** from Antwerp and **Marc Comans** from Brussels established what was probably the best of these factories in the Faubourg Saint-Marcel. The most distinguished products date from the reign of Louis XIII – *The History of Constantine* after Rubens (Philadelphia Museum of Art), *Old Testament* scenes after Simon Vouet and *The Acts of the Apostles* after Raphael (Musée Gobelins; Louvre). The troubles of the Fronde brought these workshops to a halt. In 1662 the royal GOBELINS factory was established and the subsequent history of tapestry-weaving in Paris is described under that heading. Private tapestry factories in C17 and C18 Paris were of minor importance.

Lit: R.-A. Weigert, *French Tapestry,* London 1962; H. Göbel, *Wandteppiche,* Leipzig 1923–34.

Parisot, Pierre or **Peter,** *see* FULHAM CARPET & TAPESTRY FACTORY.

Parquetry Geometrical inlay of various coloured woods or of the same wood laid to contrast the grain. *See also* MARQUETRY.

Partners' desk A late-C18 and C19 type of English desk or large writing-table with drawers on both sides, for two people sitting opposite each other.

Party gilt Silver gilded in parts.

Passarini, Filippo (*c*.1638–98). Italian ornamental designer. He was the author of *Nuove inventioni d'ornamenti, d'architettura e d'intagli diversi*, Rome 1698, which includes designs for domestic and ecclesiastical furniture, metalwork, etc. in an exuberant and sometimes fantastic Baroque style.

Lit: P. Jessen, *Der Ornamentstich*, Berlin 1920.

F. Passarini: design for console table, candlestick, etc., 1698

Passavant, Claude (*fl*.1755–60). A native of Basle who, after working at Strasbourg, settled in England and set up a serge factory at Exeter. In 1755 he bought the FULHAM TAPESTRY FACTORY and moved it to Exeter. The high quality of his work is revealed by the few surviving marked pile carpets (e.g. that in the Victoria & Albert Museum) with bold scroll ornaments and in the centre a spaniel curled up on a tasselled cushion.

Lit: W. G. Thomson, *A History of Tapestry*, London 1930; C. E. C. Tattersall and S. Reed, *A History of British Carpets*, Leigh-on-Sea 1966.

Passementerie Trimming of gold or silver lace, braid, gimp or beads applied to the edges of textiles.

Passglas A late-C16 and C17 type of German cylindrical beaker, made of green glass and decorated with equidistant threads or rings. The glass was used for communal drinking and the threads or rings mark the individual's share. A variation is decorated with a spiral thread, notched at intervals.

Paste (1) The body of pottery, as distinct from the glaze, used mainly to describe PORCELAIN (i.e., hard-paste, soft-paste). *See also* PÂTE DE VERRE.

(2) Imitations of precious stones made from a hard vitreous substance usually backed with coloured foil. *See also* Georges Frédéric STRAS(S).

Pastiglia A moulded paste used in Renaissance Italy for the decoration of furniture and, especially, small wooden boxes probably produced as cheap substitutes for caskets of precious metals. Consisting either of gesso or of white lead mixed with an egg binder, *pastiglia* was applied soft, moulded in relief with matrices and allowed to harden. It was then painted or gilded. Pastiglia decorations usually cover the whole outer surface of the box. The matrices used for the relief decorations were probably of metal since the decorations are often remarkably crisp and delicate. Many matrices were needed for the decoration of a single box and even for a single relief panel forming part of such decorations since they were composed of many separate impressions, each from a tiny matrix individually representing figures, animals, plants, arms and armour, etc. Such *pastiglia* relief decorations are sometimes comparable to the small plaques of bone by the EMBRIACHI school. They are also related, on a miniature scale, to Renaissance chests and *cassoni* decorated with stucco in relief and to frames for pictures and mirrors similarly decorated. In the C14 and early C15 the relief decorations were fairly bold, in the later C15 and C16 they became more delicate and refined and sharper in detail.

Surviving eyamples are of uncertain origin but they are thought to have been Venetian, though similarities with certain contemporary WAFERING IRONS suggest that they may also have had Umbrian connections.

Pastiglia: box, Italian, late c15 (Victoria & Albert Museum)

Lit: W. L. Hildburgh in *The Antiquaries Journal*, vol. xxvi, 1946, nos. 3, 4.

Pastille burner English term for a CASSOLETTE or perfume burner, generally reserved for one of English (rather than French) type, e.g., one made of porcelain in the form of a thatched cottage *c.*1820–50.

Patanazzi factory Notable URBINO maiolica factory active *c.*1580–1625. Its wares are similar to those of the FONTANA factory but the grotesque decorations tend to be more densely packed and the forms more richly (sometimes fussily) modelled, while such small objects as inkwells, vases and cups reveal a still more extravagant sense of fantasy.

Lit: B. Rackham, *Italian Maiolica*, London 1962; G. Liverani, *Five Centuries of Italian Maiolica*, London 1960.

Patchwork A gay, peasant textile technique used mainly for quilts and bed-covers: small pieces of varying colour and pattern being sewn together by the edges, usually in a geometrical pattern.

Pâte de riz Alternative term for PÂTE DE VERRE.

Pâte de verre Glass (usually coloured) which has been ground down and refired in a mould, often having the appearance of precious or semi-precious stones. It was first used for small objects in ancient Egypt, at least as early as the XVIIIth Dynasty (1570 B.C.). The process was developed in c19 France by the sculptor **Henri Cros** (1840–1907), to make large reliefs, and was taken up for the production of glass vessels by A.-L. DAMMOUSE from 1898 and F. DÉCORCHEMONT.

Pâte dure Hard-paste porcelain, made in France from 1768 onwards, first at SÈVRES after the discovery of kaolin at Saint-Yrieix.

Pâte tendre, *see* PORCELAIN.

Paten A shallow dish on which the bread is 'offered' at the Offertory of the Mass and on which the consecrated Host is placed after the fraction. Invariably of gold or silver it was usually made to match a chalice: normally circular, with a circular or sexfoil depression in the centre.

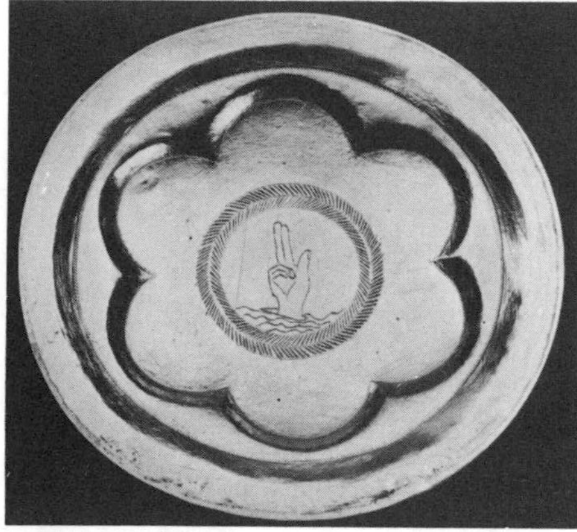

Paten, English silver, 1350, from Hamstall Ridware Church, Staffs. (Victoria & Albert Museum)

Patent furniture English early-C19 term for the ingeniously contrived pieces of transformation furniture (expanding tables, adjustable chairs, etc.) popular at the time. Some, but by no means all, were made under officially granted patents.

Patera A small flat circular or oval ornament, often decorated with acanthus leaves: much used on silver, furniture, etc., 1770–1830.

Patera

Paterna potteries Established near VALENCIA in the C14 and active into the C15, they produced plates, bowls, dishes and jugs of tin-glazed earthenware, very boldly painted in green and dark purple (sometimes almost black). The earlier pieces are decorated with stylized plant forms, the later with fishes, birds, animals or human heads with degraded Kufic lettering. The general effect is Gothic rather than Islamic and some pieces are painted with coats of arms and jousting knights. Lustred wares were produced in the later C15 but seem to be indistinguishable from those of Valencia.

Lit: J. Folch y Torres, *Noticia sobre la ceramica de Paterne,* Barcelona 1921; M. Gonzalez Marti, *Ceramica de levante español,* Barcelona 1944.

Pâte-sur-pâte A tricky and expensive method of decorating porcelain in relief, developed at SÈVRES in mid C19 and practised most ably there and at the MINTON factory by M.-L. SOLON. Designs are painted on vessels or plaques of unfired clay in successive coats of slip (each of which is allowed to dry before the next is applied), they are modelled with metal instruments, then glazed and fired.

Lit: B. Mundt, 'Pâte-sur-pâte' in *Berliner Museen,* n.f. XXIII, 1973.

Patina The effect produced, either naturally or artificially, on bronze by oxidation which turns the surface green; or, by extension, any lacquering or finishing other than gilding applied to bronze objects, especially statuettes. The term is also used figuratively for the surface texture of old furniture, silver, etc.

Pattern moulded glass Vessels made from molten glass moulded in a small form and then blown up to the desired size.

Paul, Bruno (1874–1968). German painter and industrial designer. He was one of the founders of the DEUTSCHE WERKSTÄTTEN for which he designed in 1906 some simple, practical, homely furniture of mainly rectilinear form with an occasional reminiscence of an Art Nouveau curve, intended for mass-production and termed *Typenmöbel.* At the same time he was a contributor to the periodical *Jugend* from which German *Art*

Nouveau takes its name. As principal of the Berlin School of Arts and Crafts (Kunstgewerbeschule) from 1907 and director of the Vereinigte Staatschulen für freie und angewandte Kunst in Berlin 1924–33, he exerted great influence on the development of industrial design in Germany.

Lit: J. Popp, *Bruno Paul,* n.d.; S. Günther, *Interieurs um 1900: B. Pankok, B. Paul u. R. Riemerschmied als Mitarbeit der Vereinigten Werkstatten für Kunst im Handwerk,* Munich 1971.

Paul, Nikolaus, *see* WEESP PORCELAIN FACTORY.

Pax Eucharistic tablet, usually of silver, with a projecting handle behind and often decorated on the front with a sacred symbol, scene from the Gospel (usually the Crucifixion) or lives of the saints, engraved, nielloed or enamelled.

Payne, Roger (1739–97). The leading late-C18 English bookbinder. He personally executed every detail of his bindings, including the cutting of the tools used in decorating them. His work is extremely dignified and refined. The most notable group of bindings by him was that made for the Rev. Mordaunt Cracherode.

Peachblow A type of American late-C19 (usually cased) glass coloured in emulation of the peach bloom colouring found on K'ANG HSI porcelain, generally red merging into yellow. It was made by HOBBS, BROCKUNIER AND COMPANY and other glasshouses.

Pea-pod ornament A decorative device resembling a pea-pod (though sometimes more like a leaf) used from the early C17 onwards. It is commonly but mistakenly believed that Grinling GIBBONS 'signed' his carvings with an open pea-pod.

Pearl ware An improved form of CREAM-COLOURED EARTHENWARE containing a greater quantity of flint and white clay in the body and cobalt added to the glaze to counteract the cream tone, first evolved by WEDGWOOD in 1779 and quickly adopted by several other potteries notably SPODE (1783), LEEDS (late 1780s) and SWANSEA (*c.*1800).

Peche, Dagobert (1887–1923). Austrian designer, he was closely associated with the WIENER WERKSTÄTTE. He was trained as an architect and began designing for industry (ceramics and carpets) in 1912. He joined the Wiener Werkstätte in 1915 and was director of its branch in Zurich from 1917 to 1919 when he returned to Vienna. He developed a style somewhat analogous to ART DECO but with greater emphasis on crafts and hand-made look, and a wholly original sense of fantasy. His most notable designs were for silver – fluted vases which look as if they had been folded out of paper, a fantastic tobacco box crowned by the figure of a gazelle wreathed in flowers.

Lit: H. Ankwicz-Kleehover, *Dagobert Peche,* Exh. Cat., Vienna 1923.

Peckitt, William (1731–95). The only notable English glass stainer of his day. He worked in York where he restored some old and made some new windows for the Minster. His works include biblical scenes and some small medallion portraits (Victoria & Albert Museum, London) executed in transparent enamels but retaining all the shading and modelling of the oil paintings on which they were based. He developed a palette of fine clear colours, notably a scarlet stain almost as translucent as ruby glass, which are perhaps seen at their best in his roundels of abstract geometrical design.

Lit: J. A. Knowles, *The York School of Glass Painters,* London 1936.

W. Peckitt: engraved glass, York, 1780 (Victoria & Albert Museum)

Pecs pottery A pottery started at Fünfkirchen (now Pecs) in Hungary in 1855 by **Vilmós Zsolnay** (1828–1900). It began in a very small way but by 1883 had 450 employees and by 1900 a thousand. Early products were in stoneware and in traditional Hungarian peasant styles. In the 1870s it began to go in for more refined wares, notably an imitation ISNIK ware called **'Ivoir-Fayence'** decorated in high-temperature colours with a porcelain glaze. It also produced lustred wares in an Italian Neo-Renaissance style. Art Nouveau wares were produced in the 1890s, often designed by J. RIPPL-RONAI, though by then much of the factory's production was industrial and architectural. Vilmós Zsolnay was succeeded by his son **Miklos** (1857–1925) and the factory still survives as a Hungarian State concern.

Lit: K. Csány, *Geschichte der ungarischen Keramik, der Porzellane und ihre Marken*, Budapest 1954.

Pedestal In classical architecture the base supporting a column; also, more loosely, any fairly tall base for a statue, bust, clock, etc. Pedestal tables are those supported on a single pillar or column; pedestal desks on two side sections containing drawers. *See also* TABLE, pedestal.

Pediment The low-pitched gable above the portico of a classical temple, also a similar motif used elsewhere, as on furniture (e.g., the tops of bookcases, bureaux, cabinets, long-case clocks, etc.). Since the Mannerist period the triangular form has undergone many variations both in architecture and the decorative arts. The broken pediment is, strictly, one with a central break in the base moulding though the term is often applied to an open pediment on which the sloping sides are stopped before reaching the apex. The open type, which was much used by C18 cabinet-makers, may have the sides straight or segmentally curved: if they end in scrolls it is called swan-necked.

Peg tankard An English type of silver tankard, introduced during the late C17 for communal drinking. The inside is fitted with pegs marking each individual's share.

Pein, Georg (1775–1834). Ornamentalist and teacher of perspective and architectural ornament at the academy in Vienna. He published two volumes – *Ideen zur äusseren und inneren Verzierung der Gebäude*, Vienna 1809 and 1811 – which included designs for stoves and such small objects as candlesticks in a Neo-Classical manner which hovers on the border of Biedermeier.

Lit: P. Jessen, *Der Klassizismus im Ornementstich*, Berlin 1924.

Peintre-doreur The French craftsman responsible for painting and gilding the woodwork of furniture made by the *menuisiers*. He was a member of a different gild from the *doreurs sur métaux* responsible only for gilding metalwork.

Pelikan, Franz Anton (1786–1858). The most prominent of a family of Bohemian glass-engravers working at Meistersdorf-Ulrichsthal. He engraved glass vessels with figure scenes and portraits in the Biedermeier style. He trained four of his sons to the same art: **Anton, Joseph, Franz** and **Emanuel.**

Lit: G. E. Pazaurek, *Gläser der Empire- und Biedermeierzeit*, Leipzig 1923.

Pellatt, Apsley (1791–1863). The owner of the Falcon glasshouse in Southwark, London, which had been founded in the C17 and acquired by his

A. Pellatt style scent bottle, cut glass with 'sulphide' of Princess Charlotte, 1810–20 (Victoria & Albert Museum)

father (of the same name) *c.*1790. Under his direction the factory made a wide variety of wares, specializing in the more decorative types of glass. In 1819 he introduced into England and patented a French method of decorating flasks, paper-weights, pendants, etc. with cameo-like portrait busts, classical heads, figures of *putti*, etc. made of a porcellaneous white material enclosed in the thickness of the clear crystal glass, i.e. *crystallo-céramie* or 'sulphides'. He obtained a patent for their manufacture in 1831. Later he devoted himself mainly to imitating earlier types of glassware, mainly Venetian and Islamic, and was particularly successful in reviving the various Venetian techniques of coloured glass. The factory's contributions to the Great Exhibition of 1851 included a chandelier 24 ft long, another chandelier of white, ruby and blue glass said to have been 'in the style of the Alhambra', and many cut, engraved and frosted drinking vessels, decanters, scent bottles, etc. He lectured on the history and practice of glassmaking, publishing *Curiosities of Glass Making* in London in 1849.

Lit: H. Wakefield, *Nineteenth Century British Glass*, London 1961; B. O'Looney, *Victorian Glass*, London 1973.

Pelletier, John (*fl.c.*1690–1710). He was a leading English Baroque furniture-maker. Probably of French origin, he worked in the Louis XIV Style and specialized in high quality carved and gilt pieces. There are documented *torchères* by him at Hampton Court, and tables and firescreens there have been attributed to him. The carved and gilt *torchères* were provided *c.*1700–1.

Lit: R. Edwards and M. Jourdain, *Georgian Cabinet-Makers*, London 1955.

Pellevé, Etienne-Dominique (*fl.*1750–76). Potter and painter, he was the son of and assistant to **Denis-Pierre Pellevé** who was director of the SINCENY factory 1734–50 and SAINT-DENIS-SUR-SARTHON factory from 1750. He attempted to start a faience factory at Dangau in 1753, became the director of a factory at Liège in 1757 but was subsequently engaged in making porcelain at OTTWEILER 1763–7, ETIOLLES 1768–70, and at other minor factories. A number of attractively painted pieces of faience and porcelain are signed with his initials.

Pellipario, Nicola (*fl.*1510–42). The greatest Italian maiolica painter. Began at CASTEL DURANTE *c.*1510–15 where he developed the relatively new ISTORIATO style on numerous plates and dishes painted with (often rather *recherché*) mythological scenes, notably a set of seventeen now in Museo Correr, Venice, and a

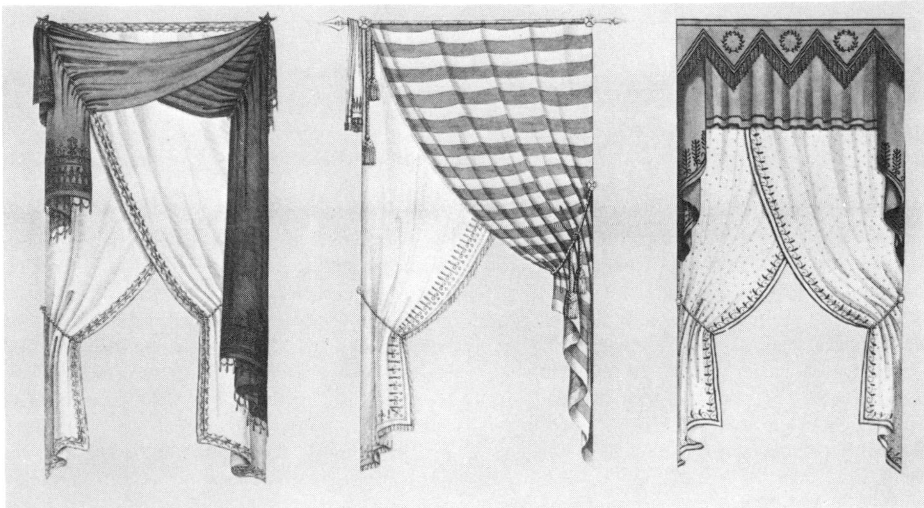

Pelmet designs, French, early c19

dinner service made for Isabella d'Este (*c*.1519, dispersed). They are characterized by their spirited, boldly drawn figures, wide Umbrian landscapes and exquisite architectural details reminiscent of Bramante. Also credited with plates painted with portrait busts of fashionably dressed girls (occasionally men) inscribed *Silvia Bella, Alda la Bela e Galanta* and such like. He employed a cool colour scheme with greens and blues predominating. In 1528 he moved to URBINO where his son **Guido** had set up the FONTANA factory. (Known as Guido Durantino or Guido da Castello Durante, he took the name Fontana.) Here he adopted a warmer palette, dominated by yellow and orange, and relied less on his imagination than on prints after Raphael. (For his mark *see* p. 886.)

Lit: O. von Falke in *Die Majolikasammlung Alfred Pringsheim* II, The Hague 1923; B. Rackham, *Italian Maiolica*, London 1952; G. C. Polidori in *Studi Urbinati*, 1953.

Pelmet A piece of cloth or board placed above a window or door to hide the top of a curtain or blind. *Illustrated previous page.*

Pelta In ornamental design, an element shaped like a type of Roman shield.

Pembroke table *see* TABLE, Pembroke.

Penicaud, Léonard or **Nardon** (*c*.1470–1543). Leading LIMOGES ENAMEL painter in whose studio the art of enamel painting in colour was perfected. His masterpiece is a Crucifixion (1503, Musée de Cluny, Paris). Most of his early paintings are copied from contemporary prints. His younger brother, **Jean** (*fl*.1510–40), used a much richer palette and gave greater attention to details, especially hair and the flowers in the foregrounds of his paintings. Three other members of the Penicaud family were notable enamellers: **Jean II** (*fl*.1530–88), a master of *grisaille* painting who did a certain amount of ecclesiastical work, especially reliquaries, besides secular work, including some fine portraits. **Jean III** and **Pierre** were active in the late C16 working much under the Mannerist influence of the School of Fontainebleau.

Lit: E. Rupin, *L'Oeuvre de Limoges*, Paris 1890; P. Verdier, *The Walters Art Gallery: Catalogue of the Painted Enamels of the Renaissance*, Baltimore 1967.

Pierre Penicaud: painted enamel plaque of Juno, late C16 (Louvre)

Penig pottery, *see* WALDENBURG POTTERIES.

Pennewitz, David, *see* PLAUE-ON-HAVEL POTTERY.

Pennsylvania Dutch style American folk-art style of decoration by German colonists in Pennsylvania between 1750 and 1850. (Dutch is merely a corruption of *Deutsch*.) Bold, cheerful and with distinctive qualities derived from the combination of English and German peasant styles. Favourite motifs, such as hearts, tulips, trees of life, parrots, peacocks, and endless variations on geometrically divided star-forms, became almost standardized and were used for decorating all types of furniture, ceramics, needlework (especially quilts and hooked rugs), and *Fractur (Frakturschriften)* or hand-lettered,

Pennsylvania Dutch chest, 1765–1800 (Courtesy of The Henry Francis du Pont Winterthur Museum)

illuminated manuscripts. Wardrobes, cupboards, and dower chests display the style at its best, with large gaily painted decorative panels surrounded by mottled or stippled texturing. But it is also effective on a small scale, e.g., turned wooden egg-cups, spice boxes and sugar pails, such pieces being sometimes called Lehn Ware, after **Joseph Long Lehn** (1798–1892) of Lancaster County who specialized in decorating such pieces in the mid C19. Very few other craftsmen are known by name. The **Seltzer-Rank family** of Jonestown, Lebanon County, signed vases; **Jacob Schelli** signed chests; **John Drissel** (*fl.*1794–97) of Bucks County, signed salt boxes, etc.; **John Maser** was the leading exponent of Mahantongo Valley furniture, 1820–40, a distinctive type characterized by borders of stencilled rosettes on the stiles.

Lit: H. J. Kauffman, *Pennsylvania Dutch American Folk Art*, New York 1964; E. A. Barber, *Tulip Ware of the Pennsylvania-German Potters*, Philadelphia 1922, New York 1970.

Penwork A type of decoration applied to JAPANNED furniture in the late C18 and early C19, mainly in England. Furniture to be treated in this way was first japanned black, then the patterns were painted on in white Japan and finally the details and shading were executed in black Indian ink with a fine quill pen. The effect is delicate and lacy, rather like an etching in reverse, with white motifs on a black ground. *Illustrated next page.*

Percier, Charles, *see* FONTAINE, Pierre-François-Léonard.

Perfume burner, *see* CASSOLETTE.

Pergamo carpets, *see* TURKISH CARPETS.

Pergolesi, Michelangelo (d.1801). Italian ornamental designer who settled in England before 1770 and worked under Robert ADAM. He published *Original Designs* (1777–1801) for ceilings, wall-panels, furniture, silver, marquetry, etc., in a bold and capricious version of the Adam style.

Perino del Vaga (Pietro Buonaccorsi) (1501–47). Florentine painter who worked mainly in Rome.

Penwork decoration, English cabinet, early c19 (Victoria & Albert Museum)

He was a prolific author of designs for goldsmiths' work in a richly sculpturesque Mannerist style akin to that of Francesco SALVIATI. He also provided designs for engravers of rock crystal, notably Giovanni BERNARDI (e.g., Cofanetto Farnese in the Museo di Capodimonte, Naples).

Period room A room in which all the furnishings and decorative objects belong to a single artistic period or alternatively are such as might have been found grouped together at some date in the past (e.g., a dining-room with late-c18 furniture and Antique statues). The vogue for such rooms is a late product of c19 Historicism and was much advocated in the 1880s by **Mrs Haweis,** an influential writer on interior decorating (e.g. *Beautiful Houses*, London 1882). The idea was soon adopted by museums.

Perrin, Pierette, known as **La Veuve** (d.1793). The directress of an outstanding faience factory in MARSEILLES which she inherited from her husband in 1748 and ran until her death. The wares that bear her mark (VP in monogram) are among the best made at Marseilles – plates, jugs and bulging Rococo tureens decorated with informally straggling sprigs of flowers, great *bouillabaisse* heaps of glittering fish or delicate landscapes.

La veuve Perrin: tureen, second half of c18 (Musée des Arts Décoratifs, Paris)

Lit: H. J. Reymond, *Faiences anciennes de Marseille XVII et XVIII siècle*, Berne 1964; E. Fabre, *Die französischen Fayencen des Mittelmeergebietes*, Cologne 1965.

Perroquet, *see* CHAIR.

Perrot(to), Bernard(o) (d.1709). The leading French glass-maker of his time. He was Italian by birth (probably from ALTARE) and a nephew of **Giovanni Castellano** who was authorized to establish a glasshouse at NEVERS in 1647. He was naturalized French in 1666 and received the first of several patents for glass-making. By 1672 he had settled in Orléans and founded a factory which passed to his family on his death. He made common *verre de fougère* and also much fine glass – a crystal glass *(façon de Venise)*, a transparent red glass, a milky white glass *(façon de porcelaine)* used mainly for figures, an agate glass and imitations of Antique cameos. Such objects as a pair of milky glass dolphins (Bayerisches Nationalmuseum, Munich) and a red glass table centre (Musée des Arts Décoratifs, Paris) illustrate his flair for exuberant Baroque forms. He invented a process of relief moulding, as used in his portrait of Louis XIV (Musée Historique d'Orléans). But his main achievement was the invention of a process for casting glass in sheets, which was exploited by **Louis-Lucas de Nehou** at Tourlaville, Normandy, in 1688 and subsequently at the SAINT-GOBAIN GLASS FACTORY for the production of looking-glass.

B. Perrot: milky glass dolphin. c.1700 (Bayerisches Nationalmuseum, Munich)

Lit: J. Barrelet, *La Verrerie en France*, Paris 1954; J. Barrelet in *Cahiers de la céramique* 36 (1964), pp. 254–85.

Perry, Edward (*fl.*1829). The owner of a notable factory producing JAPANNED metal and PAPIER MÂCHÉ wares in Wolverhampton in the early C19.

Perry, Mary Chase (1868–1961). American porcelain decorator and potter. She began by executing overglaze decorations on porcelain, at first having her wares fired in Detroit in kilns intended for making false teeth, and then, in collaboration with the owner of the kilns Horace Caulkins, setting up a small establishment called **Revelation Kilns.** This succeeded and in 1903 she founded the **Pewabic Pottery,** Detroit, to produce art pottery. Under the influence of W. GRUEBY, L. C. TIFFANY and the fine early-Chinese pottery in the collection of Charles L. Freer she produced vases at first in the Art Nouveau style but later of very simple form decorated only with rich iridescent glazes. She continued to make such wares until she was more than 90 years old.

Lit: R. Judson Clark (ed.), *The Arts and Crafts Movement in America 1876–1916*, Exh. Cat., Art Museum, Princeton University, Art Institute of Chicago, etc., 1972–3.

Persian carpets A term covering some of the finest carpets ever made, in point of technique no less than design, as well as several types of rugs woven by nomadic tribes and a large quantity of modern commercially produced floor coverings. They have a warp and weft of wool, silk or cotton and a woollen or silk pile usually tied with the PERSIAN KNOT. The earliest of importance date from the reign of Shah Tahmasp, 1524–76, and include the famous ARDABIL CARPETS. Unlike earlier TURKISH CARPETS, which were decorated with geometrical and highly stylized motifs created by weavers, they are decorated with an abund-

Persian carpet: silk pile woven at Kashan, c16, Safavid Period
(Metropolitan Museum of Art, Bequest of Benjamin Altman 1913, New York)

ance of naturalistic interlaced flower and leaf motifs sometimes incorporating figures of birds and beasts and appear to have been designed by or under the influence of Court painters. Their sophisticated subtlety and almost feminine delicacy distinguish them from all other Oriental carpets. Several different types were evolved in the C16. One has a large central medallion from the ends of which mosque lamps are, as it were, 'suspended'. The so-called 'hunting carpets' are decorated with lively figures of horsemen pursuing game across flowery meadows (notable examples in Victoria and Albert Museum, London, Poldi Pezzoli Museum, Milan, and Residenzmuseum, Munich). A group known as 'Emperor carpets' have complex arabesque designs with medallions which incorporate figures of animals (Metropolitan Museum, New York, etc.). All these carpets appear to have been made in N.W. Persia, probably in or near the capital, Tabriz.

In 1598 the capital was moved to Isfahan by Shah 'Abbas the Great who initiated another period of outstanding artistic activity. Magnificent carpets were woven for the palace and other buildings in the new capital. Compositions tended to be simpler and bolder than those of the Shah Tahmasp period but their general effect was often richer. New types include carpets of the vase pattern (probably woven at Kirman) with a progressive floral design springing from a (sometimes inconspicuous) vase. A particularly sumptuous group with a silk surface woven with flower and animal motifs seems to have been made partly as royal gifts. Many of these were exported and as the first to come to Western notice were found in Poland they are known as 'Polonaise carpets' (at first they were erroneously supposed to have been of Polish make). Another type with a silk pile has an all-over pattern of large palmettes, extensively imitated in later centuries, popularly known as the 'Shah 'Abbas design'. Two other notable types appear to have originated in the Shah 'Abbas period but in N. Persia – 'tree pattern' carpets in which stylized trees are the main motifs, and 'garden carpets' whose design is based on the plan of a Persian garden with beds of stylized flowers and trees intersected by canals. At Kashan (N. of Isfahan) silk-pile carpets were woven with naturalistic flower and leaf motifs and very lively animals from the C16 onwards.

Persian carpet: silk pile, Shah 'Abbas type, Central Persia, C17
(Museo degli Argenti, Palazzo Pitti, Florence)

Prayer rugs, sometimes with a pile of fine goat hair which has a silky sheen, decorated with many flowers and tall cypress trees on either side of the niche, were made in the South, probably around Shiraz (few surviving specimens date from before the C18). In the C17 carpets with designs incorporating little figures of sailors in ships, called 'Portuguese carpets', were woven in the South. Less sophisticated but very handsome rugs were woven in various parts of Persia by nomadic tribes, notably the Afshari (including coarser versions of the Shiraz prayer-rugs), Bachtiari or Bakhtiari (with strongly coloured bold floral and geometrical motifs) and Kaskai. Tapestry woven rugs were made in various parts of Persian Kurdistan including the city of Sehna – where pile carpets were also made from the C19 and whence the term 'Sehna knot' derives.

Although the finest Persian carpets were made in the C16–17, dated examples reveal that work of high quality was still being executed in the last years of the C18. Early patterns were repeated but tended to lose their freshness in the C19, especially after the 1850s when weavers began to work mainly for export to the West. The introduction of aniline dyes in the 1870s had a more obviously deleterious effect on colour schemes. In 1934 the Iranian government introduced legislation to prohibit the export of carpets of inferior quality. The most important carpet-producing centres of the present day are Herez (also a market for carpets made at Bakshihis, Gorevan and Serapi), Sultanabad (with Lilihan and other places in the vicinity), Tabriz (where the carpet industry was revived in the later C19) and the capital Tehran. Two European firms, Hotz & Sons and Zeigler & Co., established factories at Sultanabad in the 1880s.

A large number of place names are used for the classification of old and modern Persian carpets, sometimes indicating towns or districts of origin, sometimes types of pattern. They include: Bijar (coarse stout carpets with Persian designs, also called Sarakhs), Feraghan (with stylized flower motifs), Hamadan (originally with a pile of goat hair and camel hair in strongly coloured diapers, but also a wide range of modern commercially made and modestly priced carpets including those called 'Mosul' carpets), Herat (notable since the C16 for rather heavy carpets and the source of a fish-like decorative motif), Isfahan (with vase motifs, but not necessarily woven at Isfahan), Joshaghan (the traditional source of C17 Polonaises, making from the early C19 carpets with tight diamonds of floral motifs), Kara Dagh (with an intermixture of Caucasian motifs), Kermanshah (with medallion patterns and flower and leaf motifs), Khorassan (brilliantly coloured with human figures, animals and birds among flowers, from the early C19), Kirman (the probable source of the C17 vase pattern, making from the late C18 carpets with flower and leaf motifs more naturalistically rendered than usual, from the late C19 incorporating human figures and many birds, and from 1937 distant imitations of Aubusson), Meshed (richly coloured with flower and animal motifs), Niris (somewhat resembling TURKMAN CARPETS), Saraband (with a distinctive design of rows of pear-shaped motifs in alternating directions), Saruk (richly coloured with a velvety texture from the late C19) and Souj-Bulak (a compact, strong Kurdish type).

Lit: K. Erdmann, *Oriental Carpets*, London 1960, and *Siebenhundert Jahre Orientteppich*, Herford 1966; A. U. Pope (ed.), *A Survey of Persian Art* (1938–9), London and New York 1964–7.

Persian knot, also called the **Sehna knot** though it is not used in the village of Sehna. The knot used for the pile of most Persian, Central Asiatic, Indian and Chinese carpets. It is less a knot than a twist, with the yarn encircling one warp thread and passing under that next to it. It is used for carpets with a very close pile.

Persian pottery Some of the most beautiful early pottery was produced in Persia (*see* ISLAMIC POTTERY), but the industry suffered greatly from the Mongol invasions and did not fully recover until the C16 except for architectural decorations for mosques, madrasahs, palaces, etc. under Timur and his sons and successors. Fine examples of such tiles and ceramic mosaics date from the C15, usually painted in cobalt-blue, manganese purple, yellow and green. They are decorated with inscriptions or arabesques or a combination of the two, the arabesque patterns sometimes being so elaborate that the inscriptions can hardly be read. They are often decorated in openwork. C15 Persian ceramics also include large dishes decorated in black on a white slip (the design being incised into the black, under a transparent turquoise glaze) and a type of peasant pottery known as 'cross-hatched ware'. This was probably made in North and North-Western Iran. The body is red and decorations are confined to heavy lines and cross-hatchings, painted in black-blue and green on a white ground slip under a clear glaze.

The earliest surviving Persian blue-and-white wares also date from the C15 and were probably made at Meshed and Kirman which long remained the centres for such wares. Whether or not Persia preceded China in the production of blue-and-white wares is unknown but they were certainly being produced in C14 Persia (blue-and-white vessels of forms unknown in Chinese ceramics appear in late C14 Persian miniatures).

However, Far Eastern influence is evident in the decoration of Persian pottery under the Safavids in the early C16 and later wares sometimes adopt Chinese styles.

Apart from blue-and-white wares, pottery of the Safavid and Kajar periods (C16–C19) may be divided into five main types: GOMBROON WARES, KUBACHI WARES, lustre-painted wares, polychrome-painted wares and monochrome wares. The lustre technique appears to have been abandoned in the late C14 and was not revived until the late C17. In later lustre wares decoration is restricted to floral and plant designs, painted in lustre and reserving the ground in white. The glaze is either colourless or a deep blue. The lustre is ruby-brown or greenish-brown, with a coppery sheen. C17 polychrome wares are decorated in colours ranging from a dull red to blue, dark green and brown, with designs that often reflect Chinese Ming influence. Finally, a great variety of monochrome-glazed wares, deriving from Chinese celadon wares, were produced from the C16 to the C18, mainly at Kirman. The colours range from celadon, yellow and light brown to vermilion and deep blue. Decorations are either in relief or are painted in white or are cut through the coloured glaze down to the white body.

Lit: A. U. Pope (ed.), *A Survey of Persian Art* (1938–9), London and New York 1964–7; A. Lane, *Later Islamic Pottery*, London (rev. ed. by R. Pinder Wilson) 1971.

Peruvian pottery: Mochica Culture, vase (Nathan Cummings Collection, Chicago)

Peruvian pottery The earthenware vessels of Peru are probably the finest made in S. America and among the more notable examples of Pre-Columbian art in any medium. Utilitarian wares were made in this region from *c.*1200 B.C. (if not earlier). But by *c.*800 B.C. potters were making grey vessels with a curious stirrup-shaped spout also serving as a handle, which persisted in the region until the time of the Spanish conquest more than two millennia later. Vessels assigned to the **Mochica Culture** (*c.*200 B.C.–800 A.D.) are often modelled with extraordinary realism as human heads or animals and naturalistically painted. Later vessels of this type, of the **Chimu period** (*c.*1200–1500) were made from moulds, rather than modelled individually, and are generally grey or black without painting. A strikingly different, though equally interesting, type of vessel was made on the S. coast around **Nazca** before the C9 A.D. – of ovoid form surmounted by twin spouts linked by a bar which also served as a handle. The bodies of these vessels were richly decorated, sometimes in as many as eight different pigments, on a background of white or black slip, with highly stylized representations of plants, mythical beings and animals (especially felines). At **Tiahuanca** in the highlands fine pottery was made *c.*1000 A.D. notably bowls painted with animals or mythological beings, always stylized and sometimes broken down into geometrical patterns, as well as some zoomorphic vessels. The main **Inca** contribution to the pottery of the region was the large arabyllus or water jar with a pointed base, handles low down on the body (to enable it to be strapped to the carrier's back) and much schematic decoration, made in the C15–16.

Lit: G. H. S. Bushnell, *Ancient Arts of the Americas*, London 1965.

Pesaro potteries Maiolica factories are known to have been active from the 1480s (if not earlier) in Pesaro but none of their products has been identified. A factory owned by the **Lanfranco** (or **Lanfranchi**) family in the nearby village of Gabbice was active 1540–66 producing *istoriato* wares painted with mythological and Biblical subjects in the style of the FONTANA FACTORY at Urbino. Notable products include a large service made for one frate, Andrea da Volterra (British Museum, Victoria & Albert Museum, Museo Civico Bologna, etc.). The production of maiolica declined from the late C16. In 1757 **Giuseppe Bertolucci** started a short-lived factory. A more prominent concern was founded in 1763 by **Antonio Casali** and **Filippo Antonio Callegari** from Lodi making tin-glazed wares imitative of Chinese and European porcelain, also jugs and dishes decorated in a revived version of the C16 grotesque style of URBINO. A factory owned by **Ferruccio Mengaroni** (d.1925) in Pesaro made imitations, sometimes regarded as forgeries, of C16 maiolica.

Lit: J. Chompret, *Répertoire de la maiolique italienne*, Paris 1952; G. Liverani, *Five Centuries of Italian Majolica*, New York & London 1960.

Peterinck, François-Joseph, *see* TOURNAI POTTERIES & PORCELAIN FACTORY.

Petersdorf glasshouse A factory founded at Petersdorf near Warmbrumm in the Riesengebirge in 1866 by **Fritz Heckert,** member of a German glass-making family. It quickly became one of the most prominent producers of glass in historical styles, e.g. various kinds of enamelled *humpen*. Other pieces called *Jodhpur-gläser* were modelled on Indian metalwork. In 1923 it was amalgamated with the SCHREIBERHAU GLASSHOUSE.

Lit: B. Mundt, *Historismus*, Catalogue of the Kunstgewerbemuseum, Berlin, vol. VII, Berlin 1973.

Petit feu The French name for ENAMEL COLOURS.

Petit, Jacob (1796–1865). Porcelain painter who began his career at the SÈVRES factory and, with his brother **Mardochée,** acquired a porcelain factory at Belleville in 1830 and Fontainebleau in 1838. He transferred the latter to AVON in 1850 but returned to Fontainebleau in 1862. He produced richly decorated ornamental and useful wares (*veilleuses* in the form of human figures and sculptural clock-cases were specialities). He was also a designer in the Louis-Philippe style, publishing *Recueil de décorations intérieures*, Paris 1830–31. His wares are sometimes marked with the initials 'J.P.' in blue.

Lit: X. de Chavagnac & A. de Grollier, *Histoire des manufactures françaises de porcelaine*, Paris 1906; M. Ernould-Gandouet, *La Céramique en France au XIX siècle*, Paris 1969.

Petit, Nicolas (1732–91). He became a *maître ébéniste* in 1761. In his early work he made great use of lacquer but later developed a more restrained classical style. He is not to be confused with another **Nicolas Petit** (1736–98) who became a *maître ébéniste* in 1765 but was rather inferior to him as a craftsman. They used very similar stamps to mark their furniture.

Petit point Canvas embroidered in TENT STITCH, mainly for cushion and chair covers. A form of embroidery practised since the Middle Ages but particularly popular from the C18 onwards.

Petitpierre, Aristide, *see* NANTES COTTON PRINTING FACTORIES.

Petri-Raben, Trude, *see* BERLIN PORCELAIN FACTORY.

Petuntse The fusible feldspathic vitrifying ingredient essential for making hard-paste PORCELAIN – i.e. the white china-stone or Feldspar (a silicate of potassium and aluminium) with which the china-clay or *kaolin* is fused at a high temperature. In China the stone was pulverized and sent to the porcelain-makers in the form of small bricks – *petuntse* means, in Chinese, 'little white bricks' *pai-tun-tsŭ*.

Petzolt or **Petzoldt, Hans** (1551–1633). On JAMNITZER's death in 1585 he became the

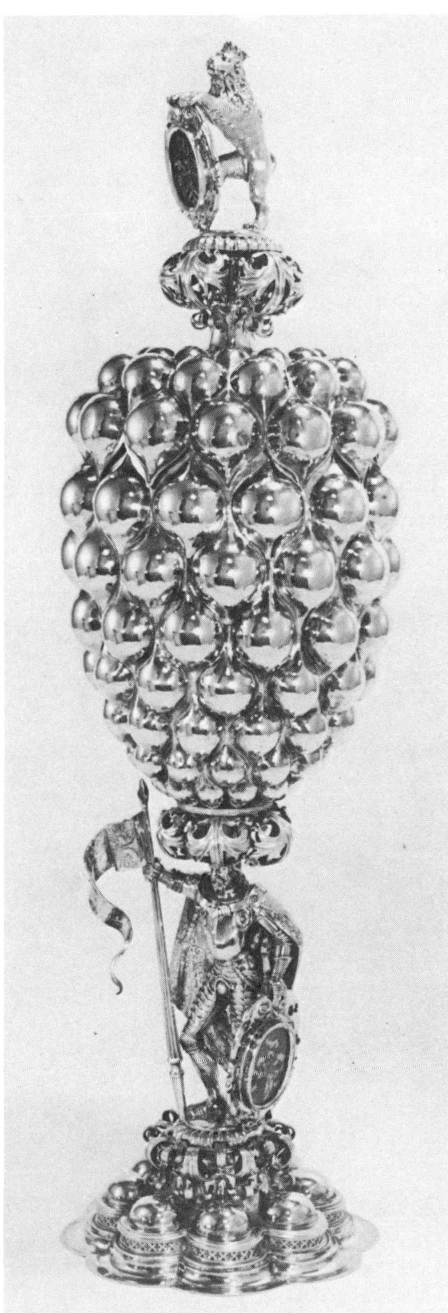

H. Petzolt: Traubenpokal *or bunch-of-grapes cup, silver gilt, Nuremberg, 1610–12 (Kunstgewerbemuseum, Berlin)*

leading goldsmith in Nuremberg. He had been made a master of the Guild in 1578 and, like Jamnitzer, was to play a prominent part in the city's council and affairs. Some 40 works by him survive, mostly cups. Apart from two visits to Prague at the invitation of Rudolf II he spent all his life in Nuremberg. Some of his work follows the Jamnitzer tradition, e.g. cup in the Royal Scottish Museum in Edinburgh, but the majority of his pieces are in a strikingly different style, notably his *Dianapokal*, 1610–20 (Kunstgewerbemuseum, West Berlin) which is one of his largest and most impressive works. But it is composed of elements associated with the early rather than the late C16. A silver double-cup in the Rijksmuseum in Amsterdam is still more obviously in the style of early-C16 Nuremberg goldsmiths. These are usually regarded as manifestations of a precocious Gothic revival and described as *Neugotik*. But it may be suggested that they were part of a Dürer revival rather than a Gothic revival, for his cups are not so much reminiscent of the Middle Ages as of the period of the revival of the arts in Germany. And this return to the early C16 may also reflect a reaction against the Mannerism of Jamnitzer and his generation.

Lit: E. Böhm, *Hans Petzolt*, Munich 1939; J. F. Hayward in *The Connoisseur*, clxv (1967), pp. 162–7; H. Honour, *Goldsmiths and Silversmiths*, London & New York 1971.

Pew groups Ornaments of salt-glazed stoneware made in STAFFORDSHIRE in the mid C18

Pew group: Staffordshire salt-glazed earthenware, c.1745 (William Rockhill Nelson Gallery of Art, Kansas City)

representing two or three stiff little figures seated on a high-backed settle – very endearing and very naïve. Some have been credited to T. ASTBURY and some to Aaron, brother of R. WOOD.

Pewabic pottery, *see* PERRY, Mary Chase.

Pewter An alloy consisting mainly of tin. The best (known as 'English pewter') contains copper or occasionally bismuth, but no lead. Ordinary pewter (known as 'test pewter' and 'low-grade pewter') contains lead in varying quantities, the more lead the poorer in quality and the more dangerous if used for eating, but also the cheaper. The colour varies according to the quantity of lead: if there is none it is very nearly as bright as silver when well polished, otherwise it tends towards a blackish grey. Pewter has been made in Europe since very early times but does not seem to have been developed until the Middle Ages. It has been used mainly for useful wares such as plates, drinking vessels, bowls, spoons, candlesticks, etc. But in the C16 a more elaborate type, known as 'display pewter', was developed, first in France and then in Germany, to be shown on dressers, sideboards, etc. Display pewter is decorated in relief. Pewter is cast in moulds either of clay or of brass or stone. On display or relief-decorated pewter, the decoration, which is sometimes extremely elaborate and refined, was cast with the object. The decoration was normally applied in brass moulds carved *intaglio* with a chisel, though it might be etched into the mould. Display pewter originated in Lyons and culminated with BRIOT. Subsequently Nuremberg became the centre, notably with Caspar ENDERLEIN, Nicholas HORCHHAIMER and Albrecht PREISSENSIN. In England William GRAINGER was outstanding. Much of the finest pewter continued to be made in France throughout the C17 and was later stimulated by the sumptuary edict of 1709 prohibiting the use of table silver. In France, also, the use of makers' marks or 'touches' was more regular than elsewhere. In N. America pewter has been made since the mid C17. The introduction of Britannia Metal and Electroplate in the C19 rendered pewter largely obsolete. But it was revived as a medium for decorative wares in England and Germany *c.*1900 by A. L. LIBERTY and E. KAYSER.

Pewter flagon, South German, C15 (Museum für Kunst and Gewerbe, Hamburg)

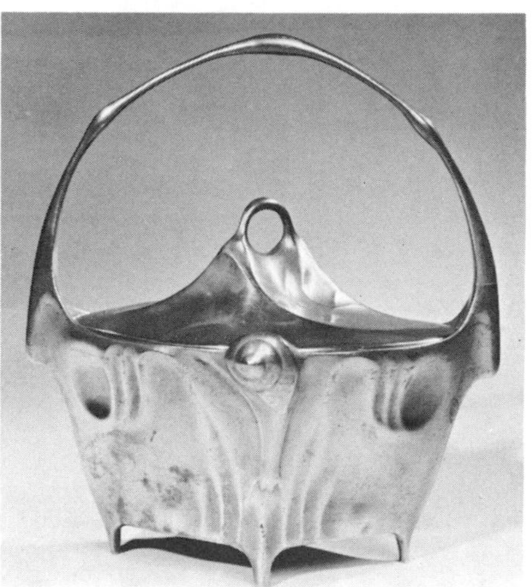

Pewter sugar bowl, designed by Hugo Leven and made by Engelbert Kayser, Krefeld, c.1900 *(Kunstgewerbemuseum, Berlin)*

Lit: J. B. Kerfoot, *American Pewter*, New York 1942; R. F. Michaelis, *Antique Pewter of the British Isles*, London 1955; A. J. G. Verster, *Old European Pewter*, London 1958; H.-U. Haedeke, *Metalwork*, London 1970; C. F. Montgomery, *A History of American Pewter*, New York and Washington 1973.

Pfalzer, Zacharias, *see* BADEN-BADEN POTTERY & PORCELAIN FACTORY.

Pfalz-Zweibrücken porcelain factory A Rhineland factory under the patronage of Duke Christian IV of Pfalz-Zweibrücken, it was founded in 1767 and directed by two potters from HÖCHST. It was active until 1775. Its products were mainly table-wares, the simpler (and technically inferior) decorated in underglaze blue, the more elaborate (made of superior ingredients) decorated in colours with flowers or landscapes. Figures are known to have been made but none has been certainly identified. (For factory mark *see* p. 886.)

Lit: E. Heuser, *Die Pfalz-Zweibrücken Porzellan-manufaktur*, Neustadt-an-der-Hardt 1907.

Pfau, Johan Ernst, *see* COPENHAGEN POTTERIES.

Pfau, Ludwig, *see* WINTERTHUR POTTERIES.

Pfeiffer, Max Adolf, *see* SCHWARZBERG PORCELAIN FACTORY.

Pharmacy vases A term used to describe the two types of drug jars, i.e. the ALBARELLO for dry drugs and the spouted vases (known as *chevrettes* in France) for liquids. Many examples, in HISPANO-MORESQUE ware, Italian MAIOLICA, French faience, etc. are inscribed with the names of drugs. But vessels of the same forms were probably made for ordinary household use as well.

Lit: C. Benito del Caño and R. Roldan y Guerrero, *Ceramica Farmaceutica: apuntes para su estudio*, Madrid 1928; L. Campanile, *I vasi di farmacia*, Milan 1973.

Philadelphia porcelain factory, *see* BONNIN AND MORRIS PORCELAIN FACTORY.

Phyfe, Duncan (1768–1854). He has been called 'the greatest of all American cabinet-makers' and is certainly the best known. He was extremely successful, eventually employing some hundred men in his New York workshops and leaving a fortune estimated at nearly $500,000. He emigrated from Scotland with his parents in 1783 or 1784, settling at Albany. In 1792 he was working in New York as a joiner, but two years later he was described in the New York Directory and Register as a 'cabinet-maker'. In 1795 he moved his shop from Broad Street, New York, (then the main centre for cabinet-makers) to the more fashionable Partition Street. By 1815 his premises had expanded to three buildings, serving as workshops, warehouse and show-rooms.

D. Phyfe: mahogany sewing-table with marble top and brass bands, c.1810–16 (Henry Francis du Pont Winterthur Museum, Winterthur)

He began by working in the Sheraton style, never straying far from the designs published in English pattern books. He also imitated the Directoire and, later, Empire styles. From about 1830 he answered the call for what he is said to have scorned as 'butcher furniture' – pieces of a more opulent massiveness. But he appears to have been either too timorous or too prudent to play the role of an innovator. Although his name has been given to the American furniture styles of a long period and he has been credited with individuality, the designs he used seem to have differed little if at all from those employed by other New York cabinet-makers of his day. And he never made any Empire style furniture comparable either in design or execution with the rare pieces which bear LANNUIER'S label.

(Lannuier's output must have been limited, whereas Phyfe's was considerable and intended for a wide public.)

Surviving pieces bearing Phyfe's label are of high quality (Museum of the City of New York and the Du Pont Winterthur Museum, Winterthur). He used the finest San Domingo mahogany – and West Indian exporters are said to have called the best wood 'Duncan Phyfe logs'. His veneers are neat, his carving is well executed and such pieces of ornamental brass-work as claw foot-tips for table legs are well made. His best furniture stands up well to comparison with that produced by the best large firms of a similar type in Europe – GILLOWS in England and JACOB-DESMALTER in France. After *c.*1830 the quality of his production declined and he began to use rosewood and other cheaper materials.

Lit: E. H. Bjerkoe, *The Cabinet Makers of America*, New York 1957; C. F. Montgomery, *American Furniture of the Federal Period in the Henry Francis Du Pont Winterthur Museum*, New York and London 1967.

Pi A type of Chinese ritual jade resembling a flat disc with a circular hole in the centre of about one third of the total diameter. It symbolizes heaven and was used at the sacrifices to Heaven until the abdication of the last of the Manchu emperors in 1912. It is not to be confused with the HUAN or with the HSÜAN-CHI. For illustration *see* JADE.

Picasso, Pablo (1881–1973). So far as the decorative arts are concerned Picasso is notable mainly for his work in and influence on ceramics. Although several other outstanding artists of his generation sometimes used pottery as a medium – including Georges Braque, Henri Matisse and Fernand Léger – none has been so deeply involved in its modelling and decoration. He began in 1947, working in the **Madoura pottery** of **Suzanne** and **Georges Ramié** at Vallauris where all his ceramics have been produced. His work in this medium comprises both original works – statuettes, figures of birds, human heads, etc. and sometimes vessels in these forms – which he modelled and painted – and also plates, jugs, etc. of normal shape made in the pottery and only painted by him. But in these two categories a distinction should be drawn between unique pieces and the replicas of them made at the Madoura pottery and issued in limited editions. These ceramics are an extension of Picasso's work in other media and many motifs from his paintings, drawings, etc. recur in them – the dove, the faun, minotaur and centaur, bull-fights, artist and model. Sometimes there are echoes of Greek vases or of Peruvian water vessels; some models of owls are reminiscent of German C16 pottery while plates painted with owls recall C17 slipwares. But they are all far more strongly marked by the individuality, vitality and wit of Picasso himself.

Lit: D.-H. Kahnweiler, *Picasso Keramik*, Hanover 1957.

Piccolpasso, Cipriano (1524–79). Italian potter of CASTEL DURANTE (now Urbania) notable mainly as the author of a treatise on maiolica technique *Li tre libri dell'arte del vasaio* written between 1556 and 1559. It is the earliest known account of POTTERY to be written in Europe (there is a Persian treatise of 1301). It was first published in Rome in 1857. Champfleury's French translation of 1860 seems to have influenced studio potters in France. The original manuscript, which is illustrated, is now in the Victoria & Albert Museum.

Lit: C. Piccolpasso, *Li tre libri dell'arte del vasaio*, tr. and ed. B. Rackham and V. van de Put, London 1934; G. Cecchini in *Archiginnasio* (Bologna), LVII (1962), pp. 299–306.

Pickled furniture Furniture with a whitish finish obtained by scraping the paint off. Furniture made of light coloured woods, such as deal, was frequently treated in this way in the early C20. The white colour is produced by the remains of the gesso base to the paint.

Picot, *see* LACE.

Pie-crust table, *see* TABLE, pie-crust.

Pie-crust ware Buff-coloured pottery pie-dishes simulating pastry, made by WEDGWOOD and other English factories from the late C18 onwards, especially after 1800 when there was such a shortage of flour that pastry became a luxury.

Pied de biche A type of foot used on cabriole legs

of chairs and other pieces of furniture. It was introduced *c.*1690 and resembles the cloven hoof of a doe or stag.

Pien-Hu, *see* HU.

Pier table, *see* TABLE, pier.

Pier-glass A tall narrow mirror made to hang against the pier, i.e. the wall between two windows. It was popular mainly in the C18.

Pieri, Giovanni Francesco, *see* NAPLES TAPESTRY FACTORY.

Pietre dure Italian term for hard or semi-precious stones such as agate, chalcedony, jasper, lapis lazuli, etc. as distinct from the various types of marble. (The singular form of the term, *pietra dura,* though sometimes used outside Italy for combinations of more than one type of stone, should correctly be reserved for a single type.) Because of their hardness they can be worked only with instruments similar to those employed for cutting precious stones. Seals, articles for personal adornment and small decorative objects have been fashioned out of such materials since very early times. The techniques of working them were highly developed in ancient Rome, and revived in Renaissance Italy especially in Milan and Florence (where the Grand Ducal studio for such work, the *Opificio delle Pietre Dure* was founded in 1588), and by Italian craftsmen (e.g. the MISERONI family) working at the Court of Rudolf II in Prague. Large vases, ewers, bowls, etc. were carved out of such stones and set in very showy gold and enamel mounts, often in the most extravagantly MANNERIST style (outstanding examples are in the Kunsthistorisches Museum, Vienna, and the Schatz-

Pietra dura:
jasper ewer with enamelled gold and silver mounts, probably by the Saracchi brothers, Milan, 1570–80 Residenzmuseum, Munich)

Pietre dure: ebony prie-dieu *with* pietre dure *decoration, designed by G. B. Foggini, Florence, 1706 (Palazzo Pitti, Florence)*

kammer of the Residenz, Munich). Occasionally statuettes and even life-size busts were made from different types of *pietre dure* (notably a bust of Vittoria della Rovere with drapery of black Flanders marble, and flesh and eyes of chalcedony and agate, *Museo dell'Opificio delle Pietre Dure*, Florence). From the C16 laminae of the stones were worked into mosaics (generally flat but sometimes in relief) for the decoration of cabinets or to serve as table-tops, altar-frontals, etc.: such work is called *commesso di pietre dure* or FLORENTINE MOSAIC.

Lit: E. Kris, *Meister und Meisterwerke der Steinschneidkunst*, Vienna 1929; L. Bartoli and E. A. Maser, *Il Museo dell'Opificio delle Pietre Dure*, Florence 1953.

Piffetti, Pietro (*c.*1700–77). He was one of the few outstanding Italian cabinet-makers. After beginning in Rome he settled in Turin in 1731, becoming cabinet-maker to the King and he continued working for the royal palaces and villas until the end of his life. Up to 1735 he worked under the influence, if not the direct guidance, of JUVARRA who provided him with designs for ecclesiastical furniture and possibly for the handsome Baroque secretaires, side-tables, etc., which he made for the Royal Palace in Turin and which may still be seen there. Then he turned to France for inspiration, developing a bold but very Italianate version of the Louis XV style. His furniture is characterized by the use of almost excessively opulent inlays of rare woods, mother-of-pearl, tortoise-shell and, especially, ivory (usually engraved with hatched shading or figure decoration). His larger pieces are encrusted with gilt-bronze or gilt-wood mounts in the form of human or animal heads, etc., sometimes by the sculptor Francesco LADATTE. Of his ecclesiastical furniture the altar frontal of 1749 for S. Filippo, Turin, remains *in situ*. Though a virtuoso craftsman unrivalled in Italy and with few equals outside France, he was unfortunately less accomplished as a designer. His furniture has an obsessive, overwrought character, the product of a belief in display, whether of rich materials or manual skill. More restrained pieces from the 1750s have been attributed to him and, if correct, suggest that he later adopted the easier manners of a Parisian *salon*.

Lit: V. Viale in *Mostra del Barocco Piemontese*, Catalogue, Turin 1963; H. Honour, *Cabinet Makers and Furniture Designers*, London & New York 1969.

P. Piffetti: marquetry cabinet with gilt-bronze mounts by F. Ladatte, 1731 (Palazzo Reale, Turin)

Pilaster A shallow pier or rectangular column. When used in conjunction with other architectural motifs on furniture it usually conforms to one of the classical ORDERS.

Pile Threads which project from a ground fabric, as in VELVET.

Pilgrim bottle A flattened globular or pear-shaped vessel with loops for suspension on the shoulders and sides, originally a dried gourd in which pilgrims carried drinking water. It is found in Chinese ceramics from the late c16 onwards, late examples in porcelain being sometimes known as 'precious moon vases'. In Europe the shape was copied for decorative objects in ceramics and silver from the c16.

Pilgrim bottle: silver, by A. Nelme, 1715 (Chatsworth House, Derbyshire)

Pilgrim furniture American term for the furniture made in the c17 for the first settlers in New England. It is very simple and very solid, derived stylistically from English furniture.

Pilgrims' badges Lead badges distributed to pilgrims at the main shrines in Medieval Europe. The shell-shaped badges of Santiago de Compostela are the most famous. They were extensively faked in the c19.

Pilkington's Royal Lancastrian pottery A factory near Manchester established in 1892 by the **Pilkington family** – owners of glasshouses and coalmines – with **William Burton** (who had previously worked as a chemist at the WEDGWOOD FACTORY) and his brother **Joseph** in charge. It began by producing tiles and from 1897 decorative vases which were shown at the Paris Exhibition of 1900. Until 1903 vases were either moulded on the premises or made elsewhere and brought to the Lancastrian factory for glazing. After many experiments the Burton brothers developed a new hard transparent glaze and a process of decorating in lustre. Production on a large scale began in 1903. Designs were provided by W. CRANE, L. F. DAY and C. F. A. VOYSEY. The factory closed in 1938.

Lit: L. Thornton in *The Connoisseur* CLXXIV (1970), pp. 10–14.

Pillement, Jean Baptiste (1728–1808). French painter and the most imaginative and fantastic of all Rococo ornamental designers. A curiously elusive figure, he worked in France, Spain, England, Poland, Austria and Portugal. He was born in Lyons, the son of a textile designer but did not himself design silks for the Lyons factories as has been supposed. He seems to have begun at the GOBELINS TAPESTRY FACTORY in Paris. But his great influence on design and the decorative arts was exerted through engravings after his designs (published in France and England) which were widely used and imitated by silk-weavers, cotton-printers, porcelain-painters, marquetry-workers, etc. The best are whimsically individual Chinoiserie scenes with little Chinamen hopping, dancing and tumbling or placidly sitting and fishing beside spindly latticed pavilions which appear to have been spun by some exotic Eastern spider. Others represent strange imaginary flowers, like the tiny blossoms of mosses and lichens magnified a thousand times. Some of his wall paintings are in a similar style which he continued to practise long after the Rococo had given way to Neo-Classicism in Europe. In France the term *le style Pillement* has been used to describe Rococo Chinoiserie decorations in general.

Lit: G. Pillement, *Jean Pillement*, Paris 1945; M. N. Benisovich in *Gazette des Beaux Arts* XXXIV (1952), p. 124.

Pillow lace, *see* LACE.

Pinchbeck An alloy of copper and zinc similar to brass but with rather more copper in it, invented by a London watchmaker **Christopher Pinchbeck** (*fl.*1695–1732). The cheaper types of watch-cases, snuff-boxes, etc. which were made of it were gilt – and when the gilding wore off at the edges the difference in colour was barely perceptible.

Pineau, Nicolas (1684–1754). Leading Rococo designer and the creator (with MEISSONNIER) of the *genre pittoresque* (1730–35), i.e. the second, more frivolous phase of the Rococo in France, characterized by asymmetrical decoration in intricate curves and C scrolls. Born in Paris and architect-trained (under J. H. Mansart and Boffrand), he began his career in Russia (1716–26). He designed *boiseries* for Peter the Great's cabinet at Peterhof *c.*1720. On his return to Paris he became one of the most fashionable designers. Contrast and the deliberate use of asymmetry distinguish his style of interior decoration in which the furniture, executed to his anti-functional designs by such cabinet-makers as CRESSENT, forms an integral part and adds to the general effect of movement, reflection and glitter. Some of his designs were engraved during his lifetime and circulated widely. (They were plagiarized in England by Thomas LANGLEY.) A collection was published in facsimile by Deshais: *Dessins originaux des Maîtres Decorateurs . . . Nicolas et Dominique Pineau.* Paris n.d. (1911).

Lit: D. Guilmard, *Les Maîtres Ornemantistes*, Paris 1880; F. Kimball, *The Creation of the Rococo*, Philadelphia 1943.

Pinewood A straight-grained yellow- or white-coloured wood from the *pinus* tree. It varies from fairly hard to very soft and was used by English furniture-makers from the early C17 onwards, especially for pieces that were to be gilded. It was used widely in the U.S. It was also used for the carcases of veneered furniture.

Pingsdorf pottery The name generally given to a group of early pieces of Rhenish stoneware, formerly supposed to have been made at Pingsdorf though their exact place of origin is unknown. They date from C12 to C14. The earliest pieces are vessels of rough unglazed stoneware often of handsome form and sometimes decorated with abstract patterns painted in reddish-brown (e.g. amphora in Römisch-Germanisches Museum, Cologne) or more usually with horizontal lines incised as the pot was revolved on the wheel. C14 pieces are usually glazed.

Lit: U. Lobbedey in *Keramos* 27 (1965), pp. 3–29.

Pink scale, *see* SCALE PATTERN.

Pintado The English C17 name (derived from Spanish) for a painted or printed calico imported from India.

Pinxton porcelain factory Established in Derbyshire by William BILLINGSLEY under the patronage of a local land-owner, John Coke, it produced from 1796 to 1801 wares of a translucent soft-paste porcelain (containing bone-ash) prettily painted with flowers in the style of DERBY. It was under the management of **John Cutts** from 1804 to 1813 when wares of a rather coarse nearly opaque porcelain sometimes decorated with landscapes were made. The factory has no recognized marks but impressed capital letters are not uncommon on early wares.

Lit: J. Haslem, *The Old Derby China Factory*, London 1876.

Piqué work Tortoise-shell or ivory inlaid with small studs and strips of gold or silver, usually made into snuff-boxes, *étuis*, etc. It was known in France as *Piqué d'or*. The tortoise-shell *piqué* technique was first developed by a Neapolitan jeweller named **Laurentini** in the mid C17 and soon adopted in Paris and London. In England M. BOULTON produced it by factory methods from the mid-1760s. *See also* POSÉ D'OR.

Piqué work: snuff-box, tortoiseshell piqué with silver, French, late C18 (Victoria & Albert Museum)

Lit: H. C. Dent, *Piqué. A Beautiful Minor Art*, London 1923.

Piranesi, Giovanni Battista (1720–78). He was an architect, designer, engraver of Roman views and a Neo-Classical polemicist of some influence. Born near Venice, he was trained there as an architect and went to Rome in 1740, settling there in 1745. His major work *Le antichità Romane*, a series of etchings of Roman buildings, began to appear in 1756 and presented a new and extremely dramatic vision of the grandeur and magnificence of Roman architecture. In 1764 he began his only building (S. Maria del Priorato, Rome) and at the same period designed some furniture, mainly for Cardinal G. B. Rezzonico (nephew of Pope Clement XIII) who commissioned him to decorate an apartment in the Quirinal Palace in Rome. His work there has been destroyed but designs for the furniture in this apartment were included in his folio published in 1769, *Diverse maniere d'adornare i cammini ed ogni altra parte degli edifici*. It includes designs for tables, chairs, picture frames, wall-lights, vases, clock-cases, etc., as well as chimney-pieces – some in a flamboyant Rococo manner but the majority distinctly Neo-Classical and dramatically overloaded with such Antique motifs as palmettes, lion monopods, bucrania, sphinxes, etc. He also made use of Egyptian motifs and designed Egyptian-style wall decorations for the English Coffee House in Rome (now destroyed). Apart from chimney-pieces (examples at Burghley House, England, and the Rijksmuseum, Amsterdam), the only surviving pieces of furniture made exactly to his designs are a pair of side-tables now in the Minneapolis Institute of Arts and the Rijksmuseum, Amsterdam. They were designed for Cardinal G. B. Rezzonico *c.*1769 and are strangely successful exercises in the use of Antique motifs, though their similarity to the bronze furniture shortly to be excavated at Pompeii is probably coincidental.

G. B. Piranesi: design for a side-table, clock, urns, sconces and caskets, 1769

Lit: H. Focillon, *Giovanni-Batista Piranesi, 1720–1778*, Paris 1918; F. J. B. Watson in *The Minneapolis Institute of Arts Bulletin*, LIV (1965).

Pirkenhammer porcelain factory Established near Carlsbad (Karlovy Vary) in Bohemia by 1802 by **Friedrich Hölke** and **J. G. List** from Budstadt in Saxony. It was acquired in 1818 by **Christian Fischer** of Erfurt who greatly improved the quality of its products. It continued to produce wares in the Empire style until the mid C19. Wares were marked 'F & R' impressed from *c.*1815 to *c.*1845 and 'CF' impressed from 1846 to 1853. Modern wares are marked with crossed hammers and sometimes the name of the place.

Lit: H. Meyer, *Böhmischer Porzellan und Steingut*, Leipzig 1927.

Pirot, Andreas, *see* WÜRZBURG TAPESTRY FACTORY.

Pirota, Casa A notable early-C16 maiolica factory in Faenza, probably owned by the **Pirotti family.** Two large dishes, one dated 1525 (private collection), the other depicting the Coronation of Charles V in 1530 (Museo Civico, Bologna), inscribed as having been made in Casa Pirota, are among the outstanding masterpieces of maiolica-ware. Many other pieces bearing the mark of a crossed circle are associated with the factory though this mark was also used elsewhere. They are painted on a ground stained light or dark blue (*a berettino*).

Lit: C. Grigioni in *Faenza* XXV (1937), pp. 38–42 and XXVI (1938), pp. 133–5. G. Liverani, *Five Centuries of Italian Majolica*, New York and London 1960.

Pirotti, *see* PIROTA, CASA.

Pistol handle The slightly curved handle of a table-knife, resembling the butt of a pistol, the most usual form throughout the C18, made of silver, pottery, porcelain, horn or wood. C18 forks sometimes have handles of the same form though they were more usually made *en suite* with spoons.

Pitkin glasshouse A factory at Manchester, Connecticut, established by **Captain Richard Pitkin** and his sons in 1783 and active until *c.*1830, making amber or green bottles and flasks.

Pitoin, Quentin-Claude (d.1777). He was a *fondeur-doreur*, became a *maître* in 1752 and was supplying the Court from 1763 onwards. Little else is known about him apart from the few signed works which survive: fire-dogs for Madame Du Barry (now in the Louvre) and candlesticks for Marie Antoinette of which two are now in the Wallace Collection in London.

Lit: S. Eriksen, *Early Neo-Classicism in France*, London 1974.

Pittsburgh Flint Glass Works, *see* BAKEWELL'S GLASS WORKS.

Planche, François de la, *see* PARIS TAPESTRY FACTORIES.

Planishing The process of flattening sheet metal with a smooth-faced hammer.

Plastics Essentially man-made substances that can be moulded. The first (cellulose nitrate or celluloid) was discovered by Alexander Parkes in Britain in 1862 and for many years remained the only example. It is still used in limited quantities – notably for table-tennis balls and spectacle frames. Cellulose acetate, patented in 1894, had the advantage over celluloid of non-flammability and today is employed in sheet form as a film base and in moulded form for cutlery handles and pen barrels. It was followed, in 1897, by casein, which

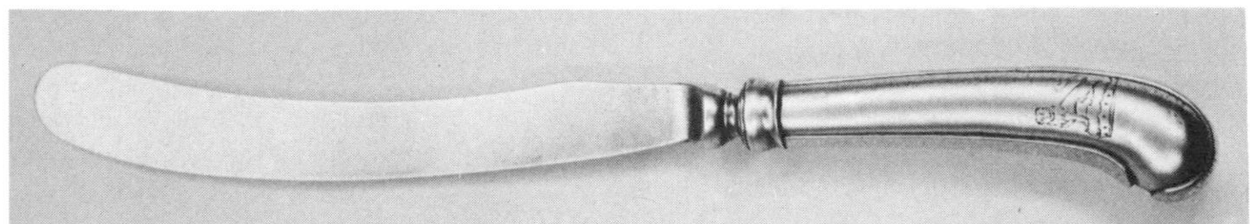

Pistol handle: silver knife by D. Willaume, 1700–1710 (Manchester City Art Gallery)

(Right) Plastic kitchen pail, by G. Colombini, 1954, manufactured by Kartell-Samco, Italy (Museum of Modern Art, New York)

Plastic kitchen containers and implements in translucent flexible plastic, by Earl S. Tupper, 1945–56, manufactured by Tupper Corporation, U.S.A. (Museum of Modern Art, New York)

Plastic chair by J. Colombo, 1963 (Musée des Arts Décoratifs, Paris)

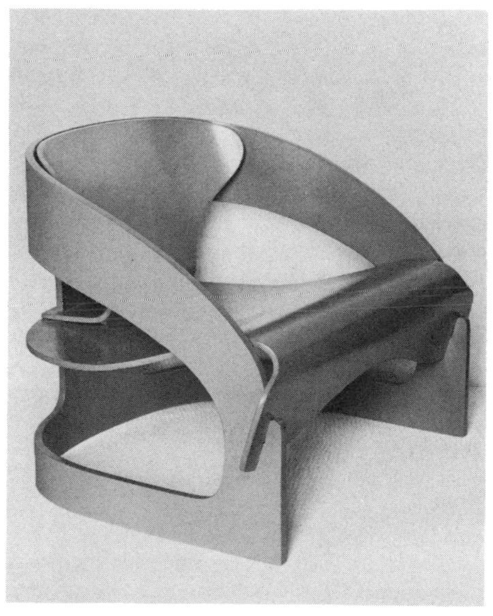

Plastic chair by V. Panton, 1967 (Musée des Arts Décoratifs, Paris)

could be readily coloured and has been used chiefly for buttons.

Both the cellulosics and casein are derived, in part, from natural raw materials. The first completely synthetic resin, phenol formaldehyde or bakelite, was developed by the Belgian chemist Baekeland and patented in 1907. This was the first thermosetting material – setting in an irreversible reaction under heat and pressure – and was used for electrical insulation. It was followed by the related urea formaldehyde (1926) which could be coloured, and melamine formaldehyde (1935) familiar today in the form of decorative laminates (e.g. FORMICA) and moulded table-ware.

The foundations of the modern plastics industry were laid in the 1930s with the development of polyvinyl chloride (pvc), polystyrene, polythene, acrylics and nylon (also of interest as a MAN-MADE FIBRE). All these materials are thermoplastic – they soften on heating to become workable and resume their original characteristics when cool. This property has greatly extended the possibilities of fabrication, in moulded, extruded or sheet form. The production of plastics – mostly thermoplastics – has increased tenfold since 1945. Intensive research has yielded more sophisticated plastics. A few, like polypropylene, are likely to be used on a large scale, but most have limited and highly specialized applications. The point is being reached where materials may be tailor-made to achieve a desired range of properties demanded by the designer.

However, plastics are still overwhelmingly used as substitutes for traditional materials and, just as POTTERY imitated the forms of more primitive materials or, for example, early motor cars were modelled on carriages, there has as yet been little innovation in basic shapes. The Charles EAMES glass-fibre chair and the tulip range by Eero SAARINEN are both hand-moulded and though their appearance may be sleekly modern the concept is still traditional (and in the latter case the design had to be modified by making the supports separately in metal, not plastic). Even Robin Day's highly successful polypropylene chair, made by Hille, is the result of finding a plastic in which a premeditated design could be economically manufactured, rather than taking the properties of a material as the starting point for the design process. W. WAGENFELD's table set for Lufthansa aeroplanes and Gino COLOMBINI's household and other equipment in plastic for Kartell of Milan display great feeling for the material and manufacturing process and are among the most successful designs for plastics to date.

Lit: A. J. Gatt, *Plastics and Synthetic Rubbers*, Oxford 1970.

Plate Generic term for wrought silver and gold, derived from the Spanish *plata* meaning silver. Not to be confused with ELECTOPLATE or SHEFFIELD PLATE.

Plate pail A bucket-shaped wooden container with slots for carrying plates from the kitchen to the dining room.

Plate warmer A stand on which plates may be placed to warm in front of a fire.

Plateau (1) An ornamental stand on a low plinth or feet for the centre of a dining table: usually made in parts so that it could be shortened or lengthened.

(2) A shallow dish on a short stem, usually of silver, i.e., a short TAZZA.

Platel, Pierre (*fl.*1699–1719). He was a French Huguenot silversmith who settled in London and became a member of the Goldsmiths' Company in 1699. His finest recorded work is a gold helmet-shaped ewer and dish with a delicately scalloped edge (1701) at Chatsworth. He was patronized by George, Prince of Wales (later George II) for whom he provided a complete service of plate. Numerous pieces of domestic plate by him are known, e.g. a very elegant two-handled cup (1705) in the Ashmolean Museum, Oxford. His apprentices included Paul de LAMERIE. (For his mark *see* p. 894.)

Lit: J. F. Hayward, *Huguenot Silver in England*, London 1959.

Plaue-on-Havel pottery Established in Brandenburg in 1713 by **Samuel Kempe,** a renegade from MEISSEN, producing imitations of BÖTTGER's red stoneware. Kempe was soon succeeded by **David Pennewitz** who appears to have run the

(Opposite) F. Plitzner: cabinet, c.1715–25 (Schloss Pommersfelden)

concern until it closed *c.*1730. Faience was also produced.

Lit: E. Zimmermann in *Monatshefte für Kunstwissenschaft* I (1908), pp. 602 ff.; K. Hüseler, *Deutsche Fayencen*, Stuttgart 1956–8.

Pliant or **Ployant** A French term for a folding stool with legs crossing as in an X-chair. It is one of the most ancient forms of seat, still surviving in the camp stool. The form came into use in France in the late C17. Previously such a stool had been called *faldesteuil* (Faldstool). It replaced the TABOURET at Court. Versailles and other royal palaces, e.g. Hampton Court in England, were largely furnished with them.

Plique à jour, *see* ENAMEL.

Plitzner, Ferdinand (1678–1724). German cabinet-maker of Franconian origin, trained under J. MATUSCH in Ansbach. His works reveal such perfect mastery of the LOUIS XIV STYLE that it seems likely that he visited Paris. From 1706 he had a workshop at Eyrichshof where he was employed by Hans Georg von Rotenhan, master of the horse to the Kurfürst Lothar Franz von Schönborn. He worked for Lothar Franz from 1709 onwards, first at Schloss Gaibach, then at Pommersfelden where he was responsible for the furnishings of the *Spiegelkabinett* (mirror room) which is among the finest of its kind. Identified works include console tables and gueridons, delicately carved wall cabinets for the display of porcelain, chests of drawers with ivory inlays, etc., all in the French style. His last work, a magnificent writing desk with Boulle-style marquetry was completed after his death by Matusch (Schloss Pommersfelden). *Illustrated previous page.*

Lit: H. Kreisel, *Die Kunst des deutschen Möbels*, vol. ii, Munich 1970.

Plumbate ware Pre-conquest Central American pottery covered with a greyish lustrous slip of leaden colour, hence the name.

Plush A cut VELVET with very long pile.

Plymouth porcelain factory The first to make hard-paste porcelain in England. Founded by COOKWORTHY (1705–80) who had discovered kaolin on the estate of Lord Camelford and took out a patent for the use of this material with PETUNTSE in 1768. In 1770 he moved the factory to Bristol and in 1774 assigned the patent to Richard CHAMPION who closed down the concern in 1782, selling the patent to the NEW HALL FACTORY. Early wares have a thick, rather bobbly glaze: the most notable are salts in the form of sea-shells, mugs and sauce-boats decorated in underglaze blue, and rather clumsy statuettes generally copied from BOW or LONGTON HALL. Many products are slightly distorted (cups have handles askew, etc.). The quality of paste and glaze was improved under Champion's directorship but most products are not very successful imitations of MEISSEN, SÈVRES or DERBY. They include numerous rather clumsy figures and some handsome richly decorated vases. (For factory mark *see* p. 886.)

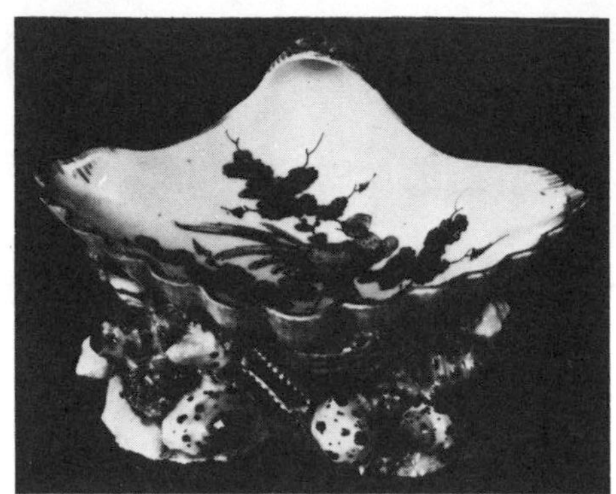

Plymouth porcelain salt cellar, late C18 (Victoria & Albert Museum)

Lit: F. S. MacKenna, *Cookworthy's Plymouth and Bristol Porcelain*, Leigh-on-Sea 1946.

Plywood Three or more layers of wood plied together with the grain running crosswise to give strength and resilience. It has been used in furniture-making since the C18, if not earlier. (It is used in the mahogany dining-room chairs designed by Robert ADAM for Osterley Park *c.*1773.) But it was not exploited until the C19 when Biedermeier craftsmen in Germany and Austria developed its use in BENTWOOD form for concave chair-backs, etc. It then found its great master in THONET who used it in the form of rods.

His contemporary BELTER used it mainly in sheet form. The only later furniture-makers of note to exploit its possibilities with imagination have been AALTO and BREUER.

Plywood tables by M. Breuer, 1935–7 (Isokon Furniture Company, England)

Pocock, William (1750–1835). English furniture-maker trained as a carpenter in London and a freeman of the Carpenters' Company from 1782. He set up a large building firm at Leyton in Essex *c.*1786 but also manufactured furniture and had a London showroom at 26 Southampton Street, 1802–24. He specialized in ingenious transformation pieces known at the time as 'patent furniture' – though he appears to have taken out a patent only for a dining-table with a system of chains or ropes and pulleys inside the framework to enable a single person to extend its length by turning a handle (1805). He advertized a 'patent elevating library or office table', a kind of wheel-chair called 'Merlin's reclining and gouty chair' and the 'boethema rising mattress'. He ceased to produce furniture and closed his London premises in 1824.

Lit: E. T. Joy in *The Connoisseur* CLXXIII (1970). pp. 88–92.

Pohl, Johann, *see* HARRACHOV GLASSHOUSE.

Point, *see* LACE.

Point d'Angleterre The finest type of pillow LACE, made in Brussels and elsewhere in Flanders (not in England) and so called from 1662 when the importation of Flemish lace into France was banned. Patterns are generally floral with *cordonnets* (i.e. raised ribs of plaited threads) outlining leaves and petals, generally on a hexagonal mesh ground, worked after the pattern. *Point d'Angleterre à brides* is a variant with BRIDES supplementing the meshed ground.

Point de France, *see* LACE.

Pointillé A technique for decorating leather, especially in bookbinding, by dots in gold instead of by a cut or impressed outline. It was first introduced *c.*1635 in France on FANFARE BINDINGS.

Pokal A German type of covered wine goblet or cup on a high stem, made of silver and rock-crystal or glass. It is usually a cup or goblet of some distinction, suitable for presentation or for ceremonial purposes.

Pole-screen A small fire-screen; usually a shield-shaped panel mounted on an upright pole so that it could be raised or lowered.

Polidoro Caldara da Caravaggio (d.1543). Italian Mannerist painter and the inventor of a type of vase and ewer which remained popular with ornamental designers, silversmiths, bronze-workers and decorative stone-carvers throughout Europe until well into the C18. It has an ovoid body richly decorated with figurative reliefs, handles in the form of wriggling snakes and, if designed as a ewer, fantastically shaped lips. He also designed basins, tazzas and other silver objects, all in a similarly fantastic and Mannerist style.

Pollaiuolo, Antonio del (*c.*1431–98). He was one of the greatest early Renaissance painters and sculptors but was equally, if not better, known in his own day as a goldsmith. In 1456 he and two other artists were commissioned to make a silver crucifix for the Florentine Baptistery and in 1457 he and Betto Betti were commissioned to make the reliquary for it. The whole work was finished in 1459 and is one of the masterpieces of early Renaissance art (now in the Museo dell'Opera del Duomo, Florence). The tabernacle is reminiscent of the lantern on Brunelleschi's cupola of Florence cathedral and it contains exquisite statuettes and silver reliefs. Originally it glittered with translucent enamels but most of these have flaked off. In 1477 he executed a silver relief of *The Birth of St John the Baptist* for the Baptistery altar, to flank the work which LEONARDO DI SER GIOVANNI had begun. This is still *in situ*. None other of Pollaiuolo's documented works in gold or silver has survived. (The candlesticks he made for the Baptistery altar in 1465 were melted down in 1539.) A reliquary bust in silver of St Octavian (Museo Diocesano, Volterra) is attributed to him. And, according to Cellini, several of Maso FINIGUERRA's *niello* panels were made after his designs. In 1466 he designed for the Florentine Baptistery what is probably the finest surviving set of

Embroidery of coloured and gold and silver thread, designed by A. Pollaiuolo and made 1466–80 (Museo dell'Opera del Duomo, Florence)

embroidered vestments (Museo dell'Opera del Duomo, Florence).

Lit: A. Sabatini, *Antonio e Piero del Pollaiuolo*, Florence 1944; L. Becherucci & G. Brunetti, *Il Museo dell'Opera del Duomo a Firenze*, vol. ii, Florence 1970.

Polonaise carpet A very fine type of PERSIAN CARPET, formerly supposed to be of Polish manufacture. It was made from the late C16 to the mid C17, with a silk pile and often with gold or silver thread inserted by the tapestry method.

Pomegranate motif A decorative device based on the fruit of the pomegranate tree (*punica granatum*) generally supposed to symbolize fertility and plenty. The device derives from the Eastern Mediterranean and is frequently found in Islamic art (especially ceramics and textiles) and in W. Europe from the early Middle Ages. It appears as a flat pattern, especially in textiles, generally in a schematic form. When used in the round – as finials for woodwork, knops, thumb-pieces or feet of silver vessels – pomegranates were often rendered naturalistically, especially in the C17.

Lit: R. Reichelt, *Das Granatapfelmotif in der Textilkunst*, Berlin 1956.

Pommel A globular boss or knob.

Pomona glass A type of American ART GLASS, blown from clear glass and partly etched and partly stained a pale amber. It was produced by the NEW ENGLAND GLASS COMPANY.

Pompeiian style A decorative style derived from the frescoed rooms unearthed at Pompeii (excavations began in 1748) and Herculaneum (systematic excavations began in 1738). It is marked by the use of rather flimsy architectural motifs of a somewhat fantastic kind and a preference for a dull dark terracotta red called 'Pompeiian red'. It first became popular in the late C18 and remained so into the mid C19, mainly for wall decorations, wallpapers, furnishing textiles, painted furniture and ceramics (especially wares made at the ROYAL NEAPOLITAN FACTORY and the WEDGWOOD FACTORY). Furniture found at Pompeii was also copied, mainly in the C19, though such pieces are stylistically indistinguishable from other Neo-Classical furniture imitated from Roman pieces which had been found elsewhere. The term is also, loosely and inaccurately, applied to all manner of GROTESQUE ornament of the type which had been popular in Italy since the C16. The Pompeiian style should not be confused with the ETRUSCAN STYLE.

Lit: P. Werner, *Pompeji und die Wanddekoration der Goethezeit*, Munich 1970.

Ponti Gio (b.1891). Italian architect and designer, he has been an influential propagandist for *avant-garde* industrial design and, especially, for standardization. He founded the periodicals

Domus in 1928 and *Stile Industria* in 1945 and is a universal designer himself, almost in the Renaissance sense, for he has designed ceramics, furniture, light-fittings, ships' interiors and many products of light industry. He began as a designer for the GINORI PORCELAIN FACTORY (1923–38) and renewed their entire range of production. For his first Montecatini building in Milan (1936) he designed all the fittings from washstands to door knobs. His most notable recent designs have been *La Pavone* espresso-coffee machine (1949), cutlery for Krupps of Essen (1951), bathroom equipment for Ideal-Standard (1953) and the dashboard bed-head for hotel bedrooms. His best known furniture design is the *Chiavari* chair (1951), a well-known vernacular chair design refined and adjusted with the greatest skill and taste for mass production. Equally elegant is his *Letizia* chair – a comfortable folding chair with leather seat and brass feet.

Pontil mark, *see* PUNTY.

Pontipool ware Japanned metalware, especially trays, resembling the products of the PONTYPOOL JAPANNING FACTORY but made elsewhere, e.g. Birmingham where **John Taylor** (1711–*c.*1775) produced such wares from 1738 onwards though he later lacquered *papier-mâché* wares and made painted enamel wares. **Wolverhampton** was also a centre for Pontipool ware.

Ponty, *see* PUNTY.

Pontypool japanning factory The source of much of the best C18 japanned tin-plated ironware: *see* JAPANNING. **Thomas Allgood** (d.*c.*1710) who settled in Pontypool, Monmouthshire, in 1660 discovered a by-product of coal which could be applied as a varnish to objects made locally of thin rolled iron plates. He appears to have founded the first Pontypool japanning factory which was developed by his sons **Edward** (1681–1763) and **John.** Products included trays, canisters, tea and coffee urns, cake baskets, candlesticks, vases, etc., japanned with numerous coats of varnish each one of which had to be fired at high temperature, making them both expensive and durable. Various colours were used for the backgrounds – brown and tortoise-shell as well as

Pontypool Japan: tea urn, late C18 (National Museum of Wales, Cardiff)

black – with gilt decorations (usually chinoiseries or flowers). Edward Allgood retired in 1760, making over his business to his three sons. Two of his sons seceded in 1763 and established a rival concern nearby at Usk which closed *c.*1862. Its products are known as **Usk Ware.** The best Pontypool products of the later C18 are large trays painted in colours with landscapes, pastoral and sporting scenes, especially those by **Benjamin Barker** and his sons. The factory closed in 1820 but a member of one Allgood family founded a japanning factory in Birmingham which became the main centre of the japanning industry in C19 England. Pontypool gave its name in popular parlance to all types of japanned metalware, but the name should be reserved for the products of the Allgood factory which were of higher quality than any made elsewhere and are inferior to French *tôle peinte* only in their painted decorations.

Lit: W. D. John & A. Simcox, *Pontypool and Usk Japanned Wares*, Newport 1966.

Poplin or **papeline** A mixture of silk and wool so called because it was first woven in Avignon, the City of the Popes.

Popp, Johann Georg Christoph, *see* ANSBACH POTTERY & PORCELAIN FACTORY.

Poppelsdorf pottery A faience factory founded near Bonn on the orders of Clemens August of Cologne in 1755. Little is known of its earlier products. But from the 1770s it was making cream-coloured earthenware. It was acquired by **Ludwig Wessel** in 1825 and is still active. No C18 factory mark is known, but an anchor was used on C19 earthenware, sometimes with a 'B'.

Lit: W. Schumacher, *Die Poppelsdorfer Porzellan- und Steingutfabrik von Ludwig Wessel in Bonn*, Bonn 1880.

Porcelain A hard, translucent and, generally, white ceramic substance. There are two main types:

1. Hard-paste (*pâte dure*) or true porcelain is made from *kaolin* (white china clay) and a feldspathic rock called chinastone or *petuntse* (chemically, silicate of potassium and aluminium) which when fired at a high temperature (1250°–1350°C.) fuse to a glassy matrix. Usually it is covered with a glaze made from powdered feldspar applied before firing, sometimes it is decorated under the glaze with paintings (the only colours available before 1800 were cobalt blue and manganese). After the first firing it may be decorated over the glaze with ENAMEL COLOURS. If left unglazed it is called BISCUIT PORCELAIN. It was first made in China in the C7 or C8 A.D. and in Europe in 1709 at MEISSEN whence the process was diffused (despite attempts to keep it secret) throughout the West, e.g. to VIENNA PORCELAIN FACTORY 1719, the VEZZI PORCELAIN FACTORY, Venice, *c.*1720 and various other factories in Germany. It was first produced in France *c.*1758 but not on any great scale until adopted at SÈVRES in 1768. In England its production began at the PLYMOUTH PORCELAIN FACTORY in 1768. Little was made in America until the foundation of the TUCKER PORCELAIN FACTORY at Philadelphia in 1826. *See also* BONE CHINA.

2. Soft-paste porcelain (*pâte tendre*) is an imitation of true porcelain invented as a substitute before the secret of true porcelain had been discovered. It was made from a wide variety of materials, mainly white clay and ground glass fired at, generally, much less than 1250°C. A type of soft-paste porcelain was made in Persia as early as the late C11 or C12 but this appears to have had no influence elsewhere. In Europe it was first produced at the MEDICI factory in Florence 1575–87, then at ROUEN 1673 and on a larger scale at SAINT CLOUD from *c.*1675, and thereafter at many European factories (notably BOW, CAPODIMONTE, CHELSEA, DERBY, MENNECY, VINCENNES, WORCESTER) until the end of the C18 (very rarely later). Glazes derived from lead were added to soft-paste porcelain after it had been fired and required a second firing at lower temperatures: pieces painted with enamel colours needed a third firing to sink the colours into the glaze (on feldspathic glazes they stand out very slightly in relief). As losses in the kilns were considerable production on a commercially satisfactory scale was rarely achieved. Soft-paste is therefore much rarer than hard-paste and for this and other reasons has often been preferred to hard-paste by collectors.

(For factory marks *see* pp. 881–9.)

Lit: E. Hannover, *Pottery and Porcelain*, London 1925; W. B. Honey, *European Ceramic Art*, London 1952; G. Savage, *Porcelain through the Ages*, Harmondsworth rev. ed. 1963; R. J. Charleston (ed.), *World Ceramics*, London 1968.

Porcellana, Alla Contemporary term for a type of decoration used on Italian maiolica in imitation of C15 Chinese wares (knowledge of which was probably conveyed through Islamic wares from Turkey or Syria) – a trailing pattern of foliage and scrolls in blue on a white ground.

Porringer A small bowl with one or two handles, generally of silver or pewter, popular in England and the U.S.A. from early C17 to the late C19.

Porringer and cover, English silver with chinoiserie *decoration, 1681 (Private Collection)*

Porrón Spanish glass drinking vessel with a long tapering spout from which the liquid may be poured into the drinker's mouth without the glass touching his lips.

Portière A curtain, often of tapestry, made to hang over a door.

Portobello pottery The main group of Scottish earthenware factories established on the Firth of Forth in 1786, producing household articles in CREAM-COLOURED EARTHENWARE and red earthenware covered with white SLIP. In C19 useful wares are rustic and rather rough, statuettes are similar to those of STAFFORDSHIRE but include several Scottish subjects – Highlanders, fish-wives, etc. STONEWARE was also made from 1830. Wares are sometimes marked 'Scott P. B.' or 'Scott Bros'.

Lit: J. A. Fleming, *Scottish Pottery*, Glasgow 1923.

Portuguese bulb A late C17 English baluster-turned chair leg with the main element like an inverted pear.

Portuguese carpets, *see* PERSIAN CARPETS.

Portuguese potteries Tin-glazed earthenware, especially tiles (AZULEJOS), was produced in Portugal from the C16 though little is known of the factories making it. In the C17 a factory, probably at Lisbon or Braga, produced outstandingly handsome blue-and-white wares, dishes, two-handled vases, narrow-necked bottles, ewers, etc., decorated with chinoiseries, which strongly influenced the makers of wares usually ascribed to HAMBURG. In the C18 faience table-wares were made at RATO, Aveiro, Coimbra, Minagaia, Santo Antonio and Viana Darque. (For factory marks *see* p. 886.)

Lit: J. Queiroz, *Ceramica Portugueza* 1907, rev. ed. Lisbon 1946; J. M. dos Santos Simoes, *Azulejos arcaicos en Portugal*, Madrid 1945; A. Klein in *Keramos* 22 (1963), pp. 7–12.

Portuguese tin-glazed earthenware jar, Lisbon, C17 (Museu de Arte Antiga, Lisbon)

Posé d'or Tortoise-shell inlaid with chased gold designs usually representing baldachins, arabesques, silhouettes, etc. It was often combined with PIQUÉ WORK and was used mainly for ornamenting snuff-boxes, etc.

Posset pot A vessel for posset (hot milk curdled with ale or wine and seasoned with spices). Made in England in the C17–C18 of slipware, stoneware, tin-glazed earthenware or glass, generally straight-sided or bell-shaped with looped handles and a spout, covered with a domed lid. Slipware specimens are often decorated with such inscriptions as 'The best is not too good for you'. The name is sometimes applied incorrectly to PORRINGERS which have no spouts.

Pot pourri vase A vessel with an openwork top (and sometimes openwork sides) to hold aromatic leaves and petals. Made in porcelain at MEISSEN from 1748 and later at many other European porcelain and faience factories. The SÈVRES *vaisseau à mat* is a distinct type.

Pot pourri: Strasbourg faience, c.*1755–60 (Kunstgewerbemuseum, Berlin)*

Pot-à-Oille A C18 type of French silver tureen, nearly spherical and generally with a stand.

Potato ring, *see* DISH RING.

Poterat, Edmé (1612–87). The founder of the ROUEN faience industry, he obtained a monopoly for making faience in Normandy for fifty years from 1644. His factory in the rue d'Elbeuf passed to his widow, then to his younger son **Michel** (d.1721) and then to **Charles Le Coq de Villeray** in 1726. His elder son **Louis** (1641–96) set up his own factory and in 1673 obtained a monopoly for porcelain-making but he is notable mainly as the originator of the characteristic Rouen style of faience decoration. His soft-paste porcelain was apparently the first to be made in France but he made very little and no specimens have been securely identified. After his death, which is said to have been caused by chemicals used in his porcelain, his factory in the rue du Pré was run by his widow and son who sold it in 1720 to **Nicolas Fouquay** (1686–1742). There is no recognized mark.

Lit: M. J. Ballot, *Nevers, Rouen et les fabriques du XVIIe et du XVIIIe siècles,* Paris 1924.

Potiche French term for a Chinese or Japanese vase or jar, generally used for a small covered vase without handles.

Potichomania Mid-C19 English term for the contemporary mania for imitating porcelain by covering the inside of glass vessels with coloured designs on paper or sheet gelatine. In 1855 several firms were advertising the necessary equipment in *The Illustrated London News.* Hutton & Co. of London offered 'new sheets of small and medium sized figures and borders for Etruscan Potichomania, glass vases of classic and artistic shapes, and every requisite for this new art.' At the 'Foreign Depot' this agreeable pastime was 'taught in a few lessons by a lady'. Books of instructions were issued by the various manufacturers.

Potschappel A porcelain factory established near Meissen in the 1870s by Carl Thieme and trading as the Sächsiche Porzellanfabrik Carl Thieme. Products included imitations of the prettier C18 MEISSEN figures and very elaborate vases, some of which are marked *Dresden.*

Potsdam glasshouse In 1674 a glasshouse was established at Drewitz near Potsdam by the 'great' Elector Friedrich Wilhelm of Brandenburg to produce crystal glass and mirror glass for his use and ordinary wares for sale. But he withdrew

625

(*Right*) *Potsdam Glasshouse: glass goblet,* c.1730–40 (*Kunstgewerbemuseum, Zurich*)

Potsdam Glasshouse: tankard mounted in silver-gilt, c.1701 (*Kunstgewerbemuseum, Berlin*)

from this concern in 1678 when he employed J. F. KUNCKEL to direct a glasshouse at an island in the Hakendam transferred in 1685 to the Pfauen Insel on the Havel. By 1680 Kunckel was producing a fine clear crystal glass and in 1687 Martin Winter's Berlin glass-engraving workshop was affiliated. Early products suffered severely from crisseling but this defect was remedied by the use of additional chalk, and wares similar to Bohemian glass were made. Other products were in white *Milchglas* and, more notably, RUBY GLASS. Forms tend to be heavy and the glass is notable mainly for its engraved decorations often executed elsewhere (e.g. by F. GONDELACH at Cassel). The quality of products seems to have declined after the death of the Elector in 1688 and, especially, the retirement of Kunckel in 1693, but the factory remained active until 1736 when it was transferred to **Zechlin** where glass was made under State control until 1890.

Lit: R. Schmidt, *Brandenburgische Gläser*, Berlin 1914; F. A. Dreier in *Jahrbuch der Preussischer Kulturbesitz* VI, 1969, p. 210 ff; R. Schmidt, *Das Glas*, Berlin and Leipzig 1922.

Potsdam pottery A faience factory was founded *c.*1739 at Potsdam by **Christian Friedrich Rewend** (d.1768) producing wares in the style of DELFT. Quality fell off after Rewend's death but the concern survived into the C19. (For factory mark *see* p. 886.)

Lit: O. von Falke, *Alt-Berliner Fayencen*, Berlin 1923; K. Hüseler, *Deutsche Fayencen*, Stuttgart 1956–8.

Potter, Christopher (*fl.* 1789–1800). An English ceramic manufacturer who established a pottery in the rue de Crussol, Paris, in 1789 and applied unsuccessfully for a monopoly of TRANSFER PRINTING on pottery and porcelain. In 1792 he acquired the CHANTILLY PORCELAIN FACTORY which was closed in 1800 when he was ruined by his speculations.

Pottery All types of ware made from baked clay can be termed pottery (though PORCELAIN is sometimes described as a distinct substance it is merely a sub-species). Clay is a natural substance formed by the decomposition of feldspathic rocks (e.g. granite and gneiss), and it is chemically termed hydrated silicate of aluminium. But it is never found without such impurities as alkalis, iron oxides, etc. The primary clays, notably kaolin or china-clay used in porcelain, are found

Pottery: Mesopotamian bowl, c.4000 B.C. *(Louvre)*

in a relatively limited number of places in China, the Ukraine, Europe and the southern U.S.A. Secondary clays – e.g. the common red-clay or earthenware clay – are very widely dispersed. Primary clays contain fewer impurities but are less plastic than secondary clays.

Pottery probably had no single origin. It was made in late Ice Age Moravia, in Mesolithic times among the forest dwellers of N. Europe and in the upper Palaeolithic Kenya Capria culture in Africa. But it was probably preceded by BASKETRY. In the pre-ceramic cultures of Peru there were various types of basketry: and among the Pueblo peoples of S.E. United States baskets caulked with clay preceded pottery. But there is no positive archaeological evidence that pottery derived from basketry. Because of its fragility pottery took the place of more permanent materials (e.g. LEATHER) only when settled life began, and its development followed the growth of urban civilizations. It is one of the four criteria of Neolithic culture (with domestication of stock, cultivation of cereals and manufacture of polished stone implements). The earliest specimens are probably

Pottery: Mycenaean vase, c.1500 B.C. *(Archaeological Museum. Athens)*

those found in Middle Neolithic levels at Jericho and at Fayum.

From the first a substitute material, pottery has no characteristic forms. The shapes we think of as being characteristic derive from the process of manufacture, not the material. And the imitation of vessels made in other materials has always been a dominant factor in pottery design. The forms of basketry, leather and natural containers such as gourds were all imitated and, later, those of metal as well. Early Minoan pottery, for example, sometimes imitates wooden cups even to the extent of having painted imitation wood graining. Basketry frequently suggested both

Pottery: Amphora, Greece, c.800 B.C. *(Archaeological Museum, Athens)*

shapes and decorations (e.g. Egyptian Neolithic Tarsian beakers). Leatherwork was imitated, notably in the otherwise inexplicably impractical shape of the tall, narrow Greek wine-jar with a pointed base, derived from wine-skins of leather. Metalwork radically transformed pottery shapes from prehistoric to modern times (e.g. the Hallstatt bronze situla or bucket which was for long a dominant form in the prehistoric pottery of the West: the common copper cooking pot, issued as equipment to the Roman army, which was the prototype for popular Iron Age ware in Gaul and Britain: much later Renaissance silver and other fine metalwork which provided models for MAIOLICA and, similarly, Baroque silver which was imitated by BÖTTGER, the discoverer of true porcelain in Europe).

Processes:

The instinctive and presumably the earliest method of shaping pottery is by 'building' i.e. by pressing the thumb into a lump of clay and thinning the walls of the pot between thumb and finger. This is sometimes called pinch-pottery or squeeze-pottery. It was used in Neolithic cultures and is still in use, e.g. for RAKU tea-bowls.

Coiling is another Neolithic method, similar to coiled basketry and familiar from N. American pottery. Sausages of clay are built into a pot spirally, each being pressed and smeared into that below. The resulting uneven surface was

Pottery: Skyphos, Greece, c.490–480 B.C. *(Louvre)*

usually smoothed by beating with a bat, as in prehistoric China and as still practised by Sindh potters whose methods descend intact from the Indus civilization of the third millennium. A final smoothing can be given with a wet cloth.

Moulding was not extensively used until modern times though the standard methods of liquid moulding or slip-casting were known to Palestinian Iron Age potters. Some Greek pottery was moulded, usually in a fired clay mould with a wooden core.

Wheel throwing was the only new pottery process invented before modern industrial methods were applied to pottery manufacture. But wheel throwing is also an ancient process which appears to have been known before 3000 B.C. in Mesopotamia. The potter's wheel is to be distinguished from a turn-table on which a pot is *built*. For the wheel introduced the technique of 'throwing', i.e. shaping the plasic clay by spinning. The wheel's function is to supply centrifugal force to a lump of clay accurately 'thrown' on its centre. When spun at a minimum of 100 revs. per second the clay needs only light guiding pressure from the potter's hand to assume any sectionally circular shape he wishes. Thus the potter merely directs the energy imparted to the clay by the wheel. The wheel was normally spun by hand or foot and kept spinning by its own momentum, like a top. The introduction of this process usually led to more elaborate shapes – to mouldings, groovings and to such refinements as heavily undercut and extravagantly curved lips – also to an emphasis on form rather than decoration. In China the virtual disappearance of decoration may have been largely due to it – combined with the simultaneous development of fine glazes.

When a pot has been formed it must be dried and fired. Clays become plastic when mixed with water and will retain whatever shape they have been given when dried in the air. When dried, either by natural or artificial heat (according to climatic conditions) to a 'leather-hard' condition (i.e. water content 3–15 per cent), the clay can be worked by scraping, cutting or turning. It may also be burnished to reduce porosity, usually after the pot has been dipped in or painted with a SLIP of the finer portions of the clay used in making it. When dried to a 'white-hard' state (i.e. water content 3 per cent) it can be fired either in a kiln or open fire. At temperatures from 450°C. to 700°C. the clay decomposes with loss of its chemically combined water and is then similar to a moderately hard stone. If fired at a higher temperature the clay becomes denser and less porous and will ultimately vitrify and fuse. Such high temperatures were rarely reached in early pottery which was seldom fired above 1000°C. And because of their impurities some clays will not withstand firing at a very great temperature. In the process of firing (sometimes in a second firing) the surface of a piece of pottery may be covered with GLAZE.

In the history of European pottery the red and black wares of Greece and Rome are unique in being an indigenous Mediterranean invention (*see* GREEK POTTERY, HELLENISTIC POTTERY, ETRUSCAN POTTERY, ROMAN POTTERY). All other developments derive directly or indirectly from the East. After the fall of the Western Empire large-scale production of good wheel-thrown pottery ceased except in a few areas of Gaul, the Rhineland and in Italy. The history of medieval and later pottery is largely that of oriental influence either direct from CHINESE POTTERY or by way of ISLAMIC POTTERY. Chinese porcelain and stonewares were reaching the Baghdad area by the C9 and continued to be imported into the Near East throughout the Middle Ages (though they did not reach Europe in significant quantities until the C17, with the founding of the Dutch East India Company in 1609 and the British East India Company in 1631). Fine T'ANG mottled stoneware and creamy porcelain imported into the Middle East in the C9 inspired attempts to imitate their texture and whiteness and led to the invention of an opaque TIN GLAZE. This was a barely passable imitation. Its great importance lay in the facilities it offered for painted decoration. Paints applied to the unfired matt surface did not run when fired, as they did when applied direct on a pottery surface under the more fusible LEAD GLAZE. The subsequent development of pottery in Europe can be traced largely from the spread of Islamic tin-glaze techniques, first to Spain where the HISPANO-MORESQUE wares were the best made in C15 Europe, then to Italy where MAIOLICA was produced and from Italy to the North. STONEWARES of great refinement were, however, made from the C15 mainly in the Rhineland. And in the C16 outstanding lead-glazed wares were made in France by B. PALISSY and his imitators. From the C16, however, attention was increasingly given to attempts to produce porcelain. Soft-paste porcelain was produced at the MEDICI PORCELAIN FACTORY in Florence before the end of the C16, but no hard-paste porcelain was made until the early C18 when the MEISSEN factory began production.

(For factory marks *see* pp. 881–9.)

Lit: A. Rieth, *5,000 Jahre Töpferscheibe*, Konstanz 1960; H. Hodges, *Artifacts*, London 1964;

R. J. Charleston (ed.), *World Ceramics*, London 1968; D. Green, *Pottery Materials and Techniques*, London 1972.

Pottier and Stymus A firm of New York cabinet-makers and interior decorators. The principals, **Auguste Pottier** and **William Pierre Stymus**, began their careers in the 1840s in a New York cabinet-making workshop, Rochefort & Skarren, on Broadway. They became foremen of it and took it over in 1859. Pottier was a cabinet-maker and Stymus an upholsterer. The concern prospered; by 1871 they had acquired a large factory on Lexington Avenue and from 1883 an office on Fifth Avenue as well. In the 1870s and 80s it was among the most fashionable firms of its type in New York, producing furniture liberally decorated with a variety of ornament derived from the historical styles from Late Empire Grecian to Renaissance (e.g. 'Henri II' style chairs in the Metropolitan Museum, New York). They were also responsible for a Moorish smoking-room executed for John D. Rockefeller, now in the Brooklyn Museum.

Lit: 19th Century America: Furniture and Other Decorative Arts, Exh. Cat., Metropolitan Museum, New York 1970.

Poudreuse French term for a dressing table, *see* TOILETTE.

Pouffe Late C19 English term for a large free-standing stuffed cushion used as a seat.

Pouffe, c20

Pounce box Box, usually of silver, containing pounce or the fine powder used to prevent ink spreading on unsized paper.

Pounced surface A matt surface, usually on silver, produced by hammering to give a powdered effect.

Poutney Pottery Co., *see* WEMYSS WARE.

Powell, James, *see* WHITEFRIARS GLASSHOUSE.

Powell, John Hardman, *see* HARDMAN, John.

Powolny, Michael (1871–1954). Austrian ceramic artist, he was the son of a stove-maker at Judenburg, attended the Fachschule für Tonindustrie in Znaim and then the Kunstgewerbeschule in Vienna. In 1906 he founded in Vienna the **'Wiener Keramik'** studio in collaboration with the graphic artist **Berthold Löffler** (1874–1960). He specialized in white faience figures generally decorated only in black (occasionally other colours) in the Viennese SECESSION style. J. HOFFMANN and D. PECHE also provided designs for this studio and its products were marketed by the WIENER WERKSTÄTTE. It was amalgamated in 1912 with a studio founded by one of his pupils, **Franz Schleiss** (b.1884) as the **'Wiener und Gmundener Keramik Werkstätte'.** (*see* GMUNDEN POTTERY). He taught pottery-making from 1909 and sculpture from 1932 at the Kunstgewerbeschule. After 1918 he established a studio for glass decoration (by grinding and cutting), working for LOBMEYR and other firms. As both teacher and craftsman he exerted great influence on the development of the decorative arts in Austria. (For his mark *see* p. 886.)

Lit: L. W. Rochowanski, *Wiener Keramik*, Vienna 1923; F. Lipp in *Keramos* 24 (1964), pp. 20–29.

Pratt, Felix (1780–1859). A Staffordshire potter who began in his father's pottery at Lane Delph, he established in 1812 with his brother a pottery at Fenton, called **F. & R. Pratt.** They produced Toby jugs, figures and domestic wares and are associated with PRATT WARE though this was certainly produced by other potteries as well as theirs. In the 1840s the firm developed the process of transfer-printing in colour (by transfer from stippled copper-plates) invented by **Jesse Austin** (1806–79), mainly for lids of pomade pots, etc., but also for table-wares. The factory mark of 'PRATT' impressed is found on c18 wares, but is rare. Mid-c19 wares are marked 'F & R Pratt'.

Pratt ware Cream-coloured earthenware painted in high-temperature colours – green, ochre, blue and brown – often over relief decorations of figures, fruits, etc. It is associated with the Staffordshire pottery of **F. & R. Pratt,** though similarly decorated pieces are known to have been made at other factories, at LEEDS and elsewhere, in the early c19.

Prayer rugs Small, often very finely worked, carpets on which Muslims pray. The central motif of the design is a conventionalized representation of the *mihrab*, the prayer niche facing Mecca in a mosque.

Precht, Christian (1706–79). He was one of the leading Rococo designers and a famous Swedish silversmith, but unfortunately no works certainly by him are known. His father, **Burchardt Precht,** was a sculptor and cabinet-maker from Bremen who went to Stockholm in 1674 to work at Drottningholm Palace. Christian was apprenticed to a goldsmith in Stockholm in 1721 and in 1727 went to London and later to Paris, Augsburg and Nuremberg before returning to Stockholm in 1731. In 1737 he obtained permission to carry on a silversmith's business without intervention from the guild. This meant that he could not stamp his products with a personal mark. They are therefore very difficult to identify. Numerous designs by him have survived in the National Museum, Stockholm, and these show silver in a richly fluid Rococo style derived from Parisian designers such as MEISSONNIER. A few pieces have been attributed to him as a designer, notably a very fine Rococo baptismal ewer and basin, with **Johan Colin**'s mark as maker and dated 1745 (Eriksberg Castle) and a coffee-pot made by **Michael Astrom** in 1764 (Nordiska Museet, Stockholm). Both are unlike other works by Colin and Astrom. In addition to working in silver Precht made medals and was also active as a jeweller and designed ceramics. In 1738 he provided designs for 'export porcelain' which were sent out to China. He may also have made designs for MARIEBERG POTTERY at which jugs, basins and tureens were made in close imitation of Rococo silver vessels.

C. Precht: design for a coffee-pot, mid c18 (National Museum, Stockholm)

Lit: Gustaf Munthe, *Konsthantwerkaren Christian Precht*, Stockholm 1957.

Preissensin, Albrecht (d.1598). He was a leading Nuremberg pewterer – *Meister* in 1564 – famous for large bowls with figure decoration cast in low relief by a technique similar to that used by his contemporary Nicholas HORCHHAIMER. Instead of engraving the decorations, Preissensin etched them on the metal or stone moulds in the same way that armourers decorate their work, but in *intaglio*. The effect was a rather flat relief reminiscent of woodcuts and was later known as the 'wood-cutting style'. The decoration is either abstract (e.g. arabesques) or of scenes from the Passion or classical mythology.

Lit: H.-U. Haedeke, *Metalwork*, London 1970.

Preissler, Daniel (1636–1733). He was a *Hausmaler* to whom some outstandingly fine decorations on glass and porcelain are generally attributed. He worked at Friedrichswalde in Silesia and is said to have introduced the SCHWARZLOT technique into Bohemia. His son, **Ignaz** (b.1676) was also a HAUSMALER and is known to have worked in Breslau before 1729 and at Kronstadt in Bohemia 1729–39. None of their works is signed, but decorations in *Schwarzlot* in red or purple monochrome and in gold on Bohemian and Silesian glass, Chinese, MEISSEN and VIENNA porcelain are ascribed to them. Subjects range from townscapes, landscapes, mythological scenes, hunting and battle pieces and genre scenes to fantastic chinoiseries sometimes with Baroque *Laub- und Bandelwerk* ornament. Most of the decorations on European porcelain are ascribed to Ignaz rather than to Daniel who is assumed to have worked mainly on glass and Oriental porcelain. This group of decorations was at one time attributed to a single painter called Preussler.

Lit: G. E. Pazaurek: *Deutsche Fayence- und Porzellan-Hausmaler* Leipzig 1925; R. von Strasser in *Journal of Glass Studies* XV (1973), pp. 135–42.

Press Old English term for a cupboard for the storage of clothes, books, linen, etc. generally qualified as clothes-press, linen-press, etc. The term is now generally reserved for a C16–C17 type of cupboard with doors enclosing a large compartment below and two smaller compartments side by side in the upper part. A type peculiar to Wales with two lower stages closed by doors and an open upper stage is called a **tridarn.** The term press-cupboard is tautological but sometimes applied to a piece of C16–C17 furniture similar to a COURT CUPBOARD but taller and with both upper and lower stages closed by doors.

Press moulding A ceramic technique. Moist clay is beaten into a flat bat and then pressed into a mould and trimmed. Moulds were of fired clay, wood, alabaster or plaster of Paris. They usually had ridged or incised patterns. Press moulding was used from the early C18 onwards in England, notably at the STAFFORDSHIRE POTTERIES where dishes were commonly press-moulded and the patterns finished with slip. Figures were also made, with two-piece moulds, the two parts being united when firm with slip. Parts of the figures were also moulded separately.

Pressed glass Vessels of glass formed in a cast-iron mould – into which the molten metal is forced by a plunger. It is an American process first adopted in 1827 at the factory of the NEW ENGLAND GLASS COMPANY, soon imitated by the BOSTON AND SANDWICH GLASS COMPANY, and in the 1830s taken up in England especially at STOURBRIDGE and on Tyneside where the glass-house of **Sowerby & Co.** at Gateshead became a leading producer. At first the mechanism was hand-operated but in 1864 a steam-operated press was patented in the U.S. The earliest pieces were made in imitation of clear CUT GLASS but coloured pieces and vessels in the form of baskets, animals, birds, etc. were also made on a very large scale.

Preuning, Paul (*fl.*1540–50). Nuremberg potter who, with his relative, **Kunz Preuning,** adapted the HAFNER WARE technique to large jugs very elaborately decorated with horizontal bands of figurative scenes in applied relief, coloured – predominantly green, blue, yellow and purple-

P. & K. Preuning: Hafner ware jug, Nuremberg, c.1550 (Kunstgewerbemuseum, Cologne)

brown – by glazes kept from mingling in the firing by threads of clay. They were prosecuted in 1541 for combining Biblical and profane subjects on the same vessel. Other members of the Preuning family were named **Andreas**, **Matthäus** and **Stefan** but seem to belong to a younger generation. Jugs with crucifixes and processions of drummers and fifers are ascribed to Kunz; those with Biblical scenes and half-length portraits of German Protestant princes to Paul; those with Biblical subjects between floral motifs to Andreas. Notable examples are in the Victoria & Albert Museum, the Kunstgewerbemuseum, Cologne and the Kunstgewerbemuseum, West Berlin. At one time these wares were incorrectly attributed to A. HIRSCHVOGEL.

Lit: A. Walcher von Molthein in *Kunst und Kunsthandwerk*, 1904, pp. 486ff, 1905, pp. 134ff.

Pricket, Limoges enamel on copper (Victoria & Albert Museum)

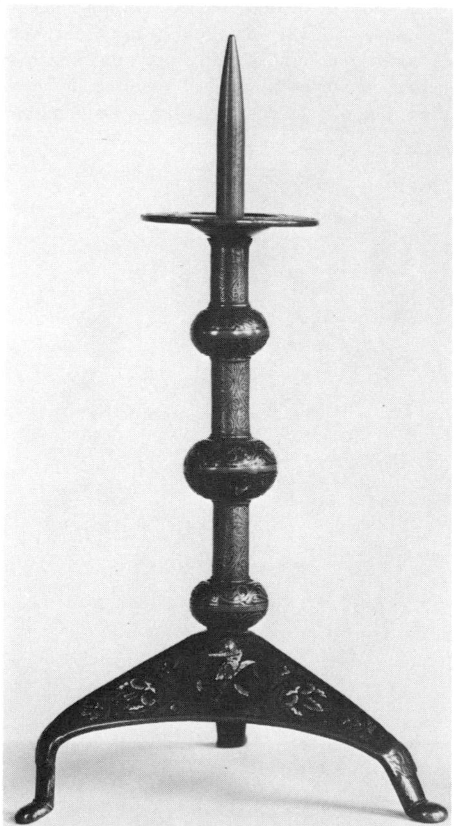

Preussler, *see* PREISSLER, Daniel.

Price, Richard (d.1683). An English chair- and bed-maker who is first recorded in London in 1662 and was extensively employed by Charles II as 'Joyner to his Great Wardrobe' from 1678 onwards. Accounts reveal that he made day-beds, upholstered chairs with tilting iron-framed backs, caned chairs, folding tables and the royal *chaise-percé* for the King's New Lodgings in Whitehall, but none survives.

Lit: P. Macquoid and R. Edwards, *Dictionary of English Furniture*, London 1954.

Pricket The earliest type of candlestick, with a metal spike on which the candle was stuck. From the C14 onwards candlesticks with sockets for the candles were more usual for domestic use. *Illustrated previous column.*

Pricking Needle-point decoration on silver, especially of the C16 and C17.

Prie-dieu A faldstool or praying desk, often in the form of a chair with a low seat and a high back with a padded top. *Illustrated next column; for additional illustration see* PIETRE DURE.

Prieur, Jean-Louis (*fl.*1765–85). He was a bronze founder, became a *maître* in 1769 and in 1783 described himself as *sculpteur, ciseleur et doreur du Roi*. He made the bronze mounts (to BELANGER's designs) for Louis XVI's coronation coach and several gilt bronze clock-cases by him are recorded. However, he is now known mainly for his designs for furniture and other decorative work. He made a great number of designs for the Polish Court at Warsaw in 1766 and many of his ornamental and other designs were engraved in Paris in the 1780s.

Lit: S. Eriksen, *Early Neo-Classicism in France*, London 1974.

Princes' metal A kind of BRASS of a golden colour made in C17 England, sometimes called **Prince Rupert's metal.** It is an alloy of approximately

Prie-dieu: style Troubadour, *early* C19 *(Musée Condé, Chantilly)*

three parts copper to one of zinc pickled in a diluted spirit of vitriol and then immersed in aquafortis before burnishing.

Print room A room decorated with etchings and engravings, especially of buildings and landscapes, glued to the wallpaper and generally surrounded by paper frames so that the whole wall surface is covered with a slightly irregular pattern of tightly packed squares and oblongs. It looks extremely pretty. The vogue for such rooms began in England in the 1760s and reached its height in the early C19. Very few now survive and the best is that at Stratfield Saye.

Printies Concave circles or ovals cut into the surface of a glass vessel.

Prismatic cutting A technique of CUT GLASS decoration with horizontal rows of prisms which catch the light, very popular in the early C19.

Proskau pottery A Silesian faience factory founded by Count Leopold von Proskau in 1763 and producing wares decorated in enamel colours in a slightly coarsened version of the STRASBOURG style. The founder was killed in a duel in 1769 and next year the factory was acquired by Count Johann Carl von Dietrichstein who appointed **Johann Joseph Reiner** as manager, under whom it produced, most notably, tureens in the form of fruits and vegetables, also figures of saints and children. The estate and factory were acquired by Frederick the Great in 1783 and the factory leased to the manager **Johann Gottlieb Leopold** who ran it from 1782 to 1812. During this period products included useful wares and vases, the latter sometimes imitated from Greek pottery. From 1793 cream-coloured earthenware was made in place of faience. In 1812 the concern was leased to, and in 1823 bought by, **J. K. Dickhut** whose descendants ran it until 1850. Wares of 1763–9 are usually marked 'P', those of 1770–83 are usually marked 'DP'. Later wares were marked with the full name impressed, though enamelled faience was again marked 'P'.

Lit: K. Hüseler, *Deutsche Fayencen*, Stuttgart 1956–8.

Proto-porcelain A term applied to early (C4–3 B.C.) Chinese wares such as YÜEH, with a feldspathic glaze for which a high firing temperature is needed. The body is fine-grained, hard and grey in colour.

Prouvé, Emile Victor (1858–1943). French Art Nouveau sculptor, painter and designer. He was born in Nancy, studied at the drawing school there and then went to the Academy in Paris. Returning to Nancy he worked under E. GALLÉ and adopted a closely similar style for the design of furniture, jewellery and glass. On Gallé's death in 1904 he took over his factory and was largely responsible for the design of its later products (signed with Gallé's name and a star to distinguish them from those made in the master's lifetime). In 1905 he went to Germany to study the work of the Munich *Werkbund* and in 1908–9 organized a congress at Nancy to discuss and publicize his and others' findings on modern German design. He was appointed director of the École des Beaux Arts in Nancy in 1918. His son **Jean** (b.1901) is an architect who has also designed some of the best modern French furniture, notably a simple, elegant and clean-lined chair of 1925. As an architect he is notable for his sensitive experimentation with new materials, especially aluminium and plastics, and this is equally evident in his furniture which is closely related to his architecture, e.g. a steel and plastic table with the top cantilevered on an irregular inverted V base which exactly repeats the structure of the building for which it was originally made.

Lit: M. Prouvé, *Victor Prouvé*, Paris 1958.

Prunt A decoration on a glass vessel, made out of an applied blob of molten glass modelled into the form of a raspberry, lion mask, etc.

Prunts, on the stem of a glass by Ravenscroft, c.1675 (Victoria & Albert Museum)

Psyche, *see* CHEVAL GLASS.

Puente A type of Spanish carved table trestle stand to carry a VARGUEÑO. It has two oblong slides which, when pulled out, support the drop-front of the vargueño.

Pugin, Augustus Welby Northmore (1812–52). Architect and designer, he became an impassioned leader and propagandist of the Gothic Revival and a strong influence on Victorian taste. His father, **Augustus Charles Pugin** (1762–1832), was a French *émigré* who was in London by 1792, and later worked as a draughtsman and water-colourist. His work includes a few designs for rather spindly Neo-Gothic furniture similar to the *style Troubadour* objects made in *Restauration* France. His son began in a similar style producing, at the age of fifteen, furniture designs for a set of chairs for Windsor Castle to be executed by Messrs Morel and Seddon. (The chairs are still at Windsor Castle.) He also designed silver for the royal goldsmiths RUNDELL and BRIDGE at the same time. But by the early 1830s he was insisting on archaeological accuracy and truth to materials. He tried to make his furniture look like medieval furniture, whereas previous designers had merely tricked out contemporary patterns with Gothic ornament, usually derived from architecture and never intended for furniture. He issued several books of designs, notably *Gothic Furniture in the style of the 15th century* (1835) and *Designs for Iron and Brass Work* (1836) and expounded his views on furniture and decoration as well as architecture in *The True Principle of Pointed or Christian Architecture* (1841). His preference was for bold, solid, rather chunky forms whether in architecture, furniture or jewellery. Most of his furniture was made for the houses which he designed and is relatively plain – massive armoires with linen-fold panelling and large iron hinges to the doors, heavy upright settles, etc. They are comely rather than elegant, with a minimum of decorative enrichments. The basic structure of the carpentry is emphasized with unusual honesty. He allowed himself greater extravagance of tracery and crocketting on the furniture designed for the Houses of Parliament (including Gothic umbrella stands) 1836–7, and also that for the Medieval Court at the Great Exhibition, 1851. He also designed Gothic ceramics for MINTONS, wallpapers of an heraldic character of J. C. CRACE and some beautiful if (to the wearer) uncomfortably heavy gold enamelled jewellery. He also designed church plate, derived from C15 patterns, for the Birmingham firm of **John Hardman & Co.** which had been founded in

Oak cabinet designed by Pugin for Abney Hall, Cheshire, c.1847 (City Art Gallery, Salford)

1838 by HARDMAN in association with Pugin. Much of the ecclesiastical plate and furnishings were of course for churches designed and built by Pugin. Examples of his furniture are in the Victoria & Albert Museum, London.

Lit: M. Trappes Lomax, *Pugin: a Medieval Victorian*, London 1933; P. Stanton, *Pugin*, London 1971.

Puiforcat, Jean (1897–1945). He was the outstanding silversmith working in the ART DECO style of the Paris 1925 exhibition. He was also a famous collector of silver, especially of the Louis XV and Louis XVI periods. (Much of his collection is now in the Louvre.) And, surprisingly, he was also a well-known athlete, being a tennis champion, a member of the French national Rugby football team and the Olympic ice-hockey team. His father was a silversmith but Jean worked independently, beginning in 1922. In 1925 he contributed silver wares to RUHLMANN's *Hôtel du Collectionneur* in the great Paris exhibition of that year. In 1926 he joined 'Les Cinq', a group including Pierre CHAREAU and Pierre LEGRAIN; and in 1928 he joined the Union des Artistes Modernes (U.A.M.) led by René Herbst and including Charlotte PERRIAND among its members. It was a SÉCESSION group in reaction to Art Deco. Puiforcat's silver was produced for the luxury market. He specialized in costly simplicity. But despite the admirable austerity of design and smooth finish his work is remote from 'machine' aesthetics. Examples are in the Musée des Arts Décoratifs, Paris, and in the Metropolitan Museum, New York.

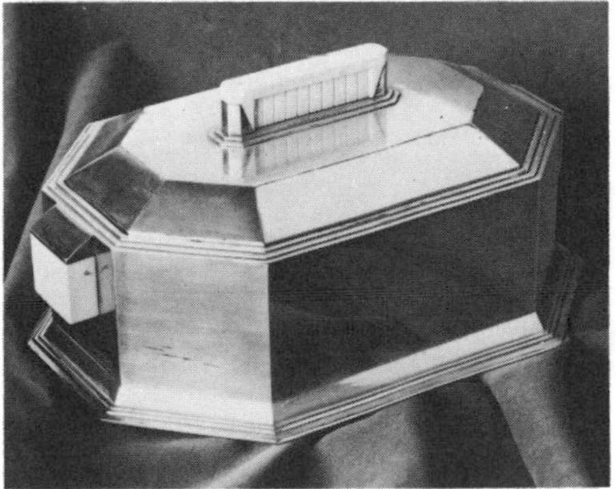

J. Puiforcat: silver soup-tureen, c.1925 *(Musée de peinture et sculpture, Grenoble)*

Lit: R. Herbst *et al.*, *Jean Puiforçat Orfèvre et Sculpteur*, Paris 1951.

Pull, Georges (1810–89). German potter who settled in Paris and set up a pottery in 1856 producing some of the best imitations of the work of B. PALISSY.

Punch bowl A type of English silver, porcelain or pottery bowl, introduced after the Restoration. It is usually wide and deep and without any moulding round the rim but resting on a plain foot rim. It sometimes has handles. After 1730 they became slightly more elaborate and were sometimes embossed with fluting. Towards the end of the C18 they were made with a tray. In ceramics, those made at the BRISTOL factories with painted ship decoration are notable.

Punct, Carl Christoph (d.1765). Sculptor and modeller at the MEISSEN PORCELAIN FACTORY 1761–5 and notable for his shepherds, allegorical figures of children in modern dress and a group of Diana and Actaeon made for Frederick the Great.

Punto in aria The first type of true needlepoint LACE made from the C15 at first in Venice. It differs from such immediate predecessors as CUTWORK, DRAWN WORK, DARNED NETTING and RETICELLA in that it is made from a single thread and not from a previously woven panel, though the designs tend to retain their geometrical rigidity.

Punty or **Ponty** The round hollow mark made on glass in breaking off the pontil or iron rod used for handling glass during manufacture. On old drinking glasses the mark is usually found on the bottom and is rough. In the C18 the roughness was usually ground smooth.

Purdonium A C19 English type of coal scuttle invented by a Mr Purdon. It has a removable sheet-metal container for the coal, and a lid or door.

Purl Fine wire closely bound with silk and coiled, much used in C16 and C17 needlework. Also a type of stitch in knitting.

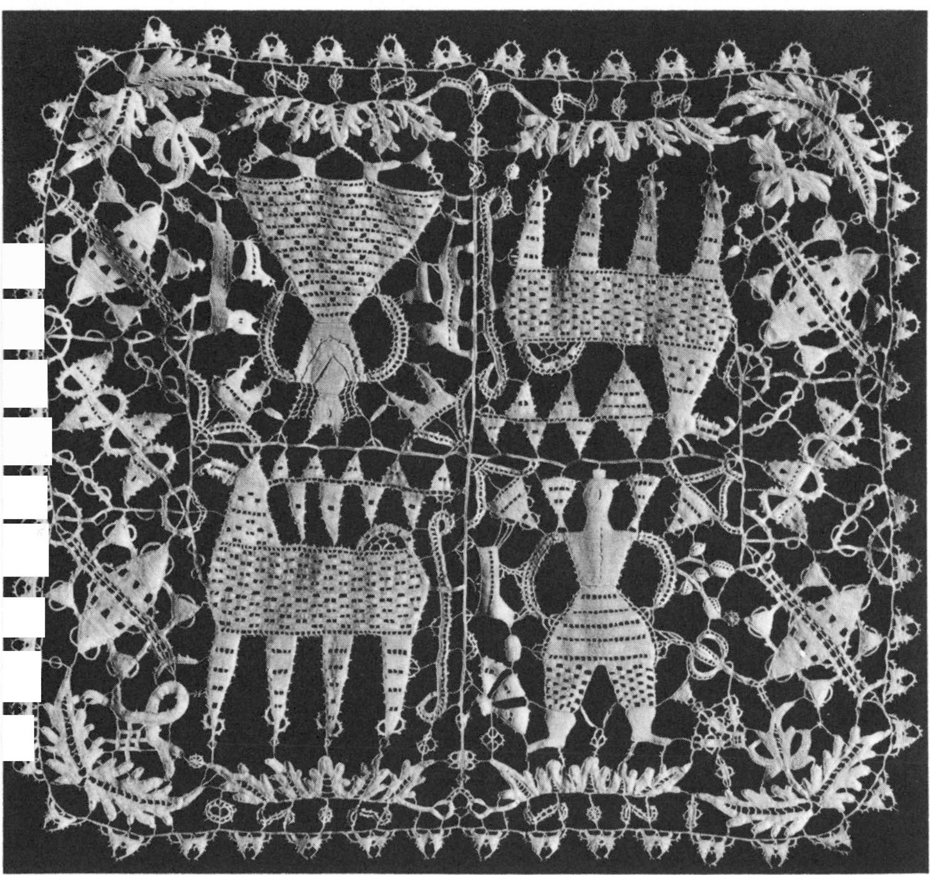

Punto in aria *chalice cover, Italian, late C16 (Courtesy of the Art Institute of Chicago)*

Purled ornament An all-over diaper pattern of moulded round or oval compartments on glass vessels.

Purple of Cassius A deep crimson pigment for painting on porcelain and faience, invented by **Andreas Cassius** of Leyden *c.*1650, and made by dissolving a gold coin in nitric acid and sal-ammoniac. Much used in C18 France and Germany, especially at MEISSEN, and transmitted to China where it gave the key to the FAMILLE ROSE colour scheme.

Puteaux, Louis-François-Laurent (1780–1864). He was one of the best *Restauration* furniture-makers, specializing in pieces in *bois clair* with elegant inlays of ebony, sometimes after designs by PERCIER and FONTAINE. He also used inlays of mother-of-pearl. He was known especially for *secrétaires*. After 1830 he appears to have gradually abandoned high quality cabinet-making for the mass-production of cheaper work. A typical example of his work at its best is the *bureau à cylindre* of *c.*1819 in the Musée Carnavalet in Paris.

Lit: D. Ledoux-Lebard, *Les ébénistes-parisiens (1795–1870)*, Paris 1965.

Puzzle jugs Vessels with perforated necks so made that the liquid in them can be drunk only by sucking through an inconspicuous tube which runs from the rim to the bottom of the bowl: made from medieval times to the C19, especially in the C17 and C18.

Pyne, Benjamin (*fl.*1684–1724). Notable London silversmith, he was patronized by Queen Anne and was one of the best practitioners of the style associated with her reign. Though among the English silversmiths who opposed the influx of Huguenot refugee craftsmen, he often adopted their style and may have employed them as journeymen in his workshop. An hexagonal plate of 1698 (Victoria & Albert Museum) which bears his mark is finely engraved with designs after Jean LE PAUTRE, probably by a French hand. Many pieces of plate bearing his mark are known. (For his mark *see* p. 894.)

Lit: J. F. Hayward, *Huguenot Silver in England*, London 1959.

Pyrex glass A heat-resistant glass largely impervious to rapid fluctuations in temperature due to the high proportion of borax used in its manufacture. It was developed in 1908 by the CORNING GLASS WORKS for lamps but is now used mainly for kitchenware and ovenware.

Pyx Small vessel in which the sacrament is carried to the sick, usually a round silver box.

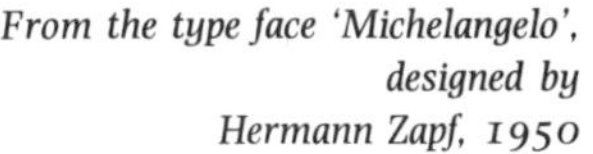

From the type face 'Michelangelo', designed by Hermann Zapf, 1950

Quaich A Scottish type of drinking bowl of shallow, circular form with two or three flat handles. It was originally made of wood (sometimes mounted in silver) but later of silver or pewter.

Quaich, silver, 1701 (Museum of Scottish Art, Edinburgh)

Quail pattern A decorative motif painted on porcelain, consisting of a pair of quails, rocks and foliage, originated by the KAKIEMON family in Japan and much imitated by C18 European decorators of porcelain and tin-glazed earthenware.

Quartering A type of veneer. Four sheets are used, two pairs sliced successively so that when two are reversed and the pairs juxtaposed they make a pattern. It was usually employed for large surfaces, especially in early C18 English furniture.

Quartetto tables Four small tables fitting one under another. The design may have been invented by SHERATON.

Quarti, Eugenio (1867–1931). One of the most notable of Italian ART NOUVEAU furniture-makers. He was born near Bergamo, began his training as a cabinet-maker as a child and at the age of 14 went to work in a furniture manufactory in Paris. Returning to Italy in 1888 he settled in Milan where after a few weeks in Carlo BUGATTI's workshop he set up on his own. At the Paris international exhibition of 1900 he won a *grand prix* for furniture. This encouraged him to take larger premises and increase his staff (he had previously employed only 3 men). He showed at the exhibition of decorative and modern art in Turin in 1902 and the Milanese exhibition of 1906, winning a prize at the latter. His furniture is finely made with much use of decorative inlays (sometimes in mother-of-pearl and silver), carved work and cast bronze ornament in an original version of Art Nouveau inspired by but not imitative of French and Austrian work. He collaborated on schemes of interior decoration with the architect Giuseppe Sommaruga (1867–1917).

Lit: Milano 70/70: 1° dall'Unità al 1914, Exh. Cat., Museo Poldi Pezzoli, Milan 1970.

Quedlinburg hangings One of the earliest sets of hangings in Europe, representing *The Marriage of Mercury and Philosophy*, made *c.*1200 by **Abbess Agnes II of Quedlinburg** and still preserved in the Stiftskirche there. The design is worked in tufts of wool knotted to the warp threads and cut to make an even pile, like an oriental carpet.

Lit: B. Kurth, *Die deutschen Bildteppiche des Mittelalters*, Vol. I, Vienna 1936.

Queen Anne style The reign of Queen Anne (1702–14) brought very few innovations in the decorative arts. The most notable were in silver due mainly to the predominance of HUGUENOT craftsmen *c.*1700. Their fancier pieces were strongly influenced by France though their household wares were usually of the greatest simplicity, without any moulded or engraved decorations. The Queen's intimate, Sarah Duchess of Marl-

Queen Anne style: silver teapot by Anthony Nelme, London, 1710 (Private Collection)

borough, expressed a widely felt wish 'to have things plain and clean, from a piece of wainscot to a lady's face', and an influential poet of the period declared his highest ambition was to own a 'private seat, built Uniform, not little nor too great', containing no objects 'but what are useful, necessary, plain'. This desire for simplicity, raised to a cult by Steele and Addison, helped to banish carved decorations and elaborate JAPANNING from furniture and to prepare the way for the Palladianism of the early GEORGIAN period. Nevertheless, the SPITALSFIELD SILK FACTORIES produced textiles of greater richness than any hitherto woven in England.

There was a Queen Anne revival in late C19 England. Norman Shaw *c.*1870 began to design houses inspired by the red brick country houses of the later C17 popularly described as Queen Anne though usually rather earlier. This led to a vogue for collecting furniture and silver of the same period and, inevitably, to the fabrication of reproductions, especially chairs and tables with cabriole legs commonly known as 'Queen Anne legs'.

Queen's pattern, *see* KING'S PATTERN.

Queen's ware The name given *c.*1765 to the improved version of **Booth**'s creamware produced by the WEDGWOOD POTTERY and, later, by other potteries. It is still produced by Wedgwood. It is a light, white earthenware with a thin, brilliant glaze.

Quervelle, Antoine-Gabriel (1789–1856). Furniture-maker who was born in Paris, emigrated to the U.S.A. and settled before 1817 in Philadelphia where he worked until his death. In 1829 he made three tables for the White House in Washington (during the presidency of Andrew Jackson). Next year he was advertising in the *United States Gazette* that 'orders from any part of the Union will be promptly executed'. His identified works are in a somewhat heavy version of the English Regency style.

Lit: R. C. Smith in *Antiques* May, July, August 1973, January 1974.

Quezal Art Glass and Decorating Company One of the first firms to imitate the iridescent glass of L. C. TIFFANY. It was established in Brooklyn, N.Y., and took its name for the gaily coloured quetzal bird of Central America. But it was very short-lived, active only 1916–18.

Quilling American term for the surface decoration of glassware with ribbons of glass pinched into pleats.

Quilt A padded coverlet, usually for a bed, made of a layer of wool, flock or down sewn between two pieces of material by stitches which pass through the three layers. The stitching generally follows a geometrical lozenge or network pattern but is sometimes much more elaborate, worked in curvilinear arabesques or floral patterns. Embroidered decorations were sometimes added. Quilts were made throughout Europe, notably in England, Italy and Portugal, from the early C17: and later became very popular in the U.S.A., especially with patchwork. The term 'corded' or 'Italian' quilting is applied to a type of decorative embroidery which is given an effect of stronger relief by the insertion of cords under the surface of the material and between rows of parallel stitches.

Quimper pottery A notable Breton faience factory founded *c.*1690 at Loc Maria near Quimper but of little importance before 1743 when it came under the direction of **Pierre-Paul Caussy** (d.1759) from Rouen and began to produce wares imitative of the ROUEN POTTERIES, decorated with chinoiseries and Rococo motifs in high-temperature colours on a rather dull white enamel ground. It remained in the hands of the same family into the c19. In 1872 it began to produce imitations of its c18 wares. Late c19 wares, from 1872 onwards, were marked 'HB'.

Lit: G. Le Breton, *Les faïences de Quimper et les faïences de Rouen,* Rouen 1876; A. Lesur and Tardy, *Les poteries et les faïences françaises,* Paris 1957–60; M. Ernould-Gandouet, *La Céramique en France au XIX siècle,* Paris 1969.

Quimper faience bénitier, *or Holy Water stoup, c18 (Musée des Arts Décoratifs, Paris)*

Wood-cut initial letter from
De Las Tablas y Escalera Spiritual,
printed by
Peter Hagenbach, Toledo, 1504

Raab, Johann Philipp (1736–1802). The son of a carpenter, he was a cabinet-maker working at Mainz where he was born and died. His masterpiece (in both senses of the word) is an outstanding bureau in a late Baroque style with geometrical marquetry and very finely carved Corinthian capitals, now in the Badisches Landesmuseum, Karlsruhe. His drawing for it, signed and dated 21 September 1764, is in the Staatlichen Kunstbibliothek, Berlin. *Illustrated next page.*

Lit: Badisches Landesmuseum: Neuerwerbungen 1952–65, Karlsruhe 1966.

Rabe, J. B. E., *see* BRUNSWICK POTTERIES.

Race, Ernest (1913–63). English furniture and textile designer, trained as an architect, studied hand-weaving in India 1937–39 and began to design furniture after the war. He sought a compromise between English traditional and Swedish modern and the results tended to appear rather genteel. His best-known designs were the Antelope chair (1951), the Flamingo easy-chair (1959) and the Sheppey settee and chair (1963). The latter is comfortable and ingenious in its design, being assembled from a set of interchangeable, mass-produced components. But Race's best design was one of his first: a demountable chair of cast aluminium (1947).

Rachette, Jean, *see* ST PETERSBURG IMPERIAL PORCELAIN FACTORY.

Racinage An acid technique for decorating leather with patterns resembling leaves, twigs, etc.

Radford, Thomas (*fl.c.*1800). He was an engraver for transfer-printing on pottery and worked for the DERBY and the Shelton and Fenton STAFFORDSHIRE POTTERIES. A signed example is in the British Museum.

Raeren potteries Established near Aachen and producing some of the best Rhenish brown (later grey) salt-glazed stoneware. The earliest products, made by the 1530s, are imitative of those of the COLOGNE POTTERIES. But from the mid 1560s until nearly the end of the century outstandingly fine wares were produced, especially by J. E. MENNICKEN and his several kinsmen – great vigorously modelled jugs decorated with cut relief friezes of religious or mythological scenes which hover between the Gothic and Renaissance styles. From *c.*1587 a grey body which permitted greater delicacy of modelling came into use though wares continued to be made in the older brown body as well. C17 wares are more elaborately decorated but much less admired today. By the C18 the potteries were producing only common beer jugs. From *c.*1887 a pottery run by Hubert Schiffer in Raeren produced imitations of C16 wares mistaken for original productions. Copies and imitations were also made in the later C19 by C. W. Fleischmann in Nuremberg.

Lit: O. von Falke, *Das rheinische Steinzeug*, Berlin 1908; K. Koetschau, *Rheinisches Steinzeug*, Munich 1924; G. Reineking von Bock in *Keramos* IL (1970), pp. 1–65 (for fakes and imitations); *idem, Kunstgewerbemuseum des Stadt Köln, Steinzeug*, Cologne 1971.

Raes, Jean, *see* BRUSSELS TAPESTRY FACTORY.

Raffaele pottery, *see* RAPHAEL'S WARE.

J. P. Raab: bureau with marquetry decoration, Mainz, 1764 (Badischer Landesmuseum, Karlsruhe)

Rafraîchissoir French term for a WINE-GLASS COOLER, WINE COOLER, and sometimes a DUMB WAITER incorporating a wine cooler.

Raising The very ancient (prehistoric) standard craftsman's process of making a hollow vessel from a sheet of fairly soft metal – e.g. gold, silver or copper – by hammering it into shape on a wood block. Hollow wares have also been made since early times by the process of SPINNING.

Raku A type of Japanese pottery made exclusively as TEA CEREMONY WARES, at first in and around KYOTO, later elsewhere. It is a moulded (not thrown) earthenware, rather soft and low fired, with a thick lead glaze generally black or rather dark in colour, sometimes salmon-red dappled with green, rarely white or yellow. Some pieces are decorated with designs composed of a few brush strokes in white slip, sepia or underglaze blue; but the majority rely for their effect on irregular shape, texture and colour. The word *raku* means 'enjoyment' and the ware takes its name from a seal engraved with this word used to mark many early pieces. The ware was first made *c.*1580 by **Chojiro** (1516–1592/5) who took the name **Raku** and was succeeded by his assistant **Jokei,** called **Raku II** (1536–1634/5).

Raku Pottery: tea-bowl, Japan, c17–18 (Musée Guimet, Paris)

The title subsequently passed from master to pupil (the latter was sometimes the son as well) to the present day and **Kichizaemon, Raku XIV,** is still working in the house of his predecessors in Kyoto. But the ware was also made by many other potters, most notably by KOETSU, and (because it needs no elaborate equipment) innumerable amateurs, including a number of tea-masters.

Lit: S. Jenyns, *Japanese Pottery,* London 1971; H. Riegger, *Raku,* London 1970.

Rambusch, Johann & Friedrich Vollrath, *see* SCHLESWIG POTTERY.

Ram's head motif, *see* AEGRICANES.

Ramsden, Omar (1873–1939). English silversmith who specialized in individually designed presentation plate. He was born in Sheffield and began his career as an apprentice in a silversmith's workshop, also attending evening classes at the Sheffield School of Art where he met his future partner **Alwyn Charles Ellison Carr** (1872–1940). After a continental tour in 1897 he and Carr set up a workshop in London and began to gather a team of assistant craftsmen. Their first commission was a mace for the city of Sheffield, completed in 1899. In the following years their workshop produced a quantity of decorative, hand-made pieces of silver and also objects in base metals, all showing the influence of the ARTS AND CRAFTS movement and many incorporating Art Nouveau motifs in their decorations. A silver-gilt monstrance encrusted with enamels in Westminster Cathedral (1907) is probably their masterpiece: other products are in Victoria & Albert Museum, London, City Museum, Birmingham, City Museum, Sheffield, etc. The designs seem to have been made mainly by Carr while Ramsden ran the firm: neither appears to have worked very much as a craftsman. In 1914 Carr joined the army and Ramsden ran the workshop alone, profiting from the new demand for war memorials. The partnership was formally dissolved in 1919. Carr continued to design silver and wrought iron on his own. Ramsden, who kept the premises in London and the team of craftsmen (which he augmented), carried on a considerable trade in liturgical, municipal and domestic plate generally in Revivalist (Elizabethan,

Queen Anne or Georgian) styles. Many pieces are inscribed *Omar Ramsden me fecit.*

Lit: Omar Ramsden 1873–1939: Centenary Exhibition of Silver, City Museum, Birmingham, 1973.

Randall, John (1810–1910). English porcelain decorator who specialized in paintings of birds, at first in the Sèvres style of the later C18 and subsequently in a very meticulous naturalistic manner of his own. He began as an apprentice to his uncle **Thomas Martin Randall** (1786–1859) who after working at the COALPORT, DERBY and PINXTON factories ran with **Richard Robins** a porcelain decorating shop in Spa Fields, London (employing Moses WEBSTER and others), and in about 1825 established a soft-paste porcelain factory and decorating shop at Madeley in Staffordshire, specializing in imitations of SÈVRES wares. From *c.*1830 John Randall worked at the ROCKINGHAM POTTERY but in 1835 returned to Staffordshire where he was employed as a decorator by the Coalport factory until 1880 when failing eyesight obliged him to retire. Vases, plates, etc. and a plaque decorated by him are in the Clive House Museum, Shrewsbury.

Lit: M. Messenger in *Country Life* (1973), pp. 11–14.

Randall, Thomas Martin, *see* RANDALL, John.

Randolph, Benjamin (*fl.*1770). Leading American cabinet-maker, he worked in Philadelphia where he issued a trade card in 1770 and became an outstanding exponent of the American Chippendale style. He was less restrained and more Rococo than his contemporary AFFLECK. Some of his mahogany chairs are among the best pieces of American furniture.

Lit: J. Downs, *American Furniture: Queen Anne and Chippendale Periods in the Henry Francis Du Pont Winterthur Museum,* New York 1952.

Rannie, James, *see* CHIPPENDALE, Thomas.

Ranson, Pierre (1736–86). A French decorative designer who published some attractive floral patterns similar to those by SALEMBIER for embroidered or tapestry chair and footstool covers in the LOUIS XVI style, and some designs for silk-hung beds. Tapestries were woven to his designs at the AUBUSSON TAPESTRY FACTORIES. Several of his watercolour designs are in the Musée des Arts Décoratifs, Paris. His furniture designs are somewhat fantastic and impractical.

Lit: H. Clouzot, *P. Ranson,* Paris 1919.

P. Ranson: decorative designs, late C18 (Musée des Arts Décoratifs, Paris)

Raphael, Raffaello Sanzio, called (1483–1520). The greatest exponent of High Renaissance classicism in architecture and painting, Raphael also had considerable influence on the decorative arts. He executed the cartoons (completed 1516) for one of the most famous sets of tapestries ever produced, the *Acts of the Apostles* first woven in BRUSSELS and copied in many other factories. But perhaps his most far-reaching influence was exerted through the GROTESQUE paintings which were painted under his direction in a room for Cardinal Bibbiena in the Vatican and the similar decorations modelled in stucco and painted in the Villa Madama, Rome. Decorations of this type were quickly taken up by the maiolica painters of URBINO (*see* RAPHAEL'S WARE) and numerous C16 ornamentalists, remaining popular until after the end of the C18.

Raphael's ware or **Raffaele pottery** A name formerly given to maiolica wares in the ISTORIATO style, many of which were painted with scenes after Raphael. Some were erroneously supposed to have been painted by Raphael himself.

Raphael's ware: Urbino maiolica (Fontana factory) with a design after Raphael (Museo Nazionale, Florence)

Rapp or **Rappoir** or **Rasp** A file for grating tobacco, usually made of bone, wood or ivory, especially in C18 France and England.

Ratafia glass English C18 type of drinking glass with a very long narrow bowl to hold a small quantity (1 to 1½ oz.) of the cordial called ratafia.

Rateau, Armand-Albert (1882–1938). Fashionable Parisian interior decorator and furniture designer. He was trained at the École Boulle, Paris, began working independently in 1898 and directed the decorative studio of Maison Alavoine 1905–14. In 1920–22 he decorated the establishment of the couturier Jeanne Lanvin with opulently elegant furnishings (now in the Musée des Arts Décoratifs, Paris), became a director of **Lanvin-Décoration** and was responsible for a number of very luxurious *ensembles* – for the Georges Blumenthals, New York; the Baronne Eugène de Rothschild, Paris; the Château de la Cröe, Cap d'Antibes; and a bathroom for the Duchess of Alba in Madrid. Although involved in the 1925 Exposition he did not exhibit in the salons and stood somewhat apart from contemporary designers. His work shows the influence of the Far East and also of Roman bronze furniture from Pompeii. Sumptuousness is the key-note of his style.

Lit: Les annèes "25", Exh. Cat., Musée des Arts Décoratifs, Paris 1966.

Rato pottery The Portuguese royal faience factory near Lisbon, founded in 1767 and directed until 1771 by **T. Brunetto** from Turin, later by Portuguese managers. It produced table-wares in the style of SAVONA often influenced by silver designs, tureens in the form of birds and large figures. (For factory mark *see* p. 887.)

Lit: J. Queiroz, *Ceramica Portugueza*, 1907, rev. ed., Lisbon 1948.

Rat-tail spoon The standard type of English late-C17 – early-C18 spoon, with a tapering rib running down the back of the bowl. *Illustrated below.*

Ratti, Giovanni Agostino, *see* SAVONA POTTERIES.

Rauenstein porcelain factory A Thuringian factory founded by three members of the **Greiner family**

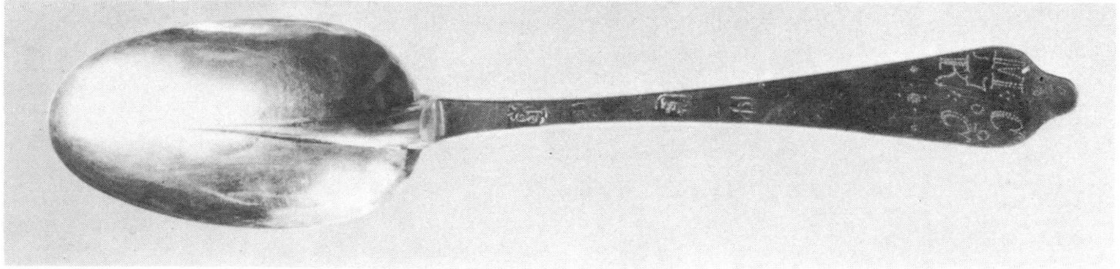

Rat-tail spoon, English silver, c.1709

(**Johann Georg, Johann Friedrich** and **Christian Daniel**) in 1783 producing mainly imitations of MEISSEN table-wares.

Lit: R. Graul and A. Kurzwelly, *Altthüringer Porzellan,* Leipzig 1909.

Rauter, Oscar, *see* EHRENFELD GLASSHOUSE.

Ravenscroft, George (1618–81). The most famous English glass-maker, important mainly as the inventor of FLINT GLASS. Employed in 1673 by the London Glass-Sellers' Company to produce a substitute for Venetian clear crystal glass made out of English materials. The first products suffered from 'crisselling' – a network of interior cracks obscuring the clarity of the glass – remedied by the use of lead oxide. By 1676 he was making jugs and goblets of fine quality, more brilliant but rather heavier than those of Venice, to German and Venetian patterns marked with a raven's head. His wares are much prized by English collectors, though more for their historical interest than their beauty.

G. Ravenscroft: ribbed goblet with hollow stem decorated with raspberry prunts, c.1675 *(Victoria & Albert Museum)*

Lit: R. J. Charleston in *Journal of Glass Studies* X (1968), 156–67.

Ravier, Jacques-Marie, *see* LYONS POTTERIES.

Ravrio, Antoine-André (1759–1814). French Empire bronze worker second only to THOMIRE. His father was a *fondeur* and his mother was the sister of Roger VANDERCRUSE and sister-in-law of OEBEN and RIESENER. He was trained as a bronze worker and in 1786 bought a *marchand-mercier* business in Paris specializing in girandoles, clocks, lamps and bronze mounts. He supplied JACOB and BENNEMAN and others with mounts. He was employed by the Crown but it was under the Empire that he flourished. He worked for Napoleon at the Tuileries, Saint-Cloud, Fontainebleau, Compiègne and Rambouillet (also for the Quirinal in Rome and for Stupinigi outside Turin). In 1806 he was awarded a silver medal at the Exposition de l'Industrie in Paris. By this time he must have been employing a hundred or more workmen. In 1810 he was appointed *'bronzier'* to the Emperor. His work is difficult to identify as he rarely signed his pieces, except clocks of which examples are in the Musée Massena, Nice; at Fontainebleau; at the Upper Belvedere, Vienna; and in the Stedelijk Museum at Lakenhal. In his clocks he displayed great ingenuity in making the dial part of a sculptural composition, e.g. the wheel of Venus's chariot. He left 3,000 francs to whoever might discover a sure way of protecting craftsmen from the harmful vapours of MERCURY GILDING. His business was carried on by his adopted son **Louis-Stanislas Lenoir** (1783–*c.*1840) who produced works in the same style, e.g. torchère in the Hermitage, Leningrad, signed 'L.Ravrio fecit 1819'.

Lit: J. Niclausse in *Gazette des Beaux Arts,* 1966, pp. 25–36.

Rayon, *see* MAN-MADE FIBRES.

Rayy pottery, *see* ISLAMIC POTTERY.

Reading chair, *see* CHAIR.

Rebate A groove of rectangular section on the edge of a door, drawer, etc.

Recessed carving The decoration of woodwork by outlining a figurative or other pattern on the flat surface and lightly carving away the surrounding areas which are stippled or punched to provide a uniformly rough background. It was executed on the simpler types of English C17 furniture.

Réchampi Ornamentation picked out in gold or in a colour different from the ground, e.g. chair frames with carved decoration gilded against a white or green ground.

Red ware American term for the simple household pottery made in N. America in the C17 and C18. It is of a soft porous reddish body covered with lead glaze in browns, yellows, orange or copper-green. Shapes are simple and derived from European pottery; decorations are bold and lively, sometimes with inscriptions in slip; the finish is distinctly rustic. Such wares were made at a number of small potteries (like that of Andrew DUCHE before he took up finer work) and sometimes by part-time potters. Improvements in technique drove most of the charm out of the ware. By the early C19 it was more or less superseded by factory-produced coarse wares for the kitchen and by English blue-and-white wares for the table. Not to be confused with red STONEWARE.

Reed, Henry Gooding (1810–1901). He was the pioneer of ELECTROPLATE in the U.S.A., the transatlantic counterpart of ELKINGTON in England and CHRISTOFLE in France. In 1834 he and three partners took over a small factory in Taunton, Mass., producing Britannia Metal wares. In 1840 it became **'Reed & Barton'** by which name it became famous and is still in business. In the 1850s it moved from Britannia Metal to electroplate production and a drawing-office was also set up to design wares for the firm though their designs continued to derive from contemporary English prototypes. Later they began to produce wares in solid silver as well as electroplate and in the 1890s, when the price of silver fell, expanded this production considerably.

Lit: G. S. Gibb, *The Whitesmiths of Taunton: A History of Reed & Barton 1834–1943*, Cambridge, Mass. 1946.

Reed & Barton, *see* REED, Henry Gooding.

Reed-and-tie moulding Reeding crossed at intervals by straps giving the appearance of rods tied together with ribbons.

Reeding Decoration with parallel convex mouldings touching one another, the opposite of fluting.

Refectory table, *see* TABLE, *Refectory.*

Régence style The first phase of the French Rococo or LOUIS XV STYLE. It began *c.*1710 and ended *c.*1730, i.e. it began earlier and lasted longer than the *Régence* of Philippe d'Orleans (1715–23).

Régence style: medal cabinet made for Louis duc d'Orléans, probably by C. Cressent, c.1725 (Bibliothèque Nationale, Paris)

Régence style: clock case (Musée des Arts Décoratifs, Paris)

WATTEAU was the outstanding artist of the period but it was the *ébéniste* CRESSENT who epitomized the style, his furniture being completely anti-classical and Rococo in form yet still retaining something of the grandeur and nobility of the LOUIS XIV STYLE. Its opulence harmonized perfectly with the richly gilt early Rococo interiors which G. M. OPPENORDT created for the Regent in the Palais Royal and Vassé at the Hotel de la Vrillière (now the Banque de France) Paris. Other typical products of the style are silver by BESNIER and SAINT CLOUD PORCELAIN. The style gave way *c.*1730–35 to the *genre pittoresque*, the second, more frivolous, phase of the Rococo in France of which N. PINEAU and J.-A. MEISSONNIER were the leading exponents.

Regency style A modern and imprecise term for the English late NEO-CLASSICAL style of the early C19. Strictly the term should be reserved for the styles current between 1811 when George Prince of Wales became Regent and 1820 when he succeeded as George IV (or 1830 when he died), but these dates are without artistic significance. The term Regency provides, however, a useful label for the predominant style in England from the 1790s until the early VICTORIAN 1840s. A reaction against the expensive ornamentation of ADAM style furniture and the spindly elegance of HEPPLEWHITE first appears in the works of Henry HOLLAND, C. H. TATHAM and T. SHERATON, together with a desire for furniture based on Antique prototypes and not merely decorated with Antique motifs. This archaeologizing tendency reached its peak in the furniture which Thomas HOPE designed for himself. His designs were popularized in a much less pedantic spirit by George SMITH. Here the Regency style came close to the EMPIRE, but with significant differences – there are no Napoleonic devices and few symbols of any kind: gilt bronze mounts are rare, but brass inlays are frequent. Fully classicizing pieces, such as Hope's and Smith's, were of course exceptional: most furniture merely aped the Antique with sabre legs, carved acanthus scrolls, inlaid palmettes or lion-paw feet. But there was a general tendency towards greater solidity and heaviness. As Sir Walter Scott remarked in 1828, 'An ordinary chair, in the most ordinary parlour, has now something of an antique cast – some-

Regency style: engraved design for a bookcase from Sheraton's Encyclopaedia, *1805*

Regency style: lacquer cabinet (Private Collection)

thing of Grecian massiveness, at once, and elegance in its forms. That of twenty or thirty years since was mounted on four tapering and tottering legs, resembling four tobacco pipes'. Mahogany remained the most popular wood, but rosewood, zebra wood, amboyna and maple veneers were also much used, especially for the small pieces of furniture (e.g. occasional tables, work tables) which began to proliferate in middle as well as upper class houses. Figurative marquetry went out of fashion and painted furniture became less popular, but there was a revival of JAPANNED furniture. The best cabinet-maker was probably Thomas CHIPPENDALE the younger though fine furniture was made by GILLOWS. But in general standards of craftsmanship fell off and furniture was made increasingly by factory processes. The most famous silversmith of the period was Paul STORR but several others were scarcely less able, e.g. Benjamin SMITH. Much silver was made in a classical style as severe as that of Empire France. But a curious Rococo revival began in 1804 and had become widely popular by *c.*1810. Textile designs owed little to Continental fashions: richly flowered chintzes seem to have been the most popular (plain striped materials much less so). In porcelain the forms were often of Neo-Classical simplicity and elegance but the painted decorations on the wares produced by the DERBY, SPODE, WEDGWOOD, COALPORT, ROCKINGHAM and other factories grew increasingly rich and florid, especially after *c.*1820.

Regensburg (Ratisbon) silks The name applied to a group of late-C13 silk fabrics with linen backing, one of which was found in the chapel of the bishop's castle near Regensburg. They are decorated with rather stocky, distinctly Romanesque religious figure subjects and seem to be German, but there is no evidence that they were woven in Regensburg. Nor is Regensburg known to have had any silk factories. Another group of silk and linen textiles woven with a pattern of lions of oriental inspiration (fragments in the museums of Berlin, Brussels and Chicago), formerly attributed to Regensburg, is Spanish.

Lit: D. G. Shepherd in *Bulletin of the Needle and Bobbin Club*, 1951.

Regnard, Louis (d.1779) and **Pierre-Louis** (d.1771). They were French Rococo silversmiths, uncle and nephew, working in Paris. Louis registered his poinçon in 1733 and Pierre-Louis registered his in 1759. Louis appears to have retired in 1769. Pierre-Louis completed several of GERMAIN's unfinished commissions after he went bankrupt in 1767. Examples of their work are in the Louvre. (For their marks *see* p. 894.)

Régulateur French name for a particularly accurate clock, usually with a very tall case to accommodate pendulum and weights; sometimes the case also incorporates a barometer. (For illustration *see* LIEUTAUD.)

Rehn pattern, *see* RÖRSTRAND POTTERY.

Reichsadlerhumpen A German type of cylindrical glass beaker with a cover. It is decorated with enamelled designs incorporating the Imperial eagle and the 56 armorial bearings of the members of the confederation composing the Holy Roman Empire, similar to an ADLERGLAS.

Lit: A. von Saldern, *German Enamelled Glass*, New York 1965.

Reiner, Johann Joseph, *see* PROSKAU POTTERY.

Reinicke, Peter (1715–1768). Sculptor born in Danzig and employed from 1743 until his death as a modeller at the MEISSEN PORCELAIN FACTORY where he assisted J. J. KÄNDLER and is known to have worked on various portrait busts (including those of Popes), chinoiserie figures and figures in the Monkey Orchestra. His independent models include figures of Turks, Chinamen, Saints, *Commedia dell'Arte* actors (inspired by Callot) and many animals.

Lit: E. Zimmermann, *Meissner Porzellan*, Leipzig 1926; C. Albiker, *Die Meissner Porzellantiere im 18 Jahrhundert*, Berlin 1959.

Reliquary A vessel made to hold a relic or relics of a saint, generally of precious metals and often very richly wrought.

Reliquary, silver partly gilt, by Oswald Ueberlinger, 1450 (Landesmuseum, Zurich)

Lit: E. G. Grimme, *Form und Bedeutung des Reliquairs von 800 bis 1500*, Cologne 1972.

Rémond, Félix (b.1779). He was apprenticed in Paris, perhaps to RIESENER, and became the most successful of all RESTAURATION furniture-makers, being patronized by the duchesse d'Angoulême and the duchesse de Berry as well as by the Bourbon Court. His first work of note was a *nécessaire* made for the Empress Josephine in 1806. During the Restauration period he worked in partnership with his mother-in-law **Mme Morillon.** She appears to have died *c.*1833 and this together with the fall of the Bourbons terminated Rémond's period of great success. Examples of his furniture are in the Grand Trianon at Versailles and the Musée des Arts Décoratifs in Paris.

Lit: D. Ledoux-Lebard, *Les ébénistes-parisiens (1795–1870)*, Paris 1965.

Renaissance style The rebirth of Ancient Roman ideals, which began to transform Italian literature and painting in the C14, sculpture from *c.*1400 and architecture from *c.*1420, originated in Florence and gradually spread across the whole of Europe eventually superseding the GOTHIC style. As knowledge of Roman art was confined almost exclusively to architecture and sculpture, decorative motifs were derived mainly from the Classical ORDERS and from Roman sarcophagi, e.g. acanthus leaves, trophies of arms and armour, urns, sphinxes, griffins and other mythological

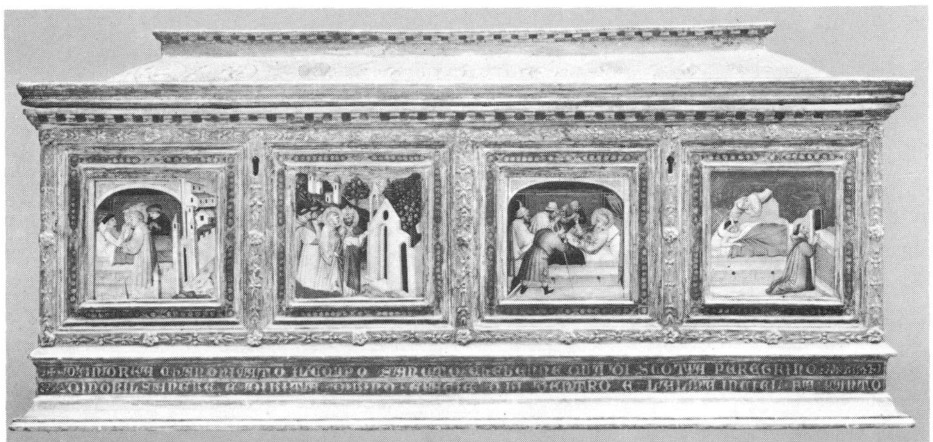

Renaissance style: reliquary casket, painted and gilt wood and gesso, Florentine, c14 (S. Martino a Mensola, Florence)

creatures, and, most popular of all, nude *putti*. At the same time, a new belief in the nobility of Man and a new interest in the visible world led

Renaissance style: detail of silver cross by Pollaiuolo, 1457–9 (Museo dell'Opera del Duomo, Florence)

to greater naturalism in painting and carving. But the goldsmith and enameller still ranked alongside the sculptor and painter. (It was not until the c16 that they began to lose this position.) Leading artists often began their careers in and continued to apply themselves to the decorative arts: Brunelleschi was a silversmith as well as sculptor and architect, POLLAIUOLO was both silversmith and embroidery designer, Luca della ROBBIA worked in tin-glazed earthenware as well as marble. But during the c15 the gulf between artist and craftsman widened, the latter following the former at a respectful distance. It is significant that none of the great maiolica painters – ANDREOLI, AVELLI, FATTORINI, PELLIPARIO – is known to have worked in any other medium although they nearly all derived their compositions from prints after the leading painters of the time. Well-known painters did, however, decorate furniture, usually bed-heads or CASSONI, with panels of religious or mythological scenes. The carved woodwork of such furniture is generally of an architectural character. But most furniture in Italian Renaissance houses would appear to have been of very simple construction indeed – benches and trestle tables covered, on special occasions, with rich textiles. Metalwork was either sculptural or architectural in inspiration, e.g. inkstands and andirons incorporating statuettes, lanterns in the

Renaissance style: cupboard with intarsia panels (one shown in detail, above right), perhaps by Giovanni da Verona, c.1502 (Monte Oliveto, Siena)

form of Renaissance temples, e.g. by Niccolo GROSSO. Furnishing and dress textiles are classified as Renaissance more by the absence of Gothic motifs than by the use of Classical ones. Tuscan (LUCCHESE or Florentine) figured silks were however influenced by contemporary painters. RAPHAEL provided cartoons for tapestries to be woven at BRUSSELS and thus helped to establish the Renaissance style in N. Europe.

The diffusion of the Renaissance style in the decorative arts was effected mainly by prints. As these were usually ornamental they influenced surface decoration rather than form. They tended to be applied profusely, e.g. PASTIGLIA, sometimes to furniture and silver of Gothic shape. The finest German Renaissance designs were for silver and were produced by the leading painters: Dürer, ALTDORFER and HOLBEIN. Nuremberg became the main German centre for silversmiths

Renaissance style: decorative design by Peter Flötner, 1533

and engraved patterns were published there by Mathis Zundt, Virgil Solis, Flötner, Ieronimus Hopf(f)er (*fl.* 1528–36) and others. Another German engraver, Brossamer, published a pattern book of silver designs which had a wide influence. Glass made at Nuremberg in the c16 imitated Venetian patterns; and the bronzes made there have a typically Renaissance nobility. In striking contrast the contemporary pottery by Preuning and others, seems hardly to have been touched by the Renaissance at all. Italian Renaissance maiolica was competently imitated in

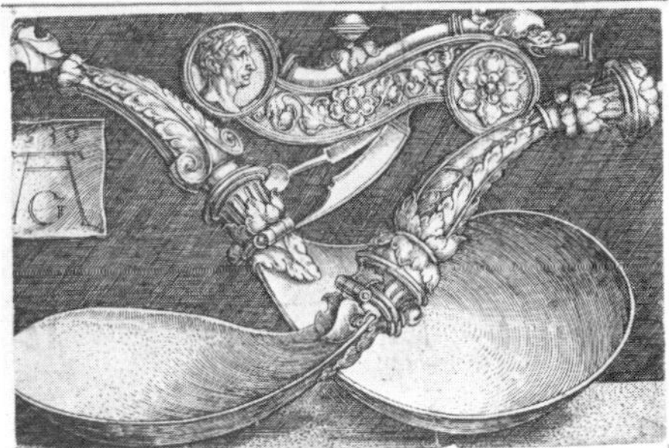

Renaissance style: design for spoons, by H. Aldegraver, 1539

(Left) Renaissance style: maiolica dish, Castel Durante, early c16 (Musée de Cluny, Paris)

Renaissance style: ivory comb, Italian, c15–c16 (Museo Nazionale, Florence)

Renaissance style: walnut cupboard. Burgundian, mid-late c16 (Philadelphia Museum of Art)

France by SIGALON. But in France the Renaissance style merged very soon with the Mannerist. Renaissance motifs were used in Spain from the early c16 but usually with Gothic profusion: the outstanding Spanish Renaissance craftsman was the silversmith Juan ARFE. The Renaissance was introduced into England by Holbein, and throughout the c16 English craftsmen acquired Renaissance motifs more frequently from Germany and the Low Countries than from Italy direct.

Rendsburg pottery A faience factory in Holstein founded by an apothecary and a merchant in 1764–5 and producing a wide variety of objects (described in a price-list of 1768) ranging from cane handles and snuff-boxes to bishop-bowls and tureens in the form of animals and birds. The few specimens that have been identified are painted in blue or, more rarely, polychrome high-temperature colours, with Chinese plants. In 1772 it abandoned faience for cream-coloured earthenware but went bankrupt in 1784. Under new management it enjoyed greater success, producing imitations of WEDGWOOD wares, including black basaltes and red stoneware, and survived until 1818.

Lit: K. Hüseler, *Geschichte der Schleswig-Holsteinischen Fayence-Manufakturen im 18.Jahrhundert,* Breslau 1929.

Rennes potteries The most notable in Brittany. A faience factory run by Italians and producing faience tiles is said to have existed in the C17 at Rennes, but two C18 factories are of greater importance. One was founded by a Florentine, **Forasassi,** in 1748 and changed hands several times. Its most notable product is a large inkstand (Musée Nationale de Céramique de Sèvres) painted in blue with Chinese flowers and landscapes and signed by **J.-B.-A. Bourgoing** who was employed at the factory from 1756 and became its manager in 1775. The other factory, in the rue Huë, was active from 1749 to 1774 or later, producing polychrome wares in the STRASBOURG style. A factory founded by **Jean Vaumont** in 1820 was run by his descendants until 1878. No factory mark was used, but inscribed pieces are known.

Lit: A. Jacquemart in *Gazette des Beaux Arts* XVIII (1865), pp. 163 ff.; A. Lesur & Tardy, *Les poteries et les faïences françaises,* Paris 1957–60; J. Giacomotti, *French Faience,* London 1963.

Rep A vague term for any fabric with a corded surface, properly called ribbed.

Repairer A craftsman, in a pottery or porcelain factory, responsible for moulding, assembling and finishing an object (figure, vessel, etc.) and preparing it for firing. In small factories repairers may also have been modellers; but in the larger the two functions were distinct. A repairer is called a *Boissierer* in German and a *repaireur* in French.

Repoussé work Relief decoration on metal, especially silver and copper, produced by hammering from the under side so that the decoration projects. The term is sometimes incorrectly applied to other types of EMBOSSED WORK. Repoussé technique was among the first to be developed by the metal-worker. Exceptionally fine early examples include the Vaphio cup made in Crete *c.*1600 B.C. (National Museum, Athens) and the Scythian animal reliefs of *c.*C6–C5 B.C. (Hermitage Museum, Leningrad).

Réseau, *see* LACE.

Resht patchwork A type of C18–C19 mosiac patchwork made at Resht in Persia with floral designs made up of small pieces of coloured felt with the outlines worked in coloured silks. The smaller elements of the pattern are inlaid in larger pieces and not applied to them (as they would be in APPLIQUÉ work). This type of patchwork was, however, imitated in appliqué work, with the smaller pieces stitched on to the ground.

Resist lustre, *see* LUSTRE.

Restauration style The style current in France from the restoration of the Bourbon monarchy in 1815 to the July Revolution of 1830. There was no abrupt departure from the style of the EMPIRE period, nor did official patronage reject the designers and craftsmen who had been employed by Napoleon and his family, e.g. FONTAINE, JACOB-DESMALTER, ODIOT and RÉMOND. The Antique revival Empire style persisted though it gradually grew coarser and heavier as in the

Restauration style: secrétaire
(Musée Carnavalet, Paris)

Restauration style: chair (Musée des Arts Décoratifs, Paris)

Restauration style: wallpapers by Dufour et Leroy, 1820–25 (Musée des Arts Décoratifs, Paris)

furniture of LEMARCHAND. The TROUBADOUR STYLE which was already well established seems to have grown more popular and several craftsmen, notably BELLANGÉ and CAHIER worked both in it and in the classicizing Empire style. Napoleonic devices were naturally avoided: the characteristic decorative motifs were swans, lyres, flowers and thick acanthus scrolls. Specifically Bourbon symbols were rare, though JACQUEMART AND BÉNARD produced a wallpaper decorated with the emblem of the Order of the Saint Esprit. Generally colours became brighter and gaudier, as in the carpet designs by SAINT-ANGE, the richly gilt and thickly painted vases and table-wares made at the SÈVRES PORCELAIN FACTORY, Lyons silks designed by DUGOURC, and the SCENIC WALL-PAPERS produced by DUFOUR and ZUBER which were extremely popular. In silver the most notable development was a sharp increase in the influence of English work. In furniture the only distinctive style to emerge was that sometimes called the *style duchesse de Berry* characterized by the use of such light-coloured woods as bird's eye maple delicately inlaid with arabesques in dark woods.

Restoration style The Restoration of Charles II in 1660 marks a break in the history of English life, manners and decorative arts. As John Evelyn remarked, the king 'brought in a politer way of living which passed to luxury and intolerable expense'. This was due partly to the influence of Royalists who had picked up Continental habits and attitudes in exile. The new fashion thus introduced might have been confined to Court circles had not the Fire of London in 1666 destroyed some ten thousand houses together with their furnishings of ponderous oak tables and buffets, uncomfortable joint stools and benches. Many replaced their losses with furniture in the latest style – lighter, more elegant and generally veneered with walnut rather than made of solid oak – thus stimulating a popular vogue which quickly spread beyond the capital to the provinces. The main foreign influence came from Holland, introducing floral marquetry, chests of drawers and cabinets on turned legs, chairs with caned seats, silver embossed with garlands of flowers (or, more rarely, decorated in the AURICULAR STYLE), and tin-glazed earthenware similar to that of DELFT. French influence was much less strong until the beginning of the WILLIAM AND MARY period (1688), though the widespread Oriental craze, which began soon after the Restoration, may have originated in France. The English East India Company imported increasing quantities of Indian CHINTZ and PINTADOS, Japanese LACQUER and Chinese porcelain. English craftsmen answered the new demand for exoticism by engraving wispy CHINOISERIE scenes on silver and by mastering the art of JAPANNING (the first English manual on japanning was published by STALKER AND PARKER in the year of James II's flight). The introduction of such exotic beverages as tea, chocolate and coffee necessitated new types of pottery and silver wares. At the same time new standards of politeness made the silver fork an essential piece of dining equipment. The development of the English glass industry, by G. RAVENSCROFT, helped to drive the silver wine goblet and beaker from the table, though silver tankards were still preferred for ale: and such was the general prosperity that silver wares were used even in taverns. A desire for splendour and courtly magnificence was reflected in furniture entirely coated with silver (e.g. surviving sets at Knole and Windsor Castle), large silver toilet sets, and an unprecedented use of gilding on woodwork, especially the florid carved Baroque bases for japanned or lacquer cabinets. Elaborate limewood carvings of fruit and flowers, by Grinling GIBBONS and others, began to appear on walls and around picture frames. Further touches of richness were added to the Restoration interior by MORTLAKE tapestry hangings and upholstery,

Restoration style: lacquer cabinet on stand (Private Collection)

Restoration style: sleeping chair, with an adjustable back – a type first made in the Restoration period (Victoria & Albert Museum)

(*Left*) *Restoration style: silver vase, from the Ashburnham garniture, London, 1675 (Victoria & Albert Museum)*

Restoration style: silver looking-glass from the Calverley toilet service, London, *1683 (Victoria & Albert Museum)*

and by CREWEL WORK bed-hangings. The demand for greater comfort was answered by the wing chair, the day-bed and the couch. But, of course, much provincial and inexpensive furniture was made on traditional patterns which had altered little, if at all, since the end of the C16. And the slipware pottery chargers of Thomas TOFT, decorated with designs of an engagingly vital rustic naïveté and among the most immediately appealing products of the period, were as untouched by foreign or courtly influence as the country squires who drove James II into exile and welcomed William and Mary in 1688.

Retable or **Retablo** or **Retablum** Strictly, the shelf for ornaments or the frame for decorative panels behind an altar but also applied to the decorative panels or altarpiece itself.

Reticella A decorative fabric made, like CUTWORK and DRAWN WORK, from panels of woven lines but with less use of the textile threads and much more free needlework. The effect is closer to that of true LACE of which it is an immediate precursor, though the designs are geometrical.

Reticello glass Glass decorated with a mesh of opaque white threads beneath the surface. First made at Murano in the early C16 and popular ever since. *Illustrated opposite page.*

Reval pottery A short-lived Estonian faience factory at Reval on the Baltic, founded in 1775 by **Karl Christian Fick**, an apothecary from Stralsund, and closed on his death in 1792. Its products included table-wares, vases with openwork decorations and figures, mainly in the Rococo style painted in enamel colours with a strong bluish or yellowish green and a brownish yellow predominating. The figures include some attractive animals. Some wares are painted with naturalistic flowers by **Hermann G. Pauel.** (For factory mark *see* p. 887.)

Lit: E. Hannover, *Pottery and Porcelain*, London 1925; K. Strauss in *Cahiers de la céramique* 40 (1968), pp. 262–9.

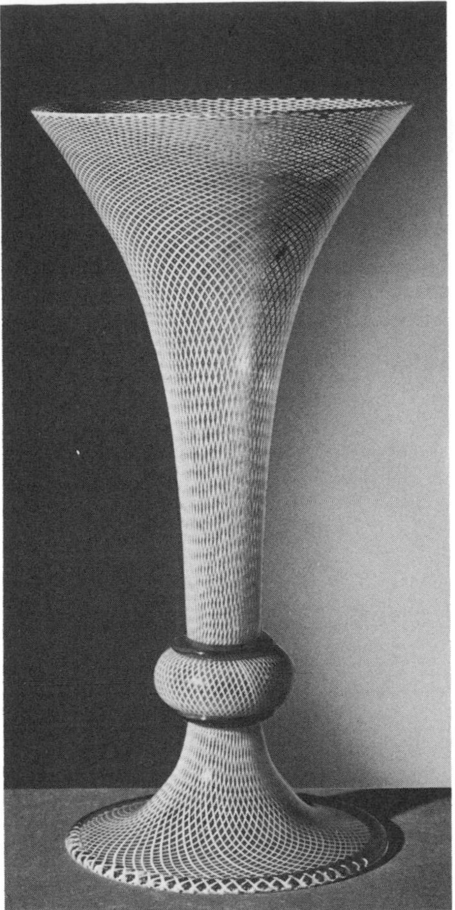

Reticello wine-glass, Venetian, c16 (Victoria & Albert Museum)

Réveillon, Jean Baptiste (d.1811). Leading Louis XVI period Parisian wallpaper manufacturer. He began *c.*1752 as a retailer marketing French and English wallpapers. In 1765 he established a factory in the Faubourg Saint-Antoine and in 1770 acquired a paper factory at Courtalin-en-Brie. Employing several notable designers including J. B. Fay, HUET, Lavallé-Poussin, he specialized in Neo-Classical papers which provided an inexpensive alternative to painted decorations in the so-called Etruscan style: in the late 1780s he produced some very attractive imitations of ancient Roman wall paintings. He also issued papers decorated with attractive naturalistic flower patterns and chinoiseries of the PILLEMENT type. From 1784 his factory was styled a *Manufacture Royale.* In 1789 it was burnt down by the Revolutionary mob and he left for England, disposing of what remained of his business to JACQUEMART AND BÉNARD.

Lit: H. Clouzot & C. Follot, *Histoire du papier peint en France,* Paris 1935; *Trois siècles de papiers peints,* Exh. Cat., Musée des Arts Décoratifs, Paris 1967.

Revel, Jean (1684–1751). Leading French silk designer mainly responsible for the taste for naturalistic figured silks, fashionable throughout Europe until the late c19. He was born in Lyons, began as a painter and by *c.*1730 had become the outstanding Lyonnais silk designer. By exploiting a new technical development in weaving, *points rentrés* (interlocking patches of colour blurring the division between neighbouring colours), he was able to abandon flat patterns for realistically shaded designs (even lighting them consistently from one point) and obtain almost *trompe l'oeil* effects. Though far from naturalistic botanically, the juicy fruits and heavy petalled flowers represented on silks woven to his designs are as naturalistic pictorially as any contemporary still-life painting. His silks were intended mainly, if not exclusively, as dress materials. Later in the century his technique was applied to furnishing fabrics, notably by LASALLE.

Lit: P. Thornton, *Baroque & Rococo Silks,* London 1965.

Revelation kilns, *see* PERRY, Mary Chase.

Revere, Paul (1734–1818). American silversmith, famous on account of his romantic role in the War of Independence and immortalized by Longfellow for his ride to Lexington on 19 April 1775 to warn the country that the regulars were out. He was the son of a Huguenot silversmith who had been apprenticed to John CONEY in Boston. Like other New Englanders (e.g. Benjamin FROTHINGHAM) he served in the war against the French in Canada. In the 1760s his silversmith business in Boston was in financial difficulties and he turned to engraving prints (mostly political) and to dentistry. After Independence he flourished and expanded his business to include bell-founding and dealing in imported clothing, paper and large quantities of Sheffield Plate. His own silver changed stylistically from a plain early Georgian style before the War of Independence to the latest English fashions afterwards, when he made delicately fluted almost fragile vessels very lightly engraved with feathery swags. The Templeman tea-set of 1792–3 (in the Minneapolis Institute of Arts) is a good example. Other

P. Revere: silver teapot, 1792–3 (Minneapolis Institute of Arts)

examples of his work are in the Metropolitan Museum, New York; Museum of Fine Arts, Boston; and the Museum of Art, Rhode Island School of Design, Providence.

Lit: E. Forbes, *Paul Revere & the World he Lived in*, Boston, Mass. 1942; H. J. Gourley, *The New England Silversmith*, Exh. Cat., Providence, Rhode Island 1965.

Réverend, Claude A potter and merchant who had lived in Delft and in 1664, together with **François Réverend,** obtained a patent granting exclusive rights for the manufacture of porcelain in and around Paris. In 1667 François Réverend was employing Dutch workmen in a factory at Saint Cloud, but its products have not been securely identified. Neither he nor Claude Réverend succeeded in making porcelain.

Lit: X. de Chavagnac & A. de Grollier, *Histoire des manufactures française de porcelaine*, Paris 1906.

Rewend, Christian Friedrich, *see* POTSDAM POTTERY.

Reymond, Pierre (*c*.1513–84). Outstanding LIMOGES ENAMEL painter, second only to LIMOSIN and no less famous in his lifetime. He was the head of a large workshop and the objects which bear his initials are therefore of somewhat variable quality. Unlike Limosin, he executed few independent enamel paintings. He specialized in caskets, vessels, cups, salts, ewers, dishes, etc.,

P. Reymond: painted enamel plaque, c.1560 *(Musée P. Dupuy, Toulouse)*

decorated with mythological scenes rendered in *grisaille* with flesh tints on dark blue grounds. Four other members of the Reymond family are known by signed enamels: **Martial I, Martial II, Jean** and **Joseph.**

Lit: W. Burger, *Abendlandische Schmelzarbeiten*, Berlin 1930; P. Verdier *The Walters Art Gallery: Catalogue of the Painted Enamels of the Renaissance*, Baltimore 1967.

Rhenish potteries, *see* COLOGNE, RAEREN and SIEGBURG POTTERIES.

Rhodes, David (d.1777). English decorator of porcelain and pottery. With Jasper Robinson, he ran a studio at Leeds *c*.1760, enamelling STAFFORDSHIRE salt-glazed stoneware and cream-coloured earthenware made at the LEEDS POTTERY. In 1763 he became the proprietor and Robinson his employee. From 1768 he worked in WEDGWOOD's London decorating studio, becoming in *c.*1770 the head of the enamelling workshop in Chelsea.

Rhodian ware A misnomer for the products of the ISNIK POTTERIES.

Rhyton A drinking vessel of pottery, stone or metal (especially of Assyrian, Minoan or Greek origin) of trumpet or horn shape, often fashioned zoomorphically (e.g. wholly or partly as a bull's head).

Rhyton, silver c5 B.C. (Museo Civico, Trieste)

Ribbon back, English mahogany chair, c.1760 (Victoria & Albert Museum)

Ribbed Of a fabric with a corded surface, commonly called 'rep'.

Ribbon back A type of carved decoration used on the splats of chair backs, especially by **Chippendale.** The wood is carved to resemble ribbons tied in bows. *Illustrated previous column.*

Riccio, Andrea Briosco, called (d.1532). The most famous Renaissance sculptor specializing in small bronzes. He was born and worked in Padua where he was trained first as a goldsmith and then as a sculptor under Bartolommeo Bellano (d.1496/7). His masterpiece is the large Paschal candlestick in the Santo, Padua (1507–15), ornamented with an extraordinary combination of pagan and Christian figures and reliefs. He executed several other works for churches but is best known for his small bronzes of satyrs, sphinxes and bucolic themes (e.g. nude shepherd milking a goat, Museo Nazionale, Florence) intended for domestic use as inkwells, fire-dogs, candlesticks or simply as decorative statuettes. They include some of the most beautiful and moving evocations of the Antique world made in the Renaissance. The libidinous attitudes and faces of his satyrs perfectly reflect the Renaissance nostalgia for pagan sensuality. In quality of execution they are equalled only by the bronzes of Antico. Numerous imitations were made by contemporary and later bronze workers, especially in Padua and Venice.

Lit: J. Pope-Hennessy, *Italian Renaissance Sculpture,* London 1958.

Ricco, Antonio, *see* ROME POTTERY & PORCELAIN FACTORIES.

Rice grain decoration Perforated decoration used in porcelain, from the C12 in Western Asia but notably in C18 Chinese and especially CH'IEN LUNG porcelain. The body of the vessel is given small oval perforations, like grains of rice, and these are filled in and sealed by the transparent glaze covering the whole piece so that they are still faintly visible. *See also* GOMBRON WARE.

Richard-Ginori, *see* DOCCIA PORCELAIN FACTORY.

Richardson, Benjamin, *see* STOURBRIDGE GLASS-HOUSES.

Richardson, George, *see* WROTHAM POTTERIES.

Richardson, Henry Hobson (1838–86). The leading U.S. architect of his generation, best known for buildings in a massive Romanesque style though he also designed private houses in the Shingle style which he initiated with the Sherman House at Newport, Rhode Island, in 1874. For some of his buildings he also designed movable furniture of an appropriately masculine character – strongly constructed, generally of solid wood and with bold carved ornament.

Lit: R. H. Randall, *The Furniture of H. H. Richardson*, Exh. Cat., Museum of Fine Arts, Boston 1962.

Ricketts glasshouse Two factories in Bristol partly or wholly owned by members of the Ricketts family. The **Phoenix glasshouse** which produced cut glass of high quality in the late c18 was owned by a partnership which included **Jacob Wilcox Ricketts** and his brother **Richard.** The former and his son **Henry** acquired in 1811 a factory known as the **Soapboilers' Glasshouse,** where they manufactured bottles. The two concerns were united under the name of **Henry Ricketts and Co.** and remained active until 1923.

Ridgway, Job (1759–1813). English potter, the son of **Ralph Ridgway** who owned a pottery at Chell near Burslem, he began by working at the SWANSEA POTTERIES and then at the LEEDS POTTERIES. With his brother **George** (*c.*1758–1823) he established a factory at Hanley in 1794, moved to Cauldon Place, Shelton, in 1802, producing stone-china and also porcelain. After his death this concern was run by his sons **John** (1786–1860), who became first mayor of Hanley in 1856, and **William** (1787–*c.*1865). Their stone-china, known as **'Cauldon ware',** became very popular; much of it was exported to the U.S.A. and some patterns were made specially for this purpose – e.g. the blue-and-white 'Beauties of America' table service, decorated with prints of notable American buildings. William set up his own establishment at Bell Bank in 1830 producing similar wares including a service decorated with views of American rivers. Both factories made polychrome as well as blue-and-white wares. The Cauldon factory made lavishly gilded porcelain table-wares and also garden fountains and what were described as 'sanitary vessels' when exhibited at the Great Exhibition of 1851. This concern was eventually absorbed by the COALPORT China Company.

Lit: G. A. Godden, *Ridgway Porcelains*, London 1972.

Rie, Lucie (b.1902). Notable studio potter, born in Austria and trained at the Kunstgewerbeschule, Vienna, she settled in England shortly before 1939 and came under the influence of Bernard LEACH. She makes very simply shaped and decorated, distinctly feminine, vases and useful wares in stoneware and an attractive thin

L. Rie: stoneware bowl and bottle, 1967 (Victoria & Albert Museum)

cream raw-glazed porcelain. Since 1947 she has shared a studio with **Hans Coper** (b.1920) who works in a much bolder, rougher, almost defiantly masculine style, sometimes reminiscent of Mycenaean and Archaic Greek pottery.

Lit: M. Rose, *Artist Potters in England*, London 1955.

Riedel, Gottlieb Friedrich (1724–84). German porcelain painter, ornamental designer and engraver, born in Dresden and trained there under J. C. Fiedler and Louis de Silvestre, director of the academy. From 1743 he worked as a painter at the MEISSEN PORCELAIN FACTORY. After a visit to Paris in 1757 he went to FRANK-

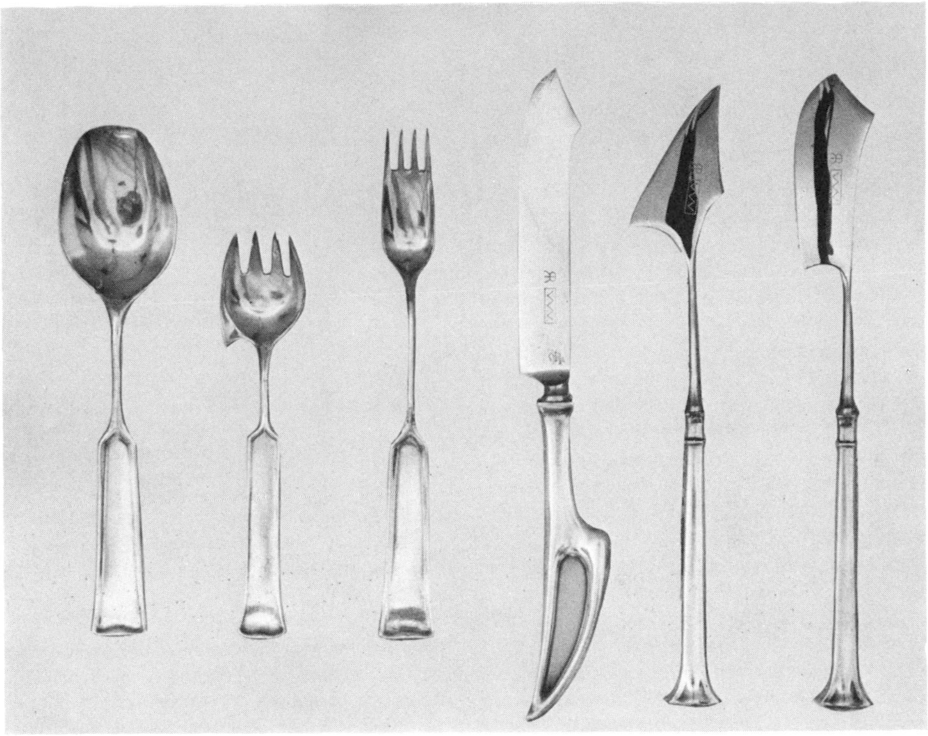

R. Riemerschmid: silver cutlery, 1900 (Württenbergisches Landesmuseum, Stuttgart)

ENTHAL as director of painting in the porcelain factory and was probably responsible for the design of some of the more exuberantly Rococo wares made there – e.g. clock-cases, inkstands and table-centres. He also executed enamel paintings on copper. But he left after two years and became director of painting at the LUDWIGSBURG PORCELAIN FACTORY from 1759 to 1779. Here he was probably responsible for the design of vases and table-wares with elaborate Rococo relief decorations similar to those of Frankenthal and may also have influenced the modelling of Rococo statuettes made during the first years of his employment. He was presumably responsible for the factory's gradual adoption of the Louis XVI style in the later 1760s. The engraved designs which he published from 1776 are entirely in this manner, e.g. *Sammlung von Feder-Vieh besonders Hausgeflügel* (1776), trophies after J. C. DELAFOSSE (1779), etc. These designs were occasionally copied on porcelain. In 1779 he settled in Augsburg where he worked mainly as an engraver.

Lit: H. Christ, *Ludwigsburger Porzellanfiguren*, Berlin 1921.

Riedl, Josef, *see* HARRACHOV GLASSHOUSE.

Riemerschmid, Richard (1868–1957). German

R. Riemerschmid: armchair, 1899 (Museum of Modern Art, New York)

architect, painter and – with BEHRENS and Bruno PAUL – one of the first designers for industrialized mass-production. He was a founder of the Munich *Vereinigte Werkstätten für Kunst im Handwerk* (arts and crafts workshop) in 1897. He designed furniture, cutlery, glass, electric light fittings, etc., at first in a modified and simplified version of Art Nouveau, but without any naturalistic ornament, and later in a purely functional manner inspired by VAN DE VELDE. One of his chairs, designed in 1899, is still in production in the U.S. and an example is in the Museum of Modern Art, New York. In 1905 he designed a set of machine-made furniture produced by the DEUTSCHE WERKSTÄTTEN at Hellerau near Dresden, slightly antedating Bruno Paul's *Typenmöbel* of the same organization. He was director of the Munich Kunstgewerbeschule 1913–24 and of the Werkschulen in Cologne from 1926.

Lit: H. Thiersch 'Im Memoriam Richard Riemerschmid' in *Baukunst und Werkreform* X (1957); *München 1869–1958*, Exh. Cat., Munich 1958; H. Selig (ed.), *Jugendstil*, Heidelberg-Munich 1959; S. Günther, *Interieurs um 1900, B. Pankok, B. Paul und R. Riemerschmid als Mitarbeiter d. Vereinigte Werkstätten für Kunst im Handwerk*, Munich 1971.

Riesener, Jean-Henri (1734–1806). He was the best LOUIS XVI STYLE furniture-maker and perhaps the best, as he was certainly the most expensive, of all French furniture-makers. Extremely versatile, he made almost every type of furniture, except chairs and other upholstered pieces. His works are distinguished for their perfection of craftsmanship no less than for their elegance of design – marquetry panels and plain veneers are of superlative quality, bronzes are applied so that no unsightly screw-heads are visible, even the carcases are treated with much greater care than usual. German by birth, he went to Paris as a youth and soon after 1754 joined OEBEN's workshop of which he became the manager on Oeben's death (1763), ousting his rival LELEU. He became a *maître ébéniste* in 1767 and married Oeben's widow in 1768. In 1769 he delivered the great *bureau du Roi*, commissioned from Oeben in 1760, which he had completed, incorporating his signature in the marquetry. (It is now at Versailles.) He also completed and

J.-H. Riesener: Bureau de Louis Quinze, *begun by Oeben 1760, completed by Riesener, 1769 (Château de Versailles)*

signed the similar roll-top desk begun by Oeben for Stansilas Lesczynski. (It is now in the Wallace Collection, London.) There were other pieces begun before Oeben died which Rieesner finished. As he was obliged to go on using Oeben's *estampille* until he became a *maître* himself (and as Oeben had used no *estampille* until shortly before his death) most of the furniture marked with Oeben's name was, in fact, partly if not wholly executed under Riesener's direction.

In 1774 he was appointed *ébéniste* to Louis XVI. Almost immediately he supplied a commode richly decorated with marquetry and gilt bronze mounts for the King's bedroom at Versailles (now in the Wallace Collection, London) and in the following year replaced it with another still richer (now in the Musée Condé, Chantilly). He kept up a steady supply of *secrétaires*. He also produced 'mechanical' pieces in collaboration with the German mechanic **Merklein,** notably a table which by pressing buttons could be transformed into a dressing-table, writing-table or dining-table (now in the Metropolitan Museum, New York). As a result of the abortive economy campaign of 1784 he was employed rather less frequently by the *Garde-meuble* but continued to be employed by Marie Antoinette making mother-of-pearl encrusted furniture for her apartments at Fontainebleau (still *in situ*) and a superb *secrétaire* and commode decorated with panels of

Japanese lacquer for her apartments at Saint Cloud in 1787 (now in the Metropolitan Museum, New York). Other patrons included several members of the Royal Family, such noblemen as the duc de Penthièvre, the duc de Rochefoucauld and the duc de Biron as well as many wealthy *fermiers généraux*.

Though he began in the chastened Rococo style of Oeben, he later produced some furniture of elegant rectilinear simplicity which borders on austerity. But there is no steady stylistic development in his work and late in his career he occasionally harked back to his earlier manner. Economy, as much as aesthetic taste, may account for the plainness of some of his later pieces – the veneers of West Indian mahogany and slender fillets of gilt bronze which he used in the 1780s were much less expensive to produce than elaborate panels of floral marquetry and richly sculptured bronzes. But he responded to late-C18 changes of fashion, abandoning Rococo curves and flourishes for straighter lines and more solid forms, producing furniture as graceful as that of the Louis XV period, faintly tinged by the new style which had begun to emerge in architecture and the figurative arts. There can be little doubt that he was responsible for the design, as well as the making, of his furniture – Antoine Vestier's portrait of him (at Versailles) shows him with a pencil and sheets of ornamental drawings. He appears to have had his bronze mounts made in his own workshop taking advantage of his position as *ébéniste du Roi* which exempted him from guild regulations.

J. H. Riesener: commode, 1784 (Louvre)

He survived the Revolution and in 1794 was employed by the Directory to remove 'insignia of feudality (i.e. royal emblems) from furniture, including the bureau he and Oeben had made for Louis XV. He bought back many of his own pieces at the Revolutionary sales and continued in business until 1801, though his work under the Directoire and Consulate lacks the distinction and fine quality of his earlier pieces.

Lit: P. Verlet, *Möbel von H. Riesener*, Darmstadt 1955, and *French Royal Furniture*, London 1963; F. J. B. Watson, *The Wrightsman Collection: Furniture*, New York 1966.

Riessner and Kessel's *Amphora* porcelain factory Established in 1892 at Turn-Teplitz in Bohemia. Its products won prizes at several international exhibitions (Chicago 1893), San Francisco (1893–4) and Antwerp (1894). Earthenware vases of fantastic Art Nouveau form with stylized leaf and flower motifs were a speciality but porcelain figures were also made.

Lit: Porzellan-Kunst, Sammlung Karl H. Bröhan, Exh. Cat., Schloss Charlottenburg, Berlin 1969, pp. 132–4.

Rietveld, Gerrit Thomas (1888–1964). Dutch architect and designer, he was the son of a joiner to whom he was apprenticed. He began in a conventional manner and does not seem to have had any contact with the modern movement until 1916 when the architect Robert van t'Hoff commissioned him to make furniture for his pioneer concrete-built house 'Huis ter Heide'. Like the house itself, the furniture was inspired by Frank Lloyd WRIGHT whose wooden chairs of 1904 composed of flat boards set in a framework of lathes provided the point of departure for Rietveld's designs. In about 1917 he designed his first chair, consisting of a framework of lathes set at right angles to one another, supporting a board for the seat, a longer board for the back and two smaller ones for the arm rests. Traditional methods of joinery were abandoned: no dovetailed joints or smoothed corners. Every member is distinct from the others and the lathes of the framework are screwed together so that they appear to adhere by magnetism. They are painted black with the ends yellow or white, as if they had just been sawn. The seat is bright blue and the back pillar-box red. The effect is like that of a Mondrian painting, though Mondrian did not begin to compose pictures of straight lines and rectangles of primary colours until later. But Rietveld was associated with Mondrain and other members of the *de Stijl* group from 1917 onwards. He produced several variations on his first chair design and also designed tables, a sideboard and even a wheelbarrow based on a combination of triangle and circle. In 1920 he designed furniture and light-fittings for a house at Maarsen and in 1923 designed a remarkable asymmetrical chair for an exhibition in Berlin. In 1924 he designed his most famous building, the Schroder House in Utrecht, and thereafter worked mainly as an architect though he continued to produce furniture occasionally – moulded plywood chairs in 1927, a cantilever chair in 1934 and an arm-chair with circular holes in the seat, back and sides in 1942.

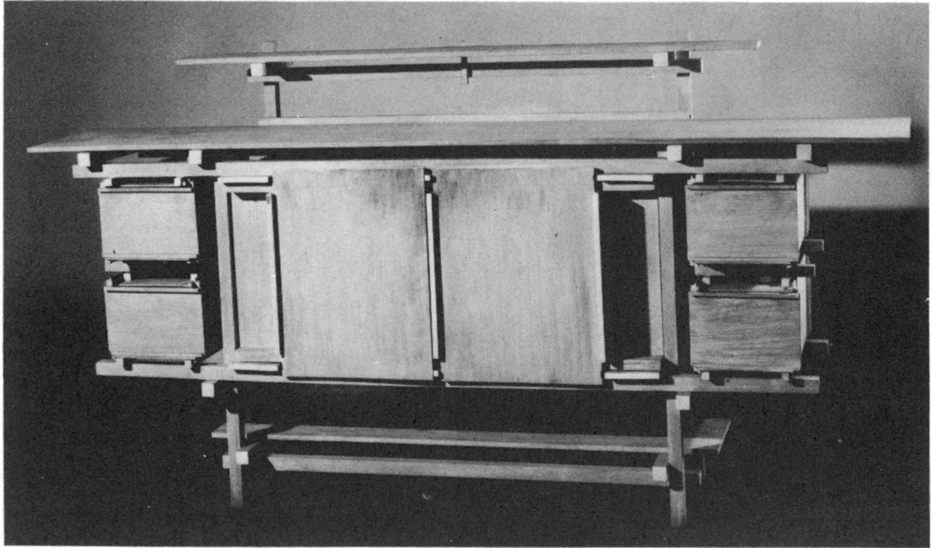

G. Rietveld: sideboard, 1919 (Collection of Mr and Mrs B. Housden, London)

Rietveld's furniture challenged all the assumptions on which theories of modern design had hitherto been based – belief in the value of simplicity, logical construction and truth to materials, not to mention fitness for purpose. His chairs are anything but simple. They are extremely illogical. And the material (wood) is masked by paint. Nothing could be further from the ideals of the Arts and Crafts Movement which had dominated the theory of design until his day. His work reasserted the role of furniture as sculpture – but as abstract sculpture. Some of his chairs can now be seen to have been among the most exciting three-dimensional works of art created at the time. They do not solve the controversy about craftsmanship and machinery – they make it irrelevant. Like van Doesburg and other members of the *de Stijl* group, he believed that by separating man from nature, the machine contributes to the spiritualization of life. Art, for them, appeared in terms of, rather than in opposition to, machinery – an idea distinct from the age-old 'utilitarian' theory of beauty. His furniture may thus be said to resemble machinery in an aesthetic rather than a practical sense. Its merits have been widely appreciated only since the rejection of functionalism in the 1950s. Examples of his furniture can be seen in the Museum of Modern Art, New York.

Lit: T. M. Brown, *The Work of G. R. Architect*, Utrecht 1958; A. Drexler & G. Daniel, *Introduction to Twentieth Century Design*, New York 1959;

R. Banham, *Theory and Design in the First Machine Age*, London 1960; H. Honour, *Cabinet Makers & Furniture Designers*, London 1969.

Rigaree trail The decoration of a blown glass vessel with threads of glass melted into its surface in parallel vertical lines and impressed with a metal wheel to form contiguous ribs.

Rinceau A French term for carved, moulded or painted decorative foliage, used mainly for the scrolls of acanthus-like leaves popular with C18 ornamental designers.

Rinceau

Ringflasche or **Ringkrug** German terms for a type of decorative vessel, bottle or jug, with the body in the form of a ring, made from the C16 onwards, usually of stone-glazed earthenware, at the RHENISH POTTERIES, but sometimes made of glass.

Ringflasche, stoneware by A. Knutgen, Siegburg, c.1570 (Kunstgewerbemuseum, Berlin)

Ringler, Joseph Jakob (1730–1804). One of the most important of the porcelain arcanists. He was born in Vienna and began as a boy by working as a painter at the VIENNA PORCELAIN FACTORY (*c.*1744) where he is said to have learned the secret of porcelain-making and kiln construction through the director's daughter. He put this technical knowledge to effect at HÖCHST (1750), STRASBOURG (*c.*1751), NYMPHENBURG (1753–7) and finally LUDWIGSBURG where he was director 1759–1802. His associates at these factories further diffused the secret (e.g. Johann Benckgraff who was with him at Höchst helped to found the BERLIN and FÜRSTENBERG factories). His son **Philipp Joseph** was employed as a painter at Ludwigsburg from 1775.

Lit: F. H. Hoffmann, *Das Porzellan*, Berlin 1932; S. Ducret in *Keramos* 30 (1965), pp. 3–47.

Ringuet le Prince & Marcotte, *see* MARCOTTE, Leon.

Ripp, Johann Caspar (1681–1726). He was a leading German arcanist and faience decorator. Apprenticed at Delft, he worked at the Frankfurt Pottery (1702–8), the Hanau Pottery (1708–10) and at the Ansbach Pottery (1710–12). He started the Nuremberg Pottery and the Bayreuth Pottery and also worked at Brunswick, Zerbst and Fulda.

Rippl-Rónai, Jozsef (1861–1927). Hungarian painter and designer who after training in Munich went in 1887 to Paris where he became an associate of the Nabis and was involved in the Art Nouveau movement. After his return to Hungary he worked mainly as a painter but also designed vases for the PECS POTTERY, tapestries, bookbindings, furniture and schemes of interior decoration, at first in a French Art Nouveau manner, later in a more self-consciously Hungarian modern style.

Risenburgh, Bernard II van or **Vanrisamburgh** (*c.*1700–1765/7). Other spellings are recorded. He was one of the most elegant and refined of French furniture-makers. He was presumably of Dutch origin though probably born in Paris where his father **Bernard I** (d.1738) was also a furniture maker. (Bernard I became a *maître ébéniste* in 1722 but none of his furniture has been identified.) Bernard II's work was known only by his stamp B.V.R.B. until his name was discovered in 1957. He seems to have worked exclusively for Parisian dealers, or *marchands-merciers*, through whom his furniture was supplied to Louis XV, the Prince de Condé, Mme de Pompadour, the German Courts and private clients. He became a *maître-ébéniste* before 1730 but his earliest known work is a commode made in 1737 for the Queen's *cabinet* at Fontainebleau, now in a French private collection. He specialized in furniture veneered with oriental or imitation Japanese gold and black lacquer, or

B. van Risenburgh: secrétaire en pente *veneered with oriental lacquer, c.1730–40 (Residenzmuseum, Munich)*

with wood marquetry of naturalistic flower sprays in *bois de rapport*. He occasionally employed VERNIS MARTIN and was the first to use Sèvres porcelain plaques on furniture, sometimes combining both materials very effectively, as on the exquisite small table now in the Louvre. His style is generally Rococo but occasionally classicising. His mounts were of very high quality and were perhaps sometimes made by his son **Bernard III** (d.1799) who was also a furniture-maker and carried on his father's business until his mother's death *c.*1775 when he devoted himself to sculpture. Examples of Bernard II's work are in the Louvre, the Wallace Collection, London, the Residenzmuseum, Munich, and the Metropolitan Museum, New York.

Lit: F. J. B. Watson, *The Wrightsman Collection: Furniture*, New York 1967.

Rising sun ornament American term for a semi-circular fan-shaped motif often carved, sometimes as the only form of decoration, on later-C18 New England furniture especially highboys.

Roanne potteries Earthenware is said to have been made at Roanne on the Loire in the C16 but the first documented faience factory is that founded by **Richard Teste** in 1632. Others were established *c.*1650. C17 products included tiles and large undecorated dishes. The faience industry was revived *c.*1760 and nine factories were active before the Revolution, making tablewares and such larger objects as stoves and wall-fountains, prettily decorated with flowers or figure subjects in underglaze colours. *Faience patriotique* was made during the Revolutionary period. Of the several factories, one of the most prominent, and the last to remain active, was the **Faïencerie Sébastian Nicolas,** in operation 1772–1866.

Lit: R. Mancey and J. Broisin in *Cahiers de la céramique* 31 (1963), pp. 171–93.

Robbia, Luca della (1399/1400–1482). The most important member of a family of Florentine Renaissance sculptors who were the first to use a ceramic medium for sculpture and gave their name to a type of large TIN-GLAZED EARTHENWARE relief – usually a representation of the Virgin and Child or other religious subject (often life-size) in a circular, semi-circular or rectangular frame formed like a wreath or swag of tightly packed fruit (oranges and lemons), leaves and flowers. He also worked in marble. But his nephew **Andrea della Robbia** (1435–1528) devoted himself exclusively to work in tin-glazed earthenware and developed the full range of this medium for decorative sculpture, producing numerous reliefs of which the most famous are those of babies in swaddling clothes on the façade of Brunelleschi's Loggia degli Innocenti, Florence

A. della Robbia: tin-glazed earthenware plaque of the Madonna and Child and St John, c.1500 (Museo Nazionale, Florence)

(1463–6). Andrea was assisted by his son **Giovanni** (1469–1529) and appears to have had several studio assistants. Della Robbia reliefs became very popular in the mid C19 when reproductions and fakes proliferated.

Lit: A. Marquand, *Luca della Robbia*, Princeton 1914; *Andrea della Robbia*, Princeton 1922; *Giovanni della Robbia*, Princeton 1920; *The Brothers of Giovanni della Robbia*, Princeton 1928; G. Cora, *Storia della maiolica di Firenze e del contado, secoli XIV e XV*, Florence 1973.

Robert, Joseph-Gaspard, *see* MARSEILLES POTTERY.

Roberts, Samuel, *see* SHEFFIELD PLATE.

Roberts, Thomas (*fl.*1685–1714). He was a prominent London cabinet-maker and supplied the royal palaces with beds, chairs, firescreens, etc., some of which were later transferred from Whitehall to Knole where some splendid gilt chairs and stools are attributed to him. He also worked at Hampton Court, Chatsworth and, perhaps, Houghton. The use of foliated scrolls on seat rails would appear to have been a distinctive feature of his work. He was succeeded at the royal palaces by a **Richard Roberts** (*fl.*1714–29), who was perhaps his son or other relative. Richard Roberts supplied walnut chairs to Hampton Court in 1717 and they can be identified there.

Lit: R. Edwards and M. Jourdain, *Georgian Cabinet-Makers*, London 1955.

Robertson, George (d.1835). He was a porcelain decorator known for his nautical scenes on DERBY porcelain *c.*1796–*c.*1820.

Robertson, Hugh C. and **Alexander,** *see* CHELSEA KERAMIC ART WORKS.

Robineau, Adelaide Alsop (1865–1929). American ceramic decorator and porcelain maker. She began by executing naturalistic overglaze paintings on porcelain and for a while taught this art in Minnesota. In 1899 she married Samuel E. Robineau with whom she bought the periodical *China Decorator* which they renamed *Keramic Studio* and published at Syracuse, N.Y. Under the influence of French ceramics and, especially, the work of T. DOAT, she soon afterwards adopted the Art Nouveau style. She began to make porcelain *c.*1903, specializing in vases of Art Nouveau form with incised decorations and very effective crystalline glazes. For a collection of 55 such pieces shown at the International Exhibition of decorative arts in Turin in 1911 she won a major award. But soon afterwards she gradually abandoned Art Nouveau for Chinese and Mayan motifs on her wares. The most notable collection of her porcelain is in the Everson Museum of Art, Syracuse.

Lit: W. Hull in *Everson Museum of Art Bulletin* XXII (1960), pp. 1–6; R. Judson Clark (ed.), *The Arts and Crafts Movement in America 1876–1916*, Exh. Cat., Art Museum, Princeton University, Art Institute of Chicago, etc. 1972–3.

Robins, Richard, *see* RANDALL, John.

Robin's egg glaze A speckled opaque turquoise and blue glaze developed in early-C18 China. The turquoise is blown through a gauze on to the all-over blue glaze.

Robinson, Gerrard (1834–91). High Victorian

wood-carver of great dexterity and nightmarish vulgarity. He was born and worked for most of his life in Newcastle-on-Tyne carving preposterously massive oak sideboards seething with a profusion of figures representing scenes from the ballad of Chevy Chase and similar romantic subjects. They are of a type called into existence by the C19 international exhibitions at which he showed and won prizes. He was the best of numerous Victorian craftsmen employed on such work.

Lit: R. W. Symonds and B. B. Whineray, *Victorian Furniture*, London 1962.

Robinson, Jasper He decorated cream-coloured earthenware and salt-glazed stoneware at Leeds with D. RHODES by whom he was employed after 1763.

Robinson, Thomas, *see* TIJOU, Jean.

Roccatagliata, Niccolo (*fl.*1593–1636). Bronze sculptor of Genoese origin, working mainly in Venice. His only documented works are statuettes of St George and St Stephen (1593) and some elaborate candlesticks (1594 & 1598) in S. Giorgio Maggiore, Venice, and a very fine altar frontal executed with his son in 1633 (S. Moise, Venice). But numerous statuettes, firedogs and other ornamental sculpture have been attributed to him.

Rock crystal cup, C16, probably Milanese (Kunsthistorisches Museum, Vienna)

Rock crystal A transparent colourless quartz found in many parts of the world and, from very early times, carved into decorative objects, bowls, etc. It is very hard and can be carved only with difficulty, usually with a lapidary's wheel. In the C16 a number of Italian artists specialized in carving this material in intaglio, notably V. BELLI, G. BERNARDI and the MISERONI FAMILY. Colourless glass was made in emulation of and named after rock crystal. *Illustrated previous column.*

Rocking chair, *see* CHAIR, *Rocking.*

Rockingham pottery and porcelain factory A factory on the estate of the Marquis of Rockingham at Swinton in Yorkshire. It produced pottery from about 1745 but was not known as the 'Rocking-

Rockingham bone china, the Rhinoceros Vase, 1830 (Victoria & Albert Museum)

ham Works' until 1826. It appears to have begun by making simple brown stoneware. From 1787 it was in partnership with the LEEDS POTTERY, producing similar wares. But two of the partners, **John** and **William Brameld,** acquired the concern in 1806 (products of the next 20 years are marked with their names). A manganese-brown glaze – known as the 'Rockingham glaze' – was developed. In addition to the usual table-wares products included CADOGANS, later imitated by other factories. Porcelain seems to have been made from 1826 when Earl Fitzwilliam (heir to the Rockingham estates) helped to finance the factory and the griffin from his family crest was adopted as a mark. The concern was named 'Manufacturer to the King' in 1830. Wares of this period were mostly in a very rich Neo-Rococo style with much floral decoration and sometimes imitative of COALPORT wares. Endearing little pastille burners in the form of cottages and romantic castles were also produced. The factory closed in 1842, (For factory mark *see* p. 887.)

Lit: A. and A. Cox, *The Rockingham Works,* Sheffield 1974; D. G. Rice, *The Illustrated Guide to Rockingham Pottery and Porcelain,* London 1971; A. A. Eaglestone and T. A. Lockett, *The Rockingham Pottery,* Newton Abbot 1973; D. G. Rice, *Rockingham Ornamental Porcelain,* 1965.

Rockingham ware American term loosely applied to a wide variety of C19 household wares usually with a mottled brown glaze. The connection, if any, between this term and the English factory is uncertain.

Rococo style The delicately light and elegant decorative style which succeeded the BAROQUE and preceded the NEO-CLASSICAL. It has been regarded by some as the last phase of the Baroque, by others as an independent style – a reaction against the pompous solemnity of the Baroque. It is characterized by freely handled S-shaped curves; bright clear colours set off by much white and gold; the harmonious combination of naturalistic motifs, e.g. sprigs of flowers, with unrepresentational ornament, often reminiscent of splashing water; a tendency towards asymmetry; and a preference for the delicately poised to the solidly square set form. CHINOISERIE and other exotic motifs were extensively used. Unlike other styles, it first appeared in the decorative arts and only later affected painting, sculpture and architecture. Its most important manifestations are schemes of interior decoration, e.g. Boffrand's Hôtel de Soubise pavilion (now the Archives Nationales) in Paris and CUVILLIÉS's Amalienburg pavilion at Nymphenburg near Munich. Many of its masterpieces are on a very small scale, e.g. statuettes by BUSTELLI. The style began to emerge in France in the late 1690s in the asymmetrical design of Pierre LE PAUTRE and in the BIZARRE SILKS woven at Lyons. This first phase was exclusively French and is often called the RÉGENCE STYLE. The rest of Europe was affected only from *c.*1730 onwards when the more exuberantly spirited and frivolous LOUIS XV STYLE was established in France. The more extreme French Rococo designs were those most influential outside France, e.g. those by MEISSONNIER, who was very little patronized by Frenchmen, TORO and PILLEMENT. The curvaceous forms of French furniture were exaggerated east of the Rhine and south of the Alps, especially in Venice where the *bombé* commode took on a

Rococo style: design for a looking-glass, by T. Johnson, 1758

Rococo style: porcelain group 'The Music Lesson', Frankenthal, c.1759, probably modelled by J. F. von Lück (Badisches Landesmuseum, Karlsruhe)

preposterously pot-bellied corpulence. In Germany the furniture designs of AUVERA, CUVILLIÉS, HABERMANN and HOPPENHAUPT were generally more *outré*, though rarely more accomplished, than those of their French contemporaries. The Scandinavians, notably the Swedish silversmith and designer, PRECHT, were perhaps the most faithful followers of French taste. Only in England were French designs toned down rather than up, though here too there were exceptions (see GEORGIAN STYLE). The Rococo period coincides with the early stages of the European porcelain industry and hard-paste porcelain proved an ideal medium for the expression of the feminine and somewhat precious elegance of the style. The main German factories, MEISSEN, NYMPHENBURG, HÖCHST, FRANKENTHAL, LUDWIGSBURG, etc., turned out a stream of delicately painted tablewares, vases and posturing statuettes which rank among the best works of art in the century. The mania for porcelain was such that whole rooms were lined with panels of it, see CAPODIMONTE and BUEN RETIRO factories. A rather bolder version of the style was developed at the potteries, notably at ALCORA. Despite its widespread popularity, especially in Court circles, the style was severely criticized by classically minded theorists under whose influence the NEO-CLASSICAL STYLE eventually emerged to supersede it from the 1750s in France, England and Italy. But in certain areas, notably Spain, Portugal and Venice, the Rococo lingered on until the 1790s.

Rococo style: cradle, Venetian, c.1750 *(Private Collection, Venice)*

Rococo style: furniture design by J. Wachsmuth, c.1760

Rodney decanters A type of English decanter, with a very broad base suitable for use at sea and made for the cabins of ships' officers. They were called after Admiral Rodney and the term, if not the type, dates from after 1780, the year of Rodney's victory at Cape St Vincent.

Roed, Jørgen (1808–88). Danish romantic painter who also designed some remarkable and very attractive Neo-Classical furniture – Grecian in inspiration, refreshingly simple in form and often painted with motifs reminiscent of Attic vases (1840–45; Kunstindustrimuseet, Copenhagen).

Roemer, *see* RÖMER.

Roentgen, David (1743–1807). He was the greatest German furniture-maker and the most successful of all C18 furniture-makers. He is usually classed among French furniture-makers though he never worked in France. Many C18 French furniture-makers were German by birth, e.g. BENNEMAN, CARLIN, MOLITOR, OEBEN, RIESENER, SCHWERDFEGER, WEISWEILER, but whereas they settled in Paris and became assimilated into French culture, Roentgen never moved his workshops from Neuwied near Coblenz and merely had a depot in Paris as he had also in Berlin and Vienna. In this way he was also the first to establish a furniture industry on a fully international basis. And in some ways he anticipated the luxury-loving furniture industrialists of the C19. His furniture is Germanic in its heaviness, in its *trompe l'oeil* pictorial marquetry, and in the elaborate clock-maker's ingenuity of its mechanical devices – doors spring open at the touch of a button, drawers rise up from concealed spaces in the interior. There are even built-in clocks in some of his pieces, usually by **Peter Kinzing** (1745–1816). But his best works have a sumptuosity and grandeur and an almost architectural monumentality that is unique. (For illustration *see* p. 553.)

He was the son of a Saxon cabinet-maker, **Abraham Roentgen** (1711–93) who worked for a time in England between 1731 and 1738, settled in Neuwied in 1750 and set up his furniture workshops there which produced attractive furniture in a restrained Rococo style which shows some influence from CHIPPENDALE. He also produced clocks, musical boxes, mechanical toys and furniture with complex locks and secret drawers. He retired in 1772 but his son David had probably taken over control of the business in 1768. In the following year David held an extremely successful sale by lottery in Hamburg which marked the beginning of the firm's great prosperity and fame. He first visited Paris in 1774. In 1779 he returned with several cart-loads of furniture and set up a depot. He was patronized by the Queen and the influential connoisseur Baron Grimm. Louis XVI bought a writing table for an unprecedented sum variously given as 80,000 and 96,000 livres and created for him the special appointment of *ébéniste-méchanicien du Roi et de la Reine*. During the next decade Roentgen's bills for furniture supplied to the Crown totalled nearly a million livres – more even than RIESENER's. Piqued by his success, the French cabinet-makers forced him to join the Paris guild of which he was made a *maître* in 1789, using the stamp *DAVID*. He travelled on business to Italy, the Low Countries and, in 1783, to Russia where he sold a great quantity of furniture to the Empress Catherine II, notably several massive *bureaux*, with Neo-Classical low-relief bronze plaques and mounted on columns set on stepped bases as if they were classical temples. They are still in the Hermitage in Leningrad. He returned to Russia on six subsequent visits. In 1791 he was appointed Court Furnisher to Frederick William II in Berlin. By this date he was recognized as *'le plus célèbre ébéniste de l'Europe entier'*. But the Revolution ruined him. His Paris depot was confiscated and his workshops at Neuwied were overrun and pillaged by the Republican troops. Only those parts of his stock stored in depots in Kassel, Gotha and Altenburg were saved. He fled to Berlin and did not return to Neuwied until 1802. He appears to have made an attempt to

D. Roentgen: mahogany cupboard with gilt-bronze mounts, 1780–90 (Musée Nissim de Camondo, Paris)

re-establish his business, but died while travelling in 1807.

Despite his membership of the Paris guild of *ébénistes*, he seldom signed or stamped his works. But his marquetry is easily recognizable by its very high technical quality and by the numerous minute inlays of different coloured woods which he used to produce effects of shading, and by the correct drawing and good composition of the floral and figure designs which were usually provided by **Januarius Zick** (1730–97). His furniture continues to fetch the highest prices, a marquetry *commode à vanteux* sold at Sothebys in 1964 for £63,000 making a world record (at that time) for a piece of furniture.

Lit: H. Kreisel, *Die Kunst des deutschen Möbels*, vol. II, Munich 1970; P. Verlet in *The Connoisseur*, October 1961, and F. Windisch-Graetz in *The Connoisseur*, November 1963; H. Huth, *Abraham und David Roentgen und ihr Neuwieder Möbelwerkstatt*, Munich 1974.

Roettiers, Jacques (1707–84). He belonged to a large family from Walloon Flanders, several of whom achieved fame as mint masters and coin-engravers. His father worked at the London mint but went to France a few years after the 1688 Revolution. The Old Pretender stood godfather to Jacques Roettiers at his baptism. In 1731 he tried to establish himself in England but returned to France by 1733 in which year he became a royal goldsmith with an apartment in the Louvre. In 1737 he succeeded his father-in-law BESNIER as *Orfèvre du Roi*. He made some of the finest Rococo silver, notably the Berkeley service of 1735–8 now in the Niarchos collection in Paris. By the 1750s he had abandoned this style for the restraint and solidity of the '*goût grec*' – e.g. candlesticks of 1762–3 in the Metropolitan Museum, New York. From this date until he retired in 1772 he was associated with his son **Jacques-Nicolas** (b.1736). Jacques-Nicolas became a *maître* in 1765, and succeeded his father as *Orfèvre du Roi* in 1772. Nearly all his large works for the Crown are destroyed. His outstanding surviving work is the vast dinner service made for Catherine the Great who gave it to her favourite, Count Orloff, in 1775. In contrast to his father's Berkeley service, the Orloff service is of an almost pompous solemnity and marmoreal monumentality. It was dispersed after the Russian Revolution and some pieces are in the Metropolitan Museum, New York. Jacques-Nicolas Roettiers retired in 1777 and appears to have turned his talents to sculpture. (For their marks *see* p. 894.)

J. Roettiers: silver tureen from the Berkeley dinner service, 1735–8 (S. Niarchos Collection, Paris)

J.-N. Roettiers: silver tureen from the Orloff dinner service, 1775 (Metropolitan Museum)

Lit: V. Advielle in *Réunion des Sociétés des Beaux-Arts des départments*, vol. xii, 1888; S. Brault and Y. Bottineau, *Les grands orfèvres*, Paris 1965; C. Corbeiller in *Metropolitan Museum Bulletin* XXVII (1969), pp. 289–298.

Roger of Helmarshausen (*fl.*1100). The Romanesque style in Germany is associated with the name of a goldsmith Roger of the abbey of

Helmarshausen who made in 1100 a portable altar of silver and niello for Bishop Henry of Werl (1084–1127). The portable altar is dedicated to St Kilian and St Liborius and survives in the Cathedral Treasury at Paderborn. Apart from this work, of which the date and authorship is documented, nothing is known about Roger. By analogy with this work a number of others have been attributed to him, including the portable altar from the abbey of Abdinghof, decorated on its sides with continuous scenes of openwork bronze-gilt (now in the Franciscan church at Paderborn), the bookcover of the Gospels from Helmarshausen (now in the Cathedral Library at Trier), a processional or altar cross (Frankfurt, Museum für Kunsthandwerk), and crucifix figures probably from this cross (St Louis Museum, Missouri). His somewhat Byzantinizing style appears to have been established throughout Lower Saxony and several works have now been attributed to his workshops, e.g. the copper-gilt back-plate of an altar cross of St Modoaldus of *c.*1107 (Cologne, Schnütgen Museum); another fragment of embossed bronze-gilt with Christ in Majesty (Cologne, Schnütgen Museum); and a gold reliquary cross for the church of St Dionysius at Enger (Berlin, Staatliche Museen). He may be identical with the priest 'Theophilus', author of *De Diversis Artibus*, a very informative treatise on painting, glassmaking and the various techniques of working in metal (cf. the edition by C. R. Dodwell, London 1961).

Lit: P. Lasko, *Ars Sacra 800–1200*, Pelican History of Art, Harmondsworth 1972; *Kunst und Kultur im Weserraum*, Exh. Cat., Corvey 1966.

Rogers brothers A company, directed by the brothers **Asa, Simeon** and **William Rogers**, which produced in 1847 at Hartford, Connecticut, the first successful electroplated wares made in the U.S.A. From 1853 it was called Rogers Brothers Manufacturing Company. The brothers separated in 1856, establishing different concerns which were gradually absorbed by the MERIDEN BRITANNIA COMPANY.

Rogers groups American plaster figures and groups made in New York from about 1859 to 1893, which became extremely popular as decorations in late C19 American parlours. They were by or, more usually, were reproductions of models by, the sculptor **John Rogers** (1829–1904). Subjects from the Civil War and from everyday life, treated in a rather sentimental fashion, are the most typical. A large collection may be seen at the New York Historical Society.

Rogers pottery Established in 1780 by **John Rogers** (1760–1816) and **George Rogers** (1762–1815) in Dale Hall, Longport, Staffordshire. From 1815 it traded as J. Rogers & Son and closed in 1836. It produced good quality cream-coloured earthenware, transfer-printed in blue. Decorations include exotic views with zebras and elephants as well as classical landscapes and ruins, etc. It was much exported to America.

Rohde, Heinrich Ludwig (1683–1755). German cabinet-maker working at Mainz, a master of inlaid work. Documented works include a table and small fall-front writing desk of *c.*1725 at Pommersfelden, a large fall-front cabinet of after 1732 at Burg Rheinstein, and a small chest of drawers inlaid with ivory in the Rheinisches Landesmuseum, Bonn – all in a late Baroque style.

Lit: H. Kreisel, *Die Kunst des deutschen Möbels*, vol. ii, Munich 1970.

Rohlfs, Charles (1853–1936). A leading figure in the U.S. Arts and Crafts movement. He was born in New York City, trained at the Cooper Union, began as a designer of cast-iron stoves and then became an actor before turning to furniture-making *c.*1890. He then set up a small workshop with a handful of assistants in Buffalo where he produced individual custom-built solid oak pieces, rather in the English Arts and Crafts manner with exposed joinery but also some abstract Art Nouveau ornament. He showed furniture at several large exhibitions (Buffalo 1901, Turin 1902, St Louis 1904, etc.), won widespread acclaim in Europe as well as the U.S.A. and was commissioned to make some pieces (though not in his usual style) for Buckingham Palace. He was a friend of Elbert HUBBARD, lectured to the Roycrofters and contributed an article on 'The grain of wood' to *House Beautiful*. He retired in the mid 1920s.

Lit: R. Judson Clark (ed.), *The Arts and Crafts Movement in America 1876–1916*, Exh. Cat., Art Museum, Princeton University, Art Institute of Chicago, etc. 1972–3.

Roll A cylindrical tool introduced in the late C15 for the decoration of leather, and used especially in bookbinding. The roll is rotated and impresses a ribbon of repeated pattern on the leather. It was frequently used for borders.

Roll work, *see* STRAPWORK.

Rolled paper work A Victorian technique for the decoration of boxes and small articles. The all-over design is formed by innumerable small scrolls of rolled paper or card of varying sizes.

Rollos, Philip (*fl.*1697–1721). He was a Huguenot silversmith working in London where he was admitted to the Goldsmiths' Company by order of the Lord Mayor in 1697. He was responsible for several very large and handsome pieces of plate in the Huguenot style with much gadrooning, cut card work and cast figurative decoration – a huge wine cooler of 1699 made for the 1st Duke of Kingston (now in the Hermitage, Leningrad), another made for the 1st Duke of Marlborough (now at Althorp), a pair of fire-dogs of 1704 formerly in the collection of the Duke of Portland, a pair of ice-pails *c.*1715–20 at Ickworth House. But he also made smaller and simpler pieces of distinction. (For his mark *see* p. 894.)

Lit: J. F. Hayward, *Huguenot Silver in England*, London 1959.

Roman pottery A term applied to ceramics made in various parts of the Roman Empire from C1 B.C. to C4 A.D. The most notable type is TERRA SIGILLATA, a ware covered with a red GLOSS made since the C3 B.C. in the E. Mediterranean, from the late C1 B.C. at the ARRETINE POTTERIES (with particular success) and subsequently in other parts of Italy (Pozzuoli, Modena, Padua), Gaul (especially at La Gramfesenque near Toulouse), the Rhineland, the Iberian peninsula, England and N. Africa. Such wares provided a cheap alternative to metal cups, bowls, etc., from which they derived in both form and decoration, but in the provinces and in the later periods the classical decorations, which had been applied to Italian wares, gradually disintegrated into abstract forms (as on coins of the same period) and in N. Europe ornament of a Celtic flavour was also used. The technique of lead-glazing was introduced from Asia Minor to Italy whence it was diffused to S. Gaul by the mid C1 A.D. when handsome jugs and other vessels with a greenish-yellow glaze were produced in the regions of St Remy-en-Rollat, Vichy and Gannat. Similar lead-glazed wares were made in the Rhineland and in England by the C3 A.D. In the Eastern provinces of the Empire pottery with a very glassy brightly coloured turquoise-blue glaze (originally developed in Egypt), made from powdered quartz and now called 'glazed quartz fritware', was produced C1 to C3 A.D. All these types of pottery were exported in quantity from their places of manufacture to other parts of the Empire.

Lit: R. J. Charleston, *Roman Pottery*, London 1955.

Romanesque style The style current until the advent of GOTHIC. Its origins are usually placed in the C10 though some historians date it from the C7 and regard the CAROLINGIAN style as merely its preliminary phase. In the decorative arts, mainly metalwork, a distinct change in emphasis is evident in the late C10 soon after the creation of the architectural style associated with the Cluniac Order in France and the establishment of the Ottonian Empire in Germany (Otto I crowned 962). It was a change from fluidity to solidity. The thin gold reliefs embossed with weightless figures and decorated with delicate tendrils of filigree so typical of the Carolingian period are replaced by solid cast bronze and engraved copper: shimmering translucent *cloisonné* enamels gave way to opaque *champlevé* enamels. The nature of Antique influence changed significantly (e.g. figures on the bronze font by Rainer of Huy in Liège appear to be derived from C5 B.C. Greek statues). Themes from pagan mythology were much more frequently used for the decoration of liturgical as well as secular objects which are often difficult to distinguish from one another (e.g. a bronze aquamanile of *c.*1125–50 in Aachen Minster is in the form of a head of Bacchus based on a Roman water jar). At the same time Byzantine influence increased, reaching its height in the early C12 as a result of the first Crusade (which had also brought N. Europeans into direct contact with the masterpieces of Antique art in Constantinople). Romanesque artists acquired Byzantine ideals of human

Romanesque style: ivory pastoral staff, English, c11–12 (Victoria & Albert Museum)

Romanesque style: reliquary, champlevé enamel, 1180–90 (Victoria & Albert Museum)

Romanesque style: chest from Valère Castle, Switzerland, c12 (Landesmuseum, Zurich)

dignity, formal order and discipline, the concept of the organic representation of the human form, as well as established canons of iconography. This undoubtedly contributed to the creation of such masterpieces as the silver head-shaped reliquary of St Alexander made by GODEFROID DE HUY in 1145 and given by Abbot Wibald to Stavelot (Musée Cinquentennaire, Brussels) – perhaps the first human head sculptured in the round since antiquity that is as expressive as a Roman portrait bust. It is typical of the age that this powerful image should be in silver and thus rank among what are now termed the minor arts. Romanesque metalworkers were, in fact, major artists (e.g. ROGER OF HELMARSHAUSEN and NICOLAS OF VERDUN). Many of the great masterpieces of Romanesque sculpture are in silver or bronze: and several of the finest Romanesque paintings are in enamel. Indeed the art of the metalworker reached a height of excellence in the Romanesque period seldom to be regained before the Renaissance. Superb textiles were also produced e.g. SICILIAN SILKS, NORWEGIAN TAPESTRIES and of course the so-called Bayeux Tapestry.

Romanesque style: textile (appliqué work), detail from the Bayeux Tapestry, c11 (Bayeux)

The period is marked by the emergence of local schools with clearly defined styles. At Hildesheim Bishop BERNWARD established at the beginning of the c11 a very important school of bronze workers whose products were sent as far afield as England. The MOSAN school of metal-workers and enamellers was still more important. Very handsome enamelled reliquaries shaped like little cruciform churches were made at Cologne in the early c12 (a good example in the Victoria & Albert Museum). Nevertheless it is difficult to assign many of the most accomplished Romanesque objects to their places of origin. The very beautiful bronze 'Trivulzio' candlestick in Milan Cathedral with athletic nudes struggling to overcome the tentacle-like scrolls of vegetation, made *c.*1200, has been variously ascribed to Milan, Lorraine and England.

The advent of the GOTHIC style in architecture had no immediate effect on the decorative arts. Indeed, some of the finest examples of Romanesque goldsmiths' work was commissioned by Abbot Suger for Saint Denis where the Gothic style in architecture may be said to have been born *c.*1140: they include various vessels of precious materials, notably a porphyry vase mounted in the form of an eagle (Louvre). But by the late c12 Gothic architectural motifs had begun to appear in metal-work, figures began to lose their rock-like monumentality and fluid surface decorations eventually drove solidity out of fashion.

Romayne work An English c16 term for Renaissance carved ornament with heads in roundels, scroll-work, foliage, vases, etc. It is an imprecise term.

Rombrich, Johann Christoph, *see* FÜRSTENBERG PORCELAIN FACTORY.

Rome potteries and porcelain factories Maiolica similar to that of ORVIETO was made in Rome in the c14–c15. Maiolica was also produced here by craftsmen from Faenza in the early c16 but no products have been identified. A group of pieces dated 1600–1623 decorated with grotesques in the Urbino style are inscribed as having been made in Rome (Victoria & Albert Museum; Ashmolean Museum). There were various c18 factories: that of **Gregorio Cerasoli** making faience from 1745; that of **Filippo Cuccumos** making porcelain 1761–84; that of **Antonio Riccò** making maiolica in 1779; that of **Lanfranco Bosio** making cream-coloured earthenware from 1780 onwards; that of **Antonio** and **Lorenzo Cialli** making cream-coloured earthenware in 1783 and porcelain from 1784 onwards; that of **Antonio**

'Sieubert' making biscuit figures after the Antique in 1790. But few products of these factories have been identified. The only Roman factory from which numerous marked specimens survive is that of G. VOLPATO.

Lit: Il Settecento a Roma, Exh. Cat., Rome 1959, pp. 425–8.

Römer German type of wine-glass made mainly in the Rhineland since the C15 and still popular for Rhenish white wine. It is of green WALDGLAS decorated with applied drops on the lower part – the earliest examples are beakers; later the bowl becomes hemispherical, the drops (sometimes moulded like raspberries) adorn the stem and the foot is formed out of a conical coil of glass thread (nowadays imitated by mould blowing).

Rontjen van Beek, Jan (b.1899). Potter of Dutch origin born in Denmark but a naturalized German. He has worked in Germany since the 1920s and specializes in making stoneware with fine glazes. In 1945 he was appointed director of the Hochschule für angewandte Kunst in Berlin.

Rookwood pottery One of the most important factories for the production of art pottery in the U.S.A., founded in Cincinnati in 1880, by **Mrs Maria Nichols** (later Mrs Storer) with financial support from her father, Joseph Longworth, a rich patron of the arts. It was named after their family home. The foundress was one of a number of Cincinnati ladies who had dabbled in ceramic decoration. But the pottery was from the start run on a commercial basis (though it supplied

Römer, German, c.1620 (Kunsthistorischesmuseum, Zurich)

Rookwood pottery: vase, 1898 (Metropolitan Museum of Art, gift of Wells M. Sawyer)

and fired pieces decorated by the Women's Pottery Club until 1883). A professional painter **Albert R. Valentien** (1862–1925) was engaged as a decorator. The administration was confided to **William Watts Taylor** (1847–1913) who took over the whole concern when the foundress withdrew on her second marriage in 1890. Only decorative wares were produced, mainly vases and ornamental jugs of simple, generally Oriental shapes, and notable mainly for their rich green or brown glazes, especially a 'tiger-eye' crystalline glaze introduced in 1884. Painted decorations often reveal Japanese influence and a Japanese artist, Kataro Shirayamadani, was employed for a time. Every piece was marked with the initials of the decorator and a symbol indicating the year in which it was made. The pottery first secured international attention at the Paris Exposition of 1890, when it won a gold medal. At the Paris Exposition of 1900 it showed Art Nouveau pieces. It is still active. (For factory mark *see* p. 887.)

Lit: H. Peck, *The Book of Rookwood Pottery*, New York 1968; ibid. in *The Connoisseur* CLXXII (1969), pp. 43–9; ibid. *Catalog of Rookwood Art Pottery Shapes*, Kingston, N.Y. 1971.

Rörstrand pottery and porcelain factory Founded near Stockholm in 1725 by the Swedish Chamber of Commerce with **Johann Wolff** as manager (until 1728). Wolff was a renegade from the COPENHAGEN POTTERIES. It began by producing blue-and-white faience similar to that of Copenhagen but with decorations derived also from ROUEN, DELFT, the German factories and Chinese porcelain. *Bianco sopra bianco* painting in opaque white on a greyish ground became a speciality. After the appointment of **Anders Fahlström** as director in 1741 the quality of products improved. Decorations were now executed in a fanciful Rococo style. But the factory's best period began slightly later, in 1753, when **Elias Magnus Ingman** became director and reorganized the whole concern. The full range of high-temperature colours was now used for the decorations of table-wares (notably tureens modelled with shell motifs), large tea-trays, stoves, etc. Products were also painted in enamel colours, in competition with those of the MARIEBERG POTTERY. The designer **Erick Rehn** supplied the factory with recent examples of French faience for copying

Rörstrand tin-glazed earthenware covered vase, c.1760 (National Museum, Stockholm)

and also introduced the 'Rehn Pattern' in the mid C18 – a central floral or fruit motif painted in blue or manganese with a border of leaf scrolls echoing the wavy edge of the plate or dish. The production of faience slowed down from *c.*1773 when the factory began to specialize in cream-coloured earthenware in the English style (called *Flintporslin*) which remained the staple product into the C19. In the 1830s products included tablewares with black-printed landscapes in the English style. Bone china was made from 1857 and hard-paste porcelain from the 1870s. Wares were in the usual range of C19 styles until 1895 when **Alf Wallender** (1862–1914) became art director and introduced Art Nouveau. He initiated the production of and provided models for vases decorated in relief with relatively large flowers and leaves painted in subdued underglaze colours, which are among the more attractive Art Nouveau ceramics. Similar vases were made after models by Anna Katarina Boberg (b.1864), Karl Lindström (b.1865) and Nils Erik Lundström (1865–1960). Figures of animals and birds were also made. The factory moved to Lidköping in 1932 and still flourishes, producing excellent table-wares in earthenware, stoneware and porcelain, some being designed by **Edward Hald** of the ORREFORS GLASSHOUSE. A subsidiary factory called ARABIA was opened near Helsinki in 1874 and split away as a separate concern in 1916. (For factory mark *see* p. 887.)

Lit: A. Baeckstrom, *Rörstrand och dese tillverkninger*, Stockholm 1930.

Roscher, Georg Michael (*fl.*1750). German ornamentalist, the author of some bold Rococo designs for various furnishings – looking-glass frames, pier-tables, chandeliers, clock-cases, etc. – which were engraved and published in Augsburg.

Lit: H. Kreisel, *Die Kunst des deutschen Möbels*, vol. ii, Munich 1970.

G. M. Roscher: furniture and other designs, c.1750 (Bayerisches Nationalmuseum, Munich)

Rose engine turned decoration A relief pattern simulating basket work, executed on pottery or porcelain by means of a lathe. *See* ENGINE TURNED.

Rose, John, *see* CAUGHLEY POTTERY & PORCELAIN FACTORY and COALPORT & COALBROOKDALE PORCELAIN FACTORY.

Rose Pompadour An opaque light rose-pink ground colour used on porcelain at SÈVRES. It is said to have been invented by the factory painter **Xhrouet** and was used there from 1757 to *c.*1765. Related to PURPLE OF CASSIUS and *famille rose* it is similarly made from a compound of gold. Various factories, including CHELSEA and WORCESTER, tried to imitate it but without complete success. It does not appear to have acquired its name until after Mme de Pompadour's death. A similar colour used on English C19 porcelain was called *rose du Barry* – a term sometimes inappropriately given to *rose Pompadour*.

Rosenthal porcelain factory (Rosenthal-Porzellan A.G.) One of the largest producers of table-wares (mainly porcelain, though the company includes factories making table-glass, silver and stainless steel). It was founded at Selb in Bavaria in 1879 by **Philipp Rosenthal** (1855–1937) and is now directed by his grandson of the same name. It first began to achieve prominence in the early years of the C20 with figures of contemporary subjects, e.g. bathing beauties, and, more notably, with table-wares in a greatly simplified version of Art Nouveau, e.g. the 'Darmstadt' service of 1905 and the 'Donatello' service of 1907, both designed by the founder. The 'Donatello' service was available either plain or with discreet underglaze painting of a bough of fruit (a motif much favoured at the factory). Other products were more traditional, some based on C18 patterns. Since 1950 it has been one of the most adventurous producers of ceramics and has employed a wide range of designers including R. LOEWY, W. WAGENFELD

Rosenthal porcelain figures modelled by R. Marcuse, c.1914 (Collection Karl H. Bröhan, Berlin)

and T. WIRKKALA. In 1960 Rosenthal opened the first of a number of 'Studio Houses' – now to be found in many European cities – to market its own wares and those of other factories, studio potters, etc. approved by the panel of artists and critics which advises the firm on design. Although it still produces some traditional patterns, most of the company's present-day wares are conspicuously modern and rely for their effect on form rather than decoration.

Lit: A.-L. Leistikow-Duchardt, *Die Entwicklung eines neuen Stiles im Porzellan*, Heidelberg 1957.

Rosette A circular PATERA usually with formalized rose-like petals.

Rosewood (Kingwood or **Palissandre).** A hard, dark purplish-red wood, sometimes streaked with black or brown, from the *Dalbergia* tree and imported into Europe and N. America from S. America and the W. Indies from the mid C18 onwards. It was used by English furniture-makers as a contrasting wood, e.g. with SATINWOOD, for both veneers and ornamental inlays, bandings, etc. In the C19 it became more popular and was widely used especially in REGENCY furniture when whole pieces were made of it. It became equally popular in France during the same period.

An E. Indian type of rosewood is called blackwood and was much used by Chinese furniture-makers.

Rosset, Elias Karl, *see* MAGDEBURG POTTERIES.

Rosset, Joseph (1706–86). Leading French sculptor and ivory-carver practising a delicate Rococo style. His work ranges from snuff-boxes and rasps to religious statuettes (e.g. St Teresa in the Louvre) and portraits of such celebrities as Voltaire, Montesquieu, Rousseau and d'Alembert, of which there are numerous versions. He was assisted by his sons **Jacques** (1741–1826) and **Antoine** (1759–1818).

Rössler, Wolf (*c.*1650–1717). Goldsmith and engraver working in Nuremberg. He is generally supposed to be identical with the *Hausmaler* who signed some of the best faience decorations of the late C17 with the initials WR, some delicately painted in *Schwarzlot*, others in richly coloured enamels and including very attractive landscapes (e.g. jug in Franks Collection, British Museum).

Lit: G. E. Pazaurek, *Deutsche Fayence- und Porzellan-Hausmaler*, Leipzig 1925, pp. 51–8.

Rosso antico A type of WEDGWOOD ware: an unglazed red stoneware, imitating that of Greek or Roman pottery, and decorated in the same manner as Wedgwood Basaltes wares or with black figures in imitation of Greek black-figure vases.

Rosso, Domenico del, *see* NAPLES TAPESTRY FACTORY.

Rosso Fiorentino, Giovanni Battista Rosso, known as (1495–1540). He was a leading Florentine Mannerist painter and, with Primaticcio, was one of the creators of the School of Fontainebleau. He appears to have invented STRAPWORK, which makes it first appearance in the stucco frieze he designed for the Gallerie de François I at Fontainebleau, 1533–5. He is also known to have designed much silver plate for François I and although none of it survives its style can be judged from René Boyvin's engravings inspired by it if not directly copied from it – e.g. very elaborate nefs, salts, etc., with frogs, tortoises or shell-fish as supports and an abundance of figurative sculpture, monstrous, contorted and sometimes overtly erotic (the stem of a standing salt is composed of two figures wriggling in coition).

Rost or **Rostel, Jan,** *see* FERRARA TAPESTRY FACTORY and FLORENCE TAPESTRY FACTORY.

Roubo, Jacob (1739–91). French furniture-maker and designer, notable for his manual *Art du Menuisier* (Paris 1769–75), the most informative c18 French book on the technique of furniture-making, illustrated with designs which are strangely behind the Neo-Classical times.

Rouen potteries A factory founded in Rouen by M. ABAQUESNE in 1526 made some of the earliest French tin-glazed earthenware in the style of Italian maiolica. It was continued by his son until the end of the c16. A new period began in 1644 when a fifty-year monopoly for making faience in Normandy was granted to Nicolas Poirel who transferred it to Edme POTERAT (on whose behalf he may have applied for it). Poterat's factory produced wares ranging from plates to wine cisterns (Musée de Cluny, Paris), decorated in blue and white (sometimes also yellow) in the style of NEVERS. His son, Louis, who established an independent factory and obtained a patent in 1673, was responsible for the development of the style associated with Rouen: he produced table-wares liberally decorated with *lambrequins* and other formal ornamental motifs in blue and white. He also obtained a monopoly for making porcelain but appears to have produced very little (a few soft-paste wares marked with the letters A.P. have been attributed to his factory but the attributions are disputed). When the Poterat monopoly expired in 1694 a large number of factories sprang up in Rouen which became one of the most important centres for the production of faience in France. As their wares are very rarely marked the products of the different factories can hardly be distinguished. They seem to have shared a common style and specialized in ewers and in other vessels modelled on silver patterns, and also in plates decorated in the STYLE RAYONNANT, often decorated with coats of arms and made for the aristocracy who had been prohibited from using silver table-wares by the sumptuary laws of 1709. With their stiff lacy decorations, there are the best examples of Louis XIV faience. They were normally painted in blue on a white ground but a dull Indian red was also used. After *c.*1720 the full range of high-

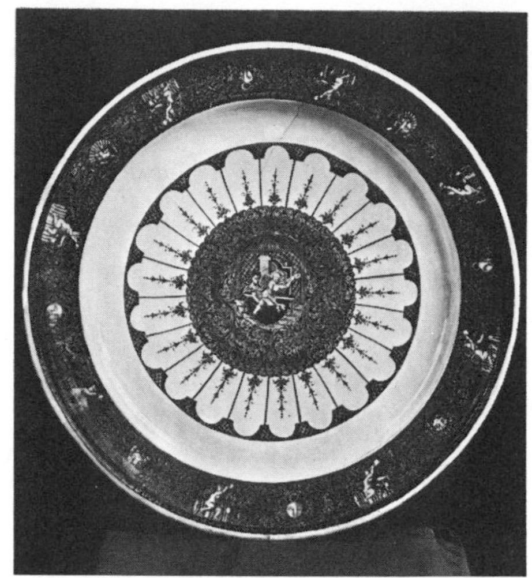

Rouen faience plate with 'style rayonnant' *decoration, early c18 (Louvre)*

temperature colours was adopted, especially for exotic floral decorations in the Chinese *famille verte* manner. (**Paul Caussy** (d.1731) is credited with the introduction of a yellow ochre ground colour.) Some of the best of these pieces are signed by **Jean-Baptiste Guillibaud** (d.1739). Some wares, especially jugs, basins and *écuelles* are decorated in a variant of the BLEU PERSAN style of Nevers with a paler ground and coloured flowers. A richer effect was produced by plates painted with Chinese-style flowers and rocks on a black ground. Some very impressive large objects were also made, notably a pair of terrestial and celestial globes on bold Baroque stands dated 1725 (Musée Céramique, Rouen) and larger-than-life-sized busts of the Seasons (Louvre) and Apollo (Victoria & Albert Museum), probably made in the factory of **Nicolas Fouquay** who succeeded Louis Poterat. Very attractive Rococo wares were made in the 1750s and 1760s, often decorated with amorous pastoral scenes surrounded by elaborate borders. Large stoves and tiles were also made. Big cider jugs were a speciality but were generally decorated in a distinctly rustic version of the Rococo. From *c.*1770 wares painted in enamel colours in imitation of porcelain were made, especially at the factory of the **Levavasseur family.** There were still eighteen factories at Rouen in 1786 but the

Rouen faience bust and pedestal, c.1740 *(Louvre)*

industry had begun to decline partly as a result of competition from English cream-coloured earthenware which was copied by some of them with little success. By 1807 only four factories were left, making simple household wares. No Rouen factory in the C17 or C18 ever adopted a recognized factory mark, but marks, presumed to be those of painters, are sometimes found.

Lit: M. J. Ballot, *Nevers, Rouen et les fabriques du XVIIe et du XVIIIe siècles,* Paris 1924; A. Lane, *French Faience,* London 1948; *Trésors de la faïence de Rouen,* Exh. Cat., Rouen 1952.

Rouleau vase A type of Chinese vase produced from the C17 onwards, with a cylinder body, short flat shoulders, a short thick neck and slightly spreading mouth.

Round glasshouse The first flint-glass factory in Ireland, founded in Dublin in the early 1690s by Capt. **Philip Roche,** advertising in the early C18 a very wide range of cut-glass vessels. But it was crippled by the Excise Act of 1745 which prohibited the export of glass and closed in 1755.

Lit: M. S. Dudley Westropp, *Irish Glass,* London 1920.

Rousseau, Eugène (1827–91). Notable French designer and decorator of glass and ceramics, and one of the first to fall under the influence of Japanese arts. Some of his works are straightforward essays in JAPONAISERIE. He also made imitations of jade in glass. But his most interesting works are large and rather heavy glass vases ornamented with crackling and splashes of colour

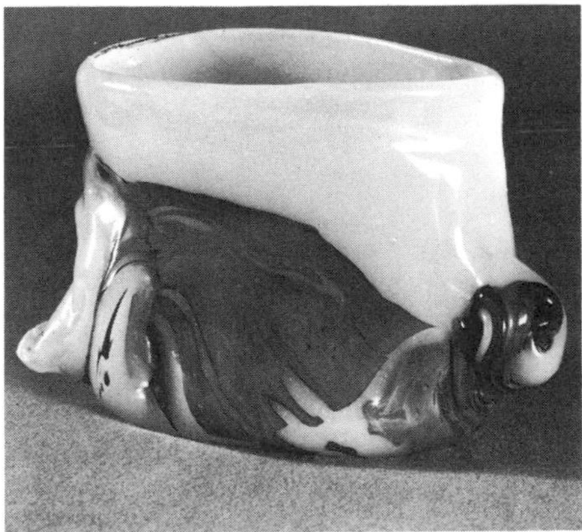
E. Rousseau, vase in glass imitating jade, c.1885 *(Musée des Arts Décoratifs, Paris)*

– early instances of the application to glass of decorative effects derived from Japanese pottery. In 1885 he handed over his studio to his pupil **Ernest-Baptiste Leveillé** who worked in a more sculpturesque but otherwise similar style.

Lit: L. Rosenthal in *Gazette des Beaux Arts* 1927 (I), pp. 55–7.

Roussel, Pierre (1723–1782). A Parisian *ébéniste*, he became a *maître* in 1745 and by 1767 was one of the leading furniture-makers in Paris. Four of his brothers were *menuisiers*. He worked in every variation of the Louis XV and Louis XVI styles, using floral and pictorial marquetry (often after Chinese prints) as well as geometrical marquetry, lacquer and simple veneers. Examples of his work are in the Musée Jacquemart-André, Paris.

Lit: F. J. B. Watson, *The Wrightsman Collection: Furniture*, New York 1966.

Roux, Alexandre (*fl.* 1837–81). French cabinet-maker working in New York from 1837, in partnership with his brother **Frederick** from 1847 to 1849, and as **Roux & Company** from 1857 to 1881 with workshops at a number of different addresses on Broadway. He made furniture in versions of a wide variety of historical styles, Gothic in the 1840s, Elizabethan, French Renaissance and Rococo in the 1850s, Grecian and Louis XVI (with ormolu and porcelain plaques) in the 1860s. The pieces were well made and clearly enjoyed some success in affluent New York society. He also imported furniture manufactured by his brother in Paris for the American market.

Lit: D. B. Hauserman in *Antiques* XCIII (1968), pp. 210–17.

A. Roux: stool, New York, c.1865 (Metropolitan Museum of Art, Edgar J. Kaufmann Charitable Foundation Fund)

Roycrofters, *see* HUBBARD, Elbert.

Rozenburg pottery and porcelain factory Founded in 1883 at Rozenburg near The Hague by Baron von Gudenberg to make DELFT style blue-and-white wares. The most important of its early products are those decorated with abstract ornament by T. A. C. COLENBRANDER who was employed from 1884 to 1889. **J. Juriaan Kok** (1861–1919), who was director from 1894 until his death, reorganized the concern, developed a type of very thin 'egg-shell' porcelain and introduced the Art Nouveau style for the design of vessels, showing a preference for angular and attenuated forms. Painted decorations, executed most notably by **J. Schellink** and **R. Sterken,** include peacocks, overblown poppies, limp pannicles of lilac and other motifs from the Art Nouveau repertory.

Lit: H. E. van Gelder, *Pottenbakkerskunst*, Rotterdam 1923.

Rubati, Pasquale, *see* MILAN POTTERIES.

Ruby glass Rich red glass made by the addition of gold chloride to the frit, invented by **J. Kunckel,** first produced at POTSDAM in 1679 and soon imitated by several other German glasshouses.

Ruhlmann, Jacques-Emile (1879–1933). He was the leading Parisian decorator and furniture designer of the 1920s, and was astonishingly quick in exploiting (and debasing) the cubist International Modern style for the luxury market. He created a comfortable, ritzy and self-consciously up-to-date style as characteristic of its period as the bobbed hair-do and the long cigarette holder. Born in Paris, he began as a painter but turned to design furniture in 1901. In 1910 he began to exhibit furniture regularly at the *salons d'automne*. After the First World War he went into partnership with **M. Laurent** and expanded the firm by adding a *maison de décoration* which became, by 1925, the most important in

Paris with workshops for *ébénisterie, menuiserie,* upholstery, japanning and *miroiterie.* They produced what was probably the best made and certainly the most expensive furniture of the time. Although he employed 16 draughtsmen Ruhlmann was himself responsible for the design of furniture made in his *ateliers.* He consistently showed a strong preference for the simplest forms and the most expensive materials – amboyna wood, macassar ebony and inlays of ivory. His favoured colour schemes, said to be '*Whistlériennes*', were gray and silver or, sometimes, black and gold like Russian cigarettes. Bureaux, sideboards and dressing-tables are lightly constructed with delicately curved and tapering legs ending

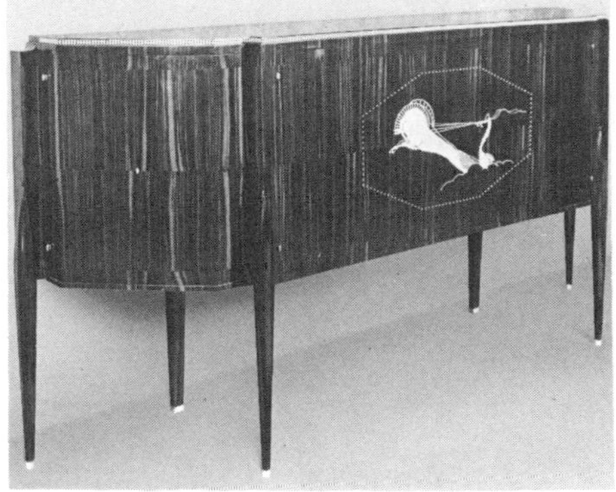

J.-E. Ruhlmann: cabinet, c.1925 (Louvre)

in little metal (often silver) shoes. Sometimes these pieces seem to have been inspired by C18 furniture. His chairs and sofas owe a more obvious debt to the First Empire. It is perhaps significant that he reverted to the C18 practice of marking his products with an *estampille.* He was a magnificent anachronism. But although his furniture played no part in the main evolution of C20 furniture design he anticipated a number of modern developments and the superb quality of the craftsmanship given to his work redeems it from the expensive vulgarity of his imitators. Examples of his furniture are in the Musée des Arts Décoratifs and Louvre, Paris, and Victoria & Albert Museum, London.

Lit: H. Honour, *Cabinet Makers and Furniture Designers,* London and New York 1969.

Rummer A capacious short-stemmed drinking glass of a type used in the late C18 and early C19 in England. It is sometimes said that they were intended for hot toddy. Early examples have

Rummer, English glass, c.1830 (Victoria & Albert Museum)

ovoid bowls of fairly thin glass, later ones are much thicker, straight sided and stand on heavy, sometimes square, feet. The name derives from the German RÖMER, and not from 'rum'.

Rumpp, Johannes (*fl.* 1740). Ornamental designer and engraver of Augsburg who published *c.*1740 *Tischler oder Schreiner Riese,* a volume of engraved designs for furniture, notably cupboards and desks, in a ponderous German late Baroque style with much marquetry and carved decoration.

Rundell, Philip (1743–1827). Proprietor of a notable and very prosperous firm of London silversmiths (he was worth £1,500,000 at his death). He was born in Bath, began as a jeweller, went to London in 1767, became a partner in a firm of goldsmiths and jewellers, Theed and Picket, in 1772 and obtained sole command of it in 1786. In 1788 he went into partnership with **John Bridge,** a man of suave manners able to deal with rich and important clients. They were appointed jewellers and goldsmiths to the Crown and given warrants by the Prince of Wales, the Duke of York and other members of the Royal Family. By 1806 they were employing 1,000 hands, including such skilled craftsmen as William Pitts, but seem to have farmed out the most important commissions for plate to independent silversmiths including Paul STORR and Benjamin SMITH. William Theed, a sculptor who had previously worked as a modeller for WEDGWOOD, joined the partnership in 1808, and Storr in 1811. The firm which traded as **Rundell, Bridge and Rundell** produced all types of silver wares from the simplest to the most elaborate, making a speciality of the vast presentation pieces which came into vogue during the last years of the Napoleonic wars. Most of their output was Antique-Revival in style – wine-coolers based on Roman marble urns, candlesticks supported by Grecian statuettes, centre-pieces incorporating architectural elements and allegorical figures – sometimes modelled by notable sculptors, including John Flaxman and Francis Chantrey. But they also succumbed occasionally to the Neo-Rococo taste, possibly under the influence of silver bought from French emigrés. Theed died in 1817 and Storr withdrew from the partnership in 1819. By this date the firm had established agencies in Paris, Vienna, St Petersburg, Constantinople, Baghdad, Calcutta, Bombay and various towns in South America. It continued to produce plate in the same style until Rundell's death and also, on one occasion, obtained designs for Gothic-Revival church plate from the young PUGIN. But the firm was dissolved in 1842 and many of the models for useful wares were sold, e.g. to G. R. Collis who put them into production in Sheffield Plate.

Lit: N. M. Penzer, *Paul Storr, the last of the Goldsmiths,* London 1954; S. Bury, 'The Lengthening Shadow of Rundell's' in *The Connoisseur* CLXI (1966), pp. 79, 152, 218; C. Oman, 'Problem of artistic responsibility: the firm of Rundell, Bridge and Rundell' in *Apollo*, March 1966.

Runner foot or **Bar foot** A type of foot common in the Renaissance for chairs, tables, etc., and later for small pieces also. Horizontal side-bars connect the front and rear legs at ground level.

Runners Long, narrow carpets usually those made in the Orient to cover the sides of tents or rooms and used in Europe and N. America as floor-covering for corridors, halls, etc.

Running circles An ornamental band composed of circles connected by tangents,

Running dog A classical ornament of repeated volutes, generally on a frieze; much used in early GEORGIAN furniture. It is also called a *Vitruvian scroll.*

Running dog

Ruolz, *see* ELECTROPLATE.

Ruskin pottery, *see* TAYLOR, W. Howson.

Rüsselbecher Tall conical or club-shaped drinking glass decorated with drawn-out hollow protuberances rather like elephants' trunks. Made in the early Middle Ages, probably in the Rhineland. *Illustrated next column.*

Russell, Sir Gordon (b.1892). English furniture designer and manufacturer who began *c.*1914 in the Cotswold ARTS AND CRAFTS tradition. The Arts and Crafts influence remained strong, but from 1925 he designed furniture of greater simplicity. In 1930 he began to design frankly modern furniture with a greater element of machine work. His company's Murphy wireless sets, the first and still among the best of their kind, also date from this year. In 1929 he opened showrooms in London to supplement those already existing in Broadway, Worcestershire, both marketing the products of his company, Gordon Russell Limited, and those of other leaders of the modern movement, e.g. bent-plywood chairs by AALTO, bentwood chairs by THONET, textiles by EDINBURGH WEAVERS, pottery by LEACH. During World War II when there was a serious timber shortage he was largely responsible, as Chairman of the Board of Trade's Design Panel, for the design of the 'utility' furniture made throughout the country – a complete range of simple modestly priced pieces of sound construction, unglamorous but by no means unattractive. He was appointed second director of the Council of Industrial Design (now the Design Council) in 1947, knighted in 1955 and retired in 1960. From 1924 **W. H. Russell** (no relation) was associated with him, first as design assistant and ultimately as chief designer for his firm. He retired in 1972 and died in 1973.

Lit: G. Russell, (autobiography) *Designer's Trade*, London 1968; G. Russell, *Looking at Furniture*, London 1964; John Gloag, *English Furniture* (6th edition), London 1973; N. Pevsner, *Studies in Art, Architecture & Design*, vol. II, London 1968; D. Joel, *Furniture Design Set Free*, London 1969.

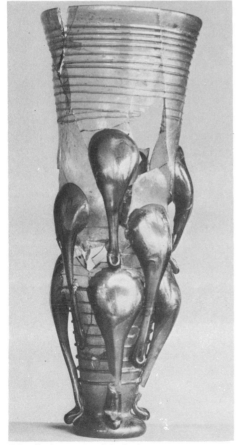

Rüsselbecher or 'trunk-beaker', Teutonic glass, c5–c6 (Victoria & Albert Museum)

Russinger, Laurentius, *see* HÖCHST FAIENCE AND PORCELAIN FACTORY.

Rustic furniture: design for a garden chair by M. Darley, 1754

Rustic furniture Literally, any type of rough furniture made for farmhouses and cottages, e.g. Windsor chairs, Yorkshire ladder-back chairs. The term is also used for a type of furniture made in the late C18, mainly in England, for use out of doors in rustic arbours, hermitages and other

Rya or Ryijy rug, 1952 (Kunstindustrimuseet, Copenhagen)

follies in a landscape park – chairs and tables cunningly (sometimes exquisitely) carved of wood to simulate roughly hewn logs, the roots of trees, etc. Designs for such furniture were published in several pattern books, notably *A New Book of Chinese Designs* by Edwards and Darley (London 1754).

Ryijy rugs Knotted pile rugs made since very early times in Denmark, Norway, Sweden and, especially, Finland, for use as bed-covers, horse cloths or sleigh rugs. They have a rather thin ground of wool or linen and an unusually long woollen pile with several shoots of weft (from ten to twenty) between each row of knots. Some are plain-coloured, others have geometrical or formalized flower patterns. The art of making them, generally practised by amateurs until the late C19, has recently been revived.

Engraved letter from
Magnum in Parvo; or, the Pens Perfection,
by Edward Cocker, London, 1672
(reduced). Courtesy Victoria & Albert Museum

Saarinen, Eero (1910–61). Son of the Finnish architect **Eliel Saarinen** who emigrated to the U.S. in 1923. Eero Saarinen studied architecture in Paris and at Yale and became one of the most adventurous and exciting post-war architects. He was equally important as a designer and pioneered, with Charles EAMES, an entirely new approach to furniture design based on the use of PLASTICS which enable a chair, for example, to be moulded in much the same way as a motor-car body is stamped out by a die-press. His work epitomizes the mid-C20 trend in design away from geometrical simplicity and angularity towards freer and more organic forms. His furniture was premiated with Eames's in 1941 by the Museum of Modern Art. Like Eames he was greatly influenced by airplane 'aesthetics' – his chairs often having a volatile, almost airborne look.

He began in association with Eames with whom he designed a notable plywood chair in 1940 – the plywood being moulded into a multi-curved shell which anticipated the forms taken by plastics after the war. In 1948 he produced an armchair in stamped-out plastic similar to the contemporary Eames chairs but with a simpler metal rod support and upholstered with foam rubber. Known as the 'womb chair', it gives maximum comfort with the minimum weight and bulk. His well-known 'Tulip' set of chairs and tables in moulded fibre-glass (manufactured by KNOLL ASSOCIATES) is eminently organic in form and yet extremely, perhaps rather affectedly, elegant. Both chairs and tables are mounted on slender, tapering pedestal supports of white lacquered cast metal, as graceful and fragile-looking as flower stems. (These supports were originally intended to be of plastic and their manufacture in metal indicates a technical 'defeat' for the designer.) The table tops are circular and made of wood, white plastic laminate or marble.

E. Saarinen: moulded plastic armchair,
reinforced with fibreglass and aluminium, 1957
(Museum of Modern Art, New York,
gift of Knoll Associates)

Though the 'Tulip' furniture could not be manufactured entirely of plastic as intended by Saarinen it is perhaps the most distinguished example to date of the use of plastic for domestic design.

Lit: R. Spade, *Eero Saarinen*, London 1971.

Sabot French term for the metal (usually gilt bronze) shoe enclosing the bottom of the leg of a piece of furniture.

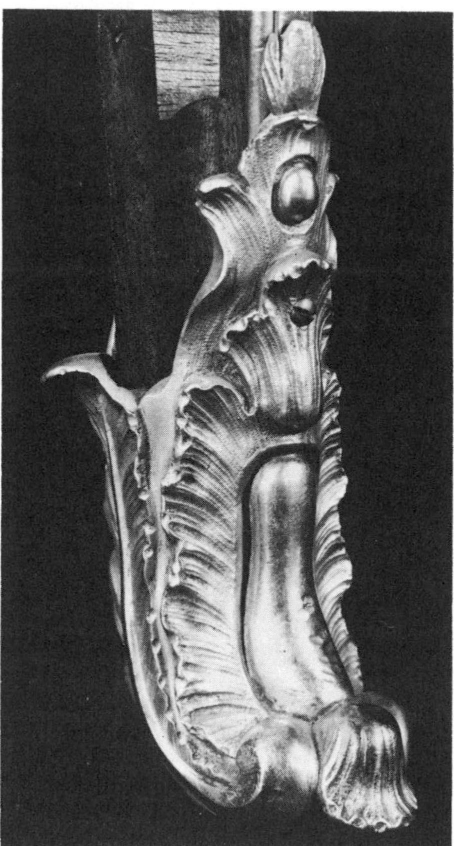

Sabot of gilt bronze from a piece of c18 furniture (Château de Versailles)

Sabre leg A leg, curved like a cavalry sabre, square or round in section and tapering gently towards the base. Derived from the Greek KLISMOS, it was much used on late-c18 and early-c19 chairs and sofas.

Saddle bar One of the small horizontal bars to which the panes of glass are attached in a window.

Saddle seat A chair seat carved and curved like a saddle, especially one on a Windsor chair, *see* CHAIR.

Sadler, John (1720–89). He was one of the earliest practitioners of TRANSFER PRINTING on porcelain and may have discovered the process. He is first recorded in 1756 when he and his partner **Guy Green** appear in an affidavit as having printed 'upwards of 1200 earthenware tiles of different patterns' at Liverpool. He decorated pottery made at several factories, notably WEDGWOOD. He retired in 1770.

Lit: E. S. Price, *John Sadler, a Liverpool Pottery Printer*, West Kirby 1949.

Sadware Pewterers' term for plates, dishes, etc.

Saint-Amand-les-Eaux potteries and porcelain factory A faience factory was founded here in 1718 by **Pierre Joseph Fauquez** (d.1741) as a branch of his factory in nearby TOURNAI, which he closed in 1725. The Saint-Amand-les-Eaux factory was run by his son and grandson until the Revolution. First ROUEN and then STRASBOURG provided the main sources for inspiration for the forms and decorations of table-wares. But from *c*.1760 an individual type of *bianco sopra bianco* decoration combined with underglaze painting of flowers, landscapes and figures in blue or manganese was adopted, mainly for plates and dishes but occasionally also for larger products (e.g. wall-fountain in Musée Nationale de Céramique de Sèvres). In the later c18 wares were sometimes decorated with enamel colours and towards the end cream-coloured earthenware was produced. Under the founder's grandson, **Jean-Baptiste-Joseph Fauquez** (1742–1804), simply decorated soft-paste porcelain was produced on a fairly small scale from 1771 to 1778. **Maximilian-Joseph de Bettignies** (d.1865), who acquired the factory after the Revolution, resumed the production of porcelain and produced forgeries of SÈVRES and other soft-paste wares. The factory closed in 1882. It is sometimes said that there was a second c18 faience factory in the town conducted by **N. A. Dorez** whose signature appears on a few pieces but he may have been a painter rather than a factory-owner. (For factory mark *see* p. 887.)

Lit: J. Houdoy, *Histoire de la céramique lilloise*, Paris 1869; A. Lane, *French Faience*, London 1948; R. Le Bacqz in *Cahiers de la céramique* 9 (1958), pp. 41–7; M. Ernould-Gandouet, *La Céramique en France au XIX siècle*, Paris 1969.

Saint-Ange, Jacques-Louis de la Hamayde de (b.1780). French designer, he began under the influence of PERCIER and BRONGNIART and worked for the SÈVRES PORCELAIN FACTORY from 1806 or earlier. After 1814 he devoted himself mainly to textiles and designed numerous carpets and some tapestries for the Garde Meuble de la Couronne. His carpet designs are characteristic of the RESTAURATION STYLE in their density of pattern and choice of motifs – swans, flowers, lyres, acanthus scrolls, etc. – no less than in their rich and occasionally jarring colours.

Saint-Clément pottery A faience factory founded in 1758 as a branch of the LUNÉVILLE factory but run independently by Charles Loyal in partnership with the architect Richard Mique and for a while with P. L. CYFFLÉ. It produced white biscuit and enamelled faience figures after models by Cyfflé, but it is known mainly for its table-wares decorated with enamel colours and/or gilding in the style of SCEAUX. After several changes of ownership it was acquired in 1824 by **Germain Thomas** whose descendants ran it until the late C19. Early wares are very rarely marked but an example marked 'S C' in blue is recorded. C19 wares have 'St Clement' stencilled in blue or 'St Ct' impressed.

Lit: H. Haug in *Archives Alsaciennes d'histoire de l'art* IX (1930) p. 160ff.; A. Lesur & Tardy, *Les poteries et les faïences françaises*, Paris 1957–60; M. Ernould-Gandouet, *La Céramique en France au XIX siècle*, Paris 1969.

Saint-Cloud pottery and porcelain factory The early history of these concerns is confused. A faience factory was active in the late C17, directed in 1667 by François RÉVEREND and employing Dutch workmen. This or another concern, conducted in 1679 by **Henri-Charles Trou**, bailiff to the duc d'Orléans, supplied drug vases for the hospital at Versailles and very simple plates for the use of servants in the royal palaces. In 1679 Trou married Berthe Coudray the widow of **Pierre Chicaneau** who had discovered a process of making soft-paste porcelain. Such porcelain was made from 1693 at Saint-Cloud and in 1702 Berthe Coudray and her children by Chicaneau were granted a privilege for the manufacture of both porcelain and faience at Saint-Cloud. A subsidiary factory was established in the rue de la Ville-L'Eveque, Paris (run independently from 1722 to 1742 when it was reunited with the original factory). Products are notable mainly for the quality of the material, of a warm tone with a satin glaze (less shiny than that of MENNECY) and the accomplishment of the modelling. They include a wide range of objects – jam-pots, butter dishes, spice-boxes, jugs in the form of men and birds, teapots with dragon-shaped handles and spouts, elaborate chinoiserie *pot pourris*, cups and saucers, tureens, cane-handles, knife-handles, snuff-boxes, etc. Many pieces are decorated in relief either with sprigs of prunus blossom, as on *blanc de Chine*, or an unusual pattern of overlapping scales. Many pieces were mounted in silver which sets off their jewel-like quality. The earlier products are either unpainted or decorated in underglaze blue with

St Cloud: soft-paste porcelain ice-pail, c.1710–20 (Musée des Arts Décoratifs, Paris)

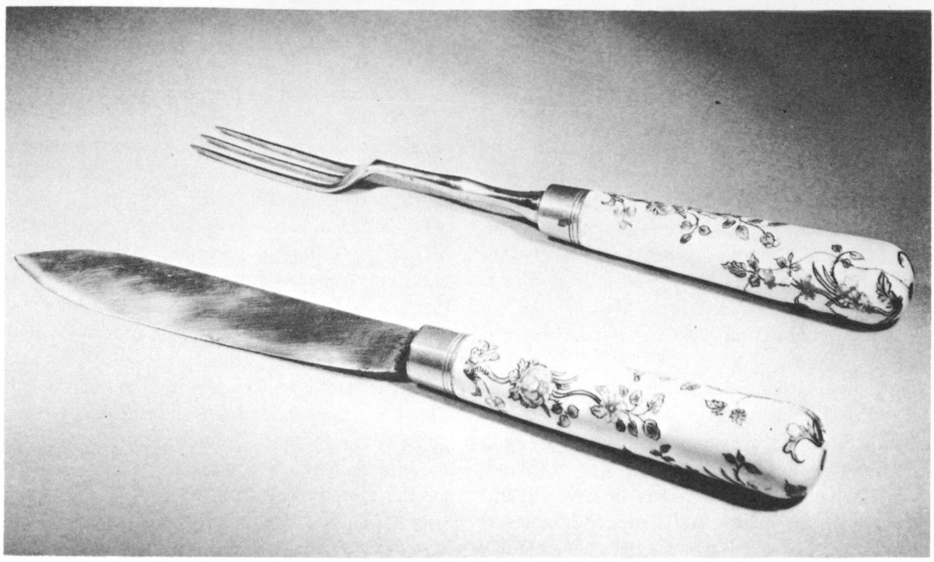

St Cloud: soft-paste porcelain knife and fork handles, c.1740 *(Musée des Arts Décoratifs, Paris)*

delicate *lambrequins*. Gilt was rarely applied. Enamel colours were used, mainly after 1730, for Kakiemon style decorations. At this time the factory began to come under the influence of MEISSEN. Standards fell off from *c.*1750 and the factory closed in 1766. (For factory mark *see* p. 887.)

Lit: P. Alfassa & J. Guérin, *Porcelaine française*, Paris 1932; W. B. Honey, *French Porcelain of the 18th Century*, London 1950.

Saint-Cyr embroideries The name generally given to panels of needlework of the Louis XIV period executed in a curious mixture of stitches, *gros point* and *petit point* in silk and silver threads; but the name is also applied, erroneously, to other embroideries of the same date. The name derives from the convent school which Mme de Maintenon established at the Château de Noisy in 1684 and transferred to Saint-Cyr near Versailles in 1686. A certain **Lherminot** was employed as embroidery instructor 1684–6 and his son also from 1685 to 1687. Other professional embroiderers were attached to the school as well. Lherminot was responsible for a set of embroideries made at Saint-Cyr and given by Louis XIV to Strasbourg Cathedral. And it seems likely that other pieces assigned to Saint-Cyr in contemporary inventories were the work of the instructors and professionals rather than the pupils at the school.

Lit: F. J. B. Watson, *The Wrightsman Collection: Furniture*, New York 1966.

Saint-Denis-sur-Sarthon pottery A small faience factory founded in 1750 with D.-P. PELLEVÉ as manager, initially producing wares similar to those of ROUEN and SINCENY where many members of the staff had previously worked. It survived until 1861, latterly producing only peasant wares. No factory mark was ever used.

Lit: G. Despierres, *Histoire de la faïence de Saint-Denis-sur-Sarthon*, Paris and Alençon 1889; A. Lesur and Tardy, *Les poteries et les faïences françaises*, Paris 1957–60.

St Gall lace, *see* LACE.

Saint-Germain, Jean-Joseph de (1719–after 1787). He was a bronze founder and became a *maître* in Paris in 1746. His father was a cabinet-maker. He made elaborate clock-cases, sometimes to models by such sculptors as Pajou. He also produced furniture mounts for cabinet-makers, notably for François LACROIX.

Lit: S. Eriksen, *Early Neo-Classicism in France*, London 1974.

Saint-Gobain glasshouse The main French glasshouse, famous for plate glass the process of which (invented by G. B. PERROT) was first practised there. Founded in 1688 at Tourlaville, Normandy, by **Louis-Lucas de Nehou** and transferred to Saint-Gobain, Picardy, in 1693 as the *Manufacture Royale des Grandes Glaces*, it amalgamated 1695 with a company originally set up in Paris (1665) by Colbert. Its large cast plate-glass LOOKING-GLASSES soon drove the smaller blown glass mirrors of Venice out of fashion. It enjoyed a monopoly for making plate glass for windows and mirrors in France until the Revolution and still survives as a national concern.

Lit: E. Frémy, *Histoire de la Manufacture Royale des Glaces de France au XVIIe et XVIIIe siècles*, Paris 1909.

Saint-Louis, Cristalleries de French glasshouse founded in the Munzthal, Lorraine, 1767 and making by 1782 fine crystal glass imitated from English patterns. It became the most important producer of fine table-glass in C19 France, also making, from 1839, coloured glass and, a little later, Venetian-style filigree glass and *millefiore* paper-weights. Mid-C19 products are notable for their unusual simplicity of outline which gives them a more modern appearance. The factory still survives.

Lit: J. Hollister, *The Encyclopedia of Glass Paperweights*, New York 1969.

Saint-Maur silk factory A Louis XIV period silk factory established by a weaver from Lyons, **Marcelin Charlier**, first in Paris, then moved to Saint-Maur on the outskirts. Its history is obscure but it is known to have made damask, lampas and very expensive velvet. It supplied sumptuous fabrics for Versailles, including *portières* to designs by BÉRAIN and white and gold brocade for the Grande Galerie.

Lit: P. Verlet, *French Royal Furniture*, London 1963.

Saint Omer pottery A faience factory founded in 1750, managed by a potter named **Levêque** from ROUEN and producing until *c.*1775 wares mainly imitative of the Rouen potteries but also some decorated in an original version of the BLEU PERSAN of NEVERS and others with *bianco sopra bianco* painting. In addition to table-wares it made some handsome large wall cisterns decorated with chinoiseries (Musée Hôtel Sandelin, Saint Omer). Wares marked 'S O' and 'A Saint-Omer 1759' are recorded.

St Omer: faience chocolate pot, c.1750–75 (Hôtel Sandelin, St Omer)

Lit: G. Mellor in *The Connoisseur* LVIII (1920), pp. 133ff.; A. Lesur & Tardy, *Les poteries et les faïences françaises*, Paris 1957–60; J. Giacomotti, *French Faience*, London 1963.

St Petersburg Imperial porcelain factory Founded 1744 and working exclusively for the Imperial Court, it survived the Revolution to become a State factory. The first arcanist was C. K. HUNGER, succeeded by a Russian 1747 and **Joseph Regensburg** from Vienna 1762 when the first objects of good quality were produced. In the early 1760s MEISSEN ROCOCO patterns for figures and tablewares were copied but under Catherine II's influence a classicising style was soon introduced. Table-wares are similar to SÈVRES but more gaudily coloured. The most attractive products are lively statuettes of Russian peasants by **Jean Rachette** who was chief modeller 1779–1804. Similar figures were made in the later C19. Table-wares, large vases, etc. were often painted with scenes from Russian history. As the factory was non-commercial it maintained high standards to the end and was barely affected by changes in taste. *Illustrated below and opposite page.* (For factory marks *see* p. 887.)

Lit: G. Lukomsky, *Russisches Porzellan*, Berlin 1924; D. Roche and I. Issaievitch, *Exposition de céramiques russes anciennes*, Exh. Cat., Sèvres 1929; M. C. Ross, *Russian Porcelains*, Norman 1968.

St Petersburg tapestry factory Founded 1716 by Peter the Great on the model of the GOBELINS and staffed mainly with French weavers. It was revived by Catherine the Great, once again with French weavers. In both periods it was occupied almost exclusively in copying French tapestries from the Gobelins.

St Petersburg: porcelain sugar-bowl, spoon and saucer, c.1760 *(Musée des Arts Décoratifs, Paris)*

Saint-Porchaire pottery A French factory certainly active before 1542 (when products from it were mentioned in an inventory) and the probable source of a highly individual type of lead-glazed earthenware. These pieces are decorative (rather than useful) objects of a finely grained off-white paste with intricate inlaid patterns of strapwork made by impressing the clay with metal punches (like book-binders' stamps) and filling the cavities with clays of contrasting colours, red, yellow and brown: they are covered with a transparent lead glaze. Some pieces are very elaborately modelled in the Mannerist style, and a few have reliefs of lizards, frogs, etc., apparently imitated from PALISSY. The simpler pieces with only abstract decorations are generally assigned to the earliest period (*c.*1525–40), the more elaborate to the succeeding years and some very extravagant but less carefully executed pieces to the years around 1560. Many pieces incorporate armorial and other devices, notably the salamander of François I (1515–47), the interlaced crescents of Diane de Poitiers, and the monogram of Henri II (1547–59). The ware is very soft and fragile and no more than 64 pieces are recorded. During the C19 numerous reproductions were made, e.g. by MINTON. It was generally known as '*Henri Deux* ware', attributed to many different places (Lyons, Beauvais, etc.) and supposed to have been made by a variety of different people (including a pupil of Benvenuto Cellini, Girolamo della Robbia and the printer Geoffrey Tory). From 1864 it was thought to have been made at

St Petersburg: porcelain vase, c.1862 *(Victoria & Albert Museum)*

Oiron (and is still sometimes called *faïence d'Oiron*) and Saint-Porchaire was not put forward as its place of origin until 1888. No factory mark is known. *Illustrated next column.*

Lit: M. J. Ballot, *Bernard Palissy et les fabriques du XVIe siècle,* Paris 1924; M. Ernould-Gandouet, *La Céramique en France au XIX siècle,* Paris 1969.

St Porchaire: lead-glazed earthenware salt, c.1545–55 *(Louvre)*

Saintes potteries Situated in the Saintonge district, which was one of the main centres for the production of French c16 and c17 lead-glazed earthenware. B. PALISSY worked here. LA-CHAPELLE-DES-POTS is nearby. A faience factory was founded *c.*1730 by **Louis Sazerac** and **Jacques Crouzat** from Bordeaux, run by the latter from 1733 and by his descendants until 1813. No factory mark is recorded.

Lit: A. Lesur & Tardy, *Les poteries et les faïences françaises,* Paris 1957–60; J. Giacomotti, *French Faience,* London 1963.

Salem secretary A large piece of late-c18 New England furniture with a glass-fronted (2- or 4-doored) cabinet or bookcase surmounting a chest of drawers (sometimes flanked by cupboards) with one 'false drawer' panel which falls forward to provide a writing platform and reveal a pigeon-hole-fitted interior.

Salem snowflake A six-pointed star often used as a background motif on furniture made in the c18 at Salem, Mass.

Salembier, Henri (*fl.c.*1770–1820). He was a Parisian ornamental designer notable for his floral arabesques and scrolls, sometimes including figures, cartouches, etc. They were intended for use on wall-paintings, tapestries, needlework and porcelain. Some thirty sets of his ornamental engravings were issued between 1777 and 1809. His floral arabesque style became very popular during the late Louis XVI period. He also made designs for furniture, vases, goldsmiths' work, etc., some of which are in the Directoire style.

Lit: Connaissance des Arts, 93, Nov. 1959, pp. 66–75.

Salt A salt-cellar. The term is generally reserved for the very elaborate salt-cellars used on the tables of the great from the Middle Ages to the late C16, e.g. CELLINI's famous gold and enamel salt.

Salt, silver gilt, London, 1576 (Goldsmiths' Company, London)

Salt, Ralph (1782–1846) and his son **Charles** (1810–64). They were potters at Hanley, Staffordshire. Ralph Salt made figures (Dr Syntax, etc.) in the style of J. WALTON and also dogs and sheep. Charles Salt made Parian Ware as well as earthenware figures similar to those of his father though with an inferior finish.

Salt-glaze A glaze with a slightly rough pitted surface applied to STONEWARE by throwing salt onto the fire of the kiln in which the pots are being baked when the temperature is at its highest. The heat splits the salt (sodium chloride) into its components, the chlorine going out through the kiln chimney and the sodium combining with the silicates in the body of the pots to form a thin glaze, *see* STONEWARE.

Salver A tray or plate for serving food or drink, usually made of silver. The earliest (C17) have a flat circular top mounted on a foot to be held by the hand of the person serving. Later they were made with three or more feet, for standing, and a top which varied greatly in shape, though it was usually given a moulded border and was often decorated in the centre with a coat-of-arms. A small salver is often called a card tray or waiter.

Salviati, Francesco (1510–63). A leading Florentine Mannerist painter who began as a goldsmith and continued to design gold, silver and bronze objects throughout his career. Numerous drawings survive: freely executed sketches from his own hand and very carefully finished drawings, often in several versions, presumably executed in his studio for sale to goldsmiths. In addition to the stock Antique grotesque motifs, his favourite devices were pairs of addorsed winged terms, nude figures in erotic postures, and friezes of marine creatures. No objects made directly according to his designs are known, but his drawings were widely imitated, both in the Low Countries and in Italy, and devices which originated with him found their way on to numerous caskets, vases, urns, etc. He also did cartoons for the FLORENCE TAPESTRY FACTORY.

Lit: J. F. Hayward in *The Connoisseur* CXLIX (1962), pp. 157–65; H. Bassmann, *Verzeichnungen Francesco Salviati*, Berlin 1969.

Salviati glasshouse A Venetian glasshouse which played a leading role in the c19 revival of the Venetian glass industry. It was founded as the **Società Salviati e Compagni** in 1866 – the year Austria ceded Venice and it joined the new kingdom of Italy – by **Antonio Salviati** (1816–90) with English support, notably that of Sir Henry Layard the discoverer of Nineveh who later lived in Venice. Salviati was a lawyer who became interested in glass for mosaics, in particular for the restoration of the mosaics in St Mark's. From 1859 he was in partnership with **Lorenzo Radi** and carried on an international business in mosaics. After 1866 the firm obtained several prominent commissions for mosaics in England, e.g. the high altar reredos in Westminster Abbey (1867) and the ceiling of the Albert Memorial Chapel in Windsor Castle, and in Germany where the mosaics in the Palatine Chapel in Aachen were carried out between 1870 and 1875. In the following year Salviati left his English associates and founded a new firm of his own. In addition to mosaics, Salviati produced ornamental and table glass, mainly in Venetian Renaissance styles and exhibited at all the great late-c19 exhibitions. He also produced imitations of ancient Roman glass in the 1870s and later. Salviati is still one of the leading Venetian glass firms.

Lit: T. Shull, *Victorian Antiques*, Rutland 1963; G. Mariacher, *Vetri di Murano*, Milan and Rome 1967.

'Schmelzglas' vase by Antonio Salviati, c.1862 (Victoria & Albert Museum)

Samadet pottery A faience factory in the Landes founded by the **Abbé de Roquépine** in 1732 (inherited by his nephew in 1754 and sold to **Jean Dyzes** or **d'Yzes** in 1785) producing blue-and-white and polychrome wares initially in the style of MOUSTIERS. Products probably include plates painted with large butterflies (sometimes ascribed to Bordeaux). It remained active until 1836 but only common household wares were made after the Revolution. No factory mark is recorded but wares were sometimes inscribed with the full name and date.

Samadet faience cruet stand, c18 (Musée Pyrénéen, Lourdes)

Lit: L. Sentex in *Bulletin de la Société de Borda*, Dax, 1900; A. Lesur & Tardy, *Les poteries et les faïences françaises*, Paris 1957–60; M. Ernould-Gandouet, *La Céramique en France au XIX siècle*, Paris 1969; J. Rouffet, *La faïencerie de Samadet et ses satellites regionaux au 18e et 19e siècles* Paris 1973.

Samarkand carpets, *see* TURKMAN CARPETS.

Sambin, Hugues (1515/20–1600/2). French architect and wood-carver. Much of the best and most elaborately carved C16 French furniture is attributed to him (e.g. examples in the Louvre; Metropolitan Museum, New York; Victoria & Albert Museum, London), but no work by him can be certainly identified and in fact there is no record that he ever made furniture at all. He lived and worked mainly in Dijon where he prepared decorations for the entry of Henri II in 1548 and was received by the guild as a *maître menuisier* in 1549. He has been credited as an architect with a number of buildings in Dijon, notably the Maison Milsand and the Hôtel Le Compasseur, and in 1583 was paid for work in the interior of the Palais de Parlement, now the Palais de Justice, where the very finely carved wooden screen in the chapel is presumably by him. His reputation

French mid-C16 cupboard attributed to H. Sambin (Louvre)

H. Sambin: design for a term figure, 1572

as a designer rests on his book of engraved TERM figures, *Oeuvre de la diversité des Termes, dont on use en Architecture,* 1572. These are extremely fanciful and display the influence of Italian Mannerists and also of the school of Fontainebleau. Term figures similar to those in Sambin's book are found on several C16 cabinets.

Lit: E. Bonaffé, *Le meuble en France au XVIe siècle,* Paris 1887; A. Castan, *L'Architecteur Hugues Sambin,* Besançon/Dijon 1891; E. Prost in *Gazette des Beaux Arts,* 1892, I, pp. 123–35; H. David, *De Sluter à Sambin,* Paris 1933.

Samian ware, *see* TERRA SIGILLATA.

Sampler An embroidered panel, originally one on which various types of stitches had been executed or motifs worked to serve as models. From the C16 the term was also applied in its still current sense to a panel worked in a variety of stitches to demonstrate the skill of an (usually young) embroidress. The earliest surviving examples date from the second quarter of the C17. They are worked in coloured silks on a linen ground with geometrical patterns, stylized birds, flowers, etc. Those embroidered by children from the early C18 usually incorporate the letters of the alphabet and pious texts, the name of the embroidress and the date of completion.

Samson, Émile (1837–1913). The most famous maker of reproduction porcelain, especially C18 Sèvres, Meissen and Chinese Export. He was extremely skilful and sensitive and his reproductions are deceptively accurate. He was the son of **Edmé Samson** (1810–91) a *Hausmaler* who specialized in romantic scenes. Émile established a factory at Montreuil which still flourishes under the direction of his grandson who employs a large staff of craftsmen to make reproduction faience, enamels, gilt-bronze mounts, etc., as well as vessels and statuettes in imitation of those produced by the best C18 factories. All their products bear one or other of the Samson marks (various arrangements of S).

Lit: M. Ernould-Gandouet, *La Céramique en France au XIX siècle,* Paris 1969.

Sand blasting A method of decorating glass by directing a stream of sand, crushed flint or powdered iron on to the surface (the parts to be left untouched are protected by a steel stencil, plate or an elastic varnish or rubber solution, to form a resist). In use since 1870 (when invented in America) mainly for large panels of glass to be used as architectural decoration and for mass-produced table-ware.

Sandbox A caster for sand to be sprinkled on wet ink – before the introduction of blotting paper – like a sugar caster in appearance, usually incorporated in a STANDISH. It is alternatively called a pouncebox.

Sanderson, Elijah (1751–1825). He was an American cabinet-maker and worked at Salem, Massachusetts, with his brother **Jacob** (1757–1810). They produced high-quality pieces, and it has been suggested that Samuel McINTIRE may have executed some of the carving on them.

Lit: C. F. Montgomery, *American Furniture: The Federal Period,* New York and London 1966.

Sanderson, Robert, *see* HULL, John.

Sandwich glass, *see* BOSTON AND SANDWICH GLASS COMPANY.

Sang, Andreas Friedrich (*fl.*1719–47). A glass engraver, noted for his landscapes within a *Laub-und-Bandelwerk* border. He worked at Erfurt, Weimar and Ilmenau. After 1747 he went to Holland where he appears to have influenced Dutch engravers.

Sang de boeuf A brilliant deep plum-red porcelain glaze, used by Chinese potters from the K'ANG HSI period onwards for monochrome vases, and imitated by European C19 potters. It is derived from copper and has the appearance of coagulated ox-blood, especially on the shoulders and bases of vases where it lies more thickly. The attractive unevenness of the glaze is due to the difficulties in firing – *sang de boeuf* has to be fired in a reducing atmosphere, ending with a strong oxidizing period. If the oxidizing period is lengthened a lighter glaze results, known as a Peach-Bloom Glaze. This is much rarer than *sang de boeuf* and is found only on small objects. *Sang de boeuf* is known in China as *lang-yao*.

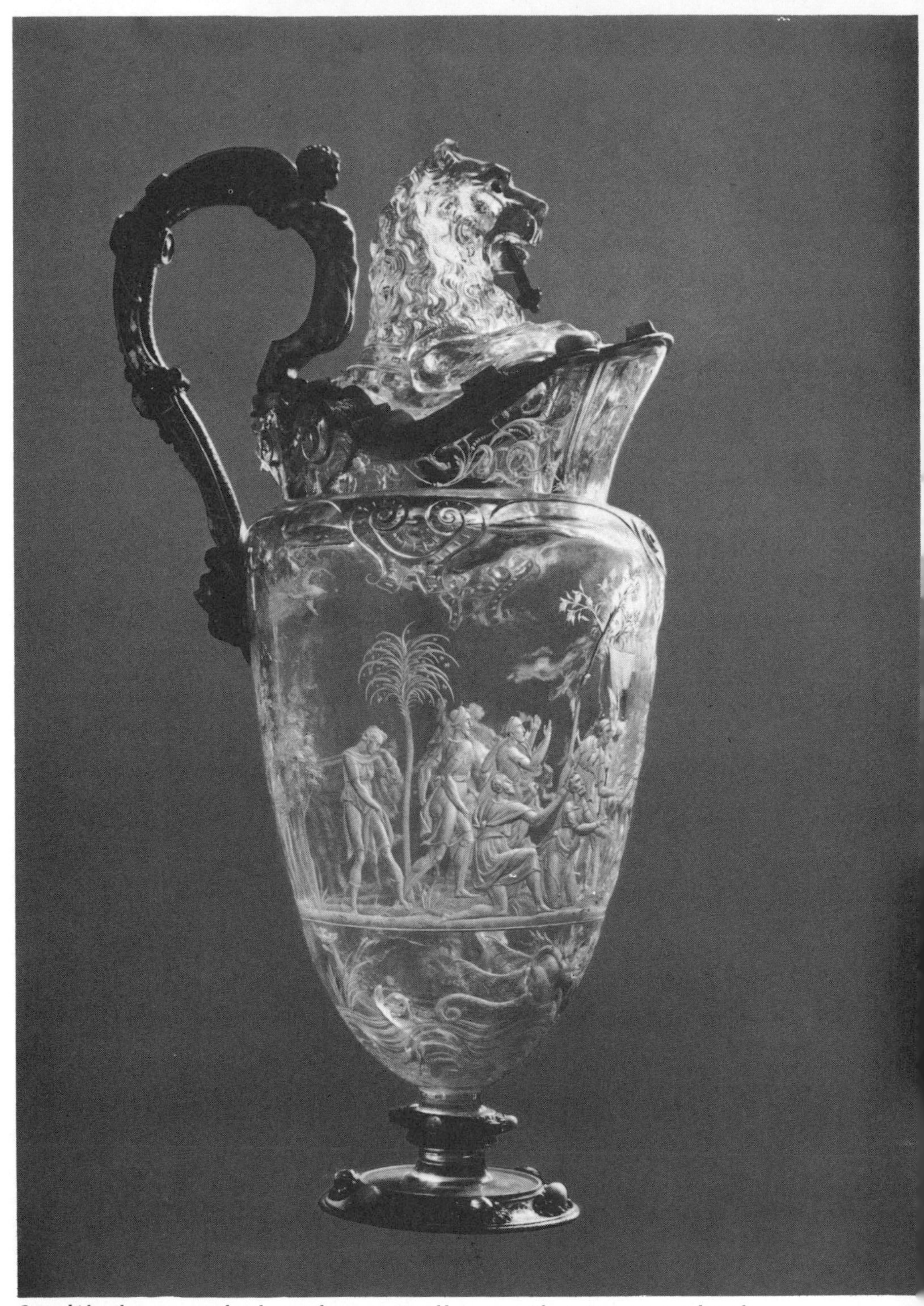

***Saracchi** brothers: engraved rock-crystal ewer set in gold mounts with precious stones and pearls, Milan, c.1570–80 (Residenzmuseum, Munich)*

Santa Barbara tapestry factory, *see* MADRID TAPESTRY FACTORY.

San-ts'ai Literally 'three colour', a Chinese term applied to stoneware and porcelain decorated with coloured lead glazes – mainly dark blue, turquoise and aubergine though other colours were also used – kept from intermingling by raised ridges like cloisons which outline the pattern. This technique of decoration was first used on T'ANG pottery and later on MING porcelain. The latter type is also called *Fa-hua*. The pieces are generally large – vases, bulb-bowls, flower pots, etc. – and the decorations very bold.

Saqui, Soqui or **Laquoi** He was a porcelain decorator who specialized in exotic birds in the Sèvres manner and painted wares from the WORCESTER, BRISTOL and PLYMOUTH factories.

Sarabend carpets, *see* PERSIAN CARPETS.

Saracchi family One of the most distinguished groups of Italian goldsmiths and hard-stone engravers of the late C16 and early C17. They worked in Milan but the products of their studio were internationally prized and acquired for the Imperial and Grand Ducal treasuries in Germany as well as Italy. The best known are vases of rock crystal exquisitely engraved with figures in a restrained Mannerist style. The family consisted of five brothers: **Giovanni Ambrogio** (employed by the Duke of Mantua from 1616 onwards), **Simone, Stefano** (d. before 1595), **Michele** and **Raffaello** (d. before 1595), and the four sons of Giovanni Ambrogio – **Gabriele** (Court Jeweller to the Duke of Mantua from 1617 onwards), **Pietro Antonio, Gasparo** and **Costanzo.** There are works reliably attributed to them in the Museo degli Argenti, Palazzo Pitti, Florence; in the Schatzkammer of the Residenzmuseum, Munich; and in the Kunsthistorisches Museum, Vienna. *Illustrated opposite page.*

Lit: E. Kris, *Die Meister und Meisterwerke der Steinschneidkunst . . . ,* Vienna 1929.

Sarakh carpets, *see* PERSIAN CARPETS.

Sarpaneva, Timo (b.1926). Leading Finnish industrial designer of the generation younger than AALTO and FRANCK. His designs for glass made by the Iittala factory have a mathematical assurance of line and a flair for unusual combinations of smoky colours.

T. Sarpaneva, glass vase by Iittala Glassworks, Finland, 1961 (Victoria & Albert Museum)

Sarreguemines pottery A large factory in Lorraine, founded *c.*1770 by **Paul Utzschneider** and run by his descendants until the end of the C19. It began by producing cream-coloured earthenware and stoneware in the style of WEDGWOOD. In 1794 it acquired the materials and models of the OTTWEILER POTTERY AND PORCELAIN FACTORY. In the C19 it produced table-wares with printed landscapes (in the English style) or distantly imitative of Italian maiolica. By 1867 it was said to be not only the largest French factory of industrial ceramics (with some 2,000 employees) but also the most notable, after MINTON, for the production of *faïence-fine.* Wares were usually marked with *'Sarguemines'* or *'Sarguemine'* or 'U C' (in a triangle) or 'U & Cie' (in an octagon) impressed or transfer-printed.

Lit: G. E. Pazaurek, *Steingut: Formgebung und Geschichte,* Stuttgart 1927; A. Lesur & Tardy, *Les poteries et les faïences françaises,* Paris 1957–60; M. Ernould-Gandouet, *La Céramique en France au XIX siècle,* Paris 1969.

Sarsenet The old English name for a very fine silk cloth. The term is descriptive of quality rather than origin or technique.

Saruk carpets, *see* PERSIAN CARPETS.

Saryk carpets, *see* TURKMAN CARPETS.

Satin A fabric with long floating warp threads on the face, tied at intervals by a single weft thread and thus appearing to be made up almost entirely of warp threads on the face of the cloth (and of weft threads on the reverse). Satin weaves are spoken of as four-end, five-end or eight-end satins. Satins with short floating wefts are often called satinettes, while those in which the floating threads are in the weft, instead of the warp, are termed sateens or reverse satins. A fabric in which a pattern is formed by areas of satin and sateen in the same weave is termed a DAMASK. The term satin is popularly applied to a variety of silk fabrics with glossy surfaces.

Satinet(te) Strictly a type of SATIN, but the term is also popularly applied to a variety of fabrics woven with a mixture of cotton and silk threads, a cotton warp and woollen weft, etc.

Satsuma potteries The source of two distinct types of Japanese pottery – very simple earthenware vessels seldom seen outside Japan and very gaudy tin-glazed wares made almost exclusively for export. They were established in Satsuma province, S. W. Kyushu, like the KARATSU POTTERIES, by Koreans in the late C16, and early wares are often directly imitative of Chinese and Korean pottery. They produced both ordinary household wares and TEA CEREMONY WARES, notably rather simple vessels with thick dark-coloured glazes sometimes irregularly combined. One group of potteries produced from early in the C17 white wares decorated in underglaze blue or reddish-brown with lightly painted landscapes, birds, etc. and with a creamy crackled glaze. Pieces were occasionally painted in enamel colours from the mid C17 and in quantity after 1795. Early C19 examples include attractive, delicately painted small objects such as incense boxes and burners, wine bottles, etc. 'Brocaded' Satsuma wares, once so extravagantly admired in the West, are of crackled cream-coloured faience very richly decorated in gold and enamel and sometimes artificially 'aged' with tea, sulphuric acid or smoke. Their production began in the mid C19 and was steadily increased from 1870 onwards. They were also imitated elsewhere in Japan.

Lit: S. Jenyns, *Japanese Pottery*, London 1971.

Saunders, Paul, *see* NORMAN, Samuel.

Saunier, Claude Charles (1735–1807). Louis XVI furniture-maker of outstanding grace and delicacy, he became a *maître-ébéniste* in 1765. He specialized in small consoles and *bureaux aux cylindres*, usually of a light-coloured wood inlaid with ebony or other dark wood, e.g. his elegant console in the Rijksmuseum, Amsterdam. But he also used lacquer and *vernis Martin* with great effect.

Lit: F. de Salverte, *Les ébénistes du XVIIIe siècle*, rev. ed., Paris 1962.

Sauvage, Charles-Gabriel, *see* LE MIRE.

Savery, William (1721–88). Leading American furniture-maker working at Philadelphia where he settled *c.*1740. A number of pieces marked with his label reveal a high standard of carving, especially on the mahogany chairs in which he appears to have specialized (though he also made case furniture). The style of his more elaborate products is derived from the pattern books of mid-C18 England, notably CHIPPENDALE and Batty LANGLEY. But he also made plain, undecorated furniture.

Lit: J. Downs, *American Furniture: Queen Anne & Chippendale Periods*, New York 1952.

Savignies potteries Earthenware was made at Savignies, near Beauvais, from the Middle Ages, but early products cannot be distinguished from those of the other BEAUVAISIS POTTERIES. When Mary of Modena, consort of James II of England, passed through Beauvais in 1689 she was given pottery made at Savignies. C18 products included inscribed brown-glazed *sgraffiato* wares (dish in Musée Nationale de Céramique, Sèvres) and probably some boldly decorated slip-ware. No factory mark is recorded, but wares were sometimes inscribed with the name of the place and painter. *Illustrated next column.*

Savona potteries A group of prolific C17 and C18 maiolica factories probably of greater importance than those in the other two Ligurian towns – ALBISSOLA and GENOA – where similar wares were made at the same time. The marks found on Ligurian wares rarely indicate the place of manufacture though some pieces are marked

Savignies slipware dish, c18 (Musée de la Vénerie, Senlis)

Savona maiolica dish, 1750 (Victoria & Albert Museum)

with the coat of arms of Savona and others are signed by potters who are known to have worked there, notably G. BOSELLI. Among the wide variety of wares produced, two-handled vases of Baroque form and boldly modelled plates and dishes based on silver designs are the most notable. c17 wares are generally painted in blue on a pearly white ground often with chinoiseries: those of the c18 in polychrome with very vigorous sketchy designs of figures, landscapes, etc. A few outstanding pieces are painted in the pictorial style of CASTELLI – notably a number of panels some of which are signed by the easel and fresco painter **Giovanni Agostino Ratti** (there is an example dated 1721 in the British Museum). In the late c18 cream-coloured earthenware was produced. There are still potteries at Savona. Certain marks have been attributed to Savona factories but they have also been claimed for other Ligurian factories.

Lit: Mostra del'antica maiolica ligure dal secolo XIV al secolo XVIII, Exh. Cat., Palazzo Reale, Genoa 1939; P. Torriti, *Giacomo Boselli e la ceramica savonese del suo tempo,* Genoa 1965.

Savonarola chair, *see* CHAIR, *X-chair.*

Savonnerie carpet factory The most important European factory of knotted-pile carpets. The name Savonnerie is often applied loosely and erroneously to French pile carpets produced in other factories. The Savonnerie factory was founded by Louis XIII in 1627 when he granted a royal 'privilege' to **Pierre Dupont** (1577–1640) and his former apprentice **Simon Lourdet** (d.1671) for a carpet-making concern. Dupont was the inventor of *tapis façon du Levant* and the author of *La Stromatourgie, ou Traité de la Fabrication des Tapis de Turquie* (1632). Lourdet had taken over an old soapworks – *savonnerie* – on the Quai de Chaillot in Paris. But Dupont and Lourdet soon quarrelled and Dupont worked mainly from his own *atelier* in the Louvre. However it was at this time that carpets woven by Dupont and Lourdet's factory, whether at the Savonnerie or at the Louvre, became known as 'Savonnerie carpets'. Until 1768 the concern worked chiefly, if not exclusively, for the Crown. Its most flourishing period was the earlier part of Louis XIV's reign. It was granted a new contract in 1664. Its most important commission was for the magnificent series of carpets for the Galerie d'Apollon and the Grande Galerie in the Louvre. The latter were never used. They numbered nearly a hundred and were made between 1664 and 1683. These magnificent carpets, probably the finest ever made in Europe, have a fine, close woollen pile tied with GHIORDES KNOTS, some 90 knots to the square inch, and were woven on upright looms similar to those used for high-warp tapestries. They were extremely costly since it took a skilled craftsman a year to make three square metres of plain carpet and correspondingly longer the more complex the pattern. Although floor carpets were the factory's staple product it also produced upholstery for furniture, coverings for screens and wall-hangings, including pictorial panels (e.g. portraits, though these mostly dated from the late C18). Designs were provided by painters many of whom, like **Blain de Fontenay**, also worked for the royal tapestry factories. They follow the main stylistic trends of their period. Louis XIV carpets are richly patterned with Baroque acanthus scrolls, classical and royal emblems, linked bars and C scrolls, against a background of deep and noble browns and blacks. From about 1690 to 1712 the factory went into eclipse due to stringent State economies, but it later revived and was much employed by Napoleon after 1805 and produced many fine carpets in the Empire style. In 1825 it was amalgamated with the GOBELINS TAPESTRY FACTORY and its independent existence came to an end. But a number of important Savonnerie carpets continued to be produced under Louis Philippe and the Second Empire though the quality of design declined noticeably. Later, because of costs, Savonneries ceased to be made as floor-coverings. They continued to be made for wall-hangings and in the early C20 panels have been produced after paintings by Monet, Manet, Van Gogh and Odilon Redon. Examples can be seen at the Mobilier National and the Louvre in Paris; The Metropolitan Museum in New York; The Philadelphia Museum of Art, Philadelphia; and Waddesdon Manor in England.

Lit: M. Jarry, *The Carpets of the Manufacture de la Savonnerie*, Leigh-on-Sea 1966.

Savoy glasshouse, *see* RAVENSCROFT, George.

Sawankhalok ware Thai pottery produced at Sawankhalok from the C14 until the potteries were abandoned in the mid C15, when the tradition was continued at potteries further north. Sawankhalok ware was exported throughout South East Asia. It is a hard, rather coarse-grained, light grey stoneware and is usually covered with a celadon glaze of a light grassy or pale sea-green tint. Some wares have a dark brown glaze and these are called 'Kaliang Ware'. Chinese influence is felt both in the celadon glazes and in the forms of jars and other vessels and in their incised decorations.

Sazerac, Bernard, *see* ANGOULÊME POTTERY.

Sazerac, Louis, *see* SAINTES POTTERIES.

Scagliola A material used since Roman times to imitate marble and, later, PIETRE DURE. It is composed of pulverized selenite, applied to a wet gesso ground, fixed under heat and highly polished. Mainly used for columns, pilasters and

Scagliola table-top by Lamberto Cristiano Gori, 1768 (Museo dell'Opificio delle Pietre Dure, Florence)

other interior architectural features, its artistic possibilities were developed from the c16 onwards for table-tops, especially in c18 Florence where Enrico Hugford and Lamberto Cristiano Gori used it for imitation FLORENTINE MOSAIC.

Lit: L. Bartoli & E. A. Maser, *Il Museo dell'Opificio delle Pietre Dure*, Florence 1953.

Scale pattern A pattern composed of overlapping circles like the scales of a fish, also called an imbricated pattern or scaling, it is one of the basic forms of decoration applied to objects in a wide variety of media in many different places and periods. A kind of scaling called MOSÄIK was painted on porcelain made at MEISSEN and other German factories from *c.*1760. In England it was especially favoured by the WORCESTER PORCELAIN FACTORY, as a background to reserved panels, in pink from 1761 and, much more frequently, in blue from 1763; the wares bearing this decoration are called pink-scale or blue-scale (occasionally scale-pink or scale-blue).

Scaling An ornament of overlapping circles, like the scales of a fish.

Scalloped An edge cut or modelled in a series of semi-circles, on textiles, glass, ceramics, metalwork, woodwork, etc. Sometimes the term is applied to other more elaborately shaped edges.

Sceaux pottery and porcelain factory A small concern just outside Paris, between Sèvres and Mennecy. It was established before 1748 (in premises where pottery had been made since *c.*1735) by **Jacques Chapelle** who began by making porcelain but was obliged to stop by the Vincennes monopoly. He consequently turned to the production of faience as delicately made and as finely painted in enamel colours as porcelain. Some pieces are of outstanding beauty, notably a dinner service (partly in the Musée des Arts Décoratifs, Paris) including plates with a scattering of naturalistic flowers surrounded by borders of fresh green leaves. Other products included *pot pourris*, flower vases, plates, etc. decorated with landscapes, birds, *putti* and pastoral scenes sometimes in the style of Boucher. Figures were also made, but these were generally imitative of Sèvres. Porcelain was again made at the factory after it had been acquired in 1763 by **Joseph Jullien** (d.1774) and **Charles-Symphorien Jacques** (d.1798) who took over the MENNECY factory in 1766 and produced similar wares in both places. In 1772 the concern was sold to **Richard Glot** who ran it until the Revolution, making wares in the Sèvres Louis XVI style. Most surviving specimens are of this type. Glot is reputed to have been a modeller of ability. The painter **Jacques Jarry**, famous for his birds and formerly at APREY POTTERY, was working at Sceaux in about 1784. It survived until after 1810 but latterly made only common household wares. (For factory mark *see* p. 887.)

Sceaux faience tureen, c.1770–80 (Musée nationale de Céramique, Sèvres)

Lit: M. J. Ballot, *La ceramique française: Nevers, Rouen et les fabriques du XVIIe et XVIIIe siècles*, Paris 1925; A. Lane, *French Faience*, London 1948; J. Giacomotti, *French Faience*, London 1963.

Scenic wallpaper A printed wallpaper of non-repetitive pictorial design made to cover the entire wall surface of a room, usually a panoramic view of a landscape or townscape, but also other scenes. The first was J. ZUBER's *Vues de Suisses*, 1804, and all the best examples were produced in France by this firm and that of J. DUFOUR, often for export to England and the U.S.A. The fashion for such papers lasted until the mid c19 and has recently been revived by the reproduction of many of the original designs.

Lit: E. A. Entwistle, *French Scenic Wallpapers 1810–50*, London 1971.

D. Schäffer: bureau, 1732
(Royal Collection, Rosenborg Castle, Copenhagen)

Schadow, Johann Gottfried, *see* BERLIN PORCELAIN FACTORY.

Schäffer, Dietrich (*fl.*1732). Cabinet-maker from Keyla in Thuringia, he was appointed official cabinet-maker to Christian VI of Denmark for whom he made one of the more elaborate pieces of North European Baroque furniture – a huge writing desk with legs in the form of spouts of water issuing from dolphins, a towering superstructure of drawers flanking a cupboard, crowned with a sculptural group representing the apotheosis of the king. It was made in 1732. *Illustrated opposite page.*

Lit: H. Kreisel, *Die Kunst des deutschen Möbels*, vol. ii, Munich 1970.

Schäper, Johann (1621–70). He was a German HAUSMALER, decorating both pottery and glass. He began as a stained-glass-window painter working at Nuremberg (from 1655) and Ratisbon (from 1664). He is notable mainly for drinking vessels decorated with very deft little decorations in black enamel or SCHWARZLOT with landscapes scratched through the surface with a needle point. The landscapes are in a curiously classicising style and are set within bands or within circular or oval frames. Glasses decorated in this manner are known as *Schäpergläser*. About a dozen faience jugs and a single dish with paintings signed by him are recorded, but many unsigned pieces have been attributed to him. The largest collection of his glasses was formerly in the Schlossmuseum, Berlin. His followers included Johann Ludwig FABER.

Lit: G. E. Pazaurek, *Deutsche Fayence- und Porzellan-Hausmaler*, Leipzig 1925; K. Pilz in *Keramos* 23 (1964), pp. 3–7.

Scharvogel, Johann Julius (1854–1938). German artist potter who began his career as an employee at the VILLEROY & BOCH factory at Mettlach. He set up his own workshop in Munich *c.*1900 making stoneware decorated with free-running mottled glazes. In 1906 he went to Darmstadt where he was appointed head of the Grand Ducal pottery. But he returned to Munich by 1913. He used a stylized bird as a mark, sometimes with the initials S. K. M. (for Scharvogel Keramik München).

J. Schäper: glass painted in Schwarzlot, *c.1660 (Victoria & Albert Museum)*

(Right) J. J. Scharvogel: stoneware vase, post-1906 (Kunstgewerbemuseum, Berlin)

Schelli, Jacob, *see* PENNSYLVANIA DUTCH STYLE.

Schellink, J., *see* ROZENBURG POTTERY & PORCELAIN FACTORY.

Scheurich, Paul (1883–1945). Sculptor, painter and book illustrator, born in New York and trained at the academy in Berlin where he later became professor. He provided figure models for several German porcelain factories, notably BERLIN, MEISSEN, NYMPHENBURG and SCHWARZBURG – dancers, blackamoors, goddesses, in a conspicuously 1920ish style.

Schick, Maria Seraphina Suzanna Magdalena, *see* LÖWENFINCK, Adam Friedrich von, and FULDA POTTERY & PORCELAIN FACTORY.

Schiffer, Hubert, *see* RAERAN POTTERIES.

Schinkel, Karl Friedrich (1781–1841). Architect, painter and designer, he settled in Berlin in 1805 after studying architecture under Friedrich Gilly and travelling in Italy and France. His first recorded pieces of furniture are a bed and toilet table in beechwood which he designed for Queen Louise in 1809 for the Charlottenburg Palace, where they still survive. They are remarkable in having none of the airs and graces of Empire furniture: they almost anticipate, with their delicate, light-coloured veneers, the BIEDERMEIER style of the post-Napoleonic period. His career as an architect began in 1815 when he was appointed Geheimes Oberbaurat in the Prussian Office of Public Works. He handled the Greek or Gothic style with equal ease and ability, but his designs, whether for architecture or furniture, differ strikingly from those of his contemporaries in England. His Grecian furniture has none of the attenuated elegance of REGENCY and none of the archaeological discomfort of Thomas HOPE. Schinkel furniture is solid and simple. But he was striving – in furniture as in architecture – for a contemporary style. Historical motifs are seldom stressed, though he made use of monopods and flamboyant tracery just as he made use of columns and pointed windows in his Grecian or Gothic buildings. The chairs he designed for Prince August's palace in Berlin in 1818–21 are in a version of the Empire style

K. F. Schinkel: armchair with book-stand, c.1820 *(Monbijou, Berlin)*

from which most of the characteristic motifs have been erased. Even more original are those he designed in 1817 for Prince Friedrich: they have curious rounded backs and are eminently practical. It is the practicality and comfort and unpretentious simplicity of his furniture that makes it outstanding. It is interesting and perhaps significant that he also had designs carried out in cast iron, a material of which he made daring use as an architect. Examples of his furniture survive in the Charlottenburg Palace and Monbijou Palace in Berlin.

Lit: J. Sievers, *K. F. Schinkel: Die Möbel,* Berlin 1950; G. Himmelheber, *Biedermeier Furniture,* London 1974.

Schleiss, Franz, *see* POWOLNY, Michael, and GMUNDEN POTTERY.

Schleswig pottery A faience factory founded in 1755 by J. C. L. von LÜCK, who left in the following year, and run by a consortium until 1758 when it was acquired by **Johann Rambusch** (d.1773). Products included boldly modelled Rococo tureens, bishop bowls, basket-shaped dishes, trays, table-tops and centre-pieces as well as the usual range of table-wares, generally decorated in manganese-purple on an off-white ground, sometimes also a greyish or yellowish green with flowers, pastoral scenes, etc. Standards declined after 1773 when the concern was inherited by **Friedrich Vollrath Rambusch** who sold it in 1801: it was closed in 1814. Wares were rarely marked with the name, more usually with 'S' with the painter's initials below, usually in manganese.

Lit: K. Hüseler, *Geschichte der Schleswig-Holsteinischen Fayence-Manufakturen im 18.Jahrhundert*, Breslau 1929.

Schmelzglas The German name for AGATE GLASS or *calcedonio*. The German word was frequently used by English and other non-German C19 makers of agate glass, e.g. Salviati.

Schmidt, Karl (1873–1948). German furniture-maker who played an important part in the development of modern industrial design. He began as a cabinet-maker under the influence of the English ARTS AND CRAFTS Movement but in 1898 founded a factory in Dresden for the production of furniture designed by leading architects, Bruno PAUL and Bruno TAUT and others. His aim was good cheap mass-produced furniture.

Schmuz-Baudiss, Theodor Hermann, *see* BERLIN PORCELAIN FACTORY.

Schnabelkrug A type of Rhenish stoneware jug with a long beak-like spout. Many of them were made at the SIEGBURG POTTERIES in the late C16 and early C17.

Schneider, Christian Gottfried (1710–73). German gem- and glass-engraver born and working at Warmbrunn. No signed works are recorded but many fine examples of Bohemian-Silesian glass engraving have been associated with a goblet, with figures personifying the Continents, traditionally ascribed to him (Kunstgewerbemuseum, Berlin).

Schnell, Martin (fl.1703–40). German furniture and porcelain (MEISSEN) painter. Born in Dresden, he worked under G. DAGLEY in Berlin 1703–9, then returned to Dresden where he was appointed lacquer-maker to Augustus the Strong (1710) and spent the rest of his life. He specialized in japanned trays – the best of their period – decorated with charmingly whimsical chinoiserie scenes, but also made larger pieces, e.g. bureaux, with elaborate japanned decorations.

M. Schnell: red and gold lacquered chair, 1715–21 (Moritzburg, Dresden)

Lit: W. Holzhausen, *Lackkunst in Europa*, Brunswick 1959; H. Kreisel, *Die Kunst des deutschen Möbels*, vol. II, Munich 1970; H. Huth, *Lacquer in the West*, Chicago and London 1971.

Schnelle A tall slender tapering tankard, usually of STONEWARE. It was a speciality of the Rhenish potteries (e.g. COLOGNE, RAEREN, SIEGBURG, WESTERWALD) in the C16 but very few were made after *c.*1600 until the C19 when imitations and fakes of the earlier ones were produced. *Illustrated next page.*

Schnelle: stoneware, Siegburg, late c16 (Kunstgewerbemuseum, Cologne)

Schofield, John (*fl.*1776–94). He was one of the best London silversmiths of his day though he was never admitted to the Goldsmiths' Company. In 1776 he and **Robert Jones** registered a joint mark and he registered his own mark two years later. He specialised in cruets and candelabra in a very elegant Adamesque style which almost anticipates in its crispness and technical mastery the Regency silver of Paul STORR.

Lit: R. Rowe, *Adam Silver*, London 1965.

Schonau, Johann Elias Zeissig called, *see* MEISSEN PORCELAIN FACTORY.

Schongauer, Martin (1430–90). One of the greatest of German late Gothic engravers. He was the son and brother of goldsmiths and executed a few very beautiful and influential designs for ecclesiastical plate, e.g. a crozier and very intricate censer composed of intertwined ogee arches. He also published several prints of scrolling Gothic foliage, similar to much painted, carved and wrought decoration of the period. Some of his figurative prints were adapted by LIMOGES ENAMEL painters of the MONVAERNI WORKSHOP.

Schouman, Aert (1710–92). Dutch glass engraver and associate of F. GREENWOOD of whom he made an engraving. His few known signed glasses are after his own compositions. *See also* STIPPLE ENGRAVING.

Schreiberhau glasshouse Glass has been made at Schreiberhau in the Riesengebirge since the c14. A new factory called the **Gräflich Schaffgottsch'sche Josephinenhütte** was founded nearby at Marienthal in 1840–42 by the local Graf – Leopold Schaffgottsch. It was under the direction of **Franz Pohl** (1813–84) who made it one of the most notable German glass factories of its time, successfully combining traditional techniques with current BIEDERMEIER forms. The virtuoso techniques of c16 Venetian glass were also imitated. It achieved international fame at the Great Exhibition in London in 1851 when a wide range of its products was shown, from huge ruby-glass vases to *millefiore* paper-weights. From the 1870s onwards it produced much enamelled glass and, in the 1880s, iridescent glass – though without developing Art Nouveau forms until after 1900. In 1923 it was amalgamated with the PETERSDORF GLASSHOUSE and with **Neumann & Staebe** in Hermsdorf under the name of **Jo-He-Ky-AG.** The factory, now in Poland, is still active.

Lit: B. Mundt, *Historismus*, Catalogue of the Kunstgewerbemuseum, Berlin, vol. VII, Berlin 1973.

Schrezheim pottery A faience factory near Ellwangen in Württemberg founded in 1752 by

Johann Baptist **Bux** (1716–1800). Its most interesting products are on an unusually large scale – a Rococo altarpiece with many angels in the chapel of St Anthony at Schrezheim (*c.*1773–5) and a statue of St John Nepomuk (Mainfrankisches Museum, Würzburg). It also produced tureens in the form of boars' heads, vegetables, etc., and plaques in the form of pictures with scrolled frames, in addition to the usual household wares. On the earlier products decorations are in high-temperature colours, on the later in enamel colours. After the founder's death the factory was carried on by his son and sons-in-law and their descendants until 1872. (For factory mark *see* p. 887.)

Lit: H. Erdner & G. K. Nagel, *Die Fayencefabrik zu Schrezheim*, Ellwangen/Jagst 1972; K. Hüseler, *Deutsche Fayencen*, Stuttgart 1956.

Schübler, Johann Jakob (1689–1741). He was a notable German Baroque furniture designer, and also a mathematician, architect, painter and sculptor. He claimed to have abandoned 'fantasy, deceptive taste and insinuating fashion' in favour of 'geometrical measurements'. His most notable inventions in furniture appear in his *Nützliche Vorstellung* . . . published in Nuremberg in 1730. It includes his ingenious designs for a dumbwaiter, a collapsible bed and a merchant's desk on a polygonal plan with projecting bookrests and writing platforms and a revolving drum in which ledgers and correspondence might be kept. But many of his other furniture designs are so heavily muffled in scrolls and furbelows that it is difficult to appreciate the nice mathematical calculations on which they were based. His designs for beds, cabinets, tables, commodes, chaises longues, etc. were first issued in Augsburg in *c.*1720 and were reissued in twenty editions. They were evidently very widely diffused and used, for Batty LANGLEY borrowed one of his designs for a dressing-table.

Lit: H. Honour, *Cabinet Makers and Furniture Designers*, London and New York 1969.

Schuchard, Georg, *see* MAGDEBURG POTTERIES.

J. J. Schübler: design for pedestal table and chair, Augsburg, 1720

M. Schumacher: chest-of-drawers and cabinet, 1736 (Schloss Nymphenburg, Munich)

Schumacher, Martin (1695–1781). German cabinet-maker working at Ansbach, he was the son of **Daniel Schumacher** (1663–1728) who was also a craftsman in the service of the Margrave. Martin Schumacher's earliest known work, dated 1736, is probably his best and is among the most notable pieces of German furniture of its period – a chest of drawers surmounted by a cabinet and crowned with a clock, very finely decorated with Boulle type marquetry. He was probably trained under J. MATUSCH whom he succeeded as Court cabinet-maker (*Hofebenist*) at Ansbach in 1737. He continued to make furniture for the Margraves of Ansbach until 1778. *Illustrated previous page.*

Lit: H. Kreisel, *Die Kunst des deutschen Möbels*, vol. ii, Munich 1970.

Schuppe, John (*fl.*1753–73). A London silversmith, presumably of Dutch origin, he specialized in cow creamers.

Schwanhardt, Georg (1601–67). German engraver of glass and rock crystal working in Nuremberg, a pupil of K. LEHMANN whose privileges he inherited in 1622. A master of the technique of wheel engraving which he generally used in combination with delicate work in diamond point, he decorated vessels and panels with portraits or figures in landscapes surrounded with formal Baroque scroll-work. His two sons **Georg the younger** (d.1676) and **Heinrich** (d.1693) and three daughters were also glass engravers. Heinrich is credited with the invention of a technique of etching on glass, and a panel decorated in this way and dated 1686 (Germanisches Nationalmuseum, Nuremberg) is attributed to him.

Lit: R. Schmidt, *Das Glas*, Berlin/Leipzig 1922; W. B. Honey, *Glass: A Handbook*, London 1946.

Schwarzburg porcelain factory A short-lived concern at Unterweissbach in Schwarzburg-Rudolfstadt, styled the *Schwarzburger Werkstätten für Porzellankunst*, founded in 1908 by **Max Adolf Pfeiffer** who directed it until 1913 when it merged with a factory in VOLKSTÄDT. It specialized in figures after models by **Ernst Barlach** (1870–1938) – notably those of stocky Russian peasants. P. SCHEURICH, Otto Thiem and others also provided models. The Barlach figures are plain white, the others sometimes decorated in underglaze or enamel colours.

Lit: O. Pelka, *Keramik der Neuzeit*, Leipzig 1924.

Schwarzlot Decorations on glass, faience and porcelain in black enamel, sometimes with iron-red and gilding. Such decorations had been used by glass painters for some time before they were first applied to faience, probably by J. SCHÄPER in Nuremberg *c.*1660. They became very popular with HAUSMALER in the late C17 and early C18. (For additional illustration *see* SCHÄPER.)

Schwarzlot decoration on a Berlin porcelain teapot, c.1768 (Berlin Porzellansammlung, Belvedere Charlottenburg, Berlin)

Schwerdfeger, Ferdinand (d.*c.*1798). German furniture-maker who settled in Paris *c.*1760 and became one of the leading craftsmen at the very end of the *ancien régime*. He became a *maître-ébéniste* in 1786 and was much patronized by the Queen. Though rather Teutonic and heavy, his furniture is of very high quality and usually of simple design with plain mahogany veneers, e.g. his commode in the Museum of Fine Arts, Boston. But his most celebrated piece, an *armoire à bijoux* made for the Queen in 1786 (now at Versailles), is anything but simple, being over-decorated with Sèvres plaques, mother-of-pearl, glass-paintings in the Pompeian manner and very elaborate sculptural gilt-bronze mounts, perhaps by THOMIRE.

Lit: F. J. B. Watson, *Louis XVI Furniture*, London 1960.

Schwinger, Hermann (1640–83). An accomplished Nuremberg glass engraver working in a style similar to that of G. SCHWANHARDT, decorating tall goblets with delicately executed mythological scenes and heraldic achievements (dated example of 1681 in the Victoria & Albert Museum, London).

Lit: W. B. Honey, *Glass: A Handbook*, London 1946.

Sciacca potteries, *see* SICILIAN POTTERIES.

Sconce A wall-light consisting of a bracket candlestick with a polished back-plate to reflect the light. From the late C17 onwards the back-plate is often a mirror. Elaborate, and especially Rococo, sconces are sometimes called 'girandoles'.

Sconce, silver wall-light by John Bodington, London, 1710 (Private Collection)

Scotch carpet, *see* DOUBLE CLOTH CARPET.

Scotia A half-rounded concave moulding, as between two torus mouldings on the base of a column.

Scratch blue ware A type of English C18 salt-glazed stoneware decorated before firing with incised designs or inscriptions into which a mixture of clay and cobalt was rubbed: dated specimens range 1724–76. It appears to have superseded the slightly earlier scratch brown ware on which the decorations were coloured with a brown pigment mixed with clay. The technique was revived by DOULTON in the 1870s using black and brown pigments.

Scratch carving Decorations consisting of simple outline drawings roughly incised on the humbler types of C16–C17 furniture.

Scrimshaw work Carvings on bone, ivory, shells or wood, made by sailors (especially American) as a pastime on long whaling and other voyages. The origin of the word is unknown. There is a reference to 'skrim shunder articles' in H. Melville's *Moby Dick* (1851).

Scroll foot The foot especially of a mid-C18 English chair-leg in the form of a tight scroll. *Illustrated next page.*

Scroll handle The handle usually of a silver or pewter vessel in the form of the letter S. *Illustrated next page.*

Scroll moulding A moulding in the form of a partly rolled scroll of paper.

Scroll salt A salt-cellar of silver or pottery surmounted by three little scrolled arms, made in C17 England.

Scroll top An American term for an open swan-necked PEDIMENT on a piece of furniture.

Scrutoire C17 English term for a desk, usually in the form of a box in which papers and writing materials could be kept. There is no clear distinction between it and the (probably later) term ESCRITOIRE.

Sculpteur French for sculptor, but the term was also used for the craftsman who executed carved decorations on chairs, tables, etc. for a MENUISIER. A C18 French chair was usually the work of four different craftsmen, each with his own

Scroll foot

Double scroll handles on a Charles II silver-gilt cup, English, c.1680–85

establishment – the *menuisier* who made the frame, the *sculpteur* who carved the ornaments on it, the *doreur* who gilded it and the *tapissier* who upholstered it.

Seal-top spoon The commonest type of English C15–C17 spoon with an hexagonal stem terminating in a little disc-capped baluster.

Seaweed marquetry Modern term for an English C17–C18 type of marquetry decoration usually composed of walnut and geometrically shaped panels of such woods as holly or boxwood which have a very richly figured grain somewhat recalling seaweed. It was much used for the fronts of long-case clocks.

Secession or **Sezession** A group of artists and architects who seceded from the conservative academy in Vienna and established a new organization called the *Wiener Sezession*. Notable among them were Gustav Klimt, Kolo MOSER, Josef HOFFMANN and J. M. OLBRICH who in 1898 designed their headquarters and exhibition premises. Though concerned mainly with architecture and the figurative arts, the Secession also played a role of great importance in the development of the decorative arts in Austria as several of its members were designers of furniture, metalwork, ceramics, textiles, etc. It also exhibited the work of foreign designers, notably C. R. MACKINTOSH and other members of the GLASGOW SCHOOL, introducing them to the Central European public. It has thus given its name to the Austrian version of ART NOUVEAU and the products of the WIENER WERKSTÄTTE founded by Hoffmann and Moser. The Secession still survives but has played little part in the decorative arts since the 1920s.

Lit: R. Weissenberger, *Die Wiener Secession*, Vienna 1972.

Second Empire style The style, or rather styles, current in France under Napoleon III (President 1848, Emperor 1852, abdicated 1870). No attempt was made to revive the first EMPIRE STYLE even though some of its practitioners still survived, notably FONTAINE. The Empress Eugenie, who was more interested in the arts than her husband, identified herself with Marie Antoinette rather than with Josephine and therefore revived the LOUIS XVI STYLE. Makers of expensive reproduction furniture flourished, notably BARBEDIENNE, BEURDELEY and GROHÉ, while CHRISTOFLE turned out similar *bronzes d'ameublement* and table-silver, usually electroplated. Wallpapers were printed in imitation of Louis XVI *boiseries*. The fashionable sculptor CARRIER-BELLEUSE designed self-consciously artistic furniture and silver: the architect VIOLLET-LE-DUC designed Gothic Revival church plate and schemes for interior decoration. There was a Renaissance

Second Empire style: sideboard or 'grand buffet' (Ministère des Finances, Paris)

Second Empire style: wallpaper by Desfossé & Karth, Le Jardin d'hiver, *1853 (Musée des Arts Décoratifs, Paris)*

revival (SAINT-PORCHAIRE POTTERY) and a Baroque revival; and the fashion for JAPONAISERIE began in the 1860s. The eclecticism, as well as the vulgar ostentation, of the period is very evident in the work of the leading designer Liénard, author of *Spécimens de la décoration et de l'ornementation au XIX siècle* (1866). Of non-Revivalist furnishings the most notable are the armchairs, sofas and *indiscrets*, of ample buxom curves, abundantly upholstered, tasselled and buttoned. The tone of the period is indicated by Guizot's remark, 'enrichissez-vous' which might well have been the watchword for the creators of its most opulent monument, the Paris Opéra (1861–75).

Secrétaire French term for various types of writing desk in which papers could be kept secret,

Secrétaire en pente *by J. Dubois (Patino Collection, Paris)*

Sécretaire à abattant *by G. Haupt, Stockholm, 1778 (Royal Collection, Tullgarn Palace, Stockholm)*

i.e. covered up and locked away. The term seems first to have been applied to the *secrétaire en pente*, otherwise called a *bureau en pente* – a free-standing desk with a lean-to fall-front which, when open and supported on struts or hinges, served as a flat platform on which to write and, when closed, as a lid for the area where papers might be left undisturbed. A double *secrétaire en pente*, like two placed back to back and thus having two flaps enabling two people to write at it facing one another, is called a *secrétaire en dos d'âne*. A *secrétaire à cylindre* also called a *bureau à cylindre*, made from *c*.1750 onwards, has a quarter cylinder roll top which covers the writing platform and a set of drawers and pigeon holes at the back. A *secrétaire à abattant* (otherwise called a *secrétaire en armoire* or *en tombeau*, in English a 'writing cabinet') was first made in the C17 and was very popular in late-C18 .France. It stands against a wall and looks like a cabinet or cupboard with the fall-front flap closed vertically. *See also* BUREAU.

Secretary Modern term for a desk, especially a fall-front writing cabinet mounted on a stand or chest of drawers. The term does not exactly correspond with the French SECRÉTAIRE. Nor is there any clear distinction in English between a secretary and a BUREAU.

Seddon, George (1727–1801). Born in Lancashire, he was apprenticed in London in 1743 and set up his own cabinet-making workshop there *c*.1760. By 1768 he was described as 'one of the most eminent of cabinet-makers of London' and his firm became one of the largest and best known. He was employing several hundred craftsmen in the 1780s and carrying a large stock of very wide range (known from accounts of his losses by fire in 1768 and 1783). In 1785 he took his elder son **George** into partnership and in 1788 his younger son **Thomas** (d.1804). In 1793 he took his son-in-law **Thomas Shackleton** into the firm which was known until 1800 as Seddon, Sons and Shackleton. In 1826 Messrs Thomas and George Seddon opened a new West End branch in London and the business continued until the mid C19. Despite the firm's very large output remarkably little furniture by Seddon is known and that is of unexceptional though good quality. In the mid C19 Gothic pieces were made to the design of W. BURGES and **John Pollard Seddon** (1827–1906). The latter also designed furniture for MORRIS, and ceramics, and published *Progress in art and architecture . . .*, London 1852.

Lit: R. Edwards and M. Jourdain, *Georgian Cabinet Makers*, London 1955; A. Coleridge, *Chippendale Furniture*, London 1968.

Seefried, P. A., *see* KELSTERBACH POTTERY & PORCELAIN FACTORY.

Seger, Herrmann, *see* BERLIN PORCELAIN FACTORY and CRYSTALLINE GLAZE and FLAMBÉ GLAZE.

Seguin, *see* VINCENNES PORCELAIN FACTORY.

Sehna carpets A type of PERSIAN CARPET woven in the village of Sehna. The pile, which is tied with the GHIORDES rather than the Sehna or PERSIAN KNOT, tends to be very short. Rather tight HERAT and cone patterns are usual.

Sehna knot, *see* PERSIAN KNOT.

Seignouret, François (1768–after 1853). French cabinet-maker who settled in New Orleans *c.*1815 with a workshop in Royal Street until 1853 when he returned to France. He specialized in massive pieces of furniture with much carved work, generally in an over-ripe Neo-Rococo style. In his later years he shared the fashionable clientèle of New Orleans with P. MALLARD.

Seltzer-Rank family, *see* PENNSYLVANIA DUTCH STYLE.

Semainier In furniture, a case, rack or other piece with seven divisions or drawers, one for each day of the week.

Semis An heraldic term also used in bookbinding for a diaper design made by the repetition of one or more small tooled ornaments.

Sené, Jean-Baptiste-Claude (1748–1803). He was the most important Louis XVI period chair-maker after JACOB whom he equalled as a craftsman though not as a designer. He did not, in fact, design most of his chairs but relied on such artists as Gondouin and DUGOURC. He was the son and grandson of *menuisiers* (examples of the work of his father **Claude I Sené** (1724–92) are in the Musée des Arts Décoratifs, Paris). He became a *maître* in 1769 and by 1784 counted among the main suppliers of the Court (appointed *fournisseur da la Couronne* in 1785), together with FOLIOT and BOULARD with whom he sometimes collaborated. His work for the Court was probably executed under the direction of HAURÉ. He collaborated with several different *sculpteurs*, notably Vallois, Laurent, Alexandre Regnier and Guérin. His work for Marie Antoinette's bedroom at Fontainebleau in 1787 was one of the last major commissions of the *ancien régime*. His style is characterized by his use of fluted columns, caryatids, fasces, etc., and by his device of placing detached columns flanking the backs of his chairs. He also favoured lyre-backs, presumably derived from England either directly or through Jacob, as was also his use of plain mahogany. In 1785 he supplied simple Louis XIII style armchairs for the Académie de France. Despite his royal patronage his work continued to be in demand after the Revolution though he was usually employed for utilitarian jobs, e.g. he supplied two hundred desks for government officials. Examples of his work are in the Louvre and the Musée des Arts Décoratifs in Paris; the Victoria & Albert Museum, London; the Metropolitan Museum, New York.

Lit: I. Verlet, *Le Mobilier royal français*, Paris 1945–55; F. J. B. Watson, *The Wrightsman Collection: Furniture*, New York 1966.

Serapi carpets, *see* PERSIAN CARPETS.

Serpentine front An undulating, Rococo type of surface, e.g. chests of drawers with convex centre and concave ends: a less exaggerated form of BOMBÉ front.

Serre papier, *see* CARTONNIER.

Serrurier-Bovy, Gustave (1858–1910). Belgian Art Nouveau designer of furniture and interiors, with a shop in Liège. He visited England in 1884 and was much impressed by the products of the ARTS AND CRAFTS movement. But by 1894 he claimed to have rid his designs 'of any reminiscences from past or English styles'. He developed a style less sculptural and plainer than that of his compatriot HORTA and influenced H. VAN DE VELDE.

Serviteur-fidèle, *see* TABLE, *serviteur-fidèle.*

Serviteur-muet, *see* TABLE, *serviteur-muet.*

Seto potteries One of the most important centres for the production of ceramics in Japan, situated in Owari province around the city of Seto (10 miles north-east of Nagoya) and active from an early date, traditionally from the C9 A.D. It is perhaps the most famous of the potteries known as the 'Six Ancient Kilns', the others being TOKONAME, SHIGARAKI, TAMBA, BIZEN and ECHIZEN. The earliest wares attributed to the Seto potteries are large globular jars with a natural ash glaze, made in the late Heian period (898–1184) but similar to the much earlier SUE POTTERY. In the Kamakura period (1185–1338) wares were made in imitation of those of T'ANG and SUNG pottery but with much coarser clay and usually with brown or brownish-green wood-ash glazes. But the most handsome products, the so-called 'flower' Seto wares, also date from the C13–C14 and include vases with incised designs of formalized flowers covered with ash glazes or iron glazes. These wares were extensively imitated and faked in later times. According to Japanese tradition the great early master potter of the district was TOSHIRO but his very existence is now doubted. Of the later products of the kilns the best known are the vessels, especially TEA CEREMONY WARES, of brown or grey stoneware occasionally decorated with paintings in iron or copper oxide and covered with thick sometimes almost opaque feldspathic glazes. But those of the C17 and C18 are difficult to distinguish from the wares of the MINO POTTERIES. In the C19 products included kitchen wares – herring plates and oil dishes – made in very large quantities but often attractively decorated with freely painted birds, landscapes, etc. in iron black or brown or underglaze blue. Blue-and-white porcelain was also made in the district. For the wares known as 'Old Seto Ware', 'Black Seto Ware' and 'Yellow Seto Ware', *see* MINO POTTERIES.

Lit: S. Jenyns, *Japanese Potteries,* London 1971.

Seto ware tea bowl (Victoria & Albert Museum)

Settee A seat with back and, usually, arms; large enough for two or more persons. More comfortable than a SETTLE and more formal than a SOFA, it invites the user to sit but not to lounge or recline upon it. It was popular in England from the early C17 onwards, though largely superseded by the sofa during the C19. There were various types, e.g. the love-seat, an armchair enlarged laterally to accommodate two persons side by side similar to the French CAUSEUSE. The **Hall Settee** is an enlarged hall chair, with a solid wood seat, made in England in the late C18 and early C19. *Illustrated opposite page.*

Settle In medieval inventories the term is interchangeable with BENCH, but it is now applied only to a bench with back and arms, a notable type of medieval furniture which continued to be made, especially for farmhouses and taverns, until the C19. The earlier form was revived by William MORRIS and his associates.

Seuter, Bartholomäus (1678–1754). Member of a notable family of Augsburg craftsmen, he was a goldsmith, engraver, silk-dyer and dealer in maiolica but is best remembered as a *Hausmaler*

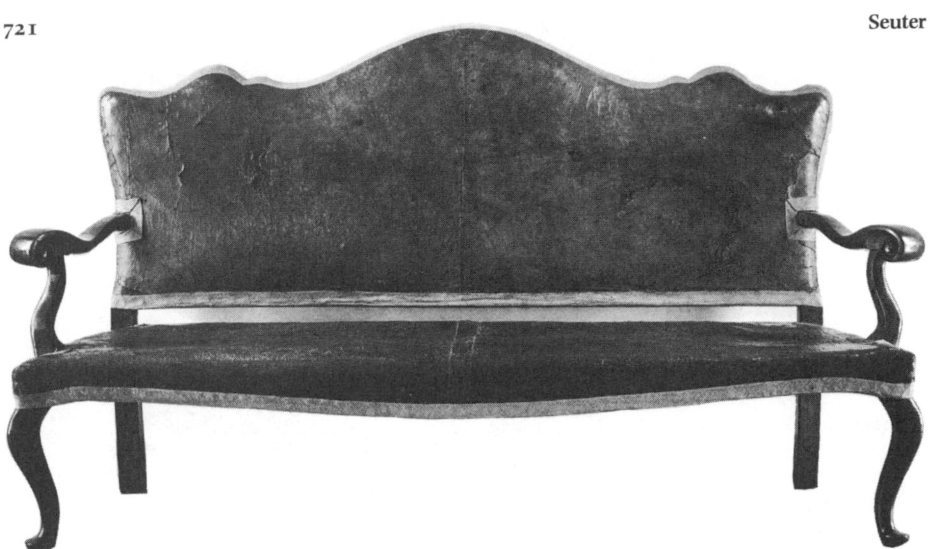

Settee, Italian, early c18 (Fondazione Giorgio Cini, Venice)

Settee, French, by L. Delanois, 1761–70 (Louvre)

working on NUREMBERG and BAYREUTH faience and MEISSEN PORCELAIN. Before 1729 he was decorating white porcelain which he acquired from Meissen. He worked in gold, *Schwarzlot* and polychrome, painting bunches of flowers, figure scenes and chinoiseries. His figure subjects are often surrounded with borders of gilt scrollwork (a row of C-shaped scrolls with a dot in the centre of each C is sometimes regarded as an identifying characteristic of his work). He appears to have employed several assistants in his studio. As an engraver he executed plates for J. W. Weinmann's *Phylanthus Iconographia* (Augsburg 1737) which provided a source for the DEUTSCHE BLUMEN on Meissen porcelain. His brother **Abraham** (1688/9–1747) was also a notable *Hausmaler* specializing in the decoration of porcelain with gold chinoiseries.

Lit: G. E. Pazaurek, *Deutsche Fayence- und Porzellan-Hausmaler*, Leipzig 1925; S. Ducret in *Keramos* 37 (1967), pp. 3–62.

Seville potteries Established under the Moors by the C11 and producing fine large well-heads, water and oil jars, and two-handled vases. But apart from a well-head of 1039 (Museo Arqueológico, Madrid) surviving specimens are difficult to date. The most important products were tiles made after the Christian reconquest of 1248 – plain coloured tiles which could be fitted together to make mosaic patterns as in the Alcazar in Seville (1350–66), CUERDA SECA from the mid C15 and CUENCA tiles from the late C15. Such tiles were exported to other parts of Europe. And tile-workers from Seville are said to have been employed in a pottery at Granada to make tiles for the Alhambra. Dishes and drug vases with decorations similar to those on *cuerda seca* tiles have been attributed to Seville. Designs are usually abstract or heraldic. Early in the C16 the Italian Renaissance style was introduced for large pictorial panels of tiles by F. NICULOSO and, rather later, the northern Renaissance manner by CRISTOBAL DE AUGUSTA. Tiles continued to be made in the C17 and C18.

Lit: A. Lane, *Victoria & Albert Museum: Guide to Tiles*, London 1939.

Seville earthenware tiles decorated with coloured glaze (cuerda seca), *C15* *(British Museum)*

Sèvres (or **Vincennes-Sèvres**) **porcelain factory** French national porcelain factory, catering for

Sèvres porcelain factory: the enamelling and gilding workshop, 1823 (from a Sèvres plate decorated by C. Develly)

Sèvres porcelain factory: modelling workshop, 1823 (from a Sèvres plate decorated by C. Develly)

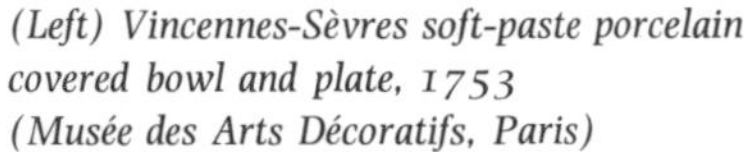
(Left) Vincennes-Sèvres soft-paste porcelain covered bowl and plate, 1753 (Musée des Arts Décoratifs, Paris)

Sèvres soft-paste porcelain sugar bowl, painted by Elisa le Guay, 1761 (Musée de Manufacture de Sèvres)

the luxury trade, it led European ceramic fashions from *c.*1760 to 1815. It was founded in 1738 in the château de Vincennes with workmen from CHANTILLY and in 1745 was granted a twenty-year monopoly for the production of 'porcelain in the style of the Saxon, that is to say, painted and gilded with human figures'. Products of this early 'Vincennes period' are in soft paste (which was to be used exclusively until 1768 and occasionally until 1800) but of uneven quality, generally inferior to those of Chantilly, MENNECY and SAINT CLOUD. The most numerous are flowers which were mounted on wire stems or gilt-bronze scrolls or applied to vases, chandeliers, jugs, etc., in the manner of MEISSEN flowers. The great period began in 1751 with the appointment of J.-J. BACHELIER as art director. Next year Louis XV became the principal shareholder (possibly under the influence of Mme de Pompadour who also had a financial interest in it). In 1753 the concern was styled the 'Manufacture royale de porcelaine' in an edict issued to strengthen its privileges and to prohibit the manufacture elsewhere in France not only of porcelain but of white pottery decorated like porcelain. The crossed Ls of the royal cipher, already used by the factory, were now officially adopted as its mark with the addition of a letter to indicate date of manufacture (thus an 'a' within the crossed Ls indicates that a piece was made in 1753). The factory was moved in 1756 to a new building at Sèvres and in 1759 it was taken over by the king who became its chief client and its chief salesman. An annual sale of Sèvres products was held from 1758 in the king's private dining-room at Versailles: and courtiers were expected to buy. Table-wares of the 1750s and 1760s are modelled in a very restrained Rococo style though some distinctly bizarre forms were launched by the factory, notably the *vaisseau-à-mât* and elephant candelabra invented by J.-L. DUPLESSIS. The best have brilliantly coloured enamel grounds, marking a sharp departure from the white backgrounds characteristic of earlier French porcelain. Similar ground colours had been used at Meissen, but those developed by the painters and chemists of the Sèvres factory are of unequalled evenness of both tone and texture. The most famous are the dark *gros bleu* used from 1749 onwards, the turquoise *bleu celeste* from 1752 onwards, *jaune jonquille* from 1753 onwards, a pea-green from 1756 onwards (these four developed by Jean Hellot (1685–1766), decorator and chemist at Sèvres from 1745 until his death), and a rose-pink (later called *rose Pompadour*) invented in 1757 but little used after 1766. These colours are decorated with delicately tooled thick gold scrolls and form the backgound to reserved white medallions or panels painted with flowers, birds, or figure subjects in the style of Boucher. The brilliance of gilding and colour give such wares an air of well-bred opulence most appealing to the wealthy. They are showy and expensive-looking without a trace of vulgarity. (These soft-paste wares are still among the most expensive in the world.) Statuettes were also produced: at first they were painted as in Germany but some were left glittering white. But the most famous by far are the biscuit figures and groups made of a paste invented by Bachelier before 1753. Whether of mythological or rustic subjects they reveal the influence of Boucher's gay Rococo paintings until 1757 when FALCONET was appointed chief modeller and introduced a gently classicising style. Pigalle, Houdon and Clodion were among the other notable sculptors who provided models. Later figures are more markedly Neo-Classical, especially those by L.-S. BOIZOT who was chief modeller 1774–1802. Hard-paste porcelain was made from 1768 when supplies of kaolin and petuntse were discovered at Saint-Yrieix and the production of soft-paste wares gradually decreased. This entailed the development of a new range of high-temperature ground colours including brown, black, tortoiseshell and a new dark blue. Designs for all products were modified to fit in with the Louis XVI style. Forms were simplified, lines were straightened, but the colour schemes tended to grow richer, gilding was still

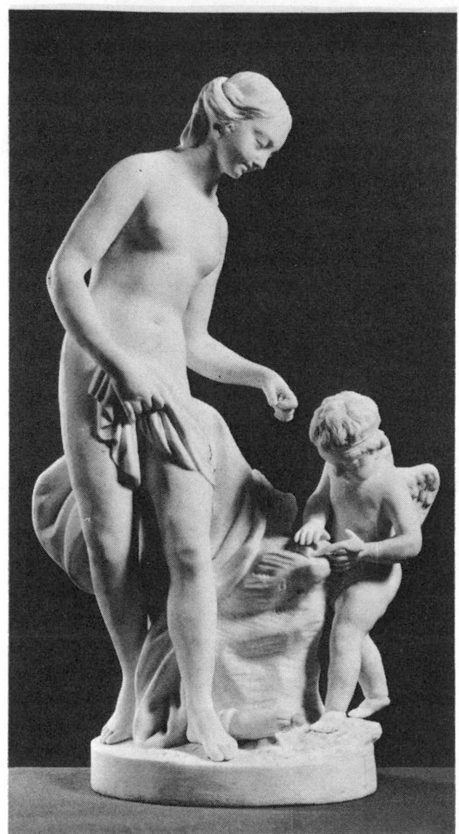

Sèvres biscuit porcelain group of Venus and Cupid, c.1765 (Victoria & Albert Museum)

more lavishly employed, the so-called JEWELLED DECORATIONS were used and painted decorations, especially of sentimental and mythological scenes, assumed greater importance. (Even after the relaxation of the Sèvres privileges in 1766 no other French factories were allowed to produce porcelain with coloured grounds or gilding.) Plaques delicately painted with sprays of flowers were made for the adornment of furniture from *c.*1760 onwards (see CARLIN and RISENBURGH). The factory employed a large staff of painters who signed their works with symbols or initials. In the 1780s some imitations of WEDGWOOD jasper wares were produced, partly to satisfy the cult of *Anglomania*, partly (and for the first time) to compete with a rival factory.

In 1793 the factory was declared state property, and the letters R.F. (République Française) were used as a mark in place of the royal cipher. Moulds of royal busts were broken and much undecorated porcelain was sold, to be bought by painters (many of them English) and decorated in their studios. The staff was greatly reduced and production nearly stopped. But in 1800 **Alexandre Brongniart** (1770–1847) was appointed director. A talented adminstrator and scientist, he quickly put the concern on its feet. He abandoned the tricky and expensive manufacture of soft paste, invented a new formula for hard paste and developed a whole new range of pigments with which it could be coloured, facilitating the production of wares as richly toned as (and often imitative of) oil paintings. The factory was extensively patronized by Napoleon for whom some of the most ambitious products were made – huge vases decorated with allegories of his victories, tables set with painted porcelain plaques, extensive dinner services. Forms were based either on antiquities (Egyptian as well as Greek and Roman) or on the geometry of cylinder and sphere, and decoration was very rich with much gilding and scenic painting. The architects PERCIER & FONTAINE were called on for designs, paintings were executed by artists as eminent as J.-B. Isabey. With these pieces the factory created an EMPIRE STYLE in ceramics which was imitated by most other porcelain factories and remained popular long after the defeat of Napoleon. But after 1815 decorations became increasingly fussy. Plaques imitating oil paintings were produced in quantity.

The factory was reorganized in 1848 and the painters who had specialized in making copies after Old Masters on porcelain were dismissed. From this time greater attention was applied to the porcelain itself, and a new emphasis on rather pale decorations (instead of those in opaque colours), which emphasized the quality of the paste, became apparent. Several C18 patterns were revived and imitations of C18 Meissen and of Chinese 'egg-shell' porcelain were made. The PÂTE-SUR-PÂTE technique of decoration was introduced and developed especially by M.-L. SOLON. The factory moved to new premises near Saint-Cloud in 1876 and a committee of artists, critics and potters was appointed to suggest ways

Sèvres porcelain urn with painted view of Sanssouci, Potsdam, by Robert, c.1805 (Château de Malmaison)

Sèvres porcelain 'artistic furniture' exhibited at the Great Exhibition, 1851

of improving standards. A notable sculptor, CARRIER-BELLEUSE, was appointed artistic director: products included very elborate vases with much sculptural ornament and also simply shaped Chinese-style vases with *flambé* glazes. Japanese influence is conspicuous in many products, especially table-wares painted by A. DAMMOUSE and F. BRACQUEMOND. In 1887

Sèvres porcelain plate decorated by Dammouse, pre-1880 (Musée des Arts Décoratifs, Paris)

T. DECK was appointed director – the first potter to hold the post – and introduced various new types of materials, notably a soft paste and a stoneware for architectural ornaments. Art Nouveau was adopted in the later 1890s and various products in this style were shown at the International Exhibition of 1900 in Paris – most notably a table decoration consisting of a dozen statuettes of girls in long dresses dancing with scarves above their heads, from models by Agathon Léonard. The ART DECO style was taken up in the 1920s (some pieces were designed by the cabinet-maker RUHLMANN), but in the present century the factory has been mainly engaged in producing copies or simplified versions of C18 wares.

No porcelain wares have been as carefully and consistently marked as those of Sèvres since 1753. The only exceptions are the biscuit figures to which no factory mark was applied until 1860. (For factory marks *see* p. 887.)

Lit: P. Verlet *et al.*, *La porcelaine de Sèvres*, Paris 1954; S. Eriksen, *The James A. Rothschild Collection at Waddesdon Manor: Sèvres Porcelain*, London 1968; M. Ernould-Gandouet, *La Céramique en France au XIX siècle*, Paris 1969; J. Terrasson, *Madame de Pompadour et la création de la porcelaine en France*, Fribourg 1969.

Sewing table A small work-table with drawers and often a cloth bag to hold needlework.

Seymour, John (*c.*1738–1818). Leading cabinet-maker working in the Federal style in Boston, Mass. He was born and trained in England and emigrated to America with his son and future partner **Thomas** in 1785, settling first in Maine and later, in 1794, in Boston. His furniture, which owes much to English design books by HEPPLEWHITE, SHERATON, etc., is notable for its fine finish, rich veneers, delicate banding and inlaid pilasters. His tambour desks with straight tapering legs, inspired by Hepplewhite (fine example in the Boston Museum of Fine Arts), appear to have been widely imitated. He may also have introduced as a decorative device the reeded colonnettes which were much used by other cabinet-makers in Boston and Salem.

Lit: V. C. Stoneman, *John and Thomas Seymour, Cabinet-makers in Boston*, Boston, Mass. 1959; C. F. Montgomery, *American Furniture: The Federal Period*, New York and London 1966.

Sgabello Italian word for a stool or bench. Although it does not denote any particular form, this word is generally used outside Italy to describe a C16 type chair with solid carved back, wooden seat and carved end-boards, front and back, instead of legs.

Sgraffiato or **Sgraffito** (Italian: *scratched*) **ware** LEAD-GLAZED POTTERY decorated in a technique which originated in China and was transmitted by way of Persia and Byzantium to Europe. Moulded or thrown clay vessels are dipped into a bath of white slip (pipe-clay mixed with water) and then fired; decorations are scratched on the surface to reveal the darker body underneath (and sometimes filled with high-temperature pigments); they are then dipped in transparent lead-glaze and fired again. The most notable examples are those made at BOLOGNA and PADUA in the C15 and C16.

Shagreen A word derived from the Turkish *saghri* (the croup of an animal) and applied to two different substances of similar surface appearance.

1. A type of untanned leather made in Persia from the hides of asses, horses and camels: seeds were trampled into the surface when it was still moist and shaken out when it had dried, leaving small granular indentations; it was then stained.

2. Finely granulated skin of sharks and ray-fish, ground flat so that the pearl-like papillae make a granulated pattern, used since the C17 for covering small boxes, tea-caddies.

Shah 'Abbas design, *see* PERSIAN CARPETS.

Shaker furniture A uniquely American style developed by the 'Shaking Quakers' or Shakers, properly the United Society of Believers in Christ's Second Appearance, a Christian communal sect founded in England 1747, in America 1774 with headquarters at New Lebanon, N.Y. Spare, clean lines give their furniture an airy elegance; its good materials, sound craftsmanship and strictly functional design, without any flaw-masking ornament, reflect Shaker ideals of plain, simple living and scrupulous honesty. Its remarkable qualities were soon recognized; the Shakers began making it commercially at an early date, establishing communal factories; and even before the end of the C19 it was being faked. Chairs have always been the best-known type of Shaker furniture – rockers, spinning, tilting, etc. – especially the so-called 'Shaker chair' (first made in the 1820s) which derives from English farmhouse patterns (e.g. Yorkshire ladder-back) but is much more elegant and attenuated, with delicate finials on the top of the posts and an extra bar across the top from which a cushion may be hung. The tilting chair, devised *c.*1852, has balls of hardwood fitted into sockets at the bottom of the rear legs.

Lit: A. D. & F. Andrews, *Shaker Furniture,* New Haven 1937.

Shaker rocking-chair from Mt Lebanon, New York, early C19 (Philadelphia Museum of Art)

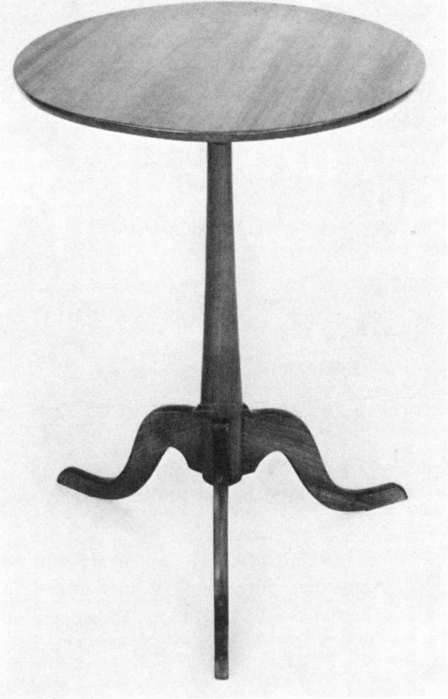

Shaker tripod table from Mt Lebanon, New York (Philadelphia Museum of Art)

Shang-Yin The earliest named Chinese dynasty, it flourished from *c.*1500 B.C. until *c.*1028 B.C. The names Shang and Yin are interchangeable. It is notable for some astonishingly accomplished and refined bronze vessels cast by the CIRE-PERDUE technique. They are of a quality seldom equalled and never surpassed at any later date or in any other country. Forms are simple, robust and massive, yet often extremely elegant, especially those of the CHÜEH and KU. The decorations, which sometimes cover most of the surface, are very rich and consist mainly of stylized animal motifs which probably had some symbolical significance. These bronzes were known from descriptions and illustrations in Chinese manuals (a selection was published in England by P. P. Thoms in 1851) but examples were first rediscovered by excavation at Anyang (Honan) in 1929 and the first to be seen in the West were those exhibited in London in 1935–6. Many have subsequently passed into European and rather more into U.S. museums, notably the Freer Gallery, Washington, and the Nelson Atkins Gallery, Kansas City. The chief types, apart from

Shang bronze vessel, lei *type (William Rockhill Nelson Gallery of Art, Kansas City)*

Shang bronze sacrificial vessel, Chüeh *type (William Rockhill Nelson Gallery of Art, Kansas City)*

the *Chüeh* and *Ku*, are the FANG-I, KUANG, TING, TSUN and YU.

Lit: B. Kalgren, *Yin and Chou Researches*, Stockholm 1935; K. E. Forster, *A Handbook of Ancient Chinese Bronzes*, Claremont, California 1949; W. Watson, *Ancient Chinese Bronzes*, London 1962.

Shaving dish, *see* BARBER'S BOWL.

Shang jade bird-dragon (William Rockhill Nelson Gallery of Art, Kansas City)

Shaving stand A stand with adjustable circular mirror and circular box with lids.

Shaw, John (1745–1829). American FEDERAL STYLE furniture-maker, born in Glasgow. He settled in Annapolis after emigrating to the U.S.A. His furniture derives from HEPPLEWHITE but is personal in style and of high quality, ranking with that of SEYMOUR and PHYFE.

Lit: C. F. Montgomery, *American Furniture: The Federal Period*, New York and London 1966.

Shearer, Thomas (*fl.*1788). He is known only because he signed most of the plates in *The Cabinet-maker's London Book of Prices*, 1788, a trade manual for the use of cabinet-makers and journeymen in estimating costs and wages (it contains detailed price schedules). But although, in contrast to HEPPLEWHITE's *Guide* issued the same year, it was not intended as a repertoire of designs it appears to have been widely used as such and a number of pieces of furniture survive which are close to Shearer's designs. His designs are in a sensible, fairly solid, unpretentiously Neo-Classical style. The book was reissued with additional plates from Hepplewhite, in 1793, 1805 and 1823.

Lit: J. Hayward in *The Connoisseur*, June 1961.

Sheerer, Mary G., *see* NEWCOMB COLLEGE POTTERY.

Sheffield plate (a) Silver wares made at Sheffield, England. (b) Wares made of copper rolled between and fused with films of silver, a cheap substitute for solid silver. The process was discovered *c.*1742 by **Thomas Boulsover** or **Bolsover** (1704–88) of Sheffield who used it for buttons and other small articles. From *c.*1760 it began to be used more extensively. Matthew BOULTON seems to have been the first to realize its great possibilities for domestic wares (coffee-pots, teapots, etc.) if the copper could be prevented from wearing through. He applied ribbons of solid silver wire at the places most liable to wear, notably along the rims and edges (this is known as 'lapping'). **Samuel Roberts the younger** (1763–1848) also developed various improvements both for silver edges and for 'rubbing in' silver shields. Boulton established high standards of quality for Sheffield plated wares and also produced them in large quantities. They gradually displaced pewter wares and remained very popular – there were factories in London, Birmingham, Dublin, Paris and elsewhere besides Sheffield – until superseded from *c.*1840 onwards by the still cheaper though less attractive ELECTROPLATE. By 1852 there was only one metal-workshop producing Sheffield Plate in Sheffield.

Sheffield Plate is usually unmarked though Boulton (two suns) and Samuel Roberts the younger (a bell) consistently marked their work. Samuel Roberts the younger was the son of a Sheffield Plate maker. Until 1823 he was in partnership with **George Cadman.** In 1826 the firm became Roberts, Smith & Co., and in 1834 Smith, Sissons & Co. Of the many other makers of Sheffield Plate the following may be mentioned: **Thomas Bradbury** (1763–1838) who was in partnership with **Thomas Watson** from 1795 to 1832; **Joseph Hancock** (*c.*1711–91); **Thomas Law** (1717–75); and **Tudor & Leader** the earliest large scale manufacturer, from *c.*1760 onwards until 1783 when it became **Tudor, Leader and Nicolson. Thomas Leader** died in 1797 and the firm split up. In Birmingham **Sir Edward Thomason** (1769–1835) founded a Sheffield Plate firm in 1793 which was taken over on his death by **George Richmond Collis** who acquired several models from **Rundell, Bridge & Rundell** in 1842 and put them into production.

Lit: Frederick Bradbury, *History of Old Sheffield Plate,* London 1912; Edward Wenham, *Old Sheffield Plate,* London 1955.

Shekwan potteries A number of southern Chinese factories in Kuantung province producing since the MING period brown stoneware vessels, especially large jars, with a thick blue, green and grey streaked and flecked glaze. They catered extensively for the export trade.

Sheldon, William (d.1570). The founder of the first important English tapestry factory, established on his estates at Barcheston (Warwickshire) and Bordesley (Worcestershire) shortly after 1560, under the direction of **Richard Hyches** (d.1612) who had learnt the art of tapestry-weaving in the Low Countries. The enterprise was continued by his son **Ralph Sheldon** (1537–1613) and his grandson **Ralph the younger.** The factory was patronized mainly by the local gentry. Its most notable products are a set of maps of English counties (1588, Bodleian Library, Oxford) and a fair number of smaller pieces such as cushion covers, all rather coarse with stiff figures, little pastoral landscapes, formalized birds and flowers, etc. but not without charm (they are as homely and unsophisticated as Elizabethan furniture). Several hangings have been attributed to the factory, a *Judgement of Paris* (Victoria & Albert Museum), four scenes from the *Story of Judah* (one in the Birmingham Museum) and a set

Sheldon tapestry factory: detail of a valance woven in wool, silk and gold threads, early c17 (Victoria & Albert Museum)

of *Four Seasons* dated 1611 at Hatfield House, Hertfordshire.

Lit: J. Humphreys, *Elizabethan Sheldon Tapestries*, London 1929.

Shell work Decorations made of seashells arranged in geometrical or floral patterns and applied to such objects as small caskets and sometimes even to whole wall-surfaces, especially grottoes. The art of shell work became a popular pastime in the late C18 and C19 and in fact was practised almost exclusively by amateurs.

Shelton pottery, *see* STAFFORDSHIRE POTTERIES.

Shemakha carpets, *see* CAUCASIAN CARPETS.

Shepherd's crook arm The arm of a chair or settee carved in a curving form reminiscent of a shepherd's crook, popular mainly in England in the early and mid C18.

Sheraton, Thomas (1751–1806). Sheraton gave his name to the last phase of English C18 furniture, the elegant and sophisticated post-HEPPLEWHITE and pre-REGENCY phase of the 1790s in which the rectilinear Adamesque Neo-Classical style reached its apogee. Though he described himself as a cabinet-maker not a single piece of furniture by him has been identified and his fame rests entirely on his books of designs, especially *The Cabinet-Maker and Upholsterer's Drawing-Book* (issued in parts 1791–4). Surprisingly few pieces can even be directly related to his designs and these 'book pieces', as they are called, are usually of a simplified or modified character. He was born in Stockton-on-Tees and settled in London *c.*1790. An ardent Baptist, he published religious tracts as well as furniture designs and put forward schemes for evangelizing the villages around London. He left London on being ordained a Baptist minister for Stockton and Marston in 1800 but seems to have returned two years later. In 1804 his mind gave way and he died in poverty.

It is highly improbable that Sheraton had a workshop or ever made any furniture. On a trade card he had printed *c.*1795 he declared that he 'Teaches Perspective, Architecture and Ornaments, makes Designs for Cabinet-Makers and sells all kinds of Drawing Books &c.' This probably gives an accurate account of his activities. He is not known to have provided designs for any particular piece of furniture except in one case – that of a somewhat preposterous grand piano in satinwood with Wedgwood and Tassie medallions, made in 1796 by John Broadwood for presentation to Queen Maria Louisa of Spain.

His *Drawing-Book* was addressed primarily to the trade and its aim was practical – to acquaint cabinet-makers with the most up-to-date designs. He remarks that 'in conversing with cabinet makers' he found 'no one individual equally experienced in every job of work. There are certain pieces made in one shop that are not manufactured in another' and he had therefore applied 'to the best workmen in different shops, to obtain their assistance in the explanation of such pieces as they have been most acquainted with'. He frequently acknowledges his indebtedness to those who had helped him. In addition, he appears to have studied the Louis XVI style furniture which had recently been brought across the Channel, and also the work recently carried out by Henry HOLLAND at Carlton House.

If Sheraton did not invent the furniture style named after him, he certainly played a leading role in formulating it. His *Drawing-Book* designs have a remarkable stylistic unity – a marked preference for simple, sometimes severe, outlines combined with flat (painted or inlaid) decoration of great delicacy and elaboration, sometimes with stringing lines and contrasting veneers in geometrical patterns, sometimes with intricate arabesques or figurative panels. Whereas many earlier designers, especially Rococo designers, seem almost to have been ashamed of using wood as their medium, Sheraton's patterns emphasize its essential qualities. The grains of veneers are carefully delineated: the forms are those which come easily to craftsmen working with saws and lathes. He made free play with antique ornaments of the type used by Adam (urns, paterae, vases and swags) but without pedantry. His designs are very elegant, very delicate and perhaps rather feminine.

His second book of designs, the *Cabinet Dictionary* (1803) was less successful than the *Drawing-Book*. His third was published incompletely, *The Cabinet-Maker, Upholsterer and*

General Artist's Encyclopaedia (1805); only the first thirty folio instalments had been completed when Sheraton's mind gave way. It owes much to the re-establishment of French influence during the brief Peace of Amiens. Antique forms are imitated, such as the sabre-legged chair derived from the Greek *klismos*; and such Regency motifs as the monopod, lion-paw feet and the heads of lions, sphinxes and rams. After his death a selection of plates from all his three pattern books was issued as *Designs for Household Furniture* (1812). For illustrations *see* pp. 649, 774.

Lit: R. Fastnedge, *Sheraton Furniture*, London 1962.

Sherratt, Obadiah (*fl.c.*1815–46). Staffordshire potter who specialized in figures and toys, with a factory at Hot Lane, Burslem, from *c.*1815 and Waterloo Road, Burslem, from 1828. After his death, *c.*1846, the firm was carried on by his widow, **Martha,** and son **Hamlet** until the 1850s. Products were unmarked.

Sheveret English type of small writing table popular *c.*1790. Characterized by having a superstructure of drawers fitted with a handle for lifting.

Shigaraki potteries A widely dispersed group of potteries in the Shiga prefecture, described as one of the 'Six Ancient Kilns' of Japan (with SETO, TOKONAME, etc.). They began in the Kamakura period (1185–1338) making seed jars and other vessels for local farmers. On account of the quality of the clay these vessels were of a rough texture, with lumps of quartz embedded in the body, which appealed to the tea-masters who ordered TEA CEREMONY WARES from the potteries and encouraged the development of mottled glazes. Household pottery is still made in the district.

Lit: S. Jenyns, *Japanese Pottery*, London 1971.

Shino wares, *see* MINO POTTERIES.

Shirayamadani, Kataro, *see* ROOKWOOD POTTERY.

Shiraz carpets, *see* PERSIAN CARPETS.

Shirvan carpets, *see* CAUCASIAN CARPETS.

Shorleyker, Richard (*fl.*1624). The author of *A schole house for the needle* (London 1624) which contains numerous embroidery designs of formalized, sometimes almost heraldic, plants.

Shorthouse, John (1768–1828). A potter at Hanley, Staffordshire, he made cream-coloured earthenware, black basaltes and, from *c.*1800, some transfer-printed porcelain. His products are marked Shorthouse & Heath *c.*1815 and Shorthouse & Co *c.*1817–1822.

Shu-fu ware A type of Chinese porcelain made for the Court of the YÜAN Emperors, some pieces being marked with the characters *shu-fu* (privy council). It is a development from the CH'ING PAI WARE of the SUNG dynasty and has a similar bluish-white glaze but is much more ornate. Bowls and dishes have incised, moulded or slip decorations of flowers, lotus leaves, birds, etc. and sometimes the characters for such words as happiness or emoluments. It appears to have been made initially at CHING-TÊ-CHÊN.

Lit: B. Gray, *Early Chinese Pottery and Porcelain*, London 1953.

Sibmacher, Johannes (d.1611). German ornamental designer, the author of *Schön Neues Modelbuch* (Nuremberg 1597) and *Neues Modelbuch* (Nuremberg 1601) which contain numerous elaborate designs for lace and drawn-threadwork, sometimes with figures in contemporary costume shown against geometrically patterned backgrounds. These designs were widely pirated, as in Boler's *The Needles Excellency* which had reached its 12th edition by 1648. *Illustrated opposite page.*

Sicilian potteries Pottery appears to have been made in Sicily from a very early date though no distinctive style was developed. The more elaborate wares were imported and a group of C13 and C14 lustred pieces found on the island and at one time described as 'Siculo-Arab' is now known to have been made in Syria. Maiolica in a style derived from CASTEL DURANTE was made from the late C16 in various places, notably Burgio, Caltagirone, Collesano, Palermo, Sciacca and Trapani. But these wares tend to be coarse in composition and decoration with a dull orange-

Embroidery designs from J. Sibmacher's Neues Modelbuch, *Nuremberg, 1601*

yellow dominating the colour scheme. *Albarelli* with rather tighter waists than usual are among the more notable products. Except for a few marked pieces, specimens can rarely be attributed to specific places or manufacture. In the late C17 and C18, however, the better wares seem to have been made at Caltagirone and in Palermo where the French style of decoration in enamel colours was practised towards the end of the C18. Tiles with floral or geometrical decorations are probably the most attractive C18 wares.

Lit: G. R. Perez in *Faenza* VIII (1920), pp. 19ff. and XXII (1934); E. Mauceri in *Faenza* XVIII (1930), pp. 5ff. and pp. 33ff.

Sicilian silks The art of silk-weaving was introduced into Sicily by the Saracen Emirs in the C10 and much developed under the Normans from the late C11. The ability of both designers and weavers (perhaps Greeks) is revealed by the coronation mantle of the Holy Roman Emperors woven in the royal workshop in Palermo in 1133–4 (Kunsthistorisches Museum, Vienna), probably the finest of all medieval textiles. It is shaped like a cope, of scarlet silk embroidered in dark blue silk and gold thread with rows of pearls and represents two addorsed lions energetically attacking camels. Documents reveal that the Palermitan weavers specialized in DIASPRUM weaves and also in rich gold borders. Many other textiles, similar to HISPANO-MORESQUE SILKS, with patterns of rows of confronted animals and birds (especially peacocks) have been ascribed without much foundation to the Palermitan weavers. When Frederick II transferred his capital to Naples in 1226 the weavers of the royal workshop probably followed him. But silk factories had already been established elsewhere in S. Italy. It is rarely

Sicilian silk: coronation mantle, Palermo, 1133–4 (Kunsthistorischesmuseum, Vienna)

possible to say where S. Italian or Sicilian silks of this period were woven and generally difficult to distinguish them from Spanish silks.

Lit: H. J. Schmidt, *Alte Seidenstoffe*, Brunswick 1958; A. Santangelo, *Tessuti d'arte italiani*, Milan 1959.

Siculo-Arab wares, *see* SICILIAN POTTERIES.

Sideboard A side-table for use as a serving table, invented in the early 1760s by Robert ADAM. The word now connotes that type of side-table which was specifically for use in a dining-room. Such sideboards were designed *en suite* with a wine-cooler, knife-boxes and the rest of the dining-room furniture. A more compact type, with drawers and cupboards for storage, came into use in the 1770s.

Siebel, Franz Anton (1777–1842). *Hausmaler* working in Vienna and at Lichtenfels, notable mainly for his silhouette portraits on glass and porcelain. His daughter **Klara** (b.1815) was also a glass painter.

Siegburg potteries One of the most important groups of stoneware potteries in the Rhineland established by the C14. From the C15 they were owned by a few families, notably the KNÜTGEN family. Products were of a nearly white stoneware with a generally thin, colourless salt-glaze. The earliest are very slender tall jugs and cups with ring handles and wide funnel-shaped mouths sometimes with incised or relief ornament in the Gothic style. STURZBECHER were a speciality in

Siegburg stoneware jug, C15
(Victoria & Albert Museum)

Siegburg stoneware flagon, late c16 (Kunstgewerbemuseum, Cologne)

the early c16. Wares with relief decorations like those of COLOGNE appear to have been made in the mid c16 and from 1559 individual types of vessel – notably the tall tankards *(Schnellen)* and long-spouted jugs *(Schnabelkannen)* – were produced, the best probably deriving from the workshop of ANNO KNÜTGEN. Pilgrim bottles, ring-flasks, owl-shaped jugs were among other products of the period. Decorative motifs, taken from the pattern books of V. SOLIS and others, are in the German Renaissance style. *Schnellen* appear to have gone out of favour *c.*1600; otherwise the products of the factories were little modified in the early c17. But the town was sacked by the Swedes in 1632 and its pottery industry never recovered. Some Siegburg types were imitated at Höhr near WESTERWALD in the early c17. In 1822 Peter Löwenick (1787–1845) began producing imitations of c16 wares.

Lit: O. von Falke, *Das rheinische Steinzeug*, Berlin 1908; G. Reineking von Bock, *Kunstgewerbemuseum der Stadt Köln: Steinzeug*, Cologne 1971.

Siena potteries Founded in the c13, they probably produced wares like those of ORVIETO (though no documented pieces are known) and were making maiolica by 1500. Among the pieces generally ascribed to the Siena potteries are some very handsome maiolica tiles made for two Sienese buildings *c.*1504–9, S. Caterina and Palazzo Petrucci (dispersed and now in the Victoria & Albert Museum, British Museum, Louvre, etc.), and some dishes and drug jars with similarly unusual decorations, minutely rendered grotesques on a black ground which is almost unique in Italian maiolica, or on a yellow ground. The outstanding products of the following decade are those from the workshop of Maestro BENEDETTO. Though the potteries continued active until the end of the c16 later wares are undistinguished. Maiolica was again made in Siena in the c18 somewhat in the style of CASTELLI – dishes and plaques painted with biblical subjects by **Ferdinando Maria Campani** dated 1733–1747 are the most interesting products.

Lit: R. Langton Douglas, *Le maioliche di Siena*, Siena 1903; J. Chompret, *Repertoire de la majolique italienne*, Paris 1949.

Sieubert, Antonio, *see* ROME POTTERIES & PORCELAIN FACTORIES.

Sigalon, Antoine (*c.*1524–90). Potter or owner of a pottery at Nîmes making from *c.*1554 very handsome faience in the Italian style. Products included plates, pilgrim bottles and *albarelli* decorated with boldly stylized foliage, grotesque motifs, heraldry and occasionally portrait heads in a colour scheme predominantly deep blue, orange and yellow. He was a Huguenot and one of his pieces (in the Pierpont Morgan collection, New York) is decorated with a satire on the Catholic ritual. After his death his nephews are said to have run the pottery until 1620.

Byzantine silk, compound twill, detail from The Emperors Hunting, *late c8–c9, probably made in Constantinople (Staatlichemuseum, Berlin)*

Lit: A. van de Put in *Burlington Magazine* LXII (1933), pp. 108ff., 157ff., LXIII (1934), pp. 16ff.; E. Fabre in *Keramos* 25 (1964), pp. 39–61.

Silesian Hafner ware, *see* HAFNER WARE.

Silk A natural fibre spun into a cocoon by the larva of the mulberry silk-moth of China, the *Bombyx mori*, first used for textiles at a very early period in China. The oldest surviving fragments date from *c.*1000 B.C. and reveal fairly advanced knowledge of the technique of WEAVING. Silk was exported to Europe from the time of the Han dynasty (220 B.C.–202 B.C.). The Romans imported not only silk textiles but silk yarn which was sometimes mixed with LINEN or WOOL. A silk-weaving industry was established in the E. Mediterranean in C2 A.D. and developed in C4 in Constantinople and Persia. From *c.*550 silk was both cultivated and woven in Syria (see BYZANTINE STYLES) whence sericulture spread to E. Europe, flourishing in Spain and Sicily in the C10 (*see* HISPANO-MORESQUE SILKS and SICILIAN SILKS), in LUCCA, VENICE and GENOA in the C12–C13. Italy and Spain produced the best European silks throughout the Middle Ages and Renaissance (both plain and in bold flat patterns, variants on the POMEGRANATE PATTERN being the most popular). Genoa continued to produce the best heavy silks and velvets suitable for furnishing fabrics until the late C18. But the lead in the production of silks for clothing passed in the late C17 to France and especially to the LYONS SILK FACTORIES which produced the first naturalistic patterns *c.*1730 and set fashions which were imitated at SPITALFIELDS, STOCKHOLM and elsewhere for silks of every kind. It was also in C18 France that the major improvements in the technique of preparing and weaving silk were accomplished.

Processes. When removed from the cocoons (which are plunged into boiling water) the filaments must first be 'reeled' – i.e. separated and dried by winding them onto open reels – and then 'thrown' or twisted into yarn by a process similar to that of spinning. By the C14 (or probably earlier) the Lucca silk manufacturers had devised water-driven mills to facilitate the process of twisting, and similar mills were soon adopted in other Italian centres of the silk industry.

Silk chasuble, Florence or Lucca, late C15 (S. Maria a Quinto, Sesto Fiorentino)

Silk panel, possibly Lucca, C15 (Courtesy of the Art Institute of Chicago)

Silk, Turkish, c16–17
(Musée des Arts Décoratifs, Paris)

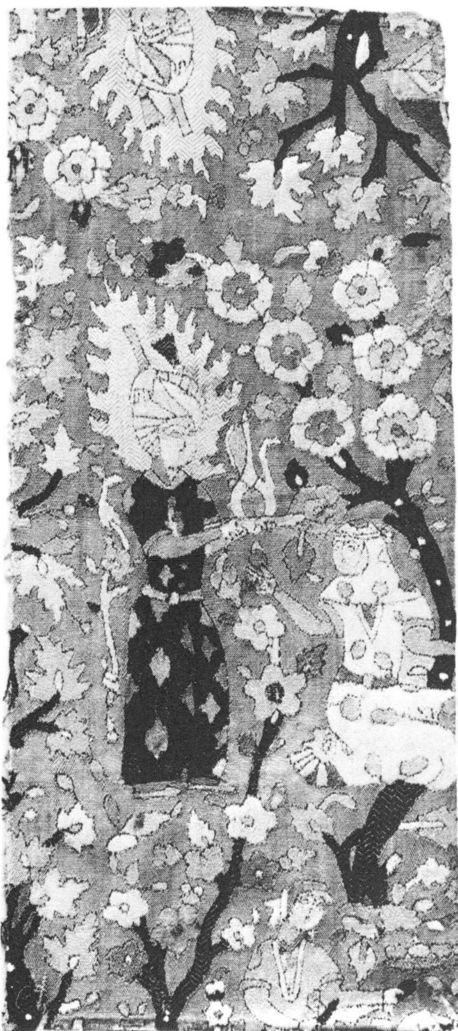

Silk panel, Persia, c17 (Musée des Arts Décoratifs, Paris)

After it had been twisted the yarn had only to be bleached and dyed to prepare it for weaving. Late c18 developments affected not only loom mechanism but also the culture of the worm and the processes of reeling and twisting. Italian scientists and agriculturalists (notably Vincenzo Dandolo) discovered how the culture of the silk worm could be improved and this led to the adoption of more scientific methods in Europe and also (through the British East India Company) in Bengal. The process of reeling was improved though it was not until 1825 that a machine was invented (by John Heathcote) to do this. Silk throwing machinery was much improved by mills invented in France and introduced into England in 1718 by John and Thomas Lombe of Derby. Great advances were also made in the treatment of waste silk – i.e. the filaments taken from damaged cocoons which will not unwind continuously or from the cocoon remains after reeling, etc. (This is sometimes called wild silk since the cocoons from which the silk moth had escaped in a natural state would be similarly damaged.) It had to be cleaned, carded and dressed in much the same way as flax or wool and was originally spun into yarn by distaff and wheel, but machinery was employed in England from the late c18 and the processing of waste silk was fully mechanized soon after the mid c19. Although both preparatory and weaving processes could be mechanized, the production of raw silk is still based mainly on hand labour and sericulture

Silk brocaded cope, detail, probably Austrian, c.1750–75 (Kunsthistorischesmuseum, Vienna)

is thus practised only where labour is cheap (mainly in the Far East). Despite competition from MAN-MADE FIBRES silk remains popular both for dresses and furnishing textiles.

Chinese silk panel, detail, c18 (Victoria & Albert Museum)

Silver ewer from the Boscoreale treasure, Roman, pre-79 A.D. *(Louvre)*

Lit: O. von Falke, *Kunstgeschichte der seidenweberei*, Berlin 1913; F. O. Howitt, *Bibliography of the Technical Literature on Silk*, London 1947.

Sillabub (or **Syllabub**) **glass** A c18 English glass vessel for sillabub (a frothy concoction of milk or cream curdled and spiced), with a fairly wide bowl, like a wine-glass or a jelly-glass.

Sillon de Caderas A medieval Spanish type of X-chair, often with inlaid decorations.

Silver A precious metal regarded as second only to gold since very early times. It occurs in its pure state and as an alloy (in ELECTRUM) and as a compound in lead ore (galena). Nowadays 80 per cent of the world's supply comes from the American continent. In its pure state it is too soft for use in metalwork so it is alloyed with another metal, generally copper, the proportions of the alloy varying according to country and period (in England the normal sterling standard is 92.5 per cent silver; the Britannia standard, compulsory from 1697 to 1719 and optional thereafter, is 95.8 per cent silver). Only slightly less malleable, ductile and permanent than gold (it melts at a temperature of about 1000°C.) it is less rare and has been more widely used as a medium for household and religious objects, varying in size from small cups and plates to large candlesticks, altar-frontals and occasionally pieces of furniture. It may be decorated by ENGRAVING, EMBOSSING, the addition of solid cast ornament, ENAMELS either applied directly to the surface or on applied plaques. (For hall-marks *see* p. 890; for makers' marks *see* p. 893.)

Silver Chinese stem cup, T'ang dynasty (618–906) (William Rockhill Nelson Gallery of Art, Kansas City)

Lit: L. Aitchison, *A History of Metals*, London 1960.

Simm, Anton (1799–1873). The best known member of a family of Bohemian glass engravers working at Gablonz. He engraved glasses with views of Teplitz, Prague, Carlsbad, etc., Italianate landscapes, mythological figures, coats of arms, etc.

Lit: G. E. Pazaurek in *Der Kunstwanderer*, 1922/3, pp. 50ff., 76ff.

Simonet, Johann, *see* FRANKFURT-AM-MAIN POTTERY.

Simpson, Ralph He was a late C17 STAFFORDSHIRE potter, a contemporary of T. TOFT. He decorated slipware, often with borders of heads and roundels.

Sinceny pottery A faience factory, near Laon, founded in 1733, run by Dennis-Pierre (father of Etienne-Dominique) PELLEVÉ from Rouen until 1737 and then by **Leopold Malériat** until 1775. Products of these years are in the style of ROUEN and very nearly as handsome – notably tablewares painted in high-temperature colours with chinoiseries, and some large cider jugs. Figures were also made, including a 78-cm high group of St Nicholas with three children (Musée nationale de Céramique de Sèvres). From 1775 to 1795 wares were decorated in enamel colours in the style of and executed by painters from STRASBOURG. The factory remained active until 1864. (For factory marks *see* p. 888.)

Lit: J. Chompret *et al.*, *Répertoire de la faïence française*, Paris 1933–5; C. Sondée-Lacomber in *Cahiers de la céramique* 36 (1964), pp. 224–51.

Singerie Decoration in which the main figures are monkeys, often dressed in human clothes and aping the actions of men, e.g. hunting, smoking, playing cards, etc. Although monkeys had figured in European art since the Middle Ages, the vogue for *singeries* did not begin much before the end of the C17 and reached its height of popularity in the C18 when it became associated with CHINOISERIE. The first decorative designer to make use of *singeries* was J. BERAIN and the best C. HUET. *Singeries* were painted on walls, on porcelain and faience, worked in piqué and in marquetry, embroidered and printed on textiles. They were chased off the scene by 1800 only to reappear later under the aegis of the C19 revival of taste for the C18.

Situla A bucket-shaped vessel, generally for liturgical use. Roman in origin, examples in silver, ivory and glass survive from the early Middle Ages.

Situla, ivory, Milan or Reichenau, c.980 (Victoria & Albert Museum)

Six ancient kilns, *see* BIZEN, ECHIZEN, SETO, SHIGARAKI, TAMBA and TOKONAME POTTERIES.

Size gilding The earliest method of applying gilt decorations to TIN-GLAZED EARTHENWARE. A sticky substance prepared by boiling linseed oil and litharge is applied to the pot and gold-leaf rubbed onto it. This form of gilding is very impermanent since the gilt is unfired.

Skillet English medieval term for a saucepan, now generally reserved for those of the earliest type – with a rounded bowl, three or four legs and a long handle, made of earthenware or metal – though the term was also applied in the C16–C17 to the straight-sided saucepan without feet which then came into use.

Slag glass Glass, of various colours, with a proportion of slag from iron foundries, etc. It was widely manufactured in the C19 and in the U.S.A. one type became greatly prized as AGATE GLASS.

Slavkov porcelain factory Founded *c.*1800 at Schlaggenwald (now Slavkov) in Bohemia. By 1842 it was owned by **Georg Lippert** under whose management it produced Neo-Rococo wares.

Slee's Modern Pottery, *see* LEEDS POTTERY.

Slip A mixture of fine clay and water originally used on vessels of coarser clay to render them less porous – before the introduction of GLAZES – and as a cement to join parts (e.g. spouts and handles) to the body of a vessel while still soft. It has also been used ornamentally. By one process, most familiar in the barbotine and trailed slip of Roman times and the slipware of C17 Staffordshire, the slip is applied as relief decoration, trailed in lines, squiggles and dots like icing on a cake, in monochrome or contrasting colours, usually white or cream on a dark body. By the other process a thinner slip mixture is painted on the vessel or the vessel is dipped in it, thus giving a piece of coarse pottery a finer surface texture. From the C9 onwards such wares were often covered with a lead glaze. They might also be decorated by the SGRAFFIATO technique, by cutting through the slip to reveal the darker body, before glazing.

Slip-top spoon A spoon with an hexagonal stem terminating in a simple bevelled end, very common from the Middle Ages to the mid C17.

Slipware The name given to LEAD-GLAZED EARTHENWARE decorated with SLIP in relief before firing. It was produced by Roman potters and by peasant potters in the Balkans, England, France and Scandinavia. The earliest notable English examples were made at Wrotham in Kent in the early C17 and are rather crude. Plates made in London in the C17 often bear pious inscriptions – 'Faste and Pray', 'Remember thy end' etc. The most attractive were made in STAFFORDSHIRE by T. TOFT.

Lit: R. G. Cooper, *English Slipware Dishes 1650–1850*, London 1968.

Sloane, Sir Hans, *see* CHELSEA PORCELAIN FACTORY.

Slodtz, Antoine-Sébastien (*c*.1695–1754). He was the son of the sculptor **Sébastien Slodtz** (1655–1726) who married a daughter of Domenico Filippo CUCCI. He was a prolific designer for the theatre and Court festivities as well as of furniture, etc., and became *dessinateur de la Chambre du Roi* in 1750. His style is typically Rococo, e.g. the commode he designed for Louis XV's bedroom at Versailles, made by GAUDREAU and CAFFIÉRI and now in the Wallace Collection, London, and the table he designed for Versailles in 1739 and still there. He was succeeded as *dessinateur* by his brother **Paul-Amboise** (1702–1758) by whom there are surviving works at Versailles. He was succeeded by **Réné Michel** known as **Michel-Ange Slodtz** (1705–64) who was a notable sculptor.

Lit: F. Souchal, *Les Slodtz sculpteurs et decorateurs du roi (1685–1764)*, Paris 1967.

Slop basin A bowl for slops (tea rinsings) which formed part of every tea-service, whether in silver or porcelain, from the early C18.

Smaltino A C16 Italian term for a nearly transparent pale blue or greyish tin-glaze on maiolica, especially that of the Venice potteries.

Smith, Benjamin (*fl.*1791–1822). London silversmith working in a style similar to that of his great rival, Paul STORR, and like him much employed by RUNDELL and Bridge, later in partnership with **Digby Scott** 1802–7, with **James Smaith** 1809, and with his son **Benjamin** from 1816. He excelled in relatively small pieces, salvers and trays with delicate open-work vine borders,

B. Smith: silver wine-coaster, London, 1810 (Goldsmiths' Company, London)

Grecian sugar-bowls, elegant tea-sets, etc. On a monumental scale he was less successful than Storr and such works as the candelabra of 1816 or the preposterous Wellington shield with myriad figures in relief of 1822 (both Apsley House, London) are of an almost Victorian fussiness and opulence.

Lit: A. Grimwade in *The Connoisseur*, June 1960; p. 30.

Smith, Benjamin the younger (1793–1850). A London silversmith, he succeeded to his father's business in 1822. He was in charge of ELKINGTON's plating works in Moorgate, London, in the 1840s until he was removed in 1849. (His son **Apsley** married Elkington's daughter). His work in silver is in an organic naturalistic style, sometimes incorporating motifs electrotyped from natural specimens.

Lit: A. Grimwade in *The Connoisseur*, June 1960.

Smith, George (*fl.*1804–28). Leading REGENCY furniture designer and the proprietor of a large cabinet-making business in London. He is important mainly for popularizing the circular dining-table and the ottoman in England: also as the vulgarizer of Thomas HOPE's Egyptian and Grecian styles. He interpreted these with a greater regard for comfort and utility than for archaeological accuracy though he had a weakness for antefixae, monopods, claw feet, sabre legs and currule chairs. Hope's influence is very evident in his first book: *A Collection of Designs for Household Furniture and Interior Decoration* (1808) though it also contains designs for Gothic and chinoiserie furniture; it is even stronger in *A Collection of Ornamental Designs after the Antique* (1812); but it had waned by the time he published *The Cabinet Maker and Upholsterer's Guide* (1826). This includes designs in the Gothic and French C18 styles as well as the Egyptian, Grecian and Roman, and often foreshadows the solemnity and heaviness of Victorian furniture.

Lit: C. Musgrave, *Regency Furniture*, London 1961; J. Harris, *Regency Furniture Designs 1803–1826*, London 1961.

Smith, Sampson (*fl.*1850). He was the owner of a pottery at Longton in Staffordshire making brightly coloured earthenware figures of the STAFFORDSHIRE type and one of the few who occasionally marked their products.

Smyrna carpets, *see* TURKISH CARPETS.

Snowman figures English porcelain figures with a thick opaque glaze made at LONGTON HALL in the 1750s. In the past they have been erroneously ascribed to other factories.

Snuffers An instrument for trimming the wicks of candles, in appearance like a pair of scissors with a box near the end of the blades, made from the late C17. The finer examples were made of silver and provided with a stand – an upright one in the C17 but more usually a tray from the early C18.

Soap box A spherical perforated container with a rounded foot to hold soap, forming part of C18 silver toilet services.

Soaprock or **soapstone** Steatite (chemically, hydrated silicate of magnesia), a soft stone found in many parts of the world and used as a medium for carving in the Far East. In England it is found in Cornwall and was first used as a substitute for FELDSPAR by Benjamin LUND at Bristol and later by some porcelain factories, notably Bristol, WORCESTER, LIVERPOOL, CAUGHLEY and SWANSEA. The porcelain of which it is a component is translucent (sometimes with a slight orange tinge when held up to the light), fine textured, strong and withstands hot water without cracking.

Socci, Giovanni (*fl.*1809–15). He was an Italian EMPIRE cabinet-maker, patronized by Napoleon's sister, Elisa Baciocchi, Grand-Duchess of Tuscany. For her he made furniture for the Palazzo Pitti in Florence, including some very attractive drum-shaped commodes and a pair of very ingenious convertible writing-desks. When closed they look like oval chests-of-drawers on legs, but a portion of the front conceals a chair which may be drawn out, and the top divides and opens laterally while a container for pens and paper rises up in the centre. Two of the writing-desks are in the Palazzo Pitti (both signed) and another is at Malmaison outside Paris. Nothing is known of Socci after the Restoration but he probably continued to work as a cabinet-maker in Florence.

Lit: H. Honour, *Cabinet Makers and Furniture Designers*, London and New York 1969.

Soda glass An early type of GLASS, made with sodium carbonate as a flux, and not with potash. It was fragile and lacked resonance and was superseded by soda-lime glass, i.e. glass made with soda and lime as alkalis.

Sofa A long, informal SETTEE, heavily upholstered and inviting the user to lounge or recline upon it. It gradually replaced the settee during the C19 in England.

Sofa and chair by Leistler & Son, Vienna, 1851

Soffit The underside of any architectural member, e.g. an arch.

Soft-paste porcelain, *see* PORCELAIN.

Soho tapestries The generic name given to English tapestries made after the MORTLAKE TAPESTRY FACTORY closed *c.*1685, though relatively few were woven in the Soho district of London. The best were woven under the direction of John VANDERBANK, chief arras worker to the Great Wardrobe which was situated in Great Queen Street, London, outside the Soho district. The only Soho factory of importance was that of Joshua MORRIS. Some attractive hangings and tapestry covers for chairs, settees and screens, after or imitative of Watteau and other French painters and signed by a certain **Bradshaw,** are usually classed as Soho – though no one knows where they were made or who Bradshaw was. A factory called the 'Soho Tapestry Works' in Poland Street, London, was active 1890–1910 making large figurative panels often of Scottish subjects.

Soho tapestry, chinoiserie scene, early c18 (Victoria & Albert Museum)

Lit: H.-C. Mariller, *English Tapestries of the Eighteenth Century,* London 1930.

Soldani, Massimiliano (1658–1740). Leading Florentine late Baroque bronze sculptor and medallist, specializing in small decorative bronzes, reliefs, ornamental urns, etc. in an exuberant Baroque style, also small copies of Antique statues. After his death his terracotta models were bought by the DOCCIA PORCELAIN FACTORY which produced porcelain versions of some of them. For illustration *see* DOCCIA PORCELAIN FACTORY.

Solis, Virgilius (1514–62). German Renaissance ornamental designer and engraver whose workshop in Nuremberg turned out some six hundred ornamental and figurative prints. They were widely used and many surviving pieces of German Renaissance silver are similar to them. He executed numerous designs for silversmiths in a variety of styles – chalices of late Gothic form decorated with classical motifs and grotesques, classically shaped ewers richly adorned with arabesque and strapwork decorations, and some bizarre experiments reminiscent of work by the JAMNITZER family, e.g. ewer in the form of a snail. His designs were used by German silversmiths until well into the C17 also by stuccoists, wood carvers and furniture-makers. His son of the same name (b.1551) worked as a draughtsman and painter for Rudolf II in Prague.

Lit: S. Jervis, *Printed Furniture Designs before 1650*, London 1974.

Solitaire, *see* CABARET.

Solon, Marc-Louis-Emanuel (1835–1913). French porcelain decorator and the most famous practitioner of the PÂTE-SUR-PÂTE technique, working at SÈVRES from 1857 to 1870 under the pseudonym *Milès*, then in England at the MINTON factory from 1870 to 1904. His decorations, usually in white against a dark ground, were generally of classical subjects inspired by Renaissance paintings and sculptures. He was widely acclaimed and commanded high prices, as much as £100 for a large vase. He published a set of fifty ornamental designs, *Inventions décoratives*, Paris 1866. After settling in England he wrote a number of books on ceramics, notably *The Ancient Art of Stoneware in the Low Countries and Germany*, 1892; *Pottery Worship*, 1898; *A History and Description of the Old French Faïence*, 1903; *A History and Description of Italian Maiolica*, 1907, all published in London. He also made a large collection of English pottery which was sold in 1912. His son **Léon Victor Solon** (1872–1957) worked for Mintons 1900–1909 designing Art Nouveau pottery, then went to the U.S. where he worked as a ceramic designer and interior decorator, providing coloured sculptural decorations for the Museum of Fine Arts, Philadelphia.

Lit: H. C. Read in *Burlington Magazine* XXIII (1913), pp. 317ff; G. Godden, *Victorian Porcelain*, London 1970.

Sölvesborg pottery Swedish faience factory founded in 1773 by Baron **Gabriel Sparre** (1724–1804) and advertising its wares in the local press from 1776. The chief painter, **Peter Ackermarck** (*c*.1731–*c*.1808) had previously been employed at MARIEBERG and STRALSUND and its products recall the wares of those factories. They are generally in a restrained Rococo style painted in underglaze blue or manganese purple, occasionally with enamel colours. Black glazed tea-wares similar to those associated with the English JACKFIELD POTTERY were also made. The founder sold the factory in 1792: it was destroyed when the town was burnt in 1800. (For factory mark *see* p. 888.)

Lit: R. J. Charleston in *The Connoisseur*, CLIII (1963), pp. 25–30.

Sommer, Johann Daniel (1643–after 1685). The most important member of a large family of German woodcarvers and furniture makers working at Künzelsau am Kocher, Württemberg. He specialized in furniture with Boulle-type marquetry and it has been suggested (not very plausibly) that he was trained in Paris. His masterpiece, a large cabinet, is destroyed. (It was formerly in Schloss Charlottenburg, Berlin.) But there is a fine inlaid table-top by him, signed and dated 1666, in the Hohenlohemuseum, Schloss Neuenstein. From 1685 he worked in the Schloss at Heidelberg. Another member of the family, **Johann Eberhard Sommer,** is known to have executed elaborate wall decorations of carved wood for the mirror room or Spiegelkabinett (1714–7) at Schloss Welkersheim as well as other pieces of furniture for the same place and for Schloss Neuenstein.

Lit: H. Kreisel, *Die Kunst des deutschen Möbels*, Munich 1970.

Sonnenschein, Valentin, *see* ZURICH POTTERY & PORCELAIN FACTORY.

Sopha French term roughly corresponding with the equally imprecise English SOFA. It is currently defined either as a CANAPÉ with the wooden structure entirely covered by upholstery, or simply as a type of *canapé* with a rounded back.

Sorgenthal, Konrad von, *see* VIENNA PORCELAIN FACTORY.

Souj-Bulak carpets, *see* PERSIAN CARPETS.

Soumak carpets, *see* CAUCASIAN CARPETS.

South Jersey glasshouses The most important in C18 America, founded in 1739 by **Caspar Wistar**

on the banks of Alloway's Creek, and originally staffed with German craftsmen. Made mainly bottles and window panes. Jugs, mugs, vases, candlesticks, often boldly decorated with applied prunts and wavy threads, were apparently made by the glass-blowers on their own account and are called 'off-hand pieces'. Although made in many other glasshouses, such objects are usually termed 'South Jersey type' in the U.S. where they are much collected. The original firm failed in 1780 and another was established by two former employees named **Stranger** in *c.*1781.

Lit: L. W. Watkins, *American Glass & Glass-making*, London 1950.

Southwark (Philadelphia) porcelain factory, *see* BONNIN AND MORRIS PORCELAIN FACTORY.

Southwark potteries The leading C17 English TIN-GLAZED EARTHENWARE factory, established in 1618 by a Dutchman, **Christian Wilhelm** (*c.*1595–*c.*1640) who obtained a 14-year monopoly for making tin-glazed earthenware in 1628. He specialized in rather heavily modelled blue-and-white wares decorated with motifs derived from Ming porcelain (notably a bird perched on a rock)

Southwark tin-glazed earthenware dish, c.1635–40 *(Victoria & Albert Museum)*

which anticipate DELFT wares of the 1660s. A few of his wares are rather clumsily painted with Biblical scenes in polychrome.

Lit: H. Tait in *The Connoisseur* CXLVI (1960), pp. 36–40 and CXLVII (1961), pp. 22–9.

Soy frame A silver or plated stand for bottles of sauce to be used at table, made from the late C18 in England, similar to but generally smaller than a cruet-stand.

Spa japanning workshops A JAPANNING industry grew up at Spa, a watering-place near Aachen, in the C17 and flourished throughout the C18. Its products, ranging from large cupboards to snuff-boxes usually decorated with gilt chinoiseries on a black ground and known as *bois de Spa,* were bought mainly by the fashionable visitors of all nationalities who flocked to Spa to take the waters and frequent the gaming rooms. They were thus dispersed throughout Europe and are now difficult to distinguish from japanned wares made in other countries.

Lit: H. Huth, *Lacquer of the West,* Chicago/London 1971.

Spade foot An English type of foot for chairs and tables, often used by HEPPLEWHITE and SHERATON. It is quadrangular, tapering slightly from the top.

Spandrel The triangular space between the side of an arch, the horizontal drawn from its apex and the vertical from its springing; or the space between one arch and another in an arcade.

Spängler, J. J., *see* DERBY PORCELAIN FACTORY.

Spanish carpets All-wool carpets with the pile tied with the SPANISH KNOT have been made in Spain since the C15. They are usually rather long and narrow, patterns are generally geometrical, often with coats of arms as central devices. Colours are bright and few, mainly yellow, blue, red and green. Few knotted pile carpets were made after the C17 but small rugs with looped pile were produced until the late C18. *See* ALCARAZ and CUENCA CARPETS.

Lit: M. Campana, *Tapetti d'occidente,* Milan 1966.

Spanish foot An English type of foot for chairs and sometimes for tables. It frequently took the place of the bun foot on William and Mary furniture.

It is a carved scroll foot with vertical grooves, the scroll turning backwards in a curve at the bottom.

Spanish knot or **single warp knot** The knot with which the pile is tied on a SPANISH CARPET. Unlike the GHIORDES and PERSIAN knots it is tied to a single warp thread. Knots are tied to alternate threads in each row with the result that the horizontal and vertical lines of the pattern are slightly serrated while the diagonals are much smoother than usual.

Sparre, Baron Gabriel, *see* SÖLVESBORG POTTERY.

Sparre, Louis, *see* FINCH, Alfred William.

Sparrow-beaked jug, *see* BIRD-BEAKED JUG.

Sparta carpets, *see* TURKISH CARPETS.

Sparver C16 and C17 type of bed curtain, hung from the ceiling above the bed.

Spatter ware, *see* SPONGED WARE.

Speckner, Lorenz (1598–after 1669). He was a German potter and appears to have served his apprenticeship in Nuremberg before settling at KREUSSEN, near Bayreuth, where he married the widow of a stoneware maker, **George Vest,** and began to produce tin-glazed earthenware of fine quality, signed with his initials, from 1618. His products include four- and six-sided flasks, cups, drinking vessels in the form of birds, drug vases, plates and dishes decorated with formalized floral motifs or heraldry (rarely figures) in light blue on a fine pure white ground. His last recorded piece is a spouted drug pot (Danske Folkmuseum, Copenhagen) of 1668. His son **Johannes Lorenz** (*fl.*1639–73) and his grandson **Georg Julius** (b.1673) were also potters at Kreussen. He sometimes signed his work, with either his initials or monogram, on the decorated part and not on the base.

Lit: R. Stettiner in *Der Cicerone* XV (1923).

L. Speckner: tin-glazed earthenware flask, Kreussen, 1618
(Museum für Kunst und Gewerbe, Hamburg)

Speculum metal An alloy of tin and copper used for making a *speculum* or mirror before silvered glass was introduced. It took a high shiny polish.

Spelter Commercial name for ZINC, generally applied to cast decorative objects, furniture mounts, etc. made as cheap substitutes for those of bronze from the mid C19. The surface was often bronzed by a process developed by M. Geiss of Berlin for statues, some of which he showed at the Great Exhibition of 1851.

Spengler, Adam, *see* ZURICH POTTERY & PORCELAIN FACTORY.

Sphinx A mythological creature with the body of a lion and head of a woman, much used in furniture decoration from the Renaissance onwards.

Spill vase A cylindrical vessel, usually of pottery or porcelain, to hold spills, i.e. thin slips of wood or folded and twisted paper for lighting candles, pipes, etc.

Spinacci, Giovanni, *see* GUBBIO POTTERIES.

Spindle and bead moulding A moulding with alternating round beads and long spindles.

Spindler, Johann Friedrich (1726–after 1799)

J. F. Spindler: commode with marquetry and gilt-bronze mounts, c.1765 (Museum der Potsdamer Rokoko, Potsdam)

and **Heinrich Wilhelm** (1738–after 1799). German furniture-makers born at Bayreuth, they were notable mainly for their work at Potsdam. They were the sons of **Johann** (1691–1770) and the brothers of **Jakob** (1724–92) with whom they collaborated in executing marquetry panelling for a room at Schloss Fantasie at Donndorf near Bayreuth from 1762 onwards. In 1764 they went to Potsdam where they made some very fine furniture for Frederick the Great, usually decorated with floral marquetry in the French style but incorporating characteristically German Rococo architectural elements. Many of their pieces have bronze mounts by J. M. KAMBLI. In 1776 they set up their workshop in Berlin which was still active in 1799.

Lit: H. Kreisel, *Die Kunst des deutschen Möbels*, vol. ii, Munich 1970.

Spinner, David (1758–1811). American potter working in Bucks County, Pennsylvania, in the Pennsylvania Dutch style. He made earthenware dishes decorated with slip trickled through a quill. Signed examples survive.

Spinning The process of fashioning sheet metal into hollow wares by pressing the sheet against a wooden core in a lathe. It has been used since prehistoric times.

Spitalfields silk factories First established on the outskirts of London in the late C17 (earlier in the century silks had been woven in Chelsea). They began by weaving plain materials. The industry was greatly stimulated by the arrival of numerous Huguenot weavers after the revocation of the Edict of Nantes in 1685. Early in the C18 the factories were producing a wide variety of materials – velvets, damasks and especially figured silk brocades often with gold and silver thread (used mainly as dress materials). The industry was assisted by laws prohibiting the import of Indian calico (1701), heavy taxes on printed cotton (1712 and 1714) and a law against the manufacture of printed cotton (1720, repealed 1774). It also profited greatly from the European wars which hampered French commerce – notably the War of the Spanish Succession 1701–13 and the Seven Years' War 1756–

63 when exports soared. But throughout its history the industry suffered from a shortage of good designers. Most patterns were strongly influenced by if not directly copied from French silks. BIZARRE designs were favoured in the early C18, giving way to lush naturalistic floral patterns in the 1730s and elegant, distinctly Rococo designs with delicate bunches of flowers and ribbons in the 1740s. Numerous designs survive (Victoria & Albert Museum) but it is rarely possible to distinguish the silks woven at Spitalfields from those made on the Continent (those of the mid C18 are the most distinctively English). Patterned silks went out of fashion, both for furnishing and dress materials, in the 1770s when the industry set into a decline from which it never recovered. Other English silk factories of the C18 were at Manchester, Macclesfield and Norwich but little is known of their products and most English silks of this period are generally attributed to the Spitalfields factories which were certainly the largest.

Lit: J. F. Flanagan, *Spitalfields Silks of the 18th and 19th Centuries*, Leigh-on-Sea 1954.

Splat The central, vertical member of a chair back, generally shaped or pierced.

Splint seat An American type of chair seat made of interlaced strips of hickory or oak, in use since the C18.

Split-turned ornament Small turned wood balusters split vertically and applied as a relief decoration to furniture in the C17.

Spode pottery and porcelain factory Founded in 1776 at Stoke-on-Trent, Staffordshire, by **Josiah Spode** (1733–97) who had been trained as a potter under T. WHIELDON. It began by producing

Spitalfields silk, designed by Anna Maria Garthwaite, 1748 (Victoria & Albert Museum)

Spode pottery wares exhibited at the Great Exhibition, 1851

CREAM-COLOURED EARTHENWARE, and from 1783 a very fine type of PEARL WARE, rather whiter than that made by WEDGWOOD and of a silky smoothness which provided an excellent ground for underglaze decorations in blue. Under the founder's son **Josiah II** (1754–1827) it achieved distinction for pearl wares, bone-porcelain (from 1800) and stone-china (from 1805) decorated with blue TRANSFER PRINTED underglaze designs of oriental or Italianate views and hunting scenes, probably the best of their type. In 1833 it was acquired by **W. T. Copeland**, who had been a partner since 1813, and T. Garrett, and was subsequently known as Copeland and Garrett (now as W. T. Copeland & Sons Ltd). Mid-C19 products included numerous PARIAN WARE figures (which were first made here), elaborate table-services decorated with meticulously painted landscapes, flowers, birds, etc., a vast quantity of ordinary household crockery and such curiosities as pieces of garden furniture. The factory still survives and is one of the best and most productive in England. Wares were marked with name, impressed or painted.

Lit: L. Whiter, *Spode, a history of the family, factory and ware from 1733–1833*, London 1970.

Sponged ware or **Spatter ware** C19 wares decorated with bright colours applied with a sponge through a stencil, usually giving a blotchy effect. The sponged decoration could be supplemented with painting, either in enamel or underglaze blue. Sponged decoration was much used in STAFFORDSHIRE POTTERIES, often on granite ware, and exported to the U.S.A.

Spool Axminster, *see* AXMINSTER CARPET.

Spoon back chair, *see* CHAIR.

Spoon tray A small oval or oblong dish used in mid-C18 England to hold tea-spoons.

Sprigged ware An C18 English type of ceramic ware decorated with applied reliefs of flowers, foliage, etc. The reliefs were pressed in intaglio moulds and fixed to the vessel with slip. There are early examples by ASTBURY and WHIELDON and in Staffordshire salt-glazed stoneware, similarly in Rhenish stoneware.

Sprimont, Nicholas (*c.*1716–71). Silversmith and porcelain manufacturer and one of the leading practitioners of the Rococo style in England. He appears to have been a Huguenot of Flemish origin, probably from Liège. He worked with PAUL CRESPIN and is thought to have been responsible for an elaborate centre-piece of 1741 in the Royal Collection which bears Crespin's mark. In 1742 he was admitted to the London Goldsmiths' Company. He specialized in objects richly decorated with shells, crabs, etc., probably cast from nature and with finely modelled human figures and dolphins, notably those made for Frederick Prince of Wales (d.1751) and still in the Royal Collection. From *c.*1745 he was involved in the CHELSEA PORCELAIN FACTORY – in partnership with **Charles Gouyn** until 1749, working under the patronage of the Duke of Cumberland 1750–56, and proprietor 1756–69 – and was responsible for some of its models including a bust of the Duke of Cumberland and several pieces similar to his silver.

Lit: H. Bellamy Gardner in *The Connoisseur* LXV (1923), p. 159; H. Bellamy Gardner in *Transactions of the English Porcelain Circle* I (1928), pp. 18–19; R. Ormond in *Country Life* CXLIII (1968), pp. 224–6.

Spruce An English medieval corruption of Preuzsen or Prussian, especially applied to furniture (e.g. chests) which were imported from the Baltic coast and generally made of oak or cypress (not necessarily the wood of the spruce-fir tree).

Spur marks Small unglazed scars on the bottom of a piece of glazed pottery or porcelain, left by the stilts or spurs on which it stood while being fired in the kiln.

Squab A removable stuffed cushion for a chair or stool.

Stabler, Harold (1872–1945). English craftsman, designer and teacher (Sir John Cass Technical Institute and Royal College of Art, London) in the ARTS AND CRAFTS tradition. At his studio in Hammersmith he and his wife Phoebe made jewellery, enamels and pottery figures. He designed tiles for the St Paul's Underground

Station, London, figures for the WORCESTER PORCELAIN FACTORY, table-wares to be hand-thrown and hand-decorated in a pottery at Poole of which he was co-founder in 1921 (still active and now called **Poole Pottery Ltd**), elaborate pieces of presentation silver and stainless steel equipment. A silver cup with ivory stem and enamelled decorations by him is in the Musée des Arts Décoratifs, Paris.

Lit: Journal of the Royal Society of Arts, XCIII (1945) p. 284ff.

Stafford pottery A pottery at Stockton-on-Tees, established in 1824 and from 1826 to 1855 trading as **William Smith & Co.** It produced imitation WEDGWOOD and in 1848 Wedgwood obtained an injunction to prevent it making Queensware marked 'Wedgwood' or 'Wedgwood & Co.'.

Staffordshire potteries The largest group of English ceramic factories producing vast quantities of useful and ornamental wares from the C17 to the present day (generally lead-glazed or salt-glazed, never tin-glazed, earthenwares but also types of porcelain especially from the early C19). They began as a purely national industry but were influencing Continental factories in the late C18 and were carrying on an export trade with all parts of the world in the C19. They are situated in the county borough of Stoke-on-Trent, in the district commonly known as The Potteries or the Five Towns (Burslem, Stoke, Hanley, Tunstall and Longton, though also including Longport, Fenton, Cobridge, Shelton, Lane Delph – now called Middle Fenton – and Lane End). The first notable products are in SLIPWARE by T. TOFT and others. STONEWARE was first produced in the late C17 by the ELERS brothers and soon became the material most frequently used, generally with a salt-glaze from *c*.1710, both for household crockery and such ornaments as PEW GROUPS. The earlier salt-glazed wares were decorated with incised ornament filled with blue colouring (known as 'scratch blue') or with moulded and applied reliefs of Tudor roses, sprays of plum blossom, naked boys, etc. (moulded wares were produced from the 1740s onwards). In the first half of the C18 the factories of J. ASTBURY and (from 1740) T. WHIELDON appear to have

Staffordshire salt-glazed stoneware tea-canister, c.1740–60 (Victoria & Albert Museum)

Staffordshire earthenware figure of 'Dick Turpin', 1840–50 (Victoria & Albert Museum)

been the best; that of R. WOOD produced attractively rustic figures and TOBY JUGS of earthenware with coloured glazes from the mid C18. The whole group of potteries was revolutionized by J. WEDGWOOD who from 1759 made the most refined wares ever produced in the district and exerted a dominant stylistic (Neo-Classical) and technical influence on most other factories. He was mainly responsible for developing CREAM-COLOURED EARTHENWARE, first made by Enoch BOOTH of Tunstall. It became the staple product from the later 1760s and was exported to and imitated on the Continent where it drove faience out of fashion. A little later Josiah SPODE began to produce attractive printed blue-and-white wares which were also much imitated. Spode set the pace for the ever increasing richness of modelling, gilding and painting practised by both pottery and porcelain factories in the C19. He was largely responsible for the introduction of porcelain-making in the district (though soft-paste had been made at LONGTON HALL and hard-paste at NEW HALL) and in 1805 began producing stone-china, to be followed in 1813 by MASONS. Later several of the more notable factories added PARIAN WARE to their types of product. But the majority of minor factories were engaged chiefly in the C19 in turning out vast quantities of simple household wares and endearingly naïve statuettes to grace cottage mantelpieces. The statuettes represent spaniels and poodles and a whole panorama of C19 notabilities – Queen Victoria, Prince Albert, John Brown, General Gordon, General Booth, Garibaldi, W. G. Grace, Maria Marten, etc. – and were made mainly from *c.*1840 to 1900. They were cast from moulds and decorated in gay enamel colours with a little glazing. The backs of figures were generally treated in a summary fashion and rarely coloured. Similar figures were made elsewhere, especially in Scotland.

Lit: B. Rackham, *Early Staffordshire Pottery*, London 1951; W. L. Little, *Staffordshire Blue*, London 1969; P. D. G. Pugh, *Victorian Staffordshire Portrait Figures*, London 1970; A. R. Mountford, *The Illustrated Guide to Staffordshire Saltglazed Stoneware*, London 1971.

Stained glass Glass stained with a colouring material throughout its substance and/or on its surface, especially that used for windows in churches and, less often, in private houses. Usually the pieces of glass of various shapes and colours are held together by a lead framework. Originally the patterns appear to have been abstract but by the mid C11 panels of glass were arranged to represent figures (e.g. five windows in Augsburg Cathedral). The art of making such windows reached its peak of excellence in the C12 and C13 in France (Cathedrals of Chartres, Saint Denis, Le Mans, Bourges, Chalons-sur-Marne, Sainte-Chapelle in Paris, etc.), and in England (Cathedrals of Canterbury and York). At this period the windows were made up of a mosaic of pieces of variously coloured CROWN GLASS (for the ruby red colour sheets of clear glass were 'flashed' with a film of red glass) onto which such details as the features of a face, the folds of a drapery or the leaves of a plant were painted in opaque black enamel. Designs were derived mainly from contemporary manuscript illuminations. The effect is rich and jewel-like though the individual scenes are often difficult to 'read'. Technical advances were made in the C14 when larger panels of coloured glass became available and the use of a transparent yellow surface stain derived from sulphide of silver was developed. The immediate result was that the

Stained glass: a grocer in his shop, Flemish, C16 (Victoria & Albert Museum)

windows became much lighter. Also, the role of the painter, who picked out detail in enamels, increased significantly. From this moment onwards the art of the glass stainer grew less and less independent and more closely associated with that of the panel and fresco painter (in c15 Italy windows were generally designed by panel or fresco painters who made few concessions to the different medium, e.g. Milan Cathedral). In the c15 the process of abrasion of sheets of flashed glass was developed, making it possible to pick out very fine details in white on a coloured ground. Finally, in the mid c16 the discovery of transparent enamel pigments which could be painted onto regularly shaped sheets of clear white glass revolutionized the art of the glass stainer who was henceforth spared the labour of cutting pieces of coloured glass and fitting them into a framework of leads. These technical improvements were not accompanied by any equivalent artistic advance: indeed rather the reverse, partly because of a decline in the demand for stained glass windows. But attractive work continued to be executed in the c16 and c17.

The early history of stained glass windows was intimately connected with the great Gothic cathedrals in which they played symbolic and didactic as well as decorative and utilitarian roles. Their character changed fundamentally as the early Gothic style merged into the Flamboyant (with greater emphasis on stone tracery) and, in England, into the Perpendicular (with greater desire for light). They first appear in domestic buildings in c14 France when heraldic panels were sometimes set in windows composed of circular 'bulls-eye' pieces of glass. By the c15 they were also to be found in houses in Germany, the Netherlands, Switzerland and England. The allegories of the Months, religious and mythological subjects as well as coats-of-arms were popular for houses and castles. In Switzerland it became a fairly common practice at this date to use stained glass panels, usually heraldic but often incorporating portraits, as gifts to mark special occasions (weddings, etc.), and the custom was perpetuated into the c17 (and peasants continued to give panels of engraved glass on similar occasions into the c19). This stimulated the art of glass-staining in Switzerland which produced many of the best c16 and c17 glass-stainers in

Stained glass: panel of Hans Wendel Scherer and his wife, by H. C. Gallati, Switzerland, 1675 (Victoria & Albert Museum)

Europe (e.g. C. and J. Murer, L. Zeiner). These and other domestic panels were intended to be seen close at hand and are thus executed with great delicacy and love of detail. But the desire for, and increased availability of, large panels of clear glass for windows led inevitably to a decline in the production of stained glass from the mid c17 onwards – though good work was still done, especially in England by H. Gyles and W. Peckitt. Stained glass windows came back into fashion with the Gothic Revival though almost exclusively for churches. In 1827 the Sèvres porcelain factory established a studio for making stained glass and employed such outstanding painters as Ingres and Delacroix to provide cartoons (e.g. Chapelle-Royale, Dreux). Other studios in Germany, Italy and England worked mainly in imitation of medieval windows and paintings. The art was revived with much greater understanding by William Morris who established a glass-staining studio in London in

1861, executing both ecclesiastical and domestic work (the latter mainly of Arthurian and Chaucerian subjects) after cartoons by the Pre-Raphaelite painters D. G. Rossetti and E. Burne-Jones. Handsome domestic stained glass was made in the U.S. by J. LA FARGE and J. L. C. TIFFANY. In France stained glass windows became very popular during the Art Nouveau period (S. BING commissioned windows to designs by Bonnard and other leading painters). More recently stained glass has been produced in France, to cartoons by such artists as Léger, Matisse, Rouault, etc.

Lit: V. Beyer, *Stained Glass Windows*, Edinburgh 1964; W. J. Drake, *A Dictionary of Glass Painters . . .*, New York 1953; J. G. Lloyd, *Stained Glass in America*, Jenkintown 1963; A. C. Sewter, *The Stained Glass of William Morris and his Circle*, New Haven 1974.

Staite Murray, William (1881–1962). English studio potter who began *c.*1919 to produce stoneware in Kensington, later at Bray. Contact with Bernard LEACH and Shoji Hamada encouraged him to adopt Japanese methods and attitudes to pottery. His most notable works are handsome, large vases (reminiscent of RAKU wares), simply decorated with painted and/or incised motifs, and often embarrassed with pretentious titles like *Vortex*, *Cadence* or *Purple Night*.

Lit: M. Rose, *Artist Potters in England*, London 1955.

Stalker, John and **Parker, George** (*fl.*1688). The authors of *A Treatise of Japanning and Varnishing* (Oxford 1688) which describes various ways of imitating Japanese lacquer, illustrated with strange chinoiserie designs for the adornment of furniture, picture frames, brush-backs, etc. The designs seem to have had more influence on silversmiths than on japanners.

Stam, Mart (b.1899). Dutch architect and designer and the inventor of the tubular steel cantilever chair. He was the first to realize that the strength of tubular steel would enable a chair to be cantilevered on two supports, instead of four legs – with the added advantage of resilience, light weight and extreme simplicity of construction. Stam's epoch-making design came in 1924 but unfortunately he did not have access to the necessary pipe-bending techniques until the following year and his chair was not realized until 1926. (A provisional 1924 version had to be made with lengths of straight tubing with standard elbow pieces, thus losing the springiness inherent in the cantilever design.) By 1926 MIES VAN DER ROHE had also produced a tubular steel cantilever chair. Stam's design was immediately taken up and popularized, notably by BREUER who designed his classic tubular steel cantilever chair in 1928.

M. Stam: cantilever chair of steel tube and webbing, 1926 (Victoria & Albert Museum)

Stamped bindings Leather bookbindings decorated with metal panel stamps or blocks cut or engraved with a pictorial or decorative device and stamped blind on the leather (usually calf or pigskin) by means of a hand-press. They were made throughout Europe in late Medieval to early Renaissance times. The process was much less laborious than that previously used, i.e. stamping by hand with small dies. Stamped bindings were made at Antwerp by 1400 and in Paris by 1450. In England they appear from the 1480s onwards. By the end of the c16 they had been superseded by gold-tooled and other types of binding. Stamped bindings were revived in the early c19, first in France and later in England and elsewhere. The revival led to the introduction of EMBOSSED BINDINGS.

Lit: J. B. Oldham, *English Blind-stamped Bindings*, Cambridge 1952.

Standing cup Medieval English term for a cup with a stem and base, especially of gold or silver, generally applied to one of a decorative character with a tall stem.

Standish Stand for ink, pens, sand and other writing materials. The earliest (late c17) are of silver, but wood, ormolu, etc. were also used.

Standish, silver gilt, by Paul de Lamerie, London 1741 (Goldsmiths' Company, London)

Stangenglas A c17 German type of tall, slim cylindrical beaker with a spreading, hollow foot and sometimes with enamelled decoration.

Steel A somewhat imprecise term for an alloy of iron and carbon, but with rather less carbon than most of the alloys commonly called IRON. Sometimes other metals are included in the alloy: mild steel contains no more than 0.25 per cent carbon but also larger proportions of other metals such as manganese. To save confusion, the term steel is now generally reserved for alloys which contain higher proportions of carbon than mild steel and which (unlike wrought iron) may be hardened and tempered. This material has been used since prehistoric times for weapons and cutting instruments – from razors and knives to saws and swords. It has also been used occasionally for decorative objects – caskets, small boxes, and items of personal adornment – decorated in a variety of ways, by combining metals of different percentages of alloy (pattern welding), DAMASCENING, inlaying, chiselling or etching. The term 'damascening' is commonly and loosely applied to the process of decorating steel with gold or silver beaten into undercut grooves, more correctly termed inlaying.

Lit: L. Aitchison, *A History of Metals*, London 1960; H. Hodges, *Artifacts*, London 1964.

Steel, stainless A steel alloy, made rust- and stainproof by the addition of chromium, first produced in Germany and England in the early c20 and developed as a medium for table-wares from the 1920s. At first it was used mainly for knife blades – soon replacing all other metals for this purpose – subsequently for spoons, forks, dishes, etc.

Steele, Thomas (1772–1850). The most prominent member of a family of English procelain decorators (others were named **Edwin** and **Horatio**). He worked for the DERBY, ROCKINGHAM, DAVENPORT and, 1825–43, MINTON factories, specializing in carefully rendered paintings of fruit.

Steeple cup An early c17 English type of decorative standing cup with a cover crowned by an obelisk or steeple-like terminal.

Steingut The German term for lead-glazed earthenware similar to English CREAM-COLOURED EARTHENWARE and French *faïence fine*.

Steinzeug The German term for STONEWARE.

Steitz, Heinrich, *see* CASSEL POTTERY & PORCELAIN FACTORY.

Stem cup A type of Chinese porcelain drinking vessel with a wide shallow bowl set on a tubular stem which spreads out slightly at the base, first made in the MING period, though the form derives from earlier metal ritual vessels. (For illustration *see* page 741.)

Stephan, Pierre, *see* DERBY PORCELAIN FACTORY.

Sterken, R., *see* ROZENBURG POTTERY & PORCELAIN FACTORY.

Sterling standard The standard of purity in English silver which has been in use since early medieval times except for a short period 1697–1720. The standard for coinage was established by statute in 1300. The Troy pound contains 11 oz. 2 dwt of pure silver and 18 dwt of alloy – that is 925 parts per 1000 pure.

Steuben Glass Works A glasshouse at Corning, New York, founded in 1903 with F. CARDER as manager and specializing in decorative pieces, notably AURENE GLASS. It was absorbed by the CORNING GLASS WORKS in 1918. In 1933 the name was revived as a department of the Corning Corporation producing absolutely clear, rather thick, glass ornamental pieces discreetly decorated with wheel engravings under the direction of Sidney Waugh (1904–63). The first of these pieces was shown at the Paris Exhibition in 1937 when they attracted the attention of Henri Matisse who agreed to make a design to be engraved on crystal. A series of pieces of glass engraved according to designs provided by contemporary European and U.S. artists were issued in editions of six examples, and also recorded in illustrated books published by the company (*A Selection of Engraved Crystal, by Steuben Glass,* 1961).

Lit: J. S. Plaut, *Steuben Glass,* New York 1951; P. Perrot, P. Gardner & J. Plant, *Steuben, Seventy Years of American Glass-making,* New York 1974.

Steuben glass: goblet, engraved after a design by P. Tchelitchew, c.1950 *(Victoria & Albert Museum)*

Stevengraphs The trade name for silk pictures made on a modified type of JACQUARD LOOM by **Thomas Stevens** of Coventry from 1879 onwards. He died in 1888 but his firm appears to have continued production until 1938. The factory was bombed in 1940.

Lit: G. A. Godden, *Stevengraphs,* London 1971.

Stevens, Alfred (1817–75). English painter, sculptor and designer. He studied in Italy where he developed a lasting passion for High Renaissance art. As a designer he is most notable for sculpturesque metal-work, especially cast-iron stoves and fireplaces, decorated profusely with figures, foliage and architectural motifs of a Renaissance flavour. His masterpiece was the interior of Dorchester House, London (1858–62, demolished 1929) for which he painted ceilings and designed chimney-pieces, doors, etc. (some now in the Walker Art Gallery, Liverpool).

Alfred Stevens: cast-iron fire-grate and bronze firedogs, made by Henry E. Hoole & Co., Sheffield, c.1862 *(Victoria & Albert Museum)*

Lit: K. R. Towndrow, *Alfred Stevens,* London 1939.

Stevens and Williams English glasshouse at Brierley Hill, Worcestershire, and one of the most notable of the STOURBRIDGE GLASSHOUSES, established under this name in 1846. It produced a wide range of decorative glass – cased glass, vessels with crackled or with silver deposit decorations, etc. Several notable cameo-glass cutters were employed including J. NORTHWOOD and F. CARDER. For many years the intaglio department was directed by **William Hodgetts** (1857–1933) who specialized in naturalistic flower patterns. In the 1930s the factory produced bowls, vases and table-wares designed by K. MURRAY in an International Modern style. The firm is still active.

Lit: W. B. Honey, *Glass: A Handbook*, London 1946; G. W. Beard, *Nineteenth Century Cameo Glass*, Newport, Mon. 1956.

Stick furniture The commonest type of stools (later chairs) and tables of the Middle Ages, still made to this day in the less advanced parts of Europe and America. The basic form is the stool with a fairly thick slab of wood to serve as the seat supported on three or four splayed-out stick-like legs of round or square section, the tops of which are driven through the seat and held tight by wedges hammered in from the top.

Stick furniture: Italian c16 chair (Palazzo Davanzati, Florence)

Stickley, Gustav(e) (1857–1942). U.S. furniture designer, maker and theorist. He was born at Osceola, Wisconsin and began as a stone mason, but soon turned to chair-making under an uncle in Pennsylvania. After working with a succession of partners making furniture in historical styles he established his own concern, the **Gustave Stickley Company** at Eastwood (a suburb of Syracuse), New York, in 1898. Also in 1898 he visited Europe where he met C. F. A. VOYSEY and other notable designers. He abandoned Revivalist styles and began to make handsome, solid plain furniture with a modicum of Art Nouveau ornament which he first exhibited at GRAND RAPIDS in 1900. To distinguish his products from those made by his two brothers, **L. and J. G. Stickley** at Fayetteville, he now adopted the trade-name 'Craftsman'. He founded in 1901 a periodical *The Craftsman*, stating in its first issue that his aim was 'to substitute the luxury of taste for the luxury of costliness; to teach that beauty does not imply elaboration or ornament; to employ only those forms and materials which make for simplicity, individuality and dignity of effect'. The notions derive from Ruskin and MORRIS, the furniture from that of the English ARTS AND CRAFTS movement – sturdy tables and cupboards, chairs with slat backs, usually made of oak, with exposed joinery (dowel pins, dove-tails, etc.) and plain leather or canvas upholstery. It became known as MISSION FURNITURE. He patented several of his designs, notably that of an arm-chair with an adjustable back, and issued catalogues of his products which were intended for and reached a wide market (unlike those of the arts-and-craftsmen in England). Such was his success that his designs were much plagiarized. In 1905 he set up an office in New York City and in 1913 acquired there a large building with offices and showrooms. But he had expanded too much and went bankrupt in 1915. A last-minute attempt to revive his fortunes by a change in style and the use of bright colours was unsuccessful.

Lit: J. C. Freeman, *The Forgotten Rebel*, Watkins Glen, N.Y. 1966; R. Judson Clark (ed.),

The Arts and Crafts Movement in America 1876–1916, Exh. Cat., Art Museum, Princeton University, Art Institute of Chicago, etc. 1972–3.

Stickwork Small objects such as chess-men, egg-cups, snuff-boxes, etc. made from sticks of various types of wood assembled by the same technique as in TUNBRIDGE WARE and then turned on a lathe. They were produced at Tunbridge Wells and also in London in the C19.

Stiegel, Henry William (1729–85). German glass manufacturer, he was in America by 1750 and founded three glasshouses in Pennsylvania in the 1760s, the best-known at Manheim in 1763, employing German, Venetian and English blowers who worked in their national styles. The **Manheim Glasshouse** is credited with some handsome pieces of crystal glass, sometimes rather crudely engraved, and much coloured and PATTERN MOULDED table-wares of a slightly rough or German peasant type. Over-rapid expansion brought about financial troubles and in 1774 the Manheim factory closed and Stiegel was imprisoned for debt. The workmen moved to various other glasshouses where they continued to work in much the same manner. The term 'Stiegel glass' is commonly applied to most C18 American pattern-moulded wares.

Lit: G. S. & H. McKearin, *American Glass*, New York 1941; B. M. Lindsey, *American Historical Glass*, London 1967.

Stile A vertical member of a framing of chest, cupboard, door, etc. Stiles have mortices cut through them to receive the tenons of the horizontal members or rails.

Stipple engraving A technique of decorating glass with designs made up of incised dots of varying density, giving an appearance of light and shade (brightest where they are most dense) and a much richer effect than line engraving, somewhat similar to a mezzotint. It is executed with a diamond point set in a handle and gently struck with a hammer against the surface of the glass. As the incisions are slight, it is particularly suitable for the decoration of thin-walled vessels. It appears to have originated in the Netherlands where it was used in conjunction with line engraving by

Stipple engraving on a glass by D. Wolff, c.1775 (Victoria & Albert Museum)

A. R. VISSCHER and others in the C17 and was first adopted as an almost independent medium (i.e. with very few if any engraved lines) by F. GREENWOOD, who is traditionally credited with its invention, in the early C18. Notable practitioners include Aert Schouman (1710–92), G. H. HOOLAART (*c.*1716–71/2), D. WOLFF, J. van den Blijk (1736–1814), L. Adams (*fl.*1806), A. Melort (1779–1849) and D. H. de Castro (d.1863). The technique is still practised by both professionals and amateurs.

Stirrup cup A drinking vessel without handle or foot, often made in the form of an animal's head, like a RHYTON, from the later C18.

Stobwasser, Johann Heinrich (1740–1829). German japanner and proprietor of one of the most important JAPANNING factories of the day. The main factory was in Brunswick and a subsidiary one, run by his brother-in-law **Jean Guérin**, was established in Berlin in 1772. They specialized in small objects, notably boxes very finely painted with portraits, landscapes, mythological scenes after Old Masters, sentimental genre scenes, satirical groups, etc. There is a large collection of them in the Stadtmuseum, Brunswick. They also produced some larger objects such as commodes.

Lit: W. Holzhausen, *Lackkunst in Europa*, Brunswick 1959; H. Huth, *Lacquer in the West*, Chicago and London 1971.

Stockamer, Balthazar (*fl.* 1666–1700). German Baroque ivory carver who worked mainly for the Medici in Florence, styling himself Ivory Turner to Cosimo III. His works include a turned cup supported by a naked youth (Victoria & Albert Museum) and a very fine Crucifixion group (Palazzo Pitti, Florence).

Stöckel, Joseph (1743–1800). He was a German furniture-maker who settled in Paris in 1769 and became a *maître ébéniste* in 1775. His work is often Neo-Roman in style, sometimes to designs by LALONDE. Some of his finer pieces were later revised by BENEMAN, e.g. the commodes he made *c.*1785 for Compiègne and now in the Louvre and Fontainebleau.

Stockelsdorf pottery A faience factory founded in 1771, near Lübeck, specializing in making stoves, at first in an ebulliently Rococo manner, all curves and scrolls painted with chinoiseries, etc. (notably by A. LEIHAMER) but later in a rather pompous Antique Revival style. Other products included large trays or tea-table tops, helmet shaped ewers with shell mouldings, wall fountains, *jardinières*, pear-shaped vases, plates with basket-work edges, etc., very attractively painted in enamel colours, especially a bluish green and clear orange yellow. Some wares painted in underglaze blue or manganese are similar to those of ECKERNFÖRDE. The quality of its products declined sharply after 1788 (when the founder **Georg Nicolaus Lübbers** died) but the concern seems to have remained active until 1811. *Illustrated next column.* (For factory mark *see* p. 888.)

Lit: K. Hüseler, *Deutsche Fayencen*, Stuttgart 1956–8; G. Lindtke in *Keramos* 14 (1961), pp. 14–24.

Stockelsdorf faience stove painted by A. Leihamer, c.1775 (Museum für Kunst und Gewerbe, Hamburg)

Stockholm silk factories The most important was that established by a French weaver, **Barthelemi Peyron**, in 1741 under state encouragement and to work mainly for the Court. Its chief designers were trained in France and its products are hardly inferior to those of LYONS. The concern seems to have petered out in the 1760s.

Stone china A very hard earthenware containing petuntse, first made in 1805 at the SPODE POTTERY in STAFFORDSHIRE. A similar material called Ironstone China was patented by MASONS in 1813.

Stoneware Very hard, non-porous and sometimes slightly translucent pottery made from a mixture of clay and a fusible stone, usually feldspar, fired at a temperature high enough to vitrify the stone but not the clay, from 1200°C. to 1400°C. It was first produced from the C4 onwards in China whence the process was transmitted to the Middle East. But in Europe its production seems to have been developed independently in the C9 in the Rhineland. This region remained the main centre for stoneware throughout the Middle Ages and into the C17 (*see* COLOGNE POTTERIES, RAEREN POTTERIES, SIEGBURG POTTERIES). From the C14 onwards Rhenish stoneware was often covered with a SALT GLAZE (although sometimes used, lead glazes are difficult to apply on account of the high temperature of firing). These wares varied from off-white to dull grey though occasionally they were coloured by the glaze, usually brown, black, purple or blue. Similar salt-glazed stoneware was produced in England from *c.*1684 by J. DWIGHT and later at the STAFFORDSHIRE POTTERIES where it was made in quantity until superseded by CREAM WARE. Red stoneware, in imitation of that of YI-HSING in China, made at DELFT and by Dwight in London in the late C17, and BÖTTGER'S red stoneware (the immediate forerunner of the hard-paste porcelain made at MEISSEN) are much softer than true stoneware of the Rhenish type. The production of stoneware was much taken up by French studio potters in the late C19. Stoneware is called *grès* in French and *Steinzeug* in German.

Stool The commonest type of seat furniture until the C19, distinct from the bench in that it seats only one person and from the chair in that it has neither arms nor back. The two main types – one supported on four straight legs, the other on four legs arranged cross-wise – were in use in Egypt at a very early period. Both types were adopted by the Greeks – who called the straight-legged type a *diphros* and the cross-legged *diphros okladias* – and later by the Romans. They passed

Stool by Pelagio Palagi, 1835–40 (Palazzo Reale, Turin)

almost unaltered into medieval use. In the later Middle Ages a three-legged type of stool with a circular or polygonal top was developed in Italy where it remained popular into the C17 (sometimes called a *Strozzi* stool). But most later stools (even those of C20 designers) are merely variants of the two basic types. Innovations occur only in the decorations of the supports and the treatment of the padded or hard top. *See also* PLIANT and TABOURET.

Store Kongensgade, *see* COPENHAGEN POTTERIES.

Storr, Paul (1771–1844). He was the leading English Regency silversmith. He was apprenticed to Andrew FOGELBERG, a silversmith of Swedish origin working in the Adam style. After obtaining his freedom he was in partnership with **William Frisbee** from 1792 to 1796 when he set up on his own. Shortly afterwards he began to work for RUNDELL and Bridge whom he joined in partnership 1811–19, apparently in charge of the workshops, making large quantities of plate, often to models provided by sculptors (notably FLAXMAN) for a wide range of patrons including the Prince Regent and members of the Royal Family. His early works are in the late C18 Antique Revival style and include monumental wine-coolers, urns, etc., with shapes derived from Greek vases, and an abundance of Greek architectural embellishments (palmettes, frets, etc.) vine-leaf ornament in relief and cast figures of allegories and ancient deities. He specialized in the pieces of presentation plate so much in demand as gifts to victorious generals and admirals during the Napoleonic wars. But he was no less successful on a small scale and such trifles as honey-pots in the form of bee-hives and little jugs wreathed in vine leaves are among the most immediately attractive pieces of English silver of their period. From the very beginning of the C19 he also produced silver in a revived version of the Rococo style, encrusted with shell-work and rock-work and sometimes incorporating figures of prancing sea-horses. Such pieces are among the earliest manifestations of reaction against Neo-classicism in England. He left Rundell in 1819 and once again set up on his own but in 1822 went into partnership with **John Mortimer.** Unfortunately over-stocking (by Mortimer) brought the firm to the edge of bankruptcy in 1826, but Storr's nephew **John Samuel Hunt** came to the rescue with £5,000. He became a partner. In the early 1830s E. H. BAILEY joined the firm as designer but generally the work produced was very similar to that made at Rundell's, with a slight tendency to effects of greater weightiness. Storr retired in 1839 but the firm was carried on under the name of **Mortimer and Hunt** until 1842, and then as **Hunt and Roskell.** The firm continued to make large richly sculptural trophies, candelabra, vases, table-centres and other pieces of presentation plate many of which were shown at the Great Exhibition in 1851, notably pieces by the sculptor Henry Hugh Armstead (*c.*1816–96) and French designer Antoine VECHTE (1799–1868) who was permanently employed by them after 1848 though he had worked on the Titan vase previously, before leaving Paris for London. *Illustrated next column.* (For his mark *see* p. 894.)

Lit: N. M. Penzer, *Paul Storr*, London 1954; C. Oman in *Apollo* LXXXIII (1966), pp. 174–83.

Stötzel, Samuel, *see* VIENNA PORCELAIN FACTORY.

Stourbridge glasshouses A large group of factories in and around Stourbridge in Worcestershire. The first were established before 1612 when members of the **Tysack** and **Henzey** families – Huguenot immigrants from Lorraine – are known to have been active in the area. They specialized

P. Storr: silver urn, after a design by Flaxman, London 1812 (Royal Collection, by gracious permission of H.M. the Queen)

The 'Titan Vase' by Storr's successors, Hunt & Roskell, designed by Antoine Vechte, silver, London 1851 (Goldsmiths' Company, London)

in flat glass but by the mid C18 were also making table-wares and decorative pieces, sometimes of coloured glass. In the C19 the area became the most important in England for the production of fine table glass and decorative glass. A boom began in 1845 when an oppressive tax on flint glass was lifted and the factories were enabled to compete with the BOHEMIAN GLASSHOUSES whose wares they often imitated. The largest and most notable factories were those of **Benjamin Richardson** (1802–87), STEVENS AND WILLIAMS and T. WEBB. But there were numerous smaller factories. Products included vases, drinking vessels, candlesticks, plates, scent-bottles, decanters, etc. in a very wide range of colours. CASED GLASS became something of a speciality (the master-craftsmen in this genre, J. NORTHWOOD and F. CARDER, worked for Stevens and Williams). From the mid C19 much decorative work was executed mechanically. In 1851 the Richardson factory introduced a pressing machine for decorating flint glass with relief ornament and in 1857 a threading machine to make Venetian-style filigree glass. Further technical developments made possible the production of CAMEO glass on a commercial scale by 1880. The products answered C19 taste for historical and exotic styles. Similar glass was made not far from Stourbridge at Birmingham where the leading factories were those of BACCHUS, Rice Harris & Son, and F. & C. Osler.

Lit: W. B. Honey, *Glass: A Handbook*, London 1946; G. W. Beard, *Nineteenth Century Cameo Glass*, Newport, Mon. 1956.

Straight banding Decoration on furniture or panelling by means of thin strips of veneer, cut with the grain. *See also* CROSS BANDING.

Stralsund pottery A Pomeranian faience factory founded by **Johann Ulrich Giese** *c.*1755–6 and directed from 1766 by **Johann Eberhardt Ludwig Ehrenreich** (1722–1803) a doctor of medicine who had founded the MARIEBERG POTTERY. For a few years it produced large Rococo vases, tureens and other wares similar to those of Marieberg. But it was partly destroyed by the explosion of a powder magazine in 1770. Although it was re-started by Giese in 1772 and survived until 1792, it produced little of interest during these later years. (For factory mark *see* p. 888.)

Lit: R. Marsson, *Die Stralsunder Fayencen*, Berlin 1928.

Strapwork or **Rollwork** Ornament consisting of interlaced bands, reminiscent of leather thongs or carved fretwork. Its origin is uncertain. It is first recorded in the wide stucco frieze serving as a frame for a series of paintings, designed by ROSSO FIORENTINO 1533–5 for the Galerie de François I at Fontainebleau. It probably derived from Antique motifs as distorted for expressive purposes by such Italian Renaissance artists as Cosimo Tura. But it became popular mainly in northern Europe, especially in the Netherlands where fantastic variations on it – typically Mannerist in their tortured, intertwining forms –

Strapwork cartouche by unknown C16 Flemish or Dutch designer

were published by numerous designers, notably **Cornelis Bos, Cornelis Floris, Vredeman de Vries** and **W. Dietterlin.** It was frequently combined with grotesques and influenced the development of GROTESQUE decorations. French designers used it with restraint, e.g. **René Boyvin** and **Du Cerceau.** It was also popular in Elizabethan England.

Lit: P. Ward-Jackson, 'Some main streams and tributaries in European ornament from 1500 to 1750', Part I, in *Victoria & Albert Museum Bulletin*, April 1967.

Strasbourg pottery and porcelain factory The source of much of the finest C18 faience and of a style of decoration in enamel colours which was widely imitated in France, Germany, Scandinavia and Italy. The faience factory was founded in 1720 by J. H. WACHENFELD who went into partnership with C.-F. HANNONG (previously a manufacturer of clay pipes) in 1721 but withdrew in 1722. Throughout the rest of its history it was run by various members of the Hannong family. In 1723 a branch factory was established near the source of clay at Haguenau (it is possible that wares were made there and only decorated at the Strasbourg workshops). Early products were unambitious, confined mainly to blue-and-white

(Below) Strasbourg faience tureen, pre-1754 (Badisches Landesmuseum, Karlsruhe)

(Right) Strasbourg faience stove by F. P. Acker, c.1760 (Historisches Museum, Basel)

(Far right) Strasbourg faience plate, c.1770 (Victoria & Albert Museum)

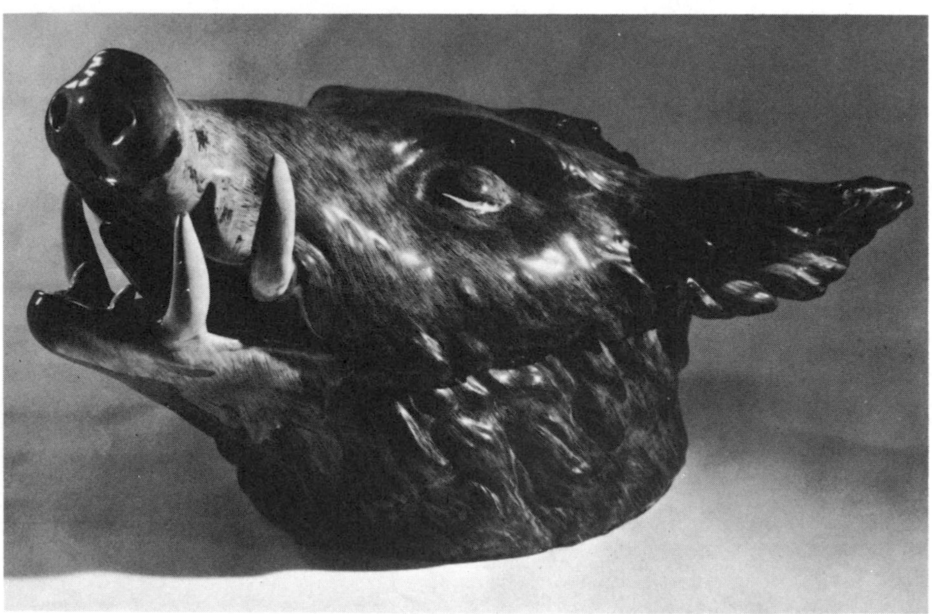

wares influenced by ROUEN. A new period began in 1732 when C.-F. Hannong retired and his sons took over the two factories, Balthasar running that at Haguenau and Paul-Antoine that at Strasbourg, though the latter directed both from 1737. Under Paul-Antoine's direction the full range of high-temperature colours was introduced for the decoration of wares, generally with *fleurs des Indes* or chinoiseries. But from the later 1740s the factory adopted the hitherto unusual practice of decorating faience in enamel colours. This may have been due partly to the employment from 1748 of Christian Wilhelm and Karl Heinrich von Löwenfinck who were followed in 1751 by their more famous brother A. F. von LÖWENFINCK. All of them had worked at porcelain factories where enamel decoration was normal. These painters also seem to have been responsible for introducing, as an alternative to *fleurs des Indes*, naturalistic flowers or *deutsche Blumen* which were soon to be known in France as *fleurs de Strasbourg*. The best Strasbourg wares are painted in this manner and date from the late 1740s and 1750s. They include table services with tureens composed of shell and flower forms or in the shape of birds or vegetables, delicate *pot-pourris*, large clock cases, sconces and wall fountains and such articles as bidets and bourda-

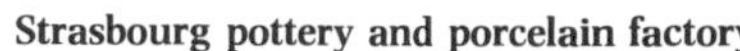

lous, modelled with the swirling curves of the high Rococo style and painted in bright enamel colours, especially purple of Cassius, pale blue, yellow and shades of violet and green on a very fine white ground. Figures of *putti*, gods and goddesses were also made both as table ornaments and for application to the large vases, fountains, etc., the best of them apparently after models by Johann Wilhelm Lanz. All these products tend to simulate, and were sold in competition with, porcelain. And with the assistance of the arcanist J. J. RINGLER porcelain was made at the factory from 1752 to 1755. But as an exclusive monopoly of porcelain-making was held by the Vincennes SÈVRES factory, P.-A. Hannong was obliged to move this part of the concern to a new factory which he established in Germany at FRANKENTHAL. (It is very hard to distinguish between Strasbourg porcelain of this period and early Frankenthal.) After the death of Paul-Antoine Hannong in 1760 the Strasbourg and Haguenau factories passed to his son Pierre-Antoine, a disastrously bad administrator, and in 1762 to another son Joseph-Adam who ran them until they closed in 1781. In this later period faience wares (but no figures) like and often from the same models as those of the 1750s continued to be made and decorated in the same brilliant palette on a still larger scale. The manufacture of

porcelain was resumed after the relaxation of the Sèvres monopoly in 1766, but the useful wares (decorated in the Louis XVI style seldom if ever used for the faience) and ornamental figures were generally imitative of other factories. The expense of the porcelain factory ruined the whole concern and in 1781 Joseph-Adam was declared bankrupt and fled to Germany. Pierre-Antoine Hannong attempted to revive the manufacture of porcelain at Haguenau in 1783–4 but without success. (For mark *see* p. 888.)

Lit: J. Terrasson, *Les Hannong et leurs manufactures Strasbourg-Frankenthal*, Paris and Lausanne 1971.

Stras(s), Georges Frédéric (1701–73). Jeweller and maker of imitation precious stones named *strass* after him. He was born at Wolfisheim near Strasbourg, the son of a Protestant pastor, apprenticed to a jeweller in Strasbourg until 1719 and settled in Paris before 1724 when he was working in a fashionable jewellery *atelier* run by the widow **Prévost.** He set up on his own *c.*1730, perfected a method of making false stones (especially diamonds) from glass and was appointed jeweller to the King in 1734. He made a fortune from his artificial stones but in 1752 he ceded the formula for their production to **Georges-Michel Bapst** (with whom he had been in partnership since 1750), and subsequently worked and dealt only in precious stones. The term *pierres de strasse* was soon applied indiscriminately to many types of paste jewellery and from 1775 to cut-glass pendants for chandeliers. Paste *bijoux en strasse* exhibited in Paris in 1819 were, however, thought to have been made by a newly discovered process recently introduced into France and later credited to a non-existent Joseph Strasser. The word *strass*, still in general use on the Continent, is first recorded in English in 1820, but the term paste is generally preferred in English.

Lit: H. Haug in *Cahiers de la céramique* 23 (1961), pp. 175–85.

Straw marquetry or **Straw-work** Decorations on caskets, mirror-frames and various small pieces of furniture, made by applying strips of bleached and coloured straw in geometrical patterns or to form landscapes, etc. It was practised in Europe from the C17 onwards, most notably in late-C18 France where furniture was occasionally veneered with it.

Strawberry dish A type of late C17–C18 English silver dish, deeper but no larger than a plate, rather thin with punched decorations in the C17, more substantial and usually with a scalloped rim in the C18. It is improbable that such dishes were used originally only for strawberries.

Stretcher Horizontal bar joining and strengthening the legs of chairs, tables, etc.

Striegau pottery A Silesian factory producing *c.*1600–39 vessels of soft red (or more usually yellowish or white covered with red colouring matter) earthenware in imitation of Roman TERRA SIGILLATA and similarly decorated with reliefs and often marked with impressed seals. Most of the surviving specimens are mounted in silver or pewter. At the time of their manufacture it was believed that liquids could acquire medicinal properties from vessels of this material. Similar wares were made from *c.*1630 at GABEL and have often been confused with those of Striegau. (For factory mark *see* p. 888.)

Lit: M. Sauerlandt, *Edelmetallfassungen in der Keramik*, Berlin 1929.

Stringing A line or lines of wood or metal inlay used as a decorative border for furniture (especially table tops from C16 onwards).

Stuart, James 'Athenian' (1713–88). English architect famed mainly as co-author with **N. Revett** of *The Antiquities of Athens* (1762, vol. ii, 1789), which exerted a profound though delayed influence on the Greek Revival. Immediately after his return from Greece in 1755 he sought commissions as an interior designer but with no apparent success until 1759 when he began to design interiors and furniture for Spencer House, London, in a classical Roman – not Grecian – style which antedates and may have had some influence on the early style of Robert ADAM. It was rather oppressively rich and ill-organized. The furniture (some now at Althorp, Northampton) shows an obsession with classical ornament, an ability to adapt Roman temple fittings, such as altars and tripods, to household use, but little invention, and suggests that he would never have achieved Adam's success even had he been less dilatory and unreliable in character.

Lit: E. Harris, *The Furniture of Robert Adam*, London 1963; P. Thornton & J. Hardy in *Apollo* LXXXVII (1968), pp. 449–50.

Stuck shank The stem of a glass vessel made separately from the bowl and welded to it.

Studio potter A potter who works by traditional methods and on a limited scale with few or no assistants – as opposed to one employed in a factory. The term is normally reserved for those of the C19 and C20 who have spurned industrialization. Most studio potters have been French, English or American. The French, e.g. E. CHAPLET and A. DAMMOUSE, began by working in the Renaissance style. The earliest English group, R. W. MARTIN and his brothers, was influenced mainly by C16 Rhenish stoneware. From the 1860s onwards the influence of JAPANESE POTTERY, especially the rough tea ceremony wares, grew steadily and is still the most important (see B. LEACH, L. RIE and W. STAITE MURRAY). GAUGUIN is the most notable artist to have made studio pottery but three French potters were closely associated with prominent artists: J. L. ARTIGAS, E. LACHENAL and A. METHEY. In the U.S.A. the most influential figure was C. F. BINNS and notable potters include W. H. GRUEBY and A. VAN BRIGGLE; *see also* CHELSEA KERAMIC ART WORKS, NEWCOMB COLLEGE POTTERY, ROOKWOOD POTTERY.

Lit: M. Rose, *Artist Potters in England*, London 1955.

Stump leg A simple thick rear leg of a chair, much stronger than the more elaborate front legs.

Stumpwork Needlework in which all or most of the ornament is raised into relief on a foundation of wool or cotton-wool.

Stumpwork panel of 'David and Bathsheba', English, 1656 (Victoria & Albert Museum)

Sturzbecher A drinking cup of pottery (frequently of SIEGBURG stoneware) or metal with a stem in the form of a human figure or head which is upright only when the cup is inverted and empty.

Sturzbecher: Hafner ware, Cologne, mid c16 (Kunstgewerbemuseum, Berlin)

Style rayonnant A manner of painting blue-and-white faience, especially early c18 ROUEN wares. Rather thick LAMBREQUIN motifs in blue, picked out in white with scrolls and formalized flowers and leaves, alternating between very lacy blue arabesque motifs, are painted around the edge of the vessel; on plates these motifs are often repeated in reverse as a star-shaped pattern in the centre. (The term is also used architecturally but in an entirely different sense.)

Sucket fork An implement with a spoon at one end and a two-pronged fork at the other, intended for eating fruit, especially *succade* (fruit either candied or preserved in syrup).

Süe, Louis (b.1875). Trained at the École des Beaux Arts in Paris, he began as a painter but from 1910 onwards worked mainly as an interior decorator and furniture designer, at first in partnership with **Paul Huillard** (b.1875) exhibiting at the Salon d'Automne furniture marked by German influence. In 1919 he founded the Compagnie des Arts Français in partnership with **André Mare** (1887–1932) who had similarly begun as a painter and began his career as a decorator in 1910. Süe and Mare published a manifesto *Architectures* to which Paul Valéry contributed in 1921. In association with a number of younger designers and craftsmen including M. MARINOT they applied themselves to the production of all types of household furnishings, generally in a style of fairly costly simplicity with unmistakably ART DECO elements. The partnership was dissolved in 1928.

Lit: Les années '25', Exh. Cat., Musée des Arts Décoratifs, Paris 1966.

Sue(ki) pottery A group of Japanese ceramics later in date than YAYOI POTTERY, found mainly in tombs dating from c3 to c6 A.D. and so called from the identification of wares as religious utensils (from the word *sueru*: to offer). The wares appear to have been made by invaders from Korea. Vessels – wheel-turned and kiln-baked at high temperature – are very regular in form, light weight, and of a thinly potted smooth grey body sometimes splashed with a greenish glaze produced by accidental contact with wood-ash in the course of firing. They include drinking bowls, stemmed dishes, wide-mouthed jars and bottles in the form of leather bags or rings. Decorations are generally sparse but some vases have a ring of little human figures around their necks. The stems of cups and vases are often pierced with triangles, etc. It has not been ascertained whether Sue wares were made for daily use as well as for tombs.

Lit: S. Jenyns, *Japanese Pottery*, London 1971.

Sullivan, Louis Henry (1856–1924). The leading architect of his day in Chicago and, indeed, the U.S. Although he did not design movable furnishings he exerted considerable influence on the decorative arts in America, both through his theoretical writings and his development of an individual style of ornament with much use of prickly stylized plant forms anticipating ART NOUVEAU, e.g. in the interior of the Chicago Auditorium (1886–9) and on the exterior of the Carson Pirie Scott Store, Chicago (1899). G. G. ELMSLIE and F. L. WRIGHT were the most successful of the several architects and designers who began their careers in his office and owed much to him.

Lit: H. R. Hope, 'Louis Sullivan's architectural ornament' in *Magazine of Art*, March 1947.

Sulphide, *see* PELLAT, Apsley.

Sultane, *see* CANAPÉ.

Summerly's Art Manufactures, *see* COLE, Henry.

Sunderland potteries The most important was that of **Dixon, Austen & Co.** which was active *c.*1800–65 and specialized in large bowls and jugs decorated in pink lustre, often splashed with white to give a marbled effect, and printed views of the district notably the cast-iron bridge at Sunderland. Wares were marked with the name, impressed, of the various companies. **William Ball** (d.1884) established the **Deptford Pottery** in 1857, whose wares are similarly decorated but with a rather orange-tinted pink lustre. They are usually unmarked.

Lit: F. Buckley in *Archaeologia Aeliana* IV (1927); J. T. Shaw, *The Potteries of Sunderland and District*, n.d.

Sung The Chinese dynasty which flourished from 960 to 1279, following on the chaotic Five Dynasties period which succeeded the T'ANG epoch. Though a period of political unrest with much of the former empire in the hands of barbarians it was, artistically, a classical age and produced paintings, sculpture and ceramics of an unequalled serenity and nobility. T'ang pottery forms were refined to an almost feminine delicacy. Incised decorations of lotus, fish and ducks became very popular especially on CELADON wares which are among the most beautiful products of the period. Similar in style are the ivory white TING WARES and the very fine

Sung dynasty: vase, Tz'û-Chou type, porcellaneous stoneware (William Rockhill Nelson Gallery of Art, Kansas City)

Sung Dynasty: jar, Chien *ware, porcellaneous stoneware (William Rockhill Nelson Gallery of Art, Kansas City)*

Sung dynasty: plate, Ting ware (William Rockhill Nelson Gallery of Art, Kansas City)

lavender-coloured JU WARES made only from 1107 to 1127 and the CHIEN wares, called Temmoku in Japan. The TZ'Û-CHOU WARES are much bolder in shape and decoration, but similarly reveal an exquisite sensibility for the subtleties and refinements of ceramic form and flat linear decoration. All these wares possess the classical qualities of simplicity, sobriety and finality. They are also classical in another sense, for they provided the prototypes to which Chinese potters were to return again and again during succeeding periods. The first Sung ceramics reached Europe in the late C19 and have ever since exerted an influence on European potters (notably the STUDIO POTTERS of France and England). Paintings reveal that the basic types of Chinese furniture design were perfected in the Sung period but few examples survive.

Supper set A set of five dishes, four open and shaped so that they form a ring round the fifth which is circular and has a cover. Such sets were made in England of silver, Sheffield plate, porcelain or pottery from the late C18 to the early C19.

Surrey enamel The name once given to brass objects decorated with *champlevé* enamel by a technique erroneously supposed to have originated in Surrey. The objects were cast with recesses for the enamel. They were made both in England and on the Continent.

Surtout de table French name for a TABLE-CENTRE.

Sussex potteries Late C18 and C19 potteries at Chailey, Brede, Rye, Cadborough, Wiston, Dicker, Burgess Hill and elsewhere made slipware, mostly of a rather crude variety but sometimes charmingly decorated with incised or impressed designs of foliage, stars or formal patterns in inlaid white slip. Raised hop-garlands are characteristic as decoration. The best were attributed to the Chailey and Brede potteries but the latter are now thought to have been made at Bethersden in Kent. Drinking vessels in the form of pigs and flat pocket flasks appear to have been a speciality of the Sussex potteries.

Swag An ornament similar to a FESTOON but of cloth instead of fruit and flowers.

Swansea potteries and porcelain factory A small concern called the **Cambrian Pottery** was active from 1765 producing wares of Staffordshire type,

Swansea porcelain plate, 1823 (Victoria & Albert Museum)

including cream-coloured earthenware, marbled wares, basaltes and blue-printed wares. But the factory owes its reputation to the fine soft-paste porcelain made from 1814, with the assistance of W. BILLINGSLEY of NANTGARW until 1817 and then to a slightly different formula until 1822. Products are of simple form and notable mainly for the quality of the paste and the delicacy of the paintings on it, especially figure subjects, birds, etc. by T. BAXTER and flowers by **Thomas Pardoe** (1770–1823). Many pieces were however sold unpainted and were decorated in London studios. After 1822 the factory produced only earthenware, the most interesting products being copies of Greek vases made by **Lewis Llewellyn Dillwyn** who was manager 1831–50. The factory closed in 1870. Another concern, the **Glamorgan Pottery,** was active at Swansea *c.*1813–39 and produced similar household wares. (For factory mark *see* p. 888.)

Lit: E. Morton Nance, *The Pottery and Porcelain of Swansea and Nantgarw,* London 1942; W. D. John, *Swansea Porcelain,* Newport 1958.

Swatow ware A misnomer for a type of Chinese export porcelain of the MING period made in the provinces of Fukien and Kwangtung (at Chaochou, Shih-ma and Ch'uan-chou) and so called because it is believed to have been shipped from the port of Swatow. Both blue-and-white and five-colour enamel wares, vigorously decorated but distinctly uncouth by courtly standards, are included under the name.

Sweetmeat glass An C18 English type of glass vessel with a stem and shallow bowl often moulded at the rim. It was intended to hold sweetmeats.

Sycamore wood The light-coloured rather soft wood of the *Acer Pseudoplatanus* used as a veneer in furniture making, especially in C18 England, and as an element in marquetry in France and Germany. When it is dyed a brownish-grey it is called **harewood.**

Syllabub glass, *see* SILLABUB.

Syng, Philip (1703–89). He was born in Cork, where his father was a goldsmith, and emigrated with his family to Annapolis in 1714. By 1720 his father had established himself in Philadelphia, but returned to Annapolis shortly after 1724 when Philip took over his silversmith workshops. He became one of the leading silversmiths of his day in Philadelphia, and is famous for the STANDISH which he made for the provincial Assembly in 1752 and which was used for the signing of the Declaration of Independence in

P. Syng: silver inkstand, made in 1752 and used at the signing of the Declaration of Independence, 1776 (Independence Hall, Philadelphia)

1776. He became a close friend of Benjamin Franklin and was a prominent citizen of Philadelphia. His few surviving pieces of silver are in styles fashionable in early- and mid-C18 England, sometimes adorned with delicate, though subdued, Rococo ornaments. Examples are in the Philadelphia Museum and the Yale University Art Gallery.

Lit: H. F. Jayne & S. W. Woodhouse in *Art in America* xl (1921), pp. 248–59; K. A. Kellock in *Dictionary of American Biography*, vol. xviii, New York; J. H. Pleasants & H. Sill, *Maryland Silversmiths 1715–1830*, Baltimore 1930 (for Philip Syng senior).

Synthetic fibres, *see* MAN-MADE FIBRES.

Hand-drawn initial from
Godfrey of Boloyne,
printed by William Caxton, London, 1481

Tabby 1. The earliest, simplest and still the commonest type of weave, also called plain weave, taffeta weave and in the U.S. cloth weave (*see* WEAVING). It is composed of wefts passing alternatively over and under warps at right angles to them. When the number of warps and wefts is equal it is termed a linen weave; when warps predominate and cover the wefts, a warp-faced weave; when the wefts predominate and cover the warps, a tapestry weave. The term is sometimes extended to include a canvas weave (ordinary hopsack or matt weave), with two or more wefts passing alternately over and under two or more warps.

2. Old English name for a silk fabric with a variegated surface, introduced in the C17. The cat is named after this material.

Tabernacle mirror American term for a Federal style vertical wall mirror of architectural form with a panel of painted glass above the mirror and a frame composed of half-columns surmounted by an entablature with balls beneath the cornice.

Table There are two basic types of table, the one with a central support, the other with supports placed under the edge of the table-top. In ancient Egypt small tables of the former type were normal. The Greeks similarly had only small tables, but generally of the latter type; those used at meal-times were generally light, with oblong tops supported on three legs (two at one end and one at the centre of the other), though four-legged tables were also made. A table for each person was placed beside the couch on which he reclined while eating. Circular tables with three monopod legs came into use after the C5 B.C. These types of Greek table survived in ancient Rome where they were sometimes provided with very elaborately wrought legs. Two new kinds of table were however developed – the decorative semi-circular topped console table attached to a wall, and the centrally placed marble table with a rectangular top resting on two upright slabs of marble, sometimes very richly carved with animals, acanthus foliage, palmettes, etc. The use of a single large communal dining-table seems to have derived from the practice of North European barbarians. Such tables were in use in the Middle Ages but appear to have been very simply made, generally consisting of no more than boards placed on trestles; and indeed this was the most usual type of dining-table until the C18. Rather more elaborately made writing-tables and games-tables began to appear in the Middle Ages. The Roman type of central table resting on two upright supports was revived during the Renaissance, though more often in wood than in marble. At this time tables that were mainly, if not purely, decorative also began to appear, though they did not became widespread until the later C17. From this moment onwards small tables began to proliferate in the richer houses. The C20 tendency towards simplicity has marked the design of tables as much as other pieces of furniture, but no new type has been invented.

Breakfast table, see Pembroke table below.

Butterfly table A C18 American type of *drop-leaf table* which owes its name to the shape of the supports for the leaves – though they more closely resemble the rudders of rowing boats. The

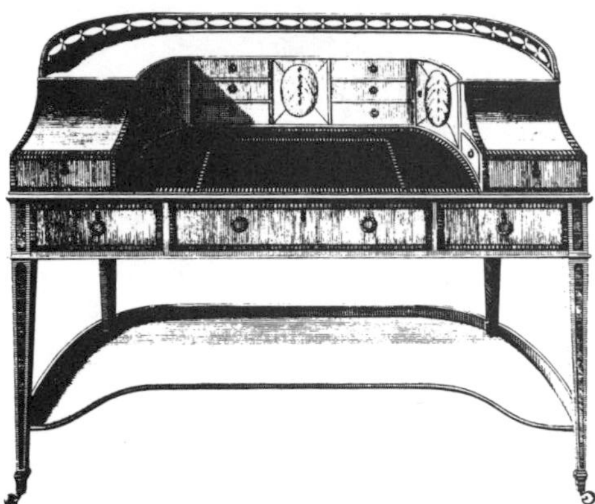

Carlton House table, from Sheraton's The Cabinet-Maker and Upholsterer's Drawing-Book, *1793*

legs are usually slanted outwards from a frame containing a single drawer.

Capstan table, see drum table.

Carlton House table A writing table with a low superstructure consisting of two or three tiers of small drawers rising from the back and curving round the sides. Presumably named after the Prince Regent's Carlton House, first illustrated in *The Cabinet Maker's Book of Prices* (1792) and first named in GILLOW's cost books in 1796.

Chair-table An armchair with a large generally rectangular back pivoted to the arms in such a way that it can be lowered onto them to convert it into a table. One of the earliest pieces of convertible furniture, made from the Middle Ages though most surviving examples date from the C17. Sometimes called a monk's chair, though this term is modern.

Console table A table fixed to a wall, the top, often of marble, being supported on bracket-shaped legs which curve back to the wall. The term is also applied to tables with legs on only the front side, but should not be used for *pier tables* and *side tables* which can stand up without being attached to a wall.

Draw table A table with flaps which may be drawn out from beneath the top to extend its length. Later-C16 and early-C17 *hall tables* are often of this type.

Dressing-table A term that refers to the purpose rather than the design of the piece. In the C18 it often took a form similar to the BUREAU, with compartments for toilet articles and sometimes a fitted looking glass.

Drop-leaf table Generic term for various types of space-saving table with leaves hinged to the top so that they can be raised to extend its surface, covering the *butterfly table, gate-leg table, handkerchief table, Pembroke table,* etc.

Drum table A round table with drawers beneath the top, on a central support which usually rises from a tripod base. It was made in late-C18 and

Centre table, probably Roman, early C18 (Private Collection)

Console table, design by T. Johnson, 1758

early-C19 England, also called a capstan table or a rent table.

Dumb waiter A wooden column, usually supported on a tripod, carrying two or more trays or shelves, one above the other in diminishing size, designed to stand by a dining-table to hold plates, food, etc. so that the diners may help themselves after the servants have left the room. First made in England *c.*1740 and later throughout Europe soon after the mid century.

Gate-leg table A *drop-leaf table* with flaps which may be supported on gate-like legs hinged to the central supports, made since the C16 especially in England and America. The top when extended is usually square, oval or circular.

Guard-room table Modern term for a Spanish type of table with splayed trestle supports and a wrought iron underbrace attaching their stretchers to the underside of the table-top.

Hall table A large table made to stand in the hall, i.e. principal room, of a medieval or C16–C17 house, used not only for eating but for general purposes. Most examples are supported on carved baluster-shaped legs.

Handkerchief table American name for a C18 type of *drop-leaf table* with an equilateral triangle top and similar leaf which, when raised, converts it into a square-topped table.

Harlequin table A more elaborate version of the *Pembroke table,* with a small nest of drawers which is concealed in the body and may be made to rise from the top by means of weights. Made in late-C18 England.

Hutch table An Elizabethan type of serving table – long, narrow, with a cupboard below the top, standing on rather stumpy legs.

Kidney table A table with a kidney-shaped top, used as a writing- or dressing-table, of a type first made in Louis XV period in France (sometimes called a *haricot*) and introduced into England in the late C18.

Library table A writing-table for use in a library, generally with a leather-covered top, often supported on a central pedestal and usually with drawers in the freize.

Gaming table, 1720–30 (Victoria & Albert Museum)

Gate-leg table, carved and turned elmwood, English, c.1700 (Victoria & Albert Museum)

Night table A small table with a cupboard to hold a chamber pot, made to stand beside a bed, from the C18 onwards.

Occasional table Modern term applied to any small easily movable table.

Pedestal table A round- or square-topped table supported on a central column with, usually, a tripod base. First made in early-C18 England, it has remained popular ever since.

Pembroke table The most elegant type of *drop-leaf table*, made from the mid C18 onwards and probably named after a Countess of Pembroke. It stands on four legs and has rectangular leaves which are supported on wooden brackets hinged to the frieze. There is no clear distinction between it and the sofa table and the breakfast table, though the basic design was varied in many ways.

Pie-crust table A modern term for a table with a circular top scalloped at the edge rather like the top of a pie. It is usually made of mahogany with a tilt-to and tripod base, popular in England and America in the mid C18 and much imitated from the late C19 onwards.

Pier table A table designed to stand against a pier, i.e. between windows, often surmounted by a looking glass, in use since the C17. It may have the form of a *console table*.

Refectory table Modern name for a *hall table*.

Rent table, see drum table.

Sawbuck table American term for a rustic type of table with X-shaped legs.

Serviteur-fidèle French C18 term for a small table with movable arms to support candlesticks, used as a work-, reading-, or bedside-table.

Serviteur-muet French C18 name for a DUMB WAITER.

Side table A table designed to stand by a wall, generally with one side undecorated.

Sofa table, see Pembroke table.

Sutherland table A swing-leg drop-leaf table with a very narrow central portion of a type made in England from the early C19.

Sofa table, by J. & A. Semfell, 1809
(Temple Newsam House, Leeds)

Pembroke table, satinwood inlaid with ebony, English, c.1800 (Victoria & Albert Museum)

Swing-leg table A drop-leaf table with two of its four legs so arranged that they may be swung out to support the flaps, distinct from a *gate-leg* table. An English type made from the early C18.

Table ambulante C18 French term for any small easily portable table.

Table de lit French term for a table with very short legs, designed to stand on a bed, straddling the thighs of the occupant. First made in C18 France, sometimes as the detachable upper part of a low chest of drawers.

Table en chiffonnière A small C18 French work-table with high galleries around the top and the shelf joining the legs, to serve as receptacles for *chiffons* and other pieces of material.

Table en crachoir French term for a table with a deep rim round the top.

Vide poche A small bedroom-table with a deeply rimmed top, designed to hold the contents of a man's pockets when he undresses. First made in France in the 1720s and popular both there and in England in the later C18.

Work-table A small low table fitted with receptacles for needlework, silks, bobbins, etc., first made in the later C18.

Writing-table A rather vague English term applied to various types of flat-topped desks especially those with drawers but without any superstructure. Writing-tables resting on two pedestal chests of drawers came into use in the late C17 and were very popular from the mid C18 onwards. This type of writing-table is called a partners' desk when the top is square allowing for two people to work at it facing one another. The basic form has remained unchanged to this day.

Table-centre An elaborate piece of silver (or porcelain or glass) to go in the centre of a dining-table, usually with holders for candles and for pepper-pots, salt-cellars, vinegar bottles, etc. It was invented in France in the 1690s and was soon imitated elsewhere. The English C18 and C19 type, known as an epergne, usually has baskets for sweetmeats. The term is also applied to such purely decorative table ornaments as the PLATEAU and the Italian DESSERT.

Table-centre, gilt bronze, by Thomire, 1810–13 (British Embassy, Paris)

Tabouret A French term for a stool, originally applied to one of drum shape, hence the term. It was later, in the C18, applied to any stool with fixed upright legs, as distinct from the PLIANT which had folding cross-legs. In the C18 *tabourets* were usually rectangular, not drum-shaped, and the seats were usually upholstered. Under Louis XIV a rigid etiquette prescribed who were and were not permitted to sit on *tabourets* at Court. The distinction of sitting on a *tabouret* was eagerly sought after.

Tabriz carpets, *see* PERSIAN CARPETS.

Taffeta or **Taffety** An imprecise name for various types of textiles, mainly a plain or patterned silk with a glossy surface used for hangings.

Tagliolini, Filippo, *see* NAPLES TAPESTRY FACTORY.

Takamakiyé Japanese term (literally: raised sewn picture) for lacquer work with decorations in high relief.

Takatori pottery One of the several Japanese potteries established with Korean workmen on Kyushu Island (like the KARATSU POTTERIES). It was founded in 1600 by a great military Daimyo, lord Kuroda Nagamasa, who had fought in Korea and brought potters back with him. As the kilns were moved from place to place, though always within the province of Chikuzen, different types of clay were used at different periods. They began by making simple household wares strongly influenced by Korean pottery and covered with brown, green or black glazes. Few TEA CEREMONY WARES were produced before 1630 when a celebrated tea-master Kobori Enshu began to influence the making of pieces (named after him *Enshu Takatori*) which have been highly prized ever since, notably tea jars with rich dark brown glazes occasionally splashed with green, purple-black or yellow. The tradition of making such pieces has been maintained to the present day.

Lit: S. Jenyns, *Japanese Pottery*, London 1971.

Talavera de la Reina potteries A group of tin-glazed earthenware factories which was established in Castile in the mid C16 and soon became one of the most important in Spain. One or more tile factories were active before 1562 when J. FLORIS, the 'royal tile maker', was appointed to design tiles to be made here for royal palaces. To improve the technique of tile-making Philip II in 1566 ordered a potter from SEVILLE, Jerónimo Montero, to instruct the craftsmen of Talavera in processes of painting and glazing. **Juan Fernandez** (*fl.*1570–1603), who seems to have run the most important of the factories, was commissioned to make for the Escorial 24,800 tiles in 1570 and 136 vessels – flower pots, vases and jars – in 1573. Tiles decorated with acanthus motifs in white on a blue ground, still *in situ* in the Escorial, and some jars painted with strapwork and grotesque motifs in yellow and shades of blue on a white ground (Museo Arqueológico Nacional, Madrid) appear

Talavera de la Reina tiles, tin-glazed earthenware, probably 1570 (Escorial, near Madrid)

to derive from the Fernandez factory. Polychrome tiles with similar foliage motifs coloured orange, olive green and blue on white are probably a little later. The factories also made large pictorial panels many of which survive in churches in and around Talavera (e.g. large altarpiece of St Anthony the Abbot in Hermitage of El Pardo). By the late C16 Talavera tiles were being sent to all parts of Spain. Early in the C17 the most important factory seems to have been that of **Alonso de Figueroa Gaintán** (d.1653) who was commissioned to execute 102,980 tiles for the Dominican convent of Porta Coeli at Valladolid – an outstandingly attractive decorative scheme with panels of formal ornament divided by simulated Tuscan pilasters. This factory is also known to have made flower pots, etc. for the garden of the ducal palace of Lerma at Valladolid. Tiles remained a major product of the factories in the C17 but the household wares of this period are generally of greater interest. They answered a demand for pottery of high quality to replace table silver, the use of which had been restricted by an edict of 1601. A great variety of wares was made, ranging from small plates to helmet-shaped ewers, globular jars, vast basins, tall vases, etc., either in blue and white or painted in the full range of high-temperature colours with green and purple predominating. The painting is usually in a very bold sketchy style: hunting scenes (often derived from prints after J. Stradanus and A. Tempesta), bull-fights and landscapes appear to have been the most popular subjects. The pottery industry declined in the C18 as the lead in Spanish faience production was taken by ALCORA, but it has survived to the present day. None of the earlier wares appears to have been marked (apart from tiles rarely inscribed with the maker's name), but modern wares made in imitation of those of the C17 are sometimes marked with the letters of the name Talavera in a monogram.

Lit: A. W. Frothingham, *Talavera Pottery*, New York 1944; A. W. Frothingham, *Tile Panels of Spain*, New York 1969; B. Martinez Caviro, *Ceramica de Talavera*, Madrid 1969.

Talbert, Bruce James (1838–81). He was a prolific and very influential designer, especially of furniture, and popularized a simple and practical style which, like that of EASTLAKE, reflected the mid-C19 reaction against the elaborate Neo-Gothic of PUGIN and BURGES. Born in Dundee, he was apprenticed to a woodcarver but was later trained as an architect in Glasgow, being awarded a medal by the Edinburgh Architectural Association in 1862. From 1862 to 1865 he was designer to Doverton, Bird & Hull, furniture manufacturers in Manchester, and from 1866 onwards to Holland & Sons, furniture manufacturers in London, for whom he gained a silver medal at the Paris Exhibition in 1867 with a 'Gothic dressoir' and some smaller pieces. This success was consolidated by the publication of his *Gothic Forms Applied to Furniture, Metal Work and Decoration for Domestic Purposes*, London 1867. His Neo-Gothic furniture is more sober and rectangular than Pugin's, with panels of inlay or very shallow reliefs instead of florid, deeply cut ornamentation. His once well-known 'Pet Sideboard' of 1867, made by GILLOWS, is a classic

B. J. Talbert: the Pet Sideboard, made by Gillows, 1867 (Victoria & Albert Museum)

B. J. Talbert: illustration from Gothic Forms Applied to Furniture, *1867*

example. But he later abandoned this style for a much less original version of Jacobean, publicized in his *Examples of Ancient & Modern Furniture*, London 1876, and made by such firms as MARSH AND JONES. He also designed wallpapers and metalwork, being awarded the Society of Arts Silver Medal for metalwork in 1871.

Lit: Peter Floud in *The Concise Encyclopaedia of Antiques*, vol. III, London 1957; Elizabeth Aslin, *19th Century English Furniture*, London 1962.

Tallboy A double chest of drawers or chest upon chest, of Dutch origin, introduced into England in the early C18 and popular until superseded by the wardrobe. Usually of walnut, it stands on plain or ogee bracket-feet and is straight fronted and rather severe, though later examples sometimes have broken pediments and canted and fluted corners. The HIGHBOY is an American variant.

Tamba potteries A group of potteries described, with SETO, TOKONAME, etc., as one of the 'Six Ancient Kilns' of Japan. Earthenware is said to have been made in the province of Tamba (W. of Yamashiro) since prehistoric times but the earliest known products date from the Kamakura period (1185–1338). TEA CEREMONY WARES of red stoneware with black or dark brown glazes were made from the C16 and greatly prized by tea-masters: the best pieces are generally dated 1660–72. Pottery is still made in the region.

Lit: S. Jenyns, *Japanese Pottery*, London 1971.

Tambour A roll front, made of narrow strips of wood glued side by side to a canvas backing; often used for roll-top desks or for sliding doors.

Tambour lace A decorative openwork fabric (not a true LACE) consisting of net which provides the support for a pattern made of threads of cotton or floss drawn through the meshes with a hooked needle. It originated in the Middle or Far East and was made in Europe (Saxony and Switzerland) from the mid C18. From 1829 it was made at Limerick in Ireland where, from the 1840s, machine-made net was used for the ground material.

Tamietti, Carlo, *see* VINOVO PORCELAIN FACTORY.

T'ang The Chinese dynasty which flourished between 618 and 906 and re-established the prestige China had enjoyed under the HAN

T'ang dynasty: pottery vase with three-colour glaze (William Rockhill Nelson Gallery of Art, Kansas City)

T'ang dynasty: silver bowl, early c8, silver-gilt and parcel-gilt, exterior (above) and interior (below)
(William Rockhill Nelson Gallery of Art, Kansas City)

Emperors. It was a period of territorial expansion during which China became, in her cultural, commercial and religious contacts, more cosmopolitan than ever before. And it nurtured a great flowering of all the arts, especially ceramics. Importations of Sassanian silver vessels and European pottery and glass helped to enlarge the potter's repertory of forms, though immediately translated into Chinese idiom. At the same time techniques were improved to increase the range of coloured glazes for earthenware – orange-red, lemon yellow, chalky blue, a rich spinach green and translucent white. Wares of great delicacy were also produced in a porcellaneous material, *see* YÜEH WARE. But the best known T'ang ceramics are the tomb figures – wonderfully spirited statuettes of camels, horses, men and women – in glazed or unglazed pottery. Such figures first appeared in Europe in 1909: their success with collectors was so great and so immediate that by 1912 an enterprising Peking factory had begun to produce fakes which are exceedingly difficult to recognize.

Tankard A tall one-handled metal drinking vessel, generally straight-sided or barrel-shaped. It is usually of silver or pewter and has been in use in N. Europe since the Middle Ages for beer and cider.

Tankard, English silver, 1678
(O. Richmond Collection, Oxford)

Tännich, Johann Samuel Friedrich (1728–after 1785). German porcelain painter who began his career at MEISSEN (1750), then went to STRASBOURG (*c.*1755) and FRANKENTHAL (1757–9). After an unsuccessful attempt to start a faience factory of his own, he became director at JEVER (1760–63) and KIEL (1763–68), HUBERTUSBERG (1770–74) and MOSBACH (1774–81). He is last recorded in 1785 making stoves at Frankenthal. He seems to have been responsible for an attractive style of naturalistic flower painting practised at the various factories where he worked though none of his own paintings has been securely identified.

Lit: O. Riesebieter, *Die deutsche Fayencen des 17 und 18 Jahrhunderts*, Leipzig 1921.

Tanqueray, David (d.*c.*1726). A London silversmith of French Huguenot origin, apprenticed in 1708 to David WILLAUME whose daughter **Anne** he married. He was admitted to the Goldsmiths' Company in 1722. Pieces of domestic plate bearing David and/or Anne Tanqueray's mark are in the HUGUENOT STYLE. A candlestick of 1720–21 by David Tanqueray is in the Victoria & Albert Museum. Anne Tanqueray made pieces for a dinner service for the Empress of Russia in 1734. (For his mark *see* p. 894.)

Tantalus A mid-C19 English type of open-work case for spirit decanters, usually of wood, with a metal bar by which they were locked in though remaining visible.

Tanzemann A C17 Swiss type of drinking vessel, known in Germany as a *Buttenmann*, it is generally of wood, carved to represent a standing peasant with a large basket on his or her back. The basket forms the bowl and is usually edged with silver. It is also detachable. The figure forms the stem.

Tapa A primitive type of paper-like fabric, sometimes known as bark cloth, made from the beaten bast of various trees (notably types of mulberry), until recently in New Zealand and the equatorial zones, especially Polynesia. It is not very durable and has seldom been produced by peoples to whom woven cloths were available. It was used for clothing, covers, etc., and often painted with decorative or symbolic patterns.

Tapestry A hand-woven fabric, usually of silk and/or wool, with a non-repetitive pattern which is woven during manufacture and thus forms an integral part of the textile. It may be made on the HIGH-WARP LOOM or LOW-WARP LOOM. It is also called Arras or Gobelins from places of manufacture. The word is also incorrectly applied to various other textiles used for wall hangings or furniture upholstery – PINTADO, APPLIQUÉ WORK (e.g. The Bayeux Tapestry), BERLIN WOOLWORK and other types of embroidery.

See: ARRAS TAPESTRY FACTORIES, AUBUSSON, BARBERINI, BATAILLE, BEAUVAIS, BERLIN, BONDOLF, BRADSHAW, BRUSSELS, ELSINORE, FLORENCE, FONTAINEBLEAU, FULHAM, GOBELINS, MADRID, MAINCY, MILLE-FLEURS, W. MORRIS, MORTLAKE, NORWEGIAN TAPESTRIES, PARIS, QUEDLINBURG HANGINGS, ST PETERSBURG, W. SHELDON, SOHO, TOURNAI, TURIN, J. VANDERBANK, WÜRZBURG.

Lit: The Art of Tapestry, ed. J. Jobe, London 1965; W. G. Thomson, *A History of Tapestry*, London (rev. ed.) 1973; D. Heinz, *Medieval Tapestries*, London 1967.

Tapestry Brussels carpet, *see* BRUSSELS CARPET.

Tapestry ingrain carpet, *see* DOUBLE CLOTH CARPET.

Tapestry velvet carpet, *see* BRUSSELS CARPET.

Tapiovaara, Ilmari (b.1914). Finnish furniture designer who has specialized in stacking chairs for offices, public halls, schools, etc. His chairs are light in weight, elegant and reasonably comfortable, notably the Lukki steel chair (1951) and the more daring and graceful Wilhelmina chair (1960) of pressure-moulded plywood.

Tapissier French term for (1) an upholsterer who makes both coverings for furniture and curtains and draperies of all kinds, and (2) a tapestry weaver.

Tappit hen A Scottish type of pewter chalice, variable in size. The largest holds three quarts.

Taquillón A Spanish type of cupboard used as a support or stand for a VARGUEÑO. It has four equal-sized compartments, either two upper drawers and two lower cupboards with doors or four of each. Two slides support the drop-front of the Vargueño. The front is often decorated with bone or ivory inlays and it stands on four short legs. *See also* PUENTE.

Taracea A Spanish type of inlay work composed of small dots of ivory resembling grains of wheat, hence its alternative name of *granos de trigo*.

Tarsia, *see* INTARSIA.

Tatham, Charles Heathcote (1772–1842). English architect and designer, he was instrumental in the creation of the REGENCY STYLE. While studying in Rome 1794–7 he supplied Henry HOLLAND with drawings of Antique (and C18 Grecian and Egyptian style) ornament which anticipated the Empire and Regency styles. He later published some thorough-going Neo-Classical *Designs for Ornamental Plate* (1806) as well as etchings of Roman architectural ornament (1799 and 1806) which provided archaeologically accurate source books for decorative artists. His elder brother, **Thomas** (1763–1817) became a partner in the cabinet-making firm of **Elward Marsh & Tatham** which supplied very handsome furniture (Grecian and Chinoiserie) to Southill, Bedfordshire, and the Brighton Pavilion.

Lit: P. Ward-Jackson, *English Furniture Designs*, London 1958.

Taylor, I. & J. (*fl.c.*1795–1802). English ornamental designers, authors of *Ornamental Ironwork* (London *c.*1795) an influential and much used book of patterns for fan-lights, staircase railings, window guards, lamp irons, fences, gates, etc., in a neat Neo-Classical style derived from Robert ADAM. They also published *Designs for Shop Fronts and Doorcases* (London 1802) which includes patterns for fan-light tracery of a cobwebby delicacy.

Lit: J. Harris, *English Decorative Ironwork*, London 1960.

Taylor, John, *see* PONTIPOOL WARE.

Taylor, W. Howson (1876–1935). English potter who was born in Lincoln and founded in 1898 the **Ruskin Pottery** at Smethwick, near Birmingham, where he specialized in making decorative vases of simple Chinese-inspired form decorated only with coloured glazes – mottled, flambé or monochrome. His work was known internationally between 1901 and 1914. The pottery officially closed in 1933 though it remained active until 1935. Examples of his work are in the Manchester City Art Gallery, Victoria & Albert Museum, London, etc.

Tazza A wine cup with a shallow circular bowl of a type made in the C16 and C17 throughout Europe. The term is often applied indiscriminately and incorrectly to dishes and salvers on a central foot.

Tazza, English silver, 1528 (Rochester Cathedral)

Tchichi carpets, *see* CAUCASIAN CARPETS.

Tea caddy A container for storing tea. Made almost exclusively in C18 and (much less) early-C19 England to a wide variety of designs – rectangular, octagonal, sarcophagus-shaped, urn-shaped, etc. Inside there are usually two or more compartments either for the tea or for tea-canisters.

Tea canister A small container for tea which might be fitted into a TEA CADDY. Made of silver, earthenware or glass.

Tea ceremony wares Pottery vessels – tea-bowls, tea-caddies, water jars, dishes, flower vases, incense boxes and burners, etc. – used in the Buddhist tea ceremony called in Japanese *cha no yu* (literally, 'hot water for tea'). The ceremony derived from China and is said to have been introduced into Japan by a Buddhist priest named Muso Koshi and first established as a ritual in 1472 by another Buddhist priest, named Murata Shuko, who won the support of the Shogun Yoshimasa. Within a century it was the centre of the main religio-aesthetic cult in Japan and has continued to play an important part in the intellectual life of the country to the present day. One of the most famous of the masters of the tea ceremony, named Sen no Rikyn, who codified its rules in 1591, declared that its essence was to boil water, make tea and sip it. The ceremony takes place in a special very simple, dimly-lit small building in a specially designed 'natural' garden with an abundance of rough stones, moss and fallen leaves. But the etiquette of making, serving and drinking tea is combined with admiration and discussion of poetry, painting and flower arrangement. And the tea-masters were regarded as both arbiters of taste and censors of behaviour (morals). The tea-masters have always taken great trouble to select for the ceremony pottery vessels which are appropriately humble in origin, subdued in colour, uneven in texture and irregular in form, preferring the peasant wares of China, Korea or Japan to the more sophisticated types of stoneware or porcelain. At first they acquired vessels intended for ordinary use but from the C16 there was an increasing tendency for Japanese potters to cater for the taste of the tea-masters, making vessels as intentionally rough and irregularly formed as RAKU wares and those of the IGA, KARATSU and MINO potteries. Tea ceremony wares are prized in Japan for their historical associations (e.g. ownership by a succession of famous tea-masters recorded in pedigrees which are sometimes of dubious reliability) as well as the aesthetic merits of form, texture and weight which few Westerners have learned to appreciate. The sophisticated cult of the unsophisticated, on which the whole tea ceremony is based, has however influenced studio potters in the West.

Lit: S. Jenyns, *Japanese Pottery*, London 1971.

Tea poy A small tripod table supported on a central pillar, sometimes with a box forming the top; for drawing-room use 'when taking refreshment' (Smith's *Household Furniture*, 1808).

Tea urn A large, usually silver, vessel in which tea could be made, shaped like an URN and provided with a tap. Made in England from the 1760s.

Tea urn, silver, by Whipham and Wright, London, 1761 (Formerly Ionides Collection, Buxted Park)

Teague, Walter Dorwin (1883–1960). The father figure of U.S. industrial designers and, with N. Bel Geddes, Henry DREYFUSS and R. LOEWY, one of the founders of the profession. Born in Indiana, he was trained as an artist in New York, joined an advertising firm and in 1911 set up his own office for graphic design. He did not begin as a consultant designer for industry until 1926 but quickly established himself, notably by his work for Eastman Kodak (e.g. the Baby Brownie camera of 1933). Profiting from the new and more enlightened attitude which industrialists took to design after the 1929 Wall Street crash, his office expanded rapidly in the 1930s. Its range was enormous, embracing furniture (a chair of aluminium and transparent Lucite), clinical equipment, interiors of railway Pullman coaches, motor-cars, aircraft interiors (e.g. the Boeing 707 Jet Airliner), glass for the CORNING GLASSWORKS (Steuben Division), etc. In the war he designed (or selected) everything, from furniture to tooth-brushes, for the 12,000 strong U.S. Air Force Academy in Colorado. He was co-founder and first president of the American Society of Industrial Designers in 1944. One of his last and best designs was for the Eastman Kodak K-100 Turret Camera. His book, *Design this Day* (1940, rev. ed. 1949) contains a statement of classic Functionalist belief which informs all his own eminently practical designs. His son **Walter Dorwin Teague Jr.** succeeded him as director of Walter Dorwin Teague Associates but has now set up his own practice.

Tebo, Mr (*fl.*1750–75). A somewhat mysterious porcelain modeller of French origin (Tebo was probably an anglicized spelling of Thibaut) working apparently at Bow *c.*1750–65, PLYMOUTH 1768–70, BRISTOL and WORCESTER *c.*1770–75. Useful wares (in a Rococo style derived from silver) and many figures made at these factories and marked with an impressed *T* or *To* are believed to be by him: unmarked pieces in a similar style are also ascribed to him. He may have worked mainly as a REPAIRER rather than as a modeller. In 1775, however, he was working as a modeller for WEDGWOOD who described him as 'incompetent'.

Lit: W. B. Honey, *Old English Porcelain*, London, rev. ed. 1948.

Tê-hua porcelain factories The source of the Chinese porcelain known in Europe as *blanc-de-chine*. The factories at Tê-hua in Fukien Province (S.E. China) made white porcelain from the SUNG period but their products were unmarked and can rarely be dated precisely. They are associated mainly with the CH'ING dynasty and most of the more notable pieces appear to have been made in the late C17 or early C18. The most notable products are statuettes, especially of the Buddhist goddess Kuan Yin, of a delicately feminine fluid elegance. Figures of animals, incense burners, and ordinary household vessels, bottles, cups, dishes, etc. were also made. They have a lustrous glaze which is pure white except where it runs very thick and shows a trace of brown. From the C17 wares were exported in ever increasing quantities to Europe where in the early C18 they exerted a very strong influence on porcelain factories. In the early C19 products tended to lose their delicacy of modelling and subtlety of glaze, acquiring the appearance of moulded blancmange.

Lit: P. J. Donnelly, *Blanc de Chine*, London 1969.

Tekke carpets, *see* TURKMAN CARPETS.

Telamone A support in the form of a carved male figure, i.e. a male caryatid. It is also called an Atlante. Such figures were used for the decoration of furniture and metalwork from the C16 onwards.

Telamone designed by H. Sambin, 1572

Temmoku Japanese term originally applied to stoneware pottery tea bowls with an iron-brown glaze imported from China. The name may be derived from the T'ien Mu mountains of Chekiang, the site of one of the Zen Buddhist monasteries in which the TEA CEREMONY originated. But the wares appear to have been made from the C10 much further south at CHIEN-AN in Fukien. The name was subsequently applied to all pottery with an iron-brown glaze whether made in China, Korea or Japan, though a wide variety of terms were applied to indicate differences of colour and texture.

Tent stitch Needlework in which the unit is a series of parallel stitches arranged diagonally across the intersections of the threads. When applied to a woven canvas ground it is usually called *petit point.*

Term A pedestal tapering towards the base and supporting a bust or merging at the top into a sculptured human, animal or mythical figure. Used as a decorative device from the C16 onwards and particularly popular in the Baroque and Rococo periods. (For illustration *see* SAMBIN.)

Terra sigillata A type of ROMAN POTTERY with a red GLOSS derived from a ware first made in the C3 B.C. in the E. Mediterranean, produced in very large quantities in various parts of the Roman Empire, most notably at the ARRETINE POTTERIES (C1 B.C.–C1 A.D.) and at La Graufesenque near Toulouse (C1 A.D.), later in the Rhineland (from *c.*180 A.D.), in Britain (C2 A.D.), etc. Many pieces were marked with the impressed seals of the owners of workshops, hence the name which is however applied also to unmarked pieces. It is decorated with moulded, trailed slip or incised ornament. It is sometimes called Samian ware. Imitations were made in the C17 at STRIEGAU and in the C18 by WEDGWOOD and others.

Lit: T. D. Price, *An Introduction to the Study of Terra Sigillata,* London 1920; R. J. Charleston, *Roman Pottery,* London 1955.

Terrazzo A flooring finish of marble chips mixed with cement, laid *in situ,* ground smooth and level and then polished. In origin an Italian technique.

Terre de Lorraine A type of cream-coloured earthenware made at LUNÉVILLE and especially for the figures of CYFFLÉ.

Terre de pipe Literally pipe clay, but the term is also applied to white-bodied earthenware especially that made at LUNÉVILLE, SAINT CLÉMENT and Bellevue and used unglazed for biscuit figures or with a lead glaze for useful wares.

Teruel potteries A group of tin-glazed earthenware factories in Aragon, producing from the C13 to the C16 handsome vessels decorated in green and dark purple on opaque white with a mixture of Islamic and Gothic motifs, similar to those of the PATERNA and VALENCIA factories. (The Gothic motifs include jousting knights, heraldry, etc.). Bell-shaped jugs and two-handled pear-shaped vases were specialities. Tiles were also made.

Lit: Archivo de Arte Valenciana XIII (1927), pp. 48–50; M. Gonzalez-Marti, *Ceramica española,* Barcelona 1933.

Terylene, *see* MAN-MADE FIBRES.

Teste, Richard, *see* ROANNE POTTERY.

Tester A canopy, especially one of carved or draped wood, over a bed. A half-tester bed (popular from the late C17 to late C18) is one with the tester supported from above the head and with no posts at the foot. *Illustrated opposite page.*

Tête-à-tête An alternative name for (a) a CABARET or (b) a CONFIDENT.

Teutonic glass The glass produced in the Rhineland C5 to C8, mainly drinking glasses with no feet on which they can stand but generally with rounded bases (sometimes terminated by a button finial), derived from an ancient Roman pattern, of poor technical quality, greenish in colour and very bubbly, but sometimes possessing a certain virile beauty.

Lit: D. Horden *et al., Masterpieces of Glass,* London 1968; I. Schlosser, *Das alte Glas,* Brunswick 1965.

Textile A woven fabric of SILK, COTTON, WOOL,

Tester on an English oak bed, c.*1610 (Victoria & Albert Museum)*

or any of the MAN-MADE FIBRES. *See also* WEAVING.

The Hague porcelain factory Established in 1776 by a German porcelain dealer **Anton Lyncker** (1718–81) and continued until 1790 by his son, making wares of good technical quality and simple form, sometimes attractively painted with *putti* in monochrome or with flowers in polychrome. (For factory mark *see* p. 888.)

Lit: H. E. von Gelder, *Catalogue van de Verzameling Haagsch Porselein,* The Hague 1916.

Thistle cup Scottish type of late-C17 – early-C18 silver cup with a single handle, lobed decoration on the bottom of the bowl and flared rim.

Thomas, Germain, *see* SAINT-CLÉMENT POTTERY.

Thomire, Pierre-Philippe (1751–1843). The outstanding Empire FONDEUR-DOREUR. He began under the sculptors Pajou and Houdon, casting portrait bronzes, then turned to work as a *ciseleur* under GOUTHIÈRE in 1774. He collaborated in the decoration of the coronation coach of Louis XVI in 1776 and in the following year started on his own. His early works are in the Louis XVI style (e.g. his gilt-bronze fire dogs with flaming urns and sphinxes of 1786 now in the Louvre) but he was already anticipating the Empire style (e.g. his bronze circular table derived from the Antique in the Musée Nissim Camondo, Paris). He is known to have supplied mounts for furniture by BENNEMAN, SCHWERDFEGER and WEISWEILER. In 1783 he joined the SÈVRES PORCELAIN FACTORY, specializing in clock-cases of bronze and porcelain. During the Revolution he prudently went over to the manufacture of arms and ammunition, but returned to decorative bronze work after the Consulate and was soon employing eight hundred men. He was much patronized by Napoleon who made him *Ciseleur de l'Empereur*. His works include some of the finest and purest expressions of the Empire style, e.g. *Vase de Marriage de l'Empereur* (Versailles) and other vast Greek-shaped urns delicately modelled with crisp foliage and figures in low relief, candelabra supported by winged victories, etc. In 1811 he collaborated with the goldsmith ODIOT in making the celebrated cradle for the King of Rome (designed by Proud'hon, now in the Schatzkammer, Vienna) and the bronzes for another Imperial cradle (Fontainebleau). He also collaborated frequently with WEISWEILER during this period, making bronze mounts for his furniture. After the Restoration he continued to work in the same style, was patronized by the Bourbons and awarded the Legion d'Honneur by Louis-Philippe. He retired in 1823 but continued to work occasionally as a sculptor. His firm, **Thomire et Cie,** survived until after 1850.

P.-P. Thomire: gilt-bronze and blued-steel candelabra, early c19
(William Rockhill Nelson Gallery of Art, Kansas City)

Lit: J. Niclausse, *Thomire Fondeur Ciseleur (1751–1843)*, Paris 1947; S. Grandjean, *Empire Furniture 1800–1825*, London 1966.

Thomsen, Christian, *see* COPENHAGEN PORCELAIN FACTORY.

Thonet, Michael (1796–1871). The most original of German furniture makers and designers, he perfected the BENTWOOD process for chair-making and pioneered the mass-production of standardized furniture. He was far in advance of his time, both technically and in design. Several of his chairs have become classics and have been in continuous production for over a hundred years. The best look extraordinarily modern, almost as if they had been designed by some early c20 'functionalist' of genius. Significantly, LE CORBUSIER recommended one of them for use in his own buildings because, he said, 'this chair, whose millions of representatives are used on the Continent and in the two Americas, possesses nobility'. Thonet was born at Boppard in Prussia, a few miles up the Rhine from Neuwied where ROENTGEN's workshops were still in production. He started his own cabinet-making business in 1819, specializing in parquetry. In 1830 he began experimenting with bentwood, at first glueing veneers together to make sections of furniture and later inventing a new process by which solid lengths of beechwood could be steamed or boiled in water and glue and then bent to form long curved rods for chair frames. This led to great simplifications, both in manufacture and design – to low costs combined with durability, lightness and flexibility. Hand-carved joints, for instance, were no longer necessary after it became possible to form the rear legs and backrest of a chair from one piece of bentwood, the front legs from another and the seat from another – the latter being simply a hoop covered with cane. Ornament was thus gradually eliminated. It was not until about

Michael Thonet: chair no. 14, 1859, (far right) chair no. B9, (below) rocking chair

1859, when he produced Chair no. 14, that Thonet developed a fully mechanized process and began to make furniture without any decoration at all. Chair no. 14 consists of no more than six parts and could therefore be transported very economically in parts and assembled with no more than 10 screws. It cost about 3s. (75 U.S. cents) in the money of the day. Thonet's early experimental chairs in bentwood had been rather BIEDERMEIER in style, but his later designs were very individual in their extreme simplicity, relieved only by the flowing curves and curls into which the bentwood rods of the chair frame were occasionally extended, most effectively in his elegant rocking-chairs.

Thonet took out patents for his bentwood process in 1841 in France, England and Belgium and exhibited examples of his bentwood chairs in Coblenz in the same year. They were admired by Prince Metternich who invited him to settle in Vienna. He established himself there in 1842 and went into partnership with the Neo-Rococo furniture-maker Carl LEISTLER with whom he supplied furniture (some of it in bentwood) to Prince Liechtenstein. But he was unable, for lack of capital, to exploit his bentwood process until 1849 when, with the help of the English architect P. H. Desvignes who was in charge of the redecoration of the Liechtenstein Palace and tried to persuade Thonet to settle in London, he finally launched his first bentwood factory. He eventually took his four sons into partnership, calling the firm **Gebrüder Thonet.** His success was immediate. In 1850 he exhibited the famous bentwood Chair no. 4, the prototype of the famous Vienna café chair which is still in production. A series was ordered immediately for the Café Daum in Vienna (one is now in the Museum of Technology in Vienna) and several hundred for a Budapest hotel. Some 50,000,000 are said to have been made since it was first devised. During the 1850s new factories were opened in the Moravian beechwoods and in Hungary, where cheap local labour could be trained and employed. By 1871 he had established salerooms not only in the main cities of Austria and Germany but also at Brussels, Marseilles, Milan, Rome, Naples, Barcelona, Madrid, St Petersburg, Moscow, Odessa, New York and Chicago. After Michael Thonet's death the still expanding business was carried on by his sons, but no important new design of chair was invented by them, except a folding theatre-seat in 1888. By the end of the century the Thonet factories were employing a staff of 6,000 and were turning out 4,000 pieces of furniture a day. After the First World War the main factory was established at Brno in Czechoslovakia and in 1923 Gebrüder Thonet merged with **Mundus.** The firm still flourishes in Austria manufacturing some excellent modern furniture, e.g. by BREUER, as well as its traditional bentwood pieces.

Lit: *Bugholzmöbel – Das Werk Michael Thonets*, Exh. Cat., Vienna 1965; G. Santoro, *Il caso Thonet*, Rome 1966; H. Kreisel & G. Himmelheber, *Die Kunst des deutschen Möbels*, Vol. III, Munich 1973.

Thouret, Nikolaus Friedrich von (1766–1845). German architect, born in Ludwigsburg and educated there. After ten years studying in Paris and Rome he returned to Germany in 1797 and began to practise as an architect. Between 1804 and 1812 he designed for the Ludwigsburg Schloss handsome solid Empire-style furniture of which several pieces survive both there and in the Württembergisches Landesmuseum, Stuttgart.

Lit: H. Kreisel & G. Himmelheber, *Die Kunst des deutschen Möbels*, vol. III, Munich 1973.

Thread and shell pattern, *see* FIDDLE PATTERN.

Thread circuit Relief decoration applied to a glass vessel by winding a thread of molten glass around it, generally on the rim of the bowl or on the neck.

Threading Narrow lines engraved round the border of the handle or a fork or spoon or other small piece of silver. Also called a threaded edge.

Three-colour ware, *see* SAN-TS'AI.

Thumb-piece A knob attached to the hinged metal lid of a flagon, tankard or other vessel, to enable the lid to be opened with the thumb while the handle is held in the fingèrs. Sometimes it is decoratively fashioned. Also called a billet.

Thursfield, Maurice, *see* JACKFIELD POTTERY.

Thuya-wood Also called Yellow Cedar. A fairly

soft, close-grained brown-coloured wood with a pronounced mottled and curled marking, from the *callitris quadrivalvis* tree. It is found in Africa and N. America and was used for inlays and veneers in furniture.

Tichelaar, Freerk Jans, *see* MAKKUM POTTERIES.

Tickenhall pottery A Derbyshire pottery active from the Middle Ages and probably the source of some C16 pieces of slipware with a red body, dark brown glaze and decorations of stags' heads, flowers, etc. cut from discs of white clay. C17–C18 wares of STAFFORDSHIRE type with trailed decorations are sometimes (but without authority) ascribed to the same place.

Lit: B. Rackham & H. Read, *English Pottery*, London 1924.

Tiefschnitt The technique of engraving glass in intaglio (rather than cameo as in HOCHSCHNITT). It was perfected in C18 Bohemia and was popular throughout Germany, especially in POTSDAM glass.

Tiffany, Charles Louis (1812–1902). He was a New York goldsmith and jeweller, but a manufacturer and vendor rather than a craftsman or designer. He began in 1837 by dealing in fancy goods and so flourished that in 1848 his firm, then called **Tiffany, Young & Ellis,** set up a workshop for making jewellery and opened a branch in Paris. In 1853 Tiffany took over sole command of the firm; in 1867 he was given an award at the Paris exhibition for his display of silver and in the following year he opened a branch in London. William Chaffers described his factory in 1883 as 'the largest devoted solely to the manufacture of silver ware in America and probably in the world. A building of five storeys in height, of which the top floor is used as a designing room . . .' By the 1890s he held official appointments to no less than twenty-three royal patrons, Queen Victoria, the Czar of Russia, the Shah of Persia, the Khedive of Egypt being among them. In the 1890s he also expanded his business to include Electroplate, thus entering into competition with REED & BARTON. Stylistically, Tiffany conformed to current taste and his products are in the usual range of historic and exotic styles. The richest are presentation pieces, such as the Adams gold vase of 1893–5, now in the Metropolitan Museum, New York. But he maintained consistently high standards of craftsmanship, for ordinary household wares as well as for special pieces. There are good examples of his work in the Museum of the

Tiffany & Co.: silver cheese scoop, manufactured by the Gorham Manufacturing Co., 1864, and silver fish-server, 1870 (Metropolitan Museum of Art, gift of Mrs D. Chester Noyes)

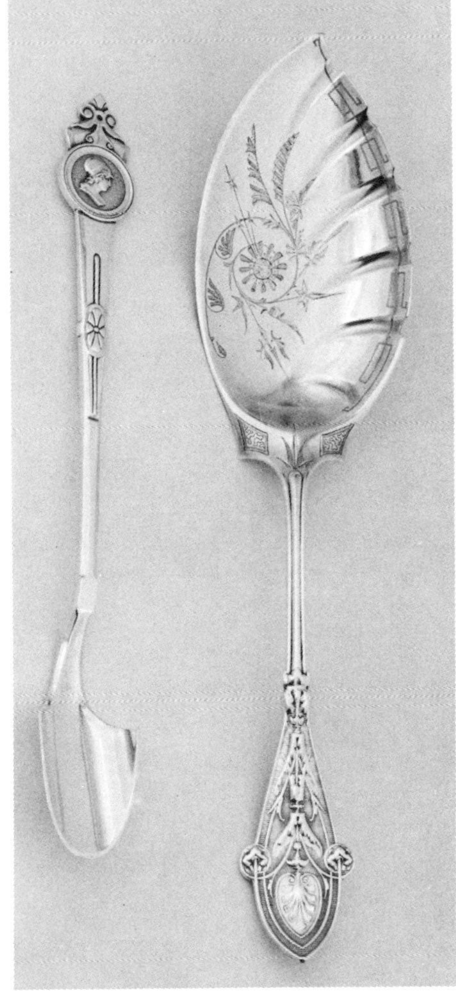

Tiffany & Co.: silver vase, designed by James H. Whitehouse, 1876, the 'Bryant Vase' (Metropolitan Museum of Art, gift of William Cullen Bryant)

City of New York. Latterly he marketed some of the Art Nouveau glass lamps and vases made by his even more famous son, Louis Comfort TIFFANY, who succeeded to his business after his death.

Lit: G. F. Heydt, *Charles L. Tiffany and the House of Tiffany & Co.*, New York 1893.

Tiffany, Louis Comfort (1848–1933). Leading American Art Nouveau designer and interior decorator. He was the son of Charles Louis TIFFANY. But whereas his father had been a keen businessman with some artistic sense, Louis Comfort Tiffany was an aesthete with an exceptionally sharp eye for business. He began as a painter studying under George Innes and later in Paris. Inspired by William MORRIS he turned to the decorative arts in 1878, established a firm of interior decorators (1879) and decorated numerous public and private buildings in New York, also some rooms in the White House, Washington (1882–3) in a curious mixture of Byzantine, Moorish and Romanesque styles. But he achieved wider and more enduring fame for his work in glass. He patented a type of hand-made iridescent glass (1880) which he called 'favrile glass', and founded the **Tiffany Furnaces** in 1892. Some works were on a large scale, e.g. a Romanesque chapel encrusted with glass mosaic for the Chicago Exhibition (1893) and stained glass

L. C. Tiffany: lamp of bronze and favrile *glass, c.1902 (Kunstgewerbemuseum, Zurich)*

windows made to designs by the Nabi painters (Vuillard, Bonnard, etc.) for S. BING's Parisian shop *L'Art Nouveau* (1895). He also produced numerous goblets and glasses very delicately shaped and decorated with flowing abstract patterns, which sometimes suggest waves, leaves or peacock feathers, in iridescent reds, greens, gold or mother-of-pearl with a unique satiny finish. He was fascinated by organic forms and utilized, with great sensibility, the fluidity of glass to suggest the growth and movement of flowers and plants. His unique iridescent colours were the result of exposing the molten glass to the fumes of vapourized metals. His wares were very popular in Europe as well as thc U.S: and much imitated, especially in BOHEMIA. He designed electric lamps with shades made of irregular mosaics of opalescent glass, furniture, wallpapers, fabrics, etc., in an individual, generally rather robust, version of Art Nouveau. After his father's death in 1902 he devoted himself largely to jewellery.

Lit: R. Koch, *Louis C. Tiffany, Rebel in Glass,* New York 1964; E. Neustadt, *The Lamps of Tiffany,* New York 1970; R. Koch, *Louis C. Tiffany's Glass, Bronzes, Lamps,* New York 1971.

Tiger ware A C16 to C17 name for stoneware with a mottled brown glaze imported into England from the Rhenish potteries (especially COLOGNE). The name is also used for English imitations of it, e.g. by John DWIGHT. *Illustrated next column.*

Tiger ware jug mounted in English silver, C17 (Victoria & Albert Museum)

Tijou, Jean (*fl.* 1689–1712). Master ironworker of French origin known only for his work in England, 1689–1712. He began at Hampton Court Palace, executing in wrought-iron the Baroque balustrade to the King's Staircase and Queen's Staircase and twelve gates for the Fountain Garden (now in the Privy Garden) composed of luxuriant scrolls of foliage and delicate interlaced tendrils. At St Paul's Cathedral (gates to the N. and S. chancel aisles) he practised a less flamboyant style, probably under Wren's influence. He published *A New Book of Drawings* (1693), the first English book of designs for ironwork, which was soon pirated in France. He had several English pupils, notably **Thomas Robinson** (gates of New College, Oxford, 1711), but Robert BAKEWELL was the best of his followers. His designs were plagiarized in France by **Louis Fordrin** who was appointed *Serrurier du Roi* in 1723.

Lit: J. Harris, *English Decorative Ironwork,* London 1960.

Till A small box or tray fitting inside a casket or chest, the predecessor of the drawer (which may be drawn out horizontally) of a chest of drawers, but surviving as the compartmented coin-tray in a money-box and as the fitted tray in a modern travelling trunk or suitcase.

Tilliard, Jean Baptiste (1685–1766). Leading

Louis XV period chair-maker, he worked largely for the Crown from about 1730 onwards and obtained many important commissions. His chairs are extremely sumptuous, with ample proportions and richly carved and gilt frames. Those he made for the Crown in the mid century were carved by Roumier and gilded by Bardou. His other patrons included the Prince de Soubise and the *fermier général* Fontaine de Cramayel. He retired in 1764 and was succeeded by his son **Jean Baptiste II** (d.1797) who had become a *maître-menuisier* in 1752. Father and son used the same stamp but the son's work is recognizable by its heavier proportions and over-elaborate ornamentation. Both favoured as a decorative motif a heart-shaped cartouche in the centre of the front rail of the seat and/or the top-rail of the back. The younger Tilliard often collaborated with the carver Chaillon and the gilder Mathon.

Lit: P. Verlet, *Le mobilièr royal français*, Paris 1945–55; F. J. B. Watson, *The Wrightsman Collection: Furniture*, New York 1966.

Tin A metal obtained since prehistoric times by smelting cassiterite, and used in alloys to make bronze, brass, pewter, etc. It has often been used as a coating for other metals, especially the interior of COPPER vessels, to protect them from oxidization or corrosion.

Ting A Chinese Bronze Age food vessel. In the SHANG-YIN and Early CHOU dynasties (*c.*1500 to 1000 B.C.) it was made in either rectangular or circular form, later only the circular form persisted, and the bowl became shallower. It has three or four feet, usually cylindrical but sometimes in animal form. The *ting* continued to be made after the Bronze Age – in pottery as well as bronze – and is often found as an incense burner in Buddhist temples.

Ting ware A type of translucent Chinese porcelain (strictly called a proto-porcelain) produced in the SÜNG and YUAN periods at Chien-tzu Ts'un in the Chu-yang district of Hopei (formerly called Chih-li) Province where white pottery had been made since the c6. It is a finely potted ware with an orange body and a highly fired ivory white glaze which appears brownish or greenish where it runs thickly. Conical bowls with small feet and deep bowls

Ting ware basin with incised decoration and copper-bound rim, Sung dynasty 960–1279 (Percival David Foundation of Chinese Art, London)

with foliate rims, fired upside down in the kiln so that the rims are unglazed (and sometimes protected with bronze sheaths) are among the more characteristic pieces. Larger vessels are ornamented with carved decorations – flowers, fish, ducks, etc. – under the glaze. Many of the ceramic forms and types of decoration of the N. Sung period appear to have been first developed in this ware. It was imitated in later periods.

Lit: B. Gray, *Early Chinese Pottery and Porcelain*, London 1953.

Tin-glazed earthenware Fine-quality pottery decorated by a technique first developed in Baghdad in the c9 in an attempt to rival the glossy whiteness of Chinese porcelain by covering earthenware with an opaque white glaze, later transmitted to Spain (HISPANO-MORESQUE POTTERY) and thence to Italy and the rest of Europe. After the pottery has been fired in a kiln from which it emerges as a brownish earthenware it is dipped in a glaze composed of oxides of lead and tin combined with silicate of potash which gives it a porous white coat. The vessel can either be left plain or decorated in pigments derived from various metallic oxides called HIGH-TEMPERATURE COLOURS. As these colours are absorbed into the glaze as soon as they are applied and no corrections are possible, the process is akin to fresco painting. The vessel is then given a second firing which fixes the glaze to the body and melts it to a glossy surface. To enhance the sheen of the surface vessels are often coated with lead-glaze before being fired. In the C18, under the influence of porcelain factories, the decorations were often applied in ENAMEL COLOURS over the already fired white tin-glaze and were then given a third firing in a low temperature or muffle kiln. Italian tin-glazed earthenware and imitations of it are called MAIOLICA; that produced in France, Germany, Scandinavia and Spain is called FAIENCE; that of Holland is known as DELFT and that of England as English Delftware.

Lit: A. Craiger-Smith, *Tin Glaze Pottery*, London 1973.

Tinworth, George (1843–1913). English wood-carver and pottery-modeller working at the DOULTON POTTERY from 1866. His works range from the sublime to the grotesque (akin to those of his friend Wallace MARTIN) including some large plaques of religious subjects which Ruskin deemed 'full of fire and zealous faculty', small figures of grinning boy musicians, and rather coy groups of animals (e.g. white mice watching a Punch and Judy show), all executed in stoneware.

Lit: D. Eyles, *Doulton News*, London 1950; G. A. Godden in *The Connoisseur* CLXIX (1968), pp. 232–4.

Toast-master's glass A drinking glass with a very thick bowl so that it holds much less than it appears to do. The toast-master had to remain sober while appearing to drink as frequently and deeply as others. The same type of glass was used by inn-keepers, for the same reason.

Tobey Furniture Company The most notable furnishing and decorating firm in Chicago at the end of the C19. It was founded in 1875 by two brothers, **Charles** and **Frank Tobey.** Charles had opened a retail furniture shop in 1856 and Frank had started a manufacturing company with **F. Porter Thayer** in 1870. In 1888 they formed a subsidiary concern, the **Tobey and Christianson Cabinet Company,** for the production of expensive furniture of high quality. Products of the latter included some pieces with carved decorations in an Art Nouveau style which owes more to the architecture of L. H. SULLIVAN than to European furniture of the same date.

Tobey Furniture Company, Chicago: dining-table, 1890 (Metropolitan Museum of Art, gift of Mrs Frank W. McCabe)

Lit: 19th Century America: Furniture and Other Decorative Arts, Exh. Cat., Metropolitan Museum, New York 1970.

Toby jug An earthenware jug in the form of a seated tippling figure in a three-cornered hat,

Toby jug in lead-glazed earthenware, by R. Wood, c.1780 (Victoria & Albert Museum)

first made at the factory of R. WOOD in the 1760s, soon imitated by many other STAFFORDSHIRE POTTERIES and later on the Continent and even in Japan. It was probably inspired by an engraving of 'Toby Philpot' to illustrate a song, 'The Brown Jug', translated from the Latin and published 1761. There are numerous variants on the original model – the drunken parson, the night-watchman, Prince Hal, etc., usually male but sometimes female (MARTHA GUNN). Those by Wood are superior to all others.

Lit: D. Eyles, *Good Sir Toby*, London 1956; J. Bedford, *Toby Jugs*, London 1968.

Toft, Charles (1832–1909). Ceramic modeller employed in the 1860s at the MINTON factory where he specialized in reproducing SAINT-PORCHAIRE wares, generally signing his work.

Toft, Thomas (d.1689). Staffordshire potter and outstanding maker of SLIPWARE known by thirty-one large dishes and three pots inscribed with his name. His method was to cover the entire unfired dish with white slip, trail the outlines of his design in dark brown slip, fill in areas (the bodies of figures or birds, etc.) with a slip which fires to an orange-brown, and add finishing touches in dots of white slip. His subjects include Adam and Eve, a mermaid, Charles II hiding in the oak protected by a prancing lion and unicorn, the pelican in her piety, etc., executed with a robust naiveté and a remarkable sense of design.

T. Toft: Adam and Eve plate, 1674 (Temple Newsam House, Leeds)

These wares were intended for decoration rather than use. Many similar plates are signed by **Ralph Toft** (from 1676), **James Toft** (1705), **George Taylor** (1660), **William Taylor** and others.

Lit: R. G. Cooper, *English Slipware Dishes*, London 1968.

Toiles de Jouy, *see* COTTON, PLATE-PRINTED and OBERKAMPF.

Toilette or **Table de toilette** French name for a dressing-table and, sometimes, all its appurtenances such as scent bottles, pomade pots, looking-glass, brushes, etc. The term *table de toilette*, first recorded in an inventory of 1705, indicates the function rather than form though at least one type acquired a descriptive name – the *toilette en papillon* which is heart-shaped with drawers springing out at each side. The terms *coiffeuse* and *poudreuse* were applied to dressing-tables in the C19.

Tokoname potteries One of the largest and most prolific of the groups of Japanese potteries known as the 'Six Ancient Kilns' (the others being SETO, SHIGARAKI, TAMBA, BIZEN and ECHIZEN). They are situated some 20 miles S. of Nagoya and appear to have been active, from the C12 to the late C16, making rather irregularly formed undecorated wares partly or wholly covered with natural wood-ash glazes. In the Muromachi period (1338–1568) they made TEA CEREMONY WARES highly prized by tea-masters. In the late C19 and early C20 good imitations of Chinese YI-HSING teapots and early Japanese wares were made. Ceramic pipes and water-jars are still produced in the area.

Lit: S. Jenyns, *Japanese Pottery*, London 1971.

Tôle peinte The French name for japanned tinware, *See* JAPANNING.

Toleware or **Tolerware** American wares of imported tin-plate decorated by JAPANNING in New York, New England, etc. They are sometimes called Pennsylvania tin-wares.

Tombac An alloy of copper and zinc used in the Far East for gongs and bells, and in Europe from the C18 for small boxes, etc.

Topino, Charles (d.*c.*1789). One of the few important French furniture-makers working in Paris during the last years of the *ancien régime* when most of the leading *ébénistes* were German. He became a *maître* in 1773. His furniture has great elegance and charm. He specialized in small pieces – *bonheurs-du-jours*, etc. – and developed a very personal style of marquetry decoration reminiscent of Coromandel lacquer because of the motifs employed (teapots, teacups and vases of flowers).

Lit: F. J. B. Watson, *Louis XVI Furniture*, London 1960.

Torchère of carved and gilt wood, French, late c17 (Musée des Arts Décoratifs, Paris)

Torchère A portable stand for a candle or lamp, usually made like a tall table with a very small top. It is known in England as a candle-stand. *Illustrated previous column.*

Toro (or **Turreau**), **Jean Bernard Honoré** (1672–1731). French sculptor and ornamental designer born in Toulon. He published in Paris between 1716 and 1719 a series of designs in a very elegant and precociously Rococo style: *Cartouches nouvellement Inventés*, *Livre de Tables de diverses Formes* (with some pretty, rather spidery engravings of console and side tables supported on slender terms with dragons, *putti*, fauns, etc.), *Desseins arabesques à plusieurs usages* and *Trophées nouvellement Inventées*. These books had great influence on Rococo furniture-designers in both France and England (e.g. Thomas JOHNSON).

Lit: H. Hayward, *Thomas Johnson and the English Rococo*, London 1964.

Tortoiseshell A hard, brittle, translucent material of mottled yellow and brown colour which may be moulded under heat and will take and retain a very high polish. The best type is taken, as thin plates, from the carapace of the Far Eastern hawksbill turtle, *Chelonia imbricata*. It was first used in Europe by the ancient Romans as a furniture veneer. It was used again on furniture by A. C. BOULLE and his imitators, but is more usually moulded into small boxes, cut into combs, or used as a veneer for such objects as caskets and mirror or picture frames, often with ebony. It is frequently imitated by staining horn and, since the c19, in celluloid.

Tortoiseshell ware A type of c18 STAFFORDSHIRE POTTERY of mottled colour made by blending metallic oxides in a clear lead glaze.

Torus A large convex moulding, e.g. at the base of a column.

Toshiro, otherwise called **Kato Shirozaemon** He is the legendary 'father' of Japanese pottery. He is traditionally said to have visited China to study the art of potting in the early C13 and on his return to Japan set up kilns at SETO where he made the first Japanese glazed wares. But the earliest written references to him date from the C16 and most of the wares ascribed to him (TEA CEREMONY WARES) seem to date from the C16 or later. Recent students of Japanese ceramics have doubted his existence.

Lit: S. Jenyns, *Japanese Pottery*, London 1971.

Tou ts'ai Literally 'contrasted colours' – the term is now used for a delicate type of porcelain first made in the Ch'êng-hua period (1465–87) and decorated with an underglaze blue outline filled in with overglaze translucent enamel colours of a wide range.

Touch mark A pewterer's trade mark, stamped on his product. It corresponds to a silversmith's 'maker's mark'. At various places and at various times local guilds enforced the application of touch marks. Sometimes touch marks were applied by the guild rather than by the individual pewterer.

Toulouse potteries The area around modern Toulouse was an important centre for the production of TERRA SIGILLATA in Roman times. Faience was made at Toulouse from 1676 until the mid C18. The few pieces that have been identified date from the C18 and are decorated with BÉRAIN style decorations in blue and white. Wares are said to have been sometimes marked with the name. For illustration *see* BARBER'S BOWL.

Lit: J. Giacomotti, *French Faïence*, Fribourg 1963.

Tournai carpet, *see* WILTON CARPET.

Tournai potteries and porcelain factory More than one faience factory seems to have been active before the mid C18. One was run by **P. J. Fauquez** from 1698 until 1725 when he moved it to SAINT-AMAND-LES-EAUX. Another was established in 1750 and taken over in 1751 by **François-Joseph Peterinck** (1719–99) but few products have been identified. With privileges granted by Maria Teresa, Peterinck also founded in 1751 what was to become the most important porcelain factory in the Low Countries. With the initial help of the arcanist Robert Dubois (b.1709) who had worked at CHANTILLY and VINCENNES it produced soft-paste porcelain (at first of a greyish colour later slightly yellowish) decorated in underglaze blue in imitation of MEISSEN. Plates with ozier borders were a speciality. Wares were also decorated in polychrome with naturalistic flowers. Henri-Joseph Duvivier (d.1771), who was chief painter 1763–71, is said to have worked in England and the exotic birds painted on many pieces during this period resemble those of WORCESTER. But the main source of influence from the 1760s was SÈVRES. Attractive figures and groups were produced from the beginning, after models by Nicolas Lecreux (1733–99), notably a charming Rococo group of bird's-nesters, and by Antoine Gillis (1702–82), Joseph

Tournai porcelain group of 'The Bird's-nesters', from a model by Nicolas Lecreux, c.1760–65 (Victoria & Albert Museum)

Willems (d.1766) who had previously worked at CHELSEA, and N.-F. GAURON who had worked at MENNECY. The Louis XVI style was adopted in the 1780s, the most notable products being tablewares painted with birds after the engravings in Buffon's *Natural History* (1786). But much porcelain was sold in the white for decoration in studios at The Hague and elsewhere. The founder F.-J. Peterinck retired in 1796, turning the factory over to his son **Charles Peterinck-Gérard** who left in 1800 to start a new factory making earthenware, which survived until 1885. The porcelain factory passed to the founder's daughter who had married **J.-M.-J. de Bettignies** the owner of the Saint-Amand-les-Eaux factory and their descendants united these two concerns which remained active until the mid C19, the factory at Tournai making simple household wares while that at Saint-Amand-les-Eaux seems to have specialized in reproductions of C18 porcelain. (For factory mark *see* p. 888.)

Lit: E. J. Soil de Moriamé and J. Deplace de Formanoir, *La Manufacture Imperiale et Royale de porcelaine de Tournay*, Tournai 1937; A. M. Marieu-Dugardin, *Les Legs. Mme Louis Solray. Porcelaines de Tournai*, Brussels 1971.

Tournai tapestry factories Established in Hainault, a province of the Duchy of Burgundy in the C14. Early products are difficult to distinguish from those of the ARRAS TAPESTRY FACTORIES. The first important commission was for *The Story of Gideon* series woven in 1449 for the Chapter Hall of the Order of the Golden Fleece (now lost). Mid-C15 sets of *The Story of St Peter* (Beauvais Cathedral; Musée de Cluny, Paris) and *The Seven Sacraments* (Metropolitan Museum, New York; Victoria & Albert Museum; a fragment in the Glasgow Art Gallery) are generally assigned to Tournai. The leading contractor and weaver was Pasquier GRENIER; other factories at Tournai produced such fine works as *The Story of Jephtha* (Saragossa Cathedral), three panels with the arms of Charles the Bold on flowered backgrounds (Historisches Museum, Berne), *The Battle of Roncevaux* (Musée Cinquantenaire, Brussels; Museo Nazionale, Florence), *The Story of Hercules* (Musée des Gobelins; Musée Cinquantenaire, Brussels) and probably *The Dance of the Wild Men and Women* (Notre Dame de Nantilly, Saumur) which depicts a group of dancing figures, some dressed in the height of late-C15 Burgundian fashion, others exotically clad in feathers and animal skins. Works of the late C15 to early C16 include moral subjects like the *Condemnation de Banquet* illustrating a story published in 1507 (Musée Lorrain, Nancy), several exotic scenes with processions of giraffes, etc., also many VERDURE panels which must have constituted a large part of the Tournai production. Reaching the height of prosperity in the early C16, the industry rapidly declined from 1512 as a result of plague and war. MILLE-FLEURS TAPESTRIES have been claimed for the Tournai tapestry factories but were more probably the work of itinerant weavers in the Loire region.

Lit: D. Heinz, *Europäische Wandteppiche*, Brunswick 1963; R. A. Weigert, *French Tapestry*, London 1962; H. Göbel, *Wandteppiche*, Leipzig 1923–34.

Tours silk factories The most notable in France from their establishment in the late C15 until overtaken by those of LYONS in the 1670s. In the C17 they were cossetted by Cardinal Richelieu who introduced protective laws to limit the importation of silk and also commissioned large quantities from Tours to furnish his own apartments. But the machinations of the Lyons weavers and the defection of numerous Huguenot craftsmen after the revocation of the Edict of Nantes contributed to a decline from which they never recovered. The C17 products appear to have been of Baroque design similar to those woven in Italy (though DU CERCEAU provided flower patterns in the 1660s), those of the C18 imitated Lyons.

Townsend, Job (1699–1765). Outstanding American furniture-maker working in Newport, Rhode Island, where he founded a dynasty of furniture-makers famous for finely carved shell decoration on BLOCKFRONT pieces. He was the father-in-law of John GODDARD. His son **Edmund** (1736–1811) carried on his business and was probably the most gifted member of the family. **John Townsend** (1732–1809) worked first in the American Chippendale and later in the Federal style.

Lit: J. Downs, *American Furniture: Queen Anne and Chippendale Periods in the Henry Francis Du Pont Winterthur Museum*, New York 1952.

Toys A word used until the C19 to describe not only the playthings of children but also a wide variety of small objects originally of slight value. Such objects were called in French *galanteries* and

Toy: a Chelsea porcelain scent-bottle, c.1758–70 *(Victoria & Albert Museum)*

included scent-bottles, snuff-boxes, *étuis, bonbonnières,* etc. made of various, generally non-precious, materials. They were made in porcelain at MEISSEN and later at many other factories, notably those of CHELSEA and MENNECY.

Lit: G. E. Bryant, *Chelsea Porcelain Toys,* London 1925.

Trac(k), F. (*fl.*1559–68). Potter working in SIEGBURG, probably in the factory of A. KNÜTGEN, who signed some of the finest known pieces of Rhenish stoneware with the initials F.T., or, rarely, with his name. He modelled reliefs for the decoration of *Schnellen,* mainly of Biblical subjects, strongly influenced by if not derived from the prints of Heinrich Aldegrever (1502–58), but adapted to the forms and material of stoneware with rare ability. His earliest recorded piece is a *Schnelle* dated 1559, with a relief of the Raising of Lazarus (Germanisches Nationalmuseum, Nuremberg). After 1568 his reliefs were copied by other potters in Siegburg.

Lit: O. von Falke, *Das rheinische Steinzeug,* Berlin 1908.

Trail ornament An ornamental band, usually a border, of leaves, often vine-leaves, and tendrils, used for the decoration of woodwork, metalwork, ceramics, etc.

Trailed decorations or **Trailing** Decorations on glass vessels formed by threads of molten glass applied to, and sometimes melted into, the surface.

Trailed slip Decoration applied to pottery by trailing lines of SLIP on the surface from a vessel with a spout which determines the width of the line.

Transfer printing A method of decorating enamels or ceramics (probably invented by John Brooks or J. SADLER), first practised at the BATTERSEA ENAMEL factory in 1753, soon afterwards at the Bow and WORCESTER PORCELAIN FACTORIES (1757), at many other English factories, notably LIVERPOOL (1756), WEDGWOOD (1760), at the Swedish RÖRSTRAND and MARIEBERG faience factories in the 1760s and throughout Europe in the C19. An engraved copper plate is inked with ceramic colour, a print is taken from it on paper then pressed to the surface of the object to be decorated leaving a monochrome impression usually in black or blue (very rarely in polychrome until the C19). The transfer could be applied either before or after glazing. The resulting

Tree of Life design on Indian painted cotton, C18 (Victoria & Albert Museum)

decoration has the appearance of an engraved print. Sometimes only an outline was printed, to be filled in by hand in colour. Stipple engravings popular in the late C18 were transferred to porcelain on bats of soft glue instead of paper. R. HANCOCK was responsible for some of the finest of the earlier prints.

Transylvanian carpets, *see* TURKISH CARPETS.

Trapani potteries, *see* SICILIAN POTTERIES.

Tree of Life design The creative force of the universe was symbolized by a tree in Indian art. A motif in the form of a large asymmetrical tree, much used for the decoration of textiles, especially bed-covers on which a single tree occupies the centre of the piece, was invented in England in the 1660s to provide a model for Indian calico printers working for the English market. The Indian printers modified it, passed it on to the Chinese who modified it further and it finally returned to Europe and N. America where it was regarded as a Chinese design. *Illustrated previous column.*

Lit: J. Irwin in *Burlington Magazine,* XCVII (1955), pp. 106–14.

Tree pattern carpet, *see* PERSIAN CARPETS.

Treen A collector's term (derived from an obsolete adjective meaning wooden) for household objects such as bowls, trenchers, spoons, boxes, stay-busks, etc., made of carved or turned wood in rustic communities throughout Europe and N. America. All types of wood were used though naturally the harder forms, especially maple and burr walnut, were preferred, particularly for vessels intended to hold liquids. Shapes are very simple and often pleasing. Carved decorations are rare except on such semi-ceremonial objects as Welsh spoons made as love tokens.

Treenail A cylindrical pin of wood used to fasten pieces of timber together, also called a dowel.

Trefid spoon, *see* TRIFID SPOON.

Trek Dutch term for the strong blue, black or manganese outlines to the decorations painted on TIN-GLAZED EARTHENWARE, especially DELFT.

Trembleuse French term for a saucer with a raised ring to hold the cup, made of silver, pottery or porcelain.

Trembleuse: Savona maiolica cup and Genoa silver saucer, 1765 (Private Collection)

Trencher A small, usually wooden, plate or dish either rectangular or circular in shape, on which cut meat was served. The joint of meat was cut on a similar but larger piece of wood known as a **charger.**

Trencher salt A small salt-cellar for the use of a single person. It takes the form of a circular, oval or polygonal block with an oval or circular concavity for the salt, made in pottery or metal (usually silver) from the early C17 to the early C18.

Trespolo Italian type of small, spindly three-legged table, especially popular in C18 Venice.

Treviso pottery and porcelain factory There were potteries at Treviso from the C15 onwards and earthenware of various types and periods has been attributed to them, but no certain examples are known. A faience factory is known to have been run by **Giovanni Rossi di Stefano** from 1766 onwards and later by **Giovanni Maria Roberti** (1771–77) but no examples of their products are certainly known. A soft-paste factory was run by two brothers **Giuseppe** and **Andrea Fontebasso** in the late C18 and early C19 and an elaborate covered tureen by them, signed and dated 1799, is in the British Museum. They also produced cream-coloured earthenware.

Lit: G. Morazzoni, *La maiolica antica Veneta,* I, Milan 1955.

Tricoteuse A C19 term for a small work table: in origin a table at which one could *tricoter* or knit.

Tridarn A Welsh PRESS CUPBOARD in three stages, the lower closed by doors, the upper one open.

Trifid or **Trefid spoon** A C17 English type of spoon with a flat handle widening towards the end which is divided into three parts by deep notches.

Trivet Strictly, a three-legged stand for utensils to be placed in front of a fire, but also any object of similar function either with legs or with a hook to attach it to the front of the grate.

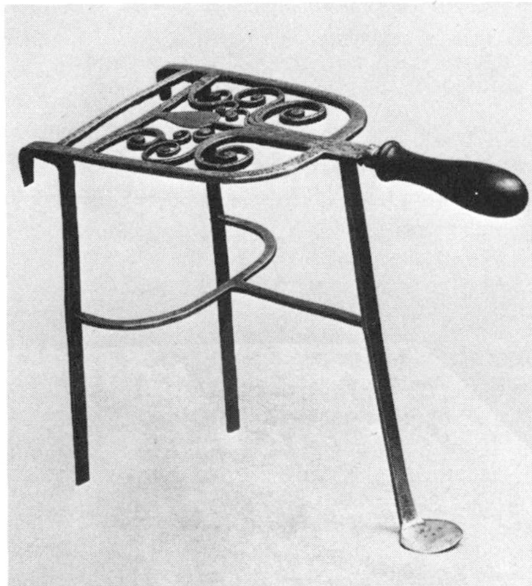

Trivet: English iron, C18 (Victoria & Albert Museum)

Trophy Originally a memorial to a victory consisting of arms and armour and other spoils taken from the enemy, hung up on a tree, pillar, etc., or erected as a monument. By extension the term is applied to similar painted or sculptural groups which were used purely decoratively, often incorporating musical instruments, etc. and with floreated motifs intermingled to form a festoon. *Illustrated next column.*

Trophy of gilt bronze, French, c.1780 (Wallace Collection, London)

Trou, Henri-Charles, *see* SAINT-CLOUD POTTERY & PORCELAIN FACTORY.

Troubadour style The French version of GOTHIC REVIVAL in the decorative arts, also called the Cathedral style. The first essays in this manner were made, surprisingly enough, under the Empire. In 1804 JACOB-DESMALTER made four Gothic *prie-dieu* for the chapel of the Petit Trianon: in 1805 the Empress Josephine had a Gothic gallery built at Malmaison; and in 1813 a writer commented: *'Naguère nous ne voulions que de l'antique, c'est du gothique qu'il nous faut maintenant'.* After the Restoration the vogue became more widespread, due partly to the writings of Chateaubriand on the Middle Ages, to the translation of Sir Walter Scott's novels and to the taste and patronage of the Duchesse de Berry. Details derived from flamboyant Gothic churches were applied to the decoration of furniture (e.g. crocketted, pinnacled and traceried chairbacks), tapestries (e.g. Aubusson *portières* with coats of arms set in Gothic canopies), *Toiles de Jouy* (e.g. armed crusaders resting under palm trees against a background of Gothic tracery), book-bindings and innumerable small objects. Characteristic products include a toilet mirror suspended from a Gothic archway, a clock in the form of a windmill with an ogee top, another with a dial forming the central rose in a traceried window with two figures in medieval costume seated beneath, a

Troubadour style: clock case of iron and gilt bronze, 1830–40 (Musée des Arts Décoratifs, Paris)

cruet with its bottles enclosed by a gilt-bronze Gothic arcade. Such trifles went out of fashion *c.*1835 when Chateaubriand himself declared that the style had become so wearisome *'qu'on meurt d'ennui'* and when archaeologically accurate imitations of medieval furniture and objects began to come in, e.g. caskets and jewellery by FROMENT MEURICE. But by the mid century reproductions of Renaissance and C18 French styles were much more popular in France.

Lit: Le Style Troubadour, Exh. Cat., Brou 1971.

Truité A type of crackle found on porcelain glazes in which the pattern suggests the scales of a trout.

Trumeau French term which originally signified the interior space between two windows, was then applied to the pier-glass which was hung in this piece of wall from the late C17 and by the mid C18 to a looking glass used as an overmantel. A secretaire with a tall superstructure is called a *Bureau trumeau* in Italian.

Tschirnhausen, Ehrenfried Walther von, *see* BÖTTGER, Johann Friedrich.

Tsun A type of Chinese Bronze Age wine vessel with sloping shoulders and a wide, flaring mouth. It was sometimes made in bird or animal form, e.g. in the form of an elephant with the opening in the centre of the back.

Tsung A type of Chinese ritual jade resembling in form a cylinder with a central rectangular section. They vary greatly in size, from a few inches to over a foot in height, and similarly in proportions. Their significance is obscure.

Tucker porcelain factory The first American porcelain factory of note, begun in 1825 by **William Ellis Tucker** (1800–1832) in Philadelphia. It became **Tucker & Hulme** in 1828 and **Tucker & Hemphill** in 1831. From 1833–6 the factory was run by **Hemphill** with Tucker's brother **Thomas** (b.1812) as manager. It closed in 1838. Early wares were decorated with painted scenes in sepia and dark brown, similar to blue-and-white Staffordshire wares; later, during the Hemphill period, they became much richer, often derived from SÈVRES patterns, with heavy gilding and brightly painted flower decorations. Some pieces were occasionally supplied with ormolu mounts. *Illustrated next page.*

Lit: Tucker China 1825–1838, Exh. Cat., Philadelphia Museum of Art, 1957.

Tudor & Leader, *see* SHEFFIELD PLATE.

Tudric pewter, *see* LIBERTY, Sir Arthur Lazenby.

Tula ironworks Founded in central Russia by Peter the Great to make small arms but partly converted into a factory for making steel

Tucker porcelain: veilleuse, c.*1836* *(Philadelphia Museum of Art)*

furniture and small ornaments before 1725. By 1736 it was producing considerable quantities of decorative objects. Later in the century it was much patronized by Catherine the Great. Some products were in traditional Russian styles, e.g. chairs on X-shaped supports with elaborate openwork scrolls on the back and sides. Others are distinctly Western and some steel chimney-pieces and fenders are similar to those designed by R. ADAM in England. Smaller objects, such as candlesticks, caskets and so on, were also made of very finely cut faceted steel, often inlaid with other metals.

Tula work Small silver objects, such as snuff-boxes, decorated with NIELLO and sometimes partly gilt, made at Tula and elsewhere in Russia from the early C19.

Tulip ware An early type of American pottery, made in Pennsylvania by German immigrants in the C17–C18, with SGRAFFIATO decorations often of formalized tulip flowers and leaves.

Tulipière A vase for tulips (and other flowers) made of tin-glazed earthenware, mainly at DELFT in the late C17 and early C18. There are two main types: fan-shaped with one or three rows of nozzles to hold the blooms, and pagoda-shaped with nozzles at the corners on each storey.

Tulipwood A hard, dense wood, light coloured with pronounced red grain so that it sometimes resembles striped tulips. It comes from the *Dalbergia* tree and is related to ROSEWOOD. It was imported into Europe in the C18 from Brazil and Peru and was often employed by French furniture-makers together with amaranth. It is known in France as *bois de rose*.

Tumbler A drinking cup without a handle or foot and originally with a rounded or pointed bottom so that it could not be put down until emptied, but later, i.e. from the C17 onwards, with a heavy flat bottom. It is normally of glass, tapering or of barrel shape, for domestic use.

Tunbridge ware Small wooden objects lavishly decorated with parquetry or marquetry patterns by a special method developed at Tunbridge Wells (Kent) in the late C17 and sometimes imitated elsewhere. Each unit of the design was built up out of sticks of various coloured woods (each about 6 ins. long) glued together so that the ends formed the pattern. The pattern could then be repeated identically on some thirty sheets by slicing the block transversely. In the early C19 the decorations were sometimes based on the floral designs used in BERLIN WOOLWORK though geometrical patterns and little pictures of buildings and landscapes in and around Tunbridge Wells were always more popular. Products included games boards, small boxes, picture frames, pin-trays, etc., and sometimes larger objects such as writing boxes and games tables. See also STICKWORK.

Lit: E. H. and E. R. Pinto, *Tunbridge and Scottish Souvenir Woodware,* London 1970.

Tureen A large, deep earthenware or, more usually, silver vessel for serving soup. It is generally oval in shape, with a loop handle at each end and with a domed lid. Late-C18 tureens often took the form of classical urns, resting on a high spreading base.

Turin potteries and porcelain factory The first of a succession of good maiolica factories was founded before 1562 with painters from URBINO but nothing is known of its products. Pierced baskets of BIANCO DI FAENZA type were made in the 1570s and blue-and-white wares similar to those of SAVONA in the C17. The most interesting factory was that founded in 1725 under royal patronage by **Giorgio Rossetti di Macello** with his nephews **Giorgio Giacinto** (who had worked at LODI) and **Giovanni Battista.** This concern survived until after 1828. Its best wares date from the 1750s and compare favourably with French faience. They are boldly painted in high-temperature colours, with blue and yellow predominating, in the Rococo style with rather juicy asymmetrical cartouches composed of shell and leaf motifs framing landscapes peopled by sprightly nymphs, peasants, *putti* and occasionally saints.

Turin maiolica plate, Rossetti factory, c.1750–75 *(Museo Civico, Turin)*

Similar wares were made in the factory of **Giovanni Antonio Ardizzone,** 1765–71. Other designs are derived from DELFT and the BÉRAIN designs used at MOUSTIERS. Rossetti's factory made porcelain 1737–43 but apparently on only a small scale and very few specimens have been identified. Another very short-lived factory was founded by **Francesco Lodovico Birago, Conte de Vische,** 1765–8. The most important porcelain factory in the neighbourhood of Turin was that of VINOVO. (For factory mark *see* p. 888.)

Lit: V. Viale in Exh, Cat., *Mostra del Barocco Piemontese* vol. iii, Turin 1963; V. Brosio, *Rossetti, Vische, Vinovo,* Milan 1971.

Turin tapestry factory The best in C18 Italy. It was set up in 1731–8 to provide hangings for the several palaces of the House of Savoy. The early products owe their distinction to the happy collaboration between the designer **Claudio Beaumont** (1694–1766) and the chief weavers, **Vittorio Demignot** (trained at Brussels, d.1743), **Antonio Dini** and **Francesco Demignot.** They are unusual for their period in two ways: they are designed to look like tapestries, not framed oil paintings, and they illustrate heroic themes which had gone out of fashion elsewhere for tapestries, e.g. Histories of Alexander, Caesar and Cyrus in Palazzo Reale, Turin, and Palazzo del Quirinale, Rome. In everything save their gay Rococo colour schemes they belong to the late Baroque style. A few hangings of classical ruins and Flemish genre scenes were also woven. Some landscapes with figures in very narrow frames were woven in the 1760's (Museo Civico, Turin). Tapestry carpets were also woven but only one survives (1782, Palazzo Reale, Turin). Standards fell off after 1775: the factory was closed in 1799, re-opened in 1823 but produced little of interest before it was finally closed in 1832.

Lit: M. Viale, *Arazzi Italiani,* Milan 1962.

Turkey work English imitations of Persian and other oriental pile carpets, sometimes made by the same process (see CARPETS). Another type has the wool drawn through a canvas ground and knotted to form a pile. First made in the early C17 but more usual for upholstery than for carpets and rugs.

Lit: C. E. C. Tattersall and S. Reed, *A History of British Carpets,* Leigh-on-Sea 1966.

Turkish carpets A term covering the several

different types of carpet made over the centuries in Asia Minor (Anatolia). They differ from PERSIAN CARPETS technically (by using the GHIORDES KNOT for the pile) and stylistically in that their designs seem invariably to have been created by weavers rather than painters. Recognizable animals and human figures made no appearance on them (until recent times) and even motifs derived from plants tend to be so geometrically stylized that their natural origins are seldom obvious. The earliest surviving fragments are of the Seljuk period and date from before the end of the C13 (Museums of Istanbul and Konya). Timurid miniature paintings and a few fragments of carpets (Benaki Museum, Athens; National Museum, Stockholm, etc.) reveal that several of the main types of design were evolved in the C14–C15. By the C16 **Ushak** (or Oushak) had emerged as an important centre of carpet-making both for home use and for export. The carpets made here are classified according to two main types of design – 'medallion Ushaks' with a prominent central medallion, and 'star Ushaks' with a dominant eight-pointed star (repeated down the centre of a long carpet) linked with diamond motifs on a background with stylized flowers sometimes arranged in an inconspicuous trellis. To some extent these are non-naturalistic versions of Persian patterns but with the use of specifically Turkish motifs. The so-called bird-pattern carpets, on which a curious motif which has been likened to a bird (though its significance and origin remain obscure) is repeated in an all-over pattern filled in with stylized flower motifs, seem to be an original creation of the area. Two other types, essentially Turkish and made in W. Anatolia, are named Holbeins and Lottos after the C16 European painters in whose works they appear (though neither artist was consistent in the type of carpet he painted) – e.g. Hans Holbein's *Madonna of Burgomaster Meyer* c.1526 (Kunstmuseum, Basel), portrait of Georg Giese of 1532 (Staatliche Museum, W. Berlin) or *The Ambassadors* of 1533 (National Gallery, London) and Lorenzo Lotto's portrait of Giovanni Giuliano c.1520 (National Gallery, London) or *St Anthony Giving Alms* of 1542 (SS. Giovanni e Paolo, Venice). Both have borders of stylized (barely legible) Kufic lettering and a red ground decorated in blues and yellows, the former with octagonal motifs, the latter with a trellis of stylized palmettes. As these paintings (and those by several other artists) reveal, many such carpets had been exported to Europe by the early C16. The designs seem to have been repeated until the end of the C17.

Turkish woollen pile carpet, C15 (Staten Historiske Museum, Stockholm)

Another group of carpets is termed **'Transylvanian'** because the first to come to the notice of Western collectors were found in the Protestant churches of Transylvania and were erroneously supposed to have been made in that district: they were in fact made in Anatolia in the C17–C18. Their colours tend to be softer and more varied than those of Ushak carpets. They are often of the 'double-niche' pattern (like two prayer rugs joined end to end) with stylized lamps 'suspended' from each arch or with a large central medallion, flower motifs in the main field and arabesques in the spandrels.

Rather thick heavy carpets made in the C18 to well established designs (including motifs used at the TURKISH COURT Manufactory) appear to have been made near Izmir (Smyrna) whence

Turkish woollen pile carpet, 'Transylvanian type', c17–18 (Victoria & Albert Museum)

they were exported, and are called **'Smyrna carpets'** (and also, confusingly, SPARTA CARPETS). Izmir is still one of the main centres of the Turkish carpet industry. Carpets of good quality and vigorous design continued to be made in Turkey according to traditional patterns until well into the c19 though from the 1870s their colour schemes were affected by the use of aniline dyes. It is rarely possible to ascertain the place of origin of any but the most recent Turkish carpets. Many are attributed to Ak-Hissar (with a pile of mohair sometimes mixed with wool), Bergama or Pergamo (the probable source of some of the Holbeins, later making carpets with strong medallion patterns), Ghiordes (prayer rugs of fine quality), Karaman (with a rather long pile), Kir-Shehr, Kulah (c18 prayer rugs with multiple borders), Meles (with Caucasian patterns) and Yorganladik (prayer rugs usually called Ladiks). The term Yuruk (literally: mountaineer) is applied to rugs with a long pile of mixed wool and goat hair. A factory at Hereke made imitations of French carpets in the early c19 and of Persian from *c.*1850. Demerdji is the source of many modern Turkish carpets.

Lit: K. Erdmann, *Oriental Carpets*, London 1960 and *700 Years of Oriental Carpets*, London 1970.

Turkish Court carpets A group of outstandingly fine woollen pile carpets dating from the mid c16 to early c18, generally assigned to the 'Turkish Court Manufactory' but also termed Ottoman, or Cairene or Ottoman-Cairene. It is not known whether they were made in Egypt under Turkish rule, or in Turkey by Egyptian workmen, or even if they all come from a single source. Technically they are akin to MAMELUKE RUGS but their designs are quite distinct. The earliest appear to date from the great revival of the arts in Turkey under Sulayman the Magnificent and their very free and delicate patterns recall contemporary woven silks and the paintings on tiles and ISNIK pottery. The main decorative motifs – curling leaves, many-petalled rosettes, rich palmettes and fragile sprays of daisy-like flowers – are symmetrically arranged without dominant central medallions.

Lit: K. Erdmann, *Oriental Carpets*, London 1960 and *700 Years of Oriental Carpets*, London 1970; J. V. McMullan, *Islamic Carpets*, New York 1965.

Turkish export wares Porcelain, especially coffee cups without handles, made for export to Turkey at MEISSEN and other German factories from the 1730s until the end of the c18. The earlier Meissen wares made for this market appear to have been marked with the so-called caduceus instead of the crossed swords which were probably mistaken in Turkey for a Christian symbol.

Lit: E. Zimmermann in *Belvedere* X (1926), p. 193.

Turkish knot, *see* GHIORDES KNOT.

Turkman (or **Turkoman**) **carpets** A large group of carpets, including those woven by the Turkman nomads of Central Asia (E. of the Caspian Sea) and also modern carpets made industrially in Turkestan. They have a woollen pile usually tied with the Sehna knot, and are generally of a warm but distinctly sombre colour scheme with a dull red and black predominating. It is from this district that the Turks who settled in Anatolia originally came and the carpets made by the nomads (who preserved their identity until recent times) are woven to patterns which may well antedate those on TURKISH CARPETS, though no existing specimens can be securely dated before the 1850s. Octagons arranged in horizontal rows or staggered are dominant motifs. The carpets are classified by the names of the tribes who wove them. Saryks often have curious stylized animal figures within the octagons. Yomuts are sometimes brighter in colour and have distinctive borders of angular meanders with palmette motifs and the Caucasian latchet motif. Afghans usually have a trefoil motif repeated within the octagons. Technically the finest are probably those made by the Tekkes with the octagons filled with small stars, trefoils and cross-shaped flowers. Similar patterns were used for the coarser rugs woven in Khiva. The Ersari tribe seems to have been more adventurous in the range of designs: they often used undyed cotton in the pile. The rugs woven in Baluchistan are distinguished by their deep webbed ends, sometimes patterned in colours. Those made in and near Kashgar, Khotan and Samarkand in E. Turkestan differ considerably in that their designs are of Chinese inspiration. Since the late C19 the main market for the sale of Turkoman carpets has been Bokhara which in popular parlance has given its name to this whole group. The term Katchlie-Bokhara is applied to a rug with crossed bands dividing the field into four sections.

Lit: A. B. Thacher, *Turkoman Rugs*, New York 1940; J. V. McMullan, *Islamic Carpets*, New York 1965.

Turner, John (d.1786). One of the best of the STAFFORDSHIRE potters who were overshadowed by the fame of WEDGWOOD. He began as an apprentice of T. WHIELDON, set up on his own at Stoke in 1755 and moved to Lane End in 1762. In 1784 he was appointed potter to the Prince of Wales. His products included cream-coloured earthenware, jasper, basaltes and blue printed wares similar in design and by no means inferior in quality to those of Wedgwood. He carried on an extensive export trade to Holland and France but after his death his sons **John** and **William** who succeeded him were ruined by the closure of these markets as a result of the French Revolution and went bankrupt in 1806, though William resumed work on his own until 1829. Wares were sometimes marked 'TURNER' or 'TURNER & Co.' impressed.

Lit: B. Hillier, *Master Potters of the Industrial Revolution: the Turners of Lane End*, London 1965.

Turner, Thomas, *see* CAUGHLEY POTTERY & PORCELAIN FACTORY.

Turnery or **turning** A method of carving the legs of chairs, tables, cabinets, etc., much in use until *c.*1700. It was executed on a foot-operated pole lathe which revolved the wood while the turner cut it to the required shape with a chisel. A turned member could take various forms, e.g. baluster, CUP AND COVER, barley-sugar. The latter is spirally fluted and known as 'twist turned'.

Turquoise, *see* CANAPÉ.

Tutania An alloy of copper, calamine, antimony and tin patented in 1770 by **William Tutin** whose Birmingham firm (Tutin & Haycroft) produced small domestic articles in it.

Tutenag A term of Indian origin used loosely in the Indian trade for zinc but more correctly for an alloy of copper, zinc and nickel, with a little iron, silver and arsenic. It resembles PAKTONG and German Silver or Nickel Silver.

Lit: A. Bonnin, *Tutenag and Paktong*, Oxford 1924.

Twill A textile woven in such a way that the weft passes over two or more and under one or more warps in each row, but with the overpass staggered from row to row producing a herring-bone or diamond pattern. In its simplest form, the 2:1 twill or prunella, one weft thread passes over two warp threads and under the next, this sequence being repeated a space to the right or left in the next row. Most twills are weft-faced, i.e. with the floating weft threads on the outer surface, but there are also warp-faced twills broken vertically, e.g. whipcord twill and cork-screw twill.

Tyg A large earthenware drinking vessel with

Tyg in slipware, Wrotham 1649 (Victoria & Albert Museum)

three or more handles dividing the rim into sections for three or more drinkers. The form was common in C17 and C18 England and the word is supposed to be of ancient origin though not used in print until the mid C19.

Tyneside potteries A number of, mainly rather small, earthenware factories active on either bank of the river Tyne, just W. of Newcastle. The earliest was established by **John Warburton** at Pandon Dean *c.*1730, producing brown ware until *c.*1750 when it moved to Carr's Hill near Gateshead where it made white earthenware. New potteries were set up from the 1780s and there were said to be some twenty of them by 1827. In the C19 they produced a wide range of household objects including blue printed wares (especially willow pattern plates and dishes), lustre wares, cream ware, mocha ware, etc. In the 1830s the firm of Richard Davis was producing tiles decorated with designs after FLAXMAN's prints. The most notable factories were those of **Thomas Fell & Co.** active 1817–90, and **C. T. Maling** founded in the 1850s and surviving until 1963. The firm of **Adams & Co.**, later called **Adamsez Ltd.**, specialized in sanitary wares from 1880 but from 1904 also produced attractive *Art Nouveau* art pottery, marketed under the trade name 'Adamesk': this is the only pottery still active in the district. In 1951 a huge factory was built with government subsidies to house the **Durham China Company** which intended to produce porcelain on a large scale, but the concern failed and closed down in 1954.

Lit: R. C. Bell, *Tyneside Pottery*, London 1971.

Tz'u-chou ware A type of Chinese STONEWARE produced in the Tz'u district of the Northern Honan Province from the SUNG period to the present day (but probably made in the Sung period also in Hopei and Shansi provinces). It is a heavily potted ware, usually adopted for wine-jars, ewers, *mei-ping* vases, brush pots and pillows, with a buff body decorated in slip which may be painted, carved or incised for decorative effect, and covered with a transparent colourless or coloured glaze. The decorations consist of sprays of leaves or flowers or bamboo shoots, often very boldly painted in brown or black on white or creamy slip. But some were painted in red, green or yellow in the Sung period and are the earliest Chinese ceramics with such underglaze decorations. On other pieces the white (occasionally black) slip is carved with close floral patterns. Large vases decorated with chrysanthemums very delicately carved through black slip and covered with a transparent green glaze are exceptionally attractive. The best wares date from the Sung period and are outstandingly beautiful in their extreme simplicity of form, vivacity of decoration and subtlety of surface texture.

Lit: B. Gray, *Early Chinese Pottery and Porcelain*, London 1953.

Ugolino di Vieri: reliquary of the Sacro Corporale, gilt brass with enamel panels, 1337–8 (Orvieto Cathedral)

Typographic ornaments used by Pierre Simon Fournier le jeune in Modèles des Caractères, *Paris, 1742*

Ugolino di Vieri (*fl.*1329–80). He was a Sienese goldsmith and his masterpiece is one of the finest pieces of Italian church plate, the large gilt brass reliquary of the Sacro Corporale or holy corporal-cloth in Orvieto cathedral (1337–8). Its Gothic form is reminiscent of the façade of the cathedral itself and it is decorated with panels of enamel which are among the masterpieces of Italian C14 art. They are of translucent enamel and executed by a process which began to supersede *champlevé* in the late C13. Each silver plaque is modelled in very low relief, the enamel colours being applied one at a time and fired after application – a process similar to that of French and Rhenish *basse taille.* The earliest dated example of Italian translucent enamel, called *lavoro di basso rilievo,* is a chalice signed by **Guccio di Mannaia** and made between 1288 and 1292 for Pope Nicholas IV, in S. Francesco, Assisi. Ugolino di Vieri's only other recorded work is the beautiful reliquary of San Savino (in the Museo dell'Opera del Duomo, Orvieto) executed in collaboration with Viva di Lando, in the form of a crocketted and pinnacled Gothic canopy sheltering a statuette of the Virgin and Child. *Illustrated opposite page.*

Lit: P. Dal Poggetto, *Ugolino di Vieri: Gli smalti di Orvieto,* Florence 1965.

Unaker Virginia china clay or Cherokee clay. It was almost certainly discovered by Andrew DUCHÉ in the 1740s, imported into England a few years later, and used at the Bow and WORCESTER factories for porcelain.

Under-glaze decorations Painted or printed decorations applied to ceramics before they have been glazed, *see* HIGH-TEMPERATURE COLOURS. The colours which will resist the heat needed to vitrify a glaze on porcelain are blue derived from cobalt, red from copper and green, brown and black from iron, but of these only the blue was used before the late C18 in Europe.

Union glass company A glasshouse at Somerville, Massachusetts, which was founded in 1851 by **Amory** and **Francis Houghton,** failed in 1860 and was incorporated as the Union Glass Company and remained active until 1924 making fine cut glass.

Union porcelain works One of the most important C19 porcelain factories in the U.S.A. It was situated at Greenpoint, New York, where soft-paste porcelain factories had been established by Charles Cartlidge & Co. in 1848 and by William Boch & Brother *c.*1850, producing table-wares prettily painted with flowers and decorated in relief (e.g. oak-leaf jug made by the former and

Union Porcelain Works: 'Liberty Cup', 1876 (Metropolitan Museum of Art, gift of Mr and Mrs Franklin M. Chace)

Bacchus jug by the latter). The Cartlidge factory closed in 1856; that of Boch & Brother was bought in 1862 by **Thomas C. Smith** who renamed it the Union Porcelain Works. At the Philadelphia Centennial Exhibition in 1876 it showed a number of impressive pieces in hard-paste porcelain from models by a German immigrant **Karl Miller,** notably a pedestal in WEDGWOOD style with Grecian reliefs, a group of *The Finding of Moses,* a coffee cup with the figure of Liberty as a handle, and the Century vase which commemorates events in American history in paintings and reliefs (all now in the Metropolitan Museum, New York). It produced luxury tablewares some of which were marketed by TIFFANY. The factory closed *c.*1910.

Lit: 19th Century America: Furniture and other Decorative Arts, Exh. Cat., Metropolitan Museum, New York, 1970.

United States Pottery Co., *see* BENNINGTON POTTERY AND PORCELAIN FACTORY.

Uranium glass Glass of a peculiar greenish opaline colour obtained from uranium oxide, made in the C19 mainly at Prague and from 1848 at Stourbridge in England. It is usually fragile.

Urbino potteries One of the most famous and important groups of C16 maiolica factories, patronized by the Dukes of Urbino, Francesco Maria della Rovere and his successor Guidobaldo II della Rovere. Though now used to describe only the factories in and around the city of Urbino itself, the term was often applied from the C16 onwards to those elsewhere in the Duchy, at CASTEL DURANTE and GUBBIO. Potteries existed

Urbino maiolica dish, Orazio Fontana factory, from the Guidobaldo service, 1565–71 (Museo Nazionale, Florence)

in the city from 1477, but seem to have made only simple wares until the 1520s when N. PELLIPARIO'S son Guido, who took the name FONTANA, set up his establishment, specializing in wares decorated in the ISTORIATO style. The finest of these pieces are probably those painted by N. Pellipario and F. X. AVELLI. But several notable *Istoriato* painters worked at Urbino, including Cesare Cari from Faenza (*c.*1536), Raffaele Ciarla and Gironimo di Tommaso (who also painted grotesque decorations). In the 1560s a new style of maiolica decoration with grotesques – derived from Raphael – painted in orange and other colours on a milky white ground was originated in the Fontana factory. A magnificent table-service in this style was made at the Fontana factory for Guidobaldo II before 1574 (many pieces in Museo Nazionale, Florence). A tendency to make vases, basins, jugs, etc. of greater sculptural richness manifested itself at the Fontana factory and was taken to greater lengths at the PATANAZZI factory which was the best of the late-C16 and early-C17 factories. Maiolica was still made at Urbino on a small scale in the C18; marked specimens include plaques in the style of CASTELLI. Antonio Maria Roletti of Turin, after working in Milan and at Borgo San Sepolcro, established a factory at Urbino 1771–5.

Lit: B. Rackham, *Italian Maiolica*, London 1963; G. C. Polidori in *Studi Urbinati*, Urbino 1953.

Urn A covered vase of rounded or ovoid form like those in which the Romans kept the ashes of the dead. The word is commonly but incorrectly applied to various other types of vase.

Ushak carpets, *see* TURKISH CARPETS.

Usk ware, *see* PONTYPOOL JAPANNING FACTORY.

Utzschneider, Paul, *see* SARREGUEMINES POTTERY.

Wood-cut letter used by Robert Estienne, Paris, 1549 (reduced)

Vaisseau à mât A boat-shaped *pot-pourri* made at the Vincennes–SÈVRES PORCELAIN FACTORY from *c.*1755, probably to the design of J.-C. DUPLESSIS, and one of its most fantastic and expensive products.

Val Saint Lambert glasshouse The most important glass factory in Belgium. It was founded in 1825 in a Cistercian monastery just outside Liège and began very modestly producing bottles and flat glass. But it was soon taken over by a chemist, François Kemlin, and greatly expanded. By 1829 it was employing 400 men. Primitive wood-firing was abandoned for coal-firing and the production of decorative and table glass was initiated. Financial support was provided by William I of Orange and, after 1830, by the newly constituted Belgian State. From the early 1830s it issued illustrated catalogues of its products which included much pressed glassware. In 1836 it was absorbed into a large combine of Belgian glass factories which has carried on an extensive export trade ever since. By 1879 it was employing 2800 men with ten furnaces and three cutting workshops. The factory exploited the large new middle-class market for elaborate glass table-services evolving characteristically C19 types of ware which were imitated extensively in Europe and the U.S.A.

Lit: J. Philippe, *Le Val-Saint-Lambert, Ses cristalleries et l'art du verre en Belgique*, Liège 1974.

Valadier, Luigi (1726–85). He was the leading Roman silversmith and bronze-founder of his day. The son of Andrea Valadier (1695–1759), a Provençal silversmith who settled in Rome in 1714 and to whom he was apprenticed. He went to Paris in 1754 to complete his training but was settled in Rome by 1756 and took over his

L. Valadier: silver chalice set with lapis lazuli, c.1760–80 (Louvre)

father's workshop in 1759. He became the official silversmith to the Sacro Palazzo Apostolico and Pope Pius VI made him a *cavaliere* in 1779. His finest surviving ecclesiastical work is the silver and gilt-bronze altar (1770) in the cathedral of Monreale. He produced a quantity of useful plate – coffee-pots, sugar-bowls, etc. – but his reputation rests on his more decorative pieces such as the clock in the form of Trajan's column (begun 1774 and finished 1780, Residenzmuseum, Munich). He also made several extremely elaborate *desserts*, which were almost anthologies of antique sculpture and architecture. Despite his fame and success Valadier does not seem to have prospered and he committed suicide. His workshop was taken over by his son **Giuseppe** (1762–1839) who was later to become famous as an architect. As a silversmith and bronze founder Giuseppe worked in a similar style to his father's, and made one of the showiest pieces of Roman Neo-classical furniture, a bronze table supported on twelve statues of Hercules (designed by Vincenzo Pacetti, 1789–90, in the Vatican Library). After 1817 he worked mainly as an architect. Luigi's younger brother **Giovanni** (1732–1805) was also a notable silversmith working in Rome and his three sons **Filippo** (b.1770), **Tommaso** (b.1772) and **Luigi II** (b.1781) all followed his calling though none was as distinguished as their uncle. (For mark *see* p. 895.)

Lit: R. Righetti in *L'Urbe*, 1940, vol. v, pp. 2–16; C. G. Bulgari, *Argentari Gemmari e Orafi d'Italia*, Rome 1958, vol. ii.

Valencia potteries The source of some of the finest HISPANO-MORESQUE WARES. Pottery is known to have been made in and around Valencia from the C14 and green and purple wares of this date are usually assigned to the suburban PATERNA factory. The C15 lustred wares for which the Valencia potteries are best known are believed to have been made in the suburb of Manisses. The finest are large (40 to 50 cm diameter) dishes decorated with vigorously painted coats of arms or prancing Gothic beasts on foliage or diaper backgrounds in rich golden or purplish LUSTRE and dark blue. Such plates were made for the aristocracies of France and Italy as well as Spain and were by far the best European

Valencia lustred earthenware vase, c.1450–75 *(Victoria & Albert Museum)*

Valencia lustred earthenware dish, c.1475–1500 *(Kunstgewerbemuseum, Berlin)*

ceramics of their day (indeed, they have seldom been surpassed for the combined excellence of technique, form and decoration). ALBARELLI and jugs were also made and similarly decorated. Tiles were produced in considerable quantities usually decorated in blue and white (and sometimes lustre), with heraldic motifs, or arabesques and inscriptions in Arabic or Gothic script. Lustred wares of fine quality, including large dishes, continued to be made in the c16 but they appear to have lost status and are rarely decorated with coats of arms. They are painted with arabesques, animals or human figures of great vitality. In the c17 and c18, however, the quality of painting declined. The lustre on the early wares is of great beauty, ranging from soft, sometimes greenish, golden tones to a rich glowing reddish purple; in the c16 it was usually tawny and in the c17 and c18 of a rather harsh burnished copper tone. There are still potteries at Valencia.

Lit: A. Van de Put, *The Valencian Styles of Hispano-Moresque Pottery*, New York 1938; A. W. Frothingham, *Lustreware of Spain*, New York 1951.

Valenciennes lace One of the finest – and, in the c18, most costly – types of linen pillow lace, the best of which is supposed to have been made at Valenciennes *c.*1725–80, though work of outstanding quality was still being produced as late as 1840 when the city of Valenciennes gave a head-dress to the duchesse de Nemours as a wedding present. It is of great delicacy with designs of scrolls and stylized flowers, differing from most other types of Flemish lace in the absence of cordonnet outlines. Similar types of lace made elsewhere in the same region were called *fausses Valenciennes*. The Valenciennes type of work and patterns were extensively imitated in the c19.

Lit: B. Palliser (rev. M. Jourdain & A. Dryden), *History of Lace*, London 1902; Laprade and A. Maletet, *La dentelle à Valenciennes*, Paris 1927.

Valentien, Albert R., *see* ROOKWOOD POTTERY.

Vallet, Odoardo, *see* BYLIVELT, Jacques.

Vallin, Eugène (1856–1922). French Art Nouveau furniture designer working at Nancy. He began in the Neo-Gothic and Neo-Rococo styles but in 1895, under the influence of GALLÉ, adopted the Art Nouveau style which he practised with great success. Early in the c20 he ironed the curves and excrescences out of his designs which now tended towards the functional.

Valvassori, Giovanni Andrea, *see* LACE.

Van Briggle, Artus (1869–1904). American art potter, born at Felicity, Ohio, trained as a painter at the Academy of Art in Cincinnati where he was employed by the ROOKWOOD POTTERY. In 1893 he was given a scholarship to study painting in Paris where he spent three years. Back in Cincinnati he resumed work as a painter of underglaze decorations at the Rookwood pottery but also began to experiment with matt glazes. Suffering from tuberculosis he left in 1899 and settled at Colorado Springs, Colorado. Here, during the few years left to him, he made a remarkable number of vases, distinctly Art Nouveau in form and decoration (birds or languid plant forms incised or modelled), covered with matt glazes of subtle texture and delicately subdued colour. Many models were cast and repeated. After his death the pottery was carried on by his widow who moved into a larger factory in 1907. It is still active and still producing copies of the original wares as well as new pieces.

Lit: D. McGraw Bogue, *The Van Briggle Story*, Colorado Springs 1968.

Van de Velde, Henry (1863–1957). Belgian architect and designer, he was one of the most important pioneers and propagandists of the modern movement. He began as a painter (studying in Paris and frequenting Impressionist and Symbolist circles). After a nervous breakdown (1889–93) he devoted himself to the decorative arts and architecture under the influence of William MORRIS's writings and VOYSEY's work. His first essay was an embroidery and *appliqué* panel *The Angels Guard* (1893, Kunstgewerbemuseum, Zurich) conceived as a painting in the style of Gauguin. His originality first became apparent in the house he built for himself at Uccle near Brussels (1894–5) for which he designed the furniture, decorative fixtures, silver,

H. Van de Velde: armchair designed 1898–9 (Kunstindustrimuseum, Trondheim)

cutlery and even the clothes for his wife to wear in it. The interior was distinctly chaste with clean-lined undecorated chairs and tables and cabinets, revealing Voysey's influence and also that of English craftsmen like Ernest GIMSON, but rather more elegant. It greatly impressed S. BING who commissioned him to design rooms for his Parisian shop, *L'Art Nouveau,* in 1896. This secured Van de Velde immediate European renown (and a fair amount of abuse as well). As a designer he thereafter applied himself to furniture, ceramics, metalwork, textiles and bookbinding. In 1897 he founded the *Société van de Velde S.A.* with workshops for the production of furniture and metalwork at Ixelles near Brussels. In 1898 he was in Berlin where he did a good deal of furnishing work for the wealthy and refined, including the shop of the Imperial barber, Haby (1901). In 1901 he was called to Weimar to co-ordinate crafts, trades and good design, and became director of the Arts School and School of Arts and Crafts in 1904. From then onwards his time was devoted mainly to architecture and theory though he continued to design furniture, simpler than before and with no more than the gentlest hint of Art Nouveau. He went to Switzerland in 1914 and to Holland in 1921. In 1925 he became principal of the *Institut supérieur des arts décoratifs* in Brussels. His few decorative designs of these years are severe and angular, rather in the Paris 1925 style. He retired to Switzerland in 1947.

As early as 1894 Van de Velde had written: 'Art must conquer the machine. In the future the role of the artist will be glorious. He will entrust his ideas to thousands of steel hands, led and refined by his immaterial and superior spirit.' He later commended the English Arts and Crafts movement for its systematic discarding of ornament but criticized it as anachronistic – producing sensitively designed objects for a few equally sensitive souls. These and other pronouncements – and his own more severe pieces of furniture – undoubtedly had their influence on industrial designers. But he remained an Arts and Craftsman at heart: 'I still prefer the handwoven tablecloth to the machine-made product, hand-made silver to machine-stamped cutlery,' he wrote in 1907. And in 1914 at a meeting of the Deutscher Werkbund he entered a discussion on the use of machinery to plead for individuality against standardization. 'As long as there are artists in the Werkbund,' he declared, 'they will protest against any proposed canon and any standardization. The artist is essentially and intimately a passionate individualist, a spontaneous creator. Never will he, of his own free will, submit to a discipline forcing upon him a norm, a canon.' This old-fashioned, romantic conception of the artist is the soft centre of all his theorizing on the decorative arts. For although he moved some way beyond Ruskin's and Morris's almost Luddite hostility to mechanization, he was unable to conceive the relationship between the artist or designer and the machine in terms other than those of conflict. However, he was directly responsible for the appointment of Gropius as his successor at Weimar in 1919 and thus, indirectly, for the BAUHAUS. Examples of his furniture and other work are in the Germanisches Nationalmuseum Nuremberg; the Karl-Ernst-Osthaus-Museum,

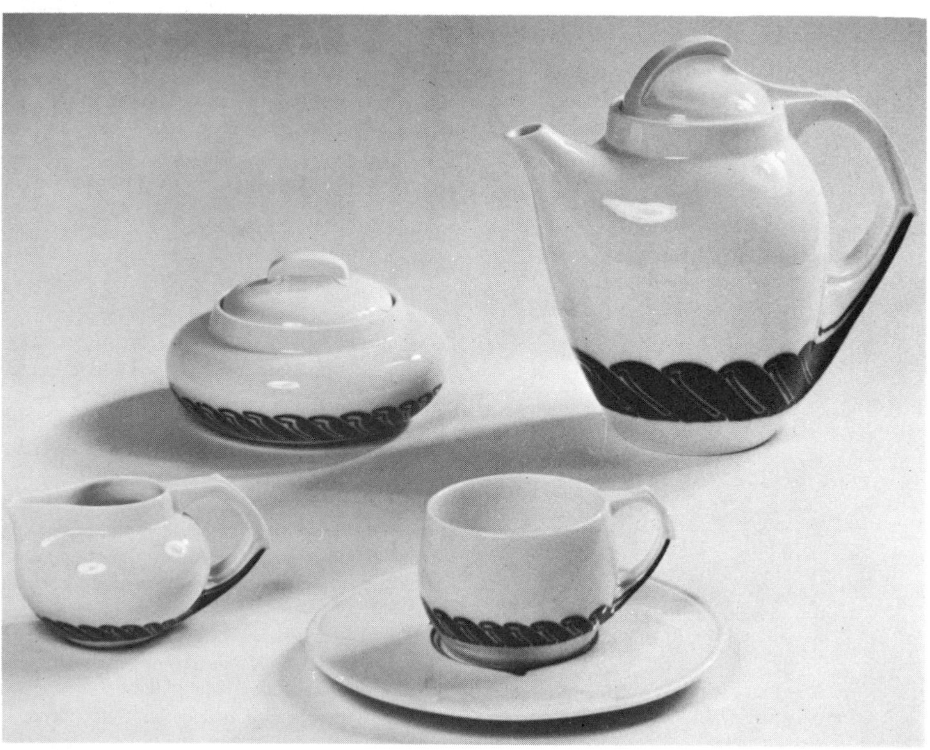

H. Van de Velde: coffee set, Meissen porcelain, c.1904 *(Badisches Landesmuseum, Karlsruhe)*

Hagen; Kunstgewerbemuseum, Zurich; the Badisches Landesmuseum, Karlsruhe; and the Kunstindustrimuseum, Trondheim.

Lit: A. M. Hammacher, *Die Welt Henry Van de Veldes,* 1967; H. Kreisel and G. Himmelheber, *Die Kunst des deutschen Möbels,* vol. III, Munich 1973.

Van der Vinne, Leonard (*fl.*1662–93). A cabinet-maker specializing in marquetry with much use of ivory, he was employed by the Medici Grand Ducal workshop in Florence from 1667 to 1693. His origin is unknown. An elaborate ebony cabinet with marquetry of various woods and ivory, supported by ten gilt blackamoors in fruit wood, and an ebony *prie-dieu* with *pietre dure* mosaic decoration are documented works still in the Palazzo Pitti, Florence. Other similar pieces have been attributed to him. He also made musical instruments and fire-arms, with inlaid wood and *pietre dure.*

Lit: K. Aschenbren Piacenti and A. Gonzalez Palacios in *The Twilight of the Medici,* Exh. Cat., Detroit-Florence 1974.

Van Erp, Dirk (1860–1933). A native of Leeuwarden, Holland, who emigrated to the U.S.A. in 1886 and settled at San Francisco working as a coppersmith in the shipyards. In his spare time he made small decorative objects in copper and this became his main activity from 1908 when he opened the Copper Shop in Oakland, moved in 1910 to San Francisco, where he worked in association with a Miss D'Arcy Gaw and later with the assistance of his two children Agatha and William. He produced table lamps with mica shades, vases, writing-table equipment, etc., making decorative use of exposed rivets, hammering, etc., simple in form and well adapted to the cosy stained-wood interior of the West Coast bungalow of the early c20.

Lit: R. Judson Clark (ed.), *The Arts and Crafts Movement in America 1876–1916*, Exh. Cat., Art Museum, Princeton University, Art Institute of Chicago, etc. 1972–3.

Vanderbank, John (d.1727). The leading tapestry weaver of his day in England and official Chief Arras Worker of the Great Wardrobe, 1689–1727. He made the best of the so-called SOHO TAPESTRIES. Most of his works derive from French or Flemish prototypes, e.g. peasant scenes after Teniers, *The Elements* after Le Brun, *Venus and Cupid* after Albani. He appears at his best and most original in a set of curious chinoiserie scenes of *c.*1700 – groups of exotically dressed Orientals as much Indian as Chinese and possibly based partly on Moghul miniatures brought back from India by the man who commissioned them, Elihu Yale (now at Yale University). These proved very popular and were repeated several times with slight differences, notably in the borders (the earlier examples have frames garlanded with flowers in the Baroque manner, the later ones are surrounded by Chinese teacups, vases, etc.).

Lit: H. C. Mariller, *English Tapestries of the Eighteenth Century*, London 1930.

Vandercruse, Roger, better known as **Lacroix** (1728–99). A leading Parisian furniture-maker, he worked in a transitional Louis XV–Louis XVI style derived from that of his celebrated brother-in-law OEBEN. He was the son of a cabinet-maker, **François Vandercruse,** of Flemish origin, and became a *maître* in 1755. Already in 1751, however, he had been working for Pierre MIGÉON and between then and 1759 he supplied Migéon with a large quantity of furniture. Later, though patronized by the Crown and by Madame du Barry, he worked mainly for the Parisian dealers and specialized in small pieces – *gueridons, bonheurs-du-jour,* etc. – with simple mounts and delicately elegant decoration whether

R. Vandercruse: secrétaire à abattant, c.1770 *(Duthuit Collection, Petit Palais, Paris)*

Vargueño, walnut inlaid with natural and coloured ivory, etc., Spanish, c.1520 (Victoria & Albert Museum)

in *vernis Martin* or floral marquetry. He also favoured the use of Sèvres porcelain plaques as decoration. Examples of his work are in the Louvre and Musée des Arts Décoratifs, Paris; Wallace Collection and Victoria & Albert Museum, London; Metropolitan Museum, New York. His son **Pierre Roger Vandercruse** (d.1789) was also a *maître-ébéniste* but seems to have worked mainly as a restorer at Versailles.

Lit: F. J. B. Watson, *The Wrightsman Collection: Furniture*, New York 1966.

Vargueño A C16–C17 Spanish type of drop-front desk resting on either a chest or a trestle stand, *see* PUENTE. The interior is often elaborately decorated with ebony, tortoiseshell, ivory or other inlays in intricate geometrical patterns. The term is C19. *Illustrated previous page.*

Varion, Giovanni Pietro, *see* ESTE POTTERY & PORCELAIN FACTORY.

Vasa diatreta The name generally given to a number of very elaborately cut Roman glass vases sometimes called cage-cups, which are among the most highly accomplished achievements of the art of glass cutting. They are of very thick glass but cut and under-cut in such a way that a network of interlacing circles, sometimes incorporating figures, stands free from the bowl which is left very thin. Their date and place of origin remain uncertain, but they seem to have been made in the late C3 to early C4 A.D. in Syria and possibly in Italy and the Rhineland. The term is something of a misnomer deriving from Winckelmann who erroneously assumed that Roman *diatretarii* were exclusively engaged in producing such pieces though they were in fact simply glass-cutters, as distinct from *vitrearii* – glass-makers and glass-blowers. The first successful attempts to imitate this type of work were made by F. CARDER.

Vasa diatreta, *late C3-early C4* *(Romisch Germanisches Museum, Cologne)*

Lit: A. Kisa, *Das Glas im Altertum*, Leipzig 1908; F. Neuburg, *Ancient Glass*, London 1962.

Vaupel, Louis, *see* NEW ENGLAND GLASS COMPANY.

Vauxhall glasshouses The most important source of plate glass in late-C17 and C18 England. The first of the glasshouses at Vauxhall – in S. London, on the right bank of the Thames opposite Westminster – was founded *c.*1663 by the Duke of Buckingham who already controlled a glasshouse at Greenwich (from 1660) and held various patents for making glass, including mirror glass. It was managed 1671–4 by John Bellingham who had previously made mirror glass at Haarlem and Amsterdam and subsequently held English patents for 'Normandy glass' (1679) and 'Crown glass' (1685). Other glasshouses were active in the same district until the late C18. No products of these factories have been identified, but mirror plates are often described as 'Vauxhall'.

Lit: H. J. Powell, *Glassmaking in England*, Cambridge 1923; F. Buckley, 'John Bellingham' in *Glass* V (1928), p. 150.

Vecellio, C., *see* LACE.

Vechte (or **Wechte**), **Antoine** (1800–1868). He was one of the best French C19 craftsmen silversmiths. He began as a bronze founder and *ciseleur* but in about 1835 came into contact with the sculptor and designer Jean-Jacques Feuchère (1807–52) under whose influence he turned to silver, rapidly acquiring extraordinary dexterity. Some of his work was bought as Renaissance silver, even by important museums (e.g. Berlin Museum). But he soon attracted important patrons such as the Duc de Luynes for his more original work and began to sign it. Later, he was employed by the leading Parisian silversmiths FROMENT-MEURICE and WAGNER. After the 1848 revolution he went to London to work for Hunt & Roskell (*see* Paul STORR) for whom he modelled display pieces and presentation plate, examples of which were shown at the Great Exhibition in 1851 and at subsequent international exhibitions. Much of his work was reproduced by the galvanoplastic process. In 1861 he retired and left England for France. (For illustration *see* Paul STORR.)

Lit: H. Marlot, *Notice sur Antoine Wechte*, Semur-en-Auxois 1908; *Historismus*, Exh. Cat., Kunstgewerbemuseum, Berlin, vol. VII, 1973.

Veilleuse An C18 contraption for keeping food and drink warm, generally of porcelain, with a covered bowl (in the C19 a small teapot) on a short drum-shaped stand which holds a lamp.

Lit: H. Newman, *Veilleuse 1750–1860*, South Brunswick, New York–London 1967.

Vellert, Dirick (*fl.* 1511–44). Painter, glass-stainer, engraver and etcher working in Antwerp. He is famous mainly as a designer of stained glass and provided cartoons for some of the windows executed by G. HONE at King's College, Cambridge (notably the very fine East window). He also painted some small glass roundels himself (Musée du Cinquantenaire, Brussels) in an early Renaissance style which owes as much to prints after Mantegna and other Italian artists as to contemporary painters in the Low Countries.

Velvet A SILK textile with a pile produced by a pile warp that, by the introduction of rods during weaving, is raised in loops. If the loops are cut it is called a *cut velvet*. It is called *solid* if the ground is entirely covered with pile, *voided* when areas of ground are left free of pile. Patterns may be made by cutting some areas of pile and leaving others uncut. In *broderie* velvet the cut pile is the same height as or lower than the uncut: in *ciselé* velvet the cut pile is higher than the uncut. *Pile on pile* velvet is woven in such a way that a pattern is formed from pile of two or more heights.

The practice of weaving velvet was probably introduced into Europe from Persia. Plain velvets were produced in Italy from the early C14 and figured velvets from the mid C14.

Lit: A. Latour in *CIBA Review* 96 (1953), pp. 3442–67; *Velvets East and West*, Exh. Cat., Los Angeles County Museum, 1966.

Veneer A very thin lamina of fine wood applied to the surface of furniture made with coarser wood. It was widely used from the second half of the C17 onwards.

Venetian carpet A cheap type of carpet woven in a simple check pattern with the weft covered by a heavy woollen warp. Such carpets were produced in many parts of Europe. It is not known why it is called Venetian.

Venetian enamels A group of late-C15 to mid-C16 copper dishes, ewers, etc. embossed with lobes and painted with opaque enamels, mainly a fine dark blue and white, and with a frequently repeated multi-petalled flower motif *(compositae)* delicately picked out in white or gold (rarely colours). A beaker in the Rothschild Collection, Paris, is inscribed: 'Dominus Bernardinus de Caramellis, plebanus fecit fieri de anno 1502'. This suggests that they were made in Italy though the precise place of origin remains unknown (the term 'Venetian enamel' is modern). There is a notable collection of such enamels in the Kunsthistorisches Museum, Vienna.

Lit: E. Steingräber in *Reallexikon zur deutschen Kunstgeschichte*, vol. v (*Email*, col. 44), Stuttgart 1967.

Venetian glasshouses There were glass-makers in Venice as early as 982; by 1255 there were enough to form a guild and in 1291 their factories were transferred from Venice to the nearby island of Murano (as a precaution against fire). By the C14 they were producing blown glass, enamelled glass and spectacle lenses. But the earliest surviving objects are C15 – notably a turquoise blue beaker enamelled with a group of gaily dressed figures (British Museum) and the dark blue 'Barovier' marriage cup enamelled with portraits and allegories (Museo Vetrario, Murano). Early in the C16 the art of making clear crystal glass was discovered and soon the factories were supplying Europe with goblets, jugs, dishes, etc. of a lightness and elegance unequalled at the time and seldom surpassed in later periods. The Venetian government protected and encouraged the industry, granting extraordinary privileges to glass-makers and threatening dire punishments to any who should attempt to transmit the secret of crystal glass elsewhere. Nevertheless several (like VERZELINI) defaulted and Venice lost the monopoly of crystal glass before the end of the c16. To compete with their new rivals the factories produced wares of ever greater fantasy and exuberance – lamps in the form of horses, jugs like ships with reticulated glass rigging, bottles with preposterously attenuated necks, goblets with stems like dragons, serpents or seahorses. During the c16 they also continued to

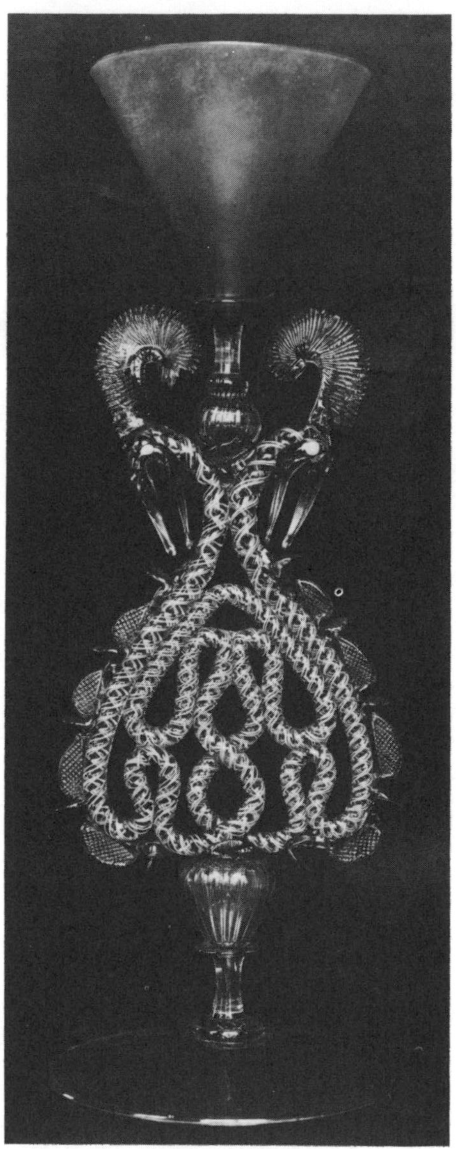

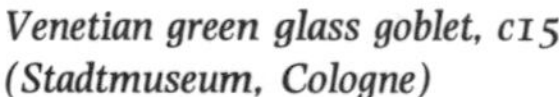

Venetian green glass goblet, c15 (Stadtmuseum, Cologne)

(Right) Venetian blue and white winged wine-glass, c16–17 (Victoria & Albert Museum)

produce opaque glass, sometimes made in imitation of hard stones like chalcedony, and they developed a new milky white glass called LATTICINO and began to make *reticello* or filigree glass for which they have ever since been renowned. Mirrors were made in the late c17 and c18,

(*Right*) *Venetian coloured and silvered glass chandelier, c18* (*Museo, Murano*)

Venetian crystal glass goblet with syphon apparatus, c16–17 (*Victoria & Albert Museum*)

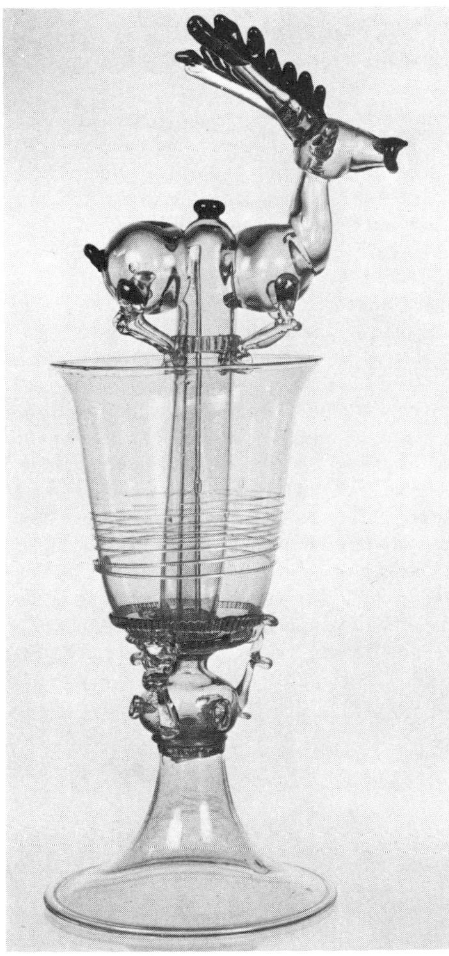

generally rather small as they were of blown glass (not, as in France, cast and ground), of interest mainly for the spirited decorations engraved on them. The most notable c18 products are large chandeliers ornamented with crystal and coloured glass flowers and fruits. But by the early c19 the factories had fallen on hard times and were producing little apart from necklaces and rosaries of glass beads (always a commercially important item of their trade). A revival began *c.*1850, inspired mainly by a factory owner, Pietro Brigaglia, (*see also* BAROVIER and SALVIATI GLASSHOUSE), but most products were adaptations if not direct imitations of c16 objects which had become immensely popular with collectors and designers. In the c20 a few factories (notably VENINI) have abandoned imitations to produce vessels which are of frankly modern design yet preserve the outstanding qualities of early Venetian glass – lightness of weight, brilliance of colour and a ductility which permits astonishing fantasy of form.

Lit: A. Gasparetto, *Il Vetro di Murano*, Venice 1958.

Venetian lace The earliest type of LACE, a needlepoint lace known as PUNTO IN ARIA, was made in Venice from *c.*1480 and pillow lace from the early c16. In the c17 two main needlepoint styles were developed: Venetian raised point, characterized by a rather thick *cordonnet* or outline to the motifs of the pattern (it looks not unlike carved ivory) and Venetian rose point which is much lighter and has the brides dotted with tiny roses which give the impression of snowflakes. (It is alternatively called *point de neige*.) Numerous lace pattern books (*see* LACE and M. PAGANO)

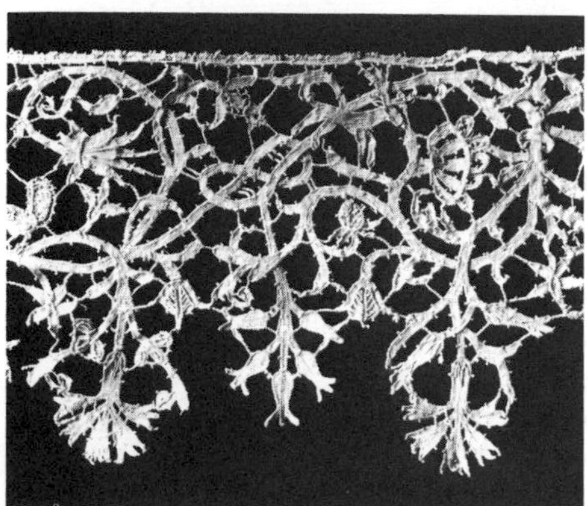

Venetian needlepoint lace, c16 (Victoria & Albert Museum)

were published in Venice in the c16 and the designs in them were widely imitated elsewhere. Lace-makers from Venice moved to other cities in Italy and also to ALENÇON in France and elsewhere. The term Venetian lace is thus used to designate style rather than the place where it was made. The latter can rarely be determined.

Lit: B. Palliser, *History of Lace*, rev. M. Jourdain and A. Dryden, London 1902; E. Ricci, *Antiche trine italiane*, Bergamo 1908; L. W. van der Meulen-Nulle, *Lace*, London 1963.

Venetian–Saracenic metalwork Engraved brass vessels, often with inlays of silver, made by a group of Persian craftsmen who settled in Venice *c*.1475 and continued to work there into the c16. Many pieces are signed by their makers, the best known being Mahmud al-Kurdi. The very delicate abstract patterns of interlaced stem and leaf forms with which they are decorated probably played a part in establishing the European vogue for ARABESQUE. On some, presumably later, pieces, however, Islamic decorations are mixed with such Italian motifs as acanthus leaves, grotesque faces and heraldic devices.

Lit: L. A. Mayer, *Islamic Metalworkers and their Works*, Geneva 1959.

Venetian silk factories Although established before 1258 little is known of their earlier products. A group of c14 silks with oriental motifs, similar to those assigned to LUCCA SILK FACTORIES, are generally but without evidence attributed to Venice where some Lucchese weavers are known to have settled at this period. Silk factories have remained active in Venice and on the Venetian mainland (notably at Vicenza and Verona) until the present day but their products seem never to have been marked by any local characteristics. In the c18 patterns for figured silks were derived from France.

Lit: C. G. E. Bunt, *Venetian Fabrics*, Leigh-on-Sea 1961.

Venice potteries and porcelain factories Maiolica factories were probably active in Venice from the c15 onwards and in 1520 Titian undertook to supervise maiolica made in Venice for Alfonso I d'Este. But the earliest known products date from *c*.1525. In the following decades a number of workshops were producing wares decorated in diverse manners but distinct from those made elsewhere in Italy on account of the quality of the *smaltino* glaze which is nearly transparent (with less tin-oxide than usual in its composition) and sometimes stained a greyish blue with cobalt. The earliest group of wares is decorated with flower and leaf motifs which seem to derive from China, probably by way of Persian ceramics. Some of these pieces were evidently made for export and bear coats-of-arms of German (Nuremberg) families. On the basis of a few signed pieces (in the Louvre, Wallace Collection and Ashmolean) some of the finest of these wares are assigned to the workshops of **Maestro Lodovico** and **Jacomo da Pesaro** functioning in the 1540s and 50s. Large dishes

Venetian maiolica dish, c.1540–50 (Victoria & Albert Museum)

(up to 43 cm diameter) signed by or attributed to the latter are painted with landscapes and in one instance (Victoria & Albert Museum) with a view of the Venetian lagoon as the background to a group of Hercules and Antaeus after an engraving by Giovanni Antonio da Brescia. Another group of wares is painted in the *Istoriato* style of URBINO and is attributed to two potters **Francesco di Pieragnolo** and **Gianantonio da Pesaro** who are known to have moved to Venice from CASTEL DURANTE. Large jugs and *albarelli* were also made, sometimes painted with busts or figure subjects. Of C17 Venetian wares the most interesting are dishes painted with landscapes surrounded by moulded borders incorporating *putti* and Baroque scrollwork with the *smaltino* glaze. A number of very distinctive late-C17 or early-C18 plates painted in pale cool colours over the entire surface with massive Roman ruins and curious loping elongated figures in wide landscapes are usually ascribed to a Venetian factory run by **Andrea** and **Pietro Bertolini** (*fl.* 1738–63), though they have also been dated rather earlier and attributed to the not very distinguished factories at ANGARANO and NOVE near Venice. Porcelain was made in Venice at the COZZI factory (which also made faience painted with flowers), at the HEWELCKE factory and the VEZZI factory. The presumed marks of the potteries include 'Venezia', 'Ven[a]' or 'V[a]' in under-glaze or enamel colour, usually red.

Lit: B. Rackham, *Italian Maiolica*, London 1963.

Venini, Paolo (1895–1959). A Venetian lawyer who gave up his profession in 1920 and turned to glass-making, buying a partnership in the Murano glasshouse of Giacomo Cappelin in 1921, acquiring control and renaming it **Venini & Co** in 1925. He abandoned the Revivalist or merely meretricious styles of the other Venetian factories without departing from the essential traditions of Venetian glass, and soon established himself as the leading manufacturer of high quality decorative and table glass in Italy. He employed several notable designers including Gio PONTI. Vessels or lamps of elegantly simple, obviously C20, form decorated with regular patterns of enamel-twist decorations are characteristic products, which won prizes at international exhibitions – and were soon imitated at other Venetian glasshouses.

Venini glass bottle, c.1968 (Kunstgewerbemuseum, Zurich)

His factory, which was taken over by his widow and son-in-law Ludovico de Santillana after his death, remains one of the best in Italy for glass designed in a modern spirit but made by traditional techniques.

Lit: A. Polak, *Modern Glass*, London 1962.

Verditure (or **Verditer**) **wallpaper** English C18 term for a plain blue-grey paper.

Verdure tapestry,
Brussels, atelier of Jan van Tiegen, 1553 (National Museum, Warsaw)

Verdure Old term for a tapestry representing leafy plants, either richly scrolled foliage or wooded landscapes, sometimes with birds and animals. Such hangings formed the main stock-in-trade of most N. European tapestry factories from the Middle Ages to the c18. *Illustrated previous column.*

Vermeil French term for Silver-Gilt.

Vermiculé A decorative pattern for gilt decorations much used at SÈVRES in the c18, sometimes similar to the 'worm-eaten' effect of vermiculated rustication in architecture but generally more like lace-work or netting.

Vernis Martin A generic name applied to all c18 French JAPANNING on wood – for panelling, carriages, furniture, small boxes, etc. It is called after Guillaume MARTIN and his brothers but covers work by other craftsmen as well.

Verre de fougère The French equivalent of WALDGLAS and WEALD GLASS.

Verre de Nevers, *see* NEVERS GLASSHOUSE.

Verre doublé, *see* CASED GLASS.

Verre églomisé Glass decorated on the back by unfired painting or, usually, by gilding, sometimes engraved with pictorial or decorative motifs. The

Verre églomisé, *medallion signed by 'Boinneri Kerami', c4 (Museo Civico dell-Età Christiana e Moderna, Brescia)*

painting or gilding is protected by another sheet of glass or by a coat of varnish or a layer of metal foil. It has been made since ancient Roman times and some outstandingly fine examples date from the early Christian period (e.g. roundel with three portraits in Museo Civico dell' Età Cristiana, Brescia, the bases of two drinking vessels in British Museum, London). Medieval and Renaissance examples are numerous. But it owes its name to a Parisian picture framer **Jean-Baptiset Glomy** (d.1786) who employed the process for decorating glass picture mounts. ZWISCHENGOLDGLÄSER were made by a similar technique.

Lit: W. B. Honey in *The Connoisseur* XCII (1933), pp. 372–82; G. Swarzenski in *The Journal of the Walters Art Galley*, 1940, p. 55; F. Zauchi Roppo, *Vetri Paleocristiani a figure d'oro*, Bologna 1969.

Verrerie de la Reine A glasshouse established under the patronage of Marie-Antoinette in 1784 at Saint Cloud but soon moved to Moncenis near Le Creusot. It specialized in the production of fine crystal glass – drinking vessels in the English style, lustres, etc. In 1806 it was named the *Manufacture de leurs Majestés Imperiales*. In 1831 it was bought by the BACCARAT and SAINT LOUIS glasshouse and closed.

Verrière, *see* MONTEITH.

Verzelini, Giacomo (1522–1606). The most important glass-maker in Elizabethan England. Born and trained in Venice, he settled first in Antwerp then in London (1571) where he is said to have been employed with other Venetians by **Jean Carré of Amiens** who was hoping to make crystal glass in the Venetian fashion. In 1575 he obtained from the Queen a monopoly of glass-making in the Venetian fashion for twenty-one years and trade protection by a nominal ban on imported Venetian glass. He prospered, bought an estate in Kent and retired in 1592, selling his patent to **Jerome Bowes** and leaving his brother **Niccolo** as manager of the factory. Only eight glasses made by him are recorded, large soda-glass goblets on stems with hollow moulded knops. The glass is clear but slightly speckled. All are decorated with diamond-point engraved ornament and some are dated (1577–90). Were it not for their inscriptions in English – e.g. *In God is al mi trust* – they could hardly be distinguished from Venetian-style glasses made in the Netherlands.

Wineglass dated 1581 and probably by G. Verzelini (Victoria & Albert Museum)

Lit: W. Buckley, *Diamond Engraved Glasses of the Sixteenth Century*, London 1929; *Burlington Magazine* CIX (1967), p. 591; E. S. Godfrey, *The Development of English Glassmaking 1560–1640*, Oxford 1975.

Vetro da trina Italian name for clear crystal glass decorated within its thickness with interlaced threads of opaque white glass, often in spirals. First used by the Romans, it became a speciality of VENETIAN GLASSHOUSES in the C16 and was later made elsewhere.

Vever, Paul (1851–1915) and **Henri** (1854–1942). The best French Art Nouveau jewellers after LALIQUE whose style they imitated, producing brooches, pendants, etc. in the form of flowers, birds and insects.

Vezzi porcelain factory The first Italian factory to make hard-paste porcelain, it was founded in Venice *c.*1720 by a prosperous goldsmith, **Francesco Vezzi** (1651–1740) with C. R. HUNGER from the MEISSEN factory as arcanist. The products are of good translucent hard-paste with a clear wet-looking glaze, strongly influenced by the Meissen and the VIENNA factories and often of the same technical quality though the decorations (especially mythological paintings) tend to be bolder and the modelling of the more ambitious pieces is sometimes rather lumpy. Forms were generally derived from European silver though some wares have reliefs of prunus blossom imitative of *blanc de Chine*. Decorations include some appealingly fantastic chinoiseries which appear to have been a speciality. Several pieces are painted with coats of arms. Few distinctly Venetian objects were made apart from a handsome gondola lantern painted in blue and gold with Bérainesque chinoiseries (Victoria & Albert Museum). The concern went bankrupt and closed down in 1727.

Lit: A. Lane, *Italian Porcelain*, London 1954; F. Stazzo, *Porcellane della casa eccellentissima Vezzi (1720–1727)*, Milan 1967.

Vianen, Paulus van (*c.*1568–1613). He was an outstanding Dutch silversmith, and the most prominent as well as one of the earliest exponents of the AURICULAR STYLE. After training under his father, a Utrecht silversmith, he spent most of his career outside Holland, at the Bavarian Court in Munich (1596–1601), at Salzburg and finally as Rudolf II's Court goldsmith at Prague (1603–13). His Auricular style work was at first limited to borders and cartouches. It emerged more strongly *c.*1607 (e.g. his *tazza* in the Rijksmuseum in Amsterdam) and was fully formed by the end of his career, e.g. the magnificent ewer and basin

Vezzi porcelain gondola-lamp, 1720–27 (Victoria & Albert Museum)

A. van Vianen: silver tazza bowl, 1618 (Rijksmuseum, Amsterdam)

made in 1613 in the Rijksmuseum in Amsterdam. He was indebted to such ornamental designers as Virgil SOLIS and perhaps to Giulio Romano's designs for silver – and also to JAMNITZER from whom he perhaps derived his taste for slithery reptilian forms. After his death his designs were probably sent back to Utrecht where his brother **Adam** (*c.*1565–1627) had remained working in the Renaissance style until 1614 when he too began to develop an Auricular style. By reference to Mannerist designs, especially by Cornelis FLORIS, he produced a bolder version of Paulus's style, embossed in higher relief, e.g. his *tazza* and ewer of 1621 in the Rijksmuseum in Amsterdam. The van Vianen tradition was carried on by Adam's son **Christiaen** (1598–after 1666) who worked mainly in Utrecht but was in England 1635–39, 1652 and again *c.*1660–66. He entered the service of Charles I in England and made 17 pieces of plate for the Royal Chapel at Windsor in 1637 but they were stolen and destroyed three years later. His Auricular, usually shell-fish, motifs tend to be slightly less fantastic than those of his father and uncle and he made greater use of human figures, especially satyrs which serve as supports for *tazzas* and salts. In 1650 he published a volume of prints of his father's and his own works, engraved by Th. van Kessel and entitled *Modelles artificiels de divers vaisseaux d'argent.* (For their marks *see* p. 895.)

Lit: J. W. Frederiks, *Dutch Silver,* The Hague 1952–6, vols. I & II.

Vicente, Gil Portuguese poet and goldsmith working at the Court of King Manuel I. He is assumed to have been responsible for making, with gold brought back by Vasco da Gama in 1503, the enamelled monstrance for the monastery at Belém and now in the Museu de Arte Antiga in Lisbon – one of the outstanding masterpieces of late Gothic art, richly decorated with pinnacles and crockets, birds, snails, sea-shells and little kneeling figures of the Apostles. It was completed in 1506. *Illustrated next column.*

Lit: A. M. Gonçalves, *A Custódia de Belém,* Lisbon 1958.

Vicker's white ware Domestic plate made of a tin alloy, polished to resemble silver, introduced in the 1780s by **John Vicker** of Sheffield.

Gil Vicente: gold and enamel custodia, 1506 (Museu Nacionale de Arte Antiga, Lisbon)

Vico, Enea (1523–67). Italian Mannerist ornamental designer, engraver and medallist. Born in Parma, he worked in Rome 1541–2 when he published prints of unusually light and airy GROTESQUE decorations which were instrumental in diffusing the Grotesque style in N. Europe. He settled in Venice in 1546 but moved to Ferrara in 1563. He issued some accomplished designs for fantastically wrought pieces of silver incorporating human figures and curious details of dolphins and leering masks which seem to anticipate the AURICULAR STYLE.

Victorian style The style current in Great Britain, and to some extent in America, during the reign of Queen Victoria (1837–1901). No great change marked the beginning of the period: many REGENCY designs remained popular but the tendency towards greater richness and elaboration of ornament (often applied by new industrial methods), a still greater love of glitter – of glass or of brass – and, in furniture, more generously upholstered curves grew steadily stronger in the 1830s and 1840s. In these years

Victorian style: Gothic Revival chair designed by Pugin and probably made by J. G. Crace, c.1840 (Victoria & Albert Museum)

the only innovating influence of importance was that of A. W. N. PUGIN who was largely responsible for changing the character of GOTHIC REVIVAL architecture and furniture design (always more popular in England than elsewhere) from the Picturesquely playful to the Romantically earnest and symbolic.

The Industrial Revolution, introducing new mechanical processes and creating a large public for cheap manufactured goods, combined with

Victorian style: ornamental vase in silver exhibited by Messrs Elkington at the Great Exhibition of 1851

the growth of middle-class prosperity and the opening of vast new markets overseas, made the large-scale manufacture of ceramics, glass, textiles, furniture, etc. extremely profitable. But few manufacturers took any interest in design. At best the designer was required merely to add surface decoration. As a result the general level of design declined steadily and the history of the decorative arts during the Victorian period is mainly the story of a series of high-minded but usually misguided attempts to impose improved standards on manufacturers and the general public alike. The pioneer was Sir Henry COLE who encouraged painters and sculptors in the 1840s to design for the big manufacturers, with dismally fussy and self-consciously artistic results. He was too much involved in, and disillusioned by, the Great Exhibition of 1851 which was both a superb manifestation of Victorian optimism and the cause of much heart-searching on the part of those few who were seriously concerned with industrial design. The worst result of this first international exhibition was to establish a new type of decorative object, the exhibition piece – gigantic porcelain vases, fountains, etc., weighty fantasies in silver, lavishly carved furniture such as the sideboards of Gerrard ROBINSON, all displaying the skill and ingenuity of the manufacturers and designed primarily as advertisements for them, to catch the eye of the exhibition visitor. Such objects eventually found their homes in museums of the decorative arts. The Victoria and Albert Museum was founded as a direct result of the Great Exhibition and was intended to encourage the improvement of design by assembling a collection of old and new examples of furniture, ceramics, metalwork, textiles, etc. But in the history of Victorian decorative arts the Exhibition of 1862 was of far greater seminal importance, for it included a number of Japanese objects which were quickly seized upon by designers searching for an alternative to the tired range of European historical styles. The example of Japan helped to simplify furniture and pottery and generally reduce the clutter in Victorian homes: *see* JAPONAISERIE, E. W. GODWIN and C. DRESSER.

Victorian style: rosewood piano by Nunns & Clark of New York, 1851 (Metropolitan Museum)

Another start, in a different direction, was made by William MORRIS who founded in 1861 the firm which was to make most of the best textiles, wallpapers and furniture (designed by P. WEBB and G. JACK) made in later C19 England. The historical importance of Morris in the decorative arts lies mainly in his textile designs for he re-introduced flat pattern and displaced the naturalistic patterns in favour for the previous hundred years. Unfortunately his hostility to the machine and industrial processes led him, despite his advanced political sympathies, to a cloud-cuckoo-land of medieval guilds and bards and joyous hand-craftsmen. The ARTS and CRAFTS movement was a direct result of his teaching. His textile designs also had some influence on the early development of ART NOUVEAU. Here he had a more important follower in the architect C. F. A. VOYSEY to whom, with Morris himself, the pioneer industrial designer on the Continent, H. VAN DE VELDE, was much indebted. But despite all the theorizing of Cole, Owen JONES, Dresser, Morris and, later, ASHBEE, and despite the valiant efforts of a few free-lance designers like Godwin, the vast majority of manufacturers went their own way. They made concessions to the theorists merely by the occasional employment of a sculptor to model figures or busts for reproduction in PARIAN WARE or bronze, or reliefs for the decoration of furniture.

Outside both the industrial world and the Arts and Crafts movement (in the U.S.A. as well as in England, *see* EASTLAKE) there were several gifted designers: William BURGES designed very colourful Gothic Revival furniture for the houses he built, Alfred STEVENS designed Renaissance-style ironwork, and R. W. MARTIN and G. TINWORTH produced 'Studio' pottery which contrasts sharply with the Frenchified porcelain of the large factories.

Victorian style: earthenware vase designed by H. Stacey Marks for Minton (Victoria & Albert Museum)

Vide poche, *see* TABLE, *vide poche.*

Vielstich, Johann Christian, *see* LESUM POTTERY.

Vienna porcelain factory After MEISSEN the first European factory to make hard-paste porcelain. It was founded in 1719 by a Court official of Dutch origin, **Claudius Innocentius Du Paquier** (d.1751) with the assistance of the arcanist C. C. HUNGER and, more important, the kiln master **Samuel Stölzel** (d.1737), both from Meissen. Early employees included the enameller J. G. HEROLD who left for Meissen in 1720 when Stölzel returned there. The products of the first, Du Paquier, period are unmarked and are identifiable mainly on account of their paste – made from Passau kaolin and of a smoky, creamy or sometimes greenish tone. They are similar to Meissen wares in form but much less so in decoration which tends to be denser, with chinoiseries, *fleurs des Indes*, naturalistic flowers (from 1725, before they appeared at Meissen) and, particularly, a lavish use of *Laub- und Bandelwerk* ornament of a Viennese Baroque cast (i.e. similar to architectural decorations in Viennese palaces) in gold and silver. One of the most interesting (and one of the few documented) early products is a very large series of plaques and tiles painted with *fleurs des Indes* and made to decorate the walls and be inset in the furniture of a 'porcelain room' in the Dubsky Palace at Brünn (now in the Österreichisches Museum für angewandte Kunst, Vienna). Several good painters were employed by the factory, notably J. K. W. ANREITER, Joseph Philipp Dannhofer (1712–90) and Anton Schultz (*fl.c.*1725–75). But many products were decorated by HAUSMALER including BOTTENGRUBER, J. HELCHIS, D. & I. PREISSLER and C. F. von WOLFSBURG. In the Du Paquier period few figures were made, notably *Commedia dell'Arte* figures and a centrepiece with an elephant surrounded by dancing peasants (Hermitage Museum, Leningrad). In 1744 Du Paquier

Vienna porcelain Commedia dell'Arte *figures (du Paquier factory),* c.1740 *(Museum für Kunsthandwerk, Frankfurt)*

relinquished the factory to the State which had been helping him with loans for some years. During the 'State period' which followed the factory adopted the Austrian shield as a mark. From 1749 a Hungarian clay of finer quality than that of Passau was used (from 1760 wares were made of a rather less satisfactory mixture of clays). As Du Paquier's financial troubles had been caused partly by over-production, no new patterns seem to have been introduced until *c.*1750 when the factory began to make attractive, if not very original, Rococo tablewares. The figures made in the State period are far more interesting, especially those of musicians, hawkers, shepherds and shepherdesses and classical gods and goddesses slightly stiffly posed on Rococo bases (for which plain bases were substituted in the 1760s) generally attributed to **Johann Josef Niedermayer** who was chief modeller from 1747 until his death in 1784. **Anton Grassi** (1755–1807) who joined the staff as a modeller in 1778 was responsible for some attractive groups of figures in fashionable contemporary costume (*The Greeting*, the *Impassioned Lover*) in a naturalistic Rococo style which he soon abandoned for the Antique Revival manner of his biscuit figures. The third period in the factory's history opens in 1784 when, after another series of financial crises, it was unsuccessfully offered for sale but taken under the direction of a cloth manufacturer **Konrad von Sorgenthal** (d.1804) who quickly transformed it into a prosperous concern. The Rococo style was entirely abandoned, simple geometrical forms were adopted (cylindrical coffee-cups with rectangular handles, urn-shaped vases, etc.) and wares were decorated in rather strong colours and with much raised gilding with Antique architectural ornament around reserved panels minutely painted with Italianate landscapes, portraits or classical subjects. Joseph Leithner, who was the chemist from 1791 onwards introduced a dark blue glaze, known by his name. Figures of the same period, nearly always in biscuit, were generally classical and included groups based on Pompeian paintings (e.g. 'The Cupid Seller') as well as antique statues. Busts of members of the Austrian Imperial family and such notabilities as Haydn were also made. In 1804 **Mathias Niedermayer** (son of the modeller) became director but the factory had already begun to decline before 1827 when he retired. It closed in 1864 and a quantity of old undecorated wares were sold off and painted in *Hausmaler* studios. (For factory mark *see* p. 888.)

Lit: J. Hayward, *Viennese Porcelain of the Du Paquier Period*, London 1952; W. Mrazek & W. Neuwirth, *Wiener Porzellan 1718–1864*, Exh. Cat., Vienna 1970; W. Neuwirth, *Porzellan aus Wien. Von Du Paquier zur Manufaktur im Augarten*, Vienna and Munich 1974, and *Wiener Keramik, Historismus–Jugendstil–Art déco*, Brunswick 1974.

Vierleger, Barnaert, *see* ANTWERP POTTERIES.

Vile & Cobb They were among the leading English furniture-makers during the decade 1755–65, when they supplied furniture to George III and Queen Charlotte. Vile was the senior partner and seems to have been responsible for the carved work which is outstanding, while Cobb attended to the upholstery side of the business. They were for long overshadowed by the fame of CHIPPENDALE, partly because they issued no pattern-book to perpetuate their names. *See* John COBB and William VILE.

Vile, William (*c.*1700–1767). He was the outstanding early George III cabinet-maker. The workshop he ran in partnership with John COBB in London maintained a standard of craftsmanship seldom equalled in England, producing furniture generally of higher quality and sometimes of rather higher price than that made by CHIPPENDALE though stylistically less adventurous. He appears to have come from the West Country. A few pieces of furniture probably dating from the 1730s have been attributed to him (at Alnwick Castle and Chatsworth), but there are no documentary references to him before 1750 when he was already in partnership with Cobb. Furniture made for the Hon. John Damer (Came House, Dorset) between 1756 and 1762 is in a muted late Baroque manner. They seem also to have been employed by the Prince of Wales who, on his accession as George III in 1761, appointed Vile cabinet-maker to the Royal Household. The most interesting of his Royal works were made for the young Queen Charlotte including a secretaire of distinctly, and probably intentionally, Germanic outline and a jewel cabinet of delicately carved mahogany with inlays of ivory and rare woods which is perhaps the finest example of English Rococo furniture. He retired in 1765 when the post of royal cabinet-maker went to his former assistant, **John Bradburn** (d.1781) who retired in 1777.

Lit: R. Edwards & M. Jourdain, *Georgian Cabinet Makers*, London 1955; A. Coleridge, *Chippendale Furniture*, London 1968.

Villeroy & Boch A large German ceramic and glass-making firm which began with a small faience factory at Audun-le-Tiche in the Meurthe-et-Moselle region (near the Luxembourg border) established in 1748 by **François Boch** and inherited by his three sons who founded a second factory at Septfontaines in Luxembourg 1766–7. In 1795 the latter was in the possession of **Jean-François Boch** who in 1809 founded a factory for cream-coloured earthenware at Mettlach in the Rhineland. The Boch factories were united in 1836 with factories belonging to the **Villeroy** family, notably that at Wallerfangen (founded 1778). The joint firm acquired a glasshouse at Wadgassen (1843), the TOURNAI PORCELAIN factory (1851) and factories at Dresden (1856), Schramberg (1883) and Torgau (1926). The concern lost its factories in E. Germany after the Second World War. It has made a wide range of products, from ornaments to sanitary wares, in a variety of materials, but has always followed rather than led stylistic tendencies. *Illustrated next column.*

Lit: Porzellan-Kunst. Sammlung Karl H. Bröhan, Exh. Cat., Schloss Charlottenburg, Berlin 1969.

Vinaigrette A small box, usually of silver or gold, to contain a perfumed sponge held in place by a

Villeroy and Boch: ornamented gilt and painted earthenware products, exhibited at the Great Exhibition, 1851

perforated grille under the lid. Different in form but similar in function to a pomander, it was held to the nose and sniffed.

Vincennes porcelain factories The French National Manufacture of soft-paste porcelain was established at Vincennes before it moved in 1756 to SÈVRES. In 1765 P.-A. HANNONG was allowed use of part of the old factory in the Château de Vincennes for faience manufacture but he surreptitiously made porcelain there: he was ejected in 1770. It was sold in 1774 to a **M. Séguin** who, under the protection of Louis-Philippe, duc de Chartres, made porcelain in the style of the PARIS factories until 1788. (For factory mark *see* p. 888.)

Lit: X. de Chavagnac & A. de Grollier, *Histoire des manufactures françaises de porcelaine,* Paris 1906.

Vinciolo, F., *see* LACE.

Vinovo porcelain factory Founded in 1776 in the castle of Vinovo near Turin under royal patronage by **Giovanni Vittorio Brodel,** in association with Pierre-Antoine HANNONG. (Brodel had previously been concerned with the short-lived Vische factory, *see* TURIN POTTERIES.) The partners quarrelled, the concern fell into debt and Hannong departed in 1780. During these four years the factory produced some simple, elegant tablewares of a pleasant creamy-coloured paste resembling soft paste (in fact a hybrid composition) of late Rococo form, prettily painted with chinoiseries or naturalistic flowers. Statuettes and groups by **Carlo Tamietti** who was chief modeller until his death in 1796 – notably a *St Hubert* of 1779 – are rather more distinguished. The factory was taken over in 1780 by a chemist, **Vittorio Amedeo Gioannetti** under whose direction it flourished, producing useful wares in the Louis XVI style decorated with landscapes, garlands of roses and, especially, tiny sprigs of flowers. A variety of figures and groups, especially rustics and *Commedia dell'Arte* actors, were made. The French invasion of 1796 brought this period of prosperity to an end and the factory never recovered. After Gioannetti's death in 1815 **Giovanni Lumello,** who had succeeded Tamietti as chief modeller, became proprietor and under

Vinovo porcelain dish with decoration by Michele Corasso, c.1780 (Museo Civico, Turin)

his control it produced some attractive classicizing statuettes. It finally closed in 1825. (For factory mark *see* p. 888.)

Lit: V. Viale in *Mostra del Barocco Piemontese*, Exh. Cat., Turin 1963, vol. iii; V. Brosio, *Rossetti, Vische, Vinovo*, Milan 1971.

Viollet-le-Duc, Eugène-Emanuel (1814–79). French architect and architectural theorist who exerted some influence on the decorative arts. His *Dictionnaire raisonné du mobilier français de l'époque Carlovingienne à la Renaissance* (Paris 1858) includes numerous accurate drawings of medieval furnishings and ends with a plea for a new style of furniture suitable to the C19 – solid, honest in the use of materials and not copied from historical styles – which anticipates the theories of William MORRIS. Nevertheless, his own work in the decorative arts, as in architecture, was obstinately Revivalist, e.g. his Gothic reliquary of the Holy Crown (1862, Notre Dame, Paris) and the railway carriage interiors in a modified C15 style for Napoleon III's train.

Lit: Eugène Viollet le Duc 1814–1879, Exh. Cat., Paris 1965.

A. Roemers Visscher: engraved glass goblet, 1621 (Rijksmuseum, Amsterdam)

Viry, Gaspard (1668–1720). French faience painter responsible for much of the best decoration of the earlier wares made at MOUSTIERS, especially pieces painted with scenes after prints by Antonio Tempesta. He was a member of a large family of faience painters, the son of **François I** (1614–89) who worked at Moustiers, brother of **François II** (1659–97) who worked at MARSEILLES factory and of **Jean-Baptiste I** (1671–1726) who worked at Moustiers. His son **Jean-Baptiste II** (1698–1750) also worked at Moustiers and **Joseph** (1709–59) worked at both Moustiers and Marseilles.

Lit: A. Lesur & Tardy, *Les poteries et les faïences françaises*, Paris 1957–60.

Visscher, Anna Roemers (1583–1651). Dutch poetess and glass engraver. She decorated many RÖMERS in diamond point with exquisite naturalistic flowers, fruit and insects, copied from contemporary prints, and inscriptions (Greek, Latin or Dutch) in very cold, graceful calligraphy. Her sister **Maria Tesselschade Roemers Visscher** (1595–1649) and **Anna Maria van Schurnan** (1607–78) worked in a similar manner. *Illustrated previous column.*

Lit: M. Pelliot in *Gazette des Beaux Arts*, 6th series vol. III (1930), pp. 302–27.

Vitrine A cabinet with glass doors and usually glass walls in which small objects may be displayed and kept free of dust, especially a showcase of the type used in museums.

Vitruvian scroll A classical ornament of repeated volutes, generally on a frieze; much used in early GEORGIAN furniture. It is also called a RUNNING DOG.

Voider or **Voyder** An obsolete term for a tray or dish for clearing scraps from table. Surviving examples from before the C18 are rare.

Voisinlieu pottery, *see* ZIEGLER, Jules-Claude.

Volkmar, Charles (1841–1914). American painter, etcher and ceramic artist who was born in Baltimore and trained in Paris under Barye and Harpignies. In 1879 he established a pottery at Greenpoint, Long Island, where he produced vases with underglaze decorations in the style of the Barbizon painters. But, under the influence of Oriental (especially Japanese) pottery, he gradually abandoned nearly all but the most stylized representational decorative motifs. His later wares are notable mainly for the colours, textures and abstract patterns of their glazes, though he continued to paint delicate atmospheric landscapes on tiles. He moved his pottery to Corona, Long Island, and then in 1903 to Metuchen, New Jersey. He also gave lessons in potting.

Lit: R. Judson Clark (ed.), *The Arts and Crafts Movement in America 1876–1916*, Exh. Cat., Art Museum, Princeton University, Art Institute of Chicago, etc., 1972–3.

Volkstedt porcelain factory A Thuringian factory founded by **Georg Heinrich Macheleid** (b.1723) at Sitzendorf *c.*1760 and moved to Volkstedt in 1762, at first making soft-paste wares, few of which survive. In 1767 it began to produce hard paste and was acquired by **Christian Nonne** who ran it under the protection of the Prince of Schwarzburg-Rudolstadt making wares most of which are imitative of MEISSEN and marked with crossed hay-forks from the Schwarzburg arms, drawn in a manner similar to the crossed swords of Meissen. The most notable products are large *pot pourris* sometimes decked with figures modelled in the round and a table service with figure paintings after prints by Chodowiecki. From 1797 it passed through many changes of ownership and for a period in the mid C19 produced forgeries of earlier wares. It still survives. Other porcelain factories were established in Volkstedt in the late C19 and early C20. (For factory mark *see* p. 888.)

Lit: R. Graul and Kurzwelly, *Altthüringer Porzellan*, Leipzig 1909.

Volpato, Giovanni (1733–1803). Notable Italian engraver who in 1785 founded a porcelain factory in via Pudenziana, Rome, specializing in biscuit figures after the most famous antique statues, urns, etc. (Many of his biscuit figures are in the Museo Capitolino, Rome.) The factory also appears to have produced cream-coloured earthenware in the English style. In 1801 he established at Civita Castellana a second factory making statuettes of inferior quality in a heavy granular clay with a very shiny yellowish glaze. The via Pudenziana factory was run mainly by his son **Giuseppe** (d.1805). His grandson **Angelo** directed

G. Volpato: biscuit porcelain figure, c.1785–1800 (Capitoline Museum, Rome)

this concern until 1818 and the Civita Castellana pottery much longer (it was still active in 1857 when sold to **Giuseppe Trocchi**).

Lit: H. Honour in *Apollo* LXXXV (1967), pp. 371–3.

Volute A spiral scroll, especially that on an Ionic capital.

Voulkos, Peter (b.1924). American studio potter working in California, he is the leader of a group of ceramic artists on the West Coast. He began with conventional hand-thrown pots and jars sometimes decorated with patterns in slip under matt glazes. But from 1957 he has made mainly abstract sculpture composed of units of thrown and slab pottery covered with rough glazes. His works have been exhibited in Los Angeles and at the Museum of Modern Art, New York.

Voyeuse, *see* CHAIR.

Voyez, John or **Jean** (*fl.*1765–91). English carver and modeller who began as a silversmith, worked for a porcelain factory and carved wood and marble ornamental sculpture for R. ADAM before 1768 when he was engaged as a modeller by WEDGWOOD for whom he executed some reliefs. Next year he was imprisoned for three months, left Wedgwood and went to work for **Humphrey Palmer** of Hanley, assisting him in the production of imitations of Wedgwood wares (notably black basaltes). In 1772 he was living at Cowbridge near Newcastle-under-Lyme making imitations of engraved gems. Later he appears to have worked for Ralph WOOD and is credited with several of the figures made at his pottery. For **Robert Garner** of Fenton he appears to have modelled 1788 the well-known jug of simulated tree-trunk form with reliefs of a rustic boy and girl and the inscription *Fair Hebe.*

Lit: R. G. Haggar, *Staffordshire Chimney Ornaments*, London 1955.

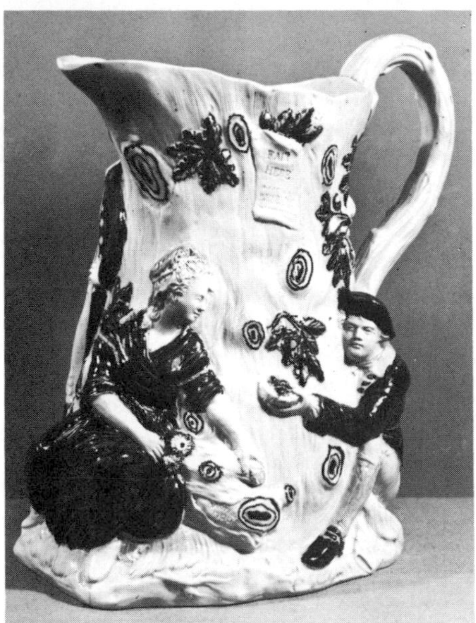

J. Voyez: 'Fair Hebe' creamware jug, 1788 (Victoria & Albert Museum)

Voysey, Charles Francis Annesley (1857–1941). Leading English architect and designer. He began under the influence of William MORRIS but soon evolved a charmingly personal style of much greater lightness and elegance. His fabrics and wallpapers, usually with patterns of birds perching on branches of stylized trees, have a freshness which made VAN DE VELDE say of their first appearance, 'it was as if spring had come all of a sudden'. His furniture – rush-seated chairs with

C. F. A. Voysey: 'The Daisy', fabric, 1898 (Victoria & Albert Museum)

heart-shaped holes in their high backs, cabinets with elaborate metal hinges – has a comely, wholesome farmhouse quality, matching his architecture and distinguishing it from the more epicene and urban products of the GLASGOW SCHOOL which owed much to him. He never advanced on the position he took up in the 1890s, either in the direction of ART NOUVEAU or functional, industrial design, though he influenced both movements.

Lit: N. Pevsner, *Studies in Art, Architecture & Design*, Vol. II, London 1968.

Vries, Hans Vredeman de (1527–1604). Painter and ornamental designer, he was born at Leeuwarden and worked in Mechlin and Antwerp. His influence on design was as extensive as that of his French contemporary DU CERCEAU, stretching to Germany, England and Scandinavia and persisting until the mid C17. He published several volumes of architectural designs, lavishly adorned with STRAPWORK and other Mannerist ornament, also *Differents pourtraicts a scavoir portaux, bancs, escabelles, tables, buffets, licts de camp propres aux menuiziers de l'invention de Jehan Vredeman dict de Vriese, mis en lumière par Philippe Galle*, Antwerp 1565. This contains the widest range of furniture designs published in the C16. They are not lavishly ornamented and are remarkable mainly for their practicability for they could all have been followed by a competent woodworker. They include everyday household objects. In fact de Vries is notable less as an inventive designer than as a codifier of the types of furniture popular in the mid C16. A stone table at Lacock Abbey, Wiltshire, of before 1553, resembles one of his designs. His son **Paul** (b.1567) issued two volumes of designs for beds, buffets, benches, chairs, chests, tables, etc. entitled *Verscheyden Schrynwerck*, 1630. They are in a similar Mannerist style but rather richer and with a greater use of figurative carving than those of his father.

Lit: P. Jessen, *Der Ornamentstich*, Berlin 1920; H. Gerson & E. H. Ter Kuile, *Art & Architecture in*

P. Vredeman de Vries: designs for cupboards, 1630

Belgium 1600–1800, Harmondsworth 1960; P. Poirier, 'Un siècle de gravure anversoise' in *Mémoires de l'Académie Royale de Belgique*, xii, I, 1967, pp. 103–115; S. Jervis, *Printed Furniture Designs before 1650*, London 1974.

Vuolvinus (*fl.*850). A relief of St Ambrose blessing a man forms part of the high altar of San Ambrogio, Milan, and is inscribed VUOLVINI MAGIST PHABER. Nothing else is known for certain about Vuolvinus, but the altar is a great masterpiece of the goldsmith's art and, indeed, of Carolingian sculpture. The front is composed of gold panels of repoussé work framed by bands of enamel and set with cabochons and antique cameos and pearls. The sides and back bear panels of silver with raised figures partly gilt. It was commissioned by Angilbert II, Bishop of Milan, 824–859, and Vuolvinus presumably flourished during these years. The altar is clearly the work of more than one man (and, according to certain scholars, was made or partly made at later periods) and Vuolvinus was probably the head of a workshop. Theories identifying him with Vussin, a pupil of Charlemagne's biographer Einhard, have been discredited. *Illustrated opposite.*

Lit: V. H. Elbern, *Der Karolingische Goldaltar von Mailand*, Bonn 1952.

Vuolvinus: silver, partly gilt, reliefs of scenes from the life of St Ambrose on the altar of S. Ambrogio, c 9 (S. Ambrogio, Milan)

From Paulus Franck's Schatzkammer, *Nuremberg, 1601*

Wachenfeld, Johann Heinrich (1694–1725). Faience painter born at Wolfshagen, near Cassel. He worked 1717–19 at the ANSBACH POTTERY where he developed a variant of the ROUEN type of decoration with neat and narrow borders of lambrequins, soon taken up at the STRASBOURG POTTERY where he was employed 1719–21. In 1722 he founded the DURLACH POTTERY which after his death three years later was continued by his widow.

Wackerle, Joseph (1880–1959). German sculptor, painter and one of the best porcelain modellers of the early C20. After training as a wood carver in his native Partenkirchen, attending the school of applied arts and academy in Munich, and travelling in Italy (he won the Rome prize in 1904), he was appointed artistic director of the NYMPHENBURG PORCELAIN FACTORY in 1906. He broke with the practice of imitating C18 models and designed some very charming statuettes of ladies dressed in the height of contemporary fashion as well as elegant sports-girls. He gave a distinctly modern look even to traditional subjects (his Pierrot and Pierrette are clearly dressed for a fancy-dress ball). Although he continued to provide models for Nymphenburg for many years on a free-lance basis, he gave up his post there in 1909 when he joined the teaching staff of the Kunstgewerbemuseum in Berlin. While in Berlin he provided models of figures in modern dress for the BERLIN PORCELAIN FACTORY. In 1917 he returned to Munich as a teacher (from 1922 he was Professor) at the Kunstgewerbeschule, also teaching at the Akademie der bildenden Künste.

Wafering irons Iron sheets used for making thin cakes and bearing in relief impressions of designs sunk in them. They are among the finest examples of Italian Renaissance popular decorative art. They were made, apparently in large quantities, in the late C15 and C16 in Umbria, possibly in Perugia, and fine examples survive with elaborate stamped decoration. The impressions on the irons were made with small punches (similar to bookbinders' stamps) each punch bearing in low relief a single figure or other ornament, often heraldic. An intricate pattern covering the whole surface of the wafering-iron was built up by combining (and repeating) several of these punches. Details of the designs are sometimes similar to decorative details on PASTIGLIA boxes.

Lit: W. L. Hildburgh in *Proceedings of the Society of Antiquaries*, 2nd series, vol. xxvii, 1915.

Wagener, Johann Heinrich, *see* MAGDEBURG POTTERIES.

Wagenfeld, Wilhelm (b.1900). A leading German industrial designer, he was born in Bremen and began by working in a local silverware factory while attending classes at the State school for arts and crafts. He later studied at the State drawing academy at Hanau and after qualifying as a journeyman silversmith and chaser went to the Weimar BAUHAUS, first as an assistant then as an instructor. At the Bauhaus he worked in a style similar to that of M. BRANDT, making a columnar tea-caddy, a handsome very simple coffee-pot, a gravy boat with two spouts (for fat and skim) and a complete tea and coffee service (1924, Schlossmuseum, Weimar). But his most notable product was a glass and chromium-plated metal table-lamp, designed in collaboration with J. K. Jucker 1923–4 (Museum of Modern Art, New York). Writing of this lamp in 1958, he remarked that it was significant for the Bauhaus that its designs were in reality craft products which, through a use of geometrically clear basic shapes, give the appearance of industrial products. On leaving the Bauhaus he abandoned its preoccupation with pure forms. From 1931 to 1935 he taught at the Berliner Kunsthochschule and from 1934 was chief designer at the FÜRSTENBURG PORCELAIN FACTORY. Since 1949 he has worked in Stuttgart where he established the Werkstatt Wagenfeld in 1954. He published his lectures on industrial design, *Wesen und Gestalt*, in 1948.

His first notable design came in 1932: a tea-service in heat-resistant glass. Simple, practical and elegant, it is still in production and still looks very up to date (manufactured by the Jena glass factory). For drinking glasses he refined on traditional shapes, especially the brandy *ballon*, with great sensitivity. Perhaps his most original work has been in reinforced kitchen glassware for which his designs have been widely imitated. In his metalwork the influence of JENSEN may be felt: he has designed some elegant sets of cutlery with short fork-prongs and knife-blades and circular spoon-bowls. More recently he has experimented with PLASTICS, designing the dining trays (with plates, cups, etc.) for Lufthansa aircraft.

W. Wagenfeld: glass tea cups and saucers and teapot, designed 1932, Jena Glasshouse 1957 (Kunstgewerbemuseum, Zurich)

Lit: Industrieware von Wilhelm Wagenfeld, 1930–1960, Exh. Cat., Kunstgewerbemuseum, Zurich 1960; W. Wagenfeld, *50 jahre Mitarbeit in Fabriken*, Exh. Cat., Cologne 1973.

Wager cups English term for various types of, usually silver, cups the contents of which were drunk for wagers on convivial occasions, e.g. the JUNGFRAUENBECHER which has two bowls which must be emptied without spilling, or the cup in the form of a windmill which must be emptied while its sails are spinning.

Wagner, Carl (1799–1841). He was a German jeweller and silversmith who revived the Renaissance NIELLO technique. Born and trained in Berlin, he settled in Paris in 1830, patented his *niello* technique and founded a firm of silversmiths **'Mention & Wagner'**. Their first products were pieces of jewellery but they also made caskets, vases, etc. decorated with *nielli*. He was patronized by Louis Philippe and was instrumental in the development of the Neo-Renaissance style in silver, influencing François-Désiré FROMENT-MEURICE, Antoine VECHTE and Lucien FALIZE.

Waiter A small salver.

Wakelin, Edward and John, *see* GARRARD, Robert.

Waldenburg potteries A group of Saxon potteries established in the Middle Ages and making from the mid C16 (if not earlier) handsome brown salt-glazed stoneware with a light brown or grey body. Tankards richly decorated with relief ornament were made in the late C16 and early C17. One of the most interesting groups of products includes two tankards each with a relief of a potter at his wheel inscribed 'Hans Glier'. But these have also been attributed to a pottery at nearby Zeitz. Stoneware was also made at Penig from 1490, and it is hardly possible to distinguish the products of this town, Zeitz, and Waldenburg from one another. After the early C17 these potteries appear to have made only simple undecorated wares.

Lit: K. Berling, *Sächsischer Steinzeug aus Waldenburg und Zeitz*, Berlin 1934.

Waldglas (Forest glass) German glass of green colour made from the early Middle Ages by the same process as WEALD GLASS, mainly in the Rhineland and the Böhmerwald on the border of Bavaria. The most notable product is the RÖMER. From the C16 very elaborate vessels were occasionally produced – but the materials were used mainly for simple household wares.

Wall, John (1708–76). A physician (M.D. 1759) practising in Worcester. He was one of the partners in the WORCESTER PORCELAIN FACTORY from 1751 until his death, and the first period of the activity of this concern is generally called after him – Dr Wall Period – although he appears to have been in personal control of it only from 1772 to 1776.

Wall pocket An C18 pottery vase for flowers or spills made to hang on a wall, often in the form of a mask or cornucopia.

Wallbaum or **Wallpaum, Matthäus** (1554–1632). He was one of the best Augsburg goldsmiths, becoming a *Meister* there in 1590. He specialized in small, portable altars (five examples in the Hofburg Schatzkammer, Vienna) and elaborate drinking cups in the form of Diana riding a stag, with clockwork mechanism, derived from Diana groups by Jac. Miller and Joachim Friess. His mark (a walnut tree) is found on many pieces of ecclesiastical and secular silver – e.g. paxes, monstances (an example in the Residenz Schatzkammer, Munich), writing-caskets, jewel caskets, etc. (For his mark *see* p. 895.)

Wallender, Alf, *see* RÖRSTRAND POTTERY & PORCELAIN FACTORY.

Wallendorf porcelain factory A Thuringian factory established by **Johann Wolfgang Hammann** in partnership with **Johann Gottfried** and **Gotthelf Greiner** and from 1764 making porcelain, mainly imitative of the simpler MEISSEN wares decorated in a dark underglaze blue, sometimes with enamel painting. Stiff figures similar to those of LIMBACH (founded by G. Greiner) and copies of Meissen figures were also made. The factory was run by Hammann's descendants until 1897 when it became a limited company: it still survives. (For factory mark *see* p. 888.)

Lit: R. Graul and A. Kurzwelly, *Altthüringer Porzellan*, Leipzig 1909.

Wallpaper A stout paper pasted to interior walls. It appears to have been in use in both France and England as an inexpensive substitute for tapestry, painted cloth or leather hangings by 1481, and to have been in fairly wide use by the end of the C16. The earliest examples were probably painted (none survives) but those of the later C16 were printed from wood blocks with heraldic devices and floral patterns in black on a white ground. In C17 England colours were sometimes added with the help of stencils, and by the end of the C17 FLOCK PAPER was in use. An advertisement records the types of paper available in England in 1702: imitations of tapestry, of 'Irish stitch, and flowered Damasks, Sprigs and Branches, others yard wide in imitation of marble . . . . Embossed work . . . flock work'. But only a few fragments of such papers have survived. Coloured papers drove black-and-white papers out of fashion in the early C18 when flowered and chinoiserie patterns became very popular. At the same time hand-painted CHINESE WALLPAPER was imported in quantity from the Orient. In France wallpaper was found only in the poorer houses until the early C18 when it became fashionable, due mainly to the work of J. PAPILLON. In mid-C18 England J. B. JACKSON attempted to elevate the art of paper-staining by introducing a more durable method of printing (with oil colours) and more 'serious' classically inspired designs. But gay sprigged papers remained popular. A variation on the normal process of papering was developed in England in the 1760s for PRINT ROOMS in which engravings were stuck on plain VERDITURE paper. The lead in wallpaper design passed from England to France in the 1770s when REVEILLON emerged as the outstanding manufacturer. He was succeeded by the firm of JACQUEMART AND BENARD. The next development was the introduction of SCENIC WALLPAPER by ZUBER and DUFOUR. The vogue for repetitive patterns (especially flowered) persisted in both France and England throughout the C19 and those produced by William MORRIS derive from this tradition. At the same time wallpaper designers were much influenced by Historicism and produced papers imitating C16 tapestries and even the *boiseries* of a Louis XVI salon, complete with 'painted' *putti*, consoles supporting vases of flowers, etc. The ART NOUVEAU style introduced papers with more elegant and refined flowers – daturas, irises, freesias – also plain-coloured papers topped with a scenic frieze. Such artists as MUCHA and GUIMARD were employed as designers for large figurative or abstract panels. Wallpapers were not employed in the interiors of houses and flats in the International Modern Style which demanded plain wall surfaces.

Lit: O. Olligs, *Tapeten: ihre Geschichte zur Gegenwart*, Brunswick 1970; E. A. Entwisle, *A Literary History of Wall Paper*, London 1960; H. Clouzot & C. Follot, *Histoire du Papier Peint en France*, Paris 1935.

Walnut A hard wood varying from light to dark brown in colour and with black or dark brown veining which produces a fine figure. It comes from the *juglans regia* tree which is found in Europe. (In the U.S. the *juglans nigra* is indigenous.) In England walnut was the most prized wood for furniture from the Restoration until the introduction of MAHOGANY in the early C18. It was equally prized on the Continent where most of the best Italian, German and French C16–C17 furniture is made of walnut. Virginia walnut was exported to Europe in the C18.

Walther, Clemens Paul, *see* MEISSEN PORCELAIN FACTORY.

Walton, George (1867–1933). Scottish architect and designer. After training at the Glasgow School of Art he set up as an 'ecclesiastical and house decorator' in Glasgow in 1888, designing metalwork which anticipates the style of C. R. MACKINTOSH on whom he exerted a seminal influence. He moved to London in 1897, designed shop-fronts and interiors for Kodaks throughout Europe, also furniture, needlework, glass and textiles – all in the GLASGOW SCHOOL manner.

Lit: N. Pevsner, *Studies in Art, Architecture and Design*, London 1968.

Walton pottery A factory at Burslem in Staffordshire run by **John Walton** from the late C18 until 1835 producing gaily painted figures with tree backgrounds marked with the name *Walton*.

Lit: H. Read, *Staffordshire Pottery Figures*, London 1929.

Wan Li porcelain Chinese porcelain made in the reign of the Emperor Wan Li (1573–1620), the last of importance produced during the MING Dynasty. Blue-and-white wares are the most numerous. Many types were designed expressly for the European market. Large fish-bowls are among the most interesting products made for the home market.

Lit: S. Jenyns, *Ming Pottery and Porcelain*, London 1953.

Wanfried-an-der-Werra pottery In Hesse, the source of a distinctive type of SLIPWARE, mainly bowls and dishes with a red body and sometimes touches of green and manganese colouring in the glaze (which covers only the front of the piece). Wares are decorated in trailed white slip with circles, arcs, festoons and formalized leaf motifs, surrounding figures (often of Saints), animals, birds, etc. Pieces are sometimes inscribed with dates – between 1584 and 1631. The wares were apparently exported to Holland and England where fragments have been found in excavations.

Lit: K. Strauss, *Alte deutsche Kunst-töpfereien*, Berlin 1923.

Wardour Street style A debased mid-C19 English GOTHIC REVIVAL furniture style, named after the ecclesiastical furnishers of Wardour Street, London. The furniture is gimcrack and overloaded with Gothic architectural detail. Subsequently the term was applied to historical writing of the 'Zounds-'Sblood-base-varlet' variety. MORRIS reacted against both the furniture and the literary convention.

Wardrobe A dressing-room or other small room in which clothes are kept and, by extension, a movable closed cupboard for storing clothes. The latter is usually fitted with hooks, pegs, etc. for hanging clothes, and also drawers, shelves, etc. From C19 onwards wardrobes often had a long mirror fitted on the outside or inside of a door.

Warp In a tapestry or other woven fabric, the thick threads extended lengthwise on the loom to form the structural basis for the thinner WEFT or woof threads which cross them to form the web. *See also* HIGH-WARP TAPESTRY and LOW-WARP TAPESTRY.

Warsaw pottery A faience factory, often called the **Belvedere Factory**, erected by King Stanislas Poniatowski in 1774, directed by Baron Franz

Schutter until 1786 and then a Saxon named Wolff. Most products were imitative of German porcelain with chinoiserie decorations, but the most notable are pieces of a large service painted in enamel colours in imitation of Japanese brocaded IMARI, said to have been made in 1776 as a present for the Sultan of Turkey. Wares were marked 'B Varsovie', the B mark (for Belvedere) being sometimes followed by three dots. Brown-enamelled vases were sometimes marked 'W' (for Wolff). Versions of the Meissen and Sèvres marks may also have been used.

Lit: F. Savery in *The Burlington Magazine* LXXXVIII (1946), p. 117.

Warwick frame A type of English silver cruet-stand made from *c.*1750 with a cinquefoil plate, supports for five bottles, and a central rod and handle.

Wassmus The best known firm of furniture-makers in Paris under Napoleon III, begun by **Jean-Henri-Chrétien Wassmus** and his brother **Jean-Henri-Christophe** who came from Hanover and settled in Paris by 1816. They were described *c.*1840 as cabinet-makers specializing in furniture in the style of Riesener, Boulle, and in that of the Louis XV and Louis XVI periods. They were joined by **Henri-Léonard Wassmus** (probably the son of Jean-Henri-Chrétien) who was perhaps largely responsible for the firm's great success. In 1862 the firm was in difficulties financially but recovered and continued until about 1868. An example of their Louis XVI style furniture is still at the Château de Compiègne for which it was made in 1859, for the *salon de famille*.

Lit: D. Ledoux-Lebard, *Les ébénistes-parisiens (1795–1870)*, Paris 1965.

Watered silk, *see* MOIRÉ.

Waterford glasshouse The most famous Irish glass factory. A flint-glass factory was established at Gurteens near Waterford 1729–39 but little is known of it. The more important Waterford glasshouse began production in 1784 with a works manager and many workmen from STOURBRIDGE. After several changes of ownership it finally closed down in 1851, a victim of English competition. Best known for very deeply cut glass vessels. Occasionally glass vessels were imported ready-made from England and merely decorated with cut ornament at Waterford. Except for a very few pieces bearing the Waterford mark products of the factory cannot be distinguished from contemporary pieces made elsewhere in Ireland (CORK and Dublin), or even in England, which often have the slightly bluish tinge formerly and incorrectly supposed to distinguish Waterford.

(Opposite) Waterford Glass: decanter, marked 'Penrose Waterford', early c19 (Victoria & Albert Museum)

Waterford Glass: chandelier (formerly in Thomastown Parish Church, County Kilkenny), late c18 (Victoria & Albert Museum)

Lit: W. A. Thorpe, *English & Irish Glass*, London 1929; Phelps Warren, *Irish Glass*, London 1970.

Water-leaf Various types of unribbed leaves used as decorative motifs from the Romanesque period onwards.

Waterloo Glasshouse Company, *see* CORK GLASSHOUSE.

Watteau, Jean Antoine (1684–1721). The great

French painter. He exerted a vital influence on the decorative arts of the early Rococo or RÉGENCE style, mainly through posthumously published engravings after his paintings and drawings. He was largely responsible for creating a new and lighter style of GROTESQUE decoration, with elegantly flimsy canopies surrounding *Commedia dell'Arte* actors or exotic orientals, widely adopted for tapestry design and decorative paintings. His *fête galante* scenes served as models for porcelain statuettes and for paintings on porcelain produced not only in French but also in German and English factories. He was also responsible, with **Gillot**, for popularizing the ESPAGNOLETTE motif.

Lit: Fiske Kimball, *The Creation of the Rococo*, Philadelphia 1943.

Waugh, Sidney, *see* CORNING GLASS WORKS and STEUBEN GLASS WORKS.

Wauters, Michel (d.1679). A weaver of Antwerp who produced tapestries of mythological, historical and biblical subjects, e.g. *Dido and Aeneas* after G. F. Romanelli (Museo Alberoni, Piacenza; Castello Sforzesco, Milan; Cleveland Museum of Arts, etc.). Several of his panels were woven after cartoons by Abraham van Diepenbeeck (1596–1675) including a nine-piece history of Moses, an eight-piece history of Solomon and a series of eight horses. He worked in collaboration with his brother **Philippe** and also with a **Pierre** or **Peeter Wauters.** The family carried on an export trade and appears to have catered specially for the English market, sometimes imitating the products of English factories, e.g. the MORTLAKE *Hero and Leander* and the *Playing Children* series.

Lit: M. Crick-Kuntziger, *Revue belge d'archéologie et d'histoire de l'art* V (1935), pp. 35–44; *Bulletin of the Detroit Institute of Arts* XIV (1934–5), pp. 44–7.

Wave pattern, *see* RUNNING DOG.

Wax-jack A stand, usually of silver, for a coil of taper which may be lit to melt sealing-wax. It was made from the mid C18 onwards, especially in England.

Weald glass The English equivalent of German WALDGLAS and French *verre de fougère*, a greenish glass made in the Weald of Kent, Surrey and Sussex from the C13 to C16. Beakers, bottles and urinals of very simple design were the main objects made, apart from window glass. Having deforested the Weald to feed their furnaces the glass-makers, joined by craftsmen from Lorraine, moved on to Gloucestershire, Hampshire, North Staffordshire and the Scottish Border. Fragments of their work found at Woodchester reveal a mixture of German and Venetian influence on design. In 1615 the use of wood for glass-making was prohibited and in 1623 Sir Robert Mansell (1573–1656) obtained an absolute monopoly for glass production in England.

Lit: W. A. Thorpe, *English & Irish Glass*, London 1929; G. H. Kenyon, *The Glass Industry of the Weald*, Leicester 1967.

Weaving The process of making a fabric by intermeshing strands of twisted or spun thread, akin to BASKETRY and similarly known to have been practised by Neolithic cultures. But whereas the basket-maker worked with simple vegetable fibres, the weaver had to prepare his by twisting or spinning them into long and stout threads. The basic practice of twisting threads may have been discovered as early as the Palaeolithic Age, and part of a fishing-net made of twined threads of plant bast survives from Mesolithic – or Middle Stone Age – Finland. The earliest known specimens of woven textiles, some pieces of LINEN, come from the Fayum in Egypt and date from soon after 5000 B.C. The first materials used appear to have been flax and other vegetable basts. COTTON first appears in India *c.*3000 B.C. and slightly later in Peru. WOOL was not used in early Egypt, where it was thought to be impure, but was used in other parts of the Near East and in Scandinavia from *c.*1150 B.C.

To weave a textile it is necessary to stretch the warp threads on some type of loom and pass the weft threads between them. The earliest loom consisted of two bars pegged to the ground – as shown in a painting on an Egyptian dish of *c.*4400 B.C. – which by *c.*3000 B.C. had been developed, by the addition of rod-heddle and shed-rod (to separate the warp threads by making a 'shed' through which the weft could be passed), into the *horizontal ground loom* still employed by nomadic people (e.g. the Bedouin) throughout the Middle East. The two other early types of loom had a vertical construction – the *vertical two-beamed loom* (in use by *c.*1500 in Egypt but perhaps earlier in Syria) on which the warp is stretched between two bars fixed in an upright frame and the weaver works from bottom to top: and the *warp-weighted loom* (in use by *c.*2500 B.C. in Troy) on which the warp is suspended from a horizontal bar and held taut by weights attached to groups of the threads, on which the weaver works from the top downwards. The basic types of loom have been varied in later times only by the development of rod-heddle and shed-rods to facilitate the weaving of patterned textiles.

The basic type of weave is the simple criss-cross of warp and weft threads. Striped and checked patterns are obtained by varying the colour of the warp and/or weft threads. By multiplying the heddles and thus varying the warp threads raised each time the weft is passed, it is possible to produce TWILL weaves. More elaborate patterns, derived from the colours rather than the system of the threads, can be obtained by the tapestry-weave technique (intoducing weft threads of a different colour for a small area) or by the practice of 'floating' either in the warp or weft, e.g. by passing coloured weft threads over three warps and under one, in the area to be distinguished. A pile is obtained by passing at intervals the weft threads round a stick to form a loop. All these techniques were brought to a high state of development in the second millennium B.C. in Egypt. Textiles from the tomb of Tutankhamen include pieces of fine linen (with 280 - 80 threads per sq. in.), a tapestry-weave robe decorated with rosettes and a lotus border, and some braids woven on a loom with at least seven heddles.

These techniques were also practised in China where SILK was being finely woven at least as early as 1000 B.C. In Europe (apart from Byzantium) the quality of weaving declined sharply after the fall of the Roman Empire but revived in the Middle Ages. The horizontal loom was much improved by raising it from the ground on legs, thus enabling the weaver to sit at it and use treadles to manipulate the heddles. This type of loom became standard for plain and simple pattern weaving (the upright loom was preferred for tapestry). For weaving figured textiles the draw-loom was introduced, probably from China, used by Italian silk weavers of the Middle Ages and then passed to France and the rest of Europe. Whereas simple looms permitted the use of no more than some twenty-four heddles, the draw-loom controlled the movement of the warp by a different means, making possible a much greater variety in the number of warp threads raised each time the weft was passed, and thus a greatly increased range of patterns. The weaver could not, however, operate it without the assistance of a draw-boy to pull the cords to open the shed each time the weft was passed.

In about 1490 Leonardo da Vinci worked out the principle of an automatic loom for weaving plain textiles. And early in the C17 looms which could be worked by unskilled men were in use in Holland, Germany and England – their introduction provoked riots by weavers who feared they would be put out of work. In the C18 various attempts were made to construct wholly automatic looms but none was used. Attempts to find a mechanical substitute for the draw-boy in working the draw-loom were more successful. In 1725 Basile Bouchon in France designed a mechanism to select the cords to be drawn automatically. This was improved upon in 1745 by Jacques de Vaucanson whose loom was too impractical for use but provided the foundation of the revolutionary JACQUARD LOOM. This made possible the weaving of the most elaborate patterns by a single operator. The machine was invented in 1801 and eleven thousand of them were in use in France by 1812. It was introduced into England *c.*1810 and by 1832 some six hundred were in operation in Coventry alone.

In the meantime considerable advances had been made in the mechanization of the various processes by which fibres were prepared for weaving. The spinning wheel was developed in Europe in the Middle Ages and after various labour- and time-saving modifications had been made spinning mechanisms driven by water were in use in England by the 1740s. Improvements were made by Hargreaves' spinning-jenny (probably 1764), Arkwright's water-frame spinning machine (1769) and Crompton's mule (1774–9) followed by a large number of different machines devised to spin various types of fibre, the most important being Richard Roberts' self-acting mule of 1830. The first successful power-operated loom for plain weaving cotton was invented by Cartwright in 1786 but was superseded by Roberts's power loom of 1822. These were suitable only for cotton and worsted, not for linen. Knowles' loom of 1863 soon became the most generally used for wool. A linen power loom came into use in 1850 and replaced the handloom in both Yorkshire and Ireland by 1890. Though America kept abreast of and contributed to these developments, Continental Europe lagged behind. But by 1900 the hand-loom survived for textile products only in the more backward parts of Europe, though it was still used for weaving short lengths of elaborate and expensive fabrics and for experimental purposes by textile designers. MAN-MADE FIBRES have, as yet, had little effect on the process of weaving.

Lit: L. Hooper, *Handloom Weaving*, London 1910; E. Flemming, *Textile Künste*, Berlin 1923; M. Dreger, *Künstlerische Entwicklung der Weberei und Stickerei*, Vienna 1904; M. E. Pritchard, *A Short Dictionary of Weaving*, London 1954; H. Hodges, *Artifacts*, London 1964.

Webb, Philip (1831–1915). Architect and designer, he was closely associated for most of his life with William MORRIS. They were together in the architect G. S. Street's office until 1858 when Webb set up on his own. He designed furniture as well as houses for his clients and he collaborated with Morris and Burne-Jones on the furniture for their house in Red Lion Square. In 1860 he designed and built the famous Red House, Bexleyheath, for Morris, and furniture was specially made for it to Webb's designs. The following year he joined the firm of **Morris, Marshall, Faulkner and Company** and from 1861 onwards worked exclusively for the Morris firm as a designer of furniture, embroideries, metalwork, jewellery and glass. Neither Morris nor Webb intended (as did PUGIN) to revive the form of medieval furniture though they looked back nostalgically to the Middle Ages as an age of social as well as artistic harmony. They tried to create a new astylar style, to make, as Lethaby wrote, 'the buildings of our own day pleasant without pretences of style'. Webb's furniture is ruthlessly honest – massively solid (veneers were anathema to him) with the joinery unconcealed and often emphasized. Generally it is of plain oak, usually stained green or black but sometimes decorated on the surface by painting, gesso work or lacquered leather. Except in his earliest pieces there is no trace of obviously Gothic ornament – no crockets, pinnacles or panels of tracery. It often looks rather gaunt, but Webb was capable of rich effects also, as in his design for pianofortes

P. Webb: oak table designed 1865–7 (Victoria & Albert Museum)

decorated with silvered and lacquered gesso relief work. He was also open to experiments with new materials and designed a bed for himself of wrought iron. Webb resigned his partnership in the Morris firm when it was reorganized in 1875, but he continued to provide the firm with designs. And by the 1890s his influence had spread beyond the Morris firm to the whole ARTS AND CRAFTS movement. Examples of his work are in the Victoria & Albert Museum, London.

Lit: W. R. Lethaby, *P. Webb and his Work*, London 1935; *Exhibition of Victorian and Edwardian Decorative Arts*, Catalogue, Victoria & Albert Museum, London 1952.

Webb, Thomas and Sons A leading STOURBRIDGE GLASSHOUSE, founded by **Thomas Webb the elder** in 1837 at The Platts, Amblecote, making the usual range of household and decorative pieces some of which were exhibited at the Great Exhibition of 1851. It was transferred to the Dennis Works in 1856. Under his sons, **Thomas Wilkes Webb** and **Charles Webb,** who inherited the concern in 1869 it became more adventurous in the production of decorative glass. At the Paris exhibition of 1878 they won a *grand prix* for a display which included some highly praised chandeliers. In 1876 they commissioned a cameo or cased-glass vase from J. NORTHWOOD, completed in 1882 and sold to TIFFANY of New York. (It is now in the Smithsonian Institution, Washington, D.C.) At about this time their employees T. and G. WOODALL began to execute the intricately carved cased-glass pieces for which the firm achieved widespread renown, employing some 70 craftsmen who specialized in such work until *c.*1906. But these pieces were exceptional (a single vase or plaque might cost more than £100) and the firm's main trade was in household glasswares of good quality which it continues to produce.

Lit: G. W. Beard, *Nineteenth-Century Cameo Glass*, Newport, Mon. 1956.

Webber, Christopher, *see* BENNINGTON POTTERY & PORCELAIN FACTORY.

Webster, Moses (1792–1870). He painted DERBY

and WORCESTER porcelain with floral decorations and also worked at R. ROBINS and T. M. RANDALL's decorating workshop in Spa Fields, London, decorating NANTGARW and SWANSEA wares.

Wechte, Antoine, *see* VECHTE, Antoine.

Wedgwood, Josiah (1730–95). The most distinguished English potter and the only one of international importance, exerting an influence as far as Russia, Italy and the U.S.A. He was born into a family of potters of Burslem, Staffordshire, and apprenticed as a pottery-thrower to his brother 1744–9. In 1754 he entered into partnership with T. WHIELDON and began to experiment with bodies and glazes. He dissolved the partnership to found the WEDGWOOD POTTERY in Burslem in 1759 and achieved such immediate success that he had to enlarge his factory in 1764. In 1769 he opened a new and larger factory, called Etruria, and went into partnership with a Liverpool merchant, Thomas Bentley (*c.*1730–80). On Bentley's death he took his own sons and nephew into partnership. His enormous success was due to a rare, if not unique, combination of scientific knowledge, artistic taste, administrative ability and business acumen. His development of CREAM-COLOURED EARTHENWARE (which, having secured royal patronage, he called Queen's Ware), JASPER WARE and BASALTES WARE enabled him to undercut the prices of the porcelain and tin-glazed earthenware factories; his early appreciation of Neo-Classicism and his eye for young artists of ability (like FLAXMAN whom he much employed) enabled him to produce ceramics nicely suited to the new style of furnishing and interior decoration; he organized his factory with modern efficiency, making use of steam power from 1782, and also sponsored a canal system connecting Staffordshire with the ports of Bristol and Liverpool to reduce carriage expenses; and he appreciated that financial success lay in supplying wares for all classes of society and not, like the porcelain factories, solely for the rich or, like the earlier Staffordshire potteries, for the indigent. Some of his designs have become classics, not for their period charm but because they still look modern in their extreme simplicity, e.g. the Queen's Ware dinner service of 1765 and the black Basaltes tea-service of 1768 which are both still in production. He was a man of advanced liberal and humanitarian views, a member of the Birmingham Lunar Society (which included Priestley, BOULTON, Watt and BASKERVILLE), a F.R.S., a supporter of the American Revolution and an advocate for the abolition of slavery.

Lit: E. Meteyard, *The Life of Josiah Wedgwood*, London 1865–6; G. Savage & A. Finer, *Selected Letters of Josiah Wedgwood*, London 1965.

Wedgwood pottery The most important English pottery, founded by Josiah WEDGWOOD at Burslem in Staffordshire in 1759. It began by covering wares made by William Greatbatch (formerly employed at WHIELDON's pottery) with a green glaze which Wedgwood had developed. But it soon turned to producing an improved version of Booth's CREAM-COLOURED EARTHENWARE, generally of simple elegant patterns which immediately appealed to buyers with a taste for Neo-Classicism. These wares (known from *c.*1765 as Queen's Ware in honour of the factory's patroness, Queen Charlotte) were left plain or decorated either with TRANSFER PRINTING by SADLER at the LIVERPOOL potteries or with painting in enamel colours. (A workshop for enamel painting was set up in Chelsea in 1769.) In a short time the painted wares were enjoying the same social status as porcelain and

Wedgwood: cream-coloured earthenware tureen, 1780–90 (Victoria & Albert Museum)

Wedgwood: mat-black basaltes ware cup and saucer, late c18 (Museum of Modern Art, New York)

a large service with English landscapes in sepia enamel was ordered by Catherine the Great of Russia and completed in 1774 (known as the 'Frog Service' from the frog in a shield on each piece, now in the Hermitage Museum, Leningrad). Wares in a vitreous red stoneware called '*rosso antico*' (made from before 1763), black BASALTES WARES (from *c.*1769) and the famous JASPER WARES (from 1774) with relief decorations in white on a blue, lavender, green or yellow ground are often based exactly on the shapes and decorations of Greek vases (then called Etruscan, hence the name of the Wedgwood factory, *Etruria*). The most famous of the Antique Revival pieces are very fine copies of the C1 B.C. Roman glass Barberini-Portland vase (copies date from 1790 onwards). In imitating antique vases the factory did not scruple to depart from the original colour schemes, to render flat orna-

Wedgwood: black basaltes ware vase (copy of a c3 B.C. urn in the British Museum), late c18 (Victoria & Albert Museum)

Wedgwood: jasper ware vase, the 'Homer Vase', c.1785 (Nottingham Castle Museum)

ment in relief or to draw inspiration as much from marble urns as from pottery. For the relief decorations of these wares and for those on useful wares such as teapots, jugs, etc., and also for busts, statuettes and plaques (especially portraits) several notable artists were employed including John FLAXMAN, George Stubbs, James Tassie, John Bacon and John Coward, a wood carver who had worked for the ADAM brothers. Models were also obtained from Italian sculptors. W. HACKWOOD was the chief modeller 1769–1832 and one of the few employees who occasionally signed his work. The range of products was prodigious including, besides the usual vases and table wares, large busts, plaques to decorate furniture (used most notably by WEISWEILER), cameos for jewellery (often mounted in cut-steel by BOULTON), shoe-buckles, chess-men, beads and mounts for snuff-boxes, watch-cases and opera glasses. Patrons included the English Royal Family, Catherine the Great, the Queen of France and the King of Naples. Wares were exported to all parts of Europe and to the U.S.A. And they were imitated not only in England (especially by the STAFFORDSHIRE potteries) but also by many continental factories, including MEISSEN, SÈVRES and VIENNA. On the founder's death in 1795 the concern was inherited by his son **Josiah II** (d.1843) and nephew **Joseph Byerley** (d.1810). It has remained in the Wedgwood family to the present day. Apart from the production of bone china for a brief period, 1812–16, few changes were made in the first years of Josiah II's direction. But in the C19 the factory followed rather than led ceramic taste. Among Victorian products the jasper-ware vases with applied reliefs of flowers are probably the most attractive. At the Great Exhibition of 1851 the firm exhibited the full range of its wares including 'statuary porcelain' (i.e. PARIAN) figures mainly of classical subjects, 'chemical earthenware, stoneware and plumber's earthenware' as well as many table-wares still made on C18 patterns. Reproductions of early types of pottery including that of SAINT PORCHAIRE were later made. New models for busts were acquired from the sculptor Edward William Wyon. From 1878 porcelain was made as well as pottery. Notable designers were occasionally employed in the late C19, including Walter CRANE and C. F. A. VOYSEY. In the 1930s some handsome simple wares were made to the design of the architect Keith Murray. Today the factory continues to produce copies (easily recognized) of its C18 jasper wares and much good earthenware and bone porcelain neatly decorated in modern style with designs after Eric Ravilious and other English painters. (For factory mark *see* p. 888.)

Wedgwood: earthenware ashtray designed by K. Murray, 1939 (Victoria & Albert Museum)

Lit: W. B. Honey, *Wedgwood Ware*, London 1948; W. Mankowitz, *Wedgwood*, London 1953; A. Kelly, *Decorative Wedgwood in Architecture and Furniture*, London 1965; R. Reilly, *Wedgwood Jasper*, London 1972.

Wednesbury enamel factories A group of enamel factories in South Staffordshire the first of which was established in 1776 by **Samuel Yardley** and the last run by his grandson until 1840. Their products were highly praised in the early C19 when they appear to have been the source of the best English enamels.

Weesp porcelain factory The first successful Dutch porcelain factory, it was founded near Amsterdam in 1757 by an Irish arcanist **D. McCarthy**, taken over in 1759 by Count Gronsveld-Diepenbroick-Impel who employed a German arcanist **Nikolaus Paul** and German craftsmen, bought in 1771 by a pastor **Johannes de Mol** and moved to Oude Loosdrecht, bought in 1782 by a company and moved to Oude Amstel, moved again in 1809 to Nieuwer Amstel where it remained active until *c.*1820. It produced hard-paste porcelain of good quality, mainly table-wares and also a few figures (in its earlier period), but did not establish an independent style. (For factory mark *see* p. 888.)

Lit: E. Schrijver, *Hollands Porcelein*, Bussum 1966.

Weft (or **woof**) In a tapestry or other woven fabric, the threads which cross from side to side at right angles to the WARP threads and out of which the pattern is generally formed.

Wegely, Wilhelm Kaspar, *see* BERLIN PORCELAIN FACTORY.

Wegner, Hans (b.1914). Danish architect and furniture designer who, with Arne JACOBSEN and Finn JUHL, has dominated the Danish furniture industry since the late 1940s. Trained as a cabinet-maker, he works out the prototype of each design at the workshop bench as well as on the drawing-board. He specializes in expensive furniture with an immaculate, satiny-smooth hand-finish, sometimes reminiscent of Chinese hard-wood furniture. Very elegant and suave yet sturdy and comfortable-looking, his style retains enough traditionalism to appeal to upper-middle-class notions of cultivated unpretentious well-being. He has a marked preference for rounded forms melting smoothly into one another which make some of his chairs look as if they had been moulded in plastic rather than carved in wood. His 1949 teak, oak and cane dining-chair is an affluent-society classic – the subtly curving top-rail has to be hand-carved.

Weiss, Georg Veit, *see* CRAILSHEIM POTTERY.

Weisweiler, Adam (*c.*1750–*c.*1810). The most refined and exquisite of the German furniture-makers who settled in Paris in the Louis XVI period, though not so sumptuous or expensive as RIESENER. He began in ROENTGEN's workshop at Nieuweid but was established in Paris by 1778 when he became a *maître ébéniste*. He worked mainly for the Parisian furniture dealers, especially Dominique Daguerre who supplied Marie Antoinette with furniture for Saint Cloud (e.g. Weisweiler's extremely elegant small ebony and lacquer table with caryatid legs, made in 1784

A. Weisweiler: writing table, 1784 (Louvre)

and now in the Louvre). Through Daguerre he also made furniture for the Prince of Wales for Carlton House in London (e.g. the side-tables from the Chinese Drawing-room now in Buckingham Palace). Despite his training under Roentgen he seldom used pictorial marquetry, preferring plain veneers, usually of mahogany or lacquer (e.g. *secrétaire* in the Rijksmuseum, Amsterdam) or, for more expensive pieces, Sèvres plaques (e.g. *secrétaire* in the Metropolitan Museum, New York) or *pietre dure* panels which were often taken from pieces of Louis XIV furniture which had been broken up for the value of the materials. He specialized in small pieces of furniture of light, almost fragile, appearance, especially *bonheurs-du-jour*, consoles, *secrétaires, guéridons*, etc. His work is characterized by impeccable execution and by elegant, clean lines and exquisitely delicate mounts, usually floral and sometimes with cupids, goats or sphinxes (sometimes perhaps by GOUTHIÈRE). He also favoured caryatids and canephorae. Especially characteristic are his curious interlacing stretchers, tapering legs inlaid with a barley-sugar pattern and, on commodes, legs like spinning-tops. Though he worked much for the royal palaces he survived the Revolution and became one of the best Empire cabinet-makers, collaborating closely with THOMIRE. In the early years of the Empire he secured the patronage of the Bonaparte family, his most notable products of this period being the beautiful jewel boxes he made for Queen Hortense in 1806. After the death of his wife in 1809 he retired; the date of his death is unknown. His business was carried on by his son **Jean** who lived until 1844.

Lit: F. J. B. Watson, *Louis XVI Furniture*, London 1960 and *The Wrightsman Collection: Furniture*, New York 1966; P. Verlet, *French Royal Furniture*, London 1963.

Weller pottery A late C19 factory at Zanesville, Ohio, run by **Samuel A. Weller** (1850–1925) and exploiting the vogue for hand-thrown wares like those made at the ROOKWOOD and NEWCOMB potteries. It employed some notable decorators including **Albert Haubrich** and a French artist **J. Sicard** who was responsible for handsome vases with iridescent glazes rather like TIFFANY glass, made from *c.*1900.

Lit: 19th Century America: Furniture and other Decorative Arts, Exh. Cat., Metropolitan Museum, New York 1970.

Wellington chest An early C19 type of English chest of drawers with a single tier of drawers (usually ten or more) which can be locked by means of a narrow hinged flap running down one side.

Welsh dresser A large but simply made cupboard usually consisting of a set of open shelves, for the display of pottery or plate, above a somewhat deeper substructure fitted with a single row of drawers (usually three) and one or more shelves sometimes enclosed by doors. The form seems to have been developed in the early C18 on the borders of Staffordshire and Shropshire and was subsequently made elsewhere in England and Wales, until well into the C19.

Welsh ware Late-C18 name for shallow earthenware meat dishes decorated with combed or feathered slip and made mainly at the STAFFORDSHIRE, SUNDERLAND and ISLEWORTH potteries.

Wemyss ware Pottery decorated with bold underglaze paintings of flowers, birds, fruit, etc., in very brilliant colours and in a cheerful cottage style, produced at the **Fife (Gallatown) Pottery**, Kirkcaldy, from *c.*1883 to 1930. The Fife Pottery was founded *c.*1790 and was run by **Robert Methven Heron** (1833–1906) during the main period of Wemyss Ware production. He brought **Karl Nekola** (d.1915) from Austria in *c.*1882 and put him in charge of the painting shop, and it was Nekola who introduced the full-blown cabbage roses and other decorative motifs so characteristic of Wemyss Ware. Products include wash-basins and jugs, large pigs for use as door-stoppers, and a variety of table-wares of which jampots were especially popular. Decorations include cherries, plums, apples, etc., as well as cottage-garden flowers, cocks and hens, etc. After 1900 the production of large pieces declined. In 1916 Edwin Sandland (b.1874) took over the painting shop, and production finally stopped in 1930. But the rights and moulds were bought by the **Bovey Tracey Pottery** and Nekola's son **Joseph** moved there and continued to paint traditional Wemyss Ware decorations until his death in 1942. Wemyss Ware is usually marked as such. But several other potteries produced similar wares,

J.-J. Werner: secrétaire, c.*1830* *(Musée des Arts Décoratifs, Paris)*

notably the nearby Kirkcaldy Pottery of **David Methven and Sons** who produced wares stamped Abbotsford Ware which are often decorated in the Wemyss style (indeed possibly by decorators from the Fife Pottery). The **Poutney Pottery Co.**, Bristol, also produced Wemyss style wares from *c.*1904 onwards.

Lit: P. H. Davis, *Wemyss Ware: The Development of a Decorative Scottish Pottery, c.1883–1930*, Exh. Cat., Edinburgh 1971.

Wennerberg, Gunnar Gunnarsson, *see* GUSTAVSBERG POTTERY.

Wenzel, Johann, *see* LOHR-AM-MAIN GLASSHOUSE.

Werner, Jean-Jacques (1791–1849). He was one of the best Restauration furniture-makers, though less successful than RÉMOND. Swiss by birth and naturalized French in 1826, he was already established in Paris by 1820. He was patronized by the Bonaparte family, the Duchesse de Berry and the King of Bavaria and his work was acclaimed at the Paris exhibitions of 1819 and 1823. Examples are in the Musée des Arts Décoratifs, Paris. *Illustrated previous page.*

Lit: D. Ledoux-Lebard, *Les ébénistes-parisiens (1795–1870)*, Paris 1965.

Wessel, Ludwig, *see* POPPELSDORF POTTERY.

Westerwald salt-glazed stoneware, the 'Prodigal Son jug', Grenzau, 1618 (Victoria & Albert Museum)

Westerwald potteries A group of stoneware factories at Grenzau, Grenzhausen, Höhr and other places in a district of the Rhineland between Cologne and Frankfurt-am-Main which was incorporated in the Duchy of Nassau in the early C19 (sometimes described anachronistically as the Nassau Potteries). The district was popularly known as the Kannenbäckerland from the number of its potteries. The earliest wares of note were made by the sons of A. KNÜTGEN who moved from SIEGBURG to Höhr in 1590: they include spouted jugs with relief decorations of the Siegburg type. A little later, members of the MENNICKEN family moved from RAEREN to Grenzhausen where they continued to make wares like those of Raeren, often using the same moulds for relief decoration. But a number of new decorative motifs were adopted – reliefs of the Prodigal Son, the good Samaritan, the 'Seven Works of Charity' and the arms of Austrian princes. Some very large jugs (nearly 1m tall) with a great deal of abstract and figurative decoration, made *c.*1630, are attributed to Johann Kalb of Grenzau. Before the mid C17 the use of figurative decorations had declined and a distinctive Westerwald type of jug began to appear – with an egg-shaped body rising from the foot ring, and a rather narrow neck, decorated with stamped reliefs (lion masks, angel heads, vases of flowers or simple rosettes and lozenges) repeated in regular patterns and partly coloured with a cobalt blue or manganese purple glaze marked off from the uncoloured parts by sharply incised lines. By the late C17 the potteries were carrying on an extensive export trade, especially with England. Many pieces are decorated with initials, arms or portraits of William III and, in the early C18, Queen Anne. In addition to the traditional stock-in-trade of jugs and tankards the potteries produced in the C18 salt-cellars, inkstands, teapots and coffee-pots sometimes similar to those made at the same time in STAFFORDSHIRE also in salt-glazed stoneware. But from this time onwards products were intended mainly for the peasant market. The district remained throughout the C19, and remains to the present day, a centre for the manufacture of simple stoneware bottles. Early in the C20 wares were made to the design of two pioneers of the modern movement who appreciated the potentialities of stoneware: H. VAN DE VELDE designed vases with figured glazes for the pottery of Reinhold Hanke at Höhr, and R. RIEMERSCHMID designed drinking vessels for Reinhold Merkelbach's pottery at Grenzhausen.

Lit: K. Koetschau, *Rheinisches Steinzeug*, Munich 1924; P. Engelmeier in *Keramos* 44 (1969) and G. Reineking von Bock, *ibid* 51 (1971), pp. 34–6; *idem, Kunstgewerbemuseum der Stadt Köln: Steinzeug*, Cologne 1971.

Whatnot A small work-table or stand with three or more shelves supported on four (sometimes three) uprights, used to hold books, ornaments, etc. It was very popular in the C19. Similar to the French ÉTAGÈRE. *Illustrated next column.*

Whatnot, English, early C19 (Victoria & Albert Museum)

Wheat ear ornament A carved motif in the form of a wheat ear, popular for the decoration of late-C18 English furniture (especially chair-backs) associated with HEPPLEWHITE.

Whieldon, Thomas (1719–95). Notable STAFFORDSHIRE potter who established a factory at Fenton Low in 1740. He began in a small way making white stoneware and AGATEWARE knife- and fork-handles for the Sheffield cutlers, to compete with the Continental porcelain ones which had become fashionable. He also made statuettes, plates and vessels similar to those of J. ASTBURY. His business expanded and he was soon making all the various types of Staffordshire pottery including attractive green or yellow glazed teapots and other vessels in the form of vegetables (the cauliflower was a favourite) and fruit, but as they are unmarked they can rarely be distinguished from those of other factories. He employed Josiah SPODE as an apprentice (1749) and was in partnership with Josiah WEDGWOOD (1754–9).

Lit: R. G. Haggar, *English Country Pottery*, London 1953; J. I. Smith in *The Connoisseur* CLXV (1967), pp. 198–204.

Whipham, Thomas (*fl.*1748–1790). London silversmith, probably the son of the Thomas Whipham who was admitted to the Goldsmiths' Company in 1739. From 1757 to 1776 he worked in partnership with Charles Wright making a wide variety of ecclesiastical and secular plate including some pieces richly embossed with Rococo decoration, (e.g. chinoiserie tea kettle and urn of 1761–6, formerly in the Ionides collection, and tea-kettle of 1767–8 in the Victoria and Albert Museum). He was elected Warden of the Goldsmiths' Company in 1772. (For illustration *see* TEA URN.)

Whistler, Laurence (b.1912). English writer (and brother of the painter Rex Whistler 1905–44) who began to engrave on glass in 1936. Since World War II he has become the leading English glass engraver and has been commissioned to execute numerous presentation pieces, usually goblets but also caskets (notable example in Royal Collection, given to George VI by his consort). Many of his pieces are engraved with views of English C18 country houses for which he has great understanding.

White metal An alternative name for BRITANNIA METAL, which is whiter in tone than pewter for which it became a cheap substitute.

Whitefriars glasshouse Established in London, between Fleet St and the Thames, in the late C17 but of little importance until 1835 when it came under the direction of **James Powell** (who was to be succeeded by his son and grandson), and began to lead a revival of the English tradition of hand-blown glass. Forms were inspired by ancient Roman, Venetian, English medieval and the simpler types of C18 glass. Cut glass was also produced. But the factory is notable mainly for the austerely simple yet very elegant glass made from 1859 for W. MORRIS probably to the design

Whitefriars Glasshouse (James Powell & Sons): tumbler and jug, the latter designed by Morris & Co., probably by P. Webb (Kunstgewerbemuseum, Zurich)

Whitefriars Glasshouse (James Powell & Sons): tumblers, 1953 (Kunstgewerbemuseum, Zurich)

of P. WEBB. Coloured flat glass was made from the 1850s and the factory maintained a studio in which windows were executed to the design of Pre-Raphaelite painters. In 1922 the factory moved to Wealdstone, Middlesex, where it remains active producing much of the best English table-glass and handsome thick vases decorated with floral or abstract designs in polished or unpolished engravings.

Lit: Harry J. Powell, *Glassmaking in England*, Cambridge 1923; W. A. Thorpe, *English Glass*, London 1935; H. Wakefield, *Nineteenth Century British Glass*, London 1961; B. O'Looney, *Victorian Glass*, London 1972.

Whitehaven potteries A number of factories were active at Whitehaven on the Cumberland coast, the first established in 1740 and one surviving until 1915. Apart from a jug made in or shortly after 1797 (Whitehaven Museum) the earliest surviving wares date from the mid C19 and are similar to those of the same time made in STAFFORDSHIRE, especially table-wares with printed decorations.

Lit: D. Hay in *Country Life*, July 13, 1972, pp. 107–8.

Whittle, James, *see* NORMAN, Samuel.

Whorl A carved motif of a type found on medieval furniture and some of the simpler pieces of later furniture (e.g. C17 English Bible Boxes). It is a circle filled with a geometrical pattern of a type which may be chip-carved with the aid of a compass and set-square.

Wickes, G., *see* GARRARD, Robert.

Wiener Keramik, *see* POWOLNY, Michael.

Wiener und Gmundener Keramik Werkstätte, *see* POWOLNY, Michael.

Wiener, René (1856–1939). French bookbinder, a member of the school of NANCY. Inherited a family bindery (1874) and in the 1890s began to work in the Art Nouveau style producing very elaborate and expensive bindings, sometimes inlaid with bronze plaques, according to designs by leading painters, notably Toulouse-Lautrec.

Wiener Werkstätte A craft studio founded in Vienna in 1903 by Josef HOFFMANN and Kolo MOSER who were members of the SECESSION. It specialized in the production of hand-made metalwork (domestic plate and jewellery), furniture, textiles and leather articles, ostensibly for a wide public but not at very popular prices. The earliest products are in the rectilinear ART NOUVEAU style often ornamented with diaper patterns in black and white or silver. Products made after the First World War are much freer and sometimes fantastic in design, e.g. silver designed by Dagobert PECHE. The workshop closed in 1932.

Lit: *Die Wiener Werkstätte,* Exh. Cat., Österreichisches Museum für angewandte Kunst, Vienna 1967.

Wiesbaden pottery A factory founded in 1770 under the protection of Prince Karl of Nassau-Usingen by **Johann Jacob Kaisin** from Popplesdorf. It began by producing tin-glazed earthenware but this was of poor quality until 1774 when **Caspar Dreste** (d.1787) took control. Products included table-wares decorated with flowers in monochrome green enamel, boxes in the form of bunches of asparagus and some rather clumsy figures of peasants. After Dreste's death it was run by his widow until 1795 when it closed. (For factory mark *see* p. 888.)

Lit: M. Oppenheim in *Keramos* 46 (1969), pp. 3–43.

Wilkes, John (*fl.c.*1700). A locksmith of Birmingham who invented a detector door-lock with a dial which records the number of times it has been opened. His locks are in latten or steel with brass decorations and are to be found on the Continent as well as in England.

Willard, Simon (1753–1848). American clockmaker working at Roxbury, Mass. He is said to have made more than 5,000 timepieces between 1802 and 1840. In 1802 he patented the BANJO CLOCK. His works are no less notable for their movements than for their forms which are often original, including one modelled on the Eddystone lighthouse. His brother **Aaron** was also a notable clockmaker.

Lit: J. W. Willard, *A History of Simon Willard,* (1911), 2nd Edition, New York 1962.

Willaume, David (1658–1741). He was one of the most prolific and successful of the Huguenot refugee silversmiths in London. There is some confusion about his birth-place which was probably Metz but possibly Mer en Blaisois. He may have reached England *c.*1674 and was certainly settled there by 1687 when he was granted papers of denization. In 1688 he registered his mark and in 1693 he was admitted to the Goldsmiths' Company. By 1720 he was also engaged in banking. His masterpiece is a magnificent wine cistern of 1708 bought for George II when Prince of Wales and now in the collection of the Duke of Brunswick. It is a very handsome example of the Huguenot style, with richly gadrooned borders and finely modelled cast-work (sea-horse handles and lion-masks). But he was equally good on a smaller scale, (e.g. helmet-shaped ewer of 1700, in the Victoria & Albert Museum, London) and his workshop also produced large quantities of excellent simple plate, especially salvers and knives, forks and spoons (examples in Manchester City Art Gallery). By 1709 he had made enough money to buy a country estate, Tingrith Manor in Bedfordshire. In 1716 his son **David** (1693–1761) took over control of the family business. (For illustrations *see* pages 614 and 860; for his mark *see* p. 895.)

Lit: J. F. Hayward, *Huguenot Silver in England 1688–1727,* London 1959; H. Honour, *Goldsmiths & Silversmiths,* London and New York 1971.

Willems, Joseph (*c.*1715–66). Sculptor and porcelain modeller, he was born in Brussels, married in Tournai in 1739 and went to England *c.*1749–50 where he worked as a modeller at the CHELSEA PORCELAIN FACTORY. He also taught drawing and modelling in London and exhibited sculpture (portrait busts and allegorical figures) at the Society of Artists between 1761 and 1766, some of which were probably models for Chelsea gold-anchor and red-anchor figures. Two terracotta figures painted in unfired oil colours and incised *Willems* with the date 1749 have survived (Ashmolean Museum, Oxford). They were presumably made shortly after his arrival in England. He was connected with the TOURNAI PORCELAIN FACTORY before and/or after his visit to England. He left London for Tournai in 1766 at the invitation of the director of the Tournai Porcelain Factory. He died there almost immediately.

Lit: A. Lane in *The Connoisseur* CXLV (1960), pp. 245–51.

Willets Manufactory Company A porcelain factory at Trenton, New Jersey, producing in the 1880s and 1890s good imitations of Irish BELLEEK ware.

William and Mary style:
silver-gilt ewer by D. Willaume, London, 1700
(Victoria & Albert Museum)

William and Mary style The reign of William III and Mary II (1688–1702) was a transitional period in the history of English decorative arts. There was no sharp break with the RESTORATION style, though elegance, lightness and comfort steadily increased during this period of growing prosperity. The main change was in the nature of foreign influence. Despite William's origin and the arrival of some Dutch cabinet-makers, notably Gerrit JENSEN, the dominant influence was no longer Dutch but French. This was due partly to the fame of Versailles which, thanks to Colbert, the GOBELINS factory and Louis XIV himself, became the cynosure of European taste,

William and Mary style: walnut chair
(Victoria & Albert Museum)

William and Mary style: settee, c.1690 *(Victoria & Albert Museum)*

but still more to an influx of Huguenot refugee craftsmen who left France on account of the revocation of the Edict of Nantes (1685) and some of whom, like MAROT, reached England by way of Holland. Their influence was at first felt mainly in the decoration of furniture, especially gilt gesso side-tables with pillar legs, scrolled stretchers and elaborate pendant aprons, chandeliers of carved and gilt wood in the style of MAROT and LE PAUTRE, and chairs with cabriole front legs and tall backs with elegantly carved central splats. The increased popularity of looking-glasses may also be attributed to French influence as much as to the growth of the VAUXHALL and other glasshouses. Several new types of furniture came into fashion, notably the swing toilet mirror on a box stand, and the fall-front writing-cabinet or bureau, both of which became still more popular in the succeeding

William and Mary style: day-bed, c.1695 *(Temple Newsam House, Leeds)*

QUEEN ANNE period. On silver the embossed decorations of fruit and flowers fell out of fashion; a simpler style was adopted for everyday pieces and a much bolder and more solid Baroque style for showy pieces such as wine cisterns, large church candlesticks, etc. So far as textiles are concerned, the vogue for tapestries declined though some very fine chinoiserie hangings were woven at the SOHO factory. Embroideries in silk and CREWEL WORK differed little from those of the Restoration period.

William and Mary style: silver candlestick by A. Nelme, 1694 (St George's Chapel, Windsor Castle)

Willow pattern A chinoiserie design for the decoration of ceramics, by TRANSFER PRINTING in underglaze blue, probably originated by Thomas MINTON *c.*1780 for the Caughley pottery in Shropshire and soon taken up by a large number of factories, especially in Staffordshire, and eventually copied even in China. The essential components are a stylized willow tree, a Chinese temple, a bridge with figures on it, a boat and a distant island. Several fanciful stories have been invented to explain its significance.

Wilms, Albert, *see* ELKINGTON, George Richard.

Wilson, Henry (1864–1934). English architect working from *c.*1895 mainly as a designer of Art Nouveau metalwork and jewellery with cabochons set in rather lumpy gold mounts. He taught metalwork at the Royal College of Art, London (from 1901) and adopted the ARTS AND CRAFTS style.

Wilton carpet A type of worsted warp-face carpet woven at Wilton and elsewhere on hand-operated JACQUARD looms until the 1850s, thereafter on the Bigelow power loom. It is similar to BRUSSELS CARPET but has more rows of pile to the inch and the pile loops are cut to form a rich velvety surface (much thicker than in Brussels tapestry-velvet carpets). It is sometimes called Tournai carpet.

Wilton Carpet Factory Founded *c.*1740 in Wiltshire, the factory began by making BRUSSELS CARPET but soon developed the WILTON CARPET technique for which it became famous. The patterns were probably very simple but no example is known to have survived. Hand-knotted carpets were produced after 1835 when the equipment of the defunct AXMINSTER CARPET FACTORY was acquired. But the factory specialized in mechanically woven carpets, called AXMINSTER CARPETS, of which 'Chenile Axminster' (first made 1839) is the best-known type. Most C19 products were undistinguished but William MORRIS provided some designs, of oriental inspiration, in the 1870s. The factory, now styled the Royal Wilton Carpet Factory, continues to flourish and specializes in simple, hard-wearing carpets.

Lit: C. E. C. Tattersall and S. Reed, *A History of British Carpets*, Leigh-on-Sea 1966.

Wincanton pottery A tin-glazed earthenware factory at Wincanton in Somerset, near Bristol, run by **Nathaniel Ireson** (1686–1769) and **Thomas Lindslee** (*fl.c.*1725–50). With the exception of a very few marked pieces, ranging in date from 1737 (plate in Royal Scottish Museum, Edinburgh) to 1748 (jug in Glaisher Collection, Fitzwilliam Museum, Cambridge), the products of this factory have not been successfully isolated from those of the BRISTOL POTTERIES. But many attractive wares, especially plates, with a speckled pinkish manganese ground and reserved white panels decorated in blue (with landscapes or chinoiseries) are commonly attributed to it.

Lit: W. J. Pountney, *The Old Bristol Potteries*, London and Bristol 1920; F. H. Garner, *English Delftware*, London 1948.

Windmill cup A late-C16 and C17 Dutch type of Wager Cup in the form of a windmill mounted on the base of the cup, usually of silver though the cup could be of glass. The sails were set spinning by blowing through a tube and the cup had to be drained before they stopped.

Window seat A bench, usually with low arms and sometimes upholstered, designed to fit into the recess beneath a window.

Windsor tapestry factory A short-lived concern founded in 1876 by H. C. T. Henry of GILLOWS with M. Brignolas and six weavers from AUBUSSON. Patronised by Queen Victoria, it became the **Royal Windsor Manufactory** in 1882 but was condemned by William Morris the same year for imitating the fluid effect of oil paint. Threads of some five thousand different shades of colour were used to obtain this effect and the tapestries were extremely expensive as a result. The concern failed and closed in 1895.

Lit: W. Hefford in *The Victoria & Albert Museum Yearbook 1969*, London 1969.

Wine cooler A container in which one or more bottles of wine may be stood among lumps of ice. The type made of wood with a lead lining and intended to hold several bottles is also called a CELLARET. The type made from the C15 and especially popular in the early C18, made of silver or other metals, is also called a wine cistern. But in the C18 these three terms – wine-cooler, wine-cistern and cellaret – were interchangeable.

Wine-glass cooler A small vessel, of silver, glass, pottery or porcelain, with one or two notches in the rim. It was intended to hold water for the cooling at table of a wine glass the stem of which could rest in the notch while the bowl was suspended in the water. It is called in French a *rafraîchissoir*. A MONTEITH is a special type of large, usually silver or glass, wine-glass cooler.

Wine-glass cooler, Bordeaux faience (perhaps Hustin factory), early C18 (Musée des Arts Décoratifs, Bordeaux)

Winslow, Edward (1669–1753). American silversmith, he worked at Boston making mainly domestic plate though he also made some church plate (e.g. paten in St Michael's Church, Bristol, R.I.). Examples of his domestic plate are in the Museum of Fine Arts, Boston.

Winter, Friedrich (*fl.* 1685–*c.*1710). Notable German glass engraver who worked from 1685 for Graf Christoph Leopold Schaffgotsch at his glasshouse near Schloss Kynast. He specialized in *Hochschnitt* (cameo relief) carving, employing a water-driven cutting mill installed by Schaffgotsch, and worked in a bold Baroque style with much use of rich scroll-work, acanthus leaves, etc. Most of his works were made for his patron and remained in the possession of the Schaffgotsch family until recently. His brother **Martin** (d.1702) was also a notable glass engraver, employed from 1680 at the POTSDAM GLASSHOUSE by the 'great' Elector of Brandenburg who installed a water-driven cutting mill there for his use. Several pieces of glass are attributed to him (Victoria & Albert Museum, etc.) but none of them is signed or otherwise documented.

Lit: R. Schmidt, *Das Glas*, Berlin and Leipzig 1922.

Winterthur potteries The most important group of Swiss faience factories which developed in the late C16 out of a stove-tile and Hafner-ware industry. Stoves were among the most important products of the factories until well into the C18. On the earlier – C16–C17 – stoves green-glazed tiles were combined with faience panels. Other wares of this period include faience plates, dishes, jugs, and rather elaborate vases painted in polychrome with Biblical subjects, heraldry, plant motifs, etc. The most notable factory appears to have been that of **Ludwig I Pfau** (d.1623) and his son **Ludwig II** (d.1683), and several pieces bear their monogram. Late C17 products include some distinctive dishes with small deep wells and wide flat rims painted with inscriptions, flowers and fruits in high-temperature colours. C18 stoves are often very rich in colour and are decorated with freely painted figure subjects. Apart from signatures on stoves no marks appear to have been used.

Lit: K. Frei in *Führer durch die Eröffnungsaustellung der Winterthur Gewerbemuseum*, Winterthur 1928; R. L. Wyss in *The Connoisseur* CLIX (1965), pp. 222–6, and *Winterthurer Keramik, Hafnerware aus d. 17 Jahrhundert*, Berne 1973.

Wirkkala, Tapio (b.1915). Finnish designer and craftsman notable, like AALTO, for his great feeling for the natural appearance and quality of wood, glass and other materials. His designs are extremely simple with elegant fluid curves, emphasized by an occasional sharp, straight edge. Hand-finished wooden platters and hand-ground crystal bowls, like chunks of ice that have just begun to melt, are typical of his style though he has also designed some remarkable 'free-form' bowls like sea anemones (manufactured by **Iittala Glasshouse**, Helsinki, of which he has been artistic director since 1947), also some porcelain for ROSENTHAL and some excellent silver wares for CHRISTOFLE.

Wistar, Caspar (1696–1752). The founder of the first important glasshouse in N. America. He was a German from Baden (son of a huntsman in the service of the Elector Palatine) who settled in Philadelphia in 1717 and set up a brass-button manufactory, which seems to have prospered. In 1739 with the help of four glassblowers brought over from Germany he established a glasshouse at a place which he named Wistarburg on Alloway's Creek in southern New Jersey. On his death both these establishments were taken over by his son **Richard** (d.1781), who ran them until 1780 when he went bankrupt as a result of the War of Independence. The Wistarburg establishment was like a European forest glasshouse with furnaces and mills surrounded by ten dwellings for the artisans, a large house for the owner and his family, and also including a farm. Products included bottles, window glass, various vessels in the *Waldglas* tradition, and apparently some ornamental pieces. After the failure of the factory two employees, the **Stanger brothers**, set up a glasshouse at a place subsequently called Glassbro which became an important glassmaking centre in the C19. Although many pieces of glass which appear to have been made in New Jersey in the C18 survive (Corning Museum of Glass, Metropolitan Museum, New York, etc.) few of them can be certainly attributed to the Wistars' factory.

Lit: H. and G. S. McKearin, *Two Hundred Years of American Blown Glass*, New York 1950.

Wolfers, Philippe (1858–1929). Leading Belgian Art Nouveau jeweller. He began in the Neo-Rococo style but abandoned it (1892) for asymmetrical Art Nouveau designs incorporating flower and insect motifs with much use of ivory, enamel and semi-precious stones. After 1900 his designs are abstract and generally symmetrical.

Wolff, David (1732–98). Dutch glass engraver. He decorated glasses in the stippled manner originated by F. GREENWOOD, sometimes with portraits of notable Dutchmen. A large number of glasses engraved in this manner have been erroneously attributed to him and all such glasses are sometimes termed 'Wolff glasses'.

Lit: H. Tait, 'Wolff Glasses in an English Collection' in *The Connoisseur* CLXVIII (1968), pp. 99–108.

Wolff, John, *see* RÖRSTRAND POTTERY & PORCELAIN FACTORY.

Wolfsburg, Carl Ferdinand von (1692–1764). A nobleman and amateur *Hausmaler*, painting on MEISSEN and VIENNA porcelain. He was a pupil of I. BOTTENGRUBER at Breslau and went with him to Vienna in 1730. His earliest work, of 1729, is in Bottengruber's style. But he developed a more individual manner, possibly under the influence of PREISSLER, painting Bacchic and similar scenes in purple monochrome with borders of angular purple and gold *Laub- und Bandelwerk*. He is also known to have painted in enamel on copper.

Lit: G. E. Pazaurek, *Deutsche Fayence- und Porzellan-Hausmaler*, Leipzig 1925.

Wood, Ralph (1715–72). The eldest member of a distinguished family of STAFFORDSHIRE potters and owner of the Hill Factory at Burslem. He specialized in the production of figures, sometimes to models by J. VOYEZ, others adapted from those by CYFFLÉ, also the true-born English TOBY JUGS, and such groups as that which shows a dozing parson and his clerk in a double-decker pulpit, robustly modelled and delicately coloured with lead glazes. His brother **Aaron** (1717–85)

R. Wood: lead-glazed earthenware jug, late c18 (Victoria & Albert Museum)

was a modeller (technically called a block-cutter) who worked for many Staffordshire potters including WHIELDON, making models for household wares as well as ornaments. Salt-glazed stoneware PEW GROUPS are often attributed to him and lead-glazed groups made by Ralph Wood are (or were) sometimes attributed to him. Ralph Wood's factory was inherited by his son **Ralph II** (1748–95) who continued to produce the same types of figures but initiated the practice of painting them in enamel colours. Aaron's son, **Enoch** (1759–1840) was a modeller of ability specializing in busts (notably of John Wesley and George Whitfield) and rather large figures. He ran a factory, in partnership with Ralph II from 1783 to 1790, with **James Caldwell** from 1790 to 1818, then with his own sons, producing the full range of Staffordshire wares including black basaltes, jasper ware and blue-printed earthenware. This concern was carried on by his sons until *c.*1846. The marks 'R. Wood' or 'Ra Wood/Burslem' or a device of four trees, all impressed, are believed to be the marks of Ralph Wood. Various marks are attributed to Enoch Wood, e.g. 'E. Wood', 'Enoch Wood & Sons', 'W (* * *)' and 'Enoch Wood & Sons Burslem' surrounding a device, all impressed.

Lit: F. Falkner, *The Wood Family of Burslem*, London 1912.

Wood, Samuel (*fl.*1721–63). He was a prominent and prolific London silversmith. Admitted to the Goldsmiths' Company in 1730, be became Warden of it in 1763. He made domestic plate mainly.

Woodall, Thomas (1849–1926) and **George** (1850–1925). Two brothers who were among the most expert and famous carvers of cameo-glass or cased-glass. They were born near Stourbridge where they were trained, as apprentices to J. NORTHWOOD and later in the Government School of Design. From *c.*1874 they both worked at the factory of T. WEBB, at first engraving designs on clear crystal glass but in the 1880s executing cameo-glass pieces which

G. Woodall: cameo-glass plaque of puce glass overlaid with white, Thomas Webb & Sons, c.1890 (Corning Museum of Glass, New York)

were shown at various exhibitions from 1884 onwards. They employed a team of up to 70 craftsmen and produced a wide variety of objects – inkwells, candlesticks, door-panels, as well as scent-bottles and vases – decorated in a wide range of styles with bunches of flowers, Chinese or Islamic motifs, classical figure subjects, etc. The works they executed on their own – mainly plaques and vases – were in the Victorian classical style. From *c.*1906 they appear to have worked without the staff of assistants. George Woodall retired from Webb's in 1911 but continued to work in his own studio.

Lit: G. W. Beard, *Nineteenth Century Cameo Glass*, Newport, Mon., 1956.

Woodin, Thomas, *see* NORMAN, Samuel.

Woodward, Ellsworth, *see* NEWCOMB COLLEGE POTTERY.

Woof, *see* WEFT.

Wool The soft hair from the coat of sheep or, more rarely, other ungulate animals. It does not seem to have been used for textile WEAVING as early as vegetable fibres and was considered unclean by the ancient Egyptians: but it was woven in Bronze Age Scandinavia (from *c.*1150 B.C.), in the lake villages of central Europe, notably Hallstatt (*c.*1000 B.C.) and in Syria and Mesopotamia. It was much used by the Greeks and Romans who improved the quality of fleeces by selective sheep-breeding. By the Middle Ages England had emerged as the most important centre for the production of fine wool which, from the C13, was exported to the manufacturing cities of Flanders and Italy. English cloth was of poor quality until the C16 when preparatory, weaving and finishing processes were improved. Although mercantile expansion diminished the importance of the industry it was zealously protected by Parliament throughout the C17 and C18.

Wool must be prepared for weaving by processes which differ from those employed for vegetable fibres. Originally it was plucked from the sheep but the Romans introduced shears, of a simple design that was to remain unchanged until recent times. It must then be graded according to texture (from fine to coarse), washed to remove the natural grease, dried, loosened and oiled and then prepared for spinning by carding or combing. Carded wool is that loosened by brushing with the head of a thistle (Latin *carduus*), more usually a teazle or some contraption with wire teeth, to produce a spongy roll of criss-crossed threads which can be spun into yarn: fabric woven from such yarn has a soft texture. The other process is to comb the wool into a mass containing only long parallel fibres, removing all the short fibres which are then used for other purposes: combed wool thus provides a yarn of even structure and fabric woven from it (worsted) has a hard clear surface. Both processes were known in antiquity but combing seems to have been discontinued after the fall of the Roman Empire, to be taken up again perhaps as early as the C9 in France though not at all widely until the C12. There was a third medieval process known as bowing which produced a yarn similar to that of carded wool.

After it is woven woollen cloth must be 'finished' – fulled, in order to felt and thicken it, by immersing and trampling it in any one of the various fulling agents (the juice of certain plants and human urine were used in the Middle Ages), then washed, beaten, brushed (originally with teazles or hedgehog skins) to raise the fibre ends, and finally cropped to an even surface.

All the preparatory and finishing, as well as weaving, processes were gradually improved during the C16, C17 and C18 and by 1800 most of them could be executed by machines. In the C19 the machines were much improved but the basic processes remained the same. Despite the introduction of many wool-like SYNTHETIC FIBRES, which need no such elaborate preparatory and finishing treatment and which are sometimes used in conjunction with wool, woollen fabrics are still among the most popular for clothing though perhaps less so for carpeting and upholstery. There is indeed widespread agreement with the advertisers that 'when the nights are growing cool there is no substitute for wool'.

Wool has been extensively used through the ages for decorative as well as utilitarian fabrics, for woven CARPETS and TAPESTRIES and as a medium for embroidery (*see* BERLIN WOOLWORK and CREWEL WORK).

Wool pictures, *see* BERLIN WOOLWORK.

Woollams and Company One of the most notable English C19 firms of wallpaper manufacturers, specializing in hand-printed pieces of high quality

Woollams & Co.: wallpaper, mid C19 (Whitworth Art Gallery, Manchester)

and resisting machine production. It was founded in London in or shortly before 1807 by **William Woollams** (1782–1840) and carried on by his sons **William** and **Henry** (d.1876). **Frederic Aumonier** who took the concern over in 1876 patented a process for making embossed flock papers in 1877. He also developed pigments which, unlike those in general use, contained no arsenic. The factory closed in 1900.

Lit: A. V. Sugden & J. L. Edmondson, *A History of English Wallpaper*, London 1926.

Worcester porcelain factory The longest-lived and one of the best English factories. It was founded in 1751 and in the following year took over the stock and secrets of Lund's BRISTOL PORCELAIN FACTORY which had been making soft-paste porcelain with Cornish soapstone (steatite) in place of the feldspathic rock used on the Continent and at PLYMOUTH. Until 1784 it used the same formula, making wares which were more thinly potted and much more durable (better able to withstand hot water) than most other types of soft paste. The first era of the factory's history is known as the 'Dr Wall Period', after J. WALL who was one of the founders and shareholders, but which extends beyond his death to 1783. During these years the manager was **William Davis.** The factory specialized in useful wares, especially for the tea-table, and decorative vases (figures were few and rather undistinguished) decorated at first with chinoiserie motifs in underglaze blue or enamel colours. From 1757 it pioneered the use of TRANSFER PRINTING, at first overglaze in black but by 1760 also underglaze in blue from prints engraved by R. HANCOCK. Many pieces were thus adorned with portraits of Frederick the Great who was regarded as a Protestant hero and whose occupation of Dresden in 1756 was a blessing for the English porcelain industry. Most products were of simple form (the most elaborate were dishes moulded like leaves, cauliflower-shaped tureens, and jugs composed of overlapping leaves) derived either from silver or Chinese porcelain. Much of the richer enamel painting of the 1760s appears to have been executed outside the factory, especially by J. GILES, sometimes on pieces with underglaze blue decoration and reserved panels to be filled with gaily coloured birds or flowers. A tendency to imitate SÈVRES began in the early 1760s with the adoption of scale pattern blue or crimson grounds and was more strongly pronounced after 1768 when a number of artists previously employed at CHELSEA joined the staff. Many of the finer products were decorated with tooled gilt ornaments (honey-gilding until the 1780s when mercury gilding was used).

In 1783 **Thomas Flight** bought the factory for his sons **Joseph** and **John.** This marked the beginning of the 'Flight period' in which the formula for the paste was modified (a more purely white body was achieved) and a somewhat severer style, influenced by the Neo-Classical movement, was adopted for both forms and decorations. In 1793 **Martin Barr** became a partner in the concern which was now called **Flight and Barr,** and younger members of the Barr family subsequently joined the firm. (It was known as Flight and Barr from 1793 to 1807, Barr, Flight and Barr 1807–13, and Flight, Barr and Barr 1813–40.) In 1840 it amalgamated with a factory founded in 1783 by R. CHAMBERLAIN and in 1847 abandoned its original

Worcester porcelain teacups and saucers, c.1760 *(Private Collection)*

Worcester porcelain mug, c.1760–70 *(Private Collection)*

workshops in favour of those of Chamberlain. This appears to have been a bad moment. But in 1850 **W. H. Kerr** joined the firm which was renamed **Kerr and Binns** and its fortunes began to revive. From 1862 it was styled the **Royal Worcester Porcelain Company.** Victorian products are elaborate, very richly gilded and painted and sometimes enriched with JEWELLED DECORATION. At the Dublin exhibition of 1858 it showed a monumental 'Shakespeare Service' with PARIAN WARE groups of Shakespearean characters, and plates, tureens, etc. of porcelain decorated

Worcester porcelain urn (Chamberlain factory), c.1815 *(Victoria & Albert Museum)*

with Renaissance motifs. A speciality was made of 'LIMOGES ware' porcelain decorated in white enamel on a dark blue ground, usually painted by T. BOTT. Statuettes were produced in a type of ivory-toned Parian ware (often glazed from 1856) and later some charming groups of children in the style of Kate Greenaway. Japanese influence marks many products of the 1870s and 80s. But the majority of C19 and early-C20 wares are decorated with rich bunches of flowers on a cream or light green ground. In 1889 it absorbed **Grainger, Lee & Co.,** a firm founded in 1801 by **Thomas Grainger** from the Chamberlain works, producing soft-paste porcelain (1815–20) but mainly bone china, Parian ware, etc. The concern prospered and grew still larger under the direction of **Charles William Dyson Perrins** 1912–53. In 1935 it began to issue very faithfully rendered American birds modelled by **Dorothy Doughty** who later modelled a series of British birds. The factory continues to produce porcelain of high quality. (For factory marks *see* pp. 888–9.)

Lit: F. A. Barrett, *Worcester Porcelain,* London 1953; H. Sandon, *The Illustrated Guide to Worcester Porcelain,* London 1969; G. Savage, *The Story of Worcester Porcelain and the Dyson Perrins Museum,* London 1969; H. Sandon, *Royal Worcester Porcelain from 1862 to the Present Day,* London 1973.

Wörflein, Johann Georg, *see* BIARELLE, Paul Amadeus.

Work-table A small table or stand for ladies' needlework, usually with drawers or shelves and/or a pouch for the silks, needles, etc. It was made from the mid C18 onwards, especially in France and England. The ÉTAGÈRE and WHATNOT were popular types of work-tables.

Worsted, *see* WOOL.

Wrigglework Zig-zag decorations engraved on pewter or silver by rocking a gouge from side to side as it is driven along the surface. It was used mainly in the late C17, generally to fill the spaces between engraved lines.

Wright, Frank Lloyd (1867–1959). The greatest American architect to date. As a designer and theorist he also exerted a profound influence on the decorative arts. He began his career in Chicago as chief draughtsman to Louis H. SULLIVAN 1888–93 then set up on his own. He soon developed a highly personal style of architecture and decoration, first for what he called the 'prairie house' with much stained woodwork (the most notable example being the Robie House, Chicago, 1908), then for buildings on a larger scale, culminating in the Midway Gardens, Chicago (1913) and the Imperial Hotel, Tokyo (1916–20; destroyed) both very heavily decorated and manifesting a taste for sharp-angled polygonal forms.

He wrote that 'the most satisfactory apartments are those in which most or all of the furniture is built in as a part of the original scheme. The whole must always be considered as an integral unit' (1908). His most notable designs for furnishings date from the early years of his career. His first furniture was designed for

F. L. Wright: armchair, 1904 (Museum of Modern Art, New York)

his own use *c.*1895 and was marked by a liking for angularity, stress on verticality and fondness for long narrow slats which was to characterize much of his later work. For his 'prairie houses' of the next few years he designed similar pieces, most of them made in oak by the Niedecken-Walbridge Company, Milwaukee, Wisconsin. He also made designs for metal grilles and lamps and stained-glass windows with elaborate geometrical leading. All this work was closely connected with the Arts and Crafts movement. But he was from an early stage an advocate of machine-made furnishings. His most important contribution to design came in 1904 with his uncompromisingly rectilinear furniture of painted metal for his Larkin Office Building in Buffalo, New York, the first building to be completely furnished with metal office chairs, desks, etc. At the same date he designed wooden-frame chairs in which the basic form is reduced to a cube: they have a similar machine-made look. These pieces are amazingly advanced for their date and were to have great influence on later

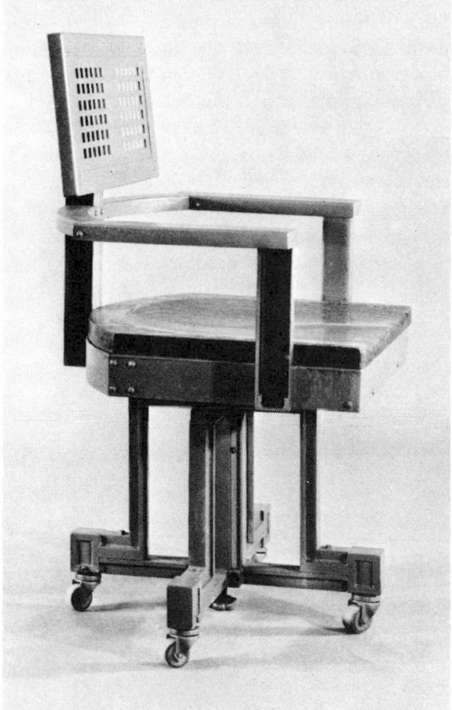

F. L. Wright: painted metal office armchair on swivel base, 1904 (Museum of Modern Art, New York)

furniture design through RIETVELD. His later furniture tended increasingly towards eccentricity – e.g. circular chairs with segmental arms for a circular-plan house, box-like furniture for a rectangular-plan house, and even polygonal chairs and beds for a hexagonal-plan house! Several of his clients found it so uncomfortable that they disposed of it.

His early writings had a seminal influence on theories of architecture and industrial design in Europe as well as the U.S.A., e.g. a lecture on *The Art and Craft of the Machine* (1901) and, more notably in Europe, an essay *In the Cause of Architecture* which appeared in *Architectural Record* (1908) and was extensively quoted by C. R. ASHBEE in the second volume of illustrations of Wright's work published by Wasmuth, Berlin, 1911.

Lit: O. Lloyd Wright, *F. L. Wright: His Life, His Work, His Words*, New York and London 1970.

Wrisbergholzen pottery A faience factory in Hanover founded 1735–7 by Baron von Wrisberg producing wares similar to those of DELFT painted in pale blue, manganese and yellow high-temperature colours – enamel colours never seem to have been used. Products also included tiles. It remained active until 1834 but latterly produced only simple household wares. (For factory mark *see* p. 889.)

Lit: O. Riesebeter, *Die deutsche Fayencen des 17. und 18. Jahrhunderts*, Leipzig 1921.

Wrotham potteries A group of Kentish potteries making, in addition to common cottage crockery, some of the best English slipware. Dated pieces range from 1612 (tyg in Liverpool Museum) to 1739 (tyg in Fitzwilliam Museum, Cambridge). Candlesticks, rarely found in slipware made in other places, were a speciality. Tygs with many handles, posset-pots, two-handled mugs but surprisingly few dishes survive. Decorations comprise *fleurs-de-lys*, roses, crosses, stars and masks in applied stamped reliefs of white clay as well as trailed flourishes and inscriptions. Several pieces are inscribed with the names or initials of potters – e.g. **Henry Ifield** (d.1673), **John Green** (*fl.*1686), **George Richardson** (d.1687), **Nicholas Hubble** (d.1689). Wares are sometimes inscribed 'Wrotham'.

Lit: A. J. B. Kiddell in *Transactions of the English Ceramic Circle*, XII, 1950.

Wrought iron, *see* IRON.

Wrythening Swirled or diagonally twisted ribbing or fluting on a glass vessel.

Wrythen-top spoon English medieval type of spoon with a stem terminating in a spirally fluted ovoid finial.

Würth, Ignaz Sebastian von (1746–1834). He was a leading Viennese goldsmith, *Meister* in 1770. The previous year he had executed an elaborate antependium for the high altar of the pilgrim church at Mariazell, unfortunately melted down in 1794. He made a great deal of excellent domestic and ecclesiastical plate, at first in the Louis XVI style and later in the Empire style.

Würth, Joseph (*fl.*1733–57). Viennese goldsmith whose most notable work was the tomb of St Johann Nepomuk in Prague Cathedral (1733–6, designed by Joseph Emanuel Fischer von Erlach and modelled by Antonio Corradini). He also executed a great deal of both ecclesiastical and domestic plate. **Ignaz Joseph Würth** (*fl.*1770–1800), who used a similar mark, was probably his son. He executed a large Louis XVI style table service for Duke Albert von Sachsen-Teschen in 1779–82. Other pieces of silver, both ecclesiastical and secular, are recorded.

Würzburg porcelain factory A very short-lived concern run *c.*1775–80 by **Johann Caspar Geyger,** producing table-wares painted with classical figures in medallions in brown monochrome, flowers or landscapes. The attribution of a number of figures to the factory is no longer maintained.

Lit: W. B. Honey in *Pantheon* XXII, 1938, p. 360; S. Ducret, *Würzburger Porzellan des 18 Jahrhunderts 1775–1780*, Brunswick 1968.

Würzburg tapestry factory Founded by the Prince Bishop of Würzburg in 1721 and directed by **Andreas Pirot** from 1728 onwards, it produced some very attractive Rococo tapestries – chinoiseries, *Commedia dell'Arte* scenes, grotesques and a very lively series of Venetian carnival scenes (Würzburg Residenz) – designed by the Court painters R. Byss and J. J. Scheubel. It closed down *c.*1775.

Lit: H. Göbel, *Wandteppiche*, Leipzig 1923–34.

Wu-ts'ai Literally 'five colours', a term applied to white Chinese porcelain painted with enamel colours on the biscuit or overglaze. This technique of decoration was developed in the MING period, probably in the reign of Hsüan-tê (1426–35) and perfected in the reign of Ch'êng-hua (1465–87). The pieces to which it was applied are generally small and the motifs consist of flowers, flowering branches, vines, etc. Sometimes the enamel colours were applied to pieces already decorated in underglaze blue.

Constructed letter from De divina proportione, *Pacioli, Venice, 1509 (reduced). Courtesy Victoria & Albert Museum*

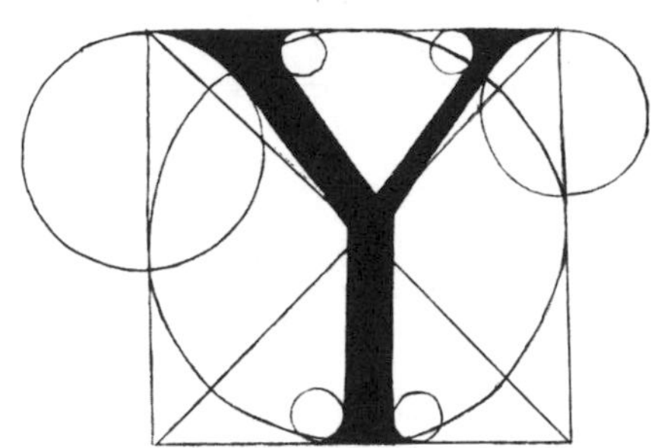

Yao The Chinese for 'ware' as in Kuan yao (KUAN WARE) or Chün yao (CHÜN WARE).

Yardley, Samuel, *see* BILSTON ENAMEL FACTORY.

Yatsushiro pottery A small Japanese pottery on Kyushu Island, begun by a Korean prisoner-of-war who had been given to the Daimyo Hosakawa Tadaoki in 1600, constructed a kiln near Agano village but after a few years moved with the Daimyo to Naraki village, Takata, Yatsushiro gun, Fukoka where he set up another kiln. TEA CEREMONY WARES with a brown glaze and decorations in brushed slip were made at Agano. The Yatsushiro wares have a grey glaze decorated in white slip with sketchy paintings of clouds, birds, etc. In 1658 the factory was moved again, to the foot of Mount Hirayama, but continued to produce similar wares until the early C20.

Lit: S. Jenyns, *Japanese Pottery*, London 1971.

Yayoi pottery A group of early Japanese ceramics, later in date than JOMON POTTERY, named after Yayoi Street, Hongo, Tokyo, where the first identified specimens were excavated. It was made in the course of 600 years after the invasion from the Continent of *c.*300 B.C. Vessels were fired at a higher temperature than Jomon wares (possibly in primitive kilns) and some may have been wheel-turned, though the practice of coiling appears to have been more usual. Shapes are simple, the range of vessels is limited to storage jars, cooking jars, bowls and high footed goblets, and decorations are usually limited to scored patterns.

Lit: S. Jenyns, *Japanese Pottery*, London 1971.

Yellow Seto wares, *see* MINO POTTERIES.

Yi-hsing potteries Factories at Yi-hsing in Kiangsu province producing the best-known type of Chinese red and brown, generally unglazed, stoneware from the late MING period onwards. The potteries are still in production. They made little vessels for the writing-table, in the form of plants, animals, etc., but are best known for teapots, generally simple but sometimes of curiously elaborate form, which were extensively exported. Their wares were imitated in Europe, notably by BÖTTGER at Meissen and ELERS in Staffordshire. They are sometimes described as BOCCARO WARES but this is misleading. Glazed wares, in imitation of Chün ware, were also made but are less well known.

Yomut carpets, *see* TURKMAN CARPETS.

Youf, Jean-Baptiste-Gilles (1762–1838). French furniture-maker who was born at Bayeux, settled in Paris by 1795 and had his own workshop by 1799. He attracted the attention of Napoleon's sister Elisa who called him to Lucca and appointed him her official cabinet-maker when she was created Grand Duchess in 1805. He provided Empire style furniture for her palace in Lucca and the Palazzo Pitti in Florence. He thus played a part in disseminating the Empire style in Italy. In 1814 he returned to Paris and supplied a very large suite of finely made but somewhat heavy furniture – tables, commodes, *torchères*, and 120 chairs – for a Norwegian client (now in Aust-Agder Museet, Arendal, Norway).

Lit: D. Ledoux-Lebard in *Arte Illustrata* 45–46 (1971), pp. 42–8.

Youghal lace Linen needlepoint LACE made from

1852 at the Convent of the Presentation at Youghal, County Cork, Ireland. It is generally imitative of C17 or C18 lace but of very fine quality.

Lit: B. Palliser, *History of Lace*, rev. M. Jourdain and A. Dryden, London 1902; P. Wardle, *Victorian Lace*, London 1968.

Yu A type of Chinese Bronze Age wine vessel in the form of a covered, rather pot-bellied, bucket with a swing handle. It varies considerably from tall to stout in general outline. It was made during the SHANG-YIN and Early CHOU dynasties, the later examples sometimes being very ornate in decoration.

Yüan The Mongol dynasty which succeeded the SUNG and ruled China from 1260 to 1368. The Emperors, especially Kublai Khan, encouraged Western visitors and China became more easily accessible to Europeans than at any time until the mid C19. Numerous silks were exported to Europe where many were made into vestments and are still preserved in church treasuries. They influenced European weavers, especially those of Italy (e.g. the so-called LUCCA SILKS). Porcelain was also exported to Europe where it was set, most inappropriately, in Gothic mounts. But little artistic influence passed back from Europe to China. In reaction to the rule of barbarian overlords, Chinese artists became more atavistic than ever and more anxious to copy the classic performances of earlier and happier times. In ceramics the only development of importance was the introduction from Persia of cobalt ore which, combined with a new technique for painting designs under the glaze, gave birth to Chinese blue-and-white porcelain though this

Yüan Dynasty: blue-and-white porcelain wine jar with red and blue relief panels, c.1300 (Percival David Foundation of Chinese Art, London)

Yüan Dynasty: celadon dish with unglazed reddish-brown relief decoration, C14 (Percival David Foundation of Chinese Art, London)

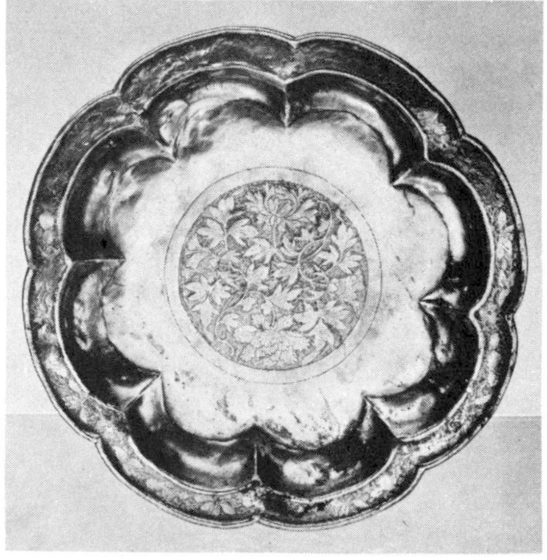

Yüan Dynasty: silver dish (William Rockhill Nelson Gallery of Art, Kansas City)

famous ware was not produced on a large scale until the MING period (the outstanding quality of early examples may however be judged from a pair of vases of 1351 in the Percival David Foundation, London). Perhaps the most handsome Yüan porcelain is SHU-FU WARE. Ceramic forms were imitated in silver vessels of which several fine specimens survive. Handsome lacquer work was also executed under the Yüan.

Lit: M. Medley, *Yüan Porcelain and Stoneware*, London 1974.

Yüeh ware The best known PROTO-PORCELAIN, it is a type of grey-bodied stoneware with an olive green to putty coloured glaze similar to Celadon. It was made as early as the c4–3 B.C. but reached its peak during the T'ANG dynasty when the best was said to have been made for the prince of Yüeh, hence the name. It was gradually displaced during the Sung dynasty by Northern Celadon ware and Lung-Ch'üan Celadon ware. It was very influential in Korean ceramics.

Lit: B. Gray, *Early Chinese Pottery and Porcelain*, London 1953.

Yung Chêng porcelain Chinese porcelain made in the reign of the CH'ING Emperor Yung Chêng (1725–35). Some of the best wares are those

Yüeh ware dish, grey stoneware with olive green glaze, c10 (Percival David Foundation of Chinese Art, London)

Yung-cheng moon flask decorated in famille rose *enamel colours, 1725–35*
(Percival David Foundation of Chinese Art, London)

decorated with a pink enamel introduced from Europe (where it is called PURPLE OF CASSIUS) which forms the basis of the FAMILLE ROSE colour scheme. The period is also notable for the revival of the SUNG and MING styles.

Lit: S. Jenyns, *Later Chinese Porcelain*, rev. ed., London 1971.

Yuruk carpets, *see* TURKISH CARPETS.

From a type face issued by the Figgin Foundry, London, c. 1820 (enlarged). Punchcutter unknown

Zanuso, Marco (b.1916). Italian architect and designer specializing in mass-production products. His Borletti 1956 sewing-machine was a precursor of NIZZOLI's classic 1960 'Mirella' model for Necchi. His furniture for Arflex of Milan includes an upholstered plastic-shell chair (1957) and several metal-frame chairs of great ingenuity and elegance, notably the 'Milord' and 'Fourlines' models. He has also designed, with Richard Sapper, an excellent clean-lined television set (1962) and small, portable transistor-television set (1964).

Zebra wood, *see* EBONY.

Zeckel, Johann (*c.*1660–1728). He was a leading Augsburg silversmith, a contemporary of BILLER and DRENTWETT. Apprenticed in Vienna, he had settled in Augsburg by 1698 and began as a journeyman with Johann MAIR. He eventually became assay-master and president of the goldsmiths' guild in Augsburg. He specialized in ecclesiastical plate (he was Roman Catholic whereas Biller and Drentwett were Lutherans) and his masterpiece is the large monstrance in St Maria Victoria, Ingolstadt, made in 1708. Of his many fine large pieces of late Baroque plate several sculptural reliquaries and altar figures are outstanding, e.g. the life-size reliquary bust of St Aquilinius made for the Marienkapelle, Würzburg, in about 1715 and the silver statue of St Joseph (with enamels by **Samuel Wolfgang**) made in 1709–10 for the cathedral of Freiburg-im-Breisgau. (For his mark *see* p. 895.)

Lit: Augsburger Barock, Exh. Cat., Augsburg 1968.

Zeiner, Lukas (*fl.*1479–1512). Glass stainer working in Zurich and specializing in small heraldic panels of a type which became very popular in Switzerland for gifts. He worked in a florid late Gothic style and was a master of fine detail, often scratched with a quill on FLASHED GLASS.

Zeissig, Johann Elias known as **Schönau,** *see* MEISSEN PORCELAIN FACTORY.

Zeitz pottery, *see* WALDENBURG POTTERIES.

Zerbst pottery A faience factory in Anhalt founded in 1720 under the patronage of the Prince of Anhalt-Zerbst by the arcanist **Johann Caspar Ripp** (1681–1726) from HANAU, who left in 1724, and **Daniel van Keyk** from Delft who was manager until 1740. It was subsequently managed by a succession of different potters. Products were mainly table-wares, decorated in the DELFT style in blue and white or high-temperature polychrome. But large baluster-shaped vases with a ground of foliage and scrolls and reserved panels painted with landscapes and figure subjects were also made. After a period in which it nearly ceased production, the concern was revived in 1793 and remained active until 1861, latterly making glazed earthenware in the English style. (For factory mark *see* p. 889.)

Lit: O. Riesebieter, *Die deutsche Fayencen des 17. und 18. Jahrhunderts,* Leipzig 1921.

Zeschinger, Johannes, *see* FÜRSTENBERG PORCELAIN FACTORY and HÖCHST FAIENCE AND PORCELAIN FACTORY.

Ziegler, Jules-Claude (1804–56). French painter (a pupil of Ingres) who in 1838 collaborated in the foundation of a pottery at Voisinlieu near Beauvais, producing salt-glazed stoneware with relief decorations. He designed wares with 'running patterns', e.g. tendrils of vine clambering round a jug. His masterpiece in this medium is the Apostle vase of 1842 (Musée nationale de céramique de Sèvres). He also provided designs for the SÈVRES PORCELAIN FACTORY 1838–42.

Lithographs of his designs were published as *Études céramiques*, Paris 1850. He also wrote one of the first books on the aesthetics of pottery: *Recherches des principes du beau dans l'art céramique*, Paris 1850.

Lit: A. Lesur and Tardy, *Les poteries et les faïences françaises*, Paris 1957–60.

J.-C. Ziegler: salt-glazed stoneware jug, Voisinlieu, near Beauvais, c.1845 (Victoria & Albert Museum)

Zinc A hard brittle bluish-white metal alloyed with copper to make BRASS. The synonym SPELTER is generally applied to objects cast from pure zinc.

Zitzmann, Friedrich, *see* KÖPPING, Karl.

Zopfstil German term (literally 'pig-tail style' i.e. style of the *ancien régime*) for the Louis XVI style and especially the German late-C18 Antique Revival style.

Zsolnay, Vilmós and **Miklos**, *see* PECS POTTERY.

Zuber, Jean (*fl.*1793–1850?). The first and, with J. DUFOUR, the best maker of SCENIC WALLPAPER. he began as salesman for a firm of textile and wallpaper printers in Mulhouse of which he obtained control in 1802. In 1804 he produced the first dated scenic wallpaper, *Vues de Suisses*, but was mainly occupied with ordinary textile-like papers in the Empire style. From 1825 he issued a number of very attractive scenic papers – horse-racing scenes in France, England and Italy (the race down the Corso in Rome), scenes from the American War of Independence, views of the Niagara Falls and Boston, Mass. He adopted mechanical printing in 1850.

Lit: E. A. Entwisle, *French Scenic Wallpapers 1810–50*, London 1971.

Zündt, Mathis (*c.*1498–1572). Leading German Renaissance goldsmith, ornamental designer and engraver, working at Nuremberg. None of his work in gold or other metals survives, but his engraved designs for jewellery and silver epitomize the classical taste of his period. Surviving Nuremberg silver includes several pieces similar to his designs. *Illustrated next column.*

Lit: J. F. Hayward in *The Connoisseur* CLXIV (1967), pp. 81–3.

Zunftbecher A late C17 German type of glass beaker with the heraldic device or other symbol of a guild enamelled on it.

Zürich pottery and porcelain factory The best in C18 Switzerland, founded in 1763 by members of a scientific society including the poet and painter **Salomon Gessner**, with **Adam Spengler** (d.1790) who had previously worked at the HÖCHST factory as technical director. It began by making faience and soft-paste porcelain but soon (*c.*1765) began to produce hard paste of great beauty with a very brilliant glaze of slightly smoky tone. The staple products were table-wares decorated in underglaze blue usually in imitation of MEISSEN patterns. But the finer wares were very delicately painted in enamels with genre scenes, Swiss landscapes (sometimes after designs by, in a few instances painted by, S. Gessner) or bouquets of naturalistic flowers. Globular teapots with

M. Zündt: design for a covered cup from his Opus craterographicum, *Hamburg, 1551*

curious scrolled handles were a speciality. A table-centre more than 60 cm high (Victoria & Albert Museum) is one of the more ambitious products: it forms part of a large table service comprising dishes with openwork rims, and plates with minutely rendered landscapes. Table-wares were also made in faience and decorated like those of porcelain. Figures of great charm were made of porcelain, the earlier (1765–75) including gardeners, huntsmen, craftsmen, hawkers, etc. and a very curious group of two slave dealers with a black slave boy, the later (1775–9) including some delicately sentimental groups from models by **Valentin Sonnenschein** (1749–1828) who had previously worked at LUDWIGSBURG. In 1778 the factory began to produce cream-coloured earthenware in the English style often decorated, from 1785, with transfer printing. After the death of Spengler in 1790 the concern was liquidated, the stock sold and in 1793 the factory was bought by his son-in-law **Mathias Nehracher** (d.1800). It subsequently passed through the hands of a number of owners, making faience and cream-coloured earthenware until 1897 when it finally closed. (For factory mark *see* p. 889.)

Lit: S. Ducret, *Die Zürcher Porzellanmanufaktur*, 2 vols., Zürich 1958–9; R. Schnyder, *Zürcher Porzellan*, Zürich 1964.

Zwiebelmuster Onion pattern – a type of porcelain decoration derived from a Chinese design of formalized leaves, flowers and peaches which were mistaken for onions by Europeans and used at the MEISSEN factory on cheaper table-wares from 1739 and much copied by other factories.

Zwischengoldglas A glass vessel engraved and decorated with gold on the outside and encased in a sheath of glass. The technique was employed in Rome C4–C6 A.D. and in Germany from the C18.

Zwischengoldglas: Bohemian glass tumbler, c.1730 (Victoria & Albert Museum)

Ceramic Marks

Marks were drawn freely and may only approximate to the version shown below.
See also MARKS ON POTTERY AND PORCELAIN, p. 512.

Alcora

Amberg

Amstel

Ansbach
1758 onwards

Aprey

Aprey
mid-C19

Arras

Baden-Baden
Pfalzer's porcelain

Baden-Baden
Amstett's faience fine

Bayreuth
Knöller period

Berlin
Wegely's factory

Berlin
Gotzowsky's factory 1761–3

Berlin
Royal factory Introduced c. *1765*

Berlin
Konigliche-Portzellan-Manufaktur

Bing & Grøndahl

Bow

Bow

Bow

Bristol

Bristol

Brunswick

Brussels
Vaume's porcelain

Buen Retiro
1760–1804

Buen Retiro

Capodimonte

Cassel
Faience

Cassel
Porcelain

Caughley

Caughley

Chantilly

Chelsea
1745–50

Chelsea
c. 1750

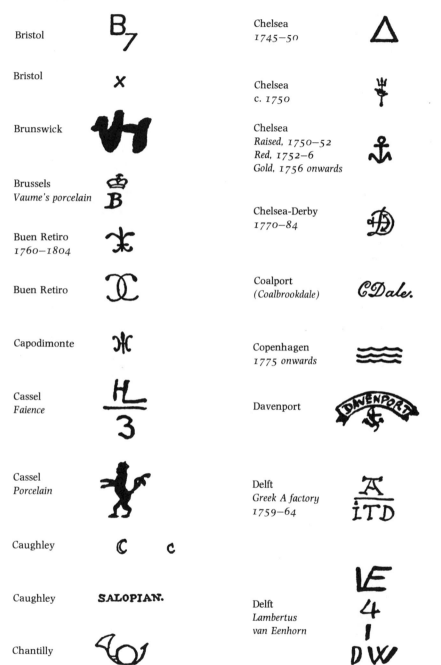

Chelsea
Raised, 1750–52
Red, 1752–6
Gold, 1756 onwards

Chelsea-Derby
1770–84

Coalport
(Coalbrookdale)

Copenhagen
1775 onwards

Davenport

Delft
Greek A factory
1759–64

Delft
Lambertus
van Eenhorn

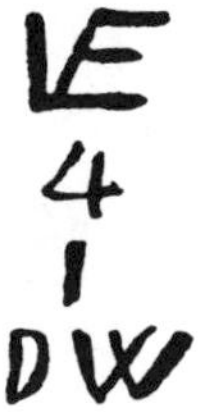

Delft
Samuel van Eenhorn

Delft
Rochus Hoppestyn

Derby
Introduced c. 1784

Derby
c. 1795

Derby
Bloor period 1811–48

Derby
Stevenson & Hancock, 1850–70

Doccia
Late c18

Dresden

Dublin

Eckenförde

Erfurt

Etiolles

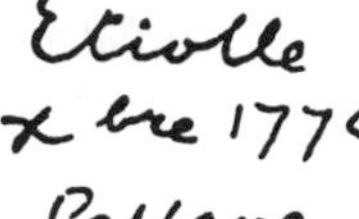

Florsheim

Frankenthal
Monogram of Carl Theodor; first used c. 1762

Fulda
From 1780, perhaps earlier

Fürstenberg

Gardner's
(Moscow)
Early c19

Gotha
1780 onwards

Gustafsberg

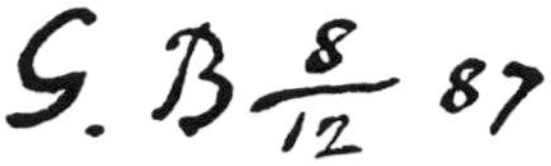

Herrebøe

Höchst

Holitsch

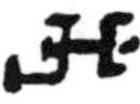

Ilmenau
From c. 1792

Kellinghusen
Behrens 1763–82

Kelsterbach
1789–1802

Kiel
Tännich und Kleffel

Kloster-Veilsdorf
1760–97

Kreussen
Lorenz Speckner

Kreussen
Vest family

Künersberg

Lenzburg

Lesum

Limbach
From c. 1772

Limoges

Longton Hall

Ludwigsburg
1758 onwards

Marieberg

Medici
(Florence)

Meissen
1724 onwards

Meissen
Monogram of Augustus the Strong, and of Augustus III

Meissen

Meissen
'Dot' period, 1763–74

Meissen
Marcolini period 1774–1814

Meissen
Inventory mark of the Johanneum Collection

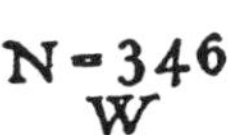

Meissen
On defective specimens sold to decorators

Mennecy

Milan
Clerici factory

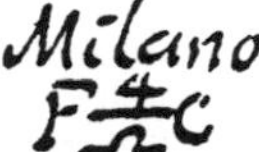

Minton
c.1800–16

Montelupo

Mosbach
After 1806

Moustiers

Naples
1771 onwards

New Hall

Niderviller
1770–93

Nove
(Venice)

Nuremberg

Nymphenburg
First used c. *1754*

Nyon
(Switzerland)

Oettingen-
Schrattenhofen

Offenbach

Orléans

Paris
de la Courtille

Paris
Rue Popincourt

Paris
Clignancourt

Paris
Rue Thiroux

Pellipario

Pfalz-Zweibrücken

Plymouth

Portuguese
Aveiro

Portuguese
Vianna do Castello

Potsdam

Powolny
with
Wiener Keramik

Rato

Reval

Rockingham

Rookwood

Rörstrand

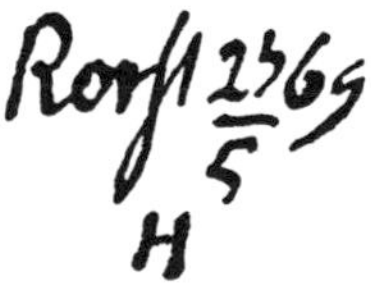

Saint-Amand-les-Eaux

Saint-Cloud

St Petersburg
1762–96

St Petersburg
1796–1801

Sceaux

Schrezheim

Sèvres
1753

Sèvres
1778

Sèvres
c. *1800–02*

Sèvres
1824–28

Sèvres
1845–8

Sèvres
Period of Napoleon III

Sinceny

Sinceny
Second period

Sölvesborg

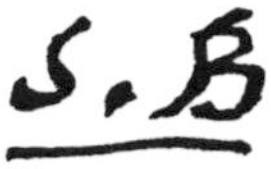

Stockelsdorf

Stralsund

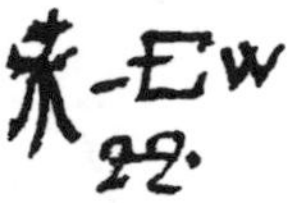

Strasbourg
Paul Hannong
1752–5

Striegau

Swansea

The Hague

Tournai

Turin

Vienna
First used c. 1744

Vincennes

Vinovo

Volkstedt
1760–99

Wallendorf

Wedgwood

Weesp
(Holland)
1759 *onwards*

Wiesbaden

Worcester

Worcester

Worcester

Worcester
Pseudo-Meissen

Worcester
Pseudo-Chinese

Worcester

Wrisbergholzen

Zerbst

Zurich

Hall-marks on Silver

Assay offices in most cities varied their marks from time to time.
Typical examples are given below, with dates.
See also HALL-MARKS, pp. 363–4.

Aachen
1573–1624

Amsterdam
c. *1606*

Antwerp
1641–2

Augsburg
1674–80

Barcelona
c16–c17

Basel
c17

Berlin
1735

Birmingham
From 1773

Brussels
1553

Chester
From 1797

Cologne
Late c17

Copenhagen
1725

Dresden
Mid c18

Dublin
1821–45

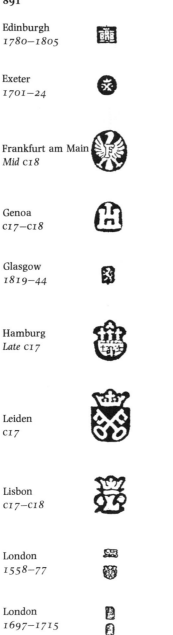

Edinburgh
1780–1805

Exeter
1701–24

Frankfurt am Main
Mid c18

Genoa
c17–c18

Glasgow
1819–44

Hamburg
Late c17

Leiden
c17

Lisbon
c17–c18

London
1558–77

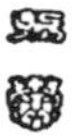

London
1697–1715

London
1856–75

Marseilles
1760

Moscow
1780

Munich
Early c18

Newcastle
1721–39

Nuremberg
1600–1700

Paris
c. 1330

Paris
1764–5

Paris
1789

Rome
Late c17

Sheffield
1824–43

St Petersburg
c. 1730–40

Strasbourg
1725

Turin
c18

Utrecht
c18

Venice
c16–c18

Vienna
1737

York
1787–1811

Zurich
c17–c18

Makers' Marks on Silver and Pewter

Peter Archambo

Robert-Joseph Auguste

Claude Ballin II

Edmé-Pierre Balzac

Hester Bateman

Nicolas Besnier

Martin Guillaume Biennais

Johann Ludwig Biller I, and II

Albrecht Biller

Johann Jacob Biller

Augustus Courtauld

Henri-Nicolas Cousinet

Paul Crespin

John Emes

Pierre Germain

Thomas Germain

François-Thomas Germain

Giovanni Giardini

Pierre Harache

Thomas Heming

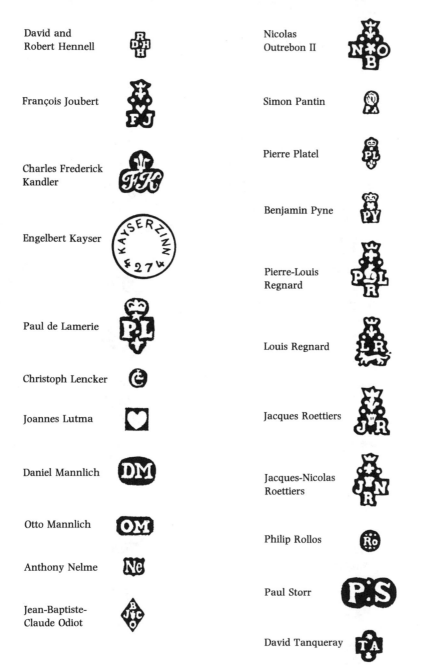

David and Robert Hennell

François Joubert

Charles Frederick Kandler

Engelbert Kayser

Paul de Lamerie

Christoph Lencker

Joannes Lutma

Daniel Mannlich

Otto Mannlich

Anthony Nelme

Jean-Baptiste-Claude Odiot

Nicolas Outrebon II

Simon Pantin

Pierre Platel

Benjamin Pyne

Pierre-Louis Regnard

Louis Regnard

Jacques Roettiers

Jacques-Nicolas Roettiers

Philip Rollos

Paul Storr

David Tanqueray

Luigi Valadier 

Paulus van Vianen 

Adam van Vianen 

Matthäus Wallbaum 

David Willaume 

Johann Zeckel 

Our thanks are due to the many galleries and museums which have kindly given permission to reproduce illustrations, and to the following (references being to pages):

A.C.L. 101, 480; Alinari 20, 67, 84, 121 bottom left, 128, 136, 137, 165 left, 297 left, 397 right, 467, 504, 579, 620, 645, 661 top, 664, 826 right; Brogi 706; G.F.N. Rome 774 bottom; Giraudon 55, 68, 92, 104, 107, 109, 114, 144 right, 147 bottom, 148, 158 left, 161 bottom, 164 top left, 165 right, 168 bottom, 170, 192, 214 left, 215, 229 left, 255 left, 273, 274 right, 275, 277 bottom, 335, 338 left, 366, 369, 393, 395, 408, 409 left, 455, 470, 472, 481, 482, 485 bottom, 490, 503 right, 509, 519, 526 left, 528, 560, 571 top, 595, 596, 603, 626 left, 627, 629, 633, 640, 643, 655, 656, 660 right, 665, 679, 685 bottom right, 687 left, 692, 693, 694, 695, 696, 699 right, 700 left, 705, 707, 717 top, 718 left, 722 right, 723, 725 left, 736, 777 right, 819 left, 826 left, 855, 863, 865; Gunderman 47, 390, 554 right, 617; Hirmer 116, 137 bottom left; Littkemann 22, 81, 82, 203 right, 251 left, 567 right, 683; Mas 135 left, 343 bottom left, 379; Philadelphia National Park Service Photo 771 bottom; Trustees of the Chatsworth Settlement 611; Victoria & Albert Museum 12, 15, 16, 18, 19, 21, 23, 30, 32, 33, 34, 37, 38, 43, 44, 48, 51, 54, 58, 60, 61, 62, 70, 71, 73, 96, 102, 103, 115, 118, 132, 140, 141, 145, 146, 147 top, 151, 155, 156, 162, 164 bottom, 166 top, 167, 173, 174, 175 left, 179, 180, 182, 183, 188, 190 right, 191 left, 193 left and bottom right, 195, 197, 198, 205, 207, 208, 209, 210, 212, 219, 220, 224, 225, 227, 230, 231, 234, 235, 244, 246, 252, 266, 267, 269, 271, 272 left, 276 right, 282, 285 bottom, 288, 293, 297 right, 302, 325, 326 right, 327 right, 329 right, 330 left, 331, 336, 343 top left, 345 top left & right, 351, 352, 381, 384, 387 right, 397, 400, 403, 405, 406, 416 left, 420, 422 left, 434 right, 446, 459, 460 left, 470 bottom, 473, 476, 486, 491, 495, 500, 503 left, 511, 515, 516, 520 right, 524, 529 right, 533 top, 534, 535, 537, 541, 551, 553 right, 558 left, 567 left, 571 bottom, 574, 576, 577, 586 right, 589, 591, 593, 594, 598, 613, 618, 632, 646, 657, 658, 659, 661 bottom, 662, 670, 678 top, 687, 689, 697, 699 left, 703, 709 left, 720, 724, 730, 734 bottom, 740, 742, 745, 747, 750 left, 752, 753, 754, 755, 757, 759, 765 right, 767, 775 bottom right, 777 left, 779, 787, 793, 795 bottom, 798, 800, 802 left, 807, 809, 815 top, 819 right, 822 right, 823 left, 824, 827, 828 left, 832, 838, 846, 847, 850, 851, 852 bottom left, 853, 856, 857, 860, 861 top, 869 right, 879.